# CUMULATIVE PROBABILITIES FOR THE STANDA

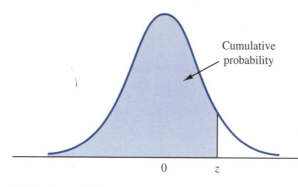

Cumulative probability

Entries in the table give the area under the curve to the left of the $z$ value. For example, for $z = 1.25$, the cumulative probability is .8944.

| z | .00 | .01 | .02 | .03 | .04 | .05 | .06 | .07 | .08 | .09 |
|---|-----|-----|-----|-----|-----|-----|-----|-----|-----|-----|
| .0 | .5000 | .5040 | .5080 | .5120 | .5160 | .5199 | .5239 | .5279 | .5319 | .5359 |
| .1 | .5398 | .5438 | .5478 | .5517 | .5557 | .5596 | .5636 | .5675 | .5714 | .5753 |
| .2 | .5793 | .5832 | .5871 | .5910 | .5948 | .5987 | .6026 | .6064 | .6103 | .6141 |
| .3 | .6179 | .6217 | .6255 | .6293 | .6331 | .6368 | .6406 | .6443 | .6480 | .6517 |
| .4 | .6554 | .6591 | .6628 | .6664 | .6700 | .6736 | .6772 | .6808 | .6844 | .6879 |
| .5 | .6915 | .6950 | .6985 | .7019 | .7054 | .7088 | .7123 | .7157 | .7190 | .7224 |
| .6 | .7257 | .7291 | .7324 | .7357 | .7389 | .7422 | .7454 | .7486 | .7517 | .7549 |
| .7 | .7580 | .7611 | .7642 | .7673 | .7704 | .7734 | .7764 | .7794 | .7823 | .7852 |
| .8 | .7881 | .7910 | .7939 | .7967 | .7995 | .8023 | .8051 | .8078 | .8106 | .8133 |
| .9 | .8159 | .8186 | .8212 | .8238 | .8264 | .8289 | .8315 | .8340 | .8365 | .8389 |
| 1.0 | .8413 | .8438 | .8461 | .8485 | .8508 | .8531 | .8554 | .8577 | .8599 | .8621 |
| 1.1 | .8643 | .8665 | .8686 | .8708 | .8729 | .8749 | .8770 | .8790 | .8810 | .8830 |
| 1.2 | .8849 | .8869 | .8888 | .8907 | .8925 | .8944 | .8962 | .8980 | .8997 | .9015 |
| 1.3 | .9032 | .9049 | .9066 | .9082 | .9099 | .9115 | .9131 | .9147 | .9162 | .9177 |
| 1.4 | .9192 | .9207 | .9222 | .9236 | .9251 | .9265 | .9279 | .9292 | .9306 | .9319 |
| 1.5 | .9332 | .9345 | .9357 | .9370 | .9382 | .9394 | .9406 | .9418 | .9429 | .9441 |
| 1.6 | .9452 | .9463 | .9474 | .9484 | .9495 | .9505 | .9515 | .9525 | .9535 | .9545 |
| 1.7 | .9554 | .9564 | .9573 | .9582 | .9591 | .9599 | .9608 | .9616 | .9625 | .9633 |
| 1.8 | .9641 | .9649 | .9656 | .9664 | .9671 | .9678 | .9686 | .9693 | .9699 | .9706 |
| 1.9 | .9713 | .9719 | .9726 | .9732 | .9738 | .9744 | .9750 | .9756 | .9761 | .9767 |
| 2.0 | .9772 | .9778 | .9783 | .9788 | .9793 | .9798 | .9803 | .9808 | .9812 | .9817 |
| 2.1 | .9821 | .9826 | .9830 | .9834 | .9838 | .9842 | .9846 | .9850 | .9854 | .9857 |
| 2.2 | .9861 | .9864 | .9868 | .9871 | .9875 | .9878 | .9881 | .9884 | .9887 | .9890 |
| 2.3 | .9893 | .9896 | .9898 | .9901 | .9904 | .9906 | .9909 | .9911 | .9913 | .9916 |
| 2.4 | .9918 | .9920 | .9922 | .9925 | .9927 | .9929 | .9931 | .9932 | .9934 | .9936 |
| 2.5 | .9938 | .9940 | .9941 | .9943 | .9945 | .9946 | .9948 | .9949 | .9951 | .9952 |
| 2.6 | .9953 | .9955 | .9956 | .9957 | .9959 | .9960 | .9961 | .9962 | .9963 | .9964 |
| 2.7 | .9965 | .9966 | .9967 | .9968 | .9969 | .9970 | .9971 | .9972 | .9973 | .9974 |
| 2.8 | .9974 | .9975 | .9976 | .9977 | .9977 | .9978 | .9979 | .9979 | .9980 | .9981 |
| 2.9 | .9981 | .9982 | .9982 | .9983 | .9984 | .9984 | .9985 | .9985 | .9986 | .9986 |
| 3.0 | .9987 | .9987 | .9987 | .9988 | .9988 | .9989 | .9989 | .9989 | .9990 | .9990 |

# Essentials of Modern Business Statistics

## With Microsoft® Office Excel® 5e

**David R. Anderson**
*University of Cincinnati*

**Dennis J. Sweeney**
*University of Cincinnati*

**Thomas A. Williams**
*Rochester Institute of Technology*

**5e**

# Essentials of Modern Business Statistics

## With Microsoft® Office Excel®

## David R. Anderson
*University of Cincinnati*

## Dennis J. Sweeney
*University of Cincinnati*

## Thomas A. Williams
*Rochester Institute of Technology*

SOUTH-WESTERN
CENGAGE Learning·

Australia • Brazil • Japan • Korea • Mexico • Singapore • Spain • United Kingdom • United States

## SOUTH-WESTERN
### CENGAGE Learning·

**Essentials of Modern Business Statistics With Microsoft® Office Excel®, Fifth Edition**

David R. Anderson

Dennis J. Sweeney

Thomas A. Williams

Vice President of Editorial, Business: Jack W. Calhoun

Editor-in-Chief: Joe Sabatino

Senior Acquisitions Editor: Charles McCormick, Jr.

Developmental Editor: Maggie Kubale

Editorial Assistant: Courtney Bavaro

Marketing Manager: Adam Marsh

Content Project Manager: Emily Nesheim

Media Editor: Chris Valentine

Manufacturing Planner: Ron J. Montgomery

Marketing Communications Manager: Libby Shipp

Production Service: MPS Limited, a Macmillan Company

Art Director: Stacy Jenkins Shirley

Internal Designer: Michael Stratton/ cmiller design

Cover Designer: Craig Ramsdell

Cover Image: © Image Source / Alamy

Rights Acquisitions Specialist: Sam Marshall

For product information and technology assistance, contact us at **Cengage Learning Customer & Sales Support, 1-800-354-9706**

For permission to use material from this text or product, submit all requests online at **www.cengage.com/permissions** Further permissions questions can be emailed to **permissionrequest@cengage.com**

Library of Congress Control Number: 2011934829

Book only ISBN-13: 978-0-8400-6239-0
Book only ISBN-10: 0-8400-6239-7
Package ISBN-13: 978-0-8400-6238-3
Package ISBN-10: 0-8400-6238-9

**South-Western**
5191 Natorp Boulevard
Mason, OH 45040
USA

Cengage Learning products are represented in Canada by Nelson Education, Ltd.

For your course and learning solutions, visit **www.cengage.com**

Purchase any of our products at your local college store or at our preferred online store **www.cengagebrain.com**

Printed in Canada
1 2 3 4 5 6 7 15 14 13 12 11

*Dedicated to*
*Krista, Justin, Mark, and Colleen*
*Mark, Linda, Brad, Tim, Scott, and Lisa*
*Cathy, David, and Kristin*

# Brief Contents

# Contents

## Chapter 5   Discrete Probability Distributions   209

## Chapter 10  Comparisons Involving Means, Experimental Design, and Analysis of Variance  414

## Chapter 13  Multiple Regression  583

## Chapter 14  Statistical Methods for Quality Control  640

# Preface

The purpose of *Essentials of Modern Business Statistics with Microsoft Office® Excel®* is to give students, primarily those in the fields of business administration and economics, a conceptual introduction to the field of statistics and its many applications. The text is applications oriented and written with the needs of the nonmathematician in mind; the mathematical prerequisite is knowledge of algebra.

Applications of data analysis and statistical methodology are an integral part of the organization and presentation of the text material. The discussion and development of each technique is presented in an applications setting, with the statistical results providing insights to decisions and solutions to problems.

Although the book is applications oriented, we have taken care to provide sound methodological development and to use notation that is generally accepted for the topic being covered. Hence, students will find that this text provides good preparation for the study of more advanced statistical material. A bibliography to guide further study is included as an appendix.

## Use of Microsoft Excel for Statistical Analysis

*Essentials of Modern Business Statistics with Microsoft Excel* is first and foremost a statistics textbook that emphasizes statistical concepts and applications. But since most practical problems are too large to be solved using hand calculations, some type of statistical software package is required to solve these problems. There are several excellent statistical packages available today. However, because most students and potential employers value spreadsheet experience, many schools now use a spreadsheet package in their statistics courses. Microsoft Excel is the most widely used spreadsheet package in business as well as in colleges and universities. We have written *Essentials of Modern Business Statistics with Microsoft Excel* especially for statistics courses in which Microsoft Excel is used as the software package.

Excel has been integrated within each of the chapters and plays an integral part in providing an application orientation. Although we assume that readers using this text are familiar with Excel basics such as selecting cells, entering formulas, copying, and so on, we do not assume that readers are familiar with Excel 2010. As a result, we have included Appendix E, which provides an introduction to Excel 2010 and tools for statistical analysis.

Throughout the text the discussion of using Excel to perform a statistical procedure appears in a subsection immediately following the discussion of the statistical procedure. We believe that this style enables us to fully integrate the use of Excel throughout the text, but still maintain the primary emphasis on the statistical methodology being discussed. In each of these subsections, we use a standard format for using Excel for statistical analysis. There are three primary tasks: Enter Data, Enter Functions and Formulas, and Apply Tools. We believe a consistent framework for applying Excel helps users to focus on the statistical methodology without getting bogged down in the details of using Excel.

In presenting worksheet figures we often use a nested approach in which the worksheet shown in the background of the figure displays the formulas and the worksheet shown in the foreground shows the values computed using the formulas. Different colors and shades of colors are used to differentiate worksheet cells containing data, highlight cells containing Excel functions and formulas, and highlight material printed by Excel as a result of using one or more data analysis tools.

# Use of StatTools

StatTools is a commercial Excel add-in which we and Palisade Corporation have made available to adopters of this text for free. StatTools extends the range of statistical and graphical options for Excel users. In an appendix to Chapter 1 we show how to download and install StatTools. Most chapters also include an appendix that shows the steps required to accomplish a statistical procedure using StatTools.

We have been very careful to make the use of StatTools completely optional. Users who want to teach using the standard tools available in Excel 2010 can continue to do so. But users who want additional statistical capabilities not available in Excel 2010 now have access to an industry standard statistics add-in that students will be able to continue to use in the workplace.

# Changes in the Fifth Edition

We appreciate the acceptance and positive response to the previous editions of *Essentials of Modern Business Statistics with Microsoft Excel*. Accordingly, in making modifications for this new edition, we have maintained the presentation style and readability of those editions. The significant changes in the new edition are summarized here.

- **Microsoft Excel 2010.** Step-by-step instructions and screen captures show how to use the latest version of Excel to implement statistical procedures.
- **Introduction to Data Mining.** A new section in Chapter 1 introduces the field of data mining. We provide a brief overview of data mining and the concept of a data warehouse. We also describe how the fields of statistics and computer science join to make data mining operational and valuable.
- **Revised Chapter 2.** We have shortened the Excel coverage by moving the discussion of how to use Excel's PivotChart report to chapter appendixes. Appendix 2.1 shows how to use Excel's PivotChart report to summarize categorical data, and Appendix 2.2 shows how to use Excel's PivotChart report to summarize quantitative data.
- **Revised Sampling Material.** The introduction of Chapter 7 has been revised and now includes the concept of a sampled population and a frame. The distinction between sampling from a finite population and an infinite population has been clarified, with sampling from a process used to illustrate the selection of a random sample from an infinite population. A practical advice section stresses the importance of obtaining close correspondence between the sampled population and the target population.
- **Revised Introduction to Hypothesis Testing.** Section 9.1, Developing Null and Alternative Hypotheses, has been revised. A better set of guidelines has been developed for identifying the null and alternative hypotheses. The context of the situation and the purpose for taking the sample are key. In situations in which the focus is on finding evidence to support a research finding, the research hypothesis is the alternative hypothesis. In situations where the focus is on challenging an assumption, the assumption is the null hypothesis.
- **Section 13.8 – "Modeling Curvilinear Relationships."** This new section shows how curvilinear relationship can easily be handled using a multiple regression model. We illustrate the use of both Excel's Chart tools and Excel's Regression tool to fit a quadratic model.
- **Chapter 15 – "Time Series Analysis and Forecasting."** This new chapter, available on the text website, focuses on using the pattern in a time series plot to select and use an appropriate forecasting method. Section 15.1 discusses time series patterns, and

Section 15.2 introduces methods for measuring forecasting accuracy. Section 15.3 discusses moving averages and exponential smoothing. Section 15.4 introduces methods appropriate for a time series that exhibits a trend. Here we illustrate how regression analysis can be used for trend projection to model nonlinear relationships involving a quadratic trend. Section 15.5 then shows how dummy variables can be used to model seasonality in a forecasting equation. Section 15.6 discusses classical time series decomposition including the concept of deseasonalizing a time series.

- **New Examples and Exercises Based on Real Data.** We have added over 170 new examples and exercises based on real data and recently referenced sources of statistical information. Using data obtained from various data collection organizations and other sources, such as *The Wall Street Journal*, *USA Today*, *Fortune*, and *Barron's*, we have drawn upon actual studies to develop explanations and to create exercises that demonstrate many uses of statistics in business and economics. We believe the use of real data helps generate more student interest in the material and enables the student to learn about both the statistical methodology and its application.

- **New Case Problems.** We have added six new case problems to this edition. The new case problems appear in the chapters on descriptive statistics, hypothesis testing, regression analysis, and forecasting. The 24 case problems in the text provide students with the opportunity to analyze somewhat larger data sets and prepare managerial reports based on the results of their analysis.

# Features and Pedagogy

Authors Anderson, Sweeney, and Williams have continued many of the features that appeared in previous editions. Important ones for students are noted here.

## Statistics in Practice

Each chapter begins with a Statistics in Practice article that describes an application of the statistical methodology to be covered in the chapter.

## Methods Exercises and Applications Exercises

The end-of-section exercises are split into two parts, Methods and Applications. The Methods exercises require students to use the formulas and make the necessary computations. The Applications exercises require students to use the chapter material in real-world situations. Thus, students first focus on the computational "nuts and bolts" and then move on to the subtleties of statistical application and interpretation.

## Self-Test Exercises

Certain exercises are identified as self-test exercises. Completely worked-out solutions for those exercises are provided in Appendix D at the back of the book. Students can attempt the self-test exercises and immediately check the solution to evaluate their understanding of the concepts presented in the chapter.

## Margin Annotations and Notes and Comments

Margin annotations that highlight key points and provide additional insights for the students are a key feature of this text. These annotations are designed to provide emphasis and enhance understanding of the terms and concepts being presented in the text.

At the end of many sections, we provide Notes and Comments designed to give the student additional insights about the statistical methodology and its application. Notes and Comments include warnings about or limitations of the methodology, recommendations for application, brief descriptions of additional technical considerations, and other matters.

## Data Files Accompany the Text

Approximately 220 data files are available on the website that accompanies this text. The data sets are available in Excel 2010 format. WEBfile logos are used in the text to identify the data sets that are available on the website. Data sets for all case problems as well as data sets for larger exercises are included.

# Engage, Prepare, and Educate with Aplia™

Aplia™ provides an interactive, auto-graded solution that improves learning by increasing student effort and engagement. Aplia's original assignments ensure that students grasp the skills and concepts presented in the textbook.

- **Problem sets.** Students stay engaged in their coursework by regularly completing interactive problem sets. Aplia offers original, auto-graded problems—each question providing instant, detailed feedback.
- **Tutorials.** Students prepare themselves to learn course concepts by using interactive tutorials that help them overcome deficiencies in necessary prerequisites.
- **Assessment and grading.** Aplia provides real-time graphical reports on student participation, progress, and performance. These can easily be downloaded, saved, manipulated, printed, and then student grades can be imported into the current grading program.
- **Course management system.** Post announcements, upload course materials, email students, and manage your grade book in Aplia's easy-to-use course management system, which works independently or in conjunction with other course management systems.

# Get Choice and Flexibility with CengageNOW™

You envisioned it, we developed it. Designed *by* instructors and students *for* instructors and students, *CengageNOW for ASW's Essentials of Modern Business Statistics with Microsoft® Office Excel®* is the most reliable, flexible, and easy-to-use online suite of services and resources. With efficient and immediate paths to success, CengageNOW delivers the results you expect.

- **Personalized learning plans.** For every chapter, personalized learning plans allow students to focus on what they still need to learn and to select the activities that best match their learning styles (such as the relevant EasyStat tutorials, animations, step-by-step problem demonstrations, and text pages).
- **More study options.** Students can choose how they read the textbook—via integrated digital eBook or by reading the print version.

# Ancillary Learning Materials for Students

- Approximately 220 data sets are available on the website that accompanies this text. The webfiles are available in Excel 2010 format. WEBfile logos are used in the text to identify the data sets that are available on the website. Data sets for all case problems, as well as data sets for larger exercises, are included.
- **EasyStat Digital Tutor for Microsoft® Excel 2010.** These focused online tutorials will make it easier for students to learn how to use one of these well-known software products to perform statistical analysis. Each digital video demonstrates how the software can be used to perform a particular statistical procedure.

    The EasyStat videos for Excel 2010 will be available in early 2012. Students may purchase an online subscription for EasyStat Digital Tutor at www.cengagebrain.com.

# Acknowledgments

A special thanks goes to our associates from business and industry who supplied the Statistics in Practice features. We recognize them individually by a credit line in each of the articles. We are also indebted to our senior acquisitions editor Charles McCormick Jr.; our developmental editor Margaret Kubale; our content project manager Emily Nesheim; our Project Manager at MPS Content Services, Lynn Lustberg; our marketing manager Adam Marsh; our media editor, Chris Valentine; and others at South-Western Cengage Learning for their editorial counsel and support during the preparation of this text.

We would like to acknowledge the work of our reviewers, who provided comments and suggestions of ways to continue to improve our text. Thanks to:

James Bang, Virginia Military Institute

Robert J. Banis, University of Missouri–St. Louis

Timothy M. Bergquist, Northwest Christian College

Gary Black, University of Southern Indiana

William Bleuel, Pepperdine University

Derrick Boone, Wake Forest University

Lawrence J. Bos, Cornerstone University

Joseph Cavanaugh, Wright State University–Lake Campus

Sheng-Kai Chang, Wayne State University

Michael Clark, University of Baltimore

Robert D. Collins, Marquette University

Ivona Contardo, Stellenbosch University

Sean Eom, Southeast Missouri State University

Samo Ghosh, Albright College

Philip A. Gibbs, Washington & Lee University

Daniel L. Gilbert, Tennessee Wesleyan College

Michael Gorman, University of Dayton

Erick Hofacker, University of Wisconsin, River Falls

David Juriga, St. Louis Community College

William Kasperski, Madonna University

Kuldeep Kumar, Bond Business School

Tenpao Lee, Niagara University

Ying Liao, Meredith College

Daniel Light, Northwest State College

Ralph Maliszewski, Waynesburg University

Saverio Manago, Salem State University

Patricia A. Mullins, University of Wisconsin–Madison

Jack Muryn, Cardinal Stritch University

Anthony Narsing, Macon State College

Robert M. Nauss, University of Missouri–St. Louis

Elizabeth L. Rankin, Centenary College of Louisiana

Surekha Rao, Indiana University, Northwest

Jim Robison, Sonoma State University

Farhad Saboori, Albright College

Susan Sandblom, Scottsdale Community College

Ahmad Saranjam, Bridgewater State University

Jeff Sarbaum, University of North Carolina at Greensboro

Robert Scott, Monmouth University

Toni Somers, Wayne State University

Jordan H. Stein, University of Arizona

Bruce Thompson, Milwaukee School of Engineering

Ahmad Vessal, California State University, Northridge

Dave Vinson, Pellissippi State

Daniel B. Widdis, Naval Postgraduate School

Sheng-Ping Yang, Black Hills State University

We would like to recognize the following individuals, who have helped us in the past and continue to influence our writing.

Glen Archibald, University of Mississippi

Darl Bien, University of Denver

Thomas W. Bolland, Ohio University

Mike Bourke, Houston Baptist University

Peter Bryant, University of Colorado

Terri L. Byczkowski, University of Cincinnati

Robert Carver, Stonehill College

Ying Chien, University of Scranton

Robert Cochran, University of Wyoming

Murray Côté, University of Florida

David W. Cravens, Texas Christian University

Eddine Dahel, Monterey Institute of International Studies

Tom Dahlstrom, Eastern College

Terry Dielman, Texas Christian University

Joan Donohue, University of South Carolina

Jianjun Du, University of Houston–Victoria

Thomas J. Dudley, Pepperdine University

Swarna Dutt, University of West Georgia

Ronald Ehresman, Baldwin-Wallace College

Mohammed A. El-Saidi, Ferris State University

Robert Escudero, Pepperdine University

Stacy Everly, Delaware County Community College

Soheila Kahkashan Fardanesh, Towson University

Nicholas Farnum, California State University–Fullerton

Abe Feinberg, California State University, Northridge

Michael Ford, Rochester Institute of Technology

Phil Fry, Boise State University

V. Daniel Guide, Duquesne University

Paul Guy, California State University–Chico

Charles Harrington, University of Southern Indiana

Carl H. Hess, Marymount University

Woodrow W. Hughes, Jr., Converse College

Alan Humphrey, University of Rhode Island

Ann Hussein, Philadelphia College of Textiles and Science

Ben Isselhardt, Rochester Institute of Technology

Jeffery Jarrett, University of Rhode Island

Barry Kadets, Bryant College

Homayoun Khamooshi, George Washington University

Kenneth Klassen, California State University Northridge

David Krueger, St. Cloud State University

June Lapidus, Roosevelt University

Martin S. Levy, University of Cincinnati

Daniel M. Light, Northwest State College

Ka-sing Man, Georgetown University

Don Marx, University of Alaska, Anchorage

Tom McCullough, University of California–Berkeley

Timothy McDaniel, Buena Vista University

Mario Miranda, The Ohio State University

Barry J. Monk, Macon State College

Mitchell Muesham, Sam Houston State University

Richard O'Connell, Miami University of Ohio

Alan Olinsky, Bryant College

Lynne Pastor, Carnegie Mellon University

Von Roderick Plessner, Northwest State University

Robert D. Potter, University of Central Florida

Tom Pray, Rochester Institute of Technology

Harold Rahmlow, St. Joseph's University

Derrick Reagle, Fordham University

Avuthu Rami Reddy, University of Wisconsin–Platteville

Tom Ryan, Case Western Reserve University

Ahmad Saranjam, Bridgewater State College

Bill Seaver, University of Tennessee

Alan Smith, Robert Morris College

William Struning, Seton Hall University

Ahmad Syamil, Arkansas State University

David Tufte, University of New Orleans

Jack Vaughn, University of Texas–El Paso

Elizabeth Wark, Springfield College

Ari Wijetunga, Morehead State University

Nancy A. Williams, Loyola College in Maryland

J. E. Willis, Louisiana State University

Larry Woodward, University of Mary Hardin–Baylor

Mustafa Yilmaz, Northeastern University

*David R. Anderson*
*Dennis J. Sweeney*
*Thomas A. Williams*

# About the Authors

**David R. Anderson**   David R. Anderson is Professor Emeritus of Quantitative Analysis in the College of Business Administration at the University of Cincinnati. Born in Grand Forks, North Dakota, he earned his B.S., M.S., and Ph.D. degrees from Purdue University. Professor Anderson has served as Head of the Department of Quantitative Analysis and Operations Management and as Associate Dean of the College of Business Administration. In addition, he was the coordinator of the College's first Executive Program.

At the University of Cincinnati, Professor Anderson has taught introductory statistics for business students as well as graduate-level courses in regression analysis, multivariate analysis, and management science. He has also taught statistical courses at the Department of Labor in Washington, D.C. He has been honored with nominations and awards for excellence in teaching and excellence in service to student organizations.

Professor Anderson has coauthored 10 textbooks in the areas of statistics, management science, linear programming, and production and operations management. He is an active consultant in the field of sampling and statistical methods.

**Dennis J. Sweeney**   Dennis J. Sweeney is Professor Emeritus of Quantitative Analysis and Founder of the Center for Productivity Improvement at the University of Cincinnati. Born in Des Moines, Iowa, he earned a B.S.B.A. degree from Drake University and his M.B.A. and D.B.A. degrees from Indiana University, where he was an NDEA Fellow. During 1978–1979, Professor Sweeney worked in the management science group at Procter & Gamble; during 1981–1982, he was a visiting professor at Duke University. Professor Sweeney served as Head of the Department of Quantitative Analysis and as Associate Dean of the College of Business Administration at the University of Cincinnati.

Professor Sweeney has published more than 30 articles and monographs in the area of management science and statistics. The National Science Foundation, IBM, Procter & Gamble, Federated Department Stores, Kroger, and Cincinnati Gas & Electric have funded his research, which has been published in *Management Science*, *Operations Research*, *Mathematical Programming*, *Decision Sciences*, and other journals.

Professor Sweeney has coauthored 10 textbooks in the areas of statistics, management science, linear programming, and production and operations management.

**Thomas A. Williams**   Thomas A. Williams is Professor Emeritus of Management Science in the College of Business at Rochester Institute of Technology. Born in Elmira, New York, he earned his B.S. degree at Clarkson University. He did his graduate work at Rensselaer Polytechnic Institute, where he received his M.S. and Ph.D. degrees.

Before joining the College of Business at RIT, Professor Williams served for seven years as a faculty member in the College of Business Administration at the University of Cincinnati, where he developed the undergraduate program in Information Systems and then served as its coordinator. At RIT he was the first chairman of the Decision Sciences Department. He teaches courses in management science and statistics, as well as graduate courses in regression and decision analysis.

Professor Williams is the coauthor of 11 textbooks in the areas of management science, statistics, production and operations management, and mathematics. He has been a consultant for numerous *Fortune* 500 companies and has worked on projects ranging from the use of data analysis to the development of large-scale regression models.

# Essentials of Modern Business Statistics

## With Microsoft® Office Excel® 5e

# CHAPTER 1

# Data and Statistics

### *BLOOMBERG BUSINESSWEEK*\*
#### *NEW YORK, NEW YORK*

With a global circulation of more than 1 million, *Bloomberg Businessweek* is one of the most widely read business magazines in the world. Bloomberg's 1700 reporters in 145 service bureaus around the world enable *Bloomberg Businessweek* to deliver a variety of articles of interest to the global business and economic community. Along with feature articles on current topics, the magazine contains articles on international business, economic analysis, information processing, and science and technology. Information in the feature articles and the regular sections helps readers stay abreast of current developments and assess the impact of those developments on business and economic conditions.

Most issues of *Bloomberg Businessweek,* formerly *BusinessWeek,* provide an in-depth report on a topic of current interest. Often, the in-depth reports contain statistical facts and summaries that help the reader understand the business and economic information. For example, the cover story for the March 3, 2011 issue discussed the impact of businesses moving their most important work to cloud computing; the May 30, 2011 issue included a report on the crisis facing the U.S. Postal Service; and the August 1, 2011 issue contained a report on why the debt crisis is even worse than you think. In addition, *Bloomberg Businessweek* provides a variety of statistics about the state of the economy, including production indexes, stock prices, mutual funds, and interest rates.

*Bloomberg Businessweek* also uses statistics and statistical information in managing its own business. For example, an annual survey of subscribers helps the company learn about subscriber demographics, reading habits, likely purchases, lifestyles, and so on. *Bloomberg Businessweek* managers use statistical summaries from the survey to provide better services to subscribers and

*Bloomberg Businessweek* uses statistical facts and summaries in many of its articles.

advertisers. One recent North American subscriber survey indicated that 90% of *Bloomberg Businessweek* subscribers use a personal computer at home and that 64% of *Bloomberg Businessweek* subscribers are involved with computer purchases at work. Such statistics alert *Bloomberg Businessweek* managers to subscriber interest in articles about new developments in computers. The results of the subscriber survey are also made available to potential advertisers. The high percentage of subscribers using personal computers at home and the high percentage of subscribers involved with computer purchases at work would be an incentive for a computer manufacturer to consider advertising in *Bloomberg Businessweek.*

In this chapter, we discuss the types of data available for statistical analysis and describe how the data are obtained. We introduce descriptive statistics and statistical inference as ways of converting data into meaningful and easily interpreted statistical information.

---

\*The authors are indebted to Charlene Trentham, Research Manager, for providing this Statistics in Practice.

Frequently, we see the following types of statements in newspapers, magazines, and websites:

- The Dow Jones Industrial Average closed at 12,639 on May 6, 2011 (*Barron's,* May 9, 2011).
- A proposed interstate highway to Myrtle Beach would pay for itself in 4 years and bring about 22,000 jobs to South Carolina (*The Sun News,* May 13, 2011).

- The average amount spent on an airline ticket for business travel in the second quarter of 2011 was $447, up 9.3% over the same period last year (*The Wall Street Journal,* August 18, 2011).
- In January 2011, 586,271 people visited Hawaii by air, which was an increase of 12% over January, 2010 (Hawaii's Business Resource website, May 13, 2011).
- As of January, 2011, China held $1,155 billion of U.S. Treasuries. This was 26% of the U.S. Treasuries owned by foreigners (*Market Insights,* J.P. Morgan Asset Management, March 31, 2011).
- Last spring the Census Bureau found that 42% of American households had an income between $50,000 and $150,000 per year (*Ad Age* website, February 25, 2011).
- The percentage of adults who report using apps on their cell phones is 29% (*Delta Sky Magazine,* March, 2011).

The numerical facts in the preceding statements (12,639, 4, 22,000, $447, 9.3%, 586,271, 12%, $1,155 billion, 26%, 42%, $50,000, $150,000, 29%) are called statistics. In this usage, the term *statistics* refers to numerical facts such as index numbers, forecasts, percents, averages, and so on that help us understand a variety of business and economic situations. However, as you will see, the field, or subject, of statistics involves much more than numerical facts. In a broader sense, **statistics** is defined as the art and science of collecting, analyzing, presenting, and interpreting data. Particularly in business and economics, the information provided by collecting, analyzing, presenting, and interpreting data gives managers and decision makers a better understanding of the business and economic environment and thus enables them to make more informed and better decisions. In this text, we emphasize the use of statistics for business and economic decision making.

Chapter 1 begins with some illustrations of the applications of statistics in business and economics. In Section 1.2 we define the term *data* and introduce the concept of a data set. This section also introduces key terms such as *variables* and *observations,* discusses the difference between quantitative and categorical data, and illustrates the uses of cross-sectional and time series data. Section 1.3 discusses how data can be obtained from existing sources or through survey and experimental studies designed to obtain new data. The important role that the Internet now plays in obtaining data is also highlighted. The uses of data in developing descriptive statistics and in making statistical inferences are described in Sections 1.4 and 1.5. Section 1.6 discusses statistical analysis using Microsoft Excel, Section 1.7 provides an introduction to data mining, and Section 1.8 discusses ethical guidelines for statistical practice. A chapter-ending appendix includes an introduction to the add-in StatTools, which can be used to extend the statistical options for users of Microsoft Excel.

## (1.1)  Applications in Business and Economics

In today's global business and economic environment, anyone can access vast amounts of statistical information. The most successful managers and decision makers understand the information and know how to use it effectively. In this section, we provide examples that illustrate some of the uses of statistics in business and economics.

### Accounting

Public accounting firms use statistical sampling procedures when conducting audits for their clients. For instance, suppose an accounting firm wants to determine whether the amount of accounts receivable shown on a client's balance sheet fairly represents the actual amount of accounts receivable. Usually the large number of individual accounts receivable makes reviewing and validating every account too time-consuming and expensive. As common practice in such situations, the audit staff selects a subset of the accounts called a sample. After reviewing the accuracy of the sampled accounts, the auditors draw a conclusion as to whether the accounts receivable amount shown on the client's balance sheet is acceptable.

## Finance

Financial analysts use a variety of statistical information to guide their investment recommendations. In the case of stocks, the analysts review a variety of financial data, including price/earnings ratios and dividend yields. By comparing the information for an individual stock with information about the stock market averages, a financial analyst can begin to draw a conclusion as to whether an individual stock is over- or underpriced. For example, *The Wall Street Journal* (November 1, 2010) reported that the average dividend yield for the 30 stocks in the Dow Jones Industrial Average was 2.54%. Chevron showed a dividend yield of 3.5%. In this case, the statistical information on dividend yield indicates a higher dividend yield for Chevron than the average for the Dow Jones stocks. Therefore, a financial analyst might conclude that Chevron was underpriced. This and other information about Chevron would help the analyst make a buy, sell, or hold recommendation for the stock.

## Marketing

Electronic scanners at retail checkout counters collect data for a variety of marketing research applications. For example, data suppliers such as ACNielsen and Information Resources, Inc., purchase point-of-sale scanner data from grocery stores, process the data, and then sell statistical summaries of the data to manufacturers. Manufacturers spend hundreds of thousands of dollars per product category to obtain this type of scanner data. Manufacturers also purchase data and statistical summaries on promotional activities such as special pricing and the use of in-store displays. Brand managers can review the scanner statistics and the promotional activity statistics to gain a better understanding of the relationship between promotional activities and sales. Such analyses often prove helpful in establishing future marketing strategies for the various products.

## Production

Today's emphasis on quality makes quality control an important application of statistics in production. A variety of statistical quality control charts are used to monitor the output of a production process. In particular, an x-bar chart can be used to monitor the average output. Suppose, for example, that a machine fills cans with 12 ounces of a soft drink. Periodically, a production worker selects a sample of cans and computes the average number of ounces in the sample. This average, or x-bar value, is plotted on an x-bar chart. A plotted value above the chart's upper control limit indicates overfilling, and a plotted value below the chart's lower control limit indicates underfilling. The process is termed "in control" and allowed to continue as long as the plotted x-bar values fall between the chart's upper and lower control limits. Properly interpreted, an x-bar chart can help determine when adjustments are necessary to correct a production process.

## Economics

Economists frequently provide forecasts about the future of the economy or some aspect of it. They use a variety of statistical information in making such forecasts. For instance, in forecasting inflation rates, economists use statistical information on such indicators as the Producer

Price Index, the unemployment rate, and manufacturing capacity utilization. Often these statistical indicators are entered into computerized forecasting models that predict inflation rates.

Applications of statistics such as those described in this section are an integral part of this text. Such examples provide an overview of the breadth of statistical applications. To supplement these examples, practitioners in the fields of business and economics provided chapter-opening Statistics in Practice articles that introduce the material covered in each chapter. The Statistics in Practice applications show the importance of statistics in a wide variety of business and economic situations.

## 1.2   Data

**Data** are the facts and figures collected, analyzed, and summarized for presentation and interpretation. All the data collected in a particular study are referred to as the **data set** for the study. Table 1.1 shows a data set containing information for 25 mutual funds that are part of the *Morningstar Funds 500* for 2008. Morningstar is a company that tracks over 7000 mutual funds and prepares in-depth analyses of 2000 of these. Its recommendations are followed closely by financial analysts and individual investors.

**WEB** file

**Morningstar**

*Data sets such as Morningstar are available on the website for this text.*

**TABLE 1.1**   DATA SET FOR 25 MUTUAL FUNDS

| Fund Name | Fund Type | Net Asset Value ($) | 5-Year Average Return (%) | Expense Ratio (%) | Morningstar Rank |
|---|---|---|---|---|---|
| American Century Intl. Disc | IE | 14.37 | 30.53 | 1.41 | 3-Star |
| American Century Tax-Free Bond | FI | 10.73 | 3.34 | 0.49 | 4-Star |
| American Century Ultra | DE | 24.94 | 10.88 | 0.99 | 3-Star |
| Artisan Small Cap | DE | 16.92 | 15.67 | 1.18 | 3-Star |
| Brown Cap Small | DE | 35.73 | 15.85 | 1.20 | 4-Star |
| DFA U.S. Micro Cap | DE | 13.47 | 17.23 | 0.53 | 3-Star |
| Fidelity Contrafund | DE | 73.11 | 17.99 | 0.89 | 5-Star |
| Fidelity Overseas | IE | 48.39 | 23.46 | 0.90 | 4-Star |
| Fidelity Sel Electronics | DE | 45.60 | 13.50 | 0.89 | 3-Star |
| Fidelity Sh-Term Bond | FI | 8.60 | 2.76 | 0.45 | 3-Star |
| Gabelli Asset AAA | DE | 49.81 | 16.70 | 1.36 | 4-Star |
| Kalmar Gr Val Sm Cp | DE | 15.30 | 15.31 | 1.32 | 3-Star |
| Marsico 21st Century | DE | 17.44 | 15.16 | 1.31 | 5-Star |
| Mathews Pacific Tiger | IE | 27.86 | 32.70 | 1.16 | 3-Star |
| Oakmark I | DE | 40.37 | 9.51 | 1.05 | 2-Star |
| PIMCO Emerg Mkts Bd D | FI | 10.68 | 13.57 | 1.25 | 3-Star |
| RS Value A | DE | 26.27 | 23.68 | 1.36 | 4-Star |
| T. Rowe Price Latin Am. | IE | 53.89 | 51.10 | 1.24 | 4-Star |
| T. Rowe Price Mid Val | DE | 22.46 | 16.91 | 0.80 | 4-Star |
| Thornburg Value A | DE | 37.53 | 15.46 | 1.27 | 4-Star |
| USAA Income | FI | 12.10 | 4.31 | 0.62 | 3-Star |
| Vanguard Equity-Inc | DE | 24.42 | 13.41 | 0.29 | 4-Star |
| Vanguard Sht-Tm TE | FI | 15.68 | 2.37 | 0.16 | 3-Star |
| Vanguard Sm Cp Idx | DE | 32.58 | 17.01 | 0.23 | 3-Star |
| Wasatch Sm Cp Growth | DE | 35.41 | 13.98 | 1.19 | 4-Star |

*Source: Morningstar Funds 500* (2008).

## Elements, Variables, and Observations

**Elements** are the entities on which data are collected. For the data set in Table 1.1 each individual mutual fund is an element: the element names appear in the first column. With 25 mutual funds, the data set contains 25 elements.

A **variable** is a characteristic of interest for the elements. The data set in Table 1.1 includes the following five variables:

- *Fund Type:* The type of mutual fund, labeled DE (Domestic Equity), IE (International Equity), and FI (Fixed Income)
- *Net Asset Value ($):* The closing price per share on December 31, 2007
- *5-Year Average Return (%):* The average annual return for the fund over the past 5 years
- *Expense Ratio:* The percentage of assets deducted each fiscal year for fund expenses
- *Morningstar Rank:* The overall risk-adjusted star rating for each fund; Morningstar ranks go from a low of 1-Star to a high of 5-Stars

Measurements collected on each variable for every element in a study provide the data. The set of measurements obtained for a particular element is called an **observation**. Referring to Table 1.1, we see that the set of measurements for the first observation (American Century Intl. Disc) is IE, 14.37, 30.53, 1.41, and 3-Star. The set of measurements for the second observation (American Century Tax-Free Bond) is FI, 10.73, 3.34, 0.49, and 4-Star, and so on. A data set with 25 elements contains 25 observations.

## Scales of Measurement

Data collection requires one of the following scales of measurement: nominal, ordinal, interval, or ratio. The scale of measurement determines the amount of information contained in the data and indicates the most appropriate data summarization and statistical analyses.

When the data for a variable consist of labels or names used to identify an attribute of the element, the scale of measurement is considered a **nominal scale**. For example, referring to the data in Table 1.1, we see that the scale of measurement for the Fund Type variable is nominal because DE, IE, and FI are labels used to identify the category or type of fund. In cases where the scale of measurement is nominal, a numerical code as well as nonnumerical labels may be used. For example, to facilitate data collection and to prepare the data for entry into a computer database, we might use a numerical code by letting 1 denote Domestic Equity, 2 denote International Equity, and 3 denote Fixed Income. In this case the numerical values 1, 2, and 3 identify the category of fund. The scale of measurement is nominal even though the data appear as numerical values.

The scale of measurement for a variable is called an **ordinal scale** if the data exhibit the properties of nominal data and the order or rank of the data is meaningful. For example, Eastside Automotive sends customers a questionnaire designed to obtain data on the quality of its automotive repair service. Each customer provides a repair service rating of excellent, good, or poor. Because the data obtained are the labels—excellent, good, or poor—the data have the properties of nominal data. In addition, the data can be ranked, or ordered, with respect to the service quality. Data recorded as excellent indicate the best service, followed by good and then poor. Thus, the scale of measurement is ordinal. As another example, note that the Morningstar Rank for the data in Table 1.1 is ordinal data. It provides a rank from 1 to 5-Stars based on Morningstar's assessment of the fund's risk-adjusted return. Ordinal data can also be provided using a numerical code, such as your class rank in school.

The scale of measurement for a variable is an **interval scale** if the data have all the properties of ordinal data and the interval between values is expressed in terms of a fixed unit of measure. Interval data are always numerical. College admission SAT scores are an example of interval-scaled data. For example, three students with SAT math scores of 620, 550, and 470 can be ranked or ordered in terms of best performance to poorest performance in math. In addition, the differences between the scores are meaningful. For instance, student 1 scored $620 - 550 = 70$ points more than student 2, while student 2 scored $550 - 470 = 80$ points more than student 3.

The scale of measurement for a variable is a **ratio scale** if the data have all the properties of interval data and the ratio of two values is meaningful. Variables such as distance, height, weight, and time use the ratio scale of measurement. This scale requires that a zero value be included to indicate that nothing exists for the variable at the zero point. For example, consider the cost of an automobile. A zero value for the cost would indicate that the automobile has no cost and is free. In addition, if we compare the cost of $30,000 for one automobile to the cost of $15,000 for a second automobile, the ratio property shows that the first automobile is $30,000/$15,000 = 2 times, or twice, the cost of the second automobile.

## Categorical and Quantitative Data

Data can be classified as either categorical or quantitative. Data that can be grouped by specific categories are referred to as **categorical data**. Categorical data use either the nominal or ordinal scale of measurement. Data that use numerical values to indicate how much or how many are referred to as **quantitative data**. Quantitative data are obtained using either the interval or ratio scale of measurement.

*The statistical method appropriate for summarizing data depends on whether the data are categorical or quantitative.*

A **categorical variable** is a variable with categorical data, and a **quantitative variable** is a variable with quantitative data. The statistical analysis appropriate for a particular variable depends on whether the variable is categorical or quantitative. If the variable is categorical, the statistical analysis is limited. We can summarize categorical data by counting the number of observations in each category or by computing the proportion of the observations in each category. However, even when the categorical data are identified by a numerical code, arithmetic operations such as addition, subtraction, multiplication, and division do not provide meaningful results. Section 2.1 discusses ways for summarizing categorical data.

Arithmetic operations provide meaningful results for quantitative variables. For example, quantitative data may be added and then divided by the number of observations to compute the average value. This average is usually meaningful and easily interpreted. In general, more alternatives for statistical analysis are possible when data are quantitative. Section 2.2 and Chapter 3 provide ways of summarizing quantitative data.

## Cross-Sectional and Time Series Data

For purposes of statistical analysis, distinguishing between cross-sectional data and time series data is important. **Cross-sectional data** are data collected at the same or approximately the same point in time. The data in Table 1.1 are cross-sectional because they describe the five variables for the 25 mutual funds at the same point in time. **Time series data** are data collected over several time periods. For example, the time series in Figure 1.1 shows the U.S. average price per gallon of regular gasoline between January 2008 and May 2011. Note that gasoline prices increased during the first half of 2008, reaching a high of $4.06 per gallon in July. However, prices decreased rapidly during the second half of 2008, reaching a low of $1.69 per gallon in December 2008. Throughout 2009 and

**FIGURE 1.1**   U.S. AVERAGE PRICE PER GALLON FOR REGULAR GASOLINE

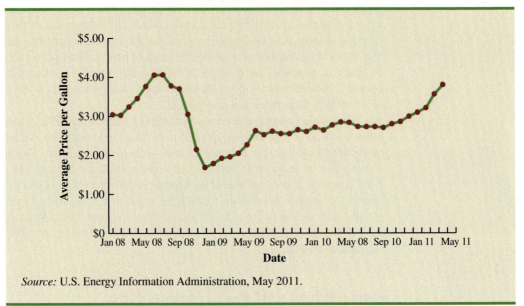

*Source:* U.S. Energy Information Administration, May 2011.

the first five months of 2010, prices generally increased before stabilizing at a price of approximately $2.75 per gallon. Prices began to rise rapidly in the fourth quarter of 2010 and first quarter of 2011.

Graphs of time series data are frequently found in business and economic publications. Such graphs help analysts understand what happened in the past, identify any trends over time, and project future levels for the time series. The graphs of time series data can take on a variety of forms, as shown in Figure 1.2. With a little study, these graphs are usually easy to understand and interpret.

For example, Panel (A) in Figure 1.2 is a graph that shows the Dow Jones Industrial Average Index from 1998 to 2011. In April 1997, the popular stock market index was near 7000. Over the next 10 years the index rose to over 14,000 in July 2007. However, notice the sharp decline in the time series after the all-time high in 2007. By March 2009, poor economic conditions had caused the Dow Jones Industrial Average Index to return to the 7000 level of 1997. This was a scary and discouraging period for investors. By February 2011, the index was showing a recovery by reaching the 12,000 level.

The graph in Panel (B) shows the net income of McDonald's Inc. from 2004 to 2010. The declining economic conditions in 2008 and 2009 were actually beneficial to McDonald's as the company's net income rose to an all-time high. The growth in McDonald's net income showed that the company was thriving during the economic downturn as people were cutting back on the more expensive sit-down restaurants and seeking less-expensive alternatives offered by McDonald's.

Panel (C) shows the time series for the occupancy rate of hotels in South Florida over a one-year period. The highest occupancy rates, 95% and 98%, occur during the months of February and March when the climate of South Florida is attractive to tourists. In fact, January to April of each year is typically the high-occupancy season for South Florida hotels. On the other hand, note the low occupancy rates during the months of August to October, with the lowest occupancy rate of 50% occurring in September. High temperatures and the hurricane season are the primary reasons for the drop in hotel occupancy during this period.

**FIGURE 1.2**    A VARIETY OF GRAPHS OF TIME SERIES DATA

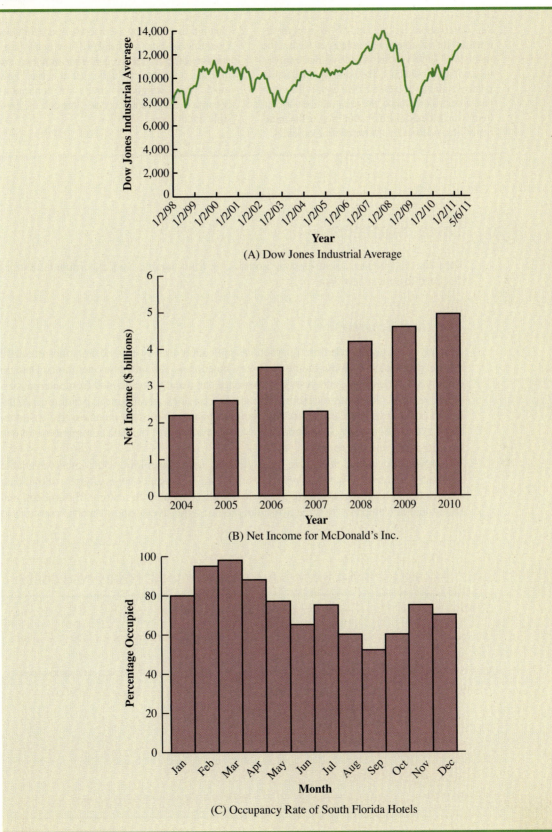

(A) Dow Jones Industrial Average

(B) Net Income for McDonald's Inc.

(C) Occupancy Rate of South Florida Hotels

1. An observation is the set of measurements obtained for each element in a data set. Hence, the number of observations is always the same as the number of elements. The number of measurements obtained for each element equals the number of variables. Hence, the total number of data items can be determined by multiplying the number of observations by the number of variables.

2. Quantitative data may be discrete or continuous. Quantitative data that measure how many (e.g., number of calls received in five minutes) are discrete. Quantitative data that measure how much (e.g., weight or time) are continuous because no separation occurs between the possible data values.

# 1.3  Data Sources

Data can be obtained from existing sources or from surveys and experimental studies designed to collect new data.

## Existing Sources

In some cases, data needed for a particular application already exist. Companies maintain a variety of databases about their employees, customers, and business operations. Data on employee salaries, ages, and years of experience can usually be obtained from internal personnel records. Other internal records contain data on sales, advertising expenditures, distribution costs, inventory levels, and production quantities. Most companies also maintain detailed data about their customers. Table 1.2 shows some of the data commonly available from internal company records.

Organizations that specialize in collecting and maintaining data make available substantial amounts of business and economic data. Companies access these external data sources through leasing arrangements or by purchase. Dun & Bradstreet, Bloomberg, and Dow Jones & Company are three firms that provide extensive business database services to

**TABLE 1.2**    EXAMPLES OF DATA AVAILABLE FROM INTERNAL COMPANY RECORDS

| Source | Some of the Data Typically Available |
|---|---|
| Employee records | Name, address, social security number, salary, number of vacation days, number of sick days, and bonus |
| Production records | Part or product number, quantity produced, direct labor cost, and materials cost |
| Inventory records | Part or product number, number of units on hand, reorder level, economic order quantity, and discount schedule |
| Sales records | Product number, sales volume, sales volume by region, and sales volume by customer type |
| Credit records | Customer name, address, phone number, credit limit, and accounts receivable balance |
| Customer profile | Age, gender, income level, household size, address, and preferences |

clients. ACNielsen and Information Resources, Inc., built successful businesses collecting and processing data that they sell to advertisers and product manufacturers.

Data are also available from a variety of industry associations and special interest organizations. The Travel Industry Association of America maintains travel-related information such as the number of tourists and travel expenditures by states. Such data would be of interest to firms and individuals in the travel industry. The Graduate Management Admission Council maintains data on test scores, student characteristics, and graduate management education programs. Most of the data from these types of sources are available to qualified users at a modest cost.

The Internet continues to grow as an important source of data and statistical information. Almost all companies maintain websites that provide general information about the company as well as data on sales, number of employees, number of products, product prices, and product specifications. In addition, a number of companies now specialize in making information available over the Internet. As a result, one can obtain access to stock quotes, meal prices at restaurants, salary data, and an almost infinite variety of information.

Government agencies are another important source of existing data. For instance, the U.S. Department of Labor maintains considerable data on employment rates, wage rates, size of the labor force, and union membership. Table 1.3 lists selected governmental agencies and some of the data they provide. Most government agencies that collect and process data also make the results available through a website. Figure 1.3 shows the homepage for the U.S. Census Bureau website.

## Statistical Studies

*The largest experimental statistical study ever conducted is believed to be the 1954 Public Health Service experiment for the Salk polio vaccine. Nearly 2 million children in grades 1, 2, and 3 were selected from throughout the United States.*

Sometimes the data needed for a particular application are not available through existing sources. In such cases, the data can often be obtained by conducting a statistical study. Statistical studies can be classified as either *experimental* or *observational*.

In an experimental study, a variable of interest is first identified. Then one or more other variables are identified and controlled so that data can be obtained about how they influence the variable of interest. For example, a pharmaceutical firm might be interested in conducting an experiment to learn about how a new drug affects blood pressure. Blood pressure is the variable of interest in the study. The dosage level of the new drug is another variable that is hoped to have a causal effect on blood pressure. To obtain data about the effect of the

**TABLE 1.3**  EXAMPLES OF DATA AVAILABLE FROM SELECTED GOVERNMENT AGENCIES

| Government Agency | Some of the Data Available |
|---|---|
| Census Bureau | Population data, number of households, and household income |
| Federal Reserve Board | Data on the money supply, installment credit, exchange rates, and discount rates |
| Office of Management and Budget | Data on revenue, expenditures, and debt of the federal government |
| Department of Commerce | Data on business activity, value of shipments by industry, level of profits by industry, and growing and declining industries |
| Bureau of Labor Statistics | Consumer spending, hourly earnings, unemployment rate, safety records, and international statistics |

**FIGURE 1.3**   U.S. CENSUS BUREAU HOMEPAGE

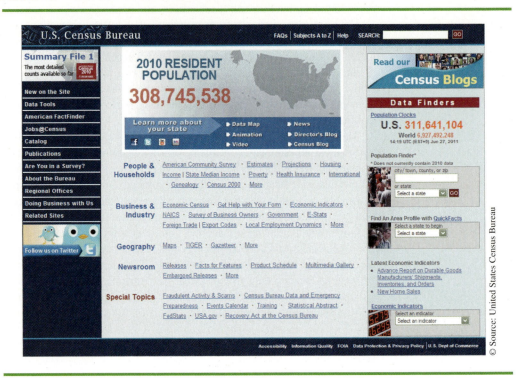

new drug, researchers select a sample of individuals. The dosage level of the new drug is controlled, as different groups of individuals are given different dosage levels. "Before" and "after" data on blood pressure are collected for each group. Statistical analysis of the experimental data can help determine how the new drug affects blood pressure.

Nonexperimental, or observational, statistical studies make no attempt to control the variables that are thought to influence the variable of interest. A survey is perhaps the most common type of observational study. For instance, in a personal interview survey, research questions are first identified. Then a questionnaire is designed and administered to a sample of individuals. Some restaurants use observational studies to obtain data about customer opinions on the quality of food, quality of service, atmosphere, and so on. A customer opinion questionnaire used by Chops City Grill in Naples, Florida, is shown in Figure 1.4. Note that the customers who fill out the questionnaire are asked to provide ratings for 12 variables, including overall experience, greeting by hostess, manager (table visit), overall service, and so on. The response categories of excellent, good, average, fair, and poor provide categorical data that enable Chops City Grill management to maintain high standards for the restaurant's food and service.

Anyone wanting to use data and statistical analysis as aids to decision making must be aware of the time and cost required to obtain the data. The use of existing data sources is desirable when data must be obtained in a relatively short period of time. If important data are not readily available from an existing source, the additional time and cost involved in obtaining the data must be taken into account. In all cases, the decision maker should consider the contribution of the statistical analysis to the decision-making process. The cost of data acquisition and the subsequent statistical analysis should not exceed the savings generated by using the information to make a better decision.

*Studies of smokers and nonsmokers are observational studies because researchers do not determine or control who will smoke and who will not smoke.*

**FIGURE 1.4** CUSTOMER OPINION QUESTIONNAIRE USED BY CHOPS CITY GRILL RESTAURANT IN NAPLES, FLORIDA

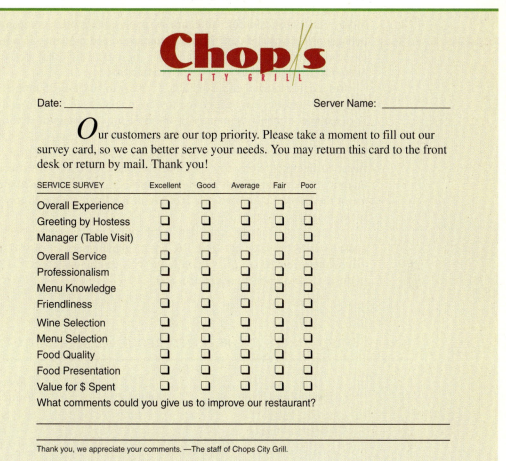

## Data Acquisition Errors

Managers should always be aware of the possibility of data errors in statistical studies. Using erroneous data can be worse than not using any data at all. An error in data acquisition occurs whenever the data value obtained is not equal to the true or actual value that would be obtained with a correct procedure. Such errors can occur in a number of ways. For example, an interviewer might make a recording error, such as a transposition in writing the age of a 24-year-old person as 42, or the person answering an interview question might misinterpret the question and provide an incorrect response.

Experienced data analysts take great care in collecting and recording data to ensure that errors are not made. Special procedures can be used to check for internal consistency of the data. For instance, such procedures would indicate that the analyst should review the accuracy of data for a respondent shown to be 22 years of age but reporting 20 years of work experience. Data analysts also review data with unusually large and small values, called outliers, which are candidates for possible data errors. In Chapter 3 we present some of the methods statisticians use to identify outliers.

Errors often occur during data acquisition. Blindly using any data that happen to be available or using data that were acquired with little care can result in misleading information and bad decisions. Thus, taking steps to acquire accurate data can help ensure reliable and valuable decision-making information.

# 1.4  Descriptive Statistics

Most of the statistical information in newspapers, magazines, company reports, and other publications consists of data that are summarized and presented in a form that is easy for the reader to understand. Such summaries of data, which may be tabular, graphical, or numerical, are referred to as **descriptive statistics**.

Refer again to the data set in Table 1.1 showing data on 25 mutual funds. Methods of descriptive statistics can be used to provide summaries of the information in this data set. For example, a tabular summary of the data for the categorical variable Fund Type is shown in Table 1.4. A graphical summary of the same data, called a bar chart, is shown in Figure 1.5. These types of tabular and graphical summaries generally make the data easier to interpret. Referring to Table 1.4 and Figure 1.5, we can see easily that the majority of the mutual funds are of the Domestic Equity type. On a percentage basis, 64% are of the Domestic Equity type, 16% are of the International Equity type, and 20% are of the Fixed Income type.

A graphical summary of the data for the quantitative variable Net Asset Value, called a histogram, is provided in Figure 1.6. The histogram makes it easy to see that the net asset values range from $0 to $75, with the highest concentration between $15 and $30. Only one of the net asset values is greater than $60.

**TABLE 1.4**   FREQUENCIES AND PERCENT FREQUENCIES FOR MUTUAL FUND TYPE

| Mutual Fund Type | Frequency | Percent Frequency |
|---|---|---|
| Domestic Equity | 16 | 64 |
| International Equity | 4 | 16 |
| Fixed Income | 5 | 20 |
| **Totals** | **25** | **100** |

**FIGURE 1.5**   BAR CHART FOR MUTUAL FUND TYPE

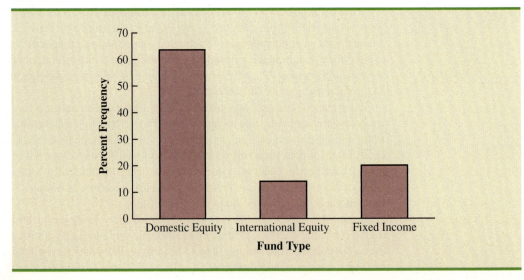

**FIGURE 1.6**   HISTOGRAM OF NET ASSET VALUE FOR 25 MUTUAL FUNDS

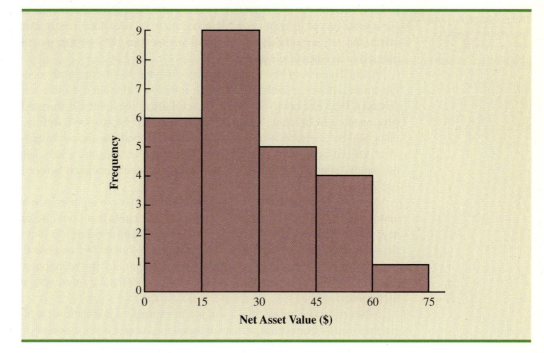

In addition to tabular and graphical displays, numerical descriptive statistics are used to summarize data. The most common numerical descriptive statistic is the average, or mean. Using the data on 5-Year Average Return for the mutual funds in Table 1.1, we can compute the average by adding the returns for all 25 mutual funds and dividing the sum by 25. Doing so provides a 5-year average return of 16.50%. This average demonstrates a measure of the central tendency, or central location, of the data for that variable.

There is a great deal of interest in effective methods for developing and presenting descriptive statistics. Chapters 2 and 3 devote attention to the tabular, graphical, and numerical methods of descriptive statistics.

## 1.5   Statistical Inference

Many situations require information about a large group of elements (individuals, companies, voters, households, products, customers, and so on). But, because of time, cost, and other considerations, data can be collected from only a small portion of the group. The larger group of elements in a particular study is called the **population**, and the smaller group is called the **sample**. Formally, we use the following definitions.

POPULATION

A population is the set of all elements of interest in a particular study.

SAMPLE

A sample is a subset of the population.

*The U.S. government conducts a census every 10 years. Market research firms conduct sample surveys every day.*

The process of conducting a survey to collect data for the entire population is called a **census**. The process of conducting a survey to collect data for a sample is called a **sample survey**. As one of its major contributions, statistics uses data from a sample to make estimates and test hypotheses about the characteristics of a population through a process referred to as **statistical inference**.

As an example of statistical inference, let us consider the study conducted by Norris Electronics. Norris manufactures a high-intensity lightbulb used in a variety of electrical products. In an attempt to increase the useful life of the lightbulb, the product design group developed a new lightbulb filament. In this case, the population is defined as all lightbulbs that could be produced with the new filament. To evaluate the advantages of the new filament, 200 bulbs with the new filament were manufactured and tested. Data collected from this sample showed the number of hours each lightbulb operated before filament burnout. See Table 1.5.

Suppose Norris wants to use the sample data to make an inference about the average hours of useful life for the population of all lightbulbs that could be produced with the new filament. Adding the 200 values in Table 1.5 and dividing the total by 200 provides the sample average lifetime for the lightbulbs: 76 hours. We can use this sample result to estimate that the average lifetime for the lightbulbs in the population is 76 hours. Figure 1.7 provides a graphical summary of the statistical inference process for Norris Electronics.

Whenever statisticians use a sample to estimate a population characteristic of interest, they usually provide a statement of the quality, or precision, associated with the estimate. For the Norris example, the statistician might state that the point estimate of the average lifetime for the population of new lightbulbs is 76 hours with a margin of error of $\pm 4$ hours. Thus, an interval estimate of the average lifetime for all lightbulbs produced with the new

**TABLE 1.5**   HOURS UNTIL BURNOUT FOR A SAMPLE OF 200 LIGHTBULBS
FOR THE NORRIS ELECTRONICS EXAMPLE

Norris

| | | | | | | | | | |
|---|---|---|---|---|---|---|---|---|---|
| 107 | 73 | 68 | 97 | 76 | 79 | 94 | 59 | 98 | 57 |
| 54 | 65 | 71 | 70 | 84 | 88 | 62 | 61 | 79 | 98 |
| 66 | 62 | 79 | 86 | 68 | 74 | 61 | 82 | 65 | 98 |
| 62 | 116 | 65 | 88 | 64 | 79 | 78 | 79 | 77 | 86 |
| 74 | 85 | 73 | 80 | 68 | 78 | 89 | 72 | 58 | 69 |
| 92 | 78 | 88 | 77 | 103 | 88 | 63 | 68 | 88 | 81 |
| 75 | 90 | 62 | 89 | 71 | 71 | 74 | 70 | 74 | 70 |
| 65 | 81 | 75 | 62 | 94 | 71 | 85 | 84 | 83 | 63 |
| 81 | 62 | 79 | 83 | 93 | 61 | 65 | 62 | 92 | 65 |
| 83 | 70 | 70 | 81 | 77 | 72 | 84 | 67 | 59 | 58 |
| 78 | 66 | 66 | 94 | 77 | 63 | 66 | 75 | 68 | 76 |
| 90 | 78 | 71 | 101 | 78 | 43 | 59 | 67 | 61 | 71 |
| 96 | 75 | 64 | 76 | 72 | 77 | 74 | 65 | 82 | 86 |
| 66 | 86 | 96 | 89 | 81 | 71 | 85 | 99 | 59 | 92 |
| 68 | 72 | 77 | 60 | 87 | 84 | 75 | 77 | 51 | 45 |
| 85 | 67 | 87 | 80 | 84 | 93 | 69 | 76 | 89 | 75 |
| 83 | 68 | 72 | 67 | 92 | 89 | 82 | 96 | 77 | 102 |
| 74 | 91 | 76 | 83 | 66 | 68 | 61 | 73 | 72 | 76 |
| 73 | 77 | 79 | 94 | 63 | 59 | 62 | 71 | 81 | 65 |
| 73 | 63 | 63 | 89 | 82 | 64 | 85 | 92 | 64 | 73 |

**FIGURE 1.7**   THE PROCESS OF STATISTICAL INFERENCE FOR THE NORRIS
ELECTRONICS EXAMPLE

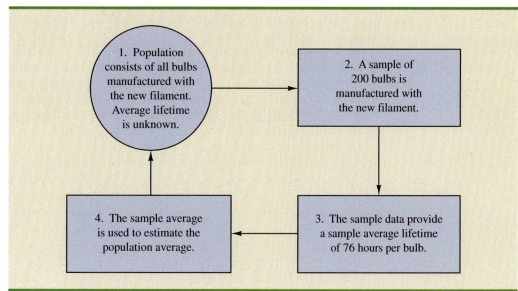

filament is 72 hours to 80 hours. The statistician can also state how confident he or she is
that the interval from 72 hours to 80 hours contains the population average.

## 1.6   Statistical Analysis Using Microsoft Excel

Because statistical analysis typically involves working with large amounts of data, computer
software is frequently used to conduct the analysis. Often the data to be analyzed reside in a
spreadsheet. Given the data management, data analysis, and presentation capabilities of
modern spreadsheet packages, it is now possible to conduct statistical analyses using them.
In this book we show how statistical analysis can be performed using Microsoft Excel. In
selected cases where Excel does not contain statistical analysis functions or data analysis
tools that can be used to perform a statistical procedure discussed in the text, we have included
chapter appendixes that show how to use StatTools, an add-in for Excel that provides an
extended range of statistical and graphical options. The appendix to Chapter 1 provides an
introduction to StatTools.

We want to emphasize that this book is about statistics; it is not a book about
spreadsheets. Thus, our focus is on showing the appropriate statistical procedures for
collecting, analyzing, presenting, and interpreting data. Because Excel is widely available
in business organizations, you can expect to put the knowledge gained here to use in the
setting where you currently, or soon will, work. If, in the process of studying this material,
you become more proficient in Excel, so much the better.

We begin most sections with an application scenario in which a statistical procedure is
useful. After showing what the statistical procedure is and how it is used, we turn to showing how to implement the procedure using Excel. Thus, you should gain an understanding
of what the procedure is, the situations in which it is useful, and how to implement it using
the capabilities of Excel.

## Data Sets and Excel Worksheets

Data sets are organized in Excel worksheets in much the same way as the data set for the 25 mutual fund companies that appears in Table 1.1. Figure 1.8 shows an Excel worksheet for that data set. Note that row 1 and column A contain labels. Cells B1:F1 contain the variable names and cells A2:A26 contain the observation names. Cells B2:F26 contain the data that were collected. A purple screen highlights the data. The data are the focus of the statistical analysis. Except for the headings in row 1, each row in the worksheet corresponds to an observation and each column corresponds to a variable. For instance, row 2 of the worksheet contains the data for the first observation, American Century Intl. Disc; row 3 contains the data for the second observation, American Century Tax-Free Bond; and so on. Thus, the names in column A provide a convenient way to refer to each of the 25 observations in the study. Note that column B of the worksheet contains the data for the variable Fund Type, column C contains the data for the variable Net Asset Value ($), and so on.

Suppose now that we want to use Excel to analyze the Norris Electronics data shown in Table 1.5. The data in Table 1.5 are organized into 10 columns with 20 data values in

**FIGURE 1.8**   EXCEL WORKSHEET FOR THE 25 MUTUAL FUNDS DATA SET

| | Fund Name | Fund Type | Net Asset Value ($) | 5 Year Average Return (%) | Expense Ratio (%) | Morningstar Rank |
|---|---|---|---|---|---|---|
| 2 | American Century Intl. Disc | IE | 14.37 | 30.53 | 1.41 | 3-Star |
| 3 | American Century Tax-Free Bond | FI | 10.73 | 3.34 | 0.49 | 4-Star |
| 4 | American Century Ultra | DE | 24.94 | 10.88 | 0.99 | 3-Star |
| 5 | Artisan Small Cap | DE | 16.92 | 15.67 | 1.18 | 3-Star |
| 6 | Brown Cap Small | DE | 35.73 | 15.85 | 1.20 | 4-Star |
| 7 | DFA U.S. Micro Cap | DE | 13.47 | 17.23 | 0.53 | 3-Star |
| 8 | Fidelity Contrafund | DE | 73.11 | 17.99 | 0.89 | 5-Star |
| 9 | Fidelity Overseas | IE | 48.39 | 23.46 | 0.90 | 4-Star |
| 10 | Fidelity Sel Electronics | DE | 45.60 | 13.50 | 0.89 | 3-Star |
| 11 | Fidelity Sh-Term Bond | FI | 8.60 | 2.76 | 0.45 | 3-Star |
| 12 | Gabelli Asset AAA | DE | 49.81 | 16.70 | 1.36 | 4-Star |
| 13 | Kalmar Gr Val Sm Cp | DE | 15.30 | 15.31 | 1.32 | 3-Star |
| 14 | Marsico 21st Century | DE | 17.44 | 15.16 | 1.31 | 5-Star |
| 15 | Mathews Pacific Tiger | IE | 27.86 | 32.70 | 1.16 | 3-Star |
| 16 | Oakmark I | DE | 40.37 | 9.51 | 1.05 | 2-Star |
| 17 | PIMCO Emerg Mkts Bd D | FI | 10.68 | 13.57 | 1.25 | 3-Star |
| 18 | RS Value A | DE | 26.27 | 23.68 | 1.36 | 4-Star |
| 19 | T. Rowe Price Latin Am. | IE | 53.89 | 51.10 | 1.24 | 4-Star |
| 20 | T. Rowe Price Mid Val | DE | 22.46 | 16.91 | 0.80 | 4-Star |
| 21 | Thornburg Value A | DE | 37.53 | 15.46 | 1.27 | 4-Star |
| 22 | USAA Income | FI | 12.10 | 4.31 | 0.62 | 3-Star |
| 23 | Vanguard Equity-Inc | DE | 24.42 | 13.41 | 0.29 | 4-Star |
| 24 | Vanguard Sht-Tm TE | FI | 15.68 | 2.37 | 0.16 | 3-Star |
| 25 | Vanguard Sm Cp Idx | DE | 32.58 | 17.01 | 0.23 | 3-Star |
| 26 | Wasatch Sm Cp Growth | DE | 35.41 | 13.98 | 1.19 | 4-Star |

**FIGURE 1.9** EXCEL WORKSHEET FOR THE NORRIS ELECTRONICS DATA SET

*Note: Rows 7–195 are hidden.*

each column so that the data would fit nicely on a single page of the text. Even though the table has several columns, it shows data for only one variable (hours until burnout). In statistical worksheets, it is customary to put all the data for each variable in a single column. Refer to the Excel worksheet shown in Figure 1.9. To make it easier to identify each observation in the data set, we entered the heading Observation into cell A1 and the numbers 1–200 into cells A2:A201. The heading Hours until Burnout has been entered into cell B1, and the data for the 200 observations have been entered into cells B2:B201. Displaying a worksheet with this many rows on a single page of a textbook is not practical. In such cases we will hide selected rows to conserve space. In the Excel worksheet for the Norris Electronics problem, we have hidden rows 7 through 195 (observations 6 through 194) to conserve space.[1]

## Using Excel for Statistical Analysis

In this text, we are careful to separate the discussion of a statistical procedure from the discussion of using Excel to implement the procedure. The material that discusses the use of Excel will usually be set apart in sections with headings such as Using Excel's COUNTIF Function to Construct a Frequency Distribution, Using Excel's Chart Tools to Construct Bar Charts and Pie Charts, and so on. In using Excel for statistical analysis, three tasks may be needed: Enter Data; Enter Functions and Formulas; and Apply Tools.

**Enter Data:** Select cell locations for the data and enter the data along with appropriate descriptive labels.

**Enter Functions and Formulas:** Select cell locations, enter Excel functions and formulas, and provide descriptive material to identify the results.

**Apply Tools:** Use Excel's tools for data management, data analysis, and presentation.

---

[1]To hide rows 7 through 195 in the Excel worksheet, first select rows 7 through 195. Then, right-click and choose the Hide option. To redisplay rows 7 through 195, just select rows 6 and 196, right-click, and select the Unhide option.

Our approach will be to describe how these tasks are performed each time we use Excel to implement a statistical procedure. It will always be necessary to enter data. But, depending on the complexity of the statistical analysis, only one of the last two tasks may be needed.

To illustrate how the discussion of using Excel will appear throughout the book, we will show how to use Excel's AVERAGE function to compute the average lifetime for the 200 burnout times in Table 1.5. Refer to Figure 1.10 as we describe the tasks involved. The worksheet shown in the foreground of Figure 1.10 displays the data for the problem and shows the results of the analysis. It is called a value worksheet. The worksheet shown in the background displays the Excel formula used to compute the average lifetime and is called the formula worksheet. A purple screen is used to highlight the data in both worksheets. In addition, a green screen is used to highlight functions and formulas in the formula worksheet and the corresponding results in the value worksheet.

**Enter Data:**   The labels Observation and Hours until Burnout are entered into cells A1:B1. The numbers 1–200 are entered into cells A2:A201 to identify each of the observations, and the data showing the hours until burnout for each observation are entered into cells B2:B201 of the worksheet.

**Enter Functions and Formulas:**   Excel's AVERAGE function can be used to compute the average lifetime for the 200 lightbulbs. We can compute the average lifetime by entering the following formula into cell E2:

$$=\text{AVERAGE(B2:B201)}$$

To identify the result, the label Average Lifetime is entered into cell D2. Note that for this problem, the Apply Tools task was not required. The value worksheet shows that the value computed using the AVERAGE function is 76 hours.

**FIGURE 1.10**   COMPUTING THE AVERAGE LIFETIME OF LIGHTBULBS FOR NORRIS ELECTRONICS USING EXCEL'S AVERAGE FUNCTION

*Note: Rows 7–195 are hidden.*

## 1.7 Data Mining

With the aid of magnetic card readers, bar code scanners, and point-of-sale terminals, most organizations obtain large amounts of data on a daily basis. And, even for a small local restaurant that uses touch screen monitors to enter orders and handle billing, the amount of data collected can be significant. For large retail companies, the sheer volume of data collected is hard to conceptualize, and figuring out how to use these data effectively to improve profitability is a challenge. For example, mass retailers such as Walmart capture data on 20 to 30 million transactions every day, telecommunication companies such as France Telecom and AT&T generate over 300 million call records per day, and Visa processes 6800 payment transactions per second or approximately 600 million transactions per day. Storing and managing the transaction data is a significant undertaking.

The term *data warehousing* is used to refer to the process of capturing, storing, and maintaining the data. Computing power and data collection tools have reached the point where it is now feasible to store and retrieve extremely large quantities of data in seconds. Analysis of the data in the warehouse may result in decisions that will lead to new strategies and higher profits for the organization.

The subject of **data mining** deals with methods for developing useful decision-making information from large databases. Using a combination of procedures from statistics, mathematics, and computer science, analysts "mine the data" in the warehouse to convert it into useful information, hence the name *data mining*. Dr. Kurt Thearling, a leading practitioner in the field, defines data mining as "the automated extraction of predictive information from (large) databases." The two key words in Dr. Thearling's definition are *automated* and *predictive*. Data mining systems that are the most effective use automated procedures to extract information from the data using only the most general or even vague queries by the user. And data mining software automates the process of uncovering hidden predictive information that in the past required hands-on analysis.

The major applications of data mining have been made by companies with a strong consumer focus, such as retail businesses, financial organizations, and communication companies. Data mining has been successfully used to help retailers such as Amazon and Barnes & Noble determine one or more related products that customers who have already purchased a specific product are also likely to purchase. Then, when a customer logs on to the company's website and purchases a product, the website uses pop-ups to alert the customer about additional products that the customer is likely to purchase. In another application, data mining may be used to identify customers who are likely to spend more than $20 on a particular shopping trip. These customers may then be identified as the ones to receive special email or regular mail discount offers to encourage them to make their next shopping trip before the discount termination date.

*Statistical methods play an important role in data mining, both in terms of discovering relationships in the data and predicting future outcomes. However, a thorough coverage of data mining and the use of statistics in data mining is outside the scope of this text.*

Data mining is a technology that relies heavily on statistical methodology such as multiple regression, logistic regression, and correlation. But it takes a creative integration of all these methods and computer science technologies involving artificial intelligence and machine learning to make data mining effective. A significant investment in time and money is required to implement commercial data mining software packages developed by firms such as Oracle, Teradata, and SAS. The statistical concepts introduced in this text will be helpful in understanding the statistical methodology used by data mining software packages and enable you to better understand the statistical information that is developed.

Because statistical models play an important role in developing predictive models in data mining, many of the concerns that statisticians deal with in developing statistical models are also applicable. For instance, a concern in any statistical study involves the issue of model reliability. Finding a statistical model that works well for a particular sample of data does not necessarily mean that it can be reliably applied to other data. One of the common statistical approaches to evaluating model reliability is to divide the sample data set into two parts: a training data set and a test data set. If the model developed using the training data is able to accurately predict values in the test data, we say that the model is reliable. One advantage that data mining has over classical statistics is that the enormous amount of data available allows the data mining software to partition the data set so that a model developed for the training data set may be tested for reliability on other data. In this sense, the partitioning of the data set allows data mining to develop models and relationships and then quickly observe if they are repeatable and valid with new and different data. On the other hand, a warning for data mining applications is that with so much data available, there is a danger of overfitting the model to the point that misleading associations and cause/effect conclusions appear to exist. Careful interpretation of data mining results and additional testing will help avoid this pitfall.

## 1.8    Ethical Guidelines for Statistical Practice

Ethical behavior is something we should strive for in all that we do. Ethical issues arise in statistics because of the important role statistics plays in the collection, analysis, presentation, and interpretation of data. In a statistical study, unethical behavior can take a variety of forms, including improper sampling, inappropriate analysis of the data, development of misleading graphs, use of inappropriate summary statistics, and/or a biased interpretation of the statistical results.

As you begin to do your own statistical work, we encourage you to be fair, thorough, objective, and neutral as you collect data, conduct analyses, make oral presentations, and present written reports containing information developed. As a consumer of statistics, you should also be aware of the possibility of unethical statistical behavior by others. When you see statistics in newspapers, on television, on the Internet, and so on, it is a good idea to view the information with some skepticism, always being aware of the source as well as the purpose and objectivity of the statistics provided.

The American Statistical Association, the nation's leading professional organization for statistics and statisticians, developed the report "Ethical Guidelines for Statistical Practice"[2] to help statistical practitioners make and communicate ethical decisions and assist students in learning how to perform statistical work responsibly. The report contains 67 guidelines organized into eight topic areas: Professionalism; Responsibilities to Funders, Clients, and Employers; Responsibilities in Publications and Testimony; Responsibilities to Research Subjects; Responsibilities to Research Team Colleagues; Responsibilities to Other Statisticians or Statistical Practitioners; Responsibilities Regarding Allegations of Misconduct; and Responsibilities of Employers Including Organizations, Individuals, Attorneys, or Other Clients Employing Statistical Practitioners.

One of the ethical guidelines in the professionalism area addresses the issue of running multiple tests until a desired result is obtained. Let us consider an example. In Section 1.5 we discussed a statistical study conducted by Norris Electronics involving a sample of 200 high-intensity lightbulbs manufactured with a new filament. The average lifetime for the sample, 76 hours, provided an estimate of the average lifetime for all lightbulbs produced with the new filament. However, consider this. Because Norris selected a sample of bulbs, it is reasonable to assume that another sample would have provided a different average lifetime.

Suppose Norris's management had hoped the sample results would enable them to claim that the average lifetime for the new lightbulbs was 80 hours or more. Suppose further that Norris's management decides to continue the study by manufacturing and testing

---

[2]American Statistical Association, "Ethical Guidelines for Statistical Practice," 1999.

repeated samples of 200 lightbulbs with the new filament until a sample mean of 80 hours or more is obtained. If the study is repeated enough times, a sample may eventually be obtained—by chance alone—that would provide the desired result and enable Norris to make such a claim. In this case, consumers would be misled into thinking the new product is better than it actually is. Clearly, this type of behavior is unethical and represents a gross misuse of statistics in practice.

Several ethical guidelines in the responsibilities and publications and testimony area deal with issues involving the handling of data. For instance, a statistician must account for all data considered in a study and explain the sample(s) actually used. In the Norris Electronics study the average lifetime for the 200 bulbs in the original sample is 76 hours; this is considerably less than the 80 hours or more that management hoped to obtain. Suppose now that after reviewing the results showing a 76-hour average lifetime, Norris discards all the observations with 70 or fewer hours until burnout, allegedly because these bulbs contain imperfections caused by startup problems in the manufacturing process. After discarding these lightbulbs, the average lifetime for the remaining lightbulbs in the sample turns out to be 82 hours. Would you be suspicious of Norris's claim that the lifetime for its lightbulbs is 82 hours?

If the Norris lightbulbs showing 70 or fewer hours until burnout were discarded to simply provide an average lifetime of 82 hours, there is no question that discarding the lightbulbs with 70 or fewer hours until burnout is unethical. But, even if the discarded lightbulbs contain imperfections due to startup problems in the manufacturing process—and, as a result, should not have been included in the analysis—the statistician who conducted the study must account for all the data that were considered and explain how the sample actually used was obtained. To do otherwise is potentially misleading and would constitute unethical behavior on the part of both the company and the statistician.

A guideline in the shared values section of the American Statistical Association report states that statistical practitioners should avoid any tendency to slant statistical work toward predetermined outcomes. This type of unethical practice is often observed when unrepresentative samples are used to make claims. For instance, in many areas of the country smoking is not permitted in restaurants. Suppose, however, a lobbyist for the tobacco industry interviews people in restaurants where smoking is permitted in order to estimate the percentage of people who are in favor of allowing smoking in restaurants. The sample results show that 90% of the people interviewed are in favor of allowing smoking in restaurants. Based on these sample results, the lobbyist claims that 90% of all people who eat in restaurants are in favor of permitting smoking in restaurants. In this case we would argue that only sampling persons eating in restaurants that allow smoking has biased the results. If only the final results of such a study are reported, readers unfamiliar with the details of the study (i.e., that the sample was collected only in restaurants allowing smoking) can be misled.

The scope of the American Statistical Association's report is broad and includes ethical guidelines that are appropriate not only for a statistician, but also for consumers of statistical information. We encourage you to read the report to obtain a better perspective of ethical issues as you continue your study of statistics and to gain the background for determining how to ensure that ethical standards are met when you start to use statistics in practice.

## Summary

Statistics is the art and science of collecting, analyzing, presenting, and interpreting data. Nearly every college student majoring in business or economics is required to take a course in statistics. We began the chapter by describing typical statistical applications for business and economics.

Data consist of the facts and figures that are collected and analyzed. Four scales of measurement used to obtain data on a particular variable include nominal, ordinal, interval, and ratio. The scale of measurement for a variable is nominal when the data are labels or names used to identify an attribute of an element. The scale is ordinal if the data demonstrate the properties of nominal data and the order or rank of the data is meaningful. The scale is interval if the data demonstrate the properties of ordinal data and the interval between values is expressed in terms of a fixed unit of measure. Finally, the scale of measurement is ratio if the data show all the properties of interval data and the ratio of two values is meaningful.

For purposes of statistical analysis, data can be classified as categorical or quantitative. Categorical data use labels or names to identify an attribute of each element. Categorical data use either the nominal or ordinal scale of measurement and may be nonnumerical or numerical. Quantitative data are numerical values that indicate how much or how many. Quantitative data use either the interval or ratio scale of measurement. Ordinary arithmetic operations are meaningful only if the data are quantitative. Therefore, statistical computations used for quantitative data are not always appropriate for categorical data.

In Sections 1.4 and 1.5 we introduced the topics of descriptive statistics and statistical inference. Descriptive statistics are the tabular, graphical, and numerical methods used to summarize data. The process of statistical inference uses data obtained from a sample to make estimates or test hypotheses about the characteristics of a population. The last three sections of the chapter provide information on the role of computers in statistical analysis, an introduction to the relative new field of data mining, and a summary of ethical guidelines for statistical practice.

## Glossary

**Statistics** The art and science of collecting, analyzing, presenting, and interpreting data.

**Data** The facts and figures collected, analyzed, and summarized for presentation and interpretation.

**Data set** All the data collected in a particular study.

**Elements** The entities on which data are collected.

**Variable** A characteristic of interest for the elements.

**Observation** The set of measurements obtained for a particular element.

**Nominal scale** The scale of measurement for a variable when the data are labels or names used to identify an attribute of an element. Nominal data may be nonnumerical or numerical.

**Ordinal scale** The scale of measurement for a variable if the data exhibit the properties of nominal data and the order or rank of the data is meaningful. Ordinal data may be nonnumerical or numerical.

**Interval scale** The scale of measurement for a variable if the data demonstrate the properties of ordinal data and the interval between values is expressed in terms of a fixed unit of measure. Interval data are always numerical.

**Ratio scale** The scale of measurement for a variable if the data demonstrate all the properties of interval data and the ratio of two values is meaningful. Ratio data are always numerical.

**Categorical data** Labels or names used to identify an attribute of each element. Categorical data use either the nominal or ordinal scale of measurement and may be nonnumerical or numerical.

**Quantitative data** Numerical values that indicate how much or how many of something. Quantitative data are obtained using either the interval or ratio scale of measurement.

**Categorical variable** A variable with categorical data.

**Quantitative variable** A variable with quantitative data.

**Cross-sectional data** Data collected at the same or approximately the same point in time.

**Time series data** Data collected over several time periods.

**Descriptive statistics** Tabular, graphical, and numerical summaries of data.

**Population** The set of all elements of interest in a particular study.

**Sample** A subset of the population.

**Census** A survey to collect data on the entire population.

**Sample survey** A survey to collect data on a sample.

**Statistical inference** The process of using data obtained from a sample to make estimates or test hypotheses about the characteristics of a population.

**Data mining** The process of using procedures from statistics and computer science to extract useful information from extremely large databases.

## Supplementary Exercises

1. Discuss the differences between statistics as numerical facts and statistics as a discipline or field of study.

2. The U.S. Department of Energy provides fuel economy information for a variety of motor vehicles. A sample of 10 automobiles is shown in Table 1.6 (Fuel Economy website, February 22, 2008). Data show the size of the automobile (compact, midsize, or large), the number of cylinders in the engine, the city driving miles per gallon, the highway driving miles per gallon, and the recommended fuel (diesel, premium, or regular).
   a. How many elements are in this data set?
   b. How many variables are in this data set?
   c. Which variables are categorical and which variables are quantitative?
   d. What type of measurement scale is used for each of the variables?

3. Refer to Table 1.6.
   a. What is the average miles per gallon for city driving?
   b. On average, how much higher is the miles per gallon for highway driving as compared to city driving?
   c. What percentage of the cars have four-cylinder engines?
   d. What percentage of the cars use regular fuel?

4. Table 1.7 shows data for seven colleges and universities. The endowment (in billions of dollars) and the percentage of applicants admitted are shown (*USA Today,* February 3, 2008). The state each school is located in, the campus setting, and the NCAA Division for

**TABLE 1.6**  FUEL ECONOMY INFORMATION FOR 10 AUTOMOBILES

| Car | Size | Cylinders | City MPG | Highway MPG | Fuel |
|---|---|---|---|---|---|
| Audi A8 | Large | 12 | 13 | 19 | Premium |
| BMW 328Xi | Compact | 6 | 17 | 25 | Premium |
| Cadillac CTS | Midsize | 6 | 16 | 25 | Regular |
| Chrysler 300 | Large | 8 | 13 | 18 | Premium |
| Ford Focus | Compact | 4 | 24 | 33 | Regular |
| Hyundai Elantra | Midsize | 4 | 25 | 33 | Regular |
| Jeep Grand Cherokee | Midsize | 6 | 17 | 26 | Diesel |
| Pontiac G6 | Compact | 6 | 15 | 22 | Regular |
| Toyota Camry | Midsize | 4 | 21 | 31 | Regular |
| Volkswagen Jetta | Compact | 5 | 21 | 29 | Regular |

**TABLE 1.7**    DATA FOR SEVEN COLLEGES AND UNIVERSITIES

| School | State | Campus Setting | Endowment ($ billions) | % Applicants Admitted | NCAA Division |
|--------|-------|----------------|------------------------|-----------------------|---------------|
| Amherst College | Massachusetts | Town: Fringe | 1.7 | 18 | III |
| Duke | North Carolina | City: Midsize | 5.9 | 21 | I-A |
| Harvard University | Massachusetts | City: Midsize | 34.6 | 9 | I-AA |
| Swarthmore College | Pennsylvania | Suburb: Large | 1.4 | 18 | III |
| University of Pennsylvania | Pennsylvania | City: Large | 6.6 | 18 | I-AA |
| Williams College | Massachusetts | Town: Fringe | 1.9 | 18 | III |
| Yale University | Connecticut | City: Midsize | 22.5 | 9 | I-AA |

varsity teams were obtained from the National Center of Education Statistics website, February 22, 2008.
   a.   How many elements are in the data set?
   b.   How many variables are in the data set?
   c.   Which of the variables are categorical and which are quantitative?

5.   Consider the data set in Table 1.7.
   a.   Compute the average endowment for the sample.
   b.   Compute the average percentage of applicants admitted.
   c.   What percentage of the schools have NCAA Division III varsity teams?
   d.   What percentage of the schools have a City: Midsize campus setting?

6.   *Foreign Affairs* magazine conducted a survey to develop a profile of its subscribers (Foreign Affairs website, February 23, 2008). The following questions were asked.
   a.   How many nights have you stayed in a hotel in the past 12 months?
   b.   Where do you purchase books? Three options were listed: Bookstore, Internet, and Book Club.
   c.   Do you own or lease a luxury vehicle? (Yes or No)
   d.   What is your age?
   e.   For foreign trips taken in the past three years, what was your destination? Seven international destinations were listed.
   Comment on whether each question provides categorical or quantitative data.

7.   The Ritz-Carlton Hotel used a customer opinion questionnaire to obtain performance data about its dining and entertainment services (The Ritz-Carlton Hotel, Naples, Florida, February 2006). Customers were asked to rate six factors: Welcome, Service, Food, Menu Appeal, Atmosphere, and Overall Experience. Data were recorded for each factor, with 1 for Fair, 2 for Average, 3 for Good, and 4 for Excellent.
   a.   The customer responses provided data for six variables. Are the variables categorical or quantitative?
   b.   What measurement scale is used?

8.   The *FinancialTimes*/Harris Poll is a monthly online poll of adults from six countries in Europe and the United States. A January poll included 1015 adults in the United States. One of the questions asked was, "How would you rate the Federal Bank in handling the credit problems in the financial markets?" Possible responses were Excellent, Good, Fair, Bad, and Terrible (Harris Interactive website, January 2008).
   a.   What was the sample size for this survey?
   b.   Are the data categorical or quantitative?
   c.   Would it make more sense to use averages or percentages as a summary of the data for this question?

    d. Of the respondents in the United States, 10% said the Federal Bank is doing a good job. How many individuals provided this response?

9. The Commerce Department reported receiving the following applications for the Malcolm Baldrige National Quality Award: 23 from large manufacturing firms, 18 from large service firms, and 30 from small businesses.
   a. Is type of business a categorical or quantitative variable?
   b. What percentage of the applications came from small businesses?

10. The Bureau of Transportation Statistics Omnibus Household Survey is conducted annually and serves as an information source for the U.S. Department of Transportation. In one part of the survey the person being interviewed was asked to respond to the following statement: "Drivers of motor vehicles should be allowed to talk on a hand-held cell phone while driving." Possible responses were strongly agree, somewhat agree, somewhat disagree, and strongly disagree. Forty-four respondents said that they strongly agree with this statement, 130 said that they somewhat agree, 165 said they somewhat disagree, and 741 said they strongly disagree with this statement (Bureau of Transportation website, August 2010).
    a. Do the responses for this statement provide categorical or quantitative data?
    b. Would it make more sense to use averages or percentages as a summary of the responses for this statement?
    c. What percentage of respondents strongly agree with allowing drivers of motor vehicles to talk on a hand-held cell phone while driving?
    d. Do the results indicate general support for or against allowing drivers of motor vehicles to talk on a hand-held cell phone while driving?

11. J.D. Power and Associates conducts vehicle quality surveys to provide automobile manufacturers with consumer satisfaction information about their products (Vehicle Quality Survey, January 2010). Using a sample of vehicle owners from recent vehicle purchase records, the survey asks the owners a variety of questions about their new vehicles, such as those shown below. For each question, state whether the data collected are categorical or quantitative and indicate the measurement scale being used.
    a. What price did you pay for the vehicle?
    b. How did you pay for the vehicle? (Cash, Lease, or Finance)
    c. How likely would you be to recommend this vehicle to a friend? (Definitely Not, Probably Not, Probably Will, and Definitely Will)
    d. What is the current mileage?
    e. What is your overall rating of your new vehicle? A 10-point scale, ranging from 1 for unacceptable to 10 for truly exceptional, was used.

12. The Hawaii Visitors Bureau collects data on visitors to Hawaii. The following questions were among 16 asked in a questionnaire handed out to passengers during incoming airline flights.
    - This trip to Hawaii is my: 1st, 2nd, 3rd, 4th, etc.
    - The primary reason for this trip is: (10 categories, including vacation, convention, honeymoon)
    - Where I plan to stay: (11 categories, including hotel, apartment, relatives, camping)
    - Total days in Hawaii
    a. What is the population being studied?
    b. Is the use of a questionnaire a good way to reach the population of passengers on incoming airline flights?
    c. Comment on each of the four questions in terms of whether it will provide categorical or quantitative data.

**SELF** test

13. Figure 1.11 provides a bar chart showing the amount of federal spending for the years 2004 to 2010 (Congressional Budget Office website, May 15, 2011).
    a. What is the variable of interest?
    b. Are the data categorical or quantitative?
    c. Are the data time series or cross-sectional?
    d. Comment on the trend in federal spending over time.

**FIGURE 1.11**    FEDERAL SPENDING

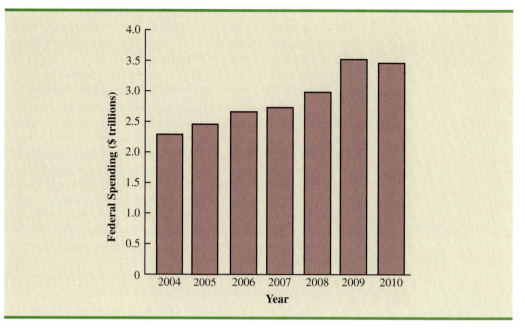

14.  The following data show the number of rental cars in service for three rental car companies: Hertz, Avis, and Dollar. The data are for the years 2007–2010 and are in thousands of vehicles (Auto Rental News website, May 15, 2011).

|  | Cars in Service (1000s) | | | |
| --- | --- | --- | --- | --- |
| **Company** | **2007** | **2008** | **2009** | **2010** |
| Hertz | 327 | 311 | 286 | 290 |
| Dollar | 167 | 140 | 106 | 108 |
| Avis | 204 | 220 | 300 | 270 |

   a.  Construct a time series graph for the years 2007 to 2010 showing the number of rental cars in service for each company. Show the time series for all three companies on the same graph.

   b.  Comment on who appears to be the market share leader and how the market shares are changing over time.

   c.  Construct a bar chart showing rental cars in service for 2010. Is this chart based on cross-sectional or time series data?

15.  Every year, the U.S. Coast Guard collects data and compiles statistics on reported recreational boating accidents. These statistics are derived from accident reports that are filed by the owners/operators of recreational vessels involved in accidents. Last year 4730 recreational boating accident reports were filed. Figure 1.12 provides a bar chart summarizing the number of accident reports that were filed each month (U.S. Coast Guard's Boating Safety Division website, August 2010).

   a.  Are the data categorical or quantitative?

   b.  Are the data time series or cross-sectional?

   c.  In what month were the most accidents reports filed? Approximately how many?

**FIGURE 1.12**  NUMBER OF RECREATIONAL BOATING ACCIDENTS

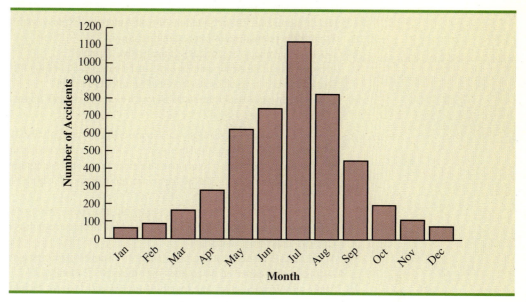

d.  There were 61 accident reports filed in January and 76 accidents reports filed in December. What percentage of the total number of accident reports for the year was filed in these two months? Does this seem reasonable?

e.  Comment on the overall shape of the bar graph.

16. The Energy Information Administration of the U.S. Department of Energy provided time series data for the U.S. average price per gallon of conventional regular gasoline between January 2008 and May 2011 (Energy Information Administration website, May 2010). Use the Internet to obtain the average price per gallon of conventional regular gasoline since May 2011.

a.  Extend the graph of the time series shown in Figure 1.1.

b.  What interpretations can you make about the average price per gallon of conventional regular gasoline since May 2011?

c.  Does the time series continue to show a summer increase in the average price per gallon? Explain.

17. A manager of a large corporation recommends a $10,000 raise be given to keep a valued subordinate from moving to another company. What internal and external sources of data might be used to decide whether such a salary increase is appropriate?

18. A random telephone survey of 1021 adults (aged 18 and older) was conducted by Opinion Research Corporation on behalf of CompleteTax, an online tax preparation and e-filing service. The survey results showed that 684 of those surveyed planned to file their taxes electronically (CompleteTax Tax Prep Survey 2010).

a.  Develop a descriptive statistic that can be used to estimate the percentage of all taxpayers who file electronically.

b.  The survey reported that the most frequently used method for preparing the tax return is to hire an accountant or professional tax preparer. If 60% of the people surveyed had their tax return prepared this way, how many people used an accountant or professional tax preparer?

c.  Other methods that the person filing the return often used include manual preparation, use of an online tax service, and use of a software tax program. Would the data for the method for preparing the tax return be considered categorical or quantitative?

19. A *Bloomberg Businessweek* North American subscriber study collected data from a sample of 2861 subscribers. Fifty-nine percent of the respondents indicated an annual income of $75,000 or more, and 50% reported having an American Express credit card.
    a. What is the population of interest in this study?
    b. Is annual income a categorical or quantitative variable?
    c. Is ownership of an American Express card a categorical or quantitative variable?
    d. Does this study involve cross-sectional or time series data?
    e. Describe any statistical inferences *Bloomberg Businessweek* might make on the basis of the survey.

20. A survey of 131 investment managers in *Barron's* Big Money poll revealed the following:
    - 43% of managers classified themselves as bullish or very bullish on the stock market.
    - The average expected return over the next 12 months for equities was 11.2%.
    - 21% selected health care as the sector most likely to lead the market in the next 12 months.
    - When asked to estimate how long it would take for technology and telecom stocks to resume sustainable growth, the managers' average response was 2.5 years.
    a. Cite two descriptive statistics.
    b. Make an inference about the population of all investment managers concerning the average return expected on equities over the next 12 months.
    c. Make an inference about the length of time it will take for technology and telecom stocks to resume sustainable growth.

21. A seven-year medical research study reported that women whose mothers took the drug DES during pregnancy were twice as likely to develop tissue abnormalities that might lead to cancer as were women whose mothers did not take the drug.
    a. This study involved the comparison of two populations. What were the populations?
    b. Do you suppose the data were obtained in a survey or an experiment?
    c. For the population of women whose mothers took the drug DES during pregnancy, a sample of 3980 women showed that 63 developed tissue abnormalities that might lead to cancer. Provide a descriptive statistic that could be used to estimate the number of women out of 1000 in this population who have tissue abnormalities.
    d. For the population of women whose mothers did not take the drug DES during pregnancy, what is the estimate of the number of women out of 1000 who would be expected to have tissue abnormalities?
    e. Medical studies often use a relatively large sample (in this case, 3980). Why?

22. The Nielsen Company surveyed consumers in 47 markets from Europe, Asia-Pacific, the Americas, and the Middle East to determine which factors are most important in determining where they buy groceries. Using a scale of 1 (low) to 5 (high), the highest rated factor was *good value for money*, with an average point score of 4.32. The second highest rated factor was *better selection of high-quality brands and products,* with an average point score of 3.78, and the lowest rated factor was *uses recyclable bags and packaging*, with an average point score of 2.71 (Nielsen website, February 24, 2008). Suppose that you have been hired by a grocery store chain to conduct a similar study to determine what factors customers at the chain's stores in Charlotte, North Carolina, think are most important in determining where they buy groceries.
    a. What is the population for the survey that you will be conducting?
    b. How would you collect the data for this study?

23. Pew Research Center is a nonpartisan polling organization that provides information about issues, attitudes, and trends shaping America. In a recent poll, Pew researchers found that 47% of American adult respondents reported getting at least some local news on their cell phone or tablet computer (Pew Research website, May 14, 2011). Further findings showed that 42% of respondents who own cell phones or tablet computers use those devices to check local weather reports and 37% use the devices to find local restaurants or other businesses.

a. One statistic reported concerned using cell phones or tablet computers for local news. What population is that finding applicable to?

b. Another statistic concerned using cell phones or tablet computers to check local weather reports and to find local restaurants. What population is this finding is applicable to?

c. Do you think the Pew researchers conducted a census or a sample survey to obtain their results? Why?

d. If you were a restaurant owner, would you find these results interesting? Why? How could you take advantage of this information?

24. A sample of midterm grades for five students showed the following results: 72, 65, 82, 90, 76. Which of the following statements are correct, and which should be challenged as being too generalized?

a. The average midterm grade for the sample of five students is 77.

b. The average midterm grade for all students who took the exam is 77.

c. An estimate of the average midterm grade for all students who took the exam is 77.

d. More than half of the students who take this exam will score between 70 and 85.

e. If five other students are included in the sample, their grades will be between 65 and 90.

25. Table 1.8 shows a data set containing information for 25 of the shadow stocks tracked by the American Association of Individual Investors. Shadow stocks are common stocks of

**TABLE 1.8**   DATA SET FOR 25 SHADOW STOCKS

Shadow02

| Company | Exchange | Ticker Symbol | Market Cap ($ millions) | Price/ Earnings Ratio | Gross Profit Margin (%) |
|---|---|---|---|---|---|
| DeWolfe Companies | AMEX | DWL | 36.4 | 8.4 | 36.7 |
| North Coast Energy | OTC | NCEB | 52.5 | 6.2 | 59.3 |
| Hansen Natural Corp. | OTC | HANS | 41.1 | 14.6 | 44.8 |
| MarineMax, Inc. | NYSE | HZO | 111.5 | 7.2 | 23.8 |
| Nanometrics Incorporated | OTC | NANO | 228.6 | 38.0 | 53.3 |
| TeamStaff, Inc. | OTC | TSTF | 92.1 | 33.5 | 4.1 |
| Environmental Tectonics | AMEX | ETC | 51.1 | 35.8 | 35.9 |
| Measurement Specialties | AMEX | MSS | 101.8 | 26.8 | 37.6 |
| SEMCO Energy, Inc. | NYSE | SEN | 193.4 | 18.7 | 23.6 |
| Party City Corporation | OTC | PCTY | 97.2 | 15.9 | 36.4 |
| Embrex, Inc. | OTC | EMBX | 136.5 | 18.9 | 59.5 |
| Tech/Ops Sevcon, Inc. | AMEX | TO | 23.2 | 20.7 | 35.7 |
| ARCADIS NV | OTC | ARCAF | 173.4 | 8.8 | 9.6 |
| Qiao Xing Universal Tele. | OTC | XING | 64.3 | 22.1 | 30.8 |
| Energy West Incorporated | OTC | EWST | 29.1 | 9.7 | 16.3 |
| Barnwell Industries, Inc. | AMEX | BRN | 27.3 | 7.4 | 73.4 |
| Innodata Corporation | OTC | INOD | 66.1 | 11.0 | 29.6 |
| Medical Action Industries | OTC | MDCI | 137.1 | 26.9 | 30.6 |
| Instrumentarium Corp. | OTC | INMRY | 240.9 | 3.6 | 52.1 |
| Petroleum Development | OTC | PETD | 95.9 | 6.1 | 19.4 |
| Drexler Technology Corp. | OTC | DRXR | 233.6 | 45.6 | 53.6 |
| Gerber Childrenswear Inc. | NYSE | GCW | 126.9 | 7.9 | 25.8 |
| Gaiam, Inc. | OTC | GAIA | 295.5 | 68.2 | 60.7 |
| Artesian Resources Corp. | OTC | ARTNA | 62.8 | 20.5 | 45.5 |
| York Water Company | OTC | YORW | 92.2 | 22.9 | 74.2 |

smaller companies that are not closely followed by Wall Street analysts. The data set is also on the website that accompanies the text in the file named Shadow02.

a.  How many variables are in the data set?
b.  Which of the variables are categorical and which are quantitative?
c.  For the Exchange variable, show the frequency and the percent frequency for AMEX, NYSE, and OTC. Construct a bar graph similar to Figure 1.5 for the Exchange variable.
d.  Show the frequency distribution for the Gross Profit Margin using the five intervals: 0–14.9, 15–29.9, 30–44.9, 45–59.9, and 60–74.9. Construct a histogram similar to Figure 1.6.
e.  What is the average price/earnings ratio?

## Appendix     An Introduction to StatTools

*StatTools is a professional add-in that expands the statistical capabilities available with Microsoft Excel. StatTools software can be downloaded from the website that accompanies this text.*

Excel does not contain statistical functions or data analysis tools to perform all the statistical procedures discussed in the text. StatTools is a Microsoft Excel statistics add-in that extends the range of statistical and graphical options for Excel users. Most chapters include a chapter appendix that shows the steps required to accomplish a statistical procedure using StatTools. For those students who want to make more extensive use of the software, StatTools offers an excellent Help facility. The StatTools Help system includes detailed explanations of the statistical and data analysis options available, as well as descriptions and definitions of the types of output provided.

### Getting Started with StatTools

StatTools software may be downloaded and installed on your computer by accessing the website that accompanies this text. After downloading and installing the software, perform the following steps to use StatTools as an Excel add-in.

**Step 1.**  Click the **Start** button on the taskbar and then point to **All Programs**
**Step 2.**  Point to the folder entitled **Palisade DecisionTools**
**Step 3.**  Click **StatTools for Excel**

These steps will open Excel and add the StatTools tab next to the Add-Ins tab on the Excel Ribbon. Alternately, if you are already working in Excel, these steps will make StatTools available.

### Using StatTools

Before conducting any statistical analysis, we must create a StatTools data set using the StatTools Data Set Manager. Let us use the Excel worksheet for the mutual funds data set in Table 1.1 to show how this is done. The following steps show how to create a StatTools data set for the mutual funds data.

**Step 1.**  Open the Excel file named Morningstar
**Step 2.**  Select any cell in the data set (for example, cell A1)
**Step 3.**  Click the **StatTools** tab on the Ribbon
**Step 4.**  In the **Data** group, click **Data Set Manager**
**Step 5.**  When StatTools asks if you want to add the range $A$1:$F$26 as a new StatTools data set, click **Yes**
**Step 6.**  When the StatTools - Data Set Manager dialog box appears, click **OK**

**FIGURE 1.13    THE STATTOOLS - DATA SET MANAGER DIALOG BOX**

Figure 1.13 shows the StatTools - Data Set Manager dialog box that appears in step 6. By default, the name of the new StatTools data set is Data Set #1. You can replace the name Data Set #1 in step 6 with a more descriptive name. And, if you select the Apply Cell Format option, the column labels will be highlighted in blue and the entire data set will have outside and inside borders. You can always select the Data Set Manager at any time in your analysis to make these types of changes.

## Recommended Application Settings

StatTools allows the user to specify some of the application settings that control such things as where statistical output is displayed and how calculations are performed. The following steps show how to access the StatTools - Application Settings dialog box.

**Step 1.**  Click the **StatTools** tab on the Ribbon
**Step 2.**  In the **Tools Group**, click **Utilities**
**Step 3.**  Choose **Application Settings** from the list of options

Figure 1.14 shows that the StatTools - Application Settings dialog box has five sections: General Settings; Reports; Utilities; Data Set Defaults; and Analyses. Let us show how to make changes in the Reports section of the dialog box.

**FIGURE 1.14** THE STATTOOLS - APPLICATION SETTINGS DIALOG BOX

Figure 1.14 shows that the Placement option currently selected is **New Workbook**. Using this option, the StatTools output will be placed in a new workbook. But suppose you would like to place the StatTools output in the current (active) workbook. If you click the words **New Workbook**, a downward-pointing arrow will appear to the right. Clicking this arrow will display a list of all the placement options, including **Active Workbook**; we recommend using this option. Figure 1.14 also shows that the Updating Preferences option in the Reports section is currently **Live - Linked to Input Data**. With live updating, anytime one or more data values are changed, StatTools will automatically change the output previously produced; we also recommend using this option. Note that there are two options available under Display Comments: **Notes and Warnings** and **Educational Comments**. Because these options provide useful notes and information regarding the output, we recommend using both options. Thus, to include educational comments as part of the StatTools output, you will have to change the value of False for Educational Comments to True.

The StatTools - Application Settings dialog box contains numerous other features that enable you to customize the way that you want StatTools to operate. You can learn more about these features by clicking the Help icon located in the lower left-hand corner of the StatTools - Application Settings dialog box. When you have finished making changes in the application settings, click OK at the bottom of the dialog box and then click Yes when StatTools asks you if you want to save the new application settings.

# CHAPTER 2

# Descriptive Statistics: Tabular and Graphical Presentations

## COLGATE-PALMOLIVE COMPANY*
*NEW YORK, NEW YORK*

The Colgate-Palmolive Company started as a small soap and candle shop in New York City in 1806. Today, Colgate-Palmolive employs more than 40,000 people working in more than 200 countries and territories around the world. Although best known for its brand names of Colgate, Palmolive, Ajax, and Fab, the company also markets Mennen, Hill's Science Diet, and Hill's Prescription Diet products.

The Colgate-Palmolive Company uses statistics in its quality assurance program for home laundry detergent products. One concern is customer satisfaction with the quantity of detergent in a carton. Every carton in each size category is filled with the same amount of detergent by weight, but the volume of detergent is affected by the density of the detergent powder. For instance, if the powder density is on the heavy side, a smaller volume of detergent is needed to reach the carton's specified weight. As a result, the carton may appear to be underfilled when opened by the consumer.

To control the problem of heavy detergent powder, limits are placed on the acceptable range of powder density. Statistical samples are taken periodically, and the density of each powder sample is measured. Data summaries are then provided for operating personnel so that corrective action can be taken if necessary to keep the density within the desired quality specifications.

A frequency distribution for the densities of 150 samples taken over a one-week period and a histogram are shown in the accompanying table and figure. Density levels above .40 are unacceptably high. The frequency distribution and histogram show that the operation is meeting its quality guidelines with all of the densities less than or equal to .40. Managers viewing these statistical summaries would be pleased with the quality of the detergent production process.

In this chapter, you will learn about tabular and graphical methods of descriptive statistics such as frequency distributions, bar charts, histograms, stem-and-

The Colgate-Palmolive Company uses statistical summaries to help maintain the quality of its products.

leaf displays, crosstabulations, and others. The goal of these methods is to summarize data so that the data can be easily understood and interpreted.

**Frequency Distribution of Density Data**

| Density | Frequency |
|---------|-----------|
| .29–.30 | 30 |
| .31–.32 | 75 |
| .33–.34 | 32 |
| .35–.36 | 9 |
| .37–.38 | 3 |
| .39–.40 | 1 |
| Total | 150 |

**Histogram of Density Data**

*The authors are indebted to William R. Fowle, Manager of Quality Assurance, Colgate-Palmolive Company, for providing this Statistics in Practice.

As indicated in Chapter 1, data can be classified as either categorical or quantitative. **Categorical data** use labels or names to identify categories of like items. **Quantitative data** are numerical values that indicate how much or how many.

This chapter introduces tabular and graphical methods commonly used to summarize both categorical and quantitative data. Tabular and graphical summaries of data can be found in annual reports, newspaper articles, and research studies. Everyone is exposed to these types of presentations. Hence, it is important to understand how they are prepared and how they should be interpreted. We begin with tabular and graphical methods for summarizing data concerning a single variable. The last section introduces methods for summarizing data when the relationship between two variables is of interest.

Excel's wide variety of statistical functions and tools will be used extensively in this chapter. We will find the chart tools and PivotTable tools to be especially helpful. These tools can be used to provide tabular and graphical summaries for a single categorical or quantitative variable as well as provide crosstabulations and graphical presentation for data sets involving more than one variable.

## 2.1   Summarizing Categorical Data

### Frequency Distribution

We begin the discussion of how tabular and graphical methods can be used to summarize categorical data with the definition of a **frequency distribution**.

> **FREQUENCY DISTRIBUTION**
>
> A frequency distribution is a tabular summary of data showing the number (frequency) of items in each of several nonoverlapping classes.

Let us use the following example to demonstrate the construction and interpretation of a frequency distribution for categorical data. Coca-Cola, Diet Coke, Dr. Pepper, Pepsi, and Sprite are five popular soft drinks. Assume that the data in Table 2.1 show the soft drink selected in a sample of 50 soft drink purchases.

**TABLE 2.1**    DATA FROM A SAMPLE OF 50 SOFT DRINK PURCHASES

| | | |
|---|---|---|
| Coca-Cola | Sprite | Pepsi |
| Diet Coke | Coca-Cola | Coca-Cola |
| Pepsi | Diet Coke | Coca-Cola |
| Diet Coke | Coca-Cola | Coca-Cola |
| Coca-Cola | Diet Coke | Pepsi |
| Coca-Cola | Coca-Cola | Dr. Pepper |
| Dr. Pepper | Sprite | Coca-Cola |
| Diet Coke | Pepsi | Diet Coke |
| Pepsi | Coca-Cola | Pepsi |
| Pepsi | Coca-Cola | Pepsi |
| Coca-Cola | Coca-Cola | Pepsi |
| Dr. Pepper | Pepsi | Pepsi |
| Sprite | Coca-Cola | Coca-Cola |
| Coca-Cola | Sprite | Dr. Pepper |
| Diet Coke | Dr. Pepper | Pepsi |
| Coca-Cola | Pepsi | Sprite |
| Coca-Cola | Diet Coke | |

**TABLE 2.2**

FREQUENCY
DISTRIBUTION OF
SOFT DRINK
PURCHASES

| Soft Drink | Frequency |
|------------|-----------|
| Coca-Cola  | 19        |
| Diet Coke  | 8         |
| Dr. Pepper | 5         |
| Pepsi      | 13        |
| Sprite     | 5         |
| Total      | 50        |

To develop a frequency distribution for these data, we count the number of times each soft drink appears in Table 2.1. Coca-Cola appears 19 times, Diet Coke appears 8 times, Dr. Pepper appears 5 times, Pepsi appears 13 times, and Sprite appears 5 times. These counts are summarized in the frequency distribution in Table 2.2.

This frequency distribution provides a summary of how the 50 soft drink purchases are distributed across the five soft drinks. This summary offers more insight than the original data shown in Table 2.1. Viewing the frequency distribution, we see that Coca-Cola is the leader, Pepsi is second, Diet Coke is third, and Sprite and Dr. Pepper are tied for fourth. The frequency distribution summarizes information about the popularity of the five soft drinks.

Let us examine how Excel can be used to count the number of times each soft drink occurs and construct a frequency distribution for the soft drink data in Table 2.1.

## Using Excel's COUNTIF Function to Construct a Frequency Distribution

Two tasks are involved in using Excel's COUNTIF function to construct a frequency distribution: Enter Data and Enter Functions and Formulas. Refer to Figure 2.1 as we describe the tasks involved. The formula worksheet is in the background; the value worksheet is in the foreground.

**Enter Data:** The label "Brand Purchased" and the data for the 50 soft drink purchases are entered into cells A1:A51.

**Enter Functions and Formulas:** Excel's COUNTIF function can be used to count the number of times each soft drink appears in cells A2:A51. We first entered a label and the soft drink names into cells C1:C6 and D1. Then, to count the number of times that Coca-Cola appears, we entered the following formula into cell D2:

$$=\text{COUNTIF}(\$A\$2:\$A\$51,C2)$$

*Appendix 2.1 shows how to use Excel's PivotChart Report to construct a frequency distribution for categorical data.*

To count the number of times the other soft drinks appear, we copied the same formula into cells D3:D6.

The value worksheet, in the foreground of Figure 2.1, shows the values computed using these cell formulas; we see that the Excel worksheet shows the same frequency distribution that we developed in Table 2.2.

## Relative Frequency and Percent Frequency Distributions

A frequency distribution shows the number (frequency) of items in each of several nonoverlapping classes. However, we are often interested in the proportion, or percentage, of items in each class. The *relative frequency* of a class equals the fraction or proportion of items belonging to a class. For a data set with $n$ observations, the relative frequency of each class can be determined as follows:

RELATIVE FREQUENCY

$$\text{Relative frequency of a class} = \frac{\text{Frequency of the class}}{n} \tag{2.1}$$

The *percent frequency* of a class is the relative frequency multiplied by 100.

**FIGURE 2.1**   FREQUENCY DISTRIBUTION FOR SOFT DRINK PURCHASES CONSTRUCTED USING
EXCEL'S COUNTIF FUNCTION

*Note: Rows 21–49
are hidden.*

A **relative frequency distribution** gives a tabular summary of data showing the relative
frequency for each class. A **percent frequency distribution** summarizes the percent frequency of the data for each class. Table 2.3 shows a relative frequency distribution and a
percent frequency distribution for the soft drink data. In Table 2.3 we see that the relative
frequency for Coca-Cola is 19/50 = .38, the relative frequency for Diet Coke is 8/50 = .16,
and so on. From the percent frequency distribution, we see that 38% of the purchases were
Coca-Cola, 16% of the purchases were Diet Coke, and so on. We can also note that
38% + 26% + 16% = 80% of the purchases were the top three soft drinks.

**TABLE 2.3**   RELATIVE FREQUENCY AND PERCENT FREQUENCY DISTRIBUTIONS
OF SOFT DRINK PURCHASES

| Soft Drink | Relative Frequency | Percent Frequency |
|---|---|---|
| Coca-Cola | .38 | 38 |
| Diet Coke | .16 | 16 |
| Dr. Pepper | .10 | 10 |
| Pepsi | .26 | 26 |
| Sprite | .10 | 10 |
| Total | 1.00 | 100 |

## Using Excel to Construct Relative Frequency and Percent Frequency Distributions

Extending the worksheet shown in Figure 2.1, we can develop the relative frequency and
percent frequency distributions shown in Table 2.3. Refer to Figure 2.2 as we describe the tasks
involved. The formula worksheet is in the background; the value worksheet is in the foreground.

**FIGURE 2.2**   RELATIVE FREQUENCY AND PERCENT FREQUENCY DISTRIBUTIONS OF
SOFT DRINK PURCHASES CONSTRUCTED USING EXCEL

Note: Rows 21–49
are hidden.

**Enter Data:**   The label "Brand Purchased" and the data for the 50 soft drink purchases are entered into cells A1:A51.

**Enter Functions and Formulas:**   The information in cells C1:D6 is the same as in Figure 2.1. Excel's SUM function is used in cell D7 to compute the sum of the frequencies in cells D2:D6. The resulting value of 50 is the number of observations in the data set. To compute the relative frequency for Coca-Cola using equation (2.1), we entered the formula =D2/$D$7 into cell E2; the result, 0.38, is the relative frequency for Coca-Cola. Copying cell E2 to cells E3:E6 computes the relative frequencies for each of the other soft drinks.

To compute the percent frequency for Coca-Cola, we entered the formula =E2*100 into cell F2. The result, 38, indicates that 38% of the soft drink purchases were Coca-Cola. Copying cell F2 to cells F3:F6 computes the percent frequencies for each of the other soft drinks. Finally, copying cell D7 to cells E7:F7 computes the total of the relative frequencies (1.00) and the total of the percent frequencies (100).

## Bar Charts and Pie Charts

*In quality control applications, bar charts are used to identify the most important causes of problems. When the bars are arranged in descending order of height from left to right with the most frequently occurring cause appearing first, the bar chart is called a* Pareto diagram. *This diagram is named for its founder, Vilfredo Pareto, an Italian economist.*

A bar chart is a graphical device for depicting categorical data summarized in a frequency, relative frequency, or percent frequency distribution. On one axis of the graph (usually the horizontal axis), we specify the labels that are used for the classes (categories). A frequency, relative frequency, or percent frequency scale can be used for the other axis of the chart (usually the vertical axis). Then, using a bar of fixed width drawn above each class label, we extend the length of the bar until we reach the frequency, relative frequency, or percent frequency of the class. For categorical data, the bars should be separated to emphasize the fact that each class is separate. Figure 2.3 shows a bar chart of the frequency distribution for the 50 soft drink purchases. Note how the graphical presentation shows Coca-Cola, Pepsi, and Diet Coke to be the most preferred brands.

The pie chart provides another graphical device for presenting relative frequency and percent frequency distributions for categorical data. To construct a pie chart, we first draw a circle to represent all the data. Then we use the relative frequencies to subdivide the circle into sectors, or parts, that correspond to the relative frequency for each class. For example, because a circle contains 360 degrees and Coca-Cola shows a relative

**FIGURE 2.3   BAR CHART OF SOFT DRINK PURCHASES**

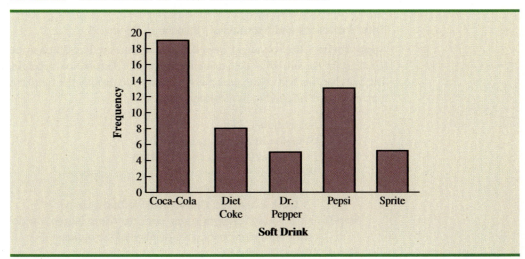

**FIGURE 2.4**    PIE CHART OF SOFT DRINK PURCHASES

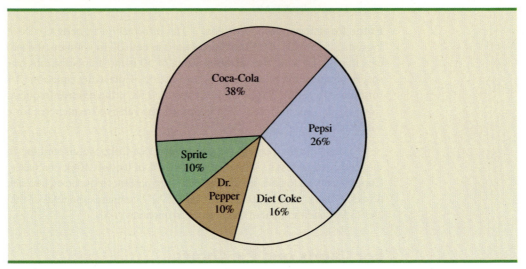

frequency of .38, the sector of the pie chart labeled Coca-Cola consists of .38(360) = 136.8 degrees. The sector of the pie chart labeled Diet Coke consists of .16(360) = 57.6 degrees. Similar calculations for the other classes yield the pie chart in Figure 2.4. The numerical values shown for each sector can be frequencies, relative frequencies, or percent frequencies.

## Using Excel's Chart Tools to Construct a Bar Chart and a Pie Chart

*Appendix 2.1 shows how to use Excel's PivotChart Report to construct a bar chart for categorical data.*

Excel's chart tools make it very easy to create a variety of graphical displays, including bar charts and pie charts. When such tools are used, a third task is needed for worksheet construction: **Apply Tools.** We illustrate by showing how to construct the bar chart for soft drink purchases. Refer to Figure 2.5 as we describe the tasks involved.

**Enter Data:**    Same as in Figure 2.1

**Enter Functions and Formulas:**    Same as in Figure 2.1

**Apply Tools:**    The following steps describe how to use Excel's chart tools to construct a bar chart for the soft drink data using the frequency distribution appearing in cells C1:D6. The bar chart we will create uses the vertical axis to display the frequencies; in Excel this type of chart is referred to as a column chart.

    **Step 1.**  Select cells C2:D6
    **Step 2.**  Click the **Insert** tab on the Ribbon
    **Step 3.**  In the **Charts** group, click **Column**
    **Step 4.**  When the list of column chart subtypes appears,
            Go to the **2-D Column** section
            Click **Clustered Column** (the leftmost chart)
    **Step 5.**  In the **Chart Layouts** group, click the **More** button (the downward pointing arrow with a line over it) to display all the options
    **Step 6.**  Choose **Layout 9**

**FIGURE 2.5** BAR CHART OF SOFT DRINK PURCHASES CONSTRUCTED USING EXCEL'S CHART TOOLS

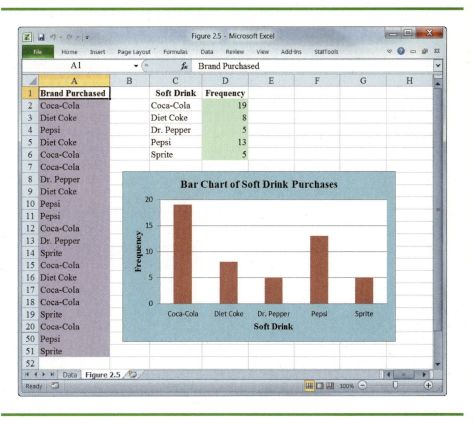

**Step 7.** Click the **Chart Title** and replace it with **Bar Chart of Soft Drink Purchases**

**Step 8.** Click the **Horizontal (Category) Axis Title** and replace it with **Soft Drink**

**Step 9.** Click the **Vertical (Value) Axis Title** and replace it with **Frequency**

**Step 10.** Right-click the **Series 1 Legend Entry** and choose **Delete** from the list of options that appears

**Step 11.** Right-click the vertical axis and choose **Format Axis** from the options that appear

**Step 12.** When the Format Axis dialog box appears,
Go to the **Axis Options** section
Select **Fixed** for **Major Unit** and enter 5.0 in the corresponding box
Click **Close**

The resulting bar chart is shown in Figure 2.5.[1] If you prefer, you can display the bars on the horizontal axis by choosing **Bar** in step 3 instead of Column.

Excel's chart tools can also be used to develop a pie chart for the soft drink data in a similar fashion. The major difference is that in step 3 we would choose **Pie** in the Charts group.

---

[1]The bar chart in Figure 2.5 is slightly different from what was provided by Excel after clicking Close. Resizing an Excel chart is not difficult. First, select the chart. Small black squares, called sizing handles, will appear on the chart border. Click on the sizing handles and drag them to resize the figure to your preference.

## NOTES AND COMMENTS

1. Often the number of classes in a frequency distribution is the same as the number of categories found in the data, as is the case for the soft drink purchase data in this section. The data involve only five soft drinks, and a separate frequency distribution class was defined for each one. Data that included all soft drinks would require many categories, most of which would have a small number of purchases. Most statisticians recommend that classes with smaller frequencies be grouped into an aggregate class called "other." Classes with frequencies of 5% or less would most often be treated in this fashion.

2. The sum of the frequencies in any frequency distribution always equals the number of observations. The sum of the relative frequencies in any relative frequency distribution always equals 1.00, and the sum of the percentages in a percent frequency distribution always equals 100.

3. Excel's PivotChart Report is a valuable tool for summarizing data and preparing charts. In Appendix 2.1, we show how it can be used to construct both a frequency distribution and a bar chart for categorical data.

## Exercises

### Methods

1. The response to a question has three alternatives: A, B, and C. A sample of 120 responses provides 60 A, 24 B, and 36 C. Show the frequency and relative frequency distributions.

2. A partial relative frequency distribution is given.

| Class | Relative Frequency |
|-------|--------------------|
| A | .22 |
| B | .18 |
| C | .40 |
| D | |

   a. What is the relative frequency of class D?
   b. The total sample size is 200. What is the frequency of class D?
   c. Show the frequency distribution.
   d. Show the percent frequency distribution.

3. A questionnaire provides 58 Yes, 42 No, and 20 no-opinion answers.
   a. In the construction of a pie chart, how many degrees would be in the section of the pie showing the Yes answers?
   b. How many degrees would be in the section of the pie showing the No answers?
   c. Construct a pie chart.
   d. Construct a bar chart.

### Applications

BestTV

4. The top four prime-time television shows were *Law & Order, CSI, Without a Trace,* and *Desperate Housewives* (Nielsen Media Research, January 1, 2007). Data indicating the preferred shows for a sample of 50 viewers follow.

| | | | | |
|------|------|-------|------|------|
| DH | CSI | DH | CSI | L&O |
| Trace | CSI | L&O | Trace | CSI |
| CSI | DH | Trace | CSI | DH |
| L&O | L&O | L&O | CSI | DH |
| CSI | DH | DH | L&O | CSI |

| DH | Trace | CSI | Trace | DH |
| DH | CSI | CSI | L&O | CSI |
| L&O | CSI | Trace | Trace | DH |
| L&O | CSI | CSI | CSI | DH |
| CSI | DH | Trace | Trace | L&O |

a. Are these data categorical or quantitative?
b. Provide frequency and percent frequency distributions.
c. Construct a bar chart and a pie chart.
d. On the basis of the sample, which television show has the largest viewing audience? Which one is second?

5. In alphabetical order, the six most common last names in the United States are Brown, Davis, Johnson, Jones, Smith, and Williams (U.S. Census Bureau website, November 1, 2010). Assume that a sample of 50 individuals with one of these last names provided the following data.

**Names**

| Brown | Williams | Williams | Williams | Brown |
| Smith | Jones | Smith | Johnson | Smith |
| Davis | Smith | Brown | Williams | Johnson |
| Johnson | Smith | Smith | Johnson | Brown |
| Williams | Davis | Johnson | Williams | Johnson |
| Williams | Johnson | Jones | Smith | Brown |
| Johnson | Smith | Smith | Brown | Jones |
| Jones | Jones | Smith | Smith | Davis |
| Davis | Jones | Williams | Davis | Smith |
| Jones | Johnson | Brown | Johnson | Davis |

Summarize the data by constructing the following:
a. Relative and percent frequency distributions
b. A bar chart
c. A pie chart
d. Based on these data, what are the three most common last names?

6. The Nielsen Media Research television rating measures the percentage of television owners who are watching a particular television program. The highest-rated television program in television history was the *M\*A\*S\*H Last Episode Special* shown on February 28, 1983. A 60.2 rating indicated that 60.2% of all television owners were watching this program. Nielsen Media Research provided the list of the 50 top-rated single shows in television history (*The New York Times Almanac,* 2006). The following data show the television network that produced each of these 50 top-rated shows.

**Networks**

| ABC | ABC | ABC | NBC | CBS |
| ABC | CBS | ABC | ABC | NBC |
| NBC | NBC | CBS | ABC | NBC |
| CBS | ABC | CBS | NBC | ABC |
| CBS | NBC | NBC | CBS | NBC |
| CBS | CBS | CBS | NBC | NBC |
| FOX | CBS | CBS | ABC | NBC |
| ABC | ABC | CBS | NBC | NBC |
| NBC | CBS | NBC | CBS | CBS |
| ABC | CBS | ABC | NBC | ABC |

a. Construct a frequency distribution, percent frequency distribution, and bar chart for the data.
b. Which network or networks have done the best in terms of presenting top-rated television shows? Compare the performance of ABC, CBS, and NBC.

**AirSurvey**

7. The Canmark Research Center Airport Customer Satisfaction Survey uses an online questionnaire to provide airlines and airports with customer satisfaction ratings for all aspects of the customers' flight experience (Airport Survey website, January 2010). After completing a flight, customers receive an email asking them to go to the website and rate a variety of factors, including the reservation process, the check-in process, luggage policy, cleanliness of gate area, service by flight attendants, food/beverage selection, on-time arrival, and so on. A five-point scale, with Excellent (E), Very Good (V), Good (G), Fair (F), and Poor (P), is used to record the customer ratings for each survey question. Assume that passengers on a Delta Airlines flight from Myrtle Beach, South Carolina, to Atlanta, Georgia, provided the following ratings for the question, "Please rate the airline based on your overall experience with this flight." The sample ratings are shown below.

| | | | | | | | | | |
|---|---|---|---|---|---|---|---|---|---|
| E | E | G | V | V | E | V | V | V | E |
| E | G | V | E | E | V | E | E | E | V |
| V | V | V | F | V | E | V | E | G | E |
| G | E | V | E | V | E | V | V | V | V |
| E | E | V | V | E | P | E | V | P | V |

a. Use a percent frequency distribution and a bar chart to summarize these data. What do these summaries indicate about the overall customer satisfaction with the Delta flight?

b. The online survey questionnaire enabled respondents to explain any aspect of the flight that failed to meet expectations. Would this be helpful information to a manager looking for ways to improve the overall customer satisfaction on Delta flights? Explain.

8. Data for a sample of 55 members of the Baseball Hall of Fame in Cooperstown, New York, are shown here. Each observation indicates the primary position played by the Hall of Famers: pitcher (P), catcher (H), 1st base (1), 2nd base (2), 3rd base (3), shortstop (S), left field (L), center field (C), and right field (R).

| | | | | | | | | | | | | | |
|---|---|---|---|---|---|---|---|---|---|---|---|---|---|
| L | P | C | H | 2 | P | R | 1 | S | S | 1 | L | P | R | P |
| P | P | P | R | C | S | L | R | P | C | C | P | P | R | P |
| 2 | 3 | P | H | L | P | 1 | C | P | P | P | S | 1 | L | R |
| R | 1 | 2 | H | S | 3 | H | 2 | L | P | | | | | |

a. Use frequency and relative frequency distributions to summarize the data.
b. What position provides the most Hall of Famers?
c. What position provides the fewest Hall of Famers?
d. What outfield position (L, C, or R) provides the most Hall of Famers?
e. Compare infielders (1, 2, 3, and S) to outfielders (L, C, and R).

9. The Pew Research Center's Social & Demographic Trends project found that 46% of U.S. adults would rather live in a different type of community than the one where they are living now (Pew Research Center, January 29, 2009). The national survey of 2260 adults asked: "Where do you live now?" and "What do you consider to be the ideal community?" Response options were City (C), Suburb (S), Small Town (T), or Rural (R). A representative portion of this survey for a sample of 100 respondents is as follows.

Where do you live now?

**LivingArea**

| | | | | | | | | | | | | | | |
|---|---|---|---|---|---|---|---|---|---|---|---|---|---|---|
| S | T | R | C | R | R | T | C | S | T | C | S | C | S | T |
| S | S | C | S | S | T | T | C | C | S | T | C | S | T | C |
| T | R | S | S | T | C | S | C | T | C | T | C | T | C | R |
| C | C | R | T | C | S | S | T | S | C | C | C | R | S | C |
| S | S | C | C | S | C | R | T | T | T | C | R | T | C | R |
| C | T | R | R | C | T | C | C | R | T | T | R | S | R | T |
| T | S | S | S | S | S | C | C | R | T | | | | | |

What do you consider to be the ideal community?

| | | | | | | | | | | | | | | | |
|---|---|---|---|---|---|---|---|---|---|---|---|---|---|---|---|
| S | C | R | R | R | S | T | S | S | T | T | S | C | S | T |
| C | C | R | T | R | S | T | T | S | S | C | C | T | T | S |
| S | R | C | S | C | C | S | C | R | C | T | S | R | R | R |
| C | T | S | T | T | T | R | R | S | C | C | R | R | S | S |
| S | T | C | T | T | C | R | T | T | T | C | T | T | R | R |
| C | S | R | T | C | T | C | C | T | T | T | R | C | R | T |
| T | C | S | S | C | S | T | S | S | R | | | | | |

a. Provide a percent frequency distribution for each question.
b. Construct a bar chart for each question.
c. Where are most adults living now?
d. Where do most adults consider the ideal community?
e. What changes in living areas would you expect to see if people moved from where they currently live to their ideal community?

**FedBank**

10. The *Financial Times*/Harris Poll is a monthly online poll of adults from six countries in Europe and the United States. The poll conducted in January 2008 included 1015 adults. One of the questions asked was, "How would you rate the Federal Bank in handling the credit problems in the financial markets?" Possible responses were Excellent, Good, Fair, Bad, and Terrible (Harris Interactive website, January 2008). The 1015 responses for this question can be found in the data file named FedBank.
a. Construct a frequency distribution.
b. Construct a percent frequency distribution.
c. Construct a bar chart for the percent frequency distribution.
d. Comment on how adults in the United States think the Federal Bank is handling the credit problems in the financial markets.
e. In Spain, 1114 adults were asked, "How would you rate the European Central Bank in handling the credit problems in the financial markets?" The percent frequency distribution obtained follows:

| Rating | Percent Frequency |
|---|---|
| Excellent | 0 |
| Good | 4 |
| Fair | 46 |
| Bad | 40 |
| Terrible | 10 |

Compare the results obtained in Spain with the results obtained in the United States.

## 2.2 Summarizing Quantitative Data

### Frequency Distribution

**TABLE 2.4**

**YEAR-END AUDIT TIMES (IN DAYS)**

| | | | |
|---|---|---|---|
| 12 | 14 | 19 | 18 |
| 15 | 15 | 18 | 17 |
| 20 | 27 | 22 | 23 |
| 22 | 21 | 33 | 28 |
| 14 | 18 | 16 | 13 |

As defined in Section 2.1, a frequency distribution is a tabular summary of data showing the number (frequency) of items in each of several nonoverlapping classes. This definition holds for quantitative as well as categorical data. However, with quantitative data we must be more careful in defining the nonoverlapping classes to be used in the frequency distribution.

For example, consider the quantitative data in Table 2.4. These data show the time in days required to complete year-end audits for a sample of 20 clients of Sanderson and

Clifford, a small public accounting firm. The three steps necessary to define the classes for a frequency distribution with quantitative data are as follows:

1. Determine the number of nonoverlapping classes.
2. Determine the width of each class.
3. Determine the class limits.

**Audit**

Let us demonstrate these steps by developing a frequency distribution for the audit time data in Table 2.4.

**Number of classes**  Classes are formed by specifying ranges that will be used to group the data. As a general guideline, we recommend using between 5 and 20 classes. For a small number of data items, as few as five or six classes may be used to summarize the data. For a larger number of data items, a larger number of classes is usually required. The goal is to use enough classes to show the variation in the data, but not so many classes that some contain only a few data items. Because the number of data items in Table 2.4 is relatively small ($n = 20$), we chose to develop a frequency distribution with five classes.

*Making the classes the same width reduces the chance of inappropriate interpretations by the user.*

**Width of the classes**  The second step in constructing a frequency distribution for quantitative data is to choose a width for the classes. As a general guideline, we recommend that the width be the same for each class. Thus the choices of the number of classes and the width of classes are not independent decisions. A larger number of classes means a smaller class width, and vice versa. To determine an approximate class width, we begin by identifying the largest and smallest data values. Then, with the desired number of classes specified, we can use the following expression to determine the approximate class width.

$$\text{Approximate class width} = \frac{\text{Largest data value} - \text{Smallest data value}}{\text{Number of classes}} \quad \textbf{(2.2)}$$

The approximate class width given by equation (2.2) can be rounded to a more convenient value based on the preference of the person developing the frequency distribution. For example, an approximate class width of 9.28 might be rounded to 10 simply because 10 is a more convenient class width to use in presenting a frequency distribution.

*No single frequency distribution is best for a data set. Different people may construct different, but equally acceptable, frequency distributions. The goal is to reveal the natural grouping and variation in the data.*

For the data involving the year-end audit times, the largest data value is 33 and the smallest data value is 12. Because we decided to summarize the data with five classes, using equation (2.2) provides an approximate class width of $(33 - 12)/5 = 4.2$. We therefore decided to round up and use a class width of five days in the frequency distribution.

In practice, the number of classes and the appropriate class width are determined by trial and error. Once a possible number of classes is chosen, equation (2.2) is used to find the approximate class width. The process can be repeated for a different number of classes. Ultimately, the analyst uses judgment to determine the combination of the number of classes and class width that provides the best frequency distribution for summarizing the data.

For the audit time data in Table 2.4, after deciding to use five classes, each with a width of five days, the next task is to specify the class limits for each of the classes.

**TABLE 2.5**

**FREQUENCY DISTRIBUTION FOR THE AUDIT TIME DATA**

| Audit Time (days) | Frequency |
|---|---|
| 10–14 | 4 |
| 15–19 | 8 |
| 20–24 | 5 |
| 25–29 | 2 |
| 30–34 | 1 |
| Total | 20 |

**Class limits**  Class limits must be chosen so that each data item belongs to one and only one class. The *lower class limit* identifies the smallest possible data value assigned to the class. The *upper class limit* identifies the largest possible data value assigned to the class. In developing frequency distributions for categorical data, we did not need to specify class limits because each data item naturally fell into a separate class. But with quantitative data, such as the audit times in Table 2.4, class limits are necessary to determine where each data value belongs.

Using the audit time data in Table 2.4, we selected 10 days as the lower class limit and 14 days as the upper class limit for the first class. This class is denoted 10–14 in Table 2.5. The smallest data value, 12, is included in the 10–14 class. We then selected 15 days as the lower class limit and 19 days as the upper class limit of the next class. We continued defining the lower and upper class limits to obtain a total of five classes: 10–14, 15–19, 20–24, 25–29, and 30–34. The largest data value, 33, is included in the 30–34 class. The difference between the lower class limits of adjacent classes is the class width. Using the first two lower class limits of 10 and 15, we see that the class width is $15 - 10 = 5$.

With the number of classes, class width, and class limits determined, a frequency distribution can be obtained by counting the number of data values belonging to each class. For example, the data in Table 2.4 show that four values—12, 14, 14, and 13—belong to the 10–14 class. Thus, the frequency for the 10–14 class is 4. Continuing this counting process for the 15–19, 20–24, 25–29, and 30–34 classes provides the frequency distribution in Table 2.5. Using this frequency distribution, we can observe the following:

1. The most frequently occurring audit times are in the class of 15–19 days. Eight of the 20 audit times belong to this class.
2. Only one audit required 30 or more days.

Other conclusions are possible, depending on the interests of the person viewing the frequency distribution. The value of a frequency distribution is that it provides insights about the data that are not easily obtained by viewing the data in their original unorganized form.

**Class midpoint** In some applications, we want to know the midpoints of the classes in a frequency distribution for quantitative data. The class midpoint is the value halfway between the lower and upper class limits. For the audit time data, the five class midpoints are 12, 17, 22, 27, and 32.

## Using Excel's PivotTable Report to Construct a Frequency Distribution

*Excel's FREQUENCY function can also be used to construct a frequency distribution for quantitative data.*

Excel's PivotTable report is a powerful tool for summarizing data. In this section we show how to use Excel's PivotTable report to construct a frequency distribution for quantitative data by showing how to construct a frequency distribution for the audit time data.

**Enter Data:** The label "Audit Time" and the 20 audit times are entered into cells A1:A21 of the Excel worksheet in Figure 2.6.

**Enter Functions and Formulas:** No functions and formulas are needed.

**Apply Tools:** The following steps describe how to use Excel's PivotTable report to construct a frequency distribution for the audit time data. When using Excel's PivotTable report, each column of data is referred to as a field. Thus, for the audit time example, the data appearing in cells A2:A21 and the corresponding label in cell A1 are referred to as the Audit Time field.

**Step 1.** Click the **Insert** tab on the Ribbon
**Step 2.** In the **Tables** group, click the icon above the word PivotTable
**Step 3.** When the **Create PivotTable** dialog box appears,
  Choose **Select a table or range**
  Enter A1:A21 in the **Table/Range** box
  Choose **Existing Worksheet** as the location for the PivotTable
  Enter C1 in the **Location** box
  Click **OK**
**Step 4.** In the **PivotTable Field List,** go to **Choose Fields to add to report,**
  Drag the **Audit Time** field to the **Row Labels** area
  Drag the **Audit Time** field to the **Values** area
**Step 5.** Click on **Sum of Audit Time** in the **Values** area
**Step 6.** Click **Value Field Settings** from the list of options that appears

**FIGURE 2.6** PIVOTTABLE FIELD LIST AND INITIAL PIVOTTABLE REPORT USED TO CONSTRUCT A FREQUENCY DISTRIBUTION FOR THE AUDIT TIME DATA

**Step 7.** When the Value Field Settings dialog appears,
> Under **Summarize value field by,** choose **Count**
> Click **OK**

Figure 2.6 shows the resulting PivotTable Field List and the corresponding PivotTable report. To construct the frequency distribution shown in Table 2.5, we must group the rows containing audit times. The following steps accomplish this.

**Step 1.** Right-click cell C2 in the PivotTable report or any other cell containing an audit time
**Step 2.** Choose **Group** from the list of options that appears
**Step 3.** When the **Grouping** dialog box appears,
> Enter 10 in the **Starting at** box
> Enter 34 in the **Ending at** box
> Enter 5 in the **By** box
> Click **OK**

Figure 2.7 shows the completed PivotTable Field List and PivotTable report. We see that with the exception of the column headings, the PivotTable report provides the same information as the frequency distribution shown in Table 2.5. And, if desired, we can change the labels to match the labels in Table 2.5 by selecting the cell and typing in the new label.

**FIGURE 2.7**   FREQUENCY DISTRIBUTION FOR THE AUDIT TIME DATA CONSTRUCTED USING EXCEL'S PIVOTTABLE REPORT

## Relative Frequency and Percent Frequency Distributions

We define the relative frequency and percent frequency distributions for quantitative data in the same manner as for qualitative data. First, recall that the relative frequency is the proportion of the observations belonging to a class. With $n$ observations,

$$\text{Relative frequency of class} = \frac{\text{Frequency of the class}}{n}$$

The percent frequency of a class is the relative frequency multiplied by 100.

Based on the class frequencies in Table 2.5 and with $n = 20$, Table 2.6 shows the relative frequency distribution and percent frequency distribution for the audit time data. Note that .40 of the audits, or 40%, required from 15 to 19 days. Only .05 of the audits, or 5%, required 30 or more days. Again, additional interpretations and insights can be obtained by using Table 2.6.

## Dot Plot

One of the simplest graphical summaries of data is a **dot plot**. A horizontal axis shows the range for the data. Each data value is represented by a dot placed above the axis. Figure 2.8 is the dot plot for the audit time data in Table 2.4. The three dots located above 18 on the horizontal axis indicate that an audit time of 18 days occurred three times. Dot plots show the details of the data and are useful for comparing the distribution of the data for two or more variables.

**TABLE 2.6**    RELATIVE FREQUENCY AND PERCENT FREQUENCY DISTRIBUTIONS FOR
THE AUDIT TIME DATA

| Audit Time (days) | Relative Frequency | Percent Frequency |
|---|---|---|
| 10–14 | .20 | 20 |
| 15–19 | .40 | 40 |
| 20–24 | .25 | 25 |
| 25–29 | .10 | 10 |
| 30–34 | .05 | 5 |
| Total | 1.00 | 100 |

**FIGURE 2.8**    DOT PLOT FOR THE AUDIT TIME DATA

## Histogram

A common graphical presentation of quantitative data is a **histogram**. This graphical summary can be prepared for data previously summarized in either a frequency, relative frequency, or percent frequency distribution. A histogram is constructed by placing the variable of interest on the horizontal axis and the frequency, relative frequency, or percent frequency on the vertical axis. The frequency, relative frequency, or percent frequency of each class is shown by drawing a rectangle whose base is determined by the class limits on the horizontal axis and whose height is the corresponding frequency, relative frequency, or percent frequency.

Figure 2.9 is a histogram for the audit time data. Note that the class with the greatest frequency is shown by the rectangle appearing above the class of 15–19 days. The height of

**FIGURE 2.9**    HISTOGRAM FOR THE AUDIT TIME DATA

the rectangle shows that the frequency of this class is 8. A histogram for the relative or percent frequency distribution of these data would look the same as the histogram in Figure 2.9 with the exception that the vertical axis would be labeled with relative or percent frequency values.

As Figure 2.9 shows, the adjacent rectangles of a histogram touch one another. Unlike a bar graph, a histogram contains no natural separation between the rectangles of adjacent classes. This format is the usual convention for histograms. Because the classes for the audit time data are stated as 10–14, 15–19, 20–24, 25–29, and 30–34, one-unit spaces of 14 to 15, 19 to 20, 24 to 25, and 29 to 30 would seem to be needed between the classes. These spaces are eliminated when constructing a histogram. Eliminating the spaces between classes in a histogram for the audit time data helps show that all values between the lower limit of the first class and the upper limit of the last class are possible.

One of the most important uses of a histogram is to provide information about the shape, or form, of a distribution. Figure 2.10 contains four histograms constructed from relative frequency distributions. Panel A shows the histogram for a set of data moderately skewed to the left. A histogram is said to be skewed to the left if its tail extends farther to the left. This histogram is typical for exam scores, with no scores above 100%, most of the scores above 70%, and only a few really low scores. Panel B shows the histogram for a set of data moderately skewed to the right. A histogram is said to be skewed to the right if its tail extends farther to the right. An example of this type of histogram would be for data such as housing prices; a few expensive houses create the skewness in the right tail.

**FIGURE 2.10**    HISTOGRAMS SHOWING DIFFERING LEVELS OF SKEWNESS

Panel C shows a symmetric histogram. In a symmetric histogram, the left tail mirrors the shape of the right tail. Histograms for data found in applications are never perfectly symmetric, but the histogram for many applications may be roughly symmetric. Data for SAT scores, heights and weights of people, and so on lead to histograms that are roughly symmetric. Panel D shows a histogram highly skewed to the right. This histogram was constructed from data on the amount of customer purchases over one day at a women's apparel store. Data from applications in business and economics often lead to histograms that are skewed to the right. For instance, data on housing prices, salaries, purchase amounts, and so on often result in histograms skewed to the right.

## Using Excel's Chart Tools to Construct a Histogram

In Section 2.1 we showed how Excel's chart tools can be used to construct a bar chart for depicting categorical data summarized in a frequency distribution. Excel's chart tools can also be used to construct a histogram for depicting quantitative data summarized in a frequency distribution. We will illustrate the use of Excel's chart tools for constructing a histogram using the frequency distribution for the audit time data constructed using Excel's PivotTable Report. Refer to Figure 2.11 as we describe the tasks involved.

**Enter Data:**   Same as in Figure 2.7

**Enter Functions and Formulas:**   No functions and formulas are needed.

**FIGURE 2.11**   USING EXCEL'S CHART TOOLS TO CONSTRUCT A HISTOGRAM FOR THE AUDIT TIME DATA

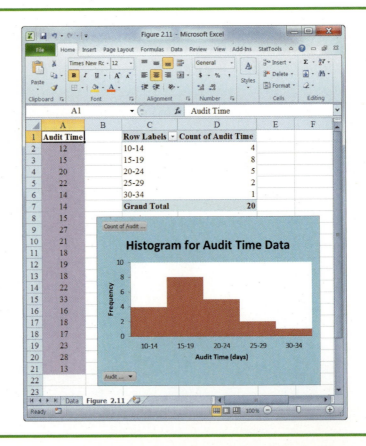

**Apply Tools:** The following steps describe how to use Excel's chart tools to construct a histogram for the audit time data using the frequency distribution appearing in cells C1:D6.

**Step 1.** Select cells C2:D6
**Step 2.** Click the **Insert** tab on the Ribbon
**Step 3.** In the **Charts** group, click **Column**
**Step 4.** When the list of column chart types appears,
Go to the **2-D Column** section
Click **Clustered Column** (the leftmost chart)
**Step 5.** In the **Chart Layouts** group, click the **More** button (the downward pointing arrow with a line over it) to display all the options
**Step 6.** Choose **Layout 8**
**Step 7.** Click the **Chart Title** and replace it with **Histogram for Audit Time Data**
**Step 8.** Click the **Horizontal (Category) Axis Title** and replace it with **Audit Time (days)**
**Step 9.** Click the **Vertical (Value) Axis Title** and replace it with **Frequency**
**Step 10.** Right-click the vertical axis and choose **Format Axis** from the list of options that appear
**Step 11.** When the Format Axis dialog box appears,
Go to the **Axis Options** section
Select Fixed for the **Major Unit** and enter 1.0 in the corresponding box
Click **Close**

Figure 2.11 shows the completed histogram for the audit time data constructed using the PivotTable report output and Excel's chart tools. Because the histogram was constructed using the frequency distribution created using Excel's PivotTable report, the resulting chart contains a Value field button in the top left part of the chart and an Axis field button in the lower left part of the chart. If you want to remove either of both of these buttons, you right-click the button and select the option to remove that button or to remove all buttons shown on the chart.

## Cumulative Distributions

A variation of the frequency distribution that provides another tabular summary of quantitative data is the cumulative frequency distribution. The cumulative frequency distribution uses the number of classes, class widths, and class limits developed for the frequency distribution. However, rather than showing the frequency of each class, the cumulative frequency distribution shows the number of data items with values *less than or equal to the upper class limit* of each class. The first two columns of Table 2.7 provide the cumulative frequency distribution for the audit time data.

**TABLE 2.7** CUMULATIVE FREQUENCY, CUMULATIVE RELATIVE FREQUENCY, AND CUMULATIVE PERCENT FREQUENCY DISTRIBUTIONS FOR THE AUDIT TIME DATA

| Audit Time (days) | Cumulative Frequency | Cumulative Relative Frequency | Cumulative Percent Frequency |
|---|---|---|---|
| Less than or equal to 14 | 4 | .20 | 20 |
| Less than or equal to 19 | 12 | .60 | 60 |
| Less than or equal to 24 | 17 | .85 | 85 |
| Less than or equal to 29 | 19 | .95 | 95 |
| Less than or equal to 34 | 20 | 1.00 | 100 |

To understand how the cumulative frequencies are determined, consider the class with the description "less than or equal to 24." The cumulative frequency for this class is simply the sum of the frequencies for all classes with data values less than or equal to 24. For the frequency distribution in Table 2.5, the sum of the frequencies for classes 10–14, 15–19, and 20–24 indicates that $4 + 8 + 5 = 17$ data values are less than or equal to 24. Hence, the cumulative frequency for this class is 17. In addition, the cumulative frequency distribution in Table 2.7 shows that four audits were completed in 14 days or less and 19 audits were completed in 29 days or less.

As a final point, we note that a **cumulative relative frequency distribution** shows the proportion of data items, and a **cumulative percent frequency distribution** shows the percentage of data items with values less than or equal to the upper limit of each class. The cumulative relative frequency distribution can be computed either by summing the relative frequencies in the relative frequency distribution or by dividing the cumulative frequencies by the total number of items. Using the latter approach, we found the cumulative relative frequencies in column 3 of Table 2.7 by dividing the cumulative frequencies in column 2 by the total number of items ($n = 20$). The cumulative percent frequencies were again computed by multiplying the relative frequencies by 100. The cumulative relative and percent frequency distributions show that .85 of the audits, or 85%, were completed in 24 days or less, .95 of the audits, or 95%, were completed in 29 days or less, and so on.

## Ogive

A graph of a cumulative distribution, called an *ogive*, shows data values on the horizontal axis and either the cumulative frequencies, the cumulative relative frequencies, or the cumulative percent frequencies on the vertical axis. Figure 2.12 illustrates an ogive for the cumulative frequencies of the audit time data in Table 2.7.

The ogive is constructed by plotting a point corresponding to the cumulative frequency of each class. Because the classes for the audit time data are 10–14, 15–19, 20–24, and so on, one-unit gaps appear from 14 to 15, 19 to 20, and so on. These gaps are eliminated by plotting points halfway between the class limits. Thus, 14.5 is used for the 10–14 class, 19.5 is used for the 15–19 class, and so on. The "less than or equal to 14" class with a cumulative

**FIGURE 2.12    OGIVE FOR THE AUDIT TIME DATA**

frequency of 4 is shown on the ogive in Figure 2.12 by the point located at 14.5 on the horizontal axis and 4 on the vertical axis. The "less than or equal to 19" class with a cumulative frequency of 12 is shown by the point located at 19.5 on the horizontal axis and 12 on the vertical axis. Note that one additional point is plotted at the left end of the ogive. This point starts the ogive by showing that no data values fall below the 10–14 class. It is plotted at 9.5 on the horizontal axis and 0 on the vertical axis. The plotted points are connected by straight lines to complete the ogive.

## NOTES AND COMMENTS

1. A bar chart and a histogram are essentially the same thing; both are graphical presentations of the data in a frequency distribution. A histogram is just a bar chart with no separation between bars. For some discrete quantitative data, a separation between bars is also appropriate. Consider, for example, the number of classes in which a college student is enrolled. The data may only assume integer values. Intermediate values such as 1.5, 2.73, and so on are not possible. With continuous quantitative data, however, such as the audit times in Table 2.4, a separation between bars is not appropriate.

2. The appropriate values for the class limits with quantitative data depend on the level of accuracy of the data. For instance, with the audit time data of Table 2.4 the limits used were integer values. If the data were rounded to the nearest tenth of a day (e.g., 12.3, 14.4, and so on), then the limits would be stated in tenths of days. For instance, the first class would be 10.0–14.9. If the data were recorded to the nearest hundredth of a day

(e.g., 12.34, 14.45, and so on), the limits would be stated in hundredths of days. For instance, the first class would be 10.00–14.99.

3. An *open-end* class requires only a lower class limit or an upper class limit. For example, in the audit time data of Table 2.4, suppose two of the audits had taken 58 and 65 days. Rather than continue with the classes of width 5 with classes 35–39, 40–44, 45–49, and so on, we could simplify the frequency distribution to show an open-end class of "35 or more." This class would have a frequency of 2. Most often the open-end class appears at the upper end of the distribution. Sometimes an open-end class appears at the lower end of the distribution, and occasionally such classes appear at both ends.

4. The last entry in a cumulative frequency distribution always equals the total number of observations. The last entry in a cumulative relative frequency distribution always equals 1.00 and the last entry in a cumulative percent frequency distribution always equals 100.

## Exercises

## Methods

11.  Consider the following data.

|     |     |     |     |     |
|-----|-----|-----|-----|-----|
| 14  | 21  | 23  | 21  | 16  |
| 19  | 22  | 25  | 16  | 16  |
| 24  | 24  | 25  | 19  | 16  |
| 19  | 18  | 19  | 21  | 12  |
| 16  | 17  | 18  | 23  | 25  |
| 20  | 23  | 16  | 20  | 19  |
| 24  | 26  | 15  | 22  | 24  |
| 20  | 22  | 24  | 22  | 20  |

**WEB** file
Frequency

a.  Develop a frequency distribution using classes of 12–14, 15–17, 18–20, 21–23, and 24–26.
b.  Develop a relative frequency distribution and a percent frequency distribution using the classes in part (a).

12. Consider the following frequency distribution.

| Class | Frequency |
|-------|-----------|
| 10–19 | 10 |
| 20–29 | 14 |
| 30–39 | 17 |
| 40–49 | 7 |
| 50–59 | 2 |

Construct a cumulative frequency distribution and a cumulative relative frequency distribution.

13. Construct a histogram and an ogive for the data in exercise 12.

14. Consider the following data.

| | | | | | | | | | |
|---|---|---|---|---|---|---|---|---|---|
| 8.9 | 10.2 | 11.5 | 7.8 | 10.0 | 12.2 | 13.5 | 14.1 | 10.0 | 12.2 |
| 6.8 | 9.5 | 11.5 | 11.2 | 14.9 | 7.5 | 10.0 | 6.0 | 15.8 | 11.5 |

a. Construct a dot plot.
b. Construct a frequency distribution.
c. Construct a percent frequency distribution.

## Applications

15. A doctor's office staff studied the waiting times for patients who arrive at the office with a request for emergency service. The following data with waiting times in minutes were collected over a one-month period.

2   5   10   12   4   4   5   17   11   8   9   8   12   21   6   8   7   13   18   3

Use classes of 0–4, 5–9, and so on in the following:
a. Show the frequency distribution.
b. Show the relative frequency distribution.
c. Show the cumulative frequency distribution.
d. Show the cumulative relative frequency distribution.
e. What proportion of patients needing emergency service wait 9 minutes or less?

16. A shortage of candidates has required school districts to pay higher salaries and offer extras to attract and retain school district superintendents. The following data show the annual base salary ($1000s) for superintendents in 20 districts in the greater Rochester, New York, area (*The Rochester Democrat and Chronicle*, February 10, 2008).

| | | | |
|-----|-----|-----|-----|
| 187 | 184 | 174 | 185 |
| 175 | 172 | 202 | 197 |
| 165 | 208 | 215 | 164 |
| 162 | 172 | 182 | 156 |
| 172 | 175 | 170 | 183 |

Use classes of 150–159, 160–169, and so on in the following.
a. Show the frequency distribution.
b. Show the percent frequency distribution.
c. Show the cumulative percent frequency distribution.
d. Develop a histogram for the annual base salary.
e. Do the data appear to be skewed? Explain.
f. What percentage of the superintendents make more than $200,000?

17. The Dow Jones Industrial Average (DJIA) underwent one of its infrequent reshufflings of companies when General Motors and Citigroup were replaced by Cisco Systems and Travelers (*The Wall Street Journal,* June 8, 2009). At the time, the prices per share for the 30 companies in the DJIA were as follows:

DJIAPrices Revised

| Company | $/Share | Company | $/Share |
|---|---|---|---|
| 3M | 61 | IBM | 107 |
| Alcoa | 11 | Intel | 16 |
| American Express | 25 | JPMorgan Chase | 35 |
| AT&T | 24 | Johnson & Johnson | 56 |
| Bank of America | 12 | Kraft Foods | 27 |
| Boeing | 52 | McDonald's | 59 |
| Caterpillar | 38 | Merck | 26 |
| Chevron | 69 | Microsoft | 22 |
| Cisco Systems | 20 | Pfizer | 14 |
| Coca-Cola | 49 | Procter & Gamble | 53 |
| DuPont | 27 | Travelers | 43 |
| ExxonMobil | 72 | United Technologies | 56 |
| General Electric | 14 | Verizon | 29 |
| Hewlett-Packard | 37 | Walmart Stores | 51 |
| Home Depot | 24 | Walt Disney | 25 |

a. What is the highest price per share? What is the lowest price per share?

b. Using a class width of 10, develop a frequency distribution for the data.

c. Prepare a histogram. Interpret the histogram, including a discussion of the general shape of the histogram, the midprice range, and the most frequent price range.

d. Use the *The Wall Street Journal* or another newspaper to find the current price per share for these companies. Prepare a histogram of the data and discuss any changes since June 2009. What company has had the largest increase in the price per share? What company has had the largest decrease in the price per share?

18. NRF/BIG research provided results of a consumer holiday spending survey (*USA Today,* December 20, 2005). The following data provide the dollar amount of holiday spending for a sample of 25 consumers.

Holiday

| | | | | |
|---|---|---|---|---|
| 1200 | 850 | 740 | 590 | 340 |
| 450 | 890 | 260 | 610 | 350 |
| 1780 | 180 | 850 | 2050 | 770 |
| 800 | 1090 | 510 | 520 | 220 |
| 1450 | 280 | 1120 | 200 | 350 |

a. What is the lowest holiday spending? The highest?

b. Use a class width of $250 to prepare a frequency distribution and a percent frequency distribution for the data.

c. Prepare a histogram and comment on the shape of the distribution.

d. What observations can you make about holiday spending?

19. *Fortune* provides a list of America's largest corporations based on annual revenue. Shown below are the 50 largest corporations, with annual revenue expressed in billions of dollars (CNN Money website, January 15, 2010).

LargeCorp

| Corporation | Revenue | Corporation | Revenue |
|---|---|---|---|
| Amerisource Bergen | 71 | Berkshire Hathaway | 108 |
| Archer Daniels Midland | 70 | Boeing | 61 |
| AT&T | 124 | Cardinal Health | 91 |
| Bank of America | 113 | Caterpillar | 51 |

(*Continued*)

| Corporation | Revenue | Corporation | Revenue |
|---|---|---|---|
| Chevron | 263 | MetLife | 55 |
| Citigroup | 112 | Microsoft | 60 |
| ConocoPhillips | 231 | Morgan Stanley | 62 |
| Costco Wholesale | 72 | Pepsico | 43 |
| CVS Caremark | 87 | Pfizer | 48 |
| Dell | 61 | Procter & Gamble | 84 |
| Dow Chemical | 58 | Safeway | 44 |
| ExxonMobil | 443 | Sears Holdings | 47 |
| Ford Motors | 146 | State Farm Insurance | 61 |
| General Electric | 149 | Sunoco | 52 |
| Goldman Sachs | 54 | Target | 65 |
| Hewlett-Packard | 118 | Time Warner | 47 |
| Home Depot | 71 | United Parcel Service | 51 |
| IBM | 104 | United Technologies | 59 |
| JPMorgan Chase | 101 | UnitedHealth Group | 81 |
| Johnson & Johnson | 64 | Valero Energy | 118 |
| Kroger | 76 | Verizon | 97 |
| Lowe's | 48 | Walgreen | 59 |
| Marathon Oil | 74 | Walmart | 406 |
| McKesson | 102 | WellPoint | 61 |
| Medco Health | 51 | Wells Fargo | 52 |

Summarize the data by constructing the following:

a.  A frequency distribution (classes 0–49, 50–99, 100–149, and so on).
b.  A relative frequency distribution.
c.  A cumulative frequency distribution.
d.  A cumulative relative frequency distribution.
e.  What do these distributions tell you about the annual revenue of the largest corporations in America?
f.  Show a histogram. Comment on the shape of the distribution.
g.  What is the largest corporation in America and what is its annual revenue?

20. The *Golf Digest 50* lists the 50 professional golfers with the highest total annual income. Total income is the sum of both on-course and off-course earnings. Tiger Woods ranked first with a total annual income of $122 million. However, almost $100 million of this total was from off-course activities such as product endorsements and personal appearances. The 10 professional golfers with the highest *off-course* income are shown in the following table (Golf Digest website, February 2008).

| Name | Off-Course Income ($1000s) |
|---|---|
| Tiger Woods | 99,800 |
| Phil Mickelson | 40,200 |
| Arnold Palmer | 29,500 |
| Vijay Singh | 25,250 |
| Ernie Els | 24,500 |
| Greg Norman | 24,000 |
| Jack Nicklaus | 20,750 |
| Sergio Garcia | 14,500 |
| Michelle Wie | 12,500 |
| Jim Furyk | 11,000 |

The off-course income of all 50 professional golfers in the *Golf Digest 50* can be found on the website that accompanies the text. The income data are in $1000s. Use classes of

0–4999, 5000–9999, 10,000–14,999, and so on to answer the following questions. Include an open-ended class of 50,000 or more as the largest income class.

OffCourse

a. Construct a frequency distribution and percent frequency distribution of the annual off-course income of the 50 professional golfers.
b. Construct a histogram for these data.
c. Comment on the shape of the distribution of off-course income.
d. What is the most frequent off-course income class for the 50 professional golfers? Using your tabular and graphical summaries, what additional observations can you make about the off-course income of these 50 professional golfers?

21. The *Nielsen Home Technology Report* provided information about home technology and its usage. The following data are the hours of personal computer usage during one week for a sample of 50 persons.

Computer

| 4.1 | 1.5 | 10.4 | 5.9 | 3.4 | 5.7 | 1.6 | 6.1 | 3.0 | 3.7 |
|-----|-----|------|------|------|-----|-----|------|------|-----|
| 3.1 | 4.8 | 2.0 | 14.8 | 5.4 | 4.2 | 3.9 | 4.1 | 11.1 | 3.5 |
| 4.1 | 4.1 | 8.8 | 5.6 | 4.3 | 3.3 | 7.1 | 10.3 | 6.2 | 7.6 |
| 10.8 | 2.8 | 9.5 | 12.9 | 12.1 | 0.7 | 4.0 | 9.2 | 4.4 | 5.7 |
| 7.2 | 6.1 | 5.7 | 5.9 | 4.7 | 3.9 | 3.7 | 3.1 | 6.1 | 3.1 |

Summarize the data by constructing the following:
a. A frequency distribution (use a class width of three hours)
b. A relative frequency distribution
c. A histogram
d. An ogive
e. Comment on what the data indicate about personal computer usage at home.

## 2.3 Exploratory Data Analysis: The Stem-and-Leaf Display

The techniques of **exploratory data analysis** consist of simple arithmetic and easy-to-draw graphs that can be used to summarize data quickly. One technique—referred to as a **stem-and-leaf display**—can be used to show both the rank order and shape of a data set simultaneously.

To illustrate the use of a stem-and-leaf display, consider the data in Table 2.8. These data result from a 150-question aptitude test given to 50 individuals recently interviewed for a position at Haskens Manufacturing. The data indicate the number of questions answered correctly.

To develop a stem-and-leaf display, we first arrange the leading digits of each data value to the left of a vertical line. To the right of the vertical line, we record the last digit for each

**TABLE 2.8  NUMBER OF QUESTIONS ANSWERED CORRECTLY ON AN APTITUDE TEST**

ApTest

| 112 | 72 | 69 | 97 | 107 |
|-----|-----|-----|-----|-----|
| 73 | 92 | 76 | 86 | 73 |
| 126 | 128 | 118 | 127 | 124 |
| 82 | 104 | 132 | 134 | 83 |
| 92 | 108 | 96 | 100 | 92 |
| 115 | 76 | 91 | 102 | 81 |
| 95 | 141 | 81 | 80 | 106 |
| 84 | 119 | 113 | 98 | 75 |
| 68 | 98 | 115 | 106 | 95 |
| 100 | 85 | 94 | 106 | 119 |

data value. Based on the top row of data in Table 2.8 (112, 72, 69, 97, and 107), the first five entries in constructing a stem-and-leaf display would be as follows:

```
 6 | 9
 7 | 2
 8 |
 9 | 7
10 | 7
11 | 2
12 |
13 |
14 |
```

For example, the data value 112 shows the leading digits 11 to the left of the line and the last digit 2 to the right of the line. Similarly, the data value 72 shows the leading digit 7 to the left of the line and last digit 2 to the right of the line. Continuing to place the last digit of each data value on the line corresponding to its leading digit(s) provides the following:

```
 6 | 9  8
 7 | 2  3  6  3  6  5
 8 | 6  2  3  1  1  0  4  5
 9 | 7  2  2  6  2  1  5  8  8  5  4
10 | 7  4  8  0  2  6  6  0  6
11 | 2  8  5  9  3  5  9
12 | 6  8  7  4
13 | 2  4
14 | 1
```

With this organization of the data, sorting the digits on each line into rank order is simple. Doing so provides the stem-and-leaf display shown here.

```
 6 | 8  9
 7 | 2  3  3  5  6  6
 8 | 0  1  1  2  3  4  5  6
 9 | 1  2  2  2  4  5  5  6  7  8  8
10 | 0  0  2  4  6  6  6  7  8
11 | 2  3  5  5  8  9  9
12 | 4  6  7  8
13 | 2  4
14 | 1
```

The numbers to the left of the vertical line (6, 7, 8, 9, 10, 11, 12, 13, and 14) form the *stem,* and each digit to the right of the vertical line is a *leaf.* For example, consider the first row with a stem value of 6 and leaves of 8 and 9.

$$6 \mid 8 \quad 9$$

This row indicates that two data values have a first digit of six. The leaves show that the data values are 68 and 69. Similarly, the second row

7 | 2  3  3  5  6  6

indicates that six data values have a first digit of seven. The leaves show that the data values are 72, 73, 73, 75, 76, and 76.

To focus on the shape indicated by the stem-and-leaf display, let us use a rectangle to contain the leaves of each stem. Doing so, we obtain the following:

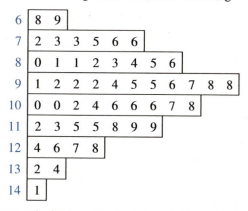

Rotating this page counterclockwise onto its side provides a picture of the data that is similar to a histogram with classes of 60–69, 70–79, 80–89, and so on.

Although the stem-and-leaf display may appear to offer the same information as a histogram, it has two primary advantages.

1. The stem-and-leaf display is easier to construct by hand.
2. Within a class interval, the stem-and-leaf display provides more information than the histogram because the stem-and-leaf shows the actual data.

Just as a frequency distribution or histogram has no absolute number of classes, neither does a stem-and-leaf display have an absolute number of rows or stems. If we believe that our original stem-and-leaf display condensed the data too much, we can easily stretch the display by using two or more stems for each leading digit. For example, to use two stems for each leading digit, we would place all data values ending in 0, 1, 2, 3, and 4 in one row and all values ending in 5, 6, 7, 8, and 9 in a second row. The following stretched stem-and-leaf display illustrates this approach.

*In a stretched stem-and-leaf display, whenever a stem value is stated twice, the first value corresponds to leaf values of 0–4, and the second value corresponds to leaf values of 5–9.*

```
 6 | 8  9
 7 | 2  3  3
 7 | 5  6  6
 8 | 0  1  1  2  3  4
 8 | 5  6
 9 | 1  2  2  2  4
 9 | 5  5  6  7  8  8
10 | 0  0  2  4
10 | 6  6  6  7  8
11 | 2  3
11 | 5  5  8  9  9
12 | 4
12 | 6  7  8
13 | 2  4
13 |
14 | 1
```

Note that values 72, 73, and 73 have leaves in the 0–4 range and are shown with the first stem value of 7. The values 75, 76, and 76 have leaves in the 5–9 range and are shown with the second stem value of 7. This stretched stem-and-leaf display is similar to a frequency distribution with intervals of 65–69, 70–74, 75–79, and so on.

The preceding example showed a stem-and-leaf display for data with as many as three digits. Stem-and-leaf displays for data with more than three digits are possible. For example, consider the following data on the number of hamburgers sold by a fast-food restaurant for each of 15 weeks.

| | | | | | | | |
|---|---|---|---|---|---|---|---|
| 1565 | 1852 | 1644 | 1766 | 1888 | 1912 | 2044 | 1812 |
| 1790 | 1679 | 2008 | 1852 | 1967 | 1954 | 1733 | |

A stem-and-leaf display of these data follows.

Leaf unit = 10

| | |
|---:|---|
| 15 | 6 |
| 16 | 4  7 |
| 17 | 3  6  9 |
| 18 | 1  5  5  8 |
| 19 | 1  5  6 |
| 20 | 0  4 |

*A single digit is used to define each leaf in a stem-and-leaf display. The leaf unit indicates how to multiply the stem-and-leaf numbers in order to approximate the original data. Leaf units may be 100, 10, 1, 0.1, and so on.*

Note that a single digit is used to define each leaf and that only the first three digits of each data value have been used to construct the display. At the top of the display we have specified Leaf unit = 10. To illustrate how to interpret the values in the display, consider the first stem, 15, and its associated leaf, 6. Combining these numbers, we obtain 156. To reconstruct an approximation of the original data value, we must multiply this number by 10, the value of the *leaf unit*. Thus, $156 \times 10 = 1560$ is an approximation of the original data value used to construct the stem-and-leaf display. Although it is not possible to reconstruct the exact data value from this stem-and-leaf display, the convention of using a single digit for each leaf enables stem-and-leaf displays to be constructed for data having a large number of digits. For stem-and-leaf displays where the leaf unit is not shown, the leaf unit is assumed to equal 1.

## Exercises

### Methods

22. Construct a stem-and-leaf display for the following data.

| | | | | | | | |
|---|---|---|---|---|---|---|---|
| 70 | 72 | 75 | 64 | 58 | 83 | 80 | 82 |
| 76 | 75 | 68 | 65 | 57 | 78 | 85 | 72 |

23. Construct a stem-and-leaf display for the following data.

| | | | | | | |
|---|---|---|---|---|---|---|
| 11.3 | 9.6 | 10.4 | 7.5 | 8.3 | 10.5 | 10.0 |
| 9.3 | 8.1 | 7.7 | 7.5 | 8.4 | 6.3 | 8.8 |

24. Construct a stem-and-leaf display for the following data. Use a leaf unit of 10.

| | | | | | | | |
|---|---|---|---|---|---|---|---|
| 1161 | 1206 | 1478 | 1300 | 1604 | 1725 | 1361 | 1422 |
| 1221 | 1378 | 1623 | 1426 | 1557 | 1730 | 1706 | 1689 |

## Applications

25. A psychologist developed a new test of adult intelligence. The test was administered to 20 individuals, and the following data were obtained.

| 114 | 99 | 131 | 124 | 117 | 102 | 106 | 127 | 119 | 115 |
|-----|-----|-----|-----|-----|-----|-----|-----|-----|-----|
| 98 | 104 | 144 | 151 | 132 | 106 | 125 | 122 | 118 | 118 |

Construct a stem-and-leaf display for the data.

26. *Money magazine* listed top career opportunities for work that is enjoyable, pays well, and will still be around 10 years from now (*Money,* November 2009). Shown below are 20 top career opportunities, with the median pay and top pay for workers with two to seven years of experience in the field. Data are shown in thousands of dollars.

**Careers**

| Career | Median Pay | Top Pay |
|--------|-----------|---------|
| Account Executive | 81 | 157 |
| Certified Public Accountant | 74 | 138 |
| Computer Security Consultant | 100 | 138 |
| Director of Communications | 78 | 135 |
| Financial Analyst | 80 | 109 |
| Finance Director | 121 | 214 |
| Financial Research Analyst | 66 | 155 |
| Hotel General Manager | 77 | 146 |
| Human Resources Manager | 72 | 111 |
| Investment Banking | 106 | 221 |
| IT Business Analyst | 83 | 119 |
| IT Project Manager | 99 | 140 |
| Marketing Manager | 77 | 126 |
| Quality-Assurance Manager | 80 | 122 |
| Sales Representative | 67 | 125 |
| Senior Internal Auditor | 76 | 106 |
| Software Developer | 79 | 116 |
| Software Program Manager | 110 | 152 |
| Systems Engineer | 87 | 130 |
| Technical Writer | 67 | 100 |

Develop a stem-and-leaf display for both the median pay and the top pay. Comment on what you learn about the pay for these careers.

27. Most major ski resorts offer family programs that provide ski and snowboarding instruction for children. The typical classes provide four to six hours on the snow with a certified instructor. The daily rate for a group lesson at 15 ski resorts follows (*The Wall Street Journal,* January 20, 2006).

| Resort | Location | Daily Rate | Resort | Location | Daily Rate |
|--------|----------|-----------|--------|----------|-----------|
| Beaver Creek | Colorado | $137 | Okemo | Vermont | $ 86 |
| Deer Valley | Utah | 115 | Park City | Utah | 145 |
| Diamond Peak | California | 95 | Butternut | Massachusetts | 75 |
| Heavenly | California | 145 | Steamboat | Colorado | 98 |
| Hunter | New York | 79 | Stowe | Vermont | 104 |
| Mammoth | California | 111 | Sugar Bowl | California | 100 |
| Mount Sunapee | New Hampshire | 96 | Whistler-Blackcomb | British Columbia | 104 |
| Mount Bachelor | Oregon | 83 | | | |

a.  Develop a stem-and-leaf display for the data.
b.  Interpret the stem-and-leaf display in terms of what it tells you about the daily rate for these ski and snowboarding instruction programs.

28. The 2004 Naples, Florida, half-marathon (13.1 miles) had 1228 registrants (*Naples Daily News,* January 17, 2004). Competition was held in six age groups. The following data show the ages for a sample of 40 individuals who participated in the marathon.

| | | | | |
|---|---|---|---|---|
| 49 | 33 | 40 | 37 | 56 |
| 44 | 46 | 57 | 55 | 32 |
| 50 | 52 | 43 | 64 | 40 |
| 46 | 24 | 30 | 37 | 43 |
| 31 | 43 | 50 | 36 | 61 |
| 27 | 44 | 35 | 31 | 43 |
| 52 | 43 | 66 | 31 | 50 |
| 72 | 26 | 59 | 21 | 47 |

**Marathon**

a.  Show a stretched stem-and-leaf display.
b.  What age group had the largest number of runners?
c.  What age occurred most frequently?
d.  A *Naples Daily News* feature article emphasized the number of runners who were "20-something." What percentage of the runners were in the 20-something age group? What do you suppose was the focus of the article?

## 2.4  Crosstabulations and Scatter Diagrams

*Crosstabulations and scatter diagrams are used to summarize data in a way that reveals the relationship between two variables.*

Thus far in this chapter, we have focused on tabular and graphical methods used to summarize the data for *one variable at a time.* Often a manager or decision maker requires tabular and graphical methods that will assist in the understanding of the *relationship between two variables.* Crosstabulation and scatter diagrams are two such methods.

### Crosstabulation

A **crosstabulation** is a tabular summary of data for two variables. Let us illustrate the use of a crosstabulation by considering the following application based on data from Zagat's Restaurant Review. The quality rating and the meal price data were collected for a sample of 300 restaurants located in the Los Angeles area. Table 2.9 shows the data for the first 10 restaurants. Data on a restaurant's quality rating and typical meal price are reported. Quality rating is a categorical variable with rating categories of good, very good, and excellent. Meal price is a quantitative variable that ranges from $10 to $49.

A crosstabulation of the data for this application is shown in Table 2.10. The left and top margin labels define the classes for the two variables. In the left margin, the row labels (good, very good, and excellent) correspond to the three classes of the quality rating variable. In the top margin, the column labels ($10–19, $20–29, $30–39, and $40–49) correspond to the four classes of the meal price variable. Each restaurant in the sample provides a quality rating and a meal price. Thus, each restaurant in the sample is associated with a cell appearing in one of the rows and one of the columns of the crosstabulation. For example, restaurant 5 is identified as having a very good quality rating and a meal price of $33. This restaurant belongs to the cell in row 2 and column 3 of Table 2.10. In constructing a crosstabulation, we simply count the number of restaurants that belong to each of the cells in the crosstabulation table.

**TABLE 2.9** QUALITY RATING AND MEAL PRICE FOR 300 LOS ANGELES RESTAURANTS

**WEB** file

**Restaurant**

| Restaurant | Quality Rating | Meal Price ($) |
|---|---|---|
| 1 | Good | 18 |
| 2 | Very Good | 22 |
| 3 | Good | 28 |
| 4 | Excellent | 38 |
| 5 | Very Good | 33 |
| 6 | Good | 28 |
| 7 | Very Good | 19 |
| 8 | Very Good | 11 |
| 9 | Very Good | 23 |
| 10 | Good | 13 |
| . | . | . |
| . | . | . |
| . | . | . |

**TABLE 2.10** CROSSTABULATION OF QUALITY RATING AND MEAL PRICE FOR 300 LOS ANGELES RESTAURANTS

| Quality Rating | Meal Price | | | | Total |
|---|---|---|---|---|---|
| | $10–19 | $20–29 | $30–39 | $40–49 | |
| Good | 42 | 40 | 2 | 0 | 84 |
| Very Good | 34 | 64 | 46 | 6 | 150 |
| Excellent | 2 | 14 | 28 | 22 | 66 |
| Total | 78 | 118 | 76 | 28 | 300 |

In reviewing Table 2.10, we see that the greatest number of restaurants in the sample (64) have a very good rating and a meal price in the $20–29 range. Only two restaurants have an excellent rating and a meal price in the $10–19 range. Similar interpretations of the other frequencies can be made. In addition, note that the right and bottom margins of the crosstabulation provide the frequency distributions for quality rating and meal price separately. From the frequency distribution in the right margin, we see that data on quality ratings show 84 good restaurants, 150 very good restaurants, and 66 excellent restaurants. Similarly, the bottom margin shows the frequency distribution for the meal price variable.

Dividing the totals in the right margin of the crosstabulation by the total for that column provides a relative and percent frequency distribution for the quality rating variable.

| Quality Rating | Relative Frequency | Percent Frequency |
|---|---|---|
| Good | .28 | 28 |
| Very Good | .50 | 50 |
| Excellent | .22 | 22 |
| Total | 1.00 | 100 |

From the percent frequency distribution we see that 28% of the restaurants were rated good, 50% were rated very good, and 22% were rated excellent.

Dividing the totals in the bottom row of the crosstabulation by the total for that row provides a relative and percent frequency distribution for the meal price variable.

| Meal Price | Relative Frequency | Percent Frequency |
|---|---|---|
| $10–19 | .26 | 26 |
| $20–29 | .39 | 39 |
| $30–39 | .25 | 25 |
| $40–49 | .09 | 9 |
| **Total** | 1.00 | 100 |

Note that the sum of the values in each column does not add exactly to the column total, because the values being summed are rounded. From the percent frequency distribution we see that 26% of the meal prices are in the lowest price class ($10–19), 39% are in the next higher class, and so on.

The frequency and relative frequency distributions constructed from the margins of a crosstabulation provide information about each of the variables individually, but they do not shed any light on the relationship between the variables. The primary value of a crosstabulation lies in the insight it offers about the relationship between the variables. A review of the crosstabulation in Table 2.10 reveals that higher meal prices are associated with the higher quality restaurants, and the lower meal prices are associated with the lower quality restaurants.

Converting the entries in a crosstabulation into row percentages or column percentages can provide more insight into the relationship between the two variables. For row percentages, the results of dividing each frequency in Table 2.10 by its corresponding row total are shown in Table 2.11. Each row of Table 2.11 is a percent frequency distribution of meal price for one of the quality rating categories. Of the restaurants with the lowest quality rating (good), we see that the greatest percentages are for the less expensive restaurants (50% have $10–19 meal prices and 47.6% have $20–29 meal prices). Of the restaurants with the highest quality rating (excellent), we see that the greatest percentages are for the more expensive restaurants (42.4% have $30–39 meal prices and 33.4% have $40–49 meal prices). Thus, we continue to see that the more expensive meals are associated with the higher quality restaurants.

A graph showing the information in a crosstabulation can also be developed to enhance the presentation. Figure 2.13 shows an Excel column chart for the results displayed in Table 2.11.

In practice, the final reports for many statistical studies include a large number of crosstabulations. In the Los Angeles restaurant survey, the crosstabulation is based on one categorical variable (quality rating) and one quantitative variable (meal price). Crosstabulations can also be developed when both variables are categorical and when both variables

**TABLE 2.11**    ROW PERCENTAGES FOR EACH QUALITY RATING CATEGORY

| Quality Rating | Meal Price $10–19 | $20–29 | $30–39 | $40–49 | Total |
|---|---|---|---|---|---|
| Good | 50.0 | 47.6 | 2.4 | 0.0 | 100 |
| Very Good | 22.7 | 42.7 | 30.6 | 4.0 | 100 |
| Excellent | 3.0 | 21.2 | 42.4 | 33.4 | 100 |

**FIGURE 2.13**    EXCEL COLUMN CHART SHOWING ROW PERCENTAGES FOR EACH
QUALITY RATING CATEGORY

are quantitative. When quantitative variables are used, however, we must first create classes for the values of the variable. For instance, in the restaurant example we grouped the meal prices into four classes ($10–19, $20–29, $30–39, and $40–49).

## Using Excel's PivotTable Report to Construct a Crosstabulation

Excel's PivotTable Report provides an excellent tool for summarizing the data for two or more variables simultaneously. We will illustrate the use of Excel's PivotTable Report by showing how to develop a crosstabulation of quality ratings and meal prices for the sample of 300 restaurants located in the Los Angeles area.

**Enter Data:**    The labels "Restaurant," "Quality Rating," and "Meal Price ($)" have been entered into cells A1:C1 of the worksheet shown in Figure 2.14. The data for each of the 300 restaurants in the sample have been entered into cells B2:C301.

**Enter Functions and Formulas:**    No functions and formulas are needed.

**Apply Tools:**    To use the PivotTable report to create a crosstabulation, we need to perform three tasks: Display the Initial PivotTable Field List and PivotTable Report; Set Up the PivotTable Field List; Finalize the PivotTable Report.

**Display the Initial PivotTable Field List and PivotTable Report:**    Three steps are needed to display the initial PivotTable Field List and PivotTable report.

> **Step 1.**  Click the **Insert** tab on the Ribbon
> **Step 2.**  In the **Tables** group, click the icon above the word PivotTable
> **Step 3.**  When the **Create PivotTable** dialog box appears,
> > Choose **Select a Table or Range**
> > Enter A1:C301 in the **Table/Range** box
> > Choose **New Worksheet** as the location for the PivotTable Report
> > Click **OK**

The resulting initial PivotTable Field List and PivotTable Report are shown in Figure 2.15.

**FIGURE 2.14**    EXCEL WORKSHEET CONTAINING RESTAURANT DATA

**WEB** file

**Restaurant**

*Note: Rows 12–291
are hidden.*

| | A | B | C | D |
|---|---|---|---|---|
| 1 | **Restaurant** | **Quality Rating** | **Meal Price ($)** | |
| 2 | 1 | Good | 18 | |
| 3 | 2 | Very Good | 22 | |
| 4 | 3 | Good | 28 | |
| 5 | 4 | Excellent | 38 | |
| 6 | 5 | Very Good | 33 | |
| 7 | 6 | Good | 28 | |
| 8 | 7 | Very Good | 19 | |
| 9 | 8 | Very Good | 11 | |
| 10 | 9 | Very Good | 23 | |
| 11 | 10 | Good | 13 | |
| 292 | 291 | Very Good | 23 | |
| 293 | 292 | Very Good | 24 | |
| 294 | 293 | Excellent | 45 | |
| 295 | 294 | Good | 14 | |
| 296 | 295 | Good | 18 | |
| 297 | 296 | Good | 17 | |
| 298 | 297 | Good | 16 | |
| 299 | 298 | Good | 15 | |
| 300 | 299 | Very Good | 38 | |
| 301 | 300 | Very Good | 31 | |
| 302 | | | | |

**FIGURE 2.15**    INITIAL PIVOTTABLE FIELD LIST AND PIVOTTABLE FIELD
REPORT FOR THE RESTAURANT DATA

**Set Up the PivotTable Field List:**    Each of the three columns in Figure 2.14 (labeled Restaurant, Quality Rating, and Meal Price ($)) is considered a field by Excel. Fields may be chosen to represent rows, columns, or values in the body of the PivotTable Report. The following steps show how to use Excel's PivotTable Field List to assign the Quality Rating field to the rows, the Meal Price ($) field to the columns, and the Restaurant field to the body of the PivotTable report.

**Step 1.**  In the **PivotTable Field List,** go to **Choose Fields to add to report**
Drag the **Quality Rating** field to the **Row Labels** area
Drag the **Meal Price ($)** field to the **Column Labels** area
Drag the **Restaurant** field to the **Values** area
**Step 2.**  Click on **Sum of Restaurant** in the **Values** area
**Step 3.**  Click **Value Field Settings** from the list of options that appear
**Step 4.**  When the Value Field Settings dialog appears,
Under **Summarize value field by,** choose **Count**
Click **OK**

Figure 2.16 shows the completed PivotTable Field List and a portion of the PivotTable worksheet as it now appears.

**Finalize the PivotTable Report:**    To complete the PivotTable Report, we need to group the columns representing meal prices and place the row labels for quality rating in the proper order. The following steps accomplish this.

**Step 1.**  Right-click in cell B4 or any cell containing meal prices
**Step 2.**  Choose **Group** from the list of options that appears

**FIGURE 2.16**    COMPLETED PIVOTTABLE FIELD LIST AND A PORTION OF THE PIVOTTABLE REPORT FOR THE RESTAURANT DATA (COLUMNS H:AK ARE HIDDEN)

**FIGURE 2.17**    FINAL PIVOTTABLE REPORT FOR THE RESTAURANT DATA

**Step 3.** When the **Grouping** dialog box appears,
Enter 10 in the **Starting at** box
Enter 49 in the **Ending at** box
Enter 10 in the **By** box
Click **OK**

**Step 4.** Right-click on **Excellent** in cell A5

**Step 5.** Choose **Move** and click **Move "Excellent" to End**

The final PivotTable Report is shown in Figure 2.17. Note that it provides the same information as the crosstabulation shown in Table 2.10. We can now use Excel's chart tools to construct the column chart shown in Figure 2.13. Alternatively, Excel's PivotChart report can be used to create both the crosstabulation and corresponding column chart at the same time.

As we have seen, Excel's PivotTable report and PivotChart report are very useful in summarizing univariate and bivariate data. Once you have used these tools to create tabular and graphical summaries for one or two data sets, we think you will find that both tools are not only very easy to use, but they provide a very powerful option for quickly summarizing very complex data sets as well.

## Simpson's Paradox

The data in two or more crosstabulations are often combined or aggregated to produce a summary crosstabulation showing how two variables are related. In such cases, we must be careful in drawing a conclusion because a conclusion based upon aggregate data can be reversed if we look at the unaggregated data. The reversal of conclusions based on aggregate and unaggregated data is called **Simpson's paradox**. To provide an illustration of Simpson's paradox, we consider an example involving the analysis of verdicts for two judges in two different courts.

Judges Ron Luckett and Dennis Kendall presided over cases in Common Pleas Court and Municipal Court during the past three years. Some of the verdicts they rendered were appealed. In most of these cases the appeals court upheld the original verdicts, but in some cases those verdicts were reversed. For each judge a crosstabulation was developed based upon two variables: Verdict (upheld or reversed) and Type of Court (Common Pleas and Municipal). Suppose that the two crosstabulations were then combined by aggregating the type of court data. The resulting aggregated crosstabulation contains two variables: Verdict (upheld or reversed) and Judge (Luckett or Kendall). This crosstabulation shows the number of appeals in which the verdict was upheld and the number in which the verdict was reversed for both judges. The following crosstabulation shows these results along with the column percentages in parentheses next to each value.

| Verdict | Judge | | Total |
|---|---|---|---|
| | **Luckett** | **Kendall** | **Total** |
| **Upheld** | 129 (86%) | 110 (88%) | 239 |
| **Reversed** | 21 (14%) | 15 (12%) | 36 |
| **Total (%)** | 150 (100%) | 125 (100%) | 275 |

A review of the column percentages shows that 86% of the verdicts were upheld for Judge Luckett, while 88% of the verdicts were upheld for Judge Kendall. From this aggregated crosstabulation, we conclude that Judge Kendall is doing the better job because a greater percentage of Judge Kendall's verdicts are being upheld.

The following unaggregated crosstabulations show the cases tried by Judge Luckett and Judge Kendall in each court; column percentages are shown in parentheses next to each value.

| | **Judge Luckett** | | | | | **Judge Kendall** | | |
|---|---|---|---|---|---|---|---|---|
| **Verdict** | **Common Pleas** | **Municipal Court** | **Total** | | **Verdict** | **Common Pleas** | **Municipal Court** | **Total** |
| **Upheld** | 29 (91%) | 100 (85%) | 129 | | **Upheld** | 90 (90%) | 20 (80%) | 110 |
| **Reversed** | 3 (9%) | 18 (15%) | 21 | | **Reversed** | 10 (10%) | 5 (20%) | 15 |
| **Total (%)** | 32 (100%) | 118 (100%) | 150 | | **Total (%)** | 100 (100%) | 25 (100%) | 125 |

From the crosstabulation and column percentages for Judge Luckett, we see that the verdicts were upheld in 91% of the Common Pleas Court cases and in 85% of the Municipal Court cases. From the crosstabulation and column percentages for Judge Kendall, we see that the verdicts were upheld in 90% of the Common Pleas Court cases and in 80% of the Municipal Court cases. Thus, when we unaggregate the data, we see that Judge Luckett has a better record because a greater percentage of Judge Luckett's verdicts are being upheld in both courts. This result contradicts the conclusion we reached with the aggregated data crosstabulation that showed Judge Kendall had the better record. This reversal of conclusions based on aggregated and unaggregated data illustrates Simpson's paradox.

The original crosstabulation was obtained by aggregating the data in the separate crosstabulations for the two courts. Note that for both judges the percentage of appeals that resulted in reversals was much higher in Municipal Court than in Common Pleas Court. Because Judge Luckett tried a much higher percentage of his cases in Municipal Court, the aggregated data favored Judge Kendall. When we look at the crosstabulations for the two courts separately, however, Judge Luckett shows the better record. Thus, for the original crosstabulation, we see that the *type of court* is a hidden variable that cannot be ignored when evaluating the records of the two judges.

Because of the possibility of Simpson's paradox, realize that the conclusion or interpretation may be reversed depending on whether you are viewing unaggregated or aggregate crosstabulation data. Before drawing a conclusion, you may want to investigate whether the aggregate or unaggregate form of the crosstabulation provides the better insight and conclusion. Especially when the crosstabulation involves aggreagrated data, you should investigate whether a hidden variable could affect the results such that separate or unaggregated crosstabulations provide a different and possibly better insight and conclusion.

## Scatter Diagram and Trendline

A scatter diagram is a graphical presentation of the relationship between two quantitative variables, and a trendline is a line that provides an approximation of the relationship. As an illustration, consider the advertising/sales relationship for a stereo and sound equipment store in San Francisco. On 10 occasions during the past three months, the store used weekend television commercials to promote sales at its stores. The managers want to investigate whether a relationship exists between the number of commercials shown and sales at the store during the following week. Sample data for the 10 weeks with sales in hundreds of dollars are shown in Table 2.12.

Figure 2.18 shows the scatter diagram and the trendline[2] for the data in Table 2.12. The number of commercials ($x$) is shown on the horizontal axis and the sales ($y$) are shown on the vertical axis. For week 1, $x = 2$ and $y = 50$. A point with those coordinates is plotted on the scatter diagram. Similar points are plotted for the other nine weeks. Note that during two of the weeks one commercial was shown, during two of the weeks two commercials were shown, and so on.

**TABLE 2.12    SAMPLE DATA FOR THE STEREO AND SOUND EQUIPMENT STORE**

**WEB** file

Stereo

| Week | Number of Commercials $x$ | Sales ($100s) $y$ |
|------|---------------------------|-------------------|
| 1 | 2 | 50 |
| 2 | 5 | 57 |
| 3 | 1 | 41 |
| 4 | 3 | 54 |
| 5 | 4 | 54 |
| 6 | 1 | 38 |
| 7 | 5 | 63 |
| 8 | 3 | 48 |
| 9 | 4 | 59 |
| 10 | 2 | 46 |

---

[2]The equation of the trendline is $y = 36.15 + 4.95x$. The slope of the trendline is 4.95 and the $y$-intercept (the point where the line intersects the $y$-axis) is 36.15. We will discuss in detail the interpretation of the slope and $y$-intercept for a linear trendline in Chapter 14 when we study simple linear regression.

**FIGURE 2.18** SCATTER DIAGRAM AND TRENDLINE FOR THE STEREO AND SOUND EQUIPMENT STORE

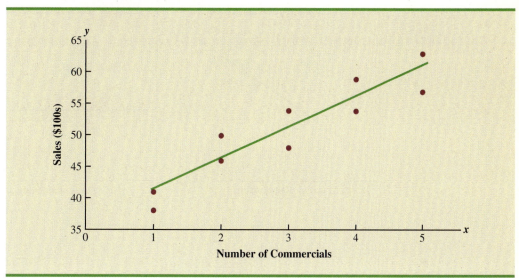

The completed scatter diagram in Figure 2.18 indicates a positive relationship between the number of commercials and sales. Higher sales are associated with a higher number of commercials. The relationship is not perfect in that all points are not on a straight line. However, the general pattern of the points and the trendline suggests that the overall relationship is positive.

Some general scatter diagram patterns and the types of relationships they suggest are shown in Figure 2.19. The top left panel depicts a positive relationship similar to the one for the number of commercials and sales example. In the top right panel, the scatter diagram shows no apparent relationship between the variables. The bottom panel depicts a negative relationship where $y$ tends to decrease as $x$ increases.

## Using Excel's Chart Tools to Construct a Scatter Diagram and a Trendline

We can use Excel's chart tools to construct a scatter diagram and a trendline for the stereo and sound equipment store data. Refer to Figures 2.20 and 2.21 as we describe the tasks involved.

**Enter Data:** Appropriate labels and the sample data have been entered into cells A1:C11 of the worksheet shown in Figure 2.20.

**Enter Functions and Formulas:** No functions and formulas are needed.

**Apply Tools:** The following steps describe how to use Excel's chart tools to produce a scatter diagram from the data in the worksheet.

 **Step 1.** Select cells B2:C11
 **Step 2.** Click the **Insert** tab on the Ribbon
 **Step 3.** In the **Charts** group, click **Scatter**
 **Step 4.** When the list of scatter diagram subtypes appears, click **Scatter with only Markers** (the chart in the upper left corner)

**FIGURE 2.19**   TYPES OF RELATIONSHIPS DEPICTED BY SCATTER DIAGRAMS

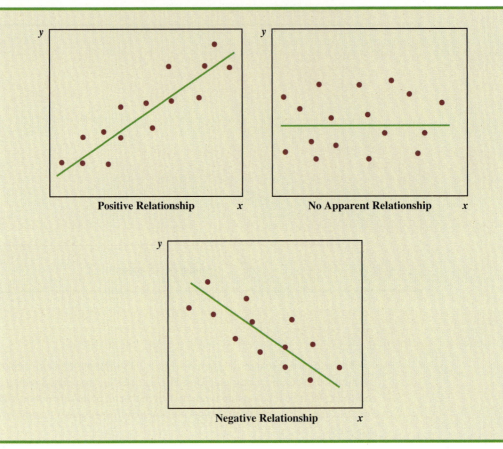

Step 5.   In the **Chart Layouts** group, click **Layout 1**
Step 6.   Select the **Chart Title** and replace it with **Scatter Diagram for the Stereo and Sound Equipment Store**
Step 7.   Select the **Horizontal (Value) Axis Title** and replace it with **Number of Commercials**
Step 8.   Select the **Vertical (Value) Axis Title** and replace it with **Sales ($100s)**
Step 9.   Right-click the **Series 1 Legend Entry** and click **Delete**

The worksheet displayed in Figure 2.20 shows the scatter diagram produced by Excel. The following steps describe how to add a trendline.

Step 1.   Position the mouse pointer over any data point in the scatter diagram and right-click to display a list of options
Step 2.   Choose **Add Trendline**
Step 3.   When the **Format Trendline** dialog box appears,
                Select **Trendline Options**
                Choose **Linear** from the **Trend/Regression Type** list
                Click **Close**

The worksheet displayed in Figure 2.21 shows the scatter diagram with the trendline added.

**FIGURE 2.20**    SCATTER DIAGRAM FOR THE STEREO AND SOUND EQUIPMENT STORE USING EXCEL'S CHART TOOLS

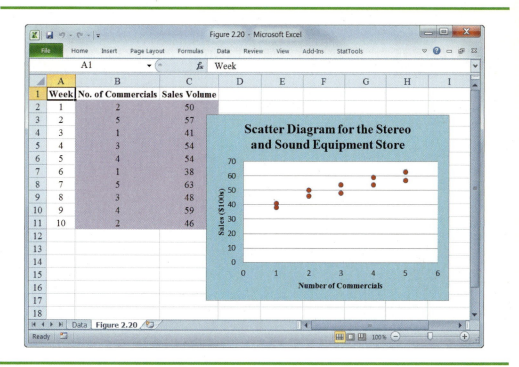

**FIGURE 2.21**    SCATTER DIAGRAM AND TRENDLINE FOR THE STEREO AND SOUND EQUIPMENT STORE USING EXCEL'S CHART TOOLS

## Exercises

### Methods

29. The following data are for 30 observations involving two qualitative variables, $x$ and $y$. The categories for $x$ are A, B, and C; the categories for $y$ are 1 and 2.

Crosstab

| Observation | $x$ | $y$ | Observation | $x$ | $y$ |
|---|---|---|---|---|---|
| 1 | A | 1 | 16 | B | 2 |
| 2 | B | 1 | 17 | C | 1 |
| 3 | B | 1 | 18 | B | 1 |
| 4 | C | 2 | 19 | C | 1 |
| 5 | B | 1 | 20 | B | 1 |
| 6 | C | 2 | 21 | C | 2 |
| 7 | B | 1 | 22 | B | 1 |
| 8 | C | 2 | 23 | C | 2 |
| 9 | A | 1 | 24 | A | 1 |
| 10 | B | 1 | 25 | B | 1 |
| 11 | A | 1 | 26 | C | 2 |
| 12 | B | 1 | 27 | C | 2 |
| 13 | C | 2 | 28 | A | 1 |
| 14 | C | 2 | 29 | B | 1 |
| 15 | C | 2 | 30 | B | 2 |

a. Develop a crosstabulation for the data, with $x$ as the row variable and $y$ as the column variable.
b. Compute the row percentages.
c. Compute the column percentages.
d. What is the relationship, if any, between $x$ and $y$?

30. The following 20 observations are for two quantitative variables, $x$ and $y$.

Scatter

| Observation | $x$ | $y$ | Observation | $x$ | $y$ |
|---|---|---|---|---|---|
| 1 | −22 | 22 | 11 | −37 | 48 |
| 2 | −33 | 49 | 12 | 34 | −29 |
| 3 | 2 | 8 | 13 | 9 | −18 |
| 4 | 29 | −16 | 14 | −33 | 31 |
| 5 | −13 | 10 | 15 | 20 | −16 |
| 6 | 21 | −28 | 16 | −3 | 14 |
| 7 | −13 | 27 | 17 | −15 | 18 |
| 8 | −23 | 35 | 18 | 12 | 17 |
| 9 | 14 | −5 | 19 | −20 | −11 |
| 10 | 3 | −3 | 20 | −7 | −22 |

a. Develop a scatter diagram for the relationship between $x$ and $y$.
b. What is the relationship, if any, between $x$ and $y$?

### Applications

31. The following crosstabulation shows household income by educational level of the head of household (*Statistical Abstract of the United States: 2008*).

| Educational Level | Household Income ($1000s) | | | | | Total |
|---|---|---|---|---|---|---|
| | Under 25 | 25.0– 49.9 | 50.0– 74.9 | 75.0– 99.9 | 100 or more | |
| Not H.S. graduate | 4207 | 3459 | 1389 | 539 | 367 | 9961 |
| H.S. graduate | 4917 | 6850 | 5027 | 2637 | 2668 | 22099 |
| Some college | 2807 | 5258 | 4678 | 3250 | 4074 | 20067 |
| Bachelor's degree | 885 | 2094 | 2848 | 2581 | 5379 | 13787 |
| Beyond bach. deg. | 290 | 829 | 1274 | 1241 | 4188 | 7822 |
| Total | 13106 | 18490 | 15216 | 10248 | 16676 | 73736 |

a. Compute the row percentages and identify the percent frequency distributions of income for households in which the head is a high school graduate and in which the head holds a bachelor's degree.

b. What percentage of households headed by high school graduates earn $75,000 or more? What percentage of households headed by bachelor's degree recipients earn $75,000 or more?

c. Construct percent frequency histograms of income for households headed by persons with a high school degree and for those headed by persons with a bachelor's degree. Is any relationship evident between household income and educational level?

32. Refer again to the crosstabulation of household income by educational level shown in exercise 31.

a. Compute column percentages and identify the percent frequency distributions displayed. What percentage of the heads of households did not graduate from high school?

b. What percentage of the households earning $100,000 or more were headed by a person having schooling beyond a bachelor's degree? What percentage of the households headed by a person with schooling beyond a bachelor's degree earned over $100,000? Why are these two percentages different?

c. Compare the percent frequency distributions for those households earning "Under 25," "100 or more," and for "Total." Comment on the relationship between household income and educational level of the head of household.

33. Recently, management at Oak Tree Golf Course received a few complaints about the condition of the greens. Several players complained that the greens are too fast. Rather than react to the comments of just a few, the Golf Association conducted a survey of 100 male and 100 female golfers. The survey results are summarized here.

**Male Golfers**

| Handicap | Greens Condition | |
|---|---|---|
| | Too Fast | Fine |
| Under 15 | 10 | 40 |
| 15 or more | 25 | 25 |

**Female Golfers**

| Handicap | Greens Condition | |
|---|---|---|
| | Too Fast | Fine |
| Under 15 | 1 | 9 |
| 15 or more | 39 | 51 |

a. Combine these two crosstabulations into one, with Male and Female as the row labels and Too Fast and Fine as the column labels. Which group shows the highest percentage saying that the greens are too fast?

b. Refer to the initial crosstabulations. For those players with low handicaps (better players), which group (male or female) shows the highest percentage saying the greens are too fast?

     c.   Refer to the initial crosstabulations. For those players with higher handicaps, which group (male or female) shows the highest percentage saying the greens are too fast?

     d.   What conclusions can you draw about the preferences of men and women concerning the speed of the greens? Are the conclusions you draw from part (a) as compared with parts (b) and (c) consistent? Explain any apparent inconsistencies.

34.   Table 2.13 shows a data set containing information for 45 mutual funds that are part of the *Morningstar Funds 500* for 2008. The data set includes the following five variables:

     Fund Type:   The type of fund, labeled DE (Domestic Equity), IE (International Equity), and FI (Fixed Income)

     Net Asset Value ($):   The closing price per share

     5-Year Average Return (%):   The average annual return for the fund over the past 5 years

     Expense Ratio (%):   The percentage of assets deducted each fiscal year for fund expenses

     Morningstar Rank:   The risk adjusted star rating for each fund; Morningstar ranks go from a low of 1-Star to a high of 5-Stars

     a.   Prepare a crosstabulation of the data on Fund Type (rows) and the average annual return over the past 5 years (columns). Use classes of 0–9.99, 10–19.99, 20–29.99, 30–39.99, 40–49.99, and 50–59.99 for the 5-Year Average Return (%).

     b.   Prepare a frequency distribution for the data on Fund Type.

     c.   Prepare a frequency distribution for the data on 5-Year Average Return (%).

     d.   How has the crosstabulation helped in preparing the frequency distributions in parts (b) and (c)?

     e.   What conclusions can you draw about the fund type and the average return over the past 5 years?

35.   Refer to the data in Table 2.13.

     a.   Prepare a crosstabulation of the data on Fund Type (rows) and the expense ratio (columns). Use classes of .25–.49, .50–.74, .75–.99, 1.00–1.24, and 1.25–1.49 for Expense Ratio (%).

     b.   Prepare a percent frequency distribution for Expense Ratio (%).

     c.   What conclusions can you draw about fund type and the expense ratio?

36.   Refer to the data in Table 2.13.

     a.   Prepare a scatter diagram with 5-Year Average Return (%) on the horizontal axis and Net Asset Value ($) on the vertical axis.

     b.   Comment on the relationship, if any, between the variables.

37.   The U.S. Department of Energy's Fuel Economy Guide provides fuel efficiency data for cars and trucks (Fuel Economy website, September 8, 2012). A portion of the data for 149 compact, midsize, and large cars is shown in Table 2.14. The data set contains the following variables:

     Size:   Compact, Midsize, and Large

     Displacement:   Engine size in liters

     Cylinders:   Number of cylinders in the engine

     Drive:   All wheel (A), front wheel (F), and rear wheel (R)

     Fuel Type:   Premium (P) or regular (R) fuel

     City MPG:   Fuel efficiency rating for city driving in terms of miles per gallon

     Hwy MPG:   Fuel efficiency rating for highway driving in terms of miles per gallon

**TABLE 2.13**   FINANCIAL DATA FOR A SAMPLE OF 45 MUTUAL FUNDS

| Fund Name | Fund Type | Net Asset Value ($) | 5-Year Average Return (%) | Expense Ratio (%) | Morningstar Rank |
|---|---|---|---|---|---|
| Amer Cent Inc & Growth Inv | DE | 28.88 | 12.39 | 0.67 | 2-Star |
| American Century Intl. Disc | IE | 14.37 | 30.53 | 1.41 | 3-Star |
| American Century Tax-Free Bond | FI | 10.73 | 3.34 | 0.49 | 4-Star |
| American Century Ultra | DE | 24.94 | 10.88 | 0.99 | 3-Star |
| Ariel | DE | 46.39 | 11.32 | 1.03 | 2-Star |
| Artisan Intl Val | IE | 25.52 | 24.95 | 1.23 | 3-Star |
| Artisan Small Cap | DE | 16.92 | 15.67 | 1.18 | 3-Star |
| Baron Asset | DE | 50.67 | 16.77 | 1.31 | 5-Star |
| Brandywine | DE | 36.58 | 18.14 | 1.08 | 4-Star |
| Brown Cap Small | DE | 35.73 | 15.85 | 1.20 | 4-Star |
| Buffalo Mid Cap | DE | 15.29 | 17.25 | 1.02 | 3-Star |
| Delafield | DE | 24.32 | 17.77 | 1.32 | 4-Star |
| DFA U.S. Micro Cap | DE | 13.47 | 17.23 | 0.53 | 3-Star |
| Dodge & Cox Income | FI | 12.51 | 4.31 | 0.44 | 4-Star |
| Fairholme | DE | 31.86 | 18.23 | 1.00 | 5-Star |
| Fidelity Contrafund | DE | 73.11 | 17.99 | 0.89 | 5-Star |
| Fidelity Municipal Income | FI | 12.58 | 4.41 | 0.45 | 5-Star |
| Fidelity Overseas | IE | 48.39 | 23.46 | 0.90 | 4-Star |
| Fidelity Sel Electronics | DE | 45.60 | 13.50 | 0.89 | 3-Star |
| Fidelity Sh-Term Bond | FI | 8.60 | 2.76 | 0.45 | 3-Star |
| Fidelity | DE | 39.85 | 14.40 | 0.56 | 4-Star |
| FPA New Income | FI | 10.95 | 4.63 | 0.62 | 3-Star |
| Gabelli Asset AAA | DE | 49.81 | 16.70 | 1.36 | 4-Star |
| Greenspring | DE | 23.59 | 12.46 | 1.07 | 3-Star |
| Janus | DE | 32.26 | 12.81 | 0.90 | 3-Star |
| Janus Worldwide | IE | 54.83 | 12.31 | 0.86 | 2-Star |
| Kalmar Gr Val Sm Cp | DE | 15.30 | 15.31 | 1.32 | 3-Star |
| Managers Freemont Bond | FI | 10.56 | 5.14 | 0.60 | 5-Star |
| Marsico 21st Century | DE | 17.44 | 15.16 | 1.31 | 5-Star |
| Mathews Pacific Tiger | IE | 27.86 | 32.70 | 1.16 | 3-Star |
| Meridan Value | DE | 31.92 | 15.33 | 1.08 | 4-Star |
| Oakmark I | DE | 40.37 | 9.51 | 1.05 | 2-Star |
| PIMCO Emerg Mkts Bd D | FI | 10.68 | 13.57 | 1.25 | 3-Star |
| RS Value A | DE | 26.27 | 23.68 | 1.36 | 4-Star |
| T. Rowe Price Latin Am. | IE | 53.89 | 51.10 | 1.24 | 4-Star |
| T. Rowe Price Mid Val | DE | 22.46 | 16.91 | 0.80 | 4-Star |
| Templeton Growth A | IE | 24.07 | 15.91 | 1.01 | 3-Star |
| Thornburg Value A | DE | 37.53 | 15.46 | 1.27 | 4-Star |
| USAA Income | FI | 12.10 | 4.31 | 0.62 | 3-Star |
| Vanguard Equity-Inc | DE | 24.42 | 13.41 | 0.29 | 4-Star |
| Vanguard Global Equity | IE | 23.71 | 21.77 | 0.64 | 5-Star |
| Vanguard GNMA | FI | 10.37 | 4.25 | 0.21 | 5-Star |
| Vanguard Sht-Tm TE | FI | 15.68 | 2.37 | 0.16 | 3-Star |
| Vanguard Sm Cp Idx | DE | 32.58 | 17.01 | 0.23 | 3-Star |
| Wasatch Sm Cp Growth | DE | 35.41 | 13.98 | 1.19 | 4-Star |

**WEB** file

MutualFunds

**TABLE 2.14**   FUEL EFFICIENCY DATA FOR 311 CARS

WEB file

FuelData2012

| Car | Size | Displacement | Cylinders | Drive | Fuel Type | City MPG | Hwy MPG |
|-----|------|--------------|-----------|-------|-----------|----------|---------|
| 1 | Compact | 2.0 | 4 | F | P | 22 | 30 |
| 2 | Compact | 2.0 | 4 | A | P | 21 | 29 |
| 3 | Compact | 2.0 | 4 | A | P | 21 | 31 |
| · | · | · | · | · | · | · | · |
| · | · | · | · | · | · | · | · |
| · | · | · | · | · | · | · | · |
| 94 | Midsize | 3.5 | 6 | A | R | 17 | 25 |
| 95 | Midsize | 2.5 | 4 | F | R | 23 | 33 |
| · | · | · | · | · | · | · | · |
| · | · | · | · | · | · | · | · |
| · | · | · | · | · | · | · | · |
| 148 | Large | 6.7 | 12 | R | P | 11 | 18 |
| 149 | Large | 6.7 | 12 | R | P | 11 | 18 |

The complete data set is contained in the file named FuelData2012.

a. Prepare a crosstabulation of the data on Size (rows) and Hwy MPG (columns). Use classes of 15–19, 20–24, 25–29, 30–34, 35–39, and 40–44 for Hwy MPG.

b. Comment on the relationship beween Size and Hwy MPG.

c. Prepare a crosstabulation of the data on Drive (rows) and City MPG (columns). Use classes of 10–14, 15–19, 20–24, 25–29, 30–34, 35–39, and 40–44 for City MPG.

d. Comment on the relationship between Drive and City MPG.

e. Prepare a crosstabulation of the data on Fuel Type (rows) and City MPG (columns). Use classes of 10–14, 15–19, 20–24, 25–29, 30–34, 35–39, and 40–44 for City MPG.

f. Comment on the relationship between Fuel Type and City MPG.

38. Refer to exercise 37 and the data in the file named FuelData2012.

a. Prepare a crosstabulation of the data on Displacement (rows) and Hwy MPG (columns). Use classes of 1–2, 2–3, 3–4, 4–5, 5–6, and 6–7 for Displacement. Use classes of 15–19, 20–24, 25–29, 30–34, and 35–39 for Hwy MPG.

b. Comment on the relationship, if any, between Displacement and Hwy MPG.

c. Develop a scatter diagram of the data on Displacement and Hwy MPG. Use the vertical axis for Hwy MPG.

d. What does the scatter diagram developed in part (c) indicate about the relationship, if any, between Displacement and Hwy MPG?

e. In investigating the relationship between Displacement and Hwy MPG you developed a tabular summary of the data (crosstabulation) and a graphical summary (scatter diagram). In this case which approach do you prefer? Explain.

## Summary

A set of data, even if modest in size, is often difficult to interpret directly in the form in which it is gathered. Tabular and graphical methods provide procedures for organizing and summarizing data so that patterns are revealed and the data are more easily interpreted. Frequency distributions, relative frequency distributions, percent frequency distributions, bar charts, and pie charts were presented as tabular and graphical procedures for summarizing categorical data. Frequency distributions, relative frequency distributions, percent frequency distributions, histograms, cumulative frequency distributions, cumulative relative

**FIGURE 2.22**    TABULAR AND GRAPHICAL METHODS FOR SUMMARIZING DATA

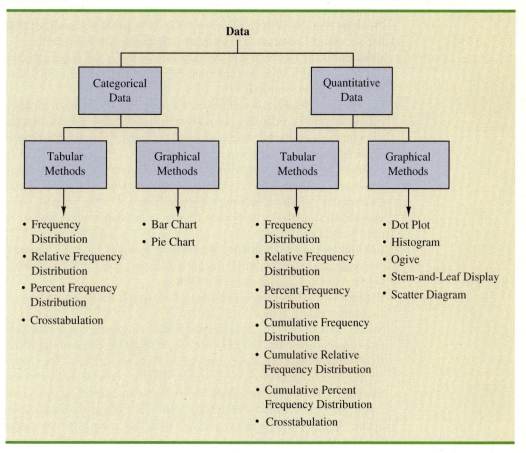

frequency distributions, cumulative percent frequency distributions, and ogives were presented as ways of summarizing quantitative data. A stem-and-leaf display provides an exploratory data analysis technique that can be used to summarize quantitative data. Crosstabulation was presented as a tabular method for summarizing data for two variables. The scatter diagram was introduced as a graphical method for showing the relationship between two quantitative variables. Figure 2.22 shows the tabular and graphical methods presented in this chapter.

With large data sets, computer software packages such as Excel and StatTools are essential in constructing tabular and graphical summaries of data.

## Glossary

**Categorical data** Labels or names used to identify categories of like items.

**Quantitative data** Numerical values that indicate how much or how many.

**Frequency distribution** A tabular summary of data showing the number (frequency) of data values in each of several nonoverlapping classes.

**Relative frequency distribution** A tabular summary of data showing the fraction or proportion of data values in each of several nonoverlapping classes.

**Percent frequency distribution** A tabular summary of data showing the percentage of data values in each of several nonoverlapping classes.

**Bar chart** A graphical device for depicting categorical data that have been summarized in a frequency, relative frequency, or percent frequency distribution.

**Pie chart** A graphical device for presenting data summaries based on subdivision of a circle into sectors that correspond to the relative frequency for each class.

**Class midpoint** The value halfway between the lower and upper class limits.

**Dot plot** A graphical device that summarizes data by the number of dots above each data value on the horizontal axis.

**Histogram** A graphical presentation of a frequency distribution, relative frequency distribution, or percent frequency distribution of quantitative data constructed by placing the class intervals on the horizontal axis and the frequencies, relative frequencies, or percent frequencies on the vertical axis.

**Cumulative frequency distribution** A tabular summary of quantitative data showing the number of data values that are less than or equal to the upper class limit of each class.

**Cumulative relative frequency distribution** A tabular summary of quantitative data showing the fraction or proportion of data values that are less than or equal to the upper class limit of each class.

**Cumulative percent frequency distribution** A tabular summary of quantitative data showing the percentage of data values that are less than or equal to the upper class limit of each class.

**Ogive** A graph of a cumulative distribution.

**Exploratory data analysis** Methods that use simple arithmetic and easy-to-draw graphs to summarize data quickly.

**Stem-and-leaf display** An exploratory data analysis technique that simultaneously rank orders quantitative data and provides insight about the shape of the distribution.

**Crosstabulation** A tabular summary of data for two variables. The classes for one variable are represented by the rows; the classes for the other variable are represented by the columns.

**Simpson's paradox** Conclusions drawn from two or more separate crosstabulations that can be reversed when the data are aggregated into a single crosstabulation.

**Scatter diagram** A graphical presentation of the relationship between two quantitative variables. One variable is shown on the horizontal axis and the other variable is shown on the vertical axis.

**Trendline** A line that provides an approximation of the relationship between two quantitative variables.

## Key Formulas

### Relative Frequency

$$\frac{\text{Frequency of the class}}{n} \tag{2.1}$$

### Approximate Class Width

$$\frac{\text{Largest data value} - \text{Smallest data value}}{\text{Number of classes}} \tag{2.2}$$

## Supplementary Exercises

39.  The Higher Education Research Institute at UCLA provides statistics on the most popular majors among incoming college freshmen. The five most popular majors are Arts and Humanities (A), Business Administration (B), Engineering (E), Professional (P), and Social Science (S) (*The New York Times Almanac,* 2006). A broad range of other (O) majors,

including biological science, physical science, computer science, and education, are grouped together. The majors selected for a sample of 64 college freshmen follow.

**Major**

| S | P | P | O | B | E | O | E | P | O | O | B | O | O | O | A |
|---|---|---|---|---|---|---|---|---|---|---|---|---|---|---|---|
| O | E | E | B | S | O | B | O | A | O | E | O | E | O | B | P |
| B | A | S | O | E | A | B | O | S | S | O | O | E | B | O | B |
| A | E | B | E | A | A | P | O | O | E | O | B | B | O | P | B |

a. Show a frequency distribution and percent frequency distribution.
b. Show a bar chart.
c. What percentage of freshmen select one of the five most popular majors?
d. What is the most popular major for incoming freshmen? What percentage of freshmen select this major?

**GMSales**

40. General Motors had a 23% share of the automobile industry with sales coming from eight divisions: Buick, Cadillac, Chevrolet, GMC, Hummer, Pontiac, Saab, and Saturn (*Forbes,* December 22, 2008). The data set GMSales shows the sales for a sample of 200 General Motors vehicles. The division for the vehicle is provided for each sale.
  a. Show the frequency distribution and the percent frequency distribution of sales by division for General Motors.
  b. Show a bar chart of the percent frequency distribution.
  c. Which General Motors division was the company leader in sales? What was the percentage of sales for this division? Was this General Motors' most important division? Explain.
  d. Due to the ongoing recession, high gasoline prices, and the decline in automobile sales, General Motors was facing bankruptcy in 2009. A government "bail-out" loan and a restructuring of the company were anticipated. Expectations were that General Motors could not continue to operate all eight divisions. Based on the percentage of sales, which of the eight divisions looked to be the best candidates for General Motors to discontinue? Which divisions looked to be the least likely candidates for General Motors to discontinue?

41. Dividend yield is the annual dividend paid by a company expressed as a percentage of the price of the stock (Dividend/Stock Price × 100). The dividend yield for the Dow Jones Industrial Average companies is shown in Table 2.15 (*The Wall Street Journal,* June 8, 2009).

**TABLE 2.15**   DIVIDEND YIELD FOR DOW JONES INDUSTRIAL AVERAGE COMPANIES

**DYield**

| Company | Dividend Yield % | Company | Dividend Yield % |
|---|---|---|---|
| 3M | 3.6 | IBM | 2.1 |
| Alcoa | 1.3 | Intel | 3.4 |
| American Express | 2.9 | JPMorgan Chase | 0.5 |
| AT&T | 6.6 | Johnson & Johnson | 3.6 |
| Bank of America | 0.4 | Kraft Foods | 4.4 |
| Boeing | 3.8 | McDonald's | 3.4 |
| Caterpillar | 4.7 | Merck | 5.5 |
| Chevron | 3.9 | Microsoft | 2.5 |
| Cisco Systems | 0.0 | Pfizer | 4.2 |
| Coca-Cola | 3.3 | Procter & Gamble | 3.4 |
| DuPont | 5.8 | Travelers | 3.0 |
| ExxonMobil | 2.4 | United Technologies | 2.9 |
| General Electric | 9.2 | Verizon | 6.3 |
| Hewlett-Packard | 0.9 | Walmart Stores | 2.2 |
| Home Depot | 3.9 | Walt Disney | 1.5 |

a. Construct a frequency distribution and percent frequency distribution.
b. Construct a histogram.
c. Comment on the shape of the distribution.
d. What do the tabular and graphical summaries tell about the dividend yields among the Dow Jones Industrial Average companies?
e. What company has the highest dividend yield? If the stock for this company currently sells for $14 per share and you purchase 500 shares, how much dividend income will this investment generate in one year?

42. Approximately 1.5 million high school students take the Scholastic Aptitude Test (SAT) each year and nearly 80% of the college and universities without open admissions policies use SAT scores in making admission decisions (College Board, March 2009). The current version of the SAT includes three parts: reading comprehension, mathematics, and writing. A perfect combined score for all three parts is 2400. A sample of SAT scores for the combined three-part SAT is as follows:

**NewSAT**

| | | | | |
|---|---|---|---|---|
| 1665 | 1525 | 1355 | 1645 | 1780 |
| 1275 | 2135 | 1280 | 1060 | 1585 |
| 1650 | 1560 | 1150 | 1485 | 1990 |
| 1590 | 1880 | 1420 | 1755 | 1375 |
| 1475 | 1680 | 1440 | 1260 | 1730 |
| 1490 | 1560 | 940 | 1390 | 1175 |

a. Show a frequency distribution and histogram. Begin with the first class starting at 800 and use a class width of 200.
b. Comment on the shape of the distribution.
c. What other observations can be made about the SAT scores based on the tabular and graphical summaries?

43. The Pittsburgh Steelers defeated the Arizona Cardinals 27 to 23 in professional football's 43rd Super Bowl. With this win, its sixth championship, the Pittsburgh Steelers became the team with the most wins in the 43-year history of the event (*Tampa Tribune,* February 2, 2009). The Super Bowl has been played in eight different states: Arizona (AZ), California (CA), Florida (FL), Georgia (GA), Louisiana (LA), Michigan (MI), Minnesota (MN), and Texas (TX). Data in the following table show the state where the Super Bowls were played and the point margin of victory for the winning team.

**WEB** file

**SuperBowl**

| Super Bowl | State | Won By Points | Super Bowl | State | Won By Points | Super Bowl | State | Won By Points |
|---|---|---|---|---|---|---|---|---|
| 1 | CA | 25 | 16 | MI | 5 | 31 | LA | 14 |
| 2 | FL | 19 | 17 | CA | 10 | 32 | CA | 7 |
| 3 | FL | 9 | 18 | FL | 19 | 33 | FL | 15 |
| 4 | LA | 16 | 19 | CA | 22 | 34 | GA | 7 |
| 5 | FL | 3 | 20 | LA | 36 | 35 | FL | 27 |
| 6 | FL | 21 | 21 | CA | 19 | 36 | LA | 3 |
| 7 | CA | 7 | 22 | CA | 32 | 37 | CA | 27 |
| 8 | TX | 17 | 23 | FL | 4 | 38 | TX | 3 |
| 9 | LA | 10 | 24 | LA | 45 | 39 | FL | 3 |
| 10 | FL | 4 | 25 | FL | 1 | 40 | MI | 11 |
| 11 | CA | 18 | 26 | MN | 13 | 41 | FL | 12 |
| 12 | LA | 17 | 27 | CA | 35 | 42 | AZ | 3 |
| 13 | FL | 4 | 28 | GA | 17 | 43 | FL | 4 |
| 14 | CA | 12 | 29 | FL | 23 | | | |
| 15 | LA | 17 | 30 | AZ | 10 | | | |

a.  Show a frequency distribution and bar chart for the state where the Super Bowl was played.

b.  What conclusions can you draw from your summary in part (a)? What percentage of Super Bowls were played in the states of Florida or California? What percentage of Super Bowls were played in northern or cold-weather states?

c.  Show a stretched stem-and-leaf display for the point margin of victory for the winning team. Show a histogram.

d.  What conclusions can you draw from your summary in part (c)? What percentage of Super Bowls have been close games with the margin of victory less than 5 points? What percentage of Super Bowls have been won by 20 or more points?

e.  The closest Super Bowl occurred when the New York Giants beat the Buffalo Bills. Where was this game played and what was the winning margin of victory? The biggest point margin in Super Bowl history occurred when the San Francisco 49ers beat the Denver Broncos. Where was this game played and what was the winning margin of victory?

44.  Data from the U.S. Census Bureau provides the population by state in millions of people (*The World Almanac,* 2006).

**Population**

| State | Population | State | Population | State | Population |
|-------|-----------|-------|-----------|-------|-----------|
| Alabama | 4.5 | Louisiana | 4.5 | Ohio | 11.5 |
| Alaska | 0.7 | Maine | 1.3 | Oklahoma | 3.5 |
| Arizona | 5.7 | Maryland | 5.6 | Oregon | 3.6 |
| Arkansas | 2.8 | Massachusetts | 6.4 | Pennsylvania | 12.4 |
| California | 35.9 | Michigan | 10.1 | Rhode Island | 1.1 |
| Colorado | 4.6 | Minnesota | 5.1 | South Carolina | 4.2 |
| Connecticut | 3.5 | Mississippi | 2.9 | South Dakota | 0.8 |
| Delaware | 0.8 | Missouri | 5.8 | Tennessee | 5.9 |
| Florida | 17.4 | Montana | 0.9 | Texas | 22.5 |
| Georgia | 8.8 | Nebraska | 1.7 | Utah | 2.4 |
| Hawaii | 1.3 | Nevada | 2.3 | Vermont | 0.6 |
| Idaho | 1.4 | New Hampshire | 1.3 | Virginia | 7.5 |
| Illinois | 12.7 | New Jersey | 8.7 | Washington | 6.2 |
| Indiana | 6.2 | New Mexico | 1.9 | West Virginia | 1.8 |
| Iowa | 3.0 | New York | 19.2 | Wisconsin | 5.5 |
| Kansas | 2.7 | North Carolina | 8.5 | Wyoming | 0.5 |
| Kentucky | 4.1 | North Dakota | 0.6 | | |

a.  Develop a frequency distribution, a percent frequency distribution, and a histogram. Use a class width of 2.5 million.

b.  Discuss the skewness in the distribution.

c.  What observations can you make about the population of the 50 states?

45.  *Drug Store News* (September 2002) provided data on annual pharmacy sales for the leading pharmacy retailers in the United States. The following data are annual sales in millions.

| Retailer | Sales | Retailer | Sales |
|----------|-------|----------|-------|
| Ahold USA | $ 1,700 | Medicine Shoppe | $ 1,757 |
| CVS | 12,700 | Rite-Aid | 8,637 |
| Eckerd | 7,739 | Safeway | 2,150 |
| Kmart | 1,863 | Walgreens | 11,660 |
| Kroger | 3,400 | Walmart | 7,250 |

a.   Show a stem-and-leaf display.
b.   Identify the annual sales levels for the smallest, medium, and largest drug retailers.
c.   What are the two largest drug retailers?

46.   The daily high and low temperatures for 20 cities follow (*USA Today,* March 3, 2006).

**CityTemp**

| City | High | Low | City | High | Low |
|------|------|-----|------|------|-----|
| Albuquerque | 66 | 39 | Los Angeles | 60 | 46 |
| Atlanta | 61 | 35 | Miami | 84 | 65 |
| Baltimore | 42 | 26 | Minneapolis | 30 | 11 |
| Charlotte | 60 | 29 | New Orleans | 68 | 50 |
| Cincinnati | 41 | 21 | Oklahoma City | 62 | 40 |
| Dallas | 62 | 47 | Phoenix | 77 | 50 |
| Denver | 60 | 31 | Portland | 54 | 38 |
| Houston | 70 | 54 | St. Louis | 45 | 27 |
| Indianapolis | 42 | 22 | San Francisco | 55 | 43 |
| Las Vegas | 65 | 43 | Seattle | 52 | 36 |

a.   Prepare a stem-and-leaf display of the high temperatures.
b.   Prepare a stem-and-leaf display of the low temperatures.
c.   Compare the two stem-and-leaf displays and make comments about the difference between the high and low temperatures.
d.   Provide a frequency distribution for both high and low temperatures.

47.   Refer to the data set for high and low temperatures for 20 cities in exercise 46.
a.   Develop a scatter diagram to show the relationship between the two variables, high temperature and low temperature.
b.   Comment on the relationship between high and low temperatures.

48.   One of the questions in a *Financial Times*/Harris Poll was, "How much do you favor or oppose a higher tax on higher carbon emission cars?" Possible responses were strongly favor, favor more than oppose, oppose more than favor, and strongly oppose. The following crosstabulation shows the responses obtained for 5372 adults surveyed in four countries in Europe and the United States (Harris Interactive website, February 27, 2008).

| | | | Country | | | |
|-------------------------|------------------|-------|-------|---------|------------------|-------|
| **Level of Support** | **Great Britain** | **Italy** | **Spain** | **Germany** | **United States** | **Total** |
| **Strongly favor** | 337 | 334 | 510 | 222 | 214 | 1617 |
| **Favor more than oppose** | 370 | 408 | 355 | 411 | 327 | 1871 |
| **Oppose more than favor** | 250 | 188 | 155 | 267 | 275 | 1135 |
| **Strongly oppose** | 130 | 115 | 89 | 211 | 204 | 749 |
| **Total** | 1087 | 1045 | 1109 | 1111 | 1020 | 5372 |

a.   Construct a percent frequency distribution for the level of support variable. Do you think the results show support for a higher tax on higher carbon emission cars?
b.   Construct a percent frequency distribution for the country variable.
c.   Does the level of support among adults in the European countries appear to be different than the level of support among adults in the United States? Explain.

49. Western University has only one women's softball scholarship remaining for the coming year. The final two players that Western is considering are Allison Fealey and Emily Janson. The coaching staff has concluded that the speed and defensive skills are virtually identical for the two players, and that the final decision will be based on which player has the best batting average. Crosstabulations of each player's batting performance in their junior and senior years of high school are as follows:

| Allison Fealey | | | Emily Janson | | |
|---|---|---|---|---|---|
| Outcome | Junior | Senior | Outcome | Junior | Senior |
| Hit | 15 | 75 | Hit | 70 | 35 |
| No Hit | 25 | 175 | No Hit | 130 | 85 |
| Total At-Bats | 40 | 250 | Total At Bats | 200 | 120 |

A player's batting average is computed by dividing the number of hits a player has by the total number of at-bats. Batting averages are represented as a decimal number with three places after the decimal.

a.  Calculate the batting average for each player in her junior year. Then calculate the batting average of each player in her senior year. Using this analysis, which player should be awarded the scholarship? Explain.

b.  Combine or aggregate the data for the junior and senior years into one crosstabulation as follows:

| | Player | |
|---|---|---|
| Outcome | Fealey | Janson |
| Hit | | |
| No Hit | | |
| Total At-Bats | | |

Calculate each player's batting average for the combined two years. Using this analysis, which player should be awarded the scholarship? Explain.

c.  Are the recommendations you made in parts (a) and (b) consistent? Explain any apparent inconsistencies.

50. A survey of commercial buildings served by the Cincinnati Gas & Electric Company asked what main heating fuel was used and what year the building was constructed. A partial crosstabulation of the findings follows.

| Year Constructed | Fuel Type | | | | |
|---|---|---|---|---|---|
| | Electricity | Natural Gas | Oil | Propane | Other |
| 1973 or before | 40 | 183 | 12 | 5 | 7 |
| 1974–1979 | 24 | 26 | 2 | 2 | 0 |
| 1980–1986 | 37 | 38 | 1 | 0 | 6 |
| 1987–1991 | 48 | 70 | 2 | 0 | 1 |

a.  Complete the crosstabulation by showing the row totals and column totals.
b.  Show the frequency distributions for year constructed and for fuel type.
c.  Prepare a crosstabulation showing column percentages.
d.  Prepare a crosstabulation showing row percentages.
e.  Comment on the relationship between year constructed and fuel type.

**TABLE 2.16**   DATA FOR A SAMPLE OF 50 *FORTUNE* 500 COMPANIES

| Company | Stockholders' Equity ($1000s) | Market Value ($1000s) | Profit ($1000s) |
|---------|------------------------------:|----------------------:|----------------:|
| AGCO | 982.1 | 372.1 | 60.6 |
| AMP | 2698.0 | 12017.6 | 2.0 |
| Apple Computer | 1642.0 | 4605.0 | 309.0 |
| Baxter International | 2839.0 | 21743.0 | 315.0 |
| Bergen Brunswick | 629.1 | 2787.5 | 3.1 |
| Best Buy | 557.7 | 10376.5 | 94.5 |
| Charles Schwab | 1429.0 | 35340.6 | 348.5 |
| . | . | . | . |
| . | . | . | . |
| . | . | . | . |
| Walgreen | 2849.0 | 30324.7 | 511.0 |
| Westvaco | 2246.4 | 2225.6 | 132.0 |
| Whirlpool | 2001.0 | 3729.4 | 325.0 |
| Xerox | 5544.0 | 35603.7 | 395.0 |

**WEB file**

*Fortune*

51. Table 2.16 contains a portion of the data in the file named Fortune. Data on stockholders' equity, market value, and profits for a sample of 50 *Fortune* 500 companies are shown.
    a. Prepare a crosstabulation for the variables Stockholders' Equity and Profit. Use classes of 0–200, 200–400, . . . , 1000–1200 for Profit, and classes of 0–1200, 1200–2400, . . . , 4800–6000 for Stockholders' Equity.
    b. Compute the row percentages for your crosstabulation in part (a).
    c. What relationship, if any, do you notice between Profit and Stockholders' Equity?

52. Refer to the data set in Table 2.16.
    a. Prepare a crosstabulation for the variables Market Value and Profit.
    b. Compute the row percentages for your crosstabulation in part (a).
    c. Comment on any relationship between the variables.

53. Refer to the data set in Table 2.16.
    a. Prepare a scatter diagram to show the relationship between the variables Profit and Stockholders' Equity.
    b. Comment on any relationship between the variables.

54. Refer to the data set in Table 2.16.
    a. Prepare a scatter diagram to show the relationship between the variables Market Value and Stockholders' Equity.
    b. Comment on any relationship between the variables.

## Case Problem 1   Pelican Stores

Pelican Stores, a division of National Clothing, is a chain of women's apparel stores operating throughout the country. The chain recently ran a promotion in which discount coupons were sent to customers of other National Clothing stores. Data collected for a sample of 100 in-store credit card transactions at Pelican Stores during one day while the promotion was running are contained in the file named PelicanStores. Table 2.17 shows a portion of the data set. The Proprietary Card method of payment refers to charges made using a National Clothing charge card. Customers who made a purchase using a discount coupon are referred to as promotional customers and customers who made a purchase but did not use a discount coupon are referred to as regular customers. Because the

**TABLE 2.17**  DATA FOR A SAMPLE OF 100 CREDIT CARD PURCHASES AT PELICAN STORES

WEB file

PelicanStores

| Customer | Type of Customer | Items | Net Sales | Method of Payment | Gender | Marital Status | Age |
|---|---|---|---|---|---|---|---|
| 1 | Regular | 1 | 39.50 | Discover | Male | Married | 32 |
| 2 | Promotional | 1 | 102.40 | Proprietary Card | Female | Married | 36 |
| 3 | Regular | 1 | 22.50 | Proprietary Card | Female | Married | 32 |
| 4 | Promotional | 5 | 100.40 | Proprietary Card | Female | Married | 28 |
| 5 | Regular | 2 | 54.00 | MasterCard | Female | Married | 34 |
| . | . | . | . | . | . | . | . |
| . | . | . | . | . | . | . | . |
| . | . | . | . | . | . | . | . |
| 96 | Regular | 1 | 39.50 | MasterCard | Female | Married | 44 |
| 97 | Promotional | 9 | 253.00 | Proprietary Card | Female | Married | 30 |
| 98 | Promotional | 10 | 287.59 | Proprietary Card | Female | Married | 52 |
| 99 | Promotional | 2 | 47.60 | Proprietary Card | Female | Married | 30 |
| 100 | Promotional | 1 | 28.44 | Proprietary Card | Female | Married | 44 |

promotional coupons were not sent to regular Pelican Stores customers, management considers the sales made to people presenting the promotional coupons as sales it would not otherwise make. Of course, Pelican also hopes that the promotional customers will continue to shop at its stores.

Most of the variables shown in Table 2.17 are self-explanatory, but two of the variables require some clarification.

Items  The total number of items purchased
Net Sales  The total amount ($) charged to the credit card

Pelican's management would like to use this sample data to learn about its customer base and to evaluate the promotion involving discount coupons.

## Managerial Report

Use the tabular and graphical methods of descriptive statistics to help management develop a customer profile and to evaluate the promotional campaign. At a minimum, your report should include the following:

1. Percent frequency distribution for key variables.
2. A bar chart or pie chart showing the number of customer purchases attributable to the method of payment.
3. A crosstabulation of type of customer (regular or promotional) versus net sales. Comment on any similarities or differences present.
4. A scatter diagram to explore the relationship between net sales and customer age.

## Case Problem 2  Motion Picture Industry

The motion picture industry is a competitive business. More than 50 studios produce a total of 300 to 400 new motion pictures each year, and the financial success of each motion picture varies considerably. The opening weekend gross sales ($millions), the total gross sales ($millions), the number of theaters the movie was shown in, and the number of weeks the motion picture was in the top 60 for gross sales are common variables used to measure

**TABLE 2.18**   PERFORMANCE DATA FOR 10 MOTION PICTURES

WEB file

Movies

| Motion Picture | Opening Gross Sales ($millions) | Total Gross Sales ($millions) | Number of Theaters | Weeks in Top 60 |
|---|---|---|---|---|
| Coach Carter | 29.17 | 67.25 | 2574 | 16 |
| Ladies in Lavender | 0.15 | 6.65 | 119 | 22 |
| Batman Begins | 48.75 | 205.28 | 3858 | 18 |
| Unleashed | 10.90 | 24.47 | 1962 | 8 |
| Pretty Persuasion | 0.06 | 0.23 | 24 | 4 |
| Fever Pitch | 12.40 | 42.01 | 3275 | 14 |
| Harry Potter and the Goblet of Fire | 102.69 | 287.18 | 3858 | 13 |
| Monster-in-Law | 23.11 | 82.89 | 3424 | 16 |
| White Noise | 24.11 | 55.85 | 2279 | 7 |
| Mr. and Mrs. Smith | 50.34 | 186.22 | 3451 | 21 |

the success of a motion picture. Data collected for a sample of 100 motion pictures produced in 2005 are contained in the file named Movies. Table 2.18 shows the data for the first 10 motion pictures in this file.

## Managerial Report

Use the tabular and graphical methods of descriptive statistics to learn how these variables contribute to the success of a motion picture. Include the following in your report.

1. Tabular and graphical summaries for each of the four variables along with a discussion of what each summary tells us about the motion picture industry.
2. A scatter diagram to explore the relationship between Total Gross Sales and Opening Weekend Gross Sales. Discuss.
3. A scatter diagram to explore the relationship between Total Gross Sales and Number of Theaters. Discuss.
4. A scatter diagram to explore the relationship between Total Gross Sales and Number of Weeks in the Top 60. Discuss.

## Appendix 2.1   Using Excel's PivotChart Report to Summarize Categorical Data

WEB file

SoftDrink

In Section 2.1 we showed how Excel's COUNTIF function can be used to develop a frequency distribution and how Excel's chart tools can be used to create bar and pie charts for categorical data. In this appendix we show how Excel's PivotChart report can also be used to develop a frequency distribution and graphical displays for categorical data. We will illustrate using the soft drink data in Figure 2.1. Refer to Figure 2.23 as we describe the tasks involved to develop a frequency distribution and a bar chart at the same time.

**Enter Data:**   Same as in Figure 2.1

**Enter Functions and Formulas:**   No functions and formulas are needed.

**Apply Tools:**   When using Excel's PivotChart report, each column of data is referred to as a field. Thus, for the soft drink purchase example, the label in cell A1 and the data appearing in cells A2:A51 are referred to as the Brand Purchased field.

**Step 1.** Click the **Insert** tab on the Ribbon
**Step 2.** In the **Tables** group, click the word **PivotTable**
**Step 3.** Choose **PivotChart** from the options that appear
**Step 4.** When the **Create PivotTable with PivotChart** dialog box appears,
    Choose **Select a table or range**
    Enter A1:A51 in the **Table/Range** box
    Choose **Existing Worksheet** as the location for the PivotTable and PivotChart
    Enter C1 in the **Location** box
    Click **OK**
**Step 5.** In the **PivotTable Field List,** go to **Choose Fields to add to report**
    Drag the **Brand Purchased** field to the **Axis Fields (Categories)** area
    Drag the **Brand Purchased** field to the **Values** area

*The PivotChart contains a Value field button in the upper left corner of the chart and an Axis field button in the lower left corner. To remove either or both of these buttons, right-click either button and select the option to remove that button or all field buttons shown on the chart.*

Figure 2.23 shows the resulting PivotTable and PivotChart. The PivotTable report (C1:D7) provides the frequency distribution for the soft drink data and the PivotChart provides the corresponding bar chart. If desired, we can change the labels in any cell in the frequency distribution by selecting the cell and typing in the new label. We can also use Excel's chart tools to reformat the bar chart.

**FIGURE 2.23**   USING EXCEL'S PIVOTCHART REPORT TO CONSTRUCT A FREQUENCY DISTRIBUTION AND A BAR CHART OF SOFT DRINK PREFERENCES

## Appendix 2.2  Using Excel's PivotChart Report to Summarize Quantitative Data

**WEB file**

**Audit**

In Section 2.2 we showed how Excel's PivotTable report can be used to construct a frequency distribution for quantitative data. Excel's PivotChart report can also be used to develop both a frequency distribution and a histogram at the same time. We will illustrate using the audit time data in Table 2.4. Refer to Figure 2.24 as we describe the tasks involved.

**Enter Data:**    The label "Audit Time" and the 20 audit times are entered into cells A1:A21 of an Excel worksheet.

**Enter Functions and Formulas:**    No functions and formulas are needed.

**Apply Tools:**    The following steps describe how to use Excel's PivotChart report to construct a frequency distribution and a histogram for the audit time data.

**Step 1.** Click the **Insert** tab on the Ribbon
**Step 2.** In the **Tables** group, click the word **PivotTable**
**Step 3.** Choose **PivotChart** from the options that appear
**Step 4.** When the **Create PivotTable with PivotChart** dialog box appears,
        Choose **Select a table or range**
        Enter A1:A21 in the **Table/Range** box

**FIGURE 2.24**    USING EXCEL'S PIVOTCHART REPORT TO CONSTRUCT A FREQUENCY DISTRIBUTION AND A HISTOGRAM FOR THE AUDIT TIME DATA

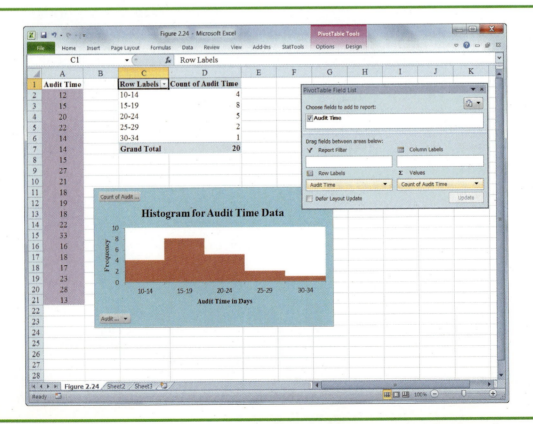

Choose **Existing Worksheet** as the location for the PivotTable and PivotChart

Enter C1 in the **Location** box

Click **OK**

**Step 5.**  In the **PivotTable Field List,** go to **Choose Fields to add to report**

Drag the **Audit Time** field to the **Axis Fields (Categories)** area

Drag the **Audit Time** field to the **Values** area

**Step 6.**  Click **Sum of Audit Time** in the **Values** area

**Step 7.**  Click **Value Field Settings** from the list of options that appears

**Step 8.**  When the Value Field Settings dialog appears,

Under **Summarize value field by,** choose **Count**

Click **OK**

**Step 9.**  Right-click cell C2 in the PivotTable report or any other cell containing an audit time

**Step 10.**  Choose **Group** from the list of options that appears

**Step 11.**  When the **Grouping** dialog box appears,

Enter 10 in the **Starting at** box

Enter 34 in the **Ending at** box

Enter 5 in the **By** box

Click **OK** (a PivotChart will appear)

**Step 12.**  Click inside the resulting PivotChart

**Step 13.**  Click the **Design** tab on the Ribbon

**Step 14.**  In the **Chart Layouts** group, click the **More** button (the downward pointing arrow with a line over it) to display all the options

**Step 15.**  Choose **Layout 8**

**Step 16.**  Select the **Chart Title** and replace it with **Histogram for Audit Time Data**

**Step 17.**  Select the **Horizontal (Category) Axis Title** and replace it with **Audit Time in Days**

**Step 18.**  Select the **Vertical (Value) Axis Title** and replace it with **Frequency**

*The PivotChart contains a Value field button in the upper left corner of the chart and an Axis field button in the lower left corner. To remove either or both of these buttons, right-click either button and select the option to remove that button or all field buttons shown on the chart.*

Figure 2.24 shows the resulting PivotTable and PivotChart. We see that the PivotTable report provides the frequency distribution for the audit time data and the PivotChart provides the corresponding histogram. If desired, we can change the labels in any cell in the frequency distribution by selecting the cell and typing in the new label. We can also use Excel's chart tools as previously described to reformat the histogram.

## Appendix 2.3   Using StatTools for Tabular and Graphical Presentations

In this appendix we show how StatTools can be used to construct a histogram and a scatter diagram.

### Histogram

We use the audit time data in Table 2.4 to illustrate. Begin by using the Data Set Manager to create a StatTools data set for these data using the procedure described in the appendix in Chapter 1. The following steps will generate a histogram.

**WEB** file

**Audit**

**Step 1.**  Click the **StatTools** tab on the Ribbon

**Step 2.**  In the **Analyses Group,** click **Summary Graphs**

**Step 3.**  Choose the **Histogram** option

**Step 4.** When the StatTools - Histogram dialog box appears,

In the **Variables** section, select **Audit Time**

In the **Options** section,

Enter 5 in the **Number of Bins** box

Enter 9.5 in the **Histogram Minimum** box

Enter 34.5 in the **Histogram Maximum** box

Choose **Categorical** in the **X-Axis** box

Choose **Frequency** in the **Y-Axis** box

Click **OK**

A histogram for the audit time data similar to the histogram shown in Figure 2.9 will appear. The only difference is the histogram developed using StatTools shows the class midpoints on the horizontal axis.

## Scatter Diagram

We use the stereo and sound equipment data in Table 2.12 to demonstrate the construction of a scatter diagram. Begin by using the Data Set Manager to create a StatTools data set for these data using the procedure described in the appendix in Chapter 1. The following steps will generate a scatter diagram.

**Stereo**

**Step 1.** Click the **StatTools** tab on the Ribbon

**Step 2.** In the **Analyses Group**, click **Summary Graphs**

**Step 3.** Choose the **Scatterplot** option

**Step 4.** When the StatTools - Scatterplot dialog box appears,

In the **Variables** section,

In the column labeled **X**, select **No. of Commercials**

In the column labeled **Y**, select **Sales Volume**

Click **OK**

A scatter diagram similar to the one shown in Figure 2.20 will appear.

# CHAPTER 3

# Descriptive Statistics: Numerical Measures

**CONTENTS**

STATISTICS IN PRACTICE:
*SMALL FRY DESIGN*

## STATISTICS *in* PRACTICE

### SMALL FRY DESIGN*
*SANTA ANA, CALIFORNIA*

Founded in 1997, Small Fry Design is a toy and accessory company that designs and imports products for infants. The company's product line includes teddy bears, mobiles, musical toys, rattles, and security blankets and features high-quality soft toy designs with an emphasis on color, texture, and sound. The products are designed in the United States and manufactured in China.

Small Fry Design uses independent representatives to sell the products to infant furnishing retailers, children's accessory and apparel stores, gift shops, upscale department stores, and major catalog companies. Currently, Small Fry Design products are distributed in more than 1000 retail outlets throughout the United States.

Cash flow management is one of the most critical activities in the day-to-day operation of this company. Ensuring sufficient incoming cash to meet both current and ongoing debt obligations can mean the difference between business success and failure. A critical factor in cash flow management is the analysis and control of accounts receivable. By measuring the average age and dollar value of outstanding invoices, management can predict cash availability and monitor changes in the status of accounts receivable. The company set the following goals: the average age for outstanding invoices should not exceed 45 days, and the dollar value of invoices more than 60 days old should not exceed 5% of the dollar value of all accounts receivable.

In a recent summary of accounts receivable status, the following descriptive statistics were provided for the age of outstanding invoices:

| | |
|---|---|
| Mean | 40 days |
| Median | 35 days |
| Mode | 31 days |

---

*The authors are indebted to John A. McCarthy, President of Small Fry Design, for providing this Statistics in Practice.

Small Fry Design uses descriptive statistics to monitor its accounts receivable and incoming cash flow.

Interpretation of these statistics shows that the mean or average age of an invoice is 40 days. The median shows that half of the invoices remain outstanding 35 days or more. The mode of 31 days, the most frequent invoice age, indicates that the most common length of time an invoice is outstanding is 31 days. The statistical summary also showed that only 3% of the dollar value of all accounts receivable was more than 60 days old. Based on the statistical information, management was satisfied that accounts receivable and incoming cash flow were under control.

In this chapter, you will learn how to compute and interpret some of the statistical measures used by Small Fry Design. In addition to the mean, median, and mode, you will learn about other descriptive statistics such as the range, variance, standard deviation, percentiles, and correlation. These numerical measures will assist in the understanding and interpretation of data.

In Chapter 2 we discussed tabular and graphical presentations used to summarize data. In this chapter, we present several numerical measures that provide additional alternatives for summarizing data.

We start by developing numerical summary measures for data sets consisting of a single variable. When a data set contains more than one variable, the same numerical measures can be computed separately for each variable. However, in the two-variable case, we will also develop measures of the relationship between the variables.

Numerical measures of location, dispersion, shape, and association are introduced. If the measures are computed for data from a sample, they are called **sample statistics**. If the measures are computed for data from a population, they are called **population parameters**. In statistical inference, a sample statistic is referred to as the **point estimator** of the corresponding population parameter. In Chapter 7 we will discuss in more detail the process of point estimation.

## 3.1  Measures of Location

### Mean

Perhaps the most important measure of location is the **mean**, or average value, for a variable. The mean provides a measure of central location for the data. If the data are for a sample, the mean is denoted by $\bar{x}$; if the data are for a population, the mean is denoted by the Greek letter $\mu$.

In statistical formulas, it is customary to denote the value of variable $x$ for the first observation by $x_1$, the value of variable $x$ for the second observation by $x_2$, and so on. In general, the value of variable $x$ for the $i$th observation is denoted by $x_i$. For a sample with $n$ observations, the formula for the sample mean is as follows.

*The sample mean $\bar{x}$ is a sample statistic.*

> **SAMPLE MEAN**
>
> $$\bar{x} = \frac{\Sigma x_i}{n} \tag{3.1}$$

In the preceding formula, the numerator is the sum of the values of the $n$ observations. That is,

$$\Sigma x_i = x_1 + x_2 + \cdots + x_n$$

The Greek letter $\Sigma$ is the summation sign.

To illustrate the computation of a sample mean, let us consider the following class size data for a sample of five college classes.

$$46 \quad 54 \quad 42 \quad 46 \quad 32$$

We use the notation $x_1, x_2, x_3, x_4, x_5$ to represent the number of students in each of the five classes.

$$x_1 = 46 \qquad x_2 = 54 \qquad x_3 = 42 \qquad x_4 = 46 \qquad x_5 = 32$$

Hence, to compute the sample mean, we can write

$$\bar{x} = \frac{\Sigma x_i}{n} = \frac{x_1 + x_2 + x_3 + x_4 + x_5}{5} = \frac{46 + 54 + 42 + 46 + 32}{5} = 44$$

The sample mean class size is 44 students.

**TABLE 3.1** MONTHLY STARTING SALARIES FOR A SAMPLE OF 12 BUSINESS SCHOOL GRADUATES

| Graduate | Monthly Starting Salary ($) | Graduate | Monthly Starting Salary ($) |
|---|---|---|---|
| 1 | 3450 | 7 | 3490 |
| 2 | 3550 | 8 | 3730 |
| 3 | 3650 | 9 | 3540 |
| 4 | 3480 | 10 | 3925 |
| 5 | 3355 | 11 | 3520 |
| 6 | 3310 | 12 | 3480 |

**WEB** file

StartSalary

Another illustration of the computation of a sample mean is given in the following situation. Suppose that a college placement office sent a questionnaire to a sample of business school graduates requesting information on monthly starting salaries. Table 3.1 shows the collected data. The mean monthly starting salary for the sample of 12 business college graduates is computed as

$$\bar{x} = \frac{\Sigma x_i}{n} = \frac{x_1 + x_2 + \cdots + x_{12}}{12}$$

$$= \frac{3450 + 3550 + \cdots + 3480}{12}$$

$$= \frac{42{,}480}{12} = 3540$$

Equation (3.1) shows how the mean is computed for a sample with $n$ observations. The formula for computing the mean of a population remains the same, but we use different notation to indicate that we are working with the entire population. The number of observations in a population is denoted by $N$ and the symbol for a population mean is $\mu$.

*The sample mean $\bar{x}$ is a point estimator of the population mean $\mu$.*

POPULATION MEAN

$$\mu = \frac{\Sigma x_i}{N} \tag{3.2}$$

## Median

The **median** is another measure of central location. The median is the value in the middle when the data are arranged in ascending order (smallest value to largest value). With an odd number of observations, the median is the middle value. An even number of observations has no single middle value. In this case, we follow convention and define the median as the average of the values for the middle two observations. For convenience the definition of the median is restated as follows.

MEDIAN

Arrange the data in ascending order (smallest value to largest value).

> **(a)** For an odd number of observations, the median is the middle value.
> **(b)** For an even number of observations, the median is the average of the two middle values.

Let us apply this definition to compute the median class size for the sample of five college classes. Arranging the data in ascending order provides the following list.

$$32 \quad 42 \quad 46 \quad 46 \quad 54$$

Because $n = 5$ is odd, the median is the middle value. Thus the median class size is 46 students. Even though this data set contains two observations with values of 46, each observation is treated separately when we arrange the data in ascending order.

Suppose we also compute the median starting salary for the 12 business college graduates in Table 3.1. We first arrange the data in ascending order.

$$3310 \quad 3355 \quad 3450 \quad 3480 \quad 3480 \quad \underbrace{3490 \quad 3520}_{\text{Middle Two Values}} \quad 3540 \quad 3550 \quad 3650 \quad 3730 \quad 3925$$

Because $n = 12$ is even, we identify the middle two values: 3490 and 3520. The median is the average of these values.

$$\text{Median} = \frac{3490 + 3520}{2} = 3505$$

*The median is the measure of location most often reported for annual income and property value data because a few extremely large incomes or property values can inflate the mean. In such cases, the median is the preferred measure of central location.*

Although the mean is the more commonly used measure of central location, in some situations the median is preferred. The mean is influenced by extremely small and large data values. For instance, suppose that one of the graduates (see Table 3.1) had a starting salary of $10,000 per month (maybe the individual's family owns the company). If we change the highest monthly starting salary in Table 3.1 from $3925 to $10,000 and recompute the mean, the sample mean changes from $3540 to $4046. The median of $3505, however, is unchanged, because $3490 and $3520 are still the middle two values. With the extremely high starting salary included, the median provides a better measure of central location than the mean. We can generalize to say that whenever a data set contains extreme values, the median is often the preferred measure of central location.

## Mode

A third measure of location is the **mode**. The mode is defined as follows.

MODE

The mode is the value that occurs with greatest frequency.

To illustrate the identification of the mode, consider the sample of five class sizes. The only value that occurs more than once is 46. Because this value, occurring with a frequency of 2, has the greatest frequency, it is the mode. As another illustration, consider the sample of starting salaries for the business school graduates. The only monthly starting salary that occurs more than once is $3480. Because this value has the greatest frequency, it is the mode.

Situations can arise for which the greatest frequency occurs at two or more different values. In these instances more than one mode exists. If the data contain exactly two modes, we say that the data are *bimodal*. If data contain more than two modes, we say that the data are *multimodal*. In multimodal cases the mode is almost never reported because listing three or more modes would not be particularly helpful in describing a location for the data.

## Using Excel to Compute the Mean, Median, and Mode

Excel provides functions for computing the mean, median, and mode. We illustrate the use of these Excel functions by computing the mean, median, and mode for the starting salary data in Table 3.1. Refer to Figure 3.1 as we describe the tasks involved. The formula worksheet is in the background; the value worksheet is in the foreground.

**Enter Data:** Labels and the starting salary data are entered into cells A1:B13 of the worksheet.

**Enter Functions and Formulas:** Excel's AVERAGE function can be used to compute the mean by entering the following formula into cell E1:

$$=\text{AVERAGE(B2:B13)}$$

*If the data are bimodal or multimodal, Excel's MODE.SNGL function will incorrectly identify a single mode.*

Similarly, the formulas =MEDIAN(B2:B13) and =MODE.SNGL(B2:B13) are entered into cells E2 and E3, respectively, to compute the median and the mode. The labels Mean, Median, and Mode are entered into cells D1:D3 to identify the output.

**FIGURE 3.1** EXCEL WORKSHEET USED TO COMPUTE THE MEAN, MEDIAN, AND MODE FOR STARTING SALARIES

The formulas in cells E1:E3 are displayed in the formula worksheet in the background of Figure 3.1. The worksheet in the foreground shows the values computed using the Excel functions. Note that the mean (3540), median (3505), and mode (3480) are the same as we computed earlier.

## Percentiles

A **percentile** provides information about how the data are spread over the interval from the smallest value to the largest value. For data that do not contain numerous repeated values, the $p$th percentile divides the data into two parts. Approximately $p$ percent of the observations have values less than the $p$th percentile; approximately $(100 - p)$ percent of the observations have values greater than the $p$th percentile. The $p$th percentile is formally defined as follows.

---

### PERCENTILE

The $p$th percentile is a value such that *at least $p$* percent of the observations are less than or equal to this value and *at least* $(100 - p)$ percent of the observations are greater than or equal to this value.

---

Colleges and universities frequently report admission test scores in terms of percentiles. For instance, suppose an applicant obtains a raw score of 54 on the verbal portion of an admission test. How this student performed in relation to other students taking the same test may not be readily apparent. However, if the raw score of 54 corresponds to the 70th percentile, we know that approximately 70% of the students scored lower than this individual and approximately 30% of the students scored higher than this individual.

The following procedure can be used to compute the $p$th percentile.

---

### CALCULATING THE $p$TH PERCENTILE

*Following these steps makes it easy to calculate percentiles.*

**Step 1.** Arrange the data in ascending order (smallest value to largest value).

**Step 2.** Compute an index $i$

$$i = \left( \frac{p}{100} \right) n$$

where $p$ is the percentile of interest and $n$ is the number of observations.

**Step 3.** (a) If $i$ *is not an integer, round up*. The next integer *greater* than $i$ denotes the position of the $p$th percentile.

(b) If $i$ *is an integer,* the $p$th percentile is the average of the values in positions $i$ and $i + 1$.

---

As an illustration of this procedure, let us determine the 85th percentile for the starting salary data in Table 3.1.

**Step 1.** Arrange the data in ascending order.

3310   3355   3450   3480   3480   3490   3520   3540   3550   3650   3730   3925

**Step 2.**

$$i = \left(\frac{p}{100}\right)n = \left(\frac{85}{100}\right)12 = 10.2$$

**Step 3.** Because $i$ is not an integer, *round up.* The position of the 85th percentile is the next integer greater than 10.2, the 11th position.

Returning to the data, we see that the 85th percentile is the data value in the 11th position, or 3730.

As another illustration of this procedure, let us consider the calculation of the 50th percentile for the starting salary data. Applying step 2, we obtain

$$i = \left(\frac{50}{100}\right)12 = 6$$

Because $i$ is an integer, step 3(b) states that the 50th percentile is the average of the sixth and seventh data values; thus the 50th percentile is $(3490 + 3520)/2 = 3505$. Note that the *50th percentile is also the median.*

## Quartiles

*Quartiles are just specific percentiles; thus, the steps for computing percentiles can be applied directly in the computation of quartiles.*

It is often desirable to divide data into four parts, with each part containing approximately one-fourth, or 25% of the observations. Figure 3.2 shows a data distribution divided into four parts. The division points are referred to as the **quartiles** and are defined as

$Q_1$ = first quartile, or 25th percentile

$Q_2$ = second quartile, or 50th percentile (also the median)

$Q_3$ = third quartile, or 75th percentile

The starting salary data are again arranged in ascending order. We already identified $Q_2$, the second quartile (median), as 3505.

3310  3355  3450  3480  3480  3490  3520  3540  3550  3650  3730  3925

The computations of quartiles $Q_1$ and $Q_3$ require the use of the rule for finding the 25th and 75th percentiles. These calculations follow.

**FIGURE 3.2**  LOCATION OF THE QUARTILES

|  | $Q_1$ | $Q_2$ | $Q_3$ |
| --- | --- | --- | --- |
|  | First Quartile (25th percentile) | Second Quartile (50th percentile) (median) | Third Quartile (75th percentile) |

For $Q_1$,

$$i = \left(\frac{p}{100}\right)n = \left(\frac{25}{100}\right)12 = 3$$

Because $i$ is an integer, step 3(b) indicates that the first quartile, or 25th percentile, is the average of the third and fourth data values; thus, $Q_1 = (3450 + 3480)/2 = 3465$.

For $Q_3$,

$$i = \left(\frac{p}{100}\right)n = \left(\frac{75}{100}\right)12 = 9$$

Again, because $i$ is an integer, step 3(b) indicates that the third quartile, or 75th percentile, is the average of the ninth and tenth data values; thus, $Q_3 = (3550 + 3650)/2 = 3600$.

The quartiles divide the starting salary data into four parts, with each part containing 25% of the observations.

| 3310 | 3355 | 3450 | 3480 | 3480 | 3490 | 3520 | 3540 | 3550 | 3650 | 3730 | 3925 |

$Q_1 = 3465$   $Q_2 = 3505$   $Q_3 = 3600$

(Median)

We defined the quartiles as the 25th, 50th, and 75th percentiles. Thus, we computed the quartiles in the same way as percentiles. However, other conventions are sometimes used to compute quartiles, and the actual values reported for quartiles may vary slightly depending on the convention used. Nevertheless, the objective of all procedures for computing quartiles is to divide the data into four equal parts.

## Using Excel to Compute Percentiles and Quartiles

Computer software packages do not all use the same method to compute percentiles and quartiles. The formula Excel uses to compute the location ($L_p$) of the $p$th percentile is

$$L_p = \left(\frac{p}{100}\right)n + \left(1 - \frac{p}{100}\right)$$

For instance, Excel would compute the location of the 85th percentile for the starting salary data as follows:

$$L_{85} = (.85)12 + (1 - .85) = 10.20 + .15 = 10.35$$

The value of $L_{85} = 10.35$ indicates that the 85th percentile is between the 10th and the 11th observations in rank order from the bottom up. It is the value of observation 10 (3650) plus .35 of the difference between observation 11 (3730) and observation 10. Therefore, the 85th percentile is $3650 + .35(3730 - 3650) = 3650 + .35(80) = 3678$.[1]

Computing percentiles and quartiles using Excel is easy. For instance, Excel's PERCENTILE.INC function can be used to compute the 85th percentile for the starting

---

[1]The value Excel computed for the 85th percentile does not strictly satisfy the definition of the 85th percentile because only 83% of the values are less than or equal to 3678. Our procedure would round up in this case to obtain 3730 as the value satisfying the definition of the 85th percentile. For larger data sets, the difference between the approximate value provided by Excel and the value computed using our three-step procedure is not of practical significance.

salary data by entering the following formula into any empty cell of the worksheet shown in Figure 3.1:

$$=\text{PERCENTILE.INC(B2:B13,.85)}$$

The value Excel provides is 3678. To compute a different percentile we simply change the value of .85. For instance, we can use Excel's PERCENTILE.INC function to compute the quartiles for the starting salary data by replacing .85 with values of .25 (25th percentile or first quartile), .50 (50th percentile or second quartile), and .75 (75th percentile or third quartile).

Alternatively, we can use Excel's QUARTILE.INC function to compute the quartiles. For example, to compute the first quartile for the starting salary data we would enter the following formula into an empty cell of the worksheet in Figure 3.1.

$$=\text{QUARTILE.INC(B2:B13,1)}$$

*If the value of 1 in the QUARTILE.INC function is changed to 0, Excel computes the minimum value in the data set. If the value of 1 is changed to 4, Excel computes the maximum value.*

The value Excel provides is 3472.5. We can compute the second quartile or median by replacing the value of 1 with 2, and the third quartile by replacing the value of 1 with 3.

Computing percentiles and quartiles is useful for a data analyst who is interested in getting a feel for how the values in a data set are distributed. However, if you are a student who wants to know how the starting salary you received ranks compared to all the other starting salaries, then what you would like to do is to take your salary and compute its rank and percentile. Or perhaps you know your raw score on an exam and would like to know its rank and percentile. Excel's Rank and Percentile tool can be used to provide this information for an entire data set.

We illustrate the use of Excel's Rank and Percentile tool by computing the ranks and percentiles for the starting salaries in Table 3.1. Refer to Figure 3.3 as we present the tasks involved.

**Enter Data:** Labels and the starting salary data are entered into cells A1:B13.

**Enter Functions and Formulas:** No functions and formulas are needed.

**FIGURE 3.3** USING EXCEL'S RANK AND PERCENTILE TOOL FOR STARTING SALARIES

**Apply Tools:**   The following steps will compute the rank and percentile for each observation.

> **Step 1.** Click the **Data** tab on the Ribbon
> **Step 2.** In the **Analysis** group, click **Data Analysis**
> **Step 3.** Choose **Rank and Percentile** from the list of Analysis Tools
> **Step 4.** When the Rank and Percentile dialog box appears,
> > Enter B1:B13 in the **Input Range** box
> > Select **Grouped by Columns**
> > Select **Labels in First Row**
> > Select **Output Range**
> > Enter D1 in the **Output Range** box
> > > (Any cell where the upper left corner of the output is desired may be entered here.)
> > Click **OK**

The output from using the Rank and Percentile tool appears in cells D1:G13. Cells F2:F13 contain the rank of each observation. The highest salary is given a rank of 1 and the lowest salary is given a rank of 12. Cells G2:G13 show the percentile each salary represents. For instance, the percentile for 3450 is 18.1% because 2 of the other 11 salaries are smaller than 3450. The lowest salary is the 0th percentile and the highest salary is the 100th percentile. The percentiles increase by $(1/11)100\%$ as we move up from the lowest salary to the highest, except for ties. In the case of a tie, Excel gives the tied values the same rank and percentile. Note that the two observations with the same value (3480) both received a rank of 8 and a percentile of 27.20%.

## NOTES AND COMMENTS

It is better to use the median than the mean as a measure of central location when a data set contains extreme values. Another measure, sometimes used when extreme values are present, is the *trimmed mean.* It is obtained by deleting a percentage of the smallest and largest values from a data set and then computing the mean of the remaining values. For example, the 5% trimmed mean is obtained by removing the smallest 5% and the largest 5% of the data values and then computing the mean of the remaining values. Using the sample with $n = 12$ starting salaries, $0.05(12) = 0.6$. Rounding this value to 1 indicates that the 5% trimmed mean would remove the 1 smallest data value and the 1 largest data value. The 5% trimmed mean using the 10 remaining observations is 3524.50.

## Exercises

## Methods

1. Consider a sample with data values of 10, 20, 12, 17, and 16. Compute the mean and median.

2. Consider a sample with data values of 10, 20, 21, 17, 16, and 12. Compute the mean and median.

3. Consider a sample with data values of 27, 25, 20, 15, 30, 34, 28, and 25. Compute the 20th, 25th, 65th, and 75th percentiles.

4. Consider a sample with data values of 53, 55, 70, 58, 64, 57, 53, 69, 57, 68, and 53. Compute the mean, median, and mode.

## Applications

5. The Dow Jones Travel Index reported what business travelers pay for hotel rooms per night in major U.S. cities (*The Wall Street Journal,* January 16, 2004). The average hotel room rates for 20 cities are as follows:

| Atlanta | $163 | Minneapolis | $125 |
|---|---|---|---|
| Boston | 177 | New Orleans | 167 |
| Chicago | 166 | New York | 245 |
| Cleveland | 126 | Orlando | 146 |
| Dallas | 123 | Phoenix | 139 |
| Denver | 120 | Pittsburgh | 134 |
| Detroit | 144 | San Francisco | 167 |
| Houston | 173 | Seattle | 162 |
| Los Angeles | 160 | St. Louis | 145 |
| Miami | 192 | Washington, D.C. | 207 |

**Hotels**

   a.  What is the mean hotel room rate?
   b.  What is the median hotel room rate?
   c.  What is the mode?
   d.  What is the first quartile?
   e.  What is the third quartile?

6. During the 2007–2008 NCAA college basketball season, men's basketball teams attempted an all-time-high number of 3-point shots, averaging 19.07 shots per game (Associated Press Sports, January 24, 2009). In an attempt to discourage so many 3-point shots and encourage more inside play, the NCAA rules committee moved the 3-point line back from 19 feet, 9 inches to 20 feet, 9 inches at the beginning of the 2008–2009 basketball season. Shown in the following table are the 3-point shots taken and the 3-point shots made for a sample of 19 NCAA basketball games during the 2008–2009 season.

| 3-Point Shots | Shots Made | 3-Point Shots | Shots Made |
|---|---|---|---|
| 23 | 4 | 17 | 7 |
| 20 | 6 | 19 | 10 |
| 17 | 5 | 22 | 7 |
| 18 | 8 | 25 | 11 |
| 13 | 4 | 15 | 6 |
| 16 | 4 | 10 | 5 |
| 8 | 5 | 11 | 3 |
| 19 | 8 | 25 | 8 |
| 28 | 5 | 23 | 7 |
| 21 | 7 | | |

**WEB** file

**3Points**

   a.  What is the mean number of 3-point shots taken per game?
   b.  What is the mean number of 3-point shots made per game?
   c.  Using the closer 3-point line, players were making 35.2% of their shots. What percentage of shots were players making from the new 3-point line?
   d.  What was the impact of the NCAA rules change that moved the 3-point line back to 20 feet, 9 inches for the 2008–2009 season? Would you agree with the Associated Press Sports article that stated, "Moving back the 3-point line hasn't changed the game dramatically"? Explain.

7. Endowment income is a critical part of the annual budgets at colleges and universities. A study by the National Association of College and University Business Officers

reported that the 435 colleges and universities surveyed held a total of $413 billion in endowments. The 10 wealthiest universities are shown below (*The Wall Street Journal*, January 27, 2009). Amounts are in billions of dollars.

| University | Endowment ($billion) | University | Endowment ($billion) |
|---|---|---|---|
| Columbia | 7.2 | Princeton | 16.4 |
| Harvard | 36.6 | Stanford | 17.2 |
| M.I.T. | 10.1 | Texas | 16.1 |
| Michigan | 7.6 | Texas A&M | 6.7 |
| Northwestern | 7.2 | Yale | 22.9 |

a. What is the mean endowment for these universities?
b. What is the median endowment?
c. What is the mode endowment?
d. Compute the first and third quartiles.
e. What is the total endowment at these 10 universities? These universities represent 2.3% of the 435 colleges and universities surveyed. What percentage of the total $413 billion in endowments is held by these 10 universities?
f. *The Wall Street Journal* reported that over a recent five-month period, a downturn in the economy has caused endowments to decline 23%. What is the estimate of the dollar amount of the decline in the total endowments held by these 10 universities? Given this situation, what are some of the steps you would expect university administrators to be considering?

8. The cost of consumer purchases such as single-family housing, gasoline, Internet services, tax preparation, and hospitalization were provided in *The Wall-Street Journal* (January 2, 2007). Sample data typical of the cost of tax-return preparation by services such as H&R Block are shown below.

**SELF** test

**WEB** file

TaxCost

| | | | | |
|---|---|---|---|---|
| 120 | 230 | 110 | 115 | 160 |
| 130 | 150 | 105 | 195 | 155 |
| 105 | 360 | 120 | 120 | 140 |
| 100 | 115 | 180 | 235 | 255 |

a. Compute the mean, median, and mode.
b. Compute the first and third quartiles.
c. Compute and interpret the 90th percentile.

9. The National Association of Realtors provided data showing that home sales were the slowest in 10 years (Associated Press, December 24, 2008). Sample data with representative sales prices for existing homes and new homes follow. Data are in thousands of dollars:

| *Existing Homes* | 315.5 | 202.5 | 140.2 | 181.3 | 470.2 | 169.9 | 112.8 | 230.0 | 177.5 |
|---|---|---|---|---|---|---|---|---|---|
| *New Homes* | 275.9 | 350.2 | 195.8 | 525.0 | 225.3 | 215.5 | 175.0 | 149.5 | |

a. What is the median sales price for existing homes?
b. What is the median sales price for new homes?
c. Do existing homes or new homes have the higher median sales price? What is the difference between the median sales prices?
d. A year earlier the median sales price for existing homes was $208.4 thousand and the median sales price for new homes was $249 thousand. Compute the percentage

change in the median sales price of existing and new homes over the one-year period. Did existing homes or new homes have the larger percentage change in median sales price?

10. A panel of economists provided forecasts of the U.S. economy for the first six months of 2007 (*The Wall Street Journal,* January 2, 2007). The percent changes in the gross domestic product (GDP) forecasted by 30 economists are as follows.

Economy

| 2.6 | 3.1 | 2.3 | 2.7 | 3.4 | 0.9 | 2.6 | 2.8 | 2.0 | 2.4 |
| 2.7 | 2.7 | 2.7 | 2.9 | 3.1 | 2.8 | 1.7 | 2.3 | 2.8 | 3.5 |
| 0.4 | 2.5 | 2.2 | 1.9 | 1.8 | 1.1 | 2.0 | 2.1 | 2.5 | 0.5 |

a. What is the minimum forecast for the percent change in the GDP? What is the maximum?
b. Compute the mean, median, and mode.
c. Compute the first and third quartiles.
d. Did the economists provide an optimistic or pessimistic outlook for the U.S. economy? Discuss.

11. In automobile mileage and gasoline-consumption testing, 13 automobiles were road tested for 300 miles in both city and highway driving conditions. The following data were recorded for miles-per-gallon performance.

*City:*      16.2  16.7  15.9  14.4  13.2  15.3  16.8  16.0  16.1  15.3  15.2  15.3  16.2
*Highway:*  19.4  20.6  18.3  18.6  19.2  17.4  17.2  18.6  19.0  21.1  19.4  18.5  18.7

Use the mean, median, and mode to make a statement about the difference in performance for city and highway driving.

12. Walt Disney Company bought Pixar Animation Studios, Inc., in a deal worth $7.4 billion (*CNN Money* website, January 24, 2006). The animated movies produced by Disney and Pixar during the previous 10 years are listed in the following table. The box office revenues are in millions of dollars. Compute the total revenue, the mean, the median, and the quartiles to compare the box office success of the movies produced by both companies. Do the statistics suggest at least one of the reasons Disney was interested in buying Pixar? Discuss.

Disney

| Disney Movies | Revenue ($millions) | Pixar Movies | Revenue ($millions) |
|---|---|---|---|
| *Pocahontas* | 346 | *Toy Story* | 362 |
| *Hunchback of Notre Dame* | 325 | *A Bug's Life* | 363 |
| *Hercules* | 253 | *Toy Story 2* | 485 |
| *Mulan* | 304 | *Monsters, Inc.* | 525 |
| *Tarzan* | 448 | *Finding Nemo* | 865 |
| *Dinosaur* | 354 | *The Incredibles* | 631 |
| *The Emperor's New Groove* | 169 | | |
| *Lilo & Stitch* | 273 | | |
| *Treasure Planet* | 110 | | |
| *The Jungle Book 2* | 136 | | |
| *Brother Bear* | 250 | | |
| *Home on the Range* | 104 | | |
| *Chicken Little* | 249 | | |

## 3.2 Measures of Variability

*The variability in the delivery time creates uncertainty for production scheduling. Methods presented in this section help measure and understand variability.*

In addition to measures of location, it is often desirable to consider measures of variability, or dispersion. For example, suppose that you are a purchasing agent for a large manufacturing firm and that you regularly place orders with two different suppliers. After several months of operation, you find that the mean number of days required to fill orders is 10 days for both of the suppliers. The histograms summarizing the number of working days required to fill orders from the suppliers are shown in Figure 3.4. Although the mean number of days is 10 for both suppliers, do the two suppliers demonstrate the same degree of reliability in terms of making deliveries on schedule? Note the dispersion, or variability, in delivery times indicated by the histograms. Which supplier would you prefer?

For most firms, receiving materials and supplies on schedule is important. The 7- or 8-day deliveries shown for J.C. Clark Distributors might be viewed favorably; however, a few of the slow 13- to 15-day deliveries could be disastrous in terms of keeping a workforce busy and production on schedule. This example illustrates a situation in which the variability in the delivery times may be an overriding consideration in selecting a supplier. For most purchasing agents, the lower variability shown for Dawson Supply, Inc., would make Dawson the preferred supplier.

We turn now to a discussion of some commonly used measures of variability.

### Range

The simplest measure of variability is the **range**.

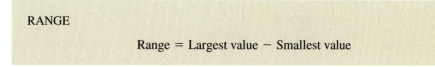

RANGE

Range = Largest value − Smallest value

**FIGURE 3.4**  HISTORICAL DATA SHOWING THE NUMBER OF DAYS REQUIRED TO FILL ORDERS

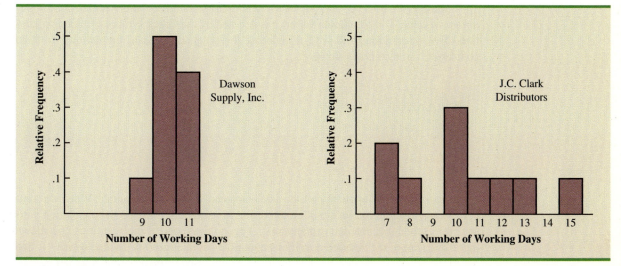

Let us refer to the data on starting salaries for business school graduates in Table 3.1. The largest starting salary is 3925 and the smallest is 3310. The range is $3925 - 3310 = 615$.

Although the range is the easiest of the measures of variability to compute, it is seldom used as the only measure. The reason is that the range is based on only two of the observations and thus is highly influenced by extreme values. Suppose one of the graduates received a starting salary of $10,000 per month. In this case, the range would be $10,000 - 3310 = 6690$ rather than 615. This large value for the range would not be especially descriptive of the variability in the data because 11 of the 12 starting salaries are closely grouped between 3310 and 3730.

## Interquartile Range

A measure of variability that overcomes the dependency on extreme values is the **interquartile range (IQR)**. This measure of variability is the difference between the third quartile, $Q_3$, and the first quartile, $Q_1$. In other words, the interquartile range is the range for the middle 50% of the data.

---

**INTERQUARTILE RANGE**

$$IQR = Q_3 - Q_1 \tag{3.3}$$

---

For the data on monthly starting salaries, the quartiles are $Q_3 = 3600$ and $Q_1 = 3465$. Thus, the interquartile range is $3600 - 3465 = 135$.

## Variance

The **variance** is a measure of variability that utilizes all the data. The variance is based on the difference between the value of each observation ($x_i$) and the mean. The difference between each $x_i$ and the mean ($\bar{x}$ for a sample, $\mu$ for a population) is called a *deviation about the mean*. For a sample, a deviation about the mean is written ($x_i - \bar{x}$); for a population, it is written ($x_i - \mu$). In the computation of the variance, the deviations about the mean are *squared*.

If the data are for a population, the average of the squared deviations is called the *population variance*. The population variance is denoted by the Greek symbol $\sigma^2$. For a population of $N$ observations and with $\mu$ denoting the population mean, the definition of the population variance is as follows.

---

**POPULATION VARIANCE**

$$\sigma^2 = \frac{\Sigma(x_i - \mu)^2}{N} \tag{3.4}$$

---

In most statistical applications, the data being analyzed are for a sample. When we compute a sample variance, we are often interested in using it to estimate the population variance $\sigma^2$. Although a detailed explanation is beyond the scope of this text, it can be shown that if the sum of the squared deviations about the sample mean is divided by $n - 1$, and not $n$, the resulting sample variance provides an unbiased estimate of the population variance. For this reason, the *sample variance,* denoted by $s^2$, is defined as follows.

**TABLE 3.2** COMPUTATION OF DEVIATIONS AND SQUARED DEVIATIONS ABOUT THE MEAN FOR THE CLASS SIZE DATA

| Number of Students in Class ($x_i$) | Mean Class Size ($\bar{x}$) | Deviation About the Mean ($x_i - \bar{x}$) | Squared Deviation About the Mean ($x_i - \bar{x})^2$ |
|---|---|---|---|
| 46 | 44 | 2 | 4 |
| 54 | 44 | 10 | 100 |
| 42 | 44 | −2 | 4 |
| 46 | 44 | 2 | 4 |
| 32 | 44 | −12 | 144 |
| | | 0 | 256 |
| | | $\Sigma(x_i - \bar{x})$ | $\Sigma(x_i - \bar{x})^2$ |

*The sample variance $s^2$ is a point estimator of the population variance $\sigma^2$.*

SAMPLE VARIANCE

$$s^2 = \frac{\Sigma(x_i - \bar{x})^2}{n - 1}$$

**(3.5)**

To illustrate the computation of the sample variance, we will use the data on class size for the sample of five college classes as presented in Section 3.1. A summary of the data, including the computation of the deviations about the mean and the squared deviations about the mean, is shown in Table 3.2. The sum of squared deviations about the mean is $\Sigma(x_i - \bar{x})^2 = 256$. Hence, with $n - 1 = 4$, the sample variance is

$$s^2 = \frac{\Sigma(x_i - \bar{x})^2}{n - 1} = \frac{256}{4} = 64$$

Before moving on, let us note that the units associated with the sample variance often cause confusion. Because the values being summed in the variance calculation, $(x_i - \bar{x})^2$, are squared, the units associated with the sample variance are also *squared*. For instance, the sample variance for the class size data is $s^2 = 64$ (students)$^2$. The squared units associated with variance make it difficult to obtain an intuitive understanding and interpretation of the numerical value of the variance. We recommend that you think of the variance as a measure useful in comparing the amount of variability for two or more variables. In a comparison of the variables, the one with the largest variance shows the most variability. Further interpretation of the value of the variance may not be necessary.

*The variance is useful in comparing the variability of two or more variables.*

As another illustration of computing a sample variance, consider the starting salaries listed in Table 3.1 for the 12 business school graduates. In Section 3.1, we showed that the sample mean starting salary was 3540. The computation of the sample variance ($s^2 = 27,440.91$) is shown in Table 3.3.

In Tables 3.2 and 3.3 we show both the sum of the deviations about the mean and the sum of the squared deviations about the mean. For any data set, the sum of the deviations about the mean will *always equal zero*. Note that in Tables 3.2 and 3.3, $\Sigma(x_i - \bar{x}) = 0$. The positive deviations and negative deviations cancel each other, causing the sum of the deviations about the mean to equal zero.

**TABLE 3.3**    COMPUTATION OF THE SAMPLE VARIANCE FOR THE STARTING SALARY DATA

| Monthly Salary $(x_i)$ | Sample Mean $(\bar{x})$ | Deviation About the Mean $(x_i - \bar{x})$ | Squared Deviation About the Mean $(x_i - \bar{x})^2$ |
|---|---|---|---|
| 3450 | 3540 | −90 | 8,100 |
| 3550 | 3540 | 10 | 100 |
| 3650 | 3540 | 110 | 12,100 |
| 3480 | 3540 | −60 | 3,600 |
| 3355 | 3540 | −185 | 34,225 |
| 3310 | 3540 | −230 | 52,900 |
| 3490 | 3540 | −50 | 2,500 |
| 3730 | 3540 | 190 | 36,100 |
| 3540 | 3540 | 0 | 0 |
| 3925 | 3540 | 385 | 148,225 |
| 3520 | 3540 | −20 | 400 |
| 3480 | 3540 | −60 | 3,600 |
| | | 0 | 301,850 |
| | | $\Sigma(x_i - \bar{x})$ | $\Sigma(x_i - \bar{x})^2$ |

Using equation (3.5),

$$s^2 = \frac{\Sigma(x_i - \bar{x})^2}{n - 1} = \frac{301,850}{11} = 27,440.91$$

## Standard Deviation

The **standard deviation** is defined to be the positive square root of the variance. Following the notation we adopted for a sample variance and a population variance, we use $s$ to denote the sample standard deviation and $\sigma$ to denote the population standard deviation. The standard deviation is derived from the variance in the following way.

*The sample standard deviation s is a point estimator of the population standard deviation $\sigma$.*

**STANDARD DEVIATION**

$$\text{Sample standard deviation} = s = \sqrt{s^2} \tag{3.6}$$

$$\text{Population standard deviation} = \sigma = \sqrt{\sigma^2} \tag{3.7}$$

Recall that the sample variance for the sample of class sizes in five college classes is $s^2 = 64$. Thus, the sample standard deviation is $s = \sqrt{64} = 8$. For the data on starting salaries, the sample standard deviation is $s = \sqrt{27,440.91} = 165.65$.

*The standard deviation is easier to interpret than the variance because the standard deviation is measured in the same units as the data.*

What is gained by converting the variance to its corresponding standard deviation? Recall that the units associated with the variance are squared. For example, the sample variance for the starting salary data of business school graduates is $s^2 = 27,440.91$ (dollars)$^2$. Because the standard deviation is the square root of the variance, the units of the variance, dollars squared, are converted to dollars in the standard deviation. Thus, the standard deviation of the starting salary data is $165.65. In other words, the standard deviation is measured in the same units as the original data. For this reason the standard deviation is more easily compared to the mean and other statistics that are measured in the same units as the original data.

## Using Excel to Compute the Sample Variance and Sample Standard Deviation

Excel provides functions for computing the sample variance and sample standard deviation, which we will illustrate using the starting salary data. Refer to Figure 3.5 as we describe the steps involved. Figure 3.5 is an extension of Figure 3.1, where we showed how to use Excel functions to compute the mean, median, and mode. The formula worksheet is in the background; the value worksheet is in the foreground.

**Enter Data:**   Labels and the starting salary data are entered into cells A1:B13 of the worksheet.

**Enter Functions and Formulas:**   The Excel AVERAGE, MEDIAN, and MODE.SNGL functions are entered into cells E1:E3 as described earlier. Excel's VAR.S function can be used to compute the sample variance by entering the following formula into cell E4:

$$=VAR.S(B2:B13)$$

Similarly, the formula =STDEV.S(B2:B13) is entered into cell E5 to compute the sample standard deviation. Appropriate labels are entered into cells D1:D5 to identify the output.

The value worksheet, in the foreground, shows the values computed using the Excel functions. Note that the sample variance and sample standard deviation are the same as we computed earlier using the definitions.

**FIGURE 3.5**   EXCEL WORKSHEET USED TO COMPUTE THE SAMPLE VARIANCE AND THE SAMPLE STANDARD DEVIATION FOR STARTING SALARIES

## Coefficient of Variation

*The coefficient of variation is a relative measure of variability; it measures the standard deviation relative to the mean.*

In some situations we may be interested in a descriptive statistic that indicates how large the standard deviation is relative to the mean. This measure is called the **coefficient of variation** and is usually expressed as a percentage.

---

COEFFICIENT OF VARIATION

$$\left(\frac{\text{Standard deviation}}{\text{Mean}} \times 100\right)\%$$    (3.8)

---

For the class size data, we found a sample mean of 44 and a sample standard deviation of 8. The coefficient of variation is $[(8/44) \times 100]\% = 18.2\%$. In words, the coefficient of variation tells us that the sample standard deviation is 18.2% of the value of the sample mean. For the starting salary data with a sample mean of 3540 and a sample standard deviation of 165.65, the coefficient of variation, $[(165.65/3540) \times 100]\% = 4.7\%$, tells us the sample standard deviation is only 4.7% of the value of the sample mean. In general, the coefficient of variation is a useful statistic for comparing the variability of variables that have different standard deviations and different means.

## Using Excel's Descriptive Statistics Tool

As we have seen, Excel provides statistical functions to compute descriptive statistics for a data set. These functions can be used to compute one statistic at a time (e.g., mean, variance, etc.). Excel also provides a variety of data analysis tools. One of these, called Descriptive Statistics, allows the user to compute a variety of descriptive statistics at once. We show here how it can be used to compute descriptive statistics for the starting salary data in Table 3.1. Refer to Figure 3.6 as we describe the tasks involved.

**FIGURE 3.6**    DIALOG BOX FOR EXCEL'S DESCRIPTIVE STATISTICS TOOL

**Enter Data:**   Labels and the starting salary data are entered into cells A1:B13 of the worksheet.

**Enter Functions and Formulas:**   No functions and formulas are needed.

**Apply Analysis Tools:**   The following steps describe how to use Excel's Descriptive Statistics tool for these data:

**Step 1.** Click the **Data** tab on the Ribbon
**Step 2.** In the **Analysis** group, click **Data Analysis**
**Step 3.** Choose **Descriptive Statistics** from the list of **Analysis Tools**
**Step 4.** When the Descriptive Statistics dialog box appears (see Figure 3.6),
   Enter B1:B13 in the **Input Range** box
   Select **Grouped By Columns**
   Select **Labels in First Row**
   Select **Output Range**
   Enter D1 in the **Output Range** box (to identify the upper left corner of the section of the worksheet where the descriptive statistics will appear)
   Select **Summary Statistics**
   Click **OK**

Cells D1:E15 of Figure 3.7 show the descriptive statistics provided by Excel. A yellow screen is used to highlight the results. The boldfaced entries are the descriptive statistics we have covered. The descriptive statistics that are not boldfaced are either covered subsequently in the text or discussed in more advanced texts.

**FIGURE 3.7**   DESCRIPTIVE STATISTICS PROVIDED BY EXCEL FOR THE STARTING SALARY DATA

## NOTES AND COMMENTS

1. The standard deviation is a commonly used measure of the risk associated with investing in stock and stock funds. It provides a measure of how monthly returns fluctuate around the long-run average return.

2. Rounding the value of the sample mean $\bar{x}$ and the values of the squared deviations $(x_i - \bar{x})^2$ may introduce errors when a calculator is used in the computation of the variance and standard deviation. To reduce rounding errors, we recommend carrying at least six significant digits during intermediate calculations. The resulting variance or standard deviation can then be rounded to fewer digits.

3. An alternative formula for the computation of the sample variance is

$$s^2 = \frac{\Sigma x_i^2 - n\bar{x}^2}{n - 1}$$

where $\Sigma x_i^2 = x_1^2 + x_2^2 + \cdots + x_n^2$.

## Exercises

### Methods

13. Consider a sample with data values of 10, 20, 12, 17, and 16. Compute the range and interquartile range.

14. Consider a sample with data values of 10, 20, 12, 17, and 16. Compute the variance and standard deviation.

15. Consider a sample with data values of 27, 25, 20, 15, 30, 34, 28, and 25. Compute the range, interquartile range, variance, and standard deviation.

### Applications

16. A bowler's scores for six games were 182, 168, 184, 190, 170, and 174. Using these data as a sample, compute the following descriptive statistics:
    a. Range                c. Standard deviation
    b. Variance             d. Coefficient of variation

17. A home theater in a box is the easiest and cheapest way to provide surround sound for a home entertainment center. A sample of prices is shown here (*Consumer Reports Buying Guide,* 2004). The prices are for models with a DVD player and for models without a DVD player.

| Models with DVD Player | Price | Models without DVD Player | Price |
|---|---|---|---|
| Sony HT-1800DP | $450 | Pioneer HTP-230 | $300 |
| Pioneer HTD-330DV | 300 | Sony HT-DDW750 | 300 |
| Sony HT-C800DP | 400 | Kenwood HTB-306 | 360 |
| Panasonic SC-HT900 | 500 | RCA RT-2600 | 290 |
| Panasonic SC-MTI | 400 | Kenwood HTB-206 | 300 |

a. Compute the mean price for models with a DVD player and the mean price for models without a DVD player. What is the additional price paid to have a DVD player included in a home theater unit?

b.    Compute the range, variance, and standard deviation for the two samples. What does this information tell you about the prices for models with and without a DVD player?

18.   Car rental rates per day for a sample of seven Eastern U.S. cities are as follows (*The Wall Street Journal,* January 16, 2004).

| City | Daily Rate |
|------|-----------|
| Boston | $43 |
| Atlanta | 35 |
| Miami | 34 |
| New York | 58 |
| Orlando | 30 |
| Pittsburgh | 30 |
| Washington, D.C. | 36 |

a.    Compute the mean, variance, and standard deviation for the car rental rates.
b.    A similar sample of seven Western U.S. cities showed a sample mean car rental rate of $38 per day. The variance and standard deviation were 12.3 and 3.5, respectively. Discuss any difference between the car rental rates in Eastern and Western U.S. cities.

19.   The *Los Angeles Times* regularly reports the air quality index for various areas of Southern California. A sample of air quality index values for Pomona provided the following data: 28, 42, 58, 48, 45, 55, 60, 49, and 50.
a.    Compute the range and interquartile range.
b.    Compute the sample variance and sample standard deviation.
c.    A sample of air quality index readings for Anaheim provided a sample mean of 48.5, a sample variance of 136, and a sample standard deviation of 11.66. What comparisons can you make between the air quality in Pomona and that in Anaheim on the basis of these descriptive statistics?

20.   The following data were used to construct the histograms of the number of days required to fill orders for Dawson Supply, Inc., and J.C. Clark Distributors (see Figure 3.4).

*Dawson Supply Days for Delivery:*    11   10    9   10   11   11   10   11   10   10
*Clark Distributors Days for Delivery:*    8   10   13    7   10   11   10    7   15   12

Use the range and standard deviation to support the previous observation that Dawson Supply provides the more consistent and reliable delivery times.

21.   How do grocery costs compare across the country? Using a market basket of 10 items including meat, milk, bread, eggs, coffee, potatoes, cereal, and orange juice, *Where to Retire* magazine calculated the cost of the market basket in six cities and in six retirement areas across the country (*Where to Retire,* November/December 2003). The data with market basket cost to the nearest dollar are as follows:

| City | Cost | Retirement Area | Cost |
|------|------|-----------------|------|
| Buffalo, NY | $33 | Biloxi-Gulfport, MS | $29 |
| Des Moines, IA | 27 | Asheville, NC | 32 |
| Hartford, CT | 32 | Flagstaff, AZ | 32 |
| Los Angeles, CA | 38 | Hilton Head, SC | 34 |
| Miami, FL | 36 | Fort Myers, FL | 34 |
| Pittsburgh, PA | 32 | Santa Fe, NM | 31 |

a.    Compute the mean, variance, and standard deviation for the sample of cities and the sample of retirement areas.
b.    What observations can be made based on the two samples?

**BackToSchool**

22. The National Retail Federation reported that college freshmen spend more on back-to-school items than any other college group (*USA Today,* August 4, 2006). Sample data comparing the back-to-school expenditures for 25 freshmen and 20 seniors are shown in the data file BackToSchool.
    a. What is the mean back-to-school expenditure for each group? Are the data consistent with the National Retail Federation's report?
    b. What is the range for the expenditures in each group?
    c. What is the interquartile range for the expenditures in each group?
    d. What is the standard deviation for expenditures in each group?
    e. Do freshmen or seniors have more variation in back-to-school expenditures?

23. Scores turned in by an amateur golfer at the Bonita Fairways Golf Course in Bonita Springs, Florida, during 2005 and 2006 are as follows:

    | *2005 Season:* | 74 | 78 | 79 | 77 | 75 | 73 | 75 | 77 |
    |---|---|---|---|---|---|---|---|---|
    | *2006 Season:* | 71 | 70 | 75 | 77 | 85 | 80 | 71 | 79 |

    a. Use the mean and standard deviation to evaluate the golfer's performance over the two-year period.
    b. What is the primary difference in performance between 2005 and 2006? What improvement, if any, can be seen in the 2006 scores?

24. The following times were recorded by the quarter-mile and mile runners of a university track team (times are in minutes).

    | *Quarter-Mile Times:* | .92 | .98 | 1.04 | .90 | .99 |
    |---|---|---|---|---|---|
    | *Mile Times:* | 4.52 | 4.35 | 4.60 | 4.70 | 4.50 |

    After viewing this sample of running times, one of the coaches commented that the quarter-milers turned in the more consistent times. Use the standard deviation and the coefficient of variation to summarize the variability in the data. Does the use of the coefficient of variation indicate that the coach's statement should be qualified?

## 3.3 Measures of Distribution Shape, Relative Location, and Detecting Outliers

We have described several measures of location and variability for data. In addition, it is often important to have a measure of the shape of a distribution. In Chapter 2 we noted that a histogram provides a graphical display showing the shape of a distribution. An important numerical measure of the shape of a distribution is called **skewness**.

### Distribution Shape

Shown in Figure 3.8 are four histograms constructed from relative frequency distributions. The histograms in Panels A and B are moderately skewed. The one in Panel A is skewed to the left; its skewness is $-.85$. The histogram in Panel B is skewed to the right; its skewness is $+.85$. The histogram in Panel C is symmetric; its skewness is zero. The histogram in Panel D is highly skewed to the right; its skewness is 1.62. The formula used to compute skewness is somewhat complex.[2] However, the skewness can be easily

---

[2]The formula for the skewness of sample data:

$$\text{Skewness} = \frac{n}{(n-1)(n-2)} \sum \left( \frac{x_i - \bar{x}}{s} \right)^3$$

**FIGURE 3.8** HISTOGRAMS SHOWING THE SKEWNESS FOR FOUR DISTRIBUTIONS

computed using statistical software. For data skewed to the left, the skewness is negative; for data skewed to the right, the skewness is positive. If the data are symmetric, the skewness is zero.

For a symmetric distribution, the mean and the median are equal. When the data are positively skewed, the mean will usually be greater than the median; when the data are negatively skewed, the mean will usually be less than the median. The data used to construct the histogram in Panel D are customer purchases at a women's apparel store. The mean purchase amount is $77.60 and the median purchase amount is $59.70. The relatively few large purchase amounts tend to increase the mean, while the median remains unaffected by the large purchase amounts. The median provides the preferred measure of location when the data are highly skewed.

## *z*-Scores

In addition to measures of location, variability, and shape, we are also interested in the relative location of values within a data set. Measures of relative location help us determine how far a particular value is from the mean.

By using both the mean and standard deviation, we can determine the relative location of any observation. Suppose we have a sample of $n$ observations, with the values denoted by $x_1, x_2, \ldots, x_n$. In addition, assume that the sample mean, $\bar{x}$, and the sample standard deviation, $s$, are already computed. Associated with each value, $x_i$, is another value called its **z-score**. Equation (3.9) shows how the z-score is computed for each $x_i$.

z-SCORE

$$z_i = \frac{x_i - \bar{x}}{s} \qquad (3.9)$$

where

$z_i$ = the z-score for $x_i$
$\bar{x}$ = the sample mean
$s$ = the sample standard deviation

The z-score is often called the *standardized value*. The z-score, $z_i$, can be interpreted as the *number of standard deviations* $x_i$ *is from the mean* $\bar{x}$. For example, $z_1 = 1.2$ would indicate that $x_1$ is 1.2 standard deviations greater than the sample mean. Similarly, $z_2 = -.5$ would indicate that $x_2$ is .5, or 1/2, standard deviation less than the sample mean. A z-score greater than zero occurs for observations with a value greater than the mean, and a z-score less than zero occurs for observations with a value less than the mean. A z-score of zero indicates that the value of the observation is equal to the mean.

The z-score for any observation can be interpreted as a measure of the relative location of the observation in a data set. Thus, observations in two different data sets with the same z-score can be said to have the same relative location in terms of being the same number of standard deviations from the mean.

The z-scores for the class size data are computed in Table 3.4. Recall the previously computed sample mean, $\bar{x} = 44$, and sample standard deviation, $s = 8$. The z-score of $-1.50$ for the fifth observation shows it is farthest from the mean; it is 1.50 standard deviations below the mean.

## Chebyshev's Theorem

**Chebyshev's theorem** enables us to make statements about the proportion of data values that must be within a specified number of standard deviations of the mean.

**TABLE 3.4**  z-SCORES FOR THE CLASS SIZE DATA

| Number of Students in Class ($x_i$) | Deviation About the Mean ($x_i - \bar{x}$) | z-Score $\left(\dfrac{x_i - \bar{x}}{s}\right)$ |
|:---:|:---:|:---:|
| 46 | 2 | 2/8 = .25 |
| 54 | 10 | 10/8 = 1.25 |
| 42 | −2 | −2/8 = −.25 |
| 46 | 2 | 2/8 = .25 |
| 32 | −12 | −12/8 = −1.50 |

> CHEBYSHEV'S THEOREM
>
> At least $(1 - 1/z^2)$ of the data values must be within $z$ standard deviations of the mean, where $z$ is any value greater than 1.

Some of the implications of this theorem, with $z = 2, 3$, and 4 standard deviations, follow.

- At least .75, or 75%, of the data values must be within $z = 2$ standard deviations of the mean.
- At least .89, or 89%, of the data values must be within $z = 3$ standard deviations of the mean.
- At least .94, or 94%, of the data values must be within $z = 4$ standard deviations of the mean.

For an example using Chebyshev's theorem, suppose that the midterm test scores for 100 students in a college business statistics course had a mean of 70 and a standard deviation of 5. How many students had test scores between 60 and 80? How many students had test scores between 58 and 82?

For the test scores between 60 and 80, we note that 60 is two standard deviations below the mean and 80 is two standard deviations above the mean. Using Chebyshev's theorem, we see that at least .75, or at least 75%, of the observations must have values within two standard deviations of the mean. Thus, at least 75% of the students must have scored between 60 and 80.

*Chebyshev's theorem requires $z > 1$; but $z$ need not be an integer.*

For the test scores between 58 and 82, we see that $(58 - 70)/5 = -2.4$ indicates 58 is 2.4 standard deviations below the mean and that $(82 - 70)/5 = +2.4$ indicates 82 is 2.4 standard deviations above the mean. Applying Chebyshev's theorem with $z = 2.4$, we have

$$\left(1 - \frac{1}{z^2}\right) = \left(1 - \frac{1}{(2.4)^2}\right) = .826$$

At least 82.6% of the students must have test scores between 58 and 82.

## Empirical Rule

*The empirical rule is based on the normal probability distribution, which will be discussed in Chapter 6. The normal distribution is used extensively throughout the text.*

One of the advantages of Chebyshev's theorem is that it applies to any data set regardless of the shape of the distribution of the data. Indeed, it could be used with any of the distributions in Figure 3.8. In many practical applications, however, data sets exhibit a symmetric mound-shaped or bell-shaped distribution like the one shown in Figure 3.9. When the data are believed to approximate this distribution, the **empirical rule** can be used to determine the percentage of data values that must be within a specified number of standard deviations of the mean.

> EMPIRICAL RULE
>
> For data having a bell-shaped distribution:
>
> - Approximately 68% of the data values will be within one standard deviation of the mean.
> - Approximately 95% of the data values will be within two standard deviations of the mean.
> - Almost all of the data values will be within three standard deviations of the mean.

**FIGURE 3.9**   A SYMMETRIC MOUND-SHAPED OR BELL-SHAPED DISTRIBUTION

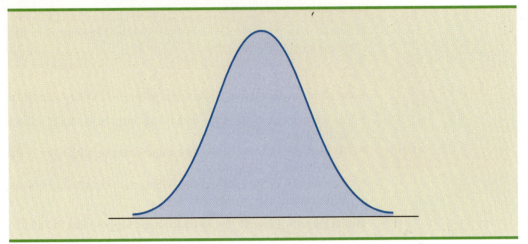

For example, liquid detergent bottles are filled automatically on a production line. Filling weights frequently have a bell-shaped distribution. If the mean filling weight is 16 ounces and the standard deviation is .25 ounces, we can use the empirical rule to draw the following conclusions.

- Approximately 68% of the filled bottles will have weights between 15.75 and 16.25 ounces (within one standard deviation of the mean).
- Approximately 95% of the filled bottles will have weights between 15.50 and 16.50 ounces (within two standard deviations of the mean).
- Almost all filled bottles will have weights between 15.25 and 16.75 ounces (within three standard deviations of the mean).

## Detecting Outliers

Sometimes a data set will have one or more observations with unusually large or unusually small values. These extreme values are called **outliers**. Experienced statisticians take steps to identify outliers and then review each one carefully. An outlier may be a data value that has been incorrectly recorded. If so, it can be corrected before further analysis. An outlier may also be from an observation that was incorrectly included in the data set; if so, it can be removed. Finally, an outlier may be an unusual data value that has been recorded correctly and belongs in the data set. In such cases it should remain.

*It is a good idea to check for outliers before making decisions based on data analysis. Errors are often made in recording data and entering data into the computer. Outliers should not necessarily be deleted, but their accuracy and appropriateness should be verified.*

Standardized values ($z$-scores) can be used to identify outliers. Recall that the empirical rule allows us to conclude that for data with a bell-shaped distribution, almost all the data values will be within three standard deviations of the mean. Hence, in using $z$-scores to identify outliers, we recommend treating any data value with a $z$-score less than $-3$ or greater than $+3$ as an outlier. Such data values can then be reviewed for accuracy and to determine whether they belong in the data set.

Refer to the $z$-scores for the class size data in Table 3.4. The $z$-score of $-1.50$ shows that the fifth class size is farthest from the mean. However, this standardized value is well within the $-3$ to $+3$ guideline for outliers. Thus, the $z$-scores do not indicate that outliers are present in the class size data.

## NOTES AND COMMENTS

1. Chebyshev's theorem is applicable for any data set and can be used to state the minimum number of data values that will be within a certain number of standard deviations of the mean. If the data are known to be approximately bell-shaped, more can be said. For instance, the empirical rule allows us to say that *approximately* 95% of the data values will be within two standard deviations of the mean; Chebyshev's theorem allows us to conclude only that at least 75% of the data values will be in that interval.

2. Before analyzing a data set, statisticians usually make a variety of checks to ensure the validity of data. In a large study it is not uncommon for errors to be made in recording data values or in entering the values into a computer. Identifying outliers is one tool used to check the validity of the data.

## Exercises

## Methods

25. Consider a sample with data values of 10, 20, 12, 17, and 16. Compute the $z$-score for each of the five observations.

26. Consider a sample with a mean of 500 and a standard deviation of 100. What are the $z$-scores for the following data values: 520, 650, 500, 450, and 280?

27. Consider a sample with a mean of 30 and a standard deviation of 5. Use Chebyshev's theorem to determine the percentage of the data within each of the following ranges:
    a.  20 to 40
    b.  15 to 45
    c.  22 to 38
    d.  18 to 42
    e.  12 to 48

28. Suppose the data have a bell-shaped distribution with a mean of 30 and a standard deviation of 5. Use the empirical rule to determine the percentage of data within each of the following ranges:
    a.  20 to 40
    b.  15 to 45
    c.  25 to 35

## Applications

29. The results of a national survey showed that on average, adults sleep 6.9 hours per night. Suppose that the standard deviation is 1.2 hours.
    a.  Use Chebyshev's theorem to calculate the percentage of individuals who sleep between 4.5 and 9.3 hours.
    b.  Use Chebyshev's theorem to calculate the percentage of individuals who sleep between 3.9 and 9.9 hours.
    c.  Assume that the number of hours of sleep follows a bell-shaped distribution. Use the empirical rule to calculate the percentage of individuals who sleep between 4.5 and 9.3 hours per day. How does this result compare to the value that you obtained using Chebyshev's theorem in part (a)?

30. The Energy Information Administration reported that the mean retail price per gallon of regular grade gasoline was $2.81 (Energy Information Administration, November 2010). Suppose that the standard deviation was $.10 and that the retail price per gallon has a bell-shaped distribution.
    a. What percentage of regular grade gasoline sold between $2.71 and $2.91 per gallon?
    b. What percentage of regular grade gasoline sold between $2.71 and $3.01 per gallon?
    c. What percentage of regular grade gasoline sold for more than $3.01 per gallon?

31. The national average for the math portion of the College Board's SAT is 515 (*The World Almanac,* 2009). The College Board periodically rescales the test scores such that the standard deviation is approximately 100. Answer the following questions using a bell-shaped distribution and the empirical rule for the verbal test scores.
    a. What percentage of students have an SAT math score greater than 615?
    b. What percentage of students have an SAT math score greater than 715?
    c. What percentage of students have an SAT math score between 415 and 515?
    d. What percentage of students have an SAT math score between 315 and 615?

32. Many families in California are using backyard structures for home offices, art studios, and hobby areas as well as for additional storage. Suppose that the mean price for a customized wooden, shingled backyard structure is $3100. Assume that the standard deviation is $1200.
    a. What is the $z$-score for a backyard structure costing $2300?
    b. What is the $z$-score for a backyard structure costing $4900?
    c. Interpret the $z$-scores in parts (a) and (b). Comment on whether either should be considered an outlier.
    d. If the cost for a backyard shed-office combination built in Albany, California, is $13,000, should this structure be considered an outlier? Explain.

33. Florida Power & Light (FP&L) Company has enjoyed a reputation for quickly fixing its electric system after storms. However, during the hurricane seasons of 2004 and 2005, a new reality was that the company's historical approach to emergency electric system repairs was no longer good enough (*The Wall Street Journal,* January 16, 2006). Data showing the days required to restore electric service after seven hurricanes during 2004 and 2005 follow.

| Hurricane | Days to Restore Service |
|-----------|-------------------------|
| Charley   | 13 |
| Frances   | 12 |
| Jeanne    | 8  |
| Dennis    | 3  |
| Katrina   | 8  |
| Rita      | 2  |
| Wilma     | 18 |

Based on this sample of seven, compute the following descriptive statistics:
    a. Mean, median, and mode
    b. Range and standard deviation
    c. Should Wilma be considered an outlier in terms of the days required to restore electric service?
    d. The seven hurricanes resulted in 10 million service interruptions to customers. Do the statistics show that FP&L should consider updating its approach to emergency electric system repairs? Discuss.

34. A sample of 10 NCAA college basketball game scores provided the following data (*USA Today*, January 26, 2004).

**NCAA**

| Winning Team | Points | Losing Team | Points | Winning Margin |
|---|---|---|---|---|
| Arizona | 90 | Oregon | 66 | 24 |
| Duke | 85 | Georgetown | 66 | 19 |
| Florida State | 75 | Wake Forest | 70 | 5 |
| Kansas | 78 | Colorado | 57 | 21 |
| Kentucky | 71 | Notre Dame | 63 | 8 |
| Louisville | 65 | Tennessee | 62 | 3 |
| Oklahoma State | 72 | Texas | 66 | 6 |
| Purdue | 76 | Michigan State | 70 | 6 |
| Stanford | 77 | Southern Cal | 67 | 10 |
| Wisconsin | 76 | Illinois | 56 | 20 |

a. Compute the mean and standard deviation for the points scored by the winning team.
b. Assume that the points scored by the winning teams for all NCAA games follow a bell-shaped distribution. Using the mean and standard deviation found in part (a), estimate the percentage of all NCAA games in which the winning team scores 84 or more points. Estimate the percentage of NCAA games in which the winning team scores more than 90 points.
c. Compute the mean and standard deviation for the winning margin. Do the data contain outliers? Explain.

35. The Associated Press Team Marketing Report listed the Dallas Cowboys as the team with the highest ticket prices in the National Football League (*USA Today*, October 20, 2009). Data showing the average ticket price for a sample of 14 teams in the National Football League are as follows.

**NFLTickets**

| Team | Ticket Price | Team | Ticket Price |
|---|---|---|---|
| Atlanta Falcons | 72 | Green Bay Packers | 63 |
| Buffalo Bills | 51 | Indianapolis Colts | 83 |
| Carolina Panthers | 63 | New Orleans Saints | 62 |
| Chicago Bears | 88 | New York Jets | 87 |
| Cleveland Browns | 55 | Pittsburgh Steelers | 67 |
| Dallas Cowboys | 160 | Seattle Seahawks | 61 |
| Denver Broncos | 77 | Tennessee Titans | 61 |

a. What is the mean ticket price?
b. The previous year, the mean ticket price was $72.20. What was the percentage increase in the mean ticket price for the one-year period?
c. Compute the median ticket price.
d. Compute the first and third quartiles.
e. Compute the standard deviation.
f. What is the $z$-score for the Dallas Cowboys ticket price? Should this price be considered an outlier? Explain.

## (3.4)  Exploratory Data Analysis

In Chapter 2 we introduced the stem-and-leaf display as a technique of exploratory data analysis. Recall that exploratory data analysis enables us to use simple arithmetic and easy-to-draw pictures to summarize data. In this section we continue exploratory data analysis by considering five-number summaries and box plots.

### Five-Number Summary

In a **five-number summary**, the following five numbers are used to summarize the data:

1. Smallest value
2. First quartile ($Q_1$)
3. Median ($Q_2$)
4. Third quartile ($Q_3$)
5. Largest value

The easiest way to develop a five-number summary is to first place the data in ascending order. Then it is easy to identify the smallest value, the three quartiles, and the largest value. The monthly starting salaries shown in Table 3.1 for a sample of 12 business school graduates are repeated here in ascending order.

$$3310 \quad 3355 \quad 3450 \quad | \quad 3480 \quad 3480 \quad 3490 \quad | \quad 3520 \quad 3540 \quad 3550 \quad | \quad 3650 \quad 3730 \quad 3925$$

$$Q_1 = 3465 \qquad Q_2 = 3505 \qquad Q_3 = 3600$$
$$\text{(Median)}$$

The median of 3505 and the quartiles $Q_1 = 3465$ and $Q_3 = 3600$ were computed in Section 3.1. Reviewing the data shows a smallest value of 3310 and a largest value of 3925. Thus the five-number summary for the salary data is 3310, 3465, 3505, 3600, 3925. Approximately one-fourth, or 25%, of the observations are between adjacent numbers in a five-number summary.

### Box Plot

A **box plot** is a graphical summary of data that is based on a five-number summary. A key to the development of a box plot is the computation of the median and the quartiles, $Q_1$ and $Q_3$. The interquartile range, IQR $= Q_3 - Q_1$, is also used. Figure 3.10 is the box plot for the monthly starting salary data. The steps used to construct the box plot follow.

1. A box is drawn with the ends of the box located at the first and third quartiles. For the salary data, $Q_1 = 3465$ and $Q_3 = 3600$. This box contains the middle 50% of the data.
2. A vertical line is drawn in the box at the location of the median (3505 for the salary data).

*Box plots provide another way to identify outliers. But they do not necessarily identify the same values as those with a z-score less than −3 or greater than +3. Either or both procedures may be used.*

3. By using the interquartile range, IQR $= Q_3 - Q_1$, *limits* are located. The limits for the box plot are 1.5(IQR) below $Q_1$ and 1.5(IQR) above $Q_3$. For the salary data, IQR $= Q_3 - Q_1 = 3600 - 3465 = 135$. Thus, the limits are $3465 - 1.5(135) = 3262.5$ and $3600 + 1.5(135) = 3802.5$. Data outside these limits are considered *outliers*.
4. The dashed lines in Figure 3.10 are called *whiskers*. The whiskers are drawn from the ends of the box to the smallest and largest values *inside the limits* computed in step 3. Thus, the whiskers end at salary values of 3310 and 3730.
5. Finally, the location of each outlier is shown with the symbol *. In Figure 3.10 we see one outlier, 3925.

**FIGURE 3.10**  BOX PLOT OF THE STARTING SALARY DATA WITH LINES SHOWING THE LOWER AND UPPER LIMITS

**FIGURE 3.11**  BOX PLOT OF MONTHLY STARTING SALARY DATA

In Figure 3.10 we included lines showing the location of the upper and lower limits. These lines were drawn to show how the limits are computed and where they are located. Although the limits are always computed, generally they are not drawn on the box plots. Figure 3.11 shows the usual appearance of a box plot for the salary data.

## Comparative Analysis Using Box Plots

**MajorSalary**

Box plots can also be used to provide a graphical summary of two or more groups and facilitate visual comparisons among the groups. For example, suppose the placement office decided to conduct a follow-up study to compare monthly starting salaries by the graduate's major: accounting, finance, information systems, management, and marketing. The major and starting salary data for a new sample of 111 recent business school graduates are shown in the data set named MajorSalary, and Figure 3.12 shows the box plots corresponding to each major. Note that major is shown on the horizontal axis and each box plot is shown vertically above the corresponding major. Displaying box plots in this manner is an excellent graphical technique for making comparisons among two or more groups.

What observations can we make about monthly starting salaries by major using the box plots in Figure 3.12? Specifically, we note the following:

- The higher salaries are in accounting; the lower salaries are in management and marketing.
- Based on the medians, accounting and information systems have similar and higher median salaries. Finance is next, with management and marketing showing lower median salaries.

**FIGURE 3.12**      BOX PLOTS OF MONTHLY STARTING SALARY BY MAJOR

- High salary outliers exist for accounting, finance, and marketing majors.
- Finance salaries appear to have the least variation, while accounting salaries appear to have the most variation.

Perhaps you can see additional interpretations based on these box plots.

## NOTES AND COMMENTS

**1.** An advantage of the exploratory data analysis procedures is that they are easy to use; few numerical calculations are necessary. We simply sort the data values into ascending order and identify the five-number summary. The box plot can then be constructed. It is not necessary to compute the mean and the standard deviation for the data.

**2.** In the chapter appendix, we show how to construct a box plot for the starting salary data using StatTools.

## Exercises

### Methods

36. Consider a sample with data values of 27, 25, 20, 15, 30, 34, 28, and 25. Provide the five-number summary for the data.

37. Show the box plot for the data in exercise 36.

38. Show the five-number summary and the box plot for the following data: 5, 15, 18, 10, 8, 12, 16, 10, 6.

39. A data set has a first quartile of 42 and a third quartile of 50. Compute the lower and upper limits for the corresponding box plot. Should a data value of 65 be considered an outlier?

### Applications

40. Some of the most well-known food franchises and the number of retail locations for each are shown below (*The New York Times Almanac*, 2010).

| Franchise | Locations | Franchise | Locations |
|---|---|---|---|
| Arby's | 2,558 | McDonald's | 24,799 |
| Baskin-Robbins | 5,889 | Papa John's | 2,615 |
| Dairy Queen | 5,619 | Pizza Hut | 10,238 |
| Domino's | 8,053 | Quiznos | 5,110 |
| Dunkin Donuts | 8,082 | Subway | 29,612 |
| Hardee's | 1,397 | Taco Bell | 4,516 |
| KFC Corp | 11,553 | | |

a. What is the largest franchise? How many retail locations does it have?
b. What is the median number of locations for the franchises?
c. Provide a five-number summary.
d. Are there any outliers?
e. Show the box plot.

41. Naples, Florida, hosts a half-marathon (13.1-mile race) in January each year. The event attracts top runners from throughout the United States as well as from around the world. In January 2009, 22 men and 31 women entered the 19–24 age class. Finish times in minutes are as follows (*Naples Daily News*, January 19, 2009). Times are shown in order of finish.

| Finish | Men | Women | Finish | Men | Women | Finish | Men | Women |
|---|---|---|---|---|---|---|---|---|
| 1 | 65.30 | 109.03 | 11 | 109.05 | 123.88 | 21 | 143.83 | 136.75 |
| 2 | 66.27 | 111.22 | 12 | 110.23 | 125.78 | 22 | 148.70 | 138.20 |
| 3 | 66.52 | 111.65 | 13 | 112.90 | 129.52 | 23 | | 139.00 |
| 4 | 66.85 | 111.93 | 14 | 113.52 | 129.87 | 24 | | 147.18 |
| 5 | 70.87 | 114.38 | 15 | 120.95 | 130.72 | 25 | | 147.35 |
| 6 | 87.18 | 118.33 | 16 | 127.98 | 131.67 | 26 | | 147.50 |
| 7 | 96.45 | 121.25 | 17 | 128.40 | 132.03 | 27 | | 147.75 |
| 8 | 98.52 | 122.08 | 18 | 130.90 | 133.20 | 28 | | 153.88 |
| 9 | 100.52 | 122.48 | 19 | 131.80 | 133.50 | 29 | | 154.83 |
| 10 | 108.18 | 122.62 | 20 | 138.63 | 136.57 | 30 | | 189.27 |
| | | | | | | 31 | | 189.28 |

a. George Towett of Marietta, Georgia, finished in first place for the men and Lauren Wald of Gainesville, Florida, finished in first place for the women. Compare the first-place finish times for men and women. If the 53 men and women runners had competed as one group, in what place would Lauren have finished?
b. What is the median time for men and women runners? Compare men and women runners based on their median times.
c. Provide a five-number summary for both the men and the women.
d. Are there outliers in either group?
e. Show the box plots for the two groups. Did men or women have the most variation in finish times? Explain.

42. *Consumer Reports* provided overall customer satisfaction scores for AT&T, Sprint, T-Mobile, and Verizon cell-phone services in major metropolitan areas throughout the United States. The rating for each service reflects the overall customer satisfaction considering a variety of factors such as cost, connectivity problems, dropped calls, static interference, and customer support. A satisfaction scale from 0 to 100 was used, with 0

indicating completely dissatisfied and 100 indicating completely satisfied. The ratings for the four cell-phone services in 20 metropolitan areas are as shown (*Consumer Reports*, January 2009).

**CellService**

| Metropolitan Area | AT&T | Sprint | T-Mobile | Verizon |
|---|---|---|---|---|
| Atlanta | 70 | 66 | 71 | 79 |
| Boston | 69 | 64 | 74 | 76 |
| Chicago | 71 | 65 | 70 | 77 |
| Dallas | 75 | 65 | 74 | 78 |
| Denver | 71 | 67 | 73 | 77 |
| Detroit | 73 | 65 | 77 | 79 |
| Jacksonville | 73 | 64 | 75 | 81 |
| Las Vegas | 72 | 68 | 74 | 81 |
| Los Angeles | 66 | 65 | 68 | 78 |
| Miami | 68 | 69 | 73 | 80 |
| Minneapolis | 68 | 66 | 75 | 77 |
| Philadelphia | 72 | 66 | 71 | 78 |
| Phoenix | 68 | 66 | 76 | 81 |
| San Antonio | 75 | 65 | 75 | 80 |
| San Diego | 69 | 68 | 72 | 79 |
| San Francisco | 66 | 69 | 73 | 75 |
| Seattle | 68 | 67 | 74 | 77 |
| St. Louis | 74 | 66 | 74 | 79 |
| Tampa | 73 | 63 | 73 | 79 |
| Washington | 72 | 68 | 71 | 76 |

a. Consider T-Mobile first. What is the median rating?

b. Develop a five-number summary for the T-Mobile service.

c. Are there outliers for T-Mobile? Explain.

d. Repeat parts (b) and (c) for the other three cell-phone services.

e. Show the box plots for the four cell-phone services on one graph. Discuss what a comparison of the box plots tells about the four services. Which service did *Consumer Reports* recommend as being best in terms of overall customer satisfaction?

43. The Philadelphia Phillies defeated the Tampa Bay Rays in the fifth game by a score of 4 to 3 to win the 2008 major league baseball World Series (*The Philadelphia Inquirer,* October 29, 2008). Earlier in the major league baseball playoffs, the Philadelphia Phillies defeated the Los Angeles Dodgers to win the National League Championship, while the Tampa Bay Rays defeated the Boston Red Sox to win the American League Championship. The file MLBSalaries contains the salaries for the 28 players on each of these four teams (USA Today Salary Database, October 2008). The data, shown in thousands of dollars, have been ordered from the highest salary to the lowest salary for each team.

**MLBSalaries**

a. Analyze the salaries for the World Champion Philadelphia Phillies. What is the total payroll for the team? What is the median salary? What is the five-number summary?

b. Were there salary outliers for the Philadelphia Phillies? If so, how many and what were the salary amounts?

c. What is the total payroll for each of the other three teams? Develop the five-number summary for each team and identify any outliers.

d. Show the box plots of the salaries for all four teams. What are your interpretations? Of these four teams, does it appear that the team with the higher salaries won the league championships and the World Series?

**TABLE 3.5** TWELVE-MONTH RETURN FOR MUTUAL FUNDS

| Mutual Fund | Return (%) | Mutual Fund | Return (%) |
|---|---|---|---|
| Alger Capital Appreciation | 23.5 | Nations Small Company | 21.4 |
| Alger LargeCap Growth | 22.8 | Nations SmallCap Index | 24.5 |
| Alger MidCap Growth | 38.3 | Nations Strategic Growth | 10.4 |
| Alger SmallCap | 41.3 | Nations Value Inv | 10.8 |
| AllianceBernstein Technology | 40.6 | One Group Diversified Equity | 10.0 |
| Federated American Leaders | 15.6 | One Group Diversified Int'l | 10.9 |
| Federated Capital Appreciation | 12.4 | One Group Diversified Mid Cap | 15.1 |
| Federated Equity-Income | 11.5 | One Group Equity Income | 6.6 |
| Federated Kaufmann | 33.3 | One Group Int'l Equity Index | 13.2 |
| Federated Max-Cap Index | 16.0 | One Group Large Cap Growth | 13.6 |
| Federated Stock | 16.9 | One Group Large Cap Value | 12.8 |
| Janus Adviser Int'l Growth | 10.3 | One Group Mid Cap Growth | 18.7 |
| Janus Adviser Worldwide | 3.4 | One Group Mid Cap Value | 11.4 |
| Janus Enterprise | 24.2 | One Group Small Cap Growth | 23.6 |
| Janus High-Yield | 12.1 | PBHG Growth | 27.3 |
| Janus Mercury | 20.6 | Putnam Europe Equity | 20.4 |
| Janus Overseas | 11.9 | Putnam Int'l Capital Opportunity | 36.6 |
| Janus Worldwide | 4.1 | Putnam International Equity | 21.5 |
| Nations Convertible Securities | 13.6 | Putnam Int'l New Opportunity | 26.3 |
| Nations Int'l Equity | 10.7 | Strong Advisor Mid Cap Growth | 23.7 |
| Nations LargeCap Enhd. Core | 13.2 | Strong Growth 20 | 11.7 |
| Nations LargeCap Index | 13.5 | Strong Growth Inv | 23.2 |
| Nation MidCap Index | 19.5 | Strong Large Cap Growth | 14.5 |

WEB file

Mutual

44. A listing of 46 mutual funds and their 12-month total return percentage is shown in Table 3.5 (*Smart Money*, February 2004).
    a. What are the mean and median return percentages for these mutual funds?
    b. What are the first and third quartiles?
    c. Provide a five-number summary.
    d. Do the data contain any outliers? Show a box plot.

## 3.5 Measures of Association Between Two Variables

Thus far we have examined numerical methods used to summarize the data for *one variable at a time.* Often a manager or decision maker is interested in the *relationship between two variables.* In this section we present covariance and correlation as descriptive measures of the relationship between two variables.

We begin by reconsidering the application concerning a stereo and sound equipment store in San Francisco as presented in Section 2.4. The store's manager wants to determine the relationship between the number of weekend television commercials shown and the sales at the store during the following week. Sample data with sales expressed in hundreds of dollars are provided in Table 3.6. It shows 10 observations ($n = 10$), one for each week. The scatter diagram in Figure 3.13 shows a positive relationship, with higher sales ($y$) associated with a greater number of commercials ($x$). In fact, the scatter diagram suggests

**TABLE 3.6**   SAMPLE DATA FOR THE STEREO AND SOUND EQUIPMENT STORE

| Week | Number of Commercials $x$ | Sales Volume ($100s) $y$ |
|------|------|------|
| 1 | 2 | 50 |
| 2 | 5 | 57 |
| 3 | 1 | 41 |
| 4 | 3 | 54 |
| 5 | 4 | 54 |
| 6 | 1 | 38 |
| 7 | 5 | 63 |
| 8 | 3 | 48 |
| 9 | 4 | 59 |
| 10 | 2 | 46 |

WEB file

Stereo

**FIGURE 3.13**   SCATTER DIAGRAM FOR THE STEREO AND SOUND EQUIPMENT STORE

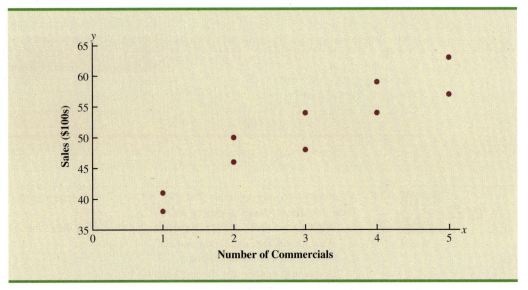

that a straight line could be used as an approximation of the relationship. In the following discussion, we introduce **covariance** as a descriptive measure of the linear association between two variables.

## Covariance

For a sample of size $n$ with the observations $(x_1, y_1)$, $(x_2, y_2)$, and so on, the sample covariance is defined as follows:

---

SAMPLE COVARIANCE

$$s_{xy} = \frac{\Sigma(x_i - \bar{x})(y_i - \bar{y})}{n - 1} \tag{3.10}$$

**TABLE 3.7   CALCULATIONS FOR THE SAMPLE COVARIANCE**

| $x_i$ | $y_i$ | $x_i - \bar{x}$ | $y_i - \bar{y}$ | $(x_i - \bar{x})(y_i - \bar{y})$ |
|---|---|---|---|---|
| 2 | 50 | $-1$ | $-1$ | 1 |
| 5 | 57 | 2 | 6 | 12 |
| 1 | 41 | $-2$ | $-10$ | 20 |
| 3 | 54 | 0 | 3 | 0 |
| 4 | 54 | 1 | 3 | 3 |
| 1 | 38 | $-2$ | $-13$ | 26 |
| 5 | 63 | 2 | 12 | 24 |
| 3 | 48 | 0 | $-3$ | 0 |
| 4 | 59 | 1 | 8 | 8 |
| 2 | 46 | $-1$ | $-5$ | 5 |
| Totals 30 | 510 | 0 | 0 | 99 |

$$s_{xy} = \frac{\Sigma(x_i - \bar{x})(y_i - \bar{y})}{n - 1} = \frac{99}{10 - 1} = 11$$

This formula pairs each $x_i$ with a $y_i$. We then sum the products obtained by multiplying the deviation of each $x_i$ from its sample mean $\bar{x}$ by the deviation of the corresponding $y_i$ from its sample mean $\bar{y}$; this sum is then divided by $n - 1$.

To measure the strength of the linear relationship between the number of commercials $x$ and the sales volume $y$ in the stereo and sound equipment store problem, we use equation (3.10) to compute the sample covariance. The calculations in Table 3.7 show the computation of $\Sigma(x_i - \bar{x})(y_i - \bar{y})$. Note that $\bar{x} = 30/10 = 3$ and $\bar{y} = 510/10 = 51$. Using equation (3.10), we obtain a sample covariance of

$$s_{xy} = \frac{\Sigma(x_i - \bar{x})(y_i - \bar{y})}{n - 1} = \frac{99}{9} = 11$$

The formula for computing the covariance of a population of size $N$ is similar to equation (3.10), but we use different notation to indicate that we are working with the entire population.

**POPULATION COVARIANCE**

$$\sigma_{xy} = \frac{\Sigma(x_i - \mu_x)(y_i - \mu_y)}{N} \qquad \textbf{(3.11)}$$

In equation (3.11) we use the notation $\mu_x$ for the population mean of the variable $x$ and $\mu_y$ for the population mean of the variable $y$. The population covariance $\sigma_{xy}$ is defined for a population of size $N$.

## Interpretation of the Covariance

To aid in the interpretation of the sample covariance, consider Figure 3.14. It is the same as the scatter diagram of Figure 3.13 with a vertical dashed line at $\bar{x} = 3$ and a horizontal dashed line at $\bar{y} = 51$. The lines divide the graph into four quadrants. Points in quadrant I correspond to $x_i$ greater than $\bar{x}$ and $y_i$ greater than $\bar{y}$, points in quadrant II correspond to $x_i$

**FIGURE 3.14**    PARTITIONED SCATTER DIAGRAM FOR THE STEREO AND SOUND
EQUIPMENT STORE

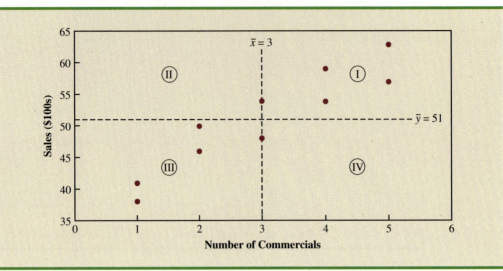

less than $\bar{x}$ and $y_i$ greater than $\bar{y}$, and so on. Thus, the value of $(x_i - \bar{x})(y_i - \bar{y})$ must be positive for points in quadrant I, negative for points in quadrant II, positive for points in quadrant III, and negative for points in quadrant IV.

*The covariance is a measure of the linear association between two variables.*

If the value of $s_{xy}$ is positive, the points with the greatest influence on $s_{xy}$ must be in quadrants I and III. Hence, a positive value for $s_{xy}$ indicates a positive linear association between $x$ and $y$; that is, as the value of $x$ increases, the value of $y$ increases. If the value of $s_{xy}$ is negative, however, the points with the greatest influence on $s_{xy}$ are in quadrants II and IV. Hence, a negative value for $s_{xy}$ indicates a negative linear association between $x$ and $y$; that is, as the value of $x$ increases, the value of $y$ decreases. Finally, if the points are evenly distributed across all four quadrants, the value of $s_{xy}$ will be close to zero, indicating no linear association between $x$ and $y$. Figure 3.15 shows the values of $s_{xy}$ that can be expected with three different types of scatter diagrams.

Referring again to Figure 3.14, we see that the scatter diagram for the stereo and sound equipment store follows the pattern in the top panel of Figure 3.15. As we should expect, the value of the sample covariance indicates a positive linear relationship with $s_{xy} = 11$.

From the preceding discussion, it might appear that a large positive value for the covariance indicates a strong positive linear relationship and that a large negative value indicates a strong negative linear relationship. However, one problem with using covariance as a measure of the strength of the linear relationship is that the value of the covariance depends on the units of measurement for $x$ and $y$. For example, suppose we are interested in the relationship between height $x$ and weight $y$ for individuals. Clearly the strength of the relationship should be the same whether we measure height in feet or inches. Measuring the height in inches, however, gives us much larger numerical values for $(x_i - \bar{x})$ than when we measure height in feet. Thus, with height measured in inches, we would obtain a larger value for the numerator $\Sigma(x_i - \bar{x})(y_i - \bar{y})$ in equation (3.10)—and hence a larger covariance—when in fact the relationship does not change. A measure of the relationship between two variables that is not affected by the units of measurement for $x$ and $y$ is the **correlation coefficient**.

**FIGURE 3.15**   INTERPRETATION OF SAMPLE COVARIANCE

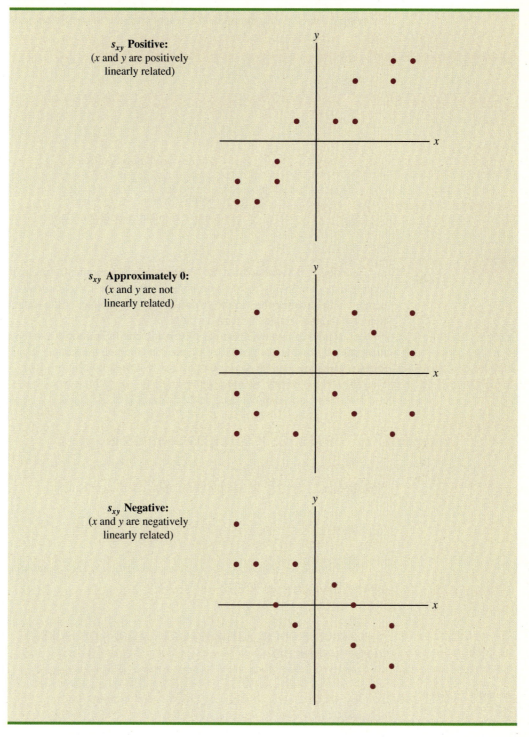

## Correlation Coefficient

For sample data, the Pearson product moment correlation coefficient is defined as follows.

PEARSON PRODUCT MOMENT CORRELATION COEFFICIENT: SAMPLE DATA

$$r_{xy} = \frac{s_{xy}}{s_x s_y} \qquad (3.12)$$

where

$r_{xy}$ = sample correlation coefficient
$s_{xy}$ = sample covariance
$s_x$ = sample standard deviation of $x$
$s_y$ = sample standard deviation of $y$

Equation (3.12) shows that the Pearson product moment correlation coefficient for sample data (commonly referred to more simply as the *sample correlation coefficient*) is computed by dividing the sample covariance by the product of the sample standard deviation of $x$ and the sample standard deviation of $y$.

Let us now compute the sample correlation coefficient for the stereo and sound equipment store. Using the data in Table 3.7, we can compute the sample standard deviations for the two variables:

$$s_x = \sqrt{\frac{\Sigma(x_i - \bar{x})^2}{n - 1}} = \sqrt{\frac{20}{9}} = 1.49$$

$$s_y = \sqrt{\frac{\Sigma(y_i - \bar{y})^2}{n - 1}} = \sqrt{\frac{566}{9}} = 7.93$$

Now, because $s_{xy} = 11$, the sample correlation coefficient equals

$$r_{xy} = \frac{s_{xy}}{s_x s_y} = \frac{11}{(1.49)(7.93)} = .93$$

The formula for computing the correlation coefficient for a population, denoted by the Greek letter $\rho_{xy}$ (rho, pronounced "row"), follows.

*The sample correlation coefficient $r_{xy}$ is a point estimator of the population correlation coefficient $\rho_{xy}$.*

PEARSON PRODUCT MOMENT CORRELATION COEFFICIENT:
POPULATION DATA

$$\rho_{xy} = \frac{\sigma_{xy}}{\sigma_x \sigma_y} \qquad (3.13)$$

where

$\rho_{xy}$ = population correlation coefficient
$\sigma_{xy}$ = population covariance
$\sigma_x$ = population standard deviation for $x$
$\sigma_y$ = population standard deviation for $y$

## Interpretation of the Correlation Coefficient

First let us consider a simple example that illustrates the concept of a perfect positive linear relationship. The scatter diagram in Figure 3.16 depicts the relationship between $x$ and $y$ based on the following sample data.

| $x_i$ | $y_i$ |
|-------|-------|
| 5     | 10    |
| 10    | 30    |
| 15    | 50    |

The straight line drawn through each of the three points shows a perfect linear relationship between $x$ and $y$. In order to apply equation (3.12) to compute the sample correlation we must first compute $s_{xy}$, $s_x$, and $s_y$. Some of the computations are shown in Table 3.8.

**FIGURE 3.16**   SCATTER DIAGRAM DEPICTING A PERFECT POSITIVE LINEAR
RELATIONSHIP

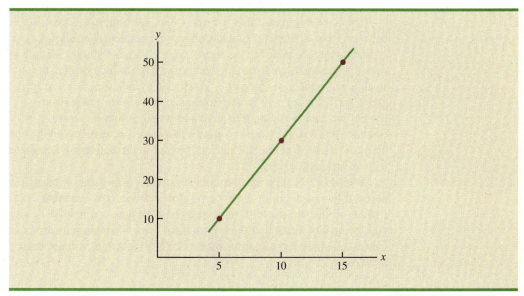

**TABLE 3.8**   COMPUTATIONS USED IN CALCULATING THE SAMPLE
CORRELATION COEFFICIENT

|        | $x_i$ | $y_i$ | $x_i - \bar{x}$ | $(x_i - \bar{x})^2$ | $y_i - \bar{y}$ | $(y_i - \bar{y})^2$ | $(x_i - \bar{x})(y_i - \bar{y})$ |
|--------|-------|-------|-----------------|---------------------|-----------------|---------------------|----------------------------------|
|        | 5     | 10    | −5              | 25                  | −20             | 400                 | 100                              |
|        | 10    | 30    | 0               | 0                   | 0               | 0                   | 0                                |
|        | 15    | 50    | 5               | 25                  | 20              | 400                 | 100                              |
| Totals | 30    | 90    | 0               | 50                  | 0               | 800                 | 200                              |

$\bar{x} = 10$   $\bar{y} = 30$

Using the results in this table, we find

$$s_{xy} = \frac{\Sigma(x_i - \bar{x})(y_i - \bar{y})}{n - 1} = \frac{200}{2} = 100$$

$$s_x = \sqrt{\frac{\Sigma(x_i - \bar{x})^2}{n - 1}} = \sqrt{\frac{50}{2}} = 5$$

$$s_y = \sqrt{\frac{\Sigma(y_i - \bar{y})^2}{n - 1}} = \sqrt{\frac{800}{2}} = 20$$

$$r_{xy} = \frac{s_{xy}}{s_x s_y} = \frac{100}{5(20)} = 1$$

*The correlation coefficient ranges from −1 to +1. Values close to −1 or +1 indicate a strong linear relationship. The closer the correlation is to zero, the weaker the relationship.*

Thus, we see that the value of the sample correlation coefficient is 1.

In general, it can be shown that if all the points in a data set fall on a positively sloped straight line, the value of the sample correlation coefficient is +1; that is, a sample correlation coefficient of +1 corresponds to a perfect positive linear relationship between $x$ and $y$. Moreover, if the points in the data set fall on a straight line having negative slope, the value of the sample correlation coefficient is −1; that is, a sample correlation coefficient of −1 corresponds to a perfect negative linear relationship between $x$ and $y$.

Let us now suppose that a certain data set indicates a positive linear relationship between $x$ and $y$ but that the relationship is not perfect. The value of $r_{xy}$ will be less than 1, indicating that the points in the scatter diagram are not all on a straight line. As the points deviate more and more from a perfect positive linear relationship, the value of $r_{xy}$ becomes smaller and smaller. A value of $r_{xy}$ equal to zero indicates no linear relationship between $x$ and $y$, and values of $r_{xy}$ near zero indicate a weak linear relationship.

For the data involving the stereo and sound equipment store, $r_{xy} = .93$. Therefore, we conclude that a strong positive linear relationship occurs between the number of commercials and sales. More specifically, an increase in the number of commercials is associated with an increase in sales.

In closing, we note that correlation provides a measure of linear association and not necessarily causation. A high correlation between two variables does not mean that changes in one variable will cause changes in the other variable. For example, we may find that the quality rating and the typical meal price of restaurants are positively correlated. However, simply increasing the meal price at a restaurant will not cause the quality rating to increase.

## Using Excel to Compute the Covariance and Correlation Coefficient

Excel provides functions that can be used to compute the covariance and correlation coefficient. We show here how these functions can be used to compute the sample covariance and the sample correlation coefficient for the stereo and sound equipment store data. Refer to Figure 3.17 as we present the steps involved. The formula worksheet is in the background; the value worksheet is in the foreground.

**Enter Data:**   Labels and data on commercials and sales are entered into cells A1:C11 of the worksheet.

**Enter Functions and Formulas:**   Excel's covariance function, COVARIANCE.S, can be used to compute the sample covariance by entering the following formula into cell F1:

=COVARIANCE.S(B2:B11,C2:C11)

**FIGURE 3.17**   EXCEL WORKSHEET USED TO COMPUTE THE COVARIANCE
AND CORRELATION COEFFICIENT

Similarly, the formula =CORREL(B2:B11,C2:C11) is entered into cell F2 to compute the sample correlation coefficient. The labels Sample Covariance and Sample Correlation are entered into cells E1 and E2 to identify the output.

The formulas in cells F1:F2 are displayed in the worksheet in the background of Figure 3.17. The worksheet in the foreground shows the values computed using the Excel functions. Note that, except for rounding, these values are the same as we computed earlier using equations (3.10) and (3.12).

## Exercises

### Methods

45. Five observations taken for two variables follow.

| $x_i$ | 4 | 6 | 11 | 3 | 16 |
|-------|----|----|----|----|----|
| $y_i$ | 50 | 50 | 40 | 60 | 30 |

   a. Develop a scatter diagram with $x$ on the horizontal axis.
   b. What does the scatter diagram developed in part (a) indicate about the relationship between the two variables?
   c. Compute and interpret the sample covariance.
   d. Compute and interpret the sample correlation coefficient.

46. Five observations taken for two variables follow.

| $x_i$ | 6 | 11 | 15 | 21 | 27 |
|-------|----|----|----|----|----|
| $y_i$ | 6 | 9 | 6 | 17 | 12 |

a.  Develop a scatter diagram for these data.
b.  What does the scatter diagram indicate about a relationship between *x* and *y*?
c.  Compute and interpret the sample covariance.
d.  Compute and interpret the sample correlation coefficient.

## Applications

47.  Ten major college football bowl games were played in January 2010, with the University of Alabama beating the University of Texas 37 to 21 to become the national champion of college football. The results of the ten bowl games are shown below (*USA Today,* January 8, 2010). The predicted winning point margin was based on Las Vegas betting odds approximately one week before the bowl games were played. For example, Auburn was predicted to beat Northwestern in the Outback Bowl by five points. The actual winning point margin for Auburn was three points. A negative predicted winning point margin means that the team that won the bowl game was an underdog and expected to lose. For example, in the Rose Bowl, Ohio State was a two-point underdog to Oregon and ended up winning by nine points.

**BowlGames**

| Bowl Game | Score | Predicted Point Margin | Actual Point Margin |
|---|---|---|---|
| Outback | Auburn 38 Northwestern 35 | 5 | 3 |
| Gator | Florida State 33 West Virginia 21 | 1 | 12 |
| Capital One | Penn State 19 LSU 17 | 3 | 2 |
| Rose | Ohio State 26 Oregon 17 | −2 | 9 |
| Sugar | Florida 51 Cincinnati 24 | 14 | 27 |
| Cotton | Mississippi State 21 Oklahoma State 7 | 3 | 14 |
| Alamo | Texas Tech 41 Michigan State 31 | 9 | 10 |
| Fiesta | Boise State 17 TCU 10 | −4 | 7 |
| Orange | Iowa 24 Georgia Tech 14 | −3 | 10 |
| Championship | Alabama 37 Texas 21 | 4 | 16 |

a.  Develop a scatter diagram with predicted point margin on the horizontal axis.
b.  What is the relationship between predicted and actual point margins?
c.  Compute and interpret the sample covariance.
d.  Compute the sample correlation coefficient. What does this value indicate about the relationship between the Las Vegas predicted point margin and the actual point margin in college football bowl games?

48.  A department of transportation's study on driving speed and miles per gallon for midsize automobiles resulted in the following data:

| Speed (Miles per Hour) | 30 | 50 | 40 | 55 | 30 | 25 | 60 | 25 | 50 | 55 |
|---|---|---|---|---|---|---|---|---|---|---|
| Miles per Gallon | 28 | 25 | 25 | 23 | 30 | 32 | 21 | 35 | 26 | 25 |

Compute and interpret the sample correlation coefficient.

49.  At the beginning of 2009, the economic downturn resulted in the loss of jobs and an increase in delinquent loans for housing. The national unemployment rate was 6.5% and the percentage of delinquent loans was 6.12% (*The Wall Street Journal*, January 27, 2009). In projecting where the real estate market was headed in the coming year, economists studied the relationship between the jobless rate and the percentage of delinquent loans. The expectation was that if the jobless rate continued to increase, there would also be an

increase in the percentage of delinquent loans. The data below show the jobless rate and the delinquent loan percentage for 27 major real estate markets.

**WEB file**

Housing

| Metro Area | Jobless Rate (%) | Delinquent Loan (%) | Metro Area | Jobless Rate (%) | Delinquent Loan (%) |
|---|---|---|---|---|---|
| Atlanta | 7.1 | 7.02 | New York | 6.2 | 5.78 |
| Boston | 5.2 | 5.31 | Orange County | 6.3 | 6.08 |
| Charlotte | 7.8 | 5.38 | Orlando | 7.0 | 10.05 |
| Chicago | 7.8 | 5.40 | Philadelphia | 6.2 | 4.75 |
| Dallas | 5.8 | 5.00 | Phoenix | 5.5 | 7.22 |
| Denver | 5.8 | 4.07 | Portland | 6.5 | 3.79 |
| Detroit | 9.3 | 6.53 | Raleigh | 6.0 | 3.62 |
| Houston | 5.7 | 5.57 | Sacramento | 8.3 | 9.24 |
| Jacksonville | 7.3 | 6.99 | St. Louis | 7.5 | 4.40 |
| Las Vegas | 7.6 | 11.12 | San Diego | 7.1 | 6.91 |
| Los Angeles | 8.2 | 7.56 | San Francisco | 6.8 | 5.57 |
| Miami | 7.1 | 12.11 | Seattle | 5.5 | 3.87 |
| Minneapolis | 6.3 | 4.39 | Tampa | 7.5 | 8.42 |
| Nashville | 6.6 | 4.78 | | | |

a. Compute the correlation coefficient. Is there a positive correlation between the jobless rate and the percentage of delinquent housing loans? What is your interpretation?

b. Show a scatter diagram of the relationship between jobless rate and the percentage of delinquent housing loans.

50. The Dow Jones Industrial Average (DJIA) and the Standard & Poor's 500 Index (S&P 500) are both used to measure the performance of the stock market. The DJIA is based on the price of stocks for 30 large companies; the S&P 500 is based on the price of stocks for 500 companies. If both the DJIA and S&P 500 measure the performance of the stock market, how are they correlated? The following data show the daily percent increase or daily percent decrease in the DJIA and S&P 500 for a sample of nine days over a three-month period (*The Wall Street Journal,* January 15 to March 10, 2006).

**WEB file**

StockMarket

| DJIA | .20 | .82 | −.99 | .04 | −.24 | 1.01 | .30 | .55 | −.25 |
|---|---|---|---|---|---|---|---|---|---|
| S&P 500 | .24 | .19 | −.91 | .08 | −.33 | .87 | .36 | .83 | −.16 |

a. Show a scatter diagram.

b. Compute the sample correlation coefficient for these data.

c. Discuss the association between the DJIA and S&P 500. Do you need to check both before having a general idea about the daily stock market performance?

51. The daily high and low temperatures for 14 cities around the world are shown (The Weather Channel, April 22, 2009).

**WEB file**

WorldTemp

| City | High | Low | City | High | Low |
|---|---|---|---|---|---|
| Athens | 68 | 50 | London | 67 | 45 |
| Beijing | 70 | 49 | Moscow | 44 | 29 |
| Berlin | 65 | 44 | Paris | 69 | 44 |
| Cairo | 96 | 64 | Rio de Janeiro | 76 | 69 |
| Dublin | 57 | 46 | Rome | 69 | 51 |
| Geneva | 70 | 45 | Tokyo | 70 | 58 |
| Hong Kong | 80 | 73 | Toronto | 44 | 39 |

a. What is the sample mean high temperature?

b. What is the sample mean low temperature?

c. What is the correlation between the high and low temperatures? Discuss.

# 3.6 The Weighted Mean and Working with Grouped Data

In Section 3.1, we presented the mean as one of the most important measures of central location. The formula for the mean of a sample with $n$ observations is restated as follows.

$$\bar{x} = \frac{\Sigma x_i}{n} = \frac{x_1 + x_2 + \cdots + x_n}{n} \qquad \text{(3.14)}$$

In this formula, each $x_i$ is given equal importance or weight. Although this practice is most common, in some instances, the mean is computed by giving each observation a weight that reflects its importance. A mean computed in this manner is referred to as a **weighted mean**.

## Weighted Mean

The weighted mean is computed as follows:

WEIGHTED MEAN

$$\bar{x} = \frac{\Sigma w_i x_i}{\Sigma w_i} \qquad \text{(3.15)}$$

where

$$x_i = \text{value of observation } i$$
$$w_i = \text{weight for observation } i$$

When the data are from a sample, equation (3.15) provides the weighted sample mean. When the data are from a population, $\mu$ replaces $\bar{x}$ and equation (3.15) provides the weighted population mean.

As an example of the need for a weighted mean, consider the following sample of five purchases of a raw material over the past three months.

| Purchase | Cost per Pound ($) | Number of Pounds |
|----------|--------------------|------------------|
| 1 | 3.00 | 1200 |
| 2 | 3.40 | 500 |
| 3 | 2.80 | 2750 |
| 4 | 2.90 | 1000 |
| 5 | 3.25 | 800 |

Note that the cost per pound varies from $2.80 to $3.40, and the quantity purchased varies from 500 to 2750 pounds. Suppose that a manager asked for information about the mean cost per pound of the raw material. Because the quantities ordered vary, we must use the formula for a weighted mean. The five cost-per-pound data values are $x_1 = 3.00, x_2 = 3.40, x_3 = 2.80,$ $x_4 = 2.90,$ and $x_5 = 3.25$. The weighted mean cost per pound is found by weighting each cost by its corresponding quantity. For this example, the weights are $w_1 = 1200, w_2 = 500,$

$w_3 = 2750$, $w_4 = 1000$, and $w_5 = 800$. Based on equation (3.15), the weighted mean is calculated as follows:

$$\bar{x} = \frac{1200(3.00) + 500(3.40) + 2750(2.80) + 1000(2.90) + 800(3.25)}{1200 + 500 + 2750 + 1000 + 800}$$

$$= \frac{18,500}{6250} = 2.96$$

Thus, the weighted mean computation shows that the mean cost per pound for the raw material is $2.96. Note that using equation (3.14) rather than the weighted mean formula would have provided misleading results. In this case, the mean of the five cost-per-pound values is $(3.00 + 3.40 + 2.80 + 2.90 + 3.25)/5 = 15.35/5 = \$3.07$, which overstates the actual mean cost per pound purchased.

*Computing a grade point average is a good example of the use of a weighted mean.*

The choice of weights for a particular weighted mean computation depends upon the application. An example that is well known to college students is the computation of a grade point average (GPA). In this computation, the data values generally used are 4 for an A grade, 3 for a B grade, 2 for a C grade, 1 for a D grade, and 0 for an F grade. The weights are the number of credits hours earned for each grade. Exercise 54 at the end of this section provides an example of this weighted mean computation. In other weighted mean computations, quantities such as pounds, dollars, or volume are frequently used as weights. In any case, when observations vary in importance, the analyst must choose the weight that best reflects the importance of each observation in the determination of the mean.

## Grouped Data

In most cases, measures of location and variability are computed by using the individual data values. Sometimes, however, data are available only in a grouped or frequency distribution form. In the following discussion, we show how the weighted mean formula can be used to obtain approximations of the mean, variance, and standard deviation for **grouped data**.

In Section 2.2 we provided a frequency distribution of the time in days required to complete year-end audits for the public accounting firm of Sanderson and Clifford. The frequency distribution of audit times is shown in Table 3.9. Based on this frequency distribution, what is the sample mean audit time?

To compute the mean using only the grouped data, we treat the midpoint of each class as being representative of the items in the class. Let $M_i$ denote the midpoint for class $i$ and let $f_i$ denote the frequency of class $i$. The weighted mean formula (3.15) is then used with the data values denoted as $M_i$ and the weights given by the frequencies $f_i$. In

**TABLE 3.9**   FREQUENCY DISTRIBUTION OF AUDIT TIMES

| Audit Time (days) | Frequency |
|---|---|
| 10–14 | 4 |
| 15–19 | 8 |
| 20–24 | 5 |
| 25–29 | 2 |
| 30–34 | 1 |
| Total | 20 |

this case, the denominator of equation (3.15) is the sum of the frequencies, which is the sample size $n$. That is, $\Sigma f_i = n$. Thus, the equation for the sample mean for grouped data is as follows.

SAMPLE MEAN FOR GROUPED DATA

$$\bar{x} = \frac{\Sigma f_i M_i}{n}$$

(3.16)

where

$$M_i = \text{the midpoint for class } i$$
$$f_i = \text{the frequency for class } i$$
$$n = \text{the sample size}$$

With the class midpoints, $M_i$, halfway between the class limits, the first class of 10–14 in Table 3.9 has a midpoint at $(10 + 14)/2 = 12$. The five class midpoints and the weighted mean computation for the audit time data are summarized in Table 3.10. As can be seen, the sample mean audit time is 19 days.

To compute the variance for grouped data, we use a slightly altered version of the formula for the variance provided in equation (3.5). In equation (3.5), the squared deviations of the data about the sample mean $\bar{x}$ were written $(x_i - \bar{x})^2$. However, with grouped data, the values are not known. In this case, we treat the class midpoint, $M_i$, as being representative of the $x_i$ values in the corresponding class. Thus, the squared deviations about the sample mean, $(x_i - \bar{x})^2$, are replaced by $(M_i - \bar{x})^2$. Then, just as we did with the sample mean calculations for grouped data, we weight each value by the frequency of the class, $f_i$. The sum of the squared deviations about the mean for all the data is approximated by $\Sigma f_i(M_i - \bar{x})^2$. The term $n - 1$ rather than $n$ appears in the denominator in order to make the sample variance the estimate of the population variance. Thus, the following formula is used to obtain the sample variance for grouped data.

SAMPLE VARIANCE FOR GROUPED DATA

$$s^2 = \frac{\Sigma f_i(M_i - \bar{x})^2}{n - 1}$$

(3.17)

**TABLE 3.10**    COMPUTATION OF THE SAMPLE MEAN AUDIT TIME FOR GROUPED DATA

| Audit Time (days) | Class Midpoint ($M_i$) | Frequency ($f_i$) | $f_i M_i$ |
|---|---|---|---|
| 10–14 | 12 | 4 | 48 |
| 15–19 | 17 | 8 | 136 |
| 20–24 | 22 | 5 | 110 |
| 25–29 | 27 | 2 | 54 |
| 30–34 | 32 | 1 | 32 |
| | | 20 | 380 |

$$\text{Sample mean } \bar{x} = \frac{\Sigma f_i M_i}{n} = \frac{380}{20} = 19 \text{ days}$$

**TABLE 3.11**  COMPUTATION OF THE SAMPLE VARIANCE OF AUDIT TIMES FOR GROUPED DATA (SAMPLE MEAN $\bar{x} = 19$)

| Audit Time (days) | Class Midpoint $(M_i)$ | Frequency $(f_i)$ | Deviation $(M_i - \bar{x})$ | Squared Deviation $(M_i - \bar{x})^2$ | $f_i(M_i - \bar{x})^2$ |
|---|---|---|---|---|---|
| 10–14 | 12 | 4 | −7 | 49 | 196 |
| 15–19 | 17 | 8 | −2 | 4 | 32 |
| 20–24 | 22 | 5 | 3 | 9 | 45 |
| 25–29 | 27 | 2 | 8 | 64 | 128 |
| 30–34 | 32 | 1 | 13 | 169 | 169 |
| | | 20 | | | 570 |

$$\Sigma f_i(M_i - \bar{x})^2$$

$$\text{Sample variance } s^2 = \frac{\Sigma f_i(M_i - \bar{x})^2}{n - 1} = \frac{570}{19} = 30$$

The calculation of the sample variance for audit times based on the grouped data is shown in Table 3.11. The sample variance is 30.

The standard deviation for grouped data is simply the square root of the variance for grouped data. For the audit time data, the sample standard deviation is $s = \sqrt{30} = 5.48$.

Before closing this section on computing measures of location and dispersion for grouped data, we note that formulas (3.16) and (3.17) are for a sample. Population summary measures are computed similarly. The grouped data formulas for a population mean and variance follow.

POPULATION MEAN FOR GROUPED DATA

$$\mu = \frac{\Sigma f_i M_i}{N} \tag{3.18}$$

POPULATION VARIANCE FOR GROUPED DATA

$$\sigma^2 = \frac{\Sigma f_i(M_i - \mu)^2}{N} \tag{3.19}$$

## NOTES AND COMMENTS

In computing descriptive statistics for grouped data, the class midpoints are used to approximate the data values in each class. As a result, the descriptive statistics for grouped data approximate the descriptive statistics that would result from using the original data directly. We therefore recommend computing descriptive statistics from the original data rather than from grouped data whenever possible.

## Exercises

### Methods

52. Consider the following data and corresponding weights.

| $x_i$ | Weight ($w_i$) |
|------|------|
| 3.2 | 6 |
| 2.0 | 3 |
| 2.5 | 2 |
| 5.0 | 8 |

a. Compute the weighted mean.
b. Compute the sample mean of the four data values without weighting. Note the difference in the results provided by the two computations.

53. Consider the sample data in the following frequency distribution.

| Class | Midpoint | Frequency |
|-------|----------|-----------|
| 3–7   | 5  | 4 |
| 8–12  | 10 | 7 |
| 13–17 | 15 | 9 |
| 18–22 | 20 | 5 |

a. Compute the sample mean.
b. Compute the sample variance and sample standard deviation.

### Applications

54. The grade point average for college students is based on a weighted mean computation. For most colleges, the grades are given the following data values: A (4), B (3), C (2), D (1), and F (0). After 60 credit hours of course work, a student at State University earned 9 credit hours of A, 15 credit hours of B, 33 credit hours of C, and 3 credit hours of D.

a. Compute the student's grade point average.
b. Students at State University must maintain a 2.5 grade point average for their first 60 credit hours of course work in order to be admitted to the business college. Will this student be admitted?

55. Morningstar tracks the total return for a large number of mutual funds. The following table shows the total return and the number of funds for four categories of mutual funds (*Morningstar Funds 500*, 2008).

| Type of Fund | Number of Funds | Total Return (%) |
|--------------|-----------------|------------------|
| Domestic Equity | 9191 | 4.65 |
| International Equity | 2621 | 18.15 |
| Specialty Stock | 1419 | 11.36 |
| Hybrid | 2900 | 6.75 |

a. Using the number of funds as weights, compute the weighted average total return for the mutual funds covered by Morningstar.

b. Is there any difficulty associated with using the "number of funds" as the weights in computing the weighted average total return for Morningstar in part (a)? Discuss. What else might be used for weights?

c. Suppose you had invested $10,000 in mutual funds at the beginning of 2007 and diversified the investment by placing $2000 in Domestic Equity funds, $4000 in International Equity funds, $3000 in Specialty Stock funds, and $1000 in Hybrid funds. What is the expected return on the portfolio?

56. Based on a survey of 425 master's programs in business administration, the *U.S. News & World Report* ranked the Indiana University Kelley Business School as the 20th best business program in the country (*America's Best Graduate Schools,* 2009). The ranking was based in part on surveys of business school deans and corporate recruiters. Each survey respondent was asked to rate the overall academic quality of the master's program on a scale from 1 "marginal" to 5 "outstanding." Use the sample of responses shown below to compute the weighted mean score for the business school deans and the corporate recruiters. Discuss.

| Quality Assessment | Business School Deans | Corporate Recruiters |
|---|---|---|
| 5 | 44 | 31 |
| 4 | 66 | 34 |
| 3 | 60 | 43 |
| 2 | 10 | 12 |
| 1 | 0 | 0 |

57. The following frequency distribution shows the price per share of the 30 companies in the Dow Jones Industrial Average (*Barron's,* February 2, 2009).

| Price per Share | Number of Companies |
|---|---|
| $0–9 | 4 |
| $10–19 | 5 |
| $20–29 | 7 |
| $30–39 | 3 |
| $40–49 | 4 |
| $50–59 | 4 |
| $60–69 | 0 |
| $70–79 | 2 |
| $80–89 | 0 |
| $90–99 | 1 |

a. Compute the mean price per share and the standard deviation of the price per share for the Dow Jones Industrial Average companies.

b. On January 16, 2006, the mean price per share was $45.83 and the standard deviation was $18.14. Comment on the changes in the price per share over the three-year period.

## Summary

In this chapter we introduced several descriptive statistics that can be used to summarize the location, variability, and shape of a data distribution. Unlike the tabular and graphical procedures introduced in Chapter 2, the measures introduced in this chapter summarize the data in terms of numerical values. When the numerical values obtained are for a sample, they are called sample statistics. When the numerical values obtained are for a population, they are called population parameters. Some of the notation used for sample statistics and population parameters follows.

*In statistical inference, the sample statistic is referred to as the point estimator of the population parameter.*

| | Sample Statistic | Population Parameter |
|---|---|---|
| Mean | $\bar{x}$ | $\mu$ |
| Variance | $s^2$ | $\sigma^2$ |
| Standard deviation | $s$ | $\sigma$ |
| Covariance | $s_{xy}$ | $\sigma_{xy}$ |
| Correlation | $r_{xy}$ | $\rho_{xy}$ |

As measures of central location, we defined the mean, median, and mode. Then the concept of percentiles was used to describe other locations in the data set. Next, we presented the range, interquartile range, variance, standard deviation, and coefficient of variation as measures of variability or dispersion. Our primary measure of the shape of a data distribution was the skewness. Negative values indicate a data distribution skewed to the left. Positive values indicate a data distribution skewed to the right. We then described how the mean and standard deviation could be used, applying Chebyshev's theorem and the empirical rule, to provide more information about the distribution of data and to identify outliers.

In Section 3.4 we showed how to develop a five-number summary and a box plot to provide simultaneous information about the location, variability, and shape of the distribution. In Section 3.5 we introduced covariance and the correlation coefficient as measures of association between two variables. In the final section, we showed how to compute a weighted mean and how to calculate a mean, variance, and standard deviation for grouped data.

## Glossary

**Sample statistic** A numerical value used as a summary measure for a sample (e.g., the sample mean, $\bar{x}$, the sample variance, $s^2$, and the sample standard deviation, $s$).

**Population parameter** A numerical value used as a summary measure for a population (e.g., the population mean, $\mu$, the population variance, $\sigma^2$, and the population standard deviation, $\sigma$).

**Point estimator** The sample statistic, such as $\bar{x}$, $s^2$, and $s$, when used to estimate the corresponding population parameter.

**Mean** A measure of central location computed by summing the data values and dividing by the number of observations.

**Median** A measure of central location provided by the value in the middle when the data are arranged in ascending order.

**Mode** A measure of location, defined as the value that occurs with greatest frequency.

**Percentile** A value such that at least $p$ percent of the observations are less than or equal to this value and at least $(100 - p)$ percent of the observations are greater than or equal to this value. The 50th percentile is the median.

**Quartiles** The 25th, 50th, and 75th percentiles are referred to as the first quartile, the second quartile (median), and third quartile, respectively. The quartiles can be used to divide a data set into four parts, with each part containing approximately 25% of the data.

**Range** A measure of variability, defined to be the largest value minus the smallest value.

**Interquartile range (IQR)** A measure of variability, defined to be the difference between the third and first quartiles.

**Variance** A measure of variability based on the squared deviations of the data values about the mean.

**Standard deviation** A measure of variability computed by taking the positive square root of the variance.

**Coefficient of variation** A measure of relative variability computed by dividing the standard deviation by the mean and multiplying by 100.

**Skewness** A measure of the shape of a data distribution. Data skewed to the left result in negative skewness; a symmetric data distribution results in zero skewness; and data skewed to the right result in positive skewness.

*z*-**score** A value computed by dividing the deviation about the mean $(x_i - \bar{x})$ by the standard deviation $s$. A $z$-score is referred to as a standardized value and denotes the number of standard deviations $x_i$ is from the mean.

**Chebyshev's theorem** A theorem that can be used to make statements about the proportion of data values that must be within a specified number of standard deviations of the mean.

**Empirical rule** A rule that can be used to compute the percentage of data values that must be within one, two, and three standard deviations of the mean for data that exhibit a bell-shaped distribution.

**Outlier** An unusually small or unusually large data value.

**Five-number summary** An exploratory data analysis technique that uses five numbers to summarize the data: smallest value, first quartile, median, third quartile, and largest value.

**Box plot** A graphical summary of data based on a five-number summary.

**Covariance** A measure of linear association between two variables. Positive values indicate a positive relationship; negative values indicate a negative relationship.

**Correlation coefficient** A measure of linear association between two variables that takes on values between $-1$ and $+1$. Values near $+1$ indicate a strong positive linear relationship; values near $-1$ indicate a strong negative linear relationship; and values near zero indicate the lack of a linear relationship.

**Weighted mean** The mean obtained by assigning each observation a weight that reflects its importance.

**Grouped data** Data available in class intervals as summarized by a frequency distribution. Individual values of the original data are not available.

## Key Formulas

**Sample Mean**

$$\bar{x} = \frac{\Sigma x_i}{n} \tag{3.1}$$

**Population Mean**

$$\mu = \frac{\Sigma x_i}{N} \tag{3.2}$$

**Interquartile Range**

$$\text{IQR} = Q_3 - Q_1 \tag{3.3}$$

**Population Variance**

$$\sigma^2 = \frac{\Sigma(x_i - \mu)^2}{N} \tag{3.4}$$

**Sample Variance**

$$s^2 = \frac{\Sigma(x_i - \bar{x})^2}{n - 1} \tag{3.5}$$

**Standard Deviation**

$$\text{Sample standard deviation} = s = \sqrt{s^2} \tag{3.6}$$

$$\text{Population standard deviation} = \sigma = \sqrt{\sigma^2} \tag{3.7}$$

**Coefficient of Variation**

$$\left( \frac{\text{Standard deviation}}{\text{Mean}} \times 100 \right)\% \tag{3.8}$$

**z-Score**

$$z_i = \frac{x_i - \bar{x}}{s} \tag{3.9}$$

**Sample Covariance**

$$s_{xy} = \frac{\Sigma(x_i - \bar{x})(y_i - \bar{y})}{n - 1} \tag{3.10}$$

**Population Covariance**

$$\sigma_{xy} = \frac{\Sigma(x_i - \mu_x)(y_i - \mu_y)}{N} \tag{3.11}$$

**Pearson Product Moment Correlation Coefficient: Sample Data**

$$r_{xy} = \frac{s_{xy}}{s_x s_y} \tag{3.12}$$

**Pearson Product Moment Correlation Coefficient: Population Data**

$$\rho_{xy} = \frac{\sigma_{xy}}{\sigma_x \sigma_y} \tag{3.13}$$

**Weighted Mean**

$$\bar{x} = \frac{\Sigma w_i x_i}{\Sigma w_i} \tag{3.15}$$

**Sample Mean for Grouped Data**

$$\bar{x} = \frac{\Sigma f_i M_i}{n} \tag{3.16}$$

### Sample Variance for Grouped Data

$$s^2 = \frac{\sum f_i(M_i - \bar{x})^2}{n - 1}$$  **(3.17)**

### Population Mean for Grouped Data

$$\mu = \frac{\sum f_i M_i}{N}$$  **(3.18)**

### Population Variance for Grouped Data

$$\sigma^2 = \frac{\sum f_i(M_i - \mu)^2}{N}$$  **(3.19)**

## Supplementary Exercises

58. According to an annual consumer spending survey, the average monthly Bank of America Visa credit card charge was $1838 (*U.S. Airways Attaché Magazine,* December 2003). A sample of monthly credit card charges provides the following data.

**Visa**

| | | | | |
|---|---|---|---|---|
| 236 | 1710 | 1351 | 825 | 7450 |
| 316 | 4135 | 1333 | 1584 | 387 |
| 991 | 3396 | 170 | 1428 | 1688 |

  a. Compute the mean and median.
  b. Compute the first and third quartiles.
  c. Compute the range and interquartile range.
  d. Compute the variance and standard deviation.
  e. The skewness measure for these data is 2.12. Comment on the shape of this distribution. Is it the shape you would expect? Why or why not?
  f. Do the data contain outliers?

59. The U.S. Census Bureau provides statistics on family life in the United States, including the age at the time of first marriage, current marital status, and size of household (U.S. Census Bureau website, March 20, 2006). The following data show the age at the time of first marriage for a sample of men and a sample of women.

**Ages**

| Men | 26 | 23 | 28 | 25 | 27 | 30 | 26 | 35 | 28 |
|---|---|---|---|---|---|---|---|---|---|
| | 21 | 24 | 27 | 29 | 30 | 27 | 32 | 27 | 25 |
| Women | 20 | 28 | 23 | 30 | 24 | 29 | 26 | 25 | |
| | 22 | 22 | 25 | 23 | 27 | 26 | 19 | | |

  a. Determine the median age at the time of first marriage for men and women.
  b. Compute the first and third quartiles for both men and women.
  c. Twenty-five years ago the median age at the time of first marriage was 25 for men and 22 for women. What insight does this information provide about the decision of when to marry among young people today?

60. Dividend yield is the annual dividend per share a company pays divided by the current market price per share expressed as a percentage. A sample of 10 large companies provided the following dividend yield data (*The Wall Street Journal,* January 16, 2004).

| Company | Yield % | Company | Yield % |
|---|---|---|---|
| Altria Group | 5.0 | General Motors | 3.7 |
| American Express | 0.8 | JPMorgan Chase | 3.5 |
| Caterpillar | 1.8 | McDonald's | 1.6 |
| Eastman Kodak | 1.9 | United Technology | 1.5 |
| ExxonMobil | 2.5 | Walmart Stores | 0.7 |

a. What are the mean and median dividend yields?
b. What are the variance and standard deviation?
c. Which company provides the highest dividend yield?
d. What is the $z$-score for McDonald's? Interpret this $z$-score.
e. What is the $z$-score for General Motors? Interpret this $z$-score.
f. Based on $z$-scores, do the data contain any outliers?

61. The U.S. Department of Education reports that about 50% of all college students use a student loan to help cover college expenses (National Center for Educational Studies, January 2006). A sample of students who graduated with student loan debt is shown here. The data, in thousands of dollars, show typical amounts of debt upon graduation.

    10.1    14.8    5.0    10.2    12.4    12.2    2.0    11.5    17.8    4.0

a. For those students who use a student loan, what is the mean loan debt upon graduation?
b. What is the variance? Standard deviation?

62. Small business owners often look to payroll service companies to handle their employee payroll. Reasons are that small business owners face complicated tax regulations and penalties for employment tax errors are costly. According to the Internal Revenue Service, 26% of all small business employment tax returns contained errors that resulted in a tax penalty to the owner (*The Wall Street Journal*, January 30, 2006). The tax penalty for a sample of 20 small business owners follows:

**WEB file**

**Penalty**

|  |  |  |  |  |  |  |  |  |  |
|---|---|---|---|---|---|---|---|---|---|
| 820 | 270 | 450 | 1010 | 890 | 700 | 1350 | 350 | 300 | 1200 |
| 390 | 730 | 2040 | 230 | 640 | 350 | 420 | 270 | 370 | 620 |

a. What is the mean tax penalty for improperly filed employment tax returns?
b. What is the standard deviation?
c. Is the highest penalty, $2040, an outlier?
d. What are some of the advantages of a small business owner hiring a payroll service company to handle employee payroll services, including the employment tax returns?

63. Public transportation and the automobile are two methods an employee can use to get to work each day. Samples of times recorded for each method are shown. Times are in minutes.

| *Public Transportation:* | 28 | 29 | 32 | 37 | 33 | 25 | 29 | 32 | 41 | 34 |
|---|---|---|---|---|---|---|---|---|---|---|
| *Automobile:* | | 29 | 31 | 33 | 32 | 34 | 30 | 31 | 32 | 35 | 33 |

a. Compute the sample mean time to get to work for each method.
b. Compute the sample standard deviation for each method.
c. On the basis of your results from parts (a) and (b), which method of transportation should be preferred? Explain.
d. Develop a box plot for each method. Does a comparison of the box plots support your conclusion in part (c)?

64. The National Association of Realtors reported the median home price in the United States and the increase in median home price over a five-year period (*The Wall Street Journal*,

January 16, 2006). Use the sample home prices shown here to answer the following questions.

**Homes**

| | | | | | | |
|---|---|---|---|---|---|---|
| 995.9 | 48.8 | 175.0 | 263.5 | 298.0 | 218.9 | 209.0 |
| 628.3 | 111.0 | 212.9 | 92.6 | 2325.0 | 958.0 | 212.5 |

a. What is the sample median home price?
b. In January 2001, the National Association of Realtors reported a median home price of $139,300 in the United States. What was the percentage increase in the median home price over the five-year period?
c. What are the first quartile and the third quartile for the sample data?
d. Provide a five-number summary for the home prices.
e. Do the data contain any outliers?
f. What is the mean home price for the sample? Why does the National Association of Realtors prefer to use the median home price in its reports?

65. The U.S. Census Bureau's American Community Survey reported the percentage of children under 18 years of age who had lived below the poverty level during the previous 12 months (U.S. Census Bureau website, August 2008). The region of the country, Northeast (NE), Southeast (SE), Midwest (MW), Southwest (SW), and West (W) and the percentage of children under 18 who had lived below the poverty level are shown for each state.

**PovertyLevel**

| State | Region | Poverty % | State | Region | Poverty % |
|---|---|---|---|---|---|
| Alabama | SE | 23.0 | Montana | W | 17.3 |
| Alaska | W | 15.1 | Nebraska | MW | 14.4 |
| Arizona | SW | 19.5 | Nevada | W | 13.9 |
| Arkansas | SE | 24.3 | New Hampshire | NE | 9.6 |
| California | W | 18.1 | New Jersey | NE | 11.8 |
| Colorado | W | 15.7 | New Mexico | SW | 25.6 |
| Connecticut | NE | 11.0 | New York | NE | 20.0 |
| Delaware | NE | 15.8 | North Carolina | SE | 20.2 |
| Florida | SE | 17.5 | North Dakota | MW | 13.0 |
| Georgia | SE | 20.2 | Ohio | MW | 18.7 |
| Hawaii | W | 11.4 | Oklahoma | SW | 24.3 |
| Idaho | W | 15.1 | Oregon | W | 16.8 |
| Illinois | MW | 17.1 | Pennsylvania | NE | 16.9 |
| Indiana | MW | 17.9 | Rhode Island | NE | 15.1 |
| Iowa | MW | 13.7 | South Carolina | SE | 22.1 |
| Kansas | MW | 15.6 | South Dakota | MW | 16.8 |
| Kentucky | SE | 22.8 | Tennessee | SE | 22.7 |
| Louisiana | SE | 27.8 | Texas | SW | 23.9 |
| Maine | NE | 17.6 | Utah | W | 11.9 |
| Maryland | NE | 9.7 | Vermont | NE | 13.2 |
| Massachusetts | NE | 12.4 | Virginia | SE | 12.2 |
| Michigan | MW | 18.3 | Washington | W | 15.4 |
| Minnesota | MW | 12.2 | West Virginia | SE | 25.2 |
| Mississippi | SE | 29.5 | Wisconsin | MW | 14.9 |
| Missouri | MW | 18.6 | Wyoming | W | 12.0 |

a. What is the median poverty level percentage for the 50 states?
b. What are the first and third quartiles? What is your interpretation of the quartiles?
c. Show a box plot for the data. Interpret the box plot in terms of what it tells you about the level of poverty for children in the United States. Are any states considered outliers? Discuss.
d. Identify the states in the lower quartile. What is your interpretation of this group and what region or regions are represented most in the lower quartile?

66. *Travel + Leisure* magazine presented its annual list of the 500 best hotels in the world (*Travel + Leisure*, January 2009). The magazine provides a rating for each hotel along with a brief description that includes the size of the hotel, amenities, and the cost per night for a double room. A sample of 12 of the top-rated hotels in the United States follows.

**WEB file**

**Travel**

| Hotel | Location | Rooms | Cost/Night |
|---|---|---|---|
| Boulders Resort & Spa | Phoenix, AZ | 220 | 499 |
| Disney's Wilderness Lodge | Orlando, FL | 727 | 340 |
| Four Seasons Hotel Beverly Hills | Los Angeles, CA | 285 | 585 |
| Four Seasons Hotel | Boston, MA | 273 | 495 |
| Hay-Adams | Washington, DC | 145 | 495 |
| Inn on Biltmore Estate | Asheville, NC | 213 | 279 |
| Loews Ventana Canyon Resort | Phoenix, AZ | 398 | 279 |
| Mauna Lani Bay Hotel | Island of Hawaii | 343 | 455 |
| Montage Laguna Beach | Laguna Beach, CA | 250 | 595 |
| Sofitel Water Tower | Chicago, IL | 414 | 367 |
| St. Regis Monarch Beach | Dana Point, CA | 400 | 675 |
| The Broadmoor | Colorado Springs, CO | 700 | 420 |

a. What is the mean number of rooms?
b. What is the mean cost per night for a double room?
c. Develop a scatter diagram with the number of rooms on the horizontal axis and the cost per night on the vertical axis. Does there appear to be a relationship between the number of rooms and the cost per night? Discuss.
d. What is the sample correlation coefficient? What does it tell you about the relationship between the number of rooms and the cost per night for a double room? Does this appear reasonable? Discuss.

67. Morningstar tracks the performance of a large number of companies and publishes an evaluation of each. Along with a variety of financial data, Morningstar includes a Fair Value estimate for the price that should be paid for a share of the company's common stock. Data for 30 companies are available in the file named FairValue. The data include the Fair Value estimate per share of common stock, the most recent price per share, and the earning per share for the company (*Morningstar Stocks 500,* 2008).

**WEB file**

**FairValue**

a. Develop a scatter diagram for the Fair Value and Share Price data with Share Price on the horizontal axis. What is the sample correlation coefficient, and what can you say about the relationship between the variables?
b. Develop a scatter diagram for the Fair Value and Earnings per Share data with Earnings per Share on the horizontal axis. What is the sample correlation coefficient, and what can you say about the relationship between the variables?

68. Does a major league baseball team's record during spring training indicate how the team will play during the regular season? Over the last six years, the correlation coefficient between a team's winning percentage in spring training and its winning percentage in the regular season is .18 (*The Wall Street Journal,* March 30, 2009). Shown are the winning percentages for the 14 American League teams during the 2008 season.

**WEB file**

**SpringTraining**

| Team | Spring Training | Regular Season | Team | Spring Training | Regular Season |
|---|---|---|---|---|---|
| Baltimore Orioles | .407 | .422 | Minnesota Twins | .500 | .540 |
| Boston Red Sox | .429 | .586 | New York Yankees | .577 | .549 |
| Chicago White Sox | .417 | .546 | Oakland A's | .692 | .466 |
| Cleveland Indians | .569 | .500 | Seattle Mariners | .500 | .377 |
| Detroit Tigers | .569 | .457 | Tampa Bay Rays | .731 | .599 |
| Kansas City Royals | .533 | .463 | Texas Rangers | .643 | .488 |
| Los Angeles Angels | .724 | .617 | Toronto Blue Jays | .448 | .531 |

a. What is the correlation coefficient between the spring training and the regular season winning percentages?

b. What is your conclusion about a team's record during spring training indicating how the team will play during the regular season? What are some of the reasons why this occurs? Discuss.

69. The days to maturity for a sample of five money market funds are shown here. The dollar amounts invested in the funds are provided. Use the weighted mean to determine the mean number of days to maturity for dollars invested in these five money market funds.

| Days to Maturity | Dollar Value ($millions) |
|---|---|
| 20 | 20 |
| 12 | 30 |
| 7 | 10 |
| 5 | 15 |
| 6 | 10 |

70. Automobiles traveling on a road with a posted speed limit of 55 miles per hour are checked for speed by a state police radar system. Following is a frequency distribution of speeds.

| Speed (miles per hour) | Frequency |
|---|---|
| 45–49 | 10 |
| 50–54 | 40 |
| 55–59 | 150 |
| 60–64 | 175 |
| 65–69 | 75 |
| 70–74 | 15 |
| 75–79 | 10 |
| Total | 475 |

a. What is the mean speed of the automobiles traveling on this road?

b. Compute the variance and the standard deviation.

## Case Problem 1   Pelican Stores

Pelican Stores, a division of National Clothing, is a chain of women's apparel stores operating throughout the country. The chain recently ran a promotion in which discount coupons were sent to customers of other National Clothing stores. Data collected for a sample of 100 in-store credit card transactions at Pelican Stores during one day while the promotion was running are contained in the file named PelicanStores. Table 3.12 shows a portion of the data set. The proprietary card method of payment refers to charges made using a National Clothing charge card. Customers who made a purchase using a discount coupon are referred to as promotional customers and customers who made a purchase but did not use a discount coupon are referred to as regular customers. Because the promotional coupons were not sent to regular Pelican Stores customers, management considers the sales made to people presenting the promotional coupons as sales it would not otherwise make. Of course, Pelican also hopes that the promotional customers will continue to shop at its stores.

**TABLE 3.12**    SAMPLE OF 100 CREDIT CARD PURCHASES AT PELICAN STORES

PelicanStores

| Customer | Type of Customer | Items | Net Sales | Method of Payment | Gender | Marital Status | Age |
|---|---|---|---|---|---|---|---|
| 1 | Regular | 1 | 39.50 | Discover | Male | Married | 32 |
| 2 | Promotional | 1 | 102.40 | Proprietary Card | Female | Married | 36 |
| 3 | Regular | 1 | 22.50 | Proprietary Card | Female | Married | 32 |
| 4 | Promotional | 5 | 100.40 | Proprietary Card | Female | Married | 28 |
| 5 | Regular | 2 | 54.00 | MasterCard | Female | Married | 34 |
| 6 | Regular | 1 | 44.50 | MasterCard | Female | Married | 44 |
| 7 | Promotional | 2 | 78.00 | Proprietary Card | Female | Married | 30 |
| 8 | Regular | 1 | 22.50 | Visa | Female | Married | 40 |
| 9 | Promotional | 2 | 56.52 | Proprietary Card | Female | Married | 46 |
| 10 | Regular | 1 | 44.50 | Proprietary Card | Female | Married | 36 |
| . | . | . | . | | . | . | . |
| . | . | . | . | | . | . | . |
| 96 | Regular | 1 | 39.50 | MasterCard | Female | Married | 44 |
| 97 | Promotional | 9 | 253.00 | Proprietary Card | Female | Married | 30 |
| 98 | Promotional | 10 | 287.59 | Proprietary Card | Female | Married | 52 |
| 99 | Promotional | 2 | 47.60 | Proprietary Card | Female | Married | 30 |
| 100 | Promotional | 1 | 28.44 | Proprietary Card | Female | Married | 44 |

Most of the variables shown in Table 3.12 are self-explanatory, but two of the variables require some clarification.

Items        The total number of items purchased
Net Sales    The total amount ($) charged to the credit card

Pelican's management would like to use this sample data to learn about its customer base and to evaluate the promotion involving discount coupons.

## Managerial Report

Use the methods of descriptive statistics presented in this chapter to summarize the data and comment on your findings. At a minimum, your report should include the following:

1. Descriptive statistics on net sales and descriptive statistics on net sales by various classifications of customers.
2. Descriptive statistics concerning the relationship between age and net sales.

## Case Problem 2    Motion Picture Industry

The motion picture industry is a competitive business. More than 50 studios produce a total of 300 to 400 new motion pictures each year, and the financial success of each motion picture varies considerably. The opening weekend gross sales, the total gross sales, the number of theaters the movie was shown in, and the number of weeks the motion picture was in the top 60 for gross sales are common variables used to measure the success of a motion picture. Data collected for a sample of 100 motion pictures produced in 2005 are

**TABLE 3.13**   PERFORMANCE DATA FOR 10 MOTION PICTURES

Movies

| Motion Picture | Opening Gross Sales ($millions) | Total Gross Sales ($millions) | Number of Theaters | Weeks in Top 60 |
|---|---|---|---|---|
| Coach Carter | 29.17 | 67.25 | 2574 | 16 |
| Ladies in Lavender | 0.15 | 6.65 | 119 | 22 |
| Batman Begins | 48.75 | 205.28 | 3858 | 18 |
| Unleashed | 10.90 | 24.47 | 1962 | 8 |
| Pretty Persuasion | 0.06 | 0.23 | 24 | 4 |
| Fever Pitch | 12.40 | 42.01 | 3275 | 14 |
| Harry Potter and the Goblet of Fire | 102.69 | 287.18 | 3858 | 13 |
| Monster-in-Law | 23.11 | 82.89 | 3424 | 16 |
| White Noise | 24.11 | 55.85 | 2279 | 7 |
| Mr. and Mrs. Smith | 50.34 | 186.22 | 3451 | 21 |

contained in the file named Movies. Table 3.13 shows the data for the first 10 motion pictures in the file.

## Managerial Report

Use the numerical methods of descriptive statistics presented in this chapter to learn how these variables contribute to the success of a motion picture. Include the following in your report.

1. Descriptive statistics for each of the four variables along with a discussion of what the descriptive statistics tell us about the motion picture industry.
2. What motion pictures, if any, should be considered high-performance outliers? Explain.
3. Descriptive statistics showing the relationship between total gross sales and each of the other variables. Discuss.

## Case Problem 3    Heavenly Chocolates Website Transactions

Heavenly Chocolates manufactures and sells quality chocolate products at its plant and retail store located in Saratoga Springs, New York. Two years ago the company developed a website and began selling its products over the Internet. Website sales have exceeded the company's expectations, and mangement is now considering stragegies to increase sales even further. To learn more about the website customers, a sample of 50 Heavenly Chocolate transactions was selected from the previous month's sales. Data showing the day of the week each transaction was made, the type of browser the customer used, the time spent on the website, the number of website pages viewed, and the amount spent by each of the 50 customers are contained in the file named Shoppers. A portion of the data is shown in Table 3.14.

Heavenly Chocolates would like to use the sample data to determine if online shoppers who spend more time and view more pages also spend more money during their visit to the website. The company would also like to investigate the effect that the day of the week and the type of browser have on sales.

**TABLE 3.14**    A SAMPLE OF 50 HEAVENLY CHOCOLATES WEBSITE TRANSACTIONS

**WEB file**

Shoppers

| Customer | Day | Browser | Time (min) | Pages Viewed | Amount Spent ($) |
|---|---|---|---|---|---|
| 1 | Mon | Internet Explorer | 12.0 | 4 | 54.52 |
| 2 | Wed | Other | 19.5 | 6 | 94.90 |
| 3 | Mon | Internet Explorer | 8.5 | 4 | 26.68 |
| 4 | Tue | Firefox | 11.4 | 2 | 44.73 |
| 5 | Wed | Internet Explorer | 11.3 | 4 | 66.27 |
| 6 | Sat | Firefox | 10.5 | 6 | 67.80 |
| 7 | Sun | Internet Explorer | 11.4 | 2 | 36.04 |
| . | . | . | . | . | . |
| . | . | . | . | . | . |
| . | . | . | . | . | . |
| 48 | Fri | Internet Explorer | 9.7 | 5 | 103.15 |
| 49 | Mon | Other | 7.3 | 6 | 52.15 |
| 50 | Fri | Internet Explorer | 13.4 | 3 | 98.75 |

## Managerial Report

Use the methods of descriptive statistics to learn about the customers who visit the Heavenly Chocolates website. Include the following in your report.

1. Graphical and numerical summaries for the length of time the shopper spends on the website, the number of pages viewed, and the mean amount spent per transaction. Discuss what you learn about Heavenly Cholcolates' online shoppers from these numerical summaries.
2. Summarize the frequency, the total dollars spent, and the mean amount spent per transaction for each day of week. What observations can you make about Heavenly Chocolates' business based on the day of the week? Discuss.
3. Summarize the frequency, the total dollars spent, and the mean amount spent per transaction for each type of browser. What observations can you make about Heavenly Chocolate's business based on the type of browser? Discuss.
4. Develop a scatter diagram and compute the sample correlation coefficient to explore the relationship between the time spent on the website and the dollar amount spent. Use the horizontal axis for the time spent on the website. Discuss.
5. Develop a scatter diagram and compute the sample correlation coefficient to explore the relationship between the the number of website pages viewed and the amount spent. Use the horizontal axis for the number of website pages viewed. Discuss.
6. Develop a scatter diagram and compute the sample correlation coefficient to explore the relationship between the time spent on the website and the number of pages viewed. Use the horizontal axis to represent the number of pages viewed. Discuss.

## Appendix    Descriptive Statistics Using StatTools

In this appendix, we describe how StatTools can be used to compute a variety of descriptive statistics and also display box plots. We then show how StatTools can be used to obtain covariance and correlation measures for two variables.

## Descriptive Statistics

**StartSalary**

We use the starting salary data in Table 3.1 to illustrate. Begin by using the Data Set Manager to create a StatTools data set for these data using the procedure described in the appendix in Chapter 1. The following steps will generate a variety of descriptive statistics.

**Step 1.** Click the **StatTools** tab on the Ribbon
**Step 2.** In the **Analyses Group,** click **Summary Statistics**
**Step 3.** Choose the **One-Variable Summary** option
**Step 4.** When the StatTools-One-Variable Summary Statistics dialog box appears,
   In the **Variables** section, select **Starting Salary**
   Click **OK**

A variety of descriptive statistics will appear.

## Box Plots

**StartSalary**

*In StatTools a box plot is referred to as a box-whisker plot.*

We use the starting salary data in Table 3.1 to illustrate. Begin by using the Data Set Manager to create a StatTools data set for the StartSalary data using the procedure described in the appendix in Chapter 1. The following steps will create the box plot for these data.

**Step 1.** Click the **StatTools** tab on the Ribbon
**Step 2.** In the **Analyses Group**, click **Summary Graphs**
**Step 3.** Choose the **Box-Whisker Plot** option
**Step 4.** When the StatTools - Box-Whisker Plot dialog box appears,
   In the Variables section, select **Starting Salary**
   Click **OK**

The box plot for the starting salary data created using StatTools has a slightly different appearance from the box plot shown in Figure 3.11. The procedure StatTools uses to compute quartiles is different from the procedure we showed in Section 3.1; this results in a different value for the interquartile range (IQR) and therefore different lower and upper limits for the box plot. In StatTools the whiskers are shown as solid lines, the location of the sample mean is shown using the symbol ✳, and two types of outliers are identified. Mild outliers, shown with the symbol □, are observations that are no more than 1.5(IQR) from the edges of the box, and extreme outliers, shown with the symbol ■, are observations that are greater than 3(IQR) from the edges of the box.

**Comparative Analysis**  StatTools can also be used to display box plots for several groups. We illustrate using the MajorSalary data set. Begin by using the Data Set Manager to create a StatTools data set for the MajorSalary data using the procedure described in the appendix to Chapter 1. The following steps will create the box plot for these data.

**Step 1.** Click the **StatTools** tab on the Ribbon
**Step 2.** In the **Analyses Group,** click **Summary Graphs**
**Step 3.** Choose the **Box-Whisker Plot** option
**Step 4.** When the StatTools - Box-Whisker Plot dialog box appears,
   Click the **Format** button and select the **Stacked** option
   In the Variables section,
      In the **Cat** column select **Major**
      In the **Val** column select **Monthly Salary**
   Click **OK**

The box plot for the monthly starting salaries by major created using StatTools has a slightly different appearance from the box plot shown in Figure 3.12; however, the interpretations based on both plots are the same.

## Covariance and Correlation

We use the stereo and sound equipment data in Table 3.7 to demonstrate the computation of the sample covariance and the sample correlation coefficient. Begin by using the Data Set Manager to create a StatTools data set for these data using the procedure described in the appendix in Chapter 1. The following steps will provide the sample covariance and sample correlation coefficient.

**Stereo**

**Step 1.** Click the **StatTools** tab on the Ribbon
**Step 2.** In the **Analyses Group,** click **Summary Statistics**
**Step 3.** Choose the **Correlation and Covariance** option
**Step 4.** When the StatTools - Correlation and Covariance dialog box appears,
    In the **Variables** section,
      Select **No. of Commercials**
      Select **Sales Volume**
    In the **Tables to Create** section,
      Select **Table of Correlations**
      Select **Table of Covariances**
    In the **Table Structure** section select **Symmetric**
    Click **OK**

A table showing the correlation coefficient and the covariance will appear.

# CHAPTER 4

# Introduction to Probability

## STATISTICS *in* PRACTICE

### OCEANWIDE SEAFOOD*
*SPRINGBORO, OHIO*

Oceanwide Seafood is the leading provider of quality seafood in southwestern Ohio. The company stocks over 90 varieties of fresh and frozen seafood products from around the world and prepares specialty cuts according to customer specifications. Customers include major restaurants and retail food stores in Ohio, Kentucky, and Indiana. Established in 2005, the company has become successful by providing superior customer service and exceptional quality seafood.

Probability and statistical information are used for both operational and marketing decisions. For instance, a time series showing monthly sales is used to track the company's growth and to set future target sales levels. Statistics such as the mean customer order size and the mean number of days a customer takes to make payments help identify the firm's best customers as well as provide benchmarks for handling accounts receivable issues. In addition, data on monthly inventory levels are used in the analysis of operating profits and trends in product sales.

Probability analysis has helped Oceanwide determine reasonable and profitable prices for its products. For example, when Oceanwide receives a whole fresh fish from one of its suppliers, the fish must be processed and cut to fill individual customer orders. A fresh 100-pound whole tuna packed in ice might cost Oceanwide $500. At first glance, the company's cost for tuna appears to be $500/100 = $5 per pound. However, due to the loss in the processing and cutting operation, a 100-pound whole tuna will not provide 100 pounds of finished product. If the processing and cutting operation yields 75% of the whole tuna, the number of pounds of finished product available for sale to customers would be .75(100) = 75 pounds, not 100 pounds. In this case, the company's actual cost of tuna would be $500/75 = $6.67 per pound. Thus, Oceanwide would need to use a cost of $6.67 per pound to determine a profitable price to charge its customers.

To help determine the yield percentage that is likely for processing and cutting whole tuna, data were

© Alaska Stock Images/PhotoLibrary

Oceanwide Seafood uses probability analysis to help determine reasonable and profitable prices for its products.

collected on the yields from a sample of whole tunas. Let $Y$ denote the yield percentage for whole tuna. Using the data, Oceanwide was able to determine that 5% of the time the yield for whole tuna was at least 90%. In conditional probability notation, this probability is written $P(Y \geq 90\% \mid \text{Tuna}) = .05$; in other words, the probability that the yield will be at least 90% given that the fish is a tuna is .05. If Oceanwide established the selling price for tuna based on a 90% yield, 95% of the time the company would realize a yield less than expected. As a result, the company would be understating its cost per pound and also understating the price of tuna for its customers. Additional conditional probability information for other yield percentages helped management select a 70% yield as the basis for determining the cost of tuna and the price to charge its customers. Similar conditional probabilities for other seafood products helped management establish pricing yield percentages for each type of seafood product. In this chapter, you will learn how to compute and interpret conditional probabilities and other probabilities that are helpful in the decision-making process.

---

*The authors are indebted to Dale Hartlage, president of Oceanwide Seafood Company, for providing this Statistics in Practice.

Managers often base their decisions on an analysis of uncertainties such as the following:

1. What are the chances that sales will decrease if we increase prices?
2. What is the likelihood a new assembly method will increase productivity?
3. How likely is it that the project will be finished on time?
4. What is the chance that a new investment will be profitable?

*Some of the earliest work on probability originated in a series of letters between Pierre de Fermat and Blaise Pascal in the 1650s.*

**Probability** is a numerical measure of the likelihood that an event will occur. Thus, probabilities can be used as measures of the degree of uncertainty associated with the four events previously listed. If probabilities are available, we can determine the likelihood of each event occurring.

Probability values are always assigned on a scale from 0 to 1. A probability near zero indicates an event is unlikely to occur; a probability near 1 indicates an event is almost certain to occur. Other probabilities between 0 and 1 represent degrees of likelihood that an event will occur. For example, if we consider the event "rain tomorrow," we understand that when the weather report indicates "a near-zero probability of rain," it means almost no chance of rain. However, if a .90 probability of rain is reported, we know that rain is likely to occur. A .50 probability indicates that rain is just as likely to occur as not. Figure 4.1 depicts the view of probability as a numerical measure of the likelihood of an event occurring.

## 4.1 Experiments, Counting Rules, and Assigning Probabilities

In discussing probability, we define an **experiment** as a process that generates well-defined outcomes. On any single repetition of an experiment, one and only one of the possible experimental outcomes will occur. Several examples of experiments and their associated outcomes follow.

| Experiment | Experimental Outcomes |
|---|---|
| Toss a coin | Head, tail |
| Select a part for inspection | Defective, nondefective |
| Conduct a sales call | Purchase, no purchase |
| Roll a die | 1, 2, 3, 4, 5, 6 |
| Play a football game | Win, lose, tie |

By specifying all possible experimental outcomes, we identify the **sample space** for an experiment.

**FIGURE 4.1**    PROBABILITY AS A NUMERICAL MEASURE OF THE LIKELIHOOD OF AN EVENT OCCURRING

Increasing Likelihood of Occurrence

Probability:    0          .5          1.0

The occurrence of the event is just as likely as it is unlikely.

> **SAMPLE SPACE**
>
> The sample space for an experiment is the set of all experimental outcomes.

*Experimental outcomes are also called sample points.*

An experimental outcome is also called a **sample point** to identify it as an element of the sample space.

Consider the first experiment in the preceding table—tossing a coin. The upward face of the coin—a head or a tail—determines the experimental outcomes (sample points). If we let $S$ denote the sample space, we can use the following notation to describe the sample space.

$$S = \{\text{Head, Tail}\}$$

The sample space for the second experiment in the table—selecting a part for inspection—can be described as follows:

$$S = \{\text{Defective, Nondefective}\}$$

Both of the experiments just described have two experimental outcomes (sample points). However, suppose we consider the fourth experiment listed in the table—rolling a die. The possible experimental outcomes, defined as the number of dots appearing on the upward face of the die, are the six points in the sample space for this experiment.

$$S = \{1, 2, 3, 4, 5, 6\}$$

## Counting Rules, Combinations, and Permutations

Being able to identify and count the experimental outcomes is a necessary step in assigning probabilities. We now discuss three useful counting rules.

**Multiple-step experiments** The first counting rule applies to multiple-step experiments. Consider the experiment of tossing two coins. Let the experimental outcomes be defined in terms of the pattern of heads and tails appearing on the upward faces of the two coins. How many experimental outcomes are possible for this experiment? The experiment of tossing two coins can be thought of as a two-step experiment in which step 1 is the tossing of the first coin and step 2 is the tossing of the second coin. If we use $H$ to denote a head and $T$ to denote a tail, $(H, H)$ indicates the experimental outcome with a head on the first coin and a head on the second coin. Continuing this notation, we can describe the sample space $(S)$ for this coin-tossing experiment as follows:

$$S = \{(H, H), (H, T), (T, H), (T, T)\}$$

Thus, we see that four experimental outcomes are possible. In this case, we can easily list all of the experimental outcomes.

The counting rule for multiple-step experiments makes it possible to determine the number of experimental outcomes without listing them.

> **COUNTING RULE FOR MULTIPLE-STEP EXPERIMENTS**
>
> If an experiment can be described as a sequence of $k$ steps with $n_1$ possible outcomes on the first step, $n_2$ possible outcomes on the second step, and so on, then the total number of experimental outcomes is given by $(n_1)(n_2) \ldots (n_k)$.

**FIGURE 4.2**   TREE DIAGRAM FOR THE EXPERIMENT OF TOSSING TWO COINS

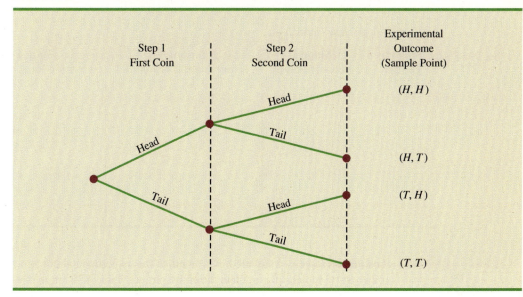

Viewing the experiment of tossing two coins as a sequence of first tossing one coin ($n_1 = 2$) and then tossing the other coin ($n_2 = 2$), we can see from the counting rule that $(2)(2) = 4$ distinct experimental outcomes are possible. As shown, they are $S = \{(H, H), (H, T), (T, H), (T, T)\}$. The number of experimental outcomes in an experiment involving tossing six coins is $(2)(2)(2)(2)(2)(2) = 64$.

*Without the tree diagram, one might think only three experimental outcomes are possible for two tosses of a coin: 0 heads, 1 head, and 2 heads.*

A **tree diagram** is a graphical representation that helps in visualizing a multiple-step experiment. Figure 4.2 shows a tree diagram for the experiment of tossing two coins. The sequence of steps moves from left to right through the tree. Step 1 corresponds to tossing the first coin, and step 2 corresponds to tossing the second coin. For each step, the two possible outcomes are head or tail. Note that for each possible outcome at step 1 two branches correspond to the two possible outcomes at step 2. Each of the points on the right end of the tree corresponds to an experimental outcome. Each path through the tree from the leftmost node to one of the nodes at the right side of the tree corresponds to a unique sequence of outcomes.

Let us now see how the counting rule for multiple-step experiments can be used in the analysis of a capacity expansion project for the Kentucky Power & Light Company (KP&L). KP&L is starting a project designed to increase the generating capacity of one of its plants in northern Kentucky. The project is divided into two sequential stages or steps: stage 1 (design) and stage 2 (construction). Even though each stage will be scheduled and controlled as closely as possible, management cannot predict beforehand the exact time required to complete each stage of the project. An analysis of similar construction projects revealed possible completion times for the design stage of 2, 3, or 4 months and possible completion times for the construction stage of 6, 7, or 8 months. In addition, because of the critical need for additional electrical power, management set a goal of 10 months for the completion of the entire project.

Because this project has three possible completion times for the design stage (step 1) and three possible completion times for the construction stage (step 2), the counting rule for multiple-step experiments can be applied here to determine a total of $(3)(3) = 9$ experimental outcomes. To describe the experimental outcomes, we use a two-number notation; for instance, $(2, 6)$ indicates that the design stage is completed in 2 months and the

**TABLE 4.1**    EXPERIMENTAL OUTCOMES (SAMPLE POINTS) FOR THE KP&L PROJECT

| Completion Time (months) | | | |
|---|---|---|---|
| Stage 1 Design | Stage 2 Construction | Notation for Experimental Outcome | Total Project Completion Time (months) |
| 2 | 6 | (2, 6) | 8 |
| 2 | 7 | (2, 7) | 9 |
| 2 | 8 | (2, 8) | 10 |
| 3 | 6 | (3, 6) | 9 |
| 3 | 7 | (3, 7) | 10 |
| 3 | 8 | (3, 8) | 11 |
| 4 | 6 | (4, 6) | 10 |
| 4 | 7 | (4, 7) | 11 |
| 4 | 8 | (4, 8) | 12 |

construction stage is completed in 6 months. This experimental outcome results in a total of $2 + 6 = 8$ months to complete the entire project. Table 4.1 summarizes the nine experimental outcomes for the KP&L problem. The tree diagram in Figure 4.3 shows how the nine outcomes (sample points) occur.

The counting rule and tree diagram help the project manager identify the experimental outcomes and determine the possible project completion times. From the information in Figure 4.3, we see that the project will be completed in 8 to 12 months, with six of the nine experimental outcomes providing the desired completion time of 10 months or less. Even though identifying the experimental outcomes may be helpful, we need to consider how probability values can be assigned to the experimental outcomes before making an assessment of the probability that the project will be completed within the desired 10 months.

**Combinations**    A second useful counting rule allows one to count the number of experimental outcomes when the experiment involves selecting $n$ objects from a (usually larger) set of $N$ objects. It is called the counting rule for combinations.

---

**COUNTING RULE FOR COMBINATIONS**

The number of combinations of $N$ objects taken $n$ at a time is

$$C_n^N = \binom{N}{n} = \frac{N!}{n!(N-n)!} \tag{4.1}$$

where
$$N! = N(N-1)(N-2)\cdots(2)(1)$$
$$n! = n(n-1)(n-2)\cdots(2)(1)$$

and, by definition,
$$0! = 1$$

---

The notation ! means *factorial;* for example, 5 factorial is $5! = (5)(4)(3)(2)(1) = 120$.

*In sampling from a finite population of size N, the counting rule for combinations is used to find the number of different samples of size n that can be selected.*

As an illustration of the counting rule for combinations, consider a quality control procedure in which an inspector randomly selects two of five parts to test for defects. In a group of five parts, how many combinations of two parts can be selected? The counting rule in equation (4.1) shows that with $N = 5$ and $n = 2$, we have

$$C_2^5 = \binom{5}{2} = \frac{5!}{2!(5-2)!} = \frac{(5)(4)(3)(2)(1)}{(2)(1)(3)(2)(1)} = \frac{120}{12} = 10$$

**FIGURE 4.3**   TREE DIAGRAM FOR THE KP&L PROJECT

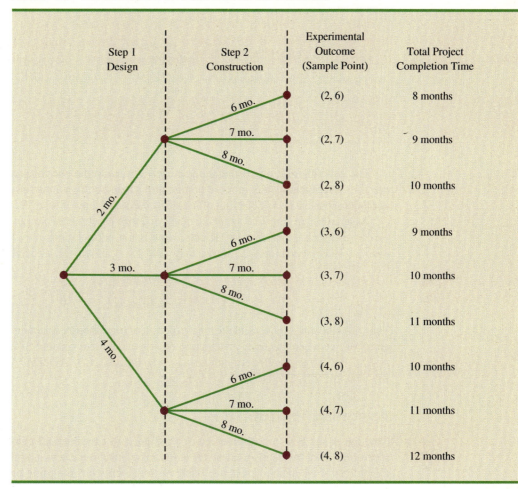

Thus, 10 outcomes are possible for the experiment of randomly selecting two parts from a group of five. If we label the five parts as A, B, C, D, and E, the 10 combinations or experimental outcomes can be identified as AB, AC, AD, AE, BC, BD, BE, CD, CE, and DE.

As another example, consider that the Florida lottery system uses the random selection of six integers from a group of 53 to determine the weekly winner. The counting rule for combinations, equation (4.1), can be used to determine the number of ways six different integers can be selected from a group of 53.

$$\binom{53}{6} = \frac{53!}{6!(53 - 6)!} = \frac{53!}{6!47!} = \frac{(53)(52)(51)(50)(49)(48)}{(6)(5)(4)(3)(2)(1)} = 22{,}957{,}480$$

*The counting rule for combinations shows that the chance of winning the lottery is very unlikely.*

The counting rule for combinations tells us that almost 23 million experimental outcomes are possible in the lottery drawing. An individual who buys a lottery ticket has 1 chance in 22,957,480 of winning.

**Permutations**   A third counting rule that is sometimes useful is the counting rule for permutations. It allows one to compute the number of experimental outcomes when *n* objects are to be selected from a set of *N* objects where the order of selection is important. The same $n$ objects selected in a different order are considered a different experimental outcome.

---

**COUNTING RULE FOR PERMUTATIONS**

The number of permutations of $N$ objects taken $n$ at a time is given by

$$P_n^N = n!\binom{N}{n} = \frac{N!}{(N-n)!} \qquad (4.2)$$

---

The counting rule for permutations closely relates to the one for combinations; however, an experiment results in more permutations than combinations for the same number of objects because every selection of $n$ objects can be ordered in $n!$ different ways.

As an example, consider again the quality control process in which an inspector selects two of five parts to inspect for defects. How many permutations may be selected? The counting rule in equation (4.2) shows that with $N = 5$ and $n = 2$, we have

$$P_2^5 = \frac{5!}{(5-2)!} = \frac{5!}{3!} = \frac{(5)(4)(3)(2)(1)}{(3)(2)(1)} = \frac{120}{6} = 20$$

Thus, 20 outcomes are possible for the experiment of randomly selecting two parts from a group of five when the order of selection must be taken into account. If we label the parts A, B, C, D, and E, the 20 permutations are AB, BA, AC, CA, AD, DA, AE, EA, BC, CB, BD, DB, BE, EB, CD, DC, CE, EC, DE, and ED.

## Assigning Probabilities

Now let us see how probabilities can be assigned to experimental outcomes. The three approaches most frequently used are the classical, relative frequency, and subjective methods. Regardless of the method used, two **basic requirements for assigning probabilities** must be met.

---

**BASIC REQUIREMENTS FOR ASSIGNING PROBABILITIES**

1. The probability assigned to each experimental outcome must be between 0 and 1, inclusively. If we let $E_i$ denote the $i$th experimental outcome and $P(E_i)$ its probability, then this requirement can be written as

$$0 \leq P(E_i) \leq 1 \text{ for all } i \qquad (4.3)$$

2. The sum of the probabilities for all the experimental outcomes must equal 1. For $n$ experimental outcomes, this requirement can be written as

$$P(E_1) + P(E_2) + \cdots + P(E_n) = 1 \qquad (4.4)$$

---

The **classical method** of assigning probabilities is appropriate when all the experimental outcomes are equally likely. If $n$ experimental outcomes are possible, a probability of $1/n$ is assigned to each experimental outcome. When using this approach, the two basic requirements for assigning probabilities are automatically satisfied.

For an example, consider the experiment of tossing a fair coin; the two experimental outcomes—head and tail—are equally likely. Because one of the two equally likely outcomes is a head, the probability of observing a head is 1/2, or .50. Similarly, the probability of observing a tail is also 1/2, or .50.

As another example, consider the experiment of rolling a die. It would seem reasonable to conclude that the six possible outcomes are equally likely, and hence each outcome is assigned a probability of 1/6. If $P(1)$ denotes the probability that one dot appears on the upward face of the die, then $P(1) = 1/6$. Similarly, $P(2) = 1/6$, $P(3) = 1/6$, $P(4) = 1/6$, $P(5) = 1/6$, and $P(6) = 1/6$. Note that these probabilities satisfy the two basic requirements of equations (4.3) and (4.4) because each of the probabilities is greater than or equal to zero and they sum to 1.

The **relative frequency method** of assigning probabilities is appropriate when data are available to estimate the proportion of the time the experimental outcome will occur if the experiment is repeated a large number of times. As an example, consider a study of waiting times in the X-ray department for a local hospital. A clerk recorded the number of patients waiting for service at 9:00 A.M. on 20 successive days and obtained the following results.

| Number Waiting | Number of Days Outcome Occurred |
|:---:|:---:|
| 0 | 2 |
| 1 | 5 |
| 2 | 6 |
| 3 | 4 |
| 4 | 3 |
| Total | 20 |

These data show that on 2 of the 20 days, zero patients were waiting for service; on 5 of the days, one patient was waiting for service; and so on. Using the relative frequency method, we would assign a probability of 2/20 = .10 to the experimental outcome of zero patients waiting for service, 5/20 = .25 to the experimental outcome of one patient waiting, 6/20 = .30 to two patients waiting, 4/20 = .20 to three patients waiting, and 3/20 = .15 to four patients waiting. As with the classical method, using the relative frequency method automatically satisfies the two basic requirements of equations (4.3) and (4.4).

The **subjective method** of assigning probabilities is most appropriate when one cannot realistically assume that the experimental outcomes are equally likely and when little relevant data are available. When the subjective method is used to assign probabilities to the experimental outcomes, we may use any information available, such as our experience or intuition. After considering all available information, a probability value that expresses our *degree of belief* (on a scale from 0 to 1) that the experimental outcome will occur is specified. Because subjective probability expresses a person's degree of belief, it is personal. Using the subjective method, different people can be expected to assign different probabilities to the same experimental outcome.

The subjective method requires extra care to ensure that the two basic requirements of equations (4.3) and (4.4) are satisfied. Regardless of a person's degree of belief, the probability value assigned to each experimental outcome must be between 0 and 1, inclusive, and the sum of all the probabilities for the experimental outcomes must equal 1.

Consider the case in which Tom and Judy Elsbernd make an offer to purchase a house. Two outcomes are possible:

$$E_1 = \text{their offer is accepted}$$
$$E_2 = \text{their offer is rejected}$$

Judy believes that the probability that their offer will be accepted is .8; thus, Judy would set $P(E_1) = .8$ and $P(E_2) = .2$. Tom, however, believes that the probability that their offer will be accepted is .6; hence, Tom would set $P(E_1) = .6$ and $P(E_2) = .4$. Note that Tom's probability estimate for $E_1$ reflects a greater pessimism that their offer will be accepted.

*Bayes' theorem (see Section 4.5) provides a means for combining subjectively determined prior probabilities with probabilities obtained by other means to obtain revised, or posterior, probabilities.*

Both Judy and Tom assigned probabilities that satisfy the two basic requirements. The fact that their probability estimates are different emphasizes the personal nature of the subjective method.

Even in business situations where either the classical or the relative frequency approach can be applied, managers may want to provide subjective probability estimates. In such cases, the best probability estimates often are obtained by combining the estimates from the classical or relative frequency approach with subjective probability estimates.

## Probabilities for the KP&L Project

To perform further analysis on the KP&L project, we must develop probabilities for each of the nine experimental outcomes listed in Table 4.1. On the basis of experience and judgment, management concluded that the experimental outcomes were not equally likely. Hence, the classical method of assigning probabilities could not be used. Management then decided to conduct a study of the completion times for similar projects undertaken by KP&L over the past three years. The results of a study of 40 similar projects are summarized in Table 4.2.

After reviewing the results of the study, management decided to employ the relative frequency method of assigning probabilities. Management could have provided subjective probability estimates, but felt that the current project was quite similar to the 40 previous projects. Thus, the relative frequency method was judged best.

In using the data in Table 4.2 to compute probabilities, we note that outcome (2, 6)—stage 1 completed in 2 months and stage 2 completed in 6 months—occurred six times in the 40 projects. We can use the relative frequency method to assign a probability of $6/40 = .15$ to this outcome. Similarly, outcome (2, 7) also occurred in six of the 40 projects, providing a $6/40 = .15$ probability. Continuing in this manner, we obtain the probability assignments for the sample points of the KP&L project shown in Table 4.3. Note that $P(2, 6)$ represents the probability of the sample point (2, 6), $P(2, 7)$ represents the probability of the sample point (2, 7), and so on.

**TABLE 4.2**   COMPLETION RESULTS FOR 40 KP&L PROJECTS

| Completion Time (months) | | | Number of Past Projects Having These |
|---|---|---|---|
| Stage 1 Design | Stage 2 Construction | Sample Point | Completion Times |
| 2 | 6 | (2, 6) | 6 |
| 2 | 7 | (2, 7) | 6 |
| 2 | 8 | (2, 8) | 2 |
| 3 | 6 | (3, 6) | 4 |
| 3 | 7 | (3, 7) | 8 |
| 3 | 8 | (3, 8) | 2 |
| 4 | 6 | (4, 6) | 2 |
| 4 | 7 | (4, 7) | 4 |
| 4 | 8 | (4, 8) | 6 |
| | | Total | 40 |

**TABLE 4.3**   PROBABILITY ASSIGNMENTS FOR THE KP&L PROJECT BASED ON THE RELATIVE FREQUENCY METHOD

| Sample Point | Project Completion Time | Probability of Sample Point |
|---|---|---|
| (2, 6) | 8 months | $P(2, 6) = 6/40 =$ .15 |
| (2, 7) | 9 months | $P(2, 7) = 6/40 =$ .15 |
| (2, 8) | 10 months | $P(2, 8) = 2/40 =$ .05 |
| (3, 6) | 9 months | $P(3, 6) = 4/40 =$ .10 |
| (3, 7) | 10 months | $P(3, 7) = 8/40 =$ .20 |
| (3, 8) | 11 months | $P(3, 8) = 2/40 =$ .05 |
| (4, 6) | 10 months | $P(4, 6) = 2/40 =$ .05 |
| (4, 7) | 11 months | $P(4, 7) = 4/40 =$ .10 |
| (4, 8) | 12 months | $P(4, 8) = 6/40 =$ .15 |
| | | Total              1.00 |

## NOTES AND COMMENTS

1. In statistics, the notion of an experiment differs somewhat from the notion of an experiment in the physical sciences. In the physical sciences, researchers usually conduct an experiment in a laboratory or a controlled environment in order to learn about cause and effect. In statistical experiments, probability determines outcomes. Even though the experiment is repeated in exactly the same way, an entirely different outcome may occur. Because of this influence of probability on the outcome, the experiments of statistics are sometimes called *random experiments*.

2. When drawing a random sample without replacement from a population of size $N$, the counting rule for combinations is used to find the number of different samples of size $n$ that can be selected.

## Exercises

## Methods

1. An experiment has three steps with three outcomes possible for the first step, two outcomes possible for the second step, and four outcomes possible for the third step. How many experimental outcomes exist for the entire experiment?

2. How many ways can three items be selected from a group of six items? Use the letters A, B, C, D, E, and F to identify the items, and list each of the different combinations of three items.

3. How many permutations of three items can be selected from a group of six? Use the letters A, B, C, D, E, and F to identify the items, and list each of the permutations of items B, D, and F.

4. Consider the experiment of tossing a coin three times.
    a. Develop a tree diagram for the experiment.
    b. List the experimental outcomes.
    c. What is the probability for each experimental outcome?

5. Suppose an experiment has five equally likely outcomes: $E_1$, $E_2$, $E_3$, $E_4$, $E_5$. Assign probabilities to each outcome and show that the requirements in equations (4.3) and (4.4) are satisfied. What method did you use?

6. An experiment with three outcomes has been repeated 50 times, and it was learned that $E_1$ occurred 20 times, $E_2$ occurred 13 times, and $E_3$ occurred 17 times. Assign probabilities to the outcomes. What method did you use?

7. A decision maker subjectively assigned the following probabilities to the four outcomes of an experiment: $P(E_1) = .10$, $P(E_2) = .15$, $P(E_3) = .40$, and $P(E_4) = .20$. Are these probability assignments valid? Explain.

## Applications

8. In the city of Milford, applications for zoning changes go through a two-step process: a review by the planning commission and a final decision by the city council. At step 1 the planning commission reviews the zoning change request and makes a positive or negative recommendation concerning the change. At step 2 the city council reviews the planning commission's recommendation and then votes to approve or to disapprove the zoning change. Suppose the developer of an apartment complex submits an application for a zoning change. Consider the application process as an experiment.

   a. How many sample points are there for this experiment? List the sample points.
   b. Construct a tree diagram for the experiment.

9. Simple random sampling uses a sample of size *n* from a population of size *N* to obtain data that can be used to make inferences about the characteristics of a population. Suppose that, from a population of 50 bank accounts, we want to take a random sample of four accounts in order to learn about the population. How many different random samples of four accounts are possible?

10. Many students accumulate debt by the time they graduate from college. Shown in the following table is the percentage of graduates with debt and the average amount of debt for these graduates at four universities and four liberal arts colleges (*U.S. News and World Report, America's Best Colleges,* 2008).

| University | % with Debt | Amount($) | College | % with Debt | Amount($) |
|---|---|---|---|---|---|
| Pace | 72 | 32,980 | Wartburg | 83 | 28,758 |
| Iowa State | 69 | 32,130 | Morehouse | 94 | 27,000 |
| Massachusetts | 55 | 11,227 | Wellesley | 55 | 10,206 |
| SUNY—Albany | 64 | 11,856 | Wofford | 49 | 11,012 |

   a. If you randomly choose a graduate of Morehouse College, what is the probability that this individual graduated with debt?
   b. If you randomly choose one of these eight institutions for a follow-up study on student loans, what is the probability that you will choose an institution with more than 60% of its graduates having debt?
   c. If you randomly choose one of these eight institutions for a follow-up study on student loans, what is the probability that you will choose an institution whose graduates with debts have an average debt of more than $30,000?
   d. What is the probability that a graduate of Pace University does not have debt?
   e. For graduates of Pace University with debt, the average amount of debt is $32,980. Considering all graduates from Pace University, what is the average debt per graduate?

11. The National Occupant Protection Use Survey (NOPUS) was conducted to provide probability-based data on motorcycle helmet use in the United States. The survey was conducted by sending observers to randomly selected roadway sites where they collected data on motorcycle helmet use, including the number of motorcyclists wearing a Department of Transportation (DOT)–compliant helmet (National Highway Traffic Safety Administration website, January 7, 2010). Sample data consistent with the most recent NOPUS are shown below:

| | Type of Helmet | |
|---|---|---|
| **Region** | **DOT-Compliant** | **Noncompliant** |
| Northeast | 96 | 62 |
| Midwest | 86 | 43 |
| South | 92 | 49 |
| West | 76 | 16 |
| Total | 350 | 170 |

a. Use the sample data to compute an estimate of the probability that a motorcyclist wears a DOT-compliant helmet.

b. The probability that a motorcyclist wore a DOT-compliant helmet five years ago was .48, and last year this probability was .63. Would the National Highway Traffic Safety Administration be pleased with the most recent survey results shown above?

c. What is the probability of DOT-compliant helmet use by region of the country? What region has the highest probability of DOT-compliant helmet use?

12. The Powerball lottery is played twice each week in 28 states, the Virgin Islands, and the District of Columbia. To play Powerball a participant must purchase a ticket and then select five numbers from the digits 1 through 55 and a Powerball number from the digits 1 through 42. To determine the winning numbers for each game, lottery officials draw five white balls out of a drum with 55 white balls, and one red ball out of a drum with 42 red balls. To win the jackpot, a participant's numbers must match the numbers on the five white balls in any order and the number on the red Powerball. Eight coworkers at the ConAgra Foods plant in Lincoln, Nebraska, claimed the record $365 million jackpot on February 18, 2006, by matching the numbers 15-17-43-44-49 and the Powerball number 29. A variety of other cash prizes are awarded each time the game is played. For instance, a prize of $200,000 is paid if the participant's five numbers match the numbers on the five white balls (Powerball website, March 19, 2006).

a. Compute the number of ways the first five numbers can be selected.

b. What is the probability of winning a prize of $200,000 by matching the numbers on the five white balls?

c. What is the probability of winning the Powerball jackpot?

13. A company that manufactures toothpaste is studying five different package designs. Assuming that one design is just as likely to be selected by a consumer as any other design, what selection probability would you assign to each of the package designs? In an actual experiment, 100 consumers were asked to pick the design they preferred. The following data were obtained. Do the data confirm the belief that one design is just as likely to be selected as another? Explain.

| Design | Number of Times Preferred |
|--------|---------------------------|
| 1 | 5 |
| 2 | 15 |
| 3 | 30 |
| 4 | 40 |
| 5 | 10 |

## 4.2    Events and Their Probabilities

In the introduction to this chapter we used the term *event* much as it would be used in everyday language. Then, in Section 4.1 we introduced the concept of an experiment and its associated experimental outcomes or sample points. Sample points and events provide the foundation for the study of probability. As a result, we must now introduce the formal definition of an **event** as it relates to sample points. Doing so will provide the basis for determining the probability of an event.

**EVENT**

An event is a collection of sample points.

For an example, let us return to the KP&L project and assume that the project manager is interested in the event that the entire project can be completed in 10 months or less. Referring to Table 4.3, we see that six sample points—(2, 6), (2, 7), (2, 8), (3, 6), (3, 7), and (4, 6)—provide a project completion time of 10 months or less. Let $C$ denote the event that the project is completed in 10 months or less; we write

$$C = \{(2, 6), (2, 7), (2, 8), (3, 6), (3, 7), (4, 6)\}$$

Event $C$ is said to occur if *any one* of these six sample points appears as the experimental outcome.

Other events that might be of interest to KP&L management include the following.

$L$ = The event that the project is completed in *less* than 10 months

$M$ = The event that the project is completed in *more* than 10 months

Using the information in Table 4.3, we see that these events consist of the following sample points.

$$L = \{(2, 6), (2, 7), (3, 6)\}$$
$$M = \{(3, 8), (4, 7), (4, 8)\}$$

A variety of additional events can be defined for the KP&L project, but in each case the event must be identified as a collection of sample points for the experiment.

Given the probabilities of the sample points shown in Table 4.3, we can use the following definition to compute the probability of any event that KP&L management might want to consider.

### PROBABILITY OF AN EVENT

The probability of any event is equal to the sum of the probabilities of the sample points in the event.

Using this definition, we calculate the probability of a particular event by adding the probabilities of the sample points (experimental outcomes) that make up the event. We can now compute the probability that the project will take 10 months or less to complete. Because this event is given by $C = \{(2, 6), (2, 7), (2, 8), (3, 6), (3, 7), (4, 6)\}$, the probability of event $C$, denoted $P(C)$, is given by

$$P(C) = P(2, 6) + P(2, 7) + P(2, 8) + P(3, 6) + P(3, 7) + P(4, 6)$$

Refer to the sample point probabilities in Table 4.3; we have

$$P(C) = .15 + .15 + .05 + .10 + .20 + .05 = .70$$

Similarly, because the event that the project is completed in less than 10 months is given by $L = \{(2, 6), (2, 7), (3, 6)\}$, the probability of this event is given by

$$P(L) = P(2, 6) + P(2, 7) + P(3, 6)$$
$$= .15 + .15 + .10 = .40$$

Finally, for the event that the project is completed in more than 10 months, we have $M = \{(3, 8), (4, 7), (4, 8)\}$ and thus

$$P(M) = P(3, 8) + P(4, 7) + P(4, 8)$$
$$= .05 + .10 + .15 = .30$$

Using these probability results, we can now tell KP&L management that there is a .70 probability that the project will be completed in 10 months or less, a .40 probability that the project will be completed in less than 10 months, and a .30 probability that the project will be completed in more than 10 months. This procedure of computing event probabilities can be repeated for any event of interest to the KP&L management.

Any time that we can identify all the sample points of an experiment and assign probabilities to each, we can compute the probability of an event using the definition. However, in many experiments the large number of sample points makes the identification of the sample points, as well as the determination of their associated probabilities, extremely cumbersome, if not impossible. In the remaining sections of this chapter, we present some basic probability relationships that can be used to compute the probability of an event without knowledge of all the sample point probabilities.

## NOTES AND COMMENTS

1. The sample space, $S$, is an event. Because it contains all the experimental outcomes, it has a probability of 1; that is, $P(S) = 1$.
2. When the classical method is used to assign probabilities, the assumption is that the experimental outcomes are equally likely. In such cases, the probability of an event can be computed by counting the number of experimental outcomes in the event and dividing the result by the total number of experimental outcomes.

## Exercises

## Methods

14. An experiment has four equally likely outcomes: $E_1$, $E_2$, $E_3$, and $E_4$.
    a. What is the probability that $E_2$ occurs?
    b. What is the probability that any two of the outcomes occur (e.g., $E_1$ or $E_3$)?
    c. What is the probability that any three of the outcomes occur (e.g., $E_1$ or $E_2$ or $E_4$)?

15. Consider the experiment of selecting a playing card from a deck of 52 playing cards. Each card corresponds to a sample point with a 1/52 probability.
    a. List the sample points in the event an ace is selected.
    b. List the sample points in the event a club is selected.
    c. List the sample points in the event a face card (jack, queen, or king) is selected.
    d. Find the probabilities associated with each of the events in parts (a), (b), and (c).

16. Consider the experiment of rolling a pair of dice. Suppose that we are interested in the sum of the face values showing on the dice.
    a. How many sample points are possible? (*Hint:* Use the counting rule for multiple-step experiments.)
    b. List the sample points.
    c. What is the probability of obtaining a value of 7?
    d. What is the probability of obtaining a value of 9 or greater?
    e. Because each roll has six possible even values (2, 4, 6, 8, 10, and 12) and only five possible odd values (3, 5, 7, 9, and 11), the dice should show even values more often than odd values. Do you agree with this statement? Explain.
    f. What method did you use to assign the probabilities requested?

## Applications

17. Refer to the KP&L sample points and sample point probabilities in Tables 4.2 and 4.3.
    a.  The design stage (stage 1) will run over budget if it takes four months to complete. List the sample points in the event the design stage is over budget.
    b.  What is the probability that the design stage is over budget?
    c.  The construction stage (stage 2) will run over budget if it takes eight months to complete. List the sample points in the event the construction stage is over budget.
    d.  What is the probability that the construction stage is over budget?
    e.  What is the probability that both stages are over budget?

18. To investigate how often families eat at home, Harris Interactive surveyed 496 adults living with children under the age of 18 (*USA Today,* January 3, 2007). The survey results are shown in the following table.

| Number of Family Meals per Week | Number of Survey Responses |
|---|---|
| 0 | 11 |
| 1 | 11 |
| 2 | 30 |
| 3 | 36 |
| 4 | 36 |
| 5 | 119 |
| 6 | 114 |
| 7 or more | 139 |

For a randomly selected family with children under the age of 18, compute the following.
    a.  The probability the family eats no meals at home during the week
    b.  The probability the family eats at least four meals at home during the week
    c.  The probability the family eats two or fewer meals at home during the week

19. Do you think the government protects investors adequately? This question was part of an online survey of investors aged less than 65 living in the United States and Great Britain (Financial Times/Harris Poll, October 1, 2009). The numbers of investors from the United States and Great Britain who answered Yes, No, or Unsure to this question are provided below.

| Response | United States | Great Britain |
|---|---|---|
| Yes | 187 | 197 |
| No | 334 | 411 |
| Unsure | 256 | 213 |

    a.  Estimate the probability that an investor in the United States thinks the government is not protecting investors adequately.
    b.  Estimate the probability that an investor in Great Britain thinks the government is not protecting investors adequately or is unsure the government is protecting investors adequately.
    c.  For a randomly selected investor from these two countries, estimate the probability that the investor thinks the government is not protecting investors adequately.
    d.  Based on the survey results, does there appear to be much difference between the perceptions of investors in the United States and investors in Great Britain regarding the issue of the government protecting investors adequately?

20. *Fortune* magazine publishes an annual list of the 500 largest companies in the United States. The following data show the five states with the largest number of *Fortune* 500 companies (*The New York Times Almanac*, 2006).

| State | Number of Companies |
|---|---|
| New York | 54 |
| California | 52 |
| Texas | 48 |
| Illinois | 33 |
| Ohio | 30 |

Suppose a *Fortune* 500 company is chosen for a follow-up questionnaire. What are the probabilities of the following events?
a. Let $N$ be the event the company is headquartered in New York. Find $P(N)$.
b. Let $T$ be the event the company is headquartered in Texas. Find $P(T)$.
c. Let $B$ be the event the company is headquartered in one of these five states. Find $P(B)$.

21. The U.S. adult population by age is as follows (*The World Almanac*, 2009). The data are in millions of people.

| Age | Number |
|---|---|
| 18 to 24 | 29.8 |
| 25 to 34 | 40.0 |
| 35 to 44 | 43.4 |
| 45 to 54 | 43.9 |
| 55 to 64 | 32.7 |
| 65 and over | 37.8 |

Assume that a person will be randomly chosen from this population.
a. What is the probability that the person is 18 to 24 years old?
b. What is the probability that the person is 18 to 34 years old?
c. What is the probability that the person is 45 or older?

## 4.3 Some Basic Relationships of Probability

### Complement of an Event

Given an event $A$, the **complement of $A$** is defined to be the event consisting of all sample points that are *not* in $A$. The complement of $A$ is denoted by $A^c$. Figure 4.4 is a diagram, known as a **Venn diagram**, which illustrates the concept of a complement. The rectangular area represents the sample space for the experiment and as such contains all possible sample points. The circle represents event $A$ and contains only the sample points that belong to $A$. The shaded region of the rectangle contains all sample points not in event $A$ and is by definition the complement of $A$.

In any probability application, either event $A$ or its complement $A^c$ must occur. Therefore, we have

$$P(A) + P(A^c) = 1$$

**FIGURE 4.4**   COMPLEMENT OF EVENT *A* IS SHADED

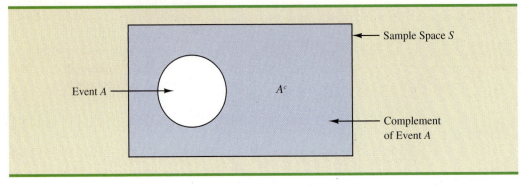

Solving for $P(A)$, we obtain the following result.

---

COMPUTING PROBABILITY USING THE COMPLEMENT

$$P(A) = 1 - P(A^c) \qquad\qquad \text{(4.5)}$$

---

Equation (4.5) shows that the probability of an event *A* can be computed easily if the probability of its complement, $P(A^c)$, is known.

As an example, consider the case of a sales manager who, after reviewing sales reports, states that 80% of new customer contacts result in no sale. By allowing *A* to denote the event of a sale and $A^c$ to denote the event of no sale, the manager is stating that $P(A^c) = .80$. Using equation (4.5), we see that

$$P(A) = 1 - P(A^c) = 1 - .80 = .20$$

We can conclude that a new customer contact has a .20 probability of resulting in a sale.

In another example, a purchasing agent states a .90 probability that a supplier will send a shipment that is free of defective parts. Using the complement, we can conclude that there is a $1 - .90 = .10$ probability that the shipment will contain defective parts.

## Addition Law

The addition law is helpful when we are interested in knowing the probability that at least one of two events occurs. That is, with events *A* and *B* we are interested in knowing the probability that event *A* or event *B* or both occur.

Before we present the addition law, we need to discuss two concepts related to the combination of events: the *union* of events and the *intersection* of events. Given two events *A* and *B*, the **union of *A* and *B*** is defined as follows.

---

UNION OF TWO EVENTS

The *union* of *A* and *B* is the event containing *all* sample points belonging to *A or B or both*. The union is denoted by $A \cup B$.

---

The Venn diagram in Figure 4.5 depicts the union of events *A* and *B*. Note that the two circles contain all the sample points in event *A* as well as all the sample points in event *B*.

**FIGURE 4.5**   UNION OF EVENTS *A* AND *B* IS SHADED

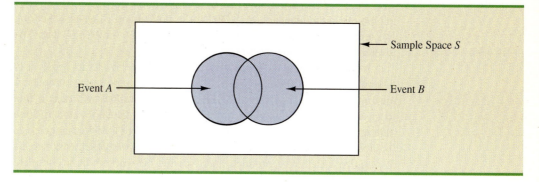

The fact that the circles overlap indicates that some sample points are contained in both *A* and *B*.

The definition of the **intersection of *A* and *B*** follows.

> INTERSECTION OF TWO EVENTS
>
> Given two events *A* and *B*, the *intersection* of *A* and *B* is the event containing the sample points belonging to *both A and B*. The intersection is denoted by $A \cap B$.

The Venn diagram depicting the intersection of events *A* and *B* is shown in Figure 4.6. The area where the two circles overlap is the intersection; it contains the sample points that are in both *A* and *B*.

Let us now continue with a discussion of the addition law. The **addition law** provides a way to compute the probability that event *A* or event *B* or both occur. In other words, the addition law is used to compute the probability of the union of two events. The addition law is written as follows.

> ADDITION LAW
>
> $$P(A \cup B) = P(A) + P(B) - P(A \cap B) \qquad \textbf{(4.6)}$$

**FIGURE 4.6**   INTERSECTION OF EVENTS *A* AND *B* IS SHADED

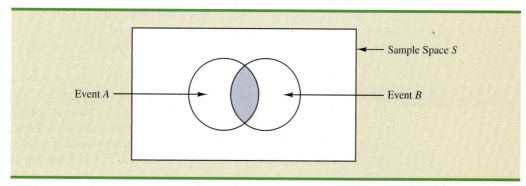

To understand the addition law intuitively, note that the first two terms in the addition law, $P(A) + P(B)$, account for all the sample points in $A \cup B$. However, because the sample points in the intersection $A \cap B$ are in both $A$ and $B$, when we compute $P(A) + P(B)$, we are in effect counting each of the sample points in $A \cap B$ twice. We correct for this overcounting by subtracting $P(A \cap B)$.

As an example of an application of the addition law, let us consider the case of a small assembly plant with 50 employees. Each worker is expected to complete work assignments on time and in such a way that the assembled product will pass a final inspection. On occasion, some of the workers fail to meet the performance standards by completing work late or assembling a defective product. At the end of a performance evaluation period, the production manager found that 5 of the 50 workers completed work late, 6 of the 50 workers assembled a defective product, and 2 of the 50 workers both completed work late *and* assembled a defective product.

Let

$$L = \text{the event that the work is completed late}$$
$$D = \text{the event that the assembled product is defective}$$

The relative frequency information leads to the following probabilities.

$$P(L) = \frac{5}{50} = .10$$

$$P(D) = \frac{6}{50} = .12$$

$$P(L \cap D) = \frac{2}{50} = .04$$

After reviewing the performance data, the production manager decided to assign a poor performance rating to any employee whose work was either late or defective; thus the event of interest is $L \cup D$. What is the probability that the production manager assigned an employee a poor performance rating?

Note that the probability question is about the union of two events. Specifically, we want to know $P(L \cup D)$. Using equation (4.6), we have

$$P(L \cup D) = P(L) + P(D) - P(L \cap D)$$

Knowing values for the three probabilities on the right side of this expression, we can write

$$P(L \cup D) = .10 + .12 - .04 = .18$$

This calculation tells us that there is a .18 probability that a randomly selected employee received a poor performance rating.

As another example of the addition law, consider a recent study conducted by the personnel manager of a major computer software company. The study showed that 30% of the employees who left the firm within two years did so primarily because they were dissatisfied with their salary, 20% left because they were dissatisfied with their work assignments, and 12% of the former employees indicated dissatisfaction with *both* their salary and their work assignments. What is the probability that an employee who leaves within two years does so because of dissatisfaction with salary, dissatisfaction with the work assignment, or both?

Let

$$S = \text{the event that the employee leaves because of salary}$$
$$W = \text{the event that the employee leaves because of work assignment}$$

We have $P(S) = .30$, $P(W) = .20$, and $P(S \cap W) = .12$. Using equation (4.6), the addition law, we have

$$P(S \cup W) = P(S) + P(W) - P(S \cap W) = .30 + .20 - .12 = .38$$

We find a .38 probability that an employee leaves for salary or work assignment reasons.

Before we conclude our discussion of the addition law, let us consider a special case that arises for **mutually exclusive events**.

---

**MUTUALLY EXCLUSIVE EVENTS**

Two events are said to be mutually exclusive if the events have no sample points in common.

---

Events $A$ and $B$ are mutually exclusive if, when one event occurs, the other cannot occur. Thus, a requirement for $A$ and $B$ to be mutually exclusive is that their intersection must contain no sample points. The Venn diagram depicting two mutually exclusive events $A$ and $B$ is shown in Figure 4.7. In this case $P(A \cap B) = 0$ and the addition law can be written as follows.

---

**ADDITION LAW FOR MUTUALLY EXCLUSIVE EVENTS**

$$P(A \cup B) = P(A) + P(B)$$

---

**FIGURE 4.7**   MUTUALLY EXCLUSIVE EVENTS

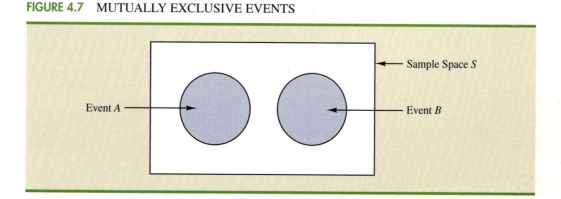

## Exercises

### Methods

22. Suppose that we have a sample space with five equally likely experimental outcomes: $E_1$, $E_2$, $E_3$, $E_4$, $E_5$. Let

$$A = \{E_1, E_2\}$$
$$B = \{E_3, E_4\}$$
$$C = \{E_2, E_3, E_5\}$$

   a. Find $P(A)$, $P(B)$, and $P(C)$.
   b. Find $P(A \cup B)$. Are $A$ and $B$ mutually exclusive?
   c. Find $A^c$, $C^c$, $P(A^c)$, and $P(C^c)$.
   d. Find $A \cup B^c$ and $P(A \cup B^c)$.
   e. Find $P(B \cup C)$.

23. Suppose that we have a sample space $S = \{E_1, E_2, E_3, E_4, E_5, E_6, E_7\}$, where $E_1, E_2, \ldots,$ $E_7$ denote the sample points. The following probability assignments apply: $P(E_1) = .05$, $P(E_2) = .20$, $P(E_3) = .20$, $P(E_4) = .25$, $P(E_5) = .15$, $P(E_6) = .10$, and $P(E_7) = .05$. Let

$$A = \{E_1, E_4, E_6\}$$
$$B = \{E_2, E_4, E_7\}$$
$$C = \{E_2, E_3, E_5, E_7\}$$

   a. Find $P(A)$, $P(B)$, and $P(C)$.
   b. Find $A \cup B$ and $P(A \cup B)$.
   c. Find $A \cap B$ and $P(A \cap B)$.
   d. Are events $A$ and $C$ mutually exclusive?
   e. Find $B^c$ and $P(B^c)$.

### Applications

24. Clarkson University surveyed alumni to learn more about what they think of Clarkson. One part of the survey asked respondents to indicate whether their overall experience at Clarkson fell short of expectations, met expectations, or surpassed expectations. The results showed that 4% of the respondents did not provide a response, 26% said that their experience fell short of expectations, and 65% of the respondents said that their experience met expectations.
   a. If we chose an alumnus at random, what is the probability that the alumnus would say their experience *surpassed* expectations?
   b. If we chose an alumnus at random, what is the probability that the alumnus would say their experience met or surpassed expectations?

25. The U.S. Census Bureau provides data on the number of young adults, ages 18–24, who are living in their parents' home.[1] Let

   $M$ = the event a male young adult is living in his parents' home

   $F$ = the event a female young adult is living in her parents' home

   If we randomly select a male young adult and a female young adult, the Census Bureau data enable us to conclude $P(M) = .56$ and $P(F) = .42$ (*The World Almanac*, 2006). The probability that both are living in their parents' home is .24.
   a. What is the probability at least one of the two young adults selected is living in his or her parents' home?
   b. What is the probability both young adults selected are living on their own (neither is living in their parents' home)?

---

[1]The data include single young adults who are living in college dormitories because it is assumed these young adults will return to their parents' home when school is not in session.

26. Information about mutual funds provided by Morningstar Investment Research includes the type of mutual fund (Domestic Equity, International Equity, or Fixed Income) and the Morningstar rating for the fund. The rating is expressed from 1-star (lowest rating) to 5-star (highest rating). A sample of 25 mutual funds was selected from *Morningstar Funds 500* (2008). The following counts were obtained:
    - Sixteen mutual funds were Domestic Equity funds.
    - Thirteen mutual funds were rated 3-star or less.
    - Seven of the Domestic Equity funds were rated 4-star.
    - Two of the Domestic Equity funds were rated 5-star.

    Assume that one of these 25 mutual funds will be randomly selected in order to learn more about the mutual fund and its investment strategy.
    a. What is the probability of selecting a Domestic Equity fund?
    b. What is the probability of selecting a fund with a 4-star or 5-star rating?
    c. What is the probability of selecting a fund that is both a Domestic Equity fund *and* a fund with a 4-star or 5-star rating?
    d. What is the probability of selecting a fund that is a Domestic Equity fund *or* a fund with a 4-star or 5-star rating?

27. What NCAA college basketball conferences have the higher probability of having a team play in college basketball's national championship game? Over the last 20 years, the Atlantic Coast Conference (ACC) ranks first by having a team in the championship game 10 times. The Southeastern Conference (SEC) ranks second by having a team in the championship game 8 times. However, these two conferences have both had teams in the championship game only one time, when Arkansas (SEC) beat Duke (ACC) 76–70 in 1994 (NCAA website, April 2009). Use these data to estimate the following probabilities.
    a. What is the probability the ACC will have a team in the championship game?
    b. What is the probability the SEC will have team in the championship game?
    c. What is the probability the ACC and SEC will both have teams in the championship game?
    d. What is the probability at least one team from these two conferences will be in the championship game? That is, what is the probability a team from the ACC or SEC will play in the championship game?
    e. What is the probability that the championship game will not a have team from one of these two conferences?

28. A survey of magazine subscribers showed that 45.8% rented a car during the past 12 months for business reasons, 54% rented a car during the past 12 months for personal reasons, and 30% rented a car during the past 12 months for both business and personal reasons.
    a. What is the probability that a subscriber rented a car during the past 12 months for business or personal reasons?
    b. What is the probability that a subscriber did not rent a car during the past 12 months for either business or personal reasons?

29. High school seniors with strong academic records apply to the nation's most selective colleges in greater numbers each year. Because the number of slots remains relatively stable, some colleges reject more early applicants. Suppose that for a recent admissions class, an Ivy League college received 2851 applications for early admission. Of this group, it admitted 1033 students early, rejected 854 outright, and deferred 964 to the regular admission pool for further consideration. In the past, this school has admitted 18% of the deferred early admission applicants during the regular admission process. Counting the students admitted early and the students admitted during the regular admission process, the total class size was 2375. Let $E, R,$ and $D$ represent the events that a student who applies for early admission is admitted early, rejected outright, or deferred to the regular admissions pool.
    a. Use the data to estimate $P(E)$, $P(R)$, and $P(D)$.
    b. Are events $E$ and $D$ mutually exclusive? Find $P(E \cap D)$.

    c. For the 2375 students that were admitted, what is the probability that a randomly selected student was accepted during early admission?

    d. Suppose a student applies for early admission. What is the probability that the student will be admitted for early admission or be deferred and later admitted during the regular admission process?

## 4.4 Conditional Probability

Often, the probability of an event is influenced by whether a related event already occurred. Suppose we have an event $A$ with probability $P(A)$. If we obtain new information and learn that a related event, denoted by $B$, already occurred, we will want to take advantage of this information by calculating a new probability for event $A$. This new probability of event $A$ is called a **conditional probability** and is written $P(A \mid B)$. We use the notation $|$ to indicate that we are considering the probability of event $A$ *given* the condition that event $B$ has occurred. Hence, the notation $P(A \mid B)$ reads "the probability of $A$ given $B$."

As an illustration of the application of conditional probability, consider the situation of the promotion status of male and female officers of a major metropolitan police force in the eastern United States. The police force consists of 1200 officers, 960 men and 240 women. Over the past two years, 324 officers on the police force received promotions. The specific breakdown of promotions for male and female officers is shown in Table 4.4.

After reviewing the promotion record, a committee of female officers raised a discrimination case on the basis that 288 male officers had received promotions but only 36 female officers had received promotions. The police administration argued that the relatively low number of promotions for female officers was due not to discrimination, but to the fact that relatively few females are members of the police force. Let us show how conditional probability could be used to analyze the discrimination charge.

Let

$$M = \text{event an officer is a man}$$
$$W = \text{event an officer is a woman}$$
$$A = \text{event an officer is promoted}$$
$$A^c = \text{event an officer is not promoted}$$

Dividing the data values in Table 4.4 by the total of 1200 officers enables us to summarize the available information with the following probability values.

$$P(M \cap A) = 288/1200 = .24 \quad \text{probability that a randomly selected officer is a man } and \text{ is promoted}$$

$$P(M \cap A^c) = 672/1200 = .56 \quad \text{probability that a randomly selected officer is a man } and \text{ is not promoted}$$

**TABLE 4.4** PROMOTION STATUS OF POLICE OFFICERS OVER THE PAST TWO YEARS

|  | Men | Women | Total |
|---|---|---|---|
| **Promoted** | 288 | 36 | 324 |
| **Not Promoted** | 672 | 204 | 876 |
| **Total** | 960 | 240 | 1200 |

**TABLE 4.5   JOINT PROBABILITY TABLE FOR PROMOTIONS**

Joint probabilities appear in the body of the table.

|  | Men (*M*) | Women (*W*) | Total |
|---|---|---|---|
| **Promoted (*A*)** | .24 | .03 | .27 |
| **Not Promoted (*A^c^*)** | .56 | .17 | .73 |
| **Total** | .80 | .20 | 1.00 |

Marginal probabilities appear in the margins of the table.

$$P(W \cap A) = 36/1200 \;\; = .03 \text{ probability that a randomly selected officer}$$
$$\text{is a woman } and \text{ is promoted}$$
$$P(W \cap A^c) = 204/1200 = .17 \text{ probability that a randomly selected officer}$$
$$\text{is a woman } and \text{ is not promoted}$$

Because each of these values gives the probability of the intersection of two events, the probabilities are called **joint probabilities**. Table 4.5, which provides a summary of the probability information for the police officer promotion situation, is referred to as a *joint probability table*.

The values in the margins of the joint probability table provide the probabilities of each event separately. That is, $P(M) = .80$, $P(W) = .20$, $P(A) = .27$, and $P(A^c) = .73$. These probabilities are referred to as **marginal probabilities** because of their location in the margins of the joint probability table. We note that the marginal probabilities are found by summing the joint probabilities in the corresponding row or column of the joint probability table. For instance, the marginal probability of being promoted is $P(A) = P(M \cap A) + P(W \cap A) = .24 + .03 = .27$. From the marginal probabilities, we see that 80% of the force is male, 20% of the force is female, 27% of all officers received promotions, and 73% were not promoted.

Let us begin the conditional probability analysis by computing the probability that an officer is promoted given that the officer is a man. In conditional probability notation, we are attempting to determine $P(A \mid M)$. To calculate $P(A \mid M)$, we first realize that this notation simply means that we are considering the probability of the event $A$ (promotion) given that the condition designated as event $M$ (the officer is a man) is known to exist. Thus $P(A \mid M)$ tells us that we are now concerned only with the promotion status of the 960 male officers. Because 288 of the 960 male officers received promotions, the probability of being promoted given that the officer is a man is 288/960 = .30. In other words, given that an officer is a man, that officer had a 30% chance of receiving a promotion over the past two years.

This procedure was easy to apply because the values in Table 4.4 show the number of officers in each category. We now want to demonstrate how conditional probabilities such as $P(A \mid M)$ can be computed directly from related event probabilities rather than the frequency data of Table 4.4.

We have shown that $P(A \mid M) = 288/960 = .30$. Let us now divide both the numerator and denominator of this fraction by 1200, the total number of officers in the study.

$$P(A \mid M) = \frac{288}{960} = \frac{288/1200}{960/1200} = \frac{.24}{.80} = .30$$

We now see that the conditional probability $P(A \mid M)$ can be computed as .24/.80. Refer to the joint probability table (Table 4.5). Note in particular that .24 is the joint probability of

$A$ and $M$; that is, $P(A \cap M) = .24$. Also note that .80 is the marginal probability that a randomly selected officer is a man; that is, $P(M) = .80$. Thus, the conditional probability $P(A \mid M)$ can be computed as the ratio of the joint probability $P(A \cap M)$ to the marginal probability $P(M)$.

$$P(A \mid M) = \frac{P(A \cap M)}{P(M)} = \frac{.24}{.80} = .30$$

The fact that conditional probabilities can be computed as the ratio of a joint probability to a marginal probability provides the following general formula for conditional probability calculations for two events $A$ and $B$.

**CONDITIONAL PROBABILITY**

$$P(A \mid B) = \frac{P(A \cap B)}{P(B)} \tag{4.7}$$

or

$$P(B \mid A) = \frac{P(A \cap B)}{P(A)} \tag{4.8}$$

The Venn diagram in Figure 4.8 is helpful in obtaining an intuitive understanding of conditional probability. The circle on the right shows that event $B$ has occurred; the portion of the circle that overlaps with event $A$ denotes the event $(A \cap B)$. We know that once event $B$ has occurred, the only way that we can also observe event $A$ is for the event $(A \cap B)$ to occur. Thus, the ratio $P(A \cap B)/P(B)$ provides the conditional probability that we will observe event $A$ given that event $B$ has already occurred.

Let us return to the issue of discrimination against the female officers. The marginal probability in row 1 of Table 4.5 shows that the probability of promotion of an officer is $P(A) = .27$ (regardless of whether that officer is male or female). However, the critical issue in the discrimination case involves the two conditional probabilities $P(A \mid M)$ and $P(A \mid W)$. That is, what is the probability of a promotion *given* that the officer is a man, and what is the probability of a promotion *given* that the officer is a woman? If these two probabilities are equal, a discrimination argument has no basis because the chances of a promotion are the same for male and female officers. However, a difference in the two conditional probabilities will support the position that male and female officers are treated differently in promotion decisions.

**FIGURE 4.8**   CONDITIONAL PROBABILITY $P(A \mid B) = P(A \cap B)/P(B)$

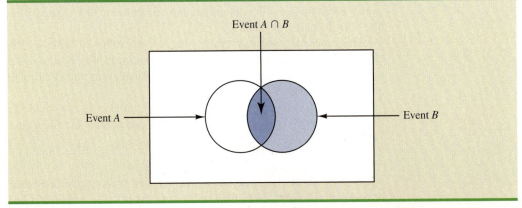

We already determined that $P(A \mid M) = .30$. Let us now use the probability values in Table 4.5 and the basic relationship of conditional probability in equation (4.7) to compute the probability that an officer is promoted given that the officer is a woman; that is, $P(A \mid W)$. Using equation (4.7), with $W$ replacing $B$, we obtain

$$P(A \mid W) = \frac{P(A \cap W)}{P(W)} = \frac{.03}{.20} = .15$$

What conclusion do you draw? The probability of a promotion given that the officer is a man is .30, twice the .15 probability of a promotion given that the officer is a woman. Although the use of conditional probability does not in itself prove that discrimination exists in this case, the conditional probability values support the argument presented by the female officers.

## Independent Events

In the preceding illustration, $P(A) = .27$, $P(A \mid M) = .30$, and $P(A \mid W) = .15$. We see that the probability of a promotion (event $A$) is affected or influenced by whether the officer is a man or a woman. Particularly, because $P(A \mid M) \neq P(A)$, we would say that events $A$ and $M$ are dependent events. That is, the probability of event $A$ (promotion) is altered or affected by knowing that event $M$ (the officer is a man) exists. Similarly, with $P(A \mid W) \neq P(A)$, we would say that events $A$ and $W$ are *dependent events*. However, if the probability of event $A$ is not changed by the existence of event $M$—that is, $P(A \mid M) = P(A)$—we would say that events $A$ and $M$ are **independent events**. This situation leads to the following definition of the independence of two events.

INDEPENDENT EVENTS

Two events $A$ and $B$ are independent if

$$P(A \mid B) = P(A) \tag{4.9}$$

or

$$P(B \mid A) = P(B) \tag{4.10}$$

Otherwise, the events are dependent.

## Multiplication Law

Whereas the addition law of probability is used to compute the probability of a union of two events, the multiplication law is used to compute the probability of the intersection of two events. The multiplication law is based on the definition of conditional probability. Using equations (4.7) and (4.8) and solving for $P(A \cap B)$, we obtain the **multiplication law**.

MULTIPLICATION LAW

$$P(A \cap B) = P(B)P(A \mid B) \tag{4.11}$$

or

$$P(A \cap B) = P(A)P(B \mid A) \tag{4.12}$$

To illustrate the use of the multiplication law, consider a newspaper circulation department where it is known that 84% of the households in a particular neighborhood subscribe to the daily edition of the paper. If we let $D$ denote the event that a household subscribes to the daily edition, $P(D) = .84$. In addition, it is known that the probability that a household that already holds a daily subscription also subscribes to the Sunday edition (event $S$) is .75; that is, $P(S \mid D) = .75$. What is the probability that a household subscribes to both the Sunday and daily editions of the newspaper? Using the multiplication law, we compute the desired $P(S \cap D)$ as

$$P(S \cap D) = P(D)P(S \mid D) = .84(.75) = .63$$

We now know that 63% of the households subscribe to both the Sunday and daily editions.

Before concluding this section, let us consider the special case of the multiplication law when the events involved are independent. Recall that events $A$ and $B$ are independent whenever $P(A \mid B) = P(A)$ or $P(B \mid A) = P(B)$. Hence, using equations (4.11) and (4.12) for the special case of independent events, we obtain the following multiplication law.

---

MULTIPLICATION LAW FOR INDEPENDENT EVENTS

$$P(A \cap B) = P(A)P(B) \qquad \textbf{(4.13)}$$

---

To compute the probability of the intersection of two independent events, we simply multiply the corresponding probabilities. Note that the multiplication law for independent events provides another way to determine whether $A$ and $B$ are independent. That is, if $P(A \cap B) = P(A)P(B)$, then $A$ and $B$ are independent; if $P(A \cap B) \neq P(A)P(B)$, then $A$ and $B$ are dependent.

As an application of the multiplication law for independent events, consider the situation of a service station manager who knows from past experience that 80% of the customers use a credit card when they purchase gasoline. What is the probability that the next two customers purchasing gasoline will each use a credit card? If we let

$$A = \text{the event that the first customer uses a credit card}$$
$$B = \text{the event that the second customer uses a credit card}$$

then the event of interest is $A \cap B$. Given no other information, we can reasonably assume that $A$ and $B$ are independent events. Thus,

$$P(A \cap B) = P(A)P(B) = (.80)(.80) = .64$$

To summarize this section, we note that our interest in conditional probability is motivated by the fact that events are often related. In such cases, we say the events are dependent and the conditional probability formulas in equations (4.7) and (4.8) must be used to compute the event probabilities. If two events are not related, they are independent; in this case neither event's probability is affected by whether the other event occurred.

## NOTES AND COMMENTS

Do not confuse the notion of mutually exclusive events with that of independent events. Two events with nonzero probabilities cannot be both mutually exclusive and independent. If one mutually exclusive event is known to occur, the other cannot occur; thus, the probability of the other event occurring is reduced to zero. They are therefore dependent.

## Exercises

### Methods

30. Suppose that we have two events, $A$ and $B$, with $P(A) = .50$, $P(B) = .60$, and $P(A \cap B) = .40$.
    a.  Find $P(A \mid B)$.
    b.  Find $P(B \mid A)$.
    c.  Are $A$ and $B$ independent? Why or why not?

31. Assume that we have two events, A and B, that are mutually exclusive. Assume further that we know P(A) = .30 and P(B) = .40.
    a.  What is P(A ∩ B)?
    b.  What is P(A | B)?
    c.  A student in statistics argues that the concepts of mutually exclusive events and independent events are really the same, and that if events are mutually exclusive they must be independent. Do you agree with this statement? Use the probability information in this problem to justify your answer.
    d.  What general conclusion would you make about mutually exclusive and independent events given the results of this problem?

## Applications

32. The automobile industry sold 657,000 vehicles in the United States during January 2009 (*The Wall Street Journal,* February 4, 2009). This volume was down 37% from January 2008 as economic conditions continued to decline. The Big Three U.S. automakers—General Motors, Ford, and Chrysler—sold 280,500 vehicles, down 48% from January 2008. A summary of sales by automobile manufacturer and type of vehicle sold is shown in the following table. Data are in thousands of vehicles. The non-U.S. manufacturers are led by Toyota, Honda, and Nissan. The category Light Truck includes pickup, minivan, SUV, and crossover models.

|  |  | Type of Vehicle | |
| --- | --- | --- | --- |
|  |  | Car | Light Truck |
| **Manufacturer** | U.S. | 87.4 | 193.1 |
|  | Non-U.S. | 228.5 | 148.0 |

    a.  Develop a joint probability table for these data and use the table to answer the remaining questions.
    b.  What are the marginal probabilities? What do they tell you about the probabilities associated with the manufacturer and the type of vehicle sold?
    c.  If a vehicle was manufactured by one of the U.S. automakers, what is the probability that the vehicle was a car? What is the probability that it was a light truck?
    d.  If a vehicle was not manufactured by one of the U.S. automakers, what is the probability that the vehicle was a car? What is the probability that it was a light truck?
    e.  If the vehicle was a light truck, what is the probability that it was manufactured by one of the U.S. automakers?
    f.  What does the probability information tell you about sales?

33. In a survey of MBA students, the following data were obtained on "students' first reason for application to the school in which they matriculated."

|  |  | Reason for Application | | | |
| --- | --- | --- | --- | --- | --- |
|  |  | School Quality | School Cost or Convenience | Other | Totals |
| **Enrollment** | **Full Time** | 421 | 393 | 76 | 890 |
| **Status** | **Part Time** | 400 | 593 | 46 | 1039 |
|  | Totals | 821 | 986 | 122 | 1929 |

    a.  Develop a joint probability table for these data.
    b.  Use the marginal probabilities of school quality, school cost or convenience, and other to comment on the most important reason for choosing a school.

    c.   If a student goes full time, what is the probability that school quality is the first reason for choosing a school?

    d.   If a student goes part time, what is the probability that school quality is the first reason for choosing a school?

    e.   Let *A* denote the event that a student is full time and let *B* denote the event that the student lists school quality as the first reason for applying. Are events *A* and *B* independent? Justify your answer.

34. The U.S. Department of Transportation reported that during November, 83.4% of Southwest Airlines' flights, 75.1% of US Airways' flights, and 70.1% of JetBlue's flights arrived on time (*USA Today,* January 4, 2007). Assume that this on-time performance is applicable for flights arriving at concourse A of the Rochester International Airport, and that 40% of the arrivals at concourse A are Southwest Airlines flights, 35% are US Airways flights, and 25% are JetBlue flights.

    a.   Develop a joint probability table with three rows (airlines) and two columns (on-time arrivals vs. late arrivals).

    b.   An announcement has just been made that Flight 1424 will be arriving at gate 20 in concourse A. What is the most likely airline for this arrival?

    c.   What is the probability that Flight 1424 will arrive on time?

    d.   Suppose that an announcement is made saying that Flight 1424 will be arriving late. What is the most likely airline for this arrival? What is the least likely airline?

35. According to the Ameriprise Financial Money Across Generations study, 9 out of 10 parents with adult children ages 20 to 35 have helped their adult children with some type of financial assistance ranging from college, a car, rent, utilities, credit-card debt, and/or down payments for houses (*Money,* January 2009). The following table, with sample data consistent with the study, shows the number of times parents have given their adult children financial assistance to buy a car and to pay rent.

|  |  | **Pay Rent** | |
|---|---|:---:|:---:|
|  |  | **Yes** | **No** |
| **Buy a Car** | **Yes** | 56 | 52 |
|  | **No** | 14 | 78 |

    a.   Develop a joint probability table and use it to answer the remaining questions.

    b.   Using the marginal probabilities for buy a car and pay rent, are parents more likely to assist their adult children with buying a car or paying rent? What is your interpretation of the marginal probabilities?

    c.   If parents provided financial assistance to buy a car, what it the probability that the parents assisted with paying rent?

    d.   If parents did not provide financial assistance to buy a car, what is the probability that the parents assisted with paying rent?

    e.   Is financial assistance to buy a car independent of financial assistance to pay rent? Use probabilities to justify your answer.

    f.   What is the probability that parents provided financial assistance for their adult children by either helping buy a car or pay rent?

36. Jerry Stackhouse of the National Basketball Association's Dallas Mavericks is the best free-throw shooter on the team, making 89% of his shots (ESPN website, July, 2008). Assume that late in a basketball game, Jerry Stackhouse is fouled and is awarded two shots.

    a.   What is the probability that he will make both shots?

    b.   What is the probability that he will make at least one shot?

    c.   What is the probability that he will miss both shots?

d. Late in a basketball game, a team often intentionally fouls an opposing player in order to stop the game clock. The usual strategy is to intentionally foul the other team's worst free-throw shooter. Assume that the Dallas Mavericks' center makes 58% of his free-throw shots. Calculate the probabilities for the center as shown in parts (a), (b), and (c), and show that intentionally fouling the Dallas Mavericks' center is a better strategy than intentionally fouling Jerry Stackhouse.

37. Visa Card USA studied how frequently young consumers, ages 18 to 24, use plastic (debit and credit) cards in making purchases (Associated Press, January 16, 2006). The results of the study provided the following probabilities.
    - The probability that a consumer uses a plastic card when making a purchase is .37.
    - Given that the consumer uses a plastic card, there is a .19 probability that the consumer is 18 to 24 years old.
    - Given that the consumer uses a plastic card, there is a .81 probability that the consumer is more than 24 years old.

    U.S. Census Bureau data show that 14% of the consumer population is 18 to 24 years old.
    a. Given that the consumer is 18 to 24 years old, what is the probability that the consumer uses a plastic card?
    b. Given that the consumer is over 24 years old, what is the probability that the consumer uses a plastic card?
    c. What is the interpretation of the probabilities shown in parts (a) and (b)?
    d. Should companies such as Visa, MasterCard, and Discover make plastic cards available to the 18- to 24-year-old age group before these consumers have had time to establish a credit history? If no, why? If yes, what restrictions might the companies place on this age group?

38. Students in grades 3 through 8 in New York State are required to take a state mathematics exam. To meet the state's proficiency standards, a student must demonstrate an understanding of the mathematics expected at his or her grade level. The following data show the number of students tested in the New York City school system for grades 3 through 8 and the number who met and did not meet the proficiency standards on the exam (New York City Department of Education website, January 16, 2010).

|       | Met Proficiency Standards? | |
|-------|-------|-------|
| Grade | Yes | No |
| 3 | 47,401 | 23,975 |
| 4 | 35,020 | 34,740 |
| 5 | 36,062 | 33,540 |
| 6 | 36,361 | 32,929 |
| 7 | 40,945 | 29,768 |
| 8 | 40,720 | 31,931 |

a. Develop a joint probability table for these data.
b. What are the marginal probabilities? What do they tell about the probabilities of a student meeting or not meeting the proficiency standards on the exam?
c. If a randomly selected student is a third grader, what is the probability that the student met the proficiency standards? If the student is a fourth grader, what is the probability that the student met the proficiency standards?
d. If a randomly selected student is known to have met the proficiency standards on the exam, what is the probability that the student is a third grader? What is the probability if the student is a fourth grader?

# 4.5 Bayes' Theorem

In the discussion of conditional probability, we indicated that revising probabilities when new information is obtained is an important phase of probability analysis. Often, we begin the analysis with initial or **prior probability** estimates for specific events of interest. Then, from sources such as a sample, a special report, or a product test, we obtain additional information about the events. Given this new information, we update the prior probability values by calculating revised probabilities, referred to as **posterior probabilities**. **Bayes' theorem** provides a means for making these probability calculations. The steps in this probability revision process are shown in Figure 4.9.

As an application of Bayes' theorem, consider a manufacturing firm that receives shipments of parts from two different suppliers. Let $A_1$ denote the event that a part is from supplier 1 and $A_2$ denote the event that a part is from supplier 2. Currently, 65% of the parts purchased by the company are from supplier 1 and the remaining 35% are from supplier 2. Hence, if a part is selected at random, we would assign the prior probabilities $P(A_1) = .65$ and $P(A_2) = .35$.

The quality of the purchased parts varies with the source of supply. Historical data suggest that the quality ratings of the two suppliers are as shown in Table 4.6. If we let $G$ denote the event that a part is good and $B$ denote the event that a part is bad, the information in Table 4.6 provides the following conditional probability values.

$$P(G \mid A_1) = .98 \quad P(B \mid A_1) = .02$$
$$P(G \mid A_2) = .95 \quad P(B \mid A_2) = .05$$

The tree diagram in Figure 4.10 depicts the process of the firm receiving a part from one of the two suppliers and then discovering that the part is good or bad as a two-step experiment. We see that four experimental outcomes are possible; two correspond to the part being good and two correspond to the part being bad.

Each of the experimental outcomes is the intersection of two events, so we can use the multiplication rule to compute the probabilities. For instance,

$$P(A_1, G) = P(A_1 \cap G) = P(A_1)P(G \mid A_1)$$

The process of computing these joint probabilities can be depicted in what is called a probability tree (see Figure 4.11). From left to right through the tree, the probabilities

**FIGURE 4.9**   PROBABILITY REVISION USING BAYES' THEOREM

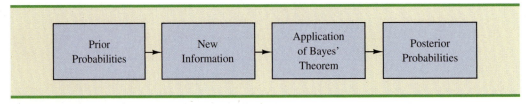

**TABLE 4.6**   HISTORICAL QUALITY LEVELS OF TWO SUPPLIERS

|  | Percentage Good Parts | Percentage Bad Parts |
|---|---|---|
| **Supplier 1** | 98 | 2 |
| **Supplier 2** | 95 | 5 |

**FIGURE 4.10** TREE DIAGRAM FOR TWO-SUPPLIER EXAMPLE

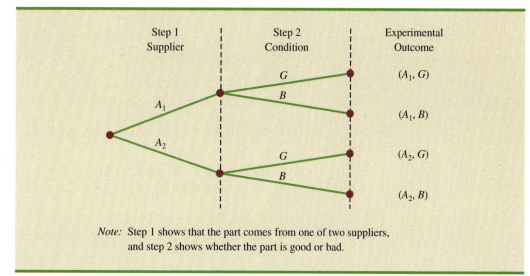

Note: Step 1 shows that the part comes from one of two suppliers, and step 2 shows whether the part is good or bad.

**FIGURE 4.11** PROBABILITY TREE FOR TWO-SUPPLIER EXAMPLE

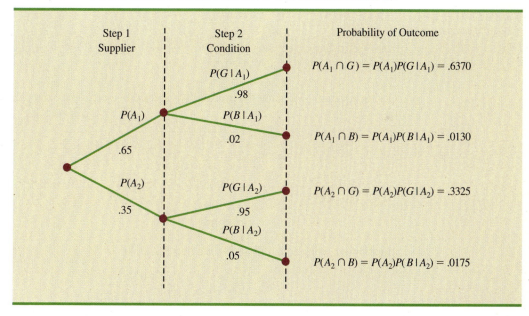

for each branch at step 1 are prior probabilities and the probabilities for each branch at step 2 are conditional probabilities. To find the probabilities of each experimental outcome, we simply multiply the probabilities on the branches leading to the outcome. Each of these joint probabilities is shown in Figure 4.11 along with the known probabilities for each branch.

Suppose now that the parts from the two suppliers are used in the firm's manufacturing process and that a machine breaks down because it attempts to process a bad part. Given the information that the part is bad, what is the probability that it came from supplier 1 and what is the probability that it came from supplier 2? With the information in the probability tree (Figure 4.11), Bayes' theorem can be used to answer these questions.

Because $B$ denotes the event that a part is bad, we are looking for the posterior probabilities $P(A_1 \mid B)$ and $P(A_2 \mid B)$. From the law of conditional probability, we know that

$$P(A_1 \mid B) = \frac{P(A_1 \cap B)}{P(B)} \qquad \textbf{(4.14)}$$

Referring to the probability tree, we see that

$$P(A_1 \cap B) = P(A_1)P(B \mid A_1) \qquad \textbf{(4.15)}$$

To find $P(B)$, we note that event $B$ can occur in only two ways: $(A_1 \cap B)$ and $(A_2 \cap B)$. Therefore, we have

$$\begin{aligned} P(B) &= P(A_1 \cap B) + P(A_2 \cap B) \\ &= P(A_1)P(B \mid A_1) + P(A_2)P(B \mid A_2) \end{aligned} \qquad \textbf{(4.16)}$$

Substituting from equations (4.15) and (4.16) into equation (4.14) and writing a similar result for $P(A_2 \mid B)$, we obtain Bayes' theorem for the case of two events.

*The Reverend Thomas Bayes (1702–1761), a Presbyterian minister, is credited with the original work leading to the version of Bayes' theorem in use today.*

**BAYES' THEOREM (TWO-EVENT CASE)**

$$P(A_1 \mid B) = \frac{P(A_1)P(B \mid A_1)}{P(A_1)P(B \mid A_1) + P(A_2)P(B \mid A_2)} \qquad \textbf{(4.17)}$$

$$P(A_2 \mid B) = \frac{P(A_2)P(B \mid A_2)}{P(A_1)P(B \mid A_1) + P(A_2)P(B \mid A_2)} \qquad \textbf{(4.18)}$$

Using equation (4.17) and the probability values provided in the example, we have

$$\begin{aligned} P(A_1 \mid B) &= \frac{P(A_1)P(B \mid A_1)}{P(A_1)P(B \mid A_1) + P(A_2)P(B \mid A_2)} \\[2mm] &= \frac{(.65)(.02)}{(.65)(.02) + (.35)(.05)} = \frac{.0130}{.0130 + .0175} \\[2mm] &= \frac{.0130}{.0305} = .4262 \end{aligned}$$

In addition, using equation (4.18), we find $P(A_2 \mid B)$.

$$\begin{aligned} P(A_2 \mid B) &= \frac{(.35)(.05)}{(.65)(.02) + (.35)(.05)} \\[2mm] &= \frac{.0175}{.0130 + .0175} = \frac{.0175}{.0305} = .5738 \end{aligned}$$

Note that in this application we started with a probability of .65 that a part selected at random was from supplier 1. However, given information that the part is bad, the probability that the part is from supplier 1 drops to .4262. In fact, if the part is bad, it has better than a 50–50 chance that it came from supplier 2; that is, $P(A_2 \mid B) = .5738$.

Bayes' theorem is applicable when the events for which we want to compute posterior probabilities are mutually exclusive and their union is the entire sample space.[2] For the case of $n$ mutually exclusive events $A_1, A_2, \ldots, A_n$, whose union is the entire sample

---

[2]If the union of events is the entire sample space, the events are said to be *collectively exhaustive.*

space, Bayes' theorem can be used to compute any posterior probability $P(A_i \mid B)$ as shown here.

**BAYES' THEOREM**

$$P(A_i \mid B) = \frac{P(A_i)P(B \mid A_i)}{P(A_1)P(B \mid A_1) + P(A_2)P(B \mid A_2) + \cdots + P(A_n)P(B \mid A_n)} \quad \textbf{(4.19)}$$

With prior probabilities $P(A_1), P(A_2), \ldots, P(A_n)$ and the appropriate conditional probabilities $P(B \mid A_1), P(B \mid A_2), \ldots, P(B \mid A_n)$, equation (4.19) can be used to compute the posterior probability of the events $A_1, A_2, \ldots, A_n$.

## Tabular Approach

A tabular approach is helpful in conducting the Bayes' theorem calculations. Such an approach is shown in Table 4.7 for the parts supplier problem. The computations shown there are done in the following steps.

**Step 1.** Prepare the following three columns:
Column 1—The mutually exclusive events $A_i$ for which posterior probabilities are desired
Column 2—The prior probabilities $P(A_i)$ for the events
Column 3—The conditional probabilities $P(B \mid A_i)$ of the new information $B$ given each event

**Step 2.** In column 4, compute the joint probabilities $P(A_i \cap B)$ for each event and the new information $B$ by using the multiplication law. These joint probabilities are found by multiplying the prior probabilities in column 2 by the corresponding conditional probabilities in column 3; that is, $P(A_i \cap B) = P(A_i)P(B \mid A_i)$.

**Step 3.** Sum the joint probabilities in column 4. The sum is the probability of the new information, $P(B)$. Thus we see in Table 4.7 that there is a .0130 probability that the part came from supplier 1 and is bad and a .0175 probability that the part came from supplier 2 and is bad. Because these are the only two ways in which a bad part can be obtained, the sum .0130 + .0175 shows an overall probability of .0305 of finding a bad part from the combined shipments of the two suppliers.

**Step 4.** In column 5, compute the posterior probabilities using the basic relationship of conditional probability.

$$P(A_i \mid B) = \frac{P(A_i \cap B)}{P(B)}$$

Note that the joint probabilities $P(A_i \cap B)$ are in column 4 and the probability $P(B)$ is the sum of column 4.

**TABLE 4.7**   TABULAR APPROACH TO BAYES' THEOREM CALCULATIONS FOR THE TWO-SUPPLIER PROBLEM

| (1) Events $A_i$ | (2) Prior Probabilities $P(A_i)$ | (3) Conditional Probabilities $P(B \mid A_i)$ | (4) Joint Probabilities $P(A_i \cap B)$ | (5) Posterior Probabilities $P(A_i \mid B)$ |
|---|---|---|---|---|
| $A_1$ | .65 | .02 | .0130 | .0130/.0305 = .4262 |
| $A_2$ | .35 | .05 | .0175 | .0175/.0305 = .5738 |
| | 1.00 | | $P(B) =$ .0305 | 1.0000 |

**FIGURE 4.12** EXCEL WORKSHEET FOR COMPUTING POSTERIOR PROBABILITIES

## Using Excel to Compute Posterior Probabilities

The tabular approach to Bayes' theorem can be easily implemented within an Excel worksheet. In this subsection we show how the Bayes' theorem calculations shown in Table 4.7 can be made. Refer to Figure 4.12 as we describe the tasks involved. The formula worksheet is in the background; the value worksheet is in the foreground.

**Enter Data:** Labels are placed in rows 1 and 2 and the two mutually exclusive events are identified in cells A3:A4. The prior probabilities were entered into cells B3:B4 and the conditional probabilities were entered into cells C3:C4.

**Enter Functions and Formulas:** The formulas in cells D3:D4 show that the joint probabilities are the product of the prior probabilities in column B and the conditional probabilities in column C. The results, shown in cells D3:D4 of the value worksheet, are the same as those shown in Table 4.7. The sum in cell D5 shows that the probability of finding a bad part is .0305. This probability is the denominator in Bayes' theorem. The formulas in cells E3:E4 provide the posterior probabilities. From the value worksheet we see that they are the same as the posterior probabilities in Table 4.7.

Note that the same worksheet could be used to find the posterior probabilities of the two suppliers given a good part is found. The prior probabilities in cells B3:B4 would not change. But we would replace the conditional probabilities in cells C3:C4 with the values .98 and .95, respectively. Doing so would provide $P(A_1 \mid G) = .6570$ and $P(A_2 \mid G) = .3430$ in cells E3:E4.

This worksheet can also be modified to handle Bayes' theorem calculations for more than two events. Just add a row for each additional event and move the sum row down.

### NOTES AND COMMENTS

1. Bayes' theorem is used extensively in decision analysis. The prior probabilities are often subjective estimates provided by a decision maker. Sample information is obtained and posterior probabilities are computed for use in choosing the best decision.

2. An event and its complement are mutually exclusive, and their union is the entire sample space. Thus, Bayes' theorem is always applicable for computing posterior probabilities of an event and its complement.

## Exercises

## Methods

39. The prior probabilities for events $A_1$ and $A_2$ are $P(A_1) = .40$ and $P(A_2) = .60$. It is also known that $P(A_1 \cap A_2) = 0$. Suppose $P(B \mid A_1) = .20$ and $P(B \mid A_2) = .05$.
    a.  Are $A_1$ and $A_2$ mutually exclusive? Explain.
    b.  Compute $P(A_1 \cap B)$ and $P(A_2 \cap B)$.
    c.  Compute $P(B)$.
    d.  Apply Bayes' theorem to compute $P(A_1 \mid B)$ and $P(A_2 \mid B)$.

40. The prior probabilities for events $A_1$, $A_2$, and $A_3$ are $P(A_1) = .20$, $P(A_2) = .50$, and $P(A_3) = .30$. The conditional probabilities of event $B$ given $A_1$, $A_2$, and $A_3$ are $P(B \mid A_1) = .50$, $P(B \mid A_2) = .40$, and $P(B \mid A_3) = .30$.
    a.  Compute $P(B \cap A_1)$, $P(B \cap A_2)$, and $P(B \cap A_3)$.
    b.  Apply Bayes' theorem, equation (4.19), to compute the posterior probability $P(A_2 \mid B)$.
    c.  Use the tabular approach to applying Bayes' theorem to compute $P(A_1 \mid B)$, $P(A_2 \mid B)$, and $P(A_3 \mid B)$.

## Applications

41. A consulting firm submitted a bid for a large research project. The firm's management initially felt they had a 50–50 chance of getting the project. However, the agency to which the bid was submitted subsequently requested additional information on the bid. Past experience indicates that for 75% of the successful bids and 40% of the unsuccessful bids, the agency requested additional information.
    a.  What is the prior probability of the bid being successful (that is, prior to the request for additional information)?
    b.  What is the conditional probability of a request for additional information given that the bid will ultimately be successful?
    c.  Compute the posterior probability that the bid will be successful given a request for additional information.

42. A local bank reviewed its credit card policy with the intention of recalling some of its credit cards. In the past approximately 5% of cardholders defaulted, leaving the bank unable to collect the outstanding balance. Hence, management established a prior probability of .05 that any particular cardholder will default. The bank also found that the probability of missing a monthly payment is .20 for customers who do not default. Of course, the probability of missing a monthly payment for those who default is 1.
    a.  Given that a customer missed one or more monthly payments, compute the posterior probability that the customer will default.
    b.  The bank would like to recall its card if the probability that a customer will default is greater than .20. Should the bank recall its card if the customer misses a monthly payment? Why or why not?

43. Two Wharton professors analyzed 1,613,234 putts by golfers on the Professional Golfers Association (PGA) Tour and found that 983,764 of the putts were made and 629,470 of the putts were missed. Further analysis showed that for putts that were made, 64.0% of the time the player was attempting to make a par putt and 18.8% of the time the player was attempting to make a birdie putt. And, for putts that were missed, 20.3% of the time the player was attempting to make a par putt and 73.4% of the time the player was attempting to make a birdie putt (*Is Tiger Woods Loss Averse? Persistent Bias in the Face of Experience, Competition, and High Stakes,* Pope, D. G., and M. E. Schweitzer, June 2009, The Wharton School, University of Pennsylvania.).

a. What is the probability that a PGA Tour player makes a putt?
b. Suppose that a PGA Tour player has a putt for par. What is the probability that the player will make the putt?
c. Suppose that a PGA Tour player has a putt for birdie. What is the probability that the player will make the putt?
d. Comment on the differences in the probabilities computed in parts (b) and (c).

44. The American Council of Education reported that 47% of college freshmen earn a degree and graduate within five years (Associated Press, May 6, 2002). Assume that graduation records show that women make up 50% of the students who graduated within five years, but only 45% of the students who did not graduate within five years. The students who had not graduated within five years either dropped out or were still working on their degrees.
    a. Let $A_1$ = the student graduated within five years
       $A_2$ = the student did not graduate within five years
       $W$ = the student is a female student
       Using the given information, what are the values for $P(A_1)$, $P(A_2)$, $P(W \mid A_1)$, and $P(W \mid A_2)$?
    b. What is the probability that a female student will graduate within five years?
    c. What is the probability that a male student will graduate within five years?
    d. Given the preceding results, what are the percentage of women and the percentage of men in the entering freshman class?

45. In an article about investment alternatives, *Money* magazine reported that drug stocks provide a potential for long-term growth, with over 50% of the adult population of the United States taking prescription drugs on a regular basis. For adults age 65 and older, 82% take prescription drugs regularly. For adults age 18 to 64, 49% take prescription drugs regularly. The age 18–64 age group accounts for 83.5% of the adult population (*Statistical Abstract of the United States*, 2008).
    a. What is the probability that a randomly selected adult is 65 or older?
    b. Given an adult takes prescription drugs regularly, what is the probability that the adult is 65 or older?

## Summary

In this chapter we introduced basic probability concepts and illustrated how probability analysis can be used to provide helpful information for decision making. We described how probability can be interpreted as a numerical measure of the likelihood that an event will occur. In addition, we saw that the probability of an event can be computed either by summing the probabilities of the experimental outcomes (sample points) comprising the event or by using the relationships established by the addition, conditional probability, and multiplication laws of probability. For cases in which additional information is available, we showed how Bayes' theorem can be used to obtain revised or posterior probabilities.

## Glossary

**Probability** A numerical measure of the likelihood that an event will occur.
**Experiment** A process that generates well-defined outcomes.
**Sample space** The set of all experimental outcomes.
**Sample point** An element of the sample space. A sample point represents an experimental outcome.
**Tree diagram** A graphical representation that helps in visualizing a multiple-step experiment.
**Basic requirements for assigning probabilities** Two requirements that restrict the manner in which probability assignments can be made: (1) for each experimental outcome $E_i$,

we must have $0 \leq P(E_i) \leq 1$; (2) considering all experimental outcomes, we must have $P(E_1) + P(E_2) + \cdots + P(E_n) = 1$.

**Classical method** A method of assigning probabilities that is appropriate when all the experimental outcomes are equally likely.

**Relative frequency method** A method of assigning probabilities that is appropriate when data are available to estimate the proportion of the time the experimental outcome will occur if the experiment is repeated a large number of times.

**Subjective method** A method of assigning probabilities on the basis of judgment.

**Event** A collection of sample points.

**Complement of A** The event consisting of all sample points that are not in $A$.

**Venn diagram** A graphical representation for showing symbolically the sample space and operations involving events in which the sample space is represented by a rectangle and events are represented as circles within the sample space.

**Union of A and B** The event containing all sample points belonging to $A$ or $B$ or both. The union is denoted $A \cup B$.

**Intersection of A and B** The event containing the sample points belonging to both $A$ and $B$. The intersection is denoted $A \cap B$.

**Addition law** A probability law used to compute the probability of the union of two events. It is $P(A \cup B) = P(A) + P(B) - P(A \cap B)$. For mutually exclusive events, $P(A \cap B) = 0$; in this case the addition law reduces to $P(A \cup B) = P(A) + P(B)$.

**Mutually exclusive events** Events that have no sample points in common; that is, $A \cap B$ is empty and $P(A \cap B) = 0$.

**Conditional probability** The probability of an event given that another event already occurred. The conditional probability of $A$ given $B$ is $P(A \mid B) = P(A \cap B)/P(B)$.

**Joint probability** The probability of two events both occurring; that is, the probability of the intersection of two events.

**Marginal probability** The values in the margins of a joint probability table that provide the probabilities of each event separately.

**Independent events** Two events $A$ and $B$ where $P(A \mid B) = P(A)$ or $P(B \mid A) = P(B)$; that is, the events have no influence on each other.

**Multiplication law** A probability law used to compute the probability of the intersection of two events. It is $P(A \cap B) = P(B)P(A \mid B)$ or $P(A \cap B) = P(A)P(B \mid A)$. For independent events it reduces to $P(A \cap B) = P(A)P(B)$.

**Prior probabilities** Initial estimates of the probabilities of events.

**Posterior probabilities** Revised probabilities of events based on additional information.

**Bayes' theorem** A method used to compute posterior probabilities.

## Key Formulas

**Counting Rule for Combinations**

$$C_n^N = \binom{N}{n} = \frac{N!}{n!(N-n)!} \qquad \text{(4.1)}$$

**Counting Rule for Permutations**

$$P_n^N = n!\binom{N}{n} = \frac{N!}{(N-n)!} \qquad \text{(4.2)}$$

**Computing Probability Using the Complement**

$$P(A) = 1 - P(A^c) \qquad \text{(4.5)}$$

**Addition Law**

$$P(A \cup B) = P(A) + P(B) - P(A \cap B) \qquad \textbf{(4.6)}$$

**Conditional Probability**

$$P(A \mid B) = \frac{P(A \cap B)}{P(B)} \qquad \textbf{(4.7)}$$

$$P(B \mid A) = \frac{P(A \cap B)}{P(A)} \qquad \textbf{(4.8)}$$

**Multiplication Law**

$$P(A \cap B) = P(B)P(A \mid B) \qquad \textbf{(4.11)}$$

$$P(A \cap B) = P(A)P(B \mid A) \qquad \textbf{(4.12)}$$

**Multiplication Law for Independent Events**

$$P(A \cap B) = P(A)P(B) \qquad \textbf{(4.13)}$$

**Bayes' Theorem**

$$P(A_i \mid B) = \frac{P(A_i)P(B \mid A_i)}{P(A_1)P(B \mid A_1) + P(A_2)P(B \mid A_2) + \cdots + P(A_n)P(B \mid A_n)} \qquad \textbf{(4.19)}$$

## Supplementary Exercises

46. *The Wall Street Journal*/Harris Personal Finance poll asked 2082 adults if they owned a home (All Business website, January 23, 2008). A total of 1249 survey respondents answered Yes. Of the 450 respondents in the 18–34 age group, 117 responded Yes.
    a. What is the probability that a respondent to the poll owned a home?
    b. What is the probability that a respondent in the 18–34 age group owned a home?
    c. What is the probability that a respondent to the poll did not own a home?
    d. What is the probability that a respondent in the 18–34 age group did not own a home?

47. A financial manager made two new investments—one in the oil industry and one in municipal bonds. After a one-year period, each of the investments will be classified as either successful or unsuccessful. Consider the making of the two investments as an experiment.
    a. How many sample points exist for this experiment?
    b. Show a tree diagram and list the sample points.
    c. Let $O$ = the event that the oil industry investment is successful and $M$ = the event that the municipal bond investment is successful. List the sample points in $O$ and in $M$.
    d. List the sample points in the union of the events $(O \cup M)$.
    e. List the sample points in the intersection of the events $(O \cap M)$.
    f. Are events $O$ and $M$ mutually exclusive? Explain.

48. Statistics from the 2009 Major League Baseball season show that there were 157 players who had at least 500 plate appearances. For this group, 42 players had a batting average of .300 or higher, 53 players hit 25 or more home runs, and 14 players had a batting average of .300 or higher and hit 25 or more home runs. Only four players had 200 or more hits (ESPN website, January 10, 2010). Use the 157 players who had at least 500 plate appearances to answer the following questions.
    a. What is the probability that a randomly selected player had a batting average of .300 or higher?
    b. What is the probability that a randomly selected player hit 25 or more home runs?
    c. Are the events "having a batting average of .300 or higher" and "hitting 25 or more home runs" mutually exclusive?

    d.   What is the probability that a randomly selected player had a batting average of .300 or higher or hit 25 or more home runs?

    e.   What is the probability that a randomly selected player had 200 or more hits? Does obtaining 200 or more hits appear to be more difficult than hitting 25 or more home runs? Explain.

49.   A study of 31,000 hospital admissions in New York State found that 4% of the admissions led to treatment-caused injuries. One-seventh of these treatment-caused injuries resulted in death, and one-fourth were caused by negligence. Malpractice claims were filed in 1 out of 7.5 cases involving negligence, and payments were made in one out of every two claims.

    a.   What is the probability that a person admitted to the hospital will suffer a treatment-caused injury due to negligence?

    b.   What is the probability that a person admitted to the hospital will die from a treatment-caused injury?

    c.   In the case of a negligent treatment-caused injury, what is the probability that a malpractice claim will be paid?

50.   A telephone survey to determine viewer response to a new television show obtained the following data.

| Rating | Frequency |
|---|---|
| Poor | 4 |
| Below average | 8 |
| Average | 11 |
| Above average | 14 |
| Excellent | 13 |

    a.   What is the probability that a randomly selected viewer will rate the new show as average or better?

    b.   What is the probability that a randomly selected viewer will rate the new show below average or worse?

51.   The following crosstabulation shows household income by educational level of the head of household (*Statistical Abstract of the United States*, 2008).

| | Household Income ($1000s) | | | | | |
|---|---|---|---|---|---|---|
| Education Level | Under 25 | 25.0– 49.9 | 50.0– 74.9 | 75.0– 99.9 | 100 or more | Total |
| Not H.S. Graduate | 4,207 | 3,459 | 1,389 | 539 | 367 | 9,961 |
| H.S. Graduate | 4,917 | 6,850 | 5,027 | 2,637 | 2,668 | 22,099 |
| Some College | 2,807 | 5,258 | 4,678 | 3,250 | 4,074 | 20,067 |
| Bachelor's Degree | 885 | 2,094 | 2,848 | 2,581 | 5,379 | 13,787 |
| Beyond Bach. Deg. | 290 | 829 | 1,274 | 1,241 | 4,188 | 7,822 |
| Total | 13,106 | 18,490 | 15,216 | 10,248 | 16,676 | 73,736 |

    a.   Develop a joint probability table.

    b.   What is the probability of a head of household not being a high school graduate?

    c.   What is the probability of a head of household having a bachelor's degree or more education?

    d.   What is the probability of a household headed by someone with a bachelor's degree earning $100,000 or more?

    e.   What is the probability of a household having income below $25,000?

f.   What is the probability of a household headed by someone with a bachelor's degree earning less than $25,000?

g.   Is household income independent of educational level?

52.  An MBA new-matriculants survey provided the following data for 2018 students.

|  |  | Applied to More Than One School | |
|---|---|---|---|
|  |  | Yes | No |
| Age Group | 23 and under | 207 | 201 |
|  | 24–26 | 299 | 379 |
|  | 27–30 | 185 | 268 |
|  | 31–35 | 66 | 193 |
|  | 36 and over | 51 | 169 |

a.   For a randomly selected MBA student, prepare a joint probability table for the experiment consisting of observing the student's age and whether the student applied to one or more schools.

b.   What is the probability that a randomly selected applicant is 23 or under?

c.   What is the probability that a randomly selected applicant is older than 26?

d.   What is the probability that a randomly selected applicant applied to more than one school?

53.  Refer again to the data from the MBA new-matriculants survey in exercise 52.

a.   Given that a person applied to more than one school, what is the probability that the person is 24–26 years old?

b.   Given that a person is in the 36-and-over age group, what is the probability that the person applied to more than one school?

c.   What is the probability that a person is 24–26 years old or applied to more than one school?

d.   Suppose a person is known to have applied to only one school. What is the probability that the person is 31 or more years old?

e.   Is the number of schools applied to independent of age? Explain.

54.  A poll conducted to learn about attitudes toward investment and retirement asked male and female respondents how important they felt level of risk was in choosing a retirement investment. The following joint probability table was constructed from the data provided. "Important" means the respondent said level of risk was either important or very important.

|  | Male | Female | Total |
|---|---|---|---|
| Important | .22 | .27 | .49 |
| Not Important | .28 | .23 | .51 |
| Total | .50 | .50 | 1.00 |

a.   What is the probability that a survey respondent will say level of risk is important?

b.   What is the probability that a male respondent will say level of risk is important?

c.   What is the probability that a female respondent will say level of risk is important?

d.   Is the level of risk independent of the gender of the respondent? Why or why not?

e.   Do male and female attitudes toward risk differ?

55. A large consumer goods company ran a television advertisement for one of its soap products. On the basis of a survey that was conducted, probabilities were assigned to the following events.

$$B = \text{individual purchased the product}$$
$$S = \text{individual recalls seeing the advertisement}$$
$$B \cap S = \text{individual purchased the product and recalls seeing the advertisement}$$

The probabilities assigned were $P(B) = .20$, $P(S) = .40$, and $P(B \cap S) = .12$.

   a. What is the probability of an individual's purchasing the product given that the individual recalls seeing the advertisement? Does seeing the advertisement increase the probability that the individual will purchase the product? As a decision maker, would you recommend continuing the advertisement (assuming that the cost is reasonable)?

   b. Assume that individuals who do not purchase the company's soap product buy from its competitors. What would be your estimate of the company's market share? Would you expect that continuing the advertisement will increase the company's market share? Why or why not?

   c. The company also tested another advertisement and assigned it values of $P(S) = .30$ and $P(B \cap S) = .10$. What is $P(B \mid S)$ for this other advertisement? Which advertisement seems to have had the bigger effect on customer purchases?

56. Cooper Realty is a small real estate company located in Albany, New York, specializing primarily in residential listings. It recently became interested in determining the likelihood of one of its listings being sold within a certain number of days. An analysis of company sales of 800 homes in previous years produced the following data.

| | | Days Listed Until Sold | | | |
|---|---|---|---|---|---|
| | | **Under 30** | **31–90** | **Over 90** | **Total** |
| | **Under $150,000** | 50 | 40 | 10 | 100 |
| **Initial Asking Price** | **$150,000–$199,999** | 20 | 150 | 80 | 250 |
| | **$200,000–$250,000** | 20 | 280 | 100 | 400 |
| | **Over $250,000** | 10 | 30 | 10 | 50 |
| | **Total** | 100 | 500 | 200 | 800 |

   a. If $A$ is defined as the event that a home is listed for more than 90 days before being sold, estimate the probability of $A$.

   b. If $B$ is defined as the event that the initial asking price is under $150,000, estimate the probability of $B$.

   c. What is the probability of $A \cap B$?

   d. Assuming that a contract was just signed to list a home with an initial asking price of less than $150,000, what is the probability that the home will take Cooper Realty more than 90 days to sell?

   e. Are events $A$ and $B$ independent?

57. A company studied the number of lost-time accidents occurring at its Brownsville, Texas, plant. Historical records show that 6% of the employees suffered lost-time accidents last year. Management believes that a special safety program will reduce such accidents to 5% during the current year. In addition, it estimates that 15% of employees who had lost-time accidents last year will experience a lost-time accident during the current year.

   a. What percentage of the employees will experience lost-time accidents in both years?

   b. What percentage of the employees will suffer at least one lost-time accident over the two-year period?

58. A survey showed that 8% of Internet users age 18 and older report keeping a blog. Referring to the 18–29 age group as young adults, the survey showed that for bloggers 54% are young adults and for nonbloggers 24% are young adults (Pew Internet & American Life Project, July 19, 2006).
    a. Develop a joint probability table for these data with two rows (bloggers vs. nonbloggers) and two columns (young adults vs. older adults).
    b. What is the probability that an Internet user is a young adult?
    c. What is the probability that an Internet user keeps a blog and is a young adult?
    d. Suppose that in a follow-up phone survey we contact someone who is 24 years old. What is the probability that this person keeps a blog?

59. An oil company purchased an option on land in Alaska. Preliminary geologic studies assigned the following prior probabilities.

$$P(\text{high-quality oil}) = .50$$
$$P(\text{medium-quality oil}) = .20$$
$$P(\text{no oil}) = .30$$

   a. What is the probability of finding oil?
   b. After 200 feet of drilling on the first well, a soil test is taken. The probabilities of finding the particular type of soil identified by the test follow.

$$P(\text{soil} \mid \text{high-quality oil}) = .20$$
$$P(\text{soil} \mid \text{medium-quality oil}) = .80$$
$$P(\text{soil} \mid \text{no oil}) = .20$$

   How should the firm interpret the soil test? What are the revised probabilities, and what is the new probability of finding oil?

60. ParFore created a website to market golf equipment and apparel. Management would like a certain offer to appear for female visitors and a different offer to appear for male visitors. From a sample of past website visits, management learned that 60% of the visitors to the website ParFore are male and 40% are female.
    a. What is the prior probability that the next visitor to the website will be female?
    b. Suppose you know that the current visitor to the website ParFore previously visited the Dillard's website, and that women are three times as likely to visit the Dillard's website as men. What is the revised probability that the current visitor to the website ParFore is female? Should you display the offer that appeals more to female visitors or the one that appeals more to male visitors?

## Case Problem   Hamilton County Judges

Hamilton County judges try thousands of cases per year. In an overwhelming majority of the cases disposed, the verdict stands as rendered. However, some cases are appealed, and of those appealed, some of the cases are reversed. Kristen DelGuzzi of *The Cincinnati Enquirer* conducted a study of cases handled by Hamilton County judges over a three-year period. Shown in Table 4.8 are the results for 182,908 cases handled (disposed) by 38 judges in Common Pleas Court, Domestic Relations Court, and Municipal Court. Two of the judges (Dinkelacker and Hogan) did not serve in the same court for the entire three-year period.

   The purpose of the newspaper's study was to evaluate the performance of the judges. Appeals are often the result of mistakes made by judges, and the newspaper wanted to know which judges were doing a good job and which were making too many mistakes. You are

**TABLE 4.8**    TOTAL CASES DISPOSED, APPEALED, AND REVERSED IN HAMILTON
COUNTY COURTS

**WEB** file

Judge

### Common Pleas Court

| Judge | Total Cases Disposed | Appealed Cases | Reversed Cases |
|---|---|---|---|
| Fred Cartolano | 3,037 | 137 | 12 |
| Thomas Crush | 3,372 | 119 | 10 |
| Patrick Dinkelacker | 1,258 | 44 | 8 |
| Timothy Hogan | 1,954 | 60 | 7 |
| Robert Kraft | 3,138 | 127 | 7 |
| William Mathews | 2,264 | 91 | 18 |
| William Morrissey | 3,032 | 121 | 22 |
| Norbert Nadel | 2,959 | 131 | 20 |
| Arthur Ney, Jr. | 3,219 | 125 | 14 |
| Richard Niehaus | 3,353 | 137 | 16 |
| Thomas Nurre | 3,000 | 121 | 6 |
| John O'Connor | 2,969 | 129 | 12 |
| Robert Ruehlman | 3,205 | 145 | 18 |
| J. Howard Sundermann | 955 | 60 | 10 |
| Ann Marie Tracey | 3,141 | 127 | 13 |
| Ralph Winkler | 3,089 | 88 | 6 |
| Total | 43,945 | 1762 | 199 |

### Domestic Relations Court

| Judge | Total Cases Disposed | Appealed Cases | Reversed Cases |
|---|---|---|---|
| Penelope Cunningham | 2,729 | 7 | 1 |
| Patrick Dinkelacker | 6,001 | 19 | 4 |
| Deborah Gaines | 8,799 | 48 | 9 |
| Ronald Panioto | 12,970 | 32 | 3 |
| Total | 30,499 | 106 | 17 |

### Municipal Court

| Judge | Total Cases Disposed | Appealed Cases | Reversed Cases |
|---|---|---|---|
| Mike Allen | 6,149 | 43 | 4 |
| Nadine Allen | 7,812 | 34 | 6 |
| Timothy Black | 7,954 | 41 | 6 |
| David Davis | 7,736 | 43 | 5 |
| Leslie Isaiah Gaines | 5,282 | 35 | 13 |
| Karla Grady | 5,253 | 6 | 0 |
| Deidra Hair | 2,532 | 5 | 0 |
| Dennis Helmick | 7,900 | 29 | 5 |
| Timothy Hogan | 2,308 | 13 | 2 |
| James Patrick Kenney | 2,798 | 6 | 1 |
| Joseph Luebbers | 4,698 | 25 | 8 |
| William Mallory | 8,277 | 38 | 9 |
| Melba Marsh | 8,219 | 34 | 7 |
| Beth Mattingly | 2,971 | 13 | 1 |
| Albert Mestemaker | 4,975 | 28 | 9 |
| Mark Painter | 2,239 | 7 | 3 |
| Jack Rosen | 7,790 | 41 | 13 |
| Mark Schweikert | 5,403 | 33 | 6 |
| David Stockdale | 5,371 | 22 | 4 |
| John A. West | 2,797 | 4 | 2 |
| Total | 108,464 | 500 | 104 |

called in to assist in the data analysis. Use your knowledge of probability and conditional probability to help with the ranking of the judges. You also may be able to analyze the likelihood of appeal and reversal for cases handled by different courts.

## Managerial Report

Prepare a report with your rankings of the judges. Also, include an analysis of the likelihood of appeal and case reversal in the three courts. At a minimum, your report should include the following:

1. The probability of cases being appealed and reversed in the three different courts.
2. The probability of a case being appealed for each judge.
3. The probability of a case being reversed for each judge.
4. The probability of reversal given an appeal for each judge.
5. Rank the judges within each court. State the criteria you used and provide a rationale for your choice.

# CHAPTER 5

# Discrete Probability Distributions

## CONTENTS

**TABLE 5.5**    CALCULATION OF THE VARIANCE FOR THE NUMBER OF AUTOMOBILES SOLD DURING A DAY AT DICARLO MOTORS

| $x$ | $x - \mu$ | $(x - \mu)^2$ | $f(x)$ | $(x - \mu)^2 f(x)$ |
|---|---|---|---|---|
| 0 | $0 - 1.50 = -1.50$ | 2.25 | .18 | $2.25(.18) = .4050$ |
| 1 | $1 - 1.50 = -.50$ | .25 | .39 | $.25(.39) = .0975$ |
| 2 | $2 - 1.50 = .50$ | .25 | .24 | $.25(.24) = .0600$ |
| 3 | $3 - 1.50 = 1.50$ | 2.25 | .14 | $2.25(.14) = .3150$ |
| 4 | $4 - 1.50 = 2.50$ | 6.25 | .04 | $6.25(.04) = .2500$ |
| 5 | $5 - 1.50 = 3.50$ | 12.25 | .01 | $12.25(.01) = \underline{.1225}$ |
|   |   |   |   | 1.2500 |

$$\sigma^2 = \Sigma(x - \mu)^2 f(x)$$

As equation (5.5) shows, an essential part of the variance formula is the deviation, $x - \mu$, which measures how far a particular value of the random variable is from the expected value, or mean, $\mu$. In computing the variance of a random variable, the deviations are squared and then weighted by the corresponding value of the probability function. The sum of these weighted squared deviations for all values of the random variable is referred to as the *variance*. The notations Var$(x)$ and $\sigma^2$ are both used to denote the variance of a random variable.

The calculation of the variance for the probability distribution of the number of automobiles sold during a day at DiCarlo Motors is summarized in Table 5.5. We see that the variance is 1.25. The **standard deviation**, $\sigma$, is defined as the positive square root of the variance. Thus, the standard deviation for the number of automobiles sold during a day is

$$\sigma = \sqrt{1.25} = 1.118$$

The standard deviation is measured in the same units as the random variable ($\sigma = 1.118$ automobiles) and therefore is often preferred in describing the variability of a random variable. The variance $\sigma^2$ is measured in squared units and is thus more difficult to interpret.

## Using Excel to Compute the Expected Value, Variance, and Standard Deviation

The calculations involved in computing the expected value and variance for a discrete random variable can easily be made in an Excel worksheet. One approach is to enter the formulas necessary to make the calculations in Tables 5.4 and 5.5. An easier way, however, is to make use of Excel's SUMPRODUCT function. In this subsection we show how to use the SUMPRODUCT function to compute the expected value and variance for daily automobile sales at DiCarlo Motors. Refer to Figure 5.2 as we describe the tasks involved. The formula worksheet is in the background; the value worksheet is in the foreground.

**Enter Data:**    The data needed are the values for the random variable and the corresponding probabilities. Labels, values for the random variable, and the corresponding probabilities are entered in cells A1:B7.

**Enter Functions and Formulas:**    The SUMPRODUCT function multiplies each value in one range by the corresponding value in another range and sums the products. To use the SUMPRODUCT function to compute the expected value of daily automobile sales at DiCarlo Motors, we entered the following formula into cell B9:

=SUMPRODUCT(A2:A7,B2:B7)

**FIGURE 5.2** EXCEL WORKSHEET FOR EXPECTED VALUE, VARIANCE, AND STANDARD DEVIATION

Note that the first range, A2:A7, contains the values for the random variable, daily automobile sales. The second range, B2:B7, contains the corresponding probabilities. Thus, the SUMPRODUCT function in cell B9 is computing A2*B2 + A3*B3 + A4*B4 + A5*B5 + A6*B6 + A7*B7; hence, it is applying the formula in equation (5.4) to compute the expected value. The result, shown in cell B9 of the value worksheet, is 1.5.

The formulas in cells C2:C7 are used to compute the squared deviations from the expected value or mean of 1.5 (the mean is in cell B9). The results, shown in the value worksheet, are the same as the results shown in Table 5.5. The formula necessary to compute the variance for daily automobile sales was entered into cell B11. It uses the SUMPRODUCT function to multiply each value in the range C2:C7 by each corresponding value in the range B2:B7 and sums the products. The result, shown in the value worksheet, is 1.25. Because the standard deviation is the square root of the variance, we entered the formula =SQRT(B11) into cell B13 to compute the standard deviation for daily automobile sales. The result, shown in the value worksheet, is 1.118034.

## Exercises

### Methods

15. The following table provides a probability distribution for the random variable $x$.

| $x$ | $f(x)$ |
|-----|--------|
| 3 | .25 |
| 6 | .50 |
| 9 | .25 |

a.   Compute $E(x)$, the expected value of $x$.
b.   Compute $\sigma^2$, the variance of $x$.
c.   Compute $\sigma$, the standard deviation of $x$.

16.  The following table provides a probability distribution for the random variable $y$.

| $y$ | $f(y)$ |
|-----|--------|
| 2 | .20 |
| 4 | .30 |
| 7 | .40 |
| 8 | .10 |

a.   Compute $E(y)$.
b.   Compute $Var(y)$ and $\sigma$.

## Applications

17.  The number of students taking the SAT has risen to an all-time high of more than 1.5 million (College Board, August 26, 2008). Students are allowed to repeat the test in hopes of improving the score that is sent to college and university admission offices. The number of times the SAT was taken and the number of students are as follows.

| Number of Times | Number of Students |
|-----------------|--------------------|
| 1 | 721,769 |
| 2 | 601,325 |
| 3 | 166,736 |
| 4 | 22,299 |
| 5 | 6,730 |

a.   Let $x$ be a random variable indicating the number of times a student takes the SAT. Show the probability distribution for this random variable.
b.   What is the probability that a student takes the SAT more than one time?
c.   What is the probability that a student takes the SAT three or more times?
d.   What is the expected value of the number of times the SAT is taken? What is your interpretation of the expected value?
e.   What is the variance and standard deviation for the number of times the SAT is taken?

18.  The American Housing Survey reported the following data on the number of bedrooms in owner-occupied and renter-occupied houses in central cities (U.S. Census Bureau website, March 31, 2003).

| | Number of Houses (1000s) | |
|---|---|---|
| Bedrooms | Renter-Occupied | Owner-Occupied |
| 0 | 547 | 23 |
| 1 | 5012 | 541 |
| 2 | 6100 | 3832 |
| 3 | 2644 | 8690 |
| 4 or more | 557 | 3783 |

a.   Define a random variable $x =$ number of bedrooms in renter-occupied houses and develop a probability distribution for the random variable. (Let $x = 4$ represent 4 or more bedrooms.)

b.   Compute the expected value and variance for the number of bedrooms in renter-occupied houses.

c.   Define a random variable $y$ = number of bedrooms in owner-occupied houses and develop a probability distribution for the random variable. (Let $y = 4$ represent 4 or more bedrooms.)

d.   Compute the expected value and variance for the number of bedrooms in owner-occupied houses.

e.   What observations can you make from a comparison of the number of bedrooms in renter-occupied versus owner-occupied homes?

19.   The National Basketball Association (NBA) records a variety of statistics for each team. Two of these statistics are the percentage of field goals made by the team and the percentage of three-point shots made by the team. For a portion of the 2004 season, the shooting records of the 29 teams in the NBA showed that the probability of scoring two points by making a field goal was .44, and the probability of scoring three points by making a three-point shot was .34 (NBA website, January 3, 2004).

a.   What is the expected value of a two-point shot for these teams?

b.   What is the expected value of a three-point shot for these teams?

c.   If the probability of making a two-point shot is greater than the probability of making a three-point shot, why do coaches allow some players to shoot the three-point shot if they have the opportunity? Use expected value to explain your answer.

20.   The probability distribution for damage claims paid by the Newton Automobile Insurance Company on collision insurance follows.

| Payment ($) | Probability |
|---|---|
| 0 | .85 |
| 500 | .04 |
| 1000 | .04 |
| 3000 | .03 |
| 5000 | .02 |
| 8000 | .01 |
| 10000 | .01 |

a.   Use the expected collision payment to determine the collision insurance premium that would enable the company to break even.

b.   The insurance company charges an annual rate of $520 for the collision coverage. What is the expected value of the collision policy for a policyholder? (*Hint:* It is the expected payments from the company minus the cost of coverage.) Why does the policyholder purchase a collision policy with this expected value?

21.   The following probability distributions of job satisfaction scores for a sample of information systems (IS) senior executives and middle managers range from a low of 1 (very dissatisfied) to a high of 5 (very satisfied).

| Job Satisfaction Score | Probability | |
|---|---|---|
| | IS Senior Executives | IS Middle Managers |
| 1 | .05 | .04 |
| 2 | .09 | .10 |
| 3 | .03 | .12 |
| 4 | .42 | .46 |
| 5 | .41 | .28 |

a.   What is the expected value of the job satisfaction score for senior executives?

b.   What is the expected value of the job satisfaction score for middle managers?

c.   Compute the variance of job satisfaction scores for executives and middle managers.
d.   Compute the standard deviation of job satisfaction scores for both probability distributions.
e.   Compare the overall job satisfaction of senior executives and middle managers.

22.   The demand for a product of Carolina Industries varies greatly from month to month. The probability distribution in the following table, based on the past two years of data, shows the company's monthly demand.

| Unit Demand | Probability |
|:-----------:|:-----------:|
| 300 | .20 |
| 400 | .30 |
| 500 | .35 |
| 600 | .15 |

a.   If the company bases monthly orders on the expected value of the monthly demand, what should Carolina's monthly order quantity be for this product?
b.   Assume that each unit demanded generates $70 in revenue and that each unit ordered costs $50. How much will the company gain or lose in a month if it places an order based on your answer to part (a) and the actual demand for the item is 300 units?

23.   The New York City Housing and Vacancy Survey showed a total of 59,324 rent-controlled housing units and 236,263 rent-stabilized units built in 1947 or later. For these rental units, the probability distributions for the number of persons living in the unit are given (U.S. Census Bureau website, January 12, 2004).

| Number of Persons | Rent-Controlled | Rent-Stabilized |
|:-----------------:|:---------------:|:---------------:|
| 1 | .61 | .41 |
| 2 | .27 | .30 |
| 3 | .07 | .14 |
| 4 | .04 | .11 |
| 5 | .01 | .03 |
| 6 | .00 | .01 |

a.   What is the expected value of the number of persons living in each type of unit?
b.   What is the variance of the number of persons living in each type of unit?
c.   Make some comparisons between the number of persons living in rent-controlled units and the number of persons living in rent-stabilized units.

24.   The J. R. Ryland Computer Company is considering a plant expansion to enable the company to begin production of a new computer product. The company's president must determine whether to make the expansion a medium- or large-scale project. Demand for the new product is uncertain, which for planning purposes may be low demand, medium demand, or high demand. The probability estimates for demand are .20, .50, and .30, respectively. Letting $x$ and $y$ indicate the annual profit in thousands of dollars, the firm's planners developed the following profit forecasts for the medium- and large-scale expansion projects.

| | | Medium-Scale Expansion Profit | | Large-Scale Expansion Profit | |
|:-------:|:------:|:----:|:------:|:---:|:------:|
| | | $x$ | $f(x)$ | $y$ | $f(y)$ |
| | Low | 50 | .20 | 0 | .20 |
| **Demand** | Medium | 150 | .50 | 100 | .50 |
| | High | 200 | .30 | 300 | .30 |

a.  Compute the expected value for the profit associated with the two expansion alternatives. Which decision is preferred for the objective of maximizing the expected profit?
b.  Compute the variance for the profit associated with the two expansion alternatives. Which decision is preferred for the objective of minimizing the risk or uncertainty?

# (5.4) Binomial Probability Distribution

The binomial probability distribution is a discrete probability distribution that provides many applications. It is associated with a multiple-step experiment that we call the binomial experiment.

## A Binomial Experiment

A **binomial experiment** exhibits the following four properties.

---

PROPERTIES OF A BINOMIAL EXPERIMENT

1. The experiment consists of a sequence of $n$ identical trials.
2. Two outcomes are possible on each trial. We refer to one outcome as a *success* and the other outcome as a *failure*.
3. The probability of a success, denoted by $p$, does not change from trial to trial. Consequently, the probability of a failure, denoted by $1 - p$, does not change from trial to trial.
4. The trials are independent.

---

*Jakob Bernoulli (1654–1705), the first of the Bernoulli family of Swiss mathematicians, published a treatise on probability that contained the theory of permutations and combinations, as well as the binomial theorem.*

If properties 2, 3, and 4 are present, we say the trials are generated by a Bernoulli process. If, in addition, property 1 is present, we say we have a binomial experiment. Figure 5.3 depicts one possible sequence of successes and failures for a binomial experiment involving eight trials.

In a binomial experiment, our interest is in the *number of successes occurring in the n trials*. If we let $x$ denote the number of successes occurring in the $n$ trials, we see that $x$ can assume the values of $0, 1, 2, 3, \ldots, n$. Because the number of values is finite, $x$ is a *discrete* random variable. The probability distribution associated with this random variable is called the **binomial probability distribution**. For example, consider the experiment of tossing a

**FIGURE 5.3**  ONE POSSIBLE SEQUENCE OF SUCCESSES AND FAILURES FOR AN EIGHT-TRIAL BINOMIAL EXPERIMENT

---

*Property 1:*  The experiment consists of $n = 8$ identical trials.

*Property 2:*  Each trial results in either success ($S$) or failure ($F$).

| Trials ⟶ | 1 | 2 | 3 | 4 | 5 | 6 | 7 | 8 |
|---|---|---|---|---|---|---|---|---|
| Outcomes ⟶ | S | F | F | S | S | F | S | S |

---

coin five times and on each toss observing whether the coin lands with a head or a tail on its upward face. Suppose we want to count the number of heads appearing over the five tosses. Does this experiment show the properties of a binomial experiment? What is the random variable of interest? Note that:

1. The experiment consists of five identical trials; each trial involves the tossing of one coin.
2. Two outcomes are possible for each trial: a head or a tail. We can designate head a success and tail a failure.
3. The probability of a head and the probability of a tail are the same for each trial, with $p = .5$ and $1 - p = .5$.
4. The trials or tosses are independent because the outcome on any one trial is not affected by what happens on other trials or tosses.

Thus, the properties of a binomial experiment are satisfied. The random variable of interest is $x =$ the number of heads appearing in the five trials. In this case, $x$ can assume the values of 0, 1, 2, 3, 4, or 5.

As another example, consider an insurance salesperson who visits 10 randomly selected families. The outcome associated with each visit is classified as a success if the family purchases an insurance policy and a failure if the family does not. From past experience, the salesperson knows the probability that a randomly selected family will purchase an insurance policy is .10. Checking the properties of a binomial experiment, we observe that:

1. The experiment consists of 10 identical trials; each trial involves contacting one family.
2. Two outcomes are possible on each trial: the family purchases a policy (success) or the family does not purchase a policy (failure).
3. The probabilities of a purchase and a nonpurchase are assumed to be the same for each sales call, with $p = .10$ and $1 - p = .90$.
4. The trials are independent because the families are randomly selected.

Because the four assumptions are satisfied, this example is a binomial experiment. The random variable of interest is the number of sales obtained in contacting the 10 families. In this case, $x$ can assume the values of 0, 1, 2, 3, 4, 5, 6, 7, 8, 9, and 10.

Property 3 of the binomial experiment is called the *stationarity assumption* and is sometimes confused with property 4, independence of trials. To see how they differ, consider again the case of the salesperson calling on families to sell insurance policies. If, as the day wore on, the salesperson got tired and lost enthusiasm, the probability of success (selling a policy) might drop to .05, for example, by the tenth call. In such a case, property 3 (stationarity) would not be satisfied, and we would not have a binomial experiment. Even if property 4 held—that is, the purchase decisions of each family were made independently—it would not be a binomial experiment if property 3 was not satisfied.

In applications involving binomial experiments, a special mathematical formula, called the *binomial probability function,* can be used to compute the probability of $x$ successes in the $n$ trials. Using probability concepts introduced in Chapter 4, we will show in the context of an illustrative problem how the formula can be developed.

## Martin Clothing Store Problem

Let us consider the purchase decisions of the next three customers who enter the Martin Clothing Store. On the basis of past experience, the store manager estimates the probability that any one customer will make a purchase is .30. What is the probability that two of the next three customers will make a purchase?

**FIGURE 5.4**   TREE DIAGRAM FOR THE MARTIN CLOTHING STORE PROBLEM

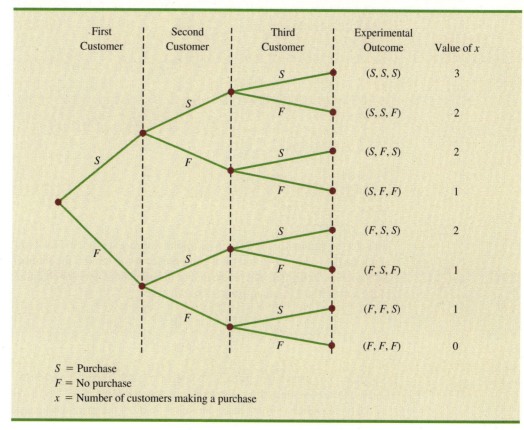

S = Purchase
F = No purchase
x = Number of customers making a purchase

Using a tree diagram (Figure 5.4), we can see that the experiment of observing the three customers each making a purchase decision has eight possible outcomes. Using *S* to denote success (a purchase) and *F* to denote failure (no purchase), we are interested in experimental outcomes involving two successes in the three trials (purchase decisions). Next, let us verify that the experiment involving the sequence of three purchase decisions can be viewed as a binomial experiment. Checking the four requirements for a binomial experiment, we note that:

1. The experiment can be described as a sequence of three identical trials, one trial for each of the three customers who will enter the store.
2. Two outcomes—the customer makes a purchase (success) or the customer does not make a purchase (failure)—are possible for each trial.
3. The probability that the customer will make a purchase (.30) or will not make a purchase (.70) is assumed to be the same for all customers.
4. The purchase decision of each customer is independent of the decisions of the other customers.

Hence, the properties of a binomial experiment are present.

The number of experimental outcomes resulting in exactly *x* successes in *n* trials can be computed using the following formula.[1]

---

[1]This formula, introduced in Chapter 4, determines the number of combinations of *n* objects selected *x* at a time. For the binomial experiment, this combinatorial formula provides the number of experimental outcomes (sequences of *n* trials) resulting in *x* successes.

NUMBER OF EXPERIMENTAL OUTCOMES PROVIDING EXACTLY $x$
SUCCESSES IN $n$ TRIALS

$$\binom{n}{x} = \frac{n!}{x!(n-x)!} \qquad (5.6)$$

where

$$n! = n(n-1)(n-2) \cdots (2)(1)$$

and, by definition,

$$0! = 1$$

Now let us return to the Martin Clothing Store experiment involving three customer purchase decisions. Equation (5.6) can be used to determine the number of experimental outcomes involving two purchases; that is, the number of ways of obtaining $x = 2$ successes in the $n = 3$ trials. From equation (5.6) we have

$$\binom{n}{x} = \binom{3}{2} = \frac{3!}{2!(3-2)!} = \frac{(3)(2)(1)}{(2)(1)(1)} = \frac{6}{2} = 3$$

Equation (5.6) shows that three of the experimental outcomes yield two successes. From Figure 5.4 we see these three outcomes are denoted by $(S, S, F)$, $(S, F, S)$, and $(F, S, S)$.

Using equation (5.6) to determine how many experimental outcomes have three successes (purchases) in the three trials, we obtain

$$\binom{n}{x} = \binom{3}{3} = \frac{3!}{3!(3-3)!} = \frac{3!}{3!0!} = \frac{(3)(2)(1)}{3(2)(1)(1)} = \frac{6}{6} = 1$$

From Figure 5.4 we see that the one experimental outcome with three successes is identified by $(S, S, S)$.

We know that equation (5.6) can be used to determine the number of experimental outcomes that result in $x$ successes. If we are to determine the probability of $x$ successes in $n$ trials, however, we must also know the probability associated with each of these experimental outcomes. Because the trials of a binomial experiment are independent, we can simply multiply the probabilities associated with each trial outcome to find the probability of a particular sequence of successes and failures.

The probability of purchases by the first two customers and no purchase by the third customer, denoted $(S, S, F)$, is given by

$$pp(1-p)$$

With a .30 probability of a purchase on any one trial, the probability of a purchase on the first two trials and no purchase on the third is given by

$$(.30)(.30)(.70) = (.30)^2(.70) = .063$$

Two other experimental outcomes also result in two successes and one failure. The probabilities for all three experimental outcomes involving two successes follow.

| **Trial Outcomes** | | | | **Probability of** |
|---|---|---|---|---|
| **1st Customer** | **2nd Customer** | **3rd Customer** | **Experimental Outcome** | **Experimental Outcome** |
| Purchase | Purchase | No purchase | $(S, S, F)$ | $pp(1-p) = p^2(1-p)$ $= (.30)^2(.70) = .063$ |
| Purchase | No purchase | Purchase | $(S, F, S)$ | $p(1-p)p = p^2(1-p)$ $= (.30)^2(.70) = .063$ |
| No purchase | Purchase | Purchase | $(F, S, S)$ | $(1-p)pp = p^2(1-p)$ $= (.30)^2(.70) = .063$ |

Observe that all three experimental outcomes with two successes have exactly the same probability. This observation holds in general. In any binomial experiment, all sequences of trial outcomes yielding $x$ successes in $n$ trials have the *same probability* of occurrence. The probability of each sequence of trials yielding $x$ successes in $n$ trials follows.

$$\text{Probability of a particular sequence of trial outcomes} = p^x(1-p)^{(n-x)} \quad \text{with } x \text{ successes in } n \text{ trials} \tag{5.7}$$

For the Martin Clothing Store, this formula shows that any experimental outcome with two successes has a probability of $p^2(1-p)^{(3-2)} = p^2(1-p)^1 = (.30)^2(.70)^1 = .063$.

Because equation (5.6) shows the number of outcomes in a binomial experiment with $x$ successes and equation (5.7) gives the probability for each sequence involving $x$ successes, we combine equations (5.6) and (5.7) to obtain the following **binomial probability function**.

### BINOMIAL PROBABILITY FUNCTION

$$f(x) = \binom{n}{x} p^x (1-p)^{(n-x)} \tag{5.8}$$

where

$$x = \text{the number of successes}$$
$$p = \text{the probability of a success on one trial}$$
$$n = \text{the number of trials}$$
$$f(x) = \text{the probability of } x \text{ successes in } n \text{ trials}$$
$$\binom{n}{x} = \frac{n!}{x!(n-x)!}$$

For the binomial probability distribution, $x$ is a discrete random variable with the probability function $f(x)$ applicable for values of $x = 0, 1, 2, \ldots, n$.

In the Martin Clothing Store example, let us use equation (5.8) to compute the probability that no customer makes a purchase, exactly one customer makes a purchase, exactly two customers make a purchase, and all three customers make a purchase. The calculations are summarized in Table 5.6, which gives the probability distribution of the number of customers making a purchase. Figure 5.5 is a graph of this probability distribution.

**TABLE 5.6**    PROBABILITY DISTRIBUTION FOR THE NUMBER OF CUSTOMERS MAKING A PURCHASE

| $x$ | $f(x)$ |
|---|---|
| 0 | $\dfrac{3!}{0!3!}(.30)^0(.70)^3 = .343$ |
| 1 | $\dfrac{3!}{1!2!}(.30)^1(.70)^2 = .441$ |
| 2 | $\dfrac{3!}{2!1!}(.30)^2(.70)^1 = .189$ |
| 3 | $\dfrac{3!}{3!0!}(.30)^3(.70)^0 = \underline{.027}$ |
|  | $1.000$ |

**FIGURE 5.5**    GRAPHICAL REPRESENTATION OF THE PROBABILITY DISTRIBUTION FOR THE NUMBER OF CUSTOMERS MAKING A PURCHASE

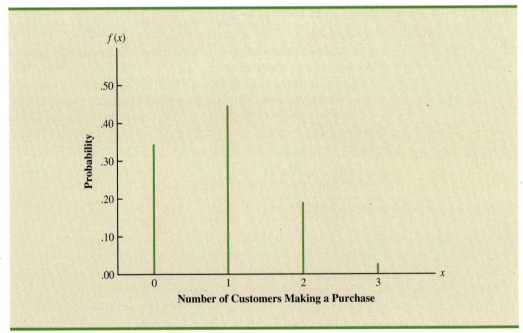

The binomial probability function can be applied to *any* binomial experiment. If we are satisfied that a situation demonstrates the properties of a binomial experiment and if we know the values of $n$ and $p$, we can use equation (5.8) to compute the probability of $x$ successes in the $n$ trials.

If we consider variations of the Martin experiment, such as 10 customers rather than three entering the store, the binomial probability function given by equation (5.8) is still applicable. Suppose we have a binomial experiment with $n = 10$, $x = 4$, and $p = .30$. The probability of making exactly four sales to 10 customers entering the store is

$$f(4) = \frac{10!}{4!6!}(.30)^4(.70)^6 = .2001$$

## Using Excel to Compute Binomial Probabilities

For many probability functions that can be specified as formulas, Excel provides functions for computing probabilities and cumulative probabilities. In this section, we show how Excel's BINOM.DIST function can be used to compute binomial probabilities and cumulative binomial probabilities. We begin by showing how to compute the binomial probabilities for the Martin Clothing Store example shown in Table 5.6. Refer to Figure 5.6 as we describe the tasks involved. The formula worksheet is in the background; the value worksheet is in the foreground.

**Enter Data:**   In order to compute a binomial probability we must know the number of trials ($n$), the probability of success ($p$), and the value of the random variable ($x$). For the Martin Clothing Store example, the number of trials is 3; this value has been entered into cell D1. The probability of success is .3; this value has been entered into cell D2. Because we want to compute the probability for $x = 0, 1, 2,$ and 3, these values were entered into cells B5:B8.

**Enter Functions and Formulas:**   The BINOM.DIST function has four inputs: the first is the value of $x$, the second is the value of $n$, the third is the value of $p$, and the fourth is FALSE or TRUE. We choose FALSE for the fourth input if a probability is desired and TRUE if a cumulative probability is desired. The formula =BINOM.DIST(B5,$D$1,$D$2,FALSE) has been entered into cell C5 to compute the probability of 0 successes in 3 trials. Note in the value worksheet that the probability computed for $f(0)$, .343, is the same as that shown in Table 5.6. The formula in cell C5 is copied to cells C6:C8 to compute the probabilities for $x = 1, 2,$ and 3 successes, respectively.

**FIGURE 5.6**   EXCEL WORKSHEET FOR COMPUTING BINOMIAL PROBABILITIES OF NUMBER OF CUSTOMERS MAKING A PURCHASE

**FIGURE 5.7**    EXCEL WORKSHEET FOR COMPUTING PROBABILITIES AND CUMULATIVE PROBABILITIES FOR NUMBER OF PURCHASES WITH 10 CUSTOMERS

We can also compute cumulative probabilities using Excel's BINOM.DIST function. To illustrate, let us consider the case of 10 customers entering the Martin Clothing Store and compute the probabilities and cumulative probabilities for the number of customers making a purchase. Recall that the cumulative probability for $x = 1$ is the probability of 1 or fewer purchases, the cumulative probability for $x = 2$ is the probability of 2 or fewer purchases, and so on. So, the cumulative probability for $x = 10$ is 1. Refer to Figure 5.7 as we describe the tasks involved in computing these cumulative probabilities. The formula worksheet is in the background; the value worksheet is in the foreground.

**Enter Data:**    We entered the number of trials (10) into cell D1, the probability of success (.3) into cell D2, and the values for the random variable into cells B5:B15.

**Enter Functions and Formulas:**    The binomial probabilities for each value of the random variable are computed in column C and the cumulative probabilities are computed in column D. We entered the formula =BINOM.DIST(B5,$D$1,$D$2,FALSE) into cell C5 to compute the probability of 0 successes in 10 trials. Note that we used FALSE as the fourth input in the BINOM.DIST function. The probability (.0282) is shown in cell C5 of the value worksheet. The formula in cell C5 is simply copied to cells C6:C15 to compute the remaining probabilities.

To compute the cumulative probabilities we start by entering the formula =BINOM.DIST (B5,$D$1,$D$2,TRUE) into cell D5. Note that we used TRUE as the fourth input in the BINOM.DIST function. The formula in cell D5 is then copied to cells D6:D15 to compute the remaining cumulative probabilities. In cell D5 of the value worksheet we see that the cumulative probability for $x = 0$ is the same as the probability for $x = 0$. Each of the remaining cumulative probabilities is the sum of the previous cumulative probability and the individual probability in column C. For instance, the cumulative probability for $x = 4$ is given by .6496 + .2001 = .8497. Note also that the cumulative probability for $x = 10$ is 1.

The cumulative probability of $x = 9$ is also 1 because the probability of $x = 10$ is zero (to four decimal places of accuracy).

## Expected Value and Variance for the Binomial Distribution

In Section 5.3 we provided formulas for computing the expected value and variance of a discrete random variable. In the special case where the random variable has a binomial distribution with a known number of trials $n$ and a known probability of success $p$, the general formulas for the expected value and variance can be simplified. The results follow.

> **EXPECTED VALUE AND VARIANCE FOR THE BINOMIAL DISTRIBUTION**
>
> $$E(x) = \mu = np \qquad\qquad\qquad \textbf{(5.9)}$$
> $$\text{Var}(x) = \sigma^2 = np(1 - p) \qquad\qquad \textbf{(5.10)}$$

For the Martin Clothing Store problem with three customers, we can use equation (5.9) to compute the expected number of customers who will make a purchase.

$$E(x) = np = 3(.30) = .9$$

Suppose that for the next month the Martin Clothing Store forecasts that 1000 customers will enter the store. What is the expected number of customers who will make a purchase? The answer is $\mu = np = (1000)(.3) = 300$. Thus, to increase the expected number of purchases, Martin's must induce more customers to enter the store and/or somehow increase the probability that any individual customer will make a purchase after entering.

For the Martin Clothing Store problem with three customers, we see that the variance and standard deviation for the number of customers who will make a purchase are

$$\sigma^2 = np(1 - p) = 3(.3)(.7) = .63$$
$$\sigma = \sqrt{.63} = .79$$

For the next 1000 customers entering the store, the variance and standard deviation for the number of customers who will make a purchase are

$$\sigma^2 = np(1 - p) = 1000(.3)(.7) = 210$$
$$\sigma = \sqrt{210} = 14.49$$

## NOTES AND COMMENTS

Statisticians have developed tables that give probabilities and cumulative probabilities for a binomial random variable. These tables can be found in some statistics textbooks. With modern calculators and the capability of the BINOM.DIST function in Excel, such tables are unnecessary.

## Exercises

### Methods

25. Consider a binomial experiment with two trials and $p = .4$.
    a. Draw a tree diagram for this experiment (see Figure 5.4).
    b. Compute the probability of one success, $f(1)$.
    c. Compute $f(0)$.
    d. Compute $f(2)$.

 e.   Compute the probability of at least one success.
 f.   Compute the expected value, variance, and standard deviation.

26.  Consider a binomial experiment with $n = 10$ and $p = .10$.
 a.   Compute $f(0)$.
 b.   Compute $f(2)$.
 c.   Compute $P(x \leq 2)$.
 d.   Compute $P(x \geq 1)$.
 e.   Compute $E(x)$.
 f.   Compute $\text{Var}(x)$ and $\sigma$.

27.  Consider a binomial experiment with $n = 20$ and $p = .70$.
 a.   Compute $f(12)$.
 b.   Compute $f(16)$.
 c.   Compute $P(x \geq 16)$.
 d.   Compute $P(x \leq 15)$.
 e.   Compute $E(x)$.
 f.   Compute $\text{Var}(x)$ and $\sigma$.

## Applications

28.  A Harris Interactive survey for InterContinental Hotels & Resorts asked respondents, "When traveling internationally, do you generally venture out on your own to experience culture, or stick with your tour group and itineraries?" The survey found that 23% of the respondents stick with their tour group (*USA Today,* January 21, 2004).
 a.   In a sample of six international travelers, what is the probability that two will stick with their tour group?
 b.   In a sample of six international travelers, what is the probability that at least two will stick with their tour group?
 c.   In a sample of 10 international travelers, what is the probability that none will stick with the tour group?

29.  In San Francisco, 30% of workers take public transportation daily (*USA Today,* December 21, 2005).
 a.   In a sample of 10 workers, what is the probability that exactly three workers take public transportation daily?
 b.   In a sample of 10 workers, what is the probability that at least three workers take public transportation daily?

30.  When a new machine is functioning properly, only 3% of the items produced are defective. Assume that we will randomly select two parts produced on the machine and that we are interested in the number of defective parts found.
 a.   Describe the conditions under which this situation would be a binomial experiment.
 b.   Draw a tree diagram similar to Figure 5.4 showing this problem as a two-trial experiment.
 c.   How many experimental outcomes result in exactly one defect being found?
 d.   Compute the probabilities associated with finding no defects, exactly one defect, and two defects.

31.  A Randstad/Harris interactive survey reported that 25% of employees said their company is loyal to them (*USA Today,* November 11, 2009). Suppose 10 employees are selected randomly and will be interviewed about company loyalty.
 a.   Is the selection of 10 employees a binomial experiment? Explain.
 b.   What is the probability that none of the 10 employees will say their company is loyal to them?
 c.   What is the probability that 4 of the 10 employees will say their company is loyal to them?

d.   What is the probability that at least 2 of the 10 employees will say their company is loyal to them?

32.   Military radar and missile detection systems are designed to warn a country of an enemy attack. A reliability question is whether a detection system will be able to identify an attack and issue a warning. Assume that a particular detection system has a .90 probability of detecting a missile attack. Use the binomial probability distribution to answer the following questions.
a.   What is the probability that a single detection system will detect an attack?
b.   If two detection systems are installed in the same area and operate independently, what is the probability that at least one of the systems will detect the attack?
c.   If three systems are installed, what is the probability that at least one of the systems will detect the attack?
d.   Would you recommend that multiple detection systems be used? Explain.

33.   Twelve of the top twenty finishers in the 2009 PGA Championship at Hazeltine National Golf Club in Chaska, Minnesota, used a Titleist brand golf ball (GolfBallTest website, November 12, 2009). Suppose these results are representative of the probability that a randomly selected PGA Tour player uses a Titleist brand golf ball. For a sample of 15 PGA Tour players, make the following calculations.
a.   Compute the probability that exactly 10 of the 15 PGA Tour players use a Titleist brand golf ball.
b.   Compute the probability that more than 10 of the 15 PGA Tour players use a Titleist brand golf ball.
c.   For a sample of 15 PGA Tour players, compute the expected number of players who use a Titleist brand golf ball.
d.   For a sample of 15 PGA Tour players, compute the variance and standard deviation of the number of players who use a Titleist brand golf ball.

34.   The Census Bureau's Current Population Survey shows that 28% of individuals, ages 25 and older, have completed four years of college (*The New York Times Almanac,* 2006). For a sample of 15 individuals, ages 25 and older, answer the following questions:
a.   What is the probability that four will have completed four years of college?
b.   What is the probability that three or more will have completed four years of college?

35.   A university found that 20% of its students withdraw without completing the introductory statistics course. Assume that 20 students registered for the course.
a.   Compute the probability that two or fewer will withdraw.
b.   Compute the probability that exactly four will withdraw.
c.   Compute the probability that more than three will withdraw.
d.   Compute the expected number of withdrawals.

36.   According to a survey conducted by TD Ameritrade, one out of four investors has exchange-traded funds in his or her portfolio (*USA Today,* January 11, 2007). Consider a sample of 20 investors.
a.   Compute the probability that exactly four investors have exchange-traded funds in their portfolios.
b.   Compute the probability that at least two of the investors have exchange-traded funds in their portfolios.
c.   If you found that exactly 12 of the investors have exchange-traded funds in their portfolios, would you doubt the accuracy of the survey results?
d.   Compute the expected number of investors who have exchange-traded funds in their portfolios.

37.   Twenty-three percent of automobiles are not covered by insurance (CNN, February 23, 2006). On a particular weekend, 35 automobiles are involved in traffic accidents.
a.   What is the expected number of these automobiles that are not covered by insurance?
b.   What are the variance and standard deviation?

# 5.5 Poisson Probability Distribution

*The Poisson probability distribution is often used to model random arrivals in waiting line situations.*

In this section we consider a discrete random variable that is often useful in estimating the number of occurrences over a specified interval of time or space. For example, the random variable of interest might be the number of arrivals at a car wash in one hour, the number of repairs needed in 10 miles of highway, or the number of leaks in 100 miles of pipeline. If the following two properties are satisfied, the number of occurrences is a random variable described by the **Poisson probability distribution**.

> **PROPERTIES OF A POISSON EXPERIMENT**
>
> 1. The probability of an occurrence is the same for any two intervals of equal length.
> 2. The occurrence or nonoccurrence in any interval is independent of the occurrence or nonoccurrence in any other interval.

The **Poisson probability function** is defined by equation (5.11).

> **POISSON PROBABILITY FUNCTION**
>
> $$f(x) = \frac{\mu^x e^{-\mu}}{x!} \tag{5.11}$$
>
> where
>
> $f(x)$ = the probability of $x$ occurrences in an interval
> $\mu$ = expected value or mean number of occurrences in an interval
> $e$ = 2.71828

*Siméon Poisson taught mathematics at the Ecole Polytechnique in Paris from 1802 to 1808. In 1837, he published a work entitled "Researches on the Probability of Criminal and Civil Verdicts," which includes a discussion of what later became known as the Poisson distribution.*

For the Poisson probability distribution, $x$ is a discrete random variable indicating the number of occurrences in the interval. Since there is no stated upper limit for the number of occurrences, the probability function $f(x)$ is applicable for values $x = 0, 1, 2, \ldots$ without limit. In practical applications, $x$ will eventually become large enough so that $f(x)$ is approximately zero and the probability of any larger values of $x$ becomes negligible.

## An Example Involving Time Intervals

*Bell Labs used the Poisson distribution to model the arrival of telephone calls.*

Suppose that we are interested in the number of arrivals at the drive-up teller window of a bank during a 15-minute period on weekday mornings. If we can assume that the probability of a car arriving is the same for any two time periods of equal length and that the arrival or nonarrival of a car in any time period is independent of the arrival or nonarrival in any other time period, the Poisson probability function is applicable. Suppose these assumptions are satisfied and an analysis of historical data shows that the average number of cars arriving in a 15-minute period of time is 10; in this case, the following probability function applies.

$$f(x) = \frac{10^x e^{-10}}{x!}$$

The random variable here is $x$ = number of cars arriving in any 15-minute period.

If management wanted to know the probability of exactly five arrivals in 15 minutes, we would set $x = 5$ and thus obtain

$$\text{Probability of exactly} \atop \text{5 arrivals in 15 minutes} = f(5) = \frac{10^5 e^{-10}}{5!} = .0378$$

The probability of five arrivals in 15 minutes was obtained by using a calculator to evaluate the probability function. Excel also provides a function called POISSON.DIST for computing Poisson probabilities and cumulative probabilities. This function is easier to use when numerous probabilities and cumulative probabilities are desired. At the end of this section, we show how to compute these probabilities with Excel.

*A property of the Poisson distribution is that the mean and variance are equal.*

In the preceding example, the mean of the Poisson distribution is $\mu = 10$ arrivals per 15-minute period. A property of the Poisson distribution is that the mean of the distribution and the variance of the distribution are *equal*. Thus, the variance for the number of arrivals during 15-minute periods is $\sigma^2 = 10$. The standard deviation is $\sigma = \sqrt{10} = 3.16$.

Our illustration involves a 15-minute period, but other time periods can be used. Suppose we want to compute the probability of one arrival in a 3-minute period. Because 10 is the expected number of arrivals in a 15-minute period, we see that $10/15 = 2/3$ is the expected number of arrivals in a 1-minute period and that $(2/3)(3 \text{ minutes}) = 2$ is the expected number of arrivals in a 3-minute period. Thus, the probability of $x$ arrivals in a 3-minute time period with $\mu = 2$ is given by the following Poisson probability function.

$$f(x) = \frac{2^x e^{-2}}{x!}$$

The probability of one arrival in a 3-minute period is calculated as follows:

$$\text{Probability of exactly} \atop \text{1 arrival in 3 minutes} = f(1) = \frac{2^1 e^{-2}}{1!} = .2707$$

Earlier we computed the probability of five arrivals in a 15-minute period; it was .0378. Note that the probability of one arrival in a three-minute period (.2707) is not the same. When computing a Poisson probability for a different time interval, we must first convert the mean arrival rate to the time period of interest and then compute the probability.

## An Example Involving Length or Distance Intervals

Let us illustrate an application not involving time intervals in which the Poisson distribution is useful. Suppose we are concerned with the occurrence of major defects in a highway one month after resurfacing. We will assume that the probability of a defect is the same for any two highway intervals of equal length and that the occurrence or nonoccurrence of a defect in any one interval is independent of the occurrence or nonoccurrence of a defect in any other interval. Hence, the Poisson distribution can be applied.

Suppose we learn that major defects one month after resurfacing occur at the average rate of two per mile. Let us find the probability of no major defects in a particular 3-mile section of the highway. Because we are interested in an interval with a length of 3 miles, $\mu = (2 \text{ defects/mile})(3 \text{ miles}) = 6$ represents the expected number of major defects over the 3-mile section of highway. Using equation (5.11), the probability of no major defects is $f(0) = 6^0 e^{-6}/0! = .0025$. Thus, it is unlikely that no major defects will occur in the 3-mile section. In fact, this example indicates a $1 - .0025 = .9975$ probability of at least one major defect in the 3-mile highway section.

## Using Excel to Compute Poisson Probabilities

The Excel function for computing Poisson probabilities and cumulative probabilities is called POISSON.DIST. It works in much the same way as the Excel function for computing binomial probabilities. Here we show how to use it to compute Poisson probabilities and cumulative probabilities. To illustrate, we use the example introduced earlier in this section; cars arrive at a bank drive-up teller window at the mean rate of 10 per 15-minute time interval. Refer to Figure 5.8 as we describe the tasks involved.

**Enter Data:**   In order to compute a Poisson probability, we must know the mean number of occurrences ($\mu$) per time period and the number of occurrences for which we want to compute the probability ($x$). For the drive-up teller window example, the occurrences of interest are the arrivals of cars. The mean arrival rate is 10, which has been entered into cell D1. Earlier in this section, we computed the probability of 5 arrivals. But suppose we now want to compute the probability of 0 up through 20 arrivals. To do so, we enter the values 0, 1, 2, . . . , 20 into cells A4:A24.

**Enter Functions and Formulas:**   The POISSON.DIST function has three inputs: the first is the value of $x$, the second is the value of $\mu$, and the third is FALSE or TRUE. We choose FALSE for the third input if a probability is desired and TRUE if a cumulative probability is

**FIGURE 5.8**   EXCEL WORKSHEET FOR COMPUTING POISSON PROBABILITIES desired. The formula =POISSON.DIST(A4,$D$1,FALSE) has been entered into cell B4 to compute the probability of 0 arrivals in a 15-minute period. The value worksheet in the foreground shows that the probability of 0 arrivals is 0.0000. The formula in cell B4 is copied to cells B5:B24 to compute the probabilities for 1 through 20 arrivals. Note, in cell B9 of the value worksheet, that the probability of 5 arrivals is .0378. This result is the same as we calculated earlier in the text.

Notice how easy it was to compute all the probabilities for 0 through 20 arrivals using the POISSON.DIST function. These calculations would take quite a bit of work using a calculator. We have also used Excel's chart tools to develop a graph of the Poisson probability distribution of arrivals. See the value worksheet in Figure 5.8. This chart gives a nice graphical presentation of the probabilities for the various number of arrival possibilities in a 15-minute interval. We can quickly see that the most likely number of arrivals is 9 or 10 and that the probabilities fall off rather smoothly for smaller and larger values.

Let us now see how cumulative probabilities are generated using Excel's POISSON.DIST function. It is really a simple extension of what we have already done. We again use the example of arrivals at a drive-up teller window. Refer to Figure 5.9 as we describe the tasks involved.

**FIGURE 5.9**   EXCEL WORKSHEET FOR COMPUTING CUMULATIVE POISSON PROBABILITIES

**Enter Data:**   To compute cumulative Poisson probabilities we must provide the mean number of occurrences ($\mu$) per time period and the values of $x$ that we are interested in. The mean arrival rate (10) has been entered into cell D1. Suppose we want to compute the cumulative probabilities for a number of arrivals ranging from zero up through 20. To do so, we enter the values 0, 1, 2, . . . , 20 into cells A4:A24.

**Enter Functions and Formulas:**   Refer to the formula worksheet in the background of Figure 5.8. The formulas we enter into cells B4:B24 of Figure 5.9 are the same as in Figure 5.8 with one exception. Instead of FALSE for the third input, we enter the word TRUE to obtain cumulative probabilities. After entering these formulas into cells B4:B24 of the worksheet in Figure 5.9, the cumulative probabilities shown were obtained.

Note, in Figure 5.9, that the probability of 5 or fewer arrivals is .0671 and that the probability of 4 or fewer arrivals is .0293. Thus, the probability of exactly 5 arrivals is the difference in these two numbers: $f(5) = .0671 - .0293 = .0378$. We computed this probability earlier in this section and in Figure 5.8. Using these cumulative probabilities, it is easy to compute the probability that a random variable lies within a certain interval. For instance, suppose we wanted to know the probability of more than 5 and fewer than 16 arrivals. We would just find the cumulative probability of 15 arrivals and subtract from that the cumulative probability for 5 arrivals. Referring to Figure 5.9 to obtain the appropriate probabilities, we obtain $.9513 - .0671 = .8842$. With such a high probability, we could conclude that 6 to 15 cars will arrive in most 15-minute intervals. Using the cumulative probability for 20 arrivals, we can also conclude that the probability of more than 20 arrivals in a 15-minute period is $1 - .9984 = .0016$; thus, there is almost no chance of more than 20 cars arriving.

## Exercises

### Methods

38.  Consider a Poisson distribution with $\mu = 3$.
  a.  Write the appropriate Poisson probability function.
  b.  Compute $f(2)$.
  c.  Compute $f(1)$.
  d.  Compute $P(x \geq 2)$.

39.  Consider a Poisson distribution with a mean of two occurrences per time period.
  a.  Write the appropriate Poisson probability function.
  b.  What is the expected number of occurrences in three time periods?
  c.  Write the appropriate Poisson probability function to determine the probability of $x$ occurrences in three time periods.
  d.  Compute the probability of two occurrences in one time period.
  e.  Compute the probability of six occurrences in three time periods.
  f.  Compute the probability of five occurrences in two time periods.

### Applications

40.  Phone calls arrive at the rate of 48 per hour at the reservation desk for Regional Airways.
  a.  Compute the probability of receiving three calls in a 5-minute interval of time.
  b.  Compute the probability of receiving exactly 10 calls in 15 minutes.
  c.  Suppose no calls are currently on hold. If the agent takes 5 minutes to complete the current call, how many callers do you expect to be waiting by that time? What is the probability that none will be waiting?
  d.  If no calls are currently being processed, what is the probability that the agent can take 3 minutes for personal time without being interrupted by a call?

41. During the period of time that a local university takes phone-in registrations, calls come in at the rate of one every two minutes.
    a. What is the expected number of calls in one hour?
    b. What is the probability of three calls in five minutes?
    c. What is the probability of no calls in a five-minute period?

42. More than 50 million guests stay at bed and breakfasts (B&Bs) each year. The website for the Bed and Breakfast Inns of North America, which averages seven visitors per minute, enables many B&Bs to attract guests (*Time,* September 2001).
    a. Compute the probability of no website visitors in a one-minute period.
    b. Compute the probability of two or more website visitors in a one-minute period.
    c. Compute the probability of one or more website visitors in a 30-second period.
    d. Compute the probability of five or more website visitors in a one-minute period.

43. Airline passengers arrive randomly and independently at the passenger-screening facility at a major international airport. The mean arrival rate is 10 passengers per minute.
    a. Compute the probability of no arrivals in a one-minute period.
    b. Compute the probability that three or fewer passengers arrive in a one-minute period.
    c. Compute the probability of no arrivals in a 15-second period.
    d. Compute the probability of at least one arrival in a 15-second period.

44. An average of 15 aircraft accidents occur each year (*The World Almanac and Book of Facts,* 2004).
    a. Compute the mean number of aircraft accidents per month.
    b. Compute the probability of no accidents during a month.
    c. Compute the probability of exactly one accident during a month.
    d. Compute the probability of more than one accident during a month.

45. The National Safety Council (NSC) estimates that off-the-job accidents cost U.S. businesses almost $200 billion annually in lost productivity (National Safety Council, March 2006). Based on NSC estimates, companies with 50 employees are expected to average three employee off-the-job accidents per year. Answer the following questions for companies with 50 employees.
    a. What is the probability of no off-the-job accidents during a one-year period?
    b. What is the probability of at least two off-the-job accidents during a one-year period?
    c. What is the expected number of off-the-job accidents during six months?
    d. What is the probability of no off-the-job accidents during the next six months?

## 5.6  Hypergeometric Probability Distribution

The **hypergeometric probability distribution** is closely related to the binomial distribution. The two probability distributions differ in two key ways. With the hypergeometric distribution, the trials are not independent, and the probability of success changes from trial to trial.

In the usual notation for the hypergeometric distribution, $r$ denotes the number of elements in the population of size $N$ labeled success, and $N - r$ denotes the number of elements in the population labeled failure. The **hypergeometric probability function** is used to compute the probability that in a random selection of $n$ elements, selected without replacement, we obtain $x$ elements labeled success and $n - x$ elements labeled failure. For this outcome to occur, we must obtain $x$ successes from the $r$ successes in the population and $n - x$ failures from the $N - r$ failures. The following hypergeometric probability function provides $f(x)$, the probability of obtaining $x$ successes in $n$ trials.

HYPERGEOMETRIC PROBABILITY FUNCTION

$$f(x) = \frac{\binom{r}{x}\binom{N-r}{n-x}}{\binom{N}{n}}$$    **(5.12)**

where

$$x = \text{the number of successes}$$
$$n = \text{the number of trials}$$
$$f(x) = \text{the probability of } x \text{ successes in } n \text{ trials}$$
$$N = \text{the number of elements in the population}$$
$$r = \text{the number of elements in the population labeled success}$$

Note that $\binom{N}{n}$ represents the number of ways $n$ elements can be selected from a population of size $N$; $\binom{r}{x}$ represents the number of ways that $x$ successes can be selected from a total of $r$ successes in the population; and $\binom{N-r}{n-x}$ represents the number of ways that $n - x$ failures can be selected from a total of $N - r$ failures in the population.

For the hypergeometric probability distribution, $x$ is a discrete random variable and the probability function $f(x)$ given by equation (5.12) is usually applicable for values of $x = 0$, 1, 2, . . . , $n$. However, only values of $x$ where the number of observed successes is *less than or equal to* the number of successes in the population ($x \le r$) and where the number of observed failures is *less than or equal to* the number of failures in the population ($n - x \le N - r$) are valid. If these two conditions do not hold for one or more values of $x$, the corresponding $f(x) = 0$, indicating that the probability of this value of $x$ is zero.

To illustrate the computations involved in using equation (5.12), let us consider the following quality control application. Electric fuses produced by Ontario Electric are packaged in boxes of 12 units each. Suppose an inspector randomly selects 3 of the 12 fuses in a box for testing. If the box contains exactly five defective fuses, what is the probability that the inspector will find exactly one of the three fuses defective? In this application, $n = 3$ and $N = 12$. With $r = 5$ defective fuses in the box, the probability of finding $x = 1$ defective fuse is

$$f(1) = \frac{\binom{5}{1}\binom{7}{2}}{\binom{12}{3}} = \frac{\left(\frac{5!}{1!4!}\right)\left(\frac{7!}{2!5!}\right)}{\left(\frac{12!}{3!9!}\right)} = \frac{(5)(21)}{220} = .4773$$

Now suppose that we wanted to know the probability of finding *at least* one defective fuse. The easiest way to answer this question is first to compute the probability that the inspector does not find any defective fuses. The probability of $x = 0$ is

$$f(0) = \frac{\binom{5}{0}\binom{7}{3}}{\binom{12}{3}} = \frac{\left(\frac{5!}{0!5!}\right)\left(\frac{7!}{3!4!}\right)}{\left(\frac{12!}{3!9!}\right)} = \frac{(1)(35)}{220} = .1591$$

With a probability of zero defective fuses $f(0) = .1591$, we conclude that the probability of finding at least one defective fuse must be $1 - .1591 = .8409$. Thus, there is a reasonably high probability that the inspector will find at least one defective fuse.

The mean and variance of a hypergeometric distribution are as follows.

$$E(x) = \mu = n\left(\frac{r}{N}\right) \tag{5.13}$$

$$\text{Var}(x) = \sigma^2 = n\left(\frac{r}{N}\right)\left(1 - \frac{r}{N}\right)\left(\frac{N-n}{N-1}\right) \tag{5.14}$$

In the preceding example $n = 3$, $r = 5$, and $N = 12$. Thus, the mean and variance for the number of defective fuses are

$$\mu = n\left(\frac{r}{N}\right) = 3\left(\frac{5}{12}\right) = 1.25$$

$$\sigma^2 = n\left(\frac{r}{N}\right)\left(1 - \frac{r}{N}\right)\left(\frac{N-n}{N-1}\right) = 3\left(\frac{5}{12}\right)\left(1 - \frac{5}{12}\right)\left(\frac{12-3}{12-1}\right) = .60$$

The standard deviation is $\sigma = \sqrt{.60} = .77$.

## Using Excel to Compute Hypergeometric Probabilities

The Excel function for computing hypergeometric probabilities is HYPGEOM.DIST. It has five inputs: the first is the value of $x$, the second is the value of $n$, the third is the value of $r$, the fourth is the value of $N$, and the fifth is FALSE or TRUE. We choose FALSE if a probability is desired and TRUE if a cumulative probability is desired. This function's usage is similar to that of BINOM.DIST for the binomial distribution and POISSON.DIST for the Poisson distribution, so we dispense with showing a worksheet figure and just explain how to use the function.

Let us reconsider the example of selecting 3 fuses for inspection from a fuse box containing 12 fuses, 5 of which are defective. We want to find the probability that 1 of the 3 fuses selected is defective. In this case, the five inputs are $x = 1$, $n = 3$, $r = 5$, $N = 12$, and FALSE. So, the appropriate formula to place in a cell of an Excel worksheet is =HYPGEOM.DIST(1,3,5,12,FALSE). Placing this formula in a cell of an Excel worksheet provides a hypergeometric probability of .4773.

If we want to know the probability that none of the 3 fuses selected is defective, the five function inputs are $x = 0$, $n = 3$, $r = 5$, $N = 12$, and FALSE. So, using the HYPGEOM.DIST function to compute the probability of randomly selecting 3 fuses without any being defective, we would enter the following formula into an Excel worksheet: =HYPGEOM.DIST(0,3,5,12,FALSE). The probability is .1591.

Cumulative probabilities can be obtained in a similar fashion by using TRUE for the fifth input. For instance, to compute the probability of finding at most 1 defective fuse, the appropriate formula is =HYPGEOM.DIST(1,3,5,12,TRUE). Placing this formula in a cell of an Excel worksheet provides a hypergeometric cumulative probability of .6364.

## NOTES AND COMMENTS

Consider a hypergeometric distribution with $n$ trials. Let $p = (r/N)$ denote the probability of a success on the first trial. If the population size is large, the term $(N-n)/(N-1)$ in equation (5.14) approaches 1. As a result, the expected value and variance can be written $E(x) = np$ and $\text{Var}(x) = np(1-p)$. Note that these expressions are the same as the expressions used to compute the expected value and variance of a binomial distribution, as in equations (5.9) and (5.10). When the population size is large, a hypergeometric distribution can be approximated by a binomial distribution with $n$ trials and a probability of success $p = (r/N)$

## Exercises

### Methods

46.   Suppose $N = 10$ and $r = 3$. Compute the hypergeometric probabilities for the following values of $n$ and $x$.
   a.   $n = 4, x = 1$
   b.   $n = 2, x = 2$
   c.   $n = 2, x = 0$
   d.   $n = 4, x = 2$
   e.   $n = 4, x = 4$

47.   Suppose $N = 15$ and $r = 4$. What is the probability of $x = 3$ for $n = 10$?

### Applications

48.   In a survey conducted by the Gallup Organization, respondents were asked, "What is your favorite sport to watch?" Football and basketball ranked number 1 and 2 in terms of preference (Gallup website, January 3, 2004). Assume that in a group of 10 individuals, seven prefer football and three prefer basketball. A random sample of three of these individuals is selected.
   a.   What is the probability that exactly two prefer football?
   b.   What is the probability that the majority (either two or three) prefer football?

49.   Blackjack, or twenty-one as it is frequently called, is a popular gambling game played in Las Vegas casinos. A player is dealt two cards. Face cards (jacks, queens, and kings) and tens have a point value of 10. Aces have a point value of 1 or 11. A 52-card deck contains 16 cards with a point value of 10 (jacks, queens, kings, and tens) and four aces.
   a.   What is the probability that both cards dealt are aces or 10-point cards?
   b.   What is the probability that both of the cards are aces?
   c.   What is the probability that both of the cards have a point value of 10?
   d.   A blackjack is a 10-point card and an ace for a value of 21. Use your answers to parts (a), (b), and (c) to determine the probability that a player is dealt blackjack. (*Hint:* Part (d) is not a hypergeometric problem. Develop your own logical relationship as to how the hypergeometric probabilities from parts (a), (b), and (c) can be combined to answer this question.)

50.   Axline Computers manufactures personal computers at two plants, one in Texas and the other in Hawaii. The Texas plant has 40 employees; the Hawaii plant has 20. A random sample of 10 employees is to be asked to fill out a benefits questionnaire.
   a.   What is the probability that none of the employees in the sample works at the plant in Hawaii?
   b.   What is the probability that one of the employees in the sample works at the plant in Hawaii?
   c.   What is the probability that two or more of the employees in the sample work at the plant in Hawaii?
   d.   What is the probability that nine of the employees in the sample work at the plant in Texas?

51.   The Zagat Restaurant Survey provides food, decor, and service ratings for some of the top restaurants across the United States. For 15 restaurants located in Boston, the average price of a dinner, including one drink and tip, was $48.60. You are leaving for a business trip to Boston and will eat dinner at three of these restaurants. Your company will reimburse you for a maximum of $50 per dinner. Business associates familiar with these restaurants have told you that the meal cost at one-third of these restaurants will exceed $50. Suppose that you randomly select three of these restaurants for dinner.

a. What is the probability that none of the meals will exceed the cost covered by your company?
b. What is the probability that one of the meals will exceed the cost covered by your company?
c. What is the probability that two of the meals will exceed the cost covered by your company?
d. What is the probability that all three of the meals will exceed the cost covered by your company?

52. The Troubled Asset Relief Program (TARP), passed by the U.S. Congress in October 2008, provided $700 billion in assistance for the struggling U.S. economy. Over $200 billion was given to troubled financial institutions with the hope that there would be an increase in lending to help jump-start the economy. But three months later, a Federal Reserve survey found that two-thirds of the banks that had received TARP funds had tightened terms for business loans (*The Wall Street Journal*, February 3, 2009). Of the 10 banks that were the biggest recipients of TARP funds, only 3 had actually increased lending during this period.

| **Increased Lending** | **Decreased Lending** |
| --- | --- |
| BB&T | Bank of America |
| Sun Trust Banks | Capital One |
| U.S. Bancorp | Citigroup |
| | Fifth Third Bancorp |
| | JPMorgan Chase |
| | Regions Financial |
| | Wells Fargo |

For the purposes of this exercise, assume that you will randomly select 3 of these 10 banks for a study that will continue to monitor bank lending practices. Let $x$ be a random variable indicating the number of banks in the study that had increased lending.
a. What is $f(0)$? What is your interpretation of this value?
b. What is $f(3)$? What is your interpretation of this value?
c. Compute $f(1)$ and $f(2)$. Show the probability distribution for the number of banks in the study that had increased lending. What value of $x$ has the highest probability?
d. What is the probability that the study will have at least one bank that had increased lending?
e. Compute the expected value, variance, and standard deviation for the random variable.

## Summary

A random variable provides a numerical description of the outcome of an experiment. The probability distribution for a random variable describes how the probabilities are distributed over the values the random variable can assume. For any discrete random variable $x$, the probability distribution is defined by a probability function, denoted by $f(x)$, which provides the probability associated with each value of the random variable. Once the probability function is defined, we can compute the expected value, variance, and standard deviation for the random variable.

The binomial distribution can be used to determine the probability of $x$ successes in $n$ trials whenever the experiment has the following properties:

1. The experiment consists of a sequence of $n$ identical trials.
2. Two outcomes are possible on each trial, one called success and the other failure.

   **3.** The probability of a success $p$ does not change from trial to trial. Consequently, the probability of failure, $1 - p$, does not change from trial to trial.
   **4.** The trials are independent.

When the four properties hold, the binomial probability function can be used to determine the probability of obtaining $x$ successes in $n$ trials. Formulas were also presented for the mean and variance of the binomial distribution.

The Poisson distribution is used when it is desirable to determine the probability of obtaining $x$ occurrences over an interval of time or space. The following assumptions are necessary for the Poisson distribution to be applicable.

   **1.** The probability of an occurrence of the event is the same for any two intervals of equal length.
   **2.** The occurrence or nonoccurrence of the event in any interval is independent of the occurrence or nonoccurrence of the event in any other interval.

A third discrete probability distribution, the hypergeometric, was introduced in Section 5.6. Like the binomial, it is used to compute the probability of $x$ successes in $n$ trials. But, in contrast to the binomial, the probability of success changes from trial to trial.

## Glossary

**Random variable** A numerical description of the outcome of an experiment.

**Discrete random variable** A random variable that may assume either a finite number of values or an infinite sequence of values.

**Continuous random variable** A random variable that may assume any numerical value in an interval or collection of intervals.

**Probability distribution** A description of how the probabilities are distributed over the values of the random variable.

**Probability function** A function, denoted by $f(x)$, that provides the probability that $x$ assumes a particular value for a discrete random variable.

**Discrete uniform probability distribution** A probability distribution for which each possible value of the random variable has the same probability.

**Expected value** A measure of the central location of a random variable.

**Variance** A measure of the variability, or dispersion, of a random variable.

**Standard deviation** The positive square root of the variance.

**Binomial experiment** An experiment having the four properties stated at the beginning of Section 5.4.

**Binomial probability distribution** A probability distribution showing the probability of $x$ successes in $n$ trials of a binomial experiment.

**Binomial probability function** The function used to compute binomial probabilities.

**Poisson probability distribution** A probability distribution showing the probability of $x$ occurrences of an event over a specified interval of time or space.

**Poisson probability function** The function used to compute Poisson probabilities.

**Hypergeometric probability distribution** A probability distribution showing the probability of $x$ successes in $n$ trials from a population with $r$ successes and $N - r$ failures.

**Hypergeometric probability function** The function used to compute hypergeometric probabilities.

## Key Formulas

**Discrete Uniform Probability Function**

$$f(x) = 1/n \tag{5.3}$$

**Expected Value of a Discrete Random Variable**

$$E(x) = \mu = \Sigma x f(x) \tag{5.4}$$

**Variance of a Discrete Random Variable**

$$\text{Var}(x) = \sigma^2 = \Sigma(x - \mu)^2 f(x) \tag{5.5}$$

**Number of Experimental Outcomes Providing Exactly $x$ Successes in $n$ Trials**

$$\binom{n}{x} = \frac{n!}{x!(n-x)!} \tag{5.6}$$

**Binomial Probability Function**

$$f(x) = \binom{n}{x} p^x (1-p)^{(n-x)} \tag{5.8}$$

**Expected Value for the Binomial Distribution**

$$E(x) = \mu = np \tag{5.9}$$

**Variance for the Binomial Distribution**

$$\text{Var}(x) = \sigma^2 = np(1-p) \tag{5.10}$$

**Poisson Probability Function**

$$f(x) = \frac{\mu^x e^{-\mu}}{x!} \tag{5.11}$$

**Hypergeometric Probability Function**

$$f(x) = \frac{\binom{r}{x}\binom{N-r}{n-x}}{\binom{N}{n}} \tag{5.12}$$

**Expected Value for the Hypergeometric Distribution**

$$E(x) = \mu = n\left(\frac{r}{N}\right) \tag{5.13}$$

**Variance for the Hypergeometric Distribution**

$$\text{Var}(x) = \sigma^2 = n\left(\frac{r}{N}\right)\left(1 - \frac{r}{N}\right)\left(\frac{N-n}{N-1}\right) \tag{5.14}$$

## Supplementary Exercises

53. The *Barron's* Big Money Poll asked 131 investment managers across the United States about their short-term investment outlook (*Barron's,* October 28, 2002). Their responses showed that 4% were very bullish, 39% were bullish, 29% were neutral, 21% were bearish, and 7% were very bearish. Let $x$ be the random variable reflecting the level of optimism about the market. Set $x = 5$ for very bullish down through $x = 1$ for very bearish.
    a. Develop a probability distribution for the level of optimism of investment managers.
    b. Compute the expected value for the level of optimism.
    c. Compute the variance and standard deviation for the level of optimism.
    d. Comment on what your results imply about the level of optimism and its variability.

54. The American Association of Individual Investors publishes an annual guide to the top mutual funds (*The Individual Investor's Guide to the Top Mutual Funds,* 22e, American Association of Individual Investors, 2003). The total risk ratings for 29 categories of mutual funds are as follows.

| Total Risk | Number of Fund Categories |
|---|---|
| Low | 7 |
| Below Average | 6 |
| Average | 3 |
| Above Average | 6 |
| High | 7 |

    a. Let $x = 1$ for low risk up through $x = 5$ for high risk, and develop a probability distribution for level of risk.
    b. What are the expected value and variance for total risk?
    c. It turns out that 11 of the fund categories were bond funds. For the bond funds, seven categories were rated low and four were rated below average. Compare the total risk of the bond funds with the 18 categories of stock funds.

55. The budgeting process for a midwestern college resulted in expense forecasts for the coming year (in $ millions) of $9, $10, $11, $12, and $13. Because the actual expenses are unknown, the following respective probabilities are assigned: .3, .2, .25, .05, and .2.
    a. Show the probability distribution for the expense forecast.
    b. What is the expected value of the expense forecast for the coming year?
    c. What is the variance of the expense forecast for the coming year?
    d. If income projections for the year are estimated at $12 million, comment on the financial position of the college.

56. A survey showed that the average commuter spends about 26 minutes on a one-way door-to-door trip from home to work. In addition, 5% of commuters reported a one-way commute of more than one hour (Bureau of Transportation Statistics website, January 12, 2004).
    a. If 20 commuters are surveyed on a particular day, what is the probability that three will report a one-way commute of more than one hour?
    b. If 20 commuters are surveyed on a particular day, what is the probability that none will report a one-way commute of more than one hour?
    c. If a company has 2000 employees, what is the expected number of employees that have a one-way commute of more than one hour?
    d. If a company has 2000 employees, what are the variance and standard deviation of the number of employees that have a one-way commute of more than one hour?

57. A political action group is planning to interview home owners to assess the impact caused by a recent slump in housing prices. According to a *Wall Street Journal*/Harris Interactive Personal Finance poll, 26% of individuals aged 18–34, 50% of individuals aged 35–44, and 88% of individuals aged 55 and over are home owners (All Business website, January 23, 2008).

    a. How many people from the 18–34 age group must be sampled to find an expected number of at least 20 home owners?

    b. How many people from the 35–44 age group must be sampled to find an expected number of at least 20 home owners?

    c. How many people from the 55 and over age group must be sampled to find an expected number of at least 20 home owners?

    d. If the number of 18–34-year-olds sampled is equal to the value identified in part (a), what is the standard deviation of the number who will be home owners?

    e. If the number of 35–44-year-olds sampled is equal to the value identified in part (b), what is the standard deviation of the number who will be home owners?

58. Many companies use a quality control technique called acceptance sampling to monitor incoming shipments of parts, raw materials, and so on. In the electronics industry, component parts are commonly shipped from suppliers in large lots. Inspection of a sample of $n$ components can be viewed as the $n$ trials of a binomial experiment. The outcome for each component tested (trial) will be that the component is classified as good or defective. Reynolds Electronics accepts a lot from a particular supplier if the defective components in the lot do not exceed 1%. Suppose a random sample of five items from a recent shipment is tested.

    a. Assume that 1% of the shipment is defective. Compute the probability that no items in the sample are defective.

    b. Assume that 1% of the shipment is defective. Compute the probability that exactly one item in the sample is defective.

    c. What is the probability of observing one or more defective items in the sample if 1% of the shipment is defective?

    d. Would you feel comfortable accepting the shipment if one item was found to be defective? Why or why not?

59. The unemployment rate in the state of Arizona is 4.1% (CNN Money website, May 2, 2007). Assume that 100 employable people in Arizona are selected randomly.

    a. What is the expected number of people who are unemployed?

    b. What are the variance and standard deviation of the number of people who are unemployed?

60. A poll conducted by Zogby International showed that of those Americans who said music plays a "very important" role in their lives, 30% said their local radio stations "always" play the kind of music they like (Zogby website, January 12, 2004). Suppose a sample is taken of 800 people who say music plays an important role in their lives.

    a. How many would you expect to say that their local radio stations always play the kind of music they like?

    b. What is the standard deviation of the number of respondents who think their local radio stations always play the kind of music they like?

    c. What is the standard deviation of the number of respondents who do not think their local radio stations always play the kind of music they like?

61. Cars arrive at a car wash randomly and independently; the probability of an arrival is the same for any two time intervals of equal length. The mean arrival rate is 15 cars per hour. What is the probability that 20 or more cars will arrive during any given hour of operation?

62. A new automated production process averages 1.5 breakdowns per day. Because of the cost associated with a breakdown, management is concerned about the possibility of having

three or more breakdowns during a day. Assume that breakdowns occur randomly, that the probability of a breakdown is the same for any two time intervals of equal length, and that breakdowns in one period are independent of breakdowns in other periods. What is the probability of having three or more breakdowns during a day?

63. A regional director responsible for business development in the state of Pennsylvania is concerned about the number of small business failures. If the mean number of small business failures per month is 10, what is the probability that exactly four small businesses will fail during a given month? Assume that the probability of a failure is the same for any two months and that the occurrence or nonoccurrence of a failure in any month is independent of failures in any other month.

64. Customer arrivals at a bank are random and independent; the probability of an arrival in any one-minute period is the same as the probability of an arrival in any other one-minute period. Answer the following questions, assuming a mean arrival rate of three customers per minute.
    a. What is the probability of exactly three arrivals in a one-minute period?
    b. What is the probability of at least three arrivals in a one-minute period?

65. A deck of playing cards contains 52 cards, four of which are aces. What is the probability that the deal of a five-card hand provides:
    a. A pair of aces?
    b. Exactly one ace?
    c. No aces?
    d. At least one ace?

66. *U.S. News & World Report*'s ranking of America's best graduate schools of business showed Harvard University and Stanford University in a tie for first place. In addition, 7 of the top 10 graduate schools of business showed students with an average undergraduate grade point average (GPA) of 3.50 or higher (*America's Best Graduate Schools, 2009 Edition, U.S. News & World Report*). Suppose that we randomly select 2 of the top 10 graduate schools of business.
    a. What is the probability that exactly one school has students with an average undergraduate GPA of 3.50 or higher?
    b. What is the probability that both schools have students with an average undergraduate GPA of 3.50 or higher?
    c. What is the probability that neither school has students with an average undergraduate GPA of 3.50 or higher?

# CHAPTER 6

# Continuous Probability Distributions

## STATISTICS *in* PRACTICE

### PROCTER & GAMBLE*
*CINCINNATI, OHIO*

Procter & Gamble (P&G) produces and markets such products as detergents, disposable diapers, over-the-counter pharmaceuticals, dentifrices, bar soaps, mouth-washes, and paper towels. Worldwide, it has the leading brand in more categories than any other consumer products company. Since its merger with Gillette, P&G also produces and markets razors, blades, and many other personal care products.

As a leader in the application of statistical methods in decision making, P&G employs people with diverse academic backgrounds: engineering, statistics, operations research, and business. The major quantitative technologies for which these people provide support are probabilistic decision and risk analysis, advanced simulation, quality improvement, and quantitative methods (e.g., linear programming, regression analysis, probability analysis).

The Industrial Chemicals Division of P&G is a major supplier of fatty alcohols derived from natural substances such as coconut oil and from petroleum-based derivatives. The division wanted to know the economic risks and opportunities of expanding its fatty-alcohol production facilities, so it called in P&G's experts in probabilistic decision and risk analysis to help. After structuring and modeling the problem, they determined that the key to profitability was the cost difference between the petroleum- and coconut-based raw materials. Future costs were unknown, but the analysts were able to approximate them with the following continuous random variables.

$x$ = the coconut oil price per pound of fatty alcohol

and

$y$ = the petroleum raw material price per pound of fatty alcohol

Because the key to profitability was the difference between these two random variables, a third random

Some of Procter & Gamble's many well-known products.

variable, $d = x - y$, was used in the analysis. Experts were interviewed to determine the probability distributions for $x$ and $y$. In turn, this information was used to develop a probability distribution for the difference in prices $d$. This continuous probability distribution showed a .90 probability that the price difference would be $.0655 or less and a .50 probability that the price difference would be $.035 or less. In addition, there was only a .10 probability that the price difference would be $.0045 or less.[†]

The Industrial Chemicals Division thought that being able to quantify the impact of raw material price differences was key to reaching a consensus. The probabilities obtained were used in a sensitivity analysis of the raw material price difference. The analysis yielded sufficient insight to form the basis for a recommendation to management.

The use of continuous random variables and their probability distributions was helpful to P&G in analyzing the economic risks associated with its fatty-alcohol production. In this chapter, you will gain an understanding of continuous random variables and their probability distributions, including one of the most important probability distributions in statistics, the normal distribution.

---

*The authors are indebted to Joel Kahn of Procter & Gamble for providing this Statistics in Practice.

[†]The price differences stated here have been modified to protect proprietary data.

In the preceding chapter we discussed discrete random variables and their probability distributions. In this chapter we turn to the study of continuous random variables. Specifically, we discuss three continuous probability distributions: the uniform, the normal, and the exponential.

A fundamental difference separates discrete and continuous random variables in terms of how probabilities are computed. For a discrete random variable, the probability function $f(x)$ provides the probability that the random variable assumes a particular value. With continuous random variables, the counterpart of the probability function is the **probability density function**, also denoted by $f(x)$. The difference is that the probability density function does not directly provide probabilities. However, the area under the graph of $f(x)$ corresponding to a given interval does provide the probability that the continuous random variable $x$ assumes a value in that interval. So when we compute probabilities for continuous random variables we are computing the probability that the random variable assumes any value in an interval.

Because the area under the graph of $f(x)$ at any particular point is zero, one of the implications of the definition of probability for continuous random variables is that the probability of any particular value of the random variable is zero. In Section 6.1 we demonstrate these concepts for a continuous random variable that has a uniform distribution.

Much of the chapter is devoted to describing and showing applications of the normal distribution. The normal distribution is of major importance because of its wide applicability and its extensive use in statistical inference. The chapter closes with a discussion of the exponential distribution. The exponential distribution is useful in applications involving such factors as waiting times and service times.

## ( 6.1 )  Uniform Probability Distribution

Consider the random variable $x$ representing the flight time of an airplane traveling from Chicago to New York. Suppose the flight time can be any value in the interval from 120 minutes to 140 minutes. Because the random variable $x$ can assume any value in that interval, $x$ is a continuous rather than a discrete random variable. Let us assume that sufficient actual flight data are available to conclude that the probability of a flight time within any 1-minute interval is the same as the probability of a flight time within any other 1-minute interval contained in the larger interval from 120 to 140 minutes. With every 1-minute interval being equally likely, the random variable $x$ is said to have a **uniform probability distribution**. The probability density function, which defines the uniform distribution for the flight-time random variable, is

*Whenever the probability is proportional to the length of the interval, the random variable is uniformly distributed.*

$$f(x) = \begin{cases} 1/20 & \text{for } 120 \le x \le 140 \\ 0 & \text{elsewhere} \end{cases}$$

Figure 6.1 is a graph of this probability density function. In general, the uniform probability density function for a random variable $x$ is defined by the following formula.

UNIFORM PROBABILITY DENSITY FUNCTION

$$f(x) = \begin{cases} \dfrac{1}{b-a} & \text{for } a \le x \le b \\[2mm] 0 & \text{elsewhere} \end{cases} \tag{6.1}$$

For the flight-time random variable, $a = 120$ and $b = 140$.

**FIGURE 6.1    UNIFORM PROBABILITY DISTRIBUTION FOR FLIGHT TIME**

As noted in the introduction, for a continuous random variable, we consider probability only in terms of the likelihood that a random variable assumes a value within a specified interval. In the flight time example, an acceptable probability question is: What is the probability that the flight time is between 120 and 130 minutes? That is, what is $P(120 \leq x \leq 130)$? Because the flight time must be between 120 and 140 minutes and because the probability is described as being uniform over this interval, we feel comfortable saying that $P(120 \leq x \leq 130) = .50$. In the following subsection we show that this probability can be computed as the area under the graph of $f(x)$ from 120 to 130 (see Figure 6.2).

## Area as a Measure of Probability

Let us make an observation about the graph in Figure 6.2. Consider the area under the graph of $f(x)$ in the interval from 120 to 130. The area is rectangular, and the area of a rectangle is simply the width multiplied by the height. With the width of the interval equal to $130 - 120 = 10$ and the height equal to the value of the probability density function $f(x) = 1/20$, we have area = width × height = $10(1/20) = 10/20 = .50$.

**FIGURE 6.2    AREA PROVIDES PROBABILITY OF A FLIGHT TIME BETWEEN 120 AND 130 MINUTES**

What observation can you make about the area under the graph of $f(x)$ and probability? They are identical! Indeed, this observation is valid for all continuous random variables. Once a probability density function $f(x)$ is identified, the probability that $x$ takes a value between some lower value $x_1$ and some higher value $x_2$ can be found by computing the area under the graph of $f(x)$ over the interval from $x_1$ to $x_2$.

Given the uniform distribution for flight time and using the interpretation of area as probability, we can answer any number of probability questions about flight times. For example, what is the probability of a flight time between 128 and 136 minutes? The width of the interval is $136 - 128 = 8$. With the uniform height of $f(x) = 1/20$, we see that $P(128 \leq x \leq 136) = 8(1/20) = .40$.

Note that $P(120 \leq x \leq 140) = 20(1/20) = 1$; that is, the total area under the graph of $f(x)$ is equal to 1. This property holds for all continuous probability distributions and is the analog of the condition that the sum of the probabilities must equal 1 for a discrete probability function. For a continuous probability density function, we must also require that $f(x) \geq 0$ for all values of $x$. This requirement is the analog of the requirement that $f(x) \geq 0$ for discrete probability functions.

Two major differences stand out between the treatment of continuous random variables and the treatment of their discrete counterparts.

*To see that the probability of any single point is 0, refer to Figure 6.2 and compute the probability of a single point, say, $x = 125$. $P(x = 125) = P(125 \leq x \leq 125) = 0(1/20) = 0$.*

1. We no longer talk about the probability of the random variable assuming a particular value. Instead, we talk about the probability of the random variable assuming a value within some given interval.

2. The probability of a continuous random variable assuming a value within some given interval from $x_1$ to $x_2$ is defined to be the area under the graph of the probability density function between $x_1$ and $x_2$. Because a single point is an interval of zero width, this implies that the probability of a continuous random variable assuming any particular value exactly is zero. It also means that the probability of a continuous random variable assuming a value in any interval is the same whether or not the endpoints are included.

The calculation of the expected value and variance for a continuous random variable is analogous to that for a discrete random variable. However, because the computational procedure involves integral calculus, we leave the derivation of the appropriate formulas to more advanced texts.

For the uniform continuous probability distribution introduced in this section, the formulas for the expected value and variance are

$$E(x) = \frac{a + b}{2}$$

$$\text{Var}(x) = \frac{(b - a)^2}{12}$$

In these formulas, $a$ is the smallest value and $b$ is the largest value that the random variable may assume.

Applying these formulas to the uniform distribution for flight times from Chicago to New York, we obtain

$$E(x) = \frac{(120 + 140)}{2} = 130$$

$$\text{Var}(x) = \frac{(140 - 120)^2}{12} = 33.33$$

The standard deviation of flight times can be found by taking the square root of the variance. Thus, $\sigma = 5.77$ minutes.

## NOTES AND COMMENTS

To see more clearly why the height of a probability density function is not a probability, think about a random variable with the following uniform probability distribution.

$$f(x) = \begin{cases} 2 & \text{for } 0 \leq x \leq .5 \\ 0 & \text{elsewhere} \end{cases}$$

The height of the probability density function, $f(x)$, is 2 for values of $x$ between 0 and .5. However, we know probabilities can never be greater than 1. Thus, we see that $f(x)$ cannot be interpreted as the probability of $x$.

## Exercises

### Methods

1. The random variable $x$ is known to be uniformly distributed between 1.0 and 1.5.
   a. Show the graph of the probability density function.
   b. Compute $P(x = 1.25)$.
   c. Compute $P(1.0 \leq x \leq 1.25)$.
   d. Compute $P(1.20 < x < 1.5)$.

2. The random variable $x$ is known to be uniformly distributed between 10 and 20.
   a. Show the graph of the probability density function.
   b. Compute $P(x < 15)$.
   c. Compute $P(12 \leq x \leq 18)$.
   d. Compute $E(x)$.
   e. Compute $\text{Var}(x)$.

### Applications

3. Delta Airlines quotes a flight time of 2 hours, 5 minutes for its flights from Cincinnati to Tampa. Suppose we believe that actual flight times are uniformly distributed between 2 hours and 2 hours, 20 minutes.
   a. Show the graph of the probability density function for flight time.
   b. What is the probability that the flight will be no more than 5 minutes late?
   c. What is the probability that the flight will be more than 10 minutes late?
   d. What is the expected flight time?

4. Most computer languages include a function that can be used to generate random numbers. In Excel, the RAND function can be used to generate random numbers between 0 and 1. If we let $x$ denote a random number generated using RAND, then $x$ is a continuous random variable with the following probability density function.

$$f(x) = \begin{cases} 1 & \text{for } 0 \leq x \leq 1 \\ 0 & \text{elsewhere} \end{cases}$$

   a. Graph the probability density function.
   b. What is the probability of generating a random number between .25 and .75?
   c. What is the probability of generating a random number with a value less than or equal to .30?
   d. What is the probability of generating a random number with a value greater than .60?
   e. Generate 50 random numbers by entering =RAND() into 50 cells of an Excel worksheet.
   f. Compute the mean and standard deviation for the random numbers in part (e).

5. The driving distance for the top 100 golfers on the PGA tour is between 284.7 and 310.6 yards (*Golfweek,* March 29, 2003). Assume that the driving distance for these golfers is uniformly distributed over this interval.

a.   Give a mathematical expression for the probability density function of driving distance.
b.   What is the probability the driving distance for one of these golfers is less than 290 yards?
c.   What is the probability the driving distance for one of these golfers is at least 300 yards?
d.   What is the probability the driving distance for one of these golfers is between 290 and 305 yards?
e.   How many of these golfers drive the ball at least 290 yards?

6.   On average, 30-minute television sitcoms have 22 minutes of programming (CNBC, February 23, 2006). Assume that the probability distribution for minutes of programming can be approximated by a uniform distribution from 18 minutes to 26 minutes.
a.   What is the probability that a sitcom will have 25 or more minutes of programming?
b.   What is the probability that a sitcom will have between 21 and 25 minutes of programming?
c.   What is the probability that a sitcom will have more than 10 minutes of commercials or other nonprogramming interruptions?

7.   Suppose we are interested in bidding on a piece of land and we know one other bidder is interested.[1] The seller announced that the highest bid in excess of $10,000 will be accepted. Assume that the competitor's bid $x$ is a random variable that is uniformly distributed between $10,000 and $15,000.
a.   Suppose you bid $12,000. What is the probability that your bid will be accepted?
b.   Suppose you bid $14,000. What is the probability that your bid will be accepted?
c.   What amount should you bid to maximize the probability that you get the property?
d.   Suppose you know someone who is willing to pay you $16,000 for the property. Would you consider bidding less than the amount in part (c)? Why or why not?

## 6.2   Normal Probability Distribution

*Abraham de Moivre, a French mathematician, published* The Doctrine of Chances *in 1733. He derived the normal distribution.*

The most important probability distribution for describing a continuous random variable is the **normal probability distribution**. The normal distribution has been used in a wide variety of practical applications in which the random variables are heights and weights of people, test scores, scientific measurements, amounts of rainfall, and other similar values. It is also widely used in statistical inference, which is the major topic of the remainder of this book. In such applications, the normal distribution provides a description of the likely results obtained through sampling.

### Normal Curve

The form, or shape, of the normal distribution is illustrated by the bell-shaped normal curve in Figure 6.3. The probability density function that defines the bell-shaped curve of the normal distribution follows.

NORMAL PROBABILITY DENSITY FUNCTION

$$f(x) = \frac{1}{\sigma\sqrt{2\pi}} e^{-(x-\mu)^2/2\sigma^2} \tag{6.2}$$

where

$\mu$ = mean
$\sigma$ = standard deviation
$\pi$ = 3.14159
$e$ = 2.71828

---

[1]This exercise is based on a problem suggested to us by Professor Roger Myerson of Northwestern University.

**FIGURE 6.3**    BELL-SHAPED CURVE FOR THE NORMAL DISTRIBUTION

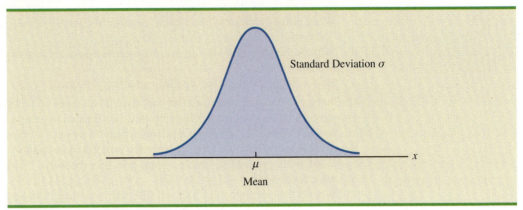

We make several observations about the characteristics of the normal distribution.

*The normal curve has two parameters, μ and σ. They determine the location and shape of the normal distribution.*

**1.** The entire family of normal distributions is differentiated by two parameters: the mean $\mu$ and the standard deviation $\sigma$.
**2.** The highest point on the normal curve is at the mean, which is also the median and mode of the distribution.
**3.** The mean of the distribution can be any numerical value: negative, zero, or positive. Three normal distributions with the same standard deviation but three different means ($-10, 0,$ and $20$) are shown here.

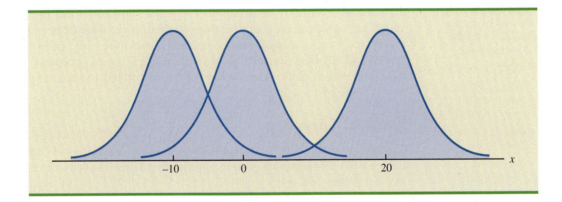

**4.** The normal distribution is symmetric, with the shape of the normal curve to the left of the mean a mirror image of the shape of the normal curve to the right of the mean. The tails of the normal curve extend to infinity in both directions and theoretically never touch the horizontal axis. Because it is symmetric, the normal distribution is not skewed; its skewness measure is zero.
**5.** The standard deviation determines how flat and wide the normal curve is. Larger values of the standard deviation result in wider, flatter curves, showing more variability in the data. Two normal distributions with the same mean but with different standard deviations are shown here.

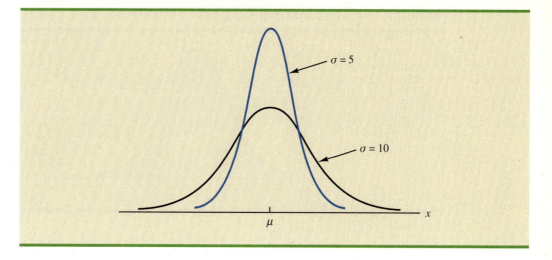

6. Probabilities for the normal random variable are given by areas under the normal curve. The total area under the curve for the normal distribution is 1. Because the distribution is symmetric, the area under the curve to the left of the mean is .50 and the area under the curve to the right of the mean is .50.

7. The percentage of values in some commonly used intervals are

   a. 68.3% of the values of a normal random variable are within plus or minus one standard deviation of its mean.

   *These percentages are the basis for the empirical rule introduced in Section 3.3.*

   b. 95.4% of the values of a normal random variable are within plus or minus two standard deviations of its mean.

   c. 99.7% of the values of a normal random variable are within plus or minus three standard deviations of its mean.

Figure 6.4 shows properties (a), (b), and (c) graphically.

**FIGURE 6.4** AREAS UNDER THE CURVE FOR ANY NORMAL DISTRIBUTION

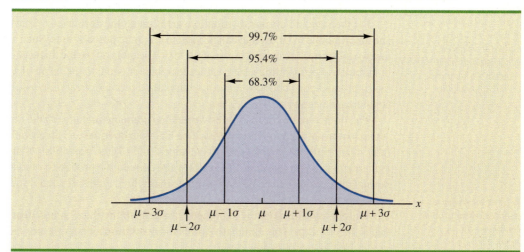

**FIGURE 6.5**    THE STANDARD NORMAL DISTRIBUTION

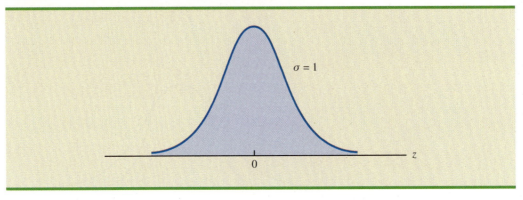

## Standard Normal Probability Distribution

A random variable that has a normal distribution with a mean of zero and a standard deviation of one is said to have a **standard normal probability distribution**. The letter $z$ is commonly used to designate this particular normal random variable. Figure 6.5 is the graph of the standard normal distribution. It has the same general appearance as other normal distributions, but with the special properties of $\mu = 0$ and $\sigma = 1$.

Because $\mu = 0$ and $\sigma = 1$, the formula for the standard normal probability density function is a simpler version of equation (6.2).

STANDARD NORMAL DENSITY FUNCTION

$$f(z) = \frac{1}{\sqrt{2\pi}} e^{-z^2/2}$$

*For the normal probability density function, the height of the normal curve varies and more advanced mathematics is required to compute the areas that represent probability.*

As with other continuous random variables, probability calculations with any normal distribution are made by computing areas under the graph of the probability density function. Thus, to find the probability that a normal random variable is within any specific interval, we must compute the area under the normal curve over that interval.

For the standard normal distribution, areas under the normal curve have been computed and are available in tables that can be used to compute probabilities. Such a table appears on the two pages inside the front cover of the text. The table on the left-hand page contains areas, or cumulative probabilities, for $z$ values less than or equal to the mean of zero. The table on the right-hand page contains areas, or cumulative probabilities, for $z$ values greater than or equal to the mean of zero.

The three types of probabilities we need to compute include (1) the probability that the standard normal random variable $z$ will be less than or equal to a given value; (2) the probability that $z$ will be between two given values; and (3) the probability that $z$ will be greater than or equal to a given value. To see how the cumulative probability table for the standard normal distribution can be used to compute these three types of probabilities, let us consider some examples.

*Because the standard normal random variable is continuous, $P(z \leq 1.00) = P(z < 1.00)$.*

We start by showing how to compute the probability that $z$ is less than or equal to 1.00; that is, $P(z \leq 1.00)$. This cumulative probability is the area under the normal curve to the left of $z = 1.00$ in the following graph.

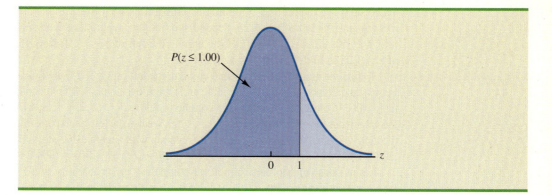

$P(z \leq 1.00)$

Refer to the right-hand page of the standard normal probability table inside the front cover of the text. The cumulative probability corresponding to $z = 1.00$ is the table value located at the intersection of the row labeled 1.0 and the column labeled .00. First we find 1.0 in the left column of the table and then find .00 in the top row of the table. By looking in the body of the table, we find that the 1.0 row and the .00 column intersect at the value of .8413; thus, $P(z \leq 1.00) = .8413$. The following excerpt from the probability table shows these steps.

| $z$ | .00 | .01 | .02 |
|-----|-----|-----|-----|
| . | | | |
| . | | | |
| . | | | |
| .9 | .8159 | .8186 | .8212 |
| 1.0 | .8413 | .8438 | .8461 |
| 1.1 | .8643 | .8665 | .8686 |
| 1.2 | .8849 | .8869 | .8888 |
| . | | | |
| . | | | |
| . | | | |

$P(z \leq 1.00)$

To illustrate the second type of probability calculation, we show how to compute the probability that $z$ is in the interval between $-.50$ and $1.25$; that is, $P(-.50 \leq z \leq 1.25)$. The following graph shows this area, or probability.

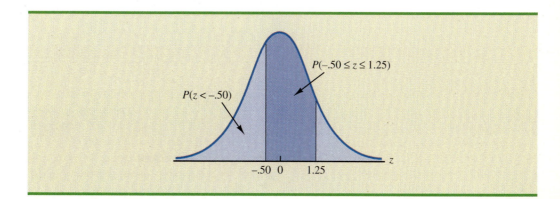

$P(z < -.50)$

$P(-.50 \leq z \leq 1.25)$

Three steps are required to compute this probability. First, we find the area under the normal curve to the left of $z = 1.25$. Second, we find the area under the normal curve to the left of $z = -.50$. Finally, we subtract the area to the left of $z = -.50$ from the area to the left of $z = 1.25$ to find $P(-.50 \leq z \leq 1.25)$.

To find the area under the normal curve to the left of $z = 1.25$, we first locate the 1.2 row in the standard normal probability table and then move across to the .05 column. Because the table value in the 1.2 row and the .05 column is .8944, $P(z \leq 1.25) = .8944$. Similarly, to find the area under the curve to the left of $z = -.50$, we use the left-hand page of the table to locate the table value in the $-.5$ row and the .00 column; with a table value of .3085, $P(z \leq -.50) = .3085$. Thus, $P(-.50 \leq z \leq 1.25) = P(z \leq 1.25) - P(z \leq -.50) = .8944 - .3085 = .5859$.

Let us consider another example of computing the probability that $z$ is in the interval between two given values. Often it is of interest to compute the probability that a normal random variable assumes a value within a certain number of standard deviations of the mean. Suppose we want to compute the probability that the standard normal random variable is within one standard deviation of the mean; that is, $P(-1.00 \leq z \leq 1.00)$. To compute this probability we must find the area under the curve between $-1.00$ and $1.00$. Earlier we found that $P(z \leq 1.00) = .8413$. Referring again to the table inside the front cover of the book, we find that the area under the curve to the left of $z = -1.00$ is .1587, so $P(z \leq -1.00) = .1587$. Therefore, $P(-1.00 \leq z \leq 1.00) = P(z \leq 1.00) - P(z \leq -1.00) = .8413 - .1587 = .6826$. This probability is shown graphically in the following figure.

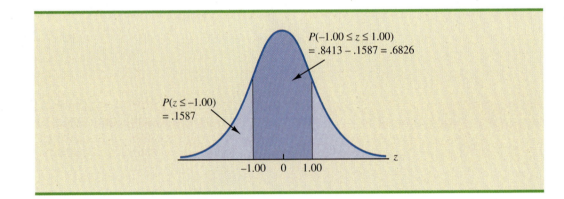

To illustrate how to make the third type of probability computation, suppose we want to compute the probability of obtaining a $z$ value of at least 1.58; that is, $P(z \geq 1.58)$. The value in the $z = 1.5$ row and the .08 column of the cumulative normal table is .9429; thus, $P(z < 1.58) = .9429$. However, because the total area under the normal curve is 1, $P(z \geq 1.58) = 1 - .9429 = .0571$. This probability is shown in the following figure.

In the preceding illustrations, we showed how to compute probabilities given specified $z$ values. In some situations, we are given a probability and are interested in working backward to find the corresponding $z$ value. Suppose we want to find a $z$ value such that the probability of obtaining a larger $z$ value is .10. The following figure shows this situation graphically.

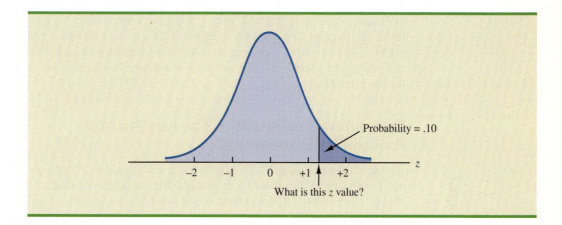

*Given a probability, we can use the standard normal table in an inverse fashion to find the corresponding z value.*

This problem is the inverse of those in the preceding examples. Previously, we specified the $z$ value of interest and then found the corresponding probability, or area. In this example, we are given the probability, or area, and asked to find the corresponding $z$ value. To do so, we use the standard normal probability table somewhat differently.

Recall that the standard normal probability table gives the area under the curve to the left of a particular $z$ value. We have been given the information that the area in the upper tail of the curve is .10. Hence, the area under the curve to the left of the unknown $z$ value must equal .9000. Scanning the body of the table, we find .8997 is the cumulative probability value closest to .9000. The section of the table providing this result follows.

| $z$ | .06 | .07 | .08 | .09 |
|-----|------|------|------|------|
| . | | | | |
| . | | | | |
| . | | | | |
| **1.0** | .8554 | .8577 | .8599 | .8621 |
| **1.1** | .8770 | .8790 | .8810 | .8830 |
| **1.2** | .8962 | .8980 | .8997 | .9015 |
| **1.3** | .9131 | .9147 | .9162 | .9177 |
| **1.4** | .9279 | .9292 | .9306 | .9319 |
| . | | | | |
| . | | Cumulative probability value | | |
| . | | closest to .9000 | | |

Reading the $z$ value from the leftmost column and the top row of the table, we find that the corresponding $z$ value is 1.28. Thus, an area of approximately .9000 (actually .8997) will be to the left of $z = 1.28$.[2] In terms of the question originally asked, there is an approximately .10 probability of a $z$ value larger than 1.28.

The examples illustrate that the table of cumulative probabilities for the standard normal probability distribution can be used to find probabilities associated with values of the standard normal random variable $z$. Two types of questions can be asked. The first type of question specifies a value, or values, for $z$ and asks us to use the table to determine the corresponding areas or probabilities. The second type of question provides an area, or probability, and asks us to use the table to determine the corresponding $z$ value. Thus, we need to be flexible in using the standard normal probability table to answer the desired probability question. In most cases, sketching a graph of the standard normal probability distribution and shading the appropriate area will help to visualize the situation and aid in determining the correct answer.

## Computing Probabilities for Any Normal Probability Distribution

The reason for discussing the standard normal distribution so extensively is that probabilities for all normal distributions are computed by using the standard normal distribution. That is, when we have a normal distribution with any mean $\mu$ and any standard deviation $\sigma$, we answer probability questions about the distribution by first converting to the standard normal distribution. Then we can use the standard normal probability table and the appropriate $z$ values to find the desired probabilities. The formula used to convert any normal random variable $x$ with mean $\mu$ and standard deviation $\sigma$ to the standard normal random variable $z$ follows.

*The formula for the standard normal random variable is similar to the formula we introduced in Chapter 3 for computing z-scores for a data set.*

CONVERTING TO THE STANDARD NORMAL RANDOM VARIABLE

$$z = \frac{x - \mu}{\sigma} \tag{6.3}$$

A value of $x$ equal to its mean $\mu$ results in $z = (\mu - \mu)/\sigma = 0$. Thus, we see that a value of $x$ equal to its mean $\mu$ corresponds to $z = 0$. Now suppose that $x$ is one standard deviation above its mean; that is, $x = \mu + \sigma$. Applying equation (6.3), we see that the corresponding $z$ value is $z = [(\mu + \sigma) - \mu]/\sigma = \sigma/\sigma = 1$. Thus, an $x$ value that is one standard deviation above its mean corresponds to $z = 1$. In other words, *we can interpret z as the number of standard deviations that the normal random variable x is from its mean $\mu$.*

To see how this conversion enables us to compute probabilities for any normal distribution, suppose we have a normal distribution with $\mu = 10$ and $\sigma = 2$. What is the probability that the random variable $x$ is between 10 and 14? Using equation (6.3), we see that at $x = 10$, $z = (x - \mu)/\sigma = (10 - 10)/2 = 0$ and that at $x = 14$, $z = (14 - 10)/2 = 4/2 = 2$. Thus, the answer to our question about the probability of $x$ being between 10 and 14 is given by the equivalent probability that $z$ is between 0 and 2 for the standard normal distribution. In other words, the probability that we are seeking is the probability that the random variable $x$ is between its mean and two standard deviations above the mean. Using $z = 2.00$ and the standard normal probability table inside the front cover of the text, we see that $P(z \leq 2) = .9772$.

---

[2] We could use interpolation in the body of the table to get a better approximation of the $z$ value that corresponds to an area of .9000. Doing so to provide one more decimal place of accuracy would yield a $z$ value of 1.282. However, in most practical situations, sufficient accuracy is obtained by simply using the table value closest to the desired probability.

Because $P(z \leq 0) = .5000$, we can compute $P(.00 \leq z \leq 2.00) = P(z \leq 2) - P(z \leq 0) = .9772 - .5000 = .4772$. Hence the probability that $x$ is between 10 and 14 is .4772.

## Grear Tire Company Problem

We turn now to an application of the normal probability distribution. Suppose the Grear Tire Company developed a new steel-belted radial tire to be sold through a national chain of discount stores. Because the tire is a new product, Grear's managers believe that the mileage guarantee offered with the tire will be an important factor in the acceptance of the product. Before finalizing the tire mileage guarantee policy, Grear's managers want probability information about $x =$ number of miles the tires will last.

From actual road tests with the tires, Grear's engineering group estimated that the mean tire mileage is $\mu = 36,500$ miles and that the standard deviation is $\sigma = 5000$. In addition, the data collected indicate that a normal distribution is a reasonable assumption. What percentage of the tires can be expected to last more than 40,000 miles? In other words, what is the probability that the tire mileage, $x$, will exceed 40,000? This question can be answered by finding the area of the darkly shaded region in Figure 6.6.

At $x = 40,000$, we have

$$z = \frac{x - \mu}{\sigma} = \frac{40,000 - 36,500}{5000} = \frac{3500}{5000} = .70$$

Refer now to the bottom of Figure 6.6. We see that a value of $x = 40,000$ on the Grear Tire normal distribution corresponds to a value of $z = .70$ on the standard normal distribution. Using the standard normal probability table, we see that the area under the standard normal curve to the left of $z = .70$ is .7580. Thus, $1.000 - .7580 = .2420$ is the probability that $z$ will exceed .70 and hence $x$ will exceed 40,000. We can conclude that about 24.2% of the tires will exceed 40,000 in mileage.

Let us now assume that Grear is considering a guarantee that will provide a discount on replacement tires if the original tires do not provide the guaranteed mileage. What should

**FIGURE 6.6** GREAR TIRE COMPANY MILEAGE DISTRIBUTION

**FIGURE 6.7**    GREAR'S DISCOUNT GUARANTEE

the guarantee mileage be if Grear wants no more than 10% of the tires to be eligible for the discount guarantee? This question is interpreted graphically in Figure 6.7.

According to Figure 6.7, the area under the curve to the left of the unknown guarantee mileage must be .10. So, we must first find the $z$ value that cuts off an area of .10 in the left tail of a standard normal distribution. Using the standard normal probability table, we see that $z = -1.28$ cuts off an area of .10 in the lower tail. Hence, $z = -1.28$ is the value of the standard normal random variable corresponding to the desired mileage guarantee on the Grear Tire normal distribution. To find the value of $x$ corresponding to $z = -1.28$, we have

*The guarantee mileage we need to find is 1.28 standard deviations below the mean. Thus, $x = \mu - 1.28\sigma$.*

$$z = \frac{x - \mu}{\sigma} = -1.28$$

$$x - \mu = -1.28\sigma$$

$$x = \mu - 1.28\sigma$$

With $\mu = 36{,}500$ and $\sigma = 5000$,

$$x = 36{,}500 - 1.28(5000) = 30{,}100$$

*With the guarantee set at 30,000 miles, the actual percentage eligible for the guarantee will be 9.68%.*

Thus, a guarantee of 30,100 miles will meet the requirement that approximately 10% of the tires will be eligible for the guarantee. Perhaps, with this information, the firm will set its tire mileage guarantee at 30,000 miles.

Again, we see the important role that probability distributions play in providing decision-making information. Namely, once a probability distribution is established for a particular application, it can be used to obtain probability information about the problem. Probability does not make a decision recommendation directly, but it provides information that helps the decision maker better understand the risks and uncertainties associated with the problem. Ultimately, this information may assist the decision maker in reaching a good decision.

## Using Excel to Compute Normal Probabilities

Excel provides two functions for computing probabilities and $z$ values for a standard normal probability distribution: NORM.S.DIST and NORM.S.INV. The NORM.S.DIST function computes the cumulative probability given a $z$ value, and the NORM.S.INV function computes the $z$ value given a cumulative probability. Two similar functions, NORM.DIST and

NORM.INV, are available for computing the cumulative probability and the $x$ value for any normal distribution. We begin by showing how to use the NORM.S.DIST and NORM.S.INV functions.

*The letter S that appears in the name of the NORM.S.DIST and NORM.S.INV functions reminds us that these functions relate to the standard normal probability distribution.*

The NORM.S.DIST function provides the area under the standard normal curve to the left of a given $z$ value; thus, it provides the same cumulative probability we would obtain if we used the standard normal probability table inside the front cover of the text. Using the NORM.S.DIST function is just like having Excel look up cumulative normal probabilities for you. The NORM.S.INV function is the inverse of the NORM.S.DIST function; it takes a cumulative probability as input and provides the $z$ value corresponding to that cumulative probability.

Let's see how both of these functions work by computing the probabilities and $z$ values obtained earlier in this section using the standard normal probability table. Refer to Figure 6.8 as we describe the tasks involved. The formula worksheet is in the background; the value worksheet is in the foreground.

**Enter Data:**   No data are entered in the worksheet. We will simply enter the appropriate $z$ values and probabilities directly into the formulas as needed.

**Enter Functions and Formulas:**   The NORM.S.DIST function has two inputs: the $z$ value and a value of TRUE or FALSE. For the second input we enter TRUE if a cumulative probability is desired, and we enter FALSE if the height of the standard normal curve is desired. Because we will always be using NORM.S.DIST to compute cumulative probabilities, we always choose TRUE for the second input. To illustrate the use of the NORM.S.DIST function, we compute the four probabilities shown in cells D3:D6 of Figure 6.8.

To compute the cumulative probability to the left of a given $z$ value (area in lower tail), we simply evaluate NORM.S.DIST at the $z$ value. For instance, to compute $P(z \leq 1)$ we entered the formula =NORM.S.DIST(1,TRUE) into cell D3. The result, .8413, is the same as obtained using the standard normal probability table.

*The probabilities in cells D4, 0.5858, and D5, 0.6827, differ from what we computed earlier due to rounding.*

To compute the probability of $z$ being in an interval we compute the value of NORM.S.DIST at the upper endpoint of the interval and subtract the value of NORM.S.DIST at the lower endpoint of the interval. For instance, to find $P(-.50 \leq z \leq 1.25)$, we entered

**FIGURE 6.8**   EXCEL WORKSHEET FOR COMPUTING PROBABILITIES AND $z$ VALUES FOR THE STANDARD NORMAL DISTRIBUTION the formula =NORM.S.DIST(1.25,TRUE)-NORM.S.DIST(-.50,TRUE) into cell D4. The interval probability in cell D5 is computed in a similar fashion.

To compute the probability to the right of a given $z$ value (upper tail area), we must subtract the cumulative probability represented by the area under the curve below the $z$ value (lower tail area) from 1. For example, to compute $P(z \geq 1.58)$ we entered the formula =1-NORM.S.DIST(1.58,TRUE) into cell D6.

To compute the $z$ value for a given cumulative probability (lower tail area), we use the NORM.S.INV function. To find the $z$ value corresponding to an upper tail probability of .10, we note that the corresponding lower tail area is .90 and enter the formula =NORM.S.INV(0.9) into cell D11. Actually, NORM.S.INV(0.9) gives us the $z$ value providing a cumulative probability (lower tail area) of .9. But it is also the $z$ value associated with an upper tail area of .10.

Two other $z$ values are computed in Figure 6.8. These $z$ values will be used extensively in succeeding chapters. To compute the $z$ value corresponding to an upper tail probability of .025, we entered the formula =NORM.S.INV(0.975) into cell D12. To compute the $z$ value corresponding to a lower tail probability of .025, we entered the formula =NORM.S.INV(0.025) into cell D13. We see that $z = 1.96$ corresponds to an upper tail probability of .025, and $z = -1.96$ corresponds to a lower tail probability of .025.

Let us now turn to the Excel functions for computing cumulative probabilities and $x$ values for any normal distribution. The NORM.DIST function provides the area under the normal curve to the left of a given value of the random variable $x$; thus it provides cumulative probabilities. The NORM.INV function is the inverse of the NORM.DIST function; it takes a cumulative probability as input and provides the value of $x$ corresponding to that cumulative probability. The NORM.DIST and NORM.INV functions do the same thing for any normal distribution that the NORM.S.DIST and NORM.S.INV functions do for the standard normal distribution.

Let's see how both of these functions work by computing probabilities and $x$ values for the Grear Tire Company example introduced earlier in this section. Recall that the lifetime of a Grear tire has a mean of 36,500 miles and a standard deviation of 5000 miles. Refer to Figure 6.9 as we describe the tasks involved. The formula worksheet is in the background; the value worksheet is in the foreground.

**Enter Data:**    No data are entered in the worksheet. We simply enter the appropriate $x$ values and probabilities directly into the formulas as needed.

**Enter Functions and Formulas:**    The NORM.DIST function has four inputs: (1) the $x$ value we want to compute the cumulative probability for, (2) the mean, (3) the standard deviation, and (4) a value of TRUE or FALSE. For the fourth input, we enter TRUE if a cumulative probability is desired, and we enter FALSE if the height of the curve is desired. Because we will always be using NORM.DIST to compute cumulative probabilities, we will always choose TRUE for the fourth input.

To compute the cumulative probability to the left of a given $x$ value (lower tail area), we simply evaluate NORM.DIST at the $x$ value. For instance, to compute the probability that a Grear tire will last 20,000 miles or less, we entered the formula =NORM.DIST(20000,36500,5000,TRUE) into cell D3. The value worksheet shows that this cumulative probability is .0005. So, we can conclude that almost all Grear tires will last at least 20,000 miles.

To compute the probability of $x$ being in an interval we compute the value of NORM.DIST at the upper endpoint of the interval and subtract the value of NORM.DIST at the lower endpoint of the interval. The formula in cell D4 provides the probability that a tire's lifetime is between 20,000 and 40,000 miles, $P(20{,}000 \leq x \leq 40{,}000)$. In the value worksheet, we see that this probability is .7576.

To compute the probability to the right of a given $x$ value (upper tail area), we must subtract the cumulative probability represented by the area under the curve below the $x$ value

**FIGURE 6.9**  EXCEL WORKSHEET FOR COMPUTING PROBABILITIES AND *x* VALUES
FOR THE NORMAL DISTRIBUTION

(lower tail area) from 1. The formula in cell D5 computes the probability that a Grear tire
will last for at least 40,000 miles. We see that this probability is .2420.

To compute the *x* value for a given cumulative probability, we use the NORM.INV function. The NORM.INV function has only three inputs. The first input is the cumulative probability; the second and third inputs are the mean and standard deviation. For instance, to
compute the tire mileage corresponding to a lower tail area of .1 for Grear Tire, we enter
the formula =NORM.INV(0.1,36500,5000) into cell D9. From the value worksheet, we see
that 10% of the Grear tires will last for 30,092.24 miles or less.

To compute the minimum tire mileage for the top 2.5% of Grear tires, we want to find
the value of *x* corresponding to an area of .025 in the upper tail. This calculation is the same
as finding the *x* value that provides a cumulative probability of .975. Thus we entered the
formula =NORM.INV(0.975,36500,5000) into cell D10 to compute this tire mileage. From
the value worksheet, we see that 2.5% of the Grear tires will last at least 46,299.82 miles.

## Exercises

## Methods

8. Using Figure 6.4 as a guide, sketch a normal curve for a random variable *x* that has a mean
   of $\mu = 100$ and a standard deviation of $\sigma = 10$. Label the horizontal axis with values of
   70, 80, 90, 100, 110, 120, and 130.

9. A random variable is normally distributed with a mean of $\mu = 50$ and a standard deviation of $\sigma = 5$.
   a.  Sketch a normal curve for the probability density function. Label the horizontal axis
       with values of 35, 40, 45, 50, 55, 60, and 65. Figure 6.4 shows that the normal curve
       almost touches the horizontal axis at three standard deviations below and at three
       standard deviations above the mean (in this case at 35 and 65).

b.  What is the probability that the random variable will assume a value between 45 and 55?

c.  What is the probability that the random variable will assume a value between 40 and 60?

10. Draw a graph for the standard normal distribution. Label the horizontal axis at values of $-3, -2, -1, 0, 1, 2,$ and $3$. Then compute the following probabilities.
    a.  $P(z \le 1.5)$
    b.  $P(z \le 1)$
    c.  $P(1 \le z \le 1.5)$
    d.  $P(0 < z < 2.5)$

11. Given that $z$ is a standard normal random variable, compute the following probabilities.
    a.  $P(z \le -1.0)$
    b.  $P(z \ge -1)$
    c.  $P(z \ge -1.5)$
    d.  $P(-2.5 \le z)$
    e.  $P(-3 < z \le 0)$

12. Given that $z$ is a standard normal random variable, compute the following probabilities.
    a.  $P(0 \le z \le .83)$
    b.  $P(-1.57 \le z \le 0)$
    c.  $P(z > .44)$
    d.  $P(z \ge -.23)$
    e.  $P(z < 1.20)$
    f.  $P(z \le -.71)$

 13. Given that $z$ is a standard normal random variable, compute the following probabilities.
    a.  $P(-1.98 \le z \le .49)$
    b.  $P(.52 \le z \le 1.22)$
    c.  $P(-1.75 \le z \le -1.04)$

14. Given that $z$ is a standard normal random variable, find $z$ for each situation.
    a.  The area to the left of $z$ is .9750.
    b.  The area between 0 and $z$ is .4750.
    c.  The area to the left of $z$ is .7291.
    d.  The area to the right of $z$ is .1314.
    e.  The area to the left of $z$ is .6700.
    f.  The area to the right of $z$ is .3300.

 15. Given that $z$ is a standard normal random variable, find $z$ for each situation.
    a.  The area to the left of $z$ is .2119.
    b.  The area between $-z$ and $z$ is .9030.
    c.  The area between $-z$ and $z$ is .2052.
    d.  The area to the left of $z$ is .9948.
    e.  The area to the right of $z$ is .6915.

16. Given that $z$ is a standard normal random variable, find $z$ for each situation.
    a.  The area to the right of $z$ is .01.
    b.  The area to the right of $z$ is .025.
    c.  The area to the right of $z$ is .05.
    d.  The area to the right of $z$ is .10.

## Applications

17. For borrowers with good credit scores, the mean debt for revolving and installment accounts is $15,015 (*BusinessWeek*, March 20, 2006). Assume the standard deviation is $3540 and that debt amounts are normally distributed.

a.   What is the probability that the debt for a borrower with good credit is more than $18,000?

b.   What is the probability that the debt for a borrower with good credit is less than $10,000?

c.   What is the probability that the debt for a borrower with good credit is between $12,000 and $18,000?

d.   What is the probability that the debt for a borrower with good credit is no more than $14,000?

18.   The average stock price for companies making up the S&P 500 is $30, and the standard deviation is $8.20 (*BusinessWeek,* Special Annual Issue, Spring 2003). Assume the stock prices are normally distributed.

a.   What is the probability that a company will have a stock price of at least $40?

b.   What is the probability that a company will have a stock price no higher than $20?

c.   How high does a stock price have to be to put a company in the top 10%?

19.   In an article about the cost of health care, *Money* magazine reported that a visit to a hospital emergency room for something as simple as a sore throat has a mean cost of $328 (*Money,* January 2009). Assume that the cost for this type of hospital emergency room visit is normally distributed with a standard deviation of $92. Answer the following questions about the cost of a hospital emergency room visit for this medical service.

a.   What is the probability that the cost will be more than $500?

b.   What is the probability that the cost will be less than $250?

c.   What is the probability that the cost will be between $300 and $400?

d.   If the cost to a patient is in the lower 8% of charges for this medical service, what was the cost of this patient's emergency room visit?

20.   In January 2003, the American worker spent an average of 77 hours logged on to the Internet while at work (CNBC, March 15, 2003). Assume that the population mean is 77 hours, the times are normally distributed, and the standard deviation is 20 hours.

a.   What is the probability that in January 2003 a randomly selected worker spent fewer than 50 hours logged on to the Internet?

b.   What percentage of workers spent more than 100 hours in January 2003 logged on to the Internet?

c.   A person is classified as a heavy user if he or she is in the upper 20% of usage. In January 2003, how many hours did a worker have to be logged on to the Internet to be considered a heavy user?

21.   A person must score in the upper 2% of the population on an IQ test to qualify for membership in Mensa, the international high-IQ society. If IQ scores are normally distributed with a mean of 100 and a standard deviation of 15, what score must a person have to qualify for Mensa?

22.   Television viewing reached a new high when the Nielsen Company reported a mean daily viewing time of 8.35 hours per household (*USA Today,* November 11, 2009). Use a normal probability distribution with a standard deviation of 2.5 hours to answer the following questions about daily television viewing per household.

a.   What is the probability that a household views television between 5 and 10 hours a day?

b.   How many hours of television viewing must a household have in order to be in the top 3% of all television viewing households?

c.   What is the probability that a household views television more than 3 hours a day?

23.   The time needed to complete a final examination in a particular college course is normally distributed with a mean of 80 minutes and a standard deviation of 10 minutes. Answer the following questions.

a.   What is the probability of completing the exam in one hour or less?

b.   What is the probability that a student will complete the exam in more than 60 minutes but less than 75 minutes?

c.  Assume that the class has 60 students and that the examination period is 90 minutes in length. How many students do you expect will be unable to complete the exam in the allotted time?

24. Trading volume on the New York Stock Exchange is heaviest during the first half hour (early morning) and last half hour (late afternoon) of the trading day. The early morning trading volumes (millions of shares) for 13 days in January and February are shown here (*Barron's,* January 23, 2006; February 13, 2006; and February 27, 2006).

| | | | | |
|---|---|---|---|---|
| 214 | 163 | 265 | 194 | 180 |
| 202 | 198 | 212 | 201 | |
| 174 | 171 | 211 | 211 | |

The probability distribution of trading volume is approximately normal.
a.  Compute the mean and standard deviation to use as estimates of the population mean and standard deviation.
b.  What is the probability that, on a randomly selected day, the early morning trading volume will be less than 180 million shares?
c.  What is the probability that, on a randomly selected day, the early morning trading volume will exceed 230 million shares?
d.  How many shares would have to be traded for the early morning trading volume on a particular day to be among the busiest 5% of days?

25. According to the Sleep Foundation, the average night's sleep is 6.8 hours (*Fortune,* March 20, 2006). Assume the standard deviation is .6 hours and that the probability distribution is normal.
a.  What is the probability that a randomly selected person sleeps more than 8 hours?
b.  What is the probability that a randomly selected person sleeps 6 hours or less?
c.  Doctors suggest getting between 7 and 9 hours of sleep each night. What percentage of the population gets this much sleep?

## 6.3    Exponential Probability Distribution

The **exponential probability distribution** may be used for random variables such as the time between arrivals at a car wash, the time required to load a truck, the distance between major defects in a highway, and so on. The exponential probability density function follows.

---

**EXPONENTIAL PROBABILITY DENSITY FUNCTION**

$$f(x) = \frac{1}{\mu} e^{-x/\mu} \qquad \text{for } x \geq 0 \qquad\qquad (6.4)$$

where

$$\mu = \text{expected value or mean}$$

$$e = 2.71828$$

---

As an example of the exponential distribution, suppose that $x$ represents the loading time for a truck at the Schips loading dock and follows such a distribution. If the mean, or

**FIGURE 6.10**   EXPONENTIAL DISTRIBUTION FOR THE SCHIPS LOADING
DOCK EXAMPLE

average, loading time is 15 minutes ($\mu = 15$), the appropriate probability density function
for $x$ is

$$f(x) = \frac{1}{15} e^{-x/15}$$

Figure 6.10 is the graph of this probability density function.

## Computing Probabilities for the Exponential Distribution

*In waiting line
applications, the
exponential distribution is
often used for service time.*

As with any continuous probability distribution, the area under the curve corresponding to
an interval provides the probability that the random variable assumes a value in that interval. In the Schips loading dock example, the probability that loading a truck will take 6 minutes or less $P(x \leq 6)$ is defined to be the area under the curve in Figure 6.10 from $x = 0$ to
$x = 6$. Similarly, the probability that the loading time will be 18 minutes or less $P(x \leq 18)$
is the area under the curve from $x = 0$ to $x = 18$. Note also that the probability that the
loading time will be between 6 minutes and 18 minutes $P(6 \leq x \leq 18)$ is given by the area
under the curve from $x = 6$ to $x = 18$.

To compute exponential probabilities such as those just described, we use the following formula. It provides the cumulative probability of obtaining a value for the exponential
random variable of less than or equal to some specific value denoted by $x_0$.

EXPONENTIAL DISTRIBUTION: CUMULATIVE PROBABILITIES

$$P(x \leq x_0) = 1 - e^{-x_0/\mu} \qquad \textbf{(6.5)}$$

For the Schips loading dock example, $x =$ loading time in minutes and $\mu = 15$ minutes. Using equation (6.5),

$$P(x \leq x_0) = 1 - e^{-x_0/15}$$

Hence, the probability that loading a truck will take 6 minutes or less is

$$P(x \leq 6) = 1 - e^{-6/15} = .3297$$

Using equation (6.5), we calculate the probability of loading a truck in 18 minutes or less.

$$P(x \leq 18) = 1 - e^{-18/15} = .6988$$

Thus, the probability that loading a truck will take between 6 minutes and 18 minutes is equal to $.6988 - .3297 = .3691$. Probabilities for any other interval can be computed similarly.

*A property of the exponential distribution is that the mean and standard deviation are equal.*

In the preceding example, the mean time it takes to load a truck is $\mu = 15$ minutes. A property of the exponential distribution is that the mean of the distribution and the standard deviation of the distribution are *equal*. Thus, the standard deviation for the time it takes to load a truck is $\sigma = 15$ minutes. The variance is $\sigma^2 = (15)^2 = 225$.

## Relationship Between the Poisson and Exponential Distributions

In Section 5.5 we introduced the Poisson distribution as a discrete probability distribution that is often useful in examining the number of occurrences of an event over a specified interval of time or space. Recall that the Poisson probability function is

$$f(x) = \frac{\mu^x e^{-\mu}}{x!}$$

where

$$\mu = \text{expected value or mean number of} \\ \text{occurrences over a specified interval}$$

*If arrivals follow a Poisson distribution, the time between arrivals must follow an exponential distribution.*

The continuous exponential probability distribution is related to the discrete Poisson distribution. If the Poisson distribution provides an appropriate description of the number of occurrences per interval, the exponential distribution provides a description of the length of the interval between occurrences.

To illustrate this relationship, suppose the number of cars that arrive at a car wash during one hour is described by a Poisson probability distribution with a mean of 10 cars per hour. The Poisson probability function that gives the probability of $x$ arrivals per hour is

$$f(x) = \frac{10^x e^{-10}}{x!}$$

Because the average number of arrivals is 10 cars per hour, the average time between cars arriving is

$$\frac{1 \text{ hour}}{10 \text{ cars}} = .1 \text{ hour/car}$$

**FIGURE 6.11**   EXCEL WORKSHEET FOR COMPUTING PROBABILITIES FOR THE EXPONENTIAL
PROBABILITY DISTRIBUTION

Thus, the corresponding exponential distribution that describes the time between the arrivals has a mean of $\mu = .1$ hour per car; as a result, the appropriate exponential probability density function is

$$f(x) = \frac{1}{.1} e^{-x/.1} = 10e^{-10x}$$

## Using Excel to Compute Exponential Probabilities

Excel's EXPON.DIST function can be used to compute exponential probabilities. We will illustrate by computing probabilities associated with the time it takes to load a truck at the Schips loading dock. This example was introduced at the beginning of the section. Refer to Figure 6.11 as we describe the tasks involved. The formula worksheet is in the background; the value worksheet is in the foreground.

**Enter Data:**   No data are entered in the worksheet. We simply enter the appropriate values for the exponential random variable into the formulas as needed. The random variable is $x =$ loading time.

**Enter Functions and Formulas:**   The EXPON.DIST function has three inputs: the first is the value of $x$, the second is $1/\mu$, and the third is TRUE or FALSE. We choose TRUE for the third input if a cumulative probability is desired and FALSE if the height of the probability density function is desired. We will always use TRUE because we will be computing cumulative probabilities.

The first probability we compute is the probability that the loading time is 18 minutes or less. For the Schips problem, $1/\mu = 1/15$, so we enter the formula =EXPON.DIST (18,1/15,TRUE) into cell D3 to compute the desired cumulative probability. From the value worksheet, we see that the probability of loading a truck in 18 minutes or less is .6988.

The second probability we compute is the probability that the loading time is between 6 and 18 minutes. To find this probability we first compute the cumulative probability for the upper endpoint of the time interval and subtract the cumulative probability for the lower endpoint of the interval. The formula we have entered into cell D4 calculates this probability. The value worksheet shows that this probability is .3691.

The last probability we calculate is the probability that the loading time is at least 8 minutes. Because the EXPON.DIST function only computes cumulative (lower tail) probabilities, we compute this probability by entering the formula =1-EXPON.DIST(8,1/15,TRUE) into cell D5. The value worksheet shows that the probability of a loading time of 8 minutes or more is .5866.

## NOTES AND COMMENTS

As we can see in Figure 6.10, the exponential distribution is skewed to the right. Indeed, the skewness measure for the exponential distributions is 2.

The exponential distribution gives us a good idea what a skewed distribution looks like.

## Exercises

### Methods

26. Consider the following exponential probability density function.

$$f(x) = \frac{1}{8} e^{-x/8} \qquad \text{for } x \geq 0$$

   a.  Find $P(x \leq 6)$.
   b.  Find $P(x \leq 4)$.
   c.  Find $P(x \geq 6)$.
   d.  Find $P(4 \leq x \leq 6)$.

27. Consider the following exponential probability density function.

$$f(x) = \frac{1}{3} e^{-x/3} \qquad \text{for } x \geq 0$$

   a.  Write the formula for $P(x \leq x_0)$.
   b.  Find $P(x \leq 2)$.
   c.  Find $P(x \geq 3)$.
   d.  Find $P(x \leq 5)$.
   e.  Find $P(2 \leq x \leq 5)$.

### Applications

28. The time required to pass through security screening at the airport can be annoying to travelers. The mean wait time during peak periods at Cincinnati/Northern Kentucky International Airport is 12.1 minutes (*The Cincinnati Enquirer,* February 2, 2006). Assume the time to pass through security screening follows an exponential distribution.
   a.  What is the probability that it will take less than 10 minutes to pass through security screening during a peak period?
   b.  What is the probability that it will take more than 20 minutes to pass through security screening during a peak period?
   c.  What is the probability that it will take between 10 and 20 minutes to pass through security screening during a peak period?
   d.  It is 8:00 A.M. (a peak period) and you just entered the security line. To catch your plane you must be at the gate within 30 minutes. If it takes 12 minutes from the time you clear security until you reach your gate, what is the probability that you will miss your flight?

29. The time between arrivals of vehicles at a particular intersection follows an exponential probability distribution with a mean of 12 seconds.
   a.  Sketch this exponential probability distribution.
   b.  What is the probability that the arrival time between vehicles is 12 seconds or less?
   c.  What is the probability that the arrival time between vehicles is 6 seconds or less?
   d.  What is the probability of 30 or more seconds between vehicle arrivals?

30. Comcast Corporation is the largest cable television company, the second largest Internet service provider, and the fourth largest telephone service provider in the United States.

Generally known for quality and reliable service, the company periodically experiences unexpected service interruptions. On January 14, 2009, such an interruption occurred for the Comcast customers living in southwest Florida. When customers called the Comcast office, a recorded message told them that the company was aware of the service outage and that it was anticipated that service would be restored in two hours. Assume that two hours is the mean time to do the repair and that the repair time has an exponential probability distribution.

  a.  What is the probability that the cable service will be repaired in one hour or less?
  b.  What is the probability that the repair will take between one hour and two hours?
  c.  For a customer who calls the Comcast office at 1:00 P.M., what is the probability that the cable service will not be repaired by 5:00 P.M.?

31. Collina's Italian Café in Houston, Texas, advertises that carryout orders take about 25 minutes (Collina's website, February 27, 2008). Assume that the time required for a carryout order to be ready for customer pickup has an exponential distribution with a mean of 25 minutes.

  a.  What is the probability than a carryout order will be ready within 20 minutes?
  b.  If a customer arrives 30 minutes after placing an order, what is the probability that the order will not be ready?
  c.  A particular customer lives 15 minutes from Collina's Italian Café. If the customer places a telephone order at 5:20 P.M., what is the probability that the customer can drive to the café, pick up the order, and return home by 6:00 P.M.?

32. Do interruptions while you are working reduce your productivity? According to a University of California–Irvine study, businesspeople are interrupted at the rate of approximately $5\frac{1}{2}$ times per hour (*Fortune*, March 20, 2006). Suppose the number of interruptions follows a Poisson probability distribution.

  a.  Show the probability distribution for the time between interruptions.
  b.  What is the probability that a businessperson will have no interruptions during a 15-minute period?
  c.  What is the probability that the next interruption will occur within 10 minutes for a particular businessperson?

## Summary

This chapter extended the discussion of probability distributions to the case of continuous random variables. The major conceptual difference between discrete and continuous probability distributions involves the method of computing probabilities. With discrete distributions, the probability function $f(x)$ provides the probability that the random variable $x$ assumes various values. With continuous distributions, the probability density function $f(x)$ does not provide probability values directly. Instead, probabilities are given by areas under the curve or graph of the probability density function $f(x)$. Because the area under the curve above a single point is zero, we observe that the probability of any particular value is zero for a continuous random variable.

Three continuous probability distributions—the uniform, normal, and exponential distributions—were treated in detail. The normal distribution is used widely in statistical inference and will be used extensively throughout the remainder of the text.

## Glossary

**Probability density function** A function used to compute probabilities for a continuous random variable. The area under the graph of a probability density function over an interval represents probability.

**Uniform probability distribution** A continuous probability distribution for which the probability that the random variable will assume a value in any interval is the same for each interval of equal length.

**Normal probability distribution** A continuous probability distribution. Its probability density function is bell-shaped and determined by its mean $\mu$ and standard deviation $\sigma$.

**Standard normal probability distribution** A normal distribution with a mean of zero and a standard deviation of one.

**Continuity correction factor** A value of .5 that is added to or subtracted from a value of $x$ when the continuous normal distribution is used to approximate the discrete binomial distribution.

**Exponential probability distribution** A continuous probability distribution that is useful in computing probabilities for the time it takes to complete a task.

## Key Formulas

### Uniform Probability Density Function

$$f(x) = \begin{cases} \dfrac{1}{b - a} & \text{for } a \leq x \leq b \\ 0 & \text{elsewhere} \end{cases}$$

(6.1)

### Normal Probability Density Function

$$f(x) = \frac{1}{\sigma \sqrt{2\pi}} e^{-(x-\mu)^2 / 2\sigma^2}$$

(6.2)

### Converting to the Standard Normal Random Variable

$$z = \frac{x - \mu}{\sigma}$$

(6.3)

### Exponential Probability Density Function

$$f(x) = \frac{1}{\mu} e^{-x/\mu} \qquad \text{for } x \geq 0$$

(6.4)

### Exponential Distribution: Cumulative Probabilities

$$P(x \leq x_0) = 1 - e^{-x_0/\mu}$$

(6.5)

## Supplementary Exercises

33.  A business executive, transferred from Chicago to Atlanta, needs to sell her house in Chicago quickly. The executive's employer has offered to buy the house for $210,000, but the offer expires at the end of the week. The executive does not currently have a better offer but can afford to leave the house on the market for another month. From conversations with her realtor, the executive believes the price she will get by leaving the house on the market for another month is uniformly distributed between $200,000 and $225,000.

   a.  If she leaves the house on the market for another month, what is the mathematical expression for the probability density function of the sales price?

b.   If she leaves it on the market for another month, what is the probability that she will get at least $215,000 for the house?

c.   If she leaves it on the market for another month, what is the probability that she will get less than $210,000?

d.   Should the executive leave the house on the market for another month? Why or why not?

34.   The U.S. Bureau of Labor Statistics reports that the average annual expenditure on food and drink for all families is $5700 (*Money,* December 2003). Assume that annual expenditure on food and drink is normally distributed and that the standard deviation is $1500.

a.   What is the range of expenditures of the 10% of families with the lowest annual spending on food and drink?

b.   What percentage of families spend more than $7000 annually on food and drink?

c.   What is the range of expenditures for the 5% of families with the highest annual spending on food and drink?

35.   Motorola used the normal distribution to determine the probability of defects and the number of defects expected in a production process. Assume a production process produces items with a mean weight of 10 ounces. Calculate the probability of a defect and the expected number of defects for a 1000-unit production run in the following situations.

a.   The process standard deviation is .15, and the process control is set at plus or minus one standard deviation. Units with weights less than 9.85 or greater than 10.15 ounces will be classified as defects.

b.   Through process design improvements, the process standard deviation can be reduced to .05. Assume the process control remains the same, with weights less than 9.85 or greater than 10.15 ounces being classified as defects.

c.   What is the advantage of reducing process variation, thereby causing process control limits to be at a greater number of standard deviations from the mean?

36.   The average annual amount American households spend for daily transportation is $6312 (*Money,* August 2001). Assume that the amount spent is normally distributed.

a.   Suppose you learn that 5% of American households spend less than $1000 for daily transportation. What is the standard deviation of the amount spent?

b.   What is the probability that a household spends between $4000 and $6000?

c.   What is the range of spending for the 3% of households with the highest daily transportation cost?

37.   *Condé Nast Traveler* publishes a Gold List of the top hotels all over the world. The Broadmoor Hotel in Colorado Springs contains 700 rooms and is on the 2004 Gold List (*Condé Nast Traveler,* January 2004). Suppose Broadmoor's marketing group forecasts a mean demand of 670 rooms for the coming weekend. Assume that demand for the upcoming weekend is normally distributed with a standard deviation of 30.

a.   What is the probability that all the hotel's rooms will be rented?

b.   What is the probability that 50 or more rooms will not be rented?

c.   Would you recommend the hotel consider offering a promotion to increase demand? What considerations would be important?

38.   Ward Doering Auto Sales is considering offering a special service contract that will cover the total cost of any service work required on leased vehicles. From experience, the company manager estimates that yearly service costs are approximately normally distributed, with a mean of $150 and a standard deviation of $25.

a.   If the company offers the service contract to customers for a yearly charge of $200, what is the probability that any one customer's service costs will exceed the contract price of $200?

b.   What is Ward's expected profit per service contract?

39.   Is lack of sleep causing traffic fatalities? A study conducted under the auspices of the National Highway Traffic Safety Administration found that the average number of fatal crashes caused

by drowsy drivers each year was 1550 (*BusinessWeek,* January 26, 2004). Assume the annual number of fatal crashes per year is normally distributed with a standard deviation of 300.

a.   What is the probability of fewer than 1000 fatal crashes in a year?

b.   What is the probability that the number of fatal crashes will be between 1000 and 2000 for a year?

c.   For a year to be in the upper 5% with respect to the number of fatal crashes, how many fatal crashes would have to occur?

40.  Assume that the test scores from a college admissions test are normally distributed, with a mean of 450 and a standard deviation of 100.

a.   What percentage of the people taking the test score between 400 and 500?

b.   Suppose someone receives a score of 630. What percentage of the people taking the test score better? What percentage score worse?

c.   If a particular university will not admit anyone scoring below 480, what percentage of the persons taking the test would be acceptable to the university?

41.  According to Salary Wizard, the average base salary for a brand manager in Houston, Texas, is $88,592 and the average base salary for a brand manager in Los Angeles, California, is $97,417 (Salary Wizard website, February 27, 2008). Assume that salaries are normally distributed, the standard deviation for brand managers in Houston is $19,900, and the standard deviation for brand managers in Los Angeles is $21,800.

a.   What is the probability that a brand manager in Houston has a base salary in excess of $100,000?

b.   What is the probability that a brand manager in Los Angeles has a base salary in excess of $100,000?

c.   What is the probability that a brand manager in Los Angeles has a base salary of less than $75,000?

d.   How much would a brand manager in Los Angeles have to make in order to have a higher salary than 99% of the brand managers in Houston?

42.  A machine fills containers with a particular product. The standard deviation of filling weights is known from past data to be .6 ounce. If only 2% of the containers hold less than 18 ounces, what is the mean filling weight for the machine? That is, what must $\mu$ equal? Assume the filling weights have a normal distribution.

43.  The Information Systems Audit and Control Association surveyed office workers to learn about the anticipated usage of office computers for personal holiday shopping (*USA Today,* November 11, 2009). Assume that the number of hours a worker spends doing holiday shopping on an office computer follows an exponential distribution.

a.   The study reported that there is a .53 probability that a worker uses the office computer for holiday shopping 5 hours or less. Is the mean time spent using an office computer for holiday shopping closest to 5.8, 6.2, 6.6, or 7 hours?

b.   Using the mean time from part (a), what is the probability that a worker uses the office computer for holiday shopping more than 10 hours?

c.   What is the probability that a worker uses the office computer for holiday shopping between four and eight hours?

44.  A website for bed and breakfast inns gets approximately seven visitors per minute. Suppose the number of website visitors per minute follows a Poisson probability distribution.

a.   What is the mean time between visits to the website?

b.   Show the exponential probability density function for the time between website visits.

c.   What is the probability that no one will access the website in a 1-minute period?

d.   What is the probability that no one will access the website in a 12-second period?

45.  The American Community Survey showed that residents of New York City have the longest travel times to get to work compared to residents of other cities in the United States (U.S. Census Bureau website, August 2008). According to the latest statistics available, the average travel time to work for residents of New York City is 38.3 minutes.

a.  Assume the exponential probability distribution is applicable and show the probability density function for the travel time to work for a resident of this city.
b.  What is the probability that it will take a resident of this city between 20 and 40 minutes to travel to work?
c.  What is the probability that it will take a resident of this city more than one hour to travel to work?

46.  The time (in minutes) between telephone calls at an insurance claims office has the following exponential probability distribution.

$$f(x) = .50e^{-.50x} \qquad \text{for } x \geq 0$$

a.  What is the mean time between telephone calls?
b.  What is the probability of having 30 seconds or less between telephone calls?
c.  What is the probability of having 1 minute or less between telephone calls?
d.  What is the probability of having 5 or more minutes without a telephone call?

## Case Problem   Specialty Toys

Specialty Toys, Inc., sells a variety of new and innovative children's toys. Management learned that the preholiday season is the best time to introduce a new toy, because many families use this time to look for new ideas for December holiday gifts. When Specialty discovers a new toy with good market potential, it chooses an October market entry date.

In order to get toys in its stores by October, Specialty places one-time orders with its manufacturers in June or July of each year. Demand for children's toys can be highly volatile. If a new toy catches on, a sense of shortage in the marketplace often increases the demand to high levels and large profits can be realized. However, new toys can also flop, leaving Specialty stuck with high levels of inventory that must be sold at reduced prices. The most important question the company faces is deciding how many units of a new toy should be purchased to meet anticipated sales demand. If too few are purchased, sales will be lost; if too many are purchased, profits will be reduced because of low prices realized in clearance sales.

For the coming season, Specialty plans to introduce a new product called Weather Teddy. This variation of a talking teddy bear is made by a company in Taiwan. When a child presses Teddy's hand, the bear begins to talk. A built-in barometer selects one of five responses that predict the weather conditions. The responses range from "It looks to be a very nice day! Have fun" to "I think it may rain today. Don't forget your umbrella." Tests with the product show that, even though it is not a perfect weather predictor, its predictions are surprisingly good. Several of Specialty's managers claimed Teddy gave predictions of the weather that were as good as many local television weather forecasters.

As with other products, Specialty faces the decision of how many Weather Teddy units to order for the coming holiday season. Members of the management team suggested order quantities of 15,000, 18,000, 24,000, or 28,000 units. The wide range of order quantities suggested indicates considerable disagreement concerning the market potential. The product management team asks you for an analysis of the stock-out probabilities for various order quantities, an estimate of the profit potential, and for help with making an order quantity recommendation. Specialty expects to sell Weather Teddy for $24 based on a cost of $16 per unit. If inventory remains after the holiday season, Specialty will sell all surplus inventory for $5 per unit. After reviewing the sales history of similar products, Specialty's senior sales forecaster predicted an expected demand of 20,000 units with a .95 probability that demand would be between 10,000 units and 30,000 units.

## Managerial Report

Prepare a managerial report that addresses the following issues and recommends an order quantity for the Weather Teddy product.

1. Use the sales forecaster's prediction to describe a normal probability distribution that can be used to approximate the demand distribution. Sketch the distribution and show its mean and standard deviation.

2. Compute the probability of a stock-out for the order quantities suggested by members of the management team.

3. Compute the projected profit for the order quantities suggested by the management team under three scenarios: worst case in which sales = 10,000 units, most likely case in which sales = 20,000 units, and best case in which sales = 30,000 units.

4. One of Specialty's managers felt that the profit potential was so great that the order quantity should have a 70% chance of meeting demand and only a 30% chance of any stock-outs. What quantity would be ordered under this policy, and what is the projected profit under the three sales scenarios?

5. Provide your own recommendation for an order quantity and note the associated profit projections. Provide a rationale for your recommendation.

# CHAPTER 7

# Sampling and Sampling Distributions

## STATISTICS *in* PRACTICE

### MEADWESTVACO CORPORATION*
*STAMFORD, CONNECTICUT*

MeadWestvaco Corporation, a leading producer of packaging, coated and specialty papers, consumer and office products, and specialty chemicals, employs more than 30,000 people. It operates worldwide in 29 countries and serves customers located in approximately 100 countries. MeadWestvaco holds a leading position in paper production, with an annual capacity of 1.8 million tons. The company's products include textbook paper, glossy magazine paper, beverage packaging systems, and office products. MeadWestvaco's internal consulting group uses sampling to provide a variety of information that enables the company to obtain significant productivity benefits and remain competitive.

For example, MeadWestvaco maintains large woodland holdings, which supply the trees, or raw material, for many of the company's products. Managers need reliable and accurate information about the timberlands and forests to evaluate the company's ability to meet its future raw material needs. What is the present volume in the forests? What is the past growth of the forests? What is the projected future growth of the forests? With answers to these important questions, MeadWestvaco's managers can develop plans for the future, including long-term planting and harvesting schedules for the trees.

How does MeadWestvaco obtain the information it needs about its vast forest holdings? Data collected from sample plots throughout the forests are the basis for learning about the population of trees owned by the company. To identify the sample plots, the timberland holdings are first divided into three sections based on location and types of trees. Using maps and random numbers, MeadWestvaco analysts identify random samples of 1/5- to 1/7-acre plots in each section of the forest.

Random sampling of its forest holdings enables MeadWestvaco Corporation to meet future raw material needs.

MeadWestvaco foresters collect data from these sample plots to learn about the forest population.

Foresters throughout the organization participate in the field data collection process. Periodically, two-person teams gather information on each tree in every sample plot. The sample data are entered into the company's continuous forest inventory (CFI) computer system. Reports from the CFI system include a number of frequency distribution summaries containing statistics on types of trees, present forest volume, past forest growth rates, and projected future forest growth and volume. Sampling and the associated statistical summaries of the sample data provide the reports essential for the effective management of MeadWestvaco's forests and timberlands.

In this chapter you will learn about simple random sampling and the sample selection process. In addition, you will learn how statistics such as the sample mean and sample proportion are used to estimate the population mean and population proportion. The important concept of a sampling distribution is also introduced.

*The authors are indebted to Dr. Edward P. Winkofsky for providing this Statistics in Practice.

In Chapter 1 we presented the following definitions of an element, a population, and a sample.

- An *element* is the entity on which data are collected.
- A *population* is the collection of all the elements of interest.
- A *sample* is a subset of the population.

The reason we select a sample is to collect data to make an inference and answer a research question about a population.

Let us begin by citing two examples in which sampling was used to answer a research question about a population.

1.  Members of a political party in Texas were considering supporting a particular candidate for election to the U.S. Senate, and party leaders wanted to estimate the proportion of registered voters in the state favoring the candidate. A sample of 400 registered voters in Texas was selected and 160 of the 400 voters indicated a preference for the candidate. Thus, an estimate of the proportion of the population of registered voters favoring the candidate is 160/400 = .40.

2.  A tire manufacturer is considering producing a new tire designed to provide an increase in mileage over the firm's current line of tires. To estimate the mean useful life of the new tires, the manufacturer produced a sample of 120 tires for testing. The test results provided a sample mean of 36,500 miles. Hence, an estimate of the mean useful life for the population of new tires was 36,500 miles.

*A sample mean provides an estimate of a population mean, and a sample proportion provides an estimate of a population proportion. With estimates such as these, some estimation error can be expected. This chapter provides the basis for determining how large that error might be.*

It is important to realize that sample results provide only *estimates* of the values of the corresponding population characteristics. We do not expect exactly .40, or 40%, of the population of registered voters to favor the candidate, nor do we expect the sample mean of 36,500 miles to exactly equal the mean mileage for the population of all new tires produced. The reason is simply that the sample contains only a portion of the population. Some sampling error is to be expected. With proper sampling methods, the sample results will provide "good" estimates of the population parameters. But how good can we expect the sample results to be? Fortunately, statistical procedures are available for answering this question.

Let us define some of the terms used in sampling. The **sampled population** is the population from which the sample is drawn, and a **frame** is a list of the elements that the sample will be selected from. In the first example, the sampled population is all registered voters in Texas, and the frame is a list of all the registered voters. Because the number of registered voters in Texas is a finite number, the first example is an illustration of sampling from a finite population. In Section 7.2, we discuss how a simple random sample can be selected when sampling from a finite population.

The sampled population for the tire mileage example is more difficult to define because the sample of 120 tires was obtained from a production process at a particular point in time. We can think of the sampled population as the conceptual population of all the tires that could have been made by the production process at that particular point in time. In this sense the sampled population is considered infinite, making it impossible to construct a frame to draw the sample from. In Section 7.2, we discuss how to select a random sample in such a situation.

In this chapter, we show how simple random sampling can be used to select a sample from a finite population and describe how a random sample can be taken from an infinite population that is generated by an ongoing process. We then show how data obtained from a sample can be used to compute estimates of a population mean, a population standard deviation, and a population proportion. In addition, we introduce the important concept of a sampling distribution. As we will show, knowledge of the appropriate sampling distribution enables us to make statements about how close the sample estimates are to the corresponding population parameters. The last section discusses some alternatives to simple random sampling that are often employed in practice.

## (7.1)  The Electronics Associates Sampling Problem

The director of personnel for Electronics Associates, Inc. (EAI), has been assigned the task of developing a profile of the company's 2500 managers. The characteristics to be identified include the mean annual salary for the managers and the proportion of managers having completed the company's management training program.

EAI

Using the 2500 managers as the population for this study, we can find the annual salary and the training program status for each individual by referring to the firm's personnel records. The data set containing this information for all 2500 managers in the population is in the file named EAI.

Using the EAI data and the formulas presented in Chapter 3, we compute the population mean and the population standard deviation for the annual salary data.

$$\text{Population mean:} \quad \mu = \$51,800$$
$$\text{Population standard deviation:} \quad \sigma = \$4000$$

The data for the training program status show that 1500 of the 2500 managers completed the training program.

Numerical characteristics of a population are called **parameters**. Letting $p$ denote the proportion of the population that completed the training program, we see that $p = 1500/2500 = .60$. The population mean annual salary ($\mu = \$51,800$), the population standard deviation of annual salary ($\sigma = \$4000$), and the population proportion that completed the training program ($p = .60$) are parameters of the population of EAI managers.

*Often the cost of collecting information from a sample is substantially less than from a population, especially when personal interviews must be conducted to collect the information.*

Now, suppose that the necessary information on all the EAI managers was not readily available in the company's database. The question we now consider is how the firm's director of personnel can obtain estimates of the population parameters by using a sample of managers rather than all 2500 managers in the population. Suppose that a sample of 30 managers will be used. Clearly, the time and the cost of developing a profile would be substantially less for 30 managers than for the entire population. If the personnel director could be assured that a sample of 30 managers would provide adequate information about the population of 2500 managers, working with a sample would be preferable to working with the entire population. Let us explore the possibility of using a sample for the EAI study by first considering how we can identify a sample of 30 managers.

## 7.2 Selecting a Sample

In this section we describe how to select a sample. We first describe how to sample from a finite population and then describe how to select a sample from an infinite population.

### Sampling from a Finite Population

*Other methods of probability sampling are described in Section 7.7.*

Statisticians recommend selecting a probability sample when sampling from a finite population because a probability sample allows them to make valid statistical inferences about the population. The simplest type of probability sample is one in which each sample of size $n$ has the same probability of being selected. It is called a simple random sample. A simple random sample of size $n$ from a finite population of size $N$ is defined as follows.

> **SIMPLE RANDOM SAMPLE (FINITE POPULATION)**
>
> A **simple random sample** of size $n$ from a finite population of size $N$ is a sample selected such that each possible sample of size $n$ has the same probability of being selected.

*The random numbers generated using Excel's RAND function follow a uniform probability distribution between 0 and 1.*

The procedures used to select a simple random sample from a finite population are based upon the use of random numbers. We can use Excel's RAND function to generate a random number between 0 and 1 by entering the formula =RAND() into any cell in a worksheet. The number generated is called a random number because the mathematical procedure used by the RAND function guarantees that every number between 0 and 1 has the same probability of being selected. Let us see how these random numbers can be used to select a simple random sample.

Our procedure for selecting a simple random sample of size $n$ from a population of size $N$ involves two steps.

**Step 1.**  Assign a random number to each element of the population.
**Step 2.**  Select the $n$ elements corresponding to the $n$ smallest random numbers.

Because each set of $n$ elements in the population has the same probability of being assigned the $n$ smallest random numbers, each set of $n$ elements has the same probability of being selected for the sample. If we select the sample using this two-step procedure, every sample of size $n$ has the same probability of being selected; thus, the sample selected satisfies the definition of a simple random sample.

Let us consider an example involving selecting a simple random sample of size $n = 5$ from a population of size $N = 16$. Table 7.1 contains a list of the 16 teams in the National Baseball League. Suppose we want to select a simple random sample of 5 teams to conduct in-depth interviews about how they manage their minor league franchises.

Step 1 of our simple random sampling procedure requires that we assign a random number to each of the 16 teams in the population. Figure 7.1 shows a worksheet used to generate a random number corresponding to each of the 16 teams in the population. The names of the baseball teams are in column A, and the random numbers generated are in column B. From the formula worksheet in the background we see that the formula =RAND() has been entered into cells B2:B17 to generate the random numbers between 0 and 1. From the value worksheet in the foreground we see that Arizona is assigned the random number .850862, Atlanta has been assigned the random number .706245, and so on.

The second step is to select the five teams corresponding to the five smallest random numbers as our sample. Looking through the random numbers in Figure 7.1, we see that the team corresponding to the smallest random number (.066942) is St. Louis, and that the four teams corresponding to the next four smallest random numbers are Washington, Houston, San Diego, and San Francisco. Thus, these five teams make up the simple random sample.

Searching through the list of random numbers in Figure 7.1 to find the five smallest random numbers is tedious, and it is easy to make mistakes. Excel's Sort procedure simplifies this step. We illustrate by sorting the list of baseball teams in Figure 7.1 to find the five teams corresponding to the five smallest random numbers. Refer to the foreground worksheet in Figure 7.1 as we describe the steps involved.

**Step 1.**  Select any cell in the range B2:B17
**Step 2.**  Click the **Home** tab on the Ribbon
**Step 3.**  In the **Editing** group, click **Sort & Filter**
**Step 4.**  Choose **Sort Smallest to Largest**

**TABLE 7.1**   NATIONAL BASEBALL LEAGUE TEAMS

| | |
|---|---|
| Arizona | Milwaukee |
| Atlanta | New York |
| Chicago | Philadelphia |
| Cincinnati | Pittsburgh |
| Colorado | San Diego |
| Florida | San Francisco |
| Houston | St. Louis |
| Los Angeles | Washington |

**FIGURE 7.1    WORKSHEET USED TO GENERATE A RANDOM NUMBER CORRESPONDING TO EACH TEAM**

**WEB** file

**National League**

After completing these steps we obtain the worksheet shown in Figure 7.2.[1] The teams listed in rows 2–6 are the ones corresponding to the smallest five random numbers; they are our simple random sample. Note that the random numbers shown in Figure 7.2 are in ascending order, and that the teams are not in their original order. For instance, St. Louis is the next to last team listed in Figure 7.1, but it is the first team selected in the simple random sample. Washington, the second team in our sample, is the sixteenth team in the original list, and so on.

We now use this simple random sampling procedure to select a simple random sample of 30 EAI managers from the population of 2500 EAI managers. We begin by generating 2500 random numbers, one for each manager in the population. Then we select 30 managers corresponding to the 30 smallest random numbers as our sample. Refer to Figure 7.3 as we describe the steps involved.

*The Excel Sort procedure for identifying the managers associated with the 30 smallest random numbers is especially valuable with such a large population.*

**Enter Data:**    The first three columns of the worksheet in the background show the annual salary data and training program status for the first 30 managers in the population of 2500 EAI managers. (The complete worksheet contains all 2500 managers.)

---

[1]In order to show the random numbers from Figure 7.1 in ascending order in this worksheet, we turned off the automatic recalculation option prior to sorting for illustrative purposes. If the recalculation option were not turned off, a new set of random numbers would have been generated when the sort was completed. But the same five teams would be selected.

**FIGURE 7.2**   USING EXCEL'S SORT PROCEDURE TO SELECT THE SIMPLE RANDOM SAMPLE OF FIVE TEAMS

**Enter Functions and Formulas:**   In the background worksheet, the label **Random Numbers** has been entered into cell D1 and the formula =RAND() has been entered into cells D2:D2501 to generate a random number between 0 and 1 for each of the 2500 EAI managers. The random number generated for the first manager is 0.613872, the random number generated for the second manager is 0.473204, and so on.

**Apply Tools:**   All that remains is to find the managers associated with the 30 smallest random numbers. To do so, we sort the data in columns A through D into ascending order by the random numbers in column D.

**Step 1.**  Select any cell in the range D2:D2501
**Step 2.**  Click the **Home** tab on the Ribbon
**Step 3.**  In the **Editing** group, click **Sort & Filter**
**Step 4.**  Choose **Sort Smallest to Largest**

After completing these steps we obtain the worksheet shown in the foreground of Figure 7.3. The managers listed in rows 2–31 are the ones corresponding to the smallest 30 random numbers that were generated. Hence, this group of 30 managers is a simple random sample. Note that the random numbers shown in the foreground of Figure 7.3 are in ascending order, and that the managers are not in their original order. For instance, manager 812 in the population is associated with the smallest random number and is the first element in the sample, and manager 13 in the population (see row 14 of the background worksheet) has been included as the 22nd observation in the sample (row 23 of the foreground worksheet).

## Sampling from an Infinite Population

Sometimes we want to select a sample from a population, but the population is infinitely large or the elements of the population are being generated by an ongoing process for

**FIGURE 7.3    USING EXCEL TO SELECT A SIMPLE RANDOM SAMPLE**

Figure 7.3 Background - Microsoft Excel

A1 — Manager

The formula in cells D2:D2501 is =RAND().

| Manager | Annual Salary | Training Program | Random Numbers |
|---|---|---|---|
| 1 | 55769.50 | No | 0.613872 |
| 2 | 50823.00 | Yes | 0.473204 |
| 3 | 48408.20 | No | 0.549011 |
| 4 | 49787.50 | No | 0.047482 |
| 5 | 52801.60 | Yes | 0.531085 |
| 6 | 51767.70 | No | 0.994296 |
| 7 | 58346.60 | Yes | 0.189065 |
| 8 | 46670.20 | No | 0.020714 |
| 9 | 50246.80 | Yes | 0.647318 |
| 10 | 51255.00 | No | 0.524341 |
| 11 | 52546.60 | No | 0.764998 |
| 12 | 49512.50 | Yes | 0.255244 |
| 13 | 51753.00 | Yes | 0.010923 |
| 14 | 53547.10 | No | 0.238003 |
| 15 | 48052.20 | No | 0.635675 |
| 16 | 44652.50 | Yes | 0.177294 |
| 17 | 51764.90 | Yes | 0.415097 |
| 18 | 45187.80 | Yes | 0.883440 |
| 19 | 49867.50 | Yes | 0.476824 |
| 20 | 53706.30 | Yes | 0.101065 |
| 21 | 52039.50 | Yes | 0.775323 |
| 22 | 52973.60 | No | 0.011729 |
| 23 | 53372.50 | No | 0.762026 |
| 24 | 54592.00 | Yes | 0.066344 |
| 25 | 55738.10 | Yes | 0.776766 |
| 26 | 52975.10 | Yes | 0.828493 |
| 27 | 52386.20 | Yes | 0.841532 |
| 28 | 51051.60 | Yes | 0.899427 |
| 29 | 52095.60 | Yes | 0.486284 |
| 30 | 44956.50 | No | 0.264628 |

Figure 7.3 Background    Ready

*Note: Rows 32–2501 are not shown.*

Figure 7.3 Foreground M.

A1 — Ma

| Manager | Annual Salary | Training Program | Random Numbers |
|---|---|---|---|
| 812 | 49094.30 | Yes | 0.000193 |
| 1411 | 53263.90 | Yes | 0.000484 |
| 1795 | 49643.50 | Yes | 0.002641 |
| 2095 | 49894.90 | Yes | 0.002763 |
| 1235 | 47621.60 | No | 0.002940 |
| 744 | 55924.00 | Yes | 0.002977 |
| 470 | 49092.30 | Yes | 0.003182 |
| 1606 | 51404.40 | Yes | 0.003448 |
| 1744 | 50957.70 | Yes | 0.004203 |
| 179 | 55109.70 | Yes | 0.005293 |
| 1387 | 45922.60 | Yes | 0.005709 |
| 1782 | 57268.40 | No | 0.005729 |
| 1006 | 55688.80 | Yes | 0.005796 |
| 278 | 51564.70 | No | 0.005966 |
| 1850 | 56188.20 | No | 0.006250 |
| 844 | 51766.00 | Yes | 0.006708 |
| 2028 | 52541.30 | No | 0.007767 |
| 1654 | 44980.00 | Yes | 0.008095 |
| 444 | 51932.60 | Yes | 0.009686 |
| 556 | 52973.00 | Yes | 0.009711 |
| 2449 | 45120.90 | Yes | 0.010595 |
| 13 | 51753.00 | Yes | 0.010923 |
| 2187 | 54391.80 | No | 0.011364 |
| 1633 | 50164.20 | No | 0.011603 |
| 22 | 52973.60 | No | 0.011729 |
| 1530 | 50241.30 | No | 0.013570 |
| 820 | 52793.90 | No | 0.013669 |
| 1258 | 50979.40 | Yes | 0.014042 |
| 2349 | 55860.90 | Yes | 0.014532 |
| 1698 | 57309.10 | No | 0.014539 |

Figure 7.3 Foreground    Ready    90%

which there is no limit on the number of elements that can be generated. Thus, it is not possible to develop a list of all the elements in the population. This is considered the infinite population case. With an infinite population, we cannot select a simple random sample because we cannot construct a frame consisting of all the elements. In the infinite population case, statisticians recommend selecting what is called a random sample.

RANDOM SAMPLE (INFINITE POPULATION)

A **random sample** of size $n$ from an infinite population is a sample selected such that the following conditions are satisfied.

  **1.** Each element selected comes from the same population.
  **2.** Each element is selected independently.

Care and judgment must be exercised in implementing the selection process for obtaining a random sample from an infinite population. Each case may require a different selection procedure. Let us consider two examples to see what we mean by the conditions (1) each element selected comes from the same population and (2) each element is selected independently.

A common quality control application involves a production process where there is no limit on the number of elements that can be produced. The conceptual population we are sampling from is all the elements that could be produced (not just the ones that are produced) by the ongoing production process. Because we cannot develop a list of all the elements that could be produced, the population is considered infinite. To be more specific, let us consider a production line designed to fill boxes of a breakfast cereal with a mean weight of 24 ounces of breakfast cereal per box. Samples of 12 boxes filled by this process are periodically selected by a quality control inspector to determine if the process is operating properly or if, perhaps, a machine malfunction has caused the process to begin underfilling or overfilling the boxes.

With a production operation such as this, the biggest concern in selecting a random sample is to make sure that condition 1, the sampled elements are selected from the same population, is satisfied. To ensure that this condition is satisfied, the boxes must be selected at approximately the same point in time. This way the inspector avoids the possibility of selecting some boxes when the process is operating properly and other boxes when the process is not operating properly and is underfilling or overfilling the boxes. With a production process such as this, the second condition, each element is selected independently, is satisfied by designing the production process so that each box of cereal is filled independently. With this assumption, the quality control inspector only needs to worry about satisfying the same population condition.

As another example of selecting a random sample from an infinite population, consider the population of customers arriving at a fast-food restaurant. Suppose an employee is asked to select and interview a sample of customers in order to develop a profile of customers who visit the restaurant. The customer arrival process is ongoing and there is no way to obtain a list of all customers in the population. So, for practical purposes, the population for this ongoing process is considered infinite. As long as a sampling procedure is designed so that all the elements in the sample are customers of the restaurant and they are selected independently, a random sample will be obtained. In this case, the employee collecting the sample needs to select the sample from people who come into the restaurant and make a purchase to ensure that the same population condition is satisfied. If, for instance, the employee selected someone for the sample who came into the restaurant just to use the restroom, that person would not be a customer and the same population condition would be violated. So, as long as the interviewer selects the sample from people making a purchase at the restaurant, condition 1 is satisfied. Ensuring that the customers are selected independently can be more difficult.

The purpose of the second condition of the random sample selection procedure (each element is selected independently) is to prevent selection bias. In this case, selection bias would occur if the interviewer were free to select customers for the sample arbitrarily. The interviewer might feel more comfortable selecting customers in a particular age group and might avoid customers in other age groups. Selection bias would also occur if the interviewer selected a group of five customers who entered the restaurant together and asked all of them to participate in the sample. Such a group of customers would be likely to exhibit similar characteristics, which might provide misleading information about the population of customers. Selection bias such as this can be avoided by ensuring that the selection of a particular customer does not influence the selection of any other customer. In other words, the elements (customers) are selected independently.

McDonald's, the fast-food restaurant leader, implemented a random sampling procedure for this situation. The sampling procedure was based on the fact that some customers presented discount coupons. Whenever a customer presented a discount coupon, the next customer served was asked to complete a customer profile questionnaire. Because arriving customers presented discount coupons randomly and independently of other customers, this sampling procedure ensured that customers were selected independently. As a result, the sample satisfied the requirements of a random sample from an infinite population.

Situations involving sampling from an infinite population are usually associated with a process that operates over time. Examples include parts being manufactured on a production line, repeated experimental trials in a laboratory, transactions occurring at a bank, telephone calls arriving at a technical support center, and customers entering a retail store. In each case, the situation may be viewed as a process that generates elements from an infinite population. As long as the sampled elements are selected from the same population and are selected independently, the sample is considered a random sample from an infinite population.

## NOTES AND COMMENTS

1. In this section we have been careful to define two types of samples: a simple random sample from a finite population and a random sample from an infinite population. In the remainder of the text, we will generally refer to both of these as either a *random sample* or simply a *sample*. We will not make a distinction of the sample being a "simple" random sample unless it is necessary for the exercise or discussion.

2. Statisticians who specialize in sample surveys from finite populations use sampling methods that provide probability samples. With a probability sample, each possible sample has a known probability of selection and a random process is used to select the elements for the sample. Simple random sampling is one of these methods. In Section 7.7, we describe some other probability sampling methods: stratified random sampling,

cluster sampling, and systematic sampling. We use the term *simple* in simple random sampling to clarify that this is the probability sampling method that assures each sample of size $n$ has the same probability of being selected.

3. The number of different simple random samples of size $n$ that can be selected from a finite population of size $N$ is

$$\frac{N!}{n!(N-n)!}$$

In this formula, $N!$ and $n!$ are the factorial formulas discussed in Chapter 4. For the EAI problem with $N = 2500$ and $n = 30$, this expression can be used to show that approximately $2.75 \times 10^{69}$ different simple random samples of 30 EAI managers can be obtained.

## Exercises

### Methods

1. Consider a finite population with five elements labeled A, B, C, D, and E. Ten possible simple random samples of size 2 can be selected.
   a.  List the 10 samples beginning with AB, AC, and so on.
   b.  Using simple random sampling, what is the probability that each sample of size 2 is selected?

c.  Suppose we use Excel's RAND function to assign random numbers to the five elements: A (.7266), B (.0476), C (.2459), D (.0957), E (.9408). List the simple random sample of size 2 that will be selected by using these random numbers.

2.  Assume a finite population has 10 elements. Number the elements from 1 to 10 and use the following 10 random numbers to select a sample of size 4.

.7545    .0936    .0341    .3242    .1449    .9060    .2420    .9773    .5428    .0729

3.  The American League consists of 14 baseball teams. Suppose a sample of 5 teams is to be selected to conduct player interviews. The following table lists the 14 teams and the random numbers assigned by Excel's RAND function. Use these random numbers to select a sample of size 5.

American League

| Team | Random Number | Team | Random Number |
|------|--------------|------|--------------|
| New York | 0.178624 | Boston | 0.290197 |
| Baltimore | 0.578370 | Tampa Bay | 0.867778 |
| Toronto | 0.965807 | Minnesota | 0.811810 |
| Chicago | 0.562178 | Cleveland | 0.960271 |
| Detroit | 0.253574 | Kansas City | 0.326836 |
| Oakland | 0.288287 | Anaheim | 0.895267 |
| Texas | 0.500879 | Seattle | 0.839071 |

4.  The 10 most active stocks on the New York Stock Exchange on March 6, 2006, are listed here (*The Wall Street Journal,* March 7, 2006).

| | | | | |
|---|---|---|---|---|
| AT&T | Lucent | Nortel | Qwest | Bell South |
| Pfizer | Texas Instruments | Gen. Elect. | iShrMsJpn | LSI Logic |

Exchange authorities decided to sample three of these stocks to investigate trading practices. Select a simple random sample of three stocks for this investigation.

EAI

5.  In this section we used a two-step procedure to select a simple random sample of 30 EAI managers. Use this procedure to select a simple random sample of 50 EAI managers.

6.  Indicate which of the following situations involve sampling from a finite population and which involve sampling from an infinite population. In cases where the sampled population is finite, describe how you would construct a frame.
    a.  Select a sample of licensed drivers in the state of New York.
    b.  Select a sample of boxes of cereal off the production line for the Breakfast Choice Company.
    c.  Select a sample of cars crossing the Golden Gate Bridge on a typical weekday.
    d.  Select a sample of students in a statistics course at Indiana University.
    e.  Select a sample of the orders being processed by a mail-order firm.

## 7.3  Point Estimation

Now that we have described how to select a simple random sample, let us return to the EAI problem. A simple random sample of 30 managers and the corresponding data on annual salary and management training program participation are as shown in Table 7.2. The notation $x_1$, $x_2$, and so on is used to denote the annual salary of the first manager in the sample, the annual salary of the second manager in the sample, and so on. Participation in the management training program is indicated by Yes in the management training program column.

**TABLE 7.2**   ANNUAL SALARY AND TRAINING PROGRAM STATUS FOR A SIMPLE
RANDOM SAMPLE OF 30 EAI MANAGERS

| Annual Salary ($) | Management Training Program | Annual Salary ($) | Management Training Program |
|---|---|---|---|
| $x_1 = 49,094.30$ | Yes | $x_{16} = 51,766.00$ | Yes |
| $x_2 = 53,263.90$ | Yes | $x_{17} = 52,541.30$ | No |
| $x_3 = 49,643.50$ | Yes | $x_{18} = 44,980.00$ | Yes |
| $x_4 = 49,894.90$ | Yes | $x_{19} = 51,932.60$ | Yes |
| $x_5 = 47,621.60$ | No | $x_{20} = 52,973.00$ | Yes |
| $x_6 = 55,924.00$ | Yes | $x_{21} = 45,120.90$ | Yes |
| $x_7 = 49,092.30$ | Yes | $x_{22} = 51,753.00$ | Yes |
| $x_8 = 51,404.40$ | Yes | $x_{23} = 54,391.80$ | No |
| $x_9 = 50,957.70$ | Yes | $x_{24} = 50,164.20$ | No |
| $x_{10} = 55,109.70$ | Yes | $x_{25} = 52,973.60$ | No |
| $x_{11} = 45,922.60$ | Yes | $x_{26} = 50,241.30$ | No |
| $x_{12} = 57,268.40$ | No | $x_{27} = 52,793.90$ | No |
| $x_{13} = 55,688.80$ | Yes | $x_{28} = 50,979.40$ | Yes |
| $x_{14} = 51,564.70$ | No | $x_{29} = 55,860.90$ | Yes |
| $x_{15} = 56,188.20$ | No | $x_{30} = 57,309.10$ | No |

To estimate the value of a population parameter, we compute a corresponding characteristic of the sample, referred to as a **sample statistic**. For example, to estimate the population mean $\mu$ and the population standard deviation $\sigma$ for the annual salary of EAI
managers, we use the data in Table 7.2 to calculate the corresponding sample statistics: the
sample mean and the sample standard deviation $s$. Using the formulas for a sample mean
and a sample standard deviation presented in Chapter 3, the sample mean is

$$\bar{x} = \frac{\Sigma x_i}{n} = \frac{1,554,420}{30} = \$51,814$$

and the sample standard deviation is

$$s = \sqrt{\frac{\Sigma(x_i - \bar{x})^2}{n - 1}} = \sqrt{\frac{325,009,260}{29}} = \$3348$$

To estimate $p$, the proportion of managers in the population who completed the management training program, we use the corresponding sample proportion $\bar{p}$. Let $x$ denote
the number of managers in the sample who completed the management training program.
The data in Table 7.2 show that $x = 19$. Thus, with a sample size of $n = 30$, the sample
proportion is

$$\bar{p} = \frac{x}{n} = \frac{19}{30} = .63$$

By making the preceding computations, we perform the statistical procedure called *point
estimation*. We refer to the sample mean $\bar{x}$ as the **point estimator** of the population mean $\mu$,
the sample standard deviation $s$ as the point estimator of the population standard deviation $\sigma$,
and the sample proportion $\bar{p}$ as the point estimator of the population proportion $p$. The
numerical value obtained for $\bar{x}$, $s$, or $\bar{p}$ is called the **point estimate**. Thus, for the simple

**TABLE 7.3**  SUMMARY OF POINT ESTIMATES OBTAINED FROM A SIMPLE RANDOM SAMPLE OF 30 EAI MANAGERS

| Population Parameter | Parameter Value | Point Estimator | Point Estimate |
|---|---|---|---|
| $\mu$ = Population mean annual salary | $51,800 | $\bar{x}$ = Sample mean annual salary | $51,814 |
| $\sigma$ = Population standard deviation for annual salary | $4000 | $s$ = Sample standard deviation for annual salary | $3348 |
| $p$ = Population proportion having completed the management training program | .60 | $\bar{p}$ = Sample proportion having completed the management training program | .63 |

random sample of 30 EAI managers shown in Table 7.2, $51,814 is the point estimate of $\mu$, $3348 is the point estimate of $\sigma$, and .63 is the point estimate of $p$. Table 7.3 summarizes the sample results and compares the point estimates to the actual values of the population parameters.

As is evident from Table 7.3, the point estimates differ somewhat from the corresponding population parameters. This difference is to be expected because a sample, and not a census of the entire population, is being used to develop the point estimates. In the next chapter, we will show how to construct an interval estimate in order to provide information about how close the point estimate is to the population parameter.

## Practical Advice

The subject matter of most of the rest of the book is concerned with statistical inference. Point estimation is a form of statistical inference. We use a sample statistic to make an inference about a population parameter. When making inferences about a population based on a sample, it is important to have a close correspondence between the sampled population and the target population. The **target population** is the population we want to make inferences about, while the sampled population is the population from which the sample is actually taken. In this section, we have described the process of drawing a simple random sample from the population of EAI managers and making point estimates of characteristics of that same population. So the sampled population and the target population are identical, which is the desired situation. But in other cases, it is not as easy to obtain a close correspondence between the sampled and target populations.

Consider the case of an amusement park selecting a sample of its customers to learn about characteristics such as age and time spent at the park. Suppose all the sample elements were selected on a day when park attendance was restricted to employees of a large company. Then the sampled population would be composed of employees of that company and members of their families. If the target population we wanted to make inferences about were typical park customers over a typical summer, then we might encounter a significant difference between the sampled population and the target population. In such a case, we would question the validity of the point estimates being made. Park management would be in the best position to know whether a sample taken on a particular day was likely to be representative of the target population.

In summary, whenever a sample is used to make inferences about a population, we should make sure that the study is designed so that the sampled population and the target population are in close agreement. Good judgment is a necessary ingredient of sound statistical practice.

## Exercises

## Methods

7. The following data are from a simple random sample.

$$5 \quad 8 \quad 10 \quad 7 \quad 10 \quad 14$$

a. What is the point estimate of the population mean?
b. What is the point estimate of the population standard deviation?

8. A survey question for a sample of 150 individuals yielded 75 Yes responses, 55 No responses, and 20 No Opinions.
a. What is the point estimate of the proportion in the population who respond Yes?
b. What is the point estimate of the proportion in the population who respond No?

## Applications

9. A simple random sample of 5 months of sales data provided the following information:

| Month: | 1 | 2 | 3 | 4 | 5 |
|---|---|---|---|---|---|
| Units Sold: | 94 | 100 | 85 | 94 | 92 |

a. Develop a point estimate of the population mean number of units sold per month.
b. Develop a point estimate of the population standard deviation.

MutualFund

10. *BusinessWeek* published information on 283 equity mutual funds (*BusinessWeek,* January 26, 2004). A sample of 40 of those funds is contained in the data set MutualFund. Use the data set to answer the following questions.
a. Develop a point estimate of the proportion of the *BusinessWeek* equity funds that are load funds.
b. Develop a point estimate of the proportion of funds that are classified as high risk.
c. Develop a point estimate of the proportion of funds that have a below-average risk rating.

11. Many drugs used to treat cancer are expensive. *BusinessWeek* reported on the cost per treatment of Herceptin, a drug used to treat breast cancer (*BusinessWeek,* January 30, 2006). Typical treatment costs (in dollars) for Herceptin are provided by a simple random sample of 10 patients.

| 4376 | 5578 | 2717 | 4920 | 4495 |
|---|---|---|---|---|
| 4798 | 6446 | 4119 | 4237 | 3814 |

a. Develop a point estimate of the mean cost per treatment with Herceptin.
b. Develop a point estimate of the standard deviation of the cost per treatment with Herceptin.

12. A sample of 50 *Fortune* 500 companies (*Fortune,* April 14, 2003) showed that 5 were based in New York, 6 in California, 2 in Minnesota, and 1 in Wisconsin.
a. Develop an estimate of the proportion of *Fortune* 500 companies based in New York.
b. Develop an estimate of the number of *Fortune* 500 companies based in Minnesota.
c. Develop an estimate of the proportion of *Fortune* 500 companies that are not based in these four states.

13. The American Association of Individual Investors (AAII) polls its subscribers on a weekly basis to determine the number who are bullish, bearish, or neutral on the short-term prospects for the stock market. Its findings for the week ending March 2, 2006, are consistent with the following sample results (AAII website, March 7, 2006).

Bullish   409        Neutral   299        Bearish   291

Develop a point estimate of the following population parameters.
a.  The proportion of all AAII subscribers who are bullish on the stock market.
b.  The proportion of all AAII subscribers who are neutral on the stock market.
c.  The proportion of all AAII subscribers who are bearish on the stock market.

14.  In this section we showed how a simple random sample of 30 EAI managers can be used to develop point estimates of the population mean annual salary, the population standard deviation for annual salary, and the population proportion having completed the management training program.
a.  Use Excel to select a simple random sample of 50 EAI managers.
b.  Develop a point estimate of the mean annual salary.
c.  Develop a point estimate of the population standard deviation for annual salary.
d.  Develop a point estimate of the population proportion having completed the management training program.

# 7.4  Introduction to Sampling Distributions

In the preceding section we said that the sample mean $\bar{x}$ is the point estimator of the population mean $\mu$, and the sample proportion $\bar{p}$ is the point estimator of the population proportion $p$. For the simple random sample of 30 EAI managers shown in Table 7.2, the point estimate of $\mu$ is $\bar{x} = \$51,814$ and the point estimate of $p$ is $\bar{p} = .63$. Suppose we select another simple random sample of 30 EAI managers and obtain the following point estimates:

$$\text{Sample mean: } \bar{x} = \$52,670$$
$$\text{Sample proportion: } \bar{p} = .70$$

Note that different values of $\bar{x}$ and $\bar{p}$ were obtained. Indeed, a second simple random sample of 30 EAI managers cannot be expected to provide the same point estimates as the first sample.

Now, suppose we repeat the process of selecting a simple random sample of 30 EAI managers over and over again, each time computing the values of $\bar{x}$ and $\bar{p}$. Table 7.4 contains a portion of the results obtained for 500 simple random samples, and Table 7.5 shows the frequency and relative frequency distributions for the 500 $\bar{x}$ values. Figure 7.4 shows the relative frequency histogram for the $\bar{x}$ values.

In Chapter 5 we defined a random variable as a numerical description of the outcome of an experiment. If we consider the process of selecting a simple random sample as an

**TABLE 7.4**   VALUES OF $\bar{x}$ AND $\bar{p}$ FROM 500 SIMPLE RANDOM SAMPLES
OF 30 EAI MANAGERS

| Sample Number | Sample Mean ($\bar{x}$) | Sample Proportion ($\bar{p}$) |
|---|---|---|
| 1 | 51,814 | .63 |
| 2 | 52,670 | .70 |
| 3 | 51,780 | .67 |
| 4 | 51,588 | .53 |
| . | . | . |
| . | . | . |
| . | . | . |
| 500 | 51,752 | .50 |

**TABLE 7.5**    FREQUENCY AND RELATIVE FREQUENCY DISTRIBUTIONS OF $\bar{x}$ FROM 500 SIMPLE RANDOM SAMPLES OF 30 EAI MANAGERS

| Mean Annual Salary ($) | Frequency | Relative Frequency |
|---|---|---|
| 49,500.00–49,999.99 | 2 | .004 |
| 50,000.00–50,499.99 | 16 | .032 |
| 50,500.00–50,999.99 | 52 | .104 |
| 51,000.00–51,499.99 | 101 | .202 |
| 51,500.00–51,999.99 | 133 | .266 |
| 52,000.00–52,499.99 | 110 | .220 |
| 52,500.00–52,999.99 | 54 | .108 |
| 53,000.00–53,499.99 | 26 | .052 |
| 53,500.00–53,999.99 | 6 | .012 |
| Totals | 500 | 1.000 |

**FIGURE 7.4**    RELATIVE FREQUENCY HISTOGRAM OF $\bar{x}$ VALUES FROM 500 SIMPLE RANDOM SAMPLES OF SIZE 30 EACH

*The ability to understand the material in subsequent chapters depends heavily on the ability to understand and use the sampling distributions presented in this chapter.*

experiment, the sample mean $\bar{x}$ is the numerical description of the outcome of the experiment. Thus, the sample mean $\bar{x}$ is a random variable. As a result, just like other random variables, $\bar{x}$ has a mean or expected value, a standard deviation, and a probability distribution. Because the various possible values of $\bar{x}$ are the result of different simple random samples, the probability distribution of $\bar{x}$ is called the **sampling distribution** of $\bar{x}$. Knowledge of this sampling distribution and its properties will enable us to make probability statements about how close the sample mean $\bar{x}$ is to the population mean $\mu$.

**FIGURE 7.5**   RELATIVE FREQUENCY HISTOGRAM OF $\bar{p}$ VALUES FROM 500 SIMPLE RANDOM SAMPLES OF SIZE 30 EACH

Let us return to Figure 7.4. We would need to enumerate every possible sample of 30 managers and compute each sample mean to completely determine the sampling distribution of $\bar{x}$. However, the histogram of 500 $\bar{x}$ values gives an approximation of this sampling distribution. From the approximation we observe the bell-shaped appearance of the distribution. We note that the largest concentration of the $\bar{x}$ values and the mean of the 500 $\bar{x}$ values is near the population mean $\mu = \$51,800$. We will describe the properties of the sampling distribution of $\bar{x}$ more fully in the next section.

The 500 values of the sample proportion $\bar{p}$ are summarized by the relative frequency histogram in Figure 7.5. As in the case of $\bar{x}$, $\bar{p}$ is a random variable. If every possible sample of size 30 were selected from the population and if a value of $\bar{p}$ were computed for each sample, the resulting probability distribution would be the sampling distribution of $\bar{p}$. The relative frequency histogram of the 500 sample values in Figure 7.5 provides a general idea of the appearance of the sampling distribution of $\bar{p}$.

In practice, we select only one simple random sample from the population. We repeated the sampling process 500 times in this section simply to illustrate that many different samples are possible and that the different samples generate a variety of values for the sample statistics $\bar{x}$ and $\bar{p}$. The probability distribution of any particular sample statistic is called the sampling distribution of the statistic. In Section 7.5 we discuss the characteristics of the sampling distribution of $\bar{x}$. In Section 7.6 we discuss the characteristics of the sampling distribution of $\bar{p}$.

# 7.5 Sampling Distribution of $\bar{x}$

In the previous section we said that the sample mean $\bar{x}$ is a random variable and its probability distribution is called the sampling distribution of $\bar{x}$.

> **SAMPLING DISTRIBUTION OF $\bar{x}$**
>
> The sampling distribution of $\bar{x}$ is the probability distribution of all possible values of the sample mean $\bar{x}$.

This section describes the properties of the sampling distribution of $\bar{x}$. Just as with other probability distributions we studied, the sampling distribution of $\bar{x}$ has an expected value or mean, a standard deviation, and a characteristic shape or form. Let us begin by considering the mean of all possible $\bar{x}$ values, which is referred to as the expected value of $\bar{x}$.

## Expected Value of $\bar{x}$

In the EAI sampling problem we saw that different simple random samples result in a variety of values for the sample mean $\bar{x}$. Because many different values of the random variable $\bar{x}$ are possible, we are often interested in the mean of all possible values of $\bar{x}$ that can be generated by the various simple random samples. The mean of the $\bar{x}$ random variable is the expected value of $\bar{x}$. Let $E(\bar{x})$ represent the expected value of $\bar{x}$ and $\mu$ represent the mean of the population from which we are selecting a simple random sample. It can be shown that with simple random sampling, $E(\bar{x})$ and $\mu$ are equal.

*The expected value of $\bar{x}$ equals the mean of the population from which the sample is selected.*

> **EXPECTED VALUE OF $\bar{x}$**
>
> $$E(\bar{x}) = \mu \qquad\qquad (7.1)$$
>
> where
>
> $$E(\bar{x}) = \text{the expected value of } \bar{x}$$
> $$\mu = \text{the population mean}$$

This result shows that with simple random sampling, the expected value or mean of the sampling distribution of $\bar{x}$ is equal to the mean of the population. In Section 7.1 we saw that the mean annual salary for the population of EAI managers is $\mu = \$51{,}800$. Thus, according to equation (7.1), the mean of all possible sample means for the EAI study is also $\$51{,}800$.

When the expected value of a point estimator equals the population parameter, we say the point estimator is **unbiased**. Thus, equation (7.1) shows that $\bar{x}$ is an unbiased estimator of the population mean $\mu$.

## Standard Deviation of $\bar{x}$

Let us define the standard deviation of the sampling distribution of $\bar{x}$. We will use the following notation.

$$\sigma_{\bar{x}} = \text{the standard deviation of } \bar{x}$$
$$\sigma = \text{the standard deviation of the population}$$
$$n = \text{the sample size}$$
$$N = \text{the population size}$$

It can be shown that the formula for the standard deviation of $\bar{x}$ depends on whether the population is finite or infinite. The two formulas for the standard deviation of $\bar{x}$ follow.

STANDARD DEVIATION OF $\bar{x}$

*Finite Population*          *Infinite Population*

$$\sigma_{\bar{x}} = \sqrt{\frac{N-n}{N-1}}\left(\frac{\sigma}{\sqrt{n}}\right) \qquad\qquad \sigma_{\bar{x}} = \frac{\sigma}{\sqrt{n}} \qquad\qquad \textbf{(7.2)}$$

In comparing the two formulas in (7.2), we see that the factor $\sqrt{(N-n)/(N-1)}$ is required for the finite population case but not for the infinite population case. This factor is commonly referred to as the **finite population correction factor**. In many practical sampling situations, we find that the population involved, although finite, is "large," whereas the sample size is relatively "small." In such cases the finite population correction factor $\sqrt{(N-n)/(N-1)}$ is close to 1. As a result, the difference between the values of the standard deviation of $\bar{x}$ for the finite and infinite population cases becomes negligible. Then, $\sigma_{\bar{x}} = \sigma/\sqrt{n}$ becomes a good approximation to the standard deviation of $\bar{x}$ even though the population is finite. This observation leads to the following general guideline, or rule of thumb, for computing the standard deviation of $\bar{x}$.

USE THE FOLLOWING EXPRESSION TO COMPUTE THE STANDARD DEVIATION OF $\bar{x}$

$$\sigma_{\bar{x}} = \frac{\sigma}{\sqrt{n}} \qquad\qquad \textbf{(7.3)}$$

whenever

1. The population is infinite; or
2. The population is finite *and* the sample size is less than or equal to 5% of the population size; that is, $n/N \leq .05$.

*Problem 17 shows that when $n/N \leq .05$, the finite population correction factor has little effect on the value of $\sigma_{\bar{x}}$.*

In cases where $n/N > .05$, the finite population version of formula (7.2) should be used in the computation of $\sigma_{\bar{x}}$. Unless otherwise noted, throughout the text we will assume that the population size is "large," $n/N \leq .05$, and expression (7.3) can be used to compute $\sigma_{\bar{x}}$.

*The term* standard error *is used throughout statistical inference to refer to the standard deviation of a point estimator.*

To compute $\sigma_{\bar{x}}$, we need to know $\sigma$, the standard deviation of the population. To further emphasize the difference between $\sigma_{\bar{x}}$ and $\sigma$, we refer to the standard deviation of $\bar{x}$, $\sigma_{\bar{x}}$, as the **standard error** of the mean. In general, the term *standard error* refers to the standard deviation of a point estimator. Later we will see that the value of the standard error of the mean is helpful in determining how far the sample mean may be from the population mean. Let us now return to the EAI example and compute the standard error of the mean associated with simple random samples of 30 EAI managers.

In Section 7.1 we saw that the standard deviation of annual salary for the population of 2500 EAI managers is $\sigma = 4000$. In this case, the population is finite, with $N = 2500$. However, with a sample size of 30, we have $n/N = 30/2500 = .012$. Because the sample size is less than 5% of the population size, we can ignore the finite population correction factor and use equation (7.3) to compute the standard error.

$$\sigma_{\bar{x}} = \frac{\sigma}{\sqrt{n}} = \frac{4000}{\sqrt{30}} = 730.3$$

## Form of the Sampling Distribution of $\bar{x}$

The preceding results concerning the expected value and standard deviation for the sampling distribution of $\bar{x}$ are applicable for any population. The final step in identifying the characteristics of the sampling distribution of $\bar{x}$ is to determine the form or shape of the sampling distribution. We will consider two cases: (1) The population has a normal distribution; and (2) the population does not have a normal distribution.

**Population has a normal distribution**     In many situations it is reasonable to assume that the population from which we are selecting a random sample has a normal, or nearly normal, distribution. When the population has a normal distribution, the sampling distribution of $\bar{x}$ is normally distributed for any sample size.

**Population does not have a normal distribution**     When the population from which we are selecting a random sample does not have a normal distribution, the **central limit theorem** is helpful in identifying the shape of the sampling distribution of $\bar{x}$. A statement of the central limit theorem as it applies to the sampling distribution of $\bar{x}$ follows.

---

CENTRAL LIMIT THEOREM

In selecting random samples of size $n$ from a population, the sampling distribution of the sample mean $\bar{x}$ can be approximated by a *normal distribution* as the sample size becomes large.

---

Figure 7.6 shows how the central limit theorem works for three different populations; each column refers to one of the populations. The top panel of the figure shows that none of the populations are normally distributed. Population I follows a uniform distribution. Population II is often called the rabbit-eared distribution. It is symmetric, but the more likely values fall in the tails of the distribution. Population III is shaped like the exponential distribution; it is skewed to the right.

The bottom three panels of Figure 7.6 show the shape of the sampling distribution for samples of size $n = 2$, $n = 5$, and $n = 30$. When the sample size is 2, we see that the shape of each sampling distribution is different from the shape of the corresponding population

**FIGURE 7.6** ILLUSTRATION OF THE CENTRAL LIMIT THEOREM
FOR THREE POPULATIONS

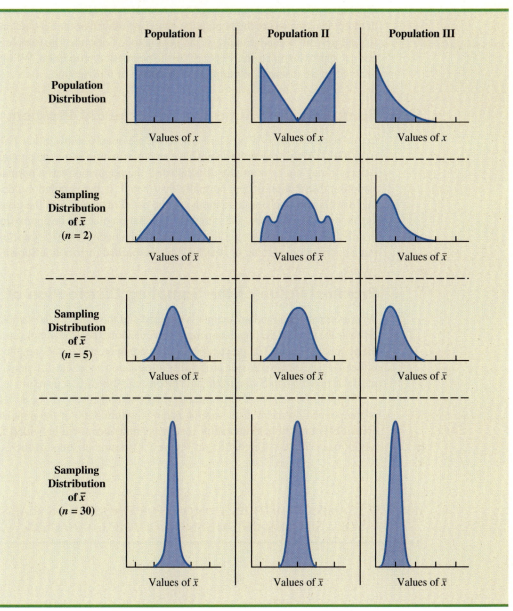

distribution. For samples of size 5, we see that the shapes of the sampling distributions for populations I and II begin to look similar to the shape of a normal distribution. Even though the shape of the sampling distribution for population III begins to look similar to the shape of a normal distribution, some skewness to the right is still present. Finally, for samples of size 30, the shapes of each of the three sampling distributions are approximately normal.

From a practitioner standpoint, we often want to know how large the sample size needs to be before the central limit theorem applies and we can assume that the shape of the sampling distribution is approximately normal. Statistical researchers have investigated this question by studying the sampling distribution of $\bar{x}$ for a variety of populations and a variety of sample sizes. General statistical practice is to assume that, for most applications, the sampling distribution of $\bar{x}$ can be approximated by a normal distribution whenever the sample is size 30 or more. In cases where the population is highly skewed or outliers are present, samples of size 50 may be needed. Finally, if the population is discrete, the sample size needed for a normal approximation often depends on the population proportion. We say more about this issue when we discuss the sampling distribution of $\bar{p}$ in Section 7.6.

## Sampling Distribution of $\bar{x}$ for the EAI Problem

Let us return to the EAI problem where we previously showed that $E(\bar{x}) = \$51,800$ and $\sigma_{\bar{x}} = 730.3$. At this point, we do not have any information about the population distribution; it may or may not be normally distributed. If the population has a normal distribution, the sampling distribution of $\bar{x}$ is normally distributed. If the population does not have a normal distribution, the simple random sample of 30 managers and the central limit theorem enable us to conclude that the sampling distribution of $\bar{x}$ can be approximated by a normal distribution. In either case, we are comfortable proceeding with the conclusion that the sampling distribution of $\bar{x}$ can be described by the normal distribution shown in Figure 7.7.

## Practical Value of the Sampling Distribution of $\bar{x}$

Whenever a simple random sample is selected and the value of the sample mean is used to estimate the value of the population mean $\mu$, we cannot expect the sample mean to exactly equal the population mean. The practical reason we are interested in the sampling distribution of $\bar{x}$ is that it can be used to provide probability information about the difference between the sample mean and the population mean. To demonstrate this use, let us return to the EAI problem.

Suppose the personnel director believes the sample mean will be an acceptable estimate of the population mean if the sample mean is within $500 of the population mean. However, it is not possible to guarantee that the sample mean will be within $500 of the population mean. Indeed, Table 7.5 and Figure 7.4 show that some of the 500 sample means

**FIGURE 7.7**    SAMPLING DISTRIBUTION OF $\bar{x}$ FOR THE MEAN ANNUAL SALARY OF A SIMPLE RANDOM SAMPLE OF 30 EAI MANAGERS

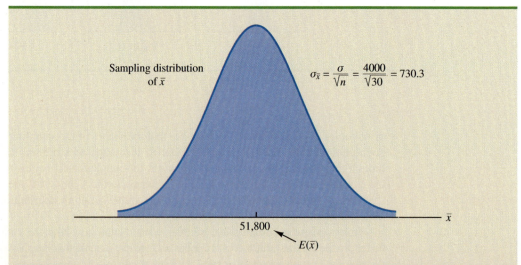

**FIGURE 7.8** PROBABILITY OF A SAMPLE MEAN BEING WITHIN $500 OF THE POPULATION MEAN FOR A SIMPLE RANDOM SAMPLE OF 30 EAI MANAGERS

differed by more than $2000 from the population mean. So we must think of the personnel director's request in probability terms. That is, the personnel director is concerned with the following question: What is the probability that the sample mean computed using a simple random sample of 30 EAI managers will be within $500 of the population mean?

Because we have identified the properties of the sampling distribution of $\bar{x}$ (see Figure 7.7), we will use this distribution to answer the probability question. Refer to the sampling distribution of $\bar{x}$ shown again in Figure 7.8. With a population mean of $51,800, the personnel director wants to know the probability that $\bar{x}$ is between $51,300 and $52,300. This probability is given by the darkly shaded area of the sampling distribution shown in Figure 7.8. Because the sampling distribution is normally distributed, with mean 51,800 and standard error of the mean 730.3, we can use the standard normal probability table to find the area or probability.

We first calculate the $z$ value at the upper endpoint of the interval (52,300) and use the table to find the cumulative probability at that point (left tail area). Then we compute the $z$ value at the lower endpoint of the interval (51,300) and use the table to find the area under the curve to the left of that point (another left tail area). Subtracting the second tail area from the first gives us the desired probability.

At $\bar{x} = 52,300$, we have

$$z = \frac{52,300 - 51,800}{730.30} = .68$$

Referring to the standard normal probability table, we find a cumulative probability (area to the left of $z = .68$) of .7517.

At $\bar{x} = 51,300$, we have

$$z = \frac{51,300 - 51,800}{730.30} = -.68$$

The area under the curve to the left of $z = -.68$ is .2483. Therefore, $P(51,300 \leq \bar{x} \leq 52,300) = P(z \leq .68) - P(z < -.68) = .7517 - .2483 = .5034.$

The desired probability can also be computed using Excel's NORM.DIST function. The advantage of using the NORM.DIST function is that we do not have to make a separate computation of the $z$ value. Evaluating the NORM.DIST function at the upper endpoint of the interval provides the cumulative probability at 52,300. Entering the formula =NORM.DIST(52300,51800,730.30,TRUE) into a cell of an Excel worksheet provides .7532 for this cumulative probability. Evaluating the NORM.DIST function at the lower endpoint of the interval provides the area under the curve to the left of 51,300. Entering the formula =NORM.DIST(51300,51800,730.30,TRUE) into a cell of an Excel worksheet provides .2468 for this cumulative probability. The probability of $\bar{x}$ being in the interval from 51,300 to 52,300 is then given by .7532 − .2468 = .5064. We note that this result is slightly different from the probability obtained using the table, because in using the normal table we rounded to two decimal places of accuracy when computing the $z$ value. The result obtained using NORM.DIST is thus more accurate.

The preceding computations show that a simple random sample of 30 EAI managers has a .5064 probability of providing a sample mean $\bar{x}$ that is within \$500 of the population mean. Thus, there is a 1 − .5064 = .4936 probability that the sampling error will be more than \$500. In other words, a simple random sample of 30 EAI managers has roughly a 50/50 chance of providing a sample mean within the allowable \$500. Perhaps a larger sample size should be considered. Let us explore this possibility by considering the relationship between the sample size and the sampling distribution of $\bar{x}$.

## Relationship Between the Sample Size and the Sampling Distribution of $\bar{x}$

Suppose that in the EAI sampling problem we select a simple random sample of 100 EAI managers instead of the 30 originally considered. Intuitively, it would seem that with more data provided by the larger sample size, the sample mean based on $n = 100$ should provide a better estimate of the population mean than the sample mean based on $n = 30$. To see how much better, let us consider the relationship between the sample size and the sampling distribution of $\bar{x}$.

First note that $E(\bar{x}) = \mu$ regardless of the sample size. Thus, the mean of all possible values of $\bar{x}$ is equal to the population mean $\mu$ regardless of the sample size $n$. However, note that the standard error of the mean, $\sigma_{\bar{x}} = \sigma/\sqrt{n}$, is related to the square root of the sample size. Whenever the sample size is increased, the standard error of the mean $\sigma_{\bar{x}}$ decreases. With $n = 30$, the standard error of the mean for the EAI problem is 730.3. However, with the increase in the sample size to $n = 100$, the standard error of the mean is decreased to

$$\sigma_{\bar{x}} = \frac{\sigma}{\sqrt{n}} = \frac{4000}{\sqrt{100}} = 400$$

The sampling distributions of $\bar{x}$ with $n = 30$ and $n = 100$ are shown in Figure 7.9. Because the sampling distribution with $n = 100$ has a smaller standard error, the values of $\bar{x}$ have less variation and tend to be closer to the population mean than the values of $\bar{x}$ with $n = 30$.

We can use the sampling distribution of $\bar{x}$ for the case with $n = 100$ to compute the probability that a simple random sample of 100 EAI managers will provide a sample mean that is within \$500 of the population mean. In this case the sampling distribution is normal with a mean of 51,800 and a standard deviation of 400 (see Figure 7.10). Again, we could compute the appropriate $z$ values and use the standard normal probability distribution table to make this probability calculation. However, Excel's NORM.DIST function is easier to use and provides more accurate results. Entering the formula =NORM.DIST(52300,51800,400,TRUE) into a cell of an Excel worksheet provides the cumulative probability corresponding to $\bar{x} = 52,300$. The value provided by Excel is .8944. Entering the formula =NORM.DIST

**FIGURE 7.9**    A COMPARISON OF THE SAMPLING DISTRIBUTIONS OF $\bar{x}$ FOR SIMPLE
RANDOM SAMPLES OF $n = 30$ AND $n = 100$ EAI MANAGERS

**FIGURE 7.10**    PROBABILITY OF A SAMPLE MEAN BEING WITHIN $500
OF THE POPULATION MEAN FOR A SIMPLE RANDOM SAMPLE
OF 100 EAI MANAGERS

(51300,51800,400,TRUE) into a cell of an Excel worksheet provides the cumulative
probability corresponding to $\bar{x} = 51,300$. The value provided by Excel is .1056. Thus, the
probability of $\bar{x}$ being in the interval from 51,300 to 52,300 is given by .8944 − .1056 = .7888.
By increasing the sample size from 30 to 100 EAI managers, we increase the probability that
the sampling error will be $500 or less; that is, the probability of obtaining a sample mean
within $500 of the population mean increases from .5064 to .7888.

   The important point in this discussion is that as the sample size increases, the standard
error of the mean decreases. As a result, a larger sample size will provide a higher probability that the sample mean falls within a specified distance of the population mean.

## NOTES AND COMMENTS

In presenting the sampling distribution of $\bar{x}$ for the EAI problem, we took advantage of the fact that the population mean $\mu = 51,800$ and the population standard deviation $\sigma = 4000$ were known. However, usually the values of the population mean $\mu$ and the population standard deviation $\sigma$ that are needed to determine the sampling distribution of $\bar{x}$ will be unknown. In Chapter 8 we show how the sample mean $\bar{x}$ and the sample standard deviation $s$ are used when $\mu$ and $\sigma$ are unknown.

## Exercises

### Methods

15. A population has a mean of 200 and a standard deviation of 50. Suppose a simple random sample of size 100 is selected and $\bar{x}$ is used to estimate $\mu$.
    a.   What is the probability that the sample mean will be within $\pm 5$ of the population mean?
    b.   What is the probability that the sample mean will be within $\pm 10$ of the population mean?

16. Assume the population standard deviation is $\sigma = 25$. Compute the standard error of the mean, $\sigma_{\bar{x}}$, for sample sizes of 50, 100, 150, and 200. What can you say about the size of the standard error of the mean as the sample size is increased?

17. Suppose a simple random sample of size 50 is selected from a population with $\sigma = 10$. Find the value of the standard error of the mean in each of the following cases (use the finite population correction factor if appropriate).
    a.   The population size is infinite.
    b.   The population size is $N = 50,000$.
    c.   The population size is $N = 5000$.
    d.   The population size is $N = 500$.

### Applications

18. Refer to the EAI sampling problem. Suppose a simple random sample of 60 managers is used.
    a.   Sketch the sampling distribution of $\bar{x}$ when simple random samples of size 60 are used.
    b.   What happens to the sampling distribution of $\bar{x}$ if simple random samples of size 120 are used?
    c.   What general statement can you make about what happens to the sampling distribution of $\bar{x}$ as the sample size is increased? Does this generalization seem logical? Explain.

19. In the EAI sampling problem (see Figure 7.8), we showed that for $n = 30$, there was .5064 probability of obtaining a sample mean within $\pm\$500$ of the population mean.
    a.   What is the probability that $\bar{x}$ is within \$500 of the population mean if a sample of size 60 is used?
    b.   Answer part (a) for a sample of size 120.

20. *Barron's* reported that the average number of weeks an individual is unemployed is 17.5 weeks (*Barron's*, February 18, 2008). Assume that for the population of all unemployed individuals the population mean length of unemployment is 17.5 weeks and that the population standard deviation is 4 weeks. Suppose you would like to select a random sample of 50 unemployed individuals for a follow-up study.
    a.   Show the sampling distribution of $\bar{x}$, the sample mean average for a sample of 50 unemployed individuals.
    b.   What is the probability that a simple random sample of 50 unemployed individuals will provide a sample mean within 1 week of the population mean?

c. What is the probability that a simple random sample of 50 unemployed individuals will provide a sample mean within 1/2 week of the population mean?

21. The College Board reported the following mean scores for the three parts of the Scholastic Aptitude Test (SAT) (*The World Almanac*, 2009):

| | |
|---|---|
| Critical Reading | 502 |
| Mathematics | 515 |
| Writing | 494 |

Assume that the population standard deviation on each part of the test is $\sigma = 100$.

a. What is the probability that a random sample of 90 test takers will provide a sample mean test score within 10 points of the population mean of 502 on the Critical Reading part of the test?

b. What is the probability that a random sample of 90 test takers will provide a sample mean test score within 10 points of the population mean of 515 on the Mathematics part of the test? Compare this probability to the value computed in part (a).

c. What is the probability that a random sample of 100 test takers will provide a sample mean test score within 10 of the population mean of 494 on the writing part of the test? Comment on the differences between this probability and the values computed in parts (a) and (b).

22. The mean annual cost of automobile insurance is $939 (*CNBC*, February 23, 2006). Assume that the standard deviation is $\sigma = \$245$.

a. What is the probability that a simple random sample of automobile insurance policies will have a sample mean within $25 of the population mean for each of the following sample sizes: 30, 50, 100, and 400?

b. What is the advantage of a larger sample size when attempting to estimate the population mean?

23. *BusinessWeek* conducted a survey of graduates from 30 top MBA programs (*BusinessWeek*, September 22, 2003). On the basis of the survey, assume that the mean annual salary for male and female graduates 10 years after graduation is $168,000 and $117,000, respectively. Assume the standard deviation for the male graduates is $40,000, and for the female graduates it is $25,000.

a. What is the probability that a simple random sample of 40 male graduates will provide a sample mean within $10,000 of the population mean, $168,000?

b. What is the probability that a simple random sample of 40 female graduates will provide a sample mean within $10,000 of the population mean, $117,000?

c. In which of the preceding two cases, part (a) or part (b), do we have a higher probability of obtaining a sample estimate within $10,000 of the population mean? Why?

d. What is the probability that a simple random sample of 100 male graduates will provide a sample mean more than $4000 below the population mean?

24. The average score for male golfers is 95 and the average score for female golfers is 106 (*Golf Digest*, April 2006). Use these values as the population means for men and women and assume that the population standard deviation is $\sigma = 14$ strokes for both. A simple random sample of 30 male golfers and another simple random sample of 45 female golfers will be taken.

a. Show the sampling distribution of $\bar{x}$ for male golfers.

b. What is the probability that the sample mean is within three strokes of the population mean for the sample of male golfers?

c. What is the probability that the sample mean is within three strokes of the population mean for the sample of female golfers?

d. In which case, part (b) or part (c), is the probability of obtaining a sample mean within three strokes of the population mean higher? Why?

25.   The average price of a gallon of unleaded regular gasoline was reported to be $2.34 in northern Kentucky (*The Cincinnati Enquirer,* January 21, 2006). Use this price as the population mean, and assume the population standard deviation is $.20.

   a.   What is the probability that the mean price for a sample of 30 service stations is within $.03 of the population mean?

   b.   What is the probability that the mean price for a sample of 50 service stations is within $.03 of the population mean?

   c.   What is the probability that the mean price for a sample of 100 service stations is within $.03 of the population mean?

   d.   Which, if any, of the sample sizes in parts (a), (b), and (c) would you recommend to have at least a .95 probability that the sample mean is within $.03 of the population mean?

26.   To estimate the mean age for a population of 4000 employees, a simple random sample of 40 employees is selected.

   a.   Would you use the finite population correction factor in calculating the standard error of the mean? Explain.

   b.   If the population standard deviation is $\sigma = 8.2$ years, compute the standard error both with and without the finite population correction factor. What is the rationale for ignoring the finite population correction factor whenever $n/N \leq .05$?

   c.   What is the probability that the sample mean age of the employees will be within $\pm 2$ years of the population mean age?

## 7.6   Sampling Distribution of $\bar{p}$

The sample proportion $\bar{p}$ is the point estimator of the population proportion $p$. The formula for computing the sample proportion is

$$\bar{p} = \frac{x}{n}$$

where

   $x$ = the number of elements in the sample that possess the characteristic of interest

   $n$ = sample size

As noted in Section 7.4, the sample proportion $\bar{p}$ is a random variable and its probability distribution is called the sampling distribution of $\bar{p}$.

> SAMPLING DISTRIBUTION OF $\bar{p}$
>
> The sampling distribution of $\bar{p}$ is the probability distribution of all possible values of the sample proportion $\bar{p}$.

   To determine how close the sample proportion $\bar{p}$ is to the population proportion $p$, we need to understand the properties of the sampling distribution of $\bar{p}$: the expected value of $\bar{p}$, the standard deviation of $\bar{p}$, and the shape or form of the sampling distribution of $\bar{p}$.

### Expected Value of $\bar{p}$

The expected value of $\bar{p}$, the mean of all possible values of $\bar{p}$, is equal to the population proportion $p$.

> EXPECTED VALUE OF $\bar{p}$
>
> $$E(\bar{p}) = p \tag{7.4}$$

where

$$E(\bar{p}) = \text{the expected value of } \bar{p}$$
$$p = \text{the population proportion}$$

Because $E(\bar{p}) = p$, $\bar{p}$ is an unbiased estimator of $p$. Recall from Section 7.1 we noted that $p = .60$ for the EAI population, where $p$ is the proportion of the population of managers who participated in the company's management training program. Thus, the expected value of $\bar{p}$ for the EAI sampling problem is .60.

## Standard Deviation of $\bar{p}$

Just as we found for the standard deviation of $\bar{x}$, the standard deviation of $\bar{p}$ depends on whether the population is finite or infinite. The two formulas for computing the standard deviation of $\bar{p}$ follow.

**STANDARD DEVIATION OF $\bar{p}$**

| *Finite Population* | *Infinite Population* | |
|---|---|---|
| $\sigma_{\bar{p}} = \sqrt{\dfrac{N-n}{N-1}} \sqrt{\dfrac{p(1-p)}{n}}$ | $\sigma_{\bar{p}} = \sqrt{\dfrac{p(1-p)}{n}}$ | **(7.5)** |

Comparing the two formulas in (7.5), we see that the only difference is the use of the finite population correction factor $\sqrt{(N-n)/(N-1)}$.

As was the case with the sample mean $\bar{x}$, the difference between the expressions for the finite population and the infinite population becomes negligible if the size of the finite population is large in comparison to the sample size. We follow the same rule of thumb that we recommended for the sample mean. That is, if the population is finite with $n/N \leq .05$, we will use $\sigma_{\bar{p}} = \sqrt{p(1-p)/n}$. However, if the population is finite with $n/N > .05$, the finite population correction factor should be used. Again, unless specifically noted, throughout the text we will assume that the population size is large in relation to the sample size and thus the finite population correction factor is unnecessary.

In Section 7.5 we used the term *standard error of the mean* to refer to the standard deviation of $\bar{x}$. We stated that in general the term *standard error* refers to the standard deviation of a point estimator. Thus, for proportions we use *standard error of the proportion* to refer to the standard deviation of $\bar{p}$. Let us now return to the EAI example and compute the standard error of the proportion associated with simple random samples of 30 EAI managers.

For the EAI study we know that the population proportion of managers who participated in the management training program is $p = .60$. With $n/N = 30/2500 = .012$, we can ignore the finite population correction factor when we compute the standard error of the proportion. For the simple random sample of 30 managers, $\sigma_{\bar{p}}$ is

$$\sigma_{\bar{p}} = \sqrt{\frac{p(1-p)}{n}} = \sqrt{\frac{.60(1-.60)}{30}} = .0894$$

## Form of the Sampling Distribution of $\bar{p}$

Now that we know the mean and standard deviation of the sampling distribution of $\bar{p}$, the final step is to determine the form or shape of the sampling distribution. The sample proportion is $\bar{p} = x/n$. For a simple random sample from a large population, the value of $x$ is a binomial random variable indicating the number of elements in the sample with the characteristic of interest. Because $n$ is a constant, the probability of $x/n$ is the same as the binomial probability of $x$, which means that the sampling distribution of $\bar{p}$ is also a discrete probability distribution and that the probability for each value of $x/n$ is the same as the probability of $x$.

In Chapter 6 we also showed that a binomial distribution can be approximated by a normal distribution whenever the sample size is large enough to satisfy the following two conditions:

$$np \geq 5 \quad \text{and} \quad n(1 - p) \geq 5$$

Assuming these two conditions are satisfied, the probability distribution of $x$ in the sample proportion, $\bar{p} = x/n$, can be approximated by a normal distribution. And because $n$ is a constant, the sampling distribution of $\bar{p}$ can also be approximated by a normal distribution. This approximation is stated as follows:

> The sampling distribution of $\bar{p}$ can be approximated by a normal distribution whenever $np \geq 5$ and $n(1 - p) \geq 5$.

In practical applications, when an estimate of a population proportion is desired, we find that sample sizes are almost always large enough to permit the use of a normal approximation for the sampling distribution of $\bar{p}$.

Recall that for the EAI sampling problem we know that the population proportion of managers who participated in the training program is $p = .60$. With a simple random sample of size 30, we have $np = 30(.60) = 18$ and $n(1 - p) = 30(.40) = 12$. Thus, the sampling distribution of $\bar{p}$ can be approximated by a normal distribution shown in Figure 7.11.

**FIGURE 7.11**    SAMPLING DISTRIBUTION OF $\bar{p}$ FOR THE PROPORTION OF EAI MANAGERS WHO PARTICIPATED IN THE MANAGEMENT TRAINING PROGRAM

**FIGURE 7.12   PROBABILITY OF OBTAINING $\bar{p}$ BETWEEN .55 AND .65**

## Practical Value of the Sampling Distribution of $\bar{p}$

The practical value of the sampling distribution of $\bar{p}$ is that it can be used to provide probability information about the difference between the sample proportion and the population proportion. For instance, suppose that in the EAI problem the personnel director wants to know the probability of obtaining a value of $\bar{p}$ that is within .05 of the population proportion of EAI managers who participated in the training program. That is, what is the probability of obtaining a sample with a sample proportion $\bar{p}$ between .55 and .65? The darkly shaded area in Figure 7.12 shows this probability. Using the fact that the sampling distribution of $\bar{p}$ can be approximated by a normal probability distribution with a mean of .60 and a standard error of $\sigma_{\bar{p}} = .0894$, we can use Excel's NORM.DIST function to make this calculation. Entering the formula =NORM.DIST(.65,.60,.0894,TRUE) into a cell of an Excel worksheet provides the cumulative probability corresponding to $\bar{p} = .65$. The value calculated by Excel is .7120. Entering the formula =NORM.DIST(.55,.60,.0894,TRUE) into a cell of an Excel worksheet provides the cumulative probability corresponding to $\bar{p} = .55$. The value calculated by Excel is .2880. Thus, the probability of $\bar{p}$ being in the interval from .55 to .65 is given by .7120 − .2880 = .4240.

If we consider increasing the sample size to $n = 100$, the standard error of the proportion becomes

$$\sigma_{\bar{p}} = \sqrt{\frac{.60(1 - .60)}{100}} = .0490$$

With a sample size of 100 EAI managers, the probability of the sample proportion having a value within .05 of the population proportion can now be computed. Because the sampling distribution is approximately normal, with mean .60 and standard deviation .0490, we can use Excel's NORM.DIST function to make this calculation. Entering the formula =NORM.DIST(.65,.60,.0490,TRUE) into a cell of an Excel worksheet provides the cumulative probability corresponding to $\bar{p} = .65$. The value calculated by Excel is .8462. Entering the formula =NORM.DIST(.55,.60,.0490,TRUE) into a cell of an Excel worksheet provides the cumulative probability corresponding to $\bar{p} = .55$. The value calculated by Excel is .1538. Thus, the probability of $\bar{p}$ being in the interval from .55 to .65 is given by .8462 − .1538 = .6924. Increasing the sample size increases the probability that the sampling error will be less than or equal to .05 by .2684 (from .4240 to .6924).

## Exercises

### Methods

27. A simple random sample of size 100 is selected from a population with $p = .40$.
    a. What is the expected value of $\bar{p}$?
    b. What is the standard error of $\bar{p}$?
    c. Show the sampling distribution of $\bar{p}$.
    d. What does the sampling distribution of $\bar{p}$ show?

28. A population proportion is .40. A simple random sample of size 200 will be taken and the sample proportion $\bar{p}$ will be used to estimate the population proportion.
    a. What is the probability that the sample proportion will be within $\pm.03$ of the population proportion?
    b. What is the probability that the sample proportion will be within $\pm.05$ of the population proportion?

29. Assume that the population proportion is .55. Compute the standard error of the proportion, $\sigma_{\bar{p}}$, for sample sizes of 100, 200, 500, and 1000. What can you say about the size of the standard error of the proportion as the sample size is increased?

30. The population proportion is .30. What is the probability that a sample proportion will be within $\pm.04$ of the population proportion for each of the following sample sizes?
    a. $n = 100$
    b. $n = 200$
    c. $n = 500$
    d. $n = 1000$
    e. What is the advantage of a larger sample size?

### Applications

31. The president of Doerman Distributors, Inc., believes that 30% of the firm's orders come from first-time customers. A random sample of 100 orders will be used to estimate the proportion of first-time customers.
    a. Assume that the president is correct and $p = .30$. What is the sampling distribution of $\bar{p}$ for this study?
    b. What is the probability that the sample proportion $\bar{p}$ will be between .20 and .40?
    c. What is the probability that the sample proportion will be between .25 and .35?

32. *The Cincinnati Enquirer* reported that, in the United States, 66% of adults and 87% of youths ages 12 to 17 use the Internet (*The Cincinnati Enquirer*, February 7, 2006). Use the reported numbers as the population proportions and assume that samples of 300 adults and 300 youths will be used to learn about attitudes toward Internet security.
    a. Show the sampling distribution of $\bar{p}$, where $\bar{p}$ is the sample proportion of adults using the Internet.
    b. What is the probability that the sample proportion of adults using the Internet will be within $\pm.04$ of the population proportion?
    c. What is the probability that the sample proportion of youths using the Internet will be within $\pm.04$ of the population proportion?
    d. Is the probability different in parts (b) and (c)? If so, why?
    e. Answer part (b) for a sample of size 600. Is the probability smaller? Why?

33. People end up tossing 12% of what they buy at the grocery store (*Reader's Digest*, March, 2009). Assume this is the true population proportion and that you plan to take a sample survey of 540 grocery shoppers to further investigate their behavior.

a. Show the sampling distribution of $\bar{p}$, the proportion of groceries thrown out by your sample respondents.
b. What is the probability that your survey will provide a sample proportion within $\pm.03$ of the population proportion?
c. What is the probability that your survey will provide a sample proportion within $\pm.015$ of the population proportion?

34. Roper ASW conducted a survey to learn about American adults' attitudes toward money and happiness (*Money,* October 2003). Fifty-six percent of the respondents said they balance their checkbook at least once a month.
   a. Suppose a sample of 400 American adults were taken. Show the sampling distribution of the proportion of adults who balance their checkbook at least once a month.
   b. What is the probability that the sample proportion will be within $\pm.02$ of the population proportion?
   c. What is the probability that the sample proportion will be within $\pm.04$ of the population proportion?

35. In 2008 the Better Business Bureau settled 75% of complaints it received (*USA Today,* March 2, 2009). Suppose you have been hired by the Better Business Bureau to investigate the complaints it received this year involving new car dealers. You plan to select a sample of new car dealer complaints to estimate the proportion of complaints the Better Business Bureau is able to settle. Assume the population proportion of complaints settled for new car dealers is .75, the same as the overall proportion of complaints settled in 2008.
   a. Suppose you select a sample of 450 complaints involving new car dealers. Show the sampling distribution of $\bar{p}$.
   b. Based upon a sample of 450 complaints, what is the probability that the sample proportion will be within .04 of the population proportion?
   c. Suppose you select a sample of 200 complaints involving new car dealers. Show the sampling distribution of $\bar{p}$.
   d. Based upon the smaller sample of only 200 complaints, what is the probability that the sample proportion will be within .04 of the population proportion?
   e. As measured by the increase in probability, how much do you gain in precision by taking the larger sample in part (b)?

36. The Grocery Manufacturers of America reported that 76% of consumers read the ingredients listed on a product's label. Assume the population proportion is $p = .76$ and a sample of 400 consumers is selected from the population.
   a. Show the sampling distribution of the sample proportion $\bar{p}$, where $\bar{p}$ is the proportion of the sampled consumers who read the ingredients listed on a product's label.
   b. What is the probability that the sample proportion will be within $\pm.03$ of the population proportion?
   c. Answer part (b) for a sample of 750 consumers.

37. The Food Marketing Institute shows that 17% of households spend more than $100 per week on groceries. Assume the population proportion is $p = .17$ and a simple random sample of 800 households will be selected from the population.
   a. Show the sampling distribution of $\bar{p}$, the sample proportion of households spending more than $100 per week on groceries.
   b. What is the probability that the sample proportion will be within $\pm.02$ of the population proportion?
   c. Answer part (b) for a sample of 1600 households.

## 7.7   Other Sampling Methods

*This section provides a brief introduction to survey sampling methods other than simple random sampling.*

We described simple random sampling as a procedure for sampling from a finite population and discussed the properties of the sampling distributions of $\bar{x}$ and $\bar{p}$ when simple random sampling is used. Other methods such as stratified random sampling, cluster sampling, and systematic sampling provide advantages over simple random sampling in some of these situations. In this section we briefly introduce these alternative sampling methods.

### Stratified Random Sampling

*Stratified random sampling works best when the variance among elements in each stratum is relatively small.*

In **stratified random sampling**, the elements in the population are first divided into groups called *strata,* such that each element in the population belongs to one and only one stratum. The basis for forming the strata, such as department, location, age, industry type, and so on, is at the discretion of the designer of the sample. However, the best results are obtained when the elements within each stratum are as much alike as possible. Figure 7.13 is a diagram of a population divided into $H$ strata.

After the strata are formed, a simple random sample is taken from each stratum. Formulas are available for combining the results for the individual stratum samples into one estimate of the population parameter of interest. The value of stratified random sampling depends on how homogeneous the elements are within the strata. If elements within strata are alike, the strata will have low variances. Thus relatively small sample sizes can be used to obtain good estimates of the strata characteristics. If strata are homogeneous, the stratified random sampling procedure provides results just as precise as those of simple random sampling by using a smaller total sample size.

### Cluster Sampling

*Cluster sampling works best when each cluster provides a small-scale representation of the population.*

In **cluster sampling**, the elements in the population are first divided into separate groups called *clusters.* Each element of the population belongs to one and only one cluster (see Figure 7.14). A simple random sample of the clusters is then taken. All elements within each sampled cluster form the sample. Cluster sampling tends to provide the best results when the elements within the clusters are not alike. In the ideal case, each cluster is a representative small-scale version of the entire population. The value of cluster sampling depends on how representative each cluster is of the entire population. If all clusters are alike in this regard, sampling a small number of clusters will provide good estimates of the population parameters.

**FIGURE 7.13**   DIAGRAM FOR STRATIFIED RANDOM SAMPLING

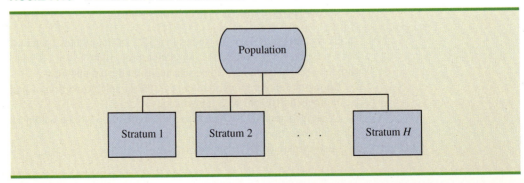

**FIGURE 7.14**   DIAGRAM FOR CLUSTER SAMPLING

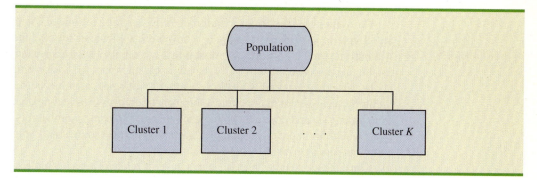

One of the primary applications of cluster sampling is area sampling, where clusters are city blocks or other well-defined areas. Cluster sampling generally requires a larger total sample size than either simple random sampling or stratified random sampling. However, it can result in cost savings because of the fact that when an interviewer is sent to a sampled cluster (e.g., a city-block location), many sample observations can be obtained in a relatively short time. Hence, a larger sample size may be obtainable with a significantly lower total cost.

## Systematic Sampling

In some sampling situations, especially those with large populations, it is time-consuming to select a simple random sample by first finding a random number and then counting or searching through the list of the population until the corresponding element is found. An alternative to simple random sampling is **systematic sampling**. For example, if a sample size of 50 is desired from a population containing 5000 elements, we will sample one element for every $5000/50 = 100$ elements in the population. A systematic sample for this case involves selecting randomly one of the first 100 elements from the population list. Other sample elements are identified by starting with the first sampled element and then selecting every 100th element that follows in the population list. In effect, the sample of 50 is identified by moving systematically through the population and identifying every 100th element after the first randomly selected element. The sample of 50 usually will be easier to identify in this way than it would be if simple random sampling were used. Because the first element selected is a random choice, a systematic sample is usually assumed to have the properties of a simple random sample. This assumption is especially applicable when the list of elements in the population is a random ordering of the elements.

## Convenience Sampling

The sampling methods discussed thus far are referred to as *probability sampling* techniques. Elements selected from the population have a known probability of being included in the sample. The advantage of probability sampling is that the sampling distribution of the appropriate sample statistic generally can be identified. Formulas such as the ones for simple random sampling presented in this chapter can be used to determine the properties of the sampling distribution. Then the sampling distribution can be used to make probability statements about the error associated with using the sample results to make inferences about the population.

**Convenience sampling** is a *nonprobability sampling* technique. As the name implies, the sample is identified primarily by convenience. Elements are included in the sample without prespecified or known probabilities of being selected. For example, a professor conducting research at a university may use student volunteers to constitute a sample simply because they are readily available and will participate as subjects for little or no cost. Similarly, an inspector may sample a shipment of oranges by selecting oranges haphazardly from among several crates. Labeling each orange and using a probability method of sampling would be impractical. Samples such as wildlife captures and volunteer panels for consumer research are also convenience samples.

Convenience samples have the advantage of relatively easy sample selection and data collection; however, it is impossible to evaluate the "goodness" of the sample in terms of its representativeness of the population. A convenience sample may provide good results or it may not; no statistically justified procedure allows a probability analysis and inference about the quality of the sample results. Sometimes researchers apply statistical methods designed for probability samples to a convenience sample, arguing that the convenience sample can be treated as though it were a probability sample. However, this argument cannot be supported, and we should be cautious in interpreting the results of convenience samples that are used to make inferences about populations.

## Judgment Sampling

One additional nonprobability sampling technique is **judgment sampling**. In this approach, the person most knowledgeable on the subject of the study selects elements of the population that he or she feels are most representative of the population. Often this method is a relatively easy way of selecting a sample. For example, a reporter may sample two or three senators, judging that those senators reflect the general opinion of all senators. However, the quality of the sample results depends on the judgment of the person selecting the sample. Again, great caution is warranted in drawing conclusions based on judgment samples used to make inferences about populations.

### NOTES AND COMMENTS

We recommend using probability sampling methods when sampling from finite populations: simple random sampling, stratified random sampling, cluster sampling, or systematic sampling. For these methods, formulas are available for evaluating the "goodness" of the sample results in terms of the closeness of the results to the population parameters being estimated. An evaluation of the goodness cannot be made with convenience or judgment sampling. Thus, great care should be used in interpreting the results based on nonprobability sampling methods.

### Summary

In this chapter we presented the concepts of sampling and sampling distributions. We demonstrated how a simple random sample can be selected from a finite population and how a random sample can be selected from an infinite population. The data collected from such samples can be used to develop point estimates of population parameters. Because different samples provide different values for the point estimators, point estimators such as $\bar{x}$ and $\bar{p}$ are random variables. The probability distribution of such a random variable is called a sampling distribution. In particular, we described in detail the sampling distributions of the sample mean $\bar{x}$ and the sample proportion $\bar{p}$.

In considering the characteristics of the sampling distributions of $\bar{x}$ and $\bar{p}$, we stated that $E(\bar{x}) = \mu$ and $E(\bar{p}) = p$. After developing the standard deviation or standard error formulas for these estimators, we described the conditions necessary for the sampling distributions of $\bar{x}$ and $\bar{p}$ to follow a normal distribution. Other sampling methods including stratified random sampling, cluster sampling, systematic sampling, convenience sampling, and judgment sampling were discussed.

## Glossary

**Sampled population** The population from which the sample is taken.

**Frame** A listing of the elements the sample will be selected from.

**Parameter** A numerical characteristic of a population, such as a population mean $\mu$, a population standard deviation $\sigma$, a population proportion $p$, and so on.

**Simple random sample** A simple random sample of size $n$ from a finite population of size $N$ is a sample selected such that each possible sample of size $n$ has the same probability of being selected.

**Random sample** A random sample from an infinite population is a sample selected such that the following conditions are satisfied: (1) Each element selected comes from the same population; (2) each element is selected independently.

**Sample statistic** A sample characteristic, such as a sample mean $\bar{x}$, a sample standard deviation $s$, a sample proportion $\bar{p}$, and so on. The value of the sample statistic is used to estimate the value of the corresponding population parameter.

**Point estimator** The sample statistic, such as $\bar{x}$, $s$, or $\bar{p}$, that provides the point estimate of the population parameter.

**Point estimate** The value of a point estimator used in a particular instance as an estimate of a population parameter.

**Target population** The population for which statistical inference such as point estimates are made. It is important for the target population to correspond as closely as possible to the sampled population.

**Sampling distribution** A probability distribution consisting of all possible values of a sample statistic.

**Unbiased** A property of a point estimator that is present when the expected value of the point estimator is equal to the population parameter it estimates.

**Finite population correction factor** The term $\sqrt{(N - n)/(N - 1)}$ that is used in the formulas for $\sigma_{\bar{x}}$ and $\sigma_{\bar{p}}$ whenever a finite population, rather than an infinite population, is being sampled. The generally accepted rule of thumb is to ignore the finite population correction factor whenever $n/N \le .05$.

**Standard error** The standard deviation of a point estimator.

**Central limit theorem** A theorem that enables one to use the normal probability distribution to approximate the sampling distribution of $\bar{x}$ whenever the sample size is large.

**Stratified random sampling** A probability sampling method in which the population is first divided into strata and a simple random sample is then taken from each stratum.

**Cluster sampling** A probability sampling method in which the population is first divided into clusters and then a simple random sample of the clusters is taken.

**Systematic sampling** A probability sampling method in which we randomly select one of the first $k$ elements and then select every $k$th element thereafter.

**Convenience sampling** A nonprobability method of sampling whereby elements are selected for the sample on the basis of convenience.

**Judgment sampling** A nonprobability method of sampling whereby elements are selected for the sample based on the judgment of the person doing the study.

## Key Formulas

**Expected Value of $\bar{x}$**

$$E(\bar{x}) = \mu \tag{7.1}$$

**Standard Deviation of $\bar{x}$ (Standard Error)**

| *Finite Population* | *Infinite Population* | |
|:---:|:---:|:---:|
| $\sigma_{\bar{x}} = \sqrt{\dfrac{N-n}{N-1}} \left( \dfrac{\sigma}{\sqrt{n}} \right)$ | $\sigma_{\bar{x}} = \dfrac{\sigma}{\sqrt{n}}$ | **(7.2)** |

**Expected Value of $\bar{p}$**

$$E(\bar{p}) = p \tag{7.4}$$

**Standard Deviation of $\bar{p}$ (Standard Error)**

| *Finite Population* | *Infinite Population* | |
|:---:|:---:|:---:|
| $\sigma_{\bar{p}} = \sqrt{\dfrac{N-n}{N-1}} \sqrt{\dfrac{p(1-p)}{n}}$ | $\sigma_{\bar{p}} = \sqrt{\dfrac{p(1-p)}{n}}$ | **(7.5)** |

## Supplementary Exercises

**WEB** file

**Dining**

38. Bob Miller, a food critic, wants to prepare an article on the quality of food at locally owned restaurants in Myrtle Beach, South Carolina. A list of 44 locally owned restaurants is contained in the data file named Dining that is on the website that accompanies this text (*Coastal Carolina Dining*, Fall 2004). Bob only has time to sample the food at 5 of these restaurants.
    a. In the data file the restaurants are listed in column A of an Excel worksheet. In column B we generated a random number for each of the restaurants in column A. Use these random numbers to select a simple random sample of five restaurants for Bob.
    b. Generate a new set of random numbers and use them to select a new simple random sample. Did you select the same restaurants?

39. Americans have become increasingly concerned about the rising cost of Medicare. In 1990, the average annual Medicare spending per enrollee was $3267; in 2003, the average

annual Medicare spending per enrollee was $6883 (*Money*, Fall 2003). Suppose you hired a consulting firm to take a sample of fifty 2003 Medicare enrollees to further investigate the nature of expenditures. Assume the population standard deviation for 2003 was $2000.

a.  Show the sampling distribution of the mean amount of Medicare spending for a sample of fifty 2003 enrollees.

b.  What is the probability that the sample mean will be within ±$300 of the population mean?

c.  What is the probability that the sample mean will be greater than $7500? If the consulting firm tells you the sample mean for the Medicare enrollees it interviewed was $7500, would you question whether the firm followed correct simple random sampling procedures? Why or why not?

40.  *BusinessWeek* surveyed MBA alumni 10 years after graduation (*BusinessWeek*, September 22, 2003). One finding was that alumni spend an average of $115.50 per week eating out socially. You have been asked to conduct a follow-up study by taking a sample of 40 of these MBA alumni. Assume the population standard deviation is $35.

a.  Show the sampling distribution of $\bar{x}$, the sample mean weekly expenditure for the 40 MBA alumni.

b.  What is the probability that the sample mean will be within $10 of the population mean?

c.  Suppose you find a sample mean of $100. What is the probability of finding a sample mean of $100 or less? Would you consider this sample to be an unusually low spending group of alumni? Why or why not?

41.  The mean television viewing time for Americans is 15 hours per week (*Money*, November 2003). Suppose a sample of 60 Americans is taken to further investigate viewing habits. Assume the population standard deviation for weekly viewing time is $\sigma = 4$ hours.

a.  What is the probability that the sample mean will be within 1 hour of the population mean?

b.  What is the probability that the sample mean will be within 45 minutes of the population mean?

42.  After deducting grants based on need, the average cost to attend the University of Southern California (USC) is $27,175 (*U.S. News & World Report, America's Best Colleges*, 2009 ed.). Assume the population standard deviation is $7400. Suppose that a random sample of 60 USC students will be taken from this population.

a.  What is the value of the standard error of the mean?

b.  What is the probability that the sample mean will be more than $27,175?

c.  What is the probability that the sample mean will be within $1000 of the population mean?

d.  How would the probability in part (c) change if the sample size were increased to 100?

43.  Three firms carry inventories that differ in size. Firm A's inventory contains 2000 items, firm B's inventory contains 5000 items, and firm C's inventory contains 10,000 items. The population standard deviation for the cost of the items in each firm's inventory is $\sigma = 144$. A statistical consultant recommends that each firm take a sample of 50 items from its inventory to provide statistically valid estimates of the average cost per item. Managers of the small firm state that because it has the smallest population, it should be able to make the estimate from a much smaller sample than that required by the larger firms. However, the consultant states that to obtain the same standard error and thus the same precision in the sample results, all firms should use the same sample size regardless of population size.

a.  Using the finite population correction factor, compute the standard error for each of the three firms given a sample of size 50.

b.  What is the probability that for each firm the sample mean $\bar{x}$ will be within ±25 of the population mean $\mu$?

44. A researcher reports survey results by stating that the standard error of the mean is 20. The population standard deviation is 500.
    a. How large was the sample used in this survey?
    b. What is the probability that the point estimate was within $\pm 25$ of the population mean?

45. A production process is checked periodically by a quality control inspector. The inspector selects simple random samples of 30 finished products and computes the sample mean product weights $\bar{x}$. If test results over a long period of time show that 5% of the $\bar{x}$ values are over 2.1 pounds and 5% are under 1.9 pounds, what are the mean and the standard deviation for the population of products produced with this process?

46. About 28% of private companies are owned by women (*The Cincinnati Enquirer,* January 26, 2006). Answer the following questions based on a sample of 240 private companies.
    a. Show the sampling distribution of $\bar{p}$, the sample proportion of companies that are owned by women.
    b. What is the probability the sample proportion will be within $\pm .04$ of the population proportion?
    c. What is the probability the sample proportion will be within $\pm .02$ of the population proportion?

47. A market research firm conducts telephone surveys with a 40% historical response rate. What is the probability that in a new sample of 400 telephone numbers, at least 150 individuals will cooperate and respond to the questions? In other words, what is the probability that the sample proportion will be at least $150/400 = .375$?

48. Advertisers contract with Internet service providers and search engines to place ads on websites. They pay a fee based on the number of potential customers who click on their ad. Unfortunately, click fraud—the practice of someone clicking on an ad solely for the purpose of driving up advertising revenue—has become a problem. Forty percent of advertisers claim they have been a victim of click fraud (*BusinessWeek,* March 13, 2006). Suppose a simple random sample of 380 advertisers will be taken to learn more about how they are affected by this practice.
    a. What is the probability that the sample proportion will be within $\pm .04$ of the population proportion experiencing click fraud?
    b. What is the probability that the sample proportion will be greater than .45?

49. The proportion of individuals insured by the All-Driver Automobile Insurance Company who received at least one traffic ticket during a five-year period is .15.
    a. Show the sampling distribution of $\bar{p}$ if a random sample of 150 insured individuals is used to estimate the proportion having received at least one ticket.
    b. What is the probability that the sample proportion will be within $\pm .03$ of the population proportion?

50. Lori Jeffrey is a successful sales representative for a major publisher of college textbooks. Historically, Lori obtains a book adoption on 25% of her sales calls. Viewing her sales calls for one month as a sample of all possible sales calls, assume that a statistical analysis of the data yields a standard error of the proportion of .0625.
    a. How large was the sample used in this analysis? That is, how many sales calls did Lori make during the month?
    b. Let $\bar{p}$ indicate the sample proportion of book adoptions obtained during the month. Show the sampling distribution of $\bar{p}$.
    c. Using the sampling distribution of $\bar{p}$, compute the probability that Lori will obtain book adoptions on 30% or more of her sales calls during a one-month period.

## Appendix    Random Sampling with StatTools

**MetAreas**

If a list of the elements in a population is available in an Excel file, StatTools Random Sample Utility can be used to select a simple random sample. For example, a list of the top 100 metropolitan areas in the United States and Canada is provided in column A of the data set MetAreas (*Places Rated Almanac—The Millennium Edition 2000*). Column B contains the overall rating of each metropolitan area. Assume that you would like to select a simple random sample of 30 metropolitan areas in order to do an in-depth study of the cost of living in the United States and Canada.

Begin by using the Data Set Manager to create a StatTools data set for these data using the procedure described in the appendix to Chapter 1. The following steps will generate a simple random sample of 30 metropolitan areas.

**Step 1.** Click the **StatTools** tab on the Ribbon
**Step 2.** In the **Data Group** click **Data Utilities**
**Step 3.** Choose the **Random Sample** option
**Step 4.** When the StatTools - Random Sample Utility dialog box appears,
   In the **Variables** section,
      Select **Metropolitan Area**
      Select **Rating**
   In the **Options** section,
      Enter 1 in the **Number of Samples** box
      Enter 30 in the **Sample Size** box
   Click **OK**

The random sample of 30 metropolitan areas will appear in columns A and B of the worksheet entitled Random Sample.

# CHAPTER 8

# Interval Estimation

**CONTENTS**

## STATISTICS *in* PRACTICE

### FOOD LION*
*SALISBURY, NORTH CAROLINA*

Founded in 1957 as Food Town, Food Lion is one of the largest supermarket chains in the United States, with 1300 stores in 11 Southeastern and Mid-Atlantic states. The company sells more than 24,000 different products and offers nationally and regionally advertised brand-name merchandise, as well as a growing number of high-quality private label products manufactured especially for Food Lion. The company maintains its low price leadership and quality assurance through operating efficiencies such as standard store formats, innovative warehouse design, energy-efficient facilities, and data synchronization with suppliers. Food Lion looks to a future of continued innovation, growth, price leadership, and service to its customers.

Being in an inventory-intense business, Food Lion made the decision to adopt the LIFO (last-in, first-out) method of inventory valuation. This method matches current costs against current revenues, which minimizes the effect of radical price changes on profit and loss results. In addition, the LIFO method reduces net income, thereby reducing income taxes during periods of inflation.

Food Lion establishes a LIFO index for each of seven inventory pools: Grocery, Paper/Household, Pet Supplies, Health & Beauty Aids, Dairy, Cigarette/Tobacco, and Beer/Wine. For example, a LIFO index of 1.008 for the Grocery pool would indicate that the company's grocery inventory value at current costs reflects a 0.8% increase due to inflation over the most recent one-year period.

A LIFO index for each inventory pool requires that the year-end inventory count for each product be valued

Fresh bread arriving at a Food Lion Store.

at the current year-end cost and at the preceding year-end cost. To avoid excessive time and expense associated with counting the inventory in all 1200 store locations, Food Lion selects a random sample of 50 stores. Year-end physical inventories are taken in each of the sample stores. The current-year and preceding-year costs for each item are then used to construct the required LIFO indexes for each inventory pool.

For a recent year, the sample estimate of the LIFO index for the Health & Beauty Aids inventory pool was 1.015. Using a 95% confidence level, Food Lion computed a margin of error of .006 for the sample estimate. Thus, the interval from 1.009 to 1.021 provided a 95% confidence interval estimate of the population LIFO index. This level of precision was judged to be very good.

In this chapter you will learn how to compute the margin of error associated with sample estimates. You will also learn how to use this information to construct and interpret interval estimates of a population mean and a population proportion.

---

*The authors are indebted to Keith Cunningham, Tax Director, and Bobby Harkey, Staff Tax Accountant, at Food Lion for providing this Statistics in Practice.

In Chapter 7, we stated that a point estimator is a sample statistic used to estimate a population parameter. For instance, the sample mean $\bar{x}$ is a point estimator of the population mean $\mu$ and the sample proportion $\bar{p}$ is a point estimator of the population proportion $p$. Because a point estimator cannot be expected to provide the exact value of the population parameter, an **interval estimate** is often computed by adding and subtracting a value, called the **margin of error**, to the point estimate. The general form of an interval estimate is as follows:

$$\text{Point estimate} \pm \text{Margin of error}$$

The purpose of an interval estimate is to provide information about how close the point estimate, provided by the sample, is to the value of the population parameter.

In this chapter we show how to compute interval estimates of a population mean $\mu$ and a population proportion $p$. The general form of an interval estimate of a population mean is

$$\bar{x} \pm \text{Margin of error}$$

Similarly, the general form of an interval estimate of a population proportion is

$$\bar{p} \pm \text{Margin of error}$$

The sampling distributions of $\bar{x}$ and $\bar{p}$ play key roles in computing these interval estimates.

## 8.1  Population Mean: $\sigma$ Known

In order to develop an interval estimate of a population mean, either the population standard deviation $\sigma$ or the sample standard deviation $s$ must be used to compute the margin of error. In most applications $\sigma$ is not known, and $s$ is used to compute the margin of error. In some applications, however, large amounts of relevant historical data are available and can be used to estimate the population standard deviation prior to sampling. Also, in quality control applications where a process is assumed to be operating correctly, or "in control," it is appropriate to treat the population standard deviation as known. We refer to such cases as **$\sigma$ known** cases. In this section we introduce an example in which it is reasonable to treat $\sigma$ as known and show how to construct an interval estimate for this case.

Each week Lloyd's Department Store selects a simple random sample of 100 customers in order to learn about the amount spent per shopping trip. With $x$ representing the amount spent per shopping trip, the sample mean $\bar{x}$ provides a point estimate of $\mu$, the mean amount spent per shopping trip for the population of all Lloyd's customers. Lloyd's has been using the weekly survey for several years. Based on the historical data, Lloyd's now assumes a known value of $\sigma = \$20$ for the population standard deviation. The historical data also indicate that the population follows a normal distribution.

**WEB file**

**Lloyd's**

During the most recent week, Lloyd's surveyed 100 customers ($n = 100$) and obtained a sample mean of $\bar{x} = \$82$. The sample mean amount spent provides a point estimate of the population mean amount spent per shopping trip, $\mu$. In the discussion that follows, we show how to compute the margin of error for this estimate and develop an interval estimate of the population mean.

### Margin of Error and the Interval Estimate

In Chapter 7 we showed that the sampling distribution of $\bar{x}$ can be used to compute the probability that $\bar{x}$ will be within a given distance of $\mu$. In the Lloyd's example, the historical data show that the population of amounts spent is normally distributed with a standard deviation of $\sigma = 20$. So, using what we learned in Chapter 7, we can conclude that the sampling distribution of $\bar{x}$ follows a normal distribution with a standard error of $\sigma_{\bar{x}} = \sigma/\sqrt{n} = 20/\sqrt{100} = 2$. This sampling distribution is shown in Figure 8.1.[1] Because the sampling distribution shows how values of $\bar{x}$ are distributed around the population mean $\mu$, the sampling distribution of $\bar{x}$ provides information about the possible differences between $\bar{x}$ and $\mu$.

---

[1]We use the fact that the population of amounts spent has a normal distribution to conclude that the sampling distribution of $\bar{x}$ has a normal distribution. If the population did not have a normal distribution, we could rely on the central limit theorem and the sample size of $n = 100$ to conclude that the sampling distribution of $\bar{x}$ is approximately normal. In either case, the sampling distribution of $\bar{x}$ would appear as shown in Figure 8.1.

**FIGURE 8.1**  SAMPLING DISTRIBUTION OF THE SAMPLE MEAN AMOUNT
SPENT FROM SIMPLE RANDOM SAMPLES OF 100 CUSTOMERS

Sampling distribution
of $\bar{x}$

$$\sigma_{\bar{x}} = \frac{\sigma}{\sqrt{n}} = \frac{20}{\sqrt{100}} = 2$$

$\mu$

$\bar{x}$

Using the standard normal probability table, we find that 95% of the values of any
normally distributed random variable are within $\pm 1.96$ standard deviations of the mean.
Thus, when the sampling distribution of $\bar{x}$ is normally distributed, 95% of the $\bar{x}$ values must
be within $\pm 1.96\sigma_{\bar{x}}$ of the mean $\mu$. In the Lloyd's example we know that the sampling
distribution of $\bar{x}$ is normally distributed with a standard error of $\sigma_{\bar{x}} = 2$. Because $\pm 1.96\sigma_{\bar{x}} =$
1.96(2) = 3.92, we can conclude that 95% of all $\bar{x}$ values obtained using a sample size
of $n = 100$ will be within $\pm 3.92$ of the population mean $\mu$. See Figure 8.2.

In the introduction to this chapter we said that the general form of an interval estimate
of the population mean $\mu$ is $\bar{x} \pm$ margin of error. For the Lloyd's example, suppose we set

**FIGURE 8.2**  SAMPLING DISTRIBUTION OF $\bar{x}$ SHOWING THE LOCATION OF SAMPLE
MEANS THAT ARE WITHIN 3.92 OF $\mu$

Sampling distribution
of $\bar{x}$

$\sigma_{\bar{x}} = 2$

95% of all
$\bar{x}$ values

$\mu$

$\bar{x}$

3.92 — 3.92

1.96 $\sigma_{\bar{x}}$

1.96 $\sigma_{\bar{x}}$

**FIGURE 8.3**    INTERVALS FORMED FROM SELECTED SAMPLE MEANS
AT LOCATIONS $\bar{x}_1$, $\bar{x}_2$, AND $\bar{x}_3$

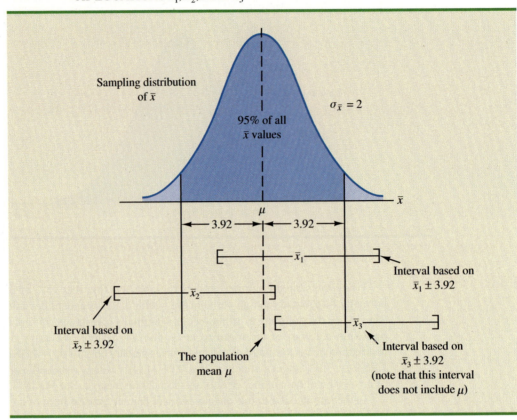

the margin of error equal to 3.92 and compute the interval estimate of $\mu$ using $\bar{x} \pm 3.92$. To provide an interpretation for this interval estimate, let us consider the values of $\bar{x}$ that could be obtained if we took three *different* simple random samples, each consisting of 100 Lloyd's customers. The first sample mean might turn out to have the value shown as $\bar{x}_1$ in Figure 8.3. In this case, Figure 8.3 shows that the interval formed by subtracting 3.92 from $\bar{x}_1$ and adding 3.92 to $\bar{x}_1$ includes the population mean $\mu$. Now consider what happens if the second sample mean turns out to have the value shown as $\bar{x}_2$ in Figure 8.3. Although this sample mean differs from the first sample mean, we see that the interval formed by subtracting 3.92 from $\bar{x}_2$ and adding 3.92 to $\bar{x}_2$ also includes the population mean $\mu$. However, consider what happens if the third sample mean turns out to have the value shown as $\bar{x}_3$ in Figure 8.3. In this case, the interval formed by subtracting 3.92 from $\bar{x}_3$ and adding 3.92 to $\bar{x}_3$ does not include the population mean $\mu$. Because $\bar{x}_3$ falls in the upper tail of the sampling distribution and is farther than 3.92 from $\mu$, subtracting and adding 3.92 to $\bar{x}_3$ forms an interval that does not include $\mu$.

Any sample mean $\bar{x}$ that is within the darkly shaded region of Figure 8.3 will provide an interval that contains the population mean $\mu$. Because 95% of all possible sample means are in the darkly shaded region, 95% of all intervals formed by subtracting 3.92 from $\bar{x}$ and adding 3.92 to $\bar{x}$ will include the population mean $\mu$.

Recall that during the most recent week, the quality assurance team at Lloyd's surveyed 100 customers and obtained a sample mean amount spent of $\bar{x} = 82$. Using $\bar{x} \pm 3.92$ to construct the interval estimate, we obtain $82 \pm 3.92$. Thus, the specific interval estimate of

*This discussion provides insight as to why the interval is called a 95% confidence interval.*

$\mu$ based on the data from the most recent week is $82 - 3.92 = 78.08$ to $82 + 3.92 = 85.92$. Because 95% of all the intervals constructed using $\bar{x} \pm 3.92$ will contain the population mean, we say that we are 95% confident that the interval 78.08 to 85.92 includes the population mean $\mu$. We say that this interval has been established at the 95% **confidence level**. The value .95 is referred to as the **confidence coefficient**, and the interval 78.08 to 85.92 is called the 95% **confidence interval**.

Another term sometimes associated with an interval estimate is the **level of significance**. The level of significance associated with an interval estimate is denoted by the Greek letter $\alpha$. The level of significance and the confidence coefficient are related as follows:

$$\alpha = \text{Level of Significance} = 1 - \text{Confidence Coefficient}$$

The level of significance is the probability that the interval estimation procedure will generate an interval that does not contain $\mu$. For example, the level of significance corresponding to a .95 confidence coefficient is $\alpha = 1 - .95 = .05$. In Lloyd's case, the level of significance ($\alpha = .05$) is the probability of drawing a sample, computing the sample mean, and finding that $\bar{x}$ lies in one of the tails of the sampling distribution (see $\bar{x}_3$ in Figure 8.3). When the sample mean happens to fall in the tail of the sampling distribution (and it will 5% of the time), the confidence interval generated will not contain $\mu$.

With the margin of error given by $z_{\alpha/2}(\sigma/\sqrt{n})$, the general form of an interval estimate of a population mean for the $\sigma$ known case follows.

---

**INTERVAL ESTIMATE OF A POPULATION MEAN: σ KNOWN**

$$\bar{x} \pm z_{\alpha/2} \frac{\sigma}{\sqrt{n}} \qquad\qquad \textbf{(8.1)}$$

where $(1 - \alpha)$ is the confidence coefficient and $z_{\alpha/2}$ is the $z$ value providing an area of $\alpha/2$ in the upper tail of the standard normal probability distribution.

---

Let us use expression (8.1) to construct a 95% confidence interval for the Lloyd's example. For a 95% confidence interval, the confidence coefficient is $(1 - \alpha) = .95$ and thus, $\alpha = .05$. Using the standard normal probability table, an area of $\alpha/2 = .05/2 = .025$ in the upper tail provides $z_{.025} = 1.96$. With the Lloyd's sample mean $\bar{x} = 82$, $\sigma = 20$, and a sample size $n = 100$, we obtain

$$82 \pm 1.96 \frac{20}{\sqrt{100}}$$

$$82 \pm 3.92$$

Thus, using expression (8.1), the margin of error is 3.92 and the 95% confidence interval is $82 - 3.92 = 78.08$ to $82 + 3.92 = 85.92$.

Although a 95% confidence level is frequently used, other confidence levels such as 90% and 99% may be considered. Values of $z_{\alpha/2}$ for the most commonly used confidence levels are shown in Table 8.1. Using these values and expression (8.1), the 90% confidence interval for the Lloyd's example is

$$82 \pm 1.645 \frac{20}{\sqrt{100}}$$

$$82 \pm 3.29$$

**TABLE 8.1**   VALUES OF $z_{\alpha/2}$ FOR THE MOST COMMONLY USED CONFIDENCE LEVELS

| Confidence Level | $\alpha$ | $\alpha/2$ | $z_{\alpha/2}$ |
|:---:|:---:|:---:|:---:|
| 90% | .10 | .05 | 1.645 |
| 95% | .05 | .025 | 1.960 |
| 99% | .01 | .005 | 2.576 |

Thus, at 90% confidence, the margin of error is 3.29 and the confidence interval is $82 - 3.29 = 78.71$ to $82 + 3.29 = 85.29$. Similarly, the 99% confidence interval is

$$82 \pm 2.576 \frac{20}{\sqrt{100}}$$

$$82 \pm 5.15$$

Thus, at 99% confidence, the margin of error is 5.15 and the confidence interval is $82 - 5.15 = 76.85$ to $82 + 5.15 = 87.15$.

Comparing the results for the 90%, 95%, and 99% confidence levels, we see that in order to have a higher degree of confidence, the margin of error and thus the width of the confidence interval must be larger.

## Using Excel

We will use the Lloyd's Department Store data to illustrate how Excel can be used to construct an interval estimate of the population mean for the $\sigma$ known case. Refer to Figure 8.4 as we describe the tasks involved. The formula worksheet is in the background; the value worksheet appears in the foreground.

**Enter Data:**   A label and the sales data are entered into cells A1:A101.

**Enter Functions and Formulas:**   The sample size and sample mean are computed in cells D4:D5 using Excel's COUNT and AVERAGE functions, respectively. The value worksheet shows that the sample size is 100 and the sample mean is 82. The value of the known population standard deviation (20) is entered into cell D7 and the desired confidence coefficient (.95) is entered into cell D8. The level of significance is computed in cell D9 by entering the formula $=1-D8$; the value worksheet shows that the level of significance associated with a confidence coefficient of .95 is .05. The margin of error is computed in cell D11 using Excel's CONFIDENCE.NORM function. The CONFIDENCE.NORM function has three inputs: the level of significance (cell D9); the population standard deviation (cell D7); and the sample size (cell D4). Thus, to compute the margin of error associated with a 95% confidence interval, the following formula is entered into cell D11:

$$=\text{CONFIDENCE.NORM(D9,D7,D4)}$$

The resulting value of 3.92 is the margin of error associated with the interval estimate of the population mean amount spent per week.

Cells D13:D15 provide the point estimate and the lower and upper limits for the confidence interval. Because the point estimate is just the sample mean, the formula $=D5$ is entered into cell D13. To compute the lower limit of the 95% confidence interval, $\bar{x} -$ (margin of error), we enter the formula $=D13-D11$ into cell D14. To compute the upper limit of the 95% confidence interval, $\bar{x} +$ (margin of error), we enter the formula $=D13+D11$ into cell D15. The value worksheet shows a lower limit of 78.08 and an upper limit of 85.92. In other words, the 95% confidence interval for the population mean is from 78.08 to 85.92.

**FIGURE 8.4** EXCEL WORKSHEET: CONSTRUCTING A 95% CONFIDENCE INTERVAL FOR LLOYD'S DEPARTMENT STORE

Note: Rows 18–99 are hidden.

**A template for other problems** To use this worksheet as a template for another problem of this type, we must first enter the new problem data in column A. Then, the cell formulas in cells D4 and D5 must be updated with the new data range and the known population standard deviation must be entered into cell D7. After doing so, the point estimate and a 95% confidence interval will be displayed in cells D13:D15. If a confidence interval with a different confidence coefficient is desired, we simply change the value in cell D8.

We can further simplify the use of Figure 8.4 as a template for other problems by eliminating the need to enter new data ranges in cells D4 and D5. To do so we rewrite the cell formulas as follows:

Cell D4: =COUNT(A:A)

Cell D5: =AVERAGE(A:A)

*The Lloyd's data set includes a worksheet entitled Template that uses the A:A method for entering the data ranges.*

With the A:A method of specifying data ranges, Excel's COUNT function will count the number of numerical values in column A and Excel's AVERAGE function will compute the average of the numerical values in column A. Thus, to solve a new problem it is only necessary to enter the new data into column A and enter the value of the known population standard deviation into cell D7.

This worksheet can also be used as a template for text exercises in which the sample size, sample mean, and the population standard deviation are given. In this type of situation we simply replace the values in cells D4, D5, and D7 with the given values of the sample size, sample mean, and the population standard deviation.

## Practical Advice

If the population follows a normal distribution, the confidence interval provided by expression (8.1) is exact. In other words, if expression (8.1) were used repeatedly to generate 95% confidence intervals, exactly 95% of the intervals generated would contain the population mean. If the population does not follow a normal distribution, the confidence interval provided by expression (8.1) will be approximate. In this case, the quality of the approximation depends on both the distribution of the population and the sample size.

In most applications, a sample size of $n \geq 30$ is adequate when using expression (8.1) to develop an interval estimate of a population mean. If the population is not normally distributed, but is roughly symmetric, sample sizes as small as 15 can be expected to provide good approximate confidence intervals. With smaller sample sizes, expression (8.1) should only be used if the analyst believes, or is willing to assume, that the population distribution is at least approximately normal.

## NOTES AND COMMENTS

1. The interval estimation procedure discussed in this section is based on the assumption that the population standard deviation $\sigma$ is known. By $\sigma$ known we mean that historical data or other information are available that permit us to obtain a good estimate of the population standard deviation prior to taking the sample that will be used to develop an estimate of the population mean. So technically we don't mean that $\sigma$ is actually known with certainty. We just mean that we obtained a good estimate of the standard deviation prior to sampling and thus we won't be using the same sample to estimate both the population mean and the population standard deviation.

2. The sample size $n$ appears in the denominator of the interval estimation expression (8.1). Thus, if a particular sample size provides too wide an interval to be of any practical use, we may want to consider increasing the sample size. With $n$ in the denominator, a larger sample size will provide a smaller margin of error, a narrower interval, and greater precision. The procedure for determining the size of a simple random sample necessary to obtain a desired precision is discussed in Section 8.3.

## Exercises

### Methods

1. A simple random sample of 40 items resulted in a sample mean of 25. The population standard deviation is $\sigma = 5$.
   a. What is the standard error of the mean, $\sigma_{\bar{x}}$?
   b. At 95% confidence, what is the margin of error?

2. A simple random sample of 50 items from a population with $\sigma = 6$ resulted in a sample mean of 32.
   a. Provide a 90% confidence interval for the population mean.

b.  Provide a 95% confidence interval for the population mean.
c.  Provide a 99% confidence interval for the population mean.

3.  A simple random sample of 60 items resulted in a sample mean of 80. The population standard deviation is $\sigma = 15$.
    a.  Compute the 95% confidence interval for the population mean.
    b.  Assume that the same sample mean was obtained from a sample of 120 items. Provide a 95% confidence interval for the population mean.
    c.  What is the effect of a larger sample size on the interval estimate?

4.  A 95% confidence interval for a population mean was reported to be 152 to 160. If $\sigma = 15$, what sample size was used in this study?

## Applications

**Restaurant**

5.  In an effort to estimate the mean amount spent per customer for dinner at an Atlanta restaurant, data were collected for a sample of 49 customers. The data collected are shown in the website file named Restaurant. Based upon past studies the population standard deviation is assumed known with $\sigma = \$5$.
    a.  At 95% confidence, what is the margin of error?
    b.  Develop a 95% confidence interval estimate of the mean amount spent for dinner.

6.  Nielsen Media Research conducted a study of household television viewing times during the 8 P.M. to 11 P.M. time period. The data contained in the file named Nielsen are consistent with the findings reported (*The World Almanac,* 2003). Based upon past studies the population standard deviation is assumed known with $\sigma = 3.5$ hours. Develop a 95% confidence interval estimate of the mean television viewing time per week during the 8 P.M. to 11 P.M. time period.

**Nielsen**

7.  *The Wall Street Journal* reported that automobile crashes cost the United States $162 billion annually (*The Wall Street Journal,* March 5, 2008). The average cost per person for crashes in the Tampa, Florida, area was reported to be $1599. Suppose this average cost was based on a sample of 50 persons who had been involved in car crashes and that the population standard deviation is $\sigma = \$600$. What is the margin of error for a 95% confidence interval? What would you recommend if the study required a margin of error of $150 or less?

8.  The National Quality Research Center at the University of Michigan provides a quarterly measure of consumer opinions about products and services (*The Wall Street Journal,* February 18, 2003). A survey of 10 restaurants in the Fast Food/Pizza group showed a sample mean customer satisfaction index of 71. Past data indicate that the population standard deviation of the index has been relatively stable with $\sigma = 5$.
    a.  What assumption should the researcher be willing to make if a margin of error is desired?
    b.  Using 95% confidence, what is the margin of error?
    c.  What is the margin of error if 99% confidence is desired?

9.  AARP reported on a study conducted to learn how long it takes individuals to prepare their federal income tax return (*AARP Bulletin,* April 2008). The data contained in the file named TaxReturn are consistent with the study results. These data provide the time in hours required for 40 individuals to complete their federal income tax returns. Using past years' data, the population standard deviation can be assumed known with $\sigma = 9$ hours. What is the 95% confidence interval estimate of the mean time it takes an individual to complete a federal income tax return?

**TaxReturn**

10. *Playbill* magazine reported that the mean annual household income of its readers is $119,155 (*Playbill,* January 2006). Assume this estimate of the mean annual household income is based on a sample of 80 households, and based on past studies, the population standard deviation is known to be $\sigma = \$30,000$.
    a.  Develop a 90% confidence interval estimate of the population mean.
    b.  Develop a 95% confidence interval estimate of the population mean.

c. Develop a 99% confidence interval estimate of the population mean.
d. Discuss what happens to the width of the confidence interval as the confidence level is increased. Does this seem reasonable? Explain.

## 8.2 Population Mean: $\sigma$ Unknown

When developing an interval estimate of a population mean we usually do not have a good estimate of the population standard deviation either. In these cases, we must use the same sample to estimate both $\mu$ and $\sigma$. This situation represents the **$\sigma$ unknown** case. When $s$ is used to estimate $\sigma$, the margin of error and the interval estimate for the population mean are based on a probability distribution known as the *t* **distribution**. Although the mathematical development of the *t* distribution is based on the assumption of a normal distribution for the population we are sampling from, research shows that the *t* distribution can be successfully applied in many situations where the population deviates significantly from normal. Later in this section we provide guidelines for using the *t* distribution if the population is not normally distributed.

*William Sealy Gosset, writing under the name "Student," is the founder of the t distribution. Gosset, an Oxford graduate in mathematics, worked for the Guinness Brewery in Dublin, Ireland. He developed the t distribution while working on small-scale materials and temperature experiments.*

The *t* distribution is a family of similar probability distributions, with a specific *t* distribution depending on a parameter known as the **degrees of freedom**. The *t* distribution with one degree of freedom is unique, as is the *t* distribution with two degrees of freedom, with three degrees of freedom, and so on. As the number of degrees of freedom increases, the difference between the *t* distribution and the standard normal distribution becomes smaller and smaller. Figure 8.5 shows *t* distributions with 10 and 20 degrees of freedom and their relationship to the standard normal probability distribution. Note that a *t* distribution with more degrees of freedom exhibits less variability and more

**FIGURE 8.5** COMPARISON OF THE STANDARD NORMAL DISTRIBUTION WITH *t* DISTRIBUTIONS HAVING 10 AND 20 DEGREES OF FREEDOM

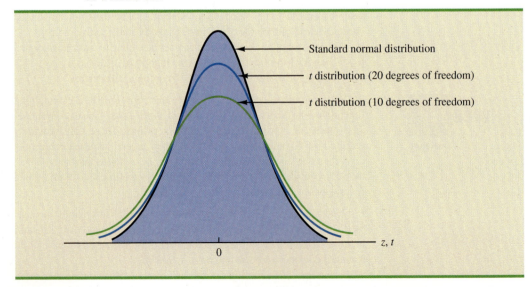

closely resembles the standard normal distribution. Note also that the mean of the $t$ distribution is zero.

We place a subscript on $t$ to indicate the area in the upper tail of the $t$ distribution. For example, just as we used $z_{.025}$ to indicate the $z$ value providing a .025 area in the upper tail of a standard normal distribution, we will use $t_{.025}$ to indicate a .025 area in the upper tail of a $t$ distribution. In general, we will use the notation $t_{\alpha/2}$ to represent a $t$ value with an area of $\alpha/2$ in the upper tail of the $t$ distribution. See Figure 8.6.

Table 2 in Appendix B contains a table for the $t$ distribution. A portion of this table is shown in Table 8.2. Each row in the table corresponds to a separate $t$ distribution with the degrees of freedom shown. For example, for a $t$ distribution with 9 degrees of freedom, $t_{.025} = 2.262$. Similarly, for a $t$ distribution with 60 degrees of freedom, $t_{.025} = 2.000$. As the degrees of freedom continue to increase, $t_{.025}$ approaches $z_{.025} = 1.96$. In fact, the standard normal distribution $z$ values can be found in the infinite degrees of freedom row (labeled $\infty$) of the $t$ distribution table. If the degrees of freedom exceed 100, the infinite degrees of freedom row can be used to approximate the actual $t$ value; in other words, for more than 100 degrees of freedom, the standard normal $z$ value provides a good approximation to the $t$ value.

*As the degrees of freedom increase, the t distribution approaches the standard normal distribution.*

## Margin of Error and the Interval Estimate

In Section 8.1 we showed that an interval estimate of a population mean for the $\sigma$ known case is

$$\bar{x} \pm z_{\alpha/2}\frac{\sigma}{\sqrt{n}}$$

To compute an interval estimate of $\mu$ for the $\sigma$ unknown case, the sample standard deviation $s$ is used to estimate $\sigma$, and $z_{\alpha/2}$ is replaced by the $t$ distribution value $t_{\alpha/2}$. The margin

**FIGURE 8.6**   $t$ DISTRIBUTION WITH $\alpha/2$ AREA OR PROBABILITY IN THE UPPER TAIL

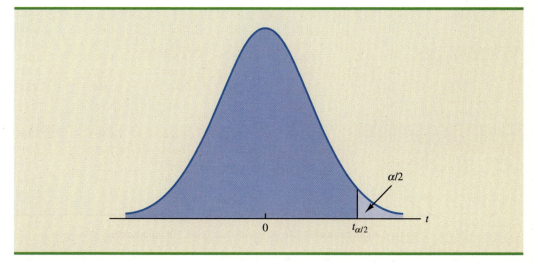

**TABLE 8.2**    SELECTED VALUES FROM THE *t* DISTRIBUTION TABLE*

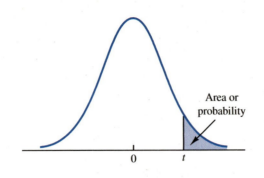

| Degrees of Freedom | Area in Upper Tail | | | | | |
|---|---|---|---|---|---|---|
| | **.20** | **.10** | **.05** | **.025** | **.01** | **.005** |
| 1 | 1.376 | 3.078 | 6.314 | 12.706 | 31.821 | 63.656 |
| 2 | 1.061 | 1.886 | 2.920 | 4.303 | 6.965 | 9.925 |
| 3 | .978 | 1.638 | 2.353 | 3.182 | 4.541 | 5.841 |
| 4 | .941 | 1.533 | 2.132 | 2.776 | 3.747 | 4.604 |
| 5 | .920 | 1.476 | 2.015 | 2.571 | 3.365 | 4.032 |
| 6 | .906 | 1.440 | 1.943 | 2.447 | 3.143 | 3.707 |
| 7 | .896 | 1.415 | 1.895 | 2.365 | 2.998 | 3.499 |
| 8 | .889 | 1.397 | 1.860 | 2.306 | 2.896 | 3.355 |
| 9 | .883 | 1.383 | 1.833 | 2.262 | 2.821 | 3.250 |
| ⋮ | ⋮ | ⋮ | ⋮ | ⋮ | ⋮ | ⋮ |
| 60 | .848 | 1.296 | 1.671 | 2.000 | 2.390 | 2.660 |
| 61 | .848 | 1.296 | 1.670 | 2.000 | 2.389 | 2.659 |
| 62 | .847 | 1.295 | 1.670 | 1.999 | 2.388 | 2.657 |
| 63 | .847 | 1.295 | 1.669 | 1.998 | 2.387 | 2.656 |
| 64 | .847 | 1.295 | 1.669 | 1.998 | 2.386 | 2.655 |
| 65 | .847 | 1.295 | 1.669 | 1.997 | 2.385 | 2.654 |
| 66 | .847 | 1.295 | 1.668 | 1.997 | 2.384 | 2.652 |
| 67 | .847 | 1.294 | 1.668 | 1.996 | 2.383 | 2.651 |
| 68 | .847 | 1.294 | 1.668 | 1.995 | 2.382 | 2.650 |
| 69 | .847 | 1.294 | 1.667 | 1.995 | 2.382 | 2.649 |
| ⋮ | ⋮ | ⋮ | ⋮ | ⋮ | ⋮ | ⋮ |
| 90 | .846 | 1.291 | 1.662 | 1.987 | 2.368 | 2.632 |
| 91 | .846 | 1.291 | 1.662 | 1.986 | 2.368 | 2.631 |
| 92 | .846 | 1.291 | 1.662 | 1.986 | 2.368 | 2.630 |
| 93 | .846 | 1.291 | 1.661 | 1.986 | 2.367 | 2.630 |
| 94 | .845 | 1.291 | 1.661 | 1.986 | 2.367 | 2.629 |
| 95 | .845 | 1.291 | 1.661 | 1.985 | 2.366 | 2.629 |
| 96 | .845 | 1.290 | 1.661 | 1.985 | 2.366 | 2.628 |
| 97 | .845 | 1.290 | 1.661 | 1.985 | 2.365 | 2.627 |
| 98 | .845 | 1.290 | 1.661 | 1.984 | 2.365 | 2.627 |
| 99 | .845 | 1.290 | 1.660 | 1.984 | 2.364 | 2.626 |
| 100 | .845 | 1.290 | 1.660 | 1.984 | 2.364 | 2.626 |
| ∞ | .842 | 1.282 | 1.645 | 1.960 | 2.326 | 2.576 |

*Note:* A more extensive table is provided as Table 2 of Appendix B.

of error is then given by $t_{\alpha/2}\, s/\sqrt{n}$. With this margin of error, the general expression for an interval estimate of a population mean when $\sigma$ is unknown follows.

---

**INTERVAL ESTIMATE OF A POPULATION MEAN: $\sigma$ UNKNOWN**

$$\bar{x} \pm t_{\alpha/2}\frac{s}{\sqrt{n}} \tag{8.2}$$

where $s$ is the sample standard deviation, $(1 - \alpha)$ is the confidence coefficient, and $t_{\alpha/2}$ is the $t$ value providing an area of $\alpha/2$ in the upper tail of the $t$ distribution with $n - 1$ degrees of freedom.

---

The reason the number of degrees of freedom associated with the $t$ value in expression (8.2) is $n - 1$ concerns the use of $s$ as an estimate of the population standard deviation $\sigma$. The expression for the sample standard deviation is

$$s = \sqrt{\frac{\Sigma(x_i - \bar{x})^2}{n - 1}}$$

Degrees of freedom refer to the number of independent pieces of information that go into the computation of $\Sigma(x_i - \bar{x})^2$. The $n$ pieces of information involved in computing $\Sigma(x_i - \bar{x})^2$ are as follows: $x_1 - \bar{x}, x_2 - \bar{x}, \ldots, x_n - \bar{x}$. In Section 3.2 we indicated that $\Sigma(x_i - \bar{x}) = 0$ for any data set. Thus, only $n - 1$ of the $x_i - \bar{x}$ values are independent; that is, if we know $n - 1$ of the values, the remaining value can be determined exactly by using the condition that the sum of the $x_i - \bar{x}$ values must be 0. Thus, $n - 1$ is the number of degrees of freedom associated with $\Sigma(x_i - \bar{x})^2$ and hence the number of degrees of freedom for the $t$ distribution in expression (8.2).

To illustrate the interval estimation procedure for the $\sigma$ unknown case, we will consider a study designed to estimate the mean credit card debt for the population of U.S. households. A sample of $n = 70$ households provided the credit card balances shown in Table 8.3. For this situation, no previous estimate of the population standard deviation $\sigma$ is available. Thus, the sample data must be used to estimate both the population mean and the population standard deviation. Using the data in Table 8.3, we compute the sample mean $\bar{x} = \$9312$ and the

**TABLE 8.3   CREDIT CARD BALANCES FOR A SAMPLE OF 70 HOUSEHOLDS**

**WEB** file

**NewBalance**

| | | | | | |
|---|---|---|---|---|---|
| 9430 | 14661 | 7159 | 9071 | 9691 | 11032 |
| 7535 | 12195 | 8137 | 3603 | 11448 | 6525 |
| 4078 | 10544 | 9467 | 16804 | 8279 | 5239 |
| 5604 | 13659 | 12595 | 13479 | 5649 | 6195 |
| 5179 | 7061 | 7917 | 14044 | 11298 | 12584 |
| 4416 | 6245 | 11346 | 6817 | 4353 | 15415 |
| 10676 | 13021 | 12806 | 6845 | 3467 | 15917 |
| 1627 | 9719 | 4972 | 10493 | 6191 | 12591 |
| 10112 | 2200 | 11356 | 615 | 12851 | 9743 |
| 6567 | 10746 | 7117 | 13627 | 5337 | 10324 |
| 13627 | 12744 | 9465 | 12557 | 8372 | |
| 18719 | 5742 | 19263 | 6232 | 7445 | |

sample standard deviation $s = \$4007$. With 95% confidence and $n - 1 = 69$ degrees of freedom, Table 8.2 can be used to obtain the appropriate value for $t_{.025}$. We want the $t$ value in the row with 69 degrees of freedom, and the column corresponding to .025 in the upper tail. The value shown is $t_{.025} = 1.995$.

We use expression (8.2) to compute an interval estimate of the population mean credit card balance.

$$9312 \pm 1.995 \frac{4007}{\sqrt{70}}$$

$$9312 \pm 955$$

The point estimate of the population mean is $9312, the margin of error is $955, and the 95% confidence interval is $9312 - 955 = \$8357$ to $9312 + 955 = \$10{,}267$. Thus, we are 95% confident that the mean credit card balance for the population of all households is between $8357 and $10,267.

## Using Excel

We will use the credit card balances in Table 8.3 to illustrate how Excel can be used to construct an interval estimate of the population mean for the $\sigma$ unknown case. We start by summarizing the data using Excel's Descriptive Statistics tool described in Chapter 3. Refer to Figure 8.7 as we describe the tasks involved. The formula worksheet is in the background; the value worksheet is in the foreground.

**Enter Data:**   A label and the credit card balances are entered into cells A1:A71.

**Apply Analysis Tools:**   The following steps describe how to use Excel's Descriptive Statistics tool for these data:

> **Step 1.** Click the **Data** tab on the Ribbon
> **Step 2.** In the **Analysis** group, click **Data Analysis**
> **Step 3.** Choose **Descriptive Statistics** from the list of Analysis Tools
> **Step 4.** When the Descriptive Statistics dialog box appears,
> > Enter A1:A71 in the **Input Range** box
> > Select **Grouped By Columns**
> > Select **Labels in First Row**
> > Select **Output Range**
> > > Enter C1 in the **Output Range** box
> > Select **Summary Statistics**
> > Select **Confidence Level for Mean**
> > > Enter 95 in the **Confidence Level for Mean** box
> > Click **OK**

The sample mean ($\bar{x}$) is in cell D3. The margin of error, labeled "Confidence Level(95%)," appears in cell D16. The value worksheet shows $\bar{x} = 9312$ and a margin of error equal to 955.

**Enter Functions and Formulas:**   Cells D18:D20 provide the point estimate and the lower and upper limits for the confidence interval. Because the point estimate is just the sample mean, the formula =D3 is entered into cell D18. To compute the lower limit of the 95% confidence interval, $\bar{x} - $ (margin of error), we enter the formula =D18−D16 into cell D19. To compute the upper limit of the 95% confidence interval, $\bar{x} + $ (margin of error), we enter the formula =D18+D16 into cell D20. The value worksheet shows a lower limit of 8357 and an upper limit of 10,267. In other words, the 95% confidence interval for the population mean is from 8357 to 10,267.

**FIGURE 8.7**    EXCEL WORKSHEET: 95% CONFIDENCE INTERVAL FOR CREDIT CARD BALANCES

*Note: Rows 21–69
are hidden.*

## Practical Advice

If the population follows a normal distribution, the confidence interval provided by expression (8.2) is exact and can be used for any sample size. If the population does not follow a normal distribution, the confidence interval provided by expression (8.2) will be approximate. In this case, the quality of the approximation depends on both the distribution of the population and the sample size.

*Larger sample sizes are needed if the distribution of the population is highly skewed or includes outliers.*

In most applications, a sample size of $n \geq 30$ is adequate when using expression (8.2) to develop an interval estimate of a population mean. However, if the population distribution is highly skewed or contains outliers, most statisticians would recommend increasing the sample size to 50 or more. If the population is not normally distributed but is roughly symmetric, sample sizes as small as 15 can be expected to provide good approximate confidence intervals. With smaller sample sizes, expression (8.2) should only be used if the analyst believes, or is willing to assume, that the population distribution is at least approximately normal.

## Using a Small Sample

In the following example we develop an interval estimate for a population mean when the sample size is small. As we already noted, an understanding of the distribution of the population becomes a factor in deciding whether the interval estimation procedure provides acceptable results.

Scheer Industries is considering a new computer-assisted program to train maintenance employees to do machine repairs. In order to fully evaluate the program, the director of

**TABLE 8.4**     TRAINING TIME IN DAYS FOR A SAMPLE OF 20 SCHEER
INDUSTRIES EMPLOYEES

**WEB** file

Scheer

| | | | |
|---|---|---|---|
| 52 | 59 | 54 | 42 |
| 44 | 50 | 42 | 48 |
| 55 | 54 | 60 | 55 |
| 44 | 62 | 62 | 57 |
| 45 | 46 | 43 | 56 |

manufacturing requested an estimate of the population mean time required for maintenance employees to complete the computer-assisted training.

A sample of 20 employees is selected, with each employee in the sample completing the training program. Data on the training time in days for the 20 employees are shown in Table 8.4. A histogram of the sample data appears in Figure 8.8. What can we say about the distribution of the population based on this histogram? First, the sample data do not support the conclusion that the distribution of the population is normal, yet we do not see any evidence of skewness or outliers. Therefore, using the guidelines in the previous subsection, we conclude that an interval estimate based on the *t* distribution appears acceptable for the sample of 20 employees.

We continue by computing the sample mean and sample standard deviation as follows.

$$\bar{x} = \frac{\Sigma x_i}{n} = \frac{1030}{20} = 51.5 \text{ days}$$

$$s = \sqrt{\frac{\Sigma(x_i - \bar{x})^2}{n - 1}} = \sqrt{\frac{889}{20 - 1}} = 6.84 \text{ days}$$

**FIGURE 8.8**     HISTOGRAM OF TRAINING TIMES FOR THE SCHEER INDUSTRIES SAMPLE

For a 95% confidence interval, we use Table 2 of Appendix B and $n - 1 = 19$ degrees of freedom to obtain $t_{.025} = 2.093$. Expression (8.2) provides the interval estimate of the population mean.

$$51.5 \pm 2.093\left(\frac{6.84}{\sqrt{20}}\right)$$

$$51.5 \pm 3.2$$

The point estimate of the population mean is 51.5 days. The margin of error is 3.2 days and the 95% confidence interval is $51.5 - 3.2 = 48.3$ days to $51.5 + 3.2 = 54.7$ days.

Using a histogram of the sample data to learn about the distribution of a population is not always conclusive, but in many cases it provides the only information available. The histogram, along with judgment on the part of the analyst, can often be used to decide whether expression (8.2) can be used to develop the interval estimate.

## Summary of Interval Estimation Procedures

We provided two approaches to developing an interval estimate of a population mean. For the $\sigma$ known case, $\sigma$ and the standard normal distribution are used in expression (8.1) to compute the margin of error and to develop the interval estimate. For the $\sigma$ unknown case, the sample standard deviation $s$ and the $t$ distribution are used in expression (8.2) to compute the margin of error and to develop the interval estimate.

A summary of the interval estimation procedures for the two cases is shown in Figure 8.9. In most applications, a sample size of $n \geq 30$ is adequate. If the population has a normal or approximately normal distribution, however, smaller sample sizes may be used.

**FIGURE 8.9**   SUMMARY OF INTERVAL ESTIMATION PROCEDURES
FOR A POPULATION MEAN

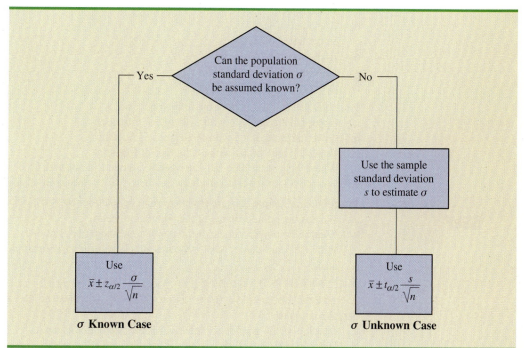

For the $\sigma$ unknown case a sample size of $n \geq 50$ is recommended if the population distribution is believed to be highly skewed or has outliers.

## NOTES AND COMMENTS

1. When $\sigma$ is known, the margin of error, $z_{\alpha/2}(\sigma/\sqrt{n})$, is fixed and is the same for all samples of size $n$. When $\sigma$ is unknown, the margin of error, $t_{\alpha/2}(s/\sqrt{n})$, varies from sample to sample. This variation occurs because the sample standard deviation $s$ varies depending upon the sample selected. A large value for $s$ provides a larger margin of error, while a small value for $s$ provides a smaller margin of error.

2. What happens to confidence interval estimates when the population is skewed? Consider a population that is skewed to the right with large data values stretching the distribution to the right. When such skewness exists, the sample mean $\bar{x}$ and the sample standard deviation $s$ are positively correlated. Larger values of $s$ tend to be associated with larger values of $\bar{x}$. Thus, when $\bar{x}$ is larger than the population mean, $s$ tends to be larger than $\sigma$. This skewness causes the margin of error, $t_{\alpha/2}(s/\sqrt{n})$, to be larger than it would be with $\sigma$ known. The confidence interval with the larger margin of error tends to include the population mean $\mu$ more often than it would if the true value of $\sigma$ were used. But when $\bar{x}$ is smaller than the population mean, the correlation between $\bar{x}$ and $s$ causes the margin of error to be small. In this case, the confidence interval with the smaller margin of error tends to miss the population mean more than it would if we knew $\sigma$ and used it. For this reason, we recommend using larger sample sizes with highly skewed population distributions.

## Exercises

## Methods

11. For a $t$ distribution with 16 degrees of freedom, find the area, or probability, in each region.
    a. To the right of 2.120
    b. To the left of 1.337
    c. To the left of $-1.746$
    d. To the right of 2.583
    e. Between $-2.120$ and 2.120
    f. Between $-1.746$ and 1.746

12. Find the $t$ value(s) for each of the following cases.
    a. Upper tail area of .025 with 12 degrees of freedom
    b. Lower tail area of .05 with 50 degrees of freedom
    c. Upper tail area of .01 with 30 degrees of freedom
    d. Where 90% of the area falls between these two $t$ values with 25 degrees of freedom
    e. Where 95% of the area falls between these two $t$ values with 45 degrees of freedom

**SELF** test

13. The following sample data are from a normal population: 10, 8, 12, 15, 13, 11, 6, 5.
    a. What is the point estimate of the population mean?
    b. What is the point estimate of the population standard deviation?
    c. With 95% confidence, what is the margin of error for the estimation of the population mean?
    d. What is the 95% confidence interval for the population mean?

14. A simple random sample with $n = 54$ provided a sample mean of 22.5 and a sample standard deviation of 4.4.
    a. Develop a 90% confidence interval for the population mean.
    b. Develop a 95% confidence interval for the population mean.

c.   Develop a 99% confidence interval for the population mean.
d.   What happens to the margin of error and the confidence interval as the confidence level is increased?

## Applications

15.   Sales personnel for Skillings Distributors submit weekly reports listing the customer contacts made during the week. A sample of 65 weekly reports showed a sample mean of 19.5 customer contacts per week. The sample standard deviation was 5.2. Provide 90% and 95% confidence intervals for the population mean number of weekly customer contacts for the sales personnel.

16.   The mean number of hours of flying time for pilots at Continental Airlines is 49 hours per month (*The Wall Street Journal,* February 25, 2003). Assume that this mean was based on actual flying times for a sample of 100 Continental pilots and that the sample standard deviation was 8.5 hours.
a.   At 95% confidence, what is the margin of error?
b.   What is the 95% confidence interval estimate of the population mean flying time for the pilots?
c.   The mean number of hours of flying time for pilots at United Airlines is 36 hours per month. Use your results from part (b) to discuss differences between the flying times for the pilots at the two airlines. *The Wall Street Journal* reported United Airlines as having the highest labor cost among all airlines. Does the information in this exercise provide insight as to why United Airlines might expect higher labor costs?

17.   The International Air Transport Association surveys business travelers to develop quality ratings for transatlantic gateway airports. The maximum possible rating is 10. Suppose a simple random sample of 50 business travelers is selected and each traveler is asked to provide a rating for the Miami International Airport. The ratings obtained from the sample of 50 business travelers follow.

| 6 | 4 | 6 | 8 | 7 | 7 | 6 | 3 | 3 | 8 | 10 | 4 | 8 |
| 7 | 8 | 7 | 5 | 9 | 5 | 8 | 4 | 3 | 8 | 5 | 5 | 4 |
| 4 | 4 | 8 | 4 | 5 | 6 | 2 | 5 | 9 | 9 | 8 | 4 | 8 |
| 9 | 9 | 5 | 9 | 7 | 8 | 3 | 10 | 8 | 9 | 6 | | |

Develop a 95% confidence interval estimate of the population mean rating for Miami.

18.   Older people often have a hard time finding work. AARP reported on the number of weeks it takes a worker aged 55 plus to find a job. The data on number of weeks spent searching for a job contained in the file JobSearch are consistent with the AARP findings (*AARP Bulletin,* April 2008).
a.   Provide a point estimate of the population mean number of weeks it takes a worker aged 55 plus to find a job.
b.   At 95% confidence, what is the margin of error?
c.   What is the 95% confidence interval estimate of the mean?
d.   Discuss the degree of skewness found in the sample data. What suggestion would you make for a repeat of this study?

19.   The average cost per night of a hotel room in New York City is $273 (*SmartMoney,* March 2009). Assume this estimate is based on a sample of 45 hotels and that the sample standard deviation is $65.
a.   With 95% confidence, what is the margin of error?
b.   What is the 95% confidence interval estimate of the population mean?
c.   Two years ago the average cost of a hotel room in New York City was $229. Discuss the change in cost over the two-year period.

*Equation (8.3) provides the minimum sample size needed to satisfy the desired margin of error requirement. If the computed sample size is not an integer, rounding up to the next integer value will provide a margin of error slightly smaller than required.*

reviewed the sample data from the previous study and found that the sample standard deviation for the daily rental cost was $9.65. Using 9.65 as the planning value for $\sigma$, we obtain

$$n = \frac{(z_{\alpha/2})^2 \sigma^2}{E^2} = \frac{(1.96)^2 (9.65)^2}{2^2} = 89.43$$

Thus, the sample size for the new study needs to be at least 89.43 midsize automobile rentals in order to satisfy the project director's $2 margin-of-error requirement. In cases where the computed $n$ is not an integer, we round up to the next integer value; hence, the recommended sample size is 90 midsize automobile rentals.

## Exercises

### Methods

23. How large a sample should be selected to provide a 95% confidence interval with a margin of error of 10? Assume that the population standard deviation is 40.

24. The range for a set of data is estimated to be 36.
    a. What is the planning value for the population standard deviation?
    b. At 95% confidence, how large a sample would provide a margin of error of 3?
    c. At 95% confidence, how large a sample would provide a margin of error of 2?

### Applications

25. Refer to the Scheer Industries example in Section 8.2. Use 6.84 days as a planning value for the population standard deviation.
    a. Assuming 95% confidence, what sample size would be required to obtain a margin of error of 1.5 days?
    b. If the precision statement was made with 90% confidence, what sample size would be required to obtain a margin of error of 2 days?

26. The average cost of a gallon of unleaded gasoline in Greater Cincinnati was reported to be $2.41 (*The Cincinnati Enquirer*, February 3, 2006). During periods of rapidly changing prices, the newspaper samples service stations and prepares reports on gasoline prices frequently. Assume the standard deviation is $.15 for the price of a gallon of unleaded regular gasoline, and recommend the appropriate sample size for the newspaper to use if they wish to report a margin of error at 95% confidence.
    a. Suppose the desired margin of error is $.07.
    b. Suppose the desired margin of error is $.05.
    c. Suppose the desired margin of error is $.03.

27. Annual starting salaries for college graduates with degrees in business administration are generally expected to be between $30,000 and $45,000. Assume that a 95% confidence interval estimate of the population mean annual starting salary is desired. What is the planning value for the population standard deviation? How large a sample should be taken if the desired margin of error is
    a. $500?
    b. $200?
    c. $100?
    d. Would you recommend trying to obtain the $100 margin of error? Explain.

28. An online survey by ShareBuilder, a retirement plan provider, and Harris Interactive reported that 60% of female business owners are not confident they are saving enough for

retirement (*SmallBiz*, Winter 2006). Suppose we would like to do a follow-up study to determine how much female business owners are saving each year toward retirement and want to use $100 as the desired margin of error for an interval estimate of the population mean. Use $1100 as a planning value for the standard deviation and recommend a sample size for each of the following situations.

a.  A 90% confidence interval is desired for the mean amount saved.
b.  A 95% confidence interval is desired for the mean amount saved.
c.  A 99% confidence interval is desired for the mean amount saved.
d.  When the desired margin of error is set, what happens to the sample size as the confidence level is increased? Would you recommend using a 99% confidence interval in this case? Discuss.

29.  The travel-to-work time for residents of the 15 largest cities in the United States is reported in the *2003 Information Please Almanac*. Suppose that a preliminary simple random sample of residents of San Francisco is used to develop a planning value of 6.25 minutes for the population standard deviation.

a.  If we want to estimate the population mean travel-to-work time for San Francisco residents with a margin of error of 2 minutes, what sample size should be used? Assume 95% confidence.
b.  If we want to estimate the population mean travel-to-work time for San Francisco residents with a margin of error of 1 minute, what sample size should be used? Assume 95% confidence.

30.  During the first quarter of 2003, the price/earnings (P/E) ratio for stocks listed on the New York Stock Exchange generally ranged from 5 to 60 (*The Wall Street Journal*, March 7, 2003). Assume that we want to estimate the population mean P/E ratio for all stocks listed on the exchange. How many stocks should be included in the sample if we want a margin of error of 3? Use 95% confidence.

## 8.4  Population Proportion

In the introduction to this chapter we said that the general form of an interval estimate of a population proportion $p$ is

$$\bar{p} \pm \text{Margin of error}$$

The sampling distribution of $\bar{p}$ plays a key role in computing the margin of error for this interval estimate.

In Chapter 7 we said that the sampling distribution of $\bar{p}$ can be approximated by a normal distribution whenever $np \geq 5$ and $n(1 - p) \geq 5$. Figure 8.10 shows the normal approximation of the sampling distribution of $\bar{p}$. The mean of the sampling distribution of $\bar{p}$ is the population proportion $p$, and the standard error of $\bar{p}$ is

$$\sigma_{\bar{p}} = \sqrt{\frac{p(1 - p)}{n}} \tag{8.4}$$

Because the sampling distribution of $\bar{p}$ is normally distributed, if we choose $z_{\alpha/2}\sigma_{\bar{p}}$ as the margin of error in an interval estimate of a population proportion, we know that $100(1 - \alpha)\%$ of the intervals generated will contain the true population proportion. But $\sigma_{\bar{p}}$ cannot be used directly in the computation of the margin of error because $p$ will not be

**FIGURE 8.10** NORMAL APPROXIMATION OF THE SAMPLING DISTRIBUTION OF $\bar{p}$

known; $p$ is what we are trying to estimate. So $\bar{p}$ is substituted for $p$ and the margin of error for an interval estimate of a population proportion is given by

$$\text{Margin of error} = z_{\alpha/2} \sqrt{\frac{\bar{p}(1 - \bar{p})}{n}} \qquad (8.5)$$

With this margin of error, the general expression for an interval estimate of a population proportion is as follows.

---

**INTERVAL ESTIMATE OF A POPULATION PROPORTION**

*When developing confidence intervals for proportions, the quantity $z_{\alpha/2}\sqrt{\bar{p}(1 - \bar{p})/n}$ provides the margin of error.*

$$\bar{p} \pm z_{\alpha/2} \sqrt{\frac{\bar{p}(1 - \bar{p})}{n}} \qquad (8.6)$$

where $1 - \alpha$ is the confidence coefficient and $z_{\alpha/2}$ is the $z$ value providing an area of $\alpha/2$ in the upper tail of the standard normal distribution.

---

**TeeTimes**

The following example illustrates the computation of the margin of error and interval estimate for a population proportion. A national survey of 900 women golfers was conducted to learn how women golfers view their treatment at golf courses in the United States. The survey found that 396 of the women golfers were satisfied with the availability of tee times. Thus, the point estimate of the proportion of the population of women golfers who are satisfied with the availability of tee times is 396/900 = .44. Using expression (8.6) and a 95% confidence level,

$$\bar{p} \pm z_{\alpha/2} \sqrt{\frac{\bar{p}(1 - \bar{p})}{n}}$$

$$.44 \pm 1.96 \sqrt{\frac{.44(1 - .44)}{900}}$$

$$.44 \pm .0324$$

Thus, the margin of error is .0324 and the 95% confidence interval estimate of the population proportion is .4076 to .4724. Using percentages, the survey results enable us to state with 95% confidence that between 40.76% and 47.24% of all women golfers are satisfied with the availability of tee times.

## Using Excel

Excel can be used to construct an interval estimate of the population proportion of women golfers who are satisfied with the availability of tee times. The responses in the survey were recorded as a Yes or No for each woman surveyed. Refer to Figure 8.11 as we describe the tasks involved in constructing a 95% confidence interval. The formula worksheet is in the background; the value worksheet appears in the foreground.

**Enter Data:**   The Yes/No data for the 900 women golfers are entered into cells A2:A901.

**Enter Functions and Formulas:**   The descriptive statistics we need and the response of interest are provided in cells D3:D6. Because Excel's COUNT function only works with numerical data, we used the COUNTA function in cell D3 to compute the sample size. The response for which we want to develop an interval estimate, Yes or No, is entered into cell D4. Figure 8.11 shows that Yes has been entered into cell D4, indicating that we want to develop an interval estimate of the population proportion of women golfers who are satisfied with the availability of tee times. If we had wanted to develop an interval estimate of the population proportion of women golfers who are not satisfied with the availability of tee times, we would have entered No in cell D4. With Yes entered in cell D4, the COUNTIF function in cell D5 counts the number of Yes responses in the sample. The sample proportion is then computed in cell D6 by dividing the number of Yes responses in cell D5 by the sample size in cell D3.

Cells D8:D10 are used to compute the appropriate $z$ value. The confidence coefficient (0.95) is entered into cell D8 and the level of significance ($\alpha$) is computed in cell D9 by entering the formula $=1-D8$. The $z$ value corresponding to an upper tail area of $\alpha/2$ is computed by entering the formula $=$NORM.S.INV$(1-D9/2)$ into cell D10. The value worksheet shows that $z_{.025} = 1.960$.

Cells D12:D13 provide the estimate of the standard error and the margin of error. In cell D12, we entered the formula $=$SQRT$(D6*(1-D6)/D3)$ to compute the standard error using the sample proportion and the sample size as inputs. The formula $=$D10*D12 is entered into cell D13 to compute the margin of error.

Cells D15:D17 provide the point estimate and the lower and upper limits for a confidence interval. The point estimate in cell D15 is the sample proportion. The lower and upper limits in cells D16 and D17 are obtained by subtracting and adding the margin of error to the point estimate. We note that the 95% confidence interval for the proportion of women golfers who are satisfied with the availability of tee times is .4076 to .4724.

**A template for other problems**   The worksheet in Figure 8.11 can be used as a template for developing confidence intervals about a population proportion $p$. To use this worksheet for another problem of this type, we must first enter the new problem data in column A. The response of interest would then be typed in cell D4 and the ranges for the formulas in cells D3 and D5 would be revised to correspond to the new data. After doing so, the point estimate and a 95% confidence interval will be displayed in cells D15:D17. If a confidence interval with a different confidence coefficient is desired, we simply change the value in cell D8.

**TABLE 8.5**    SOME POSSIBLE VALUES FOR $p^*(1 - p^*)$

| $p^*$ | $p^*(1 - p^*)$ | |
|------|----------------|---|
| .10 | $(.10)(.90) = .09$ | |
| .30 | $(.30)(.70) = .21$ | |
| .40 | $(.40)(.60) = .24$ | |
| .50 | $(.50)(.50) = .25$ | ← Largest value for $p^*(1 - p^*)$ |
| .60 | $(.60)(.40) = .24$ | |
| .70 | $(.70)(.30) = .21$ | |
| .90 | $(.90)(.10) = .09$ | |

numerator of equation (8.7) shows that the sample size is proportional to the quantity $p^*(1 - p^*)$. A larger value for the quantity $p^*(1 - p^*)$ will result in a larger sample size. Table 8.5 gives some possible values of $p^*(1 - p^*)$. Note that the largest value of $p^*(1 - p^*)$ occurs when $p^* = .50$. Thus, in case of any uncertainty about an appropriate planning value, we know that $p^* = .50$ will provide the largest sample size recommendation. In effect, we play it safe by recommending the largest necessary sample size. If the sample proportion turns out to be different from the .50 planning value, the margin of error will be smaller than anticipated. Thus, in using $p^* = .50$, we guarantee that the sample size will be sufficient to obtain the desired margin of error.

In the survey of women golfers example, a planning value of $p^* = .50$ would have provided the sample size

$$n = \frac{(z_{\alpha/2})^2 p^*(1 - p^*)}{E^2} = \frac{(1.96)^2(.50)(1 - .50)}{(.025)^2} = 1536.6$$

Thus, a slightly larger sample size of 1537 women golfers would be recommended.

## NOTES AND COMMENTS

The desired margin of error for estimating a population proportion is almost always .10 or less. In national public opinion polls conducted by organizations such as Gallup and Harris, a .03 or .04 margin of error is common. With such margins of error, equation (8.7) will almost always provide a sample size that is large enough to satisfy the requirements of $np \geq 5$ and $n(1 - p) \geq 5$ for using a normal distribution as an approximation for the sampling distribution of $\bar{x}$.

## Exercises

### Methods

**SELF** test

31. A simple random sample of 400 individuals provides 100 Yes responses.
    a. What is the point estimate of the proportion of the population that would provide Yes responses?
    b. What is your estimate of the standard error of the proportion, $\sigma_{\bar{p}}$?
    c. Compute the 95% confidence interval for the population proportion.

32. A simple random sample of 800 elements generates a sample proportion $\bar{p} = .70$.
    a. Provide a 90% confidence interval for the population proportion.
    b. Provide a 95% confidence interval for the population proportion.

33. In a survey, the planning value for the population proportion is $p^* = .35$. How large a sample should be taken to provide a 95% confidence interval with a margin of error of .05?

34. At 95% confidence, how large a sample should be taken to obtain a margin of error of .03 for the estimation of a population proportion? Assume that past data are not available for developing a planning value for $p^*$.

## Applications

35. The Consumer Reports National Research Center conducted a telephone survey of 2000 adults to learn about the major economic concerns for the future (*Consumer Reports*, January 2009). The survey results showed that 1760 of the respondents think the future health of Social Security is a major economic concern.
    a. What is the point estimate of the population proportion of adults who think the future health of Social Security is a major economic concern.
    b. At 90% confidence, what is the margin of error?
    c. Develop a 90% confidence interval for the population proportion of adults who think the future health of Social Security is a major economic concern.
    d. Develop a 95% confidence interval for this population proportion.

36. According to statistics reported on CNBC, a surprising number of motor vehicles are not covered by insurance (CNBC, February 23, 2006). Sample results, consistent with the CNBC report, showed 46 of 200 vehicles were not covered by insurance.
    a. What is the point estimate of the proportion of vehicles not covered by insurance?
    b. Develop a 95% confidence interval for the population proportion.

37. Towers Perrin, a New York human resources consulting firm, conducted a survey of 1100 employees at medium-sized and large companies to determine how dissatisfied employees were with their jobs (*The Wall Street Journal*, January 29, 2003). Representative data are shown in the file JobSatisfaction. A response of Yes indicates the employee strongly disliked the current work experience.

**WEB** file

JobSatisfaction

    a. What is the point estimate of the proportion of the population of employees who strongly dislike their current work experience?
    b. At 95% confidence, what is the margin of error?
    c. What is the 95% confidence interval for the proportion of the population of employees who strongly dislike their current work experience?
    d. Towers Perrin estimates that it costs employers one-third of an hourly employee's annual salary to find a successor and as much as 1.5 times the annual salary to find a successor for a highly compensated employee. What message did this survey send to employers?

38. According to Thomson Financial, through January 25, 2006, the majority of companies reporting profits had beaten estimates (*BusinessWeek*, February 6, 2006). A sample of 162 companies showed that 104 beat estimates, 29 matched estimates, and 29 fell short.
    a. What is the point estimate of the proportion that fell short of estimates?
    b. Determine the margin of error and provide a 95% confidence interval for the proportion that beat estimates.
    c. How large a sample is needed if the desired margin of error is .05?

39. The percentage of people not covered by health care insurance in 2003 was 15.6% (*Statistical Abstract of the United States*, 2006). A congressional committee has been charged with conducting a sample survey to obtain more current information.
    a. What sample size would you recommend if the committee's goal is to estimate the current proportion of individuals without health care insurance with a margin of error of .03? Use a 95% confidence level.
    b. Repeat part (a) using a 99% confidence level.

40. For many years businesses have struggled with the rising cost of health care. But recently, the increases have slowed due to less inflation in health care prices and employees paying for a larger portion of health care benefits. A recent Mercer survey showed that 52% of U.S. employers were likely to require higher employee contributions for health care coverage in 2009 (*BusinessWeek*, February 16, 2009). Suppose the survey was based on a sample of 800 companies. Compute the margin of error and a 95% confidence interval for the proportion of companies likely to require higher employee contributions for health care coverage in 2009.

41. America's young people are heavy Internet users; 87% of Americans ages 12 to 17 are Internet users (*The Cincinnati Enquirer*, February 7, 2006). MySpace was voted the most popular website by 9% in a sample survey of Internet users in this age group. Suppose 1400 youths participated in the survey. What is the margin of error, and what is the interval estimate of the population proportion for which MySpace is the most popular website? Use a 95% confidence level.

42. A poll for the presidential campaign sampled 491 potential voters in June. A primary purpose of the poll was to obtain an estimate of the proportion of potential voters who favored each candidate. Assume a planning value of $p^* = .50$ and a 95% confidence level.
    a. For $p^* = .50$, what was the planned margin of error for the June poll?
    b. Closer to the November election, better precision and smaller margins of error are desired. Assume the following margins of error are requested for surveys to be conducted during the presidential campaign. Compute the recommended sample size for each survey.

| Survey | Margin of Error |
|---|---|
| September | .04 |
| October | .03 |
| Early November | .02 |
| Pre-Election Day | .01 |

43. A Phoenix Wealth Management/Harris Interactive survey of 1500 individuals with net worth of $1 million or more provided a variety of statistics on wealthy people (*BusinessWeek*, September 22, 2003). The previous three-year period had been bad for the stock market, which motivated some of the questions asked.
    a. The survey reported that 53% of the respondents lost 25% or more of their portfolio value over the past three years. Develop a 95% confidence interval for the proportion of wealthy people who lost 25% or more of their portfolio value over the past three years.
    b. The survey reported that 31% of the respondents feel they have to save more for retirement to make up for what they lost. Develop a 95% confidence interval for the population proportion.
    c. Five percent of the respondents gave $25,000 or more to charity over the previous year. Develop a 95% confidence interval for the proportion who gave $25,000 or more to charity.
    d. Compare the margin of error for the interval estimates in parts (a), (b), and (c). How is the margin of error related to $\bar{p}$? When the same sample is being used to estimate a variety of proportions, which of the proportions should be used to choose the planning value $p^*$? Why do you think $p^* = .50$ is often used in these cases?

## Summary

In this chapter we presented methods for developing interval estimates of a population mean and a population proportion. A point estimator may or may not provide a good estimate of a population parameter. The use of an interval estimate provides a measure of the precision

of an estimate. Both the interval estimate of the population mean and the pop
proportion are of the form: point estimate ± margin of error.

We presented interval estimates for a population mean for two cases. In the $\sigma$ kno
case, historical data or other information is used to develop an estimate of $\sigma$ prior to taking
a sample. Analysis of new sample data then proceeds based on the assumption that $\sigma$ is
known. In the $\sigma$ unknown case, the sample data are used to estimate both the population
mean and the population standard deviation. The final choice of which interval estimation
procedure to use depends upon the analyst's understanding of which method provides the
best estimate of $\sigma$.

In the $\sigma$ known case, the interval estimation procedure is based on the assumed value
of $\sigma$ and the use of the standard normal distribution. In the $\sigma$ unknown case, the interval
estimation procedure uses the sample standard deviation $s$ and the $t$ distribution. In both
cases the quality of the interval estimates obtained depends on the distribution of the
population and the sample size. If the population is normally distributed the interval estimates will be exact in both cases, even for small sample sizes. If the population is not
normally distributed, the interval estimates obtained will be approximate. Larger sample
sizes will provide better approximations, but the more highly skewed the population is, the
larger the sample size needs to be to obtain a good approximation. Practical advice about
the sample size necessary to obtain good approximations was included in Sections 8.1 and
8.2. In most cases a sample of size 30 or more will provide good approximate confidence
intervals.

The general form of the interval estimate for a population proportion is $\bar{p}$ ± margin of
error. In practice the sample sizes used for interval estimates of a population proportion are
generally large. Thus, the interval estimation procedure is based on the standard normal
distribution.

Often a desired margin of error is specified prior to developing a sampling plan. We
showed how to choose a sample size large enough to provide the desired precision.

## Glossary

**Interval estimate** An estimate of a population parameter that provides an interval believed
to contain the value of the parameter. For the interval estimates in this chapter, it has the
form: point estimate ± margin of error.

**Margin of error** The ± value added to and subtracted from a point estimate in order to
develop an interval estimate of a population parameter.

**$\sigma$ known** The case when historical data or other information provides a good value for the
population standard deviation prior to taking a sample. The interval estimation procedure
uses this known value of $\sigma$ in computing the margin of error.

**Confidence level** The confidence associated with an interval estimate. For example, if an
interval estimation procedure provides intervals such that 95% of the intervals formed
using the procedure will include the population parameter, the interval estimate is said to
be constructed at the 95% confidence level.

**Confidence coefficient** The confidence level expressed as a decimal value. For example,
.95 is the confidence coefficient for a 95% confidence level.

**Confidence interval** Another name for an interval estimate.

**Level of significance** The probability that the interval estimation procedure will generate
an interval that does not contain $\mu$.

**$\sigma$ unknown** The more common case when no good basis exists for estimating the population standard deviation prior to taking the sample. The interval estimation procedure uses
the sample standard deviation $s$ in computing the margin of error.

*t* **distribution** A family of probability distributions that can be used to develop an interval estimate of a population mean whenever the population standard deviation $\sigma$ is unknown and is estimated by the sample standard deviation *s*.

**Degrees of freedom** A parameter of the *t* distribution. When the *t* distribution is used in the computation of an interval estimate of a population mean, the appropriate *t* distribution has $n - 1$ degrees of freedom, where *n* is the size of the simple random sample.

## Key Formulas

**Interval Estimate of a Population Mean: $\sigma$ Known**

$$\bar{x} \pm z_{\alpha/2} \frac{\sigma}{\sqrt{n}} \tag{8.1}$$

**Interval Estimate of a Population Mean: $\sigma$ Unknown**

$$\bar{x} \pm t_{\alpha/2} \frac{s}{\sqrt{n}} \tag{8.2}$$

**Sample Size for an Interval Estimate of a Population Mean**

$$n = \frac{(z_{\alpha/2})^2 \sigma^2}{E^2} \tag{8.3}$$

**Interval Estimate of a Population Proportion**

$$\bar{p} \pm z_{\alpha/2} \sqrt{\frac{\bar{p}(1 - \bar{p})}{n}} \tag{8.6}$$

**Sample Size for an Interval Estimate of a Population Proportion**

$$n = \frac{(z_{\alpha/2})^2 p^*(1 - p^*)}{E^2} \tag{8.7}$$

## Supplementary Exercises

44.  A sample survey of 54 discount brokers showed that the mean price charged for a trade of 100 shares at $50 per share was $33.77 (*AAII Journal*, February 2006). The survey is conducted annually. With the historical data available, assume a known population standard deviation of $15.

  a.  Using the sample data, what is the margin of error associated with a 95% confidence interval?

  b.  Develop a 95% confidence interval for the mean price charged by discount brokers for a trade of 100 shares at $50 per share.

45.  A survey conducted by the American Automobile Association showed that a family of four spends an average of $215.60 per day while on vacation. Suppose a sample of 64 families

of four vacationing at Niagara Falls resulted in a sample mean of $252.45 per day and a sample standard deviation of $74.50.

a. Develop a 95% confidence interval estimate of the mean amount spent per day by a family of four visiting Niagara Falls.

b. Based on the confidence interval from part (a), does it appear that the population mean amount spent per day by families visiting Niagara Falls differs from the mean reported by the American Automobile Association? Explain.

46. The 92 million Americans of age 50 and over control 50 percent of all discretionary income (*AARP Bulletin,* March 2008). AARP estimated that the average annual expenditure on restaurants and carryout food was $1873 for individuals in this age group. Suppose this estimate is based on a sample of 80 persons and that the sample standard deviation is $550.

a. At 95% confidence, what is the margin of error?

b. What is the 95% confidence interval for the population mean amount spent on restaurants and carryout food?

c. What is your estimate of the total amount spent by Americans of age 50 and over on restaurants and carryout food?

d. If the amount spent on restaurants and carryout food is skewed to the right, would you expect the median amount spent to be greater or less than $1873?

47. Many stock market observers say that when the P/E ratio for stocks gets over 20 the market is overvalued. The P/E ratio is the stock price divided by the most recent 12 months of earnings. Suppose you are interested in seeing whether the current market is overvalued and would also like to know what proportion of companies pay dividends. A random sample of 30 companies listed on the New York Stock Exchange (NYSE) is provided (*Barron's,* January 19, 2004).

NYSEStocks

| Company | Dividend | P/E Ratio | Company | Dividend | P/E Ratio |
|---|---|---|---|---|---|
| Albertsons | Yes | 14 | NY Times A | Yes | 25 |
| BRE Prop | Yes | 18 | Omnicare | Yes | 25 |
| CityNtl | Yes | 16 | PallCp | Yes | 23 |
| DelMonte | No | 21 | PubSvcEnt | Yes | 11 |
| EnrgzHldg | No | 20 | SensientTch | Yes | 11 |
| Ford Motor | Yes | 22 | SmtProp | Yes | 12 |
| Gildan A | No | 12 | TJX Cos | Yes | 21 |
| HudsnUtdBcp | Yes | 13 | Thomson | Yes | 30 |
| IBM | Yes | 22 | USB Hldg | Yes | 12 |
| JeffPilot | Yes | 16 | US Restr | Yes | 26 |
| KingswayFin | No | 6 | Varian Med | No | 41 |
| Libbey | Yes | 13 | Visx | No | 72 |
| MasoniteIntl | No | 15 | Waste Mgt | No | 23 |
| Motorola | Yes | 68 | Wiley A | Yes | 21 |
| Ntl City | Yes | 10 | Yum Brands | No | 18 |

a. What is a point estimate of the P/E ratio for the population of stocks listed on the New York Stock Exchange? Develop a 95% confidence interval.

b. Based on your answer to part (a), do you believe that the market is overvalued?

c. What is a point estimate of the proportion of companies on the NYSE that pay dividends? Is the sample size large enough to justify using the normal distribution to construct a confidence interval for this proportion? Why or why not?

Flights

48. US Airways conducted a number of studies that indicated a substantial savings could be obtained by encouraging Dividend Miles frequent flyer customers to redeem miles and

schedule award flights online (*US Airways Attaché,* February 2003). One study collected data on the amount of time required to redeem miles and schedule an award flight over the telephone. A sample showing the time in minutes required for each of 150 award flights scheduled by telephone is contained in the data set Flights. Use Excel to help answer the following questions.

a.   What is the sample mean number of minutes required to schedule an award flight by telephone?
b.   What is the 95% confidence interval for the population mean time to schedule an award flight by telephone?
c.   Assume a telephone ticket agent works 7.5 hours per day. How many award flights can one ticket agent be expected to handle a day?
d.   Discuss why this information supported US Airways' plans to use an online system to reduce costs.

**Standing**

49.   A recent article reported that there are approximately 11 minutes of actual playing time in a typical National Football League (NFL) game (*The Wall Street Journal,* January 15, 2010). The article included information about the amount of time devoted to replays, the amount of time devoted to commercials, and the amount of time the players spend standing around between plays. Data consistent with the findings published in *The Wall Street Journal* are in the file named Standing. These data provide the amount of time players spend standing around between plays for a sample of 60 NFL games.

a.   Use the Standing data set to develop a point estimate of the number of minutes during an NFL game that players are standing around between plays. Compare this to the actual playing time reported in the article. Are you surprised?
b.   What is the sample standard deviation?
c.   Develop a 95% confidence interval for the number of minutes players spend standing around between plays.

50.   Mileage tests are conducted for a particular model of automobile. If a 98% confidence interval with a margin of error of 1 mile per gallon is desired, how many automobiles should be used in the test? Assume that preliminary mileage tests indicate the standard deviation is 2.6 miles per gallon.

51.   In developing patient appointment schedules, a medical center wants to estimate the mean time that a staff member spends with each patient. How large a sample should be taken if the desired margin of error is two minutes at a 95% level of confidence? How large a sample should be taken for a 99% level of confidence? Use a planning value for the population standard deviation of eight minutes.

52.   Annual salary plus bonus data for chief executive officers are presented in the *BusinessWeek* Annual Pay Survey. A preliminary sample showed that the standard deviation is $675 with data provided in thousands of dollars. How many chief executive officers should be in a sample if we want to estimate the population mean annual salary plus bonus with a margin of error of $100,000? (*Note:* The desired margin of error would be $E = 100$ if the data are in thousands of dollars.) Use 95% confidence.

53.   The National Center for Education Statistics reported that 47% of college students work to pay for tuition and living expenses. Assume that a sample of 450 college students was used in the study.

a.   Provide a 95% confidence interval for the population proportion of college students who work to pay for tuition and living expenses.
b.   Provide a 99% confidence interval for the population proportion of college students who work to pay for tuition and living expenses.
c.   What happens to the margin of error as the confidence is increased from 95% to 99%?

54.   A *USA Today*/CNN/Gallup survey of 369 working parents found 200 who said they spend too little time with their children because of work commitments.

    a.    What is the point estimate of the proportion of the population of working parents who feel they spend too little time with their children because of work commitments?

    b.    At 95% confidence, what is the margin of error?

    c.    What is the 95% confidence interval estimate of the population proportion of working parents who feel they spend too little time with their children because of work commitments?

55. Which would be hardest for you to give up: your computer or your television? In a recent survey of 1677 U.S. Internet users, 74% of the young tech elite (average age of 22) say their computer would be very hard to give up (*PC Magazine*, February 3, 2004). Only 48% say their television would be very hard to give up.

    a.    Develop a 95% confidence interval for the proportion of the young tech elite that would find it very hard to give up their computer.

    b.    Develop a 99% confidence interval for the proportion of the young tech elite that would find it very hard to give up their television.

    c.    In which case, part (a) or part (b), is the margin of error larger? Explain why.

56. Cincinnati/Northern Kentucky International Airport had the second highest on-time arrival rate for 2005 among the nation's busiest airports (*The Cincinnati Enquirer,* February 3, 2006). Assume the findings were based on 455 on-time arrivals out of a sample of 550 flights.

    a.    Develop a point estimate of the on-time arrival rate (proportion of flights arriving on time) for the airport.

    b.    Construct a 95% confidence interval for the on-time arrival rate of the population of all flights at the airport during 2005.

57. The *2003 Statistical Abstract of the United States* reported the percentage of people 18 years of age and older who smoke. Suppose that a study designed to collect new data on smokers and nonsmokers uses a preliminary estimate of the proportion who smoke of .30.

    a.    How large a sample should be taken to estimate the proportion of smokers in the population with a margin of error of .02? Use 95% confidence.

    b.    Assume that the study uses your sample size recommendation in part (a) and finds 520 smokers. What is the point estimate of the proportion of smokers in the population?

    c.    What is the 95% confidence interval for the proportion of smokers in the population?

58. A well-known bank credit card firm wishes to estimate the proportion of credit card holders who carry a nonzero balance at the end of the month and incur an interest charge. Assume that the desired margin of error is .03 at 98% confidence.

    a.    How large a sample should be selected if it is anticipated that roughly 70% of the firm's card holders carry a nonzero balance at the end of the month?

    b.    How large a sample should be selected if no planning value for the proportion could be specified?

59. Workers in several industries were surveyed to determine the proportion of workers who feel their industry is understaffed. In the government sector, 37% of the respondents said they were understaffed, in the health care sector 33% said they were understaffed, and in the education sector 28% said they were understaffed (*USA Today,* January 11, 2010). Suppose that 200 workers were surveyed in each industry.

    a.    Construct a 95% confidence interval for the proportion of workers in each of these industries who feel their industry is understaffed.

    b.    Assuming the sample size will be the same in each industry, how large would the sample need to be to ensure that the margin of error is .05 or less for each of the three confidence intervals?

60. Although airline schedules and cost are important factors for business travelers when choosing an airline carrier, a *USA Today* survey found that business travelers list an airline's frequent flyer program as the most important factor. From a sample of $n = 1993$

business travelers who responded to the survey, 618 listed a frequent flyer program as the most important factor.

a. What is the point estimate of the proportion of the population of business travelers who believe a frequent flyer program is the most important factor when choosing an airline carrier?

b. Develop a 95% confidence interval estimate of the population proportion.

c. How large a sample would be required to report the margin of error of .01 at 95% confidence? Would you recommend that *USA Today* attempt to provide this degree of precision? Why or why not?

## Case Problem 1    *Young Professional* Magazine

*Young Professional* magazine was developed for a target audience of recent college graduates who are in their first 10 years in a business/professional career. In its two years of publication, the magazine has been fairly successful. Now the publisher is interested in expanding the magazine's advertising base. Potential advertisers continually ask about the demographics and interests of subscribers to *Young Professional*. To collect this information, the magazine commissioned a survey to develop a profile of its subscribers. The survey results will be used to help the magazine choose articles of interest and provide advertisers with a profile of subscribers. As a new employee of the magazine, you have been asked to help analyze the survey results.

**WEB** file

**Professional**

Some of the survey questions follow:

1. What is your age?
2. Are you: Male_____        Female_____
3. Do you plan to make any real estate purchases in the next two years? Yes_____ No_____
4. What is the approximate total value of financial investments, exclusive of your home, owned by you or members of your household?
5. How many stock/bond/mutual fund transactions have you made in the past year?
6. Do you have broadband access to the Internet at home? Yes_____    No_____
7. Please indicate your total household income last year.
8. Do you have children? Yes_____    No_____

The file entitled Professional contains the responses to these questions. Table 8.6 shows the portion of the file pertaining to the first five survey respondents.

### Managerial Report

Prepare a managerial report summarizing the results of the survey. In addition to statistical summaries, discuss how the magazine might use these results to attract advertisers. You

**TABLE 8.6**    PARTIAL SURVEY RESULTS FOR *YOUNG PROFESSIONAL* MAGAZINE

| Age | Gender | Real Estate Purchases | Value of Investments($) | Number of Transactions | Broadband Access | Household Income($) | Children |
|-----|--------|-----------------------|-------------------------|------------------------|------------------|---------------------|----------|
| 38 | Female | No | 12200 | 4 | Yes | 75200 | Yes |
| 30 | Male | No | 12400 | 4 | Yes | 70300 | Yes |
| 41 | Female | No | 26800 | 5 | Yes | 48200 | No |
| 28 | Female | Yes | 19600 | 6 | No | 95300 | No |
| 31 | Female | Yes | 15100 | 5 | No | 73300 | Yes |
| ⋮ | ⋮ | ⋮ | ⋮ | ⋮ | ⋮ | ⋮ | ⋮ |

might also comment on how the survey results could be used by the magazine's editors to identify topics that would be of interest to readers. Your report should address the following issues, but do not limit your analysis to just these areas.

1. Develop appropriate descriptive statistics to summarize the data.
2. Develop 95% confidence intervals for the mean age and household income of subscribers.
3. Develop 95% confidence intervals for the proportion of subscribers who have broadband access at home and the proportion of subscribers who have children.
4. Would *Young Professional* be a good advertising outlet for online brokers? Justify your conclusion with statistical data.
5. Would this magazine be a good place to advertise for companies selling educational software and computer games for young children?
6. Comment on the types of articles you believe would be of interest to readers of *Young Professional*.

## Case Problem 2    Gulf Real Estate Properties

Gulf Real Estate Properties, Inc., is a real estate firm located in southwest Florida. The company, which advertises itself as "expert in the real estate market," monitors condominium sales by collecting data on location, list price, sale price, and number of days it takes to sell each unit. Each condominium is classified as *Gulf View* if it is located directly on the Gulf of Mexico or *No Gulf View* if it is located on the bay or a golf course, near but not on the Gulf. Sample data from the Multiple Listing Service in Naples, Florida, provided recent sales data for 40 Gulf View condominiums and 18 No Gulf View condominiums.* Prices are in thousands of dollars. The data are shown in Table 8.7.

### Managerial Report

1. Use appropriate descriptive statistics to summarize each of the three variables for the 40 Gulf View condominiums.
2. Use appropriate descriptive statistics to summarize each of the three variables for the 18 No Gulf View condominiums.
3. Compare your summary results. Discuss any specific statistical results that would help a real estate agent understand the condominium market.
4. Develop a 95% confidence interval estimate of the population mean sales price and population mean number of days to sell for Gulf View condominiums. Interpret your results.
5. Develop a 95% confidence interval estimate of the population mean sales price and population mean number of days to sell for No Gulf View condominiums. Interpret your results.
6. Assume the branch manager requested estimates of the mean selling price of Gulf View condominiums with a margin of error of $40,000 and the mean selling price of No Gulf View condominiums with a margin of error of $15,000. Using 95% confidence, how large should the sample sizes be?
7. Gulf Real Estate Properties just signed contracts for two new listings: a Gulf View condominium with a list price of $589,000 and a No Gulf View condominium with a list price of $285,000. What is your estimate of the final selling price and number of days required to sell each of these units?

---

*Data based on condominium sales reported in the Naples MLS (Coldwell Banker, June 2000).

**TABLE 8.7**     SALES DATA FOR GULF REAL ESTATE PROPERTIES

| Gulf View Condominiums | | | No Gulf View Condominiums | | |
|---|---|---|---|---|---|
| List Price | Sale Price | Days to Sell | List Price | Sale Price | Days to Sell |
| 495.0 | 475.0 | 130 | 217.0 | 217.0 | 182 |
| 379.0 | 350.0 | 71 | 148.0 | 135.5 | 338 |
| 529.0 | 519.0 | 85 | 186.5 | 179.0 | 122 |
| 552.5 | 534.5 | 95 | 239.0 | 230.0 | 150 |
| 334.9 | 334.9 | 119 | 279.0 | 267.5 | 169 |
| 550.0 | 505.0 | 92 | 215.0 | 214.0 | 58 |
| 169.9 | 165.0 | 197 | 279.0 | 259.0 | 110 |
| 210.0 | 210.0 | 56 | 179.9 | 176.5 | 130 |
| 975.0 | 945.0 | 73 | 149.9 | 144.9 | 149 |
| 314.0 | 314.0 | 126 | 235.0 | 230.0 | 114 |
| 315.0 | 305.0 | 88 | 199.8 | 192.0 | 120 |
| 885.0 | 800.0 | 282 | 210.0 | 195.0 | 61 |
| 975.0 | 975.0 | 100 | 226.0 | 212.0 | 146 |
| 469.0 | 445.0 | 56 | 149.9 | 146.5 | 137 |
| 329.0 | 305.0 | 49 | 160.0 | 160.0 | 281 |
| 365.0 | 330.0 | 48 | 322.0 | 292.5 | 63 |
| 332.0 | 312.0 | 88 | 187.5 | 179.0 | 48 |
| 520.0 | 495.0 | 161 | 247.0 | 227.0 | 52 |
| 425.0 | 405.0 | 149 | | | |
| 675.0 | 669.0 | 142 | | | |
| 409.0 | 400.0 | 28 | | | |
| 649.0 | 649.0 | 29 | | | |
| 319.0 | 305.0 | 140 | | | |
| 425.0 | 410.0 | 85 | | | |
| 359.0 | 340.0 | 107 | | | |
| 469.0 | 449.0 | 72 | | | |
| 895.0 | 875.0 | 129 | | | |
| 439.0 | 430.0 | 160 | | | |
| 435.0 | 400.0 | 206 | | | |
| 235.0 | 227.0 | 91 | | | |
| 638.0 | 618.0 | 100 | | | |
| 629.0 | 600.0 | 97 | | | |
| 329.0 | 309.0 | 114 | | | |
| 595.0 | 555.0 | 45 | | | |
| 339.0 | 315.0 | 150 | | | |
| 215.0 | 200.0 | 48 | | | |
| 395.0 | 375.0 | 135 | | | |
| 449.0 | 425.0 | 53 | | | |
| 499.0 | 465.0 | 86 | | | |
| 439.0 | 428.5 | 158 | | | |

WEB file

GulfProp

## Case Problem 3     Metropolitan Research, Inc.

Metropolitan Research, Inc., a consumer research organization, conducts surveys designed to evaluate a wide variety of products and services available to consumers. In one particular study, Metropolitan looked at consumer satisfaction with the performance of automobiles produced by a major Detroit manufacturer. A questionnaire sent to owners of one of the manufacturer's full-sized cars revealed several complaints about early transmission problems. To learn more about the transmission failures, Metropolitan used a sample of actual transmission repairs provided by a transmission repair firm in the Detroit area. The following data show the actual number of miles driven for 50 vehicles at the time of transmission failure.

**WEB** file

**Auto**

| 85,092 | 32,609 | 59,465 | 77,437 | 32,534 | 64,090 | 32,464 | 59,902 |
|--------|--------|--------|--------|--------|--------|--------|--------|
| 39,323 | 89,641 | 94,219 | 116,803 | 92,857 | 63,436 | 65,605 | 85,861 |
| 64,342 | 61,978 | 67,998 | 59,817 | 101,769 | 95,774 | 121,352 | 69,568 |
| 74,276 | 66,998 | 40,001 | 72,069 | 25,066 | 77,098 | 69,922 | 35,662 |
| 74,425 | 67,202 | 118,444 | 53,500 | 79,294 | 64,544 | 86,813 | 116,269 |
| 37,831 | 89,341 | 73,341 | 85,288 | 138,114 | 53,402 | 85,586 | 82,256 |
| 77,539 | 88,798 | | | | | | |

## Managerial Report

1. Use appropriate descriptive statistics to summarize the transmission failure data.
2. Develop a 95% confidence interval for the mean number of miles driven until transmission failure for the population of automobiles with transmission failure. Provide a managerial interpretation of the interval estimate.
3. Discuss the implication of your statistical findings in terms of the belief that some owners of the automobiles experienced early transmission failures.
4. How many repair records should be sampled if the research firm wants the population mean number of miles driven until transmission failure to be estimated with a margin of error of 5000 miles? Use 95% confidence.
5. What other information would you like to gather to evaluate the transmission failure problem more fully?

## Appendix Interval Estimation with StatTools

In this appendix we show how StatTools can be used to develop an interval estimate of a population mean for the $\sigma$ unknown case and determine the sample size needed to provide a desired margin of error.

### Interval Estimation of Population Mean: $\sigma$ Unknown Case

In this case the population standard deviation $\sigma$ will be estimated by the sample standard deviation $s$. We use the credit card balance data in Table 8.3 to illustrate. Begin by using the Data Set Manager to create a StatTools data set for these data using the procedure described in the appendix to Chapter 1. The following steps can be used to compute a 95% confidence interval estimate of the population mean.

**WEB** file

**NewBalance**

**Step 1.** Click the **StatTools** tab on the Ribbon
**Step 2.** In the **Analyses** group, click **Statistical Inference**
**Step 3.** Choose the **Confidence Interval** option
**Step 4.** Choose **Mean/Std. Deviation**
**Step 5.** When the StatTools - Confidence Interval for Mean/Std. Deviation dialog box appears,
    For **Analysis Type** choose **One-Sample Analysis**
    In the **Variables** section, select **NewBalance**
    In the **Confidence Intervals to Calculate** section,
      Select the **For the Mean** option
      Select 95% for the **Confidence Level**
    Click **OK**

Some descriptive statistics and the confidence interval will appear.

## Determining the Sample Size

In Section 8.3 we showed how to determine the sample size needed to provide a desired margin of error. The example used involved a study designed to estimate the population mean daily rental cost for a midsize automobile in the United States. The project director specified that the population mean daily rental cost be estimated with a margin of error of $2 and a 95% level of confidence. Sample data from a previous study provided a sample standard deviation of $9.65; this value was used as the planning value for the population standard deviation. The following steps can be used to compute the recommended sample size required to provide a 95% confidence interval estimate of the population mean with a margin of error of $2.

**Step 1.** Click the **StatTools** tab on the Ribbon
**Step 2.** In the **Analyses** group, click **Statistical Inference**
**Step 3.** Choose the **Sample Size Selection** option
**Step 4.** When the StatTools - Sample Size Selection dialog box appears,
  In the **Parameter to Estimate** section, select **Mean**
  In the **Confidence Interval Specification** section,
    Select **95%** for the **Confidence Level**
    Enter **2** in the **Half-Length of Interval** box
    Enter **9.65** in the **Estimated Std Dev** box
  Click **OK**

*The half-length of interval is the margin of error.*

The output showing a recommended sample size of 90 will appear.

# Hypothesis Tests

## CONTENTS

*The conclusion that the research hypothesis is true is made if the sample data provide sufficient evidence to show that the null hypothesis can be rejected.*

fuel injection system increases the mean number of miles per gallon. The production of automobiles with the new fuel injection system should be considered. However, if the sample results lead to the conclusion that $H_0$ cannot be rejected, the researchers cannot conclude that the new fuel injection system is better than the current system. Production of automobiles with the new fuel injection system on the basis of better gas mileage cannot be justified. Perhaps more research and further testing can be conducted.

Successful companies stay competitive by developing new products, new methods, new systems, and the like that are better than what is currently available. Before adopting something new, it is desirable to conduct research to determine if there is statistical support for the conclusion that the new approach is indeed better. In such cases, the research hypothesis is stated as the alternative hypothesis. For example, a new teaching method is developed that is believed to be better than the current method. The alternative hypothesis is that the new method is better. The null hypothesis is that the new method is no better than the old method. A new sales force bonus plan is developed in an attempt to increase sales. The alternative hypothesis is that the new bonus plan increases sales. The null hypothesis is that the new bonus plan does not increase sales. A new drug is developed with the goal of lowering blood pressure more than an existing drug. The alternative hypothesis is that the new drug lowers blood pressure more than the existing drug. The null hypothesis is that the new drug does not provide lower blood pressure than the existing drug. In each case, rejection of the null hypothesis $H_0$ provides statistical support for the research hypothesis. We will see many examples of hypothesis tests in research situations such as these throughout this chapter and in the remainder of the text.

## The Null Hypothesis as an Assumption to Be Challenged

Of course, not all hypothesis tests involve research hypotheses. In the following discussion we consider applications of hypothesis testing where we begin with a belief or an assumption that a statement about the value of a population parameter is true. We will then use a hypothesis test to challenge the assumption and determine if there is statistical evidence to conclude that the assumption is incorrect. In these situations, it is helpful to develop the null hypothesis first. The null hypothesis $H_0$ expresses the belief or assumption about the value of the population parameter. The alternative hypothesis $H_a$ is that the belief or assumption is incorrect.

As an example, consider the situation of a manufacturer of soft drink products. The label on a soft drink bottle states that it contains 67.6 fluid ounces. We consider the label correct provided the population mean filling weight for the bottles is *at least* 67.6 fluid ounces. Without any reason to believe otherwise, we would give the manufacturer the benefit of the doubt and assume that the statement provided on the label is correct. Thus, in a hypothesis test about the population mean fluid weight per bottle, we would begin with the assumption that the label is correct and state the null hypothesis as $\mu \geq 67.6$. The challenge to this assumption would imply that the label is incorrect and the bottles are being underfilled. This challenge would be stated as the alternative hypothesis $\mu < 67.6$. Thus, the null and alternative hypotheses are:

$$H_0\!: \mu \geq 67.6$$
$$H_a\!: \mu < 67.6$$

*A manufacturer's product information is usually assumed to be true and stated as the null hypothesis. The conclusion that the information is incorrect can be made if the null hypothesis is rejected.*

A government agency with the responsibility for validating manufacturing labels could select a sample of soft drink bottles, compute the sample mean filling weight, and use the sample results to test the preceding hypotheses. If the sample results lead to the conclusion to reject $H_0$, the inference that $H_a\!: \mu < 67.6$ is true can be made. With this statistical support, the agency is justified in concluding that the label is incorrect and underfilling of the bottles is occurring. Appropriate action to force the manufacturer to comply with labeling standards would be considered. However, if the sample results indicate $H_0$ cannot be rejected, the assumption that the manufacturer's labeling is correct cannot be rejected. With this conclusion, no action would be taken.

Let us now consider a variation of the soft drink bottle-filling example by viewing the same situation from the manufacturer's point of view. The bottle-filling operation has been designed to fill soft drink bottles with 67.6 fluid ounces as stated on the label. The company does not want to underfill the containers because that could result in an underfilling complaint from customers or, perhaps, a government agency. However, the company does not want to overfill containers either because putting more soft drink than necessary into the containers would be an unnecessary cost. The company's goal would be to adjust the bottle-filling operation so that the population mean filling weight per bottle is 67.6 fluid ounces as specified on the label.

Although this is the company's goal, from time to time any production process can get out of adjustment. If this occurs in our example, underfilling or overfilling of the soft drink bottles will occur. In either case, the company would like to know about it in order to correct the situation by readjusting the bottle-filling operation to the designed 67.6 fluid ounces. In this hypothesis testing application, we would begin with the assumption that the production process is operating correctly and state the null hypothesis as $\mu = 67.6$ fluid ounces. The alternative hypothesis that challenges this assumption is that $\mu \neq 67.6$, which indicates either overfilling or underfilling is occurring. The null and alternative hypotheses for the manufacturer's hypothesis test are:

$$H_0\text{: } \mu = 67.6$$
$$H_a\text{: } \mu \neq 67.6$$

Suppose that the soft drink manufacturer uses a quality control procedure to periodically select a sample of bottles from the filling operation and computes the sample mean filling weight per bottle. If the sample results lead to the conclusion to reject $H_0$, the inference is made that $H_a\text{: } \mu \neq 67.6$ is true. We conclude that the bottles are not being filled properly and the production process should be adjusted to restore the population mean to 67.6 fluid ounces per bottle. However, if the sample results indicate $H_0$ cannot be rejected, the assumption that the manufacturer's bottle-filling operation is functioning properly cannot be rejected. In this case, no further action would be taken and the production operation would continue to run.

The two preceding forms of the soft drink manufacturing hypothesis test show that the null and alternative hypotheses may vary depending upon the point of view of the researcher or decision maker. To formulate hypotheses correctly it is important to understand the context of the situation and structure the hypotheses to provide the information the researcher or decision maker wants.

## Summary of Forms for Null and Alternative Hypotheses

The hypothesis tests in this chapter involve two population parameters: the population mean and the population proportion. Depending on the situation, hypothesis tests about a population parameter may take one of three forms: two use inequalities in the null hypothesis; the third uses an equality in the null hypothesis. For hypothesis tests involving a population mean, we let $\mu_0$ denote the hypothesized value and we must choose one of the following three forms for the hypothesis test.

*The three possible forms of hypotheses $H_0$ and $H_a$ are shown here. Note that the equality always appears in the null hypothesis $H_0$.*

$$H_0\text{: } \mu \geq \mu_0 \qquad H_0\text{: } \mu \leq \mu_0 \qquad H_0\text{: } \mu = \mu_0$$
$$H_a\text{: } \mu < \mu_0 \qquad H_a\text{: } \mu > \mu_0 \qquad H_a\text{: } \mu \neq \mu_0$$

For reasons that will be clear later, the first two forms are called one-tailed tests. The third form is called a two-tailed test.

In many situations, the choice of $H_0$ and $H_a$ is not obvious and judgment is necessary to select the proper form. However, as the preceding forms show, the equality part of the expression (either $\geq$, $\leq$, or $=$) *always* appears in the null hypothesis. In selecting the proper form of $H_0$ and $H_a$, keep in mind that the alternative hypothesis is often what the test is attempting to establish. Hence, asking whether the user is looking for evidence to support $\mu < \mu_0$, $\mu > \mu_0$, or $\mu \neq \mu_0$ will help determine $H_a$. The following exercises are designed to provide practice in choosing the proper form for a hypothesis test involving a population mean.

## Exercises

1.  The manager of the Danvers-Hilton Resort Hotel stated that the mean guest bill for a weekend is $600 or less. A member of the hotel's accounting staff noticed that the total charges for guest bills have been increasing in recent months. The accountant will use a sample of future weekend guest bills to test the manager's claim.
    a.  Which form of the hypotheses should be used to test the manager's claim? Explain.

    $$H_0: \mu \geq 600 \qquad H_0: \mu \leq 600 \qquad H_0: \mu = 600$$
    $$H_a: \mu < 600 \qquad H_a: \mu > 600 \qquad H_a: \mu \neq 600$$

    b.  What conclusion is appropriate when $H_0$ cannot be rejected?
    c.  What conclusion is appropriate when $H_0$ can be rejected?

2.  The manager of an automobile dealership is considering a new bonus plan designed to increase sales volume. Currently, the mean sales volume is 14 automobiles per month. The manager wants to conduct a research study to see whether the new bonus plan increases sales volume. To collect data on the plan, a sample of sales personnel will be allowed to sell under the new bonus plan for a one-month period.
    a.  Develop the null and alternative hypotheses most appropriate for this situation.
    b.  Comment on the conclusion when $H_0$ cannot be rejected.
    c.  Comment on the conclusion when $H_0$ can be rejected.

3.  A production line operation is designed to fill cartons with laundry detergent to a mean weight of 32 ounces. A sample of cartons is periodically selected and weighed to determine whether underfilling or overfilling is occurring. If the sample data lead to a conclusion of underfilling or overfilling, the production line will be shut down and adjusted to obtain proper filling.
    a.  Formulate the null and alternative hypotheses that will help in deciding whether to shut down and adjust the production line.
    b.  Comment on the conclusion and the decision when $H_0$ cannot be rejected.
    c.  Comment on the conclusion and the decision when $H_0$ can be rejected.

4.  Because of high production-changeover time and costs, a director of manufacturing must convince management that a proposed manufacturing method reduces costs before the new method can be implemented. The current production method operates with a mean cost of $220 per hour. A research study will measure the cost of the new method over a sample production period.
    a.  Develop the null and alternative hypotheses most appropriate for this study.
    b.  Comment on the conclusion when $H_0$ cannot be rejected.
    c.  Comment on the conclusion when $H_0$ can be rejected.

## 9.2 Type I and Type II Errors

The null and alternative hypotheses are competing statements about the population. Either the null hypothesis $H_0$ is true or the alternative hypothesis $H_a$ is true, but not both. Ideally the hypothesis testing procedure should lead to the acceptance of $H_0$ when $H_0$ is true and the rejection of $H_0$ when $H_a$ is true. Unfortunately, the correct conclusions are not always possible. Because hypothesis tests are based on sample information, we must allow for the possibility of errors. Table 9.1 illustrates the two kinds of errors that can be made in hypothesis testing.

The first row of Table 9.1 shows what can happen if the conclusion is to accept $H_0$. If $H_0$ is true, this conclusion is correct. However, if $H_a$ is true, we make a **Type II error**; that is, we accept $H_0$ when it is false. The second row of Table 9.1 shows what can happen if the conclusion is to reject $H_0$. If $H_0$ is true, we make a **Type I error**; that is, we reject $H_0$ when it is true. However, if $H_a$ is true, rejecting $H_0$ is correct.

Recall the hypothesis testing illustration discussed in Section 9.1, in which an automobile product research group developed a new fuel injection system designed to increase the miles-per-gallon rating of a particular automobile. With the current model obtaining an average of 24 miles per gallon, the hypothesis test was formulated as follows.

$$H_0: \mu \leq 24$$
$$H_a: \mu > 24$$

The alternative hypothesis, $H_a: \mu > 24$, indicates that the researchers are looking for sample evidence to support the conclusion that the population mean miles per gallon with the new fuel injection system is greater than 24.

In this application, the Type I error of rejecting $H_0$ when it is true corresponds to the researchers claiming that the new system improves the miles-per-gallon rating ($\mu > 24$) when in fact the new system is not any better than the current system. In contrast, the Type II error of accepting $H_0$ when it is false corresponds to the researchers concluding that the new system is not any better than the current system ($\mu \leq 24$) when in fact the new system improves miles-per-gallon performance.

For the miles-per-gallon rating hypothesis test, the null hypothesis is $H_0: \mu \leq 24$. Suppose the null hypothesis is true as an equality; that is, $\mu = 24$. The probability of making a Type I error when the null hypothesis is true as an equality is called the **level of significance**. Thus, for the miles-per-gallon rating hypothesis test, the level of significance is the probability of rejecting $H_0: \mu \leq 24$ when $\mu = 24$. Because of the importance of this concept, we now restate the definition of level of significance.

**TABLE 9.1** ERRORS AND CORRECT CONCLUSIONS IN HYPOTHESIS TESTING

|  |  | Population Condition | |
|---|---|---|---|
|  |  | $H_0$ True | $H_a$ True |
|  | **Accept $H_0$** | Correct Conclusion | Type II Error |
| **Conclusion** |  |  |  |
|  | **Reject $H_0$** | Type I Error | Correct Conclusion |

> **LEVEL OF SIGNIFICANCE**
>
> The level of significance is the probability of making a Type I error when the null hypothesis is true as an equality.

The Greek symbol $\alpha$ (alpha) is used to denote the level of significance, and common choices for $\alpha$ are .05 and .01.

In practice, the person responsible for the hypothesis test specifies the level of significance. By selecting $\alpha$, that person is controlling the probability of making a Type I error. If the cost of making a Type I error is high, small values of $\alpha$ are preferred. If the cost of making a Type I error is not too high, larger values of $\alpha$ are typically used. Applications of hypothesis testing that only control for the Type I error are called *significance tests*. Many applications of hypothesis testing are of this type.

*If the sample data are consistent with the null hypothesis $H_0$, we will follow the practice of concluding "do not reject $H_0$." This conclusion is preferred over "accept $H_0$," because the conclusion to accept $H_0$ puts us at risk of making a Type II error.*

Although most applications of hypothesis testing control for the probability of making a Type I error, they do not always control for the probability of making a Type II error. Hence, if we decide to accept $H_0$, we cannot determine how confident we can be with that decision. Because of the uncertainty associated with making a Type II error when conducting significance tests, statisticians usually recommend that we use the statement "do not reject $H_0$" instead of "accept $H_0$." Using the statement "do not reject $H_0$" carries the recommendation to withhold both judgment and action. In effect, by not directly accepting $H_0$, the statistician avoids the risk of making a Type II error. Whenever the probability of making a Type II error has not been determined and controlled, we will not make the statement "accept $H_0$." In such cases, only two conclusions are possible: *do not reject $H_0$ or reject $H_0$.*

Although controlling for a Type II error in hypothesis testing is not common, it can be done. More advanced texts describe procedures for determining and controlling the probability of making a Type II error.[1] If proper controls have been established for this error, action based on the "accept $H_0$" conclusion can be appropriate.

## NOTES AND COMMENTS

Walter Williams, syndicated columnist and professor of economics at George Mason University, points out that the possibility of making a Type I or a Type II error is always present in decision making (*The Cincinnati Enquirer*, August 14, 2005). He notes that the Food and Drug Administration runs the risk of making these errors in its drug approval process. The FDA must either approve a new drug or not approve it. Thus, the FDA runs the risk of approving a new drug that is not safe and effective, or failing to approve a new drug that is safe and effective. Regardless of the decision made, the possibility of making a costly error cannot be eliminated.

## Exercises

5. Nielsen reported that young men in the United States watch 56.2 minutes of prime-time TV daily (*The Wall Street Journal Europe*, November 18, 2003). A researcher believes that young men in Germany spend more time watching prime-time TV. A sample of German young men will be selected by the researcher and the time they spend watching TV in one

---

[1]See, for example, D. R. Anderson, D. J. Sweeney, and T. A. Williams, *Statistics for Business and Economics,* 11th edition (Cincinnati: South-Western, 2011).

day will be recorded. The sample results will be used to test the following null and alternative hypotheses.

$$H_0: \mu \leq 56.2$$
$$H_a: \mu > 56.2$$

    a.   What is the Type I error in this situation? What are the consequences of making this error?
    b.   What is the Type II error in this situation? What are the consequences of making this error?

6.  The label on a 3-quart container of orange juice states that the orange juice contains an average of 1 gram of fat or less. Answer the following questions for a hypothesis test that could be used to test the claim on the label.
    a.   Develop the appropriate null and alternative hypotheses.
    b.   What is the Type I error in this situation? What are the consequences of making this error?
    c.   What is the Type II error in this situation? What are the consequences of making this error?

7.  Carpetland salespersons average $8000 per week in sales. Steve Contois, the firm's vice president, proposes a compensation plan with new selling incentives. Steve hopes that the results of a trial selling period will enable him to conclude that the compensation plan increases the average sales per salesperson.
    a.   Develop the appropriate null and alternative hypotheses.
    b.   What is the Type I error in this situation? What are the consequences of making this error?
    c.   What is the Type II error in this situation? What are the consequences of making this error?

8.  Suppose a new production method will be implemented if a hypothesis test supports the conclusion that the new method reduces the mean operating cost per hour.
    a.   State the appropriate null and alternative hypotheses if the mean cost for the current production method is $220 per hour.
    b.   What is the Type I error in this situation? What are the consequences of making this error?
    c.   What is the Type II error in this situation? What are the consequences of making this error?

## 9.3   Population Mean: σ Known

In Chapter 8 we said that the σ known case corresponds to applications in which historical data and/or other information are available that enable us to obtain a good estimate of the population standard deviation prior to sampling. In such cases the population standard deviation can, for all practical purposes, be considered known. In this section we show how to conduct a hypothesis test about a population mean for the σ known case.

    The methods presented in this section are exact if the sample is selected from a population that is normally distributed. In cases where it is not reasonable to assume the population is normally distributed, these methods are still applicable if the sample size is large enough. We provide some practical advice concerning the population distribution and the sample size at the end of this section.

### One-Tailed Test

**One-tailed tests** about a population mean take one of the following two forms.

| Lower Tail Test | Upper Tail Test |
|:---:|:---:|
| $H_0: \mu \geq \mu_0$ | $H_0: \mu \leq \mu_0$ |
| $H_a: \mu < \mu_0$ | $H_a: \mu > \mu_0$ |

Let us consider an example involving a lower tail test.

The Federal Trade Commission (FTC) periodically conducts statistical studies designed to test the claims that manufacturers make about their products. For example, the label on a large can of Hilltop Coffee states that the can contains 3 pounds of coffee. The FTC knows that Hilltop's production process cannot place exactly 3 pounds of coffee in each can, even if the mean filling weight for the population of all cans filled is 3 pounds per can. However, as long as the population mean filling weight is at least 3 pounds per can, the rights of consumers will be protected. Thus, the FTC interprets the label information on a large can of coffee as a claim by Hilltop that the population mean filling weight is at least 3 pounds per can. We will show how the FTC can check Hilltop's claim by conducting a lower tail hypothesis test.

The first step is to develop the null and alternative hypotheses for the test. If the population mean filling weight is at least 3 pounds per can, Hilltop's claim is correct. This establishes the null hypothesis for the test. However, if the population mean weight is less than 3 pounds per can, Hilltop's claim is incorrect. This establishes the alternative hypothesis. With $\mu$ denoting the population mean filling weight, the null and alternative hypotheses are as follows:

$$H_0: \mu \geq 3$$
$$H_a: \mu < 3$$

Note that the hypothesized value of the population mean is $\mu_0 = 3$.

If the sample data indicate that $H_0$ cannot be rejected, the statistical evidence does not support the conclusion that a label violation has occurred. Hence, no action should be taken against Hilltop. However, if the sample data indicate that $H_0$ can be rejected, we will conclude that the alternative hypothesis, $H_a: \mu < 3$, is true. In this case a conclusion of underfilling and a charge of a label violation against Hilltop would be justified.

Suppose a sample of 36 cans of coffee is selected and the sample mean $\bar{x}$ is computed as an estimate of the population mean $\mu$. If the value of the sample mean $\bar{x}$ is less than 3 pounds, the sample results will cast doubt on the null hypothesis. What we want to know is how much less than 3 pounds must $\bar{x}$ be before we would be willing to declare the difference significant and risk making a Type I error by falsely accusing Hilltop of a label violation. A key factor in addressing this issue is the value the decision maker selects for the level of significance.

As noted in the preceding section, the level of significance, denoted by $\alpha$, is the probability of making a Type I error by rejecting $H_0$ when the null hypothesis is true as an equality. The decision maker must specify the level of significance. If the cost of making a Type I error is high, a small value should be chosen for the level of significance. If the cost is not high, a larger value is more appropriate. In the Hilltop Coffee study, the director of the FTC's testing program made the following statement: "If the company is meeting its weight specifications at $\mu = 3$, I do not want to take action against them. But, I am willing to risk a 1% chance of making such an error." From the director's statement, we set the level of significance for the hypothesis test at $\alpha = .01$. Thus, we must design the hypothesis test so that the probability of making a Type I error when $\mu = 3$ is .01.

For the Hilltop Coffee study, by developing the null and alternative hypotheses and specifying the level of significance for the test, we carry out the first two steps required in conducting every hypothesis test. We are now ready to perform the third step of hypothesis testing: collect the sample data and compute the value of what is called a test statistic.

**Test statistic**    For the Hilltop Coffee study, previous FTC tests show that the population standard deviation can be assumed known with a value of $\sigma = .18$. In addition, these tests also show that the population of filling weights can be assumed to have a normal

**FIGURE 9.1** SAMPLING DISTRIBUTION OF $\bar{x}$ FOR THE HILLTOP COFFEE STUDY WHEN THE NULL HYPOTHESIS IS TRUE AS AN EQUALITY ($\mu = 3$)

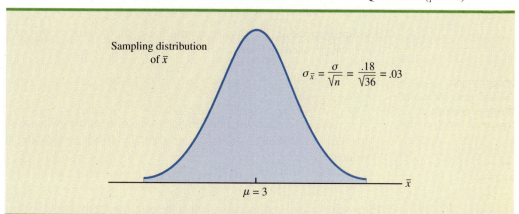

Sampling distribution of $\bar{x}$

$$\sigma_{\bar{x}} = \frac{\sigma}{\sqrt{n}} = \frac{.18}{\sqrt{36}} = .03$$

$\mu = 3$

distribution. From the study of sampling distributions in Chapter 7 we know that if the population from which we are sampling is normally distributed, the sampling distribution of $\bar{x}$ will also be normally distributed. Thus, for the Hilltop Coffee study, the sampling distribution of $\bar{x}$ is normally distributed. With a known value of $\sigma = .18$ and a sample size of $n = 36$, Figure 9.1 shows the sampling distribution of $\bar{x}$ when the null hypothesis is true as an equality, that is, when $\mu = \mu_0 = 3$.[2] Note that the standard error of $\bar{x}$ is given by $\sigma_{\bar{x}} = \sigma/\sqrt{n} = .18/\sqrt{36} = .03$.

*The standard error of $\bar{x}$ is the standard deviation of the sampling distribution of $\bar{x}$.*

Because the sampling distribution of $\bar{x}$ is normally distributed, the sampling distribution of

$$z = \frac{\bar{x} - \mu_0}{\sigma_{\bar{x}}} = \frac{\bar{x} - 3}{.03}$$

is a standard normal distribution. A value of $z = -1$ means that the value of $\bar{x}$ is one standard error below the hypothesized value of the mean, a value of $z = -2$ means that the value of $\bar{x}$ is two standard errors below the hypothesized value of the mean, and so on. We can use the standard normal probability table to find the lower tail probability corresponding to any $z$ value. For instance, the lower tail area at $z = -3.00$ is .0013. Hence, the probability of obtaining a value of $z$ that is three or more standard errors below the mean is .0013. As a result, the probability of obtaining a value of $\bar{x}$ that is 3 or more standard errors below the hypothesized population mean $\mu_0 = 3$ is also .0013. Such a result is unlikely if the null hypothesis is true.

For hypothesis tests about a population mean in the $\sigma$ known case, we use the standard normal random variable $z$ as a **test statistic** to determine whether $\bar{x}$ deviates from the hypothesized value of $\mu$ enough to justify rejecting the null hypothesis. With $\sigma_{\bar{x}} = \sigma/\sqrt{n}$, the test statistic is as follows.

TEST STATISTIC FOR HYPOTHESIS TESTS ABOUT A POPULATION MEAN: $\sigma$ KNOWN

$$z = \frac{\bar{x} - \mu_0}{\sigma/\sqrt{n}} \tag{9.1}$$

---

[2]In constructing sampling distributions for hypothesis tests, it is assumed that $H_0$ is satisfied as an equality.

The key question for a lower tail test is, How small must the test statistic $z$ be before we choose to reject the null hypothesis? Two approaches can be used to answer this question: the *p*-value approach and the critical value approach.

***p*-value approach**   The *p*-value approach uses the value of the test statistic $z$ to compute a probability called a ***p*-value**.

> *p*-VALUE
>
> A *p*-value is a probability that provides a measure of the evidence against the null hypothesis provided by the sample. Smaller *p*-values indicate more evidence against $H_0$.

The *p*-value is used to determine whether the null hypothesis should be rejected.

Let us see how the *p*-value is computed and used. The value of the test statistic is used to compute the *p*-value. The method used depends on whether the test is a lower tail, an upper tail, or a two-tailed test. For a lower tail test, the *p*-value is the probability of obtaining a value for the test statistic as small as or smaller than that provided by the sample. Thus, to compute the *p*-value for the lower tail test in the $\sigma$ known case, we must find, using the standard normal distribution, the probability that $z$ is less than or equal to the value of the test statistic. After computing the *p*-value, we must then decide whether it is small enough to reject the null hypothesis; as we will show, this decision involves comparing the *p*-value to the level of significance.

**Coffee**

Let us now compute the *p*-value for the Hilltop Coffee lower tail test. Suppose the sample of 36 Hilltop coffee cans provides a sample mean of $\bar{x} = 2.92$ pounds. Is $\bar{x} = 2.92$ small enough to cause us to reject $H_0$? Because this is a lower tail test, the *p*-value is the area under the standard normal curve for values of $z \leq$ the value of the test statistic. Using $\bar{x} = 2.92$, $\sigma = .18$, and $n = 36$, we compute the value of the test statistic $z$.

$$z = \frac{\bar{x} - \mu_0}{\sigma/\sqrt{n}} = \frac{2.92 - 3}{.18/\sqrt{36}} = -2.67$$

Thus, the *p*-value is the probability that $z$ is less than or equal to $-2.67$ (the lower tail area corresponding to the value of the test statistic).

Using the standard normal probability table, we find that the lower tail area at $z = -2.67$ is .0038. Figure 9.2 shows that $\bar{x} = 2.92$ corresponds to $z = -2.67$ and a *p*-value $= .0038$. This *p*-value indicates a small probability of obtaining a sample mean of $\bar{x} = 2.92$ (and a test statistic of $-2.67$) or smaller when sampling from a population with $\mu = 3$. This *p*-value does not provide much support for the null hypothesis, but is it small enough to cause us to reject $H_0$? The answer depends upon the level of significance for the test.

As noted previously, the director of the FTC's testing program selected a value of .01 for the level of significance. The selection of $\alpha = .01$ means that the director is willing to tolerate a probability of .01 of rejecting the null hypothesis when it is true as an equality ($\mu_0 = 3$). The sample of 36 coffee cans in the Hilltop Coffee study resulted in a *p*-value $= .0038$, which means that the probability of obtaining a value of $\bar{x} = 2.92$ or less when the null hypothesis is true as an equality is .0038. Because .0038 is less than or equal to $\alpha = .01$, we reject $H_0$. Therefore, we find sufficient statistical evidence to reject the null hypothesis at the .01 level of significance.

We can now state the general rule for determining whether the null hypothesis can be rejected when using the *p*-value approach. For a level of significance $\alpha$, the rejection rule

**FIGURE 9.2**  *p*-VALUE FOR THE HILLTOP COFFEE STUDY WHEN $\bar{x} = 2.92$ AND $z = -2.67$

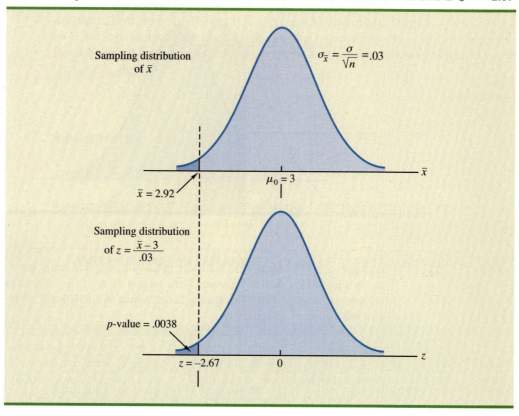

using the *p*-value approach is as follows:

---

REJECTION RULE USING *p*-VALUE

Reject $H_0$ if *p*-value $\leq \alpha$

---

In the Hilltop Coffee test, the *p*-value of .0038 resulted in the rejection of the null hypothesis. Although the basis for making the rejection decision involves a comparison of the *p*-value to the level of significance specified by the FTC director, the observed *p*-value of .0038 means that we would reject $H_0$ for any value of $\alpha \geq .0038$. For this reason, the *p*-value is also called the *observed level of significance*.

Different decision makers may express different opinions concerning the cost of making a Type I error and may choose a different level of significance. By providing the *p*-value as part of the hypothesis testing results, another decision maker can compare the reported *p*-value to his or her own level of significance and possibly make a different decision with respect to rejecting $H_0$.

**Critical value approach**  The critical value approach requires that we first determine a value for the test statistic called the **critical value**. For a lower tail test, the critical value serves as a benchmark for determining whether the value of the test statistic is small enough to reject the null hypothesis. It is the value of the test statistic that corresponds to an area of

**FIGURE 9.3**    CRITICAL VALUE = −2.33 FOR THE HILLTOP COFFEE HYPOTHESIS TEST

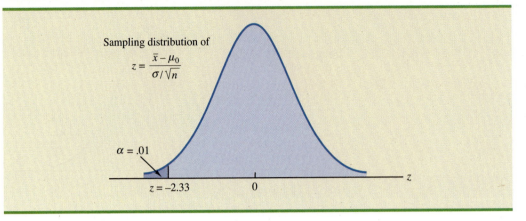

Sampling distribution of

$$z = \frac{\bar{x} - \mu_0}{\sigma / \sqrt{n}}$$

$\alpha = .01$

$z = -2.33$    $0$    $z$

$\alpha$ (the level of significance) in the lower tail of the sampling distribution of the test statistic. In other words, the critical value is the largest value of the test statistic that will result in the rejection of the null hypothesis. Let us return to the Hilltop Coffee example and see how this approach works.

In the $\sigma$ known case, the sampling distribution for the test statistic $z$ is a standard normal distribution. Therefore, the critical value is the value of the test statistic that corresponds to an area of $\alpha = .01$ in the lower tail of a standard normal distribution. Using the standard normal probability table, we find that $z = -2.33$ provides an area of .01 in the lower tail (see Figure 9.3). Thus, if the sample results in a value of the test statistic that is less than or equal to −2.33, the corresponding $p$-value will be less than or equal to .01; in this case, we should reject the null hypothesis. Hence, for the Hilltop Coffee study the critical value rejection rule for a level of significance of .01 is

$$\text{Reject } H_0 \text{ if } z \leq -2.33$$

In the Hilltop Coffee example, $\bar{x} = 2.92$ and the test statistic is $z = -2.67$. Because $z = -2.67 < -2.33$, we can reject $H_0$ and conclude that Hilltop Coffee is underfilling cans.

We can generalize the rejection rule for the critical value approach to handle any level of significance. The rejection rule for a lower tail test follows.

REJECTION RULE FOR A LOWER TAIL TEST: CRITICAL VALUE APPROACH

$$\text{Reject } H_0 \text{ if } z \leq -z_\alpha$$

where $-z_\alpha$ is the critical value; that is, the $z$ value that provides an area of $\alpha$ in the lower tail of the standard normal distribution.

**Summary**    The $p$-value approach to hypothesis testing and the critical value approach will always lead to the same rejection decision; that is, whenever the $p$-value is less than or equal to $\alpha$, the value of the test statistic will be less than or equal to the critical value. The advantage of the $p$-value approach is that the $p$-value tells us *how* significant the results are (the observed level of significance). If we use the critical value approach, we only know that the results are significant at the stated level of significance.

At the beginning of this section, we said that one-tailed tests about a population mean take one of the following two forms:

| Lower Tail Test | Upper Tail Test |
|---|---|
| $H_0\text{:}\ \mu \geq \mu_0$ | $H_0\text{:}\ \mu \leq \mu_0$ |
| $H_a\text{:}\ \mu < \mu_0$ | $H_a\text{:}\ \mu > \mu_0$ |

We used the Hilltop Coffee study to illustrate how to conduct a lower tail test. We can use the same general approach to conduct an upper tail test. The test statistic $z$ is still computed using equation (9.1). But, for an upper tail test, the $p$-value is the probability of obtaining a value for the test statistic as large as or larger than that provided by the sample. Thus, to compute the $p$-value for the upper tail test in the $\sigma$ known case, we must find, using the standard normal distribution, the probability that $z$ is greater than or equal to the value of the test statistic. Using the critical value approach causes us to reject the null hypothesis if the value of the test statistic is greater than or equal to the critical value $z_\alpha$; in other words, we reject $H_0$ if $z \geq z_\alpha$.

Let us summarize the steps involved in computing $p$-values for one-tailed hypothesis tests.

---

**COMPUTATION OF $p$-VALUES FOR ONE-TAILED TESTS**

1. Compute the value of the test statistic using equation (9.1).
2. **Lower tail test:** Using the standard normal distribution, compute the probability that $z$ is less than or equal to the value of the test statistic (area in the lower tail).
3. **Upper tail test:** Using the standard normal distribution, compute the probability that $z$ is greater than or equal to the value of the test statistic (area in the upper tail).

---

## Two-Tailed Test

In hypothesis testing, the general form for a **two-tailed test** about a population mean is as follows:

$$H_0\text{:}\ \mu = \mu_0$$
$$H_a\text{:}\ \mu \neq \mu_0$$

In this subsection we show how to conduct a two-tailed test about a population mean for the $\sigma$ known case. As an illustration, we consider the hypothesis testing situation facing MaxFlight, Inc.

The U.S. Golf Association (USGA) establishes rules that manufacturers of golf equipment must meet if their products are to be acceptable for use in USGA events. MaxFlight uses a high-technology manufacturing process to produce golf balls with a mean driving distance of 295 yards. Sometimes, however, the process gets out of adjustment and produces golf balls with a mean driving distance different from 295 yards. When the mean distance falls below 295 yards, the company worries about losing sales because the golf balls do not provide as much distance as advertised. When the mean distance passes 295 yards, MaxFlight's golf balls may be rejected by the USGA for exceeding the overall distance standard concerning carry and roll.

MaxFlight's quality control program involves taking periodic samples of 50 golf balls to monitor the manufacturing process. For each sample, a hypothesis test is conducted to determine whether the process has fallen out of adjustment. Let us develop the null and alternative hypotheses. We begin by assuming that the process is functioning correctly; that is, the golf balls being produced have a mean distance of 295 yards. This assumption establishes the null hypothesis. The alternative hypothesis is that the mean distance is not equal to 295 yards. With a hypothesized value of $\mu_0 = 295$, the null and alternative hypotheses for the MaxFlight hypothesis test are as follows:

$$H_0: \mu = 295$$
$$H_a: \mu \neq 295$$

If the sample mean $\bar{x}$ is significantly less than 295 yards or significantly greater than 295 yards, we will reject $H_0$. In this case, corrective action will be taken to adjust the manufacturing process. On the other hand, if $\bar{x}$ does not deviate from the hypothesized mean $\mu_0 = 295$ by a significant amount, $H_0$ will not be rejected and no action will be taken to adjust the manufacturing process.

The quality control team selected $\alpha = .05$ as the level of significance for the test. Data from previous tests conducted when the process was known to be in adjustment show that the population standard deviation can be assumed known with a value of $\sigma = 12$. Thus, with a sample size of $n = 50$, the standard error of $\bar{x}$ is

$$\sigma_{\bar{x}} = \frac{\sigma}{\sqrt{n}} = \frac{12}{\sqrt{50}} = 1.7$$

Because the sample size is large, the central limit theorem (see Chapter 7) allows us to conclude that the sampling distribution of $\bar{x}$ can be approximated by a normal distribution. Figure 9.4 shows the sampling distribution of $\bar{x}$ for the MaxFlight hypothesis test with a hypothesized population mean of $\mu_0 = 295$.

Suppose that a sample of 50 golf balls is selected and that the sample mean is $\bar{x} = 297.6$ yards. This sample mean provides support for the conclusion that the population mean is larger than 295 yards. Is this value of $\bar{x}$ enough larger than 295 to cause us to reject $H_0$ at the .05 level of significance? In the previous section we described two approaches that can be used to answer this question: the $p$-value approach and the critical value approach.

**WEB file**

**GolfTest**

**$p$-value approach** Recall that the $p$-value is a probability used to determine whether the null hypothesis should be rejected. For a two-tailed test, values of the test statistic in *either* tail provide evidence against the null hypothesis. For a two-tailed test, the $p$-value is the probability of obtaining a value for the test statistic *as unlikely as or more unlikely than* that provided by the sample. Let us see how the $p$-value is computed for the MaxFlight hypothesis test.

**FIGURE 9.4    SAMPLING DISTRIBUTION OF $\bar{x}$ FOR THE MAXFLIGHT HYPOTHESIS TEST**

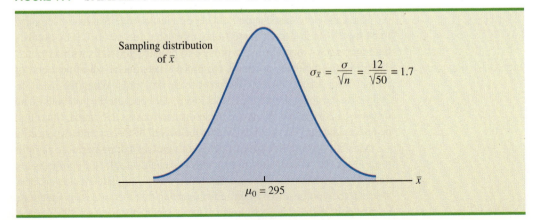

Sampling distribution of $\bar{x}$

$$\sigma_{\bar{x}} = \frac{\sigma}{\sqrt{n}} = \frac{12}{\sqrt{50}} = 1.7$$

$\mu_0 = 295$

**FIGURE 9.5**   *p*-VALUE FOR THE MAXFLIGHT HYPOTHESIS TEST

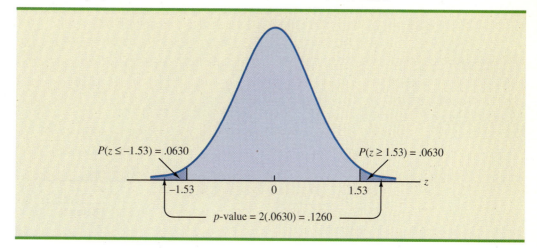

First we compute the value of the test statistic. For the $\sigma$ known case, the test statistic $z$ is a standard normal random variable. Using equation (9.1) with $\bar{x} = 297.6$, the value of the test statistic is

$$z = \frac{\bar{x} - \mu_0}{\sigma/\sqrt{n}} = \frac{297.6 - 295}{12/\sqrt{50}} = 1.53$$

Now to compute the *p*-value we must find the probability of obtaining a value for the test statistic *at least as unlikely as* $z = 1.53$. Clearly values of $z \geq 1.53$ are *at least as unlikely*. But, because this is a two-tailed test, values of $z \leq -1.53$ are also *at least as unlikely as* the value of the test statistic provided by the sample. In Figure 9.5, we see that the two-tailed *p*-value in this case is given by $P(z \leq -1.53) + P(z \geq 1.53)$. Because the normal curve is symmetric, we can compute this probability by finding $P(z \geq 1.53)$ and doubling it. The table for the standard normal distribution shows that $P(z < 1.53)$ is .9370. Thus, $P(z \geq 1.53)$ is $1.0000 - .9370 = .0630$. Doubling this, we find that the *p*-value for the MaxFlight two-tailed hypothesis test is *p*-value $= 2(.0630) = .1260$.

Next we compare the *p*-value to the level of significance to see whether the null hypothesis should be rejected. With a level of significance of $\alpha = .05$, we do not reject $H_0$ because the *p*-value $= .1260 > .05$. Because the null hypothesis is not rejected, no action will be taken to adjust the MaxFlight manufacturing process.

Let us summarize the steps involved in computing *p*-values for two-tailed hypothesis tests.

---

**COMPUTATION OF *p*-VALUES FOR TWO-TAILED TESTS**

1. Compute the value of the test statistic using equation (9.1).
2. If the value of the test statistic is in the upper tail, compute the probability that $z$ is greater than or equal to the value of the test statistic (the upper tail area). If the value of the test statistic is in the lower tail, compute the probability that $z$ is less than or equal to the value of the test statistic (the lower tail area).
3. Double the probability (or tail area) from step 2 to obtain the *p*-value.

---

**Critical value approach**   Before leaving this section, let us see how the test statistic $z$ can be compared to a critical value to make the hypothesis testing decision for a two-tailed test.

**FIGURE 9.6** CRITICAL VALUES FOR THE MAXFLIGHT HYPOTHESIS TEST

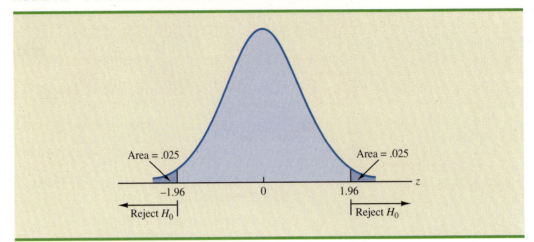

Figure 9.6 shows that the critical values for the test will occur in both the lower and upper tails of the standard normal distribution. With a level of significance of $\alpha = .05$, the area in each tail corresponding to the critical values is $\alpha/2 = .05/2 = .025$. Using the standard normal probability table, we find the critical values for the test statistic are $-z_{.025} = -1.96$ and $z_{.025} = 1.96$. Thus, using the critical value approach, the two-tailed rejection rule is

$$\text{Reject } H_0 \text{ if } z \leq -1.96 \text{ or if } z \geq 1.96 \ .$$

Because the value of the test statistic for the MaxFlight study is $z = 1.53$, the statistical evidence will not permit us to reject the null hypothesis at the .05 level of significance.

## Using Excel

Excel can be used to conduct one-tailed and two-tailed hypothesis tests about a population mean for the $\sigma$ known case using the $p$-value approach. Recall that the method used to compute a $p$-value depends upon whether the test is lower tail, upper tail, or two-tailed. Therefore, in the Excel procedure we describe we will use the sample results to compute three $p$-values: $p$-value (Lower Tail), $p$-value (Upper Tail), and $p$-value (Two Tail). The user can then choose $\alpha$ and draw a conclusion using whichever $p$-value is appropriate for the type of hypothesis test being conducted. We will illustrate using the MaxFlight two-tailed hypothesis test. Refer to Figure 9.7 as we describe the tasks involved. The formula worksheet is in the background; the value worksheet is in the foreground.

**Enter Data:**  A label and the distance data for the sample of 50 golf balls are entered into cells A1:A51.

**Enter Functions and Formulas:**  The descriptive statistics needed are provided in cells D4 and D5. Excel's COUNT and AVERAGE functions compute the sample size and the sample mean, respectively. The value of the known population standard deviation (12) is entered into cell D7, and the hypothesized value of the population mean (295) is entered into cell D8.

The standard error is obtained in cell D10 by entering the formula =D7/SQRT(D4). The formula =(D5-D8)/D10 entered into cell D11 computes the test statistic $z(1.5321)$. To compute the $p$-value for a lower tail test, we enter the formula =NORM.S.DIST(D11,TRUE) into cell D13. The $p$-value for an upper tail test is then computed in cell D14 as 1 minus the $p$-value for the lower tail test. Finally, the $p$-value for a two-tailed test is computed in cell D15

**FIGURE 9.7**   EXCEL WORKSHEET: HYPOTHESIS TEST FOR THE σ KNOWN CASE

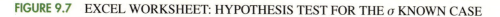

| | | Hypothesis Test about a Population Mean: σ Known Case | | |
|---|---|---|---|---|
| | | | | |
| | | Sample Size | =COUNT(A2:A51) | |
| | | Sample Mean | =AVERAGE(A2:A51) | |
| | | | | |
| | | Population Standard Deviation | 12 | |
| | | Hypothesized Value | 295 | |
| | | | | |
| | | Standard Error | =D7/SQRT(D4) | |
| | | Test Statistic z | =(D5-D8)/D10 | |
| | | | | |
| | | *p*-value (Lower Tail) | =NORM.S.DIST(D11,TRUE) | |
| | | *p*-value (Upper Tail) | =1-D13 | |
| | | *p*-value (Two Tail) | =2*(MIN(D13,D14)) | |

A column "Yards": 303, 282, 289, 298, 283, 317, 297, 308, 317, 293, 284, 290, 304, 290, 311, 301, 292

**WEB** file

**GolfTest**

Note: Rows 17–49 are hidden.

| | | Hypothesis Test about a Population Mean: σ Known Case | | |
|---|---|---|---|---|
| | | | | |
| | | Sample Size | 50 | |
| | | Sample Mean | 297.6 | |
| | | | | |
| | | Population Standard Deviation | 12 | |
| | | Hypothesized Value | 295 | |
| | | | | |
| | | Standard Error | 1.6971 | |
| | | Test Statistic z | 1.5321 | |
| | | | | |
| | | *p*-value (Lower Tail) | 0.9372 | |
| | | *p*-value (Upper Tail) | 0.0628 | |
| | | *p*-value (Two Tail) | 0.1255 | |

A column "Yards": 303, 282, 289, 298, 283, 317, 297, 308, 317, 293, 284, 290, 304, 290, 311, 301, 292

as two times the minimum of the two one-tailed *p*-values. The value worksheet shows that *p*-value (Lower Tail) = 0.9372, *p*-value (Upper Tail) = 0.0628, and *p*-value (Two Tail) = 0.1255.

The development of the worksheet is now complete. For the two-tailed MaxFlight problem we cannot reject $H_0$: $\mu = 295$ using $\alpha = .05$ because the *p*-value (Two Tail) = 0.1255 is greater than $\alpha$. Thus, the quality control manager has no reason to doubt that the manufacturing process is producing golf balls with a population mean distance of 295 yards.

**A template for other problems**  The worksheet in Figure 9.7 can be used as a template for conducting any one-tailed and two-tailed hypothesis tests for the $\sigma$ known case. Just enter the appropriate data in column A, adjust the ranges for the formulas in cells D4 and D5, enter the population standard deviation in cell D7, and enter the hypothesized value in cell D8. The standard error, the test statistic, and the three $p$-values will then appear. Depending on the form of the hypothesis test (lower tail, upper tail, or two-tailed), we can then choose the appropriate $p$-value to make the rejection decision.

We can further simplify the use of Figure 9.7 as a template for other problems by eliminating the need to enter new data ranges in cells D4 and D5. To do so we rewrite the cell formulas as follows:

$$\text{Cell D4:} \quad =\text{COUNT(A:A)}$$
$$\text{Cell D5:} \quad =\text{AVERAGE(A:A)}$$

*The GolfTest data set includes a worksheet entitled Template that uses the A:A method for entering the data ranges.*

With the A:A method of specifying data ranges, Excel's COUNT function will count the number of numerical values in column A and Excel's AVERAGE function will compute the average of the numerical values in column A. Thus, to solve a new problem it is only necessary to enter the new data in column A, enter the value of the known population standard deviation in cell D7, and enter the hypothesized value of the population mean in cell D8.

The worksheet can also be used as a template for text exercises in which $n$, $\bar{x}$, and $\sigma$ are given. Just ignore the data in column A and enter the values for $n$, $\bar{x}$, and $\sigma$ into cells D4, D5, and D7, respectively. Then enter the appropriate hypothesized value for the population mean into cell D8. The $p$-values corresponding to lower tail, upper tail, and two-tailed hypothesis tests will then appear in cells D13:D15.

## Summary and Practical Advice

We presented examples of a lower tail test and a two-tailed test about a population mean. Based upon these examples, we can now summarize the hypothesis testing procedures about a population mean for the $\sigma$ known case as shown in Table 9.2. Note that $\mu_0$ is the hypothesized value of the population mean.

The hypothesis testing steps followed in the two examples presented in this section are common to every hypothesis test.

**TABLE 9.2**   SUMMARY OF HYPOTHESIS TESTS ABOUT A POPULATION MEAN: $\sigma$ KNOWN CASE

|  | **Lower Tail Test** | **Upper Tail Test** | **Two-Tailed Test** |
|---|---|---|---|
| **Hypotheses** | $H_0: \mu \geq \mu_0$ <br> $H_a: \mu < \mu_0$ | $H_0: \mu \leq \mu_0$ <br> $H_a: \mu > \mu_0$ | $H_0: \mu = \mu_0$ <br> $H_a: \mu \neq \mu_0$ |
| **Test Statistic** | $z = \dfrac{\bar{x} - \mu_0}{\sigma/\sqrt{n}}$ | $z = \dfrac{\bar{x} - \mu_0}{\sigma/\sqrt{n}}$ | $z = \dfrac{\bar{x} - \mu_0}{\sigma/\sqrt{n}}$ |
| **Rejection Rule:** <br> **$p$-Value Approach** | Reject $H_0$ if <br> $p$-value $\leq \alpha$ | Reject $H_0$ if <br> $p$-value $\leq \alpha$ | Reject $H_0$ if <br> $p$-value $\leq \alpha$ |
| **Rejection Rule:** <br> **Critical Value** <br> **Approach** | Reject $H_0$ if <br> $z \leq -z_\alpha$ | Reject $H_0$ if <br> $z \geq z_\alpha$ | Reject $H_0$ if <br> $z \leq -z_{\alpha/2}$ <br> or if $z \geq z_{\alpha/2}$ |

STEPS OF HYPOTHESIS TESTING

**Step 1.** Develop the null and alternative hypotheses.
**Step 2.** Specify the level of significance.
**Step 3.** Collect the sample data and compute the value of the test statistic.

*p-Value Approach*

**Step 4.** Use the value of the test statistic to compute the *p*-value.
**Step 5.** Reject $H_0$ if the *p*-value $\leq \alpha$.

*Critical Value Approach*

**Step 4.** Use the level of significance to determine the critical value and the rejection rule.
**Step 5.** Use the value of the test statistic and the rejection rule to determine whether to reject $H_0$.

Practical advice about the sample size for hypothesis tests is similar to the advice we provided about the sample size for interval estimation in Chapter 8. In most applications, a sample size of $n \geq 30$ is adequate when using the hypothesis testing procedure described in this section. In cases where the sample size is less than 30, the distribution of the population from which we are sampling becomes an important consideration. If the population is normally distributed, the hypothesis testing procedure that we described is exact and can be used for any sample size. If the population is not normally distributed but is at least roughly symmetric, sample sizes as small as 15 can be expected to provide acceptable results.

## Relationship Between Interval Estimation and Hypothesis Testing

In Chapter 8 we showed how to develop a confidence interval estimate of a population mean. For the $\sigma$ known case, the $(1 - \alpha)\%$ confidence interval estimate of a population mean is given by

$$\bar{x} \pm z_{\alpha/2} \frac{\sigma}{\sqrt{n}}$$

In this chapter we showed that a two-tailed hypothesis test about a population mean takes the following form:

$$H_0: \mu = \mu_0$$
$$H_a: \mu \neq \mu_0$$

where $\mu_0$ is the hypothesized value for the population mean.

Suppose that we follow the procedure described in Chapter 8 for constructing a $100(1 - \alpha)\%$ confidence interval for the population mean. We know that $100(1 - \alpha)\%$ of the confidence intervals generated will contain the population mean and $100\alpha\%$ of the confidence intervals generated will not contain the population mean. Thus, if we reject $H_0$ whenever the confidence interval does not contain $\mu_0$, we will be rejecting the null hypothesis when it is true ($\mu = \mu_0$) with probability $\alpha$. Recall that the level of significance is the probability of rejecting the null hypothesis when it is true. So constructing a $100(1 - \alpha)\%$ confidence interval and rejecting $H_0$ whenever the interval does not contain $\mu_0$ is equivalent to conducting a two-tailed hypothesis test with $\alpha$ as the level of significance. The procedure for using a confidence interval to conduct a two-tailed hypothesis test can now be summarized.

---

**A CONFIDENCE INTERVAL APPROACH TO TESTING A HYPOTHESIS OF THE FORM**

$$H_0: \mu = \mu_0$$
$$H_a: \mu \neq \mu_0$$

1. Select a simple random sample from the population and use the value of the sample mean $\bar{x}$ to develop the confidence interval for the population mean $\mu$.

$$\bar{x} \pm z_{\alpha/2} \frac{\sigma}{\sqrt{n}}$$

*For a two-tailed hypothesis test, the null hypothesis can be rejected if the confidence interval does not include $\mu_0$.*

2. If the confidence interval contains the hypothesized value $\mu_0$, do not reject $H_0$. Otherwise, reject[3] $H_0$.

---

Let us illustrate by conducting the MaxFlight hypothesis test using the confidence interval approach. The MaxFlight hypothesis test takes the following form:

$$H_0: \mu = 295$$
$$H_a: \mu \neq 295$$

To test these hypotheses with a level of significance of $\alpha = .05$, we sampled 50 golf balls and found a sample mean distance of $\bar{x} = 297.6$ yards. Recall that the population standard deviation is $\sigma = 12$. Using these results with $z_{.025} = 1.96$, we find that the 95% confidence interval estimate of the population mean is

$$\bar{x} \pm z_{.025} \frac{\sigma}{\sqrt{n}}$$

$$297.6 \pm 1.96 \frac{12}{\sqrt{50}}$$

$$297.6 \pm 3.3$$

or

$$294.3 \text{ to } 300.9$$

This finding enables the quality control manager to conclude with 95% confidence that the mean distance for the population of golf balls is between 294.3 and 300.9 yards. Because the hypothesized value for the population mean, $\mu_0 = 295$, is in this interval, the hypothesis testing conclusion is that the null hypothesis, $H_0: \mu = 295$, cannot be rejected.

---

[3]To be consistent with the rule for rejecting $H_0$ when the $p$-value $\leq \alpha$, we would also reject $H_0$ using the confidence interval approach if $\mu_0$ happens to be equal to one of the endpoints of the $100(1 - \alpha)\%$ confidence interval.

Note that this discussion and example pertain to two-tailed hypothesis tests about a population mean. However, the same confidence interval and two-tailed hypothesis testing relationship exists for other population parameters. The relationship can also be extended to one-tailed tests about population parameters. Doing so, however, requires the development of one-sided confidence intervals, which are rarely used in practice.

## NOTES AND COMMENTS

We have shown how to use $p$-values. The smaller the $p$-value the greater the evidence against $H_0$ and the more the evidence in favor of $H_a$. Here are some guidelines statisticians suggest for interpreting small $p$-values.

- Less than .01—Overwhelming evidence to conclude that $H_a$ is true

- Between .01 and .05—Strong evidence to conclude that $H_a$ is true
- Between .05 and .10—Weak evidence to conclude that $H_a$ is true
- Greater than .10—Insufficient evidence to conclude that $H_a$ is true

## Exercises

*Note to Student:* Some of the exercises that follow ask you to use the $p$-value approach and others ask you to use the critical value approach. Both methods will provide the same hypothesis testing conclusion. We provide exercises with both methods to give you practice using both. In later sections and in following chapters, we will generally emphasize the $p$-value approach as the preferred method, but you may select either based on personal preference.

## Methods

9. Consider the following hypothesis test:

$$H_0: \mu \geq 20$$
$$H_a: \mu < 20$$

A sample of 50 provided a sample mean of 19.4. The population standard deviation is 2.
   a.   Compute the value of the test statistic.
   b.   What is the $p$-value?
   c.   Using $\alpha = .05$, what is your conclusion?
   d.   What is the rejection rule using the critical value? What is your conclusion?

10. Consider the following hypothesis test:

$$H_0: \mu \leq 25$$
$$H_a: \mu > 25$$

A sample of 40 provided a sample mean of 26.4. The population standard deviation is 6.
   a.   Compute the value of the test statistic.
   b.   What is the $p$-value?
   c.   At $\alpha = .01$, what is your conclusion?
   d.   What is the rejection rule using the critical value? What is your conclusion?

11. Consider the following hypothesis test:

$$H_0: \mu = 15$$
$$H_a: \mu \neq 15$$

A sample of 50 provided a sample mean of 14.15. The population standard deviation is 3.
a. Compute the value of the test statistic.
b. What is the $p$-value?
c. At $\alpha = .05$, what is your conclusion?
d. What is the rejection rule using the critical value? What is your conclusion?

12. Consider the following hypothesis test:

$$H_0: \mu \geq 80$$
$$H_a: \mu < 80$$

A sample of 100 is used and the population standard deviation is 12. Compute the $p$-value and state your conclusion for each of the following sample results. Use $\alpha = .01$.
a. $\bar{x} = 78.5$
b. $\bar{x} = 77$
c. $\bar{x} = 75.5$
d. $\bar{x} = 81$

13. Consider the following hypothesis test:

$$H_0: \mu \leq 50$$
$$H_a: \mu > 50$$

A sample of 60 is used and the population standard deviation is 8. Use the critical value approach to state your conclusion for each of the following sample results. Use $\alpha = .05$.
a. $\bar{x} = 52.5$
b. $\bar{x} = 51$
c. $\bar{x} = 51.8$

14. Consider the following hypothesis test:

$$H_0: \mu = 22$$
$$H_a: \mu \neq 22$$

A sample of 75 is used and the population standard deviation is 10. Compute the $p$-value and state your conclusion for each of the following sample results. Use $\alpha = .01$.
a. $\bar{x} = 23$
b. $\bar{x} = 25.1$
c. $\bar{x} = 20$

## Applications

15. Individuals filing federal income tax returns prior to March 31 received an average refund of $1056. Consider the population of "last-minute" filers who mail their tax return during the last five days of the income tax period (typically April 10 to April 15).
a. A researcher suggests that a reason individuals wait until the last five days is that on average these individuals receive lower refunds than do early filers. Develop appropriate hypotheses such that rejection of $H_0$ will support the researcher's contention.

b.    For a sample of 400 individuals who filed a tax return between April 10 and 15, the sample mean refund was $910. Based on prior experience, a population standard deviation of $\sigma$ = $1600 may be assumed. What is the $p$-value?

c.    At $\alpha$ = .05, what is your conclusion?

d.    Repeat the preceding hypothesis test using the critical value approach.

16.   In a study entitled How Undergraduate Students Use Credit Cards, it was reported that undergraduate students have a mean credit card balance of $3173 (*Sallie Mae*, April 2009). This figure was an all-time high and had increased 44% over the previous five years. Assume that a current study is being conducted to determine if it can be concluded that the mean credit card balance for undergraduate students has continued to increase compared to the April 2009 report. Based on previous studies, use a population standard deviation $\sigma$ = $1000.

a.    State the null and alternative hypotheses.

b.    What is the $p$-value for a sample of 180 undergraduate students with a sample mean credit card balance of $3325?

c.    Using a .05 level of significance, what is your conclusion?

17.   Wall Street securities firms paid out record year-end bonuses of $125,500 per employee for 2005 (*Fortune,* February 6, 2006). Suppose we would like to take a sample of employees at the Jones & Ryan securities firm to see whether the mean year-end bonus is different from the reported mean of $125,500 for the population.

a.    State the null and alternative hypotheses you would use to test whether the year-end bonuses paid by Jones & Ryan were different from the population mean.

b.    Suppose a sample of 40 Jones & Ryan employees showed a sample mean year-end bonus of $118,000. Assume a population standard deviation of $\sigma$ = $30,000 and compute the $p$-value.

c.    With $\alpha$ = .05 as the level of significance, what is your conclusion?

d.    Repeat the preceding hypothesis test using the critical value approach.

18.   The average annual total return for U.S. Diversified Equity mutual funds from 1999 to 2003 was 4.1% (*BusinessWeek,* January 26, 2004). A researcher would like to conduct a hypothesis test to see whether the returns for mid-cap growth funds over the same period are significantly different from the average for U.S. Diversified Equity funds.

a.    Formulate the hypotheses that can be used to determine whether the mean annual return for mid-cap growth funds differ from the mean for U.S. Diversified Equity funds.

b.    A sample of 40 mid-cap growth funds provides a mean return of $\bar{x}$ = 3.4%. Assume the population standard deviation for mid-cap growth funds is known from previous studies to be $\sigma$ = 2%. Use the sample results to compute the test statistic and $p$-value for the hypothesis test.

c.    At $\alpha$ = .05, what is your conclusion?

19.   The Internal Revenue Service (IRS) provides a toll-free help line for taxpayers to call in and get answers to questions as they prepare their tax returns. In recent years, the IRS has been inundated with taxpayer calls and has redesigned its phone service as well as posting answers to frequently asked questions on its website (*The Cincinnati Enquirer,* January 7, 2010). According to a report by a taxpayer advocate, callers using the new system can expect to wait on hold for an unreasonably long time of 12 minutes before being able to talk to an IRS employee. Suppose you select a sample of 50 callers after the new phone service has been implemented; the sample results show a mean waiting time of 10 minutes before an IRS employee comes on line. Based upon data from past years, you decide it is reasonable to assume that the standard deviation of waiting times is 8 minutes. Using your sample results, can you conclude that the actual mean waiting time turned out to be significantly less than the 12-minute claim made by the taxpayer advocate? Use $\alpha$ = .05.

20. For the United States, the mean monthly Internet bill is \$32.79 per household (CNBC, January 18, 2006). A sample of 50 households in a southern state showed a sample mean of \$30.63. Use a population standard deviation of $\sigma = \$5.60$.
    a. Formulate hypotheses for a test to determine whether the sample data support the conclusion that the mean monthly Internet bill in the southern state is less than the national mean of \$32.79.
    b. What is the value of the test statistic?
    c. What is the $p$-value?
    d. At $\alpha = .01$, what is your conclusion?

**Fowle**

21. Fowle Marketing Research, Inc., bases charges to a client on the assumption that telephone surveys can be completed in a mean time of 15 minutes or less. If a longer mean survey time is necessary, a premium rate is charged. A sample of 35 surveys provided the survey times shown in the file named Fowle. Based upon past studies, the population standard deviation is assumed known with $\sigma = 4$ minutes. Is the premium rate justified?
    a. Formulate the null and alternative hypotheses for this application.
    b. Compute the value of the test statistic.
    c. What is the $p$-value?
    d. At $\alpha = .01$, what is your conclusion?

22. CCN and ActMedia provided a television channel targeted to individuals waiting in supermarket checkout lines. The channel showed news, short features, and advertisements. The length of the program was based on the assumption that the population mean time a shopper stands in a supermarket checkout line is 8 minutes. A sample of actual waiting times will be used to test this assumption and determine whether actual mean waiting time differs from this standard.
    a. Formulate the hypotheses for this application.
    b. A sample of 120 shoppers showed a sample mean waiting time of 8.4 minutes. Assume a population standard deviation of $\sigma = 3.2$ minutes. What is the $p$-value?
    c. At $\alpha = .05$, what is your conclusion?
    d. Compute a 95% confidence interval for the population mean. Does it support your conclusion?

## 9.4 Population Mean: $\sigma$ Unknown

In this section we describe how to conduct hypothesis tests about a population mean for the $\sigma$ unknown case. Because the $\sigma$ unknown case corresponds to situations in which an estimate of the population standard deviation cannot be developed prior to sampling, the sample must be used to develop an estimate of both $\mu$ and $\sigma$. Thus, to conduct a hypothesis test about a population mean for the $\sigma$ unknown case, the sample mean $\bar{x}$ is used as an estimate of $\mu$ and the sample standard deviation $s$ is used as an estimate of $\sigma$.

The steps of the hypothesis testing procedure for the $\sigma$ unknown case are the same as those for the $\sigma$ known case described in Section 9.3. But, with $\sigma$ unknown, the computation of the test statistic and $p$-value is a bit different. Recall that for the $\sigma$ known case, the sampling distribution of the test statistic has a standard normal distribution. For the $\sigma$ unknown case, however, the sampling distribution of the test statistic follows the $t$ distribution; it has slightly more variability because the sample is used to develop estimates of both $\mu$ and $\sigma$.

In Section 8.2 we showed that an interval estimate of a population mean for the $\sigma$ unknown case is based on a probability distribution known as the $t$ distribution. Hypothesis tests about a population mean for the $\sigma$ unknown case are also based on the *t* distribution. For the σ unknown case, the test statistic has a *t* distribution with *n* − 1 degrees of freedom.

> **TEST STATISTIC FOR HYPOTHESIS TESTS ABOUT A POPULATION MEAN: σ UNKNOWN**
>
> $$t = \frac{\bar{x} - \mu_0}{s/\sqrt{n}}$$  (9.2)

In Chapter 8 we said that the *t* distribution is based on an assumption that the population from which we are sampling has a normal distribution. However, research shows that this assumption can be relaxed considerably when the sample size is large enough. We provide some practical advice concerning the population distribution and sample size at the end of the section.

## One-Tailed Test

**AirRating**

Let us consider an example of a one-tailed test about a population mean for the σ unknown case. A business travel magazine wants to classify transatlantic gateway airports according to the mean rating for the population of business travelers. A rating scale with a low score of 0 and a high score of 10 will be used, and airports with a population mean rating greater than 7 will be designated as superior service airports. The magazine staff surveyed a sample of 60 business travelers at each airport to obtain the ratings data. The sample for London's Heathrow Airport provided a sample mean rating of $\bar{x} = 7.25$ and a sample standard deviation of $s = 1.052$. Do the data indicate that Heathrow should be designated as a superior service airport?

We want to develop a hypothesis test for which the decision to reject $H_0$ will lead to the conclusion that the population mean rating for the Heathrow Airport is *greater* than 7. Thus, an upper tail test with $H_a$: $\mu > 7$ is required. The null and alternative hypotheses for this upper tail test are as follows:

$$H_0: \mu \leq 7$$
$$H_a: \mu > 7$$

We will use $\alpha = .05$ as the level of significance for the test.

Using equation (9.2) with $\bar{x} = 7.25, \mu_0 = 7, s = 1.052$, and $n = 60$, the value of the test statistic is

$$t = \frac{\bar{x} - \mu_0}{s/\sqrt{n}} = \frac{7.25 - 7}{1.052/\sqrt{60}} = 1.84$$

The sampling distribution of *t* has $n - 1 = 60 - 1 = 59$ degrees of freedom. Because the test is an upper tail test, the *p*-value is $P(t \geq 1.84)$, that is, the upper tail area corresponding to the value of the test statistic.

The *t* distribution table provided in most textbooks will not contain sufficient detail to determine the exact *p*-value, such as the *p*-value corresponding to $t = 1.84$. For instance, using Table 2 in Appendix B, the *t* distribution with 59 degrees of freedom provides the following information.

| Area in Upper Tail | .20 | .10 | .05 | .025 | .01 | .005 |
|---|---|---|---|---|---|---|
| *t* Value (59 *df*) | .848 | 1.296 | 1.671 | 2.001 | 2.391 | 2.662 |

$t = 1.84$

We see that $t = 1.84$ is between 1.671 and 2.001. Although the table does not provide the exact p-value, the values in the "Area in Upper Tail" row show that the p-value must be less than .05 and greater than .025. With a level of significance of $\alpha = .05$, this placement is all we need to know to make the decision to reject the null hypothesis and conclude that Heathrow should be classified as a superior service airport.

It is cumbersome to use a t table to compute p-values, and only approximate values are obtained. We describe how to compute exact p-values using Excel's T.DIST function in the Using Excel subsection which follows. The exact upper tail p-value for the Heathrow Airport hypothesis test is .0354. With .0354 < .05, we reject the null hypothesis and conclude that Heathrow should be classified as a superior service airport.

## Two-Tailed Test

To illustrate how to conduct a two-tailed test about a population mean for the $\sigma$ unknown case, let us consider the hypothesis testing situation facing Holiday Toys. The company manufactures and distributes its products through more than 1000 retail outlets. In planning production levels for the coming winter season, Holiday must decide how many units of each product to produce prior to knowing the actual demand at the retail level. For this year's most important new toy, Holiday's marketing director is expecting demand to average 40 units per retail outlet. Prior to making the final production decision based upon this estimate, Holiday decided to survey a sample of 25 retailers in order to develop more information about the demand for the new product. Each retailer was provided with information about the features of the new toy along with the cost and the suggested selling price. Then each retailer was asked to specify an anticipated order quantity.

With $\mu$ denoting the population mean order quantity per retail outlet, the sample data will be used to conduct the following two-tailed hypothesis test:

$$H_0: \mu = 40$$
$$H_a: \mu \neq 40$$

If $H_0$ cannot be rejected, Holiday will continue its production planning based on the marketing director's estimate that the population mean order quantity per retail outlet will be $\mu = 40$ units. However, if $H_0$ is rejected, Holiday will immediately reevaluate its production plan for the product. A two-tailed hypothesis test is used because Holiday wants to reevaluate the production plan if the population mean quantity per retail outlet is less than anticipated or greater than anticipated. Because no historical data are available (it's a new product), the population mean $\mu$ and the population standard deviation must both be estimated using $\bar{x}$ and $s$ from the sample data.

The sample of 25 retailers provided a mean of $\bar{x} = 37.4$ and a standard deviation of $s = 11.79$ units. Before going ahead with the use of the t distribution, the analyst constructed a histogram of the sample data in order to check on the form of the population distribution. The histogram of the sample data showed no evidence of skewness or any extreme outliers, so the analyst concluded that the use of the t distribution with $n - 1 = 24$ degrees of freedom was appropriate. Using equation (9.2) with $\bar{x} = 37.4$, $\mu_0 = 40$, $s = 11.79$, and $n = 25$, the value of the test statistic is

$$t = \frac{\bar{x} - \mu_0}{s/\sqrt{n}} = \frac{37.4 - 40}{11.79/\sqrt{25}} = -1.10$$

Because we have a two-tailed test, the p-value is two times the area under the curve of the t distribution for $t \leq -1.10$. Using Table 2 in Appendix B, the t distribution table for 24 degrees of freedom provides the following information.

| Area in Upper Tail | .20 | .10 | .05 | .025 | .01 | .005 |
|---|---|---|---|---|---|---|
| *t*-Value (24 *df*) | .857 | 1.318 | 1.711 | 2.064 | 2.492 | 2.797 |

$t = 1.10$

The *t* distribution table only contains positive *t* values (corresponding to areas in the upper tail). Because the *t* distribution is symmetric, however, the upper tail area for $t = 1.10$ is the same as the lower tail area for $t = -1.10$. We see that $t = 1.10$ is between 0.857 and 1.318. From the "Area in Upper Tail" row, we see that the area in the tail to the right of $t = 1.10$ is between .20 and .10. When we double these amounts, we see that the *p*-value must be between .40 and .20. With a level of significance of $\alpha = .05$, we now know that the *p*-value is greater than $\alpha$. Therefore, $H_0$ cannot be rejected. Sufficient evidence is not available to conclude that Holiday should change its production plan for the coming season.

In the Using Excel subsection which follows, we show how to compute the exact *p*-value for this hypothesis test using Excel. The *p*-value obtained is .2811. With a level of significance of $\alpha = .05$, we cannot reject $H_0$ because .2811 > .05.

The test statistic can also be compared to the critical value to make the two-tailed hypothesis testing decision. With $\alpha = .05$ and the *t* distribution with 24 degrees of freedom, $-t_{.025} = -2.064$ and $t_{.025} = 2.064$ are the critical values for the two-tailed test. The rejection rule using the test statistic is

$$\text{Reject } H_0 \text{ if } t \leq -2.064 \text{ or if } t \geq 2.064$$

Based on the test statistic $t = -1.10$, $H_0$ cannot be rejected. This result indicates that Holiday should continue its production planning for the coming season based on the expectation that $\mu = 40$.

## Using Excel

Excel can be used to conduct one-tailed and two-tailed hypothesis tests about a population mean for the $\sigma$ unknown case. The approach is similar to the procedure used in the $\sigma$ known case. The sample data and the test statistic (*t*) are used to compute three *p*-values: *p*-value (Lower Tail), *p*-value (Upper Tail), and *p*-value (Two Tail). The user can then choose $\alpha$ and draw a conclusion using whichever *p*-value is appropriate for the type of hypothesis test being conducted.

Let's start by showing how to use Excel's T.DIST function to compute a lower tail *p*-value. The T.DIST function has three inputs; its general form is as follows:

T.DIST(test statistic, degrees of freedom, cumulative)

For the first input, we enter the value of the test statistic, for the second input we enter the number of degrees of freedom. For the third input, we enter TRUE if we want a cumulative probability and FALSE if we want the height of the curve. When we want to compute a lower tail *p*-value, we enter TRUE.

Once the lower tail *p*-value has been computed, it is easy to compute the upper tail and the two-tailed *p*-values. The upper tail *p*-value is just 1 minus the lower tail *p*-value. And the two-tailed *p*-value is given by two times the smaller of the lower and upper tail *p*-values.

Let us now construct an Excel worksheet to conduct the two-tailed hypothesis test for the Holiday Toys study. Refer to Figure 9.8 as we describe the tasks involved. The formula worksheet is in the background; the value worksheet is in the foreground.

**FIGURE 9.8**    EXCEL WORKSHEET: HYPOTHESIS TEST FOR THE $\sigma$ UNKNOWN CASE

**WEB file**

Orders

*Note: Rows 18–24 are hidden.*

**Enter Data:**   A label and the order quantity data for the sample of 25 retailers are entered into cells A1:A26.

**Enter Functions and Formulas:**   The descriptive statistics needed are provided in cells D4:D6. Excel's COUNT, AVERAGE, and STDEV functions compute the sample size, the sample mean, and the sample standard deviation, respectively. The hypothesized value of the population mean (40) is entered into cell D8.

Using the sample standard deviation as an estimate of the population standard deviation, an estimate of the standard error is obtained in cell D10 by dividing the sample standard deviation in cell D6 by the square root of the sample size in cell D4. The formula =(D5-D8)/D10 entered into cell D11 computes the test statistic $t(-1.1026)$. The degrees of freedom are computed in cell D12 as the sample size in cell D4 minus 1.

To compute the $p$-value for a lower tail test, we enter the following formula into cell D14:

$$=T.DIST(D11,D12,TRUE)$$

The $p$-value for an upper tail test is then computed in cell D15 as 1 minus the $p$-value for the lower tail test. Finally, the $p$-value for a two-tailed test is computed in cell D16 as two times the minimum of the two one-tailed $p$-values. The value worksheet shows that the three $p$-values are $p$-value (Lower Tail) = 0.1406, $p$-value (Upper Tail) = 0.8594, and $p$-value (Two Tail) = 0.2811.

The development of the worksheet is now complete. For the two-tailed Holiday Toys problem we cannot reject $H_0$: $\mu = 40$ using $\alpha = .05$ because the $p$-value (Two Tail) = 0.2811 is greater than $\alpha$. This result indicates that Holiday should continue its production planning for the coming season based on the expectation that $\mu = 40$. The worksheet in Figure 9.8 can also be used for any one-tailed hypothesis test involving the $t$ distribution. If a lower tail test is required, compare the $p$-value (Lower Tail) with $\alpha$ to make the rejection decision. If an upper tail test is required, compare the $p$-value (Upper Tail) with $\alpha$ to make the rejection decision.

**A template for other problems**   The worksheet in Figure 9.8 can be used as a template for any hypothesis tests about a population mean for the $\sigma$ unknown case. Just enter the appropriate data in column A, adjust the ranges for the formulas in cells D4:D6, and enter the hypothesized value in cell D8. The standard error, the test statistic, and the three $p$-values will then appear. Depending on the form of the hypothesis test (lower tail, upper tail, or two-tailed), we can then choose the appropriate $p$-value to make the rejection decision.

We can further simplify the use of Figure 9.8 as a template for other problems by eliminating the need to enter new data ranges in cells D4:D6. To do so we rewrite the cell formulas as follows:

Cell D4:  =COUNT(A:A)
Cell D5:  =AVERAGE(A:A)
Cell D6:  =STDEV(A:A)

*The Orders data set includes a worksheet entitled Template that uses the A:A method for entering the data ranges.*

With the A:A method of specifying data ranges, Excel's COUNT function will count the number of numeric values in column A, Excel's AVERAGE function will compute the average of the numeric values in column A, and Excel's STDEV function will compute the standard deviation of the numeric values in Column A. Thus, to solve a new problem it is only necessary to enter the new data in column A and enter the hypothesized value of the population mean in cell D8.

**TABLE 9.3**   SUMMARY OF HYPOTHESIS TESTS ABOUT A POPULATION MEAN: $\sigma$ UNKNOWN CASE

|  | Lower Tail Test | Upper Tail Test | Two-Tailed Test |
|---|---|---|---|
| **Hypotheses** | $H_0: \mu \geq \mu_0$ <br> $H_a: \mu < \mu_0$ | $H_0: \mu \leq \mu_0$ <br> $H_a: \mu > \mu_0$ | $H_0: \mu = \mu_0$ <br> $H_a: \mu \neq \mu_0$ |
| **Test Statistic** | $t = \dfrac{\bar{x} - \mu_0}{s/\sqrt{n}}$ | $t = \dfrac{\bar{x} - \mu_0}{s/\sqrt{n}}$ | $t = \dfrac{\bar{x} - \mu_0}{s/\sqrt{n}}$ |
| **Rejection Rule:** <br> *p*-Value Approach | Reject $H_0$ if <br> $p$-value $\leq \alpha$ | Reject $H_0$ if <br> $p$-value $\leq \alpha$ | Reject $H_0$ if <br> $p$-value $\leq \alpha$ |
| **Rejection Rule:** <br> Critical Value <br> Approach | Reject $H_0$ if <br> $t \leq -t_\alpha$ | Reject $H_0$ if <br> $t \geq t_\alpha$ | Reject $H_0$ if <br> $t \leq -t_{\alpha/2}$ <br> or if $t \geq t_{\alpha/2}$ |

## Summary and Practical Advice

Table 9.3 provides a summary of the hypothesis testing procedures about a population mean for the $\sigma$ unknown case. The key difference between these procedures and the ones for the $\sigma$ known case is that $s$ is used, instead of $\sigma$, in the computation of the test statistic. For this reason, the test statistic follows the $t$ distribution.

The applicability of the hypothesis testing procedures of this section is dependent on the distribution of the population being sampled from and the sample size. When the population is normally distributed, the hypothesis tests described in this section provide exact results for any sample size. When the population is not normally distributed, the procedures are approximations. Nonetheless, we find that sample sizes of 30 or greater will provide good results in most cases. If the population is approximately normal, small sample sizes (e.g., $n < 15$) can provide acceptable results. If the population is highly skewed or contains outliers, sample sizes approaching 50 are recommended.

## Exercises

### Methods

23.  Consider the following hypothesis test:

$$H_0: \mu \leq 12$$
$$H_a: \mu > 12$$

A sample of 25 provided a sample mean $\bar{x} = 14$ and a sample standard deviation $s = 4.32$.
a.  Compute the value of the test statistic.
b.  Use the $t$ distribution table (Table 2 in Appendix B) to compute a range for the $p$-value.
c.  At $\alpha = .05$, what is your conclusion?
d.  What is the rejection rule using the critical value? What is your conclusion?

24.  Consider the following hypothesis test:

$$H_0: \mu = 18$$
$$H_a: \mu \neq 18$$

A sample of 48 provided a sample mean $\bar{x} = 17$ and a sample standard deviation $s = 4.5$.
a.   Compute the value of the test statistic.
b.   Use the $t$ distribution table (Table 2 in Appendix B) to compute a range for the $p$-value.
c.   At $\alpha = .05$, what is your conclusion?
d.   What is the rejection rule using the critical value? What is your conclusion?

25.   Consider the following hypothesis test:

$$H_0: \mu \geq 45$$
$$H_a: \mu < 45$$

A sample of 36 is used. Identify the $p$-value and state your conclusion for each of the following sample results. Use $\alpha = .01$.
a.   $\bar{x} = 44$ and $s = 5.2$
b.   $\bar{x} = 43$ and $s = 4.6$
c.   $\bar{x} = 46$ and $s = 5.0$

26.   Consider the following hypothesis test:

$$H_0: \mu = 100$$
$$H_a: \mu \neq 100$$

A sample of 65 is used. Identify the $p$-value and state your conclusion for each of the following sample results. Use $\alpha = .05$.
a.   $\bar{x} = 103$ and $s = 11.5$
b.   $\bar{x} = 96.5$ and $s = 11.0$
c.   $\bar{x} = 102$ and $s = 10.5$

## Applications

27.   The Employment and Training Administration reported that the U.S. mean unemployment insurance benefit was $238 per week (*The World Almanac*, 2003). A researcher in the state of Virginia anticipated that sample data would show evidence that the mean weekly unemployment insurance benefit in Virginia was below the national average.
a.   Develop appropriate hypotheses such that rejection of $H_0$ will support the researcher's contention.
b.   For a sample of 100 individuals, the sample mean weekly unemployment insurance benefit was $231 with a sample standard deviation of $80. What is the $p$-value?
c.   At $\alpha = .05$, what is your conclusion?
d.   Repeat the preceding hypothesis test using the critical value approach.

28.   A shareholders' group, in lodging a protest, claimed that the mean tenure for a chief executive officer (CEO) was at least nine years. A survey of companies reported in *The Wall Street Journal* found a sample mean tenure of $\bar{x} = 7.27$ years for CEOs with a standard deviation of $s = 6.38$ years (*The Wall Street Journal*, January 2, 2007).
a.   Formulate hypotheses that can be used to challenge the validity of the claim made by the shareholders' group.
b.   Assume 85 companies were included in the sample. What is the $p$-value for your hypothesis test?
c.   At $\alpha = .01$, what is your conclusion?

29.   The cost of a one-carat VS2 clarity, H color diamond from Diamond Source USA is $5600 (Diamond Source website, March 2003). A midwestern jeweler makes calls to contacts in the diamond district of New York City to see whether the mean price of diamonds there differs from $5600.

a. Formulate hypotheses that can be used to determine whether the mean price in New York City differs from $5600.

b. A sample of 25 New York City contacts provided the prices shown in the file named Diamonds. What is the *p*-value?

c. At $\alpha = .05$, can the null hypothesis be rejected? What is your conclusion?

d. Repeat the preceding hypothesis test using the critical value approach.

30. Time Warner Inc.'s CNN has been the longtime ratings leader of cable television news. Nielsen Media Research indicated that the mean CNN viewing audience was 600,000 viewers per day during 2002 (*The Wall Street Journal,* March 10, 2003). Assume that for a sample of 40 days during the first half of 2003, the daily audience was 612,000 viewers with a sample standard deviation of 65,000 viewers.

a. What are the hypotheses if CNN management would like information on any change in the CNN viewing audience?

b. What is the *p*-value?

c. Select your own level of significance. What is your conclusion?

d. What recommendation would you make to CNN management in this application?

31. The Coca-Cola Company reported that the mean per capita annual sales of its beverages in the United States was 423 eight-ounce servings (Coca-Cola Company website, February 3, 2009). Suppose you are curious whether the consumption of Coca-Cola beverages is higher in Atlanta, Georgia, the location of Coca-Cola's corporate headquarters. A sample of 36 individuals from the Atlanta area showed a sample mean annual consumption of 460.4 eight-ounce servings with a standard deviation of $s = 101.9$ ounces. Using $\alpha = .05$, do the sample results support the conclusion that mean annual consumption of Coca-Cola beverage products is higher in Atlanta?

**WEB** file

**UsedCars**

32. According to the National Automobile Dealers Association, the mean price for used cars is $10,192. A manager of a Kansas City used car dealership reviewed a sample of 50 recent used car sales at the dealership in an attempt to determine whether the population mean price for used cars at this particular dealership differed from the national mean. The prices for the sample of 50 cars are shown in the file named UsedCars.

a. Formulate the hypotheses that can be used to determine whether a difference exists in the mean price for used cars at the dealership.

b. What is the *p*-value?

c. At $\alpha = .05$, what is your conclusion?

33. Annual per capita consumption of milk is 21.6 gallons (*Statistical Abstract of the United States: 2006*). Being from the Midwest, you believe milk consumption is higher there and wish to support your opinion. A sample of 16 individuals from the midwestern town of Webster City showed a sample mean annual consumption of 24.1 gallons with a standard deviation of $s = 4.8$.

a. Develop a hypothesis test that can be used to determine whether the mean annual consumption in Webster City is higher than the national mean.

b. What is a point estimate of the difference between mean annual consumption in Webster City and the national mean?

c. At $\alpha = .05$, test for a significant difference. What is your conclusion?

34. Joan's Nursery specializes in custom-designed landscaping for residential areas. The estimated labor cost associated with a particular landscaping proposal is based on the number of plantings of trees, shrubs, and so on to be used for the project. For cost-estimating purposes, managers use two hours of labor time for the planting of a medium-sized tree. Actual times from a sample of 10 plantings during the past month follow (times in hours).

| 1.7 | 1.5 | 2.6 | 2.2 | 2.4 | 2.3 | 2.6 | 3.0 | 1.4 | 2.3 |
|-----|-----|-----|-----|-----|-----|-----|-----|-----|-----|

With a .05 level of significance, test to see whether the mean tree-planting time differs from two hours.

a.   State the null and alternative hypotheses.
b.   Compute the sample mean.
c.   Compute the sample standard deviation.
d.   What is the *p*-value?
e.   What is your conclusion?

## 9.5   Population Proportion

In this section we show how to conduct a hypothesis test about a population proportion *p*. Using $p_0$ to denote the hypothesized value for the population proportion, the three forms for a hypothesis test about a population proportion are as follows.

$$H_0: p \geq p_0 \qquad H_0: p \leq p_0 \qquad H_0: p = p_0$$
$$H_a: p < p_0 \qquad H_a: p > p_0 \qquad H_a: p \neq p_0$$

The first form is called a lower tail test, the second form is called an upper tail test, and the third form is called a two-tailed test.

Hypothesis tests about a population proportion are based on the difference between the sample proportion $\bar{p}$ and the hypothesized population proportion $p_0$. The methods used to conduct the hypothesis test are similar to those used for hypothesis tests about a population mean. The only difference is that we use the sample proportion and its standard error to compute the test statistic. The *p*-value approach or the critical value approach is then used to determine whether the null hypothesis should be rejected.

Let us consider an example involving a situation faced by Pine Creek golf course. Over the past year, 20% of the players at Pine Creek were women. In an effort to increase the proportion of women players, Pine Creek implemented a special promotion designed to attract women golfers. One month after the promotion was implemented, the course manager requested a statistical study to determine whether the proportion of women players at Pine Creek had increased. Because the objective of the study is to determine whether the proportion of women golfers increased, an upper tail test with $H_a: p > .20$ is appropriate. The null and alternative hypotheses for the Pine Creek hypothesis test are as follows:

$$H_0: p \leq .20$$
$$H_a: p > .20$$

If $H_0$ can be rejected, the test results will give statistical support for the conclusion that the proportion of women golfers increased and the promotion was beneficial. The course manager specified that a level of significance of $\alpha = .05$ be used in carrying out this hypothesis test.

The next step of the hypothesis testing procedure is to select a sample and compute the value of an appropriate test statistic. To show how this step is done for the Pine Creek upper tail test, we begin with a general discussion of how to compute the value of the test statistic for any form of a hypothesis test about a population proportion. The sampling distribution of $\bar{p}$, the point estimator of the population parameter *p*, is the basis for developing the test statistic.

When the null hypothesis is true as an equality, the expected value of $\bar{p}$ equals the hypothesized value $p_0$; that is, $E(\bar{p}) = p_0$. The standard error of $\bar{p}$ is given by

$$\sigma_{\bar{p}} = \sqrt{\frac{p_0(1 - p_0)}{n}}$$

In Chapter 7 we said that if $np \geq 5$ and $n(1 - p) \geq 5$, the sampling distribution of $\bar{p}$ can be approximated by a normal distribution.[4] Under these conditions, which usually apply in practice, the quantity

$$z = \frac{\bar{p} - p_0}{\sigma_{\bar{p}}} \tag{9.3}$$

has a standard normal probability distribution. With $\sigma_{\bar{p}} = \sqrt{p_0(1 - p_0)/n}$, the standard normal random variable $z$ is the test statistic used to conduct hypothesis tests about a population proportion.

---

**TEST STATISTIC FOR HYPOTHESIS TESTS ABOUT A POPULATION PROPORTION**

$$z = \frac{\bar{p} - p_0}{\sqrt{\dfrac{p_0(1 - p_0)}{n}}} \tag{9.4}$$

---

**WEB** file

**WomenGolf**

We can now compute the test statistic for the Pine Creek hypothesis test. Suppose a random sample of 400 players was selected, and that 100 of the players were women. The proportion of women golfers in the sample is

$$\bar{p} = \frac{100}{400} = .25$$

Using equation (9.4), the value of the test statistic is

$$z = \frac{\bar{p} - p_0}{\sqrt{\dfrac{p_0(1 - p_0)}{n}}} = \frac{.25 - .20}{\sqrt{\dfrac{.20(1 - .20)}{400}}} = \frac{.05}{.02} = 2.50$$

Because the Pine Creek hypothesis test is an upper tail test, the $p$-value is the probability that $z$ is greater than or equal to $z = 2.50$; that is, it is the upper tail area corresponding to $z \geq 2.50$. Using the standard normal probability table, we find that the lower tail area for $z = 2.50$ is .9938. Thus, the $p$-value for the Pine Creek test is $1.0000 - .9938 = .0062$. Figure 9.9 shows this $p$-value calculation.

Recall that the course manager specified a level of significance of $\alpha = .05$. A $p$-value $= .0062 < .05$ gives sufficient statistical evidence to reject $H_0$ at the .05 level of significance. Thus, the test provides statistical support for the conclusion that the special promotion increased the proportion of women players at the Pine Creek golf course.

The decision whether to reject the null hypothesis can also be made using the critical value approach. The critical value corresponding to an area of .05 in the upper tail of a normal probability distribution is $z_{.05} = 1.645$. Thus, the rejection rule using the critical value approach is to reject $H_0$ if $z \geq 1.645$. Because $z = 2.50 > 1.645$, $H_0$ is rejected.

Again, we see that the $p$-value approach and the critical value approach lead to the same hypothesis testing conclusion, but the $p$-value approach provides more information. With a $p$-value $= .0062$, the null hypothesis would be rejected for any level of significance greater than or equal to .0062.

---

[4]In most applications involving hypothesis tests of a population proportion, sample sizes are large enough to use the normal approximation. The exact sampling distribution of $\bar{p}$ is discrete, with the probability for each value of $\bar{p}$ given by the binomial distribution. So hypothesis testing is a bit more complicated for small samples when the normal approximation cannot be used.

**FIGURE 9.9**   CALCULATION OF THE *p*-VALUE FOR THE PINE CREEK HYPOTHESIS TEST

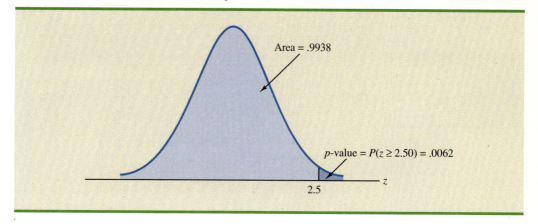

# Using Excel

Excel can be used to conduct one-tailed and two-tailed hypothesis tests about a population proportion using the *p*-value approach. The procedure is similar to the approach used with Excel in conducting hypothesis tests about a population mean. The primary difference is that the test statistic is based on the sampling distribution of $\bar{x}$ for hypothesis tests about a population mean and on the sampling distribution of $\bar{p}$ for hypothesis tests about a population proportion. Thus, although different formulas are used to compute the test statistic needed to make the hypothesis testing decision, the computations of the critical value and the *p*-value for the tests are identical.

We will illustrate the procedure by showing how Excel can be used to conduct the upper tail hypothesis test for the Pine Creek golf course study. Refer to Figure 9.10 as we describe the tasks involved. The formula worksheet is in the background; the value worksheet is in the foreground.

**Enter Data:**   A label and the gender of each golfer in the study are entered into cells A1:A401.

**Enter Functions and Formulas:**   The descriptive statistics needed are provided in cells D3, D5, and D6. Because the data are not numeric, Excel's COUNTA function, not the COUNT function, is used in cell D3 to determine the sample size. We entered Female in cell D4 to identify the response for which we wish to compute a proportion. The COUNTIF function is then used in cell D5 to determine the number of responses of the type identified in cell D4. The sample proportion is then computed in cell D6 by dividing the response count by the sample size.

The hypothesized value of the population proportion (.20) is entered into cell D8. The standard error is obtained in cell D10 by entering the formula =SQRT(D8*(1-D8)/D3). The formula =(D6-D8)/D10 entered into cell D11 computes the test statistic *z*(2.50). To compute the *p*-value for a lower tail test, we enter the formula =NORM.S.DIST(D11,TRUE) into cell D13. The *p*-value for an upper tail test is then computed in cell D14 as 1 minus the *p*-value for the lower tail test. Finally, the *p*-value for a two-tailed test is computed in cell D15 as two times the minimum of the two one-tailed *p*-values. The value worksheet shows that the three *p*-values are as follows: *p*-value (Lower Tail) = 0.9938; *p*-value (Upper Tail) = 0.0062; and *p*-value (Two Tail) = 0.0124.

The development of the worksheet is now complete. For the Pine Creek upper tail hypothesis test, we reject the null hypothesis that the population proportion is .20 or less because the *p*-value (Upper Tail) = 0.0062 is less than $\alpha = .05$. Indeed, with this *p*-value we would reject the null hypothesis for any level of significance of .0062 or greater.

**FIGURE 9.10     EXCEL WORKSHEET: HYPOTHESIS TEST FOR PINE CREEK GOLF COURSE**

**A template for other problems**  The worksheet in Figure 9.10 can be used as a template for hypothesis tests about a population proportion whenever $np \geq 5$ and $n(1 - p) \geq 5$. Just enter the appropriate data in column A, adjust the ranges for the formulas in cells D3 and D5, enter the appropriate response in cell D4, and enter the hypothesized value in cell D8. The standard error, the test statistic, and the three $p$-values will then appear. Depending on

**TABLE 9.4**   SUMMARY OF HYPOTHESIS TESTS ABOUT A POPULATION PROPORTION

| | **Lower Tail Test** | **Upper Tail Test** | **Two-Tailed Test** |
|---|---|---|---|
| **Hypotheses** | $H_0: p \geq p_0$ <br> $H_a: p < p_0$ | $H_0: p \leq p_0$ <br> $H_a: p > p_0$ | $H_0: p = p_0$ <br> $H_a: p \neq p_0$ |
| **Test Statistic** | $z = \dfrac{\bar{p} - p_0}{\sqrt{\dfrac{p_0(1 - p_0)}{n}}}$ | $z = \dfrac{\bar{p} - p_0}{\sqrt{\dfrac{p_0(1 - p_0)}{n}}}$ | $z = \dfrac{\bar{p} - p_0}{\sqrt{\dfrac{p_0(1 - p_0)}{n}}}$ |
| **Rejection Rule:** <br> **_p_-Value Approach** | Reject $H_0$ if <br> $p$-value $\leq \alpha$ | Reject $H_0$ if <br> $p$-value $\leq \alpha$ | Reject $H_0$ if <br> $p$-value $\leq \alpha$ |
| **Rejection Rule:** <br> **Critical Value** <br> **Approach** | Reject $H_0$ if <br> $z \leq -z_\alpha$ | Reject $H_0$ if <br> $z \geq z_\alpha$ | Reject $H_0$ if <br> $z \leq -z_{\alpha/2}$ <br> or if $z \geq z_{\alpha/2}$ |

the form of the hypothesis test (lower tail, upper tail, or two-tailed), we can then choose the appropriate $p$-value to make the rejection decision.

## Summary

The procedure used to conduct a hypothesis test about a population proportion is similar to the procedure used to conduct a hypothesis test about a population mean. Although we only illustrated how to conduct a hypothesis test about a population proportion for an upper tail test, similar procedures can be used for lower tail and two-tailed tests. Table 9.4 provides a summary of the hypothesis tests about a population proportion. We assume that $np \geq 5$ and $n(1 - p) \geq 5$; thus the normal probability distribution can be used to approximate the sampling distribution of $\bar{p}$.

## Exercises

### Methods

35.   Consider the following hypothesis test:

$$H_0: p = .20$$
$$H_a: p \neq .20$$

A sample of 400 provided a sample proportion $\bar{p} = .175$.
a.   Compute the value of the test statistic.
b.   What is the $p$-value?
c.   At $\alpha = .05$, what is your conclusion?
d.   What is the rejection rule using the critical value? What is your conclusion?

36.   Consider the following hypothesis test:

**SELF** test

$$H_0: p \geq .75$$
$$H_a: p < .75$$

A sample of 300 items was selected. Compute the p-value and state your conclusion for each of the following sample results. Use $\alpha = .05$.

a.   $\bar{p} = .68$        c.   $\bar{p} = .70$
b.   $\bar{p} = .72$        d.   $\bar{p} = .77$

## Applications

37.   A study found that, in 2005, 12.5% of U.S. workers belonged to unions (*The Wall Street Journal*, January 21, 2006). Suppose a sample of 400 U.S. workers is collected in 2006 to determine whether union efforts to organize have increased union membership.

a.   Formulate the hypotheses that can be used to determine whether union membership increased in 2006.

b.   If the sample results show that 52 of the workers belonged to unions, what is the p-value for your hypothesis test?

c.   At $\alpha = .05$, what is your conclusion?

38.   A study by *Consumer Reports* showed that 64% of supermarket shoppers believe supermarket brands to be as good as national name brands. To investigate whether this result applies to its own product, the manufacturer of a national name-brand ketchup asked a sample of shoppers whether they believed that supermarket ketchup was as good as the national brand ketchup.

a.   Formulate the hypotheses that could be used to determine whether the percentage of supermarket shoppers who believe that the supermarket ketchup was as good as the national brand ketchup differed from 64%.

b.   If a sample of 100 shoppers showed 52 stating that the supermarket brand was as good as the national brand, what is the p-value?

c.   At $\alpha = .05$, what is your conclusion?

d.   Should the national brand ketchup manufacturer be pleased with this conclusion? Explain.

**WEB file**

**AgeGroup**

39.   According to the Pew Internet & American Life Project, 75% of American adults use the Internet (Pew Internet website, April 19, 2008). The Pew project authors also reported on the percentage of Americans who use the Internet by age group. The data in the file AgeGroup are consistent with their findings. These data were obtained from a sample of 100 Internet users in the 30–49 age group and 200 Internet users in the 50–64 age group. A Yes indicates the survey repondent had used the Internet; a No indicates the survey repondent had not.

a.   Formulate hypotheses that could be used to determine whether the percentage of Internet users in the two age groups differs from the overall average of 75%.

b.   Estimate the proportion of Internet users in the 30–49 age group. Does this proportion differ significantly from the overall proportion of .75? Use $\alpha = .05$.

c.   Estimate the proportion of Internet users in the 50–64 age group. Does this proportion differ significantly from the overall proportion of .75? Use $\alpha = .05$.

d.   Would you expect the proportion of users in the 18–29 age group to be larger or smaller than the proportion for the 30–49 age group? Support your conclusion with the results obtained in parts (b) and (c).

40.   In 2008, 46% of business owners gave a holiday gift to their employees. A 2009 survey of business owners indicated that 35% plan to provide a holiday gift to their employees (Radio WEZV, Myrtle Beach, South Carolina, November 11, 2009). Suppose the survey results are based on a sample of 60 business owners.

a.   How many business owners in the survey plan to provide a holiday gift to their employees?

b.   Suppose the business owners in the sample do as they plan. Compute the p-value for a hypothesis test that can be used to determine if the proportion of business owners providing holiday gifts has decreased from the 2008 level.

c.   Using a .05 level of significance, would you conclude that the proportion of business owners providing gifts has decreased? What is the smallest level of significance for which you could draw such a conclusion?

41.   Speaking to a group of analysts in January 2006, a brokerage firm executive claimed that at least 70% of investors are currently confident of meeting their investment objectives. A UBS Investor Optimism Survey, conducted over the period January 2 to January 15, found that 67% of investors were confident of meeting their investment objectives (CNBC, January 20, 2006).
a.   Formulate the hypotheses that can be used to test the validity of the brokerage firm executive's claim.
b.   Assume the UBS Investor Optimism Survey collected information from 300 investors. What is the *p*-value for the hypothesis test?
c.   At $\alpha = .05$, should the executive's claim be rejected?

42.   According to the University of Nevada Center for Logistics Management, 6% of all merchandise sold in the United States gets returned (*BusinessWeek*, January 15, 2007). A Houston department store sampled 80 items sold in January and found that 12 of the items were returned.
a.   Construct a point estimate of the proportion of items returned for the population of sales transactions at the Houston store.
b.   Construct a 95% confidence interval for the porportion of returns at the Houston store.
c.   Is the proportion of returns at the Houston store significantly different from the returns for the nation as a whole? Provide statistical support for your answer.

**Eagle**

43.   Eagle Outfitters is a chain of stores specializing in outdoor apparel and camping gear. It is considering a promotion that involves mailing discount coupons to all its credit card customers. This promotion will be considered a success if more than 10% of those receiving the coupons use them. Before going national with the promotion, coupons were sent to a sample of 100 credit card customers.
a.   Develop hypotheses that can be used to test whether the population proportion of those who will use the coupons is sufficient to go national.
b.   The file Eagle contains the sample data. Develop a point estimate of the population proportion.
c.   Use $\alpha = .05$ to conduct your hypothesis test. Should Eagle go national with the promotion?

**Drowsy**

44.   In a cover story, *BusinessWeek* published information about sleep habits of Americans (*BusinessWeek*, January 26, 2004). The article noted that sleep deprivation causes a number of problems, including highway deaths. Fifty-one percent of adult drivers admit to driving while drowsy. A researcher hypothesized that this issue was an even bigger problem for night shift workers.
a.   Formulate the hypotheses that can be used to help determine whether more than 51% of the population of night shift workers admit to driving while drowsy.
b.   A sample of 400 night shift workers identified those who admitted to driving while drowsy. See the Drowsy file. What is the sample proportion? What is the *p*-value?
c.   At $\alpha = .01$, what is your conclusion?

45.   Many investors and financial analysts believe the Dow Jones Industrial Average (DJIA) provides a good barometer of the overall stock market. On January 31, 2006, 9 of the 30 stocks making up the DJIA increased in price (*The Wall Street Journal*, February 1, 2006). On the basis of this fact, a financial analyst claims we can assume that 30% of the stocks traded on the New York Stock Exchange (NYSE) went up the same day.
a.   Formulate null and alternative hypotheses to test the analyst's claim.
b.   A sample of 50 stocks traded on the NYSE that day showed that 24 went up. What is your point estimate of the population proportion of stocks that went up?
c.   Conduct your hypothesis test using $\alpha = .01$ as the level of significance. What is your conclusion?

## Summary

Hypothesis testing is a statistical procedure that uses sample data to determine whether a statement about the value of a population parameter should or should not be rejected. The hypotheses are two competing statements about a population parameter. One statement is called the null hypothesis ($H_0$), and the other statement is called the alternative hypothesis ($H_a$). In Section 9.1 we provided guidelines for developing hypotheses for situations frequently encountered in practice.

Whenever historical data or other information provides a basis for assuming that the population standard deviation is known, the hypothesis testing procedure for the population mean is based on the standard normal distribution. Whenever $\sigma$ is unknown, the sample standard deviation $s$ is used to estimate $\sigma$ and the hypothesis testing procedure is based on the $t$ distribution. In both cases, the quality of results depends on both the form of the population distribution and the sample size. If the population has a normal distribution, both hypothesis testing procedures are applicable, even with small sample sizes. If the population is not normally distributed, larger sample sizes are needed. General guidelines about the sample size were provided in Sections 9.3 and 9.4. In the case of hypothesis tests about a population proportion, the hypothesis testing procedure uses a test statistic based on the standard normal distribution.

In all cases, the value of the test statistic can be used to compute a $p$-value for the test. A $p$-value is a probability used to determine whether the null hypothesis should be rejected. If the $p$-value is less than or equal to the level of significance $\alpha$, the null hypothesis can be rejected.

Hypothesis testing conclusions can also be made by comparing the value of the test statistic to a critical value. For lower tail tests, the null hypothesis is rejected if the value of the test statistic is less than or equal to the critical value. For upper tail tests, the null hypothesis is rejected if the value of the test statistic is greater than or equal to the critical value. Two-tailed tests consist of two critical values: one in the lower tail of the sampling distribution and one in the upper tail. In this case, the null hypothesis is rejected if the value of the test statistic is less than or equal to the critical value in the lower tail or greater than or equal to the critical value in the upper tail.

## Glossary

**Null hypothesis** The hypothesis tentatively assumed true in the hypothesis testing procedure.

**Alternative hypothesis** The hypothesis concluded to be true if the null hypothesis is rejected.

**Type I error** The error of rejecting $H_0$ when it is true.

**Type II error** The error of accepting $H_0$ when it is false.

**Level of significance** The probability of making a Type I error when the null hypothesis is true as an equality.

**One-tailed test** A hypothesis test in which rejection of the null hypothesis occurs for values of the test statistic in one tail of its sampling distribution.

**Test statistic** A statistic whose value helps determine whether a null hypothesis should be rejected.

**_p_-value** A probability that provides a measure of the evidence against the null hypothesis provided by the sample. Smaller $p$-values indicate more evidence against $H_0$. For a lower tail test, the $p$-value is the probability of obtaining a value for the test statistic as small as or smaller than that provided by the sample. For an upper tail test, the $p$-value is the probability of obtaining a value for the test statistic as large as or larger than that provided by the sample. For a two-tailed test, the $p$-value is the probability of obtaining a value for the test statistic at least as unlikely as or more unlikely than that provided by the sample.

**Critical value** A value that is compared with the test statistic to determine whether $H_0$ should be rejected.

**Two-tailed test** A hypothesis test in which rejection of the null hypothesis occurs for values of the test statistic in either tail of its sampling distribution.

## Key Formulas

**Test Statistic for Hypothesis Tests About a Population Mean: $\sigma$ Known**

$$z = \frac{\bar{x} - \mu_0}{\sigma/\sqrt{n}}$$ (9.1)

**Test Statistic for Hypothesis Tests About a Population Mean: $\sigma$ Unknown**

$$t = \frac{\bar{x} - \mu_0}{s/\sqrt{n}}$$ (9.2)

**Test Statistic for Hypothesis Tests About a Population Proportion**

$$z = \frac{\bar{p} - p_0}{\sqrt{\dfrac{p_0(1 - p_0)}{n}}}$$ (9.4)

## Supplementary Exercises

46. A production line operates with a mean filling weight of 16 ounces per container. Overfilling or underfilling presents a serious problem and when detected requires the operator to shut down the production line to readjust the filling mechanism. From past data, a population standard deviation $\sigma = .8$ ounces is assumed. A quality control inspector selects a sample of 30 items every hour and at that time makes the decision of whether to shut down the line for readjustment. The level of significance is $\alpha = .05$.
    a. State the hypothesis test for this quality control application.
    b. If a sample mean of $\bar{x} = 16.32$ ounces were found, what is the $p$-value? What action would you recommend?
    c. If a sample mean of $\bar{x} = 15.82$ ounces were found, what is the $p$-value? What action would you recommend?
    d. Use the critical value approach. What is the rejection rule for the preceding hypothesis testing procedure? Repeat parts (b) and (c). Do you reach the same conclusion?

47. At Western University the historical mean of scholarship examination scores for freshman applications is 900. A historical population standard deviation $\sigma = 180$ is assumed known. Each year, the assistant dean uses a sample of applications to determine whether the mean examination score for the new freshman applications has changed.
    a. State the hypotheses.
    b. What is the 95% confidence interval estimate of the population mean examination score if a sample of 200 applications provided a sample mean of $\bar{x} = 935$?
    c. Use the confidence interval to conduct a hypothesis test. Using $\alpha = .05$, what is your conclusion?
    d. What is the $p$-value?

48. *Playbill* is a magazine distributed around the country to people attending musicals and other theatrical productions. The mean annual household income for the population of *Playbill* readers is $119,155 (*Playbill,* January 2006). Assume the standard deviation is

$\sigma = \$20,700$. A San Francisco civic group has asserted that the mean for theater goers in the Bay Area is higher. A sample of 60 theater attendees in the Bay Area showed a sample mean household income of $126,100.

a. Develop hypotheses that can be used to determine whether the sample data support the conclusion that theater attendees in the Bay Area have a higher mean household income than that for all *Playbill* readers.

b. What is the *p*-value based on the sample of 60 theater attendees in the Bay Area?

c. Use $\alpha = .01$ as the level of significance. What is your conclusion?

49. On Friday, Wall Street traders were anxiously awaiting the federal government's release of numbers on the January increase in nonfarm payrolls. The early consensus estimate among economists was for a growth of 250,000 new jobs (CNBC, February 3, 2006). However, a sample of 20 economists taken Thursday afternoon provided a sample mean of 266,000 with a sample standard deviation of 24,000. Financial analysts often call such a sample mean, based on late-breaking news, the *whisper number.* Treat the "consensus estimate" as the population mean. Conduct a hypothesis test to determine whether the whisper number justifies a conclusion of a statistically significant increase in the consensus estimate of economists. Use $\alpha = .01$ as the level of significance.

**FirstBirth**

50. Data released by the National Center for Health Statistics showed that the mean age at which women had their first child was 25.0 in 2006 (*The Wall Street Journal,* February 4, 2009). The reporter, Sue Shellenbarger, noted that this was the first decrease in the average age at which women had their first child in several years. A recent sample of 42 women provided the data in the website file named FirstBirth concerning the age at which these women had their first child. Do the data indicate a change from 2006 in the mean age at which women had their first child? Use $\alpha = .05$.

**WeeklyPay**

51. A recent issue of the *AARP Bulletin* reported that the average weekly pay for a woman with a high school diploma was $520 (*AARP Bulletin,* January–February, 2010). Suppose you would like to determine if the average weekly pay for all working women is significantly greater than that for women with a high school diploma. Data providing the weekly pay for a sample of 50 working women are available in the file named WeeklyPay. These data are consistent with the findings reported in the article mentioned above.

a. State the hypotheses that should be used to test whether the mean weekly pay for all women is significantly greater than the mean weekly pay for women with a high school diploma.

b. Use the data in the file named WeeklyPay to compute the sample mean, the test statistic, and the *p*-value.

c. Use $\alpha = .05$. What is your conclusion?

d. Repeat the hypothesis test using the critical value approach.

52. The chamber of commerce of a Florida Gulf Coast community advertises that area residential property is available at a mean cost of $125,000 or less per lot. Suppose a sample of 32 properties provided a sample mean of $130,000 per lot and a sample standard deviation of $12,500. Use a .05 level of significance to test the validity of the advertising claim.

**Gasoline**

53. The U.S. Energy Administration reported that the mean price for a gallon of regular gasoline in the United States was $2.357 (U.S. Energy Administration, January 30, 2006). Data for a sample of regular gasoline prices at 50 service stations in the Lower Atlantic states are contained in the data file named Gasoline. Conduct a hypothesis test to determine whether the mean price for a gallon of gasoline in the Lower Atlantic states is different from the national mean. Use $\alpha = .05$ for the level of significance, and state your conclusion.

54. On December 25, 2009, an airline passenger was subdued while attempting to blow up a Northwest Airlines flight headed for Detroit, Michigan. The passenger had smuggled explosives hidden in his underwear past a metal detector at an airport screening facility. As a result, the Transportation Security Administration (TSA) proposed installing full-body

scanners to replace the metal detectors at the nation's largest airports. This proposal resulted in strong objections from privacy advocates, who considered the scanners an invasion of privacy. On January 5–6, 2010, *USA Today* conducted a poll of 542 adults to learn what proportion of airline travelers approved of using full-body scanners (*USA Today*, January 11, 2010). The poll results showed that 455 of the respondents felt that full-body scanners would improve airline security and 423 indicated that they approved of using the devices.

a. Conduct a hypothesis test to determine if the results of the poll justify concluding that over 80% of airline travelers feel that the use of full-body scanners will improve airline security. Use $\alpha = .05$.

b. Suppose the TSA will go forward with the installation and mandatory use of full-body scanners if over 75% of airline travelers approve of using the devices. You have been told to conduct a statistical analysis using the poll results to determine if the TSA should go forward with mandatory use of the full-body scanners. Because this is viewed as a very sensitive decision, use $\alpha = .01$. What is your recommendation?

55. A recent article concerning bullish and bearish sentiment about the stock market reported that 41% of investors responding to an American Institute of Individual Investors (AAII) poll were bullish on the market and 26% were bearish (*USA Today*, January 11, 2010). The article also reported that the long-term average measure of bullishness is .39 or 39%. Suppose the AAII poll used a sample size of 450. Using .39 (the long-term average) as the population proportion of investors that are bullish, conduct a hypothesis test to determine if the current proportion of investors that are bullish is significantly greater than the long-term average proportion.

a. State the appropriate hypotheses for your significance test.

b. Use the sample results to compute the test statistic and the *p*-value.

c. Using $\alpha = .10$, what is your conclusion?

56. Virtual call centers are staffed by individuals working out of their homes. Most home agents earn $10 to $15 per hour without benefits versus $7 to $9 per hour with benefits at a traditional call center (*BusinessWeek*, January 23, 2006). Regional Airways is considering employing home agents, but only if a level of customer satisfaction greater than 80% can be maintained. A test was conducted with home service agents. In a sample of 300 customers, 252 reported that they were satisfied with service.

a. Develop hypotheses for a test to determine whether the sample data support the conclusion that customer service with home agents meets the Regional Airways criterion.

b. What is your point estimate of the percentage of satisfied customers?

c. What is the *p*-value provided by the sample data?

d. What is your hypothesis testing conclusion? Use $\alpha = .05$ as the level of significance.

57. During the 2004 election year, new polling results were reported daily. In an IBD/TIPP poll of 910 adults, 503 respondents reported that they were optimistic about the national outlook, and President Bush's leadership index jumped 4.7 points to 55.3 (*Investor's Business Daily*, January 14, 2004).

a. What is the sample proportion of respondents who are optimistic about the national outlook?

b. A campaign manager wants to claim that this poll indicates that the majority of adults are optimistic about the national outlook. Construct a hypothesis test so that rejection of the null hypothesis will permit the conclusion that the proportion optimistic is greater than 50%.

c. Use the polling data to compute the *p*-value for the hypothesis test in part (b). Explain to the manager what this *p*-value means about the level of significance of the results.

58. A radio station in Myrtle Beach announced that at least 90% of the hotels and motels would be full for the Memorial Day weekend. The station advised listeners to make reservations in advance if they planned to be in the resort over the weekend. On Saturday night a sample of 58 hotels and motels showed 49 with a no-vacancy sign and 9 with vacancies. What is

your reaction to the radio station's claim after seeing the sample evidence? Use $\alpha = .05$ in making the statistical test. What is the $p$-value?

59. According to the federal government, 24% of workers covered by their company's health care plan were not required to contribute to the premium (*Statistical Abstract of the United States: 2006*). A recent study found that 81 out of 400 workers sampled were not required to contribute to their company's health care plan.

   a. Develop hypotheses that can be used to test whether the percent of workers not required to contribute to their company's health care plan has declined.

   b. What is a point estimate of the proportion receiving free company-sponsored health care insurance?

   c. Has a statistically significant decline occurred in the proportion of workers receiving free company-sponsored health care insurance? Use $\alpha = .05$.

## Case Problem 1    Quality Associates, Inc.

Quality Associates, Inc., a consulting firm, advises its clients about sampling and statistical procedures that can be used to control their manufacturing processes. In one particular application, a client gave Quality Associates a sample of 800 observations taken during a time in which that client's process was operating satisfactorily. The sample standard deviation for these data was .21; hence, with so much data, the population standard deviation was assumed to be .21. Quality Associates then suggested that random samples of size 30 be taken periodically to monitor the process on an ongoing basis. By analyzing the new samples, the client could quickly learn whether the process was operating satisfactorily. When the process was not operating satisfactorily, corrective action could be taken to eliminate the problem. The design specification indicated the mean for the process should be 12. The hypothesis test suggested by Quality Associates follows.

$$H_0: \mu = 12$$
$$H_a: \mu \neq 12$$

Corrective action will be taken any time $H_0$ is rejected.

The samples below were collected at hourly intervals during the first day of operation of the new statistical process control procedure. These data are available in the data set Quality.

### Managerial Report

1. Conduct a hypothesis test for each sample at the .01 level of significance and determine what action, if any, should be taken. Provide the test statistic and $p$-value for each test.

**WEB** file

**Quality**

| Sample 1 | Sample 2 | Sample 3 | Sample 4 |
|----------|----------|----------|----------|
| 11.55 | 11.62 | 11.91 | 12.02 |
| 11.62 | 11.69 | 11.36 | 12.02 |
| 11.52 | 11.59 | 11.75 | 12.05 |
| 11.75 | 11.82 | 11.95 | 12.18 |
| 11.90 | 11.97 | 12.14 | 12.11 |

| | | | |
|---|---|---|---|
| 11.64 | 11.71 | 11.72 | 12.07 |
| 11.80 | 11.87 | 11.61 | 12.05 |
| 12.03 | 12.10 | 11.85 | 11.64 |
| 11.94 | 12.01 | 12.16 | 12.39 |
| 11.92 | 11.99 | 11.91 | 11.65 |
| 12.13 | 12.20 | 12.12 | 12.11 |
| 12.09 | 12.16 | 11.61 | 11.90 |
| 11.93 | 12.00 | 12.21 | 12.22 |
| 12.21 | 12.28 | 11.56 | 11.88 |
| 12.32 | 12.39 | 11.95 | 12.03 |
| 11.93 | 12.00 | 12.01 | 12.35 |
| 11.85 | 11.92 | 12.06 | 12.09 |
| 11.76 | 11.83 | 11.76 | 11.77 |
| 12.16 | 12.23 | 11.82 | 12.20 |
| 11.77 | 11.84 | 12.12 | 11.79 |
| 12.00 | 12.07 | 11.60 | 12.30 |
| 12.04 | 12.11 | 11.95 | 12.27 |
| 11.98 | 12.05 | 11.96 | 12.29 |
| 12.30 | 12.37 | 12.22 | 12.47 |
| 12.18 | 12.25 | 11.75 | 12.03 |
| 11.97 | 12.04 | 11.96 | 12.17 |
| 12.17 | 12.24 | 11.95 | 11.94 |
| 11.85 | 11.92 | 11.89 | 11.97 |
| 12.30 | 12.37 | 11.88 | 12.23 |
| 12.15 | 12.22 | 11.93 | 12.25 |

2. Compute the standard deviation for each of the four samples. Does the assumption of .21 for the population standard deviation appear reasonable?

3. Compute limits for the sample mean $\bar{x}$ around $\mu = 12$ such that, as long as a new sample mean is within those limits, the process will be considered to be operating satisfactorily. If $\bar{x}$ exceeds the upper limit or if $\bar{x}$ is below the lower limit, corrective action will be taken. These limits are referred to as upper and lower control limits for quality control purposes.

4. Discuss the implications of changing the level of significance to a larger value. What mistake or error could increase if the level of significance is increased?

## Case Problem 2   Ethical Behavior of Business Students at Bayview University

During the global recession of 2008 and 2009, there were many accusations of unethical behavior by Wall Street executives, financial managers, and other corporate officers. At that time, an article appeared that suggested that part of the reason for such unethical business behavior may stem from the fact that cheating has become more prevalent among business students (*Chronicle of Higher Education*, February 10, 2009). The article reported that 56% of business students admitted to cheating at some time during their academic career as compared to 47% of nonbusiness students.

Cheating has been a concern of the dean of the College of Business at Bayview University for several years. Some faculty members in the college believe that cheating is more widespread at Bayview than at other universities, while other faculty members think that cheating is not a major problem in the college. To resolve some of these issues, the dean commissioned a study to assess the current ethical behavior of business students at Bayview. As part of this study, an anonymous exit survey was administered to a sample of 90 business students from this year's graduating class. Responses to the following questions were used to obtain data regarding three types of cheating.

During your time at Bayview, did you ever present work copied off the Internet as your own?

Yes _____        No _____

During your time at Bayview, did you ever copy answers off another student's exam?

Yes _____        No _____

During your time at Bayview, did you ever collaborate with other students on projects that were supposed to be completed individually?

Yes _____        No _____

Any student who answered Yes to one or more of these questions was considered to have been involved in some type of cheating. A portion of the data collected follows. The complete data set is in the file named Bayview.

**WEB file**

**Bayview**

| Student | Copied from Internet | Copied on Exam | Collaborated on Individual Project | Gender |
|---|---|---|---|---|
| 1 | No | No | No | Female |
| 2 | No | No | No | Male |
| 3 | Yes | No | Yes | Male |
| 4 | Yes | Yes | No | Male |
| 5 | No | No | Yes | Male |
| 6 | Yes | No | No | Female |
| . | . | . | . | . |
| . | . | . | . | . |
| . | . | . | . | . |
| 88 | No | No | No | Male |
| 89 | No | Yes | Yes | Male |
| 90 | No | No | No | Female |

## Managerial Report

Prepare a report for the dean of the college that summarizes your assessment of the nature of cheating by business students at Bayview University. Be sure to include the following items in your report.

1. Use descriptive statistics to summarize the data and comment on your findings.
2. Develop 95% confidence intervals for the proportion of all students, the proportion of male students, and the proportion of female students who were involved in some type of cheating.

3. Conduct a hypothesis test to determine if the proportion of business students at Bayview University who were involved in some type of cheating is less than that of business students at other institutions as reported by the *Chronicle of Higher Education*.

4. Conduct a hypothesis test to determine if the proportion of business students at Bayview University who were involved in some form of cheating is less than that of nonbusiness students at other institutions as reported by the *Chronicle of Higher Education*.

5. What advice would you give to the dean based upon your analysis of the data?

## Appendix   Hypothesis Testing with StatTools

In this appendix we show how StatTools can be used to conduct hypothesis tests about a population mean for the $\sigma$ unknown case

### Population Mean: $\sigma$ Unknown Case

In this case the population standard deviation $\sigma$ will be estimated by the sample standard deviation $s$. We use the example discussed in Section 9.4 involving ratings that 60 business travelers gave for Heathrow Airport.

Begin by using the Data Set Manager to create a StatTools data set for these data using the procedure described in the appendix in Chapter 1. The following steps can be used to test the hypothesis $H_0$: $\mu \le 7$ against $H_a$: $\mu > 7$.

**Step 1.** Click the **StatTools** tab on the Ribbon
**Step 2.** In the **Analyses** group, click **Statistical Inference**
**Step 3.** Choose the **Hypothesis Test** option
**Step 4.** Choose **Mean/Std. Deviation . . .**
**Step 5.** When the StatTools - Hypothesis Test for Mean/Std. Deviation dialog box appears,
      For **Analysis Type,** choose **One-Sample Analysis**
      In the **Variables** section, select **Rating**
      In the **Hypothesis Tests to Perform** section,
        Select the **Mean** option
        Enter 7 in the **Null Hypothesis Value** box
        Select **Greater Than Null Value (One-Tailed Test)** in the **Alternative Hypothesis Type** box
      If selected, remove the check in the **Standard Deviation** box
      Click **OK**

The results from the hypothesis test will appear. They include the *p*-value and the value of the test statistic.

# CHAPTER 10

# Comparisons Involving Means, Experimental Design, and Analysis of Variance

## STATISTICS *in* PRACTICE

### U.S. FOOD AND DRUG ADMINISTRATION
*WASHINGTON, D.C.*

It is the responsibility of the U.S. Food and Drug Administration (FDA), through its Center for Drug Evaluation and Research (CDER), to ensure that drugs are safe and effective. But CDER does not do the actual testing of new drugs itself. It is the responsibility of the company seeking to market a new drug to test it and submit evidence that it is safe and effective. CDER statisticians and scientists then review the evidence submitted.

Companies seeking approval of a new drug conduct extensive statistical studies to support their application. The testing process in the pharmaceutical industry usually consists of three stages: (1) preclinical testing, (2) testing for long-term usage and safety, and (3) clinical efficacy testing. At each successive stage, the chance that a drug will pass the rigorous tests decreases; however, the cost of further testing increases dramatically. Industry surveys indicate that on average the research and development for one new drug costs $250 million and takes 12 years. Hence, it is important to eliminate unsuccessful new drugs in the early stages of the testing process, as well as to identify promising ones for further testing.

Statistics plays a major role in pharmaceutical research, where government regulations are stringent and rigorously enforced. In preclinical testing, a two- or three-population statistical study typically is used to determine whether a new drug should continue to be studied in the long-term usage and safety program. The populations may consist of the new drug, a control, and a standard drug. The preclinical testing process begins when a new drug is sent to the pharmacology group for evaluation of efficacy—the capacity of the drug to produce the desired effects. As part of the process, a statistician is asked to design an experiment that can be used to test the new drug. The design must specify the sample size and the statistical methods of analysis. In a two-population study, one sample is used to obtain data on the efficacy of the new drug (population 1) and a second sample is used to obtain data on the efficacy of a standard drug (population 2). Depending on the intended use, the new and standard drugs are tested in such disciplines

Statistical methods are used to test and develop new drugs.

© John Kuntz/The Plain Dealer/Landov

as neurology, cardiology, and immunology. In most studies, the statistical method involves hypothesis testing for the difference between the means of the new drug population and the standard drug population. If a new drug lacks efficacy or produces undesirable effects in comparison with the standard drug, the new drug is rejected and withdrawn from further testing. Only new drugs that show promising comparisons with the standard drugs are forwarded to the long-term usage and safety testing program.

Further data collection and multipopulation studies are conducted in the long-term usage and safety testing program and in the clinical testing programs. The FDA requires that statistical methods be defined prior to such testing to avoid data-related biases. In addition, to avoid human biases, some of the clinical trials are double or triple blind. That is, neither the subject nor the investigator knows what drug is administered to whom. If the new drug meets all requirements in relation to the standard drug, a new drug application (NDA) is filed with the FDA. The application is rigorously scrutinized by statisticians and scientists at the agency.

In this chapter you will learn how to construct interval estimates and make hypothesis tests about means with two or more populations. Techniques will be presented for analyzing independent random samples as well as matched samples.

In Chapters 8 and 9 we showed how to develop interval estimates and conduct hypothesis tests for situations involving a single population mean and a single population proportion. In Sections 10.1–10.3 we continue our discussion of statistical inference by showing how interval estimates and hypothesis tests can be developed for situations involving two populations, when the difference between the two population means is of prime importance. For example, we may want to develop an interval estimate of the difference between the mean starting salary for a population of men and the mean starting salary for a population of women or conduct a hypothesis test to determine whether any difference is present between the two population means.

In Section 10.4 we introduce the basic principles of an experimental study and show how they are used in a completely randomized design. We also provide a conceptual overview of the statistical procedure called analysis of variance (ANOVA). In Section 10.5 we show how ANOVA can be used to test for the equality of $k$ population means using data obtained from a completely randomized design as well as data obtained from an observational study. So, in this sense, ANOVA extends the statistical material in Sections 10.1–10.3 from two population means to three or more population means.

We begin our discussion of statistical inference about two populations by showing how to develop interval estimates and conduct hypothesis tests about the difference between the means of two populations when the standard deviations of the two populations are assumed known.

## 10.1   Inferences About the Difference Between Two Population Means: $\sigma_1$ and $\sigma_2$ Known

Letting $\mu_1$ denote the mean of population 1 and $\mu_2$ denote the mean of population 2, we will focus on inferences about the difference between the means: $\mu_1 - \mu_2$. To make an inference about this difference, we select a simple random sample of $n_1$ elements from population 1 and a second simple random sample of $n_2$ elements from population 2. The two samples, taken separately and independently, are referred to as **independent simple random samples**. In this section, we assume that information is available such that the two population standard deviations, $\sigma_1$ and $\sigma_2$, can be assumed known prior to collecting the samples. We refer to this situation as the $\sigma_1$ and $\sigma_2$ known case. In the following example we show how to compute a margin of error and develop an interval estimate of the difference between the two population means when $\sigma_1$ and $\sigma_2$ are known.

### Interval Estimation of $\mu_1 - \mu_2$

HomeStyle sells furniture at two stores: one is located in the inner city and the other is located in a suburban shopping center. The regional manager noticed that products that sell well in one store do not always sell well in the other. The manager believes this situation may be attributable to differences in customer demographics at the two locations. Customers may differ in age, education, income, and so on. Suppose the manager asks us to investigate the difference between the mean ages of the customers who shop at the two stores.

Let us define population 1 as all customers who shop at the inner-city store and population 2 as all customers who shop at the suburban store.

$\mu_1$ = mean of population 1 (i.e., the mean age of all customers who shop at the inner-city store)

$\mu_2$ = mean of population 2 (i.e., the mean age of all customers who shop at the suburban store)

The difference between the two population means is $\mu_1 - \mu_2$.

**FIGURE 10.1**   ESTIMATING THE DIFFERENCE BETWEEN TWO POPULATION MEANS

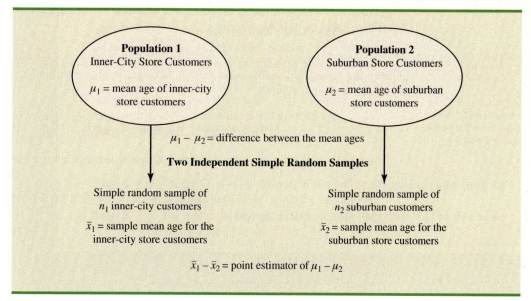

To estimate $\mu_1 - \mu_2$, we will select a simple random sample of $n_1$ customers from population 1 and a simple random sample of $n_2$ customers from population 2. We then compute the two sample means.

$\bar{x}_1 =$ sample mean age for the simple random sample of $n_1$ inner-city customers
$\bar{x}_2 =$ sample mean age for the simple random sample of $n_2$ suburban customers

The point estimator of the difference between the two population means is the difference between the two sample means.

POINT ESTIMATOR OF THE DIFFERENCE BETWEEN TWO POPULATION MEANS

$$\bar{x}_1 - \bar{x}_2 \qquad \textbf{(10.1)}$$

Figure 10.1 provides an overview of the process used to estimate the difference between two population means based on two independent simple random samples.

As with other point estimators, the point estimator $\bar{x}_1 - \bar{x}_2$ has a standard error that describes the variation in the sampling distribution of the estimator. With two independent simple random samples, the standard error of $\bar{x}_1 - \bar{x}_2$ is as follows:

*The standard error of $\bar{x}_1 - \bar{x}_2$ is the standard deviation of the sampling distribution of $\bar{x}_1 - \bar{x}_2$.*

STANDARD ERROR OF $\bar{x}_1 - \bar{x}_2$

$$\sigma_{\bar{x}_1 - \bar{x}_2} = \sqrt{\dfrac{\sigma_1^2}{n_1} + \dfrac{\sigma_2^2}{n_2}} \qquad \textbf{(10.2)}$$

If both populations have a normal distribution, or if the sample sizes are large enough that the central limit theorem enables us to conclude that the sampling distributions of $\bar{x}_1$ and $\bar{x}_2$ can be approximated by a normal distribution, the sampling distribution of $\bar{x}_1 - \bar{x}_2$ will have a normal distribution with mean given by $\mu_1 - \mu_2$.

As we showed in Chapter 8, an interval estimate is given by a point estimate ± a margin of error. When estimating the difference between two population means, the interval estimate takes the following form:

$$\bar{x}_1 - \bar{x}_2 \pm \text{Margin of error}$$

With the sampling distribution of $\bar{x}_1 - \bar{x}_2$ having a normal distribution, we can write the margin of error as follows:

*The margin of error is given by multiplying the standard error by $z_{\alpha/2}$.*

$$\text{Margin of error} = z_{\alpha/2}\sigma_{\bar{x}_1 - \bar{x}_2} = z_{\alpha/2}\sqrt{\frac{\sigma_1^2}{n_1} + \frac{\sigma_2^2}{n_2}} \qquad \textbf{(10.3)}$$

Thus, the interval estimate of the difference between two population means is as follows:

> **INTERVAL ESTIMATE OF THE DIFFERENCE BETWEEN TWO POPULATION MEANS: $\sigma_1$ AND $\sigma_2$ KNOWN**
>
> $$\bar{x}_1 - \bar{x}_2 \pm z_{\alpha/2}\sqrt{\frac{\sigma_1^2}{n_1} + \frac{\sigma_2^2}{n_2}} \qquad \textbf{(10.4)}$$
>
> where $1 - \alpha$ is the confidence coefficient.

Let us return to the HomeStyle example. Based on data from previous customer demographic studies, the two population standard deviations are assumed known with $\sigma_1 = 9$ years and $\sigma_2 = 10$ years. The data collected from the two independent simple random samples of HomeStyle customers provided the following results.

**WEB file**

**HomeStyle**

|  | Inner-City Store | Suburban Store |
|---|---|---|
| Sample Size | $n_1 = 36$ | $n_2 = 49$ |
| Sample Mean | $\bar{x}_1 = 40$ years | $\bar{x}_2 = 35$ years |

Using expression (10.1), we find that the point estimate of the difference between the mean ages of the two populations is $\bar{x}_1 - \bar{x}_2 = 40 - 35 = 5$ years. Thus, we estimate that the customers at the inner-city store have a mean age 5 years greater than the mean age of the suburban store customers. We can now use expression (10.4) to compute the margin of error and provide the interval estimate of $\mu_1 - \mu_2$. Using 95% confidence and $z_{\alpha/2} = z_{.025} = 1.96$, we have

$$\bar{x}_1 - \bar{x}_2 \pm z_{\alpha/2}\sqrt{\frac{\sigma_1^2}{n_1} + \frac{\sigma_2^2}{n_2}}$$

$$40 - 35 \pm 1.96\sqrt{\frac{9^2}{36} + \frac{10^2}{49}}$$

$$5 \pm 4.06$$

Thus, the margin of error is 4.06 years and the 95% confidence interval estimate of the difference between the two population means is $5 - 4.06 = .94$ years to $5 + 4.06 = 9.06$ years.

## Using Excel to Construct a Confidence Interval

Excel's data analysis tools do not provide a procedure for developing interval estimates involving two population means. However, we can develop an Excel worksheet that can be used as a template to construct interval estimates. We will illustrate by constructing an

**FIGURE 10.2** EXCEL WORKSHEET: CONSTRUCTING A 95% CONFIDENCE INTERVAL FOR HOMESTYLE FURNITURE STORES

Note: Rows 19–35 and 38–48 are hidden.

interval estimate of the difference between the population means in the HomeStyle Furniture Stores study. Refer to Figure 10.2 as we describe the tasks involved. The formula worksheet is in the background; the value worksheet is in the foreground.

**Enter Data:** Column A contains the age data for the simple random sample of 36 inner-city customers, and column B contains the age data for the simple random sample of 49 suburban customers.

**Enter Functions and Formulas:**    The descriptive statistics needed are provided in cells E5:F6. The known population standard deviations are entered into cells E8 and F8. Using the two population standard deviations and the sample sizes, the standard error of the point estimator, $\bar{x}_1 - \bar{x}_2$, is computed using equation (10.2) by entering the following formula into cell E9:

$$=SQRT(E8^2/E5+F8^2/F5)$$

Cells E11:E14 are used to compute the appropriate $z$ value and the margin of error. The confidence coefficient is entered into cell E11 (.95) and the corresponding level of significance ($\alpha = 1 -$ confidence coefficient) is computed in cell E12. In cell E13, we used the NORM.S.INV function to compute the $z$ value needed for the interval estimate. The margin of error is computed in cell E14 by multiplying the $z$ value by the standard error.

In cell E16 the difference in the sample means is used to compute the point estimate of the difference in the two population means. The lower limit of the confidence interval is computed in cell E17 (.94) and the upper limit is computed in cell E18 (9.06); thus, the 95% confidence interval estimate of the difference in the two population means is .94 to 9.06.

**A template for other problems**    This worksheet can be used as a template for developing interval estimates of the difference in population means when the population standard deviations are assumed known. For another problem of this type, we must first enter the new problem data in columns A and B. The data ranges in cells E5:F6 must be modified in order to compute the sample means and sample sizes for the new data. Also, the assumed known population standard deviations must be entered into cells E8 and F8. After doing so, the point estimate and a 95% confidence interval will be displayed in cells E16:E18. If a confidence interval with a different confidence coefficient is desired, we simply change the value in cell E11.

We can further simplify the use of Figure 10.2 as a template for other problems by eliminating the need to enter new data ranges in cells E5:F6. We rewrite the cell formulas as follows:

> Cell E5:  =COUNT(A:A)
>
> Cell F5:  =COUNT(B:B)
>
> Cell E6:  =AVERAGE(A:A)
>
> Cell F6:  =AVERAGE(B:B)

*The HomeStyle webfile includes a worksheet entitled Template that uses the A:A and B:B methods for entering the data ranges.*

Using the A:A method of specifying data ranges in cells E5 and E6, Excel's COUNT function will count the number of numeric values in column A and Excel's AVERAGE function will compute the average of the numeric values in column A. Similarly, using the B:B method of specifying data ranges in cells F5 and F6, Excel's COUNT function will count the number of numeric values in column B and Excel's AVERAGE function will compute the average of the numeric values in column B. Thus, to solve a new problem it is only necessary to enter the new data into columns A and B and enter the known population standard deviations in cells E8 and F8.

This worksheet can also be used as a template for text exercises in which the sample sizes, sample means, and population standard deviations are given. In this type of situation, no change in the data is necessary. We simply replace the values in cells E5:F6 and E8:F8 with the given values of the sample sizes, sample means, and population standard deviations. If something other than a 95% confidence interval is desired, the confidence coefficient in cell E11 must also be changed.

## Hypothesis Tests About $\mu_1 - \mu_2$

Let us consider hypothesis tests about the difference between two population means. Using $D_0$ to denote the hypothesized difference between $\mu_1$ and $\mu_2$, the three forms for a hypothesis test are as follows:

$$H_0: \mu_1 - \mu_2 \geq D_0 \qquad H_0: \mu_1 - \mu_2 \leq D_0 \qquad H_0: \mu_1 - \mu_2 = D_0$$
$$H_a: \mu_1 - \mu_2 < D_0 \qquad H_a: \mu_1 - \mu_2 > D_0 \qquad H_a: \mu_1 - \mu_2 \neq D_0$$

In most applications, $D_0 = 0$. Using the two-tailed test as an example, when $D_0 = 0$ the null hypothesis is $H_0: \mu_1 - \mu_2 = 0$. In this case, the null hypothesis is that $\mu_1$ and $\mu_2$ are equal. Rejection of $H_0$ leads to the conclusion that $H_a: \mu_1 - \mu_2 \neq 0$ is true; that is, $\mu_1$ and $\mu_2$ are not equal.

The steps for conducting hypothesis tests presented in Chapter 9 are applicable here. We must choose a level of significance, compute the value of the test statistic, and find the $p$-value to determine whether the null hypothesis should be rejected. With two independent simple random samples, we showed that the point estimator $\bar{x}_1 - \bar{x}_2$ has a standard error $\sigma_{\bar{x}_1 - \bar{x}_2}$ given by expression (10.2) and the sampling distribution of $\bar{x}_1 - \bar{x}_2$ can be described by a normal distribution. In this case, the test statistic for the difference between two population means when $\sigma_1$ and $\sigma_2$ are known is as follows.

TEST STATISTIC FOR HYPOTHESIS TESTS ABOUT $\mu_1 - \mu_2$: $\sigma_1$ AND $\sigma_2$ KNOWN

$$z = \frac{(\bar{x}_1 - \bar{x}_2) - D_0}{\sqrt{\dfrac{\sigma_1^2}{n_1} + \dfrac{\sigma_2^2}{n_2}}} \qquad (10.5)$$

Let us demonstrate the use of this test statistic in the following hypothesis testing example.

As part of a study to evaluate differences in education quality between two training centers, a standardized examination is given to individuals who are trained at the centers. The difference between the mean examination scores is used to assess quality differences between the centers. The population means for the two centers are as follows.

$\mu_1 =$ the mean examination score for the population of individuals trained at center A

$\mu_2 =$ the mean examination score for the population of individuals trained at center B

We begin with the tentative assumption that no difference exists between the training quality provided at the two centers. Hence, in terms of the mean examination scores, the null hypothesis is that $\mu_1 - \mu_2 = 0$. If sample evidence leads to the rejection of this hypothesis, we will conclude that the mean examination scores differ for the two populations. This conclusion indicates a quality differential between the two centers and suggests that a follow-up study investigating the reason for the differential may be warranted. The null and alternative hypotheses for this two-tailed test are written as follows.

$$H_0: \mu_1 - \mu_2 = 0$$
$$H_a: \mu_1 - \mu_2 \neq 0$$

The standardized examination given previously in a variety of settings always resulted in an examination score standard deviation near 10 points. Thus, we will use this information to assume that the population standard deviations are known with $\sigma_1 = 10$ and $\sigma_2 = 10$. An $\alpha = .05$ level of significance is specified for the study.

Independent simple random samples of $n_1 = 30$ individuals from training center A and $n_2 = 40$ individuals from training center B are taken. The respective sample means are $\bar{x}_1 = 82$ and $\bar{x}_2 = 78$. Do these data suggest a significant difference between the population means at the two training centers? To help answer this question, we compute the test statistic using equation (10.5).

$$z = \frac{(\bar{x}_1 - \bar{x}_2) - D_0}{\sqrt{\dfrac{\sigma_1^2}{n_1} + \dfrac{\sigma_2^2}{n_2}}} = \frac{(82 - 78) - 0}{\sqrt{\dfrac{10^2}{30} + \dfrac{10^2}{40}}} = 1.66$$

Next let us compute the $p$-value for this two-tailed test. Because the test statistic $z$ is in the upper tail, we first compute the upper tail area at $z = 1.66$. Using the standard normal distribution table, the area to the left of $z = 1.66$ is .9515. Thus, the area in the upper tail of the distribution is $1.0000 - .9515 = .0485$. Because this test is a two-tailed test, we must double the tail area: $p$-value $= 2(.0485) = .0970$. Following the usual rule to reject $H_0$ if $p$-value $\leq \alpha$, we see that the $p$-value of .0970 does not allow us to reject $H_0$ at the .05 level of significance. The sample results do not provide sufficient evidence to conclude that the training centers differ in quality.

In this chapter we will use the $p$-value approach to hypothesis testing as described in Chapter 9. However, if you prefer, the test statistic and the critical value rejection rule may be used. With $\alpha = .05$ and $z_{\alpha/2} = z_{.025} = 1.96$, the rejection rule employing the critical value approach would be reject $H_0$ if $z \leq -1.96$ or if $z \geq 1.96$. With $z = 1.66$, we reach the same do not reject $H_0$ conclusion.

In the preceding example, we demonstrated a two-tailed hypothesis test about the difference between two population means. Lower tail and upper tail tests can also be considered. These tests use the same test statistic as given in equation (10.5). The procedure for computing the $p$-value and the rejection rules for these one-tailed tests are the same as those presented in Chapter 9.

## Using Excel to Conduct a Hypothesis Test

The Excel tool used to conduct the hypothesis test to determine whether there is a significant difference in population means when $\sigma_1$ and $\sigma_2$ are assumed known is called *z-Test: Two Sample for Means*. We illustrate using the sample data for exam scores at center A and at center B. With an assumed known standard deviation of 10 points at each center, the known variance of exam scores for each of the two populations is equal to $10^2 = 100$. Refer to the Excel worksheets shown in Figure 10.3 and Figure 10.4 as we describe the tasks involved.

**Enter Data:**   Column A in Figure 10.3 contains the examination score data for the simple random sample of 30 individuals trained at center A, and column B contains the examination score data for the simple random sample of 40 individuals trained at center B.

**Apply Tools:**   The following steps will provide the information needed to conduct the hypothesis test to see whether there is a significant difference in test scores at the two centers.

> **Step 1.** Click the **Data** tab on the Ribbon
> **Step 2.** In the **Analysis** group, click **Data Analysis**
> **Step 3.** Choose **z-Test: Two Sample for Means** from the list of Analysis Tools
> **Step 4.** When the z-Test: Two Sample for Means dialog box appears (Figure 10.3),
> > Enter A1:A31 in the **Variable 1 Range** box
> > Enter B1:B41 in the **Variable 2 Range** box
> > Enter 0 in the **Hypothesized Mean Difference** box
> > Enter 100 in the **Variable 1 Variance (known)** box

**FIGURE 10.3    DIALOG BOX FOR EXCEL'S z-TEST: TWO SAMPLE FOR MEANS TOOL**

*Note: Rows 18–28 and 33–39 are hidden.*

Enter 100 in the **Variable 2 Variance (known)** box
Select **Labels**
Enter .05 in the **Alpha** box
Select **Output Range** and enter D4 in the box
Click **OK**

*The value of the test statistic shown here (1.6562) and the p-value (.0977) differ slightly from those shown previously, because we rounded the test statistic to two places (1.66) in the text.*

The results are shown in Figure 10.4. Descriptive statistics for the two samples are shown in cells E7:F9. The value of the test statistic, 1.6562, is shown in cell E11. The $p$-value for the test, labeled P(Z<=z) two-tail, is shown in cell E14. Because the $p$-value, .0977, is greater than the level of significance, $\alpha = .05$, we cannot conclude that the means for the two populations are different.

The z-Test: Two Sample for Means tool can also be used to conduct one-tailed hypothesis tests. The only change required to make the hypothesis testing decision is that we need to use the $p$-value for a one-tailed test, labeled P(Z<=z) one-tail (see cell E12).

## Practical Advice

In most applications of the interval estimation and hypothesis testing procedures presented in this section, random samples with $n_1 \geq 30$ and $n_2 \geq 30$ are adequate. In cases where either or both sample sizes are less than 30, the distributions of the populations become important considerations. In general, with smaller sample sizes, it is more important for the analyst to be satisfied that it is reasonable to assume that the distributions of the two populations are at least approximately normal.

**FIGURE 10.4**    EXCEL RESULTS FOR THE HYPOTHESIS TEST ABOUT EQUALITY
OF EXAM SCORES AT TWO TRAINING CENTERS

| | A | B | C | D | E | F | G |
|---|---|---|---|---|---|---|---|
| 1 | Center A | Center B | | | | | |
| 2 | 97 | 64 | | | | | |
| 3 | 95 | 85 | | | | | |
| 4 | 89 | 72 | | z-Test: Two Sample for Means | | | |
| 5 | 79 | 64 | | | | | |
| 6 | 78 | 74 | | | Center A | Center B | |
| 7 | 87 | 93 | | Mean | 82 | 78 | |
| 8 | 83 | 70 | | Known Variance | 100 | 100 | |
| 9 | 94 | 79 | | Observations | 30 | 40 | |
| 10 | 76 | 79 | | Hypothesized Mean Difference | 0 | | |
| 11 | 79 | 75 | | z | 1.6562 | | |
| 12 | 83 | 66 | | P(Z<=z) one-tail | 0.0488 | | |
| 13 | 84 | 83 | | z Critical one-tail | 1.6449 | | |
| 14 | 76 | 74 | | P(Z<=z) two-tail | 0.0977 | | |
| 15 | 82 | 70 | | z Critical two-tail | 1.9600 | | |
| 16 | 85 | 82 | | | | | |
| 17 | 85 | 82 | | | | | |
| 29 | 88 | 65 | | | | | |
| 30 | 60 | 78 | | | | | |
| 31 | 73 | 66 | | | | | |
| 32 | | 84 | | | | | |
| 40 | | 80 | | | | | |
| 41 | | 76 | | | | | |
| 42 | | | | | | | |

# Exercises

## Methods

1. The following results are for two independent random samples taken from two populations.

| Sample 1 | Sample 2 |
|---|---|
| $n_1 = 50$ | $n_2 = 35$ |
| $\bar{x}_1 = 13.6$ | $\bar{x}_2 = 11.6$ |
| $\sigma_1 = 2.2$ | $\sigma_2 = 3.0$ |

   a.   What is the point estimate of the difference between the two population means?
   b.   Provide a 90% confidence interval for the difference between the two population means.
   c.   Provide a 95% confidence interval for the difference between the two population means.

2. Consider the following hypothesis test.

$$H_0: \mu_1 - \mu_2 \leq 0$$
$$H_a: \mu_1 - \mu_2 > 0$$

The following results are for two independent samples taken from the two populations.

| Sample 1 | Sample 2 |
|---|---|
| $n_1 = 40$ | $n_2 = 50$ |
| $\bar{x}_1 = 25.2$ | $\bar{x}_2 = 22.8$ |
| $\sigma_1 = 5.2$ | $\sigma_2 = 6.0$ |

    a.    What is the value of the test statistic?
    b.    What is the *p*-value?
    c.    With $\alpha = .05$, what is your hypothesis testing conclusion?

3.   Consider the following hypothesis test.

$$H_0: \mu_1 - \mu_2 = 0$$
$$H_a: \mu_1 - \mu_2 \neq 0$$

The following results are for two independent samples taken from the two populations.

| Sample 1 | Sample 2 |
|---|---|
| $n_1 = 80$ | $n_2 = 70$ |
| $\bar{x}_1 = 104$ | $\bar{x}_2 = 106$ |
| $\sigma_1 = 8.4$ | $\sigma_2 = 7.6$ |

    a.    What is the value of the test statistic?
    b.    What is the *p*-value?
    c.    With $\alpha = .05$, what is your hypothesis testing conclusion?

## Applications

4.   *Condé Nast Traveler* conducts an annual survey in which readers rate their favorite cruise ship. All ships are rated on a 100-point scale, with higher values indicating better service. A sample of 37 ships that carry fewer than 500 passengers resulted in an average rating of 85.36, and a sample of 44 ships that carry 500 or more passengers provided an average rating of 81.40 (*Condé Nast Traveler,* February 2008). Assume that the population standard deviation is 4.55 for ships that carry fewer than 500 passengers and 3.97 for ships that carry 500 or more passengers.
    a.    What is the point estimate of the difference between the population mean rating for ships that carry fewer than 500 passengers and the population mean rating for ships that carry 500 or more passengers?
    b.    At 95% confidence, what is the margin of error?
    c.    What is a 95% confidence interval estimate of the difference between the population mean ratings for the two sizes of ships?

5.   The average expenditure on Valentine's Day was expected to be $100.89 (*USA Today,* February 13, 2006). Do male and female consumers differ in the amounts they spend? The average expenditure in a sample survey of 40 male consumers was $135.67, and the average expenditure in a sample survey of 30 female consumers was $68.64. Based on past surveys, the standard deviation for male consumers is assumed to be $35, and the standard deviation for female consumers is assumed to be $20.
    a.    What is the point estimate of the difference between the population mean expenditure for males and the population mean expenditure for females?
    b.    At 99% confidence, what is the margin of error?
    c.    Develop a 99% confidence interval for the difference between the two population means.

Hotel

6.   Suppose that you are responsible for making arrangements for a business convention. Because of budget cuts due to the recent recession, you have been charged with choosing a city for the convention that has the least expensive hotel rooms. You have narrowed your choices to Atlanta and Houston. The file named Hotel contains samples of prices for rooms in Atlanta and Houston that are consistent with the results reported by Smith Travel Research (*SmartMoney,* March 2009). Because considerable historical data on the prices of rooms in both cities are available, the population standard deviations for the prices can be assumed to be $20 in Atlanta and $25 in Houston. Based on the sample data, can you conclude that the mean price of a hotel room in Atlanta is lower than one in Houston?

7. During the 2003 season, Major League Baseball took steps to speed up the play of baseball games in order to maintain fan interest (*CNN Headline News*, September 30, 2003). The following results come from a sample of 60 games played during the summer of 2002 and a sample of 50 games played during the summer of 2003. The sample mean shows the mean duration of the games included in each sample.

| 2002 Season | 2003 Season |
|---|---|
| $n_1 = 60$ | $n_2 = 50$ |
| $\bar{x}_1 = 2$ hours, 52 minutes | $\bar{x}_2 = 2$ hours, 46 minutes |

a. A research hypothesis was that the steps taken during the 2003 season would reduce the population mean duration of baseball games. Formulate the null and alternative hypotheses.
b. What is the point estimate of the reduction in the mean duration of games during the 2003 season?
c. Historical data indicate a population standard deviation of 12 minutes is a reasonable assumption for both years. Conduct the hypothesis test and report the $p$-value. At a .05 level of significance, what is your conclusion?
d. Provide a 95% confidence interval estimate of the reduction in the mean duration of games during the 2003 season.
e. What was the percentage reduction in the mean time of baseball games during the 2003 season? Should management be pleased with the results of the statistical analysis? Discuss. Should the length of baseball games continue to be an issue in future years? Explain.

8. Will improving customer service result in higher stock prices for the companies providing the better service? "When a company's satisfaction score has improved over the prior year's results and is above the national average (currently 75.7), studies show its shares have a good chance of outperforming the broad stock market in the long run" (*Business-Week*, March 2, 2009). The following satisfaction scores of three companies for the 4th quarters of 2007 and 2008 were obtained from the American Customer Satisfaction Index. Assume that the scores are based on a poll of 60 customers from each company. Because the polling has been done for several years, the standard deviation can be assumed to equal 6 points in each case.

| Company | 2007 Score | 2008 Score |
|---|---|---|
| Rite Aid | 73 | 76 |
| Expedia | 75 | 77 |
| JC Penney | 77 | 78 |

a. For Rite Aid, is the increase in the satisfaction score from 2007 to 2008 statistically significant? Use $\alpha = .05$. What can you conclude?
b. Can you conclude that the 2008 score for Rite Aid is above the national average of 75.7? Use $\alpha = .05$.
c. For Expedia, is the increase from 2007 to 2008 statistically significant? Use $\alpha = .05$.
d. When conducting a hypothesis test with the values given for the standard deviation, sample size, and $\alpha$, how large must the increase from 2007 to 2008 be for it to be statistically significant?
e. Use the result of part (d) to state whether the increase for JC Penney from 2007 to 2008 is statistically significant.

## 10.2  Inferences About the Difference Between Two Population Means: $\boldsymbol{\sigma_1}$ and $\boldsymbol{\sigma_2}$ Unknown

In this section we extend the discussion of inferences about the difference between two population means to the case when the two population standard deviations, $\sigma_1$ and $\sigma_2$, are unknown. In this case, we will use the sample standard deviations, $s_1$ and $s_2$, to estimate the unknown population standard deviations. When we use the sample standard deviations, the interval estimation and hypothesis testing procedures will be based on the $t$ distribution rather than the standard normal distribution.

### Interval Estimation of $\mu_1 - \mu_2$

In the following example we show how to compute a margin of error and develop an interval estimate of the difference between two population means when $\sigma_1$ and $\sigma_2$ are unknown. Clearwater National Bank is conducting a study designed to identify differences between checking account practices by customers at two of its branch banks. A simple random sample of 28 checking accounts is selected from the Cherry Grove Branch and an independent simple random sample of 22 checking accounts is selected from the Beechmont Branch. The current checking account balance is recorded for each of the checking accounts. A summary of the account balances follows:

**WEB** file

**CheckAcct**

|                            | **Cherry Grove** | **Beechmont** |
|----------------------------|------------------|---------------|
| Sample Size                | $n_1 = 28$       | $n_2 = 22$    |
| Sample Mean                | $\bar{x}_1 = \$1025$ | $\bar{x}_2 = \$910$ |
| Sample Standard Deviation  | $s_1 = \$150$    | $s_2 = \$125$ |

Clearwater National Bank would like to estimate the difference between the mean checking account balance maintained by the population of Cherry Grove customers and the population of Beechmont customers. Let us develop the margin of error and an interval estimate of the difference between these two population means.

In Section 10.1, we provided the following interval estimate for the case when the population standard deviations, $\sigma_1$ and $\sigma_2$, are known.

$$\bar{x}_1 - \bar{x}_2 \pm z_{\alpha/2}\sqrt{\frac{\sigma_1^2}{n_1} + \frac{\sigma_2^2}{n_2}}$$

*When $\sigma_1$ and $\sigma_2$ are estimated by $s_1$ and $s_2$, the t distribution is used to make inferences about the difference between two population means.*

With $\sigma_1$ and $\sigma_2$ unknown, we will use the sample standard deviations $s_1$ and $s_2$ to estimate $\sigma_1$ and $\sigma_2$ and replace $z_{\alpha/2}$ with $t_{\alpha/2}$. As a result, the interval estimate of the difference between two population means is given by the following expression:

> **INTERVAL ESTIMATE OF THE DIFFERENCE BETWEEN TWO POPULATION MEANS: $\sigma_1$ AND $\sigma_2$ UNKNOWN**
>
> $$\bar{x}_1 - \bar{x}_2 \pm t_{\alpha/2}\sqrt{\frac{s_1^2}{n_1} + \frac{s_2^2}{n_2}} \tag{10.6}$$
>
> where $1 - \alpha$ is the confidence coefficient.

In this expression, the use of the $t$ distribution is an approximation, but it provides excellent results and is relatively easy to use. The only difficulty that we encounter in using expression (10.6) is determining the appropriate degrees of freedom for $t_{\alpha/2}$. The formula used is as follows:

*The Excel worksheet in Figure 10.5 makes this computation easy.*

DEGREES OF FREEDOM: $t$ DISTRIBUTION WITH TWO INDEPENDENT RANDOM SAMPLES

$$df = \frac{\left(\dfrac{s_1^2}{n_1} + \dfrac{s_2^2}{n_2}\right)^2}{\dfrac{1}{n_1 - 1}\left(\dfrac{s_1^2}{n_1}\right)^2 + \dfrac{1}{n_2 - 1}\left(\dfrac{s_2^2}{n_2}\right)^2} \tag{10.7}$$

Let us return to the Clearwater National Bank example and show how to use expression (10.6) to provide a 95% confidence interval estimate of the difference between the population mean checking account balances at the two branch banks. The sample data show $n_1 = 28$, $\bar{x}_1 = \$1025$, and $s_1 = \$150$ for the Cherry Grove Branch, and $n_2 = 22$, $\bar{x}_2 = \$910$, and $s_2 = \$125$ for the Beechmont Branch. The calculation for degrees of freedom for $t_{\alpha/2}$ is as follows:

$$df = \frac{\left(\dfrac{s_1^2}{n_1} + \dfrac{s_2^2}{n_2}\right)^2}{\dfrac{1}{n_1 - 1}\left(\dfrac{s_1^2}{n_1}\right)^2 + \dfrac{1}{n_2 - 1}\left(\dfrac{s_2^2}{n_2}\right)^2} = \frac{\left(\dfrac{150^2}{28} + \dfrac{125^2}{22}\right)^2}{\dfrac{1}{28 - 1}\left(\dfrac{150^2}{28}\right)^2 + \dfrac{1}{22 - 1}\left(\dfrac{125^2}{22}\right)^2} = 47.8$$

We round the noninteger degrees of freedom *down* to 47 to provide a larger $t$ value and a more conservative (wider) interval estimate. Using the $t$ distribution table with 47 degrees of freedom, we find $t_{.025} = 2.012$. Using expression (10.6), we develop the 95% confidence interval estimate of the difference between the two population means as follows.

$$\bar{x}_1 - \bar{x}_2 \pm t_{.025}\sqrt{\frac{s_1^2}{n_1} + \frac{s_2^2}{n_2}}$$

$$1025 - 910 \pm 2.012\sqrt{\frac{150^2}{28} + \frac{125^2}{22}}$$

$$115 \pm 78$$

The point estimate of the difference between the population mean checking account balances at the two branches is $115 and the margin of error is $78. Thus the 95% confidence interval estimate of the difference between the two population means is $115 - 78 = \$37$ to $115 + 78 = \$193$.

*This suggestion should help if you are using equation (10.7) to calculate the degrees of freedom by hand.*

The computation of the degrees of freedom in equation (10.7) is cumbersome if you are doing the calculation by hand. However, note that the expressions $s_1^2/n_1$ and $s_2^2/n_2$ appear in both expression (10.6) and equation (10.7). These values only need to be computed once in order to evaluate both (10.6) and (10.7).

## Using Excel to Construct a Confidence Interval

Excel's data analysis tools do not provide a procedure for developing interval estimates involving two population means. However, we can develop an Excel worksheet that can be used as a template to construct interval estimates. We will illustrate by constructing an interval estimate of the difference between the population means in the Clearwater National Bank study. Refer to Figure 10.5 as we describe the tasks involved. The formula worksheet is in the background; the value worksheet is in the foreground.

**FIGURE 10.5**   EXCEL WORKSHEET: CONSTRUCTING A 95% CONFIDENCE INTERVAL FOR CLEARWATER NATIONAL BANK

**Enter Data:**   Column A contains the account balances for the simple random sample of 28 customers at the Cherry Grove Branch, and column B contains the account balances for the simple random sample of 22 customers at the Beechmont Branch.

**Enter Functions and Formulas:**   The descriptive statistics needed are provided in cells E5:F7. Using the two sample standard deviations and the sample sizes, an estimate of the variance of the point estimator $\bar{x}_1 - \bar{x}_2$ is computed by entering the following formula into cell E9:

$$=E7\text{^}2/E5 + F7\text{^}2/F5$$

An estimate of the standard error is then computed in cell E10 by taking the square root of the variance.

Cells E12:E16 are used to compute the appropriate $t$ value and the margin of error. The confidence coefficient is entered into cell E12 (.95) and the corresponding level of significance is computed in cell E13 ($\alpha = .05$). In cell E14, we used formula (10.7) to compute the degrees of freedom (47.8). In cell E15, we used the T.INV.2T function to compute the $t$ value needed for the interval estimate. The margin of error is computed in cell E16 by multiplying the $t$ value by the standard error.

In cell E18 the difference in the sample means is used to compute the point estimate of the difference in the two population means (115). The lower limit of the confidence interval is computed in cell E19 (37) and the upper limit is computed in cell E20 (193); thus, the 95% confidence interval estimate of the difference in the two population means is 37 to 193.

**A template for other problems** This worksheet can be used as a template for developing interval estimates of the difference in population means when the population standard deviations are unknown. For another problem of this type, we must first enter the new problem data in columns A and B. The data ranges in cells E5:F7 must be modified in order to compute the sample means, sample sizes, and sample standard deviations for the new data. After doing so the point estimate and a 95% confidence interval will be displayed in cells E18:E20. If a confidence interval with a different confidence coefficient is desired, we simply change the value in cell E12.

We can further simplify the use of Figure 10.5 as a template for other problems by eliminating the need to enter new data ranges in cells E5:F7. We rewrite the cell formulas as follows:

Cell E5:  =COUNT(A:A)
Cell F5:  =COUNT(B:B)
Cell E6:  =AVERAGE(A:A)
Cell F6:  =AVERAGE(B:B)
Cell E7:  =STDEV.S(A:A)
Cell F7:  =STDEV.S(B:B)

*The CheckAcct data set includes a worksheet entitled Template that uses the A:A and B:B methods for entering the data ranges.*

Using the A:A method of specifying data ranges in cells E5:E7, Excel's COUNT function will count the number of numeric values in column A, Excel's AVERAGE function will compute the average of the numeric values in column A, and Excel's STDEV function will compute the standard deviation of the numeric values in column A. Similarly, using the B:B method of specifying data ranges in cells F5:F7, Excel's COUNT function will count the number of numeric values in column B, Excel's AVERAGE function will compute the average of the numeric values in column B, and Excel's STDEV function will compute the standard deviation of the numeric values in column B. Thus, to solve a new problem it is only necessary to enter the new data into columns A and B.

This worksheet can also be used as a template for text exercises in which the sample sizes, sample means, and sample standard deviations are given. In this type of situation, no change in the data is necessary. We simply replace the values in cells E5:F7 with the given values of the sample sizes, sample means, and sample standard deviations. If something other than a 95% confidence interval is desired, the confidence coefficient in cell E12 must also be changed.

## Hypothesis Tests About $\mu_1 - \mu_2$

Let us now consider hypothesis tests about the difference between the means of two populations when the population standard deviations $\sigma_1$ and $\sigma_2$ are unknown. Letting $D_0$ denote the hypothesized difference between $\mu_1$ and $\mu_2$, Section 10.1 showed that the test statistic used for the case where $\sigma_1$ and $\sigma_2$ are known is as follows.

$$z = \frac{(\bar{x}_1 - \bar{x}_2) - D_0}{\sqrt{\dfrac{\sigma_1^2}{n_1} + \dfrac{\sigma_2^2}{n_2}}}$$

The test statistic, $z$, follows the standard normal distribution.

When $\sigma_1$ and $\sigma_2$ are unknown, we use $s_1$ as an estimator of $\sigma_1$ and $s_2$ as an estimator of $\sigma_2$. Substituting these sample standard deviations for $\sigma_1$ and $\sigma_2$ provides the following test statistic when $\sigma_1$ and $\sigma_2$ are unknown.

---

**TEST STATISTIC FOR HYPOTHESIS TESTS ABOUT $\mu_1 - \mu_2$: $\sigma_1$ AND $\sigma_2$ UNKNOWN**

$$t = \frac{(\bar{x}_1 - \bar{x}_2) - D_0}{\sqrt{\dfrac{s_1^2}{n_1} + \dfrac{s_2^2}{n_2}}} \qquad \textbf{(10.8)}$$

The degrees of freedom for $t$ are given by equation (10.7).

---

Let us demonstrate the use of this test statistic in the following hypothesis testing example.

Consider a new computer software package developed to help systems analysts reduce the time required to design, develop, and implement an information system. To evaluate the benefits of the new software package, a random sample of 24 systems analysts is selected. Each analyst is given specifications for a hypothetical information system. Then 12 of the analysts are instructed to produce the information system by using current technology. The other 12 analysts are trained in the use of the new software package and then instructed to use it to produce the information system.

This study involves two populations: a population of systems analysts using the current technology and a population of systems analysts using the new software package. In terms of the time required to complete the information system design project, the population means are as follow.

$\mu_1 = $ the mean project completion time for systems analysts using the current technology

$\mu_2 = $ the mean project completion time for systems analysts using the new software package

The researcher in charge of the new software evaluation project hopes to show that the new software package will provide a shorter mean project completion time. Thus, the researcher is looking for evidence to conclude that $\mu_2$ is less than $\mu_1$; in this case, the difference between the two population means, $\mu_1 - \mu_2$, will be greater than zero. The research hypothesis $\mu_1 - \mu_2 > 0$ is stated as the alternative hypothesis. Thus, the hypothesis test becomes

$$H_0: \mu_1 - \mu_2 \leq 0$$
$$H_a: \mu_1 - \mu_2 > 0$$

We will use $\alpha = .05$ as the level of significance.

**FIGURE 10.7**    EXCEL RESULTS FOR THE HYPOTHESIS TEST ABOUT EQUALITY OF
MEAN PROJECT COMPLETION TIMES

**Step 4.** When the t-Test: Two-Sample Assuming Unequal Variances dialog box appears
(Figure 10.7),

Enter A1:A13 in the **Variable 1 Range** box
Enter B1:B13 in the **Variable 2 Range** box
Enter 0 in the **Hypothesized Mean Difference** box
Select **Labels**
Enter .05 in the **Alpha** box
Select **Output Range** and enter D1 in the box
Click **OK**

The results are shown in Figure 10.7. Descriptive statistics for the two samples are
shown in cells E4:F6. The value of the test statistic, 2.2721, is shown in cell E9. The p-value
for the test, labeled P(T<=t) one-tail, is shown in cell E10. Because the p-value, .0166, is
less than the level of significance $\alpha = .05$, we can conclude that the mean completion time
for the population using the new software package is smaller.

The t-Test: Two-Sample Assuming Unequal Variances tool can also be used to conduct
two-tailed hypothesis tests. The only change required to make the hypothesis testing
decision is that we need to use the p-value for a two-tailed test, labeled P(T<=t) two-tail
(see cell E12).

## Practical Advice

The interval estimation and hypothesis testing procedures presented in this section are ro-
bust and can be used with relatively small sample sizes. In most applications, sample sizes
that are equal or nearly equal and result in a total sample size of $n_1 + n_2 \geq 20$ will provide
very good results even if the populations are not normal. However, larger sample sizes are
recommended if the distributions of the populations are highly skewed or contain outliers.
Smaller sample sizes should only be used if the analyst is satisfied that the distributions of
the populations are at least approximately normal.

## NOTES AND COMMENTS

Another approach used to make inferences about the difference between two population means when $\sigma_1$ and $\sigma_2$ are unknown is based on the assumption that the two population standard deviations are *equal* ($\sigma_1 = \sigma_2 = \sigma$). Under this assumption, the two sample standard deviations are combined to provide the following *pooled sample variance:*

$$s_p^2 = \frac{(n_1 - 1)s_1^2 + (n_2 - 1)s_2^2}{n_1 + n_2 - 2}$$

The $t$ test statistic becomes

$$t = \frac{(\bar{x}_1 - \bar{x}_2) - D_0}{s_p\sqrt{\dfrac{1}{n_1} + \dfrac{1}{n_2}}}$$

and has $n_1 + n_2 - 2$ degrees of freedom. At this point, the computation of the $p$-value and the interpretation of the sample results are identical to the procedures discussed earlier in this section.

A difficulty with this procedure is that the assumption that the two population standard deviations are equal is usually difficult to verify. Unequal population standard deviations are frequently encountered. Using the pooled procedure may not provide satisfactory results, especially if the sample sizes $n_1$ and $n_2$ are quite different.

The $t$ procedure that we presented in this section does not require the assumption of equal population standard deviations and can be applied whether the population standard deviations are equal or not. It is a more general procedure and is recommended for most applications.

## Exercises

## Methods

9.  The following results are for independent random samples taken from two populations.

|  | Sample 1 | Sample 2 |
| --- | --- | --- |
|  | $n_1 = 20$ | $n_2 = 30$ |
|  | $\bar{x}_1 = 22.5$ | $\bar{x}_2 = 20.1$ |
|  | $s_1 = 2.5$ | $s_2 = 4.8$ |

a.  What is the point estimate of the difference between the two population means?
b.  What is the degrees of freedom for the $t$ distribution?
c.  At 95% confidence, what is the margin of error?
d.  What is the 95% confidence interval for the difference between the two population means?

10. Consider the following hypothesis test.

$$H_0: \mu_1 - \mu_2 = 0$$
$$H_a: \mu_1 - \mu_2 \neq 0$$

The following results are from independent samples taken from two populations.

|  | Sample 1 | Sample 2 |
| --- | --- | --- |
|  | $n_1 = 35$ | $n_2 = 40$ |
|  | $\bar{x}_1 = 13.6$ | $\bar{x}_2 = 10.1$ |
|  | $s_1 = 5.2$ | $s_2 = 8.5$ |

a.  What is the value of the test statistic?
b.  What is the value of the degrees of freedom for the $t$ distribution?
c.  What is the $p$-value?
d.  At $\alpha = .05$, what is your conclusion?

11. Consider the following data for two independent random samples taken from two normal populations.

| Sample 1 | 10 | 7 | 13 | 7 | 9 | 8 |
|---|---|---|---|---|---|---|
| Sample 2 | 8 | 7 | 8 | 4 | 6 | 9 |

a. Compute the two sample means.
b. Compute the two sample standard deviations.
c. What is the point estimate of the difference between the two population means?
d. What is the 90% confidence interval estimate of the difference between the two population means?

## Applications

12. The U.S. Department of Transportation provides the number of miles that residents of the 75 largest metropolitan areas travel per day in a car. Suppose that for a simple random sample of 50 Buffalo residents the mean is 22.5 miles a day and the standard deviation is 8.4 miles a day, and for an independent simple random sample of 40 Boston residents the mean is 18.6 miles a day and the standard deviation is 7.4 miles a day.
a. What is the point estimate of the difference between the mean number of miles that Buffalo residents travel per day and the mean number of miles that Boston residents travel per day?
b. What is the 95% confidence interval for the difference between the two population means?

13. FedEx and United Parcel Service (UPS) are the world's two leading cargo carriers by volume and revenue (*The Wall Street Journal,* January 27, 2004). According to the Airports Council International, the Memphis International Airport (FedEx) and the Louisville International Airport (UPS) are 2 of the 10 largest cargo airports in the world. The following random samples show the tons of cargo per day handled by these airports. Data are in thousands of tons.

**Memphis**

| 9.1 | 15.1 | 8.8 | 10.0 | 7.5 | 10.5 |
|---|---|---|---|---|---|
| 8.3 | 9.1 | 6.0 | 5.8 | 12.1 | 9.3 |

**Louisville**

| 4.7 | 5.0 | 4.2 | 3.3 | 5.5 |
|---|---|---|---|---|
| 2.2 | 4.1 | 2.6 | 3.4 | 7.0 |

a. Compute the sample mean and sample standard deviation for each airport.
b. What is the point estimate of the difference between the two population means? Interpret this value in terms of the higher-volume airport and a comparison of the volume difference between the two airports.
c. Develop a 95% confidence interval of the difference between the daily population means for the two airports.

14. Are nursing salaries in Tampa, Florida, lower than those in Dallas, Texas? Salary data provided by *http://www.salary.com* shows staff nurses in Tampa earn less than staff nurses in Dallas (*The Tampa Tribune,* January 15, 2007). Suppose that in a follow-up study of 40 staff nurses in Tampa and 50 staff nurses in Dallas you obtain the following results.

| **Tampa Bay** | **Dallas** |
|---|---|
| $n_1 = 40$ | $n_2 = 50$ |
| $\bar{x}_1 = \$56,100$ | $\bar{x}_2 = \$59,400$ |
| $s_1 = \$6000$ | $s_2 = \$7000$ |

a.  Formulate hypotheses so that, if the null hypothesis is rejected, we can conclude that salaries for staff nurses in Tampa Bay are significantly lower than for those in Dallas. Use $\alpha = .05$.
b.  What is the value of the test statistic?
c.  What is the $p$-value?
d.  What is your conclusion?

15.  Commercial real estate prices and rental rates suffered substantial declines in the past year (*Newsweek,* July 27, 2009). These declines were particularly severe in Asia; annual lease rates in Tokyo, Hong Kong, and Singapore declined by 40% or more. Even with such large declines, annual lease rates in Asia were still higher than in many cities in Europe and the United States. Annual lease rates for a sample of 30 commercial properties in Hong Kong showed an average of $1114 per square meter with a standard deviation of $230. Annual lease rates for a sample of 40 commercial properties in Paris showed an average lease rate of $989 per square meter with a standard deviation of $195.
a.  On the basis of the sample results, can we conclude that the mean annual lease rate is higher in Hong Kong than in Paris? Develop appropriate null and alternative hypotheses.
b.  Use $\alpha = .01$. What is your conclusion? Are rental rates higher in Hong Kong than in Paris?

16.  *Consumer Reports* rated 15 midpriced family sedans and 15 affordable family sedans. The following data show the road-test scores (1 to 100 scale with 100 the highest rating) for the 30 cars (*Consumer Reports,* February 2008).

**WEB** file

**RoadTest**

| Midpriced Family Sedans | Affordable Family Sedans |
|---|---|
| 89 | 85 |
| 88 | 79 |
| 87 | 78 |
| 86 | 77 |
| 84 | 76 |
| 77 | 75 |
| 77 | 74 |
| 75 | 69 |
| 70 | 69 |
| 69 | 69 |
| 64 | 64 |
| 58 | 62 |
| 56 | 59 |
| 48 | 49 |
| 46 | 44 |

a.  Formulate hypotheses so that if the null hypothesis is rejected, we can conclude that the mean road-test score for midpriced family sedans is significantly greater than the mean road-test score for affordable family sedans. Use $\alpha = .05$.
b.  What is the point estimate of the difference between the mean road-test score for midpriced family sedans and the mean road-test score for affordable family sedans?
c.  Compute the $p$-value for the hypotheses formulated in part (a).
d.  Using the $p$-value computed in part (c) and $\alpha = .05$, what is your conclusion.

17.  Periodically, Merrill Lynch customers are asked to evaluate Merrill Lynch financial consultants and services (2010 Merrill Lynch Client Satisfaction Survey). Higher ratings on the client satisfaction survey indicate better service with 7 the maximum service rating. Independent samples of service ratings for two financial consultants are summarized here. Consultant A has 10 years of experience, whereas consultant B has 1 year of experience.

Use $\alpha = .05$ and test to see whether the consultant with more experience has the higher population mean service rating.

| Consultant A | Consultant B |
|---|---|
| $n_1 = 16$ | $n_2 = 10$ |
| $\bar{x}_1 = 6.82$ | $\bar{x}_2 = 6.25$ |
| $s_1 = .64$ | $s_2 = .75$ |

a.  State the null and alternative hypotheses.
b.  Compute the value of the test statistic.
c.  What is the $p$-value?
d.  What is your conclusion?

18.  The Tire Rack, America's leading online distributor of tires and wheels, conducts extensive testing to provide customers with products that are right for their vehicle, driving style, and conditions in which they drive. In addition, they have maintained an independent consumer survey to help drivers help each other by sharing their long-term tire experiences. The data shown below show survey ratings (1 to 10 scale with 10 the highest rating) for two all-season passenger tires, the Dunlop SP60 and the Michelin MX4 (Tire Rack website, April 18, 2008).

**Dunlop**

| 7.7 | 8.1 | 9.1 | 8.6 | 7.4 | 8.3 | 9.7 | 9.5 | 9.0 | 8.2 |
|---|---|---|---|---|---|---|---|---|---|
| 9.8 | 8.0 | 10.0 | 8.5 | 9.3 | 7.7 | 8.9 | 9.6 | 7.9 | 10.0 |
| 8.3 | 8.1 | 5.1 | 7.3 | 8.0 | 8.5 | 9.4 | 7.6 | 8.4 | 4.2 |
| 7.6 | 5.9 | | | | | | | | |

**WEB file**

**TireRack**

**Michelin**

| 8.0 | 7.2 | 7.1 | 4.4 | 8.5 | 6.6 | 7.4 | 9.5 | 6.6 | 8.0 |
|---|---|---|---|---|---|---|---|---|---|
| 7.3 | 6.4 | 8.9 | 8.6 | 5.9 | 7.2 | 6.6 | 2.3 | 7.7 | 5.5 |
| 7.6 | 7.3 | 8.6 | 8.1 | 8.9 | 9.0 | 8.0 | 8.6 | 6.6 | 6.9 |
| 8.1 | 3.9 | 5.2 | 6.6 | 6.0 | 6.4 | 8.3 | 6.6 | 3.4 | 8.4 |

a.  Formulate the hypotheses that can be used to determine whether the sample data support the hypothesis that the mean rating for Dunlop SP60 tires is greater than the mean rating for Michelin MX4 tires.
b.  What is the point estimate of the difference between the means for the two populations?
c.  Compute the $p$-value for the hypothesis test.
d.  At $\alpha = .05$, what is your conclusion?

## 10.3  Inferences About the Difference Between Two Population Means: Matched Samples

Suppose employees at a manufacturing company can use two different methods to perform a production task. To maximize production output, the company wants to identify the method with the shorter population mean completion time. Let $\mu_1$ denote the population mean completion time for production method 1 and $\mu_2$ denote the population mean completion time for production method 2. With no preliminary indication of the preferred production method, we begin by tentatively assuming that the two production methods have the same population mean completion time. Thus, the null hypothesis is $H_0: \mu_1 - \mu_2 = 0$. If this hypothesis is rejected, we can conclude that the population mean completion times differ. In this case, the method providing the shorter mean completion time would be recommended. The null and alternative hypotheses are written as follows:

$$H_0: \mu_1 - \mu_2 = 0$$
$$H_a: \mu_1 - \mu_2 \neq 0$$

In choosing the sampling procedure that will be used to collect production time data and test the hypotheses, we consider two alternative designs. One is based on **independent simple random samples** and the other is based on **matched samples**.

1. *Independent sample design:* A simple random sample of workers is selected and each worker in the sample uses method 1. A second independent simple random sample of workers is selected and each worker in this sample uses method 2. The test of the difference between population means is based on the procedures in Section 10.2.
2. *Matched sample design:* One simple random sample of workers is selected. Each worker first uses one method and then uses the other method. The order of the two methods is assigned randomly to the workers, with some workers performing method 1 first and others performing method 2 first. Each worker provides a pair of data values, one value for method 1 and another value for method 2.

In the matched sample design the two production methods are tested under similar conditions (i.e., with the same workers); hence this design often leads to a smaller sampling error than the independent sample design. The primary reason is that in a matched sample design, variation between workers is eliminated because the same workers are used for both production methods.

Let us demonstrate the analysis of a matched sample design by assuming it is the method used to test the difference between population means for the two production methods. A random sample of six workers is used. The data on completion times for the six workers are given in Table 10.2. Note that each worker provides a pair of data values, one for each production method. Also note that the last column contains the difference in completion times $d_i$ for each worker in the sample.

The key to the analysis of the matched sample design is to realize that we consider only the column of differences. Therefore, we have six data values (.6, −.2, .5, .3, .0, and .6) that will be used to analyze the difference between population means of the two production methods.

Let $\mu_d$ = the mean of the *difference* values for the population of workers. With this notation, the null and alternative hypotheses are rewritten as follows:

$$H_0: \mu_d = 0$$
$$H_a: \mu_d \neq 0$$

If $H_0$ is rejected, we can conclude that the population mean completion times differ.

**TABLE 10.2    TASK COMPLETION TIMES FOR A MATCHED SAMPLE DESIGN**

| Worker | Completion Time for Method 1 (minutes) | Completion Time for Method 2 (minutes) | Difference in Completion Times ($d_i$) |
|---|---|---|---|
| 1 | 6.0 | 5.4 | .6 |
| 2 | 5.0 | 5.2 | −.2 |
| 3 | 7.0 | 6.5 | .5 |
| 4 | 6.2 | 5.9 | .3 |
| 5 | 6.0 | 6.0 | .0 |
| 6 | 6.4 | 5.8 | .6 |

WEB file

Matched

*Other than the use of the d notation, the formulas for the sample mean and sample standard deviation are the same ones used previously in the text.*

The $d$ notation is a reminder that the matched sample provides *difference* data. The sample mean and sample standard deviation for the six difference values in Table 10.2 follow.

$$\bar{d} = \frac{\Sigma d_i}{n} = \frac{1.8}{6} = .30$$

$$s_d = \sqrt{\frac{\Sigma(d_i - \bar{d})^2}{n-1}} = \sqrt{\frac{.56}{5}} = .3347$$

With the small sample of $n = 6$ workers, we need to make the assumption that the population of differences has a normal distribution. This assumption is necessary so that we may use the $t$ distribution for hypothesis testing and interval estimation procedures. Based on this assumption, the following test statistic has a $t$ distribution with $n - 1$ degrees of freedom.

*It is not necessary to make the assumption that the population has a normal distribution if the sample size is large. Sample size guidelines for using the t distribution were presented in Chapters 8 and 9.*

---

**TEST STATISTIC FOR HYPOTHESIS TESTS INVOLVING MATCHED SAMPLES**

$$t = \frac{\bar{d} - \mu_d}{s_d/\sqrt{n}} \qquad\qquad \textbf{(10.9)}$$

---

*Once the difference data are computed, the t distribution procedure for matched samples is the same as the one-population estimation and hypothesis testing procedures described in Chapters 8 and 9.*

Let us use equation (10.9) to test the hypotheses $H_0: \mu_d = 0$ and $H_a: \mu_d \neq 0$, using $\alpha = .05$. Substituting the sample results $\bar{d} = .30$, $s_d = .3347$, and $n = 6$ into equation (10.9), we compute the value of the test statistic.

$$t = \frac{\bar{d} - \mu_d}{s_d/\sqrt{n}} = \frac{.30 - 0}{.3347/\sqrt{6}} = 2.20$$

Now let us compute the $p$-value for this two-tailed test. Because $t = 2.20 > 0$, the test statistic is in the upper tail of the $t$ distribution. With $t = 2.20$, the area in the upper tail to the right of the test statistic can be found by using the $t$ distribution table with degrees of freedom $= n - 1 = 6 - 1 = 5$. Information from the 5 degrees of freedom row of the $t$ distribution table is as follows:

| Area in Upper Tail | .20 | .10 | .05 | .025 | .01 | .005 |
|---|---|---|---|---|---|---|
| $t$ Value (5 *df*) | 0.920 | 1.476 | 2.015 | 2.571 | 3.365 | 4.032 |

$t = 2.20$

Thus, we see that the area in the upper tail is between .05 and .025. Because this test is a two-tailed test, we double these values to conclude that the $p$-value is between .10 and .05. This $p$-value is greater than $\alpha = .05$. Thus, the null hypothesis $H_0: \mu_d = 0$ is not rejected. Using Excel and the data in Table 10.2, we find the exact $p$-value $= .0795$.

We can also obtain an interval estimate of the difference between the two population means by using the single population methodology of Chapter 8. At 95% confidence, the calculation follows.

$$\bar{d} \pm t_{.025} \frac{s_d}{\sqrt{n}}$$

$$.3 \pm 2.571 \left(\frac{.3347}{\sqrt{6}}\right)$$

$$.3 \pm .35$$

Thus, the margin of error is .35 and the 95% confidence interval for the difference between the population means of the two production methods is $-.05$ minute to .65 minute.

## Using Excel to Conduct a Hypothesis Test

Excel's t-Test: Paired Two Sample for Means tool can be used to conduct a hypothesis test about the difference between the population means when a matched sample design is used. We illustrate by conducting the hypothesis test involving the two production methods. Refer to the Excel worksheets shown in Figure 10.8 and Figure 10.9 as we describe the tasks involved.

**Enter Data:**    Column A in Figure 10.8 is used to identify each of the six workers who participated in the study. Column B contains the completion time data for each worker using method 1, and column C contains the completion time data for each worker using method 2.

**Apply Tools:**    The following steps describe how to use Excel's t-Test: Paired Two Sample for Means tool to conduct the hypothesis test about the difference between the means of the two production methods

**Step 1.** Click the **Data** tab on the Ribbon
**Step 2.** In the **Analysis** group, click **Data Analysis**
**Step 3.** Choose **t-Test: Paired Two Sample for Means** from the list of Analysis Tools
**Step 4.** When the t-Test: Paired Two Sample for Means dialog box appears (Figure 10.8),

>   Enter B1:B7 in the **Variable 1 Range** box
>   Enter C1:C7 in the **Variable 2 Range** box

**FIGURE 10.8**    DIALOG BOX FOR EXCEL'S t-TEST: PAIRED TWO SAMPLE FOR MEANS TOOL

**TABLE 10.3** NUMBER OF UNITS PRODUCED BY 15 WORKERS

**WEB** file

**Chemitech**

|  | Method | | |
|---|---|---|---|
|  | **A** | **B** | **C** |
|  | 58 | 58 | 48 |
|  | 64 | 69 | 57 |
|  | 55 | 71 | 59 |
|  | 66 | 64 | 47 |
|  | 67 | 68 | 49 |
| Sample mean | 62 | 66 | 52 |
| Sample variance | 27.5 | 26.5 | 31.0 |
| Sample standard deviation | 5.244 | 5.148 | 5.568 |

The real issue is whether the three sample means observed are different enough for us to conclude that the means of the populations corresponding to the three methods of assembly are different. To write this question in statistical terms, we introduce the following notation:

$\mu_1$ = mean number of units produced per week using method A

$\mu_2$ = mean number of units produced per week using method B

$\mu_3$ = mean number of units produced per week using method C

Although we will never know the actual values of $\mu_1$, $\mu_2$, and $\mu_3$, we want to use the sample means to test the following hypotheses.

$$H_0: \mu_1 = \mu_2 = \mu_3$$
$$H_a: \text{Not all population means are equal}$$

*If $H_0$ is rejected, we cannot conclude that all population means are different. Rejecting $H_0$ means that at least two population means have different values.*

As we will demonstrate shortly, ANOVA is the statistical procedure used to determine whether the observed differences in the three sample means are large enough to reject $H_0$.

## Assumptions for Analysis of Variance

Three assumptions are required to use analysis of variance.

*If the sample sizes are equal, analysis of variance is not sensitive to departures from the assumption of normally distributed populations.*

1. **For each population, the response variable is normally distributed.** Implication: In the Chemitech experiment the number of units produced per week (response variable) must be normally distributed for each assembly method.
2. **The variance of the response variable, denoted $\sigma^2$, is the same for all the populations.** Implication: In the Chemitech experiment, the variance of the number of units produced per week must be the same for each assembly method.
3. **The observations must be independent.** Implication: In the Chemitech experiment, the number of units produced per week for each employee must be independent of the number of units produced per week for any other employee.

## Analysis of Variance: A Conceptual Overview

If the means for the three populations are equal, we would expect the three sample means to be close together. In fact, the closer the three sample means are to one another, the more evidence we have for the conclusion that the population means are equal. Alternatively, the more the sample means differ, the more evidence we have for the conclusion that the population means are not equal. In other words, if the variability among the sample means is "small," it supports $H_0$; if the variability among the sample means is "large," it supports $H_a$.

**FIGURE 10.11    SAMPLING DISTRIBUTION OF $\bar{x}$ GIVEN $H_0$ IS TRUE**

If the null hypothesis, $H_0$: $\mu_1 = \mu_2 = \mu_3$, is true, we can use the variability among the sample means to develop an estimate of $\sigma^2$. First, note that if the assumptions for analysis of variance are satisfied, each sample will have come from the same normal distribution with mean $\mu$ and variance $\sigma^2$. Recall from Chapter 7 that the sampling distribution of the sample mean $\bar{x}$ for a simple random sample of size $n$ from a normal population will be normally distributed with mean $\mu$ and variance $\sigma^2/n$. Figure 10.11 illustrates such a sampling distribution.

Thus, if the null hypothesis is true, we can think of each of the three sample means, $\bar{x}_1 = 62$, $\bar{x}_2 = 66$, and $\bar{x}_3 = 52$ from Table 10.3, as values drawn at random from the sampling distribution shown in Figure 10.11. In this case, the mean and variance of the three $\bar{x}$ values can be used to estimate the mean and variance of the sampling distribution. When the sample sizes are equal, as in the Chemitech experiment, the best estimate of the mean of the sampling distribution of $\bar{x}$ is the mean or average of the sample means. Thus, in the Chemitech experiment, an estimate of the mean of the sampling distribution of $\bar{x}$ is $(62 + 66 + 52)/3 = 60$. We refer to this estimate as the *overall sample mean*. An estimate of the variance of the sampling distribution of $\bar{x}$, $\sigma_{\bar{x}}^2$, is provided by the variance of the three sample means.

$$s_{\bar{x}}^2 = \frac{(62 - 60)^2 + (66 - 60)^2 + (52 - 60)^2}{3 - 1} = \frac{104}{2} = 52$$

Because $\sigma_{\bar{x}}^2 = \sigma^2/n$, solving for $\sigma^2$ gives

$$\sigma^2 = n\sigma_{\bar{x}}^2$$

Hence,

$$\text{Estimate of } \sigma^2 = n(\text{Estimate of } \sigma_{\bar{x}}^2) = ns_{\bar{x}}^2 = 5(52) = 260$$

The result, $ns_{\bar{x}}^2 = 260$, is referred to as the *between-treatments* estimate of $\sigma^2$.

The between-treatments estimate of $\sigma^2$ is based on the assumption that the null hypothesis is true. In this case, each sample comes from the same population, and there is only one sampling distribution of $\bar{x}$. To illustrate what happens when $H_0$ is false, suppose the

**FIGURE 10.12**   SAMPLING DISTRIBUTIONS OF $\bar{x}$ GIVEN $H_0$ IS FALSE

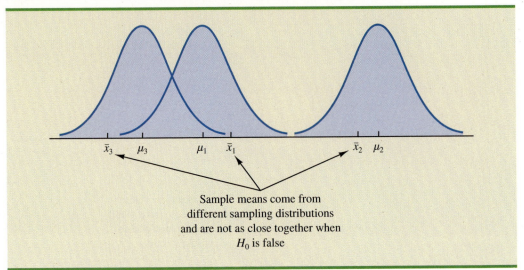

$$\bar{x}_3 \quad \mu_3 \qquad \mu_1 \quad \bar{x}_1 \qquad\qquad \bar{x}_2 \quad \mu_2$$

Sample means come from
different sampling distributions
and are not as close together when
$H_0$ is false

population means all differ. Note that because the three samples are from normal populations with different means, they will result in three different sampling distributions. Figure 10.12 shows that in this case, the sample means are not as close together as they were when $H_0$ was true. Thus, $s_{\bar{x}}^2$ will be larger, causing the between-treatments estimate of $\sigma^2$ to be larger. In general, when the population means are not equal, the between-treatments estimate will overestimate the population variance $\sigma^2$.

The variation within each of the samples also has an effect on the conclusion we reach in analysis of variance. When a simple random sample is selected from each population, each of the sample variances provides an unbiased estimate of $\sigma^2$. Hence, we can combine or pool the individual estimates of $\sigma^2$ into one overall estimate. The estimate of $\sigma^2$ obtained in this way is called the *pooled* or *within-treatments* estimate of $\sigma^2$. Because each sample variance provides an estimate of $\sigma^2$ based only on the variation within each sample, the within-treatments estimate of $\sigma^2$ is not affected by whether the population means are equal. When the sample sizes are equal, the within-treatments estimate of $\sigma^2$ can be obtained by computing the average of the individual sample variances. For the Chemitech experiment we obtain

$$\text{Within-treatments estimate of } \sigma^2 = \frac{27.5 + 26.5 + 31.0}{3} = \frac{85}{3} = 28.33$$

In the Chemitech experiment, the between-treatments estimate of $\sigma^2$ (260) is much larger than the within-treatments estimate of $\sigma^2$ (28.33). In fact, the ratio of these two estimates is $260/28.33 = 9.18$. Recall, however, that the between-treatments approach provides a good estimate of $\sigma^2$ only if the null hypothesis is true; if the null hypothesis is false, the between-treatments approach overestimates $\sigma^2$. The within-treatments approach provides a good estimate of $\sigma^2$ in either case. Thus, if the null hypothesis is true, the two estimates will be similar and their ratio will be close to 1. If the null hypothesis is false, the between-treatments estimate will be larger than the within-treatments estimate, and their ratio will be large. In the next section we will show how large this ratio must be to reject $H_0$.

In summary, the logic behind ANOVA is based on the development of two independent estimates of the common population variance $\sigma^2$. One estimate of $\sigma^2$ is based on the variability among the sample means themselves, and the other estimate of $\sigma^2$ is based on the variability of the data within each sample. By comparing these two estimates of $\sigma^2$, we will be able to determine whether the population means are equal.

## NOTES AND COMMENTS

1. Randomization in experimental design is the analog of probability sampling in an observational study.

2. In many medical experiments, potential bias is eliminated by using a double-blind experimental design. With this design, neither the physician applying the treatment nor the subject knows which treatment is being applied. Many other types of experiments could benefit from this type of design.

3. In this section we provided a conceptual overview of how analysis of variance can be used to test for the equality of $k$ population means for a completely randomized experimental design. We will see that the same procedure can also be used to test for the equality of $k$ population means for an observational or nonexperimental study.

4. In Sections 10.1 and 10.2 we presented statistical methods for testing the hypothesis that the means of two populations are equal. ANOVA can also be used to test the hypothesis that the means of two populations are equal. In practice, however, analysis of variance is usually not used except when dealing with three or more population means.

# 10.5 Analysis of Variance and the Completely Randomized Design

In this section we show how analysis of variance can be used to test for the equality of $k$ population means for a completely randomized design. The general form of the hypotheses tested is

$$H_0: \mu_1 = \mu_2 = \cdots = \mu_k$$
$$H_a: \text{Not all population means are equal}$$

where

$$\mu_j = \text{mean of the } j\text{th population}$$

We assume that a simple random sample of size $n_j$ has been selected from each of the $k$ populations or treatments. For the resulting sample data, let

$$x_{ij} = \text{value of observation } i \text{ for treatment } j$$
$$n_j = \text{number of observations for treatment } j$$
$$\bar{x}_j = \text{sample mean for treatment } j$$
$$s_j^2 = \text{sample variance for treatment } j$$
$$s_j = \text{sample standard deviation for treatment } j$$

The formulas for the sample mean and sample variance for treatment $j$ are as follows:

$$\bar{x}_j = \frac{\displaystyle\sum_{i=1}^{n_j} x_{ij}}{n_j} \tag{10.10}$$

$$s_j^2 = \frac{\displaystyle\sum_{i=1}^{n_j} (x_{ij} - \bar{x}_j)^2}{n_j - 1} \tag{10.11}$$

The overall sample mean, denoted $\bar{\bar{x}}$, is the sum of all the observations divided by the total number of observations. That is,

$$\bar{\bar{x}} = \frac{\sum\limits_{j=1}^{k} \sum\limits_{i=1}^{n_j} x_{ij}}{n_T} \tag{10.12}$$

where

$$n_T = n_1 + n_2 + \cdots + n_k \tag{10.13}$$

If the size of each sample is $n$, $n_T = kn$; in this case equation (10.12) reduces to

$$\bar{\bar{x}} = \frac{\sum\limits_{j=1}^{k} \sum\limits_{i=1}^{n_j} x_{ij}}{kn} = \frac{\sum\limits_{j=1}^{k} \sum\limits_{i=1}^{n_j} x_{ij}/n}{k} = \frac{\sum\limits_{j=1}^{k} \bar{x}_j}{k} \tag{10.14}$$

In other words, whenever the sample sizes are the same, the overall sample mean is just the average of the $k$ sample means.

Because each sample in the Chemitech experiment consists of $n = 5$ observations, the overall sample mean can be computed by using equation (10.14). For the data in Table 10.3 we obtained the following result:

$$\bar{\bar{x}} = \frac{62 + 66 + 52}{3} = 60$$

If the null hypothesis is true ($\mu_1 = \mu_2 = \mu_3 = \mu$), the overall sample mean of 60 is the best estimate of the population mean $\mu$.

## Between-Treatments Estimate of Population Variance

In the preceding section, we introduced the concept of a between-treatments estimate of $\sigma^2$ and showed how to compute it when the sample sizes were equal. This estimate of $\sigma^2$ is called the *mean square due to treatments* and is denoted MSTR. The general formula for computing MSTR is

$$\text{MSTR} = \frac{\sum\limits_{j=1}^{k} n_j(\bar{x}_j - \bar{\bar{x}})^2}{k - 1} \tag{10.15}$$

The numerator in equation (10.15) is called the *sum of squares due to treatments* and is denoted SSTR. The denominator, $k - 1$, represents the degrees of freedom associated with SSTR. Hence, the mean square due to treatments can be computed using the following formula.

MEAN SQUARE DUE TO TREATMENTS

$$\text{MSTR} = \frac{\text{SSTR}}{k - 1} \tag{10.16}$$

where

$$\text{SSTR} = \sum\limits_{j=1}^{k} n_j(\bar{x}_j - \bar{\bar{x}})^2 \tag{10.17}$$

If $H_0$ is true, MSTR provides an unbiased estimate of $\sigma^2$. However, if the means of the $k$ populations are not equal, MSTR is not an unbiased estimate of $\sigma^2$; in fact, in that case, MSTR should overestimate $\sigma^2$.

For the Chemitech data in Table 10.3, we obtain the following results:

$$\text{SSTR} = \sum_{j=1}^{k} n_j(\bar{x}_j - \bar{\bar{x}})^2 = 5(62 - 60)^2 + 5(66 - 60)^2 + 5(52 - 60)^2 = 520$$

$$\text{MSTR} = \frac{\text{SSTR}}{k - 1} = \frac{520}{2} = 260$$

## Within-Treatments Estimate of Population Variance

Earlier, we introduced the concept of a within-treatments estimate of $\sigma^2$ and showed how to compute it when the sample sizes were equal. This estimate of $\sigma^2$ is called the *mean square due to error* and is denoted MSE. The general formula for computing MSE is

$$\text{MSE} = \frac{\sum_{j=1}^{k}(n_j - 1)s_j^2}{n_T - k} \tag{10.18}$$

The numerator in equation (10.18) is called the *sum of squares due to error* and is denoted SSE. The denominator of MSE is referred to as the degrees of freedom associated with SSE. Hence, the formula for MSE can also be stated as follows.

> **MEAN SQUARE DUE TO ERROR**
>
> $$\text{MSE} = \frac{\text{SSE}}{n_T - k} \tag{10.19}$$
>
> where
>
> $$\text{SSE} = \sum_{j=1}^{k}(n_j - 1)s_j^2 \tag{10.20}$$

Note that MSE is based on the variation within each of the treatments; it is not influenced by whether the null hypothesis is true. Thus, MSE always provides an unbiased estimate of $\sigma^2$.

For the Chemitech data in Table 10.3 we obtain the following results:

$$\text{SSE} = \sum_{j=1}^{k}(n_j - 1)s_j^2 = (5 - 1)27.5 + (5 - 1)26.5 + (5 - 1)31 = 340$$

$$\text{MSE} = \frac{\text{SSE}}{n_T - k} = \frac{340}{15 - 3} = \frac{340}{12} = 28.33$$

## Comparing the Variance Estimates: The $F$ Test

If the null hypothesis is true, MSTR and MSE provide two independent, unbiased estimates of $\sigma^2$. If the ANOVA assumptions are also valid, the sampling distribution of MSTR/MSE is an **$F$ distribution** with numerator degrees of freedom equal to $k - 1$ and denominator degrees of freedom equal to $n_T - k$. The general shape of the $F$ distribution is shown in Figure 10.13. If the null hypothesis is true, the value of MSTR/MSE should appear to be from this $F$ distribution.

However, if the null hypothesis is false, the value of MSTR/MSE will be inflated because MSTR overestimates $\sigma^2$. Hence, we will reject $H_0$ if the resulting value of MSTR/MSE appears to be too large to have been selected from an $F$ distribution with $k - 1$ numerator degrees of freedom and $n_T - k$ denominator degrees of freedom. Because the decision to

**FIGURE 10.13** COMPUTATION OF $p$-VALUE USING THE SAMPLING DISTRIBUTION OF MSTR/MSE

reject $H_0$ is based on the value of MSTR/MSE, the test statistic used to test for the equality of $k$ population means is as follows.

---

**TEST STATISTIC FOR THE EQUALITY OF $k$ POPULATION MEANS**

$$F = \frac{\text{MSTR}}{\text{MSE}} \qquad \textbf{(10.21)}$$

The test statistic follows an $F$ distribution with $k - 1$ degrees of freedom in the numerator and $n_T - k$ degrees of freedom in the denominator.

---

Let us return to the Chemitech experiment and use a level of significance $\alpha = .05$ to conduct the hypothesis test. The value of the test statistic is

$$F = \frac{\text{MSTR}}{\text{MSE}} = \frac{260}{28.33} = 9.18$$

The numerator degrees of freedom is $k - 1 = 3 - 1 = 2$ and the denominator degrees of freedom is $n_T - k = 15 - 3 = 12$. Because we will only reject the null hypothesis for large values of the test statistic, the $p$-value is the upper tail area of the $F$ distribution to the right of the test statistic $F = 9.18$. Figure 10.13 shows the sampling distribution of $F = $ MSTR/MSE, the value of the test statistic, and the upper tail area that is the $p$-value for the hypothesis test.

From Table 4 of Appendix B we find the following areas in the upper tail of an $F$ distribution with 2 numerator degrees of freedom and 12 denominator degrees of freedom.

| Area in Upper Tail | .10 | .05 | .025 | .01 |
|---|---|---|---|---|
| $F$ Value ($df_1 = 2, df_2 = 12$) | 2.81 | 3.89 | 5.10 | 6.93 |

$F = 9.18$

*Using Excel, p-value = F.DIST.RT(9.18,2,12) = .004.*

Because $F = 9.18$ is greater than 6.93, the area in the upper tail at $F = 9.18$ is less than .01. Thus, the $p$-value is less than .01. Excel can be used to show that the exact $p$-value is .004. With $p$-value $\le \alpha = .05$, $H_0$ is rejected. The test provides sufficient evidence to conclude that the means of the three populations are not equal. In other words, analysis of variance supports the conclusion that the population mean number of units produced per week for the three assembly methods are not equal.

As with other hypothesis testing procedures, the critical value approach may also be used. With $\alpha = .05$, the critical $F$ value occurs with an area of .05 in the upper tail of an $F$ distribution with 2 and 12 degrees of freedom. From the $F$ distribution table, we find $F_{.05} = 3.89$. Hence, the appropriate upper tail rejection rule for the Chemitech experiment is

$$\text{Reject } H_0 \text{ if } F \geq 3.89$$

With $F = 9.18$, we reject $H_0$ and conclude that the means of the three populations are not equal. A summary of the overall procedure for testing for the equality of $k$ population means follows.

---

**TEST FOR THE EQUALITY OF $k$ POPULATION MEANS**

$$H_0: \mu_1 = \mu_2 = \cdots = \mu_k$$
$$H_a: \text{Not all population means are equal}$$

**TEST STATISTIC**

$$F = \frac{\text{MSTR}}{\text{MSE}}$$

**REJECTION RULE**

$p$-value approach:        Reject $H_0$ if $p$-value $\leq \alpha$

Critical value approach:   Reject $H_0$ if $F \geq F_\alpha$

where the value of $F_\alpha$ is based on an $F$ distribution with $k - 1$ numerator degrees of freedom and $n_T - k$ denominator degrees of freedom.

---

## ANOVA Table

The results of the preceding calculations can be displayed conveniently in a table referred to as the analysis of variance or **ANOVA table**. The general form of the ANOVA table for a completely randomized design is shown in Table 10.4; Table 10.5 is the corresponding ANOVA table for the Chemitech experiment. The sum of squares associated with the source of variation referred to as "Total" is called the total sum of squares (SST). Note that the results for the Chemitech experiment suggest that SST = SSTR + SSE, and that the degrees of freedom associated with this total sum of squares is the sum of the degrees of freedom associated with the sum of squares due to treatments and the sum of squares due to error.

We point out that SST divided by its degrees of freedom $n_T - 1$ is nothing more than the overall sample variance that would be obtained if we treated the entire set of 15 observations

**TABLE 10.4**   ANOVA TABLE FOR A COMPLETELY RANDOMIZED DESIGN

| Source of Variation | Sum of Squares | Degrees of Freedom | Mean Square | $F$ | $p$-value |
|---|---|---|---|---|---|
| Treatments | SSTR | $k - 1$ | $\text{MSTR} = \dfrac{\text{SSTR}}{k - 1}$ | $\dfrac{\text{MSTR}}{\text{MSE}}$ | |
| Error | SSE | $n_T - k$ | $\text{MSE} = \dfrac{\text{SSE}}{n_T - k}$ | | |
| Total | SST | $n_T - 1$ | | | |

**TABLE 10.5**   ANOVA TABLE FOR THE CHEMITECH EXPERIMENT

| Source of Variation | Sum of Squares | Degrees of Freedom | Mean Square | F | p-value |
|---|---|---|---|---|---|
| Treatments | 520 | 2 | 260.00 | 9.18 | .004 |
| Error | 340 | 12 | 28.33 | | |
| Total | 860 | 14 | | | |

as one data set. With the entire data set as one sample, the formula for computing the total sum of squares, SST, is

$$\text{SST} = \sum_{j=1}^{k}\sum_{i=1}^{n_j}(x_{ij} - \bar{\bar{x}})^2 \tag{10.22}$$

It can be shown that the results we observed for the analysis of variance table for the Chemitech experiment also apply to other problems. That is,

$$\text{SST} = \text{SSTR} + \text{SSE} \tag{10.23}$$

*Analysis of variance can be thought of as a statistical procedure for partitioning the total sum of squares into separate components.*

In other words, SST can be partitioned into two sums of squares: the sum of squares due to treatments and the sum of squares due to error. Note also that the degrees of freedom corresponding to SST, $n_T - 1$, can be partitioned into the degrees of freedom corresponding to SSTR, $k - 1$, and the degrees of freedom corresponding to SSE, $n_T - k$. The analysis of variance can be viewed as the process of **partitioning** the total sum of squares and the degrees of freedom into their corresponding sources: treatments and error. Dividing the sum of squares by the appropriate degrees of freedom provides the variance estimates, the F value, and the p-value used to test the hypothesis of equal population means.

## Using Excel

Excel's Anova: Single Factor tool can be used to conduct a hypothesis test about the difference between the population means for the Chemitech experiment. Refer to the Excel worksheets shown in Figure 10.14 and Figure 10.15 as we describe the tasks involved.

**Enter Data:** Columns A, B, and C in Figure 10.14 contain labels and the number of filtration systems produced per week for each method of assembly.

**Apply Tools:** The following steps describe how to use Excel's Anova: Single Factor tool to test the hypothesis that the mean number of units produced per week is the same for all three methods of assembly.

**Step 1.** Click the **Data** tab on the Ribbon
**Step 2.** In the **Analysis** group, click **Data Analysis**
**Step 3.** Choose **Anova: Single Factor** from the list of Analysis Tools
**Step 4.** When the Anova: Single Factor dialog box appears (Figure 10.14),
  Enter A1:C6 in the **Input Range** box
  Select **Grouped By: Columns**
  Select **Labels in First Row**
  Enter .05 in the **Alpha** box
  Select **Output Range**
  Enter A8 in the **Output Range** box (to identify the upper left corner of the section of the worksheet where the output will appear)
  Click **OK**

**FIGURE 10.14**   DIALOG BOX FOR EXCEL'S ANOVA: SINGLE FACTOR TOOL

The output, titled *Anova: Single Factor,* appears in cells A8:G22 of the worksheet in Figure 10.15. Cells A10:E14 provide a summary of the statistics for each method. Note that the sample mean and sample variance for each method of assembly are the same as shown in Table 10.3. The ANOVA table, shown in cells A17:G22, is basically the same as the ANOVA table shown in Table 10.5. Excel identifies the treatments source of variation using

**FIGURE 10.15**   EXCEL RESULTS FOR THE HYPOTHESIS TEST ABOUT EQUALITY OF THREE POPULATION MEANS the label *Between Groups* and the error source of variation using the label *Within Groups*. In addition, the Excel output provides the *p*-value associated with the test as well as the critical *F* value.

We can use the *p*-value shown in cell F19, 0.0038, to make the hypothesis testing decision. Thus, at the $\alpha = .05$ level of significance, we reject $H_0$ because the *p*-value $= 0.0038 < \alpha = .05$. Hence, using the *p*-value approach we still conclude that the mean number of units produced per week are not the same for the three assembly methods.

## Testing for the Equality of $k$ Population Means: An Observational Study

We have shown how analysis of variance can be used to test for the equality of $k$ population means for a completely randomized experimental design. It is important to understand that ANOVA can also be used to test for the equality of three or more population means using data obtained from an observational study. As an example, let us consider the situation at National Computer Products, Inc. (NCP).

NCP manufactures printers and fax machines at plants located in Atlanta, Dallas, and Seattle. To measure how much employees at these plants know about quality management, a random sample of 6 employees was selected from each plant and the employees selected were given a quality awareness examination. The examination scores for these 18 employees are shown in Table 10.6. The sample means, sample variances, and sample standard deviations for each group are also provided. Managers want to use these data to test the hypothesis that the mean examination score is the same for all three plants.

We define population 1 as all employees at the Atlanta plant, population 2 as all employees at the Dallas plant, and population 3 as all employees at the Seattle plant. Let

$\mu_1$ = mean examination score for population 1
$\mu_2$ = mean examination score for population 2
$\mu_3$ = mean examination score for population 3

Although we will never know the actual values of $\mu_1$, $\mu_2$, and $\mu_3$, we want to use the sample results to test the following hypotheses:

$$H_0: \mu_1 = \mu_2 = \mu_3$$
$$H_a: \text{Not all population means are equal}$$

**TABLE 10.6    EXAMINATION SCORES FOR 18 EMPLOYEES**

|  | Plant 1 Atlanta | Plant 2 Dallas | Plant 3 Seattle |
|---|---|---|---|
|  | 85 | 71 | 59 |
|  | 75 | 75 | 64 |
|  | 82 | 73 | 62 |
|  | 76 | 74 | 69 |
|  | 71 | 69 | 75 |
|  | 85 | 82 | 67 |
| Sample mean | 79 | 74 | 66 |
| Sample variance | 34 | 20 | 32 |
| Sample standard deviation | 5.83 | 4.47 | 5.66 |

*Exercise 35 will ask you to analyze the NCP data using the analysis of variance procedure.*

Note that the hypothesis test for the NCP observational study is exactly the same as the hypothesis test for the Chemitech experiment. Indeed, the same analysis of variance methodology we used to analyze the Chemitech experiment can also be used to analyze the data from the NCP observational study.

Even though the same ANOVA methodology is used for the analysis, it is worth noting how the NCP observational statistical study differs from the Chemitech experimental statistical study. The individuals who conducted the NCP study had no control over how the plants were assigned to individual employees. That is, the plants were already in operation and a particular employee worked at one of the three plants. All that NCP could do was to select a random sample of 6 employees from each plant and administer the quality awareness examination. To be classified as an experimental study, NCP would have had to be able to randomly select 18 employees and then assign the plants to each employee in a random fashion.

## NOTES AND COMMENTS

1. The overall sample mean can also be computed as a weighted average of the $k$ sample means.

$$\bar{\bar{x}} = \frac{n_1\bar{x}_1 + n_2\bar{x}_2 + \cdots + n_k\bar{x}_k}{n_T}$$

In problems where the sample means are provided, this formula is simpler than equation (10.12) for computing the overall mean.

2. If each sample consists of $n$ observations, equation (10.15) can be written as

$$\text{MSTR} = \frac{n\sum_{j=1}^{k}(\bar{x}_j - \bar{\bar{x}})^2}{k-1} = n\left[\frac{\sum_{j=1}^{k}(\bar{x}_j - \bar{\bar{x}})^2}{k-1}\right]$$
$$= ns_{\bar{x}}^2$$

Note that this result is the same as presented in Section 10.4 when we introduced the concept

of the between-treatments estimate of $\sigma^2$. Equation (10.15) is simply a generalization of this result to the unequal sample-size case.

3. If each sample has $n$ observations, $n_T = kn$; thus, $n_T - k = k(n - 1)$, and equation (10.18) can be rewritten as

$$\text{MSE} = \frac{\sum_{j=1}^{k}(n-1)s_j^2}{k(n-1)} = \frac{(n-1)\sum_{j=1}^{k}s_j^2}{k(n-1)} = \frac{\sum_{j=1}^{k}s_j^2}{k}$$

In other words, if the sample sizes are the same, MSE is just the average of the $k$ sample variances. Note that it is the same result we used in Section 10.4 when we introduced the concept of the within-treatments estimate of $\sigma^2$.

## Exercises

## Methods

28.   The following data are from a completely randomized design.

|  | Treatment | | |
| --- | --- | --- | --- |
|  | **A** | **B** | **C** |
|  | 162 | 142 | 126 |
|  | 142 | 156 | 122 |
|  | 165 | 124 | 138 |
|  | 145 | 142 | 140 |
|  | 148 | 136 | 150 |
|  | 174 | 152 | 128 |
| Sample mean | 156 | 142 | 134 |
| Sample variance | 164.4 | 131.2 | 110.4 |

a. Compute the sum of squares between treatments.
b. Compute the mean square between treatments.
c. Compute the sum of squares due to error.
d. Compute the mean square due to error.
e. Set up the ANOVA table for this problem.
f. At the $\alpha = .05$ level of significance, test whether the means for the three treatments are equal.

29. In a completely randomized design, seven experimental units were used for each of the five levels of the factor. Complete the following ANOVA table.

| Source of Variation | Sum of Squares | Degrees of Freedom | Mean Square | F | p-value |
|---|---|---|---|---|---|
| Treatments | 300 | | | | |
| Error | | | | | |
| Total | 460 | | | | |

30. Refer to exercise 29.
    a. What hypotheses are implied in this problem?
    b. At the $\alpha = .05$ level of significance, can we reject the null hypothesis in part (a)? Explain.

31. In an experiment designed to test the output levels of three different treatments, the following results were obtained: SST = 400, SSTR = 150, $n_T = 19$. Set up the ANOVA table and test for any significant difference between the mean output levels of the three treatments. Use $\alpha = .05$.

32. In a completely randomized design, 12 experimental units were used for the first treatment, 15 for the second treatment, and 20 for the third treatment. Complete the following analysis of variance. At a .05 level of significance, is there a significant difference between the treatments?

| Source of Variation | Sum of Squares | Degrees of Freedom | Mean Square | F | p-value |
|---|---|---|---|---|---|
| Treatments | 1200 | | | | |
| Error | | | | | |
| Total | 1800 | | | | |

33. Develop the analysis of variance computations for the following completely randomized design. At $\alpha = .05$, is there a significant difference between the treatment means?

**WEB** file

Exer33

| | Treatment | | |
|---|---|---|---|
| | A | B | C |
| | 136 | 107 | 92 |
| | 120 | 114 | 82 |
| | 113 | 125 | 85 |
| | 107 | 104 | 101 |
| | 131 | 107 | 89 |
| | 114 | 109 | 117 |
| | 129 | 97 | 110 |
| | 102 | 114 | 120 |
| | | 104 | 98 |
| | | 89 | 106 |
| $\bar{x}_j$ | 119 | 107 | 100 |
| $s_j^2$ | 146.86 | 96.44 | 173.78 |

# Applications

34. Three different methods for assembling a product were proposed by an industrial engineer. To investigate the number of units assembled correctly with each method, 30 employees were randomly selected and randomly assigned to the three proposed methods in such a way that each method was used by 10 workers. The number of units assembled correctly was recorded, and the analysis of variance procedure was applied to the resulting data set. The following results were obtained: SST = 10,800; SSTR = 4560.
    a.  Set up the ANOVA table for this problem.
    b.  Use $\alpha = .05$ to test for any significant difference in the means for the three assembly methods.

35. Refer to the NCP data in Table 10.6. Set up the ANOVA table and test for any significant difference in the mean examination score for the three plants. Use $\alpha = .05$.

36. To study the effect of temperature on yield, in pounds, for a chemical process, five batches were produced at each of three temperature levels. The results follow. Construct an analysis of variance table. Use a .05 level of significance to test whether the temperature level has an effect on the mean yield of the process.

| | Temperature | |
|---|---|---|
| **50°C** | **60°C** | **70°C** |
| 34 | 30 | 23 |
| 24 | 31 | 28 |
| 36 | 34 | 28 |
| 39 | 23 | 30 |
| 32 | 27 | 31 |

37. Auditors must make judgments about various aspects of an audit on the basis of their own direct experience, indirect experience, or a combination of the two. In a study, auditors were asked to make judgments about the frequency of errors to be found in an audit. The judgments by the auditors were then compared to the actual results. Suppose the following data were obtained from a similar study; lower scores indicate better judgments.

**WEB** file

AudJudg

| **Direct** | **Indirect** | **Combination** |
|---|---|---|
| 17.0 | 16.6 | 25.2 |
| 18.5 | 22.2 | 24.0 |
| 15.8 | 20.5 | 21.5 |
| 18.2 | 18.3 | 26.8 |
| 20.2 | 24.2 | 27.5 |
| 16.0 | 19.8 | 25.8 |
| 13.3 | 21.2 | 24.2 |

Use $\alpha = .05$ to test to see whether the basis for the judgment affects the quality of the judgment. What is your conclusion?

38. Four different paints are advertised as having the same drying time. To check the manufacturer's claims, five samples were tested for each of the paints. The time in minutes until the paint was dry enough for a second coat to be applied was recorded. The following data were obtained.

| Paint 1 | Paint 2 | Paint 3 | Paint 4 |
|---------|---------|---------|---------|
| 128 | 144 | 133 | 150 |
| 137 | 133 | 143 | 142 |
| 135 | 142 | 137 | 135 |
| 124 | 146 | 136 | 140 |
| 141 | 130 | 131 | 153 |

At the $\alpha = .05$ level of significance, test to see whether the mean drying time is the same for each type of paint.

39. The *Consumer Reports* Restaurant Customer Satisfaction Survey is based upon 148,599 visits to full-service restaurant chains (Consumer Reports website). One of the variables in the study is meal price, the average amount paid per person for dinner and drinks, minus the tip. Suppose a reporter for the *Sun Coast Times* thought that it would be of interest to her readers to conduct a similar study for restaurants located on the Grand Strand section in Myrtle Beach, South Carolina. The reporter selected a sample of eight seafood restaurants, eight Italian restaurants, and eight steakhouses. The following data show the meal prices ($) obtained for the 24 restaurants sampled. Use $\alpha = .05$ to test whether there is a significant difference among the mean meal price for the three types of restaurants.

| Italian | Seafood | Steakhouse |
|---------|---------|------------|
| $12 | $16 | $24 |
| 13 | 18 | 19 |
| 15 | 17 | 23 |
| 17 | 26 | 25 |
| 18 | 23 | 21 |
| 20 | 15 | 22 |
| 17 | 19 | 27 |
| 24 | 18 | 31 |

## Summary

In this chapter we discussed procedures for developing interval estimates and conducting hypothesis tests involving two populations. First, we showed how to make inferences about the difference between two population means when independent simple random samples are selected. We first considered the case where the population standard deviations $\sigma_1$ and $\sigma_2$ could be assumed known. The standard normal distribution $z$ was used to develop the interval estimate and served as the test statistic for hypothesis tests. We then considered the case where the population standard deviations were unknown and estimated by the sample standard deviations $s_1$ and $s_2$. In this case, the $t$ distribution was used to develop the interval estimate and the $t$ value served as the test statistic for hypothesis tests.

Inferences about the difference between two population means were then discussed for the matched sample design. In the matched sample design each element provides a pair of data values, one from each population. The difference between the paired data values is then used in the statistical analysis. The matched sample design is generally preferred to the independent sample design because the matched-sample procedure often improves the precision of the estimate.

In the final two sections we provided an introduction to experimental design and analysis of variance (ANOVA). Experimental studies differ from observational studies in the sense that an experiment is conducted to generate the data. The completely randomized design was described and the analysis of variance was used to test for a treatment effect. The same analysis of variance procedure can be used to test for the difference among $k$ population means in an observational study.

## Glossary

**Independent simple random samples** Samples selected from two populations in such a way that the elements making up one sample are chosen independently of the elements making up the other sample.

**Matched samples** One simple random sample of elements is selected and two data values are obtained for each element. For example, to compare two production methods, one simple random sample of $n$ workers is selected. Each worker first uses one method and then the other method. The order of the two methods is assigned randomly.

**Factor** Another word for the independent variable of interest.

**Treatments** Different levels of a factor.

**Single-factor experiment** An experiment involving only one factor with $k$ populations or treatments.

**Response variable** Another word for the dependent variable of interest.

**Experimental units** The objects of interest in the experiment.

**Completely randomized design** An experimental design in which the treatments are randomly assigned to the experimental units.

**F distribution** A probability distribution based on the ratio of two independent estimates of the variance of a normal population. The $F$ distribution is used in hypothesis tests about the equality of $k$ population means.

**ANOVA table** A table used to summarize the analysis of variance computations and results. It contains columns showing the source of variation, the sum of squares, the degrees of freedom, the mean square, the $F$ value(s), and the $p$-value(s).

## Key Formulas

**Point Estimator of the Difference Between Two Population Means**

$$\bar{x}_1 - \bar{x}_2 \tag{10.1}$$

**Standard Error of $\bar{x}_1 - \bar{x}_2$**

$$\sigma_{\bar{x}_1 - \bar{x}_2} = \sqrt{\frac{\sigma_1^2}{n_1} + \frac{\sigma_2^2}{n_2}} \tag{10.2}$$

**Interval Estimate of the Difference Between Two Population Means: $\sigma_1$ and $\sigma_2$ Known**

$$\bar{x}_1 - \bar{x}_2 \pm z_{\alpha/2} \sqrt{\frac{\sigma_1^2}{n_1} + \frac{\sigma_2^2}{n_2}} \tag{10.4}$$

**Test Statistic for Hypothesis Tests About $\mu_1 - \mu_2$: $\sigma_1$ and $\sigma_2$ Known**

$$z = \frac{(\bar{x}_1 - \bar{x}_2) - D_0}{\sqrt{\dfrac{\sigma_1^2}{n_1} + \dfrac{\sigma_2^2}{n_2}}} \tag{10.5}$$

**Interval Estimate of the Difference Between Two Population Means: $\sigma_1$ and $\sigma_2$ Unknown**

$$\bar{x}_1 - \bar{x}_2 \pm t_{\alpha/2} \sqrt{\frac{s_1^2}{n_1} + \frac{s_2^2}{n_2}} \tag{10.6}$$

**Degrees of Freedom: $t$ Distribution with Two Independent Random Samples**

$$df = \frac{\left(\dfrac{s_1^2}{n_1} + \dfrac{s_2^2}{n_2}\right)^2}{\dfrac{1}{n_1 - 1}\left(\dfrac{s_1^2}{n_1}\right)^2 + \dfrac{1}{n_2 - 1}\left(\dfrac{s_2^2}{n_2}\right)^2} \qquad \textbf{(10.7)}$$

**Test Statistic for Hypothesis Tests About $\mu_1 - \mu_2$: $\sigma_1$ and $\sigma_2$ Unknown**

$$t = \frac{(\bar{x}_1 - \bar{x}_2) - D_0}{\sqrt{\dfrac{s_1^2}{n_1} + \dfrac{s_2^2}{n_2}}} \qquad \textbf{(10.8)}$$

**Test Statistic for Hypothesis Tests Involving Matched Samples**

$$t = \frac{\bar{d} - \mu_d}{s_d/\sqrt{n}} \qquad \textbf{(10.9)}$$

**Sample Mean for Treatment $j$**

$$\bar{x}_j = \frac{\displaystyle\sum_{i=1}^{n_j} x_{ij}}{n_j} \qquad \textbf{(10.10)}$$

**Sample Variance for Treatment $j$**

$$s_j^2 = \frac{\displaystyle\sum_{i=1}^{n_j} (x_{ij} - \bar{x}_j)^2}{n_j - 1} \qquad \textbf{(10.11)}$$

**Overall Sample Mean**

$$\bar{\bar{x}} = \frac{\displaystyle\sum_{j=1}^{k}\sum_{i=1}^{n_j} x_{ij}}{n_T} \qquad \textbf{(10.12)}$$

$$n_T = n_1 + n_2 + \cdots + n_k \qquad \textbf{(10.13)}$$

**Mean Square Due to Treatments**

$$MSTR = \frac{SSTR}{k - 1} \qquad \textbf{(10.16)}$$

**Sum of Squares Due to Treatments**

$$SSTR = \sum_{j=1}^{k} n_j (\bar{x}_j - \bar{\bar{x}})^2 \qquad \textbf{(10.17)}$$

**Mean Square Due to Error**

$$MSE = \frac{SSE}{n_T - k} \qquad \textbf{(10.19)}$$

**Sum of Squares Due to Error**

$$SSE = \sum_{j=1}^{k} (n_j - 1)s_j^2 \qquad \textbf{(10.20)}$$

**Test Statistic for the Equality of $k$ Population Means**

$$F = \frac{\text{MSTR}}{\text{MSE}} \qquad\qquad \textbf{(10.21)}$$

**Total Sum of Squares**

$$\text{SST} = \sum_{j=1}^{k}\sum_{i=1}^{n_j}(x_{ij} - \bar{\bar{x}})^2 \qquad\qquad \textbf{(10.22)}$$

**Partitioning of Sum of Squares**

$$\text{SST} = \text{SSTR} + \text{SSE} \qquad\qquad \textbf{(10.23)}$$

## Supplementary Exercises

40. How much is the cost of a hospital stay increasing? The mean cost of one day in a semiprivate room was reported to be $4848 in 2005 and $5260 in 2006 (*The Wall Street Journal*, January 2, 2007). Assume the estimate for 2005 is a sample mean based on a sample size of 80 and the estimate for 2006 is a sample mean based on a sample size of 60.
    a. Develop a point estimate of the increase in the cost of a semiprivate hospital room from 2005 to 2006.
    b. Historical data indicate that a population standard deviation of $800 is a reasonable assumption for both years. Compute the margin of error for your estimate in part (a). Use 95% confidence.
    c. Develop a 95% confidence interval estimate of the increase in cost for a semiprivate room.

41. Home values tend to increase over time under normal conditions, but the recession of 2008 and 2009 has reportedly caused the resale price of existing homes to fall nationwide (*BusinessWeek*, March 9, 2009). You would like to see if the data support this conclusion. The file HomePrices contains data on 30 existing home sales in 2006 and 40 existing home sales in 2009.
    a. Provide a point estimate of the difference between the population mean prices for the two years.
    b. Develop a 99% confidence interval estimate of the difference between the resale prices of houses in 2006 and 2009.
    c. Would you feel justified in concluding that resale prices of existing homes have declined from 2006 to 2009? Why or why not?

42. Mutual funds are classified as *load* or *no-load* funds. Load funds require an investor to pay an initial fee based on a percentage of the amount invested in the fund. The no-load funds do not require this initial fee. Some financial advisors argue that the load mutual funds may be worth the extra fee because these funds provide a higher mean rate of return than the no-load mutual funds. A sample of 30 load mutual funds and a sample of 30 no-load mutual funds were selected. Data were collected on the annual return for the funds over a five-year period. The data are contained in the data set Mutual. The data for the first five load and first five no-load mutual funds are as follows.

| Mutual Funds—Load | Return | Mutual Funds—No Load | Return |
|---|---|---|---|
| American National Growth | 15.51 | Amana Income Fund | 13.24 |
| Arch Small Cap Equity | 14.57 | Berger One Hundred | 12.13 |
| Bartlett Cap Basic | 17.73 | Columbia International Stock | 12.17 |
| Calvert World International | 10.31 | Dodge & Cox Balanced | 16.06 |
| Colonial Fund A | 16.23 | Evergreen Fund | 17.61 |

a. Formulate $H_0$ and $H_a$ such that rejection of $H_0$ leads to the conclusion that the load mutual funds have a higher mean annual return over the five-year period.

b. Use the 60 mutual funds in the data set Mutual to conduct the hypothesis test. What is the $p$-value? At $\alpha = .05$, what is your conclusion?

43. The National Association of Home Builders provided data on the cost of the most popular home remodeling projects. Sample data on cost in thousands of dollars for two types of remodeling projects are as follows.

| Kitchen | Master Bedroom | Kitchen | Master Bedroom |
|---------|----------------|---------|----------------|
| 25.2 | 18.0 | 23.0 | 17.8 |
| 17.4 | 22.9 | 19.7 | 24.6 |
| 22.8 | 26.4 | 16.9 | 21.0 |
| 21.9 | 24.8 | 21.8 | |
| 19.7 | 26.9 | 23.6 | |

a. Develop a point estimate of the difference between the population mean remodeling costs for the two types of projects.

b. Develop a 90% confidence interval for the difference between the two population means.

44. In early 2009, the economy was experiencing a recession. But how was the recession affecting the stock market? Shown are data from a sample of 15 companies. Shown for each company is the price per share of stock on January 1 and April 30 (*The Wall Street Journal*, May 1, 2009).

**WEB file**

**PriceChange**

| Company | January 1 ($) | April 30 ($) |
|---------|---------------|--------------|
| Applied Materials | 10.13 | 12.21 |
| Bank of New York | 28.33 | 25.48 |
| Chevron | 73.97 | 66.10 |
| Cisco Systems | 16.30 | 19.32 |
| Coca-Cola | 45.27 | 43.05 |
| Comcast | 16.88 | 15.46 |
| Ford Motors | 2.29 | 5.98 |
| General Electric | 16.20 | 12.65 |
| Johnson & Johnson | 59.83 | 52.36 |
| JP Morgan Chase | 31.53 | 33.00 |
| Microsoft | 19.44 | 20.26 |
| Oracle | 17.73 | 19.34 |
| Pfizer | 17.71 | 13.36 |
| Philip Morris | 43.51 | 36.18 |
| Procter & Gamble | 61.82 | 49.44 |

a. What is the change in the mean price per share of stock over the four-month period?

b. Provide a 90% confident interval estimate of the change in the mean price per share of stock. Interpret the results.

c. What was the percentage change in the mean price per share of stock over the four-month period?

d. If this same percentage change were to occur for the next four months and again for the four months after that, what would be the mean price per share of stock at the end of the year 2009?

45. In a completely randomized experimental design, three brands of paper towels were tested for their ability to absorb water. Equal-size towels were used, with four sections of towels tested per brand. The absorbency rating data follow. At a .05 level of significance, does there appear to be a difference in the ability of the brands to absorb water?

| Brand | | |
|---|---|---|
| *x* | *y* | *z* |
| 91 | 99 | 83 |
| 100 | 96 | 88 |
| 88 | 94 | 89 |
| 89 | 99 | 76 |

46. A study reported in the *Journal of Small Business Management* concluded that self-employed individuals do not experience higher job satisfaction than individuals who are not self-employed. In this study, job satisfaction is measured using 18 items, each of which is rated using a Likert-type scale with 1–5 response options ranging from strong agreement to strong disagreement. A higher score on this scale indicates a higher degree of job satisfaction. The sum of the ratings for the 18 items, ranging from 18 to 90, is used as the measure of job satisfaction. Suppose that this approach was used to measure the job satisfaction for lawyers, physical therapists, cabinetmakers, and systems analysts. The results obtained for a sample of 10 individuals from each profession follow.

**WEB** file

SatisJob

| Lawyer | Physical Therapist | Cabinetmaker | Systems Analyst |
|---|---|---|---|
| 44 | 55 | 54 | 44 |
| 42 | 78 | 65 | 73 |
| 74 | 80 | 79 | 71 |
| 42 | 86 | 69 | 60 |
| 53 | 60 | 79 | 64 |
| 50 | 59 | 64 | 66 |
| 45 | 62 | 59 | 41 |
| 48 | 52 | 78 | 55 |
| 64 | 55 | 84 | 76 |
| 38 | 50 | 60 | 62 |

At the $\alpha = .05$ level of significance, test for any difference in the job satisfaction among the four professions.

47. *Money* magazine reports percentage returns and expense ratios for stock and bond funds. The following data are the expense ratios for 10 midcap stock funds, 10 small-cap stock funds, 10 hybrid stock funds, and 10 specialty stock funds (*Money*, March 2003).

**WEB** file

Funds

| Midcap | Small-Cap | Hybrid | Specialty |
|---|---|---|---|
| 1.2 | 2.0 | 2.0 | 1.6 |
| 1.1 | 1.2 | 2.7 | 2.7 |
| 1.0 | 1.7 | 1.8 | 2.6 |
| 1.2 | 1.8 | 1.5 | 2.5 |
| 1.3 | 1.5 | 2.5 | 1.9 |
| 1.8 | 2.3 | 1.0 | 1.5 |
| 1.4 | 1.9 | 0.9 | 1.6 |
| 1.4 | 1.3 | 1.9 | 2.7 |
| 1.0 | 1.2 | 1.4 | 2.2 |
| 1.4 | 1.3 | 0.3 | 0.7 |

Use $\alpha = .05$ to test for any significant difference in the mean expense ratio among the four types of stock funds.

48. The U.S. Census Bureau computes quarterly vacancy and homeownership rates by state and metropolitan statistical area. Each metropolitan statistical area (MSA) has at least one urbanized area of 50,000 or more inhabitants. The following data are the rental vacancy rates (%) for MSAs in four geographic regions of the United States for the first quarter of 2008 (U.S. Census Bureau website, January 2009).

**RentalVacancy**

| Midwest | Northeast | South | West |
|---------|-----------|-------|------|
| 16.2 | 2.7 | 16.6 | 7.9 |
| 10.1 | 11.5 | 8.5 | 6.6 |
| 8.6 | 6.6 | 12.1 | 6.9 |
| 12.3 | 7.9 | 9.8 | 5.6 |
| 10.0 | 5.3 | 9.3 | 4.3 |
| 16.9 | 10.7 | 9.1 | 15.2 |
| 16.9 | 8.6 | 5.6 | 5.7 |
| 5.4 | 5.5 | 9.4 | 4.0 |
| 18.1 | 12.7 | 11.6 | 12.3 |
| 11.9 | 8.3 | 15.6 | 3.6 |
| 11.0 | 6.7 | 18.3 | 11.0 |
| 9.6 | 14.2 | 13.4 | 12.1 |
| 7.6 | 1.7 | 6.5 | 8.7 |
| 12.9 | 3.6 | 11.4 | 5.0 |
| 12.2 | 11.5 | 13.1 | 4.7 |
| 13.6 | 16.3 | 4.4 | 3.3 |
| | | 8.2 | 3.4 |
| | | 24.0 | 5.5 |
| | | 12.2 | |
| | | 22.6 | |
| | | 12.0 | |
| | | 14.5 | |
| | | 12.6 | |
| | | 9.5 | |
| | | 10.1 | |

Use $\alpha = .05$ to test whether the mean vacancy rate is the same for each geographic region.

49. Three different assembly methods have been proposed for a new product. A completely randomized experimental design was chosen to determine which assembly method results in the greatest number of parts produced per hour, and 30 workers were randomly selected and assigned to use one of the proposed methods. The number of units produced by each worker follows.

**Assembly**

| | Method | |
|---|---|---|
| **A** | **B** | **C** |
| 97 | 93 | 99 |
| 73 | 100 | 94 |
| 93 | 93 | 87 |
| 100 | 55 | 66 |
| 73 | 77 | 59 |
| 91 | 91 | 75 |
| 100 | 85 | 84 |
| 86 | 73 | 72 |
| 92 | 90 | 88 |
| 95 | 83 | 86 |

Use these data and test to see whether the mean number of parts produced is the same with each method. Use $\alpha = .05$.

50. In a study conducted to investigate browsing activity by shoppers, each shopper was initially classified as a nonbrowser, light browser, or heavy browser. For each shopper, the study obtained a measure to determine how comfortable the shopper was in a store. Higher scores indicated greater comfort. Suppose the following data were collected.

Browsing

| Nonbrowser | Light Browser | Heavy Browser |
|---|---|---|
| 4 | 5 | 5 |
| 5 | 6 | 7 |
| 6 | 5 | 5 |
| 3 | 4 | 7 |
| 3 | 7 | 4 |
| 4 | 4 | 6 |
| 5 | 6 | 5 |
| 4 | 5 | 7 |

Use $\alpha = .05$ to test for differences among comfort levels for the three types of browsers.

## Case Problem 1   Par, Inc.

Par, Inc., is a major manufacturer of golf equipment. Management believes that Par's market share could be increased with the introduction of a cut-resistant, longer-lasting golf ball. Therefore, the research group at Par has been investigating a new golf ball coating designed to resist cuts and provide a more durable ball. The tests with the coating have been promising.

One of the researchers voiced concern about the effect of the new coating on driving distances. Par would like the new cut-resistant ball to offer driving distances comparable to those of the current-model golf ball. To compare the driving distances for the two balls, 40 balls of both the new and current models were subjected to distance tests. The testing was performed with a mechanical hitting machine so that any difference between the mean distances for the two models could be attributed to a difference in the two models. The results of the tests, with distances measured to the nearest yard, follow. These data are available on the website that accompanies this text in the file named Golf.

Golf

| Model | | Model | | Model | | Model | |
|---|---|---|---|---|---|---|---|
| Current | New | Current | New | Current | New | Current | New |
| 264 | 277 | 270 | 272 | 263 | 274 | 281 | 283 |
| 261 | 269 | 287 | 259 | 264 | 266 | 274 | 250 |
| 267 | 263 | 289 | 264 | 284 | 262 | 273 | 253 |
| 272 | 266 | 280 | 280 | 263 | 271 | 263 | 260 |
| 258 | 262 | 272 | 274 | 260 | 260 | 275 | 270 |
| 283 | 251 | 275 | 281 | 283 | 281 | 267 | 263 |
| 258 | 262 | 265 | 276 | 255 | 250 | 279 | 261 |
| 266 | 289 | 260 | 269 | 272 | 263 | 274 | 255 |
| 259 | 286 | 278 | 268 | 266 | 278 | 276 | 263 |
| 270 | 264 | 275 | 262 | 268 | 264 | 262 | 279 |

## Managerial Report

1. Formulate and present the rationale for a hypothesis test that Par could use to compare the driving distances of the current and new golf balls.
2. Analyze the data to provide the hypothesis testing conclusion. What is the *p*-value for your test? What is your recommendation for Par, Inc.?
3. Provide descriptive statistical summaries of the data for each model.
4. What is the 95% confidence interval for the population mean of each model, and what is the 95% confidence interval for the difference between the means of the two populations?
5. Do you see a need for larger sample sizes and more testing with the golf balls? Discuss.

## Case Problem 2   Wentworth Medical Center

As part of a long-term study of individuals 65 years of age or older, sociologists and physicians at the Wentworth Medical Center in upstate New York investigated the relationship between geographic location and depression. A sample of 60 individuals, all in reasonably good health, was selected; 20 individuals were residents of Florida, 20 were residents of New York, and 20 were residents of North Carolina. Each of the individuals sampled was given a standardized test to measure depression. The data collected follow; higher test scores indicate higher levels of depression. These data are available on the website that accompanies this text in the file named Medical1.

A second part of the study considered the relationship between geographic location and depression for individuals 65 years of age or older who had a chronic health condition such as arthritis, hypertension, and/or heart ailment. A sample of 60 individuals with such conditions was identified. Again, 20 were residents of Florida, 20 were residents of New York, and 20 were residents of North Carolina. The levels of depression recorded for this study follow. These data are available on the website that accompanies this text in the file named Medical2.

WEB file
Medical1

WEB file
Medical2

| Data from Medical1 | | | Data from Medical2 | | |
|---|---|---|---|---|---|
| Florida | New York | North Carolina | Florida | New York | North Carolina |
| 3 | 8 | 10 | 13 | 14 | 10 |
| 7 | 11 | 7 | 12 | 9 | 12 |
| 7 | 9 | 3 | 17 | 15 | 15 |
| 3 | 7 | 5 | 17 | 12 | 18 |
| 8 | 8 | 11 | 20 | 16 | 12 |
| 8 | 7 | 8 | 21 | 24 | 14 |
| 8 | 8 | 4 | 16 | 18 | 17 |
| 5 | 4 | 3 | 14 | 14 | 8 |
| 5 | 13 | 7 | 13 | 15 | 14 |
| 2 | 10 | 8 | 17 | 17 | 16 |
| 6 | 6 | 8 | 12 | 20 | 18 |
| 2 | 8 | 7 | 9 | 11 | 17 |
| 6 | 12 | 3 | 12 | 23 | 19 |
| 6 | 8 | 9 | 15 | 19 | 15 |
| 9 | 6 | 8 | 16 | 17 | 13 |
| 7 | 8 | 12 | 15 | 14 | 14 |
| 5 | 5 | 6 | 13 | 9 | 11 |
| 4 | 7 | 3 | 10 | 14 | 12 |
| 7 | 7 | 8 | 11 | 13 | 13 |
| 3 | 8 | 11 | 17 | 11 | 11 |

### Managerial Report

1. Use descriptive statistics to summarize the data from the two studies. What are your preliminary observations about the depression scores?
2. Use analysis of variance on both data sets. State the hypotheses being tested in each case. What are your conclusions?
3. Use inferences about individual treatment means where appropriate. What are your conclusions?

## Appendix   Comparisons Involving Means Using StatTools

In this appendix we show how StatTools can be used to develop interval estimates and conduct hypothesis tests about the difference between two population means for the $\sigma_1$ and $\sigma_2$ unknown case. We also show how StatTools can be used to test for the equality of $k$ population means for a completely randomized design.

### Interval Estimation of $\mu_1$ and $\mu_2$

**CheckAcct**

We will use the data for the checking account balances example presented in Section 10.2. Begin by using the Data Set Manager to create a StatTools data set for these data using the procedure described in the appendix in Chapter 1. The following steps can be used to compute a 95% confidence interval estimate of the difference between the two population means.

**Step 1.** Click the **StatTools** tab on the Ribbon
**Step 2.** In the **Analyses** group, click **Statistical Inference**
**Step 3.** Select the **Confidence Interval** option
**Step 4.** Choose **Mean/Std. Deviation**
**Step 5.** When the StatTools - Confidence Interval for Mean/Std. Deviation dialog box appears,

>For **Analysis Type,** choose **Two-Sample Analysis**
>In the **Variables** section,
>>Select **Cherry Grove**
>>Select **Beechmont**
>In the **Confidence Intervals to Calculate** section,
>>Select the **For the Difference of Means** option
>>Select 95% for the **Confidence Level**
>Click **OK**

Because the sample size for Cherry Grove ($n_1 = 28$) differs from the sample size for Beechmont ($n_2 = 22$), StatTools will inform you of this difference after you click OK in step 5. A dialog box will appear saying "The variable Beechmont contains missing data, which the analysis will ignore." Click OK. A Choose Variable Ordering dialog box then appears, indicating that the analysis will compare the difference between the Cherry Grove data set and the Beechmont data set. Click OK and the StatTools interval estimation output will appear.

### Hypothesis Tests About $\mu_1$ and $\mu_2$

**SoftwareTest**

We will use the software evaluation example and the completion time data presented in Table 10.1. Begin by using the Data Set Manager to create a StatTools data set for these data using the procedure described in the appendix in Chapter 1. The following steps can be used to test the hypothesis $H_0: \mu_1 - \mu_2 \leq 0$ against $H_a: \mu_1 - \mu_2 > 0$.

Step 1. Click the **StatTools** tab on the Ribbon

Step 2. In the **Analyses** group, click **Statistical Inference**

Step 3. Choose the **Hypothesis Test** option

Step 4. Choose **Mean/Std. Deviation**

Step 5. When the StatTools - Hypothesis Test for Mean/Std. Deviation dialog box appears,

> For **Analysis Type,** choose **Two-Sample Analysis**
>
> In the **Variables** section,
>> Select **Current**
>> Select **New**
>
> In the **Hypothesis Tests to Perform** section,
>> Select **Difference of Means**
>> Enter 0 in the **Null Hypothesis Value** box
>> Select **Greater Than Null Value (One-Tailed Test)** in the **Alternative Hypothesis** box
>
> Click **OK**
>
> When the Choose Variable Ordering dialog box appears, click **OK**

The results of the hypothesis test will then appear.

## Inferences About the Difference Between Two Population Means: Matched Samples

**WEB** file

**Matched**

StatTools can be used to develop interval estimates and conduct hypothesis tests for the difference between population means for the matched samples case. We will use the matched-sample completion times in Table 10.2 to illustrate.

Begin by using the Data Set Manager to create a StatTools data set for these data using the procedure described in the appendix in Chapter 1. The following steps can be used to compute a 95% confidence interval estimate of the difference between the population mean completion times.

Step 1. Click the **StatTools** tab on the Ribbon

Step 2. In the **Analyses** group, click **Statistical Inference**

Step 3. Choose the **Confidence Interval** option

Step 4. When the StatTools - Confidence Interval dialog box appears,

> For **Analysis Type,** choose **Paired-Sample Analysis**
>
> In the **Variables** section,
>> Select **Method 1**
>> Select **Method 2**
>
> In the **Confidence Intervals to Calculate** section,
>> Select the **For the Difference of Means** option
>> Select 95% for the **Confidence Level**
>> If selected, remove the check in the **For the Standard Deviation** box
>
> Click **OK**
>
> When the Choose Variable Ordering dialog box appears, click **OK**

The confidence interval will appear.

Conducting hypothesis tests for the matched samples case is very similar to conducting hypothesis tests for the difference in two means shown above. After selecting the Hypothesis Test option in step 3, select the Paired-Sample Analysis option in step 4.

## Analysis of a Completely Randomized Design

StatTools can be used to test for the equality of $k$ population means for a completely randomized design. We use the Chemitech data in Table 10.3 to illustrate. Begin by using the Data Set Manager to create a StatTools data set for these data using the procedure described in the appendix in Chapter 1. The following steps can be used to test for the equality of the three population means.

**Chemitech**

**Step 1.** Click the **StatTools** tab on the Ribbon
**Step 2.** In the **Analyses** group, click **Statistical Inference**
**Step 3.** Choose the **One-Way ANOVA** option
**Step 4.** When the One-Way ANOVA dialog box appears,
  In the **Variables** section,
    Click the **Format button** and select **Unstacked**
    Select **Method A**
    Select **Method B**
    Select **Method C**
  Select 95% in the **Confidence Level** box
  Click **OK**

Note that in step 4 we selected the Unstacked option after clicking the Format button. The Unstacked option means that the data for the three treatments appear in separate columns of the worksheet. In a stacked format, only two columns would be used. For example, the data could have been organized as shown in Figure 10.16. Data are frequently recorded in a stacked format. For stacked data, simply select the Stacked option after clicking the Format button.

**FIGURE 10.16**    CHEMITECH DATA IN STACKED FORMAT

| | A | B |
|---|---|---|
| 1 | **Method** | **Units Produced** |
| 2 | Method A | 58 |
| 3 | Method A | 64 |
| 4 | Method A | 55 |
| 5 | Method A | 66 |
| 6 | Method A | 67 |
| 7 | Method B | 58 |
| 8 | Method B | 69 |
| 9 | Method B | 71 |
| 10 | Method B | 64 |
| 11 | Method B | 68 |
| 12 | Method C | 48 |
| 13 | Method C | 57 |
| 14 | Method C | 59 |
| 15 | Method C | 47 |
| 16 | Method C | 49 |

# CHAPTER 11

# Comparisons Involving Proportions and a Test of Independence

## CONTENTS

## STATISTICS *in* PRACTICE

### UNITED WAY*
#### ROCHESTER, NEW YORK

United Way of Greater Rochester is a nonprofit organization dedicated to improving the quality of life for all people in the seven counties it serves by meeting the community's most important human care needs.

The annual United Way/Red Cross fund-raising campaign, conducted each spring, funds hundreds of programs offered by more than 200 service providers. These providers meet a wide variety of human needs—physical, mental, and social—and serve people of all ages, backgrounds, and economic means.

Because of enormous volunteer involvement, United Way of Greater Rochester is able to hold its operating costs at just eight cents of every dollar raised.

The United Way of Greater Rochester decided to conduct a survey to learn more about community perceptions of charities. Focus-group interviews were held with professional, service, and general worker groups to get preliminary information on perceptions. The information obtained was then used to help develop the questionnaire for the survey. The questionnaire was pretested, modified, and distributed to 440 individuals; 323 completed questionnaires were obtained.

A variety of descriptive statistics, including frequency distributions and crosstabulations, were provided from the data collected. An important part of the analysis involved the use of contingency tables and chi-square tests of independence. One use of such statistical tests was to determine whether perceptions of administrative expenses were independent of occupation.

The hypotheses for the test of independence were:

$H_0$: Perception of United Way administrative expenses is independent of the occupation of the respondent.

Statistical surveys help United Way adjust its program to better meet the needs of the people it serves.

$H_a$: Perception of United Way administrative expenses is not independent of the occupation of the respondent.

Two questions in the survey provided the data for the statistical test. One question obtained data on perceptions of the percentage of funds going to administrative expenses (up to 10%, 11–20%, and 21% or more). The other question asked for the occupation of the respondent.

The chi-square test at a .05 level of significance led to rejection of the null hypothesis of independence and to the conclusion that perceptions of United Way's administrative expenses did vary by occupation. Actual administrative expenses were less than 9%, but 35% of the respondents perceived that administrative expenses were 21% or more. Hence, many had inaccurate perceptions of administrative costs. In this group, production-line, clerical, sales, and professional-technical employees had more inaccurate perceptions than other groups.

The community perceptions study helped United Way of Greater Rochester to develop adjustments to its program and fund-raising activities. In this chapter, you will learn how a statistical test of independence, such as that described here, is conducted.

---

*The authors are indebted to Dr. Philip R. Tyler, Marketing Consultant to the United Way, for providing this Statistics in Practice.

Many statistical applications call for a comparison of population proportions. In Section 11.1 we describe statistical inferences concerning differences in the proportions for two populations. Two samples are required, one from each population, and the statistical inference is based on the two sample proportions. The second section looks at a hypothesis test comparing the proportions of a single multinomial population with the proportions selected in a null hypothesis. One sample from the multinomial population is used, and the hypothesis test is based on comparing the sample proportions with those stated in the null hypothesis. In the last section of the chapter, we show how contingency tables can be used to test for the independence of two variables. One sample is used for the test of independence, but measures on two variables are required for each sampled element. Both Sections 11.2 and 11.3 rely on the use of a chi-square statistical test.

## 11.1   Inferences About the Difference Between Two Population Proportions

Letting $p_1$ denote the proportion for population 1 and $p_2$ denote the proportion for population 2, we consider inferences about the difference between the two population proportions: $p_1 - p_2$. To make an inference about this difference, we will select two independent random samples consisting of $n_1$ units from population 1 and $n_2$ units from population 2.

### Interval Estimation of $p_1 - p_2$

In the following example, we show how to compute a margin of error and develop an interval estimate of the difference between two population proportions.

A tax preparation firm is interested in comparing the quality of work at two of its regional offices. By randomly selecting samples of tax returns prepared at each office and verifying the sample returns' accuracy, the firm will be able to estimate the proportion of erroneous returns prepared at each office. Of particular interest is the difference between these proportions.

$p_1$ = proportion of erroneous returns for population 1 (office 1)

$p_2$ = proportion of erroneous returns for population 2 (office 2)

$\bar{p}_1$ = sample proportion for a simple random sample from population 1

$\bar{p}_2$ = sample proportion for a simple random sample from population 2

The difference between the two population proportions is given by $p_1 - p_2$. The point estimator of $p_1 - p_2$ is as follows.

> **POINT ESTIMATOR OF THE DIFFERENCE BETWEEN TWO POPULATION PROPORTIONS**
>
> $$\bar{p}_1 - \bar{p}_2 \tag{11.1}$$

Thus, the point estimator of the difference between two population proportions is the difference between the sample proportions of two independent simple random samples.

As with other point estimators, the point estimator $\bar{p}_1 - \bar{p}_2$ has a sampling distribution that reflects the possible values of $\bar{p}_1 - \bar{p}_2$ if we repeatedly took two independent random samples. The mean of this sampling distribution is $p_1 - p_2$ and the standard error is as follows:

$$\sigma_{\bar{p}_1 - \bar{p}_2} = \sqrt{\frac{p_1(1 - p_1)}{n_1} + \frac{p_2(1 - p_2)}{n_2}} \tag{11.2}$$

*Sample sizes involving proportions are usually large enough to use this approximation.*

If the sample sizes are large enough that $n_1 p_1$, $n_1(1 - p_1)$, $n_2 p_2$, and $n_2(1 - p_2)$ are all greater than or equal to 5, the sampling distribution of $\bar{p}_1 - \bar{p}_2$ can be approximated by a normal distribution.

In the estimation of the difference between two population proportions, an interval estimate will take the following form:

$$\bar{p}_1 - \bar{p}_2 \pm \text{Margin of error}$$

With the sampling distribution of $\bar{p}_1 - \bar{p}_2$ approximated by a normal distribution, we would like to use $z_{\alpha/2}\sigma_{\bar{p}_1 - \bar{p}_2}$ as the margin of error. However, $\sigma_{\bar{p}_1 - \bar{p}_2}$ given by equation (11.2) involves the two unknown population proportions, $p_1$ and $p_2$. Thus, we use the sample proportion $\bar{p}_1$ to estimate $p_1$ and the sample proportion $\bar{p}_2$ to estimate $p_2$. The margin of error is thus:

$$\text{Margin of error} = z_{\alpha/2}\sqrt{\frac{\bar{p}_1(1 - \bar{p}_1)}{n_1} + \frac{\bar{p}_2(1 - \bar{p}_2)}{n_2}} \tag{11.3}$$

The general form of an interval estimate of the difference between two population proportions is as follows.

> **INTERVAL ESTIMATE OF THE DIFFERENCE BETWEEN TWO POPULATION PROPORTIONS**
>
> $$\bar{p}_1 - \bar{p}_2 \pm z_{\alpha/2}\sqrt{\frac{\bar{p}_1(1 - \bar{p}_1)}{n_1} + \frac{\bar{p}_2(1 - \bar{p}_2)}{n_2}} \tag{11.4}$$
>
> where $1 - \alpha$ is the confidence coefficient.

Returning to the tax preparation example, we find that independent simple random samples from the two offices provide the following information.

| Office 1 | Office 2 |
|---|---|
| $n_1 = 250$ | $n_2 = 300$ |
| Number of returns with errors = 35 | Number of returns with errors = 27 |

**WEB file**

**TaxPrep**

The sample proportions for the two offices follow.

$$\bar{p}_1 = \frac{35}{250} = .14$$

$$\bar{p}_2 = \frac{27}{300} = .09$$

The point estimate of the difference between the proportions of erroneous tax returns for the two populations is $\bar{p}_1 - \bar{p}_2 = .14 - .09 = .05$. Thus, we estimate that office 1 has a .05, or 5%, greater error rate than office 2.

Expression (11.4) can now be used to provide a margin of error and interval estimate of the difference between the two population proportions. Using a 90% confidence interval with $z_{\alpha/2} = z_{.05} = 1.645$, we have

$$\bar{p}_1 - \bar{p}_2 \pm z_{\alpha/2}\sqrt{\frac{\bar{p}_1(1 - \bar{p}_1)}{n_1} + \frac{\bar{p}_2(1 - \bar{p}_2)}{n_2}}$$

$$.14 - .09 \pm 1.645\sqrt{\frac{.14(1 - .14)}{250} + \frac{.09(1 - .09)}{300}}$$

$$.05 \pm .045$$

Thus, the margin of error is .045, and the 90% confidence interval is .005 to .095.

## Using Excel to Construct a Confidence Interval

We can create a worksheet for developing an interval estimate of the difference between population proportions. Let us illustrate by developing an interval estimate of the difference between the proportions of erroneous tax returns at the two offices of the tax preparation firm. Refer to Figure 11.1 as we describe the tasks involved. The formula worksheet is in the background; the value worksheet appears in the foreground.

**FIGURE 11.1**    CONSTRUCTING A 90% CONFIDENCE INTERVAL FOR THE DIFFERENCE
IN THE PROPORTION OF ERRONEOUS TAX RETURNS PREPARED BY TWO OFFICES

Note: Rows 20–249 and
252–299 are hidden.

**Enter Data:** Columns A and B contain Yes or No labels that indicate which of the tax returns from each office contain an error.

**Enter Functions and Formulas:** The descriptive statistics needed are provided in cells E5:F5 and E7:F8. Note that Excel's COUNTA function is used in cells E5 and F5 to count the number of observations for each of the samples. The value worksheet indicates 250 returns in the sample from office 1 and 300 returns in the sample from office 2. In cells E6 and F6, we type Yes to indicate the response of interest (an erroneous return). Excel's COUNTIF function is used in cells E7 and F7 to count the number of Yes responses from each office. Formulas entered into cells E8 and F8 compute the sample proportions. The confidence coefficient entered into cell E10 (.9) is used to compute the corresponding level of significance ($\alpha = .10$) in cell E11. In cell E12 we use the NORM.S.INV function to compute the $z$ value needed to compute the margin of error for the interval estimate.

In cell E14, a point estimate of $\sigma_{\bar{p}_1 - \bar{p}_2}$, the standard error of the point estimator $\bar{p}_1 - \bar{p}_2$, is computed based on the two sample proportions (E8 and F8) and sample sizes (E5 and F5). The margin of error is then computed in cell E15 by multiplying the $z$ value by the estimate of the standard error.

The point estimate of the difference in the two population proportions is computed in cell E17 as the difference in the sample proportions; the result, shown in the value worksheet, is .05. The lower limit of the confidence interval is computed in cell E18 by subtracting the margin of error from the point estimate. The upper limit is computed in cell E19 by adding the margin of error to the point estimate. The value worksheet shows that the 90% confidence interval estimate of the difference in the two population proportions is .0048 to .0952.

**A template for other problems** This worksheet can be used as a template for other problems requiring an interval estimate of the difference in population proportions. The new data must be entered in columns A and B. The data ranges in the cells used to compute the sample size (E5:F5) and the cells used to compute a count of the response of interest (E7:F7) must be changed to correctly indicate the location of the new data. The response of interest must be typed into cells E6:F6. The 90% confidence interval for the new data will then appear in cells E17:E19. If an interval estimate with a different confidence coefficient is desired, simply change the entry in cell E10.

This worksheet can also be used as a template for solving text exercises in which the sample data have already been summarized. No change in the data section is necessary. Simply type the values for the given sample sizes in cells E5:F5 and type the given values for the sample proportions in cells E8:F8. The 90% confidence interval will then appear in cells E17:E19. If an interval estimate with a different confidence coefficient is desired, simply change the entry in cell E10.

## Hypothesis Tests About $p_1 - p_2$

Let us now consider hypothesis tests about the difference between the proportions of two populations. We focus on tests involving no difference between the two population proportions. In this case, the three forms for a hypothesis test are as follows:

*All hypotheses considered use 0 as the difference of interest.*

$$H_0: p_1 - p_2 \geq 0 \qquad H_0: p_1 - p_2 \leq 0 \qquad H_0: p_1 - p_2 = 0$$
$$H_a: p_1 - p_2 < 0 \qquad H_a: p_1 - p_2 > 0 \qquad H_a: p_1 - p_2 \neq 0$$

When we assume $H_0$ is true as an equality, we have $p_1 - p_2 = 0$, which is the same as saying that the population proportions are equal, $p_1 = p_2$.

We will base the test statistic on the sampling distribution of the point estimator $\bar{p}_1 - \bar{p}_2$. In equation (11.2), we showed that the standard error of $\bar{p}_1 - \bar{p}_2$ is given by

$$\sigma_{\bar{p}_1 - \bar{p}_2} = \sqrt{\frac{p_1(1 - p_1)}{n_1} + \frac{p_2(1 - p_2)}{n_2}}$$

Under the assumption $H_0$ is true as an equality, the population proportions are equal and $p_1 = p_2 = p$. In this case, $\sigma_{\bar{p}_1 - \bar{p}_2}$ becomes as follows:

**STANDARD ERROR OF $\bar{p}_1 - \bar{p}_2$ WHEN $p_1 = p_2 = p$**

$$\sigma_{\bar{p}_1 - \bar{p}_2} = \sqrt{\frac{p(1 - p)}{n_1} + \frac{p(1 - p)}{n_2}} = \sqrt{p(1 - p)\left(\frac{1}{n_1} + \frac{1}{n_2}\right)} \qquad \textbf{(11.5)}$$

With $p$ unknown, we pool, or combine, the point estimators from the two samples ($\bar{p}_1$ and $\bar{p}_2$) to obtain a single point estimator of $p$ as follows:

**POOLED ESTIMATOR OF $p$ WHEN $p_1 = p_2 = p$**

$$\bar{p} = \frac{n_1 \bar{p}_1 + n_2 \bar{p}_2}{n_1 + n_2} \qquad \textbf{(11.6)}$$

This **pooled estimator of $p$** is a weighted average of $\bar{p}_1$ and $\bar{p}_2$.

Substituting $\bar{p}$ for $p$ in equation (11.5), we obtain an estimate of the standard error of $\bar{p}_1 - \bar{p}_2$. This estimate of the standard error is used in computing the test statistic. The general form of the test statistic for hypothesis tests about the difference between two population proportions is the point estimator divided by the estimate of $\sigma_{\bar{p}_1 - \bar{p}_2}$.

**TEST STATISTIC FOR HYPOTHESIS TESTS ABOUT $p_1 - p_2$**

$$z = \frac{(\bar{p}_1 - \bar{p}_2)}{\sqrt{\bar{p}(1 - \bar{p})\left(\frac{1}{n_1} + \frac{1}{n_2}\right)}} \qquad \textbf{(11.7)}$$

This test statistic applies to large sample situations where $n_1 p_1$, $n_1(1 - p_1)$, $n_2 p_2$, and $n_2(1 - p_2)$ are all greater than or equal to 5.

Let us return to the tax preparation firm example and assume that the firm wants to use a hypothesis test to determine whether the error proportions differ between the two offices. A two-tailed test is required. The null and alternative hypotheses are as follows:

$$H_0: p_1 - p_2 = 0$$
$$H_a: p_1 - p_2 \neq 0$$

If $H_0$ is rejected, the firm can conclude that the error rates at the two offices differ. We will use $\alpha = .10$ as the level of significance.

The sample data previously collected showed $\bar{p}_1 = .14$ for the $n_1 = 250$ returns sampled at office 1 and $\bar{p}_2 = .09$ for the $n_2 = 300$ returns sampled at office 2. We continue by computing the pooled estimate of $p$.

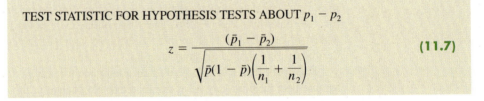

$$\bar{p} = \frac{n_1 \bar{p}_1 + n_2 \bar{p}_2}{n_1 + n_2} = \frac{250(.14) + 300(.09)}{250 + 300} = .1127$$

Using this pooled estimate and the difference between the sample proportions, the value of the test statistic is as follows.

$$z = \frac{(\bar{p}_1 - \bar{p}_2)}{\sqrt{\bar{p}(1 - \bar{p})\left(\dfrac{1}{n_1} + \dfrac{1}{n_2}\right)}} = \frac{(.14 - .09)}{\sqrt{.1127(1 - .1127)\left(\dfrac{1}{250} + \dfrac{1}{300}\right)}} = 1.85$$

In computing the $p$-value for this two-tailed test, we first note that $z = 1.85$ is in the upper tail of the standard normal distribution. Using $z = 1.85$ and the standard normal distribution table, we find the area in the upper tail is $1.0000 - .9678 = .0322$. Doubling this area for a two-tailed test, we find the $p$-value $= 2(.0322) = .0644$. With the $p$-value less than $\alpha = .10$, $H_0$ is rejected at the .10 level of significance. The firm can conclude that the error rates differ between the two offices. This hypothesis testing conclusion is consistent with the earlier 90% confidence interval results that showed the interval estimate of the difference between the population error rates at the two offices to be .005 to .095, with office 1 having the higher error rate.

## Using Excel to Conduct a Hypothesis Test

We can create a worksheet for conducting a hypothesis test about the difference between population proportions. Let us illustrate by testing to see whether there is a significant difference between the proportions of erroneous tax returns at the two offices of the tax preparation firm. Refer to Figure 11.2 as we describe the tasks involved. The formula worksheet is in the background; the value worksheet is in the foreground.

**Enter Data:**    Columns A and B contain Yes or No labels that indicate which of the tax returns from each office contain an error.

**Enter Functions and Formulas:**    The descriptive statistics needed to perform the hypothesis test are provided in cells E5:F6 and E7:F8. They are the same as the ones used for an interval estimate (see Figure 11.1). The hypothesized value of the difference between the two populations is zero; it is entered into cell E10. In cell E11, the difference in the sample proportions is used to compute a point estimate of the difference in the two population proportions. Using the two sample proportions and sample sizes, a pooled estimate of the population proportion $p$ is computed in cell E13; its value is .1127. Then, in cell E14, an estimate of $\sigma_{\bar{p}_1 - \bar{p}_2}$ is computed using equation (11.5), with the pooled estimate of $p$ and the sample sizes.

*The p-value here (.0649) differs from the one we found using the cumulative normal probability tables (.0644) due to rounding.*

The formula $=(E11\text{-}E10)/E14$ entered into cell E15 computes the test statistic $z$ (1.8462). The NORM.S.DIST function is then used to compute the $p$-value (Lower Tail) and the $p$-value (Upper Tail) in cells E17 and E18. The $p$-value (Two Tail) is computed in cell E19 as twice the minimum of the two one-tailed $p$-values. The value worksheet shows that $p$-value (Two Tail) $= .0649$. Because the $p$-value $= .0649$ is less than the level of significance, $\alpha = .10$, we have sufficient evidence to reject the null hypothesis and conclude that the population proportions are not equal.

This worksheet can be used as a template for hypothesis testing problems involving differences between population proportions. The new data can be entered into columns A and B. The ranges for the new data and the response of interest need to be revised in cells E5:F7. The remainder of the worksheet will then be updated as needed to conduct the hypothesis test. If a hypothesized difference other than 0 is to be used, the new value must be entered in cell E10.

To use this worksheet for exercises in which the sample statistics are given, just type in the given values for cells E5:F5 and E7:F8. The remainder of the worksheet will then be updated to conduct the hypothesis test. If a hypothesized difference other than 0 is to be used, the new value must be entered in cell E10.

**FIGURE 11.2**  HYPOTHESIS TEST CONCERNING DIFFERENCE IN PROPORTION OF ERRONEOUS TAX RETURNS PREPARED BY TWO OFFICES

*Note: Rows 20–249 and 252–299 are hidden.*

## Exercises

## Methods

1. Consider the following results for independent samples taken from two populations.

| Sample 1 | Sample 2 |
|---|---|
| $n_1 = 400$ | $n_2 = 300$ |
| $\bar{p}_1 = .48$ | $\bar{p}_2 = .36$ |

   a. What is the point estimate of the difference between the two population proportions?
   b. Develop a 90% confidence interval for the difference between the two population proportions.
   c. Develop a 95% confidence interval for the difference between the two population proportions.

2. Consider the hypothesis test

$$H_0: p_1 - p_2 \leq 0$$
$$H_a: p_1 - p_2 > 0$$

   The following results are for independent samples taken from the two populations.

| Sample 1 | Sample 2 |
|---|---|
| $n_1 = 200$ | $n_2 = 300$ |
| $\bar{p}_1 = .22$ | $\bar{p}_1 = .16$ |

   a. What is the $p$-value?
   b. With $\alpha = .05$, what is your hypothesis testing conclusion?

## Applications

3. The Professional Golf Association (PGA) measured the putting accuracy of professional golfers playing on the PGA Tour and the best amateur golfers playing in the World Amateur Championship (*Golf Magazine,* January 2007). A sample of 1075 6-foot putts by professional golfers found 688 made putts. A sample of 1200 6-foot putts by amateur golfers found 696 made putts.
   a. Estimate the proportion of made 6-foot putts by professional golfers. Estimate the proportion of made 6-foot putts by amateur golfers. Which group had a better putting accuracy?
   b. What is the point estimate of the difference between the proportions of the two populations? What does this estimate tell you about the percentage of putts made by the two groups of golfers?
   c. What is the 95% confidence interval for the difference between the two population proportions? Interpret this confidence interval in terms of the percentage of putts made by the two groups of golfers.

4. An American Automobile Association (AAA) study investigated the question of whether a man or a woman was more likely to stop and ask for directions (AAA, January 2006). The situation referred to in the study stated the following: "If you and your spouse are driving together and become lost, would you stop and ask for directions?" A sample representative of the data used by AAA showed 300 of 811 women said that they would stop and ask for directions, while 255 of 750 men said that they would stop and ask for directions.
   a. The AAA research hypothesis was that women would be more likely to say that they would stop and ask for directions. Formulate the null and alternative hypotheses for this study.

# 11.2 Hypothesis Test for Proportions of a Multinomial Population

In this section we consider the case in which each element of a population is assigned to one and only one of several classes or categories. Such a population is a **multinomial population**. The multinomial distribution can be thought of as an extension of the binomial distribution to the case of three or more categories of outcomes. On each trial of a multinomial experiment, one and only one of the outcomes occurs. Each trial of the experiment is assumed to be independent, and the probabilities of the outcomes remain the same for each trial.

*The assumptions for the multinomial experiment parallel those for the binomial experiment with the exception that the multinomial has three or more outcomes per trial.*

As an example, consider the market share study being conducted by Scott Marketing Research. Over the past year market shares stabilized at 30% for company A, 50% for company B, and 20% for company C. Recently company C developed a "new and improved" product to replace its current entry in the market. Company C retained Scott Marketing Research to determine whether the new product will alter market shares.

In this case, the population of interest is a multinomial population; each customer is classified as buying from company A, company B, or company C. Thus, we have a multinomial population with three outcomes. Let us use the following notation for the proportions:

$$p_A = \text{market share for company A}$$
$$p_B = \text{market share for company B}$$
$$p_C = \text{market share for company C}$$

Scott Marketing Research will conduct a sample survey and compute the proportion preferring each company's product. A hypothesis test will then be conducted to see whether the new product caused a change in market shares. For the null hypothesis, we assume that company C's new product will not alter the market shares. The null and alternative hypotheses are stated as follows:

$$H_0: p_A = .30, p_B = .50, \text{ and } p_C = .20$$
$$H_a: \text{The population proportions are not}$$
$$p_A = .30, p_B = .50, \text{ and } p_C = .20$$

If the sample results lead to the rejection of $H_0$, Scott Marketing Research will have evidence that the introduction of the new product affects market shares.

Let us assume that the market research firm has used a consumer panel of 200 customers for the study. Each individual was asked to specify a purchase preference among the three alternatives: company A's product, company B's product, and company C's new product. The 200 responses are summarized here.

*The consumer panel of 200 customers in which each individual is asked to select one of three alternatives is equivalent to a multinomial experiment consisting of 200 trials.*

| | Observed Frequency | |
| :---: | :---: | :---: |
| Company A's Product | Company B's Product | Company C's New Product |
| 48 | 98 | 54 |

We now can perform a **goodness of fit test** that will determine whether the sample of 200 customer purchase preferences is consistent with the null hypothesis. The goodness of fit test is based on a comparison of the sample of *observed* results with the *expected* results under the assumption that the null hypothesis is true. Hence, the next step is to compute expected purchase preferences for the 200 customers under the assumption that $p_A = .30$, $p_B = .50$, and $p_C = .20$. Doing so provides the expected results.

| | Expected Frequency | |
|---|---|---|
| Company A's Product | Company B's Product | Company C's New Product |
| 200(.30) = 60 | 200(.50) = 100 | 200(.20) = 40 |

Thus, we see that the expected frequency for each category is found by multiplying the sample size of 200 by the hypothesized proportion for the category.

The goodness of fit test now focuses on the differences between the observed frequencies and the expected frequencies. Large differences between observed and expected frequencies cast doubt on the assumption that the hypothesized proportions or market shares are correct. Whether the differences between the observed and expected frequencies are "large" or "small" is a question answered with the aid of the following chi-square test statistic.

**TEST STATISTIC FOR GOODNESS OF FIT**

$$\chi^2 = \sum_{i=1}^{k} \frac{(f_i - e_i)^2}{e_i} \qquad (11.8)$$

where

$f_i$ = observed frequency for category $i$

$e_i$ = expected frequency for category $i$

$k$ = the number of categories

*Note:* The test statistic has a chi-square distribution with $k - 1$ degrees of freedom provided that the expected frequencies are 5 *or more* for all categories.

Tables of areas or probabilities are readily available for the chi-square distribution. Since the test statistic for goodness of fit is known to have a chi-square distribution whenever the expected frequencies are 5 or more for all categories, we can use the chi-square distribution to conduct the hypothesis test. We will use the notation $\chi^2_\alpha$ to denote the value of the chi-square distribution that provides an area or probability of $\alpha$ to the right of the $\chi^2_\alpha$ value. For example, refer to Table 11.1 and verify that for a chi-square distribution with 2 degrees of freedom $\chi^2_{.10} = 4.605$, indicating that 10% of the chi-square values are to the right of 4.605.

Let us continue with the Scott Marketing Research example and use the sample data to test the hypothesis that the multinomial population retains the proportions $p_A = .30$, $p_B = .50$, and $p_C = .20$. We will use an $\alpha = .05$ level of significance. Let us proceed by using the observed and expected frequencies to compute the value of the test statistic. With the expected frequencies all 5 or more, the computation of the chi-square test statistic is shown in Table 11.2. At the bottom of the last column, we see that $\chi^2 = 7.34$.

*The test for goodness of fit is always a one-tailed test with the rejection occurring in the upper tail of the chi-square distribution.*

We will reject the null hypothesis if the differences between the observed and expected frequencies are *large*. Large differences between the observed and expected frequencies will result in a large value for the test statistic. Thus the test of goodness of fit will always be an upper tail test. We can use the upper tail area for the test statistic and the $p$-value approach to determine whether the null hypothesis can be rejected. With $k - 1 = 3 - 1 = 2$ degrees of freedom, the chi-square table provides the following:

| Area in Upper Tail | .10 | .05 | .025 | .01 |
|---|---|---|---|---|
| $\chi^2$ **Value (2 df)** | 4.605 | 5.991 | 7.378 | 9.210 |

$$\chi^2 = 7.34$$

**5.** Rejection rule:

$p$-value approach:        Reject $H_0$ if $p$-value $\leq \alpha$

Critical value approach:   Reject $H_0$ if $\chi^2 \geq \chi^2_\alpha$

where $\alpha$ is the level of significance for the test and there are $k - 1$ degrees of freedom.

## Using Excel to Conduct a Goodness of Fit Test

Excel can be used to conduct a goodness of fit test for the Scott Marketing Research Study. Refer to Figure 11.3 as we describe the tasks involved. The formula worksheet is in the background; the value worksheet is in the foreground.

**WEB** file

Research

**Enter Data:** Column A is used to identify each of the 200 customers who made up the consumer panel in the study. Column B shows the purchase preference (A, B, or C) for each customer. The hypothesized proportions, 0.3, 0.5, and 0.2, were entered into cells E4:E6.

**FIGURE 11.3** EXCEL WORKSHEET FOR GOODNESS OF FIT TEST CONCERNING MARKET SHARE CHANGE

*Note: Rows 16–199 are hidden.*

**Enter Functions and Formulas:** The Excel formulas in cells F4:J7 are used to compute the chi-square test statistic in a fashion parallel to that shown in Table 11.2. The result is the chi-square test statistic shown in cell J7 (7.34). The number of categories, 3, was entered into cell F9 and the two inputs used by Excel's CHISQ.DIST.RT function (test statistic and degrees of freedom) are in cells F11 and F12. The value computed in cell F14 using Excel's CHISQ.DIST.RT function is the area in the upper tail of the chi-square distribution to the right of the test statistic. So, this value is the appropriate $p$-value for our upper tail hypothesis test.

The value worksheet shows that the resulting $p$-value is 0.0255. Thus, with $\alpha = .05$, we reject $H_0$ and conclude that the introduction of the new product by company C will alter the current market share structure.

## Exercises

### Methods

11. Test the following hypotheses by using the $\chi^2$ goodness of fit test.

$$H_0: p_A = .40, p_B = .40, \text{ and } p_C = .20$$
$$H_a: \text{The population proportions are not}$$
$$p_A = .40, p_B = .40, \text{ and } p_C = .20$$

A sample of size 200 yielded 60 in category A, 120 in category B, and 20 in category C. Use $\alpha = .01$ and test to see whether the proportions are as stated in $H_0$.
   a. Use the $p$-value approach.
   b. Repeat the test using the critical value approach.

12. Suppose we have a multinomial population with four categories: A, B, C, and D. The null hypothesis is that the proportion of items is the same in every category. The null hypothesis is

$$H_0: p_A = p_B = p_C = p_D = .25$$

A sample of size 300 yielded the following results.

$$\text{A: 85} \quad \text{B: 95} \quad \text{C: 50} \quad \text{D: 70}$$

Use $\alpha = .05$ to determine whether $H_0$ should be rejected. What is the $p$-value?

### Applications

13. During the first 13 weeks of the television season, the Saturday evening 8:00 P.M. to 9:00 P.M. audience proportions were recorded as ABC 29%, CBS 28%, NBC 25%, and independents 18%. A sample of 300 homes two weeks after a Saturday night schedule revision yielded the following viewing audience data: ABC 95 homes, CBS 70 homes, NBC 89 homes, and independents 46 homes. Test with $\alpha = .05$ to determine whether the viewing audience proportions changed.

14. M&M/MARS, makers of M&M® Chocolate Candies, conducted a national poll in which consumers indicated their preference for colors. In the brochure "Colors," made available by M&M/MARS Consumer Affairs, the traditional distribution of colors for the plain candies is as follows:

| Brown | Yellow | Red | Orange | Green | Blue |
|-------|--------|-----|--------|-------|------|
| 30% | 20% | 20% | 10% | 10% | 10% |

**TABLE 11.4**   SAMPLE RESULTS FOR BEER PREFERENCES OF MALE AND FEMALE
BEER DRINKERS (OBSERVED FREQUENCIES)

| | | Beer Preference | | | |
|---|---|---|---|---|---|
| | | Light | Regular | Dark | Total |
| Gender | Male | 20 | 40 | 20 | 80 |
| | Female | 30 | 30 | 10 | 70 |
| | Total | 50 | 70 | 30 | 150 |

combinations of beer preference and gender or, in other words, listed all possible contingencies, Table 11.3 is called a **contingency table**. The test of independence uses the contingency table format and for that reason is sometimes referred to as a *contingency table test*.

Suppose a simple random sample of 150 beer drinkers is selected. After tasting each beer, the individuals in the sample are asked to state their preference or first choice. The crosstabulation in Table 11.4 summarizes the responses for the study. As we see, the data for the test of independence are collected in terms of counts or frequencies for each cell or category. Of the 150 individuals in the sample, 20 were men who favored light beer, 40 were men who favored regular beer, 20 were men who favored dark beer, and so on.

The data in Table 11.4 are the observed frequencies for the six classes or categories. If we can determine the expected frequencies under the assumption of independence between beer preference and gender of the beer drinker, we can use the chi-square distribution to determine whether there is a significant difference between observed and expected frequencies.

Expected frequencies for the cells of the contingency table are based on the following rationale. First we assume that the null hypothesis of independence between beer preference and gender of the beer drinker is true. Then we note that in the entire sample of 150 beer drinkers, a total of 50 prefer light beer, 70 prefer regular beer, and 30 prefer dark beer. In terms of fractions we conclude that $50/150 = 1/3$ of the beer drinkers prefer light beer, $70/150 = 7/15$ prefer regular beer, and $30/150 = 1/5$ prefer dark beer. If the *independence* assumption is valid, we argue that these fractions must be applicable to both male and female beer drinkers. Thus, under the assumption of independence, we would expect the sample of 80 male beer drinkers to show that $(1/3)80 = 26.67$ prefer light beer, $(7/15)80 = 37.33$ prefer regular beer, and $(1/5)80 = 16$ prefer dark beer. Application of the same fractions to the 70 female beer drinkers provides the expected frequencies shown in Table 11.5.

Let $e_{ij}$ denote the expected frequency for the contingency table category in row $i$ and column $j$. With this notation, let us reconsider the expected frequency calculation for males

**TABLE 11.5**   EXPECTED FREQUENCIES IF BEER PREFERENCE IS INDEPENDENT
OF THE GENDER OF THE BEER DRINKER

| | | Beer Preference | | | |
|---|---|---|---|---|---|
| | | Light | Regular | Dark | Total |
| Gender | Male | 26.67 | 37.33 | 16.00 | 80 |
| | Female | 23.33 | 32.67 | 14.00 | 70 |
| | Total | 50.00 | 70.00 | 30.00 | 150 |

(row $i = 1$) who prefer regular beer (column $j = 2$); that is, expected frequency $e_{12}$. Following the preceding argument for the computation of expected frequencies, we can show that

$$e_{12} = (\tfrac{7}{15})80 = 37.33$$

This expression can be written slightly differently as

$$e_{12} = (\tfrac{7}{15})80 = (\tfrac{70}{150})80 = \frac{(80)(70)}{150} = 37.33$$

Note that 80 in the expression is the total number of males (row 1 total), 70 is the total number of individuals preferring regular beer (column 2 total), and 150 is the total sample size. Hence, we see that

$$e_{12} = \frac{(\text{Row 1 Total})(\text{Column 2 Total})}{\text{Sample Size}}$$

Generalization of the expression shows that the following formula provides the expected frequencies for a contingency table in the test of independence.

> **EXPECTED FREQUENCIES FOR CONTINGENCY TABLES UNDER THE ASSUMPTION OF INDEPENDENCE**
>
> $$e_{ij} = \frac{(\text{Row } i \text{ Total})(\text{Column } j \text{ Total})}{\text{Sample Size}} \qquad \textbf{(11.9)}$$

Using equation (11.9) for male beer drinkers who prefer dark beer, we find an expected frequency of $e_{13} = (80)(30)/150 = 16.00$, as shown in Table 11.5. Use equation (11.9) to verify the other expected frequencies shown in Table 11.5.

The test procedure for comparing the observed frequencies of Table 11.4 with the expected frequencies of Table 11.5 is similar to the goodness of fit calculations made in Section 11.2. Specifically, the $\chi^2$ value based on the observed and expected frequencies is computed as follows.

> **TEST STATISTIC FOR INDEPENDENCE**
>
> $$\chi^2 = \sum_i \sum_j \frac{(f_{ij} - e_{ij})^2}{e_{ij}} \qquad \textbf{(11.10)}$$
>
> where
>
> $f_{ij}$ = observed frequency for contingency table category in row $i$ and column $j$
>
> $e_{ij}$ = expected frequency for contingency table category in row $i$ and column $j$ based on the assumption of independence
>
> *Note:* With $n$ rows and $m$ columns in the contingency table, the test statistic has a chi-square distribution with $(n - 1)(m - 1)$ degrees of freedom provided that the expected frequencies are 5 or more for all categories.

The double summation in equation (11.10) is used to indicate that the calculation must be made for all the cells in the contingency table.

**TABLE 11.6** COMPUTATION OF THE CHI-SQUARE TEST STATISTIC FOR DETERMINING WHETHER BEER PREFERENCE IS INDEPENDENT OF THE GENDER OF THE BEER DRINKER

| Gender | Beer Preference | Observed Frequency $(f_{ij})$ | Expected Frequency $(e_{ij})$ | Difference $(f_{ij} - e_{ij})$ | Squared Difference $(f_{ij} - e_{ij})^2$ | Squared Difference Divided by Expected Frequency $(f_{ij} - e_{ij})^2/e_{ij}$ |
|--------|-----------------|---------------|---------------|------------|------------|-----------|
| Male | Light | 20 | 26.67 | −6.67 | 44.44 | 1.67 |
| Male | Regular | 40 | 37.33 | 2.67 | 7.11 | 0.19 |
| Male | Dark | 20 | 16.00 | 4.00 | 16.00 | 1.00 |
| Female | Light | 30 | 23.33 | 6.67 | 44.44 | 1.90 |
| Female | Regular | 30 | 32.67 | −2.67 | 7.11 | 0.22 |
| Female | Dark | 10 | 14.00 | −4.00 | 16.00 | 1.14 |
| | **Total** | 150 | | | | $\chi^2 = 6.12$ |

By reviewing the expected frequencies in Table 11.5, we see that the expected frequencies are 5 or more for each category. We therefore proceed with the computation of the chi-square test statistic. The calculations necessary to compute the chi-square test statistic for determining whether beer preference is independent of the gender of the beer drinker are shown in Table 11.6. We see that the value of the test statistic is $\chi^2 = 6.12$.

The number of degrees of freedom for the appropriate chi-square distribution is computed by multiplying the number of rows minus 1 by the number of columns minus 1. With two rows and three columns, we have $(2 - 1)(3 - 1) = 2$ degrees of freedom. Just like the test for goodness of fit, the test for independence rejects $H_0$ if the differences between observed and expected frequencies provide a large value for the test statistic. Thus the test for independence is also an upper tail test. Using the chi-square table (Table 3 of Appendix B), we conclude that the upper tail area or $p$-value at $\chi^2 = 6.12$ is between .025 and .05. Excel can be used to show that $\chi^2 = 6.12$ provides a $p$-value $= .0468$. At the .05 level of significance, $p$-value $\leq \alpha = .05$. We reject the null hypothesis of independence and conclude that beer preference is not independent of the gender of the beer drinker.

*The test for independence is always a one-tailed test with the rejection region in the upper tail of the chi-square distribution.*

Although no further statistical conclusions can be made as a result of the test, we can compare the observed and expected frequencies informally to obtain an idea about the dependence between beer preference and gender. Refer to Tables 11.4 and 11.5. We see that male beer drinkers have higher observed than expected frequencies for both regular and dark beers, whereas female beer drinkers have a higher observed than expected frequency only for light beer. These observations give us insight about the beer preference differences between male and female beer drinkers.

Let us summarize the steps in a contingency table test of independence.

> **TEST OF INDEPENDENCE: A SUMMARY**
>
> 1. State the null and alternative hypotheses.
>
>    $H_0$: The column variable is independent of the row variable
>    $H_a$: The column variable is not independent of the row variable
>
> 2. Select a random sample and record the observed frequencies for each cell of the contingency table.
> 3. Use equation (11.9) to compute the expected frequency for each cell.
> 4. Use equation (11.10) to compute the value of the chi-square test statistic.

**5.** Rejection rule:

$p$-value approach:          Reject $H_0$ if $p$-value $\leq \alpha$

Critical value approach:   Reject $H_0$ if $\chi^2 \geq \chi_\alpha^2$

where $\alpha$ is the level of significance, with $n$ rows and $m$ columns providing $(n - 1)(m - 1)$ degrees of freedom.

*In the chapter appendix we show how StatTools can be used for a test of independence.*

## Using Excel to Conduct a Test of Independence

Excel can be used to conduct a test of independence for the Alber's Brewery example. Refer to Figure 11.4 as we describe the tasks involved. The formula worksheet is in the background; the value worksheet is in the foreground.

Alber's

**Enter Data:** Column A is used to identify each of the 150 individuals in the study. Column B shows the gender and column C shows the beer preference (Light, Regular, or Dark) for each individual.

**FIGURE 11.4   EXCEL WORKSHEET FOR THE ALBER'S BREWERY TEST OF INDEPENDENCE**

*Note: Rows 17–148 are hidden.*

**Apply Tools:**   Using Excel's PivotTable tool (see Section 2.4 for details regarding how to use this tool), we developed the crosstabulation shown in cells E3:I7. The values in cells F5:H6 are the observed frequencies for the Alber's Brewery study.

**Enter Functions and Formulas:**   To compute the expected frequencies for the Alber's Brewery contingency table under the assumption of independence, we use equation (11.9). The formulas in cells F11:H12 are used to compute these expected frequencies. Once the observed and expected frequencies have been computed, Excel's CHISQ.TEST function can be used to compute the $p$-value for a test of independence. The inputs to the CHISQ.TEST function are the range of values for the observed and expected frequencies. To compute the $p$-value for this test of independence, we entered the following function into cell H14:

$$=\text{CHISQ.TEST(F5:H6,F11:H12)}$$

The value worksheet shows that the resulting $p$-value is .0468. Thus, with $\alpha = .05$ we reject $H_0$ and conclude that beer preference is not independent of the gender of the beer drinker.

## NOTES AND COMMENTS

The test statistic for the chi-square tests in this chapter requires an expected frequency of five for each category. When a category has fewer than five, it is often appropriate to combine two adjacent categories to obtain an expected frequency of five or more in each category.

## Exercises

### Methods

19. The following 2 × 3 contingency table contains observed frequencies for a sample of 200. Test for independence of the row and column variables using the $\chi^2$ test with $\alpha = .05$.

|  | Column Variable | | |
|---|---|---|---|
| Row Variable | A | B | C |
| P | 20 | 44 | 50 |
| Q | 30 | 26 | 30 |

20. The following 3 × 3 contingency table contains observed frequencies for a sample of 240. Test for independence of the row and column variables using the $\chi^2$ test with $\alpha = .05$.

|  | Column Variable | | |
|---|---|---|---|
| Row Variable | A | B | C |
| P | 20 | 30 | 20 |
| Q | 30 | 60 | 25 |
| R | 10 | 15 | 30 |

### Applications

21. One of the questions on the *BusinessWeek* Subscriber Study was, "In the past 12 months, when traveling for business, what type of airline ticket did you purchase most often?" The data obtained are shown in the following contingency table.

| Type of Ticket | Type of Flight | |
| --- | --- | --- |
| | **Domestic Flights** | **International Flights** |
| **First class** | 29 | 22 |
| **Business/executive class** | 95 | 121 |
| **Full fare economy/coach class** | 518 | 135 |

Use $\alpha = .05$ and test for the independence of type of flight and type of ticket. What is your conclusion?

22. Visa Card USA studied how frequently consumers of various age groups use plastic cards (debit and credit cards) when making purchases (Associated Press, January 16, 2006). Sample data for 300 customers shows the use of plastic cards by four age groups.

| Payment | Age Group | | | |
| --- | --- | --- | --- | --- |
| | **18–24** | **25–34** | **35–44** | **45 and over** |
| **Plastic** | 21 | 27 | 27 | 36 |
| **Cash or Check** | 21 | 36 | 42 | 90 |

a. Test for the independence between method of payment and age group. What is the *p*-value? Using $\alpha = .05$, what is your conclusion?
b. If method of payment and age group are not independent, what observation can you make about how different age groups use plastic to make purchases?
c. What implications does this study have for companies such as Visa, MasterCard, and Discover?

23. With double-digit annual percentage increases in the cost of health insurance, more and more workers are likely to lack health insurance coverage (*USA Today*, January 23, 2004). The following sample data provide a comparison of workers with and without health insurance coverage for small, medium, and large companies. For the purposes of this study, small companies are companies that have fewer than 100 employees. Medium companies have 100 to 999 employees, and large companies have 1000 or more employees. Sample data are reported for 50 employees of small companies, 75 employees of medium companies, and 100 employees of large companies.

| Size of Company | Health Insurance | | |
| --- | --- | --- | --- |
| | **Yes** | **No** | **Total** |
| **Small** | 36 | 14 | 50 |
| **Medium** | 65 | 10 | 75 |
| **Large** | 88 | 12 | 100 |

a. Conduct a test of independence to determine whether employee health insurance coverage is independent of the size of the company. Use $\alpha = .05$. What is the *p*-value, and what is your conclusion?
b. The *USA Today* article indicated employees of small companies are more likely to lack health insurance coverage. Use percentages based on the preceding data to support this conclusion.

24. *Consumer Reports* measures owner satisfaction of various automobiles by asking the survey question, "Considering factors such as price, performance, reliability, comfort and enjoyment, would you purchase this automobile if you had it to do all over again?"

(Consumer Reports website, January 2009). Sample data for 300 owners of four popular midsize sedans are as follows.

| Purchase Again | Automobile | | | | |
| | Chevrolet Impala | Ford Taurus | Honda Accord | Toyota Camry | Total |
| --- | --- | --- | --- | --- | --- |
| Yes | 49 | 44 | 60 | 46 | 199 |
| No | 37 | 27 | 18 | 19 | 101 |

a.  Conduct a test of independence to determine if the owner's intent to purchase again is independent of the automobile. Use a .05 level of significance. What is your conclusion?

b.  *Consumer Reports* provides an owner satisfaction score for each automobile by reporting the percentage of owners who would purchase the same automobile if they could do it all over again. What are the *Consumer Reports* owner satisfaction scores for the Chevrolet Impala, Ford Taurus, Honda Accord, and Toyota Camry? Rank the four automobiles in terms of owner satisfaction.

c.  Twenty-three different automobiles were reviewed in the *Consumer Reports* midsize sedan class. The overall owner satisfaction score for all automobiles in this class was 69. How do the United States manufactured automobiles (Impala and Taurus) compare to the Japanese manufactured automobiles (Accord and Camry) in terms of owner satisfaction? What is the implication of these findings on the future market share for these automobiles?

25. FlightStats, Inc., collects data on the number of flights scheduled and the number of flights flown at major airports throughout the United States. FlightStats data showed 56% of flights scheduled at Newark, La Guardia, and Kennedy airports were flown during a three-day snowstorm (*The Wall Street Journal*, February 21, 2006). All airlines say they always operate within set safety parameters—if conditions are too poor, they don't fly. The following data show a sample of 400 scheduled flights during the snowstorm.

| Did It Fly? | Airline | | | | |
| | American | Continental | Delta | United | Total |
| --- | --- | --- | --- | --- | --- |
| Yes | 48 | 69 | 68 | 25 | 210 |
| No | 52 | 41 | 62 | 35 | 190 |

Use the chi-square test of independence with a .05 level of significance to analyze the data. What is your conclusion? Do you have a preference for which airline you would choose to fly during similar snowstorm conditions? Explain.

26. As the price of oil rises, there is increased worldwide interest in alternate sources of energy. A *Financial Times*/Harris Poll surveyed people in six countries to assess attitudes toward a variety of alternate forms of energy (*http://www.harrisinteractive.com*, February 27, 2008). The data in the table below are a portion of the poll's findings concerning whether people favor or oppose the building of new nuclear power plants.

| | Great Britain | France | Italy | Spain | Germany | United States |
| --- | --- | --- | --- | --- | --- | --- |
| **Strongly favor** | 141 | 161 | 298 | 133 | 128 | 204 |
| **Favor more than oppose** | 348 | 366 | 309 | 222 | 272 | 326 |
| **Oppose more than favor** | 381 | 334 | 219 | 311 | 322 | 316 |
| **Strongly oppose** | 217 | 215 | 219 | 443 | 389 | 174 |

a. How large was the sample in this poll?
b. Conduct a hypothesis test to determine whether people's attitude toward building new nuclear power plants is independent of country. What is your conclusion?
c. Using the percentage of respondents who "strongly favor" and "favor more than oppose," which country has the most favorable attitude toward building new nuclear power plants? Which country has the least favorable attitude?

27. The National Sleep Foundation used a survey to determine whether hours of sleeping per night are independent of age (*Newsweek,* January 19, 2004). The following table shows the hours of sleep on weeknights for a sample of individuals age 49 and younger and for a sample of individuals age 50 and older.

| | **Hours of Sleep** | | | | |
|---|---|---|---|---|---|
| **Age** | **Fewer than 6** | **6 to 6.9** | **7 to 7.9** | **8 or more** | **Total** |
| **49 or younger** | 38 | 60 | 77 | 65 | 240 |
| **50 or older** | 36 | 57 | 75 | 92 | 260 |

a. Conduct a test of independence to determine whether the hours of sleep on weeknights are independent of age. Use $\alpha = .05$. What is the $p$-value, and what is your conclusion?
b. What is your estimate of the percentage of people who sleep fewer than 6 hours, 6 to 6.9 hours, 7 to 7.9 hours, and 8 or more hours on weeknights?

28. Samples taken in three cities, Anchorage, Atlanta, and Minneapolis, were used to learn about the percentage of married couples with both the husband and the wife in the workforce (*USA Today,* January 15, 2006). Analyze the following data to see whether both the husband and wife being in the workforce is independent of location. Use a .05 level of significance. What is your conclusion? What is the overall estimate of the percentage of married couples with both the husband and the wife in the workforce?

| | **Location** | | |
|---|---|---|---|
| **In Workforce** | **Anchorage** | **Atlanta** | **Minneapolis** |
| **Both** | 57 | 70 | 63 |
| **Only One** | 33 | 50 | 90 |

## Summary

In this chapter we described statistical procedures for comparisons involving proportions and the contingency table test for independence of two variables. In the first section, we compared a proportion for one population with the same proportion from another population. We described how to construct an interval estimate for the difference between the proportions and how to conduct a hypothesis test to learn whether the difference between the proportions was statistically significant.

In the second section, we focused on a single multinomial population. There we saw how to conduct hypothesis texts to determine whether the sample proportions for the categories of the multinomial population were significantly different than the hypothesized values. The chi-square goodness of fit test was used to make the comparison.

The final section was concerned with a test of independence for two variables. A test of independence for two variables is an extension of the methodology employed in the goodness of fit test for a multinomial population. A contingency table is used to determine the observed and expected frequencies. Then a chi-square value is computed. Large chi-square values, caused by large differences between observed and expected frequencies, lead to the rejection of the null hypothesis of independence.

## Glossary

**Pooled estimator of p** An estimator of a population proportion obtained by computing a weighted average of the sample proportions obtained from two independent samples.

**Multinomial population** A population in which each element is assigned to one and only one of several categories. The multinomial distribution extends the binomial distribution from two to three or more outcomes.

**Goodness of fit test** A statistical test conducted to determine whether to reject a hypothesized probability distribution for a population.

**Contingency table** A table used to summarize observed and expected frequencies for a test of independence.

## Key Formulas

**Point Estimator of the Difference Between Two Population Proportions**

$$\bar{p}_1 - \bar{p}_2 \tag{11.1}$$

**Standard Error of $\bar{p}_1 - \bar{p}_2$**

$$\sigma_{\bar{p}_1 - \bar{p}_2} = \sqrt{\frac{p_1(1 - p_1)}{n_1} + \frac{p_2(1 - p_2)}{n_2}} \tag{11.2}$$

**Interval Estimate of the Difference Between Two Population Proportions**

$$\bar{p}_1 - \bar{p}_2 \pm z_{\alpha/2} \sqrt{\frac{\bar{p}_1(1 - \bar{p}_1)}{n_1} + \frac{\bar{p}_2(1 - \bar{p}_2)}{n_2}} \tag{11.4}$$

**Standard Error of $\bar{p}_1 - \bar{p}_2$ when $p_1 = p_2 = p$**

$$\sigma_{\bar{p}_1 - \bar{p}_2} = \sqrt{p(1 - p)\left(\frac{1}{n_1} + \frac{1}{n_2}\right)} \tag{11.5}$$

**Pooled Estimator of $p$ when $p_1 = p_2 = p$**

$$\bar{p} = \frac{n_1\bar{p}_1 + n_2\bar{p}_2}{n_1 + n_2} \tag{11.6}$$

**Test Statistic for Hypothesis Tests About $p_1 - p_2$**

$$z = \frac{(\bar{p}_1 - \bar{p}_2)}{\sqrt{\bar{p}(1 - \bar{p})\left(\frac{1}{n_1} + \frac{1}{n_2}\right)}} \tag{11.7}$$

**Test Statistic for Goodness of Fit**

$$\chi^2 = \sum_{i=1}^{k} \frac{(f_i - e_i)^2}{e_i} \tag{11.8}$$

**Expected Frequencies for Contingency Tables Under the Assumption of Independence**

$$e_{ij} = \frac{(\text{Row } i \text{ Total})(\text{Column } j \text{ Total})}{\text{Sample Size}} \tag{11.9}$$

**Test Statistic for Independence**

$$\chi^2 = \sum_i \sum_j \frac{(f_{ij} - e_{ij})^2}{e_{ij}}$$      **(11.10)**

## Supplementary Exercises

29. Jupiter Media used a survey to determine how people use their free time. Watching television was the most popular activity selected by both men and women (*The Wall Street Journal*, January 26, 2004). The proportion of men and the proportion of women who selected watching television as their most popular leisure time activity can be estimated from the following sample data.

| Gender | Sample Size | Watching Television |
|--------|-------------|---------------------|
| Men | 800 | 248 |
| Women | 600 | 156 |

    a. State the hypotheses that can be used to test for a difference between the proportion for the population of men and the proportion for the population of women who selected watching television as their most popular leisure time activity.

    b. What is the sample proportion of men who selected watching television as their most popular leisure time activity? What is the sample proportion of women?

    c. Conduct the hypothesis test and compute the *p*-value. At a .05 level of significance, what is your conclusion?

    d. What is the margin of error and 95% confidence interval estimate of the difference between the population proportions?

30. A large automobile insurance company selected samples of single and married male policyholders and recorded the number who made an insurance claim over the preceding three-year period.

| Single Policyholders | Married Policyholders |
|----------------------|-----------------------|
| $n_1 = 400$ | $n_2 = 900$ |
| Number making claims = 76 | Number making claims = 90 |

    a. Use $\alpha = .05$. Test to determine whether the claim rates differ between single and married male policyholders.

    b. Provide a 95% confidence interval for the difference between the proportions for the two populations.

31. Medical tests were conducted to learn about drug-resistant tuberculosis. Of 142 cases tested in New Jersey, 9 were found to be drug-resistant. Of 268 cases tested in Texas, 5 were found to be drug-resistant. Do these data suggest a statistically significant difference between the proportions of drug-resistant cases in the two states? Use a .02 level of significance. What is the *p*-value, and what is your conclusion?

32. Vacation occupancy rates were expected to be up during March 2008 in Myrtle Beach, South Carolina (*The Sun News*, February 29, 2008). Data in the file Occupancy will allow you to replicate the findings presented in the newspaper. The data show units rented and not rented for a random sample of vacation properties during the first week of March 2007 and March 2008.

    a. Estimate the proportion of units rented during the first week of March 2007 and the first week of March 2008.

b. Provide a 95% confidence interval for the difference in proportions.

c. On the basis of your findings, does it appear March rental rates for 2008 will be up from those a year earlier?

33. For the week ended January 15, 2009, the bullish sentiment of individual investors was 27.6% (*AAII Journal,* February 2009). The bullish sentiment was reported to be 48.7% one week earlier and 39.7% one month earlier. The sentiment measures are based on a poll conducted by the American Assocation of Individual Investors. Assume that each of the bullish sentiment measures was based on a sample size of 240.

a. Develop a 95% confidence interval for the difference between the bullish sentiment measures for the most recent two weeks.

b. Develop hypotheses so that rejection of the null hypothesis will allow us to conclude that the most recent bullish sentiment is weaker than that of one month ago.

c. Conduct a hypotheses test of part (b) using $\alpha = .01$. What is your conclusion?

34. In setting sales quotas, the marketing manager makes the assumption that order potentials are the same for each of four sales territories. A sample of 200 sales follows. Should the manager's assumption be rejected? Use $\alpha = .05$.

| **Sales Territories** | | | |
|---|---|---|---|
| **I** | **II** | **III** | **IV** |
| 60 | 45 | 59 | 36 |

35. Seven percent of mutual fund investors rate corporate stocks "very safe," 58% rate them "somewhat safe," 24% rate them "not very safe," 4% rate them "not at all safe," and 7% are "not sure." A *BusinessWeek*/Harris poll asked 529 mutual fund investors how they would rate corporate bonds on safety. The responses are as follows.

| Safety Rating | Frequency |
|---|---|
| Very safe | 48 |
| Somewhat safe | 323 |
| Not very safe | 79 |
| Not at all safe | 16 |
| Not sure | 63 |
| Total | 529 |

Do mutual fund investors' attitudes toward corporate bonds differ from their attitudes toward corporate stocks? Support your conclusion with a statistical test. Use $\alpha = .01$.

36. Since 2000, the Toyota Camry, Honda Accord, and Ford Taurus have been the three best selling passenger cars in the United States. Based on the 2003 sales data, the market shares among the top three are as follows: Toyota Camry 37%, Honda Accord 34%, and Ford Taurus 29% (*The World Almanac,* 2004). Assume a sample of 1200 sales of passenger cars during the first quarter of 2004 shows the following.

| Passenger Car | Units Sold |
|---|---|
| Toyota Camry | 480 |
| Honda Accord | 390 |
| Ford Taurus | 330 |

Can these data be used to conclude that the market shares among the top three passenger cars have changed during the first quarter of 2004? What is the *p*-value? Use a .05 level of significance. What is your conclusion?

37. A regional transit authority is concerned about the number of riders on one of its bus routes. In setting up the route, the assumption is that the number of riders is the same on every day from Monday through Friday. Using the following data, test with $\alpha = .05$ to determine whether the transit authority's assumption is correct.

| Day | Number of Riders |
|---|---|
| Monday | 13 |
| Tuesday | 16 |
| Wednesday | 28 |
| Thursday | 17 |
| Friday | 16 |

38. The results of *Computerworld*'s Annual Job Satisfaction Survey showed that 28% of information systems (IS) managers are very satisfied with their job, 46% are somewhat satisfied, 12% are neither satisfied nor dissatisfied, 10% are somewhat dissatisfied, and 4% are very dissatisfied. Suppose that a sample of 500 computer programmers yielded the following results.

| Category | Number of Respondents |
|---|---|
| Very satisfied | 105 |
| Somewhat satisfied | 235 |
| Neither | 55 |
| Somewhat dissatisfied | 90 |
| Very dissatisfied | 15 |

Use $\alpha = .05$ and test to determine whether the job satisfaction for computer programmers is different from the job satisfaction for IS managers.

39. A sample of parts provided the following contingency table data on part quality by production shift.

| Shift | Number Good | Number Defective |
|---|---|---|
| First | 368 | 32 |
| Second | 285 | 15 |
| Third | 176 | 24 |

Use $\alpha = .05$ and test the hypothesis that part quality is independent of the production shift. What is your conclusion?

40. *The Wall Street Journal* Subscriber Study showed data on the employment status of subscribers. Sample results corresponding to subscribers of the eastern and western editions are shown here.

| | Region | |
|---|---|---|
| Employment Status | Eastern Edition | Western Edition |
| Full-time | 1105 | 574 |
| Part-time | 31 | 15 |
| Self-employed/consultant | 229 | 186 |
| Not employed | 485 | 344 |

Use $\alpha = .05$ and test the hypothesis that employment status is independent of the region. What is your conclusion?

41. A lending institution supplied the following data on loan approvals by four loan officers. Use $\alpha = .05$ and test to determine whether the loan approval decision is independent of the loan officer reviewing the loan application.

| Loan Officer | Loan Approval Decision | |
|---|---|---|
| | Approved | Rejected |
| Miller | 24 | 16 |
| McMahon | 17 | 13 |
| Games | 35 | 15 |
| Runk | 11 | 9 |

42. A Pew Research Center survey asked respondents if they would rather live in a place with a slower pace of life or a place with a faster pace of life (*USA Today*, February 13, 2009). Consider the following data, which show a sample of preferences expressed by 150 men and 150 women.

| Respondent | Preferred Pace of Life | | |
|---|---|---|---|
| | Slower | No Preference | Faster |
| Men | 102 | 9 | 39 |
| Women | 111 | 12 | 27 |

a. Combine the samples of men and women. What is the overall percentage of respondents who prefer to live in a place with a slower pace of life? What is the overall percentage of respondents who prefer to live in a place with a faster pace of life? What is your conclusion?

b. Is the preferred pace of life independent of the respondent? Use $\alpha = .05$. What is your conclusion? What is your recommendation?

43. Barna Research Group collected data showing church attendance by age group (*USA Today*, November 20, 2003). Use the sample data to determine whether attending church is independent of age. Use a .05 level of significance. What is your conclusion? What conclusion can you draw about church attendance as individuals grow older?

| Age | Church Attendance | | |
|---|---|---|---|
| | Yes | No | Total |
| 20 to 29 | 31 | 69 | 100 |
| 30 to 39 | 63 | 87 | 150 |
| 40 to 49 | 94 | 106 | 200 |
| 50 to 59 | 72 | 78 | 150 |

44. The office occupancy rates were reported for four California metropolitan areas. Do the following data suggest that the office vacancies were independent of metropolitan area? Use a .05 level of significance. What is your conclusion?

| Occupancy Status | Los Angeles | San Diego | San Francisco | San Jose |
|---|---|---|---|---|
| Occupied | 160 | 116 | 192 | 174 |
| Vacant | 40 | 34 | 33 | 26 |

45. A salesperson makes four calls per day. A sample of 100 days gives the following frequencies of sales volumes.

| Number of Sales | Observed Frequency (days) |
|---|---|
| 0 | 30 |
| 1 | 32 |
| 2 | 25 |
| 3 | 10 |
| 4 | 3 |
| **Total** | 100 |

Records show sales are made to 30% of all sales calls. Assuming independent sales calls, the number of sales per day should follow a binomial distribution. The binomial probability function presented in Chapter 5 is

$$f(x) = \frac{n!}{x!(n-x)!} p^x (1-p)^{n-x}$$

For this exercise, assume that the population has a binomial distribution with $n = 4$, $p = .30$, and $x = 0, 1, 2, 3$, and 4.

a. Compute the expected frequencies for $x = 0, 1, 2, 3$, and 4 by using the binomial probability function. Combine categories if necessary to satisfy the requirement that the expected frequency is five or more for all categories.

b. Use the goodness of fit test to determine whether the assumption of a binomial distribution should be rejected. Use $\alpha = .05$. Because no parameters of the binomial distribution were estimated from the sample data, the degrees of freedom are $k - 1$ when $k$ is the number of categories.

## Case Problem   A Bipartisan Agenda for Change

A survey of 100 individuals who live in the western region of New York State was conducted in order to obtain their views of how well the state government is functioning. The party affiliation (Democrat, Independent, Republican) of each individual surveyed was recorded, as well as their responses to the following three questions.

1. Should legislative pay be cut for every day the state budget is late?
   Yes _____    No _____
2. Should there be more restrictions on lobbyists?
   Yes _____    No _____
3. Should there be term limits requiring that legislators serve a fixed number of years?
   Yes _____    No _____

**WEB** file

NYReform

The responses were coded using 1 for a Yes response and 2 for a No response. The complete data set is available on the website that accompanies the text in the data set named NYReform.

## Managerial Report

1. Use descriptive statistics to summarize the data from this study. What are your preliminary conclusions about the independence of the response (Yes or No) and party affiliation for each of the three questions in the survey?
2. With regard to question 1, test for the independence of the response (Yes and No) and party affiliation. Use $\alpha = .05$.

3. With regard to question 2, test for the independence of the response (Yes and No) and party affiliation. Use $\alpha = .05$.
4. With regard to question 3, test for the independence of the response (Yes and No) and party affiliation. Use $\alpha = .05$.
5. Does it appear that there is broad support for change across all political lines? Explain.

## Appendix    Test of Independence Using StatTools

**Alber's**

In this appendix we show how StatTools can be used to conduct a chi-square test of independence. We illustrate using the Alber's Brewery example from Section 11.3. Refer to Figure 11.5 as we describe the steps involved. We have created an Excel PivotTable for the data using the procedures described in Section 2.4. The row labels Male and Female appear in cells E5 and E6. The column labels Light, Regular, and Dark appear in cells F4, G4, and H4. The observed frequencies appear in cells F5:H6. Along with the row and column totals, this is the Alber's Brewery contingency table. The StatTools steps for conducting the test of independence follow.

**Step 1.** Click the **StatTools** tab on the Ribbon
**Step 2.** In the **Analyses Group**, click **Statistical Inference**
**Step 3.** Choose **Chi-square Independence Test**
**Step 4.** When the StatTools - Chi-square Test for Independence dialog box appears,
Enter E4:H6 in the **Contingency Table Range** box
Select **Table Includes Row and Column Headers**
Click **OK**

StatTools will create a report showing row and column percentages, expected counts, as well as the chi-square statistic and the $p$-value of .0468 for the test of independence.

**FIGURE 11.5**   CONTINGENCY TABLE FOR ALBER'S BREWERY TEST OF INDEPENDENCE

*Note: Rows 17–148 are hidden.*

| | A | B | C | D | E | F | G | H | I | J |
|---|---|---|---|---|---|---|---|---|---|---|
| 1 | Individual | Gender | Preference | | | | | | | |
| 2 | 1 | Female | Light | | | | | | | |
| 3 | 2 | Female | Regular | | Count of Individual Preference | | | | | |
| 4 | 3 | Male | Regular | | Gender | Light | Regular | Dark | Grand Total | |
| 5 | 4 | Female | Light | | Male | 20 | 40 | 20 | 80 | |
| 6 | 5 | Female | Light | | Female | 30 | 30 | 10 | 70 | |
| 7 | 6 | Female | Regular | | Grand Total | 50 | 70 | 30 | 150 | |
| 8 | 7 | Male | Regular | | | | | | | |
| 9 | 8 | Female | Dark | | | | | | | |
| 10 | 9 | Female | Regular | | | | | | | |
| 11 | 10 | Male | Dark | | | | | | | |
| 12 | 11 | Male | Regular | | | | | | | |
| 13 | 12 | Male | Regular | | | | | | | |
| 14 | 13 | Female | Regular | | | | | | | |
| 15 | 14 | Female | Regular | | | | | | | |
| 16 | 15 | Male | Light | | | | | | | |
| 149 | 148 | Male | Regular | | | | | | | |
| 150 | 149 | Female | Light | | | | | | | |
| 151 | 150 | Female | Regular | | | | | | | |
| 152 | | | | | | | | | | |

# CHAPTER 12

# Simple Linear Regression

## CONTENTS

## STATISTICS *in* PRACTICE

### ALLIANCE DATA SYSTEMS*
*DALLAS, TEXAS*

Alliance Data Systems (ADS) provides transaction processing, credit services, and marketing services for clients in the rapidly growing customer relationship management (CRM) industry. ADS clients are concentrated in four industries: retail, petroleum/convenience stores, utilities, and transportation. In 1983, Alliance began offering end-to-end credit processing services to the retail, petroleum, and casual dining industries; today Alliance employs more than 6500 employees who provide services to clients around the world. Operating more than 140,000 point-of-sale terminals in the United States alone, ADS processes in excess of 2.5 billion transactions annually. The company ranks second in the United States in private label credit services by representing 49 private label programs with nearly 72 million cardholders. In 2001, ADS made an initial public offering and is now listed on the New York Stock Exchange.

Alliance Data Systems analysts discuss use of a regression model to predict sales for a direct marketing campaign.

As one of its marketing services, ADS designs direct mail campaigns and promotions. With its database containing information on the spending habits of more than 100 million consumers, ADS can target those consumers most likely to benefit from a direct mail promotion. The Analytical Development Group uses regression analysis to build models that measure and predict the responsiveness of consumers to direct market campaigns. Some regression models predict the probability of purchase for individuals receiving a promotion, and others predict the amount spent by those consumers making a purchase.

For one particular campaign, a retail store chain wanted to attract new customers. To predict the effect of the campaign, ADS analysts selected a sample from the consumer database, sent the sampled individuals promotional materials, and then collected transaction data on the consumers' response. Sample data were collected on the amount of purchase made by the consumers responding to the campaign, as well as a variety of consumer-specific variables thought to be useful in predicting sales. The consumer-specific variable that contributed most to

predicting the amount purchased was the total amount of credit purchases at related stores over the past 39 months. ADS analysts developed an estimated regression equation relating the amount of purchase to the amount spent at related stores:

$$\hat{y} = 26.7 + 0.00205x$$

where

$$\hat{y} = \text{amount of purchase}$$
$$x = \text{amount spent at related stores}$$

Using this equation, we could predict that someone spending $10,000 over the past 39 months at related stores would spend $47.20 when responding to the direct mail promotion. In this chapter, you will learn how to develop this type of estimated regression equation.

The final model developed by ADS analysts also included several other variables that increased the predictive power of the preceding equation. Some of these variables included the absence/presence of a bank credit card, estimated income, and the average amount spent per trip at a selected store. In the following chapter, we will learn how such additional variables can be incorporated into a multiple regression model.

*The authors are indebted to Philip Clemance, Director of Analytical Development at Alliance Data Systems, for providing this Statistics in Practice.

Managerial decisions often are based on the relationship between two or more variables. For example, after considering the relationship between advertising expenditures and sales, a marketing manager might attempt to predict sales for a given level of advertising expenditures. In another case, a public utility might use the relationship between the daily high temperature and the demand for electricity to predict electricity usage on the basis of next month's anticipated daily high temperatures. Sometimes a manager will rely on intuition to judge how two variables are related. However, if data can be obtained, a statistical procedure called *regression analysis* can be used to develop an equation showing how the variables are related.

*The statistical methods used in studying the relationship between two variables were first employed by Sir Francis Galton (1822–1911). Galton was interested in studying the relationship between a father's height and the son's height. Galton's disciple, Karl Pearson (1857–1936), analyzed the relationship between the father's height and the son's height for 1078 pairs of subjects.*

In regression terminology, the variable being predicted is called the **dependent variable**. The variable or variables being used to predict the value of the dependent variable are called the **independent variables**. For example, in analyzing the effect of advertising expenditures on sales, a marketing manager's desire to predict sales would suggest making sales the dependent variable. Advertising expenditure would be the independent variable used to help predict sales. In statistical notation, $y$ denotes the dependent variable and $x$ denotes the independent variable.

In this chapter we consider the simplest type of regression analysis involving one independent variable and one dependent variable in which the relationship between the variables is approximated by a straight line. It is called **simple linear regression**. Regression analysis involving two or more independent variables is called multiple regression analysis; multiple regression and cases involving curvilinear relationships are covered in Chapter 13.

## 12.1   Simple Linear Regression Model

Armand's Pizza Parlors is a chain of Italian-food restaurants located in a five-state area. Armand's most successful locations are near college campuses. The managers believe that quarterly sales for these restaurants (denoted by $y$) are related positively to the size of the student population (denoted by $x$); that is, restaurants near campuses with a large student population tend to generate more sales than those located near campuses with a small student population. Using regression analysis, we can develop an equation showing how the dependent variable $y$ is related to the independent variable $x$.

### Regression Model and Regression Equation

In the Armand's Pizza Parlors example, the population consists of all the Armand's restaurants located near college campuses. For every restaurant in the population, there is a value of $x$ (student population) and a corresponding value of $y$ (quarterly sales). The equation that describes how $y$ is related to $x$ and an error term is called the **regression model**. The regression model used in simple linear regression follows.

---

SIMPLE LINEAR REGRESSION MODEL

$$y = \beta_0 + \beta_1 x + \epsilon \qquad\qquad \textbf{(12.1)}$$

---

$\beta_0$ and $\beta_1$ are referred to as the parameters of the model, and $\epsilon$ (the Greek letter epsilon) is a random variable referred to as the error term. The error term accounts for the variability in $y$ that cannot be explained by the linear relationship between $x$ and $y$.

The population of all Armand's restaurants can also be viewed as a collection of sub-populations, one for each distinct value of $x$. For example, one subpopulation consists of all Armand's restaurants located near college campuses with 8000 students; another subpopulation consists of all Armand's restaurants located near college campuses with 9000 students; and so on. Each subpopulation has a corresponding distribution of $y$ values. Thus, a distribution of $y$ values is associated with restaurants located near campuses with 8000 students; a distribution of $y$ values is associated with restaurants located near campuses with 9000 students; and so on. Each distribution of $y$ values has its own mean or expected value. The equation that describes how the expected value of $y$, denoted $E(y)$, is related to $x$ is called the **regression equation**. The regression equation for simple linear regression follows.

---

**SIMPLE LINEAR REGRESSION EQUATION**

$$E(y) = \beta_0 + \beta_1 x \tag{12.2}$$

---

The graph of the simple linear regression equation is a straight line; $\beta_0$ is the $y$-intercept of the regression line, $\beta_1$ is the slope, and $E(y)$ is the mean or expected value of $y$ for a given value of $x$.

Examples of possible regression lines are shown in Figure 12.1. The regression line in Panel A shows that the mean value of $y$ is related positively to $x$, with larger values of $E(y)$ associated with larger values of $x$. The regression line in Panel B shows the mean value of $y$ is related negatively to $x$, with smaller values of $E(y)$ associated with larger values of $x$. The regression line in Panel C shows the case in which the mean value of $y$ is not related to $x$; that is, the mean value of $y$ is the same for every value of $x$.

## Estimated Regression Equation

If the values of the population parameters $\beta_0$ and $\beta_1$ were known, we could use equation (12.2) to compute the mean value of $y$ for a given value of $x$. In practice, the parameter values are not known and must be estimated using sample data. Sample statistics (denoted $b_0$ and $b_1$) are computed as estimates of the population parameters $\beta_0$ and $\beta_1$. Substituting the values of the sample statistics $b_0$ and $b_1$ for $\beta_0$ and $\beta_1$ in the regression equation, we obtain the

**FIGURE 12.1**   POSSIBLE REGRESSION LINES IN SIMPLE LINEAR REGRESSION

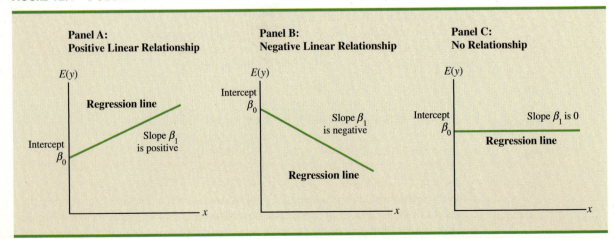

**FIGURE 12.2**   THE ESTIMATION PROCESS IN SIMPLE LINEAR REGRESSION

*The estimation of $\beta_0$ and $\beta_1$ is a statistical process much like the estimation of $\mu$ discussed in Chapter 7. $\beta_0$ and $\beta_1$ are the unknown parameters of interest, and $b_0$ and $b_1$ are the sample statistics used to estimate the parameters.*

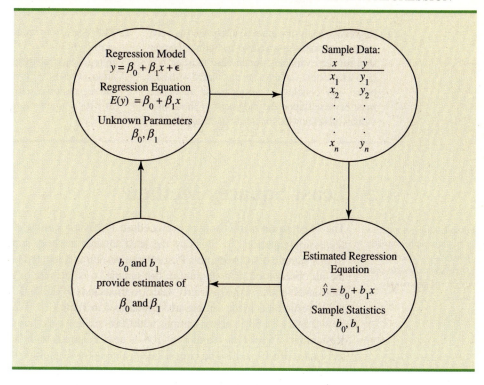

estimated regression equation. The estimated regression equation for simple linear regression follows.

ESTIMATED SIMPLE LINEAR REGRESSION EQUATION

$$\hat{y} = b_0 + b_1 x \tag{12.3}$$

Figure 12.2 provides a summary of the estimation process for simple linear regression.

The graph of the estimated simple linear regression equation is called the *estimated regression line*; $b_0$ is the $y$ intercept and $b_1$ is the slope. In the next section, we show how the least squares method can be used to compute the values of $b_0$ and $b_1$ in the estimated regression equation.

In general, $\hat{y}$ is the point estimator of $E(y)$, the mean value of $y$ for a given value of $x$. Thus, to estimate the mean or expected value of quarterly sales for all restaurants located near campuses with 10,000 students, Armand's would substitute the value of 10,000 for $x$ in equation (12.3). In some cases, however, Armand's may be more interested in predicting sales for one particular restaurant. For example, suppose Armand's would like to predict quarterly sales for a new restaurant they are considering building near Talbot College, a school with 10,000 students. As it turns out, the best predictor of $y$ for a given value of $x$ is also provided by $\hat{y}$. Thus, to predict quarterly sales for a new restaurant located near Talbot College, Armand's would also substitute the value of 10,000 for $x$ in equation (12.3).

The value of $\hat{y}$ provides both a point estimate of $E(y)$ for a given value of $x$ and a prediction of an individual value of $y$ for a given value of $x$. In most cases, we will refer to $\hat{y}$ simply as the *predicted value of y.*

## NOTES AND COMMENTS

1. Regression analysis cannot be interpreted as a procedure for establishing a cause-and-effect relationship between variables. It can only indicate how or to what extent variables are associated with each other. Any conclusions about cause and effect must be based upon the judgment of those individuals most knowledgeable about the application.

2. The regression equation in simple linear regression is $E(y) = \beta_0 + \beta_1 x$. More advanced texts in regression analysis often write the regression equation as $E(y|x) = \beta_0 + \beta_1 x$ to emphasize that the regression equation provides the mean value of $y$ for a given value of $x$.

## 12.2 Least Squares Method

*In simple linear regression, each observation consists of two values: one for the independent variable and one for the dependent variable.*

The **least squares method** is a procedure for using sample data to find the estimated regression equation. To illustrate the least squares method, suppose data were collected from a sample of 10 Armand's Pizza Parlor restaurants located near college campuses. For the $i$th observation or restaurant in the sample, $x_i$ is the size of the student population (in thousands) and $y_i$ is the quarterly sales (in thousands of dollars). The values of $x_i$ and $y_i$ for the 10 restaurants in the sample are summarized in Table 12.1. We see that restaurant 1, with $x_1 = 2$ and $y_1 = 58$, is near a campus with 2000 students and has quarterly sales of \$58,000. Restaurant 2, with $x_2 = 6$ and $y_2 = 105$, is near a campus with 6000 students and has quarterly sales of \$105,000. The largest sales value is for restaurant 10, which is near a campus with 26,000 students and has quarterly sales of \$202,000.

Figure 12.3 is a scatter diagram of the data in Table 12.1. Student population is shown on the horizontal axis and quarterly sales is shown on the vertical axis. **Scatter diagrams** for regression analysis are constructed with the independent variable $x$ on the horizontal axis and the dependent variable $y$ on the vertical axis. The scatter diagram enables us to observe the data graphically and to draw preliminary conclusions about the possible relationship between the variables.

What preliminary conclusions can be drawn from Figure 12.3? Quarterly sales appear to be higher at campuses with larger student populations. In addition, for these data the relationship between the size of the student population and quarterly sales appears to be

**TABLE 12.1    STUDENT POPULATION AND QUARTERLY SALES DATA FOR 10 ARMAND'S PIZZA PARLORS**

**WEB file**

**Armand's**

| Restaurant<br>$i$ | Student<br>Population (1000s)<br>$x_i$ | Quarterly<br>Sales (\$1000s)<br>$y_i$ |
|---|---|---|
| 1 | 2 | 58 |
| 2 | 6 | 105 |
| 3 | 8 | 88 |
| 4 | 8 | 118 |
| 5 | 12 | 117 |
| 6 | 16 | 137 |
| 7 | 20 | 157 |
| 8 | 20 | 169 |
| 9 | 22 | 149 |
| 10 | 26 | 202 |

**FIGURE 12.3**    SCATTER DIAGRAM OF STUDENT POPULATION AND QUARTERLY
SALES FOR ARMAND'S PIZZA PARLORS

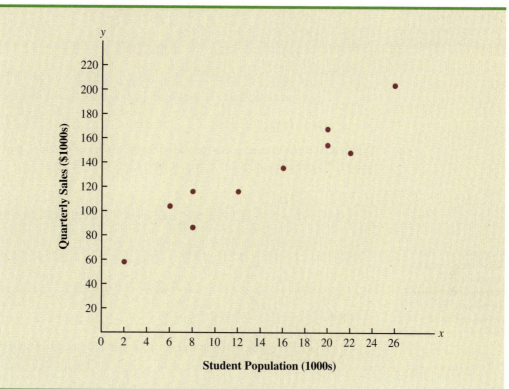

approximated by a straight line; indeed, a positive linear relationship is indicated between $x$ and $y$. We therefore choose the simple linear regression model to represent the relationship between quarterly sales and student population. Given that choice, our next task is to use the sample data in Table 12.1 to determine the values of $b_0$ and $b_1$ in the estimated simple linear regression equation. For the $i$th restaurant, the estimated regression equation provides

$$\hat{y}_i = b_0 + b_1 x_i \tag{12.4}$$

where

$\hat{y}_i$ = predicted value of quarterly sales ($1000s) for the $i$th restaurant

$b_0$ = the $y$ intercept of the estimated regression line

$b_1$ = the slope of the estimated regression line

$x_i$ = size of the student population (1000s) for the $i$th restaurant

With $y_i$ denoting the observed (actual) sales for restaurant $i$ and $\hat{y}_i$ in equation (12.4) representing the predicted value of sales for restaurant $i$, every restaurant in the sample will have an observed value of sales $y_i$ and a predicted value of sales $\hat{y}_i$. For the estimated regression line to provide a good fit to the data, we want the differences between the observed sales values and the predicted sales values to be small.

The least squares method uses the sample data to provide the values of $b_0$ and $b_1$ that minimize the *sum of the squares of the deviations* between the observed values of the dependent variable $y_i$ and the predicted values of the dependent variable $\hat{y}_i$. The criterion for the least squares method is given by expression (12.5).

*Carl Friedrich Gauss (1777–1855) proposed the least squares method.*

**LEAST SQUARES CRITERION**

$$\min \Sigma(y_i - \hat{y}_i)^2 \qquad (12.5)$$

where

$y_i$ = observed value of the dependent variable for the $i$th observation

$\hat{y}_i$ = predicted value of the dependent variable for the $i$th observation

Differential calculus can be used to show that the values of $b_0$ and $b_1$ that minimize expression (12.5) can be found by using equations (12.6) and (12.7).

**SLOPE AND $y$-INTERCEPT FOR THE ESTIMATED REGRESSION EQUATION[1]**

*In computing $b_1$ with a calculator, carry as many significant digits as possible in the intermediate calculations. We recommend carrying at least four significant digits.*

$$b_1 = \frac{\Sigma(x_i - \bar{x})(y_i - \bar{y})}{\Sigma(x_i - \bar{x})^2} \qquad (12.6)$$

$$b_0 = \bar{y} - b_1\bar{x} \qquad (12.7)$$

where

$x_i$ = value of the independent variable for the $i$th observation

$y_i$ = value of the dependent variable for the $i$th observation

$\bar{x}$ = mean value for the independent variable

$\bar{y}$ = mean value for the dependent variable

$n$ = total number of observations

Some of the calculations necessary to develop the least squares estimated regression equation for Armand's Pizza Parlors are shown in Table 12.2. With the sample of 10 restaurants, we have $n = 10$ observations. Because equations (12.6) and (12.7) require $\bar{x}$ and $\bar{y}$, we begin the calculations by computing $\bar{x}$ and $\bar{y}$.

$$\bar{x} = \frac{\Sigma x_i}{n} = \frac{140}{10} = 14$$

$$\bar{y} = \frac{\Sigma y_i}{n} = \frac{1300}{10} = 130$$

Using equations (12.6) and (12.7) and the information in Table 12.2, we can compute the slope and intercept of the estimated regression equation for Armand's Pizza Parlors. The calculation of the slope ($b_1$) proceeds as follows.

---

[1] An alternate formula for $b_1$ is

$$b_1 = \frac{\Sigma x_i y_i - (\Sigma x_i \Sigma y_i)/n}{\Sigma x_i^2 - (\Sigma x_i)^2/n}$$

This form of equation (12.6) is often recommended when using a calculator to compute $b_1$.

**TABLE 12.2**   CALCULATIONS FOR THE LEAST SQUARES ESTIMATED REGRESSION EQUATION FOR ARMAND PIZZA PARLORS

| Restaurant $i$ | $x_i$ | $y_i$ | $x_i - \bar{x}$ | $y_i - \bar{y}$ | $(x_i - \bar{x})(y_i - \bar{y})$ | $(x_i - \bar{x})^2$ |
|---|---|---|---|---|---|---|
| 1 | 2 | 58 | $-12$ | $-72$ | 864 | 144 |
| 2 | 6 | 105 | $-8$ | $-25$ | 200 | 64 |
| 3 | 8 | 88 | $-6$ | $-42$ | 252 | 36 |
| 4 | 8 | 118 | $-6$ | $-12$ | 72 | 36 |
| 5 | 12 | 117 | $-2$ | $-13$ | 26 | 4 |
| 6 | 16 | 137 | 2 | 7 | 14 | 4 |
| 7 | 20 | 157 | 6 | 27 | 162 | 36 |
| 8 | 20 | 169 | 6 | 39 | 234 | 36 |
| 9 | 22 | 149 | 8 | 19 | 152 | 64 |
| 10 | 26 | 202 | 12 | 72 | 864 | 144 |
| Totals | 140 | 1300 | | | 2840 | 568 |
| | $\Sigma x_i$ | $\Sigma y_i$ | | | $\Sigma(x_i - \bar{x})(y_i - \bar{y})$ | $\Sigma(x_i - \bar{x})^2$ |

$$b_1 = \frac{\Sigma(x_i - \bar{x})(y_i - \bar{y})}{\Sigma(x_i - \bar{x})^2}$$

$$= \frac{2840}{568}$$

$$= 5$$

The calculation of the $y$ intercept ($b_0$) follows.

$$b_0 = \bar{y} - b_1\bar{x}$$

$$= 130 - 5(14)$$

$$= 60$$

Thus, the estimated regression equation is

$$\hat{y} = 60 + 5x$$

Figure 12.4 shows the graph of this equation on the scatter diagram.

The slope of the estimated regression equation ($b_1 = 5$) is positive, implying that as student population increases, sales increase. In fact, we can conclude (based on sales measured in $1000s and student population in 1000s) that an increase in the student population of 1000 is associated with an increase of $5000 in expected sales; that is, quarterly sales are expected to increase by $5 per student.

*Using the estimated regression equation to make predictions outside the range of the values of the independent variable should be done with caution because outside that range we cannot be sure that the same relationship is valid.*

If we believe the least squares estimated regression equation adequately describes the relationship between $x$ and $y$, it would seem reasonable to use the estimated regression equation to predict the value of $y$ for a given value of $x$. For example, if we wanted to predict quarterly sales for a restaurant to be located near a campus with 16,000 students, we would compute

$$\hat{y} = 60 + 5(16) = 140$$

Hence, we would predict quarterly sales of $140,000 for this restaurant. In the following sections we will discuss methods for assessing the appropriateness of using the estimated regression equation for estimation and prediction.

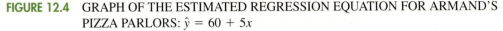

**FIGURE 12.4**    GRAPH OF THE ESTIMATED REGRESSION EQUATION FOR ARMAND'S PIZZA PARLORS: $\hat{y} = 60 + 5x$

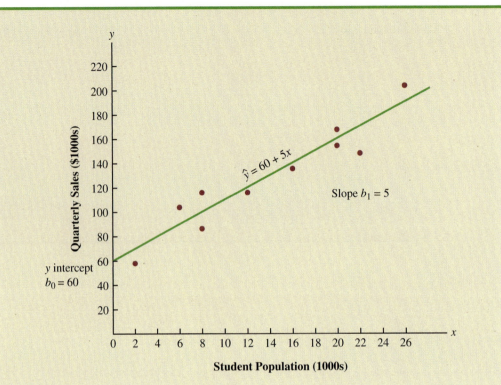

## Using Excel's Chart Tools to Construct a Scatter Diagram and Compute the Estimated Regression Equation

We can use Excel's chart tools to construct a scatter diagram and compute the estimated regression equation for the Armand's Pizza Parlors data appearing in Table 12.1. Refer to Figure 12.5 as we describe the tasks involved.

**Enter Data:**  Appropriate labels and the sample data have been entered into cells A1:C11 of the worksheet shown in Figure 12.5.

**Apply Tools:**  The following steps describe how to use Excel's chart tools to construct a scatter diagram and compute the estimated regression equation using the data in the worksheet.

**Step 1.**  Select cells B2:C11
**Step 2.**  Click the **Insert** tab on the Ribbon
**Step 3.**  In the **Charts** group, click **Scatter**
**Step 4.**  When the list of scatter diagram subtypes appears,
        Click **Scatter with only Markers** (the chart in the upper left corner)
**Step 5.**  In the **Chart Layouts** group, click **Layout 1**
**Step 6.**  Right-click on the **Chart Title** to display a list of options; choose **Delete**
**Step 7.**  Select the **Horizontal (Value) Axis Title** and replace it with **Student Population (1000s)**
**Step 8.**  Select the **Vertical (Value) Axis Title** and replace it with **Quarterly Sales ($1000s)**

**FIGURE 12.5**   SCATTER DIAGRAM, ESTIMATED REGRESSION EQUATION, AND THE ESTIMATED
REGRESSION LINE FOR ARMAND'S PIZZA PARLORS

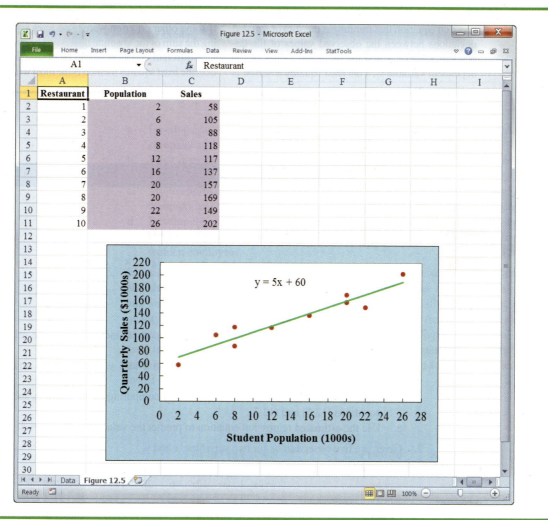

**Step 9.**  Right-click on the **Series 1 Legend Entry** to display a list of options; choose **Delete**

**Step 10.**  Position the mouse pointer over any **Vertical (Value) Axis Major Gridline** in the scatter diagram and right-click to display a list of options; choose **Delete**

**Step 11.**  Position the mouse pointer over any data point in the scatter diagram and right-click to display a list of options; choose **Add Trendline**

**Step 12.**  When the **Format Trendline** dialog box appears,
    Select **Trendline Options** and then
        Choose **Linear** from the **Trend/Regression Type** list
        Choose **Display Equation on chart**
        Click **Close**

The worksheet displayed in Figure 12.5 shows the scatter diagram, the estimated regression line, and the estimated regression equation.

seller. To investigate the relationship between the car's mileage and the sales price, data were collected on the mileage and the sale price for 10 private sales of model year 2000 Honda Accords (PriceHub website, October 2008).

WEB file

HondaAccord

| Miles (1000s) | Price ($1000s) |
|---|---|
| 90 | 7.0 |
| 59 | 7.5 |
| 66 | 6.6 |
| 87 | 7.2 |
| 90 | 7.0 |
| 106 | 5.4 |
| 94 | 6.4 |
| 57 | 7.0 |
| 138 | 5.1 |
| 87 | 7.2 |

a. Develop a scatter diagram with miles as the independent variable.
b. What does the scatter diagram developed in part (a) indicate about the relationship between the two variables?
c. Use the least squares method to develop the estimated regression equation.
d. Provide an interpretation for the slope of the estimated regression equation.
e. Predict the sales price for a 2000 Honda Accord with 100,000 miles.

7. A sales manager collected the following data on annual sales and years of experience.

WEB file

Sales

| Salesperson | Years of Experience | Annual Sales ($1000s) |
|---|---|---|
| 1 | 1 | 80 |
| 2 | 3 | 97 |
| 3 | 4 | 92 |
| 4 | 4 | 102 |
| 5 | 6 | 103 |
| 6 | 8 | 111 |
| 7 | 10 | 119 |
| 8 | 10 | 123 |
| 9 | 11 | 117 |
| 10 | 13 | 136 |

a. Develop a scatter diagram for these data with years of experience as the independent variable.
b. Develop an estimated regression equation that can be used to predict annual sales given the years of experience.
c. Use the estimated regression equation to predict annual sales for a salesperson with 9 years of experience.

8. Bergans of Norway has been making outdoor gear since 1908. The following data show the temperature rating (F°) and the price ($) for 11 models of sleeping bags produced by Bergans (*Backpacker* 2006 Gear Guide).

| Model | Temperature Rating (F°) | Price ($) |
|---|---|---|
| Ranger 3-Seasons | 12 | 319 |
| Ranger Spring | 24 | 289 |
| Ranger Winter | 3 | 389 |
| Rondane 3-Seasons | 13 | 239 |
| Rondane Summer | 38 | 149 |
| Rondane Winter | 4 | 289 |
| Senja Ice | 5 | 359 |
| Senja Snow | 15 | 259 |
| Senja Zero | 25 | 229 |
| Super Light | 45 | 129 |
| Tight & Light | 25 | 199 |

**WEB** file

**SleepingBags**

a. Develop a scatter diagram for these data with temperature rating (F°) as the independent variable.
b. What does the scatter diagram developed in part (a) indicate about the relationship between temperature rating (F°) and price?
c. Use the least squares method to develop the estimated regression equation.
d. Predict the price for a sleeping bag with a temperature rating (F°) of 20.

9. To avoid extra checked-bag fees, airline travelers often pack as much as they can into their suitcase. Finding a rolling suitcase that is durable, has good capacity, and is easy to pull can be difficult. The following table shows the results of tests conducted by *Consumer Reports* for 10 rolling suitcases; higher scores indicate better overall test results (Consumer Reports website, October 2008).

| Brand | Price ($) | Score |
|---|---|---|
| Briggs & Riley | 325 | 72 |
| Hartman | 350 | 74 |
| Heys | 67 | 54 |
| Kenneth Cole Reaction | 120 | 54 |
| Liz Claiborne | 85 | 64 |
| Samsonite | 180 | 57 |
| Titan | 360 | 66 |
| TravelPro | 156 | 67 |
| Tumi | 595 | 87 |
| Victorinox | 400 | 77 |

**WEB** file

**Suitcases**

a. Develop a scatter diagram with price as the independent variable.
b. What does the scatter diagram developed in part (a) indicate about the relationship between the two variables?
c. Use the least squares method to develop the estimated regression equation.
d. Provide an interpretation for the slope of the estimated regression equation.
e. The Eagle Creek Hovercraft suitcase has a price of $225. Predict the score for this suitcase using the estimated regression equation developed in part (c).

10. According to *Advertising Age*'s annual salary review, Mark Hurd, the 49-year-old chairman, president, and CEO of Hewlett-Packard Co., received an annual salary of $817,000, a bonus of more than $5 million, and other compensation exceeding $17 million. His total compensation was slightly better than the average CEO total pay of $12.4 million. The following table shows the age and annual salary (in thousands of dollars) for Mark Hurd and 14 other executives who led publicly held companies (*Advertising Age*, December 5, 2006).

| Executive | Title | Company | Age | Salary ($1000s) |
|-----------|-------|---------|-----|-----------------|
| Charles Prince | Chmn/CEO | Citigroup | 56 | 1000 |
| Harold McGraw III | Chmn/Pres/CEO | McGraw-Hill Cos. | 57 | 1172 |
| James Dimon | Pres/CEO | JP Morgan Chase & Co. | 50 | 1000 |
| K. Rupert Murdoch | Chmn/CEO | News Corp. | 75 | 4509 |
| Kenneth D. Lewis | Chmn/Pres/CEO | Bank of America | 58 | 1500 |
| Kenneth I. Chenault | Chmn/CEO | American Express Co. | 54 | 1092 |
| Louis C. Camilleri | Chmn/CEO | Altria Group | 51 | 1663 |
| Mark V. Hurd | Chmn/Pres/CEO | Hewlett-Packard Co. | 49 | 817 |
| Martin S. Sorrell | CEO | WPP Group | 61 | 1562 |
| Robert L. Nardelli | Chmn/Pres/CEO | Home Depot | 57 | 2164 |
| Samuel J. Palmisano | Chmn/Pres/CEO | IBM Corp. | 55 | 1680 |
| David C. Novak | Chmn/Pres/CEO | Yum Brands | 53 | 1173 |
| Henry R. Silverman | Chmn/CEO | Cendant Corp. | 65 | 3300 |
| Robert C. Wright | Chmn/CEO | NBC Universal | 62 | 2500 |
| Sumner Redstone | Exec Chmn/Founder | Viacom | 82 | 5807 |

ExecSalary

a. Develop a scatter diagram for these data with the age of the executive as the independent variable.
b. What does the scatter diagram developed in part (a) indicate about the relationship between the two variables?
c. Develop the least squares estimated regression equation.
d. Suppose Bill Gustin is the 72-year-old chairman, president, and CEO of a major electronics company. Predict the annual salary for Bill Gustin.

11. Sporty cars are designed to provide better handling, acceleration, and a more responsive driving experience than a typical sedan. But, even within this select group of cars, performance as well as price can vary. *Consumer Reports* provided road-test scores and prices for the following 12 sporty cars (Consumer Reports website, October 2008). Prices are in thousands of dollars and road-test scores are based on a 0–100 rating scale, with higher values indicating better performance.

SportyCars

| Car | Price ($1000s) | Road-Test Score |
|-----|----------------|-----------------|
| Chevrolet Cobalt SS | 24.5 | 78 |
| Dodge Caliber SRT4 | 24.9 | 56 |
| Ford Mustang GT (V8) | 29.0 | 73 |
| Honda Civic Si | 21.7 | 78 |
| Mazda RX-8 | 31.3 | 86 |
| Mini Cooper S | 26.4 | 74 |
| Mitsubishi Lancer Evolution GSR | 38.1 | 83 |
| Nissan Sentra SE-R Spec V | 23.3 | 66 |
| Suburu Impreza WRX | 25.2 | 81 |
| Suburu Impreza WRX Sti | 37.6 | 89 |
| Volkswagen GTI | 24.0 | 83 |
| Volkswagen R32 | 33.6 | 83 |

a. Develop a scatter diagram with price as the independent variable.
b. What does the scatter diagram developed in part (a) indicate about the relationship between the two variables?
c. Use the least squares method to develop the estimated regression equation.
d. Provide an interpretation for the slope of the estimated regression equation.

e.   Another sporty car that *Consumer Reports* tested is the BMW 135i; the price for this car was $36,700. Predict the road-test score for the BMW 135i using the estimated regression equation developed in part (c).

12.   A personal watercraft (PWC) is a vessel propelled by water jets, designed to be operated by a person sitting, standing, or kneeling on the vessel. In the early 1970s, Kawasaki Motors Corp. U.S.A. introduced the JET SKI® watercraft, the first commercially success-ful PWC. Today, *jet ski* is commonly used as a generic term for personal watercraft. The following data show the weight (rounded to the nearest 10 lbs.) and the price (rounded to the nearest $50) for 10 three-seater personal watercraft (Jetski News website, 2006).

**WEB** file

**JetSki**

| Make and Model | Weight (lbs.) | Price ($) |
|---|---|---|
| Honda AquaTrax F-12 | 750 | 9500 |
| Honda AquaTrax F-12X | 790 | 10500 |
| Honda AquaTrax F-12X GPScape | 800 | 11200 |
| Kawasaki STX-12F Jetski | 740 | 8500 |
| Yamaha FX Cruiser Waverunner | 830 | 10000 |
| Yamaha FX High Output Waverunner | 770 | 10000 |
| Yamaha FX Waverunner | 830 | 9300 |
| Yamaha VX110 Deluxe Waverunner | 720 | 7700 |
| Yamaha VX110 Sport Waverunner | 720 | 7000 |
| Yamaha XLT1200 Waverunner | 780 | 8500 |

a.   Develop a scatter diagram for these data with weight as the independent variable.
b.   What does the scatter diagram developed in part (a) indicate about the relationship between weight and price?
c.   Use the least squares method to develop the estimated regression equation.
d.   Predict the price for a three-seater PWC with a weight of 750 pounds.
e.   The Honda AquaTrax F-12 weighs 750 pounds and has a price of $9500. Shouldn't the predicted price you developed in part (d) for a PWC with a weight of 750 pounds also be $9500?
f.   The Kawasaki SX-R 800 Jetski has a seating capacity of one and weighs 350 pounds. Do you think the estimated regression equation developed in part (c) should be used to predict the price for this model?

13.   To the Internal Revenue Service, the reasonableness of total itemized deductions depends on the taxpayer's adjusted gross income. Large deductions, which include charity and medical deductions, are more reasonable for taxpayers with large adjusted gross incomes. If a taxpayer claims larger than average itemized deductions for a given level of income, the chances of an IRS audit are increased. Data (in thousands of dollars) on adjusted gross income and the average or reasonable amount of total itemized deductions follow.

| Adjusted Gross Income ($1000s) | Reasonable Amount of Itemized Deductions ($1000s) |
|---|---|
| 22 | 9.6 |
| 27 | 9.6 |
| 32 | 10.1 |
| 48 | 11.1 |
| 65 | 13.5 |
| 85 | 17.7 |
| 120 | 25.5 |

a. Develop a scatter diagram for these data with adjusted gross income as the independent variable.
b. Use the least squares method to develop the estimated regression equation.
c. Predict a reasonable level of total itemized deductions for a taxpayer with an adjusted gross income of $52,500. If this taxpayer claimed itemized deductions of $20,400, would the IRS agent's request for an audit appear justified? Explain.

14. *PCWorld* rated four component characteristics for 10 ultraportable laptop computers: features, performance, design, and price. Each characteristic was rated using a 0–100 point scale. An overall rating, referred to as the *PC World* Rating, was then developed for each laptop. The following table shows the features rating and the *PC World* Rating for the 10 laptop computers (PC World website, February 5, 2009).

| Model | Features Rating | PC World Rating |
|---|---|---|
| Thinkpad X200 | 87 | 83 |
| VGN-Z598U | 85 | 82 |
| U6V | 80 | 81 |
| Elitebook 2530P | 75 | 78 |
| X360 | 80 | 78 |
| Thinkpad X300 | 76 | 78 |
| Ideapad U110 | 81 | 77 |
| Micro Express JFT2500 | 73 | 75 |
| Toughbook W7 | 79 | 73 |
| HP Voodoo Envy133 | 68 | 72 |

Laptop

a. Develop a scatter diagram with the features rating as the independent variable.
b. What does the scatter diagram developed in part (a) indicate about the relationship between the two variables?
c. Use the least squares method to develop the estimated regression equation.
d. Predict the *PC World* Rating for a new laptop computer that has a features rating of 70.

## 12.3 Coefficient of Determination

For the Armand's Pizza Parlors example, we developed the estimated regression equation $\hat{y} = 60 + 5x$ to approximate the linear relationship between the size of the student population $x$ and quarterly sales $y$. A question now is: How well does the estimated regression equation fit the data? In this section, we show that the **coefficient of determination** provides a measure of the goodness of fit for the estimated regression equation.

For the $i$th observation, the difference between the observed value of the dependent variable, $y_i$, and the predicted value of the dependent variable, $\hat{y}_i$, is called the **$i$th residual**. The $i$th residual represents the error in using $\hat{y}_i$ to predict $y_i$. Thus, for the $i$th observation, the residual is $y_i - \hat{y}_i$. The sum of squares of these residuals or errors is the quantity that is minimized by the least squares method. This quantity, also known as the *sum of squares due to error,* is denoted by SSE.

**SUM OF SQUARES DUE TO ERROR**

$$SSE = \Sigma(y_i - \hat{y}_i)^2 \tag{12.8}$$

**TABLE 12.3**   CALCULATION OF SSE FOR ARMAND'S PIZZA PARLORS

| Restaurant $i$ | $x_i$ = Student Population (1000s) | $y_i$ = Quarterly Sales ($1000s) | Predicted Sales $\hat{y}_i = 60 + 5x_i$ | Error $y_i - \hat{y}_i$ | Squared Error $(y_i - \hat{y}_i)^2$ |
|---|---|---|---|---|---|
| 1 | 2 | 58 | 70 | −12 | 144 |
| 2 | 6 | 105 | 90 | 15 | 225 |
| 3 | 8 | 88 | 100 | −12 | 144 |
| 4 | 8 | 118 | 100 | 18 | 324 |
| 5 | 12 | 117 | 120 | −3 | 9 |
| 6 | 16 | 137 | 140 | −3 | 9 |
| 7 | 20 | 157 | 160 | −3 | 9 |
| 8 | 20 | 169 | 160 | 9 | 81 |
| 9 | 22 | 149 | 170 | −21 | 441 |
| 10 | 26 | 202 | 190 | 12 | 144 |
| | | | | | SSE = 1530 |

The value of SSE is a measure of the error in using the estimated regression equation to predict the values of the dependent variable in the sample.

In Table 12.3 we show the calculations required to compute the sum of squares due to error for the Armand's Pizza Parlors example. For instance, for restaurant 1 the values of the independent and dependent variables are $x_1 = 2$ and $y_1 = 58$. Using the estimated regression equation, we find that the predicted value of quarterly sales for restaurant 1 is $\hat{y}_1 = 60 + 5(2) = 70$. Thus, the error in using $\hat{y}_1$ to estimate $y_1$ for restaurant 1 is $y_1 - \hat{y}_1 = 58 - 70 = -12$. The squared error, $(-12)^2 = 144$, is shown in the last column of Table 12.3. After computing and squaring the residuals for each restaurant in the sample, we sum them to obtain SSE = 1530. Thus, SSE = 1530 measures the error in using the estimated regression equation $\hat{y} = 60 + 5x$ to predict sales.

Now suppose we are asked to predict quarterly sales without knowledge of the size of the student population. Without knowledge of any related variables, we would use the sample mean as a predictor of quarterly sales at any given restaurant. Table 12.2 showed that for the sales data, $\Sigma y_i = 1300$. Hence, the mean value of quarterly sales for the sample of 10 Armand's restaurants is $\bar{y} = \Sigma y_i / n = 1300/10 = 130$. In Table 12.4 we show the sum of squared deviations obtained by using the sample mean $\bar{y} = 130$ to predict the value of quarterly sales for each restaurant in the sample. For the $i$th restaurant in the sample, the difference $y_i - \bar{y}$ provides a measure of the error involved in using $\bar{y}$ to predict sales. The corresponding sum of squares, called the *total sum of squares*, is denoted SST.

TOTAL SUM OF SQUARES

$$SST = \Sigma(y_i - \bar{y})^2 \qquad\qquad \textbf{(12.9)}$$

The sum at the bottom of the last column in Table 12.4 is the total sum of squares for Armand's Pizza Parlors; it is SST = 15,730.

In Figure 12.6 we show the estimated regression line $\hat{y} = 60 + 5x$ and the line corresponding to $\bar{y} = 130$. Note that the points cluster more closely around the estimated

    a.   Compute the mean square error using equation (12.15).
    b.   Compute the standard error of the estimate using equation (12.16).
    c.   Compute the estimated standard deviation of $b_1$ using equation (12.18).
    d.   Use the $t$ test to test the following hypotheses ($\alpha = .05$):

$$H_0: \beta_1 = 0$$
$$H_a: \beta_1 \neq 0$$

    e.   Use the $F$ test to test the hypotheses in part (d) at a .05 level of significance. Present the results in the analysis of variance table format.

25.   The data from exercise 3 follow.

| $x_i$ | 2 | 6 | 9 | 13 | 20 |
|-------|---|---|---|----|----|
| $y_i$ | 7 | 18 | 9 | 26 | 23 |

    a.   What is the value of the standard error of the estimate?
    b.   Test for a significant relationship by using the $t$ test. Use $\alpha = .05$.
    c.   Use the $F$ test to test for a significant relationship. Use $\alpha = .05$. What is your conclusion?

## Applications

26.   In exercise 18 the data on grade point average and monthly salary were as follows.

| GPA | Monthly Salary ($) | GPA | Monthly Salary ($) |
|-----|--------------------|-----|--------------------|
| 2.6 | 3300 | 3.2 | 3500 |
| 3.4 | 3600 | 3.5 | 3900 |
| 3.6 | 4000 | 2.9 | 3600 |

    a.   Does the $t$ test indicate a significant relationship between grade point average and monthly salary? What is your conclusion? Use $\alpha = .05$.
    b.   Test for a significant relationship using the $F$ test. What is your conclusion? Use $\alpha = .05$.
    c.   Show the ANOVA table.

27.   The number of megapixels in a digital camera is one of the most important factors in determining picture quality. But, do digital cameras with more megapixels cost more? The following data show the number of megapixels and the price ($) for 10 digital cameras (*Consumer Reports*, March 2009).

**DigitalCameras**

| Brand and Model | Megapixels | Price ($) |
|-----------------|------------|-----------|
| Canon PowerShot SD1100 IS | 8 | 180 |
| Casio Exilim Card EX-510 | 10 | 200 |
| Sony Cyber-shot DSC-T70 | 7 | 230 |
| Pentax Optio M50 | 8 | 120 |
| Canon PowerShot G10 | 15 | 470 |
| Canon PowerShot A590 IS | 8 | 140 |
| Canon PowerShot E1 | 10 | 180 |
| Fujifilm FinePix F00FD | 12 | 310 |
| Sony Cyber-shot DSC-W170 | 10 | 250 |
| Canon PowerShot A470 | 7 | 110 |

a.   Use these data to develop an estimated regression equation that can be used to predict the price of a digital camera given the number of megapixels.

b.   At the .05 level of significance, are the number of megapixels and the price related? Explain.

c.   Would you feel comfortable using the estimated regression equation developed in part (a) to predict the price of a digital camera given the number of megapixels? Explain.

d.   The Kodak EasyShare Z1012 IS digital camera has 10 megapixels. Predict the price of this camera using the estimated regression equation developed in part (a).

28.  In exercise 8, data on $x$ = temperature rating (F°) and $y$ = price ($) for 11 sleeping bags manufactured by Bergans of Norway provided the estimated regression equation $\hat{y}$ = 359.2668 − 5.2772$x$. At the .05 level of significance, test whether temperature rating and price are related. Show the ANOVA table. What is your conclusion?

SleepingBags

29.  Refer to exercise 21, where data on production volume and cost were used to develop an estimated regression equation relating production volume and cost for a particular manufacturing operation. Use $\alpha$ = .05 to test whether the production volume is significantly related to the total cost. Show the ANOVA table. What is your conclusion?

30.  Refer to excercise 5, where the following data were used to investigate whether higher prices are generally associated with higher ratings for elliptical trainers (*Consumer Reports*, February 2008).

WEB file

Ellipticals

| Brand and Model | Price ($) | Rating |
|---|---|---|
| Precor 5.31 | 3700 | 87 |
| Keys Fitness CG2 | 2500 | 84 |
| Octane Fitness Q37e | 2800 | 82 |
| LifeFitness X1 Basic | 1900 | 74 |
| NordicTrack AudioStrider 990 | 1000 | 73 |
| Schwinn 430 | 800 | 69 |
| Vision Fitness X6100 | 1700 | 68 |
| ProForm XP 520 Razor | 600 | 55 |

With $x$ = price ($) and $y$ = rating, the estimated regression equation is $\hat{y}$ = 58.158 + .008449$x$. For these data, SSE = 173.88 and SST = 756. Does the evidence indicate a significant relationship between price and rating?

31.  In exercise 20, data on $x$ = price ($) and $y$ = overall score for ten 42-inch plasma televisions tested by *Consumer Reports* provided the estimated regression equation $\hat{y}$ = 12.0169 + .0127$x$. For these data SSE = 540.04 and SST = 982.40. Use the $F$ test to determine whether the price for a 42-inch plasma television and the overall score are related at the .05 level of significance.

# 12.6   Using the Estimated Regression Equation for Estimation and Prediction

When using the simple linear regression model, we are making an assumption about the relationship between $x$ and $y$. We then use the least squares method to obtain the estimated simple linear regression equation. If a significant relationship exists between $x$ and $y$ and the coefficient of determination shows that the fit is good, the estimated regression equation should be useful for estimation and prediction.

For the Armand's Pizza Parlors example, the estimated regression equation is $\hat{y} = 60 + 5x$. At the end of Section 12.1 we stated that $\hat{y}$ can be used as a *point estimator* of $E(y)$, the mean or expected value of $y$ for a given value of $x$, and as a predictor of an individual value of $y$. For example, suppose Armand's managers want to estimate the mean quarterly sales for *all* restaurants located near college campuses with 10,000 students. Using the estimated regression equation $\hat{y} = 60 + 5x$, we see that for $x = 10$ (10,000 students), $\hat{y} = 60 + 5(10) = 110$. Thus, a *point estimate* of the mean quarterly sales for all restaurant locations near campuses with 10,000 students is $110,000. In this case we are using $\hat{y}$ as the point estimator of the mean value of $y$ when $x = 10$.

We can also use the estimated regression equation to *predict* an individual value of $y$ for a given value of $x$. For example, to predict quarterly sales for a new restaurant Armand's is considering building near Talbot College, a campus with 10,000 students, we would compute $\hat{y} = 60 + 5(10) = 110$. Hence, we would predict quarterly sales of $110,000 for such a new restaurant. In this case, we are using $\hat{y}$ as the *predictor* of $y$ for a new observation when $x = 10$.

When we are using the estimated regression equation to estimate the mean value of $y$ or to predict an individual value of $y$, it is clear that the estimate or prediction depends on the given value of $x$. For this reason, as we discuss in more depth the issues concerning estimation and prediction, the following notation will help clarify matters.

$x^*$ = the given value of the independent variable $x$

$y^*$ = the random variable denoting the possible values of the dependent variable $y$ when $x = x^*$

$E(y^*)$ = the mean or expected value of the dependent variable $y$ when $x = x^*$

$\hat{y}^* = b_0 + b_1x^*$ = the point estimator of $E(y^*)$ and the predictor of an individual value of $y^*$ when $x = x^*$

To illustrate the use of this notation, suppose we want to estimate the mean value of quarterly sales for *all* Armand's restaurants located near a campus with 10,000 students. For this case, $x^* = 10$ and $E(y^*)$ denotes the unknown mean value of quarterly sales for all restaurants where $x^* = 10$. Thus, the point estimate of $E(y^*)$ is provided by $\hat{y}^* = 60 + 5(10) = 110$, or $110,000. But, using this notation, $\hat{y}^* = 110$ is also the predictor of quarterly sales for the new restaurant located near Talbot College, a school with 10,000 students.

## Interval Estimation

*Confidence intervals and prediction intervals show the precision of the regression results. Narrower intervals provide a higher degree of precision.*

Point estimators and predictors do not provide any information about the precision associated with the estimate and/or prediction. For that we must develop confidence intervals and prediction intervals. A **confidence interval** is an interval estimate of the *mean value of y* for a given value of $x$. A **prediction interval** is used whenever we want to *predict an individual value of y* for a new observation corresponding to a given value of $x$. Although the predictor of $y$ for a given value of $x$ is the same as the point estimator of the mean value of $y$ for a given value of $x$, the interval estimates we obtain for the two cases are different. As we will show, the margin of error is larger for a prediction interval. We begin by showing how to develop an interval estimate of the mean value of $y$.

## Confidence Interval for the Mean Value of $y$

In general, we cannot expect $\hat{y}^*$ to equal $E(y^*)$ exactly. If we want to make an inference about how close $\hat{y}^*$ is to the true mean value $E(y^*)$, we will have to estimate the variance of $\hat{y}^*$. The formula for estimating the variance of $\hat{y}^*$, denoted by $s_{\hat{y}^*}^2$, is

$$s_{\hat{y}^*}^2 = s^2 \left[ \frac{1}{n} + \frac{(x^* - \bar{x})^2}{\Sigma(x_i - \bar{x})^2} \right] \qquad \textbf{(12.22)}$$

The estimate of the standard deviation of $\hat{y}^*$ is given by the square root of equation (12.22).

$$s_{\hat{y}^*} = s \sqrt{\frac{1}{n} + \frac{(x^* - \bar{x})^2}{\Sigma(x_i - \bar{x})^2}} \qquad \textbf{(12.23)}$$

The computational results for Armand's Pizza Parlors in Section 12.5 provided $s = 13.829$. With $x^* = 10$, $\bar{x} = 14$, and $\Sigma(x_i - \bar{x})^2 = 568$, we can use equation (12.23) to obtain

$$s_{\hat{y}^*} = 13.829 \sqrt{\frac{1}{10} + \frac{(10 - 14)^2}{568}}$$

$$= 13.829 \sqrt{.1282} = 4.95$$

The general expression for a confidence interval follows.

*The margin of error associated with this confidence interval is $t_{\alpha/2} s_{\hat{y}^*}$.*

**CONFIDENCE INTERVAL FOR $E(y^*)$**

$$\hat{y}^* \pm t_{\alpha/2} s_{\hat{y}^*} \qquad \textbf{(12.24)}$$

where the confidence coefficient is $1 - \alpha$ and $t_{\alpha/2}$ is based on the $t$ distribution with $n - 2$ degrees of freedom.

Using expression (12.24) to develop a 95% confidence interval of the mean quarterly sales for all Armand's restaurants located near campuses with 10,000 students, we need the value of $t$ for $\alpha/2 = .025$ and $n - 2 = 10 - 2 = 8$ degrees of freedom. Using Table 2 of Appendix B, we have $t_{.025} = 2.306$. Thus, with $\hat{y}^* = 110$ and a margin of error of $t_{\alpha/2} s_{\hat{y}^*} = 2.306(4.95) = 11.415$, the 95% confidence interval estimate is

$$110 \pm 11.415$$

In dollars, the 95% confidence interval for the mean quarterly sales of all restaurants near campuses with 10,000 students is \$110,000 $\pm$ \$11,415. Therefore, the 95% confidence interval for the mean quarterly sales when the student population is 10,000 is \$98,585 to \$121,415.

Note that the estimated standard deviation of $\hat{y}^*$ given by equation (12.23) is smallest when $x^* - \bar{x} = 0$. In this case the estimated standard deviation of $\hat{y}^*$ becomes

$$s_{\hat{y}^*} = s \sqrt{\frac{1}{n} + \frac{(\bar{x} - \bar{x})^2}{\Sigma(x_i - \bar{x})^2}} = s \sqrt{\frac{1}{n}}$$

This result implies that we can make the best or most precise estimate of the mean value of $y$ whenever $x^* = \bar{x}$. In fact, the further $x^*$ is from $\bar{x}$, the larger $x^* - \bar{x}$ becomes. As a result, the confidence interval for the mean value of $y$ will become wider as $x^*$ deviates more from $\bar{x}$. This pattern is shown graphically in Figure 12.10.

**FIGURE 12.10**  CONFIDENCE INTERVALS FOR THE MEAN SALES $y$ AT GIVEN VALUES OF STUDENT POPULATION $x$

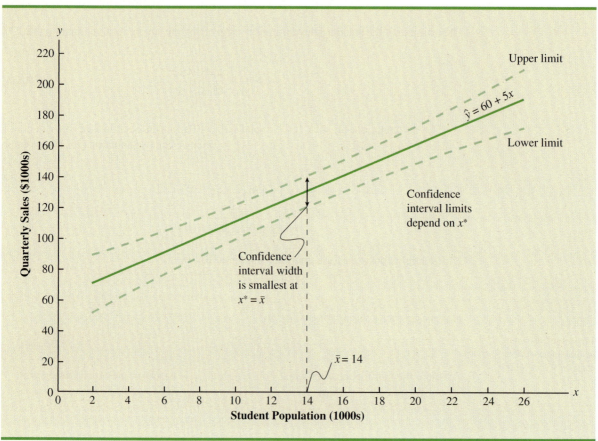

## Prediction Interval for an Individual Value of $y$

Instead of estimating the mean value of quarterly sales for all Armand's restaurants located near campuses with 10,000 students, suppose we want to predict quarterly sales for a new restaurant Armand's is considering building near Talbot College, a campus with 10,000 students. As noted previously, the predictor of $y^*$, the value of $y$ corresponding to the given $x^*$, is $\hat{y}^* = b_0 + b_1 x^*$. For the new restaurant located near Talbot College, $x^* = 10$ and the prediction of quarterly sales is $\hat{y}^* = 60 + 5(10) = 110$, or \$110,000. Note that the prediction of quarterly sales for the new Armand's restaurant near Talbot College is the same as the point estimate of the mean sales for all Armand's restaurants located near campuses with 10,000 students.

To develop a prediction interval, let us first determine the variance associated with using $\hat{y}^*$ as a predictor of $y$ when $x = x^*$. This variance is made up of the sum of the following two components.

1. The variance of the $y^*$ values about the mean $E(y^*)$, an estimate of which is given by $s^2$
2. The variance associated with using $\hat{y}^*$ to estimate $E(y^*)$, an estimate of which is given by $s_{\hat{y}^*}^2$

The formula for estimating the variance corresponding to the prediction of the value of $y$ when $x = x^*$, denoted $s^2_{pred}$, is

$$s^2_{pred} = s^2 + s^2_{\hat{y}^*}$$

$$= s^2 + s^2\left[\frac{1}{n} + \frac{(x^* - \bar{x})^2}{\Sigma(x_i - \bar{x})^2}\right]$$

$$= s^2\left[1 + \frac{1}{n} + \frac{(x^* - \bar{x})^2}{\Sigma(x_i - \bar{x})^2}\right] \tag{12.25}$$

Hence, an estimate of the standard deviation corresponding to the prediction of the value of $y^*$ is

$$s_{pred} = s\sqrt{1 + \frac{1}{n} + \frac{(x^* - \bar{x})^2}{\Sigma(x_i - \bar{x})^2}} \tag{12.26}$$

For Armand's Pizza Parlors, the estimated standard deviation corresponding to the prediction of quarterly sales for a new restaurant located near Talbot College, a campus with 10,000 students, is computed as follows.

$$s_{pred} = 13.829\sqrt{1 + \frac{1}{10} + \frac{(10 - 14)^2}{568}}$$

$$= 13.829\sqrt{1.282}$$

$$= 14.69$$

The general expression for a prediction interval follows.

**PREDICTION INTERVAL FOR $y^*$**

$$\hat{y}^* \pm t_{\alpha/2}s_{pred} \tag{12.27}$$

where the confidence coefficient is $1 - \alpha$ and $t_{\alpha/2}$ is based on a $t$ distribution with $n - 2$ degrees of freedom.

The 95% prediction interval for quarterly sales for the new Armand's restaurant located near Talbot College can be found using $t_{\alpha/2} = t_{.025} = 2.306$ and $s_{pred} = 14.69$. Thus, with $\hat{y}^* = 110$ and a margin of error of $t_{.025}s_{pred} = 2.306(14.69) = 33.875$, the 95% prediction interval is

$$110 \pm 33.875$$

In dollars, this prediction interval is $110,000 \pm \$33,875$ or $76,125 to \$143,875. Note that the prediction interval for the new restaurant located near Talbot College, a campus with 10,000 students, is wider than the confidence interval for the mean quarterly sales of all restaurants located near campuses with 10,000 students. The difference reflects the fact that we are able to estimate the mean value of $y$ more precisely than we can predict an individual value of $y$.

**FIGURE 12.11** CONFIDENCE AND PREDICTION INTERVALS FOR SALES $y$ AT GIVEN VALUES OF STUDENT POPULATION $x$

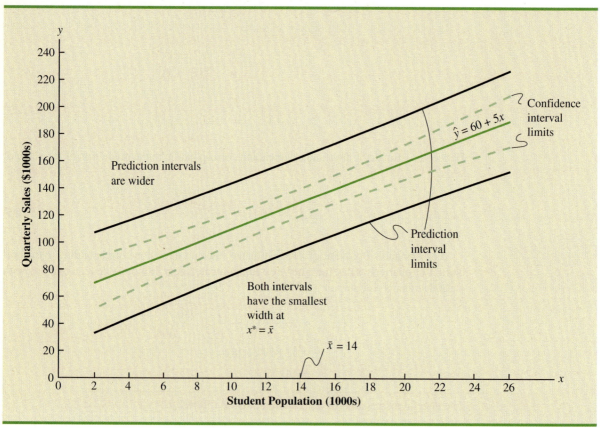

In general, the lines for the confidence interval limits and the prediction interval limits both have curvature.

Confidence intervals and prediction intervals are both more precise when the value of the independent variable $x^*$ is closer to $\bar{x}$. The general shapes of confidence intervals and the wider prediction intervals are shown together in Figure 12.11.

## NOTES AND COMMENTS

A prediction interval is used to predict the value of the dependent variable $y$ for a *new observation*. As an illustration, we showed how to develop a prediction interval of quarterly sales for a new restaurant that Armand's is considering building near Talbot College, a campus with 10,000 students. The fact that the value of $x = 10$ is not one of the values of student population for the Armand's sample data in Table 12.1 is not meant to imply that prediction intervals cannot be developed for values of $x$ in the sample data. But, for the ten restaurants that make up the data in Table 12.1, developing a prediction interval for quarterly sales for *one of these restaurants* does not make any sense because we already know the value of quarterly sales for each of these restaurants. In other words, a prediction interval only has meaning for something new, in this case a new observation corresponding to a particular value of $x$ that may or may not equal one of the values of $x$ in the sample.

## Exercises

### Methods

32. The data from exercise 1 follow.

| $x_i$ | 1 | 2 | 3 | 4 | 5 |
|-------|---|---|---|---|---|
| $y_i$ | 3 | 7 | 5 | 11 | 14 |

   a. Use equation (12.23) to compute an estimate the standard deviation of $\hat{y}^*$ when $x = 4$.
   b. Use expression (12.24) to develop a 95% confidence interval for the expected value of $y$ when $x = 4$.
   c. Use equation (12.26) to estimate the standard deviation of an individual value of $y$ when $x = 4$.
   d. Use expression (12.27) to develop a 95% prediction interval for $y$ when $x = 4$.

33. The data from exercise 2 follow.

| $x_i$ | 3 | 12 | 6 | 20 | 14 |
|-------|---|----|---|----|----|
| $y_i$ | 55 | 40 | 55 | 10 | 15 |

   a. Compute an estimate of the standard deviation of $\hat{y}^*$ when $x = 8$.
   b. Develop a 95% confidence interval for the expected value of $y$ when $x = 8$.
   c. Estimate the standard deviation of an individual value of $y$ when $x = 8$.
   d. Develop a 95% prediction interval for $y$ when $x = 8$.

34. The data from exercise 3 follow.

| $x_i$ | 2 | 6 | 9 | 13 | 20 |
|-------|---|---|---|----|----|
| $y_i$ | 7 | 18 | 9 | 26 | 23 |

   Develop the 95% confidence and prediction intervals when $x = 12$. Explain why these two intervals are different.

### Applications

35. In exercise 18, the data on grade point average $x$ and monthly salary $y$ provided the estimated regression equation $\hat{y} = 1790.5 + 581.1x$.
   a. Develop a 95% confidence interval for the mean starting salary for all students with a 3.0 GPA.
   b. Develop a 95% prediction interval for the starting salary for Joe Heller, a student with a GPA of 3.0.

**SleepingBags**

36. In exercise 8, data on $x$ = temperature rating (F°) and $y$ = price ($) for 11 sleeping bags manufactured by Bergans of Norway provided the estimated regression equation $\hat{y} = 359.2668 - 5.2772x$. For these data $s = 37.9372$.
   a. Develop a point estimate of the mean price for all sleeping bags with a temperature rating of 30.
   b. Develop a 95% confidence interval for the mean price for all sleeping bags with a temperature rating of 30.
   c. Suppose that Bergans developed a new model with a temperature rating of 30. Develop a 95% prediction interval for the price of this new model.
   d. Discuss the differences in your answers to parts (b) and (c).

37. In exercise 13, data were given on the adjusted gross income $x$ and the average or reasonable amount of total itemized deductions taken by taxpayers. Data were reported in thousands of dollars. With the estimated regression equation $\hat{y} = 4.68 + .16x$, the point

estimate of the mean reasonable level of total itemized deductions for a taxpayer with an adjusted gross income of $52,500 is $13,080.

a.   Develop a 95% confidence interval for the mean amount of total itemized deductions for all taxpayers with an adjusted gross income of $52,500.

b.   Develop a 95% prediction interval estimate for the amount of total itemized deductions for a particular taxpayer with an adjusted gross income of $52,500.

c.   If the particular taxpayer referred to in part (b) claimed total itemized deductions of $20,400, would the IRS agent's request for an audit appear to be justified?

d.   Use your answer to part (b) to give the IRS agent a guideline as to the amount of total itemized deductions a taxpayer with an adjusted gross income of $52,500 should claim before an audit is recommended.

38.   Refer to exercise 21, where data on the production volume $x$ and total cost $y$ for a particular manufacturing operation were used to develop the estimated regression equation $\hat{y} = 1246.67 + 7.6x$.

a.   The company's production schedule shows that 500 units must be produced next month. What is the point estimate of the mean total cost for next month?

b.   Develop a 99% prediction interval for the total cost for next month.

c.   If an accounting cost report at the end of next month shows that the actual production cost during the month was $6000, should managers be concerned about incurring such a high total cost for the month? Discuss.

39.   Almost all U.S. light-rail systems use electric cars that run on tracks built at street level. The Federal Transit Administration claims light-rail is one of the safest modes of travel, with an accident rate of .99 accidents per million passenger miles as compared to 2.29 for buses. The following data show the miles of track and the weekday ridership in thousands of passengers for six light-rail systems (*USA Today*, January 7, 2003).

| City | Miles of Track | Ridership (1000s) |
|---|---|---|
| Cleveland | 15 | 15 |
| Denver | 17 | 35 |
| Portland | 38 | 81 |
| Sacramento | 21 | 31 |
| San Diego | 47 | 75 |
| San Jose | 31 | 30 |
| St. Louis | 34 | 42 |

a.   Use these data to develop an estimated regression equation that could be used to predict the ridership given the miles of track.

b.   Did the estimated regression equation provide a good fit? Explain.

c.   Develop a 95% confidence interval for the mean weekday ridership for all light-rail systems with 30 miles of track.

d.   Suppose that Charlotte is considering construction of a light-rail system with 30 miles of track. Develop a 95% prediction interval for the weekday ridership for the Charlotte system. Do you think that the prediction interval you developed would be of value to Charlotte planners in anticipating the number of weekday riders for their new light-rail system? Explain.

## 12.7    Excel's Regression Tool

In previous sections of this chapter we have shown how Excel's chart tools can be used for various tasks in a regression analysis. Excel also has a more comprehensive Regression tool. In this section we will illustrate how Excel's Regression tool can be used to perform a complete regression analysis, including statistical tests of significance for the Armand's Pizza Parlors data in Table 12.1. We also show how StatTools can be used to develop prediction interval estimates.

**FIGURE 12.12**   REGRESSION TOOL DIALOG BOX FOR THE ARMAND'S PIZZA PARLORS EXAMPLE

## Using Excel's Regression Tool for the Armand's Pizza Parlors Example

*In the chapter appendix we show how to use StatTools to perform the regression analysis computations for the Armand's Pizza Parlors data. The regression analysis capabilities of StatTools are more comprehensive than those available using Excel's Regression tool.*

Refer to Figures 12.12 and 12.13 as we describe the tasks involved to use Excel's Regression tool to perform the regression analysis computations for the Armand's data.

**Enter Data:**  The labels Restaurant, Population, and Sales are entered into cells A1:C1 of the worksheet. To identify each of the 10 observations, we entered the numbers 1 through 10 into cells A2:A11. The sample data are entered into cells B2:C11.

**Apply Tools:**  The following steps describe how to use Excel's Regression tool to perform the regression analysis computations performed in Sections 12.2–12.5.

**Step 1.**  Click the **Data** tab on the Ribbon

**Step 2.**  In the **Analysis** group, click **Data Analysis**

**Step 3.**  Choose **Regression** from the list of Analysis Tools

**Step 4.**  When the Regression dialog box appears (see Figure 12.12),
Enter C1:C11 in the **Input Y Range** box
Enter B1:B11 in the **Input X Range** box
Select **Labels**
Select **Confidence Level**
Enter 99 in the **Confidence Level** box
Select **Output Range**
Enter A13 in the **Output Range** box (to identify the upper left corner of the section of the worksheet where the output will appear)
Click **OK**

**FIGURE 12.13**    REGRESSION TOOL OUTPUT FOR ARMAND'S PIZZA PARLORS

*The Excel output can be reformatted to improve readability.*

The regression output, titled SUMMARY OUTPUT, begins with row 13 in Figure 12.13. Because Excel initially displays the output using standard column widths, many of the row and column labels are unreadable. In several places we have reformatted to improve readability. We have also reformatted cells displaying numerical values to a maximum of four decimal places. Numbers displayed using scientific notation have not been modified. Regression output in future figures will be similarly reformatted to improve readability.

The first section of the summary output, titled *Regression Statistics,* contains summary statistics such as the coefficient of determination (R Square). The second section of the output, titled ANOVA, contains the analysis of variance table. The last section of the output, which is not titled, contains the estimated regression coefficients and related information. Let us begin our interpretation of the regression output with the information contained in rows 29 and 30.

## Interpretation of Estimated Regression Equation Output

Row 29 contains information about the $y$-intercept of the estimated regression line. Row 30 contains information about the slope of the estimated regression line. The $y$-intercept of the estimated regression line, $b_0 = 60$, is shown in cell B29, and the slope of the estimated regression line, $b_1 = 5$, is shown in cell B30. The label Intercept in cell A29 and the label Population in cell A30 are used to identify these two values.

In Section 12.5 we showed that the estimated standard deviation of $b_1$ is $s_{b_1} = .5803$. Cell C30 contains the estimated standard deviation of $b_1$. As we indicated previously, the standard deviation of $b_1$ is also referred to as the standard error of $b_1$. Thus, $s_{b_1}$ provides an estimate of the standard error of $b_1$. The label Standard Error in cell C28 is Excel's way of indicating that the value in cell C30 is the estimate of the standard error, or standard deviation, of $b_1$.

In Section 12.5 we stated that the form of the null and alternative hypotheses needed to test for a significant relationship between population and sales are as follows:

$$H_0: \beta_1 = 0$$
$$H_a: \beta_1 \neq 0$$

Recall that the $t$ test for a significant relationship required the computation of the $t$ statistic, $t = b_1/s_{b_1}$. For the Armand's data, the value of $t$ that we computed was $t = 5/.5803 = 8.62$. Note that after rounding, the value in cell D30 is 8.62. The label in cell D28, $t$ Stat, reminds us that cell D30 contains the value of the $t$ test statistic.

**$t$ Test**   The information in cell E30 provides a means for conducting a test of significance. The value in cell E30 is the $p$-value associated with the $t$ test for significance. Excel has displayed the $p$-value using scientific notation. To obtain the decimal equivalent, we move the decimal point 5 places to the left; we obtain a $p$-value of .0000255. Thus, the $p$-value associated with the $t$ test for significance is .0000255. Given the level of significance $\alpha$, the decision of whether to reject $H_0$ can be made as follows:

$$\text{Reject } H_0 \text{ if } p\text{-value} \leq \alpha$$

Suppose the level of significance is $\alpha = .01$. Because the $p$-value $= .0000255 < \alpha = .01$, we can reject $H_0$ and conclude that we have a significant relationship between student population and sales. Because $p$-values are provided as part of the computer output for regression analysis, the $p$-value approach is most often used for hypothesis tests in regression analysis.

The information in cells F28:I30 can be used to develop confidence interval estimates of the $y$-intercept and slope of the estimated regression equation. Excel always provides the lower and upper limits for a 95% confidence interval. Recall that in the Regression dialog box (see Figure 12.12) we selected Confidence Level and entered 99 in the Confidence Level box. As a result, Excel's Regression tool also provides the lower and upper limits for a 99% confidence interval. For instance, the value in cell H30 is the lower limit for the 99% confidence interval estimate of $\beta_1$ and the value in cell I30 is the upper limit. Thus, after rounding, the 99% confidence interval estimate of $\beta_1$ is 3.05 to 6.95. The values in cells F30 and G30 provide the lower and upper limits for the 95% confidence interval. Thus, the 95% confidence interval is 3.66 to 6.34.

## Interpretation of ANOVA Output

The information in cells A22:F26 summarizes the analysis of variance computations for the Armand's data. The three sources of variation are labeled Regression, Residual, and Total. The label *df* in cell B23 stands for degrees of freedom, the label *SS* in cell C23 stands for sum of squares, and the label *MS* in cell D23 stands for mean square. Looking at cells C24:C26, we see that the regression sum of squares is 14200, the residual or error sum

*Excel refers to the error sum of squares as the residual sum of squares.*

of squares is 1530, and the total sum of squares is 15730. The values in cells B24:B26 are the degrees of freedom corresponding to each sum of squares. Thus, the regression sum of squares has 1 degree of freedom, the residual or error sum of squares has 8 degrees of freedom, and the total sum of squares has 9 degrees of freedom. As we discussed previously, the regression degrees of freedom plus the residual degrees of freedom are equal to the total degrees of freedom, and the regression sum of squares plus the residual sum of squares are equal to the total sum of squares.

In Section 12.5 we stated that the mean square error, obtained by dividing the error or residual sum of squares by its degrees of freedom, provides an estimate of $\sigma^2$. The value in cell D25, 191.25, is the mean square error for the Armand's regression output. We also stated that the mean square regression is the sum of squares due to regression divided by the regression degrees of freedom. The value in cell D24, 14200, is the mean square regression.

*F* **Test**    In Section 12.5 we showed that an $F$ test, based upon the $F$ probability distribution, could also be used to test for significance in regression. The value in cell F24, .0000255, is the $p$-value associated with the $F$ test for significance. Suppose the level of significance is $\alpha = .01$. Because the $p$-value = .0000255 < $\alpha$ = .01, we can reject $H_0$ and conclude that we have a significant relationship between student population and sales. Note that it is the same conclusion that we obtained using the $p$-value approach for the $t$ test for significance. In fact, because the $t$ test for significance is equivalent to the $F$ test for significance in simple linear regression, the $p$-values provided by both approaches are identical. The label Excel uses to identify the $p$-value for the $F$ test for significance, shown in cell F23, is *Significance F*. In Chapter 9 we also stated that the $p$-value is often referred to as the observed level of significance. Thus, the label *Significance F* may be more meaningful if you think of the value in cell F24 as the observed level of significance for the $F$ test.

## Interpretation of Regression Statistics Output

The output in cells A15:B20 summarizes the regression statistics. The number of observations in the data set, 10, is shown in cell B20. The coefficient of determination, .9027, appears in cell B17; the corresponding label, R Square, is shown in cell A17. The square root of the coefficient of determination provides the sample correlation coefficient of 0.9501 shown in cell B16. Note that Excel uses the label Multiple R (cell A16) to identify this value. In cell A19, the label Standard Error is used to identify the value of $s$, the estimate of $\sigma$. Cell B19 shows that the value of $s$ is 13.8293. We caution the reader to keep in mind that in the Excel output, the label Standard Error appears in two different places. In the Regression Statistics section of the output the label Standard Error refers to $s$, the estimate of $\sigma$. In the Estimated Regression Equation section of the output, the label Standard Error refers to $s_{b_1}$, the estimated standard deviation of the sampling distribution of $b_1$.

## Using StatTools to Compute Prediction Intervals

*In the chapter appendix we show how to use StatTools to compute prediction intervals.*

In Section 12.6 we showed how to estimate quarterly sales for an individual Armand's restaurant located near Talbot College, a school with 10,000 students. With $x = 10$, the 95% prediction interval is $76,125 to $143,875. Hand computation of such intervals is not practical. Unfortunately, Excel's Regression Tool does not have an option for computing prediction intervals. However, StatTools can be used to compute prediction intervals. To illustrate, suppose we would like to compute prediction intervals corresponding to three particular Armand's restaurants: the proposed restaurant located near Talbot College, a

**FIGURE 12.14**   USING STATTOOLS TO COMPUTE PREDICTION INTERVALS

| | A | B | C | D | E | F | G | H | I |
|---|---|---|---|---|---|---|---|---|---|
| 1 | **Restaurant** | **Population** | **Sales** | | **Population** | **Sales** | **LowerLimit95** | **UpperLimit95** | |
| 2 | 1 | 2 | 58 | | 10 | 110 | 76.127 | 143.873 | |
| 3 | 2 | 6 | 105 | | 14 | 130 | 96.553 | 163.447 | |
| 4 | 3 | 8 | 88 | | 18 | 150 | 116.127 | 183.873 | |
| 5 | 4 | 8 | 118 | | | | | | |
| 6 | 5 | 12 | 117 | | | | | | |
| 7 | 6 | 16 | 137 | | | | | | |
| 8 | 7 | 20 | 157 | | | | | | |
| 9 | 8 | 20 | 169 | | | | | | |
| 10 | 9 | 22 | 149 | | | | | | |
| 11 | 10 | 26 | 202 | | | | | | |
| 12 | | | | | | | | | |

school with 10,000 students; another Armand's restaurant located near a school with 14,000 students; and a third Armand's restaurant located near a school with 18,000 students. The chapter appendix describes how StatTools can be used to compute prediction intervals for these three cases; the results are shown in Figure 12.14.

Refer to Figure 12.14. The usual Armand's data appears in cells A1:C11 of the worksheet. In addition, we also entered the label Population in cell E1 and the values of Population for the three Armand's restaurants for which we want to compute prediction intervals in cells E2:E4. The StatTools prediction interval output appears in cells F1:H4. The predicted values of Sales corresponding to the three values of Population are shown in cells F2:F4 in the worksheet, and the lower and upper limits for the three prediction intervals are shown in cells G2:H4. For instance, the value in cell F2 shows that the predicted value of sales for the Armand's restaurant located near Talbot college, a school with 10,000 students, is 110 or $110,000. The value in cell G2 shows that the lower limit for the 95% prediction interval for this Armand's restaurant is 76.127 or $76,127. And the value in cell H2 shows that the upper limit is 143.873 or $143,875. The slight differences between these limits and the limits shown previously using hand calculation are due to rounding. Note that for the Armand's restaurant located near a school with 14,000 students, the 95% prediction interval is $96,553 to $163,447. And, for the Armand's restaurant located near a school with 18,000 students, the 95% prediction interval is $116,127 to $183,873.

## Exercises

### Applications

40.   The commercial division of a real estate firm conducted a study to determine the extent of the relationship between annual gross rents ($1000s) and the selling price ($1000s) for apartment buildings. Data were collected on several properties sold, and Excel's Regression tool was used to develop an estimated regression equation. A portion of the regression output follows.

**ANOVA**

|  | df | SS | MS | F |
|---|---|---|---|---|
| Regression | 1 | 41587.3 |  |  |
| Residual | 7 |  |  |  |
| Total | 8 | 51984.1 |  |  |

|  | Coefficients | Standard Error | t Stat |
|---|---|---|---|
| Intercept | 20.000 | 3.2213 | 6.21 |
| Annual Gross Rents | 7.210 | 1.3626 | 5.29 |

a. How many apartment buildings were in the sample?
b. Write the estimated regression equation.
c. Use the $t$ test to determine whether the selling price is related to annual gross rents. Use $\alpha = .05$.
d. Use the $F$ test to determine whether the selling price is related to annual gross rents. Use $\alpha = .05$.
e. Predict the selling price of an apartment building with gross annual rents of $50,000.

41. Following is a portion of the regression output for an application relating maintenance expense (dollars per month) to usage (hours per week) for a particular brand of computer terminal.

**ANOVA**

|  | df | SS |
|---|---|---|
| Regression | 1 | 1575.76 |
| Residual | 8 | 349.14 |
| Total | 9 | 1924.90 |

|  | Coefficients | Standard Error | t Stat |
|---|---|---|---|
| Intercept | 6.1092 | .9361 |  |
| Usage | 0.8951 | .149 |  |

a. Write the estimated regression equation.
b. Use a $t$ test to determine whether monthly maintenance expense is related to usage at the .05 level of significance.
c. Did the estimated regression equation provide a good fit? Explain.

42. A regression model relating the number of salespersons at a branch office to annual sales at the office (in thousands of dollars) provided the following regression output.

**ANOVA**

|  | df | SS | MS | F |
|---|---|---|---|---|
| Regression |  | 6828.6 |  |  |
| Residual |  |  |  |  |
| Total |  | 9127.4 |  |  |

|  | Coefficients | Standard Error | t Stat | P-value |
|---|---|---|---|---|
| Intercept | 80.0 | 11.333 |  |  |
| Number of Salespersons | 50.0 | 5.482 |  |  |

a. Write the estimated regression equation.
b. Compute the $F$ statistic and test the significance of the relationship at the .05 level of significance.

    c. Compute the *t* statistic and test the significance of the relationship at the .05 level of significance.

    d. Predict the annual sales at the Memphis branch office. This branch employs 12 salespersons.

43. Out-of-state tuition and fees at the top graduate schools of business can be very expensive, but the starting salary and bonus paid to graduates from many of these schools can be substantial. The following data show the out-of-state tuition and fees (rounded to the nearest $1000) and the average starting salary and bonus paid to recent graduates (rounded to the nearest $1000) for a sample of 20 graduate schools of business (*U.S. News & World Report 2009 Edition America's Best Graduate Schools*).

**BusinessSchools**

| School | Tuition & Fees ($1000s) | Salary & Bonus ($1000s) |
|---|---|---|
| Arizona State University | 28 | 98 |
| Babson College | 35 | 94 |
| Cornell University | 44 | 119 |
| Georgetown University | 40 | 109 |
| Georgia Institute of Technology | 30 | 88 |
| Indiana University–Bloomington | 35 | 105 |
| Michigan State University | 26 | 99 |
| Northwestern University | 44 | 123 |
| Ohio State University | 35 | 97 |
| Purdue University–West Lafayette | 33 | 96 |
| Rice University | 36 | 102 |
| Stanford University | 46 | 135 |
| University of California–Davis | 35 | 89 |
| University of Florida | 23 | 71 |
| University of Iowa | 25 | 78 |
| University of Minnesota–Twin Cities | 37 | 100 |
| University of Notre Dame | 36 | 95 |
| University of Rochester | 38 | 99 |
| University of Washington | 30 | 94 |
| University of Wisconsin–Madison | 27 | 93 |

    a. Develop a scatter diagram with salary and bonus as the dependent variable.

    b. Does there appear to be any relationship between these variables? Explain.

    c. Develop an estimated regression equation that can be used to predict the starting salary and bonus paid to graduates given the cost of out-of-state tuition and fees at the school.

    d. Test for a significant relationship at the .05 level of significance. What is your conclusion?

    e. Did the estimated regression equation provide a good fit? Explain.

    f. Suppose that we randomly select a recent graduate of the University of Virginia graduate school of business. The school has an out-of-state tuition and fees of $43,000. Predict the starting salary and bonus for this graduate.

44. Automobile racing, high-performance driving schools, and driver education programs run by automobile clubs continue to grow in popularity. All these activities require the participant to wear a helmet that is certified by the Snell Memorial Foundation, a not-for-profit organization dedicated to research, education, testing, and development of helmet safety standards. Snell "SA" (Sports Application) rated professional helmets are designed for auto racing and provide extreme impact resistance and high fire protection. One of the key factors in selecting a helmet is weight, since lower weight helmets tend to place less stress on the neck. The following data show the weight and price for 18 SA helmets (SoloRacer website, April 20, 2008).

| Helmet | Weight (oz) | Price ($) |
|---|---|---|
| Pyrotect Pro Airflow | 64 | 248 |
| Pyrotect Pro Airflow Graphics | 64 | 278 |
| RCi Full Face | 64 | 200 |
| RaceQuip RidgeLine | 64 | 200 |
| HJC AR-10 | 58 | 300 |
| HJC Si-12 | 47 | 700 |
| HJC HX-10 | 49 | 900 |
| Impact Racing Super Sport | 59 | 340 |
| Zamp FSA-1 | 66 | 199 |
| Zamp RZ-2 | 58 | 299 |
| Zamp RZ-2 Ferrari | 58 | 299 |
| Zamp RZ-3 Sport | 52 | 479 |
| Zamp RZ-3 Sport Painted | 52 | 479 |
| Bell M2 | 63 | 369 |
| Bell M4 | 62 | 369 |
| Bell M4 Pro | 54 | 559 |
| G Force Pro Force 1 | 63 | 250 |
| G Force Pro Force 1 Grafx | 63 | 280 |

**WEB** file

**RaceHelmets**

a. Develop a scatter diagram with weight as the independent variable.
b. Does there appear to be any relationship between these two variables?
c. Develop the estimated regression equation that could be used to predict the price given the weight.
d. Test for the significance of the relationship at the .05 level of significance.
e. Did the estimated regression equation provide a good fit? Explain.

## 12.8 Residual Analysis: Validating Model Assumptions

*Residual analysis is the primary tool for determining whether the assumed regression model is appropriate.*

As we noted previously, the *residual* for observation $i$ is the difference between the observed value of the dependent variable ($y_i$) and the estimated value of the dependent variable ($\hat{y}_i$).

---

**RESIDUAL FOR OBSERVATION $i$**

$$y_i - \hat{y}_i \tag{12.28}$$

where

$y_i$ is the observed value of the dependent variable
$\hat{y}_i$ is the predicted value of the dependent variable

---

In other words, the $i$th residual is the error resulting from using the estimated regression equation to predict the value of the dependent variable. The residuals for the Armand's Pizza Parlors example are computed in Table 12.7. The observed values of the dependent variable are in the second column and the estimated values of the dependent variable, obtained using the estimated regression equation $\hat{y} = 60 + 5x$, are in the third column. An

**TABLE 12.7    RESIDUALS FOR ARMAND'S PIZZA PARLORS**

| Student Population $x_i$ | Sales $y_i$ | Predicted Sales $\hat{y}_i = 60 + 5x_i$ | Residuals $y_i - \hat{y}_i$ |
|:---:|:---:|:---:|:---:|
| 2 | 58 | 70 | −12 |
| 6 | 105 | 90 | 15 |
| 8 | 88 | 100 | −12 |
| 8 | 118 | 100 | 18 |
| 12 | 117 | 120 | −3 |
| 16 | 137 | 140 | −3 |
| 20 | 157 | 160 | −3 |
| 20 | 169 | 160 | 9 |
| 22 | 149 | 170 | −21 |
| 26 | 202 | 190 | 12 |

analysis of the corresponding residuals in the fourth column will help determine whether the assumptions made about the regression model are appropriate.

Let us now review the regression assumptions for the Armand's Pizza Parlors example. A simple linear regression model was assumed.

$$y = \beta_0 + \beta_1 x + \epsilon \qquad \textbf{(12.29)}$$

This model indicates that we assumed quarterly sales ($y$) to be a linear function of the size of the student population ($x$) plus an error term $\epsilon$. In Section 12.4 we made the following assumptions about the error term $\epsilon$.

1. $E(\epsilon) = 0$.
2. The variance of $\epsilon$, denoted by $\sigma^2$, is the same for all values of $x$.
3. The values of $\epsilon$ are independent.
4. The error term $\epsilon$ has a normal distribution.

These assumptions provide the theoretical basis for the $t$ test and the $F$ test used to determine whether the relationship between $x$ and $y$ is significant, and for the confidence and prediction interval estimates presented in Section 12.6. If the assumptions about the error term $\epsilon$ appear questionable, the hypothesis tests about the significance of the regression relationship and the interval estimation results may not be valid.

The residuals provide the best information about $\epsilon$; hence an analysis of the residuals is an important step in determining whether the assumptions for $\epsilon$ are appropriate. Much of residual analysis is based on an examination of graphical plots. In this section, we discuss the following residual plots: a plot of the residuals against values of the independent variable $x$, and a plot of residuals against the predicted values of the dependent variable $\hat{y}$.

## Residual Plot Against $x$

A **residual plot** against the independent variable $x$ is a graph in which the values of the independent variable are represented by the horizontal axis and the corresponding residual values are represented by the vertical axis. A point is plotted for each residual. The first coordinate for each point is given by the value of $x_i$ and the second coordinate is given by the corresponding value of the residual $y_i - \hat{y}_i$. For a residual plot against $x$ with the Armand's Pizza Parlors data from Table 12.7, the coordinates of the first point are $(2, -12)$, corresponding to

**FIGURE 12.15**    PLOT OF THE RESIDUALS AGAINST THE INDEPENDENT VARIABLE $x$
FOR ARMAND'S PIZZA PARLORS

$x_1 = 2$ and $y_1 - \hat{y}_1 = -12$; the coordinates of the second point are (6, 15), corresponding
to $x_2 = 6$ and $y_2 - \hat{y}_2 = 15$; and so on. Figure 12.15 shows the resulting residual plot.

Before interpreting the results for this residual plot, let us consider some general patterns that might be observed in any residual plot. Three examples appear in Figure 12.16.
If the assumption that the variance of $\epsilon$ is the same for all values of $x$ and the assumed regression model is an adequate representation of the relationship between the variables, the
residual plot should give an overall impression of a horizontal band of points such as the
one in Panel A of Figure 12.16. However, if the variance of $\epsilon$ is not the same for all values
of $x$—for example, if variability about the regression line is greater for larger values of $x$—
a pattern such as the one in Panel B of Figure 12.16 could be observed. In this case, the
assumption of a constant variance of $\epsilon$ is violated. Another possible residual plot is shown
in Panel C. In this case, we would conclude that the assumed regression model is not an
adequate representation of the relationship between the variables. A curvilinear regression
model or multiple regression model should be considered.

Now let us return to the residual plot for Armand's Pizza Parlors shown in Figure 12.15.
The residuals appear to approximate the horizontal pattern in Panel A of Figure 12.16.
Hence, we conclude that the residual plot does not provide evidence that the assumptions
made for Armand's regression model should be challenged. At this point, we are confident
in the conclusion that Armand's simple linear regression model is valid.

Experience and good judgment are always factors in the effective interpretation of
residual plots. Seldom does a residual plot conform precisely to one of the patterns in Figure 12.16. Yet analysts who frequently conduct regression studies and frequently review
residual plots become adept at understanding the differences between patterns that are reasonable and patterns that indicate the assumptions of the model should be questioned. A
residual plot provides one technique to assess the validity of the assumptions for a regression model.

**FIGURE 12.16**   RESIDUAL PLOTS FROM THREE REGRESSION STUDIES

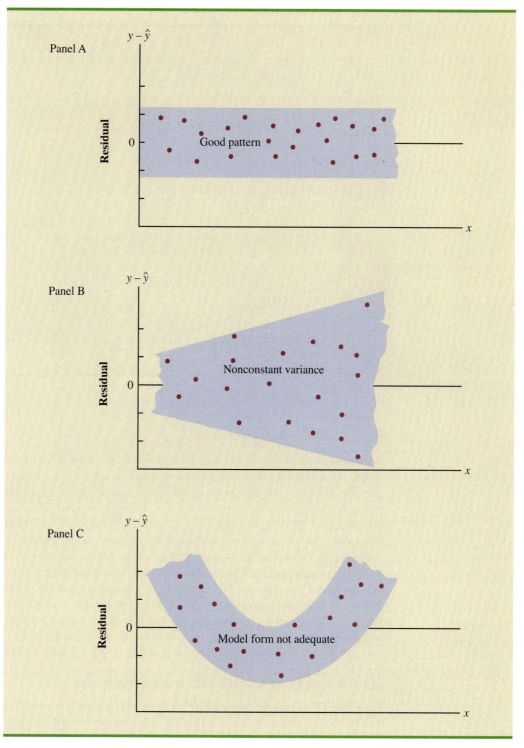

**FIGURE 12.17**   PLOT OF THE RESIDUALS AGAINST THE PREDICTED VALUES $\hat{y}$ FOR ARMAND'S PIZZA PARLORS

## Residual Plot Against $\hat{y}$

Another residual plot represents the predicted value of the dependent variable $\hat{y}$ on the horizontal axis and the residual values on the vertical axis. A point is plotted for each residual. The first coordinate for each point is given by $\hat{y}_i$ and the second coordinate is given by the corresponding value of the $i$th residual $y_i - \hat{y}_i$. With the Armand's data from Table 12.7, the coordinates of the first point are (70, $-12$), corresponding to $\hat{y}_1 = 70$ and $y_1 - \hat{y}_1 = -12$; the coordinates of the second point are (90, 15); and so on. Figure 12.17 provides the residual plot. Note that the pattern of this residual plot is the same as the pattern of the residual plot against the independent variable $x$. It is not a pattern that would lead us to question the model assumptions. For simple linear regression, both the residual plot against $x$ and the residual plot against $\hat{y}$ provide the same pattern. For multiple regression analysis, the residual plot against $\hat{y}$ is more widely used because of the presence of more than one independent variable.

## Using Excel to Construct a Residual Plot

In Section 12.7 we showed how Excel's Regression tool could be used for regression analysis. The Regression tool also provides the capability to obtain a residual plot against the independent variable $x$ and, when used with Excel's Chart tool, the Regression tool residual output can also be used to construct a residual plot against $\hat{y}$.

**Residual plot against $x$**   To obtain a residual plot against $x$, the steps that we describe in Section 12.7 in order to obtain the regression output are performed with one change. When the Regression tool dialog box appears (see Figure 12.12), we must also select the Residual

**FIGURE 12.18**   REGRESSION TOOL RESIDUAL OUTPUT FOR THE ARMAND'S PIZZA PARLORS PROBLEM

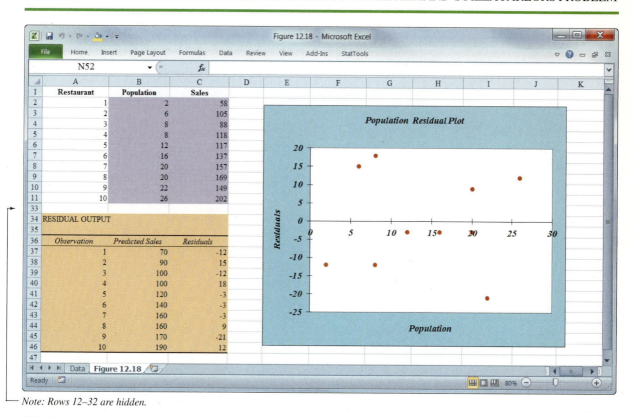

*Note: Rows 12–32 are hidden.*

Plots option in the Residual section. The regression output will appear as described previously, and the worksheet will also contain a chart showing a plot of the residuals against the independent variable Population. In addition, a list of predicted values of $y$ and the corresponding residual values are provided below the regression output. Figure 12.18 shows the residual output for the Armand's Pizza Parlors problem; note that rows 12–32, containing the standard Regression tool output, have been hidden to better focus on the residual portion of the output. We see that the shape of this plot is the same as shown previously in Figure 12.15.

**Residual plot against $\hat{y}$**   Using Excel's chart tools and the residual output provided in Figure 12.18, we can easily construct a residual plot against $\hat{y}$. The following steps describe how to use Excel's chart tools to construct the residual plot using the regression tool output in the worksheet.

**Step 1.** Select cells B37:C46
**Step 2.** Click the **Insert** tab on the Ribbon
**Step 3.** In the **Chart** group, click **Scatter**
**Step 4.** When the list of scatter diagram subtypes appears,
        Click **Scatter with only Markers** (the chart in the upper left corner)

The resulting chart will look similar to the residual plot shown in Figure 12.17. Adding a chart title, labels for the horizontal and vertical axes, as well as other formatting options can be easily done. Note that except for using different data to construct the chart as well as different labels for the chart output, the steps describing how to use Excel's chart tools to construct a residual plot against $\hat{y}$ are the same as the steps we used to construct a scatter diagram in Section 12.2.

## Exercises

## Methods

45. Given are data for two variables, $x$ and $y$.

| $x_i$ | 6 | 11 | 15 | 18 | 20 |
|-------|---|----|----|----|----|
| $y_i$ | 6 | 8 | 12 | 20 | 30 |

   a. Develop an estimated regression equation for these data.
   b. Compute the residuals.
   c. Develop a plot of the residuals against the independent variable $x$. Do the assumptions about the error term seem to be satisfied?

46. The following data were used in a regression study.

| Observation | $x_i$ | $y_i$ | Observation | $x_i$ | $y_i$ |
|-------------|-------|-------|-------------|-------|-------|
| 1 | 2 | 4 | 6 | 7 | 6 |
| 2 | 3 | 5 | 7 | 7 | 9 |
| 3 | 4 | 4 | 8 | 8 | 5 |
| 4 | 5 | 6 | 9 | 9 | 11 |
| 5 | 7 | 4 | | | |

   a. Develop an estimated regression equation for these data.
   b. Construct a plot of the residuals. Do the assumptions about the error term seem to be satisfied?

## Applications

47. Data on advertising expenditures and revenue (in thousands of dollars) for the Four Seasons Restaurant follow.

| Advertising Expenditures | Revenue |
|--------------------------|---------|
| 1 | 19 |
| 2 | 32 |
| 4 | 44 |
| 6 | 40 |
| 10 | 52 |
| 14 | 53 |
| 20 | 54 |

   a. Let $x$ equal advertising expenditures and $y$ equal revenue. Use the method of least squares to develop a straight line approximation of the relationship between the two variables.
   b. Test whether revenue and advertising expenditures are related at a .05 level of significance.

c. Prepare a residual plot of $y - \hat{y}$ versus $\hat{y}$. Use the result from part (a) to obtain the values of $\hat{y}$.

d. What conclusions can you draw from residual analysis? Should this model be used, or should we look for a better one?

48. Refer to exercise 9, where an estimated regression equation relating years of experience and annual sales was developed.

a. Compute the residuals and construct a residual plot for this problem.

b. Do the assumptions about the error terms seem reasonable in light of the residual plot?

49. Recent family home sales in San Antonio provided the following data (San Antonio Realty Watch website, November 2008).

**WEB** file

**HomePrices**

| Square Footage | Price ($) |
|---|---|
| 1580 | 142,500 |
| 1572 | 145,000 |
| 1352 | 115,000 |
| 2224 | 155,900 |
| 1556 | 95,000 |
| 1435 | 128,000 |
| 1438 | 100,000 |
| 1089 | 55,000 |
| 1941 | 142,000 |
| 1698 | 115,000 |
| 1539 | 115,000 |
| 1364 | 105,000 |
| 1979 | 155,000 |
| 2183 | 132,000 |
| 2096 | 140,000 |
| 1400 | 85,000 |
| 2372 | 145,000 |
| 1752 | 155,000 |
| 1386 | 80,000 |
| 1163 | 100,000 |

a. Develop the estimated regression equation that can be used to predict the sales prices given the square footage.

b. Construct a residual plot against the independent variable.

c. Do the assumptions about the error term and model form seem reasonable in light of the residual plot?

## Summary

In this chapter we showed how regression analysis can be used to determine how a dependent variable $y$ is related to an independent variable $x$. In simple linear regression, the regression model is $y = \beta_0 + \beta_1 x + \epsilon$. The simple linear regression equation $E(y) = \beta_0 + \beta_1 x$ describes how the mean or expected value of $y$ is related to $x$. We used sample data and the least squares method to develop the estimated regression equation $\hat{y} = b_0 + b_1 x$. In effect, $b_0$ and $b_1$ are the sample statistics used to estimate the unknown model parameters $\beta_0$ and $\beta_1$.

The coefficient of determination was presented as a measure of the goodness of fit for the estimated regression equation; it can be interpreted as the proportion of the variation in the dependent variable $y$ that can be explained by the estimated regression equation. We reviewed correlation as a descriptive measure of the strength of a linear relationship between two variables.

The assumptions about the regression model and its associated error term $\epsilon$ were discussed, and $t$ and $F$ tests, based on those assumptions, were presented as a means for determining whether the relationship between two variables is statistically significant. We showed how to use the estimated regression equation to develop confidence interval estimates of the mean value of $y$ and prediction interval estimates of individual values of $y$.

The chapter concluded with a section on the computer solution of regression problems and a section on the use of residual analysis to validate the model assumptions.

## Glossary

**Dependent variable** The variable that is being predicted or explained. It is denoted by $y$.

**Independent variable** The variable that is doing the predicting or explaining. It is denoted by $x$.

**Simple linear regression** Regression analysis involving one independent variable and one dependent variable in which the relationship between the variables is approximated by a straight line.

**Regression model** The equation that describes how $y$ is related to $x$ and an error term; in simple linear regression, the regression model is $y = \beta_0 + \beta_1 x + \epsilon$.

**Regression equation** The equation that describes how the mean or expected value of the dependent variable is related to the independent variable; in simple linear regression, $E(y) = \beta_0 + \beta_1 x$.

**Estimated regression equation** The estimate of the regression equation developed from sample data by using the least squares method. For simple linear regression, the estimated regression equation is $\hat{y} = b_0 + b_1 x$.

**Least squares method** A procedure used to develop the estimated regression equation. The objective is to minimize $\Sigma(y_i - \hat{y}_i)^2$.

**Scatter diagram** A graph of bivariate data in which the independent variable is on the horizontal axis and the dependent variable is on the vertical axis.

**Coefficient of determination** A measure of the goodness of fit of the estimated regression equation. It can be interpreted as the proportion of the variability in the dependent variable $y$ that is explained by the estimated regression equation.

**$i$th residual** The difference between the observed value of the dependent variable and the value predicted using the estimated regression equation; for the $i$th observation the $i$th residual is $y_i - \hat{y}_i$.

**Correlation coefficient** A measure of the strength of the linear relationship between two variables (previously discussed in Chapter 3).

**Mean square error** The unbiased estimate of the variance of the error term $\sigma^2$. It is denoted by MSE or $s^2$.

**Standard error of the estimate** The square root of the mean square error, denoted by $s$. It is the estimate of $\sigma$, the standard deviation of the error term $\epsilon$.

**ANOVA table** The analysis of variance table used to summarize the computations associated with the $F$ test for significance.

**Confidence interval** The interval estimate of the mean value of $y$ for a given value of $x$.

**Prediction interval** The interval estimate of an individual value of $y$ for a given value of $x$.

**Residual analysis** The analysis of the residuals used to determine whether the assumptions made about the regression model appear to be valid. Residual analysis is also used to identify outliers and influential observations.

**Residual plot** Graphical representation of the residuals that can be used to determine whether the assumptions made about the regression model appear to be valid.

## Key Formulas

**Simple Linear Regression Model**

$$y = \beta_0 + \beta_1 x + \epsilon \tag{12.1}$$

**Simple Linear Regression Equation**

$$E(y) = \beta_0 + \beta_1 x \tag{12.2}$$

**Estimated Simple Linear Regression Equation**

$$\hat{y} = b_0 + b_1 x \tag{12.3}$$

**Least Squares Criterion**

$$\min \Sigma(y_i - \hat{y}_i)^2 \tag{12.5}$$

**Slope and *y*-Intercept for the Estimated Regression Equation**

$$b_1 = \frac{\Sigma(x_i - \bar{x})(y_i - \bar{y})}{\Sigma(x_i - \bar{x})^2} \tag{12.6}$$

$$b_0 = \bar{y} - b_1\bar{x} \tag{12.7}$$

**Sum of Squares Due to Error**

$$SSE = \Sigma(y_i - \hat{y}_i)^2 \tag{12.8}$$

**Total Sum of Squares**

$$SST = \Sigma(y_i - \bar{y})^2 \tag{12.9}$$

**Sum of Squares Due to Regression**

$$SSR = \Sigma(\hat{y}_i - \bar{y})^2 \tag{12.10}$$

**Relationship Among SST, SSR, and SSE**

$$SST = SSR + SSE \tag{12.11}$$

**Coefficient of Determination**

$$r^2 = \frac{SSR}{SST} \tag{12.12}$$

**Sample Correlation Coefficient**

$$r_{xy} = (\text{sign of } b_1)\sqrt{\text{Coefficient of determination}}$$
$$= (\text{sign of } b_1)\sqrt{r^2} \tag{12.13}$$

**Mean Square Error (Estimate of $\sigma^2$)**

$$s^2 = MSE = \frac{SSE}{n - 2} \tag{12.15}$$

**Standard Error of the Estimate**

$$s = \sqrt{\text{MSE}} = \sqrt{\frac{\text{SSE}}{n-2}} \qquad \text{(12.16)}$$

**Standard Deviation of $b_1$**

$$\sigma_{b_1} = \frac{\sigma}{\sqrt{\Sigma(x_i - \bar{x})^2}} \qquad \text{(12.17)}$$

**Estimated Standard Deviation of $b_1$**

$$s_{b_1} = \frac{s}{\sqrt{\Sigma(x_i - \bar{x})^2}} \qquad \text{(12.18)}$$

**$t$ Test Statistic**

$$t = \frac{b_1}{s_{b_1}} \qquad \text{(12.19)}$$

**Mean Square Regression**

$$\text{MSR} = \frac{\text{SSR}}{\text{Number of independent variables}} \qquad \text{(12.20)}$$

**$F$ Test Statistic**

$$F = \frac{\text{MSR}}{\text{MSE}} \qquad \text{(12.21)}$$

**Estimated Standard Deviation of $\hat{y}^*$**

$$s_{\hat{y}^*} = s\sqrt{\frac{1}{n} + \frac{(x^* - \bar{x})^2}{\Sigma(x_i - \bar{x})^2}} \qquad \text{(12.23)}$$

**Confidence Interval for $E(y^*)$**

$$\hat{y}^* \pm t_{\alpha/2}s_{\hat{y}^*} \qquad \text{(12.24)}$$

**Estimated Standard Deviation of an Individual Value**

$$s_{\text{pred}} = s\sqrt{1 + \frac{1}{n} + \frac{(x^* - \bar{x})^2}{\Sigma(x_i - \bar{x})^2}} \qquad \text{(12.26)}$$

**Prediction Interval for $y^*$**

$$\hat{y}^* \pm t_{\alpha/2}s_{\text{pred}} \qquad \text{(12.27)}$$

**Residual for Observation $i$**

$$y_i - \hat{y}_i \qquad \text{(12.28)}$$

## Supplementary Exercises

50. The data in the following table show the number of shares selling (millions) and the expected price (average of projected low price and projected high price) for 10 selected initial public stock offerings.

**IPO**

| Company | Shares Selling (millions) | Expected Price ($) |
|---|---|---|
| American Physician | 5.0 | 15 |
| Apex Silver Mines | 9.0 | 14 |
| Dan River | 6.7 | 15 |
| Franchise Mortgage | 8.75 | 17 |
| Gene Logic | 3.0 | 11 |
| International Home Foods | 13.6 | 19 |
| PRT Group | 4.6 | 13 |
| Rayovac | 6.7 | 14 |
| RealNetworks | 3.0 | 10 |
| Software AG Systems | 7.7 | 13 |

a. Develop an estimated regression equation with the number of shares selling as the independent variable and the expected price as the dependent variable.

b. At the .05 level of significance, is there a significant relationship between the two variables?

c. Did the estimated regression equation provide a good fit? Explain.

d. Use the estimated regression equation to predict the expected price for a firm considering an initial public offering of 6 million shares.

51. The following data show Morningstar's Fair Value estimate and the Share Price for 28 companies. Fair Value is an estimate of a company's value per share that takes into account estimates of the company's growth, profitability, riskiness, and other factors over the next five years (*Morningstar Stocks 500*, 2008 edition).

**Stocks500**

| Company | Fair Value ($) | Share Price ($) |
|---|---|---|
| Air Products and Chemicals | 80 | 98.63 |
| Allied Waste Industries | 17 | 11.02 |
| America Mobile | 83 | 61.39 |
| AT&T | 35 | 41.56 |
| Bank of America | 70 | 41.26 |
| Barclays PLC | 68 | 40.37 |
| Citigroup | 53 | 29.44 |
| Costco Wholesale Corp. | 75 | 69.76 |
| Covidien, Ltd. | 58 | 44.29 |
| Darden Restaurants | 52 | 27.71 |
| Dun & Bradstreet | 87 | 88.63 |
| Equifax | 42 | 36.36 |
| Gannett Co. | 38 | 39.00 |
| Genuine Parts | 48 | 46.30 |
| GlaxoSmithKline PLC | 57 | 50.39 |
| Iron Mountain | 33 | 37.02 |
| ITT Corporation | 83 | 66.04 |
| Johnson & Johnson | 80 | 66.70 |
| Las Vegas Sands | 98 | 103.05 |
| Macrovision | 23 | 18.33 |
| Marriott International | 39 | 34.18 |
| Nalco Holding Company | 29 | 24.18 |
| National Interstate | 25 | 33.10 |
| Portugal Telecom | 15 | 13.02 |
| Qualcomm | 48 | 39.35 |
| Royal Dutch Shell Ltd. | 87 | 84.20 |
| SanDisk | 60 | 33.17 |
| Time Warner | 42 | 27.60 |

a. Develop the estimated regression equation that could be used to estimate the Share Price given the Fair Value.
b. At the .05 level of significance, is there a significant relationship between the two variables?
c. Use the estimated regression equation to predict the Share Price for a company that has a Fair Value of $50.
d. Do you believe the estimated regression equation would provide a good prediction of the share price? Use $r^2$ to support your answer.

52. One of the biggest changes in higher education in recent years has been the growth of online universities. The Online Education Database is an independent organization whose mission is to build a comprehensive list of the top accredited online colleges. The following table shows the retention rate (%) and the graduation rate (%) for 29 online colleges (Online Education Database website, January 2009).

**WEB file**

OnlineEdu

| College | Retention Rate (%) | Graduation Rate (%) |
|---|---|---|
| Western International University | 7 | 25 |
| South University | 51 | 25 |
| University of Phoenix | 4 | 28 |
| American InterContinental University | 29 | 32 |
| Franklin University | 33 | 33 |
| Devry University | 47 | 33 |
| Tiffin University | 63 | 34 |
| Post University | 45 | 36 |
| Peirce College | 60 | 36 |
| Everest University | 62 | 36 |
| Upper Iowa University | 67 | 36 |
| Dickinson State University | 65 | 37 |
| Western Governors University | 78 | 37 |
| Kaplan University | 75 | 38 |
| Salem International University | 54 | 39 |
| Ashford University | 45 | 41 |
| ITT Technical Institute | 38 | 44 |
| Berkeley College | 51 | 45 |
| Grand Canyon University | 69 | 46 |
| Nova Southeastern University | 60 | 47 |
| Westwood College | 37 | 48 |
| Everglades University | 63 | 50 |
| Liberty University | 73 | 51 |
| LeTourneau University | 78 | 52 |
| Rasmussen College | 48 | 53 |
| Keiser University | 95 | 55 |
| Herzing College | 68 | 56 |
| National University | 100 | 57 |
| Florida National College | 100 | 61 |

a. Develop a scatter diagram with retention rate as the independent variable. What does the scatter diagram indicate about the relationship between the two variables?
b. Develop the estimated regression equation.
c. Test for a significant relationship. Use $\alpha = .05$.
d. Did the estimated regression equation provide a good fit?
e. Suppose you were the president of South University. After reviewing the results, would you have any concerns about the performance of your university as compared to other online universities?

f.  Suppose you were the president of the University of Phoenix. After reviewing the results, would you have any concerns about the performance of your university as compared to other online universities?

53. Jensen Tire & Auto is in the process of deciding whether to purchase a maintenance contract for its new computer wheel alignment and balancing machine. Managers feel that maintenance expense should be related to usage, and they collected the following information on weekly usage (hours) and annual maintenance expense (in hundreds of dollars).

**WEB file**

Jensen

| Weekly Usage (hours) | Annual Maintenance Expense |
|---|---|
| 13 | 17.0 |
| 10 | 22.0 |
| 20 | 30.0 |
| 28 | 37.0 |
| 32 | 47.0 |
| 17 | 30.5 |
| 24 | 32.5 |
| 31 | 39.0 |
| 40 | 51.5 |
| 38 | 40.0 |

a.  Develop the estimated regression equation that relates annual maintenance expense to weekly usage.
b.  Test the significance of the relationship in part (a) at a .05 level of significance.
c.  Jensen expects to use the new machine 30 hours per week. Develop a 95% prediction interval for the company's annual maintenance expense.
d.  If the maintenance contract costs $3000 per year, would you recommend purchasing it? Why or why not?

54. In a manufacturing process the assembly line speed (feet per minute) was thought to affect the number of defective parts found during the inspection process. To test this theory, managers devised a situation in which the same batch of parts was inspected visually at a variety of line speeds. They collected the following data.

| Line Speed | Number of Defective Parts Found |
|---|---|
| 20 | 21 |
| 20 | 19 |
| 40 | 15 |
| 30 | 16 |
| 60 | 14 |
| 40 | 17 |

a.  Develop the estimated regression equation that relates line speed to the number of defective parts found.
b.  At a .05 level of significance, determine whether line speed and number of defective parts found are related.
c.  Did the estimated regression equation provide a good fit to the data?
d.  Develop a 95% confidence interval to predict the mean number of defective parts for a line speed of 50 feet per minute.

55. A sociologist was hired by a large city hospital to investigate the relationship between the number of unauthorized days that employees are absent per year and the distance (miles) between home and work for the employees. A sample of 10 employees was chosen, and the following data were collected.

**Absent**

| Distance to Work (miles) | Number of Days Absent |
|:---:|:---:|
| 1 | 8 |
| 3 | 5 |
| 4 | 8 |
| 6 | 7 |
| 8 | 6 |
| 10 | 3 |
| 12 | 5 |
| 14 | 2 |
| 14 | 4 |
| 18 | 2 |

   a. Develop a scatter diagram for these data. Does a linear relationship appear reasonable? Explain.

   b. Develop the least squares estimated regression equation.

   c. Is there a significant relationship between the two variables? Use $\alpha = .05$.

   d. Did the estimated regression equation provide a good fit? Explain.

   e. Use the estimated regression equation developed in part (b) to develop a 95% confidence interval for the expected number of days absent for employees living 5 miles from the company.

56. The regional transit authority for a major metropolitan area wants to determine whether there is any relationship between the age of a bus and the annual maintenance cost. A sample of 10 buses resulted in the following data.

**WEB** file

**AgeCost**

| Age of Bus (years) | Maintenance Cost ($) |
|:---:|:---:|
| 1 | 350 |
| 2 | 370 |
| 2 | 480 |
| 2 | 520 |
| 2 | 590 |
| 3 | 550 |
| 4 | 750 |
| 4 | 800 |
| 5 | 790 |
| 5 | 950 |

   a. Develop the least squares estimated regression equation.

   b. Test to see whether the two variables are significantly related with $\alpha = .05$.

   c. Did the least squares line provide a good fit to the observed data? Explain.

   d. Develop a 95% prediction interval for the maintenance cost for a specific bus that is 4 years old.

57. A marketing professor at Givens College is interested in the relationship between hours spent studying and total points earned in a course. Data collected on 10 students who took the course last quarter follow.

| Hours Spent Studying | Total Points Earned |
|---|---|
| 45 | 40 |
| 30 | 35 |
| 90 | 75 |
| 60 | 65 |
| 105 | 90 |
| 65 | 50 |
| 90 | 90 |
| 80 | 80 |
| 55 | 45 |
| 75 | 65 |

HoursPts

a. Develop an estimated regression equation showing how total points earned is related to hours spent studying.
b. Test the significance of the model with $\alpha = .05$.
c. Predict the total points earned by Mark Sweeney. He spent 95 hours studying.
d. Develop a 95% prediction interval for the total points earned by Mark Sweeney.

58. Reuters reported the market beta for Xerox was 1.22 (Reuters website, January 30, 2009). Market betas for individual stocks are determined by simple linear regression. For each stock, the dependent variable is its quarterly percentage return (capital appreciation plus dividends) minus the percentage return that could be obtained from a risk-free investment (the Treasury bill rate is used as the risk-free rate). The independent variable is the quarterly percentage return (capital appreciation plus dividends) for the stock market (S&P 500) minus the percentage return from a risk-free investment. An estimated regression equation is developed with quarterly data; the market beta for the stock is the slope of the estimated regression equation ($b_1$). The value of the market beta is often interpreted as a measure of the risk associated with the stock. Market betas greater than 1 indicate that the stock is more volatile than the market average; market betas less than 1 indicate that the stock is less volatile than the market average. Suppose that the following figures are the differences between the percentage return and the risk-free return for 10 quarters for the S&P 500 and Horizon Technology.

| S&P 500 | Horizon |
|---|---|
| 1.2 | −0.7 |
| −2.5 | −2.0 |
| −3.0 | −5.5 |
| 2.0 | 4.7 |
| 5.0 | 1.8 |
| 1.2 | 4.1 |
| 3.0 | 2.6 |
| −1.0 | 2.0 |
| .5 | −1.3 |
| 2.5 | 5.5 |

MktBeta

a. Develop an estimated regression equation that can be used to determine the market beta for Horizon Technology. What is Horizon Technology's market beta?
b. Test for a significant relationship at the .05 level of significance.
c. Did the estimated regression equation provide a good fit? Explain.
d. Use the market betas of Xerox and Horizon Technology to compare the risk associated with the two stocks.

59. The Transactional Records Access Clearinghouse at Syracuse University reported data showing the odds of an Internal Revenue Service audit. The following table shows the average adjusted gross income reported and the percent of the returns that were audited for 20 selected IRS districts.

**IRSAudit**

| District | Adjusted Gross Income ($) | Percent Audited |
|---|---|---|
| Los Angeles | 36,664 | 1.3 |
| Sacramento | 38,845 | 1.1 |
| Atlanta | 34,886 | 1.1 |
| Boise | 32,512 | 1.1 |
| Dallas | 34,531 | 1.0 |
| Providence | 35,995 | 1.0 |
| San Jose | 37,799 | 0.9 |
| Cheyenne | 33,876 | 0.9 |
| Fargo | 30,513 | 0.9 |
| New Orleans | 30,174 | 0.9 |
| Oklahoma City | 30,060 | 0.8 |
| Houston | 37,153 | 0.8 |
| Portland | 34,918 | 0.7 |
| Phoenix | 33,291 | 0.7 |
| Augusta | 31,504 | 0.7 |
| Albuquerque | 29,199 | 0.6 |
| Greensboro | 33,072 | 0.6 |
| Columbia | 30,859 | 0.5 |
| Nashville | 32,566 | 0.5 |
| Buffalo | 34,296 | 0.5 |

a. Develop the estimated regression equation that could be used to predict the percent audited given the average adjusted gross income reported.
b. At the .05 level of significance, determine whether the adjusted gross income and the percent audited are related.
c. Did the estimated regression equation provide a good fit? Explain.
d. Use the estimated regression equation developed in part (a) to calculate a 95% confidence interval for the expected percent audited for districts with an average adjusted gross income of $35,000.

60. The Australian Public Service Commission's State of the Service Report 2002–2003 reported job satisfaction ratings for employees. One of the survey questions asked employees to choose the five most important workplace factors (from a list of factors) that most affected how satisfied they were with their job. Respondents were then asked to indicate their level of satisfaction with their top five factors. The following data show the percentage of employees who nominated the factor in their top five, and a corresponding satisfaction rating measured using the percentage of employees who nominated the factor in the top five and who were "very satisfied" or "satisfied" with the factor in their current workplace (*www.apsc.gov.au/stateoftheservice*).

**JobSat**

| Workplace Factor | Top Five (%) | Satisfaction Rating (%) |
|---|---|---|
| Appropriate workload | 30 | 49 |
| Chance to be creative/innovative | 38 | 64 |
| Chance to make a useful contribution to society | 40 | 67 |
| Duties/expectations made clear | 40 | 69 |
| Flexible working arrangements | 55 | 86 |
| Good working relationships | 60 | 85 |
| Interesting work provided | 48 | 74 |

| Workplace Factor | Top Five (%) | Satisfaction Rating (%) |
|---|---|---|
| Opportunities for career development | 33 | 43 |
| Opportunities to develop my skills | 46 | 66 |
| Opportunities to utilize my skills | 50 | 70 |
| Regular feedback/recognition for effort | 42 | 53 |
| Salary | 47 | 62 |
| Seeing tangible results from my work | 42 | 69 |

  a.  Develop a scatter diagram with Top Five (%) on the horizontal axis and Satisfaction Rating (%) on the vertical axis.
  b.  What does the scatter diagram developed in part (a) indicate about the relationship between the two variables?
  c.  Develop the estimated regression equation that could be used to predict the Satisfaction Rating (%) given the Top Five (%).
  d.  Test for a significant relationship at the .05 level of significance.
  e.  Did the estimated regression equation provide a good fit? Explain.
  f.  What is the value of the sample correlation coefficient?

## Case Problem 1   Measuring Stock Market Risk

One measure of the risk or volatility of an individual stock is the standard deviation of the total return (capital appreciation plus dividends) over several periods of time. Although the standard deviation is easy to compute, it does not take into account the extent to which the price of a given stock varies as a function of a standard market index, such as the S&P 500. As a result, many financial analysts prefer to use another measure of risk referred to as *beta*.

Betas for individual stocks are determined by simple linear regression. The dependent variable is the total return for the stock and the independent variable is the total return for the stock market.* For this case problem we will use the S&P 500 index as the measure of the total return for the stock market, and an estimated regression equation will be developed using monthly data. The beta for the stock is the slope of the estimated regression equation ($b_1$). The data contained in the file named Beta provides the total return (capital appreciation plus dividends) over 36 months for eight widely traded common stocks and the S&P 500.

**Beta**

The value of beta for the stock market will always be 1; thus, stocks that tend to rise and fall with the stock market will also have a beta close to 1. Betas greater than 1 indicate that the stock is more volatile than the market, and betas less than 1 indicate that the stock is less volatile than the market. For instance, if a stock has a beta of 1.4, it is 40% *more* volatile than the market, and if a stock has a beta of .4, it is 60% *less* volatile than the market.

### Managerial Report

You have been assigned to analyze the risk characteristics of these stocks. Prepare a report that includes but is not limited to the following items.

  a.  Compute descriptive statistics for each stock and the S&P 500. Comment on your results. Which stocks are the most volatile?
  b.  Compute the value of beta for each stock. Which of these stocks would you expect to perform best in an up market? Which would you expect to hold their value best in a down market?
  c.  Comment on how much of the return for the individual stocks is explained by the market.

---

*Various sources use different approaches for computing betas. For instance, some sources subtract the return that could be obtained from a risk-free investment (e.g., T-bills) from the dependent variable and the independent variable before computing the estimated regression equation. Some also use different indexes for the total return of the stock market; for instance, *Value Line* computes betas using the New York Stock Exchange composite index.

**Case Problem 2**    # U.S. Department of Transportation

As part of a study on transportation safety, the U.S. Department of Transportation collected data on the number of fatal accidents per 1000 licenses and the percentage of licensed drivers under the age of 21 in a sample of 42 cities. Data collected over a one-year period follow. These data are contained in the file named Safety.

**WEB** file

Safety

| Percent Under 21 | Fatal Accidents per 1000 Licenses | Percent Under 21 | Fatal Accidents per 1000 Licenses |
|---|---|---|---|
| 13 | 2.962 | 17 | 4.100 |
| 12 | 0.708 | 8 | 2.190 |
| 8 | 0.885 | 16 | 3.623 |
| 12 | 1.652 | 15 | 2.623 |
| 11 | 2.091 | 9 | 0.835 |
| 17 | 2.627 | 8 | 0.820 |
| 18 | 3.830 | 14 | 2.890 |
| 8 | 0.368 | 8 | 1.267 |
| 13 | 1.142 | 15 | 3.224 |
| 8 | 0.645 | 10 | 1.014 |
| 9 | 1.028 | 10 | 0.493 |
| 16 | 2.801 | 14 | 1.443 |
| 12 | 1.405 | 18 | 3.614 |
| 9 | 1.433 | 10 | 1.926 |
| 10 | 0.039 | 14 | 1.643 |
| 9 | 0.338 | 16 | 2.943 |
| 11 | 1.849 | 12 | 1.913 |
| 12 | 2.246 | 15 | 2.814 |
| 14 | 2.855 | 13 | 2.634 |
| 14 | 2.352 | 9 | 0.926 |
| 11 | 1.294 | 17 | 3.256 |

## Managerial Report

1. Develop numerical and graphical summaries of the data.
2. Use regression analysis to investigate the relationship between the number of fatal accidents and the percentage of drivers under the age of 21. Discuss your findings.
3. What conclusion and recommendations can you derive from your analysis?

**Case Problem 3**    # Alumni Giving

Alumni donations are an important source of revenue for colleges and universities. If administrators could determine the factors that influence increases in the percentage of alumni who make a donation, they might be able to implement policies that could lead to increased revenues. Research shows that students who are more satisfied with their contact with teachers are more likely to graduate. As a result, one might suspect that smaller class sizes and lower student-faculty ratios might lead to a higher percentage of satisfied graduates, which in turn might lead to increases in the percentage of alumni who make a donation. Table 12.8 shows data for 48 national universities (*America's Best Colleges,* Year 2000 ed.). The column labeled % of Classes Under 20 shows the percentage of classes offered with

**TABLE 12.8**    DATA FOR 48 NATIONAL UNIVERSITIES

Alumni

| | % of Classes Under 20 | Student/Faculty Ratio | Alumni Giving Rate |
|---|---|---|---|
| Boston College | 39 | 13 | 25 |
| Brandeis University | 68 | 8 | 33 |
| Brown University | 60 | 8 | 40 |
| California Institute of Technology | 65 | 3 | 46 |
| Carnegie Mellon University | 67 | 10 | 28 |
| Case Western Reserve Univ. | 52 | 8 | 31 |
| College of William and Mary | 45 | 12 | 27 |
| Columbia University | 69 | 7 | 31 |
| Cornell University | 72 | 13 | 35 |
| Dartmouth College | 61 | 10 | 53 |
| Duke University | 68 | 8 | 45 |
| Emory University | 65 | 7 | 37 |
| Georgetown University | 54 | 10 | 29 |
| Harvard University | 73 | 8 | 46 |
| Johns Hopkins University | 64 | 9 | 27 |
| Lehigh University | 55 | 11 | 40 |
| Massachusetts Inst. of Technology | 65 | 6 | 44 |
| New York University | 63 | 13 | 13 |
| Northwestern University | 66 | 8 | 30 |
| Pennsylvania State Univ. | 32 | 19 | 21 |
| Princeton University | 68 | 5 | 67 |
| Rice University | 62 | 8 | 40 |
| Stanford University | 69 | 7 | 34 |
| Tufts University | 67 | 9 | 29 |
| Tulane University | 56 | 12 | 17 |
| U. of California–Berkeley | 58 | 17 | 18 |
| U. of California–Davis | 32 | 19 | 7 |
| U. of California–Irvine | 42 | 20 | 9 |
| U. of California–Los Angeles | 41 | 18 | 13 |
| U. of California–San Diego | 48 | 19 | 8 |
| U. of California–Santa Barbara | 45 | 20 | 12 |
| U. of Chicago | 65 | 4 | 36 |
| U. of Florida | 31 | 23 | 19 |
| U. of Illinois–Urbana Champaign | 29 | 15 | 23 |
| U. of Michigan–Ann Arbor | 51 | 15 | 13 |
| U. of North Carolina–Chapel Hill | 40 | 16 | 26 |
| U. of Notre Dame | 53 | 13 | 49 |
| U. of Pennsylvania | 65 | 7 | 41 |
| U. of Rochester | 63 | 10 | 23 |
| U. of Southern California | 53 | 13 | 22 |
| U. of Texas–Austin | 39 | 21 | 13 |
| U. of Virginia | 44 | 13 | 28 |
| U. of Washington | 37 | 12 | 12 |
| U. of Wisconsin–Madison | 37 | 13 | 13 |
| Vanderbilt University | 68 | 9 | 31 |
| Wake Forest University | 59 | 11 | 38 |
| Washington University–St. Louis | 73 | 7 | 33 |
| Yale University | 77 | 7 | 50 |

fewer than 20 students. The column labeled Student/Faculty Ratio is the number of students enrolled divided by the total number of faculty. Finally, the column labeled Alumni Giving Rate is the percentage of alumni that made a donation to the university.

## Managerial Report

1.  Develop numerical and graphical summaries of the data.
2.  Use regression analysis to develop an estimated regression equation that could be used to predict the alumni giving rate given the percentage of classes with fewer than 20 students.
3.  Use regression analysis to develop an estimated regression equation that could be used to predict the alumni giving rate given the student-faculty ratio.
4.  Which of the two estimated regression equations provides the best fit? For this estimated regression equation, perform an analysis of the residuals and discuss your findings and conclusions.
5.  What conclusions and recommendations can you derive from your analysis?

## Case Problem 4    PGA Tour Statistics

The Professional Golfers Association (PGA) maintains data on performance and earnings for members of the PGA Tour. The top 125 players based on total earnings in PGA Tour events are exempt for the following season. Making the top 125 money list is important because a player who is "exempt" has qualified to be a full-time member of the PGA tour for the following season.

**PGATour**

During recent years on the PGA Tour there have been significant advances in the technology of golf balls and golf clubs, and this technology has been one of the major reasons for the increase in the average driving distance of PGA Tour players. In 1992, the average driving distance was 260 yards, but in 2003 this increased to 286 yards. PGA Tour pros are hitting the ball farther than ever before, but how important is driving distance in terms of a player's performance? And what effect has this increased distance had on the players' accuracy? To investigate these issues, year-end performance data for the 125 players who had the highest total earnings in PGA Tour events for 2008 are contained in the file named PGA-Tour (PGA Tour website, 2009). Each row of the data set corresponds to a PGA Tour player, and the data have been sorted based upon total earnings. Descriptions for the data follow.

Money: Total earnings in PGA Tour events.

Scoring Average: The average number of strokes per completed round.

DrDist (Driving Distance): DrDist is the average number of yards per measured drive. On the PGA Tour, driving distance is measured on two holes per round. Care is taken to select two holes which face in opposite directions to counteract the effect of wind. Drives are measured to the point at which they come to rest regardless of whether they are in the fairway or not.

DrAccu (Driving Accuracy): The percentage of time a tee shot comes to rest in the fairway (regardless of club). Driving accuracy is measured on every hole, excluding par 3's.

GIR (Greens in Regulation): The percentage of time a player was able to hit the green in regulation. A green is considered hit in regulation if any portion of the ball is touching the putting surface after the GIR stroke has been taken. The GIR stroke is determined by subtracting 2 from par (first stroke on a par 3, second on a par 4, third on a par 5). In other words, a green is considered hit in regulation if the player has reached the putting surface in par minus two strokes.

## Managerial Report

1. Develop numerical and graphical summaries of the data.
2. Use regression analysis to investigate the relationship between Scoring Average and DrDist. Does it appear that players who drive the ball farther have lower average scores?
3. Use regression analysis to investigate the relationship between Scoring Average and DrAccu. Does it appear that players who are more accurate in hitting the fairway have lower average scores?
4. Use regression analysis to investigate the relationship between Scoring Average and GIR. Does it appear that players who are more accurate in hitting greens in regulation have lower average scores?
5. Which of the three variables (DrDist, DrAccu, and GIR) appears to be the most significant factor in terms of a player's average score?
6. Treating DrDist as the independent variable and DrAccu as the dependent variable, investigate the relationship between driving distance and driving accuracy.

## Appendix    Regression Analysis Using StatTools

In this appendix we show how StatTools can be used to perform a regression analysis and compute prediction intervals for the Armand's Pizza Parlors problem. We will begin by showing how to use StatTools to perform the regression analysis computations for the Armand's Pizza Parlors problem. We will then illustrate how to use the prediction interval option.

### Regression Analysis for the Armand's Pizza Parlors Problem

To perform a regression analysis for the Armand's Pizza Parlors problem we begin by using the Data Set Manager to create a StatTools data set for the Armand's data using the procedure described in the appendix in Chapter 1. The label for the independent variable in the Excel worksheet is "Population" and the label for the dependent variable is "Sales." The default name StatTools uses for the Armand's data set is "Data Set #1." The following steps describe how StatTools can be used to provide the regression results.

**Step 1.** Click the **StatTools** tab on the Ribbon
**Step 2.** In the **Analyses** group, click **Regression and Classification**
**Step 3.** Choose the **Regression** option
**Step 4.** When the StatTools - Regression dialog box appears,
      Select **Multiple** in the **Regression Type** box
      In the **Variables** section,
         Click the **Format button** and select **Unstacked**
         In the column labeled **I**, select **Population** as the independent variable
         In the column labeled **D**, select **Sales** as the dependent variable
      Click **OK**

*Multiple is used for both simple linear and multiple regression.*

The regression output will appear.

The StatTools - Regression dialog box contains a number of options that can be used to construct several types of residual plots as well as compute prediction intervals. Let us see how the prediction interval option can be used to compute prediction interval estimates for the Armand's Pizza Parlor problem.

*The StatTools Help facility provides information on using all of the options shown in the StatTools - Regression dialog box.*

## Computing Prediction Intervals for the Armand's Pizza Parlors Problem

In Section 12.7 we showed the results of using StatTools to compute prediction intervals corresponding to three values of the independent variable Population: 10, 14, and 18. Refer to Figure 12.14 as we describe how the StatTools regression procedure can be extended to perform both a regression analysis *and* compute the prediction intervals corresponding to these three values.

In the preceding subsection, we created a StatTools data set for the Armand's data shown in cells A1:C11 and the StatTools name for these data is "Data Set #1." To use the StatTools regression option to compute prediction intervals for values of Population equal to 10, 14, and 18, we must also create a new StatTools data set that contains the label "Population" and the values 10, 14, and 18. As in Figure 12.14, we enter the label "Population" into cell E1 and the values 10, 14, and 18 into cells E1:E4. Using the StatTools Data Set Manager, we now create a new StatTools data set corresponding to the values in cells E1:E4. The default name StatTools uses for this new data set is "Data Set #2."

The following steps describe how StatTools can be used to provide the regression results (as shown in the previous subsection) *and* compute the prediction intervals corresponding to three the three values (10, 14, and 18) of the independent variable.

**Step 1.** Click the **StatTools** tab on the Ribbon
**Step 2.** In the **Analyses** group, click **Regression and Classification**
**Step 3.** Choose the **Regression** option
**Step 4.** When the StatTools - Regression dialog box appears,
    Select **Multiple** in the **Regression Type** box
    In the **Variables** section,
        Click the **Format** button and select **Unstacked**
        In the column labeled **I**, select **Population**
        In the column labeled **D**, select **Sales**
    In the **Advanced Options** section,
        Select **Include Prediction for Data Set** and choose **Data Set #2** in the corresponding box
        Choose **95%** in the **Confidence Level** box
    Click **OK**

After clicking OK in step 4, StatTools will display a series of three dialog boxes, each of which contains a question involving the prediction interval output; click Yes in response to each of these questions.

Matching variable not found in prediction data set for dependent variable Sales. Do you want to insert new variable in data set?

Matching variable not found in prediction data set for lower limit variable. Do you want to insert new variable in data set?

Matching variable not found in prediction data set for upper limit variable. Do you want to insert new variable in data set?

The StatTools prediction interval output is shown in cells F1:H8 of the worksheet shown in Figure 12.14. In addition, the standard regression output for the Armand's Pizza Parlors problem is provided in a new worksheet.

# CHAPTER 13

# Multiple Regression

## INTERNATIONAL PAPER*
### PURCHASE, NEW YORK

International Paper is the world's largest paper and forest products company. The company employs more than 117,000 people in its operations in nearly 50 countries, and exports its products to more than 130 nations. International Paper produces building materials such as lumber and plywood; consumer packaging materials such as disposable cups and containers; industrial packaging materials such as corrugated boxes and shipping containers; and a variety of papers for use in photocopiers, printers, books, and advertising materials.

To make paper products, pulp mills process wood chips and chemicals to produce wood pulp. The wood pulp is then used at a paper mill to produce paper products. In the production of white paper products, the pulp must be bleached to remove any discoloration. A key bleaching agent used in the process is chlorine dioxide, which, because of its combustible nature, is usually produced at a pulp mill facility and then piped in solution form into the bleaching tower of the pulp mill. To improve one of the processes used to produce chlorine dioxide, researchers studied the process's control and efficiency. One aspect of the study looked at the chemical feed rate for chlorine dioxide production.

To produce the chlorine dioxide, four chemicals flow at metered rates into the chlorine dioxide generator. The chlorine dioxide produced in the generator flows to an absorber where chilled water absorbs the chlorine dioxide gas to form a chlorine dioxide solution. The solution is then piped into the paper mill. A key part of controlling the process involves the chemical feed rates. Historically, experienced operators set the chemical feed rates, but this approach led to overcontrol by the operators. Consequently, chemical engineers at the mill requested that a set of control equations, one for each

© Prisma Bildagentur AG/Alamy

Multiple regression analysis assisted in the development of a better bleaching process for making white paper products.

chemical feed, be developed to aid the operators in setting the rates.

Using multiple regression analysis, statistical analysts developed an estimated multiple regression equation for each of the four chemicals used in the process. Each equation related the production of chlorine dioxide to the amount of chemical used and the concentration level of the chlorine dioxide solution. The resulting set of four equations was programmed into a microcomputer at each mill. In the new system, operators enter the concentration of the chlorine dioxide solution and the desired production rate; the computer software then calculates the chemical feed needed to achieve the desired production rate. After the operators began using the control equations, the chlorine dioxide generator efficiency increased, and the number of times the concentrations fell within acceptable ranges increased significantly.

This example shows how multiple regression analysis can be used to develop a better bleaching process for producing white paper products. In this chapter we will show how Excel can be used for such purposes. Most of the concepts introduced in Chapter 12 for simple linear regression can be directly extended to the multiple regression case.

---

*The authors are indebted to Marian Williams and Bill Griggs for providing this Statistics in Practice. This application was originally developed at Champion International Corporation, which became part of International Paper in 2000.

In Chapter 12 we presented simple linear regression and demonstrated its use in developing an estimated regression equation that describes the relationship between two variables. Recall that the variable being predicted or explained is called the dependent variable and the variable being used to predict or explain the dependent variable is called the independent variable. In this chapter we continue our study of regression analysis by considering situations involving two or more independent variables. This subject area, called **multiple regression analysis**, enables us to consider more factors and thus obtain better estimates than are possible with simple linear regression.

## 13.1 Multiple Regression Model

Multiple regression analysis is the study of how a dependent variable $y$ is related to two or more independent variables. In the general case, we will use $p$ to denote the number of independent variables.

### Regression Model and Regression Equation

The concepts of a regression model and a regression equation introduced in the preceding chapter are applicable in the multiple regression case. The equation that describes how the dependent variable $y$ is related to the independent variables $x_1, x_2, \ldots, x_p$ and an error term is called the **multiple regression model**. We begin with the assumption that the multiple regression model takes the following form.

**MULTIPLE REGRESSION MODEL**

$$y = \beta_0 + \beta_1 x_1 + \beta_2 x_2 + \cdots + \beta_p x_p + \epsilon \tag{13.1}$$

In the multiple regression model, $\beta_0, \beta_1, \beta_2, \ldots, \beta_p$ are the parameters and the error term $\epsilon$ (the Greek letter epsilon) is a random variable. A close examination of this model reveals that $y$ is a linear function of $x_1, x_2, \ldots, x_p$ (the $\beta_0 + \beta_1 x_1 + \beta_2 x_2 + \cdots + \beta_p x_p$ part) plus the error term $\epsilon$. The error term accounts for the variability in $y$ that cannot be explained by the linear effect of the $p$ independent variables.

In Section 13.4 we will discuss the assumptions for the multiple regression model and $\epsilon$. One of the assumptions is that the mean or expected value of $\epsilon$ is zero. A consequence of this assumption is that the mean or expected value of $y$, denoted $E(y)$, is equal to $\beta_0 + \beta_1 x_1 + \beta_2 x_2 + \cdots + \beta_p x_p$. The equation that describes how the mean value of $y$ is related to $x_1, x_2, \ldots, x_p$ is called the **multiple regression equation**.

**MULTIPLE REGRESSION EQUATION**

$$E(y) = \beta_0 + \beta_1 x_1 + \beta_2 x_2 + \cdots + \beta_p x_p \tag{13.2}$$

### Estimated Multiple Regression Equation

If the values of $\beta_0, \beta_1, \beta_2, \ldots, \beta_p$ were known, equation (13.2) could be used to compute the mean value of $y$ at given values of $x_1, x_2, \ldots, x_p$. Unfortunately, these parameter values will not, in general, be known and must be estimated from sample data. A simple random sample is used to compute sample statistics $b_0, b_1, b_2, \ldots, b_p$ that are used as the point

**FIGURE 13.1    THE ESTIMATION PROCESS FOR MULTIPLE REGRESSION**

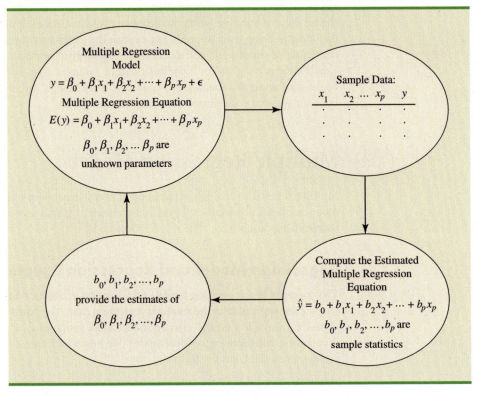

*In simple linear regression, $b_0$ and $b_1$ were the sample statistics used to estimate the parameters $\beta_0$ and $\beta_1$. Multiple regression parallels this statistical inference process, with $b_0$, $b_1, b_2, \ldots, b_p$ denoting the sample statistics used to estimate the parameters $\beta_0, \beta_1, \beta_2, \ldots, \beta_p$.*

estimators of the parameters $\beta_0, \beta_1, \beta_2, \ldots, \beta_p$. These sample statistics provide the following **estimated multiple regression equation**.

---

ESTIMATED MULTIPLE REGRESSION EQUATION

$$\hat{y} = b_0 + b_1 x_1 + b_2 x_2 + \cdots + b_p x_p \qquad (13.3)$$

where

$b_0, b_1, b_2, \ldots, b_p$ are the estimates of $\beta_0, \beta_1, \beta_2, \ldots, \beta_p$
$\hat{y}$ = predicted value of the dependent variable

---

The estimation process for multiple regression is shown in Figure 13.1.

## 13.2  Least Squares Method

In Chapter 12 we used the **least squares method** to develop the estimated regression equation that best approximated the straight-line relationship between the dependent and independent variables. This same approach is used to develop the estimated multiple regression equation. The least squares criterion is restated as follows.

---

LEAST SQUARES CRITERION

$$\min \Sigma (y_i - \hat{y}_i)^2 \qquad (13.4)$$

where

$y_i$ = observed value of the dependent variable for the $i$th observation

$\hat{y}_i$ = predicted value of the dependent variable for the $i$th observation

The predicted values of the dependent variable are computed by using the estimated multiple regression equation,

$$\hat{y} = b_0 + b_1 x_1 + b_2 x_2 + \cdots + b_p x_p$$

As expression (13.4) shows, the least squares method uses sample data to provide the values of $b_0, b_1, b_2, \ldots, b_p$ that make the sum of squared residuals [the deviations between the observed values of the dependent variable ($y_i$) and the predicted values of the dependent variable ($\hat{y}_i$)] a minimum.

In Chapter 12 we presented formulas for computing the least squares estimators $b_0$ and $b_1$ for the estimated simple linear regression equation $\hat{y} = b_0 + b_1 x$. With relatively small data sets, we were able to use those formulas to compute $b_0$ and $b_1$ by manual calculations. In multiple regression, however, the presentation of the formulas for the regression coefficients $b_0, b_1, b_2, \ldots, b_p$ involves the use of matrix algebra and is beyond the scope of this text. Therefore, in presenting multiple regression, we focus on how Excel's Regression tool can be used to obtain the estimated regression equation and other information. The emphasis will be on how to interpret the Excel output rather than on how to make the multiple regression computations.

## An Example: Butler Trucking Company

As an illustration of multiple regression analysis, we will consider a problem faced by the Butler Trucking Company, an independent trucking company in southern California. A major portion of Butler's business involves deliveries throughout its local area. To develop better work schedules, the managers want to estimate the total daily travel time for their drivers.

Initially the managers believed that the total daily travel time would be closely related to the number of miles traveled in making the daily deliveries. A simple random sample of 10 driving assignments provided the data shown in Table 13.1 and the scatter diagram shown in Figure 13.2. After reviewing this scatter diagram, the managers hypothesized that

**TABLE 13.1**  PRELIMINARY DATA FOR BUTLER TRUCKING

| Driving Assignment | $x_1$ = Miles Traveled | $y$ = Travel Time (hours) |
|---|---|---|
| 1 | 100 | 9.3 |
| 2 | 50 | 4.8 |
| 3 | 100 | 8.9 |
| 4 | 100 | 6.5 |
| 5 | 50 | 4.2 |
| 6 | 80 | 6.2 |
| 7 | 75 | 7.4 |
| 8 | 65 | 6.0 |
| 9 | 90 | 7.6 |
| 10 | 90 | 6.1 |

**FIGURE 13.2**   SCATTER DIAGRAM OF PRELIMINARY DATA FOR BUTLER TRUCKING

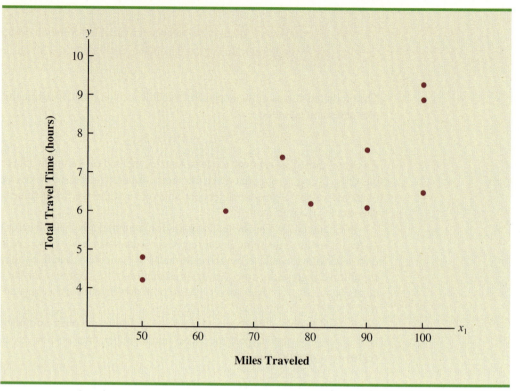

the simple linear regression model $y = \beta_0 + \beta_1 x_1 + \epsilon$ could be used to describe the relationship between the total travel time ($y$) and the number of miles traveled ($x_1$). To estimate the parameters $\beta_0$ and $\beta_1$, the least squares method was used to develop the estimated regression equation.

$$\hat{y} = b_0 + b_1 x_1 \qquad \textbf{(13.5)}$$

In Figure 13.3, we show the Excel Regression tool output[1] from applying simple linear regression to the data in Table 13.1. The estimated regression equation is

$$\hat{y} = 1.2739 + .0678 x_1$$

At the .05 level of significance, the $F$ value of 15.8146 and its corresponding $p$-value of .0041 indicate that the relationship is significant; that is, we can reject $H_0: \beta_1 = 0$ because the $p$-value is less than $\alpha = .05$. Note that the same conclusion is obtained from the $t$ value of 3.9768 and its associated $p$-value of .0041. Thus, we can conclude that the relationship between the total travel time and the number of miles traveled is significant; longer travel times are associated with more miles traveled. With a coefficient of determination of R Square = .6641, we see that 66.41% of the variability in travel time can be explained by the linear effect of the number of miles traveled. This finding is fairly good, but the managers might want to consider adding a second independent variable to explain some of the remaining variability in the dependent variable.

---

[1]Excel's Regression tool was used to obtain the output. Section 12.7 describes how to use Excel's Regression tool for simple linear regression.

**FIGURE 13.3**   REGRESSION TOOL OUTPUT FOR BUTLER TRUCKING WITH ONE INDEPENDENT VARIABLE

|  | A | B | C | D | E | F | G | H | I | J |
|---|---|---|---|---|---|---|---|---|---|---|
| 1 | **Assignment** | **Miles** | **Time** |  |  |  |  |  |  |  |
| 2 |  | 1 | 100 | 9.3 |  |  |  |  |  |  |
| 3 |  | 2 | 50 | 4.8 |  |  |  |  |  |  |
| 4 |  | 3 | 100 | 8.9 |  |  |  |  |  |  |
| 5 |  | 4 | 100 | 6.5 |  |  |  |  |  |  |
| 6 |  | 5 | 50 | 4.2 |  |  |  |  |  |  |
| 7 |  | 6 | 80 | 6.2 |  |  |  |  |  |  |
| 8 |  | 7 | 75 | 7.4 |  |  |  |  |  |  |
| 9 |  | 8 | 65 | 6 |  |  |  |  |  |  |
| 10 |  | 9 | 90 | 7.6 |  |  |  |  |  |  |
| 11 |  | 10 | 90 | 6.1 |  |  |  |  |  |  |
| 12 |  |  |  |  |  |  |  |  |  |  |
| 13 | SUMMARY OUTPUT |  |  |  |  |  |  |  |  |  |
| 14 |  |  |  |  |  |  |  |  |  |  |
| 15 | *Regression Statistics* |  |  |  |  |  |  |  |  |  |
| 16 | Multiple R | 0.8149 |  |  |  |  |  |  |  |  |
| 17 | R Square | 0.6641 |  |  |  |  |  |  |  |  |
| 18 | Adjusted R Square | 0.6221 |  |  |  |  |  |  |  |  |
| 19 | Standard Error | 1.0018 |  |  |  |  |  |  |  |  |
| 20 | Observations | 10 |  |  |  |  |  |  |  |  |
| 21 |  |  |  |  |  |  |  |  |  |  |
| 22 | ANOVA |  |  |  |  |  |  |  |  |  |
| 23 |  | *df* | *SS* | *MS* | *F* | *Significance F* |  |  |  |  |
| 24 | Regression | 1 | 15.8713 | 15.8713 | 15.8146 | 0.0041 |  |  |  |  |
| 25 | Residual | 8 | 8.0287 | 1.0036 |  |  |  |  |  |  |
| 26 | Total | 9 | 23.9 |  |  |  |  |  |  |  |
| 27 |  |  |  |  |  |  |  |  |  |  |
| 28 |  | *Coefficients* | *Standard Error* | *t Stat* | *P-value* | *Lower 95%* | *Upper 95%* | *Lower 99.0%* | *Upper 99.0%* |  |
| 29 | Intercept | 1.2739 | 1.4007 | 0.9095 | 0.3897 | -1.9562 | 4.5040 | -3.4261 | 5.9739 |  |
| 30 | Miles | 0.0678 | 0.0171 | 3.9768 | 0.0041 | 0.0285 | 0.1072 | 0.0106 | 0.1251 |  |
| 31 |  |  |  |  |  |  |  |  |  |  |

In attempting to identify another independent variable, the managers felt that the number of deliveries could also contribute to the total travel time. The Butler Trucking data, with the number of deliveries added, are shown in Table 13.2. To develop the estimated multiple regression equation with both miles traveled ($x_1$) and number of deliveries ($x_2$) as independent variables, we will use Excel's Regression tool.

**TABLE 13.2**   DATA FOR BUTLER TRUCKING WITH MILES TRAVELED ($x_1$) AND NUMBER OF DELIVERIES ($x_2$) AS THE INDEPENDENT VARIABLES

**WEB** file

Butler

| Driving Assignment | $x_1$ = Miles Traveled | $x_2$ = Number of Deliveries | $y$ = Travel Time (hours) |
|---|---|---|---|
| 1 | 100 | 4 | 9.3 |
| 2 | 50 | 3 | 4.8 |
| 3 | 100 | 4 | 8.9 |
| 4 | 100 | 2 | 6.5 |
| 5 | 50 | 2 | 4.2 |
| 6 | 80 | 2 | 6.2 |
| 7 | 75 | 3 | 7.4 |
| 8 | 65 | 4 | 6.0 |
| 9 | 90 | 3 | 7.6 |
| 10 | 90 | 2 | 6.1 |

## Using Excel's Regression Tool to Develop the Estimated Multiple Regression Equation

In Section 12.7 we showed how Excel's Regression tool could be used to determine the estimated regression equation for Armand's Pizza Parlors. We can use the same procedure with minor modifications to develop the estimated multiple regression equation for Butler Trucking. Refer to Figures 13.4 and 13.5 as we describe the tasks involved.

**Enter Data:** The labels Assignment, Miles, Deliveries, and Time are entered into cells A1:D1 of the worksheet, and the sample data are entered into cells B2:D11. The numbers 1–10 are entered into cells A2:A11 to identify each observation.

**Apply Tools:** The following steps describe how to use Excel's Regression tool for multiple regression analysis.

**Step 1.** Select the **Tools** menu
**Step 2.** Choose the **Data Analysis** option
**Step 3.** Choose **Regression** from the list of Analysis Tools
**Step 4.** When the Regression dialog box appears (see Figure 13.4),
Enter D1:D11 in the **Input Y Range** box
Enter B1:C11 in the **Input X Range** box
Select **Labels**
Select **Confidence Level**

**FIGURE 13.4**  REGRESSION TOOL DIALOG BOX FOR THE BUTLER TRUCKING EXAMPLE

**FIGURE 13.5**   REGRESSION TOOL OUTPUT FOR BUTLER TRUCKING WITH TWO INDEPENDENT
VARIABLES

| | A | B | C | D | E | F | G | H | I | J |
|---|---|---|---|---|---|---|---|---|---|---|
| 1 | **Assignment** | **Miles** | **Deliveries** | **Time** | | | | | | |
| 2 | 1 | 100 | 4 | 9.3 | | | | | | |
| 3 | 2 | 50 | 3 | 4.8 | | | | | | |
| 4 | 3 | 100 | 4 | 8.9 | | | | | | |
| 5 | 4 | 100 | 2 | 6.5 | | | | | | |
| 6 | 5 | 50 | 2 | 4.2 | | | | | | |
| 7 | 6 | 80 | 2 | 6.2 | | | | | | |
| 8 | 7 | 75 | 3 | 7.4 | | | | | | |
| 9 | 8 | 65 | 4 | 6 | | | | | | |
| 10 | 9 | 90 | 3 | 7.6 | | | | | | |
| 11 | 10 | 90 | 2 | 6.1 | | | | | | |
| 12 | | | | | | | | | | |
| 13 | SUMMARY OUTPUT | | | | | | | | | |
| 14 | | | | | | | | | | |
| 15 | *Regression Statistics* | | | | | | | | | |
| 16 | Multiple R | 0.9507 | | | | | | | | |
| 17 | R Square | 0.9038 | | | | | | | | |
| 18 | Adjusted R Square | 0.8763 | | | | | | | | |
| 19 | Standard Error | 0.5731 | | | | | | | | |
| 20 | Observations | 10 | | | | | | | | |
| 21 | | | | | | | | | | |
| 22 | ANOVA | | | | | | | | | |
| 23 | | *df* | *SS* | *MS* | *F* | *Significance F* | | | | |
| 24 | Regression | 2 | 21.6006 | 10.8003 | 32.8784 | 0.0003 | | | | |
| 25 | Residual | 7 | 2.2994 | 0.3285 | | | | | | |
| 26 | Total | 9 | 23.9 | | | | | | | |
| 27 | | | | | | | | | | |
| 28 | | *Coefficients* | *Standard Error* | *t Stat* | *P-value* | *Lower 95%* | *Upper 95%* | *Lower 99.0%* | *Upper 99.0%* | |
| 29 | Intercept | -0.8687 | 0.9515 | -0.9129 | 0.3916 | -3.1188 | 1.3813 | -4.1986 | 2.4612 | |
| 30 | Miles | 0.0611 | 0.0099 | 6.1824 | 0.0005 | 0.0378 | 0.0845 | 0.0265 | 0.0957 | |
| 31 | Deliveries | 0.9234 | 0.2211 | 4.1763 | 0.0042 | 0.4006 | 1.4463 | 0.1496 | 1.6972 | |

Enter 99 in the **Confidence Level** box
Select **Output Range**
Enter A13 in the **Output Range** box (to identify the upper left corner of the
    section of the worksheet where the output will appear)
Click **OK**

In the Excel output shown in Figure 13.5 the label for the independent variable $x_1$ is Miles
(see cell A30), and the label for the independent variable $x_2$ is Deliveries (see cell A31). The
estimated regression equation is

$$\hat{y} = -.8687 + .0611x_1 + .9234x_2 \tag{13.6}$$

Note that using Excel's Regression tool for multiple regression is almost the same as
using it for simple linear regression. The major difference is that in the multiple
regression case a larger range of cells has to be provided in order to identify the independent variables.

   In the next section we will discuss the use of the coefficient of multiple determination in
measuring how good a fit is provided by this estimated regression equation. Before doing so,
let us examine more carefully the values of $b_1 = .0611$ and $b_2 = .9234$ in equation (13.6).

## Note on Interpretation of Coefficients

One observation can be made at this point about the relationship between the estimated regression equation with only the miles traveled as an independent variable and the equation that includes the number of deliveries as a second independent variable. The value of $b_1$ is not the same in both cases. In simple linear regression, we interpret $b_1$ as an estimate of the change in $y$ for a one-unit change in the independent variable. In multiple regression analysis, this interpretation must be modified somewhat. That is, in multiple regression analysis, we interpret each regression coefficient as follows: $b_i$ represents an estimate of the change in $y$ corresponding to a one-unit change in $x_i$ when all other independent variables are held constant. In the Butler Trucking example involving two independent variables, $b_1 = .0611$. Thus, .0611 hours is an estimate of the expected increase in travel time corresponding to an increase of one mile in the distance traveled when the number of deliveries is held constant. Similarly, because $b_2 = .9234$, an estimate of the expected increase in travel time corresponding to an increase of one delivery when the number of miles traveled is held constant is .9234 hours.

## NOTES AND COMMENTS

In the appendix to this chapter we show how to use StatTools to perform multiple regression analysis for the Butler Trucking data. The regression analysis capabilities of StatTools are more comprehensive than those available using Excel's Regression tool.

## Exercises

*Note to student:* The exercises involving data in this and subsequent sections were designed to be solved using Excel.

## Methods

1. The estimated regression equation for a model involving two independent variables and 10 observations follows.

$$\hat{y} = 29.1270 + .5906x_1 + .4980x_2$$

   a. Interpret $b_1$ and $b_2$ in this estimated regression equation.
   b. Predict $y$ when $x_1 = 180$ and $x_2 = 310$.

2. Consider the following data for a dependent variable $y$ and two independent variables, $x_1$ and $x_2$.

Exer2

| $x_1$ | $x_2$ | $y$ |
|-------|-------|-----|
| 30 | 12 | 94 |
| 47 | 10 | 108 |
| 25 | 17 | 112 |
| 51 | 16 | 178 |
| 40 | 5 | 94 |
| 51 | 19 | 175 |
| 74 | 7 | 170 |
| 36 | 12 | 117 |
| 59 | 13 | 142 |
| 76 | 16 | 211 |

a.   Develop an estimated regression equation relating $y$ to $x_1$. Estimate $y$ if $x_1 = 45$.
b.   Develop an estimated regression equation relating $y$ to $x_2$. Estimate $y$ if $x_2 = 15$.
c.   Develop an estimated regression equation relating $y$ to $x_1$ and $x_2$. Estimate $y$ if $x_1 = 45$ and $x_2 = 15$.

3.   In a regression analysis involving 30 observations, the following estimated regression equation was obtained.

$$\hat{y} = 17.6 + 3.8x_1 - 2.3x_2 + 7.6x_3 + 2.7x_4$$

a.   Interpret $b_1$, $b_2$, $b_3$, and $b_4$ in this estimated regression equation.
b.   Predict $y$ when $x_1 = 10$, $x_2 = 5$, $x_3 = 1$, and $x_4 = 2$.

## Applications

4.   A shoe store developed the following estimated regression equation relating sales to inventory investment and advertising expenditures.

$$\hat{y} = 25 + 10x_1 + 8x_2$$

where

$$x_1 = \text{inventory investment (\$1000s)}$$
$$x_2 = \text{advertising expenditures (\$1000s)}$$
$$y = \text{sales (\$1000s)}$$

a.   Predict the sales resulting from a \$15,000 investment in inventory and an advertising budget of \$10,000.
b.   Interpret $b_1$ and $b_2$ in this estimated regression equation.

5.   The owner of Showtime Movie Theaters, Inc., would like to estimate weekly gross revenue as a function of advertising expenditures. Historical data for a sample of eight weeks follow.

**SELF** test

Showtime

| Weekly Gross Revenue ($1000s) | Television Advertising ($1000s) | Newspaper Advertising ($1000s) |
|---|---|---|
| 96 | 5.0 | 1.5 |
| 90 | 2.0 | 2.0 |
| 95 | 4.0 | 1.5 |
| 92 | 2.5 | 2.5 |
| 95 | 3.0 | 3.3 |
| 94 | 3.5 | 2.3 |
| 94 | 2.5 | 4.2 |
| 94 | 3.0 | 2.5 |

a.   Develop an estimated regression equation with the amount of television advertising as the independent variable.
b.   Develop an estimated regression equation with both television advertising and newspaper advertising as the independent variables.
c.   Is the estimated regression equation coefficient for television advertising expenditures the same in part (a) and in part (b)? Interpret the coefficient in each case.

d.  Predict the weekly gross revenue for a week when $3500 is spent on television advertising and $1800 is spent on newspaper advertising.

6.  Out-of-state tuition and fees at the top graduate schools of business can be very expensive. However, the starting salary and bonus paid to graduates from many of these schools can be very high. The following data show the recruiter assessment score (highest = 5), the out-of-state tuition and fees (rounded to the nearest $1000), and the average starting salary and bonus paid to recent graduates (rounded to the nearest $1000) for a sample of 20 graduate schools of business (*U.S. News & World Report 2009 Edition America's Best Graduate Schools*).

**BusinessSchools2**

| School | Recruiter Score | Tuition & Fees ($) | Salary & Bonus ($) |
|---|---|---|---|
| Arizona State University | 3.4 | 28 | 98 |
| Babson College | 3.5 | 35 | 94 |
| Cornell University | 3.8 | 44 | 119 |
| Georgetown University | 3.7 | 40 | 109 |
| Georgia Institute of Technology | 3.6 | 30 | 88 |
| Indiana University–Bloomington | 3.7 | 35 | 105 |
| Michigan State University | 3.2 | 26 | 99 |
| Northwestern University | 4.3 | 44 | 123 |
| Ohio State University | 3.1 | 35 | 97 |
| Purdue University–West Lafayette | 3.6 | 33 | 96 |
| Rice University | 3.4 | 36 | 102 |
| Stanford University | 4.4 | 46 | 135 |
| University of California–Davis | 3.3 | 35 | 89 |
| University of Florida | 3.5 | 23 | 71 |
| University of Iowa | 3.1 | 25 | 78 |
| University of Minnesota–Twin Cities | 3.5 | 37 | 100 |
| University of Notre Dame | 3.4 | 36 | 95 |
| University of Rochester | 3.5 | 38 | 99 |
| University of Washington | 3.4 | 30 | 94 |
| University of Wisconsin–Madison | 3.3 | 27 | 93 |

a.  Develop an estimated regression equation that can be used to predict the starting salary and bonus paid to graduates given the recruiter assessment score.
b.  Develop an estimated regression equation that can be used to predict the starting salary and bonus paid to graduates given both the recruiter assessment score and the out-of-state tuition and fees.
c.  Is the estimated regression coefficient for the recruiter score the same in part (a) and in part (b)? Interpret the coefficient in each case.
d.  Suppose that we randomly select a recent graduate of the University of Virginia graduate school of business. This school has a recruiter assessment score of 4.1 and an out-of-state tuition and fees of $43,000. Predict the starting salary and bonus for this graduate.

7.  *PC World* rated four component characteristics for 10 ultraportable laptop computers: features; performance; design; and price. Each characteristic was rated using a 0–100 point scale. An overall rating, referred to as the *PC World* Rating, was then developed for each laptop. The following table shows the performance rating, features rating, and the *PC World* Rating for the 10 laptop computers (PC World website, February 5, 2009).

| Model | Performance | Features | *PC* Rating |
|---|---|---|---|
| Thinkpad X200 | 77 | 87 | 83 |
| VGN-Z598U | 97 | 85 | 82 |
| U6V | 83 | 80 | 81 |
| Elitebook 2530P | 77 | 75 | 78 |
| X360 | 64 | 80 | 78 |
| Thinkpad X300 | 56 | 76 | 78 |
| Ideapad U110 | 55 | 81 | 77 |
| Micro Express JFT2500 | 76 | 73 | 75 |
| Toughbook W7 | 46 | 79 | 73 |
| HP Voodoo Envy133 | 54 | 68 | 72 |

**Laptop**

a. Determine the estimated regression equation that can be used to predict the *PC World* Rating using the performance rating as the independent variable.
b. Determine the estimated regression equation that can be used to predict the *PC World* Rating using both the performance rating and the features rating.
c. Predict the *PC World* Rating for a laptop computer that has a performance rating of 80 and a features rating of 70.

8. Would you expect more reliable and better performing cars to cost more? *Consumer Reports* provided reliability ratings, overall road-test scores, and prices for affordable family sedans, midpriced family sedans, and large sedans (*Consumer Reports*, February 2008). A portion of the data follows. Reliability was rated on a 5-point scale from poor (1) to excellent (5). The road-test score was rated on a 100-point scale, with higher values indicating better performance. The complete data set is contained in the file named Sedans.

| Make and Model | Road-Test Score | Reliability | Price ($) |
|---|---|---|---|
| Nissan Altima 2.5 S | 85 | 4 | 22,705 |
| Honda Accord LX-P | 79 | 4 | 22,795 |
| Kia Optima EX (4-cyl.) | 78 | 4 | 22,795 |
| Toyota Camry LE | 77 | 4 | 21,080 |
| Hyundai Sonata SE | 76 | 3 | 22,995 |
| . | . | . | . |
| . | . | . | . |
| . | . | . | . |
| Chrysler 300 Touring | 60 | 2 | 30,255 |
| Dodge Charger SXT | 58 | 4 | 28,860 |

**Sedans**

a. Develop an estimated regression equation that can be used to predict the price of the car given the reliability rating. Test for significance using $\alpha = .05$.
b. Consider the addition of the independent variable overall road-test score. Develop the estimated regression equation that can be used to predict the price of the car given the road-test score and the reliability rating.
c. Predict the price for a car with a road-test score of 80 and a reliability rating of 4.

9. Waterskiing and wakeboarding are two popular water-sports. Finding a model that best suits your intended needs, whether it is waterskiing, wakeboading, or general boating, can be a difficult task. *WaterSki* magazine did extensive testing for 88 boats and provided a wide variety of information to help consumers select the best boat. A portion of the data they reported for 20 boats with a length of between 20 and 22 feet follows (*WaterSki*, January/February 2006). Beam is the maximum width of the boat in inches, HP is the horsepower of the boat's engine, and TopSpeed is the top speed in miles per hour (mph).

| Make and Model | Beam | HP | TopSpeed |
|---|---|---|---|
| Calabria Cal Air Pro V-2 | 100 | 330 | 45.3 |
| Correct Craft Air Nautique 210 | 91 | 330 | 47.3 |
| Correct Craft Air Nautique SV-211 | 93 | 375 | 46.9 |
| Correct Craft Ski Nautique 206 Limited | 91 | 330 | 46.7 |
| Gekko GTR 22 | 96 | 375 | 50.1 |
| Gekko GTS 20 | 83 | 375 | 52.2 |
| Malibu Response LXi | 93.5 | 340 | 47.2 |
| Malibu Sunsetter LXi | 98 | 400 | 46 |
| Malibu Sunsetter 21 XTi | 98 | 340 | 44 |
| Malibu Sunscape 21 LSV | 98 | 400 | 47.5 |
| Malibu Wakesetter 21 XTi | 98 | 340 | 44.9 |
| Malibu Wakesetter VLX | 98 | 400 | 47.3 |
| Malibu vRide | 93.5 | 340 | 44.5 |
| Malibu Ride XTi | 93.5 | 320 | 44.5 |
| Mastercraft ProStar 209 | 96 | 350 | 42.5 |
| Mastercraft X-1 | 90 | 310 | 45.8 |
| Mastercraft X-2 | 94 | 310 | 42.8 |
| Mastercraft X-9 | 96 | 350 | 43.2 |
| MB Sports 190 Plus | 92 | 330 | 45.3 |
| Svfara SVONE | 91 | 330 | 47.7 |

**Boats**

a. Using these data, develop an estimated regression equation relating the top speed with the boat's beam and horsepower rating.

b. The Svfara SV609 has a beam of 85 inches and an engine with a 330 horsepower rating. Use the estimated regression equation developed in part (a) to estimate the mean top speed for the Svfara SV609.

10. The National Basketball Association (NBA) records a variety of statistics for each team. Four of these statistics are the proportion of games won (PCT), the proportion of field goals made by the team (FG%), the proportion of three-point shots made by the team's opponent (Opp 3 Pt%), and the number of turnovers committed by the team's opponent (Opp TO). The following data show the values of these statistics for the 29 teams in the NBA for a portion of the 2004 season (NBA website, January 3, 2004).

**NBA**

| Team | PCT | FG% | Opp 3 Pt% | Opp TO | Team | PCT | FG% | Opp 3 Pt% | Opp TO |
|---|---|---|---|---|---|---|---|---|---|
| Atlanta | 0.265 | 0.435 | 0.346 | 13.206 | Minnesota | 0.677 | 0.473 | 0.348 | 13.839 |
| Boston | 0.471 | 0.449 | 0.369 | 16.176 | New Jersey | 0.563 | 0.435 | 0.338 | 17.063 |
| Chicago | 0.313 | 0.417 | 0.372 | 15.031 | New Orleans | 0.636 | 0.421 | 0.330 | 16.909 |
| Cleveland | 0.303 | 0.438 | 0.345 | 12.515 | New York | 0.412 | 0.442 | 0.330 | 13.588 |
| Dallas | 0.581 | 0.439 | 0.332 | 15.000 | Orlando | 0.242 | 0.417 | 0.360 | 14.242 |
| Denver | 0.606 | 0.431 | 0.366 | 17.818 | Philadelphia | 0.438 | 0.428 | 0.364 | 16.938 |
| Detroit | 0.606 | 0.423 | 0.262 | 15.788 | Phoenix | 0.364 | 0.438 | 0.326 | 16.515 |
| Golden State | 0.452 | 0.445 | 0.384 | 14.290 | Portland | 0.484 | 0.447 | 0.367 | 12.548 |
| Houston | 0.548 | 0.426 | 0.324 | 13.161 | Sacramento | 0.724 | 0.466 | 0.327 | 15.207 |
| Indiana | 0.706 | 0.428 | 0.317 | 15.647 | San Antonio | 0.688 | 0.429 | 0.293 | 15.344 |
| L.A. Clippers | 0.464 | 0.424 | 0.326 | 14.357 | Seattle | 0.533 | 0.436 | 0.350 | 16.767 |
| L.A. Lakers | 0.724 | 0.465 | 0.323 | 16.000 | Toronto | 0.516 | 0.424 | 0.314 | 14.129 |
| Memphis | 0.485 | 0.432 | 0.358 | 17.848 | Utah | 0.531 | 0.456 | 0.368 | 15.469 |
| Miami | 0.424 | 0.410 | 0.369 | 14.970 | Washington | 0.300 | 0.411 | 0.341 | 16.133 |
| Milwaukee | 0.500 | 0.438 | 0.349 | 14.750 | | | | | |

a. Determine the estimated regression equation that can be used to predict the proportion of games won given the proportion of field goals made by the team.
b. Provide an interpretation for the slope of the estimated regression equation developed in part (a).
c. Determine the estimated regression equation that can be used to predict the proportion of games won given the proportion of field goals made by the team, the proportion of three-point shots made by the team's opponent, and the number of turnovers committed by the team's opponent.
d. Discuss the practical implications of the estimated regression equation developed in part (c).
e. Predict the proportion of games won for a team with the following values for the three independent variables: FG% = .45, Opp 3 Pt% = .34, and Opp TO = 17.

## 13.3 Multiple Coefficient of Determination

In simple linear regression we showed that the total sum of squares can be partitioned into two components: the sum of squares due to regression and the sum of squares due to error. The same procedure applies to the sum of squares in multiple regression.

RELATIONSHIP AMONG SST, SSR, AND SSE

$$SST = SSR + SSE \qquad \text{(13.7)}$$

where

$$SST = \text{total sum of squares} = \Sigma(y_i - \bar{y})^2$$
$$SSR = \text{sum of squares due to regression} = \Sigma(\hat{y}_i - \bar{y})^2$$
$$SSE = \text{sum of squares due to error} = \Sigma(y_i - \hat{y}_i)^2$$

Because of the computational difficulty in computing the three sums of squares, we rely on computer packages to determine those values. The analysis of variance part of the Excel output in Figure 13.5 shows the three values for the Butler Trucking problem with two independent variables: SST = 23.9, SSR = 21.6006, and SSE = 2.2994. With only one independent variable (number of miles traveled), the Excel output in Figure 13.3 shows that SST = 23.9, SSR = 15.8713, and SSE = 8.0287. The value of SST is the same in both cases because it does not depend on $\hat{y}$, but SSR increases and SSE decreases when a second independent variable (number of deliveries) is added. The implication is that the estimated multiple regression equation provides a better fit for the observed data.

In Chapter 12 we used the coefficient of determination, $r^2 = SSR/SST$, to measure the goodness of fit for the estimated regression equation. The same concept applies to multiple regression. The term **multiple coefficient of determination** indicates that we are measuring the goodness of fit for the estimated multiple regression equation. The multiple coefficient of determination, denoted $R^2$, is computed as follows.

*In the Excel Regression tool output the label R Square is used to identify the value of $R^2$.*

MULTIPLE COEFFICIENT OF DETERMINATION

$$R^2 = \frac{SSR}{SST} \qquad \text{(13.8)}$$

The multiple coefficient of determination can be interpreted as the proportion of the variability in the dependent variable that can be explained by the estimated multiple regression equation. Hence, when multiplied by 100, it can be interpreted as the percentage of the variability in $y$ that can be explained by the estimated regression equation.

In the two-independent-variable Butler Trucking example, with SSR = 21.6006 and SST = 23.9, we have

$$R^2 = \frac{21.6006}{23.9} = .9038$$

Therefore, 90.38% of the variability in travel time $y$ is explained by the estimated multiple regression equation with miles traveled and number of deliveries as the independent variables. In Figure 13.5, we see that the multiple coefficient of determination is also provided by the Excel output; it is denoted by R Square = .9038 (see cell B17).

*Adding independent variables causes the prediction errors (residuals) to become smaller, thus reducing the sum of squares due to error, SSE. Because SSR = SST − SSE, when SSE becomes smaller, SSR becomes larger, causing $R^2$ = SSR/SST to increase.*

Figure 13.3 shows that the R Square value for the estimated regression equation with only one independent variable, number of miles traveled ($x_1$), is .6641. Thus, the percentage of the variability in travel time that is explained by the estimated regression equation increases from 66.41% to 90.38% when number of deliveries is added as a second independent variable. In general, $R^2$ always increases as independent variables are added to the model.

Many analysts prefer adjusting $R^2$ for the number of independent variables to avoid overestimating the impact of adding an independent variable on the amount of variability explained by the estimated regression equation. With $n$ denoting the number of observations and $p$ denoting the number of independent variables, the **adjusted multiple coefficient of determination** is computed as follows.

*If a variable is added to the model, $R^2$ becomes larger even if the variable added is not statistically significant. The adjusted multiple coefficient of determination compensates for the number of independent variables in the model.*

ADJUSTED MULTIPLE COEFFICIENT OF DETERMINATION

$$R_a^2 = 1 - (1 - R^2)\frac{n - 1}{n - p - 1} \tag{13.9}$$

For the Butler Trucking example with $n = 10$ and $p = 2$, we have

$$R_a^2 = 1 - (1 - .9038)\frac{10 - 1}{10 - 2 - 1} = .8763$$

Thus, after adjusting for the two independent variables, we have an adjusted multiple coefficient of determination of .8763. This value is provided by the Excel output in Figure 13.5 as Adjusted R Square = .8763 (see cell B18).

## Exercises

### Methods

11. In exercise 1, the following estimated regression equation based on 10 observations was presented.

$$\hat{y} = 29.1270 + .5906x_1 + .4980x_2$$

The values of SST and SSR are 6724.125 and 6216.375, respectively.
a. Find SSE.
b. Compute $R^2$.
c. Compute $R_a^2$.
d. Comment on the goodness of fit.

12. In exercise 2, 10 observations were provided for a dependent variable $y$ and two independent variables $x_1$ and $x_2$; for these data SST $= 15,182.9$ and SSR $= 14,052.2$.
a. Compute $R^2$.
b. Compute $R_a^2$.
c. Does the estimated regression equation explain a large amount of the variability in the data? Explain.

13. In exercise 3, the following estimated regression equation based on 30 observations was presented.

$$\hat{y} = 17.6 + 3.8x_1 - 2.3x_2 + 7.6x_3 + 2.7x_4$$

The values of SST and SSR are 1805 and 1760, respectively.
a. Compute $R^2$.
b. Compute $R_a^2$.
c. Comment on the goodness of fit.

## Applications

14. In exercise 4, the following estimated regression equation relating sales to inventory investment and advertising expenditures was given.

$$\hat{y} = 25 + 10x_1 + 8x_2$$

The data used to develop the model came from a survey of 10 stores; for those data, SST $= 16,000$ and SSR $= 12,000$.
a. For the estimated regression equation given, compute $R^2$.
b. Compute $R_a^2$.
c. Does the model appear to explain a large amount of variability in the data? Explain.

15. In exercise 5, the owner of Showtime Movie Theaters, Inc., used multiple regression analysis to predict gross revenue ($y$) as a function of television advertising ($x_1$) and newspaper advertising ($x_2$). The estimated regression equation was

$$\hat{y} = 83.2 + 2.29x_1 + 1.30x_2$$

**WEB** file

Showtime

The computer solution provided SST $= 25.5$ and SSR $= 23.435$.
a. Compute and interpret $R^2$ and $R_a^2$.
b. When television advertising was the only independent variable, $R^2 = .653$ and $R_a^2 = .595$. Do you prefer the multiple regression results? Explain.

16. In exercise 6, data were given on the recruiter assessment score (highest $= 5$), the out-of-state tuition and fees (rounded to the nearest $1000), and the average starting salary and bonus (rounded to the nearest $1000) for a sample of 20 graduate schools of business (*U.S. News & World Report 2009 Edition America's Best Graduate Schools*).

**WEB** file

BusinessSchools2

a. Did the estimated regression equation that uses only the recruiter assessment score as the independent variable to predict the starting salary and bonus provide a good fit? Explain.
b. Discuss the benefits of using both the recruiter assessment score and the out-of-state tuition and fees to predict the starting salary and bonus.

17. In exercise 9, an estimated regression equation was developed relating the top speed for a boat to the boat's beam and horsepower rating.

**WEB** file

Boats

a. Compute and interpret and $R^2$ and $R_a^2$.
b. Does the estimated regression equation provide a good fit to the data? Explain.

18. Refer to exercise 10, where data were reported on a variety of statistics for the 29 teams in the National Basketball Association for a portion of the 2004 season (NBA website, January 3, 2004).

   a. In part (c) of exercise 10, an estimated regression equation was developed relating the proportion of games won given the percentage of field goals made by the team, the proportion of three-point shots made by the team's opponent, and the number of turnovers committed by the team's opponent. What are the values of $R^2$ and $R_a^2$?

   b. Does the estimated regression equation provide a good fit to the data? Explain.

## (13.4) Model Assumptions

In Section 13.1 we introduced the following multiple regression model.

---

**MULTIPLE REGRESSION MODEL**

$$y = \beta_0 + \beta_1 x_1 + \beta_2 x_2 + \cdots + \beta_p x_p + \epsilon \qquad \textbf{(13.10)}$$

---

The assumptions about the error term $\epsilon$ in the multiple regression model parallel those for the simple linear regression model.

---

**ASSUMPTIONS ABOUT THE ERROR TERM $\epsilon$ IN THE MULTIPLE REGRESSION MODEL** $y = \beta_0 + \beta_1 x_1 + \cdots + \beta_p x_p + \epsilon$

1. The error term $\epsilon$ is a random variable with mean or expected value of zero; that is, $E(\epsilon) = 0$.

   *Implication:* For given values of $x_1, x_2, \ldots, x_p$, the expected, or average, value of $y$ is given by

   $$E(y) = \beta_0 + \beta_1 x_1 + \beta_2 x_2 + \cdots + \beta_p x_p \qquad \textbf{(13.11)}$$

   Equation (13.11) is the multiple regression equation we introduced in Section 13.1. In this equation, $E(y)$ represents the average of all possible values of $y$ that might occur for the given values of $x_1, x_2, \ldots, x_p$.

2. The variance of $\epsilon$ is denoted by $\sigma^2$ and is the same for all values of the independent variables $x_1, x_2, \ldots, x_p$.

   *Implication:* The variance of $y$ about the regression line equals $\sigma^2$ and is the same for all values of $x_1, x_2, \ldots, x_p$.

3. The values of $\epsilon$ are independent.

   *Implication:* The value of $\epsilon$ for a particular set of values for the independent variables is not related to the value of $\epsilon$ for any other set of values.

4. The error term $\epsilon$ is a normally distributed random variable reflecting the deviation between the $y$ value and the expected value of $y$ given by $\beta_0 + \beta_1 x_1 + \beta_2 x_2 + \cdots + \beta_p x_p$.

   *Implication:* Because $\beta_0, \beta_1, \ldots, \beta_p$ are constants for the given values of $x_1, x_2, \ldots, x_p$, the dependent variable $y$ is also a normally distributed random variable.

---

To obtain more insight about the form of the relationship given by equation (13.11), consider the following two-independent-variable multiple regression equation:

$$E(y) = \beta_0 + \beta_1 x_1 + \beta_2 x_2$$

**FIGURE 13.6** GRAPH OF THE REGRESSION EQUATION FOR MULTIPLE REGRESSION ANALYSIS WITH TWO INDEPENDENT VARIABLES

The graph of this equation is a plane in three-dimensional space. Figure 13.6 provides an example of such a graph. Note that the value of $\epsilon$ shown is the difference between the actual $y$ value and the expected value of $y$, $E(y)$, when $x_1 = x_1^*$ and $x_2 = x_2^*$.

In regression analysis, the term *response variable* is often used in place of the term *dependent variable*. Furthermore, since the multiple regression equation generates a plane or surface, its graph is called a *response surface*.

## 13.5 Testing for Significance

In this section we show how to conduct significance tests for a multiple regression relationship. The significance tests we used in simple linear regression were a $t$ test and an $F$ test. In simple linear regression, both tests provide the same conclusion; that is, if the null hypothesis is rejected, we conclude that $\beta_1 \neq 0$. In multiple regression, the $t$ test and the $F$ test have different purposes.

1. The $F$ test is used to determine whether a significant relationship exists between the dependent variable and the set of all the independent variables; we will refer to the $F$ test as the test for *overall significance*.
2. If the $F$ test shows an overall significance, the $t$ test is used to determine whether each of the individual independent variables is significant. A separate $t$ test is conducted for each of the independent variables in the model; we refer to each of these $t$ tests as a test for *individual significance*.

In the material that follows, we will explain the $F$ test and the $t$ test and apply each to the Butler Trucking Company example.

### $F$ Test

The multiple regression model as defined in Section 13.4 is

$$y = \beta_0 + \beta_1 x_1 + \beta_2 x_2 + \cdots + \beta_p x_p + \epsilon$$

The hypotheses for the $F$ test involve the parameters of the multiple regression model.

$$H_0: \beta_1 = \beta_2 = \cdots = \beta_p = 0$$
$$H_a: \text{One or more of the parameters is not equal to zero}$$

If $H_0$ is rejected, the test gives us sufficient statistical evidence to conclude that one or more of the parameters is not equal to zero and that the overall relationship between $y$ and the set of independent variables $x_1, x_2, \ldots, x_p$ is significant. However, if $H_0$ cannot be rejected, we do not have sufficient evidence to conclude that a significant relationship is present.

Before describing the steps of the $F$ test, we need to review the concept of *mean square*. A mean square is a sum of squares divided by its corresponding degrees of freedom. In the multiple regression case, the total sum of squares has $n - 1$ degrees of freedom, the sum of squares due to regression has $p$ degrees of freedom, and the sum of squares due to error has $n - p - 1$ degrees of freedom. Hence, the mean square due to regression (MSR) is SSR/$p$ and the mean square due to error (MSE) is SSE/$(n - p - 1)$.

$$\text{MSR} = \frac{\text{SSR}}{p} \qquad (13.12)$$

and

$$\text{MSE} = \frac{\text{SSE}}{n - p - 1} \qquad (13.13)$$

As discussed in Chapter 12, MSE provides an unbiased estimate of $\sigma^2$, the variance of the error term $\epsilon$. If $H_0: \beta_1 = \beta_2 = \cdots = \beta_p = 0$ is true, MSR also provides an unbiased estimate of $\sigma^2$, and the value of MSR/MSE should be close to 1. However, if $H_0$ is false, MSR overestimates $\sigma^2$ and the value of MSR/MSE becomes larger. To determine how large the value of MSR/MSE must be to reject $H_0$, we make use of the fact that if $H_0$ is true and the assumptions about the multiple regression model are valid, the sampling distribution of MSR/MSE is an $F$ distribution with $p$ degrees of freedom in the numerator and $n - p - 1$ degrees of freedom in the denominator. A summary of the $F$ test for significance in multiple regression follows.

---

*F* TEST FOR OVERALL SIGNIFICANCE

$$H_0: \beta_1 = \beta_2 = \cdots = \beta_p = 0$$
$$H_a: \text{One or more of the parameters is not equal to zero}$$

TEST STATISTIC

$$F = \frac{\text{MSR}}{\text{MSE}} \qquad (13.14)$$

REJECTION RULE

$p$-value approach:        Reject $H_0$ if $p$-value $\leq \alpha$
Critical value approach:    Reject $H_0$ if $F \geq F_\alpha$

where $F_\alpha$ is based on an $F$ distribution with $p$ degrees of freedom in the numerator and $n - p - 1$ degrees of freedom in the denominator.

---

Let us apply the $F$ test to the Butler Trucking Company multiple regression problem. With two independent variables, the hypotheses are written as follows:

$$H_0: \beta_1 = \beta_2 = 0$$
$$H_a: \beta_1 \text{ and/or } \beta_2 \text{ is not equal to zero}$$

**FIGURE 13.7**  REGRESSION TOOL OUTPUT FOR THE BUTLER TRUCKING EXAMPLE WITH TWO INDEPENDENT VARIABLES

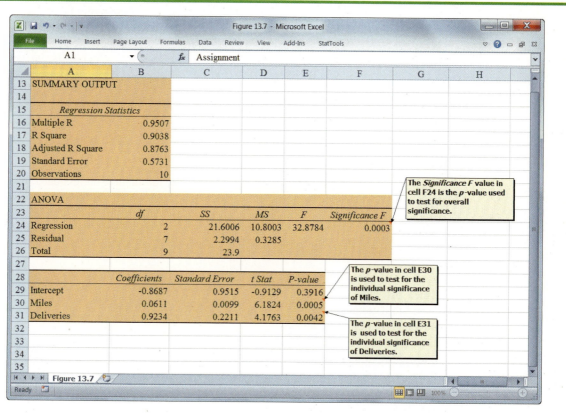

*Note: Rows 1–12 are hidden.*

Figure 13.7 shows a portion of the Excel Regression tool output shown previously in Figure 13.5 with miles traveled $(x_1)$ and number of deliveries $(x_2)$ as the two independent variables. In the analysis of variance part of the output, we see that MSR = 10.8003 and MSE = .3285. Using equation (13.14), we obtain the test statistic.

$$F = \frac{10.8003}{.3285} = 32.9$$

*The label Significance F in cell F23 is used to identify the p-value in cell F24.*

Note that the $F$ value in the Excel output is $F = 32.8784$; the value we calculated differs because we used rounded values for MSR and MSE in the calculation. Using $\alpha = .01$, the $p$-value = 0.0003 in cell F24 indicates that we can reject $H_0: \beta_1 = \beta_2 = 0$ because the $p$-value is less than $\alpha = .01$. Alternatively, Table 4 of Appendix B shows that with two degrees of freedom in the numerator and seven degrees of freedom in the denominator, $F_{.01} = 9.55$. With $32.9 > 9.55$, we reject $H_0: \beta_1 = \beta_2 = 0$ and conclude that a significant relationship is present between travel time $y$ and the two independent variables, miles traveled and number of deliveries.

As noted previously, MSE provides an unbiased estimate of $\sigma^2$, the variance of the error term $\epsilon$. Thus, the estimate of $\sigma^2$ is MSE = .3285. The square root of MSE is the estimate of the standard deviation of the error term. As defined in Section 12.5, this standard deviation is called the standard error of the estimate and is denoted $s$. Hence, we have $s = \sqrt{\text{MSE}} = \sqrt{.3285} = .5731$. Note that the value of the standard error of the estimate appears in cell B19 of Figure 13.7.

**TABLE 13.3**  GENERAL FORM OF THE ANOVA TABLE FOR MULTIPLE REGRESSION WITH $p$ INDEPENDENT VARIABLES

| Source | Sum of Squares | Degrees of Freedom | Mean Square | F | p-value |
|---|---|---|---|---|---|
| Regression | SSR | $p$ | $MSR = \dfrac{SSR}{p}$ | $F = \dfrac{MSR}{MSE}$ | |
| Error | SSE | $n - p - 1$ | $MSE = \dfrac{SSE}{n - p - 1}$ | | |
| Total | SST | $n - 1$ | | | |

Table 13.3 is the general form of the ANOVA table for multiple regression. The value of the $F$ test statistic and its corresponding $p$-value in the last column can be used to make the hypothesis test conclusion. By reviewing the Excel output for Butler Trucking Company in Figure 13.7, we see that Excel's analysis of variance table contains this information.

## $t$ Test

If the $F$ test shows that the multiple regression relationship is significant, a $t$ test can be conducted to determine the significance of each of the individual parameters. The $t$ test for individual significance follows.

---

$t$ TEST FOR INDIVIDUAL SIGNIFICANCE

For any parameter $\beta_i$

$$H_0\colon \beta_i = 0$$
$$H_a\colon \beta_i \neq 0$$

TEST STATISTIC

$$t = \frac{b_i}{s_{b_i}} \tag{13.15}$$

REJECTION RULE

$p$-value approach:  Reject $H_0$ if $p$-value $\leq \alpha$

Critical value approach:  Reject $H_0$ if $t \leq -t_{\alpha/2}$ or if $t \geq t_{\alpha/2}$

where $t_{\alpha/2}$ is based on a $t$ distribution with $n - p - 1$ degrees of freedom.

---

In the test statistic, $s_{b_i}$ is the estimate of the standard deviation of $b_i$. The value of $s_{b_i}$ will be provided by the computer software package.

Let us conduct the $t$ test for the Butler Trucking regression problem. Refer to the section of Figure 13.7 that shows the Excel output for the $t$-ratio calculations. Values of $b_1$, $b_2$, $s_{b_1}$, and $s_{b_2}$ are as follows.

$$b_1 = .0611 \quad s_{b_1} = .0099$$
$$b_2 = .9234 \quad s_{b_2} = .2211$$

Using equation (13.15), we obtain the test statistic for the hypotheses involving parameters $\beta_1$ and $\beta_2$.

$$t = .0611/.0099 = 6.1717$$
$$t = .9234/.2211 = 4.1764$$

*The t values in the Regression tool output are 6.1824 and 4.1763. The difference is due to rounding.*

Note that both of these $t$-ratio values and the corresponding $p$-values are provided by the Excel Regression tool output in Figure 13.7. Using $\alpha = .01$, the $p$-values of .0005 and .0042 on the Excel output indicate that we can reject $H_0$: $\beta_1 = 0$ and $H_0$: $\beta_2 = 0$. Hence, both parameters are statistically significant. Alternatively, Table 2 of Appendix B shows that with $n - p - 1 = 10 - 2 - 1 = 7$ degrees of freedom, $t_{.005} = 3.499$. Because $6.1717 > 3.499$, we reject $H_0$: $\beta_1 = 0$. Similarly, with $4.1763 > 3.499$, we reject $H_0$: $\beta_2 = 0$.

## Multicollinearity

We use the term *independent variable* in regression analysis to refer to any variable being used to predict or explain the value of the dependent variable. The term does not mean, however, that the independent variables themselves are independent in any statistical sense. On the contrary, most independent variables in a multiple regression problem are correlated to some degree with one another. For example, in the Butler Trucking example involving the two independent variables $x_1$ (miles traveled) and $x_2$ (number of deliveries), we could treat the miles traveled as the dependent variable and the number of deliveries as the independent variable to determine whether those two variables are themselves related. We could then compute the sample correlation coefficient $r_{x_1 x_2}$ to determine the extent to which the variables are related. Doing so yields $r_{x_1 x_2} = .16$. Thus, we find some degree of linear association between the two independent variables. In multiple regression analysis, **multicollinearity** refers to the correlation among the independent variables.

To provide a better perspective of the potential problems of multicollinearity, let us consider a modification of the Butler Trucking example. Instead of $x_2$ being the number of deliveries, let $x_2$ denote the number of gallons of gasoline consumed. Clearly, $x_1$ (the miles traveled) and $x_2$ are related; that is, we know that the number of gallons of gasoline used depends on the number of miles traveled. Hence, we would conclude logically that $x_1$ and $x_2$ are highly correlated independent variables.

*When the independent variables are highly correlated, it is not possible to determine the separate effect of any particular independent variable on the dependent variable.*

Assume that we obtain the equation $\hat{y} = b_0 + b_1 x_1 + b_2 x_2$ and find that the $F$ test shows the relationship to be significant. Then suppose we conduct a $t$ test on $\beta_1$ to determine whether $\beta_1 \neq 0$, and we cannot reject $H_0$: $\beta_1 = 0$. Does this result mean that travel time is not related to miles traveled? Not necessarily. What it probably means is that with $x_2$ already in the model, $x_1$ does not make a significant contribution to determining the value of $y$. This interpretation makes sense in our example; if we know the amount of gasoline consumed, we do not gain much additional information useful in predicting $y$ by knowing the miles traveled. Similarly, a $t$ test might lead us to conclude $\beta_2 = 0$ on the grounds that, with $x_1$ in the model, knowledge of the amount of gasoline consumed does not add much.

To summarize, in $t$ tests for the significance of individual parameters, the difficulty caused by multicollinearity is that it is possible to conclude that none of the individual parameters are significantly different from zero when an $F$ test on the overall multiple regression equation indicates a significant relationship. This problem is avoided when there is little correlation among the independent variables.

*A sample correlation coefficient greater than +.7 or less than −.7 for two independent variables is a rule of thumb warning of potential problems with multicollinearity.*

Statisticians have developed several tests for determining whether multicollinearity is high enough to cause problems. According to the rule of thumb test, multicollinearity is a potential problem if the absolute value of the sample correlation coefficient exceeds .7 for any two of the independent variables. The other types of tests are more advanced and beyond the scope of this text.

If possible, every attempt should be made to avoid including independent variables that are highly correlated. In practice, however, strict adherence to this policy is rarely possible. When decision makers have reason to believe substantial multicollinearity is present, they must realize that separating the effects of the individual independent variables on the dependent variable is difficult.

## NOTES AND COMMENTS

Ordinarily, multicollinearity does not affect the way in which we perform our regression analysis or interpret the output from a study. However, when multicollinearity is severe—that is, when two or more of the independent variables are highly correlated with one another—we can have difficulty interpreting the results of $t$ tests on the individual parameters. In addition to the type of problem illustrated in this section, severe cases of multicollinearity have been shown to result in least squares estimates that have the wrong sign. That is,

in simulated studies where researchers created the underlying regression model and then applied the least squares technique to develop estimates of $\beta_0$, $\beta_1$, $\beta_2$, and so on, it has been shown that under conditions of high multicollinearity the least squares estimates can have a sign opposite that of the parameter being estimated. For example, $\beta_2$ might actually be $+10$ and $b_2$, its estimate, might turn out to be $-2$. Thus, little faith can be placed in the individual coefficients if multicollinearity is present to a high degree.

## Exercises

### Methods

19.  In exercise 1, the following estimated regression equation based on 10 observations was presented.

$$\hat{y} = 29.1270 + .5906x_1 + .4980x_2$$

Here SST = 6724.125, SSR = 6216.375, $s_{b_1}$ = .0813, and $s_{b_2}$ = .0567.
  a.  Compute MSR and MSE.
  b.  Compute $F$ and perform the appropriate $F$ test. Use $\alpha = .05$.
  c.  Perform a $t$ test for the significance of $\beta_1$. Use $\alpha = .05$.
  d.  Perform a $t$ test for the significance of $\beta_2$. Use $\alpha = .05$.

20.  Refer to the data presented in exercise 2. The estimated regression equation for these data is

$$\hat{y} = -18.4 + 2.01x_1 + 4.74x_2$$

Here SST = 15,182.9, SSR = 14,052.2, $s_{b_1}$ = .2471, and $s_{b_2}$ = .9484.
  a.  Test for a significant relationship among $x_1$, $x_2$, and $y$. Use $\alpha = .05$.
  b.  Is $\beta_1$ significant? Use $\alpha = .05$.
  c.  Is $\beta_2$ significant? Use $\alpha = .05$.

21.  The following estimated regression equation was developed for a model involving two independent variables.

$$\hat{y} = 40.7 + 8.63x_1 + 2.71x_2$$

After $x_2$ was dropped from the model, the least squares method was used to obtain an estimated regression equation involving only $x_1$ as an independent variable.

$$\hat{y} = 42.0 + 9.01x_1$$

a.   Give an interpretation of the coefficient of $x_1$ in both models.
b.   Could multicollinearity explain why the coefficient of $x_1$ differs in the two models? If so, how?

## Applications

22.   In exercise 4, the following estimated regression equation relating sales to inventory investment and advertising expenditures was given.

$$\hat{y} = 25 + 10x_1 + 8x_2$$

The data used to develop the model came from a survey of 10 stores; for these data SST = 16,000 and SSR = 12,000.
a.   Compute SSE, MSE, and MSR.
b.   Use an $F$ test and a .05 level of significance to determine whether there is a relationship among the variables.

23.   Refer to exercise 5.

a.   Use $\alpha = .01$ to test the hypotheses

$$H_0: \beta_1 = \beta_2 = 0$$
$$H_a: \beta_1 \text{ and/or } \beta_2 \text{ is not equal to zero}$$

for the model $y = \beta_0 + \beta_1x_1 + \beta_2x_2 + \epsilon$, where

$$x_1 = \text{television advertising (\$1000s)}$$
$$x_2 = \text{newspaper advertising (\$1000s)}$$

b.   Use $\alpha = .05$ to test the significance of $\beta_1$. Should $x_1$ be dropped from the model?
c.   Use $\alpha = .05$ to test the significance of $\beta_2$. Should $x_2$ be dropped from the model?

24.   *The Wall Street Journal* conducted a study of basketball spending at top colleges. A portion of the data showing the revenue ($ millions), percentage of wins, and the coach's salary ($ millions) for 39 of the country's top basketball programs follows (*The Wall Street Journal*, March 11–12, 2006).

| School | Revenue | % Wins | Salary |
|---|---|---|---|
| Alabama | 6.5 | 61 | 1.00 |
| Arizona | 16.6 | 63 | 0.70 |
| Arkansas | 11.1 | 72 | 0.80 |
| Boston College | 3.4 | 80 | 0.53 |
| . | . | . | . |
| . | . | . | . |
| . | . | . | . |
| Washington | 5.0 | 83 | 0.89 |
| West Virginia | 4.9 | 67 | 0.70 |
| Wichita State | 3.1 | 75 | 0.41 |
| Wisconsin | 12.0 | 66 | 0.70 |

a.  Develop the estimated regression equation that can be used to predict the coach's salary given the revenue generated by the program and the percentage of wins.
b.  Use the $F$ test to determine the overall significance of the relationship. What is your conclusion at the .05 level of significance?
c.  Use the $t$ test to determine the significance of each independent variable. What is your conclusion at the .05 level of significance?

25.  Small cars offer higher fuel efficiency, are easy to maneuver and park, and have generally performed well in road tests. The following data show the overall fuel efficiency rating (miles per gallon), predicted reliability (highest = 5), safety rating (highest = 5), and the price ($) for 20 small cars (*Consumer Reports*, March 2009).

WEB file

SmallCars

| Make & Model | MPG | Reliability | Safety | Price ($) |
|---|---|---|---|---|
| Chevrolet Aveo LT | 25 | 2 | 2 | 16,205 |
| Chevrolet Cobalt LT | 24 | 3 | 3 | 17,450 |
| Ford Focus SES | 26 | 4 | 3 | 18,490 |
| Ford Focus SES (MT) | 29 | 4 | 3 | 17,440 |
| Honda Civic EX | 28 | 5 | 4 | 19,610 |
| Honda Civic EX (MT) | 31 | 5 | 4 | 18,810 |
| Honda Fit Sport (MT) | 33 | 5 | 4 | 16,730 |
| Hyundai Accent GLS | 28 | 4 | 2 | 14,230 |
| Hyundai Elantra GLS | 27 | 5 | 3 | 17,555 |
| Hyundai Elantra SE | 27 | 5 | 4 | 17,980 |
| Kia Spectra EX | 25 | 4 | 2 | 16,185 |
| Kia Spectra EX (MT) | 28 | 4 | 2 | 15,185 |
| Nissan Versa 1.8 SL | 28 | 3 | 3 | 16,675 |
| Nissan Versa 1.85 | 27 | 1 | 3 | 16,130 |
| Scion xD | 29 | 5 | 3 | 16,620 |
| Scion xD (MT) | 34 | 5 | 3 | 15,820 |
| Suzuki SX4 LE | 26 | 5 | 3 | 17,378 |
| Toyota Corolla (base, MT) | 32 | 4 | 4 | 16,419 |
| Toyota Corolla LE | 32 | 4 | 4 | 18,404 |
| Toyota Yaris Hatchback | 30 | 5 | 3 | 16,095 |

a.  Determine the estimated regression equation that can be used to predict the price of a small car given its overall fuel efficiency rating, predicted reliability, and safety rating.
b.  Use the $F$ test to determine the overall significance of the relationship. What is the conclusion at the .05 level of significance?
c.  Use the $t$ test to determine the significance of each independent variable. What is your conclusion at the .05 level of significance?
d.  Remove any independent variable that is not significant from the estimated regression equation. What is your recommended estimated regression equation? Compare the value of $R^2$ for this estimated regression equation with the value of $R^2$ for the estimated regression equation from part (a). Discuss the differences.

26.  In exercise 10 an estimated regression equation was developed relating the proportion of games won given the proportion of field goals made by the team, the proportion of three-point shots made by the team's opponent, and the number of turnovers committed by the team's opponent.

WEB file

NBA

a.  Use the $F$ test to determine the overall significance of the relationship. What is your conclusion at the .05 level of significance?
b.  Use the $t$ test to determine the significance of each independent variable. What is your conclusion at the .05 level of significance?

# Using the Estimated Regression Equation for Estimation and Prediction

The procedures for estimating the mean value of $y$ and predicting an individual value of $y$ in multiple regression are similar to those in regression analysis involving one independent variable. First, recall that in Chapter 12 we showed that the estimated regression equation $\hat{y} = b_0 + b_1 x$ can be used to estimate the mean value of $y$ for a given value of $x$ as well as to predict an individual value of $y$ for a given value of $x$. In multiple regression we use the same procedure. That is, we substitute the value of $x_1, x_2, \ldots, x_p$ into the estimated regression equation and use the corresponding value of $\hat{y}$ to estimate the mean value of $y$ given $x_1, x_2, \ldots, x_p$ as well as to predict an individual of $y$ given $x_1, x_2, \ldots, x_p$.

To illustrate the procedure in multiple regression, suppose that for the Butler Trucking example we want to use the estimated regression equation involving $x_1$ (miles traveled) and $x_2$ (number of deliveries) to develop two interval estimates:

1. A *confidence interval* of the mean travel time for all trucks that travel 100 miles and make two deliveries
2. A *prediction interval* of the travel time for *one specific* truck that travels 100 miles and makes two deliveries

The Excel output in Figure 13.5 showed the estimated regression equation is

$$\hat{y} = -.8687 + .0611x_1 + .9234x_2$$

With $x_1 = 100$ and $x_2 = 2$, we obtain the following value of $\hat{y}$:

$$\hat{y} = -.8687 + .0611(100) + .9234(2) = 7.09$$

Hence a point estimate of the mean travel time for all trucks that travel 100 miles and make two deliveries is approximately seven hours. And a prediction of the travel time for one specific truck that travels 100 miles and makes two deliveries is also seven hours.

*In the appendix to Chapter 12 we showed how to compute prediction intervals using StatTools.*

The formulas required to develop confidence and prediction intervals for multiple regression are beyond the scope of the text. And in multiple regression hand computation is simply not practical. Although Excel's Regression Tool does not have an option for computing interval estimates, StatTools—the Excel add-in provided with the text—can be used to compute prediction intervals. Table 13.4 shows the 95% prediction intervals for the

**TABLE 13.4**   THE 95% PREDICTION INTERVALS FOR BUTLER TRUCKING

| Value of $x_1$ | Value of $x_2$ | Prediction Interval | |
|---|---|---|---|
| | | Lower Limit | Upper Limit |
| 50 | 2 | 2.414 | 5.656 |
| 50 | 3 | 3.368 | 6.548 |
| 50 | 4 | 4.157 | 7.607 |
| 100 | 2 | 5.500 | 8.683 |
| 100 | 3 | 6.520 | 9.510 |
| 100 | 4 | 7.362 | 10.515 |

Butler Trucking problem for selected values of $x_1$ and $x_2$. We see that the prediction interval of the travel time for *one specific* truck that travels 100 miles and makes two deliveries is approximately 5.5 to 8.7 hours.

## Exercises

### Methods

27. In exercise 1, the following estimated regression equation based on 10 observations was presented.

$$\hat{y} = 29.1270 + .5906x_1 + .4980x_2$$

   a. Develop a point estimate of the mean value of $y$ when $x_1 = 180$ and $x_2 = 310$.
   b. Predict an individual value of $y$ when $x_1 = 180$ and $x_2 = 310$.

28. Refer to the data in exercise 2. The estimated regression equation for those data is

$$\hat{y} = -18.4 + 2.01x_1 + 4.74x_2$$

   a. Develop a point estimate of the mean value of $y$ when $x_1 = 45$ and $x_2 = 15$.
   b. Develop a 95% prediction interval for $y$ when $x_1 = 45$ and $x_2 = 15$.

### Applications

29. In exercise 5, the owner of Showtime Movie Theaters, Inc., used multiple regression analysis to predict gross revenue ($y$) as a function of television advertising ($x_1$) and newspaper advertising ($x_2$). The estimated regression equation was

$$\hat{y} = 83.2 + 2.29x_1 + 1.30x_2$$

   a. What is the gross revenue expected for a week when $3500 is spent on television advertising ($x_1 = 3.5$) and $1800 is spent on newspaper advertising ($x_2 = 1.8$)?
   b. Provide a 95% prediction interval for next week's revenue, assuming that the advertising expenditures will be allocated as in part (a).

30. In exercise 9 an estimated regression equation was developed relating the top speed for a boat to the boat's beam and horsepower rating.

**WEB file**

**Boats**

   a. Develop a point estimate for the mean top speed of a boat with a beam of 85 inches and an engine with a 330 horsepower rating.
   b. The Svfara SV609 has a beam of 85 inches and an engine with a 330 horsepower rating. Develop a 95% prediction interval for the mean top speed for the Svfara SV609.

31. The Buyer's Guide section of the website for *Car and Driver* magazine provides reviews and road tests for cars, trucks, SUVs, and vans. The average ratings of overall quality, vehicle styling, braking, handling, fuel economy, interior comfort, acceleration, dependability, fit and finish, transmission, and ride are summarized for each vehicle using a scale ranging from 1 (worst) to 10 (best). A portion of the data for 14 Sports/GT cars is shown here (Car and Driver website, January 7, 2004).

| Sports/GT | Overall | Handling | Dependability | Fit and Finish |
|---|---|---|---|---|
| Acura 3.2CL | 7.80 | 7.83 | 8.17 | 7.67 |
| Acura RSX | 9.02 | 9.46 | 9.35 | 8.97 |
| Audi TT | 9.00 | 9.58 | 8.74 | 9.38 |
| BMW 3-Series/M3 | 8.39 | 9.52 | 8.39 | 8.55 |
| Chevrolet Corvette | 8.82 | 9.64 | 8.54 | 7.87 |
| Ford Mustang | 8.34 | 8.85 | 8.70 | 7.34 |
| Honda Civic Si | 8.92 | 9.31 | 9.50 | 7.93 |
| Infiniti G35 | 8.70 | 9.34 | 8.96 | 8.07 |
| Mazda RX-8 | 8.58 | 9.79 | 8.96 | 8.12 |
| Mini Cooper | 8.76 | 10.00 | 8.69 | 8.33 |
| Mitsubishi Eclipse | 8.17 | 8.95 | 8.25 | 7.36 |
| Nissan 350Z | 8.07 | 9.35 | 7.56 | 8.21 |
| Porsche 911 | 9.55 | 9.91 | 8.86 | 9.55 |
| Toyota Celica | 8.77 | 9.29 | 9.04 | 7.97 |

**SportsCar**

a.  Develop an estimated regression equation using handling, dependability, and fit and finish to predict overall quality.

b.  Another Sports/GT car rated by *Car and Driver* is the Honda Accord. The ratings for handling, dependability, and fit and finish for the Honda Accord were 8.28, 9.06, and 8.07, respectively. Estimate the overall rating for this car.

c.  Provide a 95% prediction interval for overall quality for the Honda Accord described in part (b).

d.  The overall rating reported by *Car and Driver* for the Honda Accord was 8.65. How does this rating compare to the estimates you developed in parts (b) and (d)?

## 13.7   Categorical Independent Variables

*The independent variables may be categorical or quantitative.*

Thus far, the examples we have considered involved quantitative independent variables such as student population, distance traveled, and number of deliveries. In many situations, however, we must work with **categorical independent variables** such as gender (male, female), method of payment (cash, credit card, check), and so on. The purpose of this section is to show how categorical variables are handled in regression analysis. To illustrate the use and interpretation of a categorical independent variable, we will consider a problem facing the managers of Johnson Filtration, Inc.

### An Example: Johnson Filtration, Inc.

Johnson Filtration, Inc., provides maintenance service for water-filtration systems throughout southern Florida. Customers contact Johnson with requests for maintenance service on their water-filtration systems. To estimate the service time and the service cost, Johnson's managers want to predict the repair time necessary for each maintenance request. Hence, repair time in hours is the dependent variable. Repair time is believed to be related to two factors, the number of months since the last maintenance service and the type of repair problem (mechanical or electrical). Data for a sample of 10 service calls are reported in Table 13.5.

Let $y$ denote the repair time in hours and $x_1$ denote the number of months since the last maintenance service. The regression model that uses only $x_1$ to predict $y$ is

$$y = \beta_0 + \beta_1 x_1 + \epsilon$$

**TABLE 13.5** DATA FOR THE JOHNSON FILTRATION EXAMPLE

| Service Call | Months Since Last Service | Type of Repair | Repair Time in Hours |
|---|---|---|---|
| 1 | 2 | electrical | 2.9 |
| 2 | 6 | mechanical | 3.0 |
| 3 | 8 | electrical | 4.8 |
| 4 | 3 | mechanical | 1.8 |
| 5 | 2 | electrical | 2.9 |
| 6 | 7 | electrical | 4.9 |
| 7 | 9 | mechanical | 4.2 |
| 8 | 8 | mechanical | 4.8 |
| 9 | 4 | electrical | 4.4 |
| 10 | 6 | electrical | 4.5 |

Using Excel's Regression tool to develop the estimated regression equation, we obtained the Excel output shown in Figure 13.8. The estimated regression equation is

$$\hat{y} = 2.1473 + .3041x_1 \tag{13.16}$$

At the .05 level of significance, the $p$-value of .0163 for the $t$ (or $F$) test indicates that the number of months since the last service is significantly related to repair time. R Square = .5342 indicates that $x_1$ alone explains 53.42% of the variability in repair time.

**FIGURE 13.8** REGRESSION TOOL OUTPUT FOR THE JOHNSON FILTRATION EXAMPLE WITH MONTHS SINCE LAST SERVICE CALL AS THE INDEPENDENT VARIABLE

*The Excel Regression tool output appears in a new worksheet because we selected New Worksheet Ply as the Output option in the Regression dialog box.*

| | A | B | C | D | E | F | G |
|---|---|---|---|---|---|---|---|
| 1 | SUMMARY OUTPUT | | | | | | |
| 2 | | | | | | | |
| 3 | *Regression Statistics* | | | | | | |
| 4 | Multiple R | 0.7309 | | | | | |
| 5 | R Square | 0.5342 | | | | | |
| 6 | Adjusted R Square | 0.4759 | | | | | |
| 7 | Standard Error | 0.7810 | | | | | |
| 8 | Observations | 10 | | | | | |
| 9 | | | | | | | |
| 10 | ANOVA | | | | | | |
| 11 | | *df* | *SS* | *MS* | *F* | *Significance F* | |
| 12 | Regression | 1 | 5.5960 | 5.5960 | 9.1739 | 0.0163 | |
| 13 | Residual | 8 | 4.8800 | 0.61 | | | |
| 14 | Total | 9 | 10.476 | | | | |
| 15 | | | | | | | |
| 16 | | *Coefficients* | *Standard Error* | *t Stat* | *P-value* | | |
| 17 | Intercept | 2.1473 | 0.6050 | 3.5493 | 0.0075 | | |
| 18 | Months | 0.3041 | 0.1004 | 3.0288 | 0.0163 | | |
| 19 | | | | | | | |

**TABLE 13.6**   DATA FOR THE JOHNSON FILTRATION EXAMPLE WITH TYPE OF REPAIR
INDICATED BY A DUMMY VARIABLE ($x_2 = 0$ FOR MECHANICAL; $x_2 = 1$
FOR ELECTRICAL)

| Customer | Months Since Last Service ($x_1$) | Type of Repair ($x_2$) | Repair Time in Hours ($y$) |
|---|---|---|---|
| 1 | 2 | 1 | 2.9 |
| 2 | 6 | 0 | 3.0 |
| 3 | 8 | 1 | 4.8 |
| 4 | 3 | 0 | 1.8 |
| 5 | 2 | 1 | 2.9 |
| 6 | 7 | 1 | 4.9 |
| 7 | 9 | 0 | 4.2 |
| 8 | 8 | 0 | 4.8 |
| 9 | 4 | 1 | 4.4 |
| 10 | 6 | 1 | 4.5 |

To incorporate the type of repair into the regression model, we define the following variable.

$$x_2 = \begin{cases} 0 \text{ if the type of repair is mechanical} \\ 1 \text{ if the type of repair is electrical} \end{cases}$$

In regression analysis $x_2$ is called a **dummy** or *indicator* **variable**. Using this dummy variable, we can write the multiple regression model as

$$y = \beta_0 + \beta_1 x_1 + \beta_2 x_2 + \epsilon$$

Table 13.6 is the revised data set that includes the values of the dummy variable. Using Excel and the data in Table 13.6, we can develop estimates of the model parameters. The Excel Regression tool output in Figure 13.9 shows that the estimated multiple regression equation is

$$\hat{y} = .9305 + .3876x_1 + 1.2627x_2 \tag{13.17}$$

At the .05 level of significance, the $p$-value of .0010 associated with the $F$ test ($F = 21.357$) indicates that the regression relationship is significant. The $t$ test part of the printout in Figure 13.9 shows that both months since last service ($p$-value = .0004) and type of repair ($p$-value = .0051) are statistically significant. In addition, R Square = 0.8952 and Adjusted R Square = 0.8190 indicate that the estimated regression equation does a good job of explaining the variability in repair times. Thus, equation (13.17) should prove helpful in estimating the repair time necessary for the various service calls.

## Interpreting the Parameters

The multiple regression equation for the Johnson Filtration example is

$$E(y) = \beta_0 + \beta_1 x_1 + \beta_2 x_2 \tag{13.18}$$

**FIGURE 13.9**    REGRESSION TOOL OUTPUT FOR THE JOHNSON FILTRATION EXAMPLE
WITH MONTHS SINCE LAST SERVICE CALL AND TYPE OF REPAIR
AS THE INDEPENDENT VARIABLES

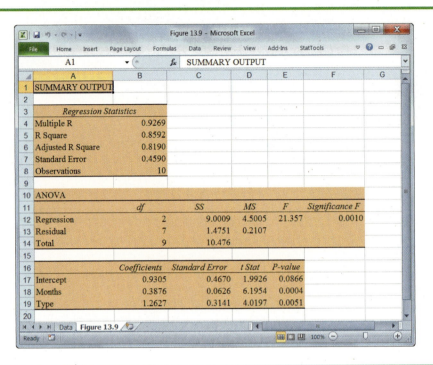

To understand how to interpret the parameters $\beta_0$, $\beta_1$, and $\beta_2$ when a categorical variable is
present, consider the case when $x_2 = 0$ (mechanical repair). Using $E(y \mid \text{mechanical})$ to
denote the mean or expected value of repair time *given* a mechanical repair, we have

$$E(y \mid \text{mechanical}) = \beta_0 + \beta_1 x_1 + \beta_2(0) = \beta_0 + \beta_1 x_1 \qquad \textbf{(13.19)}$$

Similarly, for an electrical repair ($x_2 = 1$), we have

$$E(y \mid \text{electrical}) = \beta_0 + \beta_1 x_1 + \beta_2(1) = \beta_0 + \beta_1 x_1 + \beta_2 \qquad \textbf{(13.20)}$$
$$= (\beta_0 + \beta_2) + \beta_1 x_1$$

Comparing equations (13.19) and (13.20), we see that the mean repair time is a linear function of $x_1$ for both mechanical and electrical repairs. The slope of both equations is $\beta_1$, but
the y-intercept differs. The y-intercept is $\beta_0$ in equation (13.19) for mechanical repairs and
$(\beta_0 + \beta_2)$ in equation (13.20) for electrical repairs. The interpretation of $\beta_2$ is that it indicates the difference between the mean repair time for an electrical repair and the mean repair
time for a mechanical repair.

    If $\beta_2$ is positive, the mean repair time for an electrical repair will be greater than that for
a mechanical repair; if $\beta_2$ is negative, the mean repair time for an electrical repair will be
less than that for a mechanical repair. Finally, if $\beta_2 = 0$, there is no difference in the mean
repair time between electrical and mechanical repairs and the type of repair is not related
to the repair time.

Using the estimated multiple regression equation $\hat{y} = .9305 + .3876x_1 + 1.2627x_2$, we see that .9305 is the estimate of $\beta_0$, .3876 is the estimate of $\beta_1$, and 1.2627 is the estimate of $\beta_2$. Thus, when $x_2 = 0$ (mechanical repair)

$$\hat{y} = .9305 + .3876x_1 \qquad \textbf{(13.21)}$$

and when $x_2 = 1$ (electrical repair)

$$\hat{y} = .9305 + .3876x_1 + 1.2627(1) \qquad \textbf{(13.22)}$$
$$= 2.1932 + .3876x_1$$

In effect, the use of a dummy variable for type of repair provides two estimated regression equations that can be used to predict the repair time, one corresponding to mechanical repairs and one corresponding to electrical repairs. In addition, with $b_2 = 1.2627$, we learn that, on average, electrical repairs require 1.2627 hours longer than mechanical repairs.

Figure 13.10 is the plot of the Johnson data from Table 13.6. Repair time in hours ($y$) is represented by the vertical axis and months since last service ($x_1$) is represented by the horizontal axis. A data point for a mechanical repair is indicated by an M and a data point for an electrical repair is indicated by an E. Equations (13.21) and (13.22) are plotted on the graph to show graphically the two equations that can be used to predict the repair time, one corresponding to mechanical repairs and one corresponding to electrical repairs.

**FIGURE 13.10   SCATTER DIAGRAM FOR THE JOHNSON FILTRATION REPAIR DATA FROM TABLE 13.6**

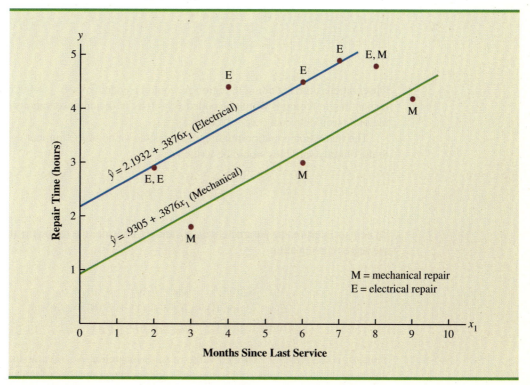

## More Complex Categorical Variables

Because the categorical variable for the Johnson Filtration example had two levels (mechanical and electrical), defining a dummy variable with zero indicating a mechanical repair and one indicating an electrical repair was easy. However, when a categorical variable has more than two levels, care must be taken in both defining and interpreting the dummy variables. As we will show, if a categorical variable has $k$ levels, $k - 1$ dummy variables are required, with each dummy variable being coded as 0 or 1.

*A categorical variable with k levels must be modeled using k − 1 dummy variables. Care must be taken in defining and interpreting the dummy variables.*

For example, suppose a manufacturer of copy machines organized the sales territories for a particular state into three regions: A, B, and C. The managers want to use regression analysis to help predict the number of copiers sold per week. With the number of units sold as the dependent variable, they are considering several independent variables (the number of sales personnel, advertising expenditures, and so on). Suppose the managers believe sales region is also an important factor in predicting the number of copiers sold. Because sales region is a categorical variable with three levels, A, B and C, we will need $3 - 1 = 2$ dummy variables to represent the sales region. Each variable can be coded 0 or 1 as follows.

$$x_1 = \begin{cases} 1 \text{ if sales region B} \\ 0 \text{ otherwise} \end{cases}$$

$$x_2 = \begin{cases} 1 \text{ if sales region C} \\ 0 \text{ otherwise} \end{cases}$$

With this definition, we have the following values of $x_1$ and $x_2$.

| Region | $x_1$ | $x_2$ |
|--------|-------|-------|
| A | 0 | 0 |
| B | 1 | 0 |
| C | 0 | 1 |

Observations corresponding to region A would be coded $x_1 = 0$, $x_2 = 0$; observations corresponding to region B would be coded $x_1 = 1$, $x_2 = 0$; and observations corresponding to region C would be coded $x_1 = 0$, $x_2 = 1$.

The regression equation relating the expected value of the number of units sold, $E(y)$, to the dummy variables would be written as

$$E(y) = \beta_0 + \beta_1 x_1 + \beta_2 x_2$$

To help us interpret the parameters $\beta_0$, $\beta_1$, and $\beta_2$, consider the following three variations of the regression equation.

$$E(y \mid \text{region A}) = \beta_0 + \beta_1(0) + \beta_2(0) = \beta_0$$
$$E(y \mid \text{region B}) = \beta_0 + \beta_1(1) + \beta_2(0) = \beta_0 + \beta_1$$
$$E(y \mid \text{region C}) = \beta_0 + \beta_1(0) + \beta_2(1) = \beta_0 + \beta_2$$

Thus, $\beta_0$ is the mean or expected value of sales for region A; $\beta_1$ is the difference between the mean number of units sold in region B and the mean number of units sold in region A;

and $\beta_2$ is the difference between the mean number of units sold in region C and the mean number of units sold in region A.

Two dummy variables were required because sales region is a categorical variable with three levels. But the assignment of $x_1 = 0$, $x_2 = 0$ to indicate region A, $x_1 = 1$, $x_2 = 0$ to indicate region B, and $x_1 = 0$, $x_2 = 1$ to indicate region C was arbitrary. For example, we could have chosen $x_1 = 1$, $x_2 = 0$ to indicate region A, $x_1 = 0$, $x_2 = 0$ to indicate region B, and $x_1 = 0$, $x_2 = 1$ to indicate region C. In that case, $\beta_1$ would have been interpreted as the mean difference between regions A and B and $\beta_2$ as the mean difference between regions C and B.

The important point to remember is that when a categorical variable has $k$ levels, $k - 1$ dummy variables are required in the multiple regression analysis. Thus, if the sales region example had a fourth region, labeled D, three dummy variables would be necessary. For example, the three dummy variables can be coded as follows.

$$x_1 = \begin{cases} 1 \text{ if sales region B} \\ 0 \text{ otherwise} \end{cases} \qquad x_2 = \begin{cases} 1 \text{ if sales region C} \\ 0 \text{ otherwise} \end{cases} \qquad x_3 = \begin{cases} 1 \text{ if sales region D} \\ 0 \text{ otherwise} \end{cases}$$

## Exercises

### Methods

32. Consider a regression study involving a dependent variable $y$, a quantitative independent variable $x_1$, and a categorical variable with two levels (level 1 and level 2).
    a.  Write a multiple regression equation relating $x_1$ and the categorical variable to $y$.
    b.  What is the expected value of $y$ corresponding to level 1 of the categorical variable?
    c.  What is the expected value of $y$ corresponding to level 2 of the categorical variable?
    d.  Interpret the parameters in your regression equation.

33. Consider a regression study involving a dependent variable $y$, a quantitative independent variable $x_1$, and a categorical independent variable with three possible levels (level 1, level 2, and level 3).
    a.  How many dummy variables are required to represent the categorical variable?
    b.  Write a multiple regression equation relating $x_1$ and the categorical variable to $y$.
    c.  Interpret the parameters in your regression equation.

### Applications

34. Management proposed the following regression model to predict sales at a fast-food outlet.

$$y = \beta_0 + \beta_1 x_1 + \beta_2 x_2 + \beta_3 x_3 + \epsilon$$

where

$$x_1 = \text{number of competitors within one mile}$$
$$x_2 = \text{population within one mile (1000s)}$$
$$x_3 = \begin{cases} 1 \text{ if drive-up window present} \\ 0 \text{ otherwise} \end{cases}$$
$$y = \text{sales (\$1000s)}$$

The following estimated regression equation was developed after 20 outlets were surveyed.

$$\hat{y} = 10.1 - 4.2x_1 + 6.8x_2 + 15.3x_3$$

a.  What is the expected amount of sales attributable to the drive-up window?
b.  Predict sales for a store with two competitors, a population of 8000 within one mile, and no drive-up window.
c.  Predict sales for a store with one competitor, a population of 3000 within one mile, and a drive-up window.

35. Refer to the Johnson Filtration problem introduced in this section. Suppose that in addition to information on the number of months since the machine was serviced and whether a mechanical or an electrical repair was necessary, the managers obtained a list showing which repairperson performed the service. The revised data follow.

| Repair Time in Hours | Months Since Last Service | Type of Repair | Repairperson |
|---|---|---|---|
| 2.9 | 2 | Electrical | Dave Newton |
| 3.0 | 6 | Mechanical | Dave Newton |
| 4.8 | 8 | Electrical | Bob Jones |
| 1.8 | 3 | Mechanical | Dave Newton |
| 2.9 | 2 | Electrical | Dave Newton |
| 4.9 | 7 | Electrical | Bob Jones |
| 4.2 | 9 | Mechanical | Bob Jones |
| 4.8 | 8 | Mechanical | Bob Jones |
| 4.4 | 4 | Electrical | Bob Jones |
| 4.5 | 6 | Electrical | Dave Newton |

a.  Ignore for now the months since the last maintenance service ($x_1$) and the repairperson who performed the service. Develop the estimated simple linear regression equation to predict the repair time ($y$) given the type of repair ($x_2$). Recall that $x_2 = 0$ if the type of repair is mechanical and 1 if the type of repair is electrical.
b.  Does the equation that you developed in part (a) provide a good fit for the observed data? Explain.
c.  Ignore for now the months since the last maintenance service and the type of repair associated with the machine. Develop the estimated simple linear regression equation to predict the repair time given the repairperson who performed the service. Let $x_3 = 0$ if Bob Jones performed the service and $x_3 = 1$ if Dave Newton performed the service.
d.  Does the equation that you developed in part (c) provide a good fit for the observed data? Explain.

36. This problem is an extension of the situation described in exercise 35.
a.  Develop the estimated regression equation to predict the repair time given the number of months since the last maintenance service, the type of repair, and the repairperson who performed the service.
b.  At the .05 level of significance, test whether the estimated regression equation developed in part (a) represents a significant relationship between the independent variables and the dependent variable.
c.  Is the addition of the independent variable $x_3$, the repairperson who performed the service, statistically significant? Use $\alpha = .05$. What explanation can you give for the results observed?

37. The *Consumer Reports* Restaurant Customer Satisfaction Survey is based upon 148,599 visits to full-service restaurant chains (Consumer Reports website, February 11, 2009). Assume the following data are representative of the results reported. The variable Type indicates whether the restaurant is an Italian restaurant or a seafood/steakhouse. Price indicates the average amount paid per person for dinner and drinks, minus the tip. Score reflects diners' overall satisfaction, with higher values indicating greater overall satisfaction. A score of 80 can be interpreted as very satisfied.

RestaurantRatings

| Restaurant | Type | Price ($) | Score |
|---|---|---|---|
| Bertucci's | Italian | 16 | 77 |
| Black Angus Steakhouse | Seafood/Steakhouse | 24 | 79 |
| Bonefish Grill | Seafood/Steakhouse | 26 | 85 |
| Bravo! Cucina Italiana | Italian | 18 | 84 |
| Buca di Beppo | Italian | 17 | 81 |
| Bugaboo Creek Steak House | Seafood/Steakhouse | 18 | 77 |
| Carrabba's Italian Grill | Italian | 23 | 86 |
| Charlie Brown's Steakhouse | Seafood/Steakhouse | 17 | 75 |
| Il Fornaio | Italian | 28 | 83 |
| Joe's Crab Shack | Seafood/Steakhouse | 15 | 71 |
| Johnny Carino's Italian | Italian | 17 | 81 |
| Lone Star Steakhouse & Saloon | Seafood/Steakhouse | 17 | 76 |
| LongHorn Steakhouse | Seafood/Steakhouse | 19 | 81 |
| Maggiano's Little Italy | Italian | 22 | 83 |
| McGrath's Fish House | Seafood/Steakhouse | 16 | 81 |
| Olive Garden | Italian | 19 | 81 |
| Outback Steakhouse | Seafood/Steakhouse | 20 | 80 |
| Red Lobster | Seafood/Steakhouse | 18 | 78 |
| Romano's Macaroni Grill | Italian | 18 | 82 |
| The Old Spaghetti Factory | Italian | 12 | 79 |
| Uno Chicago Grill | Italian | 16 | 76 |

a. Develop the estimated regression equation to show how overall customer satisfaction is related to the independent variable average meal price.
b. At the .05 level of significance, test whether the estimated regression equation developed in part (a) indicates a significant relationship between overall customer satisfaction and average meal price.
c. Develop a dummy variable that will account for the type of restaurant (Italian or seafood/steakhouse).
d. Develop the estimated regression equation to show how overall customer satisfaction is related to the average meal price and the type of restaurant.
e. Is type of restaurant a significant factor in overall customer satisfaction?
f. Predict the *Consumer Reports* customer satisfaction score for a seafood/steakhouse that has an average meal price of $20. How much would the predicted score have changed for an Italian restaurant?

38. A 10-year study conducted by the American Heart Association provided data on how age, blood pressure, and smoking relate to the risk of strokes. Assume that the following data are from a portion of this study. Risk is interpreted as the probability (times 100) that the patient will have a stroke over the next 10-year period. For the smoking variable, define a dummy variable with 1 indicating a smoker and 0 indicating a nonsmoker.

Stroke

| Risk | Age | Pressure | Smoker |
|------|-----|----------|--------|
| 12 | 57 | 152 | No |
| 24 | 67 | 163 | No |
| 13 | 58 | 155 | No |
| 56 | 86 | 177 | Yes |
| 28 | 59 | 196 | No |
| 51 | 76 | 189 | Yes |
| 18 | 56 | 155 | Yes |
| 31 | 78 | 120 | No |
| 37 | 80 | 135 | Yes |
| 15 | 78 | 98 | No |
| 22 | 71 | 152 | No |
| 36 | 70 | 173 | Yes |
| 15 | 67 | 135 | Yes |
| 48 | 77 | 209 | Yes |
| 15 | 60 | 199 | No |
| 36 | 82 | 119 | Yes |
| 8 | 66 | 166 | No |
| 34 | 80 | 125 | Yes |
| 3 | 62 | 117 | No |
| 37 | 59 | 207 | Yes |

a. Develop an estimated regression equation that relates risk of a stroke to the person's age, blood pressure, and whether the person is a smoker.

b. Is smoking a significant factor in the risk of a stroke? Explain. Use $\alpha = .05$.

c. What is the probability of a stroke over the next 10 years for Art Speen, a 68-year-old smoker who has blood pressure of 175? What action might the physician recommend for this patient?

# 13.8   Modeling Curvilinear Relationships

Curvilinear relationships can be easily handled using a multiple regression model. To illustrate let us consider the problem facing Reynolds, Inc., a manufacturer of industrial scales and laboratory equipment. Mangers at Reynolds want to investigate the relationship between length of employment of their salespeople and the number of electronic laboratory scales sold. Table 13.7 gives the number of months each salesperson has been employed by the firm ($x$) and the number of scales sold ($y$) by 15 randomly selected salespeople for the most recent sales period. In Chapter 12 we showed how Excel's chart tools can be used to construct a scatter diagram and compute the estimated regression equation and the coefficient of determination for simple linear regression. Figure 13.11 shows the results of using Excel's chart tools to fit a line to the Reynolds data. The chart tools output shows that the estimated regression equation is

$$\hat{y} = 111.23 + 2.3768x$$

where

$$\hat{y} = \text{predicted number of electronic laboratory scales sold}$$

$$x = \text{the number of months the salesperson has been employed}$$

Although the chart tools output shows that a linear relationship explains a high percentage of the variability in sales ($r^2 = 0.7812$), the scatter diagram indicates a possible curvilinear relationship between the length of time employed and the number of units sold.

**TABLE 13.7**   DATA FOR THE REYNOLDS EXAMPLE

| Months Employed (x) | Scales Sold (y) |
|:---:|:---:|
| 41 | 275 |
| 106 | 296 |
| 76 | 317 |
| 104 | 376 |
| 22 | 162 |
| 12 | 150 |
| 85 | 367 |
| 111 | 308 |
| 40 | 189 |
| 51 | 235 |
| 9 | 83 |
| 12 | 112 |
| 6 | 67 |
| 56 | 325 |
| 19 | 189 |

**FIGURE 13.11**   CHART TOOLS OUTPUT FOR THE REYNOLDS EXAMPLE: SIMPLE LINEAR REGRESSION

**FIGURE 13.12**   CHART TOOLS FORMAT TRENDLINE DIALOG BOX FOR THE
REYNOLDS EXAMPLE: SECOND-ORDER MODEL

To account for the curvilinear relationship, we will use a multiple regression model with two independent variables: $x$ and $x^2$.

$$y = \beta_0 + \beta_1 x + \beta_1 x^2 + \epsilon$$

This model is commonly referred to as a second-order polynomial or a quadratic model. Refer to Figure 13.12 as we describe how to use Excel's chart tools to fit a polynomial curve to the data. The estimated multiple regression equation and multiple coefficient of determination for this second-order model are also obtained.

**Step 1.** Position the mouse pointer over any data point in the scatter diagram and right-click to display a list of options; choose **Add Trendline**
**Step 2.** When the Format Trendline dialog box appears (Figure 13.12),
Select **Trendline Options** and then
Choose **Polynomial** from the Trend/Regression Type list and enter 2 in the **Order** box
Choose **Display Equation on chart**
Choose **Display R-squared value on chart**
Click **Close**

The results are shown in Figure 13.13. The estimated multiple regression equation is

$$\hat{y} = 45.348 + 6.3448x - 0.0345x^2$$

and the multiple coefficient of determination is $R^2 = 0.9022$.

Excel's chart tools make fitting curvilinear functions very easy. But the output does not provide any means for testing the significance of the results. To do so, we need to use Excel's Regression tool.

**FIGURE 13.13**    CHART TOOLS OUTPUT FOR THE REYNOLDS EXAMPLE: SECOND-ORDER MODEL

To use Excel's Regression tool for this polynomial model we treat the values of $x^2$ as a second independent variable. In Figure 13.14 we show the values of $x$ as Month and the values of $x^2$ as MonthsSq. Then we run the Regression tool just as if Month and MonthSq are two separate independent variables. The Regression tool output is shown in Figure 13.14. The estimated multiple regression equation is

$$\hat{y} = 45.3476 + 6.3448 \text{ Months} - .0345 \text{ MonthsSq}$$

where

   MonthsSq = the square of the number of months the salesperson has been employed

At the .05 level of significance, the Excel output shows that the overall model is significant (*p*-value for the *F* test is 8.75E-07). Note also that the *p*-value = .0023, corresponding to the *t*Stat value for MonthsSq, is less than .05. Thus, we can conclude that adding MonthsSq to the model involving Months is significant. With an Adjusted R Square value of .8859, we should be pleased with the fit provided by this estimated multiple regression equation.

   Many types of curvilinear relationships can be modeled in a similar fashion. The regression techniques with which we have been working are definitely not limited to linear, or straight-line, relationships. In multiple regression analysis the word *linear* refers only to the fact that $\beta_0, \beta_1, \ldots, \beta_p$ all have exponents of 1; it does not imply that the relationship between $y$ and the underlying $x_i$ variables is linear. Indeed, in this section we have seen one example of how regression analysis can be used to model a curvilinear relationship.

**FIGURE 13.14**    REGRESSION TOOL OUTPUT FOR THE REYNOLDS EXAMPLE: SECOND-
ORDER MODEL

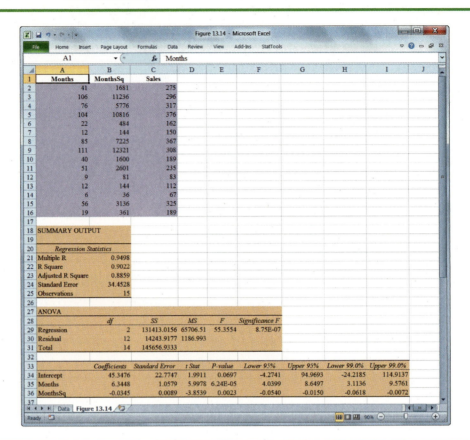

## Exercises

## Methods

39.    Consider the following data for two variables, $x$ and $y$.

| $x$ | 22 | 24 | 26 | 30 | 35 | 40 |
|---|---|---|---|---|---|---|
| $y$ | 12 | 21 | 33 | 35 | 40 | 36 |

   a.    Develop an estimated regression equation for the data of the form $\hat{y} = b_0 + b_1 x$.
   b.    Using the results from part (a), test for a significant relationship between $x$ and $y$;
       use $\alpha = .05$.
   c.    Develop a scatter diagram for the data. Does the scatter diagram suggest an estimated
       regression equation of the form $\hat{y} = b_0 + b_1 x + b_2 x^2$? Explain.
   d.    Develop an estimated regression equation for the data of the form $\hat{y} = b_0 + b_1 x + b_2 x^2$.
   e.    Refer to part (d). Is the relationship between $x$, $x^2$, and $y$ significant? Use $\alpha = .05$.
   f.    Predict the value of $y$ when $x = 25$.

40. Consider the following data for two variables, $x$ and $y$.

| $x$ | 9 | 32 | 18 | 15 | 26 |
|---|---|---|---|---|---|
| $y$ | 10 | 20 | 21 | 16 | 22 |

a. Develop an estimated regression equation for the data of the form $\hat{y} = b_0 + b_1x$. Comment on the adequacy of this equation for predicting $y$.
b. Develop an estimated regression equation for the data of the form $\hat{y} = b_0 + b_1x + b_2x^2$. Comment on the adequacy of this equation for predicting $y$.
c. Predict the value of $y$ when $x = 20$.

## Applications

41. A highway department is studying the relationship between traffic flow and speed. The following model has been hypothesized.

$$y = \beta_0 + \beta_1x + \epsilon$$

where

$$y = \text{traffic flow in vehicles per hour}$$
$$x = \text{vehicle speed in miles per hour}$$

The following data were collected during rush hour for six highways leading out of the city.

| Traffic Flow ($y$) | Vehicle Speed ($x$) |
|---|---|
| 1256 | 35 |
| 1329 | 40 |
| 1226 | 30 |
| 1335 | 45 |
| 1349 | 50 |
| 1124 | 25 |

a. Develop an estimated regression equation for the data of the form $\hat{y} = b_0 + b_1x$ and test for a significant relationship using $\alpha = .01$.
b. Develop an estimated multiple regression equation of the form $\hat{y} = b_0 + b_1x + b_2x^2$ and test for a significant relationship using $\alpha = .01$.
c. Predict the traffic flow in vehicles per hour at a speed of 38 miles per hour.

42. A study of emergency service facilities investigated the relationship between the number of facilities and the average distance traveled to provide the emergency service. The following table gives the data collected.

| Number of Facilities | Average Distance (miles) |
|---|---|
| 9 | 1.66 |
| 11 | 1.12 |
| 16 | .83 |
| 21 | .62 |
| 27 | .51 |
| 30 | .47 |

a. Develop a scatter diagram for these data, treating average distance traveled as the dependent variable.

b. Does a simple linear model appear to be appropriate? Explain.

c. Develop an estimated multiple regression equation for the data of the form $\hat{y} = b_0 + b_1 x + b_1 x^2$.

43. Corvette, Ferrari, and Jaguar produced a variety of classic cars that continue to increase in value. The following data, based upon the Martin Rating System for Collectible Cars, show the rarity rating (1–20) and the high price ($1000) for 15 classic cars (BusinessWeek website, February 2006).

**ClassicCars**

| Year | Make | Model | Rating | Price ($1000) |
|------|------|-------|--------|---------------|
| 1984 | Chevrolet | Corvette | 18 | 1600 |
| 1956 | Chevrolet | Corvette 265/225-hp | 19 | 4000 |
| 1963 | Chevrolet | Corvette coupe (340-bhp 4-speed) | 18 | 1000 |
| 1978 | Chevrolet | Corvette coupe Silver Anniversary | 19 | 1300 |
| 1960–1963 | Ferrari | 250 GTE 2+2 | 16 | 350 |
| 1962–1964 | Ferrari | 250 GTL Lusso | 19 | 2650 |
| 1962 | Ferrari | 250 GTO | 18 | 375 |
| 1967–1968 | Ferrari | 275 GTB/4 NART Spyder | 17 | 450 |
| 1968–1973 | Ferrari | 365 GTB/4 Daytona | 17 | 140 |
| 1962–1967 | Jaguar | E-type OTS | 15 | 77.5 |
| 1969–1971 | Jaguar | E-type Series II OTS | 14 | 62 |
| 1971–1974 | Jaguar | E-type Series III OTS | 16 | 125 |
| 1951–1954 | Jaguar | XK 120 roadster (steel) | 17 | 400 |
| 1950–1953 | Jaguar | XK C-type | 16 | 250 |
| 1956–1957 | Jaguar | XKSS | 13 | 70 |

a. Develop a scatter diagram of the data using the rarity rating as the independent variable and price as the independent variable. Does a simple linear regression model appear to be appropriate?

b. Develop an estimated multiple regression equation with $x$ = rarity rating and $x^2$ as the two independent variables.

## Summary

In this chapter, we introduced multiple regression analysis as an extension of simple linear regression analysis presented in Chapter 12. Multiple regression analysis enables us to understand how a dependent variable is related to two or more independent variables. The regression equation $E(y) = \beta_0 + \beta_1 x_1 + \beta_2 x_2 + \cdots + \beta_p x_p$ shows that the expected value or mean value of the dependent variable $y$ is related to the values of the independent variables $x_1$, $x_2, \ldots, x_p$. Sample data and the least squares method are used to develop the estimated regression equation $\hat{y} = b_0 + b_1 x_1 + b_2 x_2 + \cdots + b_p x_p$. In effect $b_0, b_1, b_2, \ldots, b_p$ are sample statistics used to estimate the unknown model parameters $\beta_0, \beta_1, \beta_2, \ldots, \beta_p$. Excel output was used throughout the chapter to emphasize the fact that computer software packages are the only realistic means of performing the numerous computations required in multiple regression analysis.

The multiple coefficient of determination was presented as a measure of the goodness of fit of the estimated regression equation. It determines the proportion of the variation of $y$ that can be explained by the estimated regression equation. The adjusted multiple coefficient of determination is a similar measure of goodness of fit that adjusts for the number of independent variables and thus avoids overestimating the impact of adding more independent variables.

An $F$ test and a $t$ test were presented as ways to determine statistically whether the relationship among the variables is significant. The $F$ test is used to determine whether there is a significant overall relationship between the dependent variable and the set of all independent variables. The $t$ test is used to determine whether there is a significant relationship between the dependent variable and an individual independent variable given the other independent variables in the regression model. Correlation among the independent variables, known as multicollinearity, was discussed.

The section on categorical independent variables showed how dummy variables can be used to incorporate categorical data into multiple regression analysis. And, the last section showed how curvilinear relationships can be easily handled using a multiple regression model.

## Glossary

**Multiple regression analysis** Regression analysis involving two or more independent variables.

**Multiple regression model** The mathematical equation that describes how the dependent variable $y$ is related to the independent variables $x_1, x_2, \ldots, x_p$ and an error term $\epsilon$.

**Multiple regression equation** The mathematical equation relating the expected value or mean value of the dependent variable to the values of the independent variables; that is, $E(y) = \beta_0 + \beta_1 x_1 + \beta_2 x_2 + \cdots + \beta_p x_p$.

**Estimated multiple regression equation** The estimate of the multiple regression equation based on sample data and the least squares method; it is $\hat{y} = b_0 + b_1 x_1 + b_2 x_2 + \cdots + b_p x_p$.

**Least squares method** The method used to develop the estimated regression equation. It minimizes the sum of squared residuals (the deviations between the observed values of the dependent variable, $y_i$, and the estimated values of the dependent variable, $\hat{y}_i$).

**Multiple coefficient of determination** A measure of the goodness of fit of the estimated multiple regression equation. It can be interpreted as the proportion of the variability in the dependent variable that is explained by the estimated regression equation.

**Adjusted multiple coefficient of determination** A measure of the goodness of fit of the estimated multiple regression equation that adjusts for the number of independent variables in the model and thus avoids overestimating the impact of adding more independent variables.

**Multicollinearity** The term used to describe the correlation among the independent variables.

**Categorical independent variable** An independent variable with categorical data.

**Dummy variable** A variable used to model the effect of categorical independent variables. A dummy variable may take only the value zero or one.

## Key Formulas

### Multiple Regression Model

$$y = \beta_0 + \beta_1 x_1 + \beta_2 x_2 + \cdots + \beta_p x_p + \epsilon \tag{13.1}$$

**Multiple Regression Equation**

$$E(y) = \beta_0 + \beta_1 x_1 + \beta_2 x_2 + \cdots + \beta_p x_p \qquad \textbf{(13.2)}$$

**Estimated Multiple Regression Equation**

$$\hat{y} = b_0 + b_1 x_1 + b_2 x_2 + \cdots + b_p x_p \qquad \textbf{(13.3)}$$

**Least Squares Criterion**

$$\min \Sigma (y_i - \hat{y}_i)^2 \qquad \textbf{(13.4)}$$

**Relationship Among SST, SSR, and SSE**

$$\text{SST} = \text{SSR} + \text{SSE} \qquad \textbf{(13.7)}$$

**Multiple Coefficient of Determination**

$$R^2 = \frac{\text{SSR}}{\text{SST}} \qquad \textbf{(13.8)}$$

**Adjusted Multiple Coefficient of Determination**

$$R_a^2 = 1 - (1 - R^2)\frac{n-1}{n-p-1} \qquad \textbf{(13.9)}$$

**Mean Square Regression**

$$\text{MSR} = \frac{\text{SSR}}{p} \qquad \textbf{(13.12)}$$

**Mean Square Error**

$$\text{MSE} = \frac{\text{SSE}}{n-p-1} \qquad \textbf{(13.13)}$$

***F* Test Statistic**

$$F = \frac{\text{MSR}}{\text{MSE}} \qquad \textbf{(13.14)}$$

***t* Test Statistic**

$$t = \frac{b_i}{s_{b_i}} \qquad \textbf{(13.15)}$$

## Supplementary Exercises

44. The admissions officer for Clearwater College developed the following estimated regression equation relating the final college GPA to the student's SAT mathematics score and high-school GPA.

$$\hat{y} = -1.41 + .0235x_1 + .00486x_2$$

where

$$x_1 = \text{high-school grade point average}$$
$$x_2 = \text{SAT mathematics score}$$
$$y = \text{final college grade point average}$$

a. Interpret the coefficients in this estimated regression equation.
b. Predict the final college GPA for a student who has a high-school average of 84 and a score of 540 on the SAT mathematics test.

45. The personnel director for Electronics Associates developed the following estimated regression equation relating an employee's score on a job satisfaction test to his or her length of service and wage rate.

$$\hat{y} = 14.4 - 8.69x_1 + 13.5x_2$$

where

$$x_1 = \text{length of service (years)}$$
$$x_2 = \text{wage rate (dollars)}$$
$$y = \text{job satisfaction test score (higher scores indicate greater job satisfaction)}$$

a. Interpret the coefficients in this estimated regression equation.
b. Predict the job satisfaction test score for an employee who has four years of service and makes $6.50 per hour.

46. A partial computer output from a regression analysis follows.

| SUMMARY OUTPUT | | | | | | |
|---|---|---|---|---|---|---|
| | | | | | | |
| *Regression Statistics* | | | | | | |
| Multiple R | | | | | | |
| R Square | 0.923 | | | | | |
| Adjusted R Square | | | | | | |
| Standard Error | 3.35 | | | | | |
| Observations | | | | | | |
| | | | | | | |
| ANOVA | | | | | | |
| | *df* | *SS* | *MS* | *F* | *Significance F* | |
| Regression | | 1612 | | | | |
| Residual | 12 | | | | | |
| Total | | | | | | |
| | | | | | | |
| | *Coefficients* | *Standard Error* | *t Stat* | *P-value* | | |
| Intercept | 8.103 | 2.667 | | | | |
| X1 | 7.602 | 2.105 | | | | |
| X2 | 3.111 | 0.613 | | | | |

a. Compute the missing entries in this output.
b. Using $\alpha = .05$, test for overall significance.
c. Use the $t$ test and $\alpha = .05$ to test $H_0: \beta_1 = 0$ and $H_0: \beta_2 = 0$.

47. Recall that in exercise 44, the admissions officer for Clearwater College developed the following estimated regression equation relating final college GPA to the student's SAT mathematics score and high-school GPA.

$$\hat{y} = -1.41 + .0235x_1 + .00486x_2$$

where

$$x_1 = \text{high-school grade point average}$$
$$x_2 = \text{SAT mathematics score}$$
$$y = \text{final college grade point average}$$

A portion of the regression output follows.

| | A | B | C | D | E | F | G |
|---|---|---|---|---|---|---|---|
| 1 | SUMMARY OUTPUT | | | | | | |
| 2 | | | | | | | |
| 3 | *Regression Statistics* | | | | | | |
| 4 | Multiple R | | | | | | |
| 5 | R Square | | | | | | |
| 6 | Adjusted R Square | | | | | | |
| 7 | Standard Error | | | | | | |
| 8 | Observations | | | | | | |
| 9 | | | | | | | |
| 10 | ANOVA | | | | | | |
| 11 | | *df* | *SS* | *MS* | *F* | *Significance F* | |
| 12 | Regression | | 1.76209 | | | | |
| 13 | Residual | | | | | | |
| 14 | Total | 9 | 1.88 | | | | |
| 15 | | | | | | | |
| 16 | | *Coefficients* | *Standard Error* | *t Stat* | *P-value* | | |
| 17 | Intercept | -1.4053 | 0.4848 | | | | |
| 18 | X1 | 0.023467 | 0.0086666 | | | | |
| 19 | X2 | 0.00486 | 0.001077 | | | | |
| 20 | | | | | | | |

a. Complete the missing entries in this output.
b. Using $\alpha = .05$, test for overall significance.
c. Did the estimated regression equation provide a good fit to the data? Explain.
d. Use the $t$ test and $\alpha = .05$ to test $H_0: \beta_1 = 0$ and $H_0: \beta_2 = 0$.

48. Recall that in exercise 45 the personnel director for Electronics Associates developed the following estimated regression equation relating an employee's score on a job satisfaction test to length of service and wage rate.

$$\hat{y} = 14.4 - 8.69x_1 + 13.5x_2$$

where

$$x_1 = \text{length of service (years)}$$
$$x_2 = \text{wage rate (dollars)}$$
$$y = \text{job satisfaction test score (higher scores indicate greater job satisfaction)}$$

A portion of the regression output follows.

| | A | B | C | D | E | F | G |
|---|---|---|---|---|---|---|---|
| 1 | SUMMARY OUTPUT | | | | | | |
| 2 | | | | | | | |
| 3 | *Regression Statistics* | | | | | | |
| 4 | Multiple R | | | | | | |
| 5 | R Square | | | | | | |
| 6 | Adjusted R Square | | | | | | |
| 7 | Standard Error | 3.773 | | | | | |
| 8 | Observations | | | | | | |
| 9 | | | | | | | |
| 10 | ANOVA | | | | | | |
| 11 | | *df* | *SS* | *MS* | *F* | *Significance F* | |
| 12 | Regression | | | | | | |
| 13 | Residual | | 77.17 | | | | |
| 14 | Total | | 720 | | | | |
| 15 | | | | | | | |
| 16 | | *Coefficients* | *Standard Error* | *t Stat* | *P-value* | | |
| 17 | Intercept | 14.4 | 8.191 | | | | |
| 18 | X1 | -8.69 | 1.555 | | | | |
| 19 | X2 | 13.517 | 2.085 | | | | |
| 20 | | | | | | | |

a. Complete the missing entries in this output.
b. Using $\alpha = .05$, test for overall significance.
c. Did the estimated regression equation provide a good fit to the data? Explain.
d. Use the $t$ test and $\alpha = .05$ to test $H_0: \beta_1 = 0$ and $H_0: \beta_2 = 0$.

49. The Tire Rack, America's leading online distributor of tires and wheels, conducts extensive testing to provide customers with products that are right for their vehicle, driving style, and driving conditions. In addition, the Tire Rack maintains an independent consumer survey to help drivers help each other by sharing their long-term tire experiences. The following data show survey ratings (1 to 10 scale with 10 the highest rating) for 18 maximum performance summer tires (Tire Rack website, February 3, 2009). The variable Steering rates the tire's steering responsiveness, Tread Wear rates quickness of wear based on the driver's expectations, and Buy Again rates the driver's overall tire satisfaction and desire to purchase the same tire again.

**WEB** file

**TireRack**

| Tire | Steering | Tread Wear | Buy Again |
|---|---|---|---|
| Goodyear Assurance TripleTred | 8.9 | 8.5 | 8.1 |
| Michelin HydroEdge | 8.9 | 9.0 | 8.3 |
| Michelin Harmony | 8.3 | 8.8 | 8.2 |
| Dunlop SP 60 | 8.2 | 8.5 | 7.9 |
| Goodyear Assurance ComforTred | 7.9 | 7.7 | 7.1 |
| Yokohama Y372 | 8.4 | 8.2 | 8.9 |
| Yokohama Aegis LS4 | 7.9 | 7.0 | 7.1 |
| Kumho Power Star 758 | 7.9 | 7.9 | 8.3 |
| Goodyear Assurance | 7.6 | 5.8 | 4.5 |
| Hankook H406 | 7.8 | 6.8 | 6.2 |
| Michelin Energy LX4 | 7.4 | 5.7 | 4.8 |
| Michelin MX4 | 7.0 | 6.5 | 5.3 |
| Michelin Symmetry | 6.9 | 5.7 | 4.2 |
| Kumho 722 | 7.2 | 6.6 | 5.0 |
| Dunlop SP 40 A/S | 6.2 | 4.2 | 3.4 |
| Bridgestone Insignia SE200 | 5.7 | 5.5 | 3.6 |
| Goodyear Integrity | 5.7 | 5.4 | 2.9 |
| Dunlop SP20 FE | 5.7 | 5.0 | 3.3 |

a.  Develop an estimated regression equation that can be used to predict the Buy Again rating given based on the Steering rating. At the .05 level of significance, test for a significant relationship.

b.  Did the estimated regression equation developed in part (a) provide a good fit to the data? Explain.

c.  Develop an estimated regression equation that can be used to predict the Buy Again rating given the Steering rating and the Tread Wear rating.

d.  Is the addition of the Tread Wear independent variable significant? Use $\alpha = .05$.

50.  *Consumer Reports* provided extensive testing and ratings for 24 treadmills. An overall score, based primarily on ease of use, ergonomics, exercise range, and quality, was developed for each treadmill tested. In general, a higher overall score indicates better performance. The following data show the price, the quality rating, and overall score for the 24 treadmills (*Consumer Reports*, February 2006).

**Treadmills**

| Brand & Model | Price | Quality | Score |
|---|---|---|---|
| Landice L7 | 2900 | Excellent | 86 |
| NordicTrack S3000 | 3500 | Very good | 85 |
| SportsArt 3110 | 2900 | Excellent | 82 |
| Precor | 3500 | Excellent | 81 |
| True Z4 HRC | 2300 | Excellent | 81 |
| Vision Fitness T9500 | 2000 | Excellent | 81 |
| Precor M 9.31 | 3000 | Excellent | 79 |
| Vision Fitness T9200 | 1300 | Very good | 78 |
| Star Trac TR901 | 3200 | Very good | 72 |
| Trimline T350HR | 1600 | Very good | 72 |
| Schwinn 820p | 1300 | Very good | 69 |
| Bowflex 7-Series | 1500 | Excellent | 83 |
| NordicTrack S1900 | 2600 | Very good | 83 |
| Horizon Fitness PST8 | 1600 | Very good | 82 |
| Horizon Fitness 5.2T | 1800 | Very good | 80 |
| Evo by Smooth Fitness FX30 | 1700 | Very good | 75 |
| ProForm 1000S | 1600 | Very good | 75 |
| Horizon Fitness CST4.5 | 1000 | Very good | 74 |
| Keys Fitness 320t | 1200 | Very good | 73 |
| Smooth Fitness 7.1HR Pro | 1600 | Very good | 73 |
| NordicTrack C2300 | 1000 | Good | 70 |
| Spirit Inspire | 1400 | Very good | 70 |
| ProForm 750 | 1000 | Good | 67 |
| Image 19.0 R | 600 | Good | 66 |

a.  Use these data to develop an estimated regression equation that could be used to estimate the overall score given the price.

b.  Use $\alpha = .05$ to test for overall significance.

c.  To incorporate the effect of quality, a categorical variable with three levels, we used two dummy variables, Quality-E and Quality-VG. Each variable is coded 0 or 1 as follows.

$$\text{Quality-E} = \begin{cases} 1 \text{ if quality rating is excellent} \\ 0 \text{ otherwise} \end{cases}$$

$$\text{Quality-VG} = \begin{cases} 1 \text{ if quality rating is very good} \\ 0 \text{ otherwise} \end{cases}$$

Develop an estimated regression equation that could be used to estimate the overall score given the price and the quality rating.

d. For the estimated regression equation developed in part (c), test for overall signifi-cance using $\alpha = .10$.

e. For the estimated regression equation developed in part (c), use the $t$ test to determine the significance of each independent variable. Use $\alpha = .10$.

f. Predict the overall score for a treadmill with a price of $2000 and a good quality rating. How much would the prediction change if the quality rating were very good? Explain.

51. A portion of a data set containing information for 45 mutual funds that are part of the *Morningstar Funds 500* for 2008 follows. The complete data set is available in the file named MutualFunds. The data set includes the following five variables:

Type: The type of fund, labeled DE (Domestic Equity), IE (International Equity), and FI (Fixed Income).

Net Asset Value ($): The closing price per share on December 31, 2007.

5-Year Average Return (%): The average annual return for the fund over the past five years.

Expense Ratio (%): The percentage of assets deducted each fiscal year for fund expenses.

Morningstar Rank: The risk adjusted star rating for each fund; Morningstar ranks go from a low of 1-Star to a high of 5-Stars.

**WEB** file

**MutualFunds**

| Fund Name | Fund Type | Net Asset Value ($) | Five-Year Average Return (%) | Expense Ratio (%) | Morningstar Rank |
|---|---|---|---|---|---|
| Amer Cent Inc & Growth Inv | DE | 28.88 | 12.39 | 0.67 | 2-Star |
| American Century Intl. Disc | IE | 14.37 | 30.53 | 1.41 | 3-Star |
| American Century Tax-Free Bond | FI | 10.73 | 3.34 | 0.49 | 4-Star |
| American Century Ultra | DE | 24.94 | 10.88 | 0.99 | 3-Star |
| Ariel | DE | 46.39 | 11.32 | 1.03 | 2-Star |
| Artisan Intl Val | IE | 25.52 | 24.95 | 1.23 | 3-Star |
| Artisan Small Cap | DE | 16.92 | 15.67 | 1.18 | 3-Star |
| Baron Asset | DE | 50.67 | 16.77 | 1.31 | 5-Star |
| Brandywine | DE | 36.58 | 18.14 | 1.08 | 4-Star |
| ⋮ | ⋮ | ⋮ | ⋮ | ⋮ | ⋮ |

a. Develop an estimated regression equation that can be used to predict the five-year average return given fund type. At the .05 level of significance, test for a significant relationship.

b. Did the estimated regression equation developed in part (a) provide a good fit to the data? Explain.

c. Develop the estimated regression equation that can be used to predict the five-year average return given the type of fund, the net asset value, and the expense ratio. At the .05 level of significance, test for a significant relationship. Do you think any variables should be deleted from the estimated regression equation? Explain.

d. Morningstar Rank is a categorical variable. Because the data set contains only funds with four ranks (2-Star through 5-Star), use the following dummy variables: 3Star-Rank = 1 for a 3-Star fund, 0 otherwise; 4StarRank = 1 for a 4-Star fund, 0 other-wise; and 5StarRank = 1 for a 5-Star fund, 0 otherwise. Develop an estimated regression equation that can be used to predict the five-year average return given the type of fund, the expense ratio, and the Morningstar Rank. Using $\alpha = .05$, remove any independent variables that are not significant.

e. Use the estimated regression equation developed in part (d) to predict the five-year average return for a domestic equity fund with an expense ratio of 1.05% and a 3-Star Morningstar Rank.

52. The U.S. Department of Energy's Fuel Economy Guide provides fuel efficiency data for cars and trucks (U.S. Department of Energy website, February 22, 2008). A portion of the data for 311 compact, midsize, and large cars follows. The column labeled Class identifies the size of the car: Compact, Midsize, or Large. The column labeled Displacement shows the engine's displacement in liters. The column labeled Fuel Type shows whether the car uses premium (P) or regular (R) fuel, and the column labeled Hwy MPG shows the fuel efficiency rating for highway driving in terms of miles per gallon. The complete data set is contained in the file named FuelData.

**FuelData**

| Car | Class | Displacement | Fuel Type | Hwy MPG |
|-----|-------|--------------|-----------|---------|
| 1 | Compact | 3.1 | P | 25 |
| 2 | Compact | 3.1 | P | 25 |
| 3 | Compact | 3 | P | 25 |
| . | . | . | . | . |
| . | . | . | . | . |
| . | . | . | . | . |
| 161 | Midsize | 2.4 | R | 30 |
| 162 | Midsize | 2 | P | 29 |
| . | . | . | . | . |
| . | . | . | . | . |
| . | . | . | . | . |
| 310 | Large | 3 | R | 25 |
| 311 | Large | 3 | R | 25 |

a. Develop an estimated regression equation that can be used to predict the fuel efficiency for highway driving given the engine's displacement. Test for significance using $\alpha = .05$.

b. Consider the addition of the dummy variables ClassMidsize and ClassLarge. The value of ClassMidsize is 1 if the car is a midsize car and 0 otherwise; the value of ClassLarge is 1 if the car is a large car and 0 otherwise. Thus, for a compact car, the value of ClassMidsize and the value of ClassLarge is 0. Develop the estimated regression equation that can be used to predict the fuel efficiency for highway driving given the engine's displacement and the dummy variables ClassMidsize and ClassLarge.

c. Use $\alpha = .05$ to determine whether the dummy variables added in part (b) are significant.

d. Consider the addition of the dummy variable FuelPremium, where the value of FuelPremium is 1 if the car uses premium fuel and 0 if the car uses regular fuel. Develop the estimated regression equation that can be used to predict the fuel efficiency for highway driving given the engine's displacement, the dummy variables ClassMidsize and ClassLarge, and the dummy variable FuelPremium.

e. For the estimated regression equation developed in part (d), test for overall significance and individual significance using $\alpha = .05$.

## Case Problem 1    Consumer Research, Inc.

Consumer Research, Inc., is an independent agency that conducts research on consumer attitudes and behaviors for a variety of firms. In one study, a client asked for an investigation of consumer characteristics that can be used to predict the amount charged by credit card users. Data were collected on annual income, household size, and annual credit card charges for a sample of 50 consumers. The following data appear in the file named Consumer.

| Income ($1000s) | Household Size | Amount Charged ($) | Income ($1000s) | Household Size | Amount Charged ($) |
|---|---|---|---|---|---|
| 54 | 3 | 4016 | 54 | 6 | 5573 |
| 30 | 2 | 3159 | 30 | 1 | 2583 |
| 32 | 4 | 5100 | 48 | 2 | 3866 |
| 50 | 5 | 4742 | 34 | 5 | 3586 |
| 31 | 2 | 1864 | 67 | 4 | 5037 |
| 55 | 2 | 4070 | 50 | 2 | 3605 |
| 37 | 1 | 2731 | 67 | 5 | 5345 |
| 40 | 2 | 3348 | 55 | 6 | 5370 |
| 66 | 4 | 4764 | 52 | 2 | 3890 |
| 51 | 3 | 4110 | 62 | 3 | 4705 |
| 25 | 3 | 4208 | 64 | 2 | 4157 |
| 48 | 4 | 4219 | 22 | 3 | 3579 |
| 27 | 1 | 2477 | 29 | 4 | 3890 |
| 33 | 2 | 2514 | 39 | 2 | 2972 |
| 65 | 3 | 4214 | 35 | 1 | 3121 |
| 63 | 4 | 4965 | 39 | 4 | 4183 |
| 42 | 6 | 4412 | 54 | 3 | 3730 |
| 21 | 2 | 2448 | 23 | 6 | 4127 |
| 44 | 1 | 2995 | 27 | 2 | 2921 |
| 37 | 5 | 4171 | 26 | 7 | 4603 |
| 62 | 6 | 5678 | 61 | 2 | 4273 |
| 21 | 3 | 3623 | 30 | 2 | 3067 |
| 55 | 7 | 5301 | 22 | 4 | 3074 |
| 42 | 2 | 3020 | 46 | 5 | 4820 |
| 41 | 7 | 4828 | 66 | 4 | 5149 |

**WEB** file

Consumer

## Managerial Report

1. Use methods of descriptive statistics to summarize the data. Comment on the findings.
2. Develop estimated regression equations, first using annual income as the independent variable and then using household size as the independent variable. Which variable is the better predictor of annual credit card charges? Discuss your findings.
3. Develop an estimated regression equation with annual income and household size as the independent variables. Discuss your findings.
4. What is the predicted annual credit card charge for a three-person household with an annual income of $40,000?
5. Discuss the need for other independent variables that could be added to the model. What additional variables might be helpful?

## Case Problem 2    Alumni Giving

Alumni donations are an important source of revenue for colleges and universities. If administrators could determine the factors that could lead to increases in the percentage of alumni who make a donation, they might be able to implement policies that could lead to increased revenues. Research shows that students who are more satisfied with their contact with teachers are more likely to graduate. As a result, one might suspect that smaller class sizes and lower student-faculty ratios might lead to a higher percentage of satisfied graduates, which in turn might lead to increases in the percentage of alumni who make a donation. Table 13.8 shows data for 48 national universities (*America's Best Colleges,* Year 2000 Edition). The column labeled Graduation Rate is the percentage of students who initially enrolled at the university and graduated. The column labeled % of Classes Under 20 shows the percentage of classes offered with fewer than 20 students. The column labeled Student-Faculty Ratio is the number of students enrolled divided by the total number of faculty. Finally, the column labeled Alumni Giving Rate is the percentage of alumni who made a donation to the university.

## Managerial Report

1. Use methods of descriptive statistics to summarize the data.
2. Develop an estimated regression equation that can be used to predict the alumni giving rate given the number of students who graduate. Discuss your findings.
3. Develop an estimated regression equation that could be used to predict the alumni giving rate using the data provided.
4. What conclusions and recommendations can you derive from your analysis?

## Case Problem 3   PGA Tour Statistics

The Professional Golfers Association (PGA) maintains data on performance and earnings for members of the PGA Tour. The top 125 players based on total earnings in PGA Tour events are exempt for the following season. Making the top 125 money list is important because a player who is "exempt" has qualified to be a full-time member of the PGA tour for the following season.

Scoring average is generally considered the most important statistic in terms of success on the PGA Tour. To investigate the effect that variables such as driving distance, driving accuracy, greens in regulation, sand saves, and average putts per round have on average score, year-end performance data for the 125 players who had the highest total earnings in PGA Tour events for 2008 are contained in the file named PGATour (PGA Tour website, 2009). Each row of the data set corresponds to a PGA Tour player, and the data have been sorted based upon total earnings. Descriptions for the variables in the data set follow.

Money:   Total earnings in PGA Tour events.

Scoring Average:   The average number of strokes per completed round.

DrDist (Driving Distance):   The average number of yards per measured drive. On the PGA Tour driving distance is measured on two holes per round. Care is taken to select two holes which face in opposite directions to counteract the effect of wind. Drives are measured to the point at which they come to rest regardless of whether they are in the fairway or not.

DrAccu (Driving Accuracy):   The percentage of time a tee shot comes to rest in the fairway (regardless of club). Driving accuracy is measured on every hole, excluding par 3s.

GIR (Greens in Regulation):   The percentage of time a player was able to hit the green in regulation. A green is considered hit in regulation if any portion of the ball is touching the putting surface after the GIR stroke has been taken. The GIR stroke is determined by subtracting 2 from par (1st stroke on a par 3, 2nd on a par 4, 3rd on a par 5). In other words, a green is considered hit in regulation if the player has reached the putting surface in par minus two strokes.

**TABLE 13.8**   DATA FOR 48 NATIONAL UNIVERSITIES

**WEB** file

Alumni

| | State | Graduation Rate | % of Classes Under 20 | Student-Faculty Ratio | Alumni Giving Rate |
|---|---|---|---|---|---|
| Boston College | MA | 85 | 39 | 13 | 25 |
| Brandeis University | MA | 79 | 68 | 8 | 33 |
| Brown University | RI | 93 | 60 | 8 | 40 |
| California Institute of Technology | CA | 85 | 65 | 3 | 46 |
| Carnegie Mellon University | PA | 75 | 67 | 10 | 28 |
| Case Western Reserve Univ. | OH | 72 | 52 | 8 | 31 |
| College of William and Mary | VA | 89 | 45 | 12 | 27 |
| Columbia University | NY | 90 | 69 | 7 | 31 |
| Cornell University | NY | 91 | 72 | 13 | 35 |
| Dartmouth College | NH | 94 | 61 | 10 | 53 |
| Duke University | NC | 92 | 68 | 8 | 45 |
| Emory University | GA | 84 | 65 | 7 | 37 |
| Georgetown University | DC | 91 | 54 | 10 | 29 |
| Harvard University | MA | 97 | 73 | 8 | 46 |
| Johns Hopkins University | MD | 89 | 64 | 9 | 27 |
| Lehigh University | PA | 81 | 55 | 11 | 40 |
| Massachusetts Inst. of Technology | MA | 92 | 65 | 6 | 44 |
| New York University | NY | 72 | 63 | 13 | 13 |
| Northwestern University | IL | 90 | 66 | 8 | 30 |
| Pennsylvania State Univ. | PA | 80 | 32 | 19 | 21 |
| Princeton University | NJ | 95 | 68 | 5 | 67 |
| Rice University | TX | 92 | 62 | 8 | 40 |
| Stanford University | CA | 92 | 69 | 7 | 34 |
| Tufts University | MA | 87 | 67 | 9 | 29 |
| Tulane University | LA | 72 | 56 | 12 | 17 |
| U. of California–Berkeley | CA | 83 | 58 | 17 | 18 |
| U. of California–Davis | CA | 74 | 32 | 19 | 7 |
| U. of California–Irvine | CA | 74 | 42 | 20 | 9 |
| U. of California–Los Angeles | CA | 78 | 41 | 18 | 13 |
| U. of California–San Diego | CA | 80 | 48 | 19 | 8 |
| U. of California–Santa Barbara | CA | 70 | 45 | 20 | 12 |
| U. of Chicago | IL | 84 | 65 | 4 | 36 |
| U. of Florida | FL | 67 | 31 | 23 | 19 |
| U. of Illinois–Urbana Champaign | IL | 77 | 29 | 15 | 23 |
| U. of Michigan–Ann Arbor | MI | 83 | 51 | 15 | 13 |
| U. of North Carolina–Chapel Hill | NC | 82 | 40 | 16 | 26 |
| U. of Notre Dame | IN | 94 | 53 | 13 | 49 |
| U. of Pennsylvania | PA | 90 | 65 | 7 | 41 |
| U. of Rochester | NY | 76 | 63 | 10 | 23 |
| U. of Southern California | CA | 70 | 53 | 13 | 22 |
| U. of Texas–Austin | TX | 66 | 39 | 21 | 13 |
| U. of Virginia | VA | 92 | 44 | 13 | 28 |
| U. of Washington | WA | 70 | 37 | 12 | 12 |
| U. of Wisconsin–Madison | WI | 73 | 37 | 13 | 13 |
| Vanderbilt University | TN | 82 | 68 | 9 | 31 |
| Wake Forest University | NC | 82 | 59 | 11 | 38 |
| Washington University–St. Louis | MO | 86 | 73 | 7 | 33 |
| Yale University | CT | 94 | 77 | 7 | 50 |

Sand Saves:    The percentage of time a player was able to get "up and down" once in a greenside sand bunker (regardless of score). "Up and down" indicates it took the player two shots or less to put the ball in the hole from a greenside sand bunker.

PPR (Putts Per Round):    The average number of putts per round.

Scrambling:    The percentage of time a player missed the green in regulation but still made par or better.

## Managerial Report

1. To predict Scoring Average, develop estimated regression equations, first using DrDist as the independent variable and then using DrAccu as the independent variable. Which variable is the better predictor of Scoring Average? Discuss your findings.
2. Develop an estimated regression equation with GIR as the independent variable. Compare your findings with the results obtained using DrDist and DrAccu.
3. Develop an estimated regression equation with GIR and Sand Saves as the independent variables. Discuss your findings.
4. Develop an estimated regression equation with GIR and PPR as the independent variables. Discuss your findings.
5. Develop an estimated regression equation with GIR and Scrambling as the independent variables. Discuss your findings.
6. Compare the results obtained for the estimated regression equations that use GIR and Sand Saves, GIR and PPR, and GIR and Scrambling as the two independent variables. If you had to select one of these two-independent-variable estimated regression equations to predict Scoring Average, which estimated regression equation would you use? Explain.
7. Develop the estimated regression equation that uses GIR, Sand Saves, and PPR to predict Scoring Average. Compare the results to an estimated regression equation that uses GIR, PPR, and Scrambling as the independent variables.
8. Develop an estimated regression equation that uses GIR, Sand Saves, PPR, and Scrambling to predict Scoring Average. Discuss your results.

## Case Problem 4    Predicting Winning Percentage for the NFL

**NFLStats**

The National Football League (NFL) records a variety of performance data for individuals and teams (NFL website). Some of the year-end performance data for the 2005 season appear in the file named NFLStats. Each row of the data set corresponds to an NFL team, and the teams are ranked by winning percentage. Descriptions for the data follow:

WinPct        Percentage of games won

DefYds/G      Average number of yards per game given up on defense

RushYds/G     Average number of rushing yards per game

PassYds/G     Average number of passing yards per game

FGPct         Percentage of field goals made

TakeInt       Takeaway interceptions; the total number of interceptions made by the team's defense

TakeFum       Takeaway fumbles; the total number of fumbles recovered by the team's defense

GiveInt       Giveaway interceptions; the total number of interceptions thrown by the team's offense

GiveFum       Giveaway fumbles; the total number of fumbles lost by the team's offense

## Managerial Report

1. Use methods of descriptive statistics to summarize the data. Comment on the findings.
2. Develop an estimated regression equation that can be used to predict WinPct using DefYds/G, RushYds/G, PassYds/G, and FGPct. Discuss your findings.
3. Starting with the estimated regression equation developed in part (2), delete any independent variables that are not significant and develop a new estimated regression equation that can be used to predict WinPct. Use $\alpha = .05$.
4. Some football analysts believe that turnovers are one of the most important factors in determining a team's success. With Takeaways = TakeInt + TakeFum and Giveaways = GiveInt + GiveFum, let NetDiff = Takeaways − Giveaways. Develop an estimated regression equation that can be used to predict WinPct using NetDiff. Compare your results with the estimated regression equation developed in part (3).
5. Develop an estimated regression equation that can be used to predict WinPct using all the data provided.

## Appendix   Multiple Regression Analysis Using StatTools

**Butler**

In this appendix we show how StatTools can be used to perform the regression analysis computations for the Butler Trucking problem. Begin by using the Data Set Manager to create a StatTools data set for these data using the procedure described in the appendix in Chapter 1. The following steps describe how StatTools can be used to provide the regression results.

**Step 1.** Click the **StatTools** tab on the Ribbon
**Step 2.** In the **Analyses** group, click **Regression and Classification**
**Step 3.** Choose the **Regression** option
**Step 4.** When the StatTools - Regression dialog box appears,
　　　　　Select **Multiple** in the **Regression Type** box
　　　　　In the **Variables** section:
　　　　　　　Click the **Format** button and select **Unstacked**
　　　　　　　In the column labeled **I** select **Miles**
　　　　　　　In the column labeled **I** select **Deliveries**
　　　　　　　In the column labeled **D** select **Time**
　　　　　Click **OK**

*In the appendix to Chapter 12 we showed how to compute prediction intervals using StatTools.*

The regression analysis output will appear in a new worksheet.

　　The StatTools - Regression dialog box contains a number of more advanced options for developing prediction interval estimates and producing residual plots. The StatTools Help facility provides information on using all of these options.

# CHAPTER 14

# Statistical Methods for Quality Control

**CONTENTS**

**STATISTICS** *in* PRACTICE

### DOW CHEMICAL COMPANY*
*FREEPORT, TEXAS*

In 1940 the Dow Chemical Company purchased 800 acres of Texas land on the Gulf Coast to build a magnesium production facility. That original site has expanded to cover more than 5000 acres and holds one of the largest petrochemical complexes in the world. Among the products from Dow Texas Operations are magnesium, styrene, plastics, adhesives, solvent, glycol, and chlorine. Some products are made solely for use in other processes, but many end up as essential ingredients in products such as pharmaceuticals, toothpastes, dog food, water hoses, ice chests, milk cartons, garbage bags, shampoos, and furniture.

Dow's Texas Operations produce more than 30% of the world's magnesium, an extremely lightweight metal used in products ranging from tennis racquets to suitcases to "mag" wheels. The Magnesium Department was the first group in Texas Operations to train its technical people and managers in the use of statistical quality control. Some of the earliest successful applications of statistical quality control were in chemical processing.

In one application involving the operation of a drier, samples of the output were taken at periodic intervals; the average value for each sample was computed and recorded on a chart called an $\bar{x}$ chart. Such a chart enabled Dow analysts to monitor trends in the output that might indicate the process was not operating correctly. In one instance, analysts began to observe values for the sample mean that were not indicative of a process operating within its design

© PRNewsFoto/The Dow Chemical Company

Statistical quality control has enabled Dow Chemical Company to improve its processing methods and output.

limits. On further examination of the control chart and the operation itself, the analysts found that the variation could be traced to problems involving one operator. The $\bar{x}$ chart recorded after retraining the operator showed a significant improvement in the process quality.

Dow achieves quality improvements everywhere it applies statistical quality control. Documented savings of several hundred thousand dollars per year are realized, and new applications are continually being discovered.

In this chapter we will show how an $\bar{x}$ chart such as the one used by Dow can be developed. Such charts are a part of statistical quality control known as statistical process control. We will also discuss methods of quality control for situations in which a decision to accept or reject a group of items is based on a sample.

---

*The authors are indebted to Clifford B. Wilson, Magnesium Technical Manager, The Dow Chemical Company, for providing this Statistics in Practice.

*ASQ's Vision: "By making quality a global priority, an organizational imperative, and a personal ethic, the American Society for Quality becomes the community for everyone who seeks quality concepts, technology, and tools to improve themselves and their world" (ASQ website).*

The American Society for Quality (ASQ) defines quality as "the totality of features and characteristics of a product or service that bears on its ability to satisfy given needs." In other words, quality measures how well a product or service meets customer needs. Organizations recognize that to be competitive in today's global economy, they must strive for a high level of quality. As a result, they place increased emphasis on methods for monitoring and maintaining quality.

Today, the customer-driven focus that is fundamental to high-performing organizations has changed the scope that quality issues encompass, from simply eliminating defects on a production line to developing broad-based corporate quality strategies. Broadening the scope of quality naturally leads to the concept of **total quality (TQ)**.

Total Quality (TQ) is a people-focused management system that aims at continual increase in customer satisfaction at continually lower real cost. TQ is a total system approach (not a separate area or work program) and an integral part of high-level strategy; it works horizontally across function and departments, involves all employees, top to bottom, and extends backward and forward to include the supply chain and the customer chain. TQ stresses learning and adaptation to continual change as keys to organization success.[1]

Regardless of how it is implemented in different organizations, total quality is based on three fundamental principles: a focus on customers and stakeholders; participation and teamwork throughout the organization; and a focus on continuous improvement and learning. In the first section of the chapter we provide a brief introduction to three quality management frameworks: the Malcolm Baldrige Quality Award, ISO 9000 standards, and the Six Sigma philosophy. In the last two sections we introduce two statistical tools that can be used to monitor quality: statistical process control and acceptance sampling.

## 14.1  Philosophies and Frameworks

*After World War II, Dr. W. Edwards Deming became a consultant to Japanese industry; he is credited with being the person who convinced top managers in Japan to use the methods of statistical quality control.*

In the early twentieth century, quality control practices were limited to inspecting finished products and removing defective items. But this all changed as the result of the pioneering efforts of a young engineer named Walter A. Shewhart. After completing his doctorate in physics from the University of California in 1917, Dr. Shewhart joined the Western Electric Company, working in the inspection engineering department. In 1924 Dr. Shewhart prepared a memorandum that included a set of principles that are the basis for what is known today as process control. And his memo also contained a diagram that would be recognized as a statistical control chart. Continuing his work in quality at Bell Telephone Laboratories until his retirement in 1956, he brought together the disciplines of statistics, engineering, and economics and in doing so changed the course of industrial history. Dr. Shewhart is recognized as the father of statistical quality control and was the first honorary member of the ASQ.

Two other individuals who have had great influence on quality are Dr. W. Edwards Deming, a student of Dr. Shewhart, and Joseph Juran. These men helped educate the Japanese in quality management shortly after World War II. Although quality is everybody's job, Deming stressed that the focus on quality must be led by managers. He developed a list of 14 points that he believed represent the key responsibilities of managers. For instance, Deming stated that managers must cease dependence on mass inspection; must end the practice of awarding business solely on the basis of price; must seek continual improvement in all production processes and service; must foster a team-oriented environment; and must eliminate goals, slogans, and work standards that prescribe numerical quotas. Perhaps most important, managers must create a work environment in which a commitment to quality and productivity is maintained at all times.

Juran proposed a simple definition of quality: *fitness for use*. Juran's approach to quality focused on three quality processes: quality planning, quality control, and quality improvement. In contrast to Deming's philosophy, which required a major cultural change in the organization, Juran's programs were designed to improve quality by working within the current organizational system. Nonetheless, the two philosophies are similar in that they both focus on the need for top management to be involved and stress the need for continuous improvement, the importance of training, and the use of quality control techniques.

Many other individuals played significant roles in the quality movement, including Philip B. Crosby, A. V. Feigenbaum, Karou Ishikawa, and Genichi Taguchi. More specialized texts dealing exclusively with quality provide details of the contributions of each of

---

[1]J. R. Evans and W. M. Lindsay, *Managing for Quality and Performance Excellence*, 8th ed. (Cincinnati, OH: South-Western, 2011), p. 11.

these individuals. The contributions of all individuals involved in the quality movement helped define a set of best practices and led to numerous awards and certification programs. The two most significant programs are the U.S. Malcolm Baldrige National Quality Award and the international ISO 9000 certification process. In recent years, use of Six Sigma—a methodology for improving organizational performance based on rigorous data collection and statistical analysis—has also increased.

## Malcolm Baldrige National Quality Award

*The U.S. Commerce Department's National Institute of Standards and Technology (NIST) manages the Baldrige National Quality Program. More information can be obtained at the NIST website.*

The Malcolm Baldrige National Quality Award is given by the president of the United States to organizations that apply and are judged to be outstanding in seven areas: leadership; strategic planning; customer and market focus; measurement, analysis, and knowledge management; human resource focus; process management; and business results. Congress established the award program in 1987 to recognize U.S. organizations for their achievements in quality and performance and to raise awareness about the importance of quality as a competitive edge. The award is named for Malcolm Baldrige, who served as secretary of commerce from 1981 until his death in 1987.

*2004 was the final year for the Baldrige Stock Study because of the increase in the number of recipients that are either nonprofit or privately held businesses.*

Since the presentation of the first awards in 1988, the Baldrige National Quality Program (BNQP) has grown in stature and impact. Approximately 2 million copies of the criteria have been distributed since 1988, and wide-scale reproduction by organizations and electronic access add to that number significantly. For eight years in a row, a hypothetical stock index, made up of publicly traded U.S. companies that had received the Baldrige Award, outperformed the Standard & Poor's 500. In one year, the "Baldrige Index" outperformed the S&P 500 by 4.4 to 1. Bob Barnett, executive vice president of Motorola, Inc., said, "We applied for the Award, not with the idea of winning, but with the goal of receiving the evaluation of the Baldrige Examiners. That evaluation was comprehensive, professional, and insightful . . . making it perhaps the most cost-effective, value-added business consultation available anywhere in the world today."

## ISO 9000

*ISO 9000 standards are revised periodically to improve the quality of the standard.*

ISO 9000 is a series of five international standards published in 1987 by the International Organization for Standardization (ISO), Geneva, Switzerland. Companies can use the standards to help determine what is needed to maintain an efficient quality conformance system. For example, the standards describe the need for an effective quality system, for ensuring that measuring and testing equipment is calibrated regularly, and for maintaining an adequate record-keeping system. ISO 9000 registration determines whether a company complies with its own quality system. Overall, ISO 9000 registration covers less than 10% of the Baldrige Award criteria.

## Six Sigma

In the late 1980s Motorola recognized the need to improve the quality of its products and services; their goal was to achieve a level of quality so good that for every million opportunities no more than 3.4 defects will occur. This level of quality is referred to as the six sigma level of quality, and the methodology created to reach this quality goal is referred to as **Six Sigma**.

An organization may undertake two kinds of Six Sigma projects:

- DMAIC (Define, Measure, Analyze, Improve, and Control) to help redesign existing processes
- DFSS (Design for Six Sigma) to design new products, processes, or services

In helping to redesign existing processes and design new processes, Six Sigma places a heavy emphasis on statistical analysis and careful measurement. Today, Six Sigma is a major tool in helping organizations achieve Baldrige levels of business performance and process quality. Many Baldrige examiners view Six Sigma as the ideal approach for implementing Baldrige improvement programs.

**Six Sigma limits and defects per million opportunities** In Six Sigma terminology, a *defect* is any mistake or error that is passed on to the customer. The Six Sigma process defines quality performance as defects per million opportunities (dpmo). As we indicated previously, Six Sigma represents a quality level of at most 3.4 dpmo. To illustrate how this quality level is measured, let us consider the situation at KJW Packaging.

KJW operates a production line where boxes of cereal are filled. The filling process has a mean of $\mu = 16.05$ ounces and a standard deviation of $\sigma = .10$ ounces. It is reasonable to assume the filling weights are normally distributed. The distribution of filling weights is shown in Figure 14.1. Suppose management considers 15.45 to 16.65 ounces to be acceptable quality limits for the filling process. Thus, any box of cereal that contains less than 15.45 or more than 16.65 ounces is considered to be a defect. Using Excel, it can be shown that 99.9999998% of the boxes filled will have between $16.05 - 6(.10) = 15.45$ ounces and $16.05 + 6(.10) = 16.65$ ounces. In other words, only .0000002% of the boxes filled will contain less than 15.45 ounces or more than 16.65 ounces. Thus, the likelihood of obtaining a defective box of cereal from the filling process appears to be extremely unlikely, because on average only two boxes in 10 million will be defective.

*Using Excel, NORM.S.DIST (6,TRUE)−NORM.S.DIST (−6,TRUE) = .999999998.*

Motorola's early work on Six Sigma convinced them that a process mean can shift on average by as much as 1.5 standard deviations. For instance, suppose that the process mean for KJW increases by 1.5 standard deviations or $1.5(.10) = .15$ ounces. With such a shift, the normal distribution of filling weights would now be centered at $\mu = 16.05 + .15 = 16.20$ ounces. With a process mean of $\mu = 16.05$ ounces, the probability of obtaining a box of cereal with more than 16.65 ounces is extremely small. But how does this probability

*Using Excel, 1−NORM.S.DIST (4.5,TRUE) = .0000034.*

**FIGURE 14.1** NORMAL DISTRIBUTION OF CEREAL BOX FILLING WEIGHTS WITH A PROCESS MEAN $\mu = 16.05$

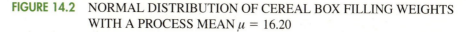

**FIGURE 14.2**   NORMAL DISTRIBUTION OF CEREAL BOX FILLING WEIGHTS
WITH A PROCESS MEAN $\mu = 16.20$

change if the mean of the process shifts up to $\mu = 16.20$ ounces? Figure 14.2 shows that for this case, the upper quality limit of 16.65 is 4.5 standard deviations to the right of the new mean $\mu = 16.20$ ounces. Using this mean and Excel, we find that the probability of obtaining a box with more than 16.65 ounces is .0000034. Thus, if the process mean shifts up by 1.5 standard deviations, approximately 1,000,000(.0000034) = 3.4 boxes of cereal will exceed the upper limit of 16.65 ounces. In Six Sigma terminology, the quality level of the process is said to be 3.4 defects per million opportunities. If management of KJW considers 15.45 to 16.65 ounces to be acceptable quality limits for the filling process, the KJW filling process would be considered a Six Sigma process. Thus, if the process mean stays within 1.5 standard deviations of its target value $\mu = 16.05$ ounces, a maximum of only 3.4 defects per million boxes filled can be expected.

Organizations that want to achieve and maintain a Six Sigma level of quality must emphasize methods for monitoring and maintaining quality. *Quality assurance* refers to the entire system of policies, procedures, and guidelines established by an organization to achieve and maintain quality. Quality assurance consists of two principal functions: quality engineering and quality control. The object of *quality engineering* is to include quality in the design of products and processes and to identify quality problems prior to production. **Quality control** consists of a series of inspections and measurements used to determine whether quality standards are being met. If quality standards are not being met, corrective or preventive action can be taken to achieve and maintain conformance. In the next two sections we present two statistical methods used in quality control. The first method, *statistical process control,* uses graphical displays known as control charts to monitor a process; the goal is to determine whether the process can be continued or whether corrective action should be taken to achieve a desired quality level. The second method, *acceptance sampling,* is used in situations where a decision to accept or reject a group of items must be based on the quality found in a sample.

# 14.2  Statistical Process Control

In this section we consider quality control procedures for a production process whereby goods are manufactured continuously. On the basis of sampling and inspection of production output, a decision will be made to either continue the production process or adjust it to bring the items or goods being produced up to acceptable quality standards.

*Continuous improvement is one of the most important concepts of the total quality management movement. The most important use of a control chart is in improving the process.*

Despite high standards of quality in manufacturing and production operations, machine tools will invariably wear out, vibrations will throw machine settings out of adjustment, purchased materials will be defective, and human operators will make mistakes. Any or all of these factors can result in poor quality output. Fortunately, procedures are available for monitoring production output so that poor quality can be detected early and the production process can be adjusted or corrected.

If the variation in the quality of the production output is due to **assignable causes** such as tools wearing out, incorrect machine settings, poor quality raw materials, or operator error, the process should be adjusted or corrected as soon as possible. Alternatively, if the variation is due to what are called **common causes**—that is, randomly occurring variations in materials, temperature, humidity, and so on, which the manufacturer cannot possibly control—the process does not need to be adjusted. The main objective of statistical process control is to determine whether variations in output are due to assignable causes or common causes.

Whenever assignable causes are detected, we conclude that the process is *out of control.* In that case, corrective action will be taken to bring the process back to an acceptable level of quality. However, if the variation in the output of a production process is due only to common causes, we conclude that the process is *in statistical control,* or simply *in control;* in such cases, no changes or adjustments are necessary.

*Process control procedures are closely related to hypothesis testing procedures discussed earlier in this text. Control charts provide an ongoing test of the hypothesis that the process is in control.*

The statistical procedures for process control are based on the hypothesis testing methodology presented in Chapter 9. The null hypothesis $H_0$ is formulated in terms of the production process being in control. The alternative hypothesis $H_a$ is formulated in terms of the production process being out of control. Table 14.1 shows that correct decisions to continue an in-control process and adjust an out-of-control process are possible. However, as with other hypothesis testing procedures, both a Type I error (adjusting an in-control process) and a Type II error (allowing an out-of-control process to continue) are also possible.

## Control Charts

A **control chart** provides a basis for deciding whether the variation in the output is due to common causes (in control) or assignable causes (out of control). Whenever an

**TABLE 14.1**   THE OUTCOMES OF STATISTICAL PROCESS CONTROL

| | | State of Production Process | |
|---|---|---|---|
| | | $H_0$ **True**<br>**Process in Control** | $H_0$ **False**<br>**Process Out of Control** |
| **Decision** | **Continue Process** | Correct decision | Type II error<br>(allowing an out-of-control<br>process to continue) |
| | **Adjust Process** | Type I error<br>(adjusting an in-control process) | Correct decision |

**FIGURE 14.3**   $\bar{x}$ CHART STRUCTURE

out-of-control situation is detected, adjustments or other corrective action will be taken to bring the process back into control.

*Control charts based on data that can be measured on a continuous scale are called variables control charts. The $\bar{x}$ chart is a variables control chart.*

Control charts can be classified by the type of data they contain. An **$\bar{x}$ chart** is used if the quality of the output of the process is measured in terms of a variable such as length, weight, temperature, and so on. In that case, the decision to continue or to adjust the production process will be based on the mean value found in a sample of the output. To introduce some of the concepts common to all control charts, let us consider some specific features of an $\bar{x}$ chart.

Figure 14.3 shows the general structure of an $\bar{x}$ chart. The center line of the chart corresponds to the mean of the process when the process is *in control.* The vertical line identifies the scale of measurement for the variable of interest. Each time a sample is taken from the production process, a value of the sample mean $\bar{x}$ is computed and a data point showing the value of $\bar{x}$ is plotted on the control chart.

The two lines labeled UCL and LCL are important in determining whether the process is in control or out of control. The lines are called the *upper control limit* and the *lower control limit,* respectively. They are chosen so that when the process is in control, there will be a high probability that the value of $\bar{x}$ will be between the two control limits. Values outside the control limits provide strong statistical evidence that the process is out of control and corrective action should be taken.

Over time, more and more data points will be added to the control chart. The order of the data points will be from left to right as the process is sampled. In essence, every time a point is plotted on the control chart, we are carrying out a hypothesis test to determine whether the process is in control.

In addition to the $\bar{x}$ chart, other control charts can be used to monitor the range of the measurements in the sample (**$R$ chart**), the proportion defective in the sample (**$p$ chart**), and the number of defective items in the sample (**$np$ chart**). In each case, the control chart has a LCL, a center line, and an UCL similar to the $\bar{x}$ chart in Figure 14.3. The major difference among the charts is what the vertical axis measures; for instance, in a $p$ chart the measurement scale denotes the proportion of defective items in the sample instead of the sample mean. In the following discussion, we will illustrate the construction and use of the $\bar{x}$ chart, $R$ chart, $p$ chart, and $np$ chart.

## $\bar{x}$ Chart: Process Mean and Standard Deviation Known

To illustrate the construction of an $\bar{x}$ chart, let us reconsider the situation at KJW Packaging. Recall that KJW operates a production line where cartons of cereal are filled. When the process

**FIGURE 14.4**    NORMAL DISTRIBUTION OF CEREAL CARTON FILLING WEIGHTS

is operating correctly—and hence the system is in control—the mean filling weight is $\mu = 16.05$ ounces, and the process standard deviation is $\sigma = .10$ ounces. In addition, the filling weights are assumed to be normally distributed. This distribution is shown in Figure 14.4.

The sampling distribution of $\bar{x}$, as presented in Chapter 7, can be used to determine the variation that can be expected in $\bar{x}$ values for a process that is in control. Let us first briefly review the properties of the sampling distribution of $\bar{x}$. First, recall that the expected value or mean of $\bar{x}$ is equal to $\mu$, the mean filling weight when the production line is in control. For samples of size $n$, the equation for the standard deviation of $\bar{x}$, called the standard error of the mean, is

$$\sigma_{\bar{x}} = \frac{\sigma}{\sqrt{n}} \tag{14.1}$$

In addition, because the filling weights are normally distributed, the sampling distribution of $\bar{x}$ is normally distributed for any sample size. Thus, the sampling distribution of $\bar{x}$ is a normal distribution with mean $\mu$ and standard deviation $\sigma_{\bar{x}}$. This distribution is shown in Figure 14.5.

The sampling distribution of $\bar{x}$ is used to determine what values of $\bar{x}$ are reasonable if the process is in control. The general practice in quality control is to define as reasonable any value of $\bar{x}$ that is within 3 standard deviations, or standard errors, above or below the mean value. Recall from the study of the normal probability distribution that approximately 99.7% of the values of a normally distributed random variable are within $\pm 3$ standard deviations of its mean value. Thus, if a value of $\bar{x}$ is within the interval $\mu - 3\sigma_{\bar{x}}$ to $\mu + 3\sigma_{\bar{x}}$, we will assume that the process is in control. In summary, then, the control limits for an $\bar{x}$ chart are as follows.

**CONTROL LIMITS FOR AN $\bar{x}$ CHART: PROCESS MEAN AND STANDARD DEVIATION KNOWN**

$$\text{UCL} = \mu + 3\sigma_{\bar{x}} \tag{14.2}$$
$$\text{LCL} = \mu - 3\sigma_{\bar{x}} \tag{14.3}$$

**FIGURE 14.5**   SAMPLING DISTRIBUTION OF $\bar{x}$ FOR A SAMPLE OF $n$ FILLING WEIGHTS

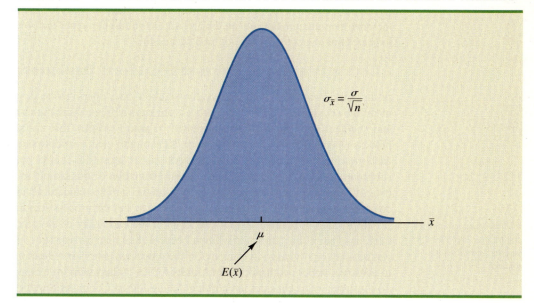

$$\sigma_{\bar{x}} = \frac{\sigma}{\sqrt{n}}$$

$E(\bar{x})$

**FIGURE 14.6**   THE $\bar{x}$ CHART FOR THE CEREAL CARTON FILLING PROCESS

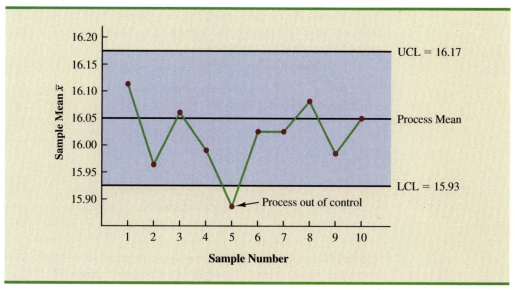

Reconsider the KJW Packaging example with the process distribution of filling weights shown in Figure 14.4 and the sampling distribution of $\bar{x}$ shown in Figure 14.5. Assume that a quality control inspector periodically samples six cartons and uses the sample mean filling weight to determine whether the process is in control or out of control. Using equation (14.1), we find that the standard error of the mean is $\sigma_{\bar{x}} = \sigma/\sqrt{n} = .10/\sqrt{6} = .04$. Thus, with the process mean at 16.05, the control limits are UCL $= 16.05 + 3(.04) = 16.17$ and LCL $= 16.05 - 3(.04) = 15.93$. Figure 14.6 is the control chart with the results of 10 samples taken over a 10-hour period. For ease of reading, the sample numbers 1 through 10 are listed below the chart.

Note that the mean for the fifth sample in Figure 14.6 shows there is strong evidence that the process is out of control. The fifth sample mean is below the LCL, indicating that assignable causes of output variation are present and that underfilling is occurring. As a result, corrective action was taken at this point to bring the process back into control. The fact that the remaining points on the $\bar{x}$ chart are within the upper and lower control limits indicates that the corrective action was successful.

## $\bar{x}$ Chart: Process Mean and Standard Deviation Unknown

In the KJW Packaging example, we showed how an $\bar{x}$ chart can be developed when the mean and standard deviation of the process are known. In most situations, the process mean and standard deviation must be estimated by using samples that are selected from the process when it is in control. For instance, KJW might select a random sample of five boxes each morning and five boxes each afternoon for 10 days of in-control operation. For each subgroup, or sample, the mean and standard deviation of the sample are computed. The overall averages of both the sample means and the sample standard deviations are used to construct control charts for both the process mean and the process standard deviation.

*It is important to maintain control over both the mean and the variability of a process.*

In practice, it is more common to monitor the variability of the process by using the range instead of the standard deviation because the range is easier to compute. The range can be used to provide good estimates of the process standard deviation; thus it can be used to construct upper and lower control limits for the $\bar{x}$ chart with little computational effort. To illustrate, let us consider the problem facing Jensen Computer Supplies, Inc.

Jensen Computer Supplies (JCS) manufactures 3.5-inch-diameter solid-state drives; they just finished adjusting their production process so that it is operating in control. Suppose random samples of five drives were selected during the first hour of operation, five drives were selected during the second hour of operation, and so on, until 20 samples were obtained. Table 14.2 provides the diameter of each drive sampled as well as the mean $\bar{x}_j$ and range $R_j$ for each of the samples.

The estimate of the process mean $\mu$ is given by the overall sample mean.

**OVERALL SAMPLE MEAN**

$$\bar{\bar{x}} = \frac{\bar{x}_1 + \bar{x}_2 + \cdots + \bar{x}_k}{k} \tag{14.4}$$

where

$\bar{x}_j$ = mean of the $j$th sample $j = 1, 2, \ldots, k$
$k$ = number of samples

For the JCS data in Table 14.2, the overall sample mean is $\bar{\bar{x}} = 3.4995$. This value will be the center line for the $\bar{x}$ chart. The range of each sample, denoted $R_j$, is simply the difference between the largest and smallest values in each sample. The average range for $k$ samples is computed as follows.

**AVERAGE RANGE**

$$\bar{R} = \frac{R_1 + R_2 + \cdots + R_k}{k} \tag{14.5}$$

where

$R_j$ = range of the $j$th sample, $j = 1, 2, \ldots, k$
$k$ = number of samples

**TABLE 14.2**   DATA FOR THE JENSEN COMPUTER SUPPLIES PROBLEM

| Sample Number | Observations | | | | | Sample Mean $\bar{x}_j$ | Sample Range $R_j$ |
|---|---|---|---|---|---|---|---|
| 1 | 3.5056 | 3.5086 | 3.5144 | 3.5009 | 3.5030 | 3.5065 | .0135 |
| 2 | 3.4882 | 3.5085 | 3.4884 | 3.5250 | 3.5031 | 3.5026 | .0368 |
| 3 | 3.4897 | 3.4898 | 3.4995 | 3.5130 | 3.4969 | 3.4978 | .0233 |
| 4 | 3.5153 | 3.5120 | 3.4989 | 3.4900 | 3.4837 | 3.5000 | .0316 |
| 5 | 3.5059 | 3.5113 | 3.5011 | 3.4773 | 3.4801 | 3.4951 | .0340 |
| 6 | 3.4977 | 3.4961 | 3.5050 | 3.5014 | 3.5060 | 3.5012 | .0099 |
| 7 | 3.4910 | 3.4913 | 3.4976 | 3.4831 | 3.5044 | 3.4935 | .0213 |
| 8 | 3.4991 | 3.4853 | 3.4830 | 3.5083 | 3.5094 | 3.4970 | .0264 |
| 9 | 3.5099 | 3.5162 | 3.5228 | 3.4958 | 3.5004 | 3.5090 | .0270 |
| 10 | 3.4880 | 3.5015 | 3.5094 | 3.5102 | 3.5146 | 3.5047 | .0266 |
| 11 | 3.4881 | 3.4887 | 3.5141 | 3.5175 | 3.4863 | 3.4989 | .0312 |
| 12 | 3.5043 | 3.4867 | 3.4946 | 3.5018 | 3.4784 | 3.4932 | .0259 |
| 13 | 3.5043 | 3.4769 | 3.4944 | 3.5014 | 3.4904 | 3.4935 | .0274 |
| 14 | 3.5004 | 3.5030 | 3.5082 | 3.5045 | 3.5234 | 3.5079 | .0230 |
| 15 | 3.4846 | 3.4938 | 3.5065 | 3.5089 | 3.5011 | 3.4990 | .0243 |
| 16 | 3.5145 | 3.4832 | 3.5188 | 3.4935 | 3.4989 | 3.5018 | .0356 |
| 17 | 3.5004 | 3.5042 | 3.4954 | 3.5020 | 3.4889 | 3.4982 | .0153 |
| 18 | 3.4959 | 3.4823 | 3.4964 | 3.5082 | 3.4871 | 3.4940 | .0259 |
| 19 | 3.4878 | 3.4864 | 3.4960 | 3.5070 | 3.4984 | 3.4951 | .0206 |
| 20 | 3.4969 | 3.5144 | 3.5053 | 3.4985 | 3.4885 | 3.5007 | .0259 |

**WEB** file

Jensen

For the JCS data in Table 14.2, the average range is $\bar{R} = .0253$.

In the preceding section we showed that the upper and lower control limits for the $\bar{x}$ chart are

$$\bar{x} \pm 3 \frac{\sigma}{\sqrt{n}} \tag{14.6}$$

*The overall sample mean $\bar{\bar{x}}$ is used to estimate $\mu$ and the sample ranges are used to develop an estimate of $\sigma$.*

Hence, to construct the control limits for the $\bar{x}$ chart, we need to estimate $\mu$ and $\sigma$, the mean and standard deviation of the process. An estimate of $\mu$ is given by $\bar{\bar{x}}$. An estimate of $\sigma$ can be developed by using the range data.

It can be shown that an estimator of the process standard deviation $\sigma$ is the average range divided by $d_2$, a constant that depends on the sample size $n$. That is,

$$\text{Estimator of } \sigma = \frac{\bar{R}}{d_2} \tag{14.7}$$

The *American Society for Testing and Materials Manual on Presentation of Data and Control Chart Analysis* provides values for $d_2$ as shown in Table 14.3. For instance, when $n = 5$, $d_2 = 2.326$, and the estimate of $\sigma$ is the average range divided by 2.326. If we substitute $\bar{R}/d_2$ for $\sigma$ in expression (14.6), we can write the control limits for the $\bar{x}$ chart as

$$\bar{\bar{x}} \pm 3 \frac{\bar{R}/d_2}{\sqrt{n}} = \bar{\bar{x}} \pm \frac{3}{d_2\sqrt{n}} \bar{R} = \bar{\bar{x}} \pm A_2\bar{R} \tag{14.8}$$

**TABLE 14.3** FACTORS FOR $\bar{x}$ AND $R$ CONTROL CHARTS

| Observations in Sample, $n$ | $d_2$ | $A_2$ | $d_3$ | $D_3$ | $D_4$ |
|---|---|---|---|---|---|
| 2 | 1.128 | 1.880 | 0.853 | 0 | 3.267 |
| 3 | 1.693 | 1.023 | 0.888 | 0 | 2.574 |
| 4 | 2.059 | 0.729 | 0.880 | 0 | 2.282 |
| 5 | 2.326 | 0.577 | 0.864 | 0 | 2.114 |
| 6 | 2.534 | 0.483 | 0.848 | 0 | 2.004 |
| 7 | 2.704 | 0.419 | 0.833 | 0.076 | 1.924 |
| 8 | 2.847 | 0.373 | 0.820 | 0.136 | 1.864 |
| 9 | 2.970 | 0.337 | 0.808 | 0.184 | 1.816 |
| 10 | 3.078 | 0.308 | 0.797 | 0.223 | 1.777 |
| 11 | 3.173 | 0.285 | 0.787 | 0.256 | 1.744 |
| 12 | 3.258 | 0.266 | 0.778 | 0.283 | 1.717 |
| 13 | 3.336 | 0.249 | 0.770 | 0.307 | 1.693 |
| 14 | 3.407 | 0.235 | 0.763 | 0.328 | 1.672 |
| 15 | 3.472 | 0.223 | 0.756 | 0.347 | 1.653 |
| 16 | 3.532 | 0.212 | 0.750 | 0.363 | 1.637 |
| 17 | 3.588 | 0.203 | 0.744 | 0.378 | 1.622 |
| 18 | 3.640 | 0.194 | 0.739 | 0.391 | 1.608 |
| 19 | 3.689 | 0.187 | 0.734 | 0.403 | 1.597 |
| 20 | 3.735 | 0.180 | 0.729 | 0.415 | 1.585 |
| 21 | 3.778 | 0.173 | 0.724 | 0.425 | 1.575 |
| 22 | 3.819 | 0.167 | 0.720 | 0.434 | 1.566 |
| 23 | 3.858 | 0.162 | 0.716 | 0.443 | 1.557 |
| 24 | 3.895 | 0.157 | 0.712 | 0.451 | 1.548 |
| 25 | 3.931 | 0.153 | 0.708 | 0.459 | 1.541 |

*Source:* Reprinted with permission from Table 27 of ASTM STP 15D, *ASTM Manual on Presentation of Data and Control Chart Analysis,* Copyright ASTM International, 100 Barr Harbor Drive, West Conshohocken, PA 19428.

Note that $A_2 = 3/(d_2\sqrt{n})$ is a constant that depends only on the sample size. Values for $A_2$ are provided in Table 14.3. For $n = 5$, $A_2 = .577$; thus, the control limits for the $\bar{x}$ chart are

$$3.4995 \pm (.577)(.0253) = 3.4995 \pm .0146$$

Hence, UCL = 3.514 and LCL = 3.485.

*In the chapter appendix, we show how to contract $\bar{x}$ and R charts using StatTools.*

Figure 14.7 shows the $\bar{x}$ chart for the Jensen Computer Supplies problem. We used the data in Table 14.2 and StatTools' X/R Charts routine to construct the chart. The center line is shown at the overall sample mean $\bar{\bar{x}} = 3.4995$. The upper control limit (UCL) is 3.514 and the lower control (LCL) is 3.485. The $\bar{x}$ chart shows the 20 sample means plotted over time. Because all 20 sample means are within the control limits, we confirm that the process mean was in control during the sampling period.

## $R$ Chart

Let us now consider a range chart ($R$ chart) that can be used to control the variability of a process. To develop the $R$ chart, we need to think of the range of a sample as a random variable with its own mean and standard deviation. The average range $\bar{R}$ provides an estimate

**FIGURE 14.7** $\bar{x}$ CHART FOR THE JENSEN COMPUTER SUPPLIES PROBLEM

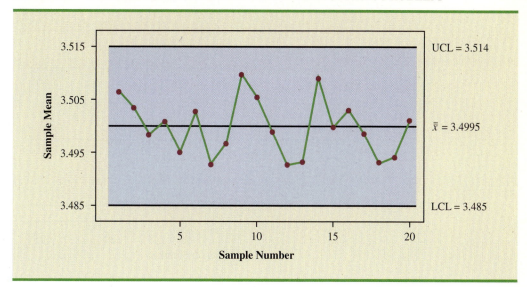

of the mean of this random variable. Moreover, it can be shown that an estimate of the standard deviation of the range is

$$\hat{\sigma}_R = d_3 \frac{\bar{R}}{d_2} \tag{14.9}$$

where $d_2$ and $d_3$ are constants that depend on the sample size; values of $d_2$ and $d_3$ are provided in Table 14.3. Thus, the UCL for the $R$ chart is given by

$$\bar{R} + 3\hat{\sigma}_R = \bar{R}\left(1 + 3\frac{d_3}{d_2}\right) \tag{14.10}$$

and the LCL is

$$\bar{R} - 3\hat{\sigma}_R = \bar{R}\left(1 - 3\frac{d_3}{d_2}\right) \tag{14.11}$$

If we let

$$D_4 = 1 + 3\frac{d_3}{d_2} \tag{14.12}$$

$$D_3 = 1 - 3\frac{d_3}{d_2} \tag{14.13}$$

we can write the control limits for the $R$ chart as

$$\text{UCL} = \bar{R}D_4 \tag{14.14}$$

$$\text{LCL} = \bar{R}D_3 \tag{14.15}$$

**FIGURE 14.8**    *R* CHART FOR THE JENSEN COMPUTER SUPPLIES PROBLEM

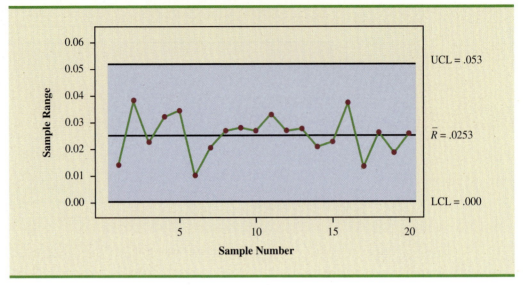

Values for $D_3$ and $D_4$ are also provided in Table 14.3. Note that for $n = 5$, $D_3 = 0$ and $D_4 = 2.114$. Thus, with $\bar{R} = .0253$, the control limits are

$$UCL = .0253(2.114) = .053$$
$$LCL = .0253(0) = 0$$

*If the R chart indicates that the process is out of control, the x̄ chart should not be interpreted until the R chart indicates the process variability is in control.*

Figure 14.8 shows the *R* chart for the Jensen Computer Supplies problem. We used the data in Table 14.2 and StatTools' X/R Charts routine to construct the chart. The center line is shown at the overall mean of the 20 sample ranges, $\bar{R} = .0253$. The UCL is .053 and the LCL is .000. The *R* chart shows the 20 sample ranges plotted over time. Because all 20 sample ranges are within the control limits, we confirm that the process variability was in control during the sampling period.

## *p* **Chart**

*Control charts that are based on data indicating the presence of a defect or a number of defects are called attributes control charts. A p chart is an attributes control chart.*

Let us consider the case in which the output quality is measured by either nondefective or defective items. The decision to continue or to adjust the production process will be based on $\bar{p}$, the proportion of defective items found in a sample. The control chart used for proportion-defective data is called a *p* chart.

To illustrate the construction of a *p* chart, consider the use of automated mail-sorting machines in a post office. These automated machines scan the zip codes on letters and divert each letter to its proper carrier route. Even when a machine is operating properly, some letters are diverted to incorrect routes. Assume that when a machine is operating correctly, or in a state of control, 3% of the letters are incorrectly diverted. Thus *p*, the proportion of letters incorrectly diverted when the process is in control, is .03.

The sampling distribution of $\bar{p}$, as presented in Chapter 7, can be used to determine the variation that can be expected in $\bar{p}$ values for a process that is in control. Recall that the expected value or mean of $\bar{p}$ is *p*, the proportion defective when the process is in control. With

**FIGURE 14.9** SAMPLING DISTRIBUTION OF $\bar{p}$

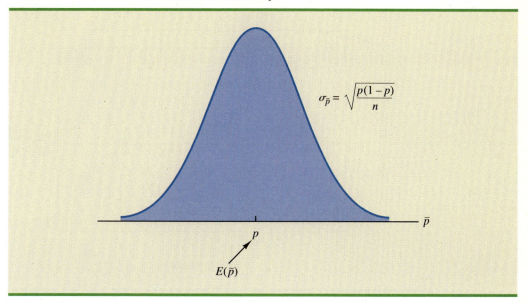

samples of size $n$, the formula for the standard deviation of $\bar{p}$, called the standard error of the proportion, is

$$\sigma_{\bar{p}} = \sqrt{\frac{p(1 - p)}{n}} \qquad \textbf{(14.16)}$$

We also learned in Chapter 7 that the sampling distribution of $\bar{p}$ can be approximated by a normal distribution whenever the sample size is large. With $\bar{p}$, the sample size can be considered large whenever the following two conditions are satisfied.

$$np \geq 5$$
$$n(1 - p) \geq 5$$

In summary, whenever the sample size is large, the sampling distribution of $\bar{p}$ can be approximated by a normal distribution with mean $p$ and standard deviation $\sigma_{\bar{p}}$. This distribution is shown in Figure 14.9.

To establish control limits for a $p$ chart, we follow the same procedure we used to establish control limits for an chart. That is, the limits for the control chart are set at 3 standard deviations, or standard errors, above and below the proportion defective when the process is in control. Thus, we have the following control limits.

---

**CONTROL LIMITS FOR A $p$ CHART**

$$\text{UCL} = p + 3\sigma_{\bar{p}} \qquad \textbf{(14.17)}$$
$$\text{LCL} = p - 3\sigma_{\bar{p}} \qquad \textbf{(14.18)}$$

---

With $p = .03$ and samples of size $n = 200$, equation (14.16) shows that the standard error is

$$\sigma_{\bar{p}} = \sqrt{\frac{.03(1 - .03)}{200}} = .0121$$

**FIGURE 14.10**    *p* CHART FOR THE PROPORTION DEFECTIVE IN A MAIL-SORTING PROCESS

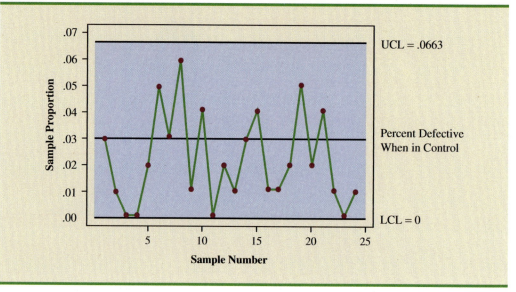

Hence, the control limits are UCL = .03 + 3(.0121) = .0663 and LCL = .03 − 3(.0121) = −.0063. Whenever equation (14.18) provides a negative value for LCL, LCL is set equal to zero in the control chart.

Figure 14.10 is the *p* chart for the mail-sorting process. The points plotted show the sample proportion defective found in samples of letters taken from the process. All points are within the control limits, providing no evidence to conclude that the sorting process is out of control.

If the proportion of defective items for a process that is in control is not known, that value is first estimated by using sample data. Suppose, for example, that *k* different samples, each of size *n*, are selected from a process that is in control. The fraction or proportion of defective items in each sample is then determined. Treating all the data collected as one large sample, we can compute the proportion of defective items for all the data; that value can then be used to estimate *p*, the proportion of defective items observed when the process is in control. Note that this estimate of *p* also enables us to estimate the standard error of the proportion; upper and lower control limits can then be established.

## *np* **Chart**

An *np* chart is a control chart developed for the number of defective items in a sample. In this case, *n* is the sample size and *p* is the probability of observing a defective item when the process is in control. Whenever the sample size is large, that is, when $np \geq 5$ and $n(1 − p) \geq 5$, the distribution of the number of defective items observed in a sample of size *n* can be approximated by a normal distribution with mean *np* and standard deviation $\sqrt{np(1 − p)}$. Thus, for the mail-sorting example, with $n = 200$ and $p = .03$, the number of defective items observed in a sample of 200 letters can be approximated by a normal distribution with a mean of 200(.03) = 6 and a standard deviation of $\sqrt{200(.03)(.97)} = 2.4125$.

The control limits for an *np* chart are set at 3 standard deviations above and below the expected number of defective items observed when the process is in control. Thus, we have the following control limits.

CONTROL LIMITS FOR AN *np* CHART

$$\text{UCL} = np + 3\sqrt{np(1 - p)} \qquad \textbf{(14.19)}$$
$$\text{LCL} = np - 3\sqrt{np(1 - p)} \qquad \textbf{(14.20)}$$

For the mail-sorting process example, with $p = .03$ and $n = 200$, the control limits are UCL = $6 + 3(2.4125) = 13.2375$ and LCL = $6 - 3(2.4125) = -1.2375$. When LCL is negative, LCL is set equal to zero in the control chart. Hence, if the number of letters diverted to incorrect routes is greater than 13, the process is concluded to be out of control.

The information provided by an *np* chart is equivalent to the information provided by the *p* chart; the only difference is that the *np* chart is a plot of the number of defective items observed, whereas the *p* chart is a plot of the proportion of defective items observed. Thus, if we were to conclude that a particular process is out of control on the basis of a *p* chart, the process would also be concluded to be out of control on the basis of an *np* chart.

## Interpretation of Control Charts

The location and pattern of points in a control chart enable us to determine, with a small probability of error, whether a process is in statistical control. A primary indication that a process may be out of control is a data point outside the control limits, such as point 5 in Figure 14.6. Finding such a point is statistical evidence that the process is out of control; in such cases, corrective action should be taken as soon as possible.

In addition to points outside the control limits, certain patterns of the points within the control limits can be warning signals of quality control problems. For example, assume that all the data points are within the control limits but that a large number of points are on one side of the center line. This pattern may indicate that an equipment problem, a change in materials, or some other assignable cause of a shift in quality has occurred. Careful investigation of the production process should be undertaken to determine whether quality has changed.

*Even if all points are within the upper and lower control limits, a process may not be in control. Trends in the sample data points or unusually long runs above or below the center line may also indicate out-of-control conditions.*

Another pattern to watch for in control charts is a gradual shift, or trend, over time. For example, as tools wear out, the dimensions of machined parts will gradually deviate from their designed levels. Gradual changes in temperature or humidity, general equipment deterioration, dirt buildup, or operator fatigue may also result in a trend pattern in control charts. Six or seven points in a row that indicate either an increasing or decreasing trend should be cause for concern, even if the data points are all within the control limits. When such a pattern occurs, the process should be reviewed for possible changes or shifts in quality. Corrective action to bring the process back into control may be necessary.

## NOTES AND COMMENTS

1. Because the control limits for the $\bar{x}$ chart depend on the value of the average range, these limits will not have much meaning unless the process variability is in control. In practice, the $R$ chart is usually constructed before the $\bar{x}$ chart; if the $R$ chart indicates that the process variability is in control, then the $\bar{x}$ chart is constructed. The StatTools X/R Charts option provides the $\bar{x}$ chart and the $R$ chart simultaneously. The steps of this procedure are described in the chapter appendix.

2. An *np* chart is used to monitor a process in terms of the number of defects. The Motorola Six Sigma Quality Level sets a goal of producing no more than 3.4 defects per million operations; this goal implies $p = .0000034$.

## Exercises

## Methods

1. A process that is in control has a mean of $\mu = 12.5$ and a standard deviation of $\sigma = .8$.
   a. Construct the $\bar{x}$ control chart for this process if samples of size 4 are to be used.
   b. Repeat part (a) for samples of size 8 and 16.
   c. What happens to the limits of the control chart as the sample size is increased? Discuss why this is reasonable.

2. Twenty-five samples, each of size 5, were selected from a process that was in control. The sum of all the data collected was 677.5 pounds.
   a. What is an estimate of the process mean (in terms of pounds per unit) when the process is in control?
   b. Develop the $\bar{x}$ control chart for this process if samples of size 5 will be used. Assume that the process standard deviation is .5 when the process is in control, and that the mean of the process is the estimate developed in part (a).

3. Twenty-five samples of 100 items each were inspected when a process was considered to be operating satisfactorily. In the 25 samples, a total of 135 items were found to be defective.
   a. What is an estimate of the proportion defective when the process is in control?
   b. What is the standard error of the proportion if samples of size 100 will be used for statistical process control?
   c. Compute the upper and lower control limits for the control chart.

4. A process sampled 20 times with a sample of size 8 resulted in $\bar{\bar{x}} = 28.5$ and $\bar{R} = 1.6$. Compute the upper and lower control limits for the $\bar{x}$ and $R$ charts for this process.

## Applications

5. Temperature is used to measure the output of a production process. When the process is in control, the mean of the process is $\mu = 128.5$ and the standard deviation is $\sigma = .4$.
   a. Construct the $\bar{x}$ chart for this process if samples of size 6 are to be used.
   b. Is the process in control for a sample providing the following data?

   | 128.8 | 128.2 | 129.1 | 128.7 | 128.4 | 129.2 |
   |---|---|---|---|---|---|

   c. Is the process in control for a sample providing the following data?

   | 129.3 | 128.7 | 128.6 | 129.2 | 129.5 | 129.0 |
   |---|---|---|---|---|---|

6. A quality control process monitors the weight per carton of laundry detergent. Control limits are set at UCL = 20.12 ounces and LCL = 19.90 ounces. Samples of size 5 are used for the sampling and inspection process. What are the process mean and process standard deviation for the manufacturing operation?

7. The Goodman Tire and Rubber Company periodically tests its tires for tread wear under simulated road conditions. To study and control the manufacturing process, 20 samples, each containing three radial tires, were chosen from different shifts over several days of operation, with the following results. Assuming that these data were collected when the manufacturing process was believed to be operating in control, develop the $R$ and $\bar{x}$ charts.

| Sample | Tread Wear* | | |
|--------|------|------|------|
| 1 | 31 | 42 | 28 |
| 2 | 26 | 18 | 35 |
| 3 | 25 | 30 | 34 |
| 4 | 17 | 25 | 21 |
| 5 | 38 | 29 | 35 |
| 6 | 41 | 42 | 36 |
| 7 | 21 | 17 | 29 |
| 8 | 32 | 26 | 28 |
| 9 | 41 | 34 | 33 |
| 10 | 29 | 17 | 30 |
| 11 | 26 | 31 | 40 |
| 12 | 23 | 19 | 25 |
| 13 | 17 | 24 | 32 |
| 14 | 43 | 35 | 17 |
| 15 | 18 | 25 | 29 |
| 16 | 30 | 42 | 31 |
| 17 | 28 | 36 | 32 |
| 18 | 40 | 29 | 31 |
| 19 | 18 | 29 | 28 |
| 20 | 22 | 34 | 26 |

*Hundredths of an inch

Tires

8. Over several weeks of normal, or in-control, operation, 20 samples of 150 packages each of synthetic-gut tennis strings were tested for breaking strength. A total of 141 packages of the 3000 tested failed to conform to the manufacturer's specifications.
   a. What is an estimate of the process proportion defective when the system is in control?
   b. Compute the upper and lower control limits for a $p$ chart.
   c. With the results of part (b), what conclusion should be made about the process if tests on a new sample of 150 packages find 12 defective? Do there appear to be assignable causes in this situation?
   d. Compute the upper and lower control limits for an $np$ chart.
   e. Answer part (c) using the results of part (d).
   f. Which control chart would be preferred in this situation? Explain.

9. An automotive industry supplier produces pistons for several models of automobiles. Twenty samples, each consisting of 200 pistons, were selected when the process was known to be operating correctly. The numbers of defective pistons found in the samples follow.

| | | | | | | | | | |
|---|---|---|---|---|---|---|---|---|---|
| 8 | 10 | 6 | 4 | 5 | 7 | 8 | 12 | 8 | 15 |
| 14 | 10 | 10 | 7 | 5 | 8 | 6 | 10 | 4 | 8 |

   a. What is an estimate of the proportion defective for the piston manufacturing process when it is in control?
   b. Construct the $p$ chart for the manufacturing process, assuming each sample has 200 pistons.
   c. With the results of part (b), what conclusion should be made if a sample of 200 has 20 defective pistons?
   d. Compute the upper and lower control limits for an $np$ chart.
   e. Answer part (c) using the results of part (d).

# 14.3  Acceptance Sampling

In acceptance sampling, the items of interest can be incoming shipments of raw materials or purchased parts as well as finished goods from final assembly. Suppose we want to decide whether to accept or reject a group of items on the basis of specified quality characteristics. In quality control terminology, the group of items is a **lot**, and **acceptance sampling** is a statistical method that enables us to base the accept-reject decision on the inspection of a sample of items from the lot.

The general steps of acceptance sampling are shown in Figure 14.11. After a lot is received, a sample of items is selected for inspection. The results of the inspection are compared to specified quality characteristics. If the quality characteristics are satisfied, the lot is accepted and sent to production or shipped to customers. If the lot is rejected, managers must decide on its disposition. In some cases, the decision may be to keep the lot and remove the unacceptable or nonconforming items. In other cases, the lot may be returned to the supplier at the supplier's expense; the extra work and cost placed on the supplier can motivate the supplier to provide high-quality lots. Finally, if the rejected lot consists of finished goods, the goods must be scrapped or reworked to meet acceptable quality standards.

**FIGURE 14.11    ACCEPTANCE SAMPLING PROCEDURE**

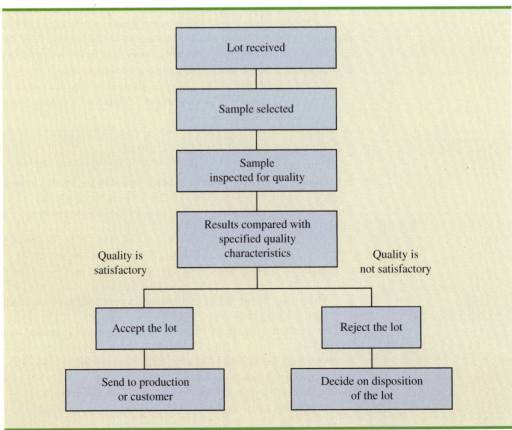

**TABLE 14.4**   THE OUTCOMES OF ACCEPTANCE SAMPLING

|  |  | State of the Lot | |
| --- | --- | --- | --- |
|  |  | $H_0$ True<br>Good-Quality Lot | $H_0$ False<br>Poor-Quality Lot |
| **Decision** | **Accept the Lot** | Correct decision | Type II error<br>(accepting a poor-quality lot) |
|  | **Reject the Lot** | Type I error<br>(rejecting a good-quality lot) | Correct decision |

*Acceptance sampling has the following advantages over 100% inspection:*
*1. Usually less expensive*
*2. Less product damage due to less handling and testing*
*3. Fewer inspectors required*
*4. The only approach possible if destructive testing must be used*

The statistical procedure of acceptance sampling is based on the hypothesis testing methodology presented in Chapter 9. The null and alternative hypotheses are stated as follows.

$$H_0: \text{Good-quality lot}$$
$$H_a: \text{Poor-quality lot}$$

Table 14.4 shows the results of the hypothesis testing procedure. Note that correct decisions correspond to accepting a good-quality lot and rejecting a poor-quality lot. However, as with other hypothesis testing procedures, we need to be aware of the possibilities of making a Type I error (rejecting a good-quality lot) or a Type II error (accepting a poor-quality lot).

The probability of a Type I error creates a risk for the producer of the lot and is known as the **producer's risk**. For example, a producer's risk of .05 indicates a 5% chance that a good-quality lot will be erroneously rejected. The probability of a Type II error, on the other hand, creates a risk for the consumer of the lot and is known as the **consumer's risk**. For example, a consumer's risk of .10 means a 10% chance that a poor-quality lot will be erroneously accepted and thus used in production or shipped to the customer. Specific values for the producer's risk and the consumer's risk can be controlled by the person designing the acceptance sampling procedure. To illustrate how to assign risk values, let us consider the problem faced by KALI, Inc.

## KALI, Inc.: An Example of Acceptance Sampling

KALI, Inc., manufactures home appliances that are marketed under a variety of trade names. However, KALI does not manufacture every component used in its products. Several components are purchased directly from suppliers. For example, one of the components that KALI purchases for use in home air conditioners is an overload protector, a device that turns off the compressor if it overheats. The compressor can be seriously damaged if the overload protector does not function properly, and therefore KALI is concerned about the quality of the overload protectors. One way to ensure quality would be to test every component received through an approach known as 100% inspection. However, to determine proper functioning of an overload protector, the device must be subjected to time-consuming and expensive tests, and KALI cannot justify testing every overload protector it receives.

Instead, KALI uses an acceptance sampling plan to monitor the quality of the overload protectors. The acceptance sampling plan requires that KALI's quality control inspectors select and test a sample of overload protectors from each shipment. If very few defective units are found in the sample, the lot is probably of good quality and should be accepted. However, if a large number of defective units are found in the sample, the lot is probably of poor quality and should be rejected.

An acceptance sampling plan consists of a sample size $n$ and an acceptance criterion $c$. The **acceptance criterion** is the maximum number of defective items that can be found in the sample and still indicate an acceptable lot. For example, for the KALI problem let us assume that a sample of 15 items will be selected from each incoming shipment or lot. Furthermore, assume that the manager of quality control states that the lot can be accepted only if no defective items are found. In this case, the acceptance sampling plan established by the quality control manager is $n = 15$ and $c = 0$.

This acceptance sampling plan is easy for the quality control inspector to implement. The inspector simply selects a sample of 15 items, performs the tests, and reaches a conclusion based on the following decision rule.

- *Accept the lot* if zero defective items are found.
- *Reject the lot* if one or more defective items are found.

Before implementing this acceptance sampling plan, the quality control manager wants to evaluate the risks or errors possible under the plan. The plan will be implemented only if both the producer's risk (Type I error) and the consumer's risk (Type II error) are controlled at reasonable levels.

## Computing the Probability of Accepting a Lot

The key to analyzing both the producer's risk and the consumer's risk is a "what-if" type of analysis. That is, we will assume that a lot has some known percentage of defective items and compute the probability of accepting the lot for a given sampling plan. By varying the assumed percentage of defective items, we can examine the effect of the sampling plan on both types of risks.

Let us begin by assuming that a large shipment of overload protectors has been received and that 5% of the overload protectors in the shipment are defective. For a shipment or lot with 5% of the items defective, what is the probability that the $n = 15, c = 0$ sampling plan will lead us to accept the lot? Because each overload protector tested will be either defective or nondefective and because the lot size is large, the number of defective items in a sample of 15 has a *binomial distribution*. The binomial probability function, which was presented in Chapter 5, follows.

---

BINOMIAL PROBABILITY FUNCTION FOR ACCEPTANCE SAMPLING

$$f(x) = \frac{n!}{x!(n-x)!} p^x (1-p)^{(n-x)} \qquad \textbf{(14.21)}$$

where

$$n = \text{the sample size}$$
$$p = \text{the proportion of defective items in the lot}$$
$$x = \text{the number of defective items in the sample}$$
$$f(x) = \text{the probability of } x \text{ defective items in the sample}$$

---

For the KALI acceptance sampling plan, $n = 15$; thus, for a lot with 5% defective ($p = .05$), we have

$$f(x) = \frac{15!}{x!(15-x)!} (.05)^x (1 - .05)^{(15-x)} \qquad \textbf{(14.22)}$$

**TABLE 14.5** PROBABILITY OF ACCEPTING THE LOT FOR THE KALI PROBLEM WITH $n = 15$ AND $c = 0$

| Percent Defective in the Lot | Probability of Accepting the Lot |
|:---:|:---:|
| 1 | .8601 |
| 2 | .7386 |
| 3 | .6333 |
| 4 | .5421 |
| 5 | .4633 |
| 10 | .2059 |
| 15 | .0874 |
| 20 | .0352 |
| 25 | .0134 |

Using equation (14.22), $f(0)$ will provide the probability that zero overload protectors will be defective and the lot will be accepted. In using equation (14.22), recall that $0! = 1$. Thus, the probability computation for $f(0)$ is

$$f(0) = \frac{15!}{0!(15 - 0)!}(.05)^0(1 - .05)^{(15-0)}$$

$$= \frac{15!}{0!(15)!}(.05)^0(.95)^{15} = (.95)^{15} = .4633$$

We now know that the $n = 15$, $c = 0$ sampling plan has a .4633 probability of accepting a lot with 5% defective items. Hence, there must be a corresponding $1 - .4633 = .5367$ probability of rejecting a lot with 5% defective items.

*Binomial probabilities can be easily computed using Excel. See Chapter 5.*

Excel's BINOM.DIST function can be used to simplify making these binomial probability calculations. Using this function, we can determine that if the lot contains 10% defective items, there is a .2059 probability that the $n = 15$, $c = 0$ sampling plan will indicate an acceptable lot. The probability that the $n = 15$, $c = 0$ sampling plan will lead to the acceptance of lots with 1%, 2%, 3%, . . . defective items is summarized in Table 14.5.

Using the probabilities in Table 14.5, a graph of the probability of accepting the lot versus the percent defective in the lot can be drawn as shown in Figure 14.12. This graph, or curve, is called the **operating characteristic (OC) curve** for the $n = 15$, $c = 0$ acceptance sampling plan.

Perhaps we should consider other sampling plans, ones with different sample sizes $n$ or different acceptance criteria $c$. First consider the case in which the sample size remains $n = 15$ but the acceptance criterion increases from $c = 0$ to $c = 1$. That is, we will now accept the lot if zero or one defective component is found in the sample. For a lot with 5% defective items ($p = .05$), the binomial probability function in equation (14.21), or Excel's BINOM.DIST function, can be used to compute $f(0) = .4633$ and $f(1) = .3658$. Thus, there is a $.4633 + .3658 = .8291$ probability that the $n = 15$, $c = 1$ plan will lead to the acceptance of a lot with 5% defective items.

Continuing these calculations, we obtain Figure 14.13, which shows the operating characteristic curves for four alternative acceptance sampling plans for the KALI problem. Samples of size 15 and 20 are considered. Note that regardless of the proportion defective in the lot, the $n = 15$, $c = 1$ sampling plan provides the highest probabilities of accepting the lot. The $n = 20$, $c = 0$ sampling plan provides the lowest probabilities of accepting the lot; however, that plan also provides the highest probabilities of rejecting the lot.

**FIGURE 14.12**     OPERATING CHARACTERISTIC CURVE FOR THE $n = 15, c = 0$
ACCEPTANCE SAMPLING PLAN

**FIGURE 14.13**     OPERATING CHARACTERISTIC CURVES FOR FOUR ACCEPTANCE
SAMPLING PLANS

## Selecting an Acceptance Sampling Plan

Now that we know how to use the binomial distribution to compute the probability of accepting a lot with a given proportion defective, we are ready to select the values of $n$ and $c$ that determine the desired acceptance sampling plan for the application being studied. To develop this plan, managers must specify two values for the fraction defective in the lot. One value, denoted $p_0$, will be used to control for the producer's risk, and the other value, denoted $p_1$, will be used to control for the consumer's risk.

We will use the following notation.

$\alpha$ = the producer's risk; the probability of rejecting a lot with $p_0$ defective items
$\beta$ = the consumer's risk; the probability of accepting a lot with $p_1$ defective items

Suppose that for the KALI problem, the managers specify that $p_0 = .03$ and $p_1 = .15$. From the OC curve for $n = 15$, $c = 0$ in Figure 14.14, we see that $p_0 = .03$ provides a producer's risk of approximately $1 - .63 = .37$, and $p_1 = .15$ provides a consumer's risk of approximately .09. Thus, if the managers are willing to tolerate both a .37 probability of rejecting a lot with 3% defective items (producer's risk) and a .09 probability of accepting a lot with 15% defective items (consumer's risk), the $n = 15$, $c = 0$ acceptance sampling plan would be acceptable.

Suppose, however, that the managers request a producer's risk of $\alpha = .10$ and a consumer's risk of $\beta = .19$. We see that now the $n = 15$, $c = 0$ sampling plan has a better-than-desired consumer's risk but an unacceptably large producer's risk. The fact that

**FIGURE 14.14**   OPERATING CHARACTERISTIC CURVE FOR $n = 15$, $c = 0$ WITH $p_0 = .03$
AND $p_1 = .15$

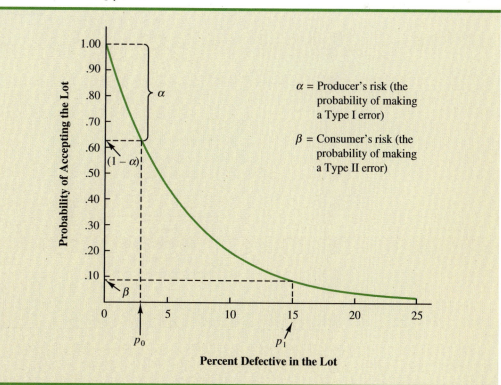

*Exercise 13 at the end of this section will ask you to compute the producer's risk and the consumer's risk for the $n = 20$, $c = 1$ sampling plan.*

$\alpha = .37$ indicates that 37% of the lots will be erroneously rejected when only 3% of the items in them are defective. The producer's risk is too high, and a different acceptance sampling plan should be considered.

Using $p_0 = .03$, $\alpha = .10$, $p_1 = .15$, and $\beta = .20$, Figure 14.13 shows that the acceptance sampling plan with $n = 20$ and $c = 1$ comes closest to meeting both the producer's and the consumer's risk requirements.

As shown in this section, several computations and several operating characteristic curves may need to be considered to determine the sampling plan with the desired producer's and consumer's risk. Fortunately, tables of sampling plans are published. For example, the American Military Standard Table, MIL-STD-105D, provides information

**FIGURE 14.15**     A TWO-STAGE ACCEPTANCE SAMPLING PLAN

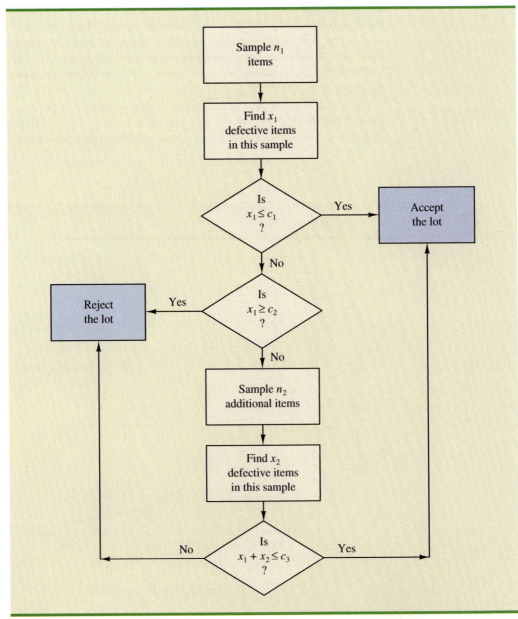

helpful in designing acceptance sampling plans. More advanced texts on quality control, such as those listed in the bibliography, describe the use of such tables. The advanced texts also discuss the role of sampling costs in determining the optimal sampling plan.

## Multiple Sampling Plans

The acceptance sampling procedure we presented for the KALI problem is a *single-sample plan*. It is called a single-sample plan because only one sample or sampling stage is used. After the number of defective components in the sample is determined, a decision must be made to accept or reject the lot. An alternative to the single-sample plan is a **multiple sampling plan**, in which two or more stages of sampling are used. At each stage a decision is made among three possibilities: stop sampling and accept the lot, stop sampling and reject the lot, or continue sampling. Although more complex, multiple sampling plans often result in a smaller total sample size than single-sample plans with the same $\alpha$ and $\beta$ probabilities.

The logic of a two-stage, or double-sample, plan is shown in Figure 14.15. Initially a sample of $n_1$ items is selected. If the number of defective components $x_1$ is less than or equal to $c_1$, accept the lot. If $x_1$ is greater than or equal to $c_2$, reject the lot. If $x_1$ is between $c_1$ and $c_2$ ($c_1 < x_1 < c_2$), select a second sample of $n_2$ items. Determine the combined, or total, number of defective components from the first sample ($x_1$) and the second sample ($x_2$). If $x_1 + x_2 \leq c_3$, accept the lot; otherwise reject the lot. The development of the double-sample plan is more difficult because the sample sizes $n_1$ and $n_2$ and the acceptance numbers $c_1$, $c_2$, and $c_3$ must meet both the producer's and consumer's risks desired.

## NOTES AND COMMENTS

1. The use of the binomial distribution for acceptance sampling is based on the assumption of large lots. If the lot size is small, the hypergeometric distribution is appropriate.

2. In the MIL-ST-105D sampling tables, $p_0$ is called the acceptable quality level (AQL). In some sampling tables, $p_1$ is called the lot tolerance percent defective (LTPD) or the rejectable quality level (RQL). Many of the published sampling plans also use quality indexes such as the indifference quality level (IQL) and the average outgoing quality limit (AOQL). The more advanced texts listed in the bibliography provide a complete discussion of these other indexes.

3. In this section we provided an introduction to *attributes sampling plans*. In these plans each item sampled is classified as nondefective or defective. In *variables sampling plans*, a sample is taken and a measurement of the quality characteristic is taken. For example, for gold jewelry a measurement of quality may be the amount of gold it contains. A simple statistic such as the average amount of gold in the sample jewelry is computed and compared with an allowable value to determine whether to accept or reject the lot.

## Exercises

## Methods

10. For an acceptance sampling plan with $n = 25$ and $c = 0$, find the probability of accepting a lot that has a defect rate of 2%. What is the probability of accepting the lot if the defect rate is 6%?

11. Consider an acceptance sampling plan with $n = 20$ and $c = 0$. Compute the producer's risk for each of the following cases.
    a. The lot has a defect rate of 2%.
    b. The lot has a defect rate of 6%.

12. Repeat exercise 11 for the acceptance sampling plan with $n = 20$ and $c = 1$. What happens to the producer's risk as the acceptance number $c$ is increased? Explain.

## Applications

13. Refer to the KALI problem presented in this section. The quality control manager requested a producer's risk of .10 when $p_0$ was .03 and a consumer's risk of .20 when $p_1$ was .15. Consider the acceptance sampling plan based on a sample size of 20 and an acceptance number of 1. Answer the following questions.
    a. What is the producer's risk for the $n = 20$, $c = 1$ sampling plan?
    b. What is the consumer's risk for the $n = 20$, $c = 1$ sampling plan?
    c. Does the $n = 20$, $c = 1$ sampling plan satisfy the risks requested by the quality control manager? Discuss.

14. To inspect incoming shipments of raw materials, a manufacturer is considering samples of sizes 10, 15, and 19. Use the binomial probabilities from Table 5 of Appendix B to select a sampling plan that provides a producer's risk of $\alpha = .03$ when $p_0$ is .05 and a consumer's risk of $\beta = .12$ when $p_1$ is .30.

15. A domestic manufacturer of watches purchases quartz crystals from a Swiss firm. The crystals are shipped in lots of 1000. The acceptance sampling procedure uses 20 randomly selected crystals.
    a. Construct operating characteristic curves for acceptance numbers of 0, 1, and 2.
    b. If $p_0$ is .01 and $p_1 = .08$, what are the producer's and consumer's risks for each sampling plan in part (a)?

## Summary

In this chapter we discussed how statistical methods can be used to assist in the control of quality. We first presented the $\bar{x}$, $R$, $p$, and $np$ control charts as graphical aids in monitoring process quality. Control limits are established for each chart; samples are selected periodically, and the data points plotted on the control chart. Data points outside the control limits indicate that the process is out of control and that corrective action should be taken. Patterns of data points within the control limits can also indicate potential quality control problems and suggest that corrective action may be warranted.

We also considered the technique known as acceptance sampling. With this procedure, a sample is selected and inspected. The number of defective items in the sample provides the basis for accepting or rejecting the lot. The sample size and the acceptance criterion can be adjusted to control both the producer's risk (Type I error) and the consumer's risk (Type II error).

## Glossary

**Total quality (TQ)** A total system approach to improving customer satisfaction and lowering real cost through a strategy of continuous improvement and learning.
**Six Sigma** A methodology that uses measurement and statistical analysis to achieve a level of quality so good that for every million opportunities no more than 3.4 defects will occur.
**Quality control** A series of inspections and measurements that determine whether quality standards are being met.
**Assignable causes** Variations in process outputs that are due to factors such as machine tools wearing out, incorrect machine settings, poor-quality raw materials, operator error,

and so on. Corrective action should be taken when assignable causes of output variation are detected.

**Common causes** Normal or natural variations in process outputs that are due purely to chance. No corrective action is necessary when output variations are due to common causes.

**Control chart** A graphical tool used to help determine whether a process is in control or out of control.

**$\bar{x}$ chart** A control chart used when the quality of the output of a process is measured in terms of the mean value of a variable such as a length, weight, temperature, and so on.

**$R$ chart** A control chart used when the quality of the output of a process is measured in terms of the range of a variable.

**$p$ chart** A control chart used when the quality of the output of a process is measured in terms of the proportion defective.

**$np$ chart** A control chart used to monitor the quality of the output of a process in terms of the number of defective items.

**Lot** A group of items such as incoming shipments of raw materials or purchased parts as well as finished goods from final assembly.

**Acceptance sampling** A statistical method in which the number of defective items found in a sample is used to determine whether a lot should be accepted or rejected.

**Producer's risk** The risk of rejecting a good-quality lot; a Type I error.

**Consumer's risk** The risk of accepting a poor-quality lot; a Type II error.

**Acceptance criterion** The maximum number of defective items that can be found in the sample and still indicate an acceptable lot.

**Operating characteristic (OC) curve** A graph showing the probability of accepting the lot as a function of the percentage defective in the lot. This curve can be used to help determine whether a particular acceptance sampling plan meets both the producer's and the consumer's risk requirements.

**Multiple sampling plan** A form of acceptance sampling in which more than one sample or stage is used. On the basis of the number of defective items found in a sample, a decision will be made to accept the lot, reject the lot, or continue sampling.

## Key Formulas

### Standard Error of the Mean

$$\sigma_{\bar{x}} = \frac{\sigma}{\sqrt{n}} \qquad (14.1)$$

### Control Limits for an $\bar{x}$ Chart: Process Mean and Standard Deviation Known

$$\text{UCL} = \mu + 3\sigma_{\bar{x}} \qquad (14.2)$$
$$\text{LCL} = \mu - 3\sigma_{\bar{x}} \qquad (14.3)$$

### Overall Sample Mean

$$\bar{\bar{x}} = \frac{\bar{x}_1 + \bar{x}_2 + \cdots + \bar{x}_k}{k} \qquad (14.4)$$

### Average Range

$$\bar{R} = \frac{R_1 + R_2 + \cdots + R_k}{k} \qquad (14.5)$$

**Control Limits for an $\bar{x}$ Chart: Process Mean and Standard Deviation Unknown**

$$\bar{\bar{x}} \pm A_2\bar{R} \qquad \text{(14.8)}$$

**Control Limits for an $R$ Chart**

$$\text{UCL} = \bar{R}D_4 \qquad \text{(14.14)}$$
$$\text{LCL} = \bar{R}D_3 \qquad \text{(14.15)}$$

**Standard Error of the Proportion**

$$\sigma_{\bar{p}} = \sqrt{\frac{p(1 - p)}{n}} \qquad \text{(14.16)}$$

**Control Limits for a $p$ Chart**

$$\text{UCL} = p + 3\sigma_{\bar{p}} \qquad \text{(14.17)}$$
$$\text{LCL} = p - 3\sigma_{\bar{p}} \qquad \text{(14.18)}$$

**Control Limits for an $np$ Chart**

$$\text{UCL} = np + 3\sqrt{np(1 - p)} \qquad \text{(14.19)}$$
$$\text{LCL} = np - 3\sqrt{np(1 - p)} \qquad \text{(14.20)}$$

**Binomial Probability Function for Acceptance Sampling**

$$f(x) = \frac{n!}{x!(n - x)!} p^x(1 - p)^{(n-x)} \qquad \text{(14.21)}$$

## Supplementary Exercises

16. Samples of size 5 provided the following 20 sample means for a production process that is believed to be in control.

| | | |
|---|---|---|
| 95.72 | 95.24 | 95.18 |
| 95.44 | 95.46 | 95.32 |
| 95.40 | 95.44 | 95.08 |
| 95.50 | 95.80 | 95.22 |
| 95.56 | 95.22 | 95.04 |
| 95.72 | 94.82 | 95.46 |
| 95.60 | 95.78 | |

   a. Based on these data, what is an estimate of the mean when the process is in control?
   b. Assume that the process standard deviation is $\sigma = .50$. Develop the $\bar{x}$ control chart for this production process. Assume that the mean of the process is the estimate developed in part (a).
   c. Do any of the 20 sample means indicate that the process was out of control?

17. Product filling weights are normally distributed with a mean of 350 grams and a standard deviation of 15 grams.
   a. Develop the control limits for the $\bar{x}$ chart for samples of size 10, 20, and 30.
   b. What happens to the control limits as the sample size is increased?
   c. What happens when a Type I error is made?

d.  What happens when a Type II error is made?
e.  What is the probability of a Type I error for samples of size 10, 20, and 30?
f.  What is the advantage of increasing the sample size for control chart purposes? What error probability is reduced as the sample size is increased?

18.  Twenty-five samples of size 5 resulted in $\bar{\bar{x}} = 5.42$ and $\bar{R} = 2.0$. Compute control limits for the $\bar{x}$ and $R$ charts, and estimate the standard deviation of the process.

19.  The following are quality control data for a manufacturing process at Kensport Chemical Company. The data show the temperature in degrees centigrade at five points in time during a manufacturing cycle. The company is interested in using control charts to monitor the temperature of its manufacturing process. Construct the $\bar{x}$ chart and $R$ chart. What conclusions can be made about the quality of the process?

| Sample | $\bar{x}$ | $R$ | Sample | $\bar{x}$ | $R$ |
|--------|-----------|------|--------|-----------|------|
| 1 | 95.72 | 1.0 | 11 | 95.80 | .6 |
| 2 | 95.24 | .9 | 12 | 95.22 | .2 |
| 3 | 95.18 | .8 | 13 | 95.56 | 1.3 |
| 4 | 95.44 | .4 | 14 | 95.22 | .5 |
| 5 | 95.46 | .5 | 15 | 95.04 | .8 |
| 6 | 95.32 | 1.1 | 16 | 95.72 | 1.1 |
| 7 | 95.40 | .9 | 17 | 94.82 | .6 |
| 8 | 95.44 | .3 | 18 | 95.46 | .5 |
| 9 | 95.08 | .2 | 19 | 95.60 | .4 |
| 10 | 95.50 | .6 | 20 | 95.74 | .6 |

20.  The following were collected for the Master Blend Coffee production process. The data show the filling weights based on samples of 3-pound cans of coffee. Use these data to construct the $\bar{x}$ and $R$ charts. What conclusions can be made about the quality of the production process?

| | | Observations | | | |
|--------|------|------|------|------|------|
| Sample | 1 | 2 | 3 | 4 | 5 |
| 1 | 3.05 | 3.08 | 3.07 | 3.11 | 3.11 |
| 2 | 3.13 | 3.07 | 3.05 | 3.10 | 3.10 |
| 3 | 3.06 | 3.04 | 3.12 | 3.11 | 3.10 |
| 4 | 3.09 | 3.08 | 3.09 | 3.09 | 3.07 |
| 5 | 3.10 | 3.06 | 3.06 | 3.07 | 3.08 |
| 6 | 3.08 | 3.10 | 3.13 | 3.03 | 3.06 |
| 7 | 3.06 | 3.06 | 3.08 | 3.10 | 3.08 |
| 8 | 3.11 | 3.08 | 3.07 | 3.07 | 3.07 |
| 9 | 3.09 | 3.09 | 3.08 | 3.07 | 3.09 |
| 10 | 3.06 | 3.11 | 3.07 | 3.09 | 3.07 |

**WEB** file

Coffee

21.  Consider the following situations. Comment on whether the situation might cause concern about the quality of the process.
a.  A $p$ chart has LCL = 0 and UCL = .068. When the process is in control, the proportion defective is .033. Plot the following seven sample results: .035, .062, .055, .049, .058, .066, and .055. Discuss.

b.   An $\bar{x}$ chart has LCL = 22.2 and UCL = 24.5. The mean is $\mu$ = 23.35 when the process is in control. Plot the following seven sample results: 22.4, 22.6, 22.65, 23.2, 23.4, 23.85, and 24.1. Discuss.

22.   Managers of 1200 different retail outlets make twice-a-month restocking orders from a central warehouse. Past experience shows that 4% of the orders result in one or more errors such as wrong item shipped, wrong quantity shipped, and item requested but not shipped. Random samples of 200 orders are selected monthly and checked for accuracy.
a.   Construct a control chart for this situation.
b.   Six months of data show the following numbers of orders with one or more errors: 10, 15, 6, 13, 8, and 17. Plot the data on the control chart. What does your plot indicate about the order process?

23.   An $n$ = 10, $c$ = 2 acceptance sampling plan is being considered; assume that $p_0$ = .05 and $p_1$ = .20.
a.   Compute both producer's and consumer's risk for this acceptance sampling plan.
b.   Would the producer, the consumer, or both be unhappy with the proposed sampling plan?
c.   What change in the sampling plan, if any, would you recommend?

24.   An acceptance sampling plan with $n$ = 15 and $c$ = 1 has been designed with a producer's risk of .075.
a.   Was the value of $p_0$ .01, .02, .03, .04, or .05? What does this value mean?
b.   What is the consumer's risk associated with this plan if $p_1$ is .25?

25.   A manufacturer produces lots of a canned food product. Let $p$ denote the proportion of the lots that do not meet the product quality specifications. An $n$ = 25, $c$ = 0 acceptance sampling plan will be used.
a.   Compute points on the operating characteristic curve when $p$ = .01, .03, .10, and .20.
b.   Plot the operating characteristic curve.
c.   What is the probability that the acceptance sampling plan will reject a lot containing .01 defective?

## Appendix   Control Charts Using StatTools

**Jensen**

In this appendix we show how StatTools can be used to construct an $\bar{x}$ chart and an $R$ chart for the Jensen Computer Supplies data shown in Table 14.2. Figure 14.16 is an Excel worksheet containing the Jensen data with the StatTools - Xbar and R Control Charts dialog box in the foreground. Begin by using the Data Set Manager to create a StatTools data set for these data using the procedure described in the appendix in Chapter 1. The following steps describe how StatTools can be used to provide both control charts.

**Step 1.**  Click the **StatTools** tab on the Ribbon
**Step 2.**  In the **Analyses** group, click **Quality Control**
**Step 3.**  Choose the **X/R Charts** option
**Step 4.**  When the StatTools - Xbar and R Control Charts dialog box appears (Figure 14.16),
          Select **X-Bar/R Chart** in the **Chart Type** box
          In the **Variables** section, select **Observation 1, Observation 2, Observation 3, Observation 4,** and **Observation 5**
     Click **OK**

An $\bar{x}$ chart similar to the one in Figure 14.7 will appear. It will be followed by an $R$ chart similar to the one in Figure 14.8.

**FIGURE 14.16**    EXCEL DATA WORKSHEET FOR JENSEN COMPUTER SUPPLIES

# APPENDIXES

# Appendix A:  References and Bibliography

## General

Freedman, D., R. Pisani, and R. Purves. *Statistics,* 4th ed. W. W. Norton, 2007.

Hogg, R. V., J. W. McKean, and A. T. Craig. *Introduction to Mathematical Statistics,* 6th ed. Pearson, 2004.

Hogg, R. V., and E. A. Tanis. *Probability and Statistical Inference,* 7th ed. Pearson, 2005.

Miller, I., and M. Miller. *John E. Freund's Mathematical Statistics,* 7th ed. Pearson, 2003.

Moore, D. S., G. P. McCabe, and B. Craig. *Introduction to the Practice of Statistics,* 6th ed. Freeman, 2007.

Wackerly, D. D., W. Mendenhall, and R. L. Scheaffer. *Mathematical Statistics with Applications,* 7th ed. Cengage Learning, 2007.

## Probability

Hogg, R. V., and E. A. Tanis. *Probability and Statistical Inference,* 7th ed. Pearson, 2005.

Ross, S. M. *Introduction to Probability Models,* 9th ed. Elsevier, 2006.

Wackerly, D. D., W. Mendenhall, and R. L. Scheaffer. *Mathematical Statistics with Applications,* 7th ed. Cengage Learning, 2007.

## Sampling

Cochran, W. G. *Sampling Techniques,* 3rd ed. Wiley, 1977.

Hansen, M. H., W. N. Hurwitz, W. G. Madow, and M. N. Hanson. *Sample Survey Methods and Theory.* Wiley, 1993.

Kish, L. *Survey Sampling.* Wiley, 2008.

Levy, P. S., and S. Lemeshow. *Sampling of Populations: Methods and Applications,* 4th ed. Wiley, 2008.

Scheaffer, R. L., W. Mendenhall, and L. Ott. *Elementary Survey Sampling,* 6th ed. Cengage Learning, 2005.

## Experimental Design

Cochran, W. G., and G. M. Cox. *Experimental Designs,* 2nd ed. Wiley, 1992.

Hicks, C. R., and K. V. Turner. *Fundamental Concepts in the Design of Experiments,* 5th ed. Oxford University Press, 1999.

Montgomery, D. C. *Design and Analysis of Experiments,* 6th ed. Wiley, 2004.

Winer, B. J., K. M. Michels, and D. R. Brown. *Statistical Principles in Experimental Design,* 3rd ed. McGraw-Hill, 1991.

Wu, C. F. Jeff, and M. Hamada. *Experiments: Planning, Analysis, and Parameter Optimization,* 2nd ed. Wiley, 2009.

## Regression Analysis

Chatterjee, S., and A. S. Hadi. *Regression Analysis by Example,* 4th ed. Wiley, 2006.

Draper, N. R., and H. Smith. *Applied Regression Analysis,* 3rd ed. Wiley, 1998.

Graybill, F. A., and H. K. Iyer. *Regression Analysis: Concepts and Applications.* Wadsworth, 1994.

Hosmer, D. W., and S. Lemeshow. *Applied Logistic Regression,* 2nd ed. Wiley, 2000.

Kleinbaum, D. G., L. L. Kupper, and K. E. Muller. *Applied Regression Analysis and Multivariate Methods,* 4th ed. Cengage Learning, 2007.

Neter, J., W. Wasserman, M. H. Kutner, and C. Nashtsheim. *Applied Linear Statistical Models,* 4th ed. McGraw-Hill, 1996.

Mendenhall, M., T. Sincich., and T. R. Dye. *A Second Course in Statistics: Regression Analysis,* 6th ed. Pearson, 1996.

## Quality Control

Evans, J. R., and W. M. Lindsay. *Managing for Quality and Performance Excellence,* 8th ed. South-Western, 2011.

Juran, J. M., and A. B. Godfrey. *Juran's Quality Handbook,* 5th ed. McGraw-Hill, 1999.

Montgomery, D. C. *Introduction to Statistical Quality Control,* 6th ed. Wiley, 2008.

## Time Series and Forecasting

Bowerman, B. L., and R. T. O'Connell. *Forecasting and Time Series: An Applied Approach,* 3rd ed. Brooks/Cole, 2000.

Box, G. E. P., G. M. Jenkins, and G. C. Reinsel. *Time Series Analysis: Forecasting and Control,* 4th ed. Wiley, 2008.

Makridakis, S. G., S. C. Wheelwright, and R. J. Hyndman. *Forecasting Methods and Applications,* 3rd ed. Wiley, 1998.

Wilson, J. H., B. Keating, and John Galt Solutions, Inc. *Business Forecasting with Accompanying Excel-Based Forecast $X^{TM}$,* 5th ed. McGraw-Hill/Irwin, 2007.

### TABLE 1   CUMULATIVE PROBABILITIES FOR THE STANDARD NORMAL DISTRIBUTION

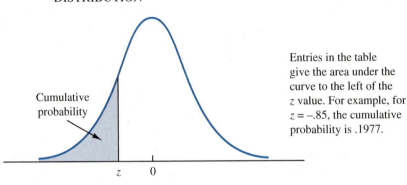

Entries in the table give the area under the curve to the left of the $z$ value. For example, for $z = -.85$, the cumulative probability is .1977.

Cumulative probability

| $z$ | .00 | .01 | .02 | .03 | .04 | .05 | .06 | .07 | .08 | .09 |
|------|------|------|------|------|------|------|------|------|------|------|
| −3.0 | .0013 | .0013 | .0013 | .0012 | .0012 | .0011 | .0011 | .0011 | .0010 | .0010 |
| −2.9 | .0019 | .0018 | .0018 | .0017 | .0016 | .0016 | .0015 | .0015 | .0014 | .0014 |
| −2.8 | .0026 | .0025 | .0024 | .0023 | .0023 | .0022 | .0021 | .0021 | .0020 | .0019 |
| −2.7 | .0035 | .0034 | .0033 | .0032 | .0031 | .0030 | .0029 | .0028 | .0027 | .0026 |
| −2.6 | .0047 | .0045 | .0044 | .0043 | .0041 | .0040 | .0039 | .0038 | .0037 | .0036 |
| −2.5 | .0062 | .0060 | .0059 | .0057 | .0055 | .0054 | .0052 | .0051 | .0049 | .0048 |
| −2.4 | .0082 | .0080 | .0078 | .0075 | .0073 | .0071 | .0069 | .0068 | .0066 | .0064 |
| −2.3 | .0107 | .0104 | .0102 | .0099 | .0096 | .0094 | .0091 | .0089 | .0087 | .0084 |
| −2.2 | .0139 | .0136 | .0132 | .0129 | .0125 | .0122 | .0119 | .0116 | .0113 | .0110 |
| −2.1 | .0179 | .0174 | .0170 | .0166 | .0162 | .0158 | .0154 | .0150 | .0146 | .0143 |
| −2.0 | .0228 | .0222 | .0217 | .0212 | .0207 | .0202 | .0197 | .0192 | .0188 | .0183 |
| −1.9 | .0287 | .0281 | .0274 | .0268 | .0262 | .0256 | .0250 | .0244 | .0239 | .0233 |
| −1.8 | .0359 | .0351 | .0344 | .0336 | .0329 | .0322 | .0314 | .0307 | .0301 | .0294 |
| −1.7 | .0446 | .0436 | .0427 | .0418 | .0409 | .0401 | .0392 | .0384 | .0375 | .0367 |
| −1.6 | .0548 | .0537 | .0526 | .0516 | .0505 | .0495 | .0485 | .0475 | .0465 | .0455 |
| −1.5 | .0668 | .0655 | .0643 | .0630 | .0618 | .0606 | .0594 | .0582 | .0571 | .0559 |
| −1.4 | .0808 | .0793 | .0778 | .0764 | .0749 | .0735 | .0721 | .0708 | .0694 | .0681 |
| −1.3 | .0968 | .0951 | .0934 | .0918 | .0901 | .0885 | .0869 | .0853 | .0838 | .0823 |
| −1.2 | .1151 | .1131 | .1112 | .1093 | .1075 | .1056 | .1038 | .1020 | .1003 | .0985 |
| −1.1 | .1357 | .1335 | .1314 | .1292 | .1271 | .1251 | .1230 | .1210 | .1190 | .1170 |
| −1.0 | .1587 | .1562 | .1539 | .1515 | .1492 | .1469 | .1446 | .1423 | .1401 | .1379 |
| −.9 | .1841 | .1814 | .1788 | .1762 | .1736 | .1711 | .1685 | .1660 | .1635 | .1611 |
| −.8 | .2119 | .2090 | .2061 | .2033 | .2005 | .1977 | .1949 | .1922 | .1894 | .1867 |
| −.7 | .2420 | .2389 | .2358 | .2327 | .2296 | .2266 | .2236 | .2206 | .2177 | .2148 |
| −.6 | .2743 | .2709 | .2676 | .2643 | .2611 | .2578 | .2546 | .2514 | .2483 | .2451 |
| −.5 | .3085 | .3050 | .3015 | .2981 | .2946 | .2912 | .2877 | .2843 | .2810 | .2776 |
| −.4 | .3446 | .3409 | .3372 | .3336 | .3300 | .3264 | .3228 | .3192 | .3156 | .3121 |
| −.3 | .3821 | .3783 | .3745 | .3707 | .3669 | .3632 | .3594 | .3557 | .3520 | .3483 |
| −.2 | .4207 | .4168 | .4129 | .4090 | .4052 | .4013 | .3974 | .3936 | .3897 | .3859 |
| −.1 | .4602 | .4562 | .4522 | .4483 | .4443 | .4404 | .4364 | .4325 | .4286 | .4247 |
| −.0 | .5000 | .4960 | .4920 | .4880 | .4840 | .4801 | .4761 | .4721 | .4681 | .4641 |

**TABLE 1**    CUMULATIVE PROBABILITIES FOR THE STANDARD NORMAL
DISTRIBUTION (*Continued*)

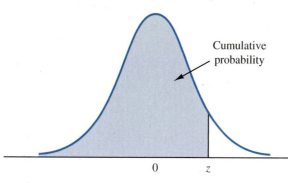

Cumulative
probability

Entries in the table
give the area under the
curve to the left of the
*z* value. For example, for
*z* = 1.25, the cumulative
probability is .8944.

| z | .00 | .01 | .02 | .03 | .04 | .05 | .06 | .07 | .08 | .09 |
|---|---|---|---|---|---|---|---|---|---|---|
| .0 | .5000 | .5040 | .5080 | .5120 | .5160 | .5199 | .5239 | .5279 | .5319 | .5359 |
| .1 | .5398 | .5438 | .5478 | .5517 | .5557 | .5596 | .5636 | .5675 | .5714 | .5753 |
| .2 | .5793 | .5832 | .5871 | .5910 | .5948 | .5987 | .6026 | .6064 | .6103 | .6141 |
| .3 | .6179 | .6217 | .6255 | .6293 | .6331 | .6368 | .6406 | .6443 | .6480 | .6517 |
| .4 | .6554 | .6591 | .6628 | .6664 | .6700 | .6736 | .6772 | .6808 | .6844 | .6879 |
| .5 | .6915 | .6950 | .6985 | .7019 | .7054 | .7088 | .7123 | .7157 | .7190 | .7224 |
| .6 | .7257 | .7291 | .7324 | .7357 | .7389 | .7422 | .7454 | .7486 | .7517 | .7549 |
| .7 | .7580 | .7611 | .7642 | .7673 | .7704 | .7734 | .7764 | .7794 | .7823 | .7852 |
| .8 | .7881 | .7910 | .7939 | .7967 | .7995 | .8023 | .8051 | .8078 | .8106 | .8133 |
| .9 | .8159 | .8186 | .8212 | .8238 | .8264 | .8289 | .8315 | .8340 | .8365 | .8389 |
| 1.0 | .8413 | .8438 | .8461 | .8485 | .8508 | .8531 | .8554 | .8577 | .8599 | .8621 |
| 1.1 | .8643 | .8665 | .8686 | .8708 | .8729 | .8749 | .8770 | .8790 | .8810 | .8830 |
| 1.2 | .8849 | .8869 | .8888 | .8907 | .8925 | .8944 | .8962 | .8980 | .8997 | .9015 |
| 1.3 | .9032 | .9049 | .9066 | .9082 | .9099 | .9115 | .9131 | .9147 | .9162 | .9177 |
| 1.4 | .9192 | .9207 | .9222 | .9236 | .9251 | .9265 | .9279 | .9292 | .9306 | .9319 |
| 1.5 | .9332 | .9345 | .9357 | .9370 | .9382 | .9394 | .9406 | .9418 | .9429 | .9441 |
| 1.6 | .9452 | .9463 | .9474 | .9484 | .9495 | .9505 | .9515 | .9525 | .9535 | .9545 |
| 1.7 | .9554 | .9564 | .9573 | .9582 | .9591 | .9599 | .9608 | .9616 | .9625 | .9633 |
| 1.8 | .9641 | .9649 | .9656 | .9664 | .9671 | .9678 | .9686 | .9693 | .9699 | .9706 |
| 1.9 | .9713 | .9719 | .9726 | .9732 | .9738 | .9744 | .9750 | .9756 | .9761 | .9767 |
| 2.0 | .9772 | .9778 | .9783 | .9788 | .9793 | .9798 | .9803 | .9808 | .9812 | .9817 |
| 2.1 | .9821 | .9826 | .9830 | .9834 | .9838 | .9842 | .9846 | .9850 | .9854 | .9857 |
| 2.2 | .9861 | .9864 | .9868 | .9871 | .9875 | .9878 | .9881 | .9884 | .9887 | .9890 |
| 2.3 | .9893 | .9896 | .9898 | .9901 | .9904 | .9906 | .9909 | .9911 | .9913 | .9916 |
| 2.4 | .9918 | .9920 | .9922 | .9925 | .9927 | .9929 | .9931 | .9932 | .9934 | .9936 |
| 2.5 | .9938 | .9940 | .9941 | .9943 | .9945 | .9946 | .9948 | .9949 | .9951 | .9952 |
| 2.6 | .9953 | .9955 | .9956 | .9957 | .9959 | .9960 | .9961 | .9962 | .9963 | .9964 |
| 2.7 | .9965 | .9966 | .9967 | .9968 | .9969 | .9970 | .9971 | .9972 | .9973 | .9974 |
| 2.8 | .9974 | .9975 | .9976 | .9977 | .9977 | .9978 | .9979 | .9979 | .9980 | .9981 |
| 2.9 | .9981 | .9982 | .9982 | .9983 | .9984 | .9984 | .9985 | .9985 | .9986 | .9986 |
| 3.0 | .9987 | .9987 | .9987 | .9988 | .9988 | .9989 | .9989 | .9989 | .9990 | .9990 |

**TABLE 2**    *t* DISTRIBUTION

Area or probability

Entries in the table give *t* values for an area or probability in the upper tail of the *t* distribution. For example, with 10 degrees of freedom and a .05 area in the upper tail, $t_{.05} = 1.812$.

| Degrees of Freedom | Area in Upper Tail | | | | | |
|---|---|---|---|---|---|---|
| | .20 | .10 | .05 | .025 | .01 | .005 |
| 1 | 1.376 | 3.078 | 6.314 | 12.706 | 31.821 | 63.656 |
| 2 | 1.061 | 1.886 | 2.920 | 4.303 | 6.965 | 9.925 |
| 3 | .978 | 1.638 | 2.353 | 3.182 | 4.541 | 5.841 |
| 4 | .941 | 1.533 | 2.132 | 2.776 | 3.747 | 4.604 |
| 5 | .920 | 1.476 | 2.015 | 2.571 | 3.365 | 4.032 |
| 6 | .906 | 1.440 | 1.943 | 2.447 | 3.143 | 3.707 |
| 7 | .896 | 1.415 | 1.895 | 2.365 | 2.998 | 3.499 |
| 8 | .889 | 1.397 | 1.860 | 2.306 | 2.896 | 3.355 |
| 9 | .883 | 1.383 | 1.833 | 2.262 | 2.821 | 3.250 |
| 10 | .879 | 1.372 | 1.812 | 2.228 | 2.764 | 3.169 |
| 11 | .876 | 1.363 | 1.796 | 2.201 | 2.718 | 3.106 |
| 12 | .873 | 1.356 | 1.782 | 2.179 | 2.681 | 3.055 |
| 13 | .870 | 1.350 | 1.771 | 2.160 | 2.650 | 3.012 |
| 14 | .868 | 1.345 | 1.761 | 2.145 | 2.624 | 2.977 |
| 15 | .866 | 1.341 | 1.753 | 2.131 | 2.602 | 2.947 |
| 16 | .865 | 1.337 | 1.746 | 2.120 | 2.583 | 2.921 |
| 17 | .863 | 1.333 | 1.740 | 2.110 | 2.567 | 2.898 |
| 18 | .862 | 1.330 | 1.734 | 2.101 | 2.552 | 2.878 |
| 19 | .861 | 1.328 | 1.729 | 2.093 | 2.539 | 2.861 |
| 20 | .860 | 1.325 | 1.725 | 2.086 | 2.528 | 2.845 |
| 21 | .859 | 1.323 | 1.721 | 2.080 | 2.518 | 2.831 |
| 22 | .858 | 1.321 | 1.717 | 2.074 | 2.508 | 2.819 |
| 23 | .858 | 1.319 | 1.714 | 2.069 | 2.500 | 2.807 |
| 24 | .857 | 1.318 | 1.711 | 2.064 | 2.492 | 2.797 |
| 25 | .856 | 1.316 | 1.708 | 2.060 | 2.485 | 2.787 |
| 26 | .856 | 1.315 | 1.706 | 2.056 | 2.479 | 2.779 |
| 27 | .855 | 1.314 | 1.703 | 2.052 | 2.473 | 2.771 |
| 28 | .855 | 1.313 | 1.701 | 2.048 | 2.467 | 2.763 |
| 29 | .854 | 1.311 | 1.699 | 2.045 | 2.462 | 2.756 |
| 30 | .854 | 1.310 | 1.697 | 2.042 | 2.457 | 2.750 |
| 31 | .853 | 1.309 | 1.696 | 2.040 | 2.453 | 2.744 |
| 32 | .853 | 1.309 | 1.694 | 2.037 | 2.449 | 2.738 |
| 33 | .853 | 1.308 | 1.692 | 2.035 | 2.445 | 2.733 |
| 34 | .852 | 1.307 | 1.691 | 2.032 | 2.441 | 2.728 |

**TABLE 2**    *t* DISTRIBUTION (*Continued*)

| Degrees of Freedom | Area in Upper Tail | | | | | |
|---|---|---|---|---|---|---|
| | **.20** | **.10** | **.05** | **.025** | **.01** | **.005** |
| 35 | .852 | 1.306 | 1.690 | 2.030 | 2.438 | 2.724 |
| 36 | .852 | 1.306 | 1.688 | 2.028 | 2.434 | 2.719 |
| 37 | .851 | 1.305 | 1.687 | 2.026 | 2.431 | 2.715 |
| 38 | .851 | 1.304 | 1.686 | 2.024 | 2.429 | 2.712 |
| 39 | .851 | 1.304 | 1.685 | 2.023 | 2.426 | 2.708 |
| 40 | .851 | 1.303 | 1.684 | 2.021 | 2.423 | 2.704 |
| 41 | .850 | 1.303 | 1.683 | 2.020 | 2.421 | 2.701 |
| 42 | .850 | 1.302 | 1.682 | 2.018 | 2.418 | 2.698 |
| 43 | .850 | 1.302 | 1.681 | 2.017 | 2.416 | 2.695 |
| 44 | .850 | 1.301 | 1.680 | 2.015 | 2.414 | 2.692 |
| 45 | .850 | 1.301 | 1.679 | 2.014 | 2.412 | 2.690 |
| 46 | .850 | 1.300 | 1.679 | 2.013 | 2.410 | 2.687 |
| 47 | .849 | 1.300 | 1.678 | 2.012 | 2.408 | 2.685 |
| 48 | .849 | 1.299 | 1.677 | 2.011 | 2.407 | 2.682 |
| 49 | .849 | 1.299 | 1.677 | 2.010 | 2.405 | 2.680 |
| 50 | .849 | 1.299 | 1.676 | 2.009 | 2.403 | 2.678 |
| 51 | .849 | 1.298 | 1.675 | 2.008 | 2.402 | 2.676 |
| 52 | .849 | 1.298 | 1.675 | 2.007 | 2.400 | 2.674 |
| 53 | .848 | 1.298 | 1.674 | 2.006 | 2.399 | 2.672 |
| 54 | .848 | 1.297 | 1.674 | 2.005 | 2.397 | 2.670 |
| 55 | .848 | 1.297 | 1.673 | 2.004 | 2.396 | 2.668 |
| 56 | .848 | 1.297 | 1.673 | 2.003 | 2.395 | 2.667 |
| 57 | .848 | 1.297 | 1.672 | 2.002 | 2.394 | 2.665 |
| 58 | .848 | 1.296 | 1.672 | 2.002 | 2.392 | 2.663 |
| 59 | .848 | 1.296 | 1.671 | 2.001 | 2.391 | 2.662 |
| 60 | .848 | 1.296 | 1.671 | 2.000 | 2.390 | 2.660 |
| 61 | .848 | 1.296 | 1.670 | 2.000 | 2.389 | 2.659 |
| 62 | .847 | 1.295 | 1.670 | 1.999 | 2.388 | 2.657 |
| 63 | .847 | 1.295 | 1.669 | 1.998 | 2.387 | 2.656 |
| 64 | .847 | 1.295 | 1.669 | 1.998 | 2.386 | 2.655 |
| 65 | .847 | 1.295 | 1.669 | 1.997 | 2.385 | 2.654 |
| 66 | .847 | 1.295 | 1.668 | 1.997 | 2.384 | 2.652 |
| 67 | .847 | 1.294 | 1.668 | 1.996 | 2.383 | 2.651 |
| 68 | .847 | 1.294 | 1.668 | 1.995 | 2.382 | 2.650 |
| 69 | .847 | 1.294 | 1.667 | 1.995 | 2.382 | 2.649 |
| 70 | .847 | 1.294 | 1.667 | 1.994 | 2.381 | 2.648 |
| 71 | .847 | 1.294 | 1.667 | 1.994 | 2.380 | 2.647 |
| 72 | .847 | 1.293 | 1.666 | 1.993 | 2.379 | 2.646 |
| 73 | .847 | 1.293 | 1.666 | 1.993 | 2.379 | 2.645 |
| 74 | .847 | 1.293 | 1.666 | 1.993 | 2.378 | 2.644 |
| 75 | .846 | 1.293 | 1.665 | 1.992 | 2.377 | 2.643 |
| 76 | .846 | 1.293 | 1.665 | 1.992 | 2.376 | 2.642 |
| 77 | .846 | 1.293 | 1.665 | 1.991 | 2.376 | 2.641 |
| 78 | .846 | 1.292 | 1.665 | 1.991 | 2.375 | 2.640 |
| 79 | .846 | 1.292 | 1.664 | 1.990 | 2.374 | 2.639 |

**TABLE 2**    *t* DISTRIBUTION (*Continued*)

| Degrees of Freedom | Area in Upper Tail | | | | | |
|---|---|---|---|---|---|---|
| | **.20** | **.10** | **.05** | **.025** | **.01** | **.005** |
| 80 | .846 | 1.292 | 1.664 | 1.990 | 2.374 | 2.639 |
| 81 | .846 | 1.292 | 1.664 | 1.990 | 2.373 | 2.638 |
| 82 | .846 | 1.292 | 1.664 | 1.989 | 2.373 | 2.637 |
| 83 | .846 | 1.292 | 1.663 | 1.989 | 2.372 | 2.636 |
| 84 | .846 | 1.292 | 1.663 | 1.989 | 2.372 | 2.636 |
| 85 | .846 | 1.292 | 1.663 | 1.988 | 2.371 | 2.635 |
| 86 | .846 | 1.291 | 1.663 | 1.988 | 2.370 | 2.634 |
| 87 | .846 | 1.291 | 1.663 | 1.988 | 2.370 | 2.634 |
| 88 | .846 | 1.291 | 1.662 | 1.987 | 2.369 | 2.633 |
| 89 | .846 | 1.291 | 1.662 | 1.987 | 2.369 | 2.632 |
| 90 | .846 | 1.291 | 1.662 | 1.987 | 2.368 | 2.632 |
| 91 | .846 | 1.291 | 1.662 | 1.986 | 2.368 | 2.631 |
| 92 | .846 | 1.291 | 1.662 | 1.986 | 2.368 | 2.630 |
| 93 | .846 | 1.291 | 1.661 | 1.986 | 2.367 | 2.630 |
| 94 | .845 | 1.291 | 1.661 | 1.986 | 2.367 | 2.629 |
| 95 | .845 | 1.291 | 1.661 | 1.985 | 2.366 | 2.629 |
| 96 | .845 | 1.290 | 1.661 | 1.985 | 2.366 | 2.628 |
| 97 | .845 | 1.290 | 1.661 | 1.985 | 2.365 | 2.627 |
| 98 | .845 | 1.290 | 1.661 | 1.984 | 2.365 | 2.627 |
| 99 | .845 | 1.290 | 1.660 | 1.984 | 2.364 | 2.626 |
| 100 | .845 | 1.290 | 1.660 | 1.984 | 2.364 | 2.626 |
| ∞ | .842 | 1.282 | 1.645 | 1.960 | 2.326 | 2.576 |

**TABLE 3**   CHI-SQUARE DISTRIBUTION

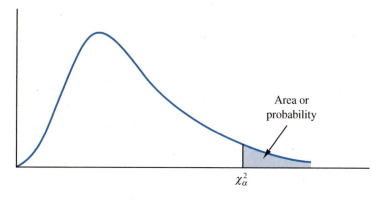

Area or
probability

$\chi_\alpha^2$

Entries in the table give $\chi_\alpha^2$ values, where $\alpha$ is the area or probability in the upper tail of the chi-square distribution. For example, with 10 degrees of freedom and a .01 area in the upper tail, $\chi_{.01}^2 = 23.209$.

| Degrees of Freedom | Area in Upper Tail | | | | | | | | | |
|---|---|---|---|---|---|---|---|---|---|---|
| | .995 | .99 | .975 | .95 | .90 | .10 | .05 | .025 | .01 | .005 |
| 1 | .000 | .000 | .001 | .004 | .016 | 2.706 | 3.841 | 5.024 | 6.635 | 7.879 |
| 2 | .010 | .020 | .051 | .103 | .211 | 4.605 | 5.991 | 7.378 | 9.210 | 10.597 |
| 3 | .072 | .115 | .216 | .352 | .584 | 6.251 | 7.815 | 9.348 | 11.345 | 12.838 |
| 4 | .207 | .297 | .484 | .711 | 1.064 | 7.779 | 9.488 | 11.143 | 13.277 | 14.860 |
| 5 | .412 | .554 | .831 | 1.145 | 1.610 | 9.236 | 11.070 | 12.832 | 15.086 | 16.750 |
| 6 | .676 | .872 | 1.237 | 1.635 | 2.204 | 10.645 | 12.592 | 14.449 | 16.812 | 18.548 |
| 7 | .989 | 1.239 | 1.690 | 2.167 | 2.833 | 12.017 | 14.067 | 16.013 | 18.475 | 20.278 |
| 8 | 1.344 | 1.647 | 2.180 | 2.733 | 3.490 | 13.362 | 15.507 | 17.535 | 20.090 | 21.955 |
| 9 | 1.735 | 2.088 | 2.700 | 3.325 | 4.168 | 14.684 | 16.919 | 19.023 | 21.666 | 23.589 |
| 10 | 2.156 | 2.558 | 3.247 | 3.940 | 4.865 | 15.987 | 18.307 | 20.483 | 23.209 | 25.188 |
| 11 | 2.603 | 3.053 | 3.816 | 4.575 | 5.578 | 17.275 | 19.675 | 21.920 | 24.725 | 26.757 |
| 12 | 3.074 | 3.571 | 4.404 | 5.226 | 6.304 | 18.549 | 21.026 | 23.337 | 26.217 | 28.300 |
| 13 | 3.565 | 4.107 | 5.009 | 5.892 | 7.041 | 19.812 | 22.362 | 24.736 | 27.688 | 29.819 |
| 14 | 4.075 | 4.660 | 5.629 | 6.571 | 7.790 | 21.064 | 23.685 | 26.119 | 29.141 | 31.319 |
| 15 | 4.601 | 5.229 | 6.262 | 7.261 | 8.547 | 22.307 | 24.996 | 27.488 | 30.578 | 32.801 |
| 16 | 5.142 | 5.812 | 6.908 | 7.962 | 9.312 | 23.542 | 26.296 | 28.845 | 32.000 | 34.267 |
| 17 | 5.697 | 6.408 | 7.564 | 8.672 | 10.085 | 24.769 | 27.587 | 30.191 | 33.409 | 35.718 |
| 18 | 6.265 | 7.015 | 8.231 | 9.390 | 10.865 | 25.989 | 28.869 | 31.526 | 34.805 | 37.156 |
| 19 | 6.844 | 7.633 | 8.907 | 10.117 | 11.651 | 27.204 | 30.144 | 32.852 | 36.191 | 38.582 |
| 20 | 7.434 | 8.260 | 9.591 | 10.851 | 12.443 | 28.412 | 31.410 | 34.170 | 37.566 | 39.997 |
| 21 | 8.034 | 8.897 | 10.283 | 11.591 | 13.240 | 29.615 | 32.671 | 35.479 | 38.932 | 41.401 |
| 22 | 8.643 | 9.542 | 10.982 | 12.338 | 14.041 | 30.813 | 33.924 | 36.781 | 40.289 | 42.796 |
| 23 | 9.260 | 10.196 | 11.689 | 13.091 | 14.848 | 32.007 | 35.172 | 38.076 | 41.638 | 44.181 |
| 24 | 9.886 | 10.856 | 12.401 | 13.848 | 15.659 | 33.196 | 36.415 | 39.364 | 42.980 | 45.558 |
| 25 | 10.520 | 11.524 | 13.120 | 14.611 | 16.473 | 34.382 | 37.652 | 40.646 | 44.314 | 46.928 |
| 26 | 11.160 | 12.198 | 13.844 | 15.379 | 17.292 | 35.563 | 38.885 | 41.923 | 45.642 | 48.290 |
| 27 | 11.808 | 12.878 | 14.573 | 16.151 | 18.114 | 36.741 | 40.113 | 43.195 | 46.963 | 49.645 |
| 28 | 12.461 | 13.565 | 15.308 | 16.928 | 18.939 | 37.916 | 41.337 | 44.461 | 48.278 | 50.994 |
| 29 | 13.121 | 14.256 | 16.047 | 17.708 | 19.768 | 39.087 | 42.557 | 45.722 | 49.588 | 52.335 |

**TABLE 3**   CHI-SQUARE DISTRIBUTION (*Continued*)

| Degrees of Freedom | Area in Upper Tail | | | | | | | | | |
|---|---|---|---|---|---|---|---|---|---|---|
| | .995 | .99 | .975 | .95 | .90 | .10 | .05 | .025 | .01 | .005 |
| 30 | 13.787 | 14.953 | 16.791 | 18.493 | 20.599 | 40.256 | 43.773 | 46.979 | 50.892 | 53.672 |
| 35 | 17.192 | 18.509 | 20.569 | 22.465 | 24.797 | 46.059 | 49.802 | 53.203 | 57.342 | 60.275 |
| 40 | 20.707 | 22.164 | 24.433 | 26.509 | 29.051 | 51.805 | 55.758 | 59.342 | 63.691 | 66.766 |
| 45 | 24.311 | 25.901 | 28.366 | 30.612 | 33.350 | 57.505 | 61.656 | 65.410 | 69.957 | 73.166 |
| 50 | 27.991 | 29.707 | 32.357 | 34.764 | 37.689 | 63.167 | 67.505 | 71.420 | 76.154 | 79.490 |
| 55 | 31.735 | 33.571 | 36.398 | 38.958 | 42.060 | 68.796 | 73.311 | 77.380 | 82.292 | 85.749 |
| 60 | 35.534 | 37.485 | 40.482 | 43.188 | 46.459 | 74.397 | 79.082 | 83.298 | 88.379 | 91.952 |
| 65 | 39.383 | 41.444 | 44.603 | 47.450 | 50.883 | 79.973 | 84.821 | 89.177 | 94.422 | 98.105 |
| 70 | 43.275 | 45.442 | 48.758 | 51.739 | 55.329 | 85.527 | 90.531 | 95.023 | 100.425 | 104.215 |
| 75 | 47.206 | 49.475 | 52.942 | 56.054 | 59.795 | 91.061 | 96.217 | 100.839 | 106.393 | 110.285 |
| 80 | 51.172 | 53.540 | 57.153 | 60.391 | 64.278 | 96.578 | 101.879 | 106.629 | 112.329 | 116.321 |
| 85 | 55.170 | 57.634 | 61.389 | 64.749 | 68.777 | 102.079 | 107.522 | 112.393 | 118.236 | 122.324 |
| 90 | 59.196 | 61.754 | 65.647 | 69.126 | 73.291 | 107.565 | 113.145 | 118.136 | 124.116 | 128.299 |
| 95 | 63.250 | 65.898 | 69.925 | 73.520 | 77.818 | 113.038 | 118.752 | 123.858 | 129.973 | 134.247 |
| 100 | 67.328 | 70.065 | 74.222 | 77.929 | 82.358 | 118.498 | 124.342 | 129.561 | 135.807 | 140.170 |

**TABLE 4**  *F* DISTRIBUTION

Entries in the table give $F_\alpha$ values, where $\alpha$ is the area or probability in the upper tail of the $F$ distribution. For example, with 4 numerator degrees of freedom, 8 denominator degrees of freedom, and a .05 area in the upper tail, $F_{.05} = 3.84$.

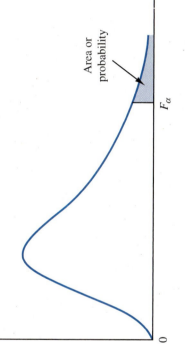

Area or probability

| Denominator Degrees of Freedom | Area in Upper Tail | 1 | 2 | 3 | 4 | 5 | 6 | 7 | 8 | 9 | 10 | 15 | 20 | 25 | 30 | 40 | 60 | 100 | 1000 |
|---|---|---|---|---|---|---|---|---|---|---|---|---|---|---|---|---|---|---|---|
| | | | | | | | | | Numerator Degrees of Freedom | | | | | | | | | | |
| 1 | .10 | 39.86 | 49.50 | 53.59 | 55.83 | 57.24 | 58.20 | 58.91 | 59.44 | 59.86 | 60.19 | 61.22 | 61.74 | 62.05 | 62.26 | 62.53 | 62.79 | 63.01 | 63.30 |
| | .05 | 161.45 | 199.50 | 215.71 | 224.58 | 230.16 | 233.99 | 236.77 | 238.88 | 240.54 | 241.88 | 245.95 | 248.02 | 249.26 | 250.10 | 251.14 | 252.20 | 253.04 | 254.19 |
| | .025 | 647.79 | 799.48 | 864.15 | 899.60 | 921.83 | 937.11 | 948.20 | 956.64 | 963.28 | 968.63 | 984.87 | 993.08 | 998.09 | 1001.40 | 1005.60 | 1009.79 | 1013.16 | 1017.76 |
| | .01 | 4052.18 | 4999.34 | 5403.53 | 5624.26 | 5763.96 | 5858.95 | 5928.33 | 5980.95 | 6022.40 | 6055.93 | 6156.97 | 6208.66 | 6239.86 | 6260.35 | 6286.43 | 6312.97 | 6333.92 | 6362.80 |
| 2 | .10 | 8.53 | 9.00 | 9.16 | 9.24 | 9.29 | 9.33 | 9.35 | 9.37 | 9.38 | 9.39 | 9.42 | 9.44 | 9.45 | 9.46 | 9.47 | 9.47 | 9.48 | 9.49 |
| | .05 | 18.51 | 19.00 | 19.16 | 19.25 | 19.30 | 19.33 | 19.35 | 19.37 | 19.38 | 19.40 | 19.43 | 19.45 | 19.46 | 19.46 | 19.47 | 19.48 | 19.49 | 19.49 |
| | .025 | 38.51 | 39.00 | 39.17 | 39.25 | 39.30 | 39.33 | 39.36 | 39.37 | 39.39 | 39.40 | 39.43 | 39.45 | 39.46 | 39.46 | 39.47 | 39.48 | 39.49 | 39.50 |
| | .01 | 98.50 | 99.00 | 99.16 | 99.25 | 99.30 | 99.33 | 99.36 | 99.38 | 99.39 | 99.40 | 99.43 | 99.45 | 99.46 | 99.47 | 99.48 | 99.48 | 99.49 | 99.50 |
| 3 | .10 | 5.54 | 5.46 | 5.39 | 5.34 | 5.31 | 5.28 | 5.27 | 5.25 | 5.24 | 5.23 | 5.20 | 5.18 | 5.17 | 5.17 | 5.16 | 5.15 | 5.14 | 5.13 |
| | .05 | 10.13 | 9.55 | 9.28 | 9.12 | 9.01 | 8.94 | 8.89 | 8.85 | 8.81 | 8.79 | 8.70 | 8.66 | 8.63 | 8.62 | 8.59 | 8.57 | 8.55 | 8.53 |
| | .025 | 17.44 | 16.04 | 15.44 | 15.10 | 14.88 | 14.73 | 14.62 | 14.54 | 14.47 | 14.42 | 14.25 | 14.17 | 14.12 | 14.08 | 14.04 | 13.99 | 13.96 | 13.91 |
| | .01 | 34.12 | 30.82 | 29.46 | 28.71 | 28.24 | 27.91 | 27.67 | 27.49 | 27.34 | 27.23 | 26.87 | 26.69 | 26.58 | 26.50 | 26.41 | 26.32 | 26.24 | 26.14 |
| 4 | .10 | 4.54 | 4.32 | 4.19 | 4.11 | 4.05 | 4.01 | 3.98 | 3.95 | 3.94 | 3.92 | 3.87 | 3.84 | 3.83 | 3.82 | 3.80 | 3.79 | 3.78 | 3.76 |
| | .05 | 7.71 | 6.94 | 6.59 | 6.39 | 6.26 | 6.16 | 6.09 | 6.04 | 6.00 | 5.96 | 5.86 | 5.80 | 5.77 | 5.75 | 5.72 | 5.69 | 5.66 | 5.63 |
| | .025 | 12.22 | 10.65 | 9.98 | 9.60 | 9.36 | 9.20 | 9.07 | 8.98 | 8.90 | 8.84 | 8.66 | 8.56 | 8.50 | 8.46 | 8.41 | 8.36 | 8.32 | 8.26 |
| | .01 | 21.20 | 18.00 | 16.69 | 15.98 | 15.52 | 15.21 | 14.98 | 14.80 | 14.66 | 14.55 | 14.20 | 14.02 | 13.91 | 13.84 | 13.75 | 13.65 | 13.58 | 13.47 |
| 5 | .10 | 4.06 | 3.78 | 3.62 | 3.52 | 3.45 | 3.40 | 3.37 | 3.34 | 3.32 | 3.30 | 3.324 | 3.21 | 3.19 | 3.17 | 3.16 | 3.14 | 3.13 | 3.11 |
| | .05 | 6.61. | 5.79 | 5.41 | 5.19 | 5.05 | 4.95 | 4.88 | 4.82 | 4.77 | 4.74 | 4.62 | 4.56 | 4.52 | 4.50 | 4.46 | 4.43 | 4.41 | 4.37 |
| | .025 | 10.01 | 8.43 | 7.76 | 7.39 | 7.15 | 6.98 | 6.85 | 6.76 | 6.68 | 6.62 | 6.43 | 6.33 | 6.27 | 6.23 | 6.18 | 6.12 | 6.08 | 6.02 |
| | .01 | 16.26 | 13.27 | 12.06 | 11.39 | 10.97 | 10.67 | 10.46 | 10.29 | 10.16 | 10.05 | 9.72 | 9.55 | 9.45 | 9.38 | 9.29 | 9.20 | 9.13 | 9.03 |

**TABLE 4  F DISTRIBUTION (Continued)**

Numerator Degrees of Freedom

| Denominator Degrees of Freedom | Area in Upper Tail | 1 | 2 | 3 | 4 | 5 | 6 | 7 | 8 | 9 | 10 | 15 | 20 | 25 | 30 | 40 | 60 | 100 | 1000 |
|---|---|---|---|---|---|---|---|---|---|---|---|---|---|---|---|---|---|---|---|
| 6 | .10 | 3.78 | 3.46 | 3.29 | 3.18 | 3.11 | 3.05 | 3.01 | 2.98 | 2.96 | 2.94 | 2.87 | 2.84 | 2.81 | 2.80 | 2.78 | 2.76 | 2.75 | 2.72 |
|  | .05 | 5.99 | 5.14 | 4.76 | 4.53 | 4.39 | 4.28 | 4.21 | 4.15 | 4.10 | 4.06 | 3.94 | 3.87 | 3.83 | 3.81 | 3.77 | 3.74 | 3.71 | 3.67 |
|  | .025 | 8.81 | 7.26 | 6.60 | 6.23 | 5.99 | 5.82 | 5.70 | 5.60 | 5.52 | 5.46 | 5.27 | 5.17 | 5.11 | 5.07 | 5.01 | 4.96 | 4.92 | 4.86 |
|  | .01 | 13.75 | 10.92 | 9.78 | 9.15 | 8.75 | 8.47 | 8.26 | 8.10 | 7.98 | 7.87 | 7.56 | 7.40 | 7.30 | 7.23 | 7.14 | 7.06 | 6.99 | 6.89 |
| 7 | .10 | 3.59 | 3.26 | 3.07 | 2.96 | 2.88 | 2.83 | 2.78 | 2.75 | 2.72 | 2.70 | 2.63 | 2.59 | 2.57 | 2.56 | 2.54 | 2.51 | 2.50 | 2.47 |
|  | .05 | 5.59 | 4.74 | 4.35 | 4.12 | 3.97 | 3.87 | 3.79 | 3.73 | 3.68 | 3.64 | 3.51 | 3.44 | 3.40 | 3.38 | 3.34 | 3.30 | 3.27 | 3.23 |
|  | .025 | 8.07 | 6.54 | 5.89 | 5.52 | 5.29 | 5.12 | 4.99 | 4.90 | 4.82 | 4.76 | 4.57 | 4.47 | 4.40 | 4.36 | 4.31 | 4.25 | 4.21 | 4.15 |
|  | .01 | 12.25 | 9.55 | 8.45 | 7.85 | 7.46 | 7.19 | 6.99 | 6.84 | 6.72 | 6.62 | 6.31 | 6.16 | 6.06 | 5.99 | 5.91 | 5.82 | 5.75 | 5.66 |
| 8 | .10 | 3.46 | 3.11 | 2.92 | 2.81 | 2.73 | 2.67 | 2.62 | 2.59 | 2.56 | 2.54 | 2.46 | 2.42 | 2.40 | 2.38 | 2.36 | 2.34 | 2.32 | 2.30 |
|  | .05 | 5.32 | 4.46 | 4.07 | 3.84 | 3.69 | 3.58 | 3.50 | 3.44 | 3.39 | 3.35 | 3.22 | 3.15 | 3.11 | 3.08 | 3.04 | 3.01 | 2.97 | 2.93 |
|  | .025 | 7.57 | 6.06 | 5.42 | 5.05 | 4.82 | 4.65 | 4.53 | 4.43 | 4.36 | 4.30 | 4.10 | 4.00 | 3.94 | 3.89 | 3.84 | 3.78 | 3.74 | 3.68 |
|  | .01 | 11.26 | 8.65 | 7.59 | 7.01 | 6.63 | 6.37 | 6.18 | 6.03 | 5.91 | 5.81 | 5.52 | 5.36 | 5.26 | 5.20 | 5.12 | 5.03 | 4.96 | 4.87 |
| 9 | .10 | 3.36 | 3.01 | 2.81 | 2.69 | 2.61 | 2.55 | 2.51 | 2.47 | 2.44 | 2.42 | 2.34 | 2.30 | 2.27 | 2.25 | 2.23 | 2.21 | 2.19 | 2.16 |
|  | .05 | 5.12 | 4.26 | 3.86 | 3.63 | 3.48 | 3.37 | 3.29 | 3.23 | 3.18 | 3.14 | 3.01 | 2.94 | 2.89 | 2.86 | 2.83 | 2.79 | 2.76 | 2.71 |
|  | .025 | 7.21 | 5.71 | 5.08 | 4.72 | 4.48 | 4.32 | 4.20 | 4.10 | 4.03 | 3.96 | 3.77 | 3.67 | 3.60 | 3.56 | 3.51 | 3.45 | 3.40 | 3.34 |
|  | .01 | 10.56 | 8.02 | 6.99 | 6.42 | 6.06 | 5.80 | 5.61 | 5.47 | 5.35 | 5.26 | 4.96 | 4.81 | 4.71 | 4.65 | 4.57 | 4.48 | 4.41 | 4.32 |
| 10 | .10 | 3.29 | 2.92 | 2.73 | 2.61 | 2.52 | 2.46 | 2.41 | 2.38 | 2.35 | 2.32 | 2.24 | 2.20 | 2.17 | 2.16 | 2.13 | 2.11 | 2.09 | 2.06 |
|  | .05 | 4.96 | 4.10 | 3.71 | 3.48 | 3.33 | 3.22 | 3.14 | 3.07 | 3.02 | 2.98 | 2.85 | 2.77 | 2.73 | 2.70 | 2.66 | 2.62 | 2.59 | 2.54 |
|  | .025 | 6.94 | 5.46 | 4.83 | 4.47 | 4.24 | 4.07 | 3.95 | 3.85 | 3.78 | 3.72 | 3.52 | 3.42 | 3.35 | 3.31 | 3.26 | 3.20 | 3.15 | 3.09 |
|  | .01 | 10.04 | 7.56 | 6.55 | 5.99 | 5.64 | 5.39 | 5.20 | 5.06 | 4.94 | 4.85 | 4.56 | 4.41 | 4.31 | 4.25 | 4.17 | 4.08 | 4.01 | 3.92 |
| 11 | .10 | 3.23 | 2.86 | 2.66 | 2.54 | 2.45 | 2.39 | 2.34 | 2.30 | 2.27 | 2.25 | 2.17 | 2.12 | 2.10 | 2.08 | 2.05 | 2.03 | 2.01 | 1.98 |
|  | .05 | 4.84 | 3.98 | 3.59 | 3.36 | 3.20 | 3.09 | 3.01 | 2.95 | 2.90 | 2.85 | 2.72 | 2.65 | 2.60 | 2.57 | 2.53 | 2.49 | 2.46 | 2.41 |
|  | .025 | 6.72 | 5.26 | 4.63 | 4.28 | 4.04 | 3.88 | 3.76 | 3.66 | 3.59 | 3.53 | 3.33 | 3.23 | 3.16 | 3.12 | 3.06 | 3.00 | 2.96 | 2.89 |
|  | .01 | 9.65 | 7.21 | 6.22 | 5.67 | 5.32 | 5.07 | 4.89 | 4.74 | 4.63 | 4.54 | 4.25 | 4.10 | 4.01 | 3.94 | 3.86 | 3.78 | 3.71 | 3.61 |
| 12 | .10 | 3.18 | 2.81 | 2.61 | 2.48 | 2.39 | 2.33 | 2.28 | 2.24 | 2.21 | 2.19 | 2.10 | 2.06 | 2.03 | 2.01 | 1.99 | 1.96 | 1.94 | 1.91 |
|  | .05 | 4.75 | 3.89 | 3.49 | 3.26 | 3.11 | 3.00 | 2.91 | 2.85 | 2.80 | 2.75 | 2.62 | 2.54 | 2.50 | 2.47 | 2.43 | 2.38 | 2.35 | 2.30 |
|  | .025 | 6.55 | 5.10 | 4.47 | 4.12 | 3.89 | 3.73 | 3.61 | 3.51 | 3.44 | 3.37 | 3.18 | 3.07 | 3.01 | 2.96 | 2.91 | 2.85 | 2.80 | 2.73 |
|  | .01 | 9.33 | 6.93 | 5.95 | 5.41 | 5.06 | 4.82 | 4.64 | 4.50 | 4.39 | 4.30 | 4.01 | 3.86 | 3.76 | 3.70 | 3.62 | 3.54 | 3.47 | 3.37 |
| 13 | .10 | 3.14 | 2.76 | 2.56 | 2.43 | 2.35 | 2.28 | 2.23 | 2.20 | 2.16 | 2.14 | 2.05 | 2.01 | 1.98 | 1.96 | 1.93 | 1.90 | 1.88 | 1.85 |
|  | .05 | 4.67 | 3.81 | 3.41 | 3.18 | 3.03 | 2.92 | 2.83 | 2.77 | 2.71 | 2.67 | 2.53 | 2.46 | 2.41 | 2.38 | 2.34 | 2.30 | 2.26 | 2.21 |
|  | .025 | 6.41 | 4.97 | 4.35 | 4.00 | 3.77 | 3.60 | 3.48 | 3.39 | 3.31 | 3.25 | 3.05 | 2.95 | 2.88 | 2.84 | 2.78 | 2.72 | 2.67 | 2.60 |
|  | .01 | 9.07 | 6.70 | 5.74 | 5.21 | 4.86 | 4.62 | 4.44 | 4.30 | 4.19 | 4.10 | 3.82 | 3.66 | 3.57 | 3.51 | 3.43 | 3.34 | 3.27 | 3.18 |
| 14 | .10 | 3.10 | 2.73 | 2.52 | 2.39 | 2.31 | 2.24 | 2.19 | 2.15 | 2.12 | 2.10 | 2.01 | 1.96 | 1.93 | 1.91 | 1.89 | 1.86 | 1.83 | 1.80 |
|  | .05 | 4.60 | 3.74 | 3.34 | 3.11 | 2.96 | 2.85 | 2.76 | 2.70 | 2.65 | 2.60 | 2.46 | 2.39 | 2.34 | 2.31 | 2.27 | 2.22 | 2.19 | 2.14 |
|  | .025 | 6.30 | 4.86 | 4.24 | 3.89 | 3.66 | 3.50 | 3.38 | 3.29 | 3.21 | 3.15 | 2.95 | 2.84 | 2.78 | 2.73 | 2.67 | 2.61 | 2.56 | 2.50 |
|  | .01 | 8.86 | 6.51 | 5.56 | 5.04 | 4.69 | 4.46 | 4.28 | 4.14 | 4.03 | 3.94 | 3.66 | 3.51 | 3.41 | 3.35 | 3.27 | 3.18 | 3.11 | 3.02 |
| 15 | .10 | 3.07 | 2.70 | 2.49 | 2.36 | 2.27 | 2.21 | 2.16 | 2.12 | 2.09 | 2.06 | 1.97 | 1.92 | 1.89 | 1.87 | 1.85 | 1.82 | 1.79 | 1.76 |
|  | .05 | 4.54 | 3.68 | 3.29 | 3.06 | 2.90 | 2.79 | 2.71 | 2.64 | 2.59 | 2.54 | 2.40 | 2.33 | 2.28 | 2.25 | 2.20 | 2.16 | 2.12 | 2.07 |
|  | .025 | 6.20 | 4.77 | 4.15 | 3.80 | 3.58 | 3.41 | 3.29 | 3.20 | 3.12 | 3.06 | 2.86 | 2.76 | 2.69 | 2.64 | 2.59 | 2.52 | 2.47 | 2.40 |
|  | .01 | 8.68 | 6.36 | 5.42 | 4.89 | 4.56 | 4.32 | 4.14 | 4.00 | 3.89 | 3.80 | 3.52 | 3.37 | 3.28 | 3.21 | 3.13 | 3.05 | 2.98 | 2.88 |

Numerator Degrees of Freedom

| Denominator Degrees of Freedom | Area in Upper Tail | 1 | 2 | 3 | 4 | 5 | 6 | 7 | 8 | 9 | 10 | 15 | 20 | 25 | 30 | 40 | 60 | 100 | 1000 |
|---|---|---|---|---|---|---|---|---|---|---|---|---|---|---|---|---|---|---|---|
| 16 | .10 | 3.05 | 2.67 | 2.46 | 2.33 | 2.24 | 2.18 | 2.13 | 2.09 | 2.06 | 2.03 | 1.94 | 1.89 | 1.86 | 1.84 | 1.81 | 1.78 | 1.76 | 1.72 |
|  | .05 | 4.49 | 3.63 | 3.24 | 3.01 | 2.85 | 2.74 | 2.66 | 2.59 | 2.54 | 2.49 | 2.35 | 2.28 | 2.23 | 2.19 | 2.15 | 2.11 | 2.07 | 2.02 |
|  | .025 | 6.12 | 4.69 | 4.08 | 3.73 | 3.50 | 3.34 | 3.22 | 3.12 | 3.05 | 2.99 | 2.79 | 2.68 | 2.61 | 2.57 | 2.51 | 2.45 | 2.40 | 2.32 |
|  | .01 | 8.53 | 6.23 | 5.29 | 4.77 | 4.44 | 4.20 | 4.03 | 3.89 | 3.78 | 3.69 | 3.41 | 3.26 | 3.16 | 3.10 | 3.02 | 2.93 | 2.86 | 2.76 |
| 17 | .10 | 3.03 | 2.64 | 2.44 | 2.31 | 2.22 | 2.15 | 2.10 | 2.06 | 2.03 | 2.00 | 1.91 | 1.86 | 1.83 | 1.81 | 1.78 | 1.75 | 1.73 | 1.69 |
|  | .05 | 4.45 | 3.59 | 3.20 | 2.96 | 2.81 | 2.70 | 2.61 | 2.55 | 2.49 | 2.45 | 2.31 | 2.23 | 2.18 | 2.15 | 2.10 | 2.06 | 2.02 | 1.97 |
|  | .025 | 6.04 | 4.62 | 4.01 | 3.66 | 3.44 | 3.28 | 3.16 | 3.06 | 2.98 | 2.92 | 2.72 | 2.62 | 2.55 | 2.50 | 2.44 | 2.38 | 2.33 | 2.26 |
|  | .01 | 8.40 | 6.11 | 5.19 | 4.67 | 4.34 | 4.10 | 3.93 | 3.79 | 3.68 | 3.59 | 3.31 | 3.16 | 3.07 | 3.00 | 2.92 | 2.83 | 2.76 | 2.66 |
| 18 | .10 | 3.01 | 2.62 | 2.42 | 2.29 | 2.20 | 2.13 | 2.08 | 2.04 | 2.00 | 1.98 | 1.89 | 1.84 | 1.80 | 1.78 | 1.75 | 1.72 | 1.70 | 1.66 |
|  | .05 | 4.41 | 3.55 | 3.16 | 2.93 | 2.77 | 2.66 | 2.58 | 2.51 | 2.46 | 2.41 | 2.27 | 2.19 | 2.14 | 2.11 | 2.06 | 2.02 | 1.98 | 1.92 |
|  | .025 | 5.98 | 4.56 | 3.95 | 3.61 | 3.38 | 3.22 | 3.10 | 3.01 | 2.93 | 2.87 | 2.67 | 2.56 | 2.49 | 2.44 | 2.38 | 2.32 | 2.27 | 2.20 |
|  | .01 | 8.29 | 6.01 | 5.09 | 4.58 | 4.25 | 4.01 | 3.84 | 3.71 | 3.60 | 3.51 | 3.23 | 3.08 | 2.98 | 2.92 | 2.84 | 2.75 | 2.68 | 2.58 |
| 19 | .10 | 2.99 | 2.61 | 2.40 | 2.27 | 2.18 | 2.11 | 2.06 | 2.02 | 1.98 | 1.96 | 1.86 | 1.81 | 1.78 | 1.76 | 1.73 | 1.70 | 1.67 | 1.64 |
|  | .05 | 4.38 | 3.52 | 3.13 | 2.90 | 2.74 | 2.63 | 2.54 | 2.48 | 2.42 | 2.38 | 2.23 | 2.16 | 2.11 | 2.07 | 2.03 | 1.98 | 1.94 | 1.88 |
|  | .025 | 5.92 | 4.51 | 3.90 | 3.56 | 3.33 | 3.17 | 3.05 | 2.96 | 2.88 | 2.82 | 2.62 | 2.51 | 2.44 | 2.39 | 2.33 | 2.27 | 2.22 | 2.14 |
|  | .01 | 8.18 | 5.93 | 5.01 | 4.50 | 4.17 | 3.94 | 3.77 | 3.63 | 3.52 | 3.43 | 3.15 | 3.00 | 2.91 | 2.84 | 2.76 | 2.67 | 2.60 | 2.50 |
| 20 | .10 | 2.97 | 2.59 | 2.38 | 2.25 | 2.16 | 2.09 | 2.04 | 2.00 | 1.96 | 1.94 | 1.84 | 1.79 | 1.76 | 1.74 | 1.71 | 1.68 | 1.65 | 1.61 |
|  | .05 | 4.35 | 3.49 | 3.10 | 2.87 | 2.71 | 2.60 | 2.51 | 2.45 | 2.39 | 2.35 | 2.20 | 2.12 | 2.07 | 2.04 | 1.99 | 1.95 | 1.91 | 1.85 |
|  | .025 | 5.87 | 4.46 | 3.86 | 3.51 | 3.29 | 3.13 | 3.01 | 2.91 | 2.84 | 2.77 | 2.57 | 2.46 | 2.40 | 2.35 | 2.29 | 2.22 | 2.17 | 2.09 |
|  | .01 | 8.10 | 5.85 | 4.94 | 4.43 | 4.10 | 3.87 | 3.70 | 3.56 | 3.46 | 3.37 | 3.09 | 2.94 | 2.84 | 2.78 | 2.69 | 2.61 | 2.54 | 2.43 |
| 21 | .10 | 2.96 | 2.57 | 2.36 | 2.23 | 2.14 | 2.08 | 2.02 | 1.98 | 1.95 | 1.92 | 1.83 | 1.78 | 1.74 | 1.72 | 1.69 | 1.66 | 1.63 | 1.59 |
|  | .05 | 4.32 | 3.47 | 3.07 | 2.84 | 2.68 | 2.57 | 2.49 | 2.42 | 2.37 | 2.32 | 2.18 | 2.10 | 2.05 | 2.01 | 1.96 | 1.92 | 1.88 | 1.82 |
|  | .025 | 5.83 | 4.42 | 3.82 | 3.48 | 3.25 | 3.09 | 2.97 | 2.87 | 2.80 | 2.73 | 2.53 | 2.42 | 2.36 | 2.31 | 2.25 | 2.18 | 2.13 | 2.05 |
|  | .01 | 8.02 | 5.78 | 4.87 | 4.37 | 4.04 | 3.81 | 3.64 | 3.51 | 3.40 | 3.31 | 3.03 | 2.88 | 2.79 | 2.72 | 2.64 | 2.55 | 2.48 | 2.37 |
| 22 | .10 | 2.95 | 2.56 | 2.35 | 2.22 | 2.13 | 2.06 | 2.01 | 1.97 | 1.93 | 1.90 | 1.81 | 1.76 | 1.73 | 1.70 | 1.67 | 1.64 | 1.61 | 1.57 |
|  | .05 | 4.30 | 3.44 | 3.05 | 2.82 | 2.66 | 2.55 | 2.46 | 2.40 | 2.34 | 2.30 | 2.15 | 2.07 | 2.02 | 1.98 | 1.94 | 1.89 | 1.85 | 1.79 |
|  | .025 | 5.79 | 4.38 | 3.78 | 3.44 | 3.22 | 3.05 | 2.93 | 2.84 | 2.76 | 2.70 | 2.50 | 2.39 | 2.32 | 2.27 | 2.21 | 2.14 | 2.09 | 2.01 |
|  | .01 | 7.95 | 5.72 | 4.82 | 4.31 | 3.99 | 3.76 | 3.59 | 3.45 | 3.35 | 3.26 | 2.98 | 2.83 | 2.73 | 2.67 | 2.58 | 2.50 | 2.42 | 2.32 |
| 23 | .10 | 2.94 | 2.55 | 2.34 | 2.21 | 2.11 | 2.05 | 1.99 | 1.95 | 1.92 | 1.89 | 1.80 | 1.74 | 1.71 | 1.69 | 1.66 | 1.62 | 1.59 | 1.55 |
|  | .05 | 4.28 | 3.42 | 3.03 | 2.80 | 2.64 | 2.53 | 2.44 | 2.37 | 2.32 | 2.27 | 2.13 | 2.05 | 2.00 | 1.96 | 1.91 | 1.86 | 1.82 | 1.76 |
|  | .025 | 5.75 | 4.35 | 3.75 | 3.41 | 3.18 | 3.02 | 2.90 | 2.81 | 2.73 | 2.67 | 2.47 | 2.36 | 2.29 | 2.24 | 2.18 | 2.11 | 2.06 | 1.98 |
|  | .01 | 7.88 | 5.66 | 4.76 | 4.26 | 3.94 | 3.71 | 3.54 | 3.41 | 3.30 | 3.21 | 2.93 | 2.78 | 2.69 | 2.62 | 2.54 | 2.45 | 2.37 | 2.27 |
| 24 | .10 | 2.93 | 2.54 | 2.33 | 2.19 | 2.10 | 2.04 | 1.98 | 1.94 | 1.91 | 1.88 | 1.78 | 1.73 | 1.70 | 1.67 | 1.64 | 1.61 | 1.58 | 1.54 |
|  | .05 | 4.26 | 3.40 | 3.01 | 2.78 | 2.62 | 2.51 | 2.42 | 2.36 | 2.30 | 2.25 | 2.11 | 2.03 | 1.97 | 1.94 | 1.89 | 1.84 | 1.80 | 1.74 |
|  | .025 | 5.72 | 4.32 | 3.72 | 3.38 | 3.15 | 2.99 | 2.87 | 2.78 | 2.70 | 2.64 | 2.44 | 2.33 | 2.26 | 2.21 | 2.15 | 2.08 | 2.02 | 1.94 |
|  | .01 | 7.82 | 5.61 | 4.72 | 4.22 | 3.90 | 3.67 | 3.50 | 3.36 | 3.26 | 3.17 | 2.89 | 2.74 | 2.64 | 2.58 | 2.49 | 2.40 | 2.33 | 2.22 |

**TABLE 4** $F$ DISTRIBUTION (Continued)

| Denominator Degrees of Freedom | Area in Upper Tail | Numerator Degrees of Freedom | | | | | | | | | | | | | | | | | |
|---|---|---|---|---|---|---|---|---|---|---|---|---|---|---|---|---|---|---|---|
| | | 1 | 2 | 3 | 4 | 5 | 6 | 7 | 8 | 9 | 10 | 15 | 20 | 25 | 30 | 40 | 60 | 100 | 1000 |
| 25 | .10 | 2.92 | 2.53 | 2.32 | 2.18 | 2.09 | 2.02 | 1.97 | 1.93 | 1.89 | 1.87 | 1.77 | 1.72 | 1.68 | 1.66 | 1.63 | 1.59 | 1.56 | 1.52 |
| | .05 | 4.24 | 3.39 | 2.99 | 2.76 | 2.60 | 2.49 | 2.40 | 2.34 | 2.28 | 2.24 | 2.09 | 2.01 | 1.96 | 1.92 | 1.87 | 1.82 | 1.78 | 1.72 |
| | .025 | 5.69 | 4.29 | 3.69 | 3.35 | 3.13 | 2.97 | 2.85 | 2.75 | 2.68 | 2.61 | 2.41 | 2.30 | 2.23 | 2.18 | 2.12 | 2.05 | 2.00 | 1.91 |
| | .01 | 7.77 | 5.57 | 4.68 | 4.18 | 3.85 | 3.63 | 3.46 | 3.32 | 3.22 | 3.13 | 2.85 | 2.70 | 2.60 | 2.54 | 2.45 | 2.36 | 2.29 | 2.18 |
| 26 | .10 | 2.91 | 2.52 | 2.31 | 2.17 | 2.08 | 2.01 | 1.96 | 1.92 | 1.88 | 1.86 | 1.76 | 1.71 | 1.67 | 1.65 | 1.61 | 1.58 | 1.55 | 1.51 |
| | .05 | 4.23 | 3.37 | 2.98 | 2.74 | 2.59 | 2.47 | 2.39 | 2.32 | 2.27 | 2.22 | 2.07 | 1.99 | 1.94 | 1.90 | 1.85 | 1.80 | 1.76 | 1.70 |
| | .025 | 5.66 | 4.27 | 3.67 | 3.33 | 3.10 | 2.94 | 2.82 | 2.73 | 2.65 | 2.59 | 2.39 | 2.28 | 2.21 | 2.16 | 2.09 | 2.03 | 1.97 | 1.89 |
| | .01 | 7.72 | 5.53 | 4.64 | 4.14 | 3.82 | 3.59 | 3.42 | 3.29 | 3.18 | 3.09 | 2.81 | 2.66 | 2.57 | 2.50 | 2.42 | 2.33 | 2.25 | 2.14 |
| 27 | .10 | 2.90 | 2.51 | 2.30 | 2.17 | 2.07 | 2.00 | 1.95 | 1.91 | 1.87 | 1.85 | 1.75 | 1.70 | 1.66 | 1.64 | 1.60 | 1.57 | 1.54 | 1.50 |
| | .05 | 4.21 | 3.35 | 2.96 | 2.73 | 2.57 | 2.46 | 2.37 | 2.31 | 2.25 | 2.20 | 2.06 | 1.97 | 1.92 | 1.88 | 1.84 | 1.79 | 1.74 | 1.68 |
| | .025 | 5.63 | 4.24 | 3.65 | 3.31 | 3.08 | 2.92 | 2.80 | 2.71 | 2.63 | 2.57 | 2.36 | 2.25 | 2.18 | 2.13 | 2.07 | 2.00 | 1.94 | 1.86 |
| | .01 | 7.68 | 5.49 | 4.60 | 4.11 | 3.78 | 3.56 | 3.39 | 3.26 | 3.15 | 3.06 | 2.78 | 2.63 | 2.54 | 2.47 | 2.38 | 2.29 | 2.22 | 2.11 |
| 28 | .10 | 2.89 | 2.50 | 2.29 | 2.16 | 2.06 | 2.00 | 1.94 | 1.90 | 1.87 | 1.84 | 1.74 | 1.69 | 1.65 | 1.63 | 1.59 | 1.56 | 1.53 | 1.48 |
| | .05 | 4.20 | 3.34 | 2.95 | 2.71 | 2.56 | 2.45 | 2.36 | 2.29 | 2.24 | 2.19 | 2.04 | 1.96 | 1.91 | 1.87 | 1.82 | 1.77 | 1.73 | 1.66 |
| | .025 | 5.61 | 4.22 | 3.63 | 3.29 | 3.06 | 2.90 | 2.78 | 2.69 | 2.61 | 2.55 | 2.34 | 2.23 | 2.16 | 2.11 | 2.05 | 1.98 | 1.92 | 1.84 |
| | .01 | 7.64 | 5.45 | 4.57 | 4.07 | 3.75 | 3.53 | 3.36 | 3.23 | 3.12 | 3.03 | 2.75 | 2.60 | 2.51 | 2.44 | 2.35 | 2.26 | 2.19 | 2.08 |
| 29 | .10 | 2.89 | 2.50 | 2.28 | 2.15 | 2.06 | 1.99 | 1.93 | 1.89 | 1.86 | 1.83 | 1.73 | 1.68 | 1.64 | 1.62 | 1.58 | 1.55 | 1.52 | 1.47 |
| | .05 | 4.18 | 3.33 | 2.93 | 2.70 | 2.55 | 2.43 | 2.35 | 2.28 | 2.22 | 2.18 | 2.03 | 1.94 | 1.89 | 1.85 | 1.81 | 1.75 | 1.71 | 1.65 |
| | .025 | 5.59 | 4.20 | 3.61 | 3.27 | 3.04 | 2.88 | 2.76 | 2.67 | 2.59 | 2.53 | 2.32 | 2.21 | 2.14 | 2.09 | 2.03 | 1.96 | 1.90 | 1.82 |
| | .01 | 7.60 | 5.42 | 4.54 | 4.04 | 3.73 | 3.50 | 3.33 | 3.20 | 3.09 | 3.00 | 2.73 | 2.57 | 2.48 | 2.41 | 2.33 | 2.23 | 2.16 | 2.05 |
| 30 | .10 | 2.88 | 2.49 | 2.28 | 2.14 | 2.05 | 1.98 | 1.93 | 1.88 | 1.85 | 1.82 | 1.72 | 1.67 | 1.63 | 1.61 | 1.57 | 1.54 | 1.51 | 1.46 |
| | .05 | 4.17 | 3.32 | 2.92 | 2.69 | 2.53 | 2.42 | 2.33 | 2.27 | 2.21 | 2.16 | 2.01 | 1.93 | 1.88 | 1.84 | 1.79 | 1.74 | 1.70 | 1.63 |
| | .025 | 5.57 | 4.18 | 3.59 | 3.25 | 3.03 | 2.87 | 2.75 | 2.65 | 2.57 | 2.51 | 2.31 | 2.20 | 2.12 | 2.07 | 2.01 | 1.94 | 1.88 | 1.80 |
| | .01 | 7.56 | 5.39 | 4.51 | 4.02 | 3.70 | 3.47 | 3.30 | 3.17 | 3.07 | 2.98 | 2.70 | 2.55 | 2.45 | 2.39 | 2.30 | 2.21 | 2.13 | 2.02 |
| 40 | .10 | 2.84 | 2.44 | 2.23 | 2.09 | 2.00 | 1.93 | 1.87 | 1.83 | 1.79 | 1.76 | 1.66 | 1.61 | 1.57 | 1.54 | 1.51 | 1.47 | 1.43 | 1.38 |
| | .05 | 4.08 | 3.23 | 2.84 | 2.61 | 2.45 | 2.34 | 2.25 | 2.18 | 2.12 | 2.08 | 1.92 | 1.84 | 1.78 | 1.74 | 1.69 | 1.64 | 1.59 | 1.52 |
| | .025 | 5.42 | 4.05 | 3.46 | 3.13 | 2.90 | 2.74 | 2.62 | 2.53 | 2.45 | 2.39 | 2.18 | 2.07 | 1.99 | 1.94 | 1.88 | 1.80 | 1.74 | 1.65 |
| | .01 | 7.31 | 5.18 | 4.31 | 3.83 | 3.51 | 3.29 | 3.12 | 2.99 | 2.89 | 2.80 | 2.52 | 2.37 | 2.27 | 2.20 | 2.11 | 2.02 | 1.94 | 1.82 |
| 60 | .10 | 2.79 | 2.39 | 2.18 | 2.04 | 1.95 | 1.87 | 1.82 | 1.77 | 1.74 | 1.71 | 1.60 | 1.54 | 1.50 | 1.48 | 1.44 | 1.40 | 1.36 | 1.30 |
| | .05 | 4.00 | 3.15 | 2.76 | 2.53 | 2.37 | 2.25 | 2.17 | 2.10 | 2.04 | 1.99 | 1.84 | 1.75 | 1.69 | 1.65 | 1.59 | 1.53 | 1.48 | 1.40 |
| | .025 | 5.29 | 3.93 | 3.34 | 3.01 | 2.79 | 2.63 | 2.51 | 2.41 | 2.33 | 2.27 | 2.06 | 1.94 | 1.87 | 1.82 | 1.74 | 1.67 | 1.60 | 1.49 |
| | .01 | 7.08 | 4.98 | 4.13 | 3.65 | 3.34 | 3.12 | 2.95 | 2.82 | 2.72 | 2.63 | 2.35 | 2.20 | 2.10 | 2.03 | 1.94 | 1.84 | 1.75 | 1.62 |
| 100 | .10 | 2.76 | 2.36 | 2.14 | 2.00 | 1.91 | 1.83 | 1.78 | 1.73 | 1.69 | 1.66 | 1.56 | 1.49 | 1.45 | 1.42 | 1.38 | 1.34 | 1.29 | 1.22 |
| | .05 | 3.94 | 3.09 | 2.70 | 2.46 | 2.31 | 2.19 | 2.10 | 2.03 | 1.97 | 1.93 | 1.77 | 1.68 | 1.62 | 1.57 | 1.52 | 1.45 | 1.39 | 1.30 |
| | .025 | 5.18 | 3.83 | 3.25 | 2.92 | 2.70 | 2.54 | 2.42 | 2.32 | 2.24 | 2.18 | 1.97 | 1.85 | 1.77 | 1.71 | 1.64 | 1.56 | 1.48 | 1.36 |
| | .01 | 6.90 | 4.82 | 3.98 | 3.51 | 3.21 | 2.99 | 2.82 | 2.69 | 2.59 | 2.50 | 2.22 | 2.07 | 1.97 | 1.89 | 1.80 | 1.69 | 1.60 | 1.45 |
| 1000 | .10 | 2.71 | 2.31 | 2.09 | 1.95 | 1.85 | 1.78 | 1.72 | 1.68 | 1.64 | 1.61 | 1.49 | 1.43 | 1.38 | 1.35 | 1.30 | 1.25 | 1.20 | 1.08 |
| | .05 | 3.85 | 3.00 | 2.61 | 2.38 | 2.22 | 2.11 | 2.02 | 1.95 | 1.89 | 1.84 | 1.68 | 1.58 | 1.52 | 1.47 | 1.41 | 1.33 | 1.26 | 1.11 |
| | .025 | 5.04 | 3.70 | 3.13 | 2.80 | 2.58 | 2.42 | 2.30 | 2.20 | 2.13 | 2.06 | 1.85 | 1.72 | 1.64 | 1.58 | 1.50 | 1.41 | 1.32 | 1.13 |
| | .01 | 6.66 | 4.63 | 3.80 | 3.34 | 3.04 | 2.82 | 2.66 | 2.53 | 2.43 | 2.34 | 2.06 | 1.90 | 1.79 | 1.72 | 1.61 | 1.50 | 1.38 | 1.16 |

## Summations

*Definition*

$$\sum_{i=1}^{n} x_i = x_1 + x_2 + \cdots + x_n \tag{C.1}$$

Example for $x_1 = 5$, $x_2 = 8$, $x_3 = 14$:

$$\sum_{i=1}^{3} x_i = x_1 + x_2 + x_3$$
$$= 5 + 8 + 14$$
$$= 27$$

*Result 1*

For a constant $c$:

$$\sum_{i=1}^{n} c = \underbrace{(c + c + \cdots + c)}_{n \text{ times}} = nc \tag{C.2}$$

Example for $c = 5$, $n = 10$:

$$\sum_{i=1}^{10} 5 = 10(5) = 50$$

Example for $c = \bar{x}$:

$$\sum_{i=1}^{n} \bar{x} = n\bar{x}$$

*Result 2*

$$\sum_{i=1}^{n} cx_i = cx_1 + cx_2 + \cdots + cx_n$$
$$= c(x_1 + x_2 + \cdots + x_n) = c\sum_{i=1}^{n} x_i \tag{C.3}$$

Example for $x_1 = 5$, $x_2 = 8$, $x_3 = 14$, $c = 2$:

$$\sum_{i=1}^{3} 2x_i = 2\sum_{i=1}^{3} x_i = 2(27) = 54$$

*Result 3*

$$\sum_{i=1}^{n} (ax_i + by_i) = a\sum_{i=1}^{n} x_i + b\sum_{i=1}^{n} y_i \tag{C.4}$$

Example for $x_1 = 5$, $x_2 = 8$, $x_3 = 14$, $a = 2$, $y_1 = 7$, $y_2 = 3$, $y_3 = 8$, $b = 4$:

$$\sum_{i=1}^{3}(2x_i + 4y_i) = 2\sum_{i=1}^{3}x_i + 4\sum_{i=1}^{3}y_i$$
$$= 2(27) + 4(18)$$
$$= 54 + 72$$
$$= 126$$

## Double Summations

Consider the following data involving the variable $x_{ij}$, where $i$ is the subscript denoting the row position and $j$ is the subscript denoting the column position:

|  |  | Column | | |
|---|---|---|---|---|
|  |  | 1 | 2 | 3 |
| Row | 1 | $x_{11} = 10$ | $x_{12} = 8$ | $x_{13} = 6$ |
|  | 2 | $x_{21} = 7$ | $x_{22} = 4$ | $x_{23} = 12$ |

*Definition*

$$\sum_{i=1}^{n}\sum_{j=1}^{m}x_{ij} = (x_{11} + x_{12} + \cdots + x_{1m}) + (x_{21} + x_{22} + \cdots + x_{2m})$$
$$+ (x_{31} + x_{32} + \cdots + x_{3m}) + \cdots + (x_{n1} + x_{n2} + \cdots + x_{nm}) \qquad \textbf{(C.5)}$$

Example:

$$\sum_{i=1}^{2}\sum_{j=1}^{3}x_{ij} = x_{11} + x_{12} + x_{13} + x_{21} + x_{22} + x_{23}$$
$$= 10 + 8 + 6 + 7 + 4 + 12$$
$$= 47$$

*Definition*

$$\sum_{i=1}^{n}x_{ij} = x_{1j} + x_{2j} + \cdots + x_{nj} \qquad \textbf{(C.6)}$$

Example:

$$\sum_{i=1}^{2}x_{i2} = x_{12} + x_{22}$$
$$= 8 + 4$$
$$= 12$$

## Shorthand Notation

Sometimes when a summation is for all values of the subscript, we use the following shorthand notations:

$$\sum_{i=1}^{n}x_i = \sum x_i \qquad \textbf{(C.7)}$$

$$\sum_{i=1}^{n}\sum_{j=1}^{m}x_{ij} = \sum\sum x_{ij} \qquad \textbf{(C.8)}$$

$$\sum_{i=1}^{n}x_{ij} = \sum_{i}x_{ij} \qquad \textbf{(C.9)}$$

## Chapter 1

**2. a.** 10

  **b.** 5

  **c.** Categorical variables: Size and Fuel
Quantitiative variables: Cylinders, City MPG, and Highway MPG

  **d.**

| Variable | Measurement Scale |
|----------|-------------------|
| Size | Ordinal |
| Cylinders | Ratio |
| City MPG | Ratio |
| Highway MPG | Ratio |
| Fuel | Nominal |

**3. a.** Average for city driving = 182/10 = 18.2 mpg

  **b.** Average for highway driving = 261/10 = 26.1 mpg
On average, the miles per gallon for highway driving is 7.9 mpg greater than for city driving

  **c.** 3 of 10 or 30% have four-cylinder engines

  **d.** 6 of 10 or 60% use regular fuel

**4. a.** 7

  **b.** 5

  **c.** Categorical variables: State, Campus Setting, and NCAA Division

  **d.** Quantitiative variables: Endowment and Applicants Admitted

**6. a.** Quantitative

  **b.** Categorical

  **c.** Categorical

  **d.** Quantitative

  **e.** Categorical

**8. a.** 1015

  **b.** Categorical

  **c.** Percentages

  **d.** .10(1015) = 101.5; 101 or 102 respondents

**10. a.** Categorical

  **b.** Percentages

  **c.** 15%

  **d.** Support against

**12. a.** All visitors to Hawaii

  **b.** Yes

  **c.** First and fourth questions provide quantitative data
Second and third questions provide categorical data

**13. a.** Federal spending ($ trillions)

  **b.** Quantitative

  **c.** Time series

  **d.** Federal spending has increased over time

**14. a.** Graph with a time series line for each manufacturer

  **b.** Toyota surpasses General Motors in 2006 to become the leading auto manufacturer

  **c.** A bar chart would show cross-sectional data for 2007; bar heights would be GM 8.8, Ford 7.9, DC 4.6, and Toyota 9.6

**18. a.** 67%

  **b.** 612

  **c.** Categorical

**20. a.** 43% of managers were bullish or very bullish, and 21% of managers expected health care to be the leading industry over the next 12 months

  **b.** The average 12-month return estimate is 11.2% for the population of investment managers

  **c.** The sample average of 2.5 years is an estimate of how long the population of investment managers think it will take to resume sustainable growth

**22. a.** The population consists of all customers of the chain stores in Charlotte, North Carolina

  **b.** Some of the ways the grocery store chain could use to collect the data are

    • Customers entering or leaving the store could be surveyed

    • A survey could be mailed to customers who have a shopper's club card

    • Customers could be given a printed survey when they check out

    • Customers could be given a coupon that asks them to complete a brief online survey; if they do, they will receive a 5% discount on their next shopping trip

**24. a.** Correct

  **b.** Incorrect

  **c.** Correct

  **d.** Incorrect

  **e.** Incorrect

## Chapter 2

**2. a.** .20

  **b.** 40

  **c/d.**

| Class | Frequency | Percent Frequency |
|-------|-----------|-------------------|
| A | 44 | 22 |
| B | 36 | 18 |
| C | 80 | 40 |
| D | 40 | 20 |
| Total | 200 | 100 |

**3. a.** $360° \times 58/120 = 174°$
   **b.** $360° \times 42/120 = 126°$
   **c.**

48.3%

16.7%

35%

   **d.**

**4. a.** Categorical
   **b.**

| TV Show | Frequency | Percent Frequency |
|---|---|---|
| *Law & Order* | 10 | 20% |
| *CSI* | 18 | 36% |
| *Without a Trace* | 9 | 18% |
| *Desp Housewives* | 13 | 26% |
| Total: | 50 | 100% |

   **d.** *CSI* had the largest viewing audience; *Desperate House-wives* was in second place

**6. a.**

| Network | Frequency | Percent Frequency |
|---|---|---|
| ABC | 15 | 30 |
| CBS | 17 | 34 |
| FOX | 1 | 2 |
| NBC | 17 | 34 |

   **b.** CBS and NBC tied for first; ABC is close with 15

**7. a.**

| Rating | Frequency | Percent Frequency |
|---|---|---|
| Excellent | 20 | 40 |
| Very Good | 23 | 46 |
| Good | 4 | 8 |
| Fair | 1 | 2 |
| Poor | 2 | 4 |
| Total | 50 | 100 |

Management should be very pleased; 86% of the ratings are very good or excellent.

   **b.** Review explanations from the three with Fair or Poor ratings to identify reasons for the low ratings

**8. a.**

| Position | Frequency | Relative Frequency |
|---|---|---|
| P | 17 | .309 |
| H | 4 | .073 |
| 1 | 5 | .091 |
| 2 | 4 | .073 |
| 3 | 2 | .036 |
| S | 5 | .091 |
| L | 6 | .109 |
| C | 5 | .091 |
| R | 7 | .127 |
| Totals | 55 | 1.000 |

   **b.** Pitcher
   **c.** 3rd base
   **d.** Right field
   **e.** Infielders 16 to outfielders 18

**10. a/b.**

| Rating | Frequency | Percent Frequency |
|---|---|---|
| Excellent | 20 | 2 |
| Good | 101 | 10 |
| Fair | 528 | 52 |
| Bad | 244 | 24 |
| Terrible | 122 | 12 |
| Total | 1015 | 100 |

   **c.**

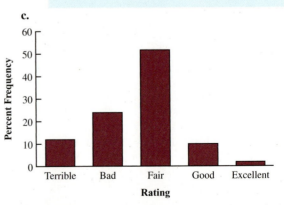

   **d.** 36% a bad or a terrible job
       12% a good or excellent job

**e.** 50% a bad or a terrible job
  4% a good or excellent job
  More pessimism in Spain

**12.**

| Class | Cumulative Frequency | Cumulative Relative Frequency |
|---|---|---|
| ≤19 | 10 | .20 |
| ≤29 | 24 | .48 |
| ≤39 | 41 | .82 |
| ≤49 | 48 | .96 |
| ≤59 | 50 | 1.00 |

**14. b/c.**

| Class | Frequency | Percent Frequency |
|---|---|---|
| 6.0–7.9 | 4 | 20 |
| 8.0–9.9 | 2 | 10 |
| 10.0–11.9 | 8 | 40 |
| 12.0–13.9 | 3 | 15 |
| 14.0–15.9 | 3 | 15 |
| Totals | 20 | 100 |

**15. a/b.**

| Waiting Time | Frequency | Relative Frequency |
|---|---|---|
| 0–4 | 4 | .20 |
| 5–9 | 8 | .40 |
| 10–14 | 5 | .25 |
| 15–19 | 2 | .10 |
| 20–24 | 1 | .05 |
| Totals | 20 | 1.00 |

**c/d.**

| Waiting Time | Cumulative Frequency | Cumulative Relative Frequency |
|---|---|---|
| ≤4 | 4 | .20 |
| ≤9 | 12 | .60 |
| ≤14 | 17 | .85 |
| ≤19 | 19 | .95 |
| ≤24 | 20 | 1.00 |

**e.** 12/20 = .60

**16. a.**

| Salary | Frequency |
|---|---|
| 150–159 | 1 |
| 160–169 | 3 |
| 170–179 | 7 |
| 180–189 | 5 |
| 190–199 | 1 |
| 200–209 | 2 |
| 210–219 | 1 |
| Total | 20 |

**b.**

| Salary | Percent Frequency |
|---|---|
| 150–159 | 5 |
| 160–169 | 15 |
| 170–179 | 35 |
| 180–189 | 25 |
| 190–199 | 5 |
| 200–209 | 10 |
| 210–219 | 5 |
| Total | 100 |

**c.**

| Salary | Cumulative Percent Frequency |
|---|---|
| Less than or equal to 159 | 5 |
| Less than or equal to 169 | 20 |
| Less than or equal to 179 | 55 |
| Less than or equal to 189 | 80 |
| Less than or equal to 199 | 85 |
| Less than or equal to 209 | 95 |
| Less than or equal to 219 | 100 |
| Total | 100 |

**e.** There is skewness to the right
**f.** 15%

**18. a.** Lowest $180; highest $2050

**b.**

| Spending | Frequency | Percent Frequency |
|---|---|---|
| $0–249 | 3 | 12 |
| 250–499 | 6 | 24 |
| 500–749 | 5 | 20 |
| 750–999 | 5 | 20 |
| 1000–1249 | 3 | 12 |
| 1250–1499 | 1 | 4 |
| 1500–1749 | 0 | 0 |
| 1750–1999 | 1 | 4 |
| 2000–2249 | 1 | 4 |
| Total | 25 | 100 |

**c.** The distribution shows a positive skewness
**d.** Majority (64%) of consumers spend between $250 and $1000; the middle value is about $750; and two high spenders are above $1750

**20. a.**

| Off-Course Income ($1000s) | Frequency | Percent Frequency |
|---|---|---|
| 0–4,999 | 30 | 60 |
| 5,000–9,999 | 9 | 18 |
| 10,000–14,999 | 4 | 8 |
| 15,000–19,999 | 0 | 0 |
| 20,000–24,999 | 3 | 6 |
| 25,000–29,999 | 2 | 4 |
| 30,000–34,999 | 0 | 0 |
| 35,000–39,999 | 0 | 0 |
| 40,000–44,999 | 1 | 2 |
| 45,000–49,999 | 0 | 0 |
| Over 50,000 | 1 | 2 |
| Total | 50 | 100 |

**c.** Off-course income is skewed to the right; only Tiger Woods earns over $50 million

**d.** The majority (60%) earn less that $5 million; 78% earn less than $10 million; five golfers (10%) earn between $20 million and $30 million; only Tiger Woods and Phil Mickelson earn more than $40 million

**22.**
```
5 | 7  8
6 | 4  5  8
7 | 0  2  2  5  5  6  8
8 | 0  2  3  5
```

**23.** Leaf unit = .1
```
 6 | 3
 7 | 5  5  7
 8 | 1  3  4  8
 9 | 3  6
10 | 0  4  5
11 | 3
```

**24.** Leaf unit = 10
```
11 | 6
12 | 0  2
13 | 0  6  7
14 | 2  2  7
15 | 5
16 | 0  2  8
17 | 0  2  3
```

**25.**
```
 9 | 8  9
10 | 2  4  6  6
11 | 4  5  7  8  8  9
12 | 2  4  5  7
13 | 1  2
14 | 4
15 | 1
```

**26.** Median Pay
```
 6 | 6  7  7
 7 | 2  4  6  7  7  8  9
 8 | 0  0  1  3  7
 9 | 9
10 | 0  6
11 | 0
12 | 1
```

Top Pay
```
10 | 0  6  9
11 | 1  6  9
12 | 2  5  6
13 | 0  5  8  8
14 | 0  6
15 | 2  5  7
16 |
17 |
18 |
19 |
20 |
21 | 4
22 | 1
```

**28. a.**
```
2 | 14
2 | 67
3 | 011123
3 | 5677
4 | 003333344
4 | 6679
5 | 00022
5 | 5679
6 | 14
6 | 6
7 | 2
```

**b.** 40–44 with 9

**c.** 43 with 5

**d.** 10%; relatively small participation in the race

**29. a.**

|   |   | $y$ |   |   |
|---|---|---|---|---|
|   |   | 1 | 2 | Total |
| $x$ | A | 5 | 0 | 5 |
|   | B | 11 | 2 | 13 |
|   | C | 2 | 10 | 12 |
|   | Total | 18 | 12 | 30 |

**b.**

|   |   | $y$ |   |   |
|---|---|---|---|---|
|   |   | 1 | 2 | Total |
| $x$ | A | 100.0 | 0.0 | 100.0 |
|   | B | 84.6 | 15.4 | 100.0 |
|   | C | 16.7 | 83.3 | 100.0 |

**c.**

|   |   | $y$ |   |
|---|---|---|---|
|   |   | 1 | 2 |
| $x$ | A | 27.8 | 0.0 |
|   | B | 61.1 | 16.7 |
|   | C | 11.1 | 83.3 |
|   | Total | 100.0 | 100.0 |

**d.** $A$ values are always in $y = 1$
$B$ values are most often in $y = 1$
$C$ values are most often in $y = 2$

**30. a.**

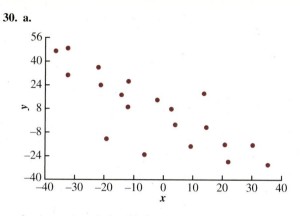

**b.** A negative relationship between $x$ and $y$; $y$ decreases as $x$ increases

**32. a.**

| Education Level | Household Income ($1000s) | | | | | |
| --- | --- | --- | --- | --- | --- | --- |
| | Under 25 | 25.0– 49.9 | 50.0– 74.9 | 75.0– 99.9 | 100 or more | Total |
| Not H.S. Graduate | 32.10 | 18.71 | 9.13 | 5.26 | 2.20 | 13.51 |
| H.S. Graduate | 37.52 | 37.05 | 33.04 | 25.73 | 16.00 | 29.97 |
| Some College | 21.42 | 28.44 | 30.74 | 31.71 | 24.43 | 27.21 |
| Bachelor's Degree | 6.75 | 11.33 | 18.72 | 25.19 | 32.26 | 18.70 |
| Beyond Bach. Deg. | 2.21 | 4.48 | 8.37 | 12.11 | 25.11 | 10.61 |
| Total | 100.00 | 100.00 | 100.00 | 100.00 | 100.00 | 100.00 |

13.51% of the heads of households did not graduate from high school

**b.** 25.11%, 53.54%

**c.** Positive relationship between income and education level

**34. a.**

| Fund Type | 5-Year Average Return | | | | | | |
| --- | --- | --- | --- | --- | --- | --- | --- |
| | 0– 9.99 | 10– 19.99 | 20– 29.99 | 30– 39.99 | 40– 49.99 | 50– 59.99 | Total |
| DE | 1 | 25 | 1 | 0 | 0 | 0 | 27 |
| FI | 9 | 1 | 0 | 0 | 0 | 0 | 10 |
| IE | 0 | 2 | 3 | 2 | 0 | 1 | 8 |
| Total | 10 | 28 | 4 | 2 | 0 | 1 | 45 |

**b.**

| 5-Year Average Return | Frequency |
| --- | --- |
| 0–9.99 | 10 |
| 10–19.99 | 28 |
| 20–29.99 | 4 |
| 30–39.99 | 2 |
| 40–49.99 | 0 |
| 50–59.99 | 1 |
| Total | 45 |

**c.**

| Fund Type | Frequency |
| --- | --- |
| DE | 27 |
| FI | 10 |
| IE | 8 |
| Total | 45 |

**d.** The margin of the crosstabulation shows these frequency distributions

**e.** Higher returns—International Equity funds
Lower returns—Fixed Income funds

**36. b.** Higher 5-year returns are associated with higher net asset values.

**38. a.**

| Displacement | Highway MPG | | | | | | Total |
| --- | --- | --- | --- | --- | --- | --- | --- |
| | 15–19 | 20–24 | 25–29 | 30–34 | 35–39 | 40–44 | |
| 1–2 | 0 | 0 | 0 | 0 | 7 | 7 | 14 |
| 2–3 | 0 | 0 | 14 | 41 | 9 | 1 | 65 |
| 3–4 | 0 | 1 | 34 | 4 | 0 | 0 | 39 |
| 4–5 | 0 | 10 | 4 | 0 | 0 | 0 | 14 |
| 5–6 | 0 | 3 | 2 | 0 | 0 | 0 | 5 |
| 6–7 | 8 | 4 | 0 | 0 | 0 | 0 | 12 |
| Total | 8 | 18 | 54 | 45 | 16 | 8 | 149 |

**b.** Higher fuel efficiencies are associated with smaller displacement engines
Lower fuel efficiencies are associated with larger displacement engines

**d.** Lower fuel efficiencies are associated with larger displacement engines

**e.** Scatter diagram

**40. a.**

| Division | Frequency | Percent |
| --- | --- | --- |
| Buick | 10 | 5 |
| Cadillac | 10 | 5 |
| Chevrolet | 122 | 61 |
| GMC | 24 | 12 |
| Hummer | 2 | 1 |
| Pontiac | 18 | 9 |
| Saab | 2 | 1 |
| Saturn | 12 | 6 |
| Total | 200 | 100 |

**b.** Chevrolet, 61%

**c.** Hummer and Saab, both only 1%
Maintain Chevrolet and GMC

**42. a.**

| SAT Score | Frequency |
| --- | --- |
| 800–999 | 1 |
| 1000–1199 | 3 |
| 1200–1399 | 6 |
| 1400–1599 | 10 |
| 1600–1799 | 7 |
| 1800–1999 | 2 |
| 2000–2199 | 1 |
| Total | 30 |

**b.** Nearly symmetrical

**c.** 33% of the scores fall between 1400 and 1599
A score below 800 or above 2200 is unusual
The average is near or slightly above 1500

**44. a.**

| Population | Frequency | Percent Frequency |
|---|---|---|
| 0.0–2.4 | 17 | 34 |
| 2.5–4.9 | 12 | 24 |
| 5.0–7.4 | 9 | 18 |
| 7.5–9.9 | 4 | 8 |
| 10.0–12.4 | 3 | 6 |
| 12.5–14.9 | 1 | 2 |
| 15.0–17.4 | 1 | 2 |
| 17.5–19.9 | 1 | 2 |
| 20.0–22.4 | 0 | 0 |
| 22.5–24.9 | 1 | 2 |
| 25.0–27.4 | 0 | 0 |
| 27.5–29.9 | 0 | 0 |
| 30.0–32.4 | 0 | 0 |
| 32.5–34.9 | 0 | 0 |
| 35.0–37.4 | 1 | 2 |
| Total | 50 | 100 |

**c.** High positive skewness

**d.** 17 (34%) with population less than 2.5 million
29 (58%) with population less than 5 million
8 (16%) with population greater than 10 million
Largest 35.9 million (California)
Smallest .5 million (Wyoming)

**46. a. High Temperatures**

```
1 |
2 |
3 | 0
4 | 1 2 2 5
5 | 2 4 5
6 | 0 0 0 1 2 2 5 6 8
7 | 0 7
8 | 4
```

**b. Low Temperatures**

```
1 | 1
2 | 1 2 6 7 9
3 | 1 5 6 8 9
4 | 0 3 3 6 7
5 | 0 0 4
6 | 5
7 |
8 |
```

**c.** The most frequent range for high is in 60s (9 of 20)
with only one low temperature above 54
High temperatures range mostly from 41 to 68, while
low temperatures range mostly from 21 to 47
Low was 11; high was 84

**d.**

| High Temp | Frequency | Low Temp | Frequency |
|---|---|---|---|
| 10–19 | 0 | 10–19 | 1 |
| 20–29 | 0 | 20–29 | 5 |
| 30–39 | 1 | 30–39 | 5 |
| 40–49 | 4 | 40–49 | 5 |
| 50–59 | 3 | 50–59 | 3 |
| 60–69 | 9 | 60–69 | 1 |
| 70–79 | 2 | 70–79 | 0 |
| 80–89 | 1 | 80–89 | 0 |
| Total | 20 | Total | 20 |

**48. a.**

| Level of Support | Percent Frequency |
|---|---|
| Strongly favor | 30.10 |
| Favor more than oppose | 34.83 |
| Oppose more than favor | 21.13 |
| Strongly oppose | 13.94 |
| Total | 100.00 |

Overall favor higher tax = 30.10% + 34.83%
$$= 64.93\%$$

**b.** 20.2, 19.5, 20.6, 20.7, 19.0
Roughly 20% per country

**c.** The crosstabulation with column percentages:

| Support | Country | | | | |
|---|---|---|---|---|---|
| | Great Britain | Italy | Spain | Germany | United States |
| Strongly favor | 31.00 | 31.96 | 45.99 | 19.98 | 20.98 |
| Favor more than oppose | 34.04 | 39.04 | 32.01 | 36.99 | 32.06 |
| Oppose more than favor | 23.00 | 17.99 | 13.98 | 24.03 | 26.96 |
| Strongly oppose | 11.96 | 11.01 | 8.03 | 18.99 | 20.00 |
| Total | 100.00 | 100.00 | 100.00 | 100.00 | 100.00 |

Considering the percentage of respondents who favor the higher tax by either saying "strongly favor" or "favor more than oppose," 65.04%, 71.00%, 78.00%, 56.97%, and 53.04% for the five countries; all show more than 50% support, but all European countries show more support for the tax than the United States; Italy and Spain show the highest level of support.

**50. a.** Row totals: 247; 54; 82; 121
Column totals: 149; 317; 17; 7; 14

**b.**

| Year | Freq. | Fuel | Freq. |
|---|---|---|---|
| 1973 or before | 247 | Elect. | 149 |
| 1974–79 | 54 | Nat. Gas | 317 |
| 1980–86 | 82 | Oil | 17 |
| 1987–91 | 121 | Propane | 7 |
| Total | 504 | Other | 14 |
| | | Total | 504 |

**c.** Crosstabulation of column percentages

| Year Constructed | Fuel Type | | | | |
|---|---|---|---|---|---|
| | Elect. | Nat. Gas | Oil | Propane | Other |
| 1973 or before | 26.9 | 57.7 | 70.5 | 71.4 | 50.0 |
| 1974–1979 | 16.1 | 8.2 | 11.8 | 28.6 | 0.0 |
| 1980–1986 | 24.8 | 12.0 | 5.9 | 0.0 | 42.9 |
| 1987–1991 | 32.2 | 22.1 | 11.8 | 0.0 | 7.1 |
| **Total** | 100.0 | 100.0 | 100.0 | 100.0 | 100.0 |

**d.** Crosstabulation of row percentages

| Year Constructed | Fuel Type | | | | | |
|---|---|---|---|---|---|---|
| | Elect. | Nat. Gas | Oil | Propane | Other | Total |
| 1973 or before | 16.2 | 74.1 | 4.9 | 2.0 | 2.8 | 100.0 |
| 1974–1979 | 44.5 | 48.1 | 3.7 | 3.7 | 0.0 | 100.0 |
| 1980–1986 | 45.1 | 46.4 | 1.2 | 0.0 | 7.3 | 100.0 |
| 1987–1991 | 39.7 | 57.8 | 1.7 | 0.0 | 0.8 | 100.0 |

**52. a.** Crosstabulation of market value and profit

| Market Value ($1000s) | Profit ($1000s) | | | | |
|---|---|---|---|---|---|
| | 0–300 | 300–600 | 600–900 | 900–1200 | Total |
| 0–8000 | 23 | 4 | | | 27 |
| 8000–16,000 | 4 | 4 | 2 | 2 | 12 |
| 16,000–24,000 | | 2 | 1 | 1 | 4 |
| 24,000–32,000 | | 1 | 2 | 1 | 4 |
| 32,000–40,000 | | 2 | 1 | | 3 |
| **Total** | 27 | 13 | 6 | 4 | 50 |

**b.** Crosstabulation of row percentages

| Market Value ($1000s) | Profit ($1000s) | | | | |
|---|---|---|---|---|---|
| | 0–300 | 300–600 | 600–900 | 900–1200 | Total |
| 0–8000 | 85.19 | 14.81 | 0.00 | 0.00 | 100 |
| 8000–16,000 | 33.33 | 33.33 | 16.67 | 16.67 | 100 |
| 16,000–24,000 | 0.00 | 50.00 | 25.00 | 25.00 | 100 |
| 24,000–32,000 | 0.00 | 25.00 | 50.00 | 25.00 | 100 |
| 32,000–40,000 | 0.00 | 66.67 | 33.33 | 0.00 | 100 |

**c.** A positive relationship is indicated between profit and market value; as profit goes up, market value goes up

**54. b.** A positive relationship is demonstrated between market value and stockholders' equity

# Chapter 3

**2.** 16, 16.5

**3.** Arrange data in order: 15, 20, 25, 25, 27, 28, 30, 34

$i = \dfrac{20}{100}(8) = 1.6$; round up to position 2

20th percentile = 20

$i = \dfrac{25}{100}(8) = 2$; use positions 2 and 3

25th percentile $= \dfrac{20 + 25}{2} = 22.5$

$i = \dfrac{65}{100}(8) = 5.2$; round up to position 6

65th percentile = 28

$i = \dfrac{75}{100}(8) = 6$; use positions 6 and 7

75th percentile $= \dfrac{28 + 30}{2} = 29$

**4.** 59.73, 57, 53

**6. a.** 18.42
   **b.** 6.32
   **c.** 34.3%
   **d.** Reductions of only .65 shots and .9% made shots per game
   Yes, agree but not dramatically

**8. a.** $\bar{x} = \dfrac{\Sigma x_i}{n} = \dfrac{3200}{20} = 160$

Order the data from low 100 to high 360

Median: $i = \left(\dfrac{50}{100}\right)20 = 10$; use 10th and 11th positions

Median $= \left(\dfrac{130 + 140}{2}\right) = 135$

Mode = 120 (occur 3 times)

**b.** $i = \left(\dfrac{25}{100}\right)20 = 5$; use 5th and 6th positions

$Q_1 = \left(\dfrac{115 + 115}{2}\right) = 115$

$i = \left(\dfrac{75}{100}\right)20 = 15$; use 15th and 16th positions

$Q_3 = \left(\dfrac{180 + 195}{2}\right) = 187.5$

**c.** $i = \left(\dfrac{90}{100}\right)20 = 18$; use 18th and 19th positions

90th percentile $= \left(\dfrac{235 + 255}{2}\right) = 245$

90% of the tax returns cost $245 or less

**10. a.** .4%, 3.5%
   **b.** 2.3%, 2.5%, 2.7%
   **c.** 2.0%, 2.8%
   **d.** optimistic

**12.** Disney: 3321, 255.5, 253, 169, 325
   Pixar: 3231, 538.5, 505, 363, 631
   Pixar films generate approximately twice as much box office revenue per film

**14.** 16, 4

**15.** Range = 34 − 15 = 19
   Arrange data in order: 15, 20, 25, 25, 27, 28, 30, 34

$i = \dfrac{25}{100}(8) = 2$; $Q_1 = \dfrac{20 + 25}{2} = 22.5$

$i = \dfrac{75}{100}(8) = 6$; $Q_3 = \dfrac{28 + 30}{2} = 29$

$IQR = Q_3 - Q_1 = 29 - 22.5 = 6.5$

$\bar{x} = \dfrac{\Sigma x_i}{n} = \dfrac{204}{8} = 25.5$

| $x_i$ | $(x_i - \bar{x})$ | $(x_i - \bar{x})^2$ |
|-------|-------------------|---------------------|
| 27    | 1.5               | 2.25                |
| 25    | −.5               | .25                 |
| 20    | −5.5              | 30.25               |
| 15    | −10.5             | 110.25              |
| 30    | 4.5               | 20.25               |
| 34    | 8.5               | 72.25               |
| 28    | 2.5               | 6.25                |
| 25    | −.5               | .25                 |
|       |                   | 242.00              |

$$s^2 = \frac{\Sigma(x_i - \bar{x})^2}{n-1} = \frac{242}{8-1} = 34.57$$

$$s = \sqrt{34.57} = 5.88$$

**16. a.** Range $= 190 - 168 = 22$

**b.** $\bar{x} = \dfrac{\Sigma x_i}{n} = \dfrac{1068}{6} = 178$

$s^2 = \dfrac{\Sigma(x_i - \bar{x})^2}{n-1}$

$= \dfrac{4^2 + (-10)^2 + 6^2 + 12^2 + (-8)^2 + (-4)^2}{6-1}$

$= \dfrac{376}{5} = 75.2$

**c.** $s = \sqrt{75.2} = 8.67$

**d.** $\dfrac{s}{\bar{x}}(100) = \dfrac{8.67}{178}(100\%) = 4.87\%$

**18. a.** 38, 97, 9.85

**b.** Eastern shows more variation

**20.** *Dawson:* range $= 2$, $s = .67$
   *Clark:* range $= 8$, $s = 2.58$

**22. a.** 1285, 433
   Freshmen spend more

**b.** 1720, 352

**c.** 404, 131.5

**d.** 367.04, 96.96

**e.** Freshmen have more variability

**24.** *Quarter-milers:* $s = .0564$, Coef. of Var. $= 5.8\%$
   *Milers:* $s = .1295$, Coef. of Var. $= 2.9\%$

**26.** .20, 1.50, 0, −.50, −2.20

**27.** Chebyshev's theorem: *at least* $(1 - 1/z^2)$

**a.** $z = \dfrac{40 - 30}{5} = 2$; $1 - \dfrac{1}{(2)^2} = .75$

**b.** $z = \dfrac{45 - 30}{5} = 3$; $1 - \dfrac{1}{(3)^2} = .89$

**c.** $z = \dfrac{38 - 30}{5} = 1.6$; $1 - \dfrac{1}{(1.6)^2} = .61$

**d.** $z = \dfrac{42 - 30}{5} = 2.4$; $1 - \dfrac{1}{(2.4)^2} = .83$

**e.** $z = \dfrac{48 - 30}{5} = 3.6$; $1 - \dfrac{1}{(3.6)^2} = .92$

**28. a.** 95%

**b.** Almost all

**c.** 68%

**29. a.** $z = 2$ standard deviations

$1 - \dfrac{1}{z^2} = 1 - \dfrac{1}{2^2} = \dfrac{3}{4}$; at least 75%

**b.** $z = 2.5$ standard deviations

$1 - \dfrac{1}{z^2} = 1 - \dfrac{1}{2.5^2} = .84$; at least 84%

**c.** $z = 2$ standard deviations
   Empirical rule: 95%

**30. a.** 68%

**b.** 81.5%

**c.** 2.5%

**32. a.** −.67

**b.** 1.50

**c.** Neither an outlier

**d.** Yes; $z = 8.25$

**34. a.** 76.5, 7

**b.** 16%, 2.5%

**c.** 12.2, 7.89; no

**36.** 15, 22.5, 26, 29, 34

**38.** Arrange data in order: 5, 6, 8, 10, 10, 12, 15, 16, 18

$i = \dfrac{25}{100}(9) = 2.25$; round up to position 3

$Q_1 = 8$
Median (5th position) $= 10$

$i = \dfrac{75}{100}(9) = 6.75$; round up to position 7

$Q_3 = 15$
5-number summary: 5, 8, 10, 15, 18

**40. a.** Subway with 29,612 locations

**b.** Order data smallest to largest
   Median (middle value) $= 5889$

**c.** Smallest $= 1397$; Largest $= 29,612$

$i = \dfrac{25}{100}(13) = 3.25$   Round to 4th position

$Q_1 = 4516$

$i = \dfrac{75}{100}(13) = 9.75$   Round to 10th position

$Q_3 = 10,238$
5-number summary: 1397  4516  5889  10,238  29,612

**d.** $IQR = Q_3 - Q_1 = 10,238 - 4516 = 5722$
   Lower: $Q_1 - 1.5\,(IQR) = 4516 - 1.5(5722) = -4067$

Upper: $Q_3 + 1.5\,(IQR) = 10{,}238 + 1.5(5722) = 18{,}821$

Subway and McDonald's are outliers

**e.**

41. **a.** Arrange data in order low to high

$i = \dfrac{25}{100}(21) = 5.25$; round up to 6th position

$Q_1 = 1872$

Median (11th position) = 4019

$i = \dfrac{75}{100}(21) = 15.75$; round up to 16th position

$Q_3 = 8305$

5-number summary: 608, 1872, 4019, 8305, 14,138

**b.** $IQR = Q_3 - Q_1 = 8305 - 1872 = 6433$

Lower limit: $1872 - 1.5(6433) = -7777.5$

Upper limit: $8305 + 1.5(6433) = 17{,}955$

**c.** No; data are within limits

**d.** $41{,}138 > 27{,}604$; 41,138 would be an outlier; data value would be reviewed and corrected

**e.**

42. **a.** 73.5

**b.** 68, 71.5, 73.5, 74.5, 77

**c.** Limits: 67 and 79; no outliers

**d.** 66, 68, 71, 73, 75; 60.5 and 80.5
63, 65, 66, 67.6, 69; 61.25 and 71.25
75, 77, 78.5, 79.5, 81; 73.25 and 83.25
No outliers for any of the services

**e.** Verizon is highest rated
Sprint is lowest rated

44. **a.** 18.2, 15.35

**b.** 11.7, 23.5

**c.** 3.4, 11.7, 15.35, 23.5, 41.3

**d.** Yes; Alger Small Cap 41.3

45. **b.** There appears to be a negative linear relationship between $x$ and $y$

**c.**

| $x_i$ | $y_i$ | $x_i - \bar{x}$ | $y_i - \bar{y}$ | $(x_i - \bar{x})(y_i - \bar{y})$ |
|---|---|---|---|---|
| 4 | 50 | −4 | 4 | −16 |
| 6 | 50 | −2 | 4 | −8 |
| 11 | 40 | 3 | −6 | −18 |
| 3 | 60 | −5 | 14 | −70 |
| 16 | 30 | 8 | −16 | −128 |
| 40 | 230 | 0 | 0 | −240 |

$\bar{x} = 8$; $\bar{y} = 46$

$s_{xy} = \dfrac{\Sigma(x_i - \bar{x})(y_i - \bar{y})}{n-1} = \dfrac{-240}{4} = -60$

The sample covariance indicates a negative linear association between $x$ and $y$

**d.** $r_{xy} = \dfrac{s_{xy}}{s_x s_y} = \dfrac{-60}{(5.43)(11.40)} = -.969$

The sample correlation coefficient of $-.969$ is indicative of a strong negative linear relationship

46. **b.** There appears to be a positive linear relationship between $x$ and $y$

**c.** $s_{xy} = 26.5$

**d.** $r_{xy} = .693$

48. $-.91$; negative relationship

50. **b.** .910

**c.** Strong positive linear relationship; no

52. **a.** 3.69

**b.** 3.175

53. **a.**

| $f_i$ | $M_i$ | $f_i M_i$ |
|---|---|---|
| 4 | 5 | 20 |
| 7 | 10 | 70 |
| 9 | 15 | 135 |
| 5 | 20 | 100 |
| 25 | | 325 |

$\bar{x} = \dfrac{\Sigma f_i M_i}{n} = \dfrac{325}{25} = 13$

**b.**

| $f_i$ | $M_i$ | $(M_i - \bar{x})$ | $(M_i - \bar{x})^2$ | $f_i(M_i - \bar{x})^2$ |
|---|---|---|---|---|
| 4 | 5 | −8 | 64 | 256 |
| 7 | 10 | −3 | 9 | 63 |
| 9 | 15 | 2 | 4 | 36 |
| 5 | 20 | 7 | 49 | 245 |
| 25 | | | | 600 |

$s^2 = \dfrac{\Sigma f_i(M_i - \bar{x})^2}{n-1} = \dfrac{600}{25-1} = 25$

$s = \sqrt{25} = 5$

54. **a.**

| Grade $x_i$ | Weight $w_i$ |
|---|---|
| 4 (A) | 9 |
| 3 (B) | 15 |
| 2 (C) | 33 |
| 1 (D) | 3 |
| 0 (F) | 0 |
| | 60 credit hours |

$\bar{x} = \dfrac{\Sigma w_i x_i}{\Sigma w_i} = \dfrac{9(4) + 15(3) + 33(2) + 3(1)}{9 + 15 + 33 + 3}$

$= \dfrac{150}{60} = 2.5$

**b.** Yes

56. 3.8, 3.7

58. **a.** 1800, 1351

**b.** 387, 1710

**c.** 7280, 1323

**d.** 3,675,303, 1917

**e.** High positive skewness

**f.** Using a box plot: 4135 and 7450 are outliers

**60. a.** 2.3, 1.85

**b.** 1.90, 1.38

**c.** Altria Group 5%

**d.** $-.51$, below mean

**e.** 1.02, above mean

**f.** No

**62. a.** $670

**b.** $456

**c.** $z = 3$; yes

**d.** Save time and prevent a penalty cost

**64. a.** 215.9

**b.** 55%

**c.** 175.0, 628.3

**d.** 48.8, 175.0, 215.9, 628.3, 2325.0

**e.** Yes, any price over 1308.25

**f.** 482.1; prefer median

**66. a.** 364 rooms

**b.** $457

**c.** $-.293$; slight negative correlation
Higher cost per night tends to be associated with smaller hotels

**68. a.** .268, low or weak positive correlation

**b.** Very poor predictor; spring training is practice and does not count toward standings or playoffs

**70. a.** 60.68

**b.** $s^2 = 31.23$; $s = 5.59$

## Chapter 4

**2.** $\binom{6}{3} = \dfrac{6!}{3!3!} = \dfrac{6 \cdot 5 \cdot 4 \cdot 3 \cdot 2 \cdot 1}{(3 \cdot 2 \cdot 1)(3 \cdot 2 \cdot 1)} = 20$

| | | | |
|---|---|---|---|
| ABC | ACE | BCD | BEF |
| ABD | ACF | BCE | CDE |
| ABE | ADE | BCF | CDF |
| ABF | ADF | BDE | CEF |
| ACD | AEF | BDF | DEF |

**4. b.** (H,H,H), (H,H,T), (H,T,H), (H,T,T), (T,H,H), (T,H,T), (T,T,H), (T,T,T)

**c.** $\frac{1}{8}$

**6.** $P(E_1) = .40$, $P(E_2) = .26$, $P(E_3) = .34$
The relative frequency method was used

**8. a.** 4: Commission Positive—Council Approves
Commission Positive—Council Disapproves
Commission Negative—Council Approves
Commission Negative—Council Disapproves

**9.** $\binom{50}{4} = \dfrac{50!}{4!46!} = \dfrac{50 \cdot 49 \cdot 48 \cdot 47}{4 \cdot 3 \cdot 2 \cdot 1} = 230{,}300$

**10. a.** Using the table, $P(\text{Debt}) = .94$

**b.** Five of the 8 institutions, $P(\text{over } 60\%) = 5/8 = .625$

**c.** Two of the 8 institutions, $P(\text{more than } \$30{,}000) = 2/8 = .25$

**d.** $P(\text{No debt}) = 1 - P(\text{debt}) = 1 - .72 = .28$

**e.** A weighted average with 72% having average debt of $32,980 and 28% having no debt

$$\text{Average debt per graduate} = \frac{.72(\$32{,}980) + .28(\$0)}{.72 + .28}$$
$$= \$23{,}746$$

**12. a.** 3,478,761

**b.** 1/3,478,761

**c.** 1/146,107,962

**14. a.** $\frac{1}{4}$

**b.** $\frac{1}{2}$

**c.** $\frac{3}{4}$

**15. a.** $S = \{$ace of clubs, ace of diamonds, ace of hearts, ace of spades$\}$

**b.** $S = \{$2 of clubs, 3 of clubs, . . . , 10 of clubs, J of clubs, Q of clubs, K of clubs, A of clubs$\}$

**c.** There are 12; jack, queen, or king in each of the four suits

**d.** For (a): 4/52 = 1/13 = .08
For (b): 13/52 = 1/4 = .25
For (c): 12/52 = .23

**16. a.** 36

**c.** $\frac{1}{6}$

**d.** $\frac{5}{18}$

**e.** No; $P(\text{odd}) = P(\text{even}) = \frac{1}{2}$

**f.** Classical

**17. a.** (4, 6), (4, 7), (4, 8)

**b.** $.05 + .10 + .15 = .30$

**c.** (2, 8), (3, 8), (4, 8)

**d.** $.05 + .05 + .15 = .25$

**e.** .15

**18. a.** .0222

**b.** .8226

**c.** .1048

**20. a.** .108

**b.** .096

**c.** .434

**22. a.** .40, .40, .60

**b.** .80, yes

**c.** $A^c = \{E_3, E_4, E_5\}$; $C^c = \{E_1, E_4\}$;
$P(A^c) = .60$; $P(C^c) = .40$

**d.** $(E_1, E_2, E_5)$; .60

**e.** .80

**23. a.** $P(A) = P(E_1) + P(E_4) + P(E_6)$
$= .05 + .25 + .10 = .40$
$P(B) = P(E_2) + P(E_4) + P(E_7)$
$= .20 + .25 + .05 = .50$
$P(C) = P(E_2) + P(E_3) + P(E_5) + P(E_7)$
$= .20 + .20 + .15 + .05 = .60$

**b.** $A \cup B = \{E_1, E_2, E_4, E_6, E_7\}$;
$P(A \cup B) = P(E_1) + P(E_2) + P(E_4) + P(E_6) + P(E_7)$
$= .05 + .20 + .25 + .10 + .05$
$= .65$

**c.** $A \cap B = \{E_4\}$; $P(A \cap B) = P(E_4) = .25$

**d.** Yes, they are mutually exclusive

**e.** $B^c = \{E_1, E_3, E_5, E_6\}$;
$P(B^c) = P(E_1) + P(E_3) + P(E_5) + P(E_6)$
$\phantom{P(B^c)} = .05 + .20 + .15 + .10$
$\phantom{P(B^c)} = .50$

**24. a.** .05
   **b.** .70

**26. a.** .64
   **b.** .48
   **c.** .36
   **d.** .76

**28.** Let $B$ = rented a car for business reasons
   $P$ = rented a car for personal reasons
   **a.** $P(B \cup P) = P(B) + P(P) - P(B \cap P)$
   $\phantom{P(B \cup P)} = .540 + .458 - .300$
   $\phantom{P(B \cup P)} = .698$
   **b.** $P(\text{Neither}) = 1 - .698 = .302$

**30. a.** $P(A \mid B) = \dfrac{P(A \cap B)}{P(B)} = \dfrac{.40}{.60} = .6667$

   **b.** $P(B \mid A) = \dfrac{P(A \cap B)}{P(A)} = \dfrac{.40}{.50} = .80$

   **c.** No, because $P(A \mid B) \neq P(A)$

**32. a.**

|  | Car | Light Truck | Total |
|---|---|---|---|
| **U.S.** | .1330 | .2939 | .4269 |
| **Non-U.S.** | .3478 | .2253 | .5731 |
| **Total** | .4808 | .5192 | 1.0000 |

   **b.** .4269, .5731 Non-U.S. higher
   .4808, .5192 Light Truck slightly higher
   **c.** .3115, .6885 Light Truck higher
   **d.** .6909, .3931 Car higher
   **e.** .5661, U.S. higher for Light Trucks

**33. a.**

| | Reason for Applying | | | |
|---|---|---|---|---|
| | **Cost/** | | | |
| | **Quality** | **Convenience** | **Other** | **Total** |
| **Full-time** | .218 | .204 | .039 | .461 |
| **Part-time** | .208 | .307 | .024 | .539 |
| **Total** | .426 | .511 | .063 | 1.000 |

   **b.** A student is most likely to cite cost or convenience as the first reason (probability = .511); school quality is the reason cited by the second largest number of students (probability = .426)
   **c.** $P(\text{quality} \mid \text{full-time}) = .218/.461 = .473$
   **d.** $P(\text{quality} \mid \text{part-time}) = .208/.539 = .386$
   **e.** For independence, we must have $P(A)P(B) = P(A \cap B)$; from the table
   $P(A \cap B) = .218, P(A) = .461, P(B) = .426$
   $P(A)P(B) = (.461)(.426) = .196$
   Because $P(A)P(B) \neq P(A \cap B)$, the events are not independent

**34. a.**

| | On Time | Late | Total |
|---|---|---|---|
| **Southwest** | .3336 | .0664 | .40 |
| **US Airways** | .2629 | .0871 | .35 |
| **JetBlue** | .1753 | .0747 | .25 |
| **Total** | .7718 | .2282 | 1.00 |

   **b.** Southwest (.40)
   **c.** .7718
   **d.** US Airways (.3817); Southwest (.2910)

**36. a.** .7921
   **b.** .9879
   **c.** .0121
   **d.** .3364, .8236, .1764
   Don't foul Jerry Stackhouse

**38. a.**

| | Met Proficiency Standards | | |
|---|---|---|---|
| **Grade** | **Yes** | **No** | **Total** |
| 3 | .11196 | .05663 | 0.16858 |
| 4 | .08271 | .08205 | 0.16476 |
| 5 | .08517 | .07922 | 0.16439 |
| 6 | .08588 | .07777 | 0.16365 |
| 7 | .09671 | .07031 | 0.16702 |
| 8 | .09618 | .07542 | 0.17159 |
| Total | .55861 | .44139 | 1.00000 |

   **b.** The column marginal probabilities are .55861 and .44139; the row marginal probabilities are .16858, .16476, and so on
   **c.** .6651; .5020
   **d.** .2004; .1481

**39. a.** Yes, because $P(A_1 \cap A_2) = 0$
   **b.** $P(A_1 \cap B) = P(A_1)P(B \mid A_1) = .40(.20) = .08$
   $P(A_2 \cap B) = P(A_2)P(B \mid A_2) = .60(.05) = .03$
   **c.** $P(B) = P(A_1 \cap B) + P(A_2 \cap B) = .08 + .03 = .11$
   **d.** $P(A_1 \mid B) = \dfrac{.08}{.11} = .7273$

   $\phantom{d.}\ P(A_2 \mid B) = \dfrac{.03}{.11} = .2727$

**40. a.** .10, .20, .09
   **b.** .51
   **c.** .26, .51, .23

**42.** $M$ = missed payment
   $D_1$ = customer defaults
   $D_2$ = customer does not default
   $P(D_1) = .05, P(D_2) = .95, P(M \mid D_2) = .2, P(M \mid D_1) = 1$
   **a.** $P(D_1 \mid M) = \dfrac{P(D_1)P(M \mid D_1)}{P(D_1)P(M \mid D_1) + P(D_2)P(M \mid D_2)}$

   $\phantom{P(D_1 \mid M)} = \dfrac{(.05)(1)}{(.05)(1) + (.95)(.2)} = \dfrac{.05}{.24} = .21$

   **b.** Yes, the probability of default is greater than .20

**44. a.** .47, .53, .50, .45
   **b.** .4963
   **c.** .4463
   **d.** 47%, 53%

**46. a.** .60
  **b.** .26
  **c.** .40
  **d.** .74

**48. a.** .2675
  **b.** .3376
  **c.** .0892
  **d.** .5159
  **e.** .0255

**50. a.** .76
  **b.** .24

**52. b.** .2022
  **c.** .4618
  **d.** .4005

**54. a.** .49
  **b.** .44
  **c.** .54
  **d.** No
  **e.** Yes

**56. a.** .25
  **b.** .125
  **c.** .0125
  **d.** .10
  **e.** No

**58. a.**

|  | Young Adult | Older Adult | Total |
|---|---|---|---|
| **Blogger** | .0432 | .0368 | .08 |
| **Nonblogger** | .2208 | .6992 | .92 |
| **Total** | .2640 | .7360 | 1.00 |

  **b.** .2640
  **c.** .0432
  **d.** .1636

**60. a.** .40
  **b.** .67

## Chapter 5

**1. a.** Head, Head ($H, H$)
  Head, Tail ($H, T$)
  Tail, Head ($T, H$)
  Tail, Tail ($T, T$)
  **b.** $x$ = number of heads on two coin tosses
  **c.**

| Outcome | Values of $x$ |
|---|---|
| ($H, H$) | 2 |
| ($H, T$) | 1 |
| ($T, H$) | 1 |
| ($T, T$) | 0 |

  **d.** Discrete; 0, 1, and 2

**2. a.** $x$ = time in minutes to assemble product
  **b.** Any positive value: $x > 0$
  **c.** Continuous

**3.** Let $Y$ = position is offered
  $N$ = position is not offered
  **a.** $S = \{(Y, Y, Y), (Y, Y, N), (Y, N, Y), (Y, N, N), (N, Y, Y), (N, Y, N), (N, N, Y), (N, N, N)\}$
  **b.** Let $N$ = number of offers made; $N$ is a discrete random variable
  **c.**

| Experimental Outcome | (Y, Y, Y) | (Y, Y, N) | (Y, N, Y) | (Y, N, N) | (N, Y, Y) | (N, Y, N) | (N, N, Y) | (N, N, N) |
|---|---|---|---|---|---|---|---|---|
| Value of $N$ | 3 | 2 | 2 | 1 | 2 | 1 | 1 | 0 |

**4.** $x = 0, 1, 2, \ldots, 9$

**6. a.** 0, 1, 2, ..., 20; discrete
  **b.** 0, 1, 2, ...; discrete
  **c.** 0, 1, 2, ..., 50; discrete
  **d.** $0 \leq x \leq 8$; continuous
  **e.** $x > 0$; continuous

**7. a.** $f(x) \geq 0$ for all values of $x$
  $\Sigma f(x) = 1$; therefore, it is a valid probability distribution
  **b.** Probability $x = 30$ is $f(30) = .25$
  **c.** Probability $x \leq 25$ is $f(20) + f(25) = .20 + .15 = .35$
  **d.** Probability $x > 30$ is $f(35) = .40$

**8. a.**

| $x$ | $f(x)$ |
|---|---|
| 1 | 3/20 = .15 |
| 2 | 5/20 = .25 |
| 3 | 8/20 = .40 |
| 4 | 4/20 = .20 |
|  | Total    1.00 |

  **b.**

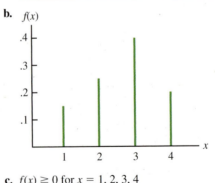

  **c.** $f(x) \geq 0$ for $x = 1, 2, 3, 4$
  $\Sigma f(x) = 1$

**10. a.**

| $x$ | 1 | 2 | 3 | 4 | 5 |
|---|---|---|---|---|---|
| $f(x)$ | .05 | .09 | .03 | .42 | .41 |

  **b.**

| $x$ | 1 | 2 | 3 | 4 | 5 |
|---|---|---|---|---|---|
| $f(x)$ | .04 | .10 | .12 | .46 | .28 |

  **c.** .83
  **d.** .28
  **e.** Senior executives are more satisfied

**12. a.** Yes
  **b.** .15
  **c.** .10

**14. a.** .05
   **b.** .70
   **c.** .40

**16. a.**

| y | f(y) | yf(y) |
|---|---|---|
| 2 | .20 | .4 |
| 4 | .30 | 1.2 |
| 7 | .40 | 2.8 |
| 8 | .10 | .8 |
| Totals | 1.00 | 5.2 |

$$E(y) = \mu = 5.2$$

**b.**

| y | $y - \mu$ | $(y - \mu)^2$ | f(y) | $(y - \mu)^2 f(y)$ |
|---|---|---|---|---|
| 2 | −3.20 | 10.24 | .20 | 2.048 |
| 4 | −1.20 | 1.44 | .30 | .432 |
| 7 | 1.80 | 3.24 | .40 | 1.296 |
| 8 | 2.80 | 7.84 | .10 | .784 |
|   |   |   | Total | 4.560 |

$$\text{Var}(y) = 4.56$$
$$\sigma = \sqrt{4.56} = 2.14$$

**18. a/b.**

| x | f(x) | xf(x) | $x - \mu$ | $(x - \mu)^2$ | $(x - \mu)^2 f(x)$ |
|---|---|---|---|---|---|
| 0 | 0.04 | 0.00 | −1.84 | 3.39 | 0.12 |
| 1 | 0.34 | 0.34 | −0.84 | 0.71 | 0.24 |
| 2 | 0.41 | 0.82 | 0.16 | 0.02 | 0.01 |
| 3 | 0.18 | 0.53 | 1.16 | 1.34 | 0.24 |
| 4 | 0.04 | 0.15 | 2.16 | 4.66 | 0.17 |
| Total | 1.00 | 1.84 ↑ $E(x)$ |  |  | 0.79 ↑ Var(x) |

**c/d.**

| y | f(y) | yf(y) | $y - \mu$ | $(y - \mu)^2$ | $y - \mu^2 f(y)$ |
|---|---|---|---|---|---|
| 0 | 0.00 | 0.00 | −2.93 | 8.58 | 0.01 |
| 1 | 0.03 | 0.03 | −1.93 | 3.72 | 0.12 |
| 2 | 0.23 | 0.45 | −0.93 | 0.86 | 0.20 |
| 3 | 0.52 | 1.55 | 0.07 | 0.01 | 0.00 |
| 4 | 0.22 | 0.90 | 1.07 | 1.15 | 0.26 |
| Total | 1.00 | 2.93 ↑ $E(y)$ |  |  | 0.59 ↑ Var(y) |

**e.** The number of bedrooms in owner-occupied houses is greater than in renter-occupied houses; the expected number of bedrooms is 2.93 − 1.84 = 1.09 greater; and the variability in the number of bedrooms is less for the owner-occupied houses

**20. a.** 430
   **b.** −90; concern is to protect against the expense of a large loss

**22. a.** 445
   **b.** $1250 loss

**24. a.** Medium: 145; large: 140
   **b.** Medium: 2725; large: 12,400

**25. a.**

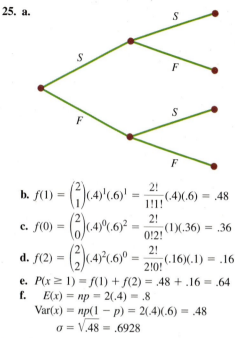

**b.** $f(1) = \binom{2}{1}(.4)^1(.6)^1 = \frac{2!}{1!1!}(.4)(.6) = .48$

**c.** $f(0) = \binom{2}{0}(.4)^0(.6)^2 = \frac{2!}{0!2!}(1)(.36) = .36$

**d.** $f(2) = \binom{2}{2}(.4)^2(.6)^0 = \frac{2!}{2!0!}(.16)(.1) = .16$

**e.** $P(x \geq 1) = f(1) + f(2) = .48 + .16 = .64$

**f.** $E(x) = np = 2(.4) = .8$
   $\text{Var}(x) = np(1 - p) = 2(.4)(.6) = .48$
   $\sigma = \sqrt{.48} = .6928$

**26. a.** .3487
   **b.** .1937
   **c.** .9298
   **d.** .6513
   **e.** 1
   **f.** .9, .95

**28. a.** .2789
   **b.** .4181
   **c.** .0733

**30. a.** Probability of a defective part being produced must be .03 for each part selected; parts must be selected independently
   **b.** Let $D$ = defective
      $G$ = not defective

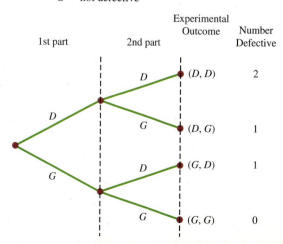

| 1st part | 2nd part | Experimental Outcome | Number Defective |
|---|---|---|---|
|  |  | (D, D) | 2 |
|  |  | (D, G) | 1 |
|  |  | (G, D) | 1 |
|  |  | (G, G) | 0 |

c. Two outcomes result in exactly one defect

d. $P(\text{no defects}) = (.97)(.97) = .9409$
$P(1\ \text{defect}) = 2(.03)(.97) = .0582$
$P(2\ \text{defects}) = (.03)(.03) = .0009$

**32. a.** .90
  **b.** .99
  **c.** .999
  **d.** Yes

**34. a.** .2262
  **b.** .8355

**36. a.** .1897
  **b.** .9757
  **c.** $f(12) = .0008$; yes
  **d.** 5

**38. a.** $f(x) = \dfrac{3^x e^{-3}}{x!}$
  **b.** .2241
  **c.** .1494
  **d.** .8008

**39. a.** $f(x) = \dfrac{2^x e^{-2}}{x!}$
  **b.** $\mu = 6$ for 3 time periods
  **c.** $f(x) = \dfrac{6^x e^{-6}}{x!}$
  **d.** $f(2) = \dfrac{2^2 e^{-2}}{2!} = \dfrac{4(.1353)}{2} = .2706$
  **e.** $f(6) = \dfrac{6^6 e^{-6}}{6!} = .1606$
  **f.** $f(5) = \dfrac{4^5 e^{-4}}{5!} = .1563$

**40. a.** .1952
  **b.** .1048
  **c.** .0183
  **d.** .0907

**42. a.** $f(0) = \dfrac{7^0 e^{-7}}{0!} = e^{-7} = .0009$
  **b.** probability $= 1 - [f(0) + f(1)]$
  $f(1) = \dfrac{7^1 e^{-7}}{1!} = 7e^{-7} = .0064$
  probability $= 1 - [.0009 + .0064] = .9927$
  **c.** $\mu = 3.5$
  $f(0) = \dfrac{3.5^0 e^{-3.5}}{0!} = e^{-3.5} = .0302$
  probability $= 1 - f(0) = 1 - .0302 = .9698$
  **d.**
  probability $= 1 - [f(0) + f(1) + f(2) + f(3) + f(4)]$
  $= 1 - [.0009 + .0064 + .0223 + .0521 + .0912]$
  $= .8271$

**44. a.** $\mu = 1.25$
  **b.** .2865
  **c.** .3581
  **d.** .3554

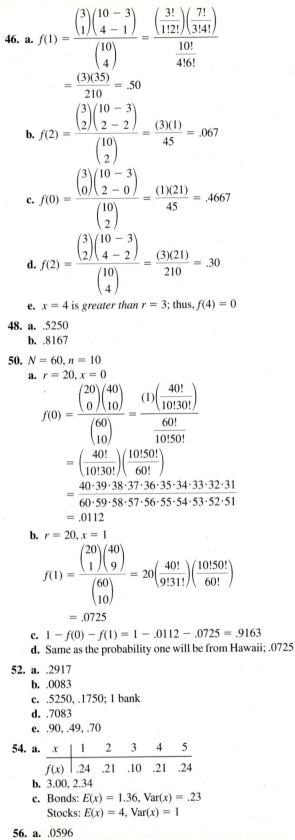

**46. a.** $f(1) = \dfrac{\binom{3}{1}\binom{10-3}{4-1}}{\binom{10}{4}} = \dfrac{\left(\frac{3!}{1!2!}\right)\left(\frac{7!}{3!4!}\right)}{\frac{10!}{4!6!}}$
  $= \dfrac{(3)(35)}{210} = .50$
  **b.** $f(2) = \dfrac{\binom{3}{2}\binom{10-3}{2-2}}{\binom{10}{2}} = \dfrac{(3)(1)}{45} = .067$
  **c.** $f(0) = \dfrac{\binom{3}{0}\binom{10-3}{2-0}}{\binom{10}{2}} = \dfrac{(1)(21)}{45} = .4667$
  **d.** $f(2) = \dfrac{\binom{3}{2}\binom{10-3}{4-2}}{\binom{10}{4}} = \dfrac{(3)(21)}{210} = .30$
  **e.** $x = 4$ is *greater than* $r = 3$; thus, $f(4) = 0$

**48. a.** .5250
  **b.** .8167

**50.** $N = 60, n = 10$
  **a.** $r = 20, x = 0$
  $f(0) = \dfrac{\binom{20}{0}\binom{40}{10}}{\binom{60}{10}} = \dfrac{(1)\left(\frac{40!}{10!30!}\right)}{\frac{60!}{10!50!}}$
  $= \left(\dfrac{40!}{10!30!}\right)\left(\dfrac{10!50!}{60!}\right)$
  $= \dfrac{40\cdot39\cdot38\cdot37\cdot36\cdot35\cdot34\cdot33\cdot32\cdot31}{60\cdot59\cdot58\cdot57\cdot56\cdot55\cdot54\cdot53\cdot52\cdot51}$
  $= .0112$
  **b.** $r = 20, x = 1$
  $f(1) = \dfrac{\binom{20}{1}\binom{40}{9}}{\binom{60}{10}} = 20\left(\dfrac{40!}{9!31!}\right)\left(\dfrac{10!50!}{60!}\right)$
  $= .0725$
  **c.** $1 - f(0) - f(1) = 1 - .0112 - .0725 = .9163$
  **d.** Same as the probability one will be from Hawaii; .0725

**52. a.** .2917
  **b.** .0083
  **c.** .5250, .1750; 1 bank
  **d.** .7083
  **e.** .90, .49, .70

**54. a.**

| $x$ | 1 | 2 | 3 | 4 | 5 |
|---|---|---|---|---|---|
| $f(x)$ | .24 | .21 | .10 | .21 | .24 |

  **b.** 3.00, 2.34
  **c.** Bonds: $E(x) = 1.36$, $\text{Var}(x) = .23$
  Stocks: $E(x) = 4$, $\text{Var}(x) = 1$

**56. a.** .0596
  **b.** .3585

**c.** 100

**d.** 95, 9.75

**58. a.** .9510

**b.** .0480

**c.** .0490

**60. a.** 240

**b.** 12.96

**c.** 12.96

**62.** .1912

**64. a.** .2240

**b.** .5767

**66. a.** .4667

**b.** .4667

**c.** .0667

# Chapter 6

**1. a.**

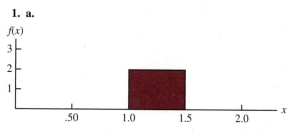

**b.** $P(x = 1.25) = 0$; the probability of any single point is zero because the area under the curve above any single point is zero

**c.** $P(1.0 \leq x \leq 1.25) = 2(.25) = .50$

**d.** $P(1.20 < x < 1.5) = 2(.30) = .60$

**2. b.** .50

**c.** .60

**d.** 15

**e.** 8.33

**4. a.**

**b.** $P(.25 < x < .75) = 1(.50) = .50$

**c.** $P(x \leq .30) = 1(.30) = .30$

**d.** $P(x > .60) = 1(.40) = .40$

**6. a.** .125

**b.** .50

**c.** .25

**10. a.** .9332

**b.** .8413

**c.** .0919

**d.** .4938

**12. a.** .2967

**b.** .4418

**c.** .3300

**d.** .5910

**e.** .8849

**f.** .2389

**13. a.** $P(-1.98 \leq z \leq .49) = P(z \leq .49) - P(z < -1.98)$
$= .6879 - .0239 = .6640$

**b.** $P(.52 \leq z \leq 1.22) = P(z \leq 1.22) - P(z < .52)$
$= .8888 - .6985 = .1903$

**c.** $P(-1.75 \leq z \leq -1.04) = P(z \leq -1.04) - P(z < -1.75) = .1492 - .0401 = .1091$

**14. a.** $z = 1.96$

**b.** $z = 1.96$

**c.** $z = .61$

**d.** $z = 1.12$

**e.** $z = .44$

**f.** $z = .44$

**15. a.** The $z$ value corresponding to a cumulative probability of .2119 is $z = -.80$

**b.** Compute $.9030/2 = .4515$; the cumulative probability of $.5000 + .4515 = .9515$ corresponds to $z = 1.66$

**c.** Compute $.2052/2 = .1026$; $z$ corresponds to a cumulative probability of $.5000 + .1026 = .6026$, so $z = .26$

**d.** The $z$ value corresponding to a cumulative probability of .9948 is $z = 2.56$

**e.** The area to the left of $z$ is $1 - .6915 = .3085$, so $z = -.50$

**16. a.** $z = 2.33$

**b.** $z = 1.96$

**c.** $z = 1.645$

**d.** $z = 1.28$

**18.** $\mu = 30$ and $\sigma = 8.2$

**a.** At $x = 40$, $z = \dfrac{40 - 30}{8.2} = 1.22$

$P(z \leq 1.22) = .8888$
$P(x \geq 40) = 1.000 - .8888 = .1112$

**b.** At $x = 20$, $z = \dfrac{20 - 30}{8.2} = -1.22$

$P(z \leq -1.22) = .1112$
$P(x \leq 20) = .1112$

**c.** A $z$ value of 1.28 cuts off an area of approximately 10% in the upper tail

$x = 30 + 8.2(1.28)$
$= 40.50$

A stock price of $40.50 or higher will put a company in the top 10%

**20. a.** .6553

**b.** 13.05 hours

**c.** .9838

**22. a.** .6553

**b.** 13.05 hours

**c.** .9838

**24. a.** 200, 26.04

**b.** .2206

  **c.** .1251

  **d.** 242.84 million

**26. a.** .5276

  **b.** .3935

  **c.** .4724

  **d.** .1341

**27. a.** $P(x \leq x_0) = 1 - e^{-x_0/3}$

  **b.** $P(x \leq 2) = 1 - e^{-2/3} = 1 - .5134 = .4866$

  **c.** $P(x \geq 3) = 1 - P(x \leq 3) = 1 - (1 - e^{-3/3})$
$$= e^{-1} = .3679$$

  **d.** $P(x \leq 5) = 1 - e^{-5/3} = 1 - .1889 = .8111$

  **e.** $P(2 \leq x \leq 5) = P(x \leq 5) - P(x \leq 2)$
$$= .8111 - .4866 = .3245$$

**28. a.** .5624

  **b.** .1915

  **c.** .2461

  **d.** .2259

**29. a.**

  **b.** $P(x \leq 12) = 1 - e^{-12/12} = 1 - .3679 = .6321$

  **c.** $P(x \leq 6) = 1 - e^{-6/12} = 1 - .6065 = .3935$

  **d.** $P(x \geq 30) = 1 - P(x < 30)$
$$= 1 - (1 - e^{-30/12})$$
$$= .0821$$

**30. a.** .3935

  **b.** .2386

  **c.** .1353

**32. a.** $f(x) = 5.5e^{-5.5x}$

  **b.** .2528

  **c.** .6002

**34. a.** $3780 or less

  **b.** 19.22%

  **c.** $8167.50

**36. a.** 3229

  **b.** .2244

  **c.** $12,382 or more

**38. a.** .0228

  **b.** $50

**40. a.** 38.3%

  **b.** 3.59% better, 96.41% worse

  **c.** 38.21%

**42.** $\mu = 19.23$ ounces

**44. a.** $\frac{1}{7}$ minute

  **b.** $7e^{-7x}$

  **c.** .0009

  **d.** .2466

**46. a.** 2 minutes

  **b.** .2212

  **c.** .3935

  **d.** .0821

# Chapter 7

**1. a.** AB, AC, AD, AE, BC, BD, BE, CD, CE, DE

  **b.** With 10 samples, each has a $\frac{1}{10}$ probability

  **c.** B and D because the two smallest random numbers are .0476 and .0957

**2.** Elements 2, 3, 5, and 10

**3.** The simple random sample consists of New York, Detroit, Oakland, Boston, and Kansas City

**4.** Step 1. Generate a random number for each stock
Step 2. Sort with respect to random numbers and select the first three stocks

**6. a.** finite

  **b.** infinite

  **c.** infinite

  **d.** finite

  **e.** infinite

**7. a.** $\bar{x} = \dfrac{\Sigma x_i}{n} = \dfrac{54}{6} = 9$

  **b.** $s = \sqrt{\dfrac{\Sigma(x_i - \bar{x})^2}{n-1}}$
$$\Sigma(x_i - \bar{x})^2 = (-4)^2 + (-1)^2 + 1^2 + (-2)^2 + 1^2 + 5^2$$
$$= 48$$
$$s = \sqrt{\dfrac{48}{6-1}} = 3.1$$

**8. a.** .50

  **b.** .3667

**9. a.** $\bar{x} = \dfrac{\Sigma x_i}{n} = \dfrac{465}{5} = 93$

  **b.**

| $x_i$ | $(x_i - \bar{x})$ | $(x_i - \bar{x})^2$ |
|---|---|---|
| 94 | +1 | 1 |
| 100 | +7 | 49 |
| 85 | −8 | 64 |
| 94 | +1 | 1 |
| 92 | −1 | 1 |
| Totals 465 | 0 | 116 |

$$s = \sqrt{\dfrac{\Sigma(x_i - \bar{x})^2}{n-1}} = \sqrt{\dfrac{116}{4}} = 5.39$$

**10. a.** .45
   **b.** .15
   **c.** .45

**12. a.** .10
   **b.** 20
   **c.** .72

**15. a.** The sampling distribution is normal with:

$$E(\bar{x}) = \mu = 200$$

$$\sigma_{\bar{x}} = \frac{\sigma}{\sqrt{n}} = \frac{50}{\sqrt{100}} = 5$$

For $+5$, $(\bar{x} - \mu) = 5$,

$$z = \frac{\bar{x} - \mu}{\sigma_{\bar{x}}} = \frac{5}{5} = 1$$

$$\text{Area} = .8413 - .1587 = .6826$$

   **b.** For $\pm 10$, $(\bar{x} - \mu) = 10$,

$$z = \frac{\bar{x} - \mu}{\sigma_{\bar{x}}} = \frac{10}{5} = 2$$

$$\text{Area} = .9772 - .0228 = .9544$$

**16.** 3.54, 2.50, 2.04, 1.77
   $\sigma_{\bar{x}}$ decreases as $n$ increases

**18. a.** Normal with $E(\bar{x}) = 51,800$ and $\sigma_{\bar{x}} = 516.40$
   **b.** $\sigma_{\bar{x}}$ decreases to 365.15
   **c.** $\sigma_{\bar{x}}$ decreases as $n$ increases

**19. a.**

$$\sigma_{\bar{x}} = \frac{\sigma}{\sqrt{n}} = \frac{4000}{\sqrt{60}} = 516.40$$

At $\bar{x} = 52,300$, $z = \dfrac{52,300 - 51,800}{516.40} = .97$

$$P(\bar{x} \le 52,300) = P(z \le .97) = .8340$$

At $\bar{x} = 51,300$, $z = \dfrac{51,300 - 51,800}{516.40} = -.97$

$$P(\bar{x} < 51,300) = P(z < -.97) = .1660$$
$$P(51,300 \le \bar{x} \le 52,300) = .8340 - .1660 = .6680$$

**Using Excel:**
NORM.DIST(52300,51800,516.40,TRUE)-
  NORM.DIST(51300,51800,516.40,TRUE) = .6671

**b.** $\sigma_{\bar{x}} = \dfrac{\sigma}{\sqrt{n}} = \dfrac{4000}{\sqrt{120}} = 365.15$

At $\bar{x} = 52,300$, $z = \dfrac{52,300 - 51,800}{365.15} = 1.37$

$$P(\bar{x} \le 52,300) = P(z \le 1.37) = .9147$$

At $\bar{x} = 51,300$, $z = \dfrac{51,300 - 51,800}{365.15} = -1.37$

$$P(\bar{x} < 51,300) = P(z < -1.37) = .0853$$
$$P(51,300 \le \bar{x} \le 52,300) = .9147 - .0853 = .8294$$

**Using Excel:**
NORM.DIST(52300,51800,365.15,TRUE)-
  NORM.DIST(51300,51800,365.15,TRUE) = .8291

**20. a.** Normal with $E(\bar{x}) = 17.5$ and $\sigma_{\bar{x}} = .57$
   **b.** .9198
   **c.** .6212

**22. a.** Using table: .4246, .5284, .6922, .9586
   **b.** Higher probability with a larger sample size

**24. a.** Normal with $E(\bar{x}) = 95$ and $\sigma_{\bar{x}} = 2.56$
   **b.** Using table: .7580; using NORM.DIST: .7595
   **c.** Using table: .8502; using NORM.DIST: .8494
   **d.** Part (c) because of the larger sample size

**26. a.** $n/N = .01$; no
   **b.** 1.29, 1.30; little difference
   **c.** Using table: .8764

**28. a.** $E(\bar{p}) = .40$

$$\sigma_{\bar{p}} = \sqrt{\frac{p(1-p)}{n}} = \sqrt{\frac{(.40)(.60)}{200}} = .0346$$

Within $\pm.03$ means $.37 \le \bar{p} \le .43$

**Using table:** $z = \dfrac{\bar{p} - p}{\sigma_{\bar{p}}} = \dfrac{.03}{.0346} = .87$

$$P(.37 \le \bar{p} \le .43) = P(-.87 \le z \le .87)$$
$$= .8078 - .1922$$
$$= .6156$$

**Using Excel:**
NORM.DIST(.43,.40,.0346,TRUE)-
  NORM.DIST(.37,.40,.0346,TRUE) = .6141

**b. Using table:** $z = \dfrac{\bar{p} - p}{\sigma_{\bar{p}}} = \dfrac{.05}{.0346} = 1.44$

$$P(.35 \le \bar{p} \le .45) = P(-1.44 \le z \le 1.44)$$
$$= .9251 - .0749$$
$$= .8502$$

**Using Excel:**
NORM.DIST(.45,.40,.0346,TRUE)-
  NORM.DIST(.35,.40,.0346,TRUE) = .8516

**30. a.** Using table: .6156; using NORM.DIST: .6175
   **b.** Using table: .7814; using NORM.DIST: .7830
   **c.** Using table: .9488; using NORM.DIST: .9490
   **d.** Using table: .9942; using NORM.DIST: .9942
   **e.** Higher probability with larger $n$

**31. a.**

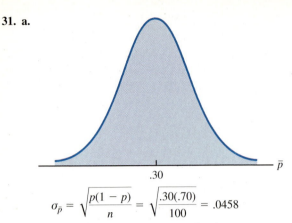

$$\sigma_{\bar{p}} = \sqrt{\frac{p(1-p)}{n}} = \sqrt{\frac{.30(.70)}{100}} = .0458$$

The normal distribution is appropriate because $np = 100(.30) = 30$ and $n(1-p) = 100(.70) = 70$ are both greater than 5

**b.** $P(.20 \leq \bar{p} \leq .40) = ?$

$$z = \frac{.40 - .30}{.0458} = 2.18$$

$$P(.20 \leq \bar{p} \leq .40) = P(-2.18 \leq z \leq 2.18)$$
$$= .9854 - .0146$$
$$= .9708$$

**Using Excel:**

NORM.DIST(.40,.30,.0458,TRUE)-
        NORM.DIST(.20,.30,.0458,TRUE) = .9710

**c.** $P(.25 \leq \bar{p} \leq .35) = ?$

$$z = \frac{.35 - .30}{.0458} = 1.09$$

$$P(.25 \leq \bar{p} \leq .35) = P(-1.09 \leq z \leq 1.09)$$
$$= .8621 - .1379$$
$$= .7242$$

**Using Excel:**

NORM.DIST(.35,.30,.0458,TRUE)-
        NORM.DIST(.25,.30,.0458,TRUE) = .7250

**32. a.** Normal with $E(\bar{p}) = .66$ and $\sigma_{\bar{p}} = .0273$
  **b.** Using table: .8584; using NORM.DIST: .8571
  **c.** Using table: .9606; using NORM.DIST: .9608
  **d.** Yes, standard error is smaller for youth population
  **e.** Using table: .9616; using NORM.DIST: .9618

**34. a.** Normal with $E(\bar{p}) = .56$ and $\sigma_{\bar{p}} = .0248$
  **b.** Using table: .5820; using NORM.DIST: .5800
  **c.** Using table: .8926; using NORM.DIST: .8932

**36. a.** Normal with $E(\bar{p}) = .76$ and $\sigma_{\bar{p}} = .0214$
  **b.** Using table: .8384; using NORM.DIST: .8390
  **c.** Using table: .9452; using NORM.DIST: .9455

**38.** Thoroughbreds, The Marker, Officers Club, SeaBlue, Crickets

**40. a.** Normal with $E(\bar{x}) = 115.50$ and $\sigma_{\bar{x}} = 5.53$
  **b.** Using table: .9298; using NORM.DIST: .9292
  **c.** Using table: $z = -2.80$, .0026;
        using NORM.DIST: .0025

**42. a.** 955
  **b.** .50

**c.** Using table: $z = \pm 1.05$, .7062;
        using NORM.DIST: .7050
**d.** .8230
        using NORM.DIST: .8234

**44. a.** 625
  **b.** .7888

**46. a.** Normal with $E(\bar{p}) = .28$ and $\sigma_{\bar{p}} = .0290$
  **b.** Using table: $z = \pm 1.38$, .8324;
        using NORM.DIST: .8322
  **c.** Using table: $z = \pm .69$, .5098;
        using NORM.DIST: .5096

**48. a.** Using table: $z = \pm 1.59$, .8882; using NORM.DIST: .8900
  **b.** Using table: $z = +1.99$, .0233; using NORM.DIST: .0232

**50. a.** 48
  **b.** Normal, $E(\bar{p}) = .25$, $\sigma_{\bar{p}} = .0625$
  **c.** .2119

# Chapter 8

**2.** Use $\bar{x} \pm z_{\alpha/2}(\sigma/\sqrt{n})$
  **a.** $32 \pm 1.645(6/\sqrt{50})$
        $32 \pm 1.4$; 30.6 to 33.4
  **b.** $32 \pm 1.96(6/\sqrt{50})$
        $32 \pm 1.66$; 30.34 to 33.66
  **c.** $32 \pm 2.576(6/\sqrt{50})$
        $32 \pm 2.19$; 29.81 to 34.19

**4.** 54

**5. a.** $1.96\sigma/\sqrt{n} = 1.96(5/\sqrt{49}) = 1.40$
  **b.** $24.80 \pm 1.40$; 23.40 to 26.20

**6.** 8.1 to 8.9

**8. a.** Population is at least approximately normal
  **b.** 3.1
  **c.** 4.1

**10. a.** \$113,638 to \$124,672
  **b.** \$112,581 to \$125,729
  **c.** \$110,515 to \$127,795
  **d.** Width increases as confidence level increases

**12. a.** 2.179
  **b.** $-1.676$
  **c.** 2.457
  **d.** $-1.708$ and 1.708
  **e.** $-2.014$ and 2.014

**13. a.** $\bar{x} = \dfrac{\Sigma x_i}{n} = \dfrac{80}{8} = 10$

  **b.** $s = \sqrt{\dfrac{\Sigma(x_i - \bar{x})^2}{n-1}} = \sqrt{\dfrac{84}{7}} = 3.46$

  **c.** $t_{.025}\left(\dfrac{s}{\sqrt{n}}\right) = 2.365\left(\dfrac{3.46}{\sqrt{8}}\right) = 2.9$

**d.** $\bar{x} \pm t_{.025}\left(\dfrac{s}{\sqrt{n}}\right)$

   $10 \pm 2.9$ (7.1 to 12.9)

**14. a.** 21.5 to 23.5
   **b.** 21.3 to 23.7
   **c.** 20.9 to 24.1
   **d.** A larger margin of error and a wider interval

**15.** $\bar{x} \pm t_{a/2}(s/\sqrt{n})$

   90% confidence: $df = 64$ and $t_{.05} = 1.669$

   $19.5 \pm 1.669\left(\dfrac{5.2}{\sqrt{65}}\right)$

   $19.5 \pm 1.08$ (18.42 to 20.58)
   95% confidence: $df = 64$ and $t_{.025} = 1.998$

   $19.5 \pm 1.998\left(\dfrac{5.2}{\sqrt{65}}\right)$

   $19.5 \pm 1.29$ (18.21 to 20.79)

**16. a.** 1.69
   **b.** 47.31 to 50.69
   **c.** Fewer hours and higher cost for United

**18. a.** 22
   **b.** 3.8014
   **c.** 18.20 to 25.80
   **d.** Larger $n$ next time

**20.** $\bar{x} = 22$; 21.48 to 22.52

**22. a.** $9269.52 to $12,540.48
   **b.** 1523
   **c.** 4,748,714; 434 million

**24. a.** Planning value of $\sigma = \dfrac{\text{Range}}{4} = \dfrac{36}{4} = 9$

   **b.** $n = \dfrac{z_{.025}^2 \sigma^2}{E^2} = \dfrac{(1.96)^2(9)^2}{(3)^2} = 34.57$; use $n = 35$

   **c.** $n = \dfrac{(1.96)^2(9)^2}{(2)^2} = 77.79$; use $n = 78$

**25. a.** Use $n = \dfrac{z_{a/2}^2 \sigma^2}{E^2}$

   $n = \dfrac{(1.96)^2(6.84)^2}{(1.5)^2} = 79.88$; use $n = 80$

   **b.** $n = \dfrac{(1.645)^2(6.84)^2}{(2)^2} = 31.65$; use $n = 32$

**26. a.** 18
   **b.** 35
   **c.** 97

**28. a.** 328
   **b.** 465
   **c.** 803
   **d.** $n$ gets larger; no to 99% confidence

**30.** 81

**31. a.** $\bar{p} = \dfrac{100}{400} = .25$

   **b.** $\sqrt{\dfrac{\bar{p}(1 - \bar{p})}{n}} = \sqrt{\dfrac{.25(.75)}{400}} = .0217$

**c.** $\bar{p} \pm z_{.025}\sqrt{\dfrac{\bar{p}(1 - \bar{p})}{n}}$

   $.25 \pm 1.96(.0217)$
   $.25 \pm .0424$; .2076 to .2924

**32. a.** .6733 to .7267
   **b.** .6682 to .7318

**34.** 1068

**35. a.** $\bar{p} = \dfrac{1760}{2000} = .88$

   **b.** Margin of error

   $z_{.05}\sqrt{\dfrac{\bar{p}(1 - \bar{p})}{n}} = 1.645\sqrt{\dfrac{.88(1 - .88)}{2000}} = .0120$

   **c.** Confidence interval:
   $.88 \pm .0120$
   or .868 to .892

   **d.** Margin of error

   $z_{.025}\sqrt{\dfrac{\bar{p}(1 - \bar{p})}{n}} = 1.96\sqrt{\dfrac{.88(1 - .88)}{2000}} = .0142$

   95% Confidence interval
   $.88 \pm .0142$ or .8658 to .8942

**36. a.** .23
   **b.** .1716 to .2884

**38. a.** .1790
   **b.** .0738; .5682 to .7158
   **c.** 354

**39. a.** $n = \dfrac{1.96^2 p^*(1 - p^*)}{E^2}$

   $n = \dfrac{1.96^2(.156)(1 - .156)}{(.03)^2} = 562$

   **b.** $n = \dfrac{2.576^2(.156)(1 - .156)}{(.03)^2} = 970.77$; use $n = 971$

**40.** .0346; .4854 to .5546

**42. a.** .0442
   **b.** 601, 1068, 2401, 9604

**44. a.** 4.00
   **b.** 29.77 to 37.77

**46. a.** 122
   **b.** $1751 to $1995
   **c.** $172.316 billion
   **d.** Less than $1873

**48. a.** 14 minutes
   **b.** 13.38 to 14.62
   **c.** 32 per day
   **d.** Staff reduction

**50.** 37

**52.** 176

**54. a.** .5420
   **b.** .0508
   **c.** .4912 to .5928

**56. a.** .8273
   **b.** .7957 to .8589
**58. a.** 1267
   **b.** 1509
**60. a.** .3101
   **b.** .2898 to .3304
   **c.** 8219; no, this sample size is unnecessarily large

## Chapter 9

**2. a.** $H_0: \mu \leq 14$
     $H_a: \mu > 14$
   **b.** No evidence that the new plan increases sales
   **c.** The research hypothesis $\mu > 14$ is supported; the new plan increases sales

**4. a.** $H_0: \mu \geq 220$
     $H_a: \mu < 220$

**5. a.** Rejecting $H_0: \mu \leq 56.2$ when it is true
   **b.** Accepting $H_0: \mu \leq 56.2$ when it is false

**6. a.** $H_0: \mu \leq 1$
     $H_a: \mu > 1$
   **b.** Claiming $\mu > 1$ when it is not true
   **c.** Claiming $\mu \leq 1$ when it is not true

**8. a.** $H_0: \mu \geq 220$
     $H_a: \mu < 220$
   **b.** Claiming $\mu < 220$ when it is not true
   **c.** Claiming $\mu \geq 220$ when it is not true

**10. a.** $z = \dfrac{\bar{x} - \mu_0}{\sigma/\sqrt{n}} = \dfrac{26.4 - 25}{6/\sqrt{40}} = 1.48$
   **b.** Using normal table with $z = 1.48$: $p$-value = $1.0000 - .9306 = .0694$
     Using Excel: $p$-value
       $= 1 - \text{NORM.S.DIST}(1.48,\text{TRUE})$
       $= .0694$
   **c.** $p$-value $> .01$, do not reject $H_0$
   **d.** Reject $H_0$ if $z \geq 2.33$
     $1.48 < 2.33$, do not reject $H_0$

**11. a.** $z = \dfrac{\bar{x} - \mu_0}{\sigma/\sqrt{n}} = \dfrac{14.15 - 15}{3/\sqrt{50}} = -2.00$
   **b.** $p$-value $= 2(.0228) = .0456$
   **c.** $p$-value $\leq .05$, reject $H_0$
   **d.** Reject $H_0$ if $z \leq -1.96$ or $z \geq 1.96$
     $-2.00 \leq -1.96$, reject $H_0$

**12. a.** .1056; do not reject $H_0$
   **b.** .0062; reject $H_0$
   **c.** $\approx 0$; reject $H_0$
   **d.** .7967; do not reject $H_0$

**14. a.** .3844; do not reject $H_0$
   **b.** .0074; reject $H_0$
   **c.** .0836; do not reject $H_0$

**15. a.** $H_0: \mu \geq 1056$
     $H_a: \mu < 1056$

**b.** $z = \dfrac{\bar{x} - \mu_0}{\sigma/\sqrt{n}} = \dfrac{910 - 1056}{1600/\sqrt{400}} = -1.83$
   $p$-value $= .0336$
   **c.** $p$-value $\leq .05$, reject $H_0$; the mean refund of "last-minute" filers is less than \$1056
   **d.** Reject $H_0$ if $z \leq -1.645$
     $-1.83 \leq -1.645$; reject $H_0$

**16. a.** $H_0: \mu \leq 3173$
     $H_a: \mu > 3173$
   **b.** .0207
   **c.** Reject $H_0$; the mean credit card balance has increased

**18. a.** $H_0: \mu = 4.1$
     $H_a: \mu \neq 4.1$
   **b.** $-2.21$, .0272
   **c.** Reject $H_0$

**20. a.** $H_0: \mu \geq 32.79$
     $H_a: \mu < 32.79$
   **b.** $-2.73$
   **c.** .0032
   **d.** Reject $H_0$; mean monthly bill in southern state is less

**22. a.** $H_0: \mu = 8$
     $H_a: \mu \neq 8$
   **b.** .1706
   **c.** Do not reject $H_0$
   **d.** 7.83 to 8.97; yes

**24. a.** $t = \dfrac{\bar{x} - \mu_0}{s/\sqrt{n}} = \dfrac{17 - 18}{4.5/\sqrt{48}} = -1.54$
   **b.** Degrees of freedom $= n - 1 = 47$
     Area in lower tail is between .05 and .10
     $p$-value (two-tail) is between .10 and .20
     Using Excel: $p$-value $= 2*\text{T.DIST}(-1.54,47,\text{TRUE})$
       $= .1303$
   **c.** $p$-value $> .05$; do not reject $H_0$
   **d.** With $df = 47$, $t_{.025} = 2.012$
     Reject $H_0$ if $t \leq -2.012$ or $t \geq 2.012$
     $t = -1.54$; do not reject $H_0$

**26. a.** Between .02 and .05; using Excel: $p$-value $= 2*[1-\text{T.DIST}(2.10,64,\text{TRUE})] = .0397$; reject $H_0$
   **b.** Between .01 and .02; using Excel: $p$-value $= 2*\text{T.DIST}(-2.57,64,\text{TRUE}) = .0125$; reject $H_0$
   **c.** Between .10 and .20; using Excel: $p$-value $= 2*[1-\text{T.DIST}(1.54,64,\text{TRUE})] = .1285$;
     do not reject $H_0$

**27. a.** $H_0: \mu \geq 238$
     $H_a: \mu < 238$
   **b.** $t = \dfrac{\bar{x} - \mu_0}{s/\sqrt{n}} = \dfrac{231 - 238}{80/\sqrt{100}} = -.88$
     Degrees of freedom $= n - 1 = 99$
     $p$-value is between .10 and .20
     Using Excel: $p$-value $= \text{T.DIST}(-.88,99,\text{TRUE}) = .1905$
   **c.** $p$-value $> .05$; do not reject $H_0$
     Cannot conclude mean weekly benefit in Virginia is less than the national mean

**d.** $df = 99$, $t_{.05} = -1.66$
Reject $H_0$ if $t \leq -1.66$
$-.88 > -1.66$; do not reject $H_0$

**28. a.** $H_0: \mu \geq 9$
$H_a: \mu < 9$

**b.** Between .005 and .01
Using Excel: $p$-value = T.DIST($-2.50$,84,TRUE)
   $= .0072$

**c.** Reject $H_0$

**30. a.** $H_0: \mu = 600$
$H_a: \mu \neq 600$

**b.** Between .20 and .40
Using Excel: $p$-value = 2*[1$-$T.DIST(1.17,39,TRUE)]
   $= .2491$

**c.** Do not reject $H_0$

**d.** A larger sample size

**32. a.** $H_0: \mu = 10{,}192$
$H_a: \mu \neq 10{,}192$

**b.** Between .02 and .05
Using Excel: $p$-value = T.DIST($-2.23$,49,TRUE)
   $= .0304$

**c.** Reject $H_0$

**34. a.** $H_0: \mu = 2$
$H_a: \mu \neq 2$

**b.** 2.2

**c.** .52

**d.** Between .20 and .40
Using Excel: $p$-value = 2*[1$-$T.DIST(1.22,9,TRUE)]
   $= .2535$

**e.** Do not reject $H_0$

**36. a.** $z = \dfrac{\bar{p} - p_0}{\sqrt{\dfrac{p_0(1 - p_0)}{n}}} = \dfrac{.68 - .75}{\sqrt{\dfrac{.75(1 - .75)}{300}}} = -2.80$

$p$-value $= .0026$
$p$-value $\leq .05$; reject $H_0$

**b.** $z = \dfrac{.72 - .75}{\sqrt{\dfrac{.75(1 - .75)}{300}}} = -1.20$

$p$-value $= .1151$
$p$-value $> .05$; do not reject $H_0$

**c.** $z = \dfrac{.70 - .75}{\sqrt{\dfrac{.75(1 - .75)}{300}}} = -2.00$

$p$-value $= .0228$
$p$-value $\leq .05$; reject $H_0$

**d.** $z = \dfrac{.77 - .75}{\sqrt{\dfrac{.75(1 - .75)}{300}}} = .80$

$p$-value $= .7881$
$p$-value $> .05$; do not reject $H_0$

**38. a.** $H_0: p = .64$
$H_a: p \neq .64$

**b.** $\bar{p} = 52/100 = .52$

$z = \dfrac{\bar{p} - p_0}{\sqrt{\dfrac{p_0(1 - p_0)}{n}}} = \dfrac{.52 - .64}{\sqrt{\dfrac{.64(1 - .64)}{100}}} = -2.50$

Area $= .4938$
$p$-value $= 2(.0062) = .0124$

**c.** $p$-value $\leq .05$; reject $H_0$
Proportion differs from the reported .64

**d.** Yes, because $\bar{p} = .52$ indicates that fewer believe the supermarket brand is as good as the name brand

**40. a.** .35

**b.** $H_0: p \geq .46$
$H_a: p < .46$
$p$-value $= .0436$

**c.** Proportion providing gifts has decreased

**42. a.** $\bar{p} = .15$

**b.** .0718 to .2218

**c.** Houston proportion is different

**44. a.** $H_0: p \leq .51$
$H_a: p > .51$

**b.** $p$-value $= 1-$NORM.S.DIST(2.80,TRUE) $= .0026$

**c.** reject $H_0$

**46. a.** $H_0: \mu = 16$
$H_a: \mu \neq 16$

**b.** .0286; reject $H_0$
Readjust line

**c.** .2186; do not reject $H_0$
Continue operation

**d.** $z = 2.19$; reject $H_0$
$z = -1.23$; do not reject $H_0$
Yes, same conclusion

**48. a.** $H_0: \mu \leq 119{,}155$
$H_a: \mu > 119{,}155$

**b.** .0047

**c.** Reject $H_0$

**50.** $t = -.93$
$p$-value between .20 and .40
Using Excel: $p$-value = 2*T.DIST($-1.05$,41,TRUE)
   $= .2999$
Do not reject $H_0$

**52.** $t = 2.26$
$p$-value between .01 and .025
Using Excel: $p$-value = 1$-$T.DIST(2.26,31,TRUE)
   $= .0155$
Reject $H_0$

**54. a.** $H_0: p \leq .80$
$H_a: p > .80$
$p$-value $= .0099$
Over 80% feel body scanners will improve security

**b.** $H_0: p \leq .75$
$H_a: p > .75$
$p$-value $= .0537$
Cannot conclude that over 75% approve using

**56. a.** $H_0: p \leq .80$
$H_a: p > .80$
**b.** .84
**c.** .0418; reject $H_0$; more than 80% are satisfied with service

**58.** $H_0: p \geq .90$
$H_a: p < .90$
p-value = .0808
Do not reject $H_0$

# Chapter 10

**1. a.** $\bar{x}_1 - \bar{x}_2 = 13.6 - 11.6 = 2$
**b.** $z_{\alpha/2} = z_{.05} = 1.645$

$$\bar{x}_1 - \bar{x}_2 \pm 1.645\sqrt{\frac{\sigma_1^2}{n_1} + \frac{\sigma_2^2}{n_2}}$$

$$2 \pm 1.645\sqrt{\frac{(2.2)^2}{50} + \frac{(3)^2}{35}}$$

$$2 \pm .98 \quad (1.02 \text{ to } 2.98)$$

**c.** $z_{\alpha/2} = z_{.05} = 1.96$

$$2 \pm 1.96\sqrt{\frac{(2.2)^2}{50} + \frac{(3)^2}{35}}$$

$$2 \pm 1.17 \ (.83 \text{ to } 3.17)$$

**2. a.** $z = \dfrac{(\bar{x}_1 - \bar{x}_2) - D_0}{\sqrt{\dfrac{\sigma_1^2}{n_1} + \dfrac{\sigma_2^2}{n_2}}} = \dfrac{(25.2 - 22.8) - 0}{\sqrt{\dfrac{(5.2)^2}{40} + \dfrac{(6)^2}{50}}} = 2.03$

**b.** p-value = 1.0000 − .9788 = .0212
**c.** p-value ≤ .05; reject $H_0$

**4. a.** $\bar{x}_1 - \bar{x}_2 = 85.36 - 81.40 = 3.96$

**b.** $z_{.025}\sqrt{\dfrac{\sigma_1^2}{n_1} + \dfrac{\sigma_2^2}{n_2}}$

$$1.96\sqrt{\frac{(4.55)^2}{37} + \frac{(3.97)^2}{44}} = 1.88$$

**c.** $3.96 \pm 1.88 \quad (2.08 \text{ to } 5.84)$

**6.** p-value = .0351
Reject $H_0$; mean price in Atlanta is lower than in Houston

**8. a.** $z = 2.74$, p-value = .0031
Conclude that customer service has improved for RiteAid
**b.** $z = .39$, p-value = .3483
Difference is not statistically significant
**c.** $z = 1.83$, p-value = .0336
Conclude customer service has improved
**d.** Increase must be 1.80 or more for the difference to be statistically significant
**e.** Not statistically significant

**9. a.** $\bar{x}_1 - \bar{x}_2 = 22.5 - 20.1 = 2.4$

**b.** $df = \dfrac{\left(\dfrac{s_1^2}{n_1} + \dfrac{s_2^2}{n_2}\right)^2}{\dfrac{1}{n_1 - 1}\left(\dfrac{s_1^2}{n_1}\right)^2 + \dfrac{1}{n_2 - 1}\left(\dfrac{s_2^2}{n_2}\right)^2}$

$$= \frac{\left(\dfrac{2.5^2}{20} + \dfrac{4.8^2}{30}\right)^2}{\dfrac{1}{19}\left(\dfrac{2.5^2}{20}\right)^2 + \dfrac{1}{29}\left(\dfrac{4.8^2}{30}\right)^2} = 45.8$$

**c.** $df = 45$, $t_{.025} = 2.014$

$$t_{.025}\sqrt{\frac{s_1^2}{n_1} + \frac{s_2^2}{n_2}} = 2.014\sqrt{\frac{2.5^2}{20} + \frac{4.8^2}{30}} = 2.1$$

**d.** $2.4 \pm 2.1 \ (.3 \text{ to } 4.5)$

**10. a.** $t = \dfrac{(\bar{x}_1 - \bar{x}_2) - 0}{\sqrt{\dfrac{s_1^2}{n_1} + \dfrac{s_2^2}{n_2}}} = \dfrac{(13.6 - 10.1) - 0}{\sqrt{\dfrac{5.2^2}{35} + \dfrac{8.5^2}{40}}} = 2.18$

**b.** $df = \dfrac{\left(\dfrac{s_1^2}{n_1} + \dfrac{s_2^2}{n_2}\right)^2}{\dfrac{1}{n_1 - 1}\left(\dfrac{s_1^2}{n_1}\right)^2 + \dfrac{1}{n_2 - 1}\left(\dfrac{s_2^2}{n_2}\right)^2}$

$$= \frac{\left(\dfrac{5.2^2}{35} + \dfrac{8.5^2}{40}\right)^2}{\dfrac{1}{34}\left(\dfrac{5.2^2}{35}\right)^2 + \dfrac{1}{39}\left(\dfrac{8.5^2}{40}\right)^2} = 65.7$$

Use $df = 65$
**c.** $df = 65$, area in tail is between .01 and .025;
two-tailed p-value is between .02 and .05
Exact p-value = .0329
**d.** p-value ≤ .05; reject $H_0$

**12. a.** $\bar{x}_1 - \bar{x}_2 = 22.5 - 18.6 = 3.9$ miles

**b.** $df = \dfrac{\left(\dfrac{s_1^2}{n_1} + \dfrac{s_2^2}{n_2}\right)^2}{\dfrac{1}{n_1 - 1}\left(\dfrac{s_1^2}{n_1}\right)^2 + \dfrac{1}{n_2 - 1}\left(\dfrac{s_2^2}{n_2}\right)^2}$

$$= \frac{\left(\dfrac{8.4^2}{50} + \dfrac{7.4^2}{40}\right)^2}{\dfrac{1}{49}\left(\dfrac{8.4^2}{50}\right)^2 + \dfrac{1}{39}\left(\dfrac{7.4^2}{40}\right)^2} = 87.1$$

Use $df = 87$, $t_{.025} = 1.988$

$$3.9 \pm 1.988\sqrt{\frac{8.4^2}{50} + \frac{7.4^2}{40}}$$

$$3.9 \pm 3.3 \ (.6 \text{ to } 7.2)$$

**14. a.** $H_0: \mu_1 - \mu_2 \geq 0$
$H_a: \mu_1 - \mu_2 < 0$
**b.** −2.41
**c.** Using t table, p-value is between .005 and .01
Exact p-value = .009
**d.** Reject $H_0$; conclude salaries of staff nurses are lower in Tampa

**16. a.** $H_0: \mu_1 - \mu_2 \leq 0$
$H_a: \mu_1 - \mu_2 > 0$
**b.** 3 points higher for midpriced family sedans
**c.** Using t table, p-value is greater than .20
Exact p-value is .2671
**d.** p-value > .05; we cannot conclude that the mean road-test score for midpriced family sedans is significantly greater

**18. a.** $H_0: \mu_1 - \mu_2 \geq 120$
   $H_a: \mu_1 - \mu_2 < 120$
   **b.** $-2.10$
   Using $t$ table, $p$-value is between .01 and .025
   Exact $p$-value $= .0195$
   **c.** 32 to 118
   **d.** Larger sample size

**19. a.** 1, 2, 0, 0, 2
   **b.** $\bar{d} = \Sigma d_i/n = 5/5 = 1$
   **c.** $s_d = \sqrt{\dfrac{\Sigma(d_i - \bar{d})^2}{n - 1}} = \sqrt{\dfrac{4}{5 - 1}} = 1$
   **d.** $t = \dfrac{\bar{d} - \mu}{s_d/\sqrt{n}} = \dfrac{1 - 0}{1/\sqrt{5}} = 2.24$
   $df = n - 1 = 4$
   Using $t$ table, $p$-value is between .025 and .05
   Exact $p$-value $= .0443$
   $p$-value $\leq .05$; reject $H_0$

**20. a.** 3, $-1$, 3, 5, 3, 0, 1
   **b.** 2
   **c.** 2.08
   **d.** 2
   **e.** .07 to 3.93

**21.** $H_0: \mu_d \leq 0$
   $H_a: \mu_d > 0$
   $\bar{d} = .625$
   $s_d = 1.30$
   $t = \dfrac{\bar{d} - \mu_d}{s_d/\sqrt{n}} = \dfrac{.625 - 0}{1.30/\sqrt{8}} = 1.36$
   $df = n - 1 = 7$
   Using $t$ table, $p$-value is between .10 and .20
   Exact $p$-value $= .1080$
   $p$-value $> .05$; do not reject $H_0$

**22.** $.10$ to $.32$

**24.** $t = 1.32$
   Using $t$ table, $p$-value is greater than .10
   Exact $p$-value $= .1142$
   Do not reject $H_0$

**26. a.** $H_0: \mu_d = 0$
   $H_a: \mu_d \neq 0$
   $t = -1.42$, $p$-value $= .1718$
   Conclude there is no significant difference between first and fourth round scores
   **b.** $\bar{d} = -1.05$, first round scores lower
   **c.** 1.28, yes

**28. a.** $\bar{\bar{x}} = (156 + 142 + 134)/3 = 144$
   $$\text{SSTR} = \sum_{j=1}^{k} n_j(\bar{x}_j - \bar{\bar{x}})^2$$
   $$= 6(156 - 144)^2 + 6(142 - 144)^2 + 6(134 - 144)^2$$
   $$= 1488$$
   **b.** $\text{MSTR} = \dfrac{\text{SSTR}}{k - 1} = \dfrac{1488}{2} = 744$

**c.** $s_1^2 = 164.4$,   $s_2^2 = 131.2$,   $s_3^2 = 110.4$
   $$\text{SSE} = \sum_{j=1}^{k} (n_j - 1)s_j^2$$
   $$= 5(164.4) + 5(131.2) + 5(110.4)$$
   $$= 2030$$
   **d.** $\text{MSE} = \dfrac{\text{SSE}}{n_T - k} = \dfrac{2030}{18 - 3} = 135.3$
   **e.**

| Source of Variation | Sum of Squares | Degrees of Freedom | Mean Square | F | p-value |
|---|---|---|---|---|---|
| Treatments | 1488 | 2 | 744 | 5.50 | .0162 |
| Error | 2030 | 15 | 135.3 | | |
| Total | 3518 | 17 | | | |

**f.** $F = \dfrac{\text{MSTR}}{\text{MSE}} = \dfrac{744}{135.3} = 5.50$
   From the $F$ table (2 numerator degrees of freedom and 15 denominator), $p$-value is between .01 and .025
   Using Excel, the $p$-value corresponding to $F = 5.50$ is .0162
   Because $p$-value $\leq \alpha = .05$, we reject the hypothesis that the means for the three treatments are equal

**30. a.** $H_0: \mu_1 = \mu_2 = \mu_3 = \mu_4 = \mu_5$
   $H_a$: Not all the population means are equal
   **b.** Yes; $p$-value $= .0000$

**32. a.**

| Source of Variation | Sum of Squares | Degrees of Freedom | Mean Square | F | p-value |
|---|---|---|---|---|---|
| Treatments | 1200 | 2 | 600 | 43.99 | .0000 |
| Error | 600 | 44 | 13.64 | | |
| Total | 1800 | 46 | | | |

Significant relationship

**34. a.**

| Source of Variation | Sum of Squares | Degrees of Freedom | Mean Square | F | p-value |
|---|---|---|---|---|---|
| Treatments | 4560 | 2 | 2280 | 9.87 | .0006 |
| Error | 6240 | 27 | 231.11 | | |
| Total | 10800 | 29 | | | |

**b.** Significant relationship

**36.** No significant relationship: $p$-value $= .2104$

**38.** $p$-value $= .0931$; at the .05 level of significance we cannot reject the null hypothesis that the mean drying times for the four paints are equal

**40. a.** 412
   **b.** 267.79
   **c.** $412 \pm 267.79$

**42. a.** $H_0: \mu_1 - \mu_2 \leq 0$
$H_a: \mu_1 - \mu_2 > 0$

   **b.** $t = .60$, $df = 57$
Using $t$ table, $p$-value is greater than .20
Exact $p$-value = .2754
Do not reject $H_0$

**44. a.** $\bar{d} = 2.45$
   **b.** \$.30 to \$4.60
   **c.** 8% decrease
   **d.** \$23.93

**46.** Significant relationship; $p$-value = .0061

**48.** Significant difference; $p$-value = .0002

**50.** Significant relationship; $p$-value = .0340

## Chapter 11

**1. a.** $\bar{p}_1 - \bar{p}_2 = .48 - .36 = .12$

   **b.** $\bar{p}_1 - \bar{p}_2 \pm z_{.05} \sqrt{\dfrac{\bar{p}_1(1 - \bar{p}_1)}{n_1} + \dfrac{\bar{p}_2(1 - \bar{p}_2)}{n_2}}$

$.12 \pm 1.645 \sqrt{\dfrac{.48(1 - .48)}{400} + \dfrac{.36(1 - .36)}{300}}$

$.12 \pm .0614$ (.0586 to .1814)

   **c.** $.12 \pm 1.96 \sqrt{\dfrac{.48(1 - .48)}{400} + \dfrac{.36(1 - .36)}{300}}$

$.12 \pm .0731$ (.0469 to .1931)

**2. a.** $\bar{p} = \dfrac{n_1 \bar{p}_1 + n_2 \bar{p}_2}{n_1 + n_2} = \dfrac{200(.22) + 300(.16)}{200 + 300} = .1840$

$z = \dfrac{\bar{p}_1 - \bar{p}_2}{\sqrt{\bar{p}(1 - \bar{p})\left(\dfrac{1}{n_1} + \dfrac{1}{n_2}\right)}}$

$= \dfrac{.22 - .16}{\sqrt{.1840(1 - .1840)\left(\dfrac{1}{200} + \dfrac{1}{300}\right)}} = 1.70$

$p$-value = $1.0000 - .9554 = .0446$

   **b.** $p$-value $\leq .05$; reject $H_0$

**3. a.** Professional Golfers: $\bar{p}_1 = 688/1075 = .64$
Amateur Golfers: $\bar{p}_2 = 696/1200 = .58$
Professional golfers have the better putting accuracy

   **b.** $\bar{p}_1 - \bar{p}_2 = .64 - .58 = .06$
Professional golfers make 6% more 6-foot putts than the very best amateur golfers

   **c.** $\bar{p}_1 - \bar{p}_2 \pm z_{.025} \sqrt{\dfrac{\bar{p}_1(1 - \bar{p}_1)}{n_1} + \dfrac{\bar{p}_2(1 - \bar{p}_2)}{n_2}}$

$.64 - .58 \pm 1.96 \sqrt{\dfrac{.64(1 - .64)}{1075} + \dfrac{.58(1 - .58)}{1200}}$

$.06 \pm .04$ (.02 to .10)

The confidence interval shows that professional golfers make from 2% to 10% more 6-foot putts than the best amateur golfers

**4. a.** $H_0: p_w \leq p_m$
$H_a: p_w > p_m$

   **b.** $\bar{p}_w = .3699$
   **c.** $\bar{p}_m = .3400$
   **d.** $p$-value = .1093
Do not reject $H_0$

**6. a.** $H_0: p_1 - p_2 = 0$
$H_a: p_1 - p_2 \neq 0$

   **b.** .28
   **c.** .26
   **d.** .3078, do not reject

**8. a.** $H_0: p_1 - p_2 = 0$
$H_a: p_1 - p_2 \neq 0$

   **b.** .13
   **c.** $p$-value = .0404

**10. a.** $H_0: p_1 - p_2 = 0$
$H_a: p_1 - p_2 \neq 0$

   **b.** .27, .17
   **c.** $p$-value $\approx 0$
Difference is significant

**11. a.** Expected frequencies: $e_1 = 200(.40) = 80$
$e_2 = 200(.40) = 80$
$e_3 = 200(.20) = 40$
Actual frequencies: $f_1 = 60, f_2 = 120, f_3 = 20$

$\chi^2 = \dfrac{(60 - 80)^2}{80} + \dfrac{(120 - 80)^2}{80} + \dfrac{(20 - 40)^2}{40}$

$= \dfrac{400}{80} + \dfrac{1600}{80} + \dfrac{400}{40}$

$= 5 + 20 + 10 = 35$

Degrees of freedom: $k - 1 = 2$
$\chi^2 = 35$ shows $p$-value is less than .005
$p$-value $\leq .01$; reject $H_0$

   **b.** Reject $H_0$ if $\chi^2 \geq 9.210$
$\chi^2 = 35$; reject $H_0$

**12.** $\chi^2 = 15.33$, $df = 3$
$p$-value less than .005
Reject $H_0$

**13.** $H_0: p_{ABC} = .29, p_{CBS} = .28, p_{NBC} = .25, p_{IND} = .18$
$H_a$: The proportions are not
$p_{ABC} = .29, p_{CBS} = .28, p_{NBC} = .25, p_{IND} = .18$
Expected frequencies: $300(.29) = 87, 300(.28) = 84$
$300(.25) = 75, 300(.18) = 54$
$e_1 = 87, e_2 = 84, e_3 = 75, e_4 = 54$
Actual frequencies: $f_1 = 95, f_2 = 70, f_3 = 89, f_4 = 46$

$\chi^2 = \dfrac{(95 - 87)^2}{87} + \dfrac{(70 - 84)^2}{84} + \dfrac{(89 - 75)^2}{75}$

$+ \dfrac{(46 - 54)^2}{54} = 6.87$

Degrees of freedom: $k - 1 = 3$
$\chi^2 = 6.87$, $p$-value between .05 and .10
Do not reject $H_0$

**14.** $\chi^2 = 29.51$, $df = 5$
$p$-value is less than .005
Reject $H_0$

**16. a.** $\chi^2 = 12.21$, $df = 3$
$p$-value is between .005 and .01
Conclude difference for 2003
**b.** 21%, 30%, 15%, 34%
Increased use of debit card
**c.** 51%

**18.** $\chi^2 = 16.31$, $df = 3$
$p$-value less than .005
Reject $H_0$

**19.** $H_0$: The column variable is independent of the row variable
$H_a$: The column variable is not independent of the row variable

Expected frequencies:

|   | A | B | C |
|---|---|---|---|
| P | 28.5 | 39.9 | 45.6 |
| Q | 21.5 | 30.1 | 34.4 |

$$\chi^2 = \frac{(20 - 28.5)^2}{28.5} + \frac{(44 - 39.9)^2}{39.9} + \frac{(50 - 45.6)^2}{45.6}$$
$$+ \frac{(30 - 21.5)^2}{21.5} + \frac{(26 - 30.1)^2}{30.1} + \frac{(30 - 34.4)^2}{34.4}$$
$$= 7.86$$

Degrees of freedom: $(2 - 1)(3 - 1) = 2$
$\chi^2 = 7.86$, $p$-value between .01 and .025
Reject $H_0$

**20.** $\chi^2 = 19.77$, $df = 4$
$p$-value less than .005
Reject $H_0$

**21.** $H_0$: Type of ticket purchased is independent of the type of flight
$H_a$: Type of ticket purchased is not independent of the type of flight

Expected frequencies:

$e_{11} = 35.59$      $e_{12} = 15.41$
$e_{21} = 150.73$    $e_{22} = 65.27$
$e_{31} = 455.68$    $e_{32} = 197.32$

| Ticket | Flight | Observed Frequency ($f_i$) | Expected Frequency ($e_i$) | $(f_i - e_i)^2/e_i$ |
|---|---|---|---|---|
| First | Domestic | 29 | 35.59 | 1.22 |
| First | International | 22 | 15.41 | 2.82 |
| Business | Domestic | 95 | 150.73 | 20.61 |
| Business | International | 121 | 65.27 | 47.59 |
| Full-fare | Domestic | 518 | 455.68 | 8.52 |
| Full-fare | International | 135 | 197.32 | 19.68 |
| Totals | | 920 | | $\chi^2 = 100.43$ |

Degrees of freedom: $(3 - 1)(2 - 1) = 2$
$\chi^2 = 100.43$, $p$-value is less than .005
Reject $H_0$

**22. a.** $\chi^2 = 7.95$, $df = 3$
$p$-value is between .025 and .05
Reject $H_0$
**b.** 18 to 24 use most

**24. a.** $\chi^2 = 8.47$; $p$-value is between .025 and .05
Reject $H_0$; intent to purchase again is not independent of the automobile
**b.** Accord 77, Camry 71, Taurus 62, Impala 57
**c.** Impala and Taurus below, Accord and Camry above; Accord and Camry have greater owner satisfaction, which may help future market share

**26. a.** 6448
**b.** $\chi^2 = 424.6674$
$p$-value $\approx 0$
Reject $H_0$
**c.** Italy

**28.** $\chi^2 = 3.01$, $df = 2$
$p$-value is greater than .10
Do not reject $H_0$; 63.3%

**30. a.** $p$-value $\approx 0$; reject $H_0$
**b.** .0468 to .1332

**32. a.** .35, .47
**b.** .0163 to .2237
**c.** Yes

**34.** $\chi^2 = 8.04$, $df = 3$
$p$-value between .025 and .05
Reject $H_0$

**36.** $\chi^2 = 4.64$, $df = 2$
$p$-value between .05 and .10
Do not reject $H_0$

**38.** $\chi^2 = 42.53$, $df = 4$
$p$-value is less than .005
Reject $H_0$

**40.** $\chi^2 = 23.37$, $df = 3$
$p$-value is less than .005
Reject $H_0$

**42. a.** 71%, 22%, slower preferred
**b.** $\chi^2 = 2.99$, $df = 2$
$p$-value greater than .10
Do not reject $H_0$; cannot conclude men and women differ in preference

**44.** $\chi^2 = 7.75$, $df = 3$
$p$-value is between .05 and .10
Do not reject $H_0$

# Chapter 12

**1. a.**

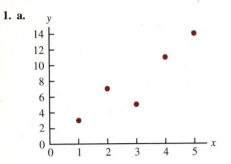

**b.** There appears to be a positive linear relationship between $x$ and $y$

**c.** Many different straight lines can be drawn to provide a linear approximation of the relationship between $x$ and $y$; in part (d) we will determine the equation of a straight line that "best" represents the relationship according to the least squares criterion

**d.** Summations needed to compute the slope and $y$-intercept:

$$\bar{x} = \frac{\Sigma x_i}{n} = \frac{15}{5} = 3, \quad \bar{y} = \frac{\Sigma y_i}{n} = \frac{40}{5} = 8,$$

$$\Sigma(x_i - \bar{x})(y_i - \bar{y}) = 26, \quad \Sigma(x_i - \bar{x})^2 = 10$$

$$b_1 = \frac{\Sigma(x_i - \bar{x})(y_i - \bar{y})}{\Sigma(x_i - \bar{x})^2} = \frac{26}{10} = 2.6$$

$$b_0 = \bar{y} - b_1\bar{x} = 8 - (2.6)(3) = 0.2$$

$$\hat{y} = 0.2 - 2.6x$$

**e.** $\hat{y} = .2 + 2.6x = .2 + 2.6(4) = 10.6$

**2. b.** There appears to be a negative linear relationship between $x$ and $y$

**d.** $\hat{y} = 68 - 3x$

**e.** 38

**4. a.**

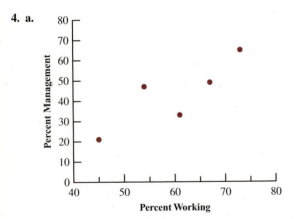

**b.** There appears to be a positive linear relationship between the percentage of women working in the five companies ($x$) and the percentage of management jobs held by women in that company ($y$)

**c.** Many different straight lines can be drawn to provide a linear approximation of the relationship between $x$ and $y$; in part (d) we will determine the equation of a straight line that "best" represents the relationship according to the least squares criterion.

**d.** $\bar{x} = \dfrac{\Sigma x_i}{n} = \dfrac{300}{5} = 60 \quad \bar{y} = \dfrac{\Sigma y_i}{n} = \dfrac{215}{5} = 43$

$$\Sigma(x_i - \bar{x})(y_i - \bar{y}) = 624 \quad \Sigma(x_i - \bar{x})^2 = 480$$

$$b_1 = \frac{\Sigma(x_i - \bar{x})(y_i - \bar{y})}{\Sigma(x_i - \bar{x})^2} = \frac{624}{480} = 1.3$$

$$b_0 = \bar{y} - b_1\bar{x} = 43 - 1.3(60) = -35$$

$$\hat{y} = -35 + 1.3x$$

**e.** $\hat{y} = -35 + 1.3x = -35 + 1.3(60) = 43\%$

**6. c.** $\hat{y} = 8.9412 - .02633x$

**e.** 6.3 or approximately $6300

**8. c.** $\hat{y} = 359.2668 - 5.2772x$

**d.** $254

**10. c.** $\hat{y} = -6,745.44 + 149.29x$

**d.** 4003 or $4,003,000

**12. c.** $\hat{y} = -8129.4439 + 22.4443x$

**d.** $8704

**14. c.** $\hat{y} = 37.1217 + .51758x$

**d.** 73

**15. a.** $\hat{y}_i = .2 + 2.6x_i$ and $\bar{y} = 8$

| $x_i$ | $y_i$ | $\hat{y}_i$ | $y_i - \hat{y}_i$ | $(y_i - \hat{y}_i)^2$ | $y_i - \bar{y}$ | $(y_i - \bar{y})^2$ |
|---|---|---|---|---|---|---|
| 1 | 3 | 2.8 | .2 | .04 | -5 | 25 |
| 2 | 7 | 5.4 | 1.6 | 2.56 | -1 | 1 |
| 3 | 5 | 8.0 | -3.0 | 9.00 | -3 | 9 |
| 4 | 11 | 10.6 | .4 | .16 | 3 | 9 |
| 5 | 14 | 13.2 | .8 | .64 | 6 | 36 |
| | | | SSE = | 12.40 | SST = | 80 |

$$\text{SSR} = \text{SST} - \text{SSE} = 80 - 12.4 = 67.6$$

**b.** $r^2 = \dfrac{\text{SSR}}{\text{SST}} = \dfrac{67.6}{80} = .845$

The least squares line provided a good fit; 84.5% of the variability in $y$ has been explained by the least squares line

**c.** $r_{xy} = \sqrt{.845} = +.9192$

**16. a.** SSE = 230, SST = 1850, SSR = 1620

**b.** $r^2 = .876$

**c.** $r_{xy} = -.936$

**18. a.** The estimated regression equation and the mean for the dependent variable:

$$\hat{y} = 1790.5 + 581.1x, \quad \bar{y} = 3650$$

The sum of squares due to error and the total sum of squares:

$$\text{SSE} = \Sigma(y_i - \hat{y}_i)^2 = 85,135.14$$

$$\text{SST} = \Sigma(y_i - \bar{y})^2 = 335,000$$

Thus, SSR = SST - SSE

$$= 335,000 - 85,135.14 = 249,864.86$$

**b.** $r^2 = \dfrac{\text{SSR}}{\text{SST}} = \dfrac{249{,}864.86}{335{,}000} = .746$

The least squares line accounted for 74.6% of the total sum of squares

**c.** $r_{xy} = \sqrt{.746} = +.8637$

**20. a.** $\hat{y} = 12.0169 + .0127x$

**b.** $r^2 = .4503$

**c.** 53

**22. a.** .77

**b.** Yes

**c.** $r_{xy} = +.88$, strong

**23. a.** $s^2 = \text{MSE} = \dfrac{\text{SSE}}{n-2} = \dfrac{12.4}{3} = 4.133$

**b.** $s = \sqrt{\text{MSE}} = \sqrt{4.133} = 2.033$

**c.** $\Sigma(x_i - \bar{x})^2 = 10$

$$s_{b_1} = \dfrac{s}{\sqrt{\Sigma(x_i - \bar{x})^2}} = \dfrac{2.033}{\sqrt{10}} = .643$$

**d.** $t = \dfrac{b_1 - \beta_1}{s_{b_1}} = \dfrac{2.6 - 0}{.643} = 4.044$

From the $t$ table (3 degrees of freedom), area in tail is between .01 and .025

$p$-value is between .02 and .05

Using Excel, the $p$-value corresponding to $t = 4.04$ is .0272

Because $p$-value $\leq \alpha$, we reject $H_0$: $\beta_1 = 0$

**e.** $\text{MSR} = \dfrac{\text{SSR}}{1} = 67.6$

$$F = \dfrac{\text{MSR}}{\text{MSE}} = \dfrac{67.6}{4.133} = 16.36$$

From the $F$ table (1 numerator degree of freedom and 3 denominator), $p$-value is between .025 and .05

Using Excel, the $p$-value corresponding to $F = 16.36$ is .0272

Because $p$-value $\leq \alpha$, we reject $H_0$: $\beta_1 = 0$

| Source of Variation | Sum of Squares | Degrees of Freedom | Mean Square | F | p-value |
|---|---|---|---|---|---|
| Regression | 67.6 | 1 | 67.6 | 16.36 | .0272 |
| Error | 12.4 | 3 | 4.133 | | |
| Total | 80 | 4 | | | |

**24. a.** 76.6667

**b.** 8.7560

**c.** .6526

**d.** Significant; $p$-value $= .0193$

**e.** Significant; $p$-value $= .0193$

**26. a.** $s^2 = \text{MSE} = \dfrac{\text{SSE}}{n-2} = \dfrac{85{,}135.14}{4} = 21{,}283.79$

$s = \sqrt{\text{MSE}} = \sqrt{21{,}283.79} = 145.89$

$\Sigma(x_i - \bar{x})^2 = .74$

$$s_{b_1} = \dfrac{s}{\sqrt{\Sigma(x_i - \bar{x})^2}} = \dfrac{145.89}{\sqrt{.74}} = 169.59$$

$$t = \dfrac{b_1 - \beta_1}{s_{b_1}} = \dfrac{581.08 - 0}{169.59} = 3.43$$

From the $t$ table (4 degrees of freedom), area in tail is between .01 and .025

$p$-value is between .02 and .05

Using Excel, the $p$-value corresponding to $t = 3.43$ is .0266

Because $p$-value $\leq \alpha$, we reject $H_0$: $\beta_1 = 0$

**b.** $\text{MSR} = \dfrac{\text{SSR}}{1} = \dfrac{249{,}864.86}{1} = 249{,}864.86$

$$F = \dfrac{\text{MSR}}{\text{MSE}} = \dfrac{249{,}864.86}{21{,}283.79} = 11.74$$

From the $F$ table (1 numerator degree of freedom and 4 denominator), $p$-value is between .025 and .05

Using Excel, the $p$-value corresponding to $F = 11.74$ is .0266

Because $p$-value $\leq \alpha$, we reject $H_0$: $\beta_1 = 0$

**c.**

| Source of Variation | Sum of Squares | Degrees of Freedom | Mean Square | F | p-value |
|---|---|---|---|---|---|
| Regression | 249,864.86 | 1 | 249,864.86 | 11.74 | .0266 |
| Error | 85,135.14 | 4 | 21,283.79 | | |
| Total | 335,000 | 5 | | | |

**28.** They are related; $p$-value $= .000$

**30.** Significant; $p$-value $= .0042$

**32. a.** $s = 2.033$

$\bar{x} = 3$, $\Sigma(x_i - \bar{x})^2 = 10$

$$s_{\hat{y}^*} = s\sqrt{\dfrac{1}{n} + \dfrac{(x^* - \bar{x})^2}{\Sigma(x_i - \bar{x})^2}}$$

$$= 2.033\sqrt{\dfrac{1}{5} + \dfrac{(4 - 3)^2}{10}} = 1.11$$

**b.** $\hat{y}^* = .2 + 2.6x^* = .2 + 2.6(4) = 10.6$

$\hat{y}^* \pm t_{\alpha/2}s_{\hat{y}^*}$

$10.6 \pm 3.182(1.11)$

$10.6 \pm 3.53$, or 7.07 to 14.13

**c.** $s_{\text{pred}} = s\sqrt{1 + \dfrac{1}{n} + \dfrac{(x^* - \bar{x})^2}{\Sigma(x_i - \bar{x})^2}}$

$$= 2.033\sqrt{1 + \dfrac{1}{5} + \dfrac{(4 - 3)^2}{10}} = 2.32$$

**d.** $\hat{y}^* \pm t_{\alpha/2}s_{\text{pred}}$

$10.6 \pm 3.182(2.32)$

$10.6 \pm 7.38$, or 3.22 to 17.98

**34.** Confidence interval: 8.65 to 21.15
Prediction interval: −4.50 to 41.30

**35. a.** $s = 145.89$, $\bar{x} = 3.2$, $\Sigma(x_i - \bar{x})^2 = .74$

$$\hat{y}^* = 1790.5 + 581.1x^* = 1790.5 + 581.1(3)$$
$$= 3533.8$$

$$s_{\hat{y}^*} = s\sqrt{\frac{1}{n} + \frac{(x^* - \bar{x})^2}{\Sigma(x_i - \bar{x})^2}}$$

$$= 145.89\sqrt{\frac{1}{6} + \frac{(3 - 3.2)^2}{.74}} = 68.54$$

$$\hat{y}^* \pm t_{\alpha/2}s_{\hat{y}^*}$$

$$3533.8 \pm 2.776(68.54)$$

$$3533.8 \pm 190.27, \text{ or } \$3343.53 \text{ to } \$3724.07$$

**b.** $s_{\text{pred}} = s\sqrt{1 + \frac{1}{n} + \frac{(x^* - \bar{x})^2}{\Sigma(x_i - \bar{x})^2}}$

$$= 145.89\sqrt{1 + \frac{1}{6} + \frac{(3 - 3.2)^2}{.74}} = 161.19$$

$$\hat{y}^* \pm t_{\alpha/2}s_{\text{pred}}$$
$$3533.8 \pm 2.776(161.19)$$
$$3533.8 \pm 447.46, \text{ or } \$3086.34 \text{ to } \$3981.26$$

**36. a.** $201
**b.** 167.25 to 234.65
**c.** 108.75 to 293.15

**38. a.** $5046.67
**b.** $3815.10 to $6278.24
**c.** Not out of line

**40. a.** 9
**b.** $\hat{y} = 20.0 + 7.21x$
**c.** $t = 5.29$
From the $t$ table (7 degrees of freedom), area in tail is less than .005
$p$-value is less than .01
Actual $p$-value = .000
Because $p$-value $\leq \alpha$, we reject $H_0: \beta_1 = 0$
**d.** SSE = SST − SSR = 51,984.1 − 41,587.3 = 10,396.8
MSE = 10,396.8/7 = 1485.3

$$F = \frac{\text{MSR}}{\text{MSE}} = \frac{41,587.3}{1485.3} = 28.00$$

From the $F$ table (1 degree of freedom numerator and 7 denominator), $p$-value is less than .01

Actual $p$-value = .001

Because $p$-value $\leq \alpha$, we reject $H_0: \beta_1 = 0$
**e.** $\hat{y} = 20.0 + 7.21x = 20.0 + 7.21(50)$
$= 380.5$ or $380,500

**42. a.** $\hat{y} = 80.0 + 50.0x$
**b.** $F = 83.17$; significant ($p$-value = .000)
**c.** $t = 9.12$; significant ($p$-value = .000)
**d.** $680,000

**44. b.** Yes
**c.** $\hat{y} = 2044.38 - 28.35$ Weight
**d.** Significant; $p$-value = .000
**e.** $r^2 = .774$; a good fit

**45. a.** $\bar{x} = \dfrac{\Sigma x_i}{n} = \dfrac{70}{5} = 14$, $\bar{y} = \dfrac{\Sigma y_i}{n} = \dfrac{76}{5} = 15.2$,

$\Sigma(x_i - \bar{x})(y_i - \bar{y}) = 200$, $\Sigma(x_i - \bar{x})^2 = 126$

$$b_1 = \frac{\Sigma(x_i - \bar{x})(y_i - \bar{y})}{\Sigma(x_i - \bar{x})^2} = \frac{200}{126} = 1.5873$$

$b_0 = \bar{y} - b_1\bar{x} = 15.2 - (1.5873)(14) = -7.0222$
$\hat{y} = -7.02 + 1.59x$

**b.**

| $x_i$ | $y_i$ | $\hat{y}_i$ | $y_i - \hat{y}_i$ |
|-------|-------|-------------|-------------------|
| 6 | 6 | 2.52 | 3.48 |
| 11 | 8 | 10.47 | −2.47 |
| 15 | 12 | 16.83 | −4.83 |
| 18 | 20 | 21.60 | −1.60 |
| 20 | 30 | 24.78 | 5.22 |

**c.**

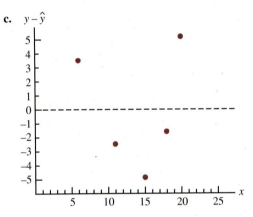

With only five observations, it is difficult to determine whether the assumptions are satisfied; however, the plot does suggest curvature in the residuals, which would indicate that the error term assumptions are not satisfied; the scatter diagram for these data also indicates that the underlying relationship between $x$ and $y$ may be curvilinear

**46. a.** $\hat{y} = 2.32 + .64x$
**b.** No; the variance appears to increase for larger values of $x$

**47. a.** Let $x$ = advertising expenditures and $y$ = revenue
$\hat{y} = 29.4 + 1.55x$
**b.** SST = 1002, SSE = 310.28, SSR = 691.72

$$\text{MSR} = \frac{\text{SSR}}{1} = 691.72$$

$$\text{MSE} = \frac{\text{SSE}}{n - 2} = \frac{310.28}{5} = 62.0554$$

$$F = \frac{\text{MSR}}{\text{MSE}} = \frac{691.72}{62.0554} = 11.15$$

From the $F$ table (1 numerator degree of freedom and 5 denominator), $p$-value is between .01 and .025

Using Excel, $p$-value = .0206

Because $p$-value $\leq \alpha = .05$, we conclude that the two variables are related

**c.**

| $x_i$ | $y_i$ | $\hat{y}_i = 29.40 + 1.55x_i$ | $y_i - \hat{y}_i$ |
|---|---|---|---|
| 1 | 19 | 30.95 | −11.95 |
| 2 | 32 | 32.50 | −.50 |
| 4 | 44 | 35.60 | 8.40 |
| 6 | 40 | 38.70 | 1.30 |
| 10 | 52 | 44.90 | 7.10 |
| 14 | 53 | 51.10 | 1.90 |
| 20 | 54 | 60.40 | −6.40 |

**d.** The residual plot leads us to question the assumption of a linear relationship between $x$ and $y$; even though the relationship is significant at the $\alpha = .05$ level, it would be extremely dangerous to extrapolate beyond the range of the data

**48. b.** Yes

**50. a.** $\hat{y} = 9.26 + .711x$
   **b.** Significant; $p$-value $= .0013$
   **c.** $r^2 = .744$; good fit
   **d.** $13.53

**52. b.** GR(%) $= 25.4229 + .2845$ RR(%)
   **c.** Significant; $p$-value $= .000$
   **d.** No; $r^2 = .4492$
   **e.** Yes
   **f.** Yes

**54. a.** $\hat{y} = 2.1739 - .1478x$
   **b.** Significant relationship; $p$-value $= .0281$
   **c.** Good fit; $r^2 = .739$
   **d.** 12.294 to 17.271

**56. a.** $\hat{y} = 220 + 131.6667x$
   **b.** Significant; $p$-value $= .000$
   **c.** $r^2 = .873$; very good fit
   **d.** $559.50 to $933.90

**58. a.** Market beta $= .95$
   **b.** Significant; $p$-value $= .029$
   **c.** $r^2 = .470$; not a good fit
   **d.** Xerox has a higher risk

**60. b.** There appears to be a positive linear relationship between the two variables
   **c.** $\hat{y} = 9.3742 + 1.2875$ Top Five (%)
   **d.** Significant; $p$-value $= .0002$
   **e.** $r^2 = .7413$; good fit
   **f.** $r_{xy} = .86$

# Chapter 13

**2. a.** The estimated regression equation is
   $\hat{y} = 45.0594 + 1.9436x_1$
   An estimate of $y$ when $x_1 = 45$ is
   $\hat{y} = 45.0594 + 1.9436(45) = 132.52$
   **b.** The estimated regression equation is
   $\hat{y} = 85.2171 + 4.3215x_2$
   An estimate of $y$ when $x_2 = 15$ is
   $\hat{y} = 85.2171 + 4.3215(15) = 150.04$
   **c.** The estimated regression equation is
   $\hat{y} = -18.3683 + 2.0102x_1 + 4.7378x_2$
   An estimate of $y$ when $x_1 = 45$ and $x_2 = 15$ is
   $\hat{y} = -18.3683 + 2.0102(45) + 4.7378(15) = 143.16$

**4. a.** $255,000

**5. a.** A portion of the Excel output is shown in Figure D13.5a
   **b.** A portion of the Excel output is shown in Figure D13.5b
   **c.** It is 1.6039 in part (a) and 2.2902 in part (b); in part (a) the coefficient is an estimate of the change in revenue due to a one-unit change in television advertising expenditures; in part (b) it represents an estimate of the change in revenue due to a one-unit change in television advertising expenditures when the amount of newspaper advertising is held constant
   **d.** Revenue $= 83.2301 + 2.2902(3.5) + 1.3010(1.8)$
   $= 93.59$ or $93,590

**6. a.** $\hat{y} = -20.0228 + 33.7264$ Recruiter Score
   **b.** $\hat{y} = 0.8790 + 14.5907$ Recruiter Score
   $+ 1.3687$ Tuition & Fees ($1000s)
   **c.** No
   **d.** 119.5550 or approximately $120,000

**8. a.** $\hat{y} = 31054.26 - 1328.722$ Reliability
   **b.** $\hat{y} = 21,312.9147 + 136.6908$ Road-Test Score
   $- 1446.3449$ Reliability
   **c.** 26,462.7991 or approximately $26,463

**10. a.** $\hat{y} = -1.2207 + 3.9576$ FG%
   **b.** .04
   **c.** $\hat{y} = -1.2346 + 4.8166$ FG% $- 2.5895$ Opp 3 Pt%
   $+ .0344$ Opp TO
   **e.** .6372

**12. a.** $R^2 = \dfrac{\text{SSR}}{\text{SST}} = \dfrac{14,052.2}{15,182.9} = .926$

   **b.** $R_a^2 = 1 - (1 - R^2)\dfrac{n - 1}{n - p - 1}$

   $= 1 - (1 - .926)\dfrac{10 - 1}{10 - 2 - 1} = .905$

   **c.** Yes; after adjusting for the number of independent variables in the model, we see that 90.5% of the variability in $y$ has been accounted for

**14. a.** .75
   **b.** .68

**FIGURE D13.5a**

| | A | B | C | D | E | F | G |
|---|---|---|---|---|---|---|---|
| 10 | | | | | | | |
| 11 | SUMMARY OUTPUT | | | | | | |
| 12 | | | | | | | |
| 13 | *Regression Statistics* | | | | | | |
| 14 | Multiple R | 0.8078 | | | | | |
| 15 | R Square | 0.6526 | | | | | |
| 16 | Adjusted R Square | 0.5946 | | | | | |
| 17 | Standard Error | 1.2152 | | | | | |
| 18 | Observations | 8 | | | | | |
| 19 | | | | | | | |
| 20 | ANOVA | | | | | | |
| 21 | | *df* | *SS* | *MS* | *F* | *Significance F* | |
| 22 | Regression | 1 | 16.6401 | 16.6401 | 11.2688 | 0.0153 | |
| 23 | Residual | 6 | 8.8599 | 1.4767 | | | |
| 24 | Total | 7 | 25.5 | | | | |
| 25 | | | | | | | |
| 26 | | *Coefficients* | *Standard Error* | *t Stat* | *P-value* | | |
| 27 | Intercept | 88.6377 | 1.5824 | 56.0159 | 2.174E-09 | | |
| 28 | Televison Advertising ($1000s) | 1.6039 | 0.4778 | 3.3569 | 0.0153 | | |
| 29 | | | | | | | |

**FIGURE D13.5b**

| | A | B | C | D | E | F | G |
|---|---|---|---|---|---|---|---|
| 10 | | | | | | | |
| 11 | SUMMARY OUTPUT | | | | | | |
| 12 | | | | | | | |
| 13 | *Regression Statistics* | | | | | | |
| 14 | Multiple R | 0.9587 | | | | | |
| 15 | R Square | 0.9190 | | | | | |
| 16 | Adjusted R Square | 0.8866 | | | | | |
| 17 | Standard Error | 0.6426 | | | | | |
| 18 | Observations | 8 | | | | | |
| 19 | | | | | | | |
| 20 | ANOVA | | | | | | |
| 21 | | *df* | *SS* | *MS* | *F* | *Significance F* | |
| 22 | Regression | 2 | 23.4354 | 11.7177 | 28.3778 | 0.0019 | |
| 23 | Residual | 5 | 2.0646 | 0.4129 | | | |
| 24 | Total | 7 | 25.5 | | | | |
| 25 | | | | | | | |
| 26 | | *Coefficients* | *Standard Error* | *t Stat* | *P-value* | | |
| 27 | Intercept | 83.2301 | 1.5739 | 52.8825 | 4.5717E-08 | | |
| 28 | Televison Advertising ($1000s) | 2.2902 | 0.3041 | 7.5319 | 0.0007 | | |
| 29 | Newspaper Advertising ($1000s) | 1.3010 | 0.3207 | 4.0567 | 0.0098 | | |
| 30 | | | | | | | |

**15. a.** $R^2 = \dfrac{\text{SSR}}{\text{SST}} = \dfrac{23.435}{25.5} = .919$

$R_a^2 = 1 - (1 - R^2)\dfrac{n-1}{n-p-1}$

$= 1 - (1 - .919)\dfrac{8-1}{8-2-1} = .887$

**b.** Multiple regression analysis is preferred because both $R^2$ and $R_a^2$ show an increased percentage of the variability of $y$ explained when both independent variables are used

**16. a.** $r^2 = .6133$; not too bad a fit using only one independent variable

**b.** $R^2 = .793$ and $R_a^2 = .768$
The multiple linear regression equation will provide a better estimate of the starting salary and bonus of the graduates

**18. a.** $R^2 = .5638$, $R_a^2 = .5114$

**b.** The fit is not very good; but it does explain over 50% of the variability in $y$

**19. a.** $\text{MSR} = \dfrac{\text{SSR}}{p} = \dfrac{6216.375}{2} = 3108.188$

$\text{MSE} = \dfrac{\text{SSE}}{n-p-1} = \dfrac{507.75}{10-2-1} = 72.536$

**b.** $F = \dfrac{\text{MSR}}{\text{MSE}} = \dfrac{3108.188}{72.536} = 42.85$

$p$-value (2 degrees of freedom numerator and 7 denominator) $= .0001$

Because the $p$-value $\leq \alpha = .05$, the overall model is significant

**c.** $t = \dfrac{b_1}{s_{b_1}} = \dfrac{.5906}{.0813} = 7.26$

$p$-value (7 degrees of freedom) $= .0002$
Because the $p$-value $\leq \alpha = .05$, $\beta_1$ is significant

**d.** $t = \dfrac{b_2}{s_{b_2}} = \dfrac{.4980}{.0567} = 8.78$

$p$-value (7 degrees of freedom) $= .0001$
Because the $p$-value $\leq \alpha = .05$, $\beta_2$ is significant

**20. a.** Significant; $p$-value $= .0001$
**b.** Significant; $p$-value $= .0000$
**c.** Significant; $p$-value $= .0016$

**22. a.** SSE $= 4000$, MSE $= 571.43$,
MSR $= 6000$
**b.** Significant; $p$-value $= .0078$

**23. a.** $F = 28.38$
$p$-value (2 degrees of freedom numerator and 1 denominator) $= .0019$
Because the $p$-value $\leq \alpha = .01$, reject $H_0$
**b.** $t = 7.53$
$p$-value $= .0007$
Because $p$-value $\leq \alpha = .05$, $\beta_1$ is significant and $x_1$ should not be dropped from the model

**c.** $t = 4.06$
$t_{.025} = 2.571$
With $t > t_{.025} = 2.571$, $\beta_2$ is significant and $x_2$ should not be dropped from the model

**24. a.** $\hat{y} = -.6820 + .0498$ Revenue $+ .0147$ %Wins
**b.** Significant; $p$-value $= .001$
**c.** Revenue is significant; $p$-value $= .0007$
%Wins is significant; $p$-value $= .0063$

**26. a.** Significant; $p$-value $= .0000$
**b.** All of the independent variables are significant

**28. a.** $143.15$
**b.** Using StatTools, the 95% prediction interval is 111.16 to 175.16

**29. a.** See Excel output in Figure D13.5b.
$\hat{y} = 83.2 + 2.29(3.5) + 1.30(1.8) = 93.555$
or $\$93,555$
**b.** Using StatTools, 91.774 to 95.401, or \$91,774 to \$95,401

**30. a.** $49$
**b.** 44.815 to 52.589

**32. a.** $E(y) = \beta_0 + \beta_1 x_1 + \beta_2 x_2$
where $x_2 = \begin{cases} 0 \text{ if level } 1 \\ 1 \text{ if level } 2 \end{cases}$
**b.** $E(y) = \beta_0 + \beta_1 x_1 + \beta_2(0) = \beta_0 + \beta_1 x_1$
**c.** $E(y) = \beta_0 + \beta_1 x_1 + \beta_2(1) = \beta_0 + \beta_1 x_1 + \beta_2$
**d.** $\beta_2 = E(y \mid \text{level } 2) - E(y \mid \text{level } 1)$
$\beta_1$ is the change in $E(y)$ for a one-unit change in $x_1$ holding $x_2$ constant

**34. a.** $\$15,300$
**b.** $\hat{y} = 10.1 - 4.2(2) + 6.8(8) + 15.3(0) = 56.1$
Sales prediction: $\$56,100$
**c.** $\hat{y} = 10.1 - 4.2(1) + 6.8(3) + 15.3(1) = 41.6$
Sales prediction: $\$41,600$

**36. a.** $\hat{y} = 1.8602 + 0.2914$ Months $+ 1.1024$ Type $- 0.6091$ Person
**b.** Significant; $p$-value $= .0021 < \alpha = .05$
**c.** Person is not significant

**38. a.** $\hat{y} = -91.7595 + 1.0767$ Age $+ .2518$ Pressure $+ 8.7399$ Smoker
**b.** Significant; $p$-value $= .0102 < \alpha = .05$
**c.** 95% prediction interval is 21.35 to 47.18 or a probability of .2135 to .4718; quit smoking and begin some type of treatment to reduce his blood pressure

**39. a.** A portion of the Excel output is shown in Figure D13.39a
**b.** The $p$-value corresponding to $F = 6.8530$ is $.0589 > \alpha = .05$; therefore, the relationship is not significant

**FIGURE D13.39a**

| | A | B | C | D | E | F | G |
|---|---|---|---|---|---|---|---|
| 8 | | | | | | | |
| 9 | SUMMARY OUTPUT | | | | | | |
| 10 | | | | | | | |
| 11 | *Regression Statistics* | | | | | | |
| 12 | Multiple R | 0.7946 | | | | | |
| 13 | R Square | 0.6314 | | | | | |
| 14 | Adjusted R Square | 0.5393 | | | | | |
| 15 | Standard Error | 7.2693 | | | | | |
| 16 | Observations | 6 | | | | | |
| 17 | | | | | | | |
| 18 | ANOVA | | | | | | |
| 19 | | *df* | *SS* | *MS* | *F* | *Significance F* | |
| 20 | Regression | 1 | 362.1305 | 362.1305 | 6.8530 | 0.0589 | |
| 21 | Residual | 4 | 211.3695 | 52.8424 | | | |
| 22 | Total | 5 | 573.5 | | | | |
| 23 | | | | | | | |
| 24 | | *Coefficients* | *Standard Error* | *t Stat* | *P-value* | | |
| 25 | Intercept | -6.7745 | 14.1709 | -0.4781 | 0.6576 | | |
| 26 | x | 1.2296 | 0.4697 | 2.6178 | 0.0589 | | |
| 27 | | | | | | | |

**c.**

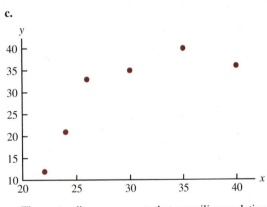

The scatter diagram suggests that a curvilinear relationship may be appropriate

**d.** A portion of the Excel output is shown in Figure D13.39d

**e.** The $p$-value corresponding to $F = 25.6778$ is $.013 < \alpha = .05$; therefore, the relationship is significant

**f.** $\hat{y} = -168.8848 + 12.1870(25) - .1770(25)^2 = 25.165$

**40. a.** $\hat{y} = 9.3152 + .4242x$; $p$-value $= .1171$ indicates that the relationship between $x$ and $y$ is not significant

**b.** $\hat{y} = -8.1014 + 2.4127x - .0480x^2$
$R_a^2 = .9324$; good fit

**c.** 20.953

**42. b.** No, the relationship appears to be curvilinear

**c.** $\hat{y} = 2.90 - .185x + .00351x^2$

**44. b.** 3.19

**46. a.** $\hat{y} = 8.103 + 7.602\,x_1 + 3.111x_2$

**b.** Significant; $p$-value $= .000$

**c.** $\beta_1$ is significant; $p$-value $= .0036$
$\beta_2$ is significant; $p$-value $= .0003$

**48. a.** $\hat{y} = 14.4 - 8.69\,x_1 + 13.517x_2$

**b.** Significant; $p$-value $= .0031$

**c.** Good fit

**d.** $\beta_1$ is significant; $p$-value $= .0025$
$\beta_2$ is significant; $p$-value $= .0013$

**50. a.** $\hat{y} = 67.6762 + .0046$ Price

**b.** Significant; $p$-value $= .0004$

**c.** $\hat{y} = 65.6597 + .0023$ Price $+ 10.2097$ Quality-E $+ 5.9246$ Quality-VG

**d.** Significant; $p$-value $= .0002$

**e.** All significant

**f.** 70; 6

**52. a.** $\hat{y} = 35.3950 - 2.8821$ Displacement
$p$-value $= .0000 < \alpha = .05$; significant relationship

**b.** $\hat{y} = 35.2289 + 3.4563$ ClassMidsize
$+ 1.7078$ ClassLarge $- 1.9347$ Displacement

**c.** ClassMidsize: $p$-value $= .000 < \alpha = .05$; significant
ClassLarge: $p$-value $= .000 < \alpha = .05$

**d.** $\hat{y} = 30.9548 + 2.9832$ ClassMidsize
$+ 1.5088$ ClassLarge $- 1.8533$ Displacement
$- 1.4306$ FuelPremium

**e.** $p$-value corresponding to $F = 317.1329$ is $.0000 < \alpha = .05$; there is a significant overall relationship
Because the $p$-values for each independent variable are also $< \alpha = .05$, each of the independent variables is significant

**FIGURE D13.39d**

# Chapter 14

**2. a.** 5.42

 **b.** UCL = 6.09, LCL = 4.75

**4.** *R chart:*

 UCL = $\bar{R}D_4$ = 1.6(1.864) = 2.98

 LCL = $\bar{R}D_3$ = 1.6(.136) = .22

 $\bar{x}$ chart:

 UCL = $\bar{\bar{x}} + A_2\bar{R}$ = 28.5 + .373(1.6) = 29.10

 LCL = $\bar{\bar{x}} - A_2\bar{R}$ = 28.5 − .373(1.6) = 27.90

**6.** 20.01, .082

**8. a.** .0470

 **b.** UCL = .0989, LCL = −0.0049 (use LCL = 0)

 **c.** $\bar{p}$ = .08; in control

 **d.** UCL = 14.826, LCL = −0.726 (use LCL = 0)

 Process is out of control if more than 14 defective

 **e.** In control with 12 defective

 **f.** *np* chart

**10.** $f(x) = \dfrac{n!}{x!(n-x)!} p^x(1-p)^{n-x}$

 When $p$ = .02, the probability of accepting the lot is

 $f(0) = \dfrac{25!}{0!(25-0)!}(.02)^0(1-.02)^{25} = .6035$

 When $p$ = .06, the probability of accepting the lot is

 $f(0) = \dfrac{25!}{0!(25-0)!}(.06)^0(1-.06)^{25} = .2129$

**12.** $p_0$ = .02; producer's risk = .0599

 $p_0$ = .06; producer's risk = .3396

 Producer's risk decreases as the acceptance number $c$ is increased

**14.** $n$ = 20, $c$ = 3

**16. a.** 95.4

 **b.** UCL = 96.07, LCL = 94.73

 **c.** No

**18.**

|  | *R* Chart | $\bar{x}$ Chart |
|---|---|---|
| UCL | 4.23 | 6.57 |
| LCL | 0 | 4.27 |

 Estimate of standard deviation = .86

**20.**

|  | *R* Chart | $\bar{x}$ Chart |
|---|---|---|
| UCL | .1121 | 3.112 |
| LCL | 0 | 3.051 |

**22. a.** UCL = .0817, LCL = −.0017 (use LCL = 0)

**24. a.** .03

 **b.** $\beta$ = .0802

# Chapter 15

**1.** The following table shows the calculations for parts (a), (b), and (c):

| Week | Time Series Value | Forecast | Forecast Error | Absolute Value of Forecast Error | Squared Forecast Error | Percentage Error | Absolute Value of Percentage Error |
|------|------|------|------|------|------|------|------|
| 1 | 18 | | | | | | |
| 2 | 13 | 18 | −5 | 5 | 25 | −38.46 | 38.46 |
| 3 | 16 | 13 | 3 | 3 | 9 | 18.75 | 18.75 |
| 4 | 11 | 16 | −5 | 5 | 25 | −45.45 | 45.45 |
| 5 | 17 | 11 | 6 | 6 | 36 | 35.29 | 35.29 |
| 6 | 14 | 17 | −3 | 3 | 9 | −21.43 | 21.43 |
| | | | Totals | 22 | 104 | −51.30 | 159.38 |

**a.** $\text{MAE} = \dfrac{22}{5} = 4.4$

**b.** $\text{MSE} = \dfrac{104}{5} = 20.8$

**c.** $\text{MAPE} = \dfrac{159.38}{5} = 31.88$

**d.** Forecast for week 7 is 14

**2.** The following table shows the calculations for parts (a), (b), and (c):

| Week | Time Series Value | Forecast | Forecast Error | Absolute Value of Forecast Error | Squared Forecast Error | Percentage Error | Absolute Value of Percentage Error |
|------|------|------|------|------|------|------|------|
| 1 | 18 | | | | | | |
| 2 | 13 | 18.00 | −5.00 | 5.00 | 25.00 | −38.46 | 38.46 |
| 3 | 16 | 15.50 | 0.50 | 0.50 | 0.25 | 3.13 | 3.13 |
| 4 | 11 | 15.67 | −4.67 | 4.67 | 21.81 | −42.45 | 42.45 |
| 5 | 17 | 14.50 | 2.50 | 2.50 | 6.25 | 14.71 | 14.71 |
| 6 | 14 | 15.00 | −1.00 | 1.00 | 1.00 | −7.14 | 7.14 |
| | | | Totals | 13.67 | 54.31 | −70.21 | 105.86 |

**a.** $\text{MAE} = \dfrac{13.67}{5} = 2.73$

**b.** $\text{MSE} = \dfrac{54.31}{5} = 10.86$

**c.** $\text{MAPE} = \dfrac{105.89}{5} = 21.18$

**d.** Forecast for week 7 is

$$\frac{18 + 13 + 16 + 11 + 17 + 14}{6} = 14.83$$

**4. a.** $\text{MSE} = \dfrac{363}{6} = 60.5$

Forecast for month 8 is 15

**b.** $\text{MSE} = \dfrac{216.72}{6} = 36.12$

Forecast for month 8 is 18

**c.** The average of all the previous values is better because MSE is smaller

**5. a.** The data appear to follow a horizontal pattern

**b.** Three-week moving average

| Week | Time Series Value | Forecast | Forecast Error | Squared Forecast Error |
|------|------|------|------|------|
| 1 | 18 | | | |
| 2 | 13 | | | |
| 3 | 16 | | | |
| 4 | 11 | 15.67 | −4.67 | 21.78 |
| 5 | 17 | 13.33 | 3.67 | 13.44 |
| 6 | 14 | 14.67 | −0.67 | 0.44 |
| | | | Total | 35.67 |

$$\text{MSE} = \frac{35.67}{3} = 11.89$$

The forecast for week 7 $= \dfrac{(11 + 17 + 14)}{3} = 14$

**c.** Smoothing constant = .2

| Week | Time Series Value | Forecast | Forecast Error | Squared Forecast Error |
|------|-------------------|----------|----------------|------------------------|
| 1 | 18 | | | |
| 2 | 13 | 18.00 | −5.00 | 25.00 |
| 3 | 16 | 17.00 | −1.00 | 1.00 |
| 4 | 11 | 16.80 | −5.80 | 33.64 |
| 5 | 17 | 15.64 | 1.36 | 1.85 |
| 6 | 14 | 15.91 | −1.91 | 3.66 |
| | | | Total | 65.15 |

$$MSE = \frac{65.15}{5} = 13.03$$

The forecast for week 7 is $.2(14) + (1 − .2)15.91$ = 15.53

**d.** The three-week moving average provides a better forecast since it has a smaller MSE

**e.** Smoothing constant = .4

| Week | Time Series Value | Forecast | Forecast Error | Squared Forecast Error |
|------|-------------------|----------|----------------|------------------------|
| 1 | 18 | | | |
| 2 | 13 | 18.00 | −5.00 | 25.00 |
| 3 | 16 | 16.00 | 0.00 | 0.00 |
| 4 | 11 | 16.00 | −5.00 | 25.00 |
| 5 | 17 | 14.00 | 3.00 | 9.00 |
| 6 | 14 | 15.20 | −1.20 | 1.44 |
| | | | Total | 60.44 |

$$MSE = \frac{60.44}{5} = 12.09$$

The exponential smoothing forecast using $\alpha = .4$ provides a better forecast than the exponential smoothing forecast using $\alpha = .2$ since it has a smaller MSE

**6. a.** The data appear to follow a horizontal pattern

**b.** $MSE = \frac{110}{4} = 27.5$

The forecast for week 8 is 19

**c.** $MSE = \frac{252.87}{6} = 42.15$

The forecast for week 7 is 19.12

**d.** The three-week moving average provides a better forecast since it has a smaller MSE

**e.** MSE = 39.79

The exponential smoothing forecast using $\alpha = .4$ provides a better forecast than the exponential smoothing forecast using $\alpha = .2$ since it has a smaller MSE

**8. a.**

| Week | 4 | 5 | 6 | 7 | 8 | 9 | 10 | 11 | 12 |
|------|---|---|---|---|---|---|----|----|----|
| Forecast | 19.33 | 21.33 | 19.83 | 17.83 | 18.33 | 18.33 | 20.33 | 20.33 | 17.83 |

**b.** MSE = 11.49

Prefer the unweighted moving average here; it has a smaller MSE

**c.** You could always find a weighted moving average at least as good as the unweighted one; actually the unweighted moving average is a special case of the weighted ones where the weights are equal

**10. b.** The more recent data receive the greater weight or importance in determining the forecast; the moving averages method weights the last $n$ data values equally in determining the forecast

**12. a.** The data appear to follow a horizontal pattern

**b.** MSE(3-Month) = .12
MSE(4-Month) = .14
Use 3-Month moving averages

**c.** 9.63

**13. a.** The data appear to follow a horizontal pattern

**b.**

| Month | Time-Series Value | 3-Month Moving Average Forecast | (Error)² | $\alpha = .2$ Forecast | (Error)² |
|-------|-------------------|--------------------------------|----------|------------------------|----------|
| 1 | 240 | | | | |
| 2 | 350 | | | 240.00 | 12100.00 |
| 3 | 230 | | | 262.00 | 1024.00 |
| 4 | 260 | 273.33 | 177.69 | 255.60 | 19.36 |
| 5 | 280 | 280.00 | 0.00 | 256.48 | 553.19 |
| 6 | 320 | 256.67 | 4010.69 | 261.18 | 3459.79 |
| 7 | 220 | 286.67 | 4444.89 | 272.95 | 2803.70 |
| 8 | 310 | 273.33 | 1344.69 | 262.36 | 2269.57 |
| 9 | 240 | 283.33 | 1877.49 | 271.89 | 1016.97 |
| 10 | 310 | 256.67 | 2844.09 | 265.51 | 1979.36 |
| 11 | 240 | 286.67 | 2178.09 | 274.41 | 1184.05 |
| 12 | 230 | 263.33 | 1110.89 | 267.53 | 1408.50 |
| | Totals | | 17,988.52 | | 27,818.49 |

MSE(3-Month) = 17,988.52/9 = 1998.72

MSE($\alpha = .2$) = 27,818.49/11 = 2528.95

Based on the preceding MSE values, the 3-Month moving averages appear better; however, exponential smoothing was penalized by including month 2, which was difficult for any method to forecast; using only the errors for months 4 to 12, the MSE for exponential smoothing is

MSE($\alpha = .2$) = 14,694.49/9 = 1632.72

Thus, exponential smoothing was better considering months 4 to 12

**c.** Using exponential smoothing,

$$F_{13} = \alpha Y_{12} + (1 − \alpha)F_{12}$$
$$= .20(230) + .80(267.53) = 260$$

**14. a.** The data appear to follow a horizontal pattern

**b.** Values for months 2–12 are as follows:

105.00    114.00    115.80    112.56    105.79    110.05
120.54    126.38    118.46    106.92    104.85

$$MSE = 510.29$$

**c.** Values for months 2–12 are as follows:

105.00   120.00   120.00   112.50   101.25   110.63
127.81   133.91   116.95   98.48   99.24

$$MSE = 540.55$$

Conclusion: A smoothing constant of .3 is better than a smoothing constant of .5 since the MSE is less for 0.3

**16. a.** The time series plot indicates a possible linear trend in the data; this could be due to decreasing viewer interest in watching the Masters, but closer inspection of the data indicates that the two highest ratings correspond to years 1997 and 2001, years in which Tiger Woods won the tournament; the pattern observed may be simply due to the effect Tiger Woods has on ratings and not necessarily on any long-term decrease in viewer interest

**b.** The methods discussed in this section are only applicable for a time series that has a horizontal pattern, so if there is a really a long-term linear trend in the data, the methods discussed in this section are not appropriate

**c.** The time series plot for the data for years 2002–2008 exhibits a horizontal pattern; it seems reasonable to conclude that the extreme values observed in 1997 and 2001 are more attributable to viewer interest in the performance of Tiger Woods; basing the forecast on years 2002–2008 does seem reasonable, but, because of the injury that Tiger Woods experienced in the 2008 reason, if he is able to play in the 2009 Masters, then the rating for 2009 may be significantly higher than suggested by the data for years 2002–2008

**17. a.** The time series plot shows a linear trend

**b.** $\bar{t} = \dfrac{\sum\limits_{t=1}^{n} t}{n} = \dfrac{15}{5} = 3$    $\bar{Y} = \dfrac{\sum\limits_{t=1}^{n} Y_t}{n} = \dfrac{55}{5} = 11$

$\Sigma(t - \bar{t})(Y_t - \bar{Y}) = 21$    $\Sigma(t - \bar{t})^2 = 10$

$b_1 = \dfrac{\sum\limits_{t=1}^{n}(t - \bar{t})(Y_t - \bar{Y})}{\sum\limits_{t=1}^{n}(t - \bar{t})^2} = \dfrac{21}{10} = 2.1$

$b_0 = \bar{Y} - b_1\bar{t} = 11 - (2.1)(3) = 4.7$

$T_t = 4.7 + 2.1t$

**c.** $T_6 = 4.7 + 2.1(6) = 17.3$

**18. a.** The time series plot exhibits a curvilinear trend

**b.** Using Excel's chart tools, the quadratic trend equation is $T_t = 1.1429 + 5.3571t - .5714t^2$

**c.** Forecast for $t = 8$ is $T_8 = 1.1429 + 5.3571(8) - .5714(8)^2 = 7.4$

**d.** $T_8 = 4.7 + 2.1(8) = 21.5$

The forecast obtained using the linear trend equation provides a much different forecast because it has not picked

up the change that has occurred in the time series in periods 7 and 8; each time a new time series value becomes available we need to develop a new time series plot and make a new decision as to what the underlying pattern of the time series is

**20. a.** The time series plot exhibits a curvilinear trend

**b.** $T_t = 107.857 - 28.9881t + 2.65476t^2$

**c.** 45.86

**21. a.** The time series plot shows a linear trend

**b.** $\bar{t} = \dfrac{\sum\limits_{t=1}^{n} t}{n} = \dfrac{45}{9} = 5$    $\bar{Y} = \dfrac{\sum\limits_{t=1}^{n} Y_t}{n} = \dfrac{108}{9} = 12$

$\Sigma(t - \bar{t})(Y_t - \bar{Y}) = 87.4$    $\Sigma(t - \bar{t})^2 = 60$

$b_1 = \dfrac{\sum\limits_{t=1}^{n}(t - \bar{t})(Y_t - \bar{Y})}{\sum\limits_{t=1}^{n}(t - \bar{t})^2} = \dfrac{87.4}{60} = 1.4567$

$b_0 = \bar{Y} - b_1\bar{t} = 12 - (1.4567)(5) = 4.7165$

$T_t = 4.7165 + 1.4567t$

**c.** $T_{10} = 4.7165 + 1.4567(10) = 19.28$

**22. a.** The time series plot shows a downward linear trend

**b.** $T_t = 13.8 - .7t$

**c.** 8.2

**d.** If SCF can continue to decrease the percentage of funds spent on administrative and fund-raising by .7% per year, the forecast of expenses for 2018 is 4.70%

**24. a.** The time series plot shows a linear trend

**b.** $T_t = 7.5623 - .07541t$

**c.** 6.7328

**d.** Given the uncertainty in global market conditions, making a prediction for December using only time is not recommended

**26. a.** A linear trend is not appropriate

**b.** $T_t = 5.702 + 2.889t - 1618t^2$

**c.** 17.90

**28. a.** The time series plot shows a horizontal pattern, but there is a seasonal pattern in the data; for instance, in each year the lowest value occurs in quarter 2 and the highest value occurs in quarter 4

**b.** The estimated multiple regression equation is

```
Value = 77.0 - 10.0 Qtr1 - 30.0
        Qtr2 - 20.0 Qtr3
```

**c.** The quarterly forecasts for next year are as follows:

Quarter 1 forecast $= 77.0 - 10.0(1) - 30.0(0) - 20.0(0) = 67$

Quarter 2 forecast $= 77.0 - 10.0(0) - 30.0(1) - 20.0(0) = 47$

Quarter 3 forecast $= 77.0 - 10.0(0) - 30.0(0)$
$$- 20.0(1) = 57$$
Quarter 4 forecast $= 77.0 - 10.0(0) - 30.0(0)$
$$- 20.0(0) = 77$$

**30. a.** There appears to be a seasonal pattern in the data and perhaps a moderate upward linear trend
 **b.** The estimated multiple regression equation is

> Value = 2492 - 712 Qtr1 - 1512
>          Qtr2 + 327 Qtr3

 **c.** The quarterly forecasts for next year are as follows:

Quarter 1 forecast is 1780
Quarter 2 forecast is 980
Quarter 3 forecast is 2819
Quarter 4 forecast is 2492

 **d.** The estimated multiple regression equation is

> Value = 2307 - 642 Qtr1 - 1465
>          Qtr2 + 350 Qtr3 + 23.1 t

The quarterly forecasts for next year are as follows:

Quarter 1 forecast is 2058
Quarter 2 forecast is 1258
Quarter 3 forecast is 3096
Quarter 4 forecast is 2769

**32. a.** The time series plot shows both a linear trend and seasonal effects
 **b.** The estimated multiple regression equation is

> Revenue = 70.0 + 10.0 Qtr1 + 105
>            Qtr2 + 245 Qtr3

Quarter 1 forecast is 80
Quarter 2 forecast is 175
Quarter 3 forecast is 315
Quarter 4 forecast is 70

 **c.** The estimated multiple regression equation is

> Revenue = -70.1 + 45.0 Qtr1 + 128
>            Qtr2 + 257 Qtr3 + 11.7 Period

Quarter 1 forecast = is 221
Quarter 2 forecast = is 315
Quarter 3 forecast = is 456
Quarter 4 forecast = is 211

**34. a.** The time series plot shows seasonal and linear trend effects
 **b.** *Note*: Jan $= 1$ if January, 0 otherwise; Feb $= 1$ if February, 0 otherwise; and so on

The estimated multiple regression equation is

> Expense = 175 - 18.4 Jan - 3.72 Feb +
>            12.7 Mar + 45.7 Apr + 57.1
>            May + 135 Jun + 181 Jul + 105
>            Aug + 47.6 Sep + 50.6 Oct +
>            35.3 Nov + 1.96 Period

 **c.** *Note*: The next time period in the time series is Period $= 37$ (January of Year 4); the forecasts for January–December are 229; 246; 264; 299; 312; 392; 440; 366; 311; 316; 302; 269

**35. a.** The time series plot indicates a linear trend and a seasonal pattern
 **b.**

| Year | Quarter | Time Series Value | Four-Quarter Moving Average | Centered Moving Average |
|------|---------|-------------------|-----------------------------|-------------------------|
| 1 | 1 | 4 | | |
|   | 2 | 2 | | |
|   |   |   | 3.50 | |
|   | 3 | 3 | | 3.750 |
|   |   |   | 4.00 | |
|   | 4 | 5 | | 4.125 |
|   |   |   | 4.25 | |
| 2 | 1 | 6 | | 4.500 |
|   |   |   | 4.75 | |
|   | 2 | 3 | | 5.000 |
|   |   |   | 5.25 | |
|   | 3 | 5 | | 5.375 |
|   |   |   | 5.50 | |
|   | 4 | 7 | | 5.875 |
|   |   |   | 6.25 | |
| 3 | 1 | 7 | | 6.375 |
|   |   |   | 6.50 | |
|   | 2 | 6 | | 6.625 |
|   |   |   | 6.75 | |
|   | 3 | 6 | | |
|   | 4 | 8 | | |

 **c.**

| Year | Quarter | Time Series Value | Centered Moving Average | Seasonal-Irregular Component |
|------|---------|-------------------|-------------------------|------------------------------|
| 1 | 1 | 4 | | |
|   | 2 | 2 | | |
|   | 3 | 3 | 3.750 | 0.800 |
|   | 4 | 5 | 4.125 | 1.212 |
| 2 | 1 | 6 | 4.500 | 1.333 |
|   | 2 | 3 | 5.000 | 0.600 |
|   | 3 | 5 | 5.375 | 0.930 |
|   | 4 | 7 | 5.875 | 1.191 |
| 3 | 1 | 7 | 6.375 | 1.098 |
|   | 2 | 6 | 6.625 | 0.906 |
|   | 3 | 6 | | |
|   | 4 | 8 | | |

| Quarter | Seasonal-Irregular Values | | Seasonal Index | Adjusted Seasonal Index |
|---|---|---|---|---|
| 1 | 1.333 | 1.098 | 1.216 | 1.205 |
| 2 | 0.600 | 0.906 | 0.752 | 0.746 |
| 3 | 0.800 | 0.930 | 0.865 | 0.857 |
| 4 | 1.212 | 1.191 | 1.201 | 1.191 |
| | | Total | 4.036 | |

$$\text{Adjustment for seasonal index} = \frac{4.000}{4.036} = 0.991$$

**36. a.**

| Year | Quarter | Deseasonalized Value |
|---|---|---|
| 1 | 1 | 3.320 |
| | 2 | 2.681 |
| | 3 | 3.501 |
| | 4 | 4.198 |
| 2 | 1 | 4.979 |
| | 2 | 4.021 |
| | 3 | 5.834 |
| | 4 | 5.877 |
| 3 | 1 | 5.809 |
| | 2 | 8.043 |
| | 3 | 7.001 |
| | 4 | 6.717 |

**b.** Let Period = 1 denote the time series value in Year 1—Quarter 1; Period = 2 denote the time series value in Year 1—Quarter 2; and so on; treating Period as the independent variable and the Deseasonlized Values as the values of the dependent variable, the estimated regression equation is

```
Deseasonalized Value = 2.42 + 0.422
                                Period
```

**c.** The quarterly deseasonalized trend forecasts for Year 4 (Periods 13, 14, 15, and 16) are as follows:

Forecast for quarter 1 is 7.906
Forecast for quarter 2 is 8.328
Forecast for quarter 3 is 8.750
Forecast for quarter 4 is 9.172

**d.** Adjusting the quarterly deseasonalized trend forecasts provides the following quarterly estimates:

Forecast for quarter 1 is 9.527
Forecast for quarter 2 is 6.213
Forecast for quarter 3 is 7.499
Forecast for quarter 4 is 10.924

**38. a.** The time series plot shows a linear trend and seasonal effects

**b.** 0.71   0.78   0.83   0.97   1.02   1.30   1.50   1.23
0.98   0.99   0.93   0.79

**c.**

| Month | Deseasonalized Expense |
|---|---|
| 1 | 239.44 |
| 2 | 230.77 |
| 3 | 246.99 |
| 4 | 237.11 |
| 5 | 235.29 |
| 6 | 242.31 |
| 7 | 240.00 |
| 8 | 235.77 |
| 9 | 244.90 |
| 10 | 242.42 |
| 11 | 247.31 |
| 12 | 246.84 |
| 13 | 253.52 |
| 14 | 262.82 |
| 15 | 259.04 |
| 16 | 252.58 |
| 17 | 259.80 |
| 18 | 253.85 |
| 19 | 266.67 |
| 20 | 272.36 |
| 21 | 265.31 |
| 22 | 272.73 |
| 23 | 274.19 |
| 24 | 278.48 |
| 25 | 274.65 |
| 26 | 269.23 |
| 27 | 277.11 |
| 28 | 288.66 |
| 29 | 284.31 |
| 30 | 300.00 |
| 31 | 280.00 |
| 32 | 268.29 |
| 33 | 295.92 |
| 34 | 297.98 |
| 35 | 301.08 |
| 36 | 316.46 |

**d.** Let Period = 1 denote the time series value in January—Year 1; Period = 2 denote the time series value in February—Year 2; and so on; treating Period as the independent variable and the Deseasonlized Values as the values of the dependent variable the estimated regression equation is

```
Deseasonalized Expense = 228 + 1.96
                                 Period
```

**e.**

| Month | Monthly Forecast |
|-------|-----------------|
| January | 213.37 |
| February | 235.93 |
| March | 252.69 |
| April | 297.21 |
| May | 314.53 |
| June | 403.42 |
| July | 486.42 |
| August | 386.52 |
| September | 309.88 |
| October | 314.98 |
| November | 297.71 |
| December | 254.44 |

**40. a.** The time series plot indicates a seasonal effect; power consumption is lowest in the time period 12–4 A.M., steadily increases to the highest value in the 12–4 P.M. time period, and then decreases again. There may also be some linear trend in the data

**b.**

| Time Period | Adjusted Seasonal Index |
|-------------|------------------------|
| 12–4 A.M. | 0.3256 |
| 4–8 A.M. | 0.4476 |
| 8–12 noon | 1.3622 |
| 12–4 P.M. | 1.6959 |
| 4–8 P.M. | 1.4578 |
| 8–12 midnight | 0.7109 |

**c.** The following estimated regression equation shows the results of fitting a linear trend equation to the deseasonalized time series:

```
Deseasonalized Power = 63108 + 1854 t
```

Deaseasonalized Power ($t = 19$) = 63,108 + 1854(19) = 98,334

Forecast for 12–4 P.M. = 1.6959(98,334) = 166,764.63 or approximately 166,765 kWh

Deaseasonalized Power ($t = 20$) = 63,108 + 1854(20) = 100,188

Forecast for 4–8 P.M. = 1.4578(100,188) = 146,054.07 or approximately 146,054 kWh

Thus, the forecast of power consumption from noon to 8 P.M. is 166,765 + 146,054 = 312,819 kWh

**42. a.** The time series plot indicates a horizontal pattern

**b.**
$$\text{MSE}(\alpha = .2) = 1.40$$
$$\text{MSE}(\alpha = .3) = 1.27$$
$$\text{MSE}(\alpha = .4) = 1.23$$

A smoothing constant of $\alpha = .4$ provides the best forecast because it has a smaller MSE

**c.** 31.00

**44. a.** There appears to be an increasing trend in the data

**b.** *Note*: $t = 1$ corresponds to 2001, $t = 2$ corresponds to 2002, and so on. The estimated regression equation is

```
Balance($) = 1984 + 146 t
```

The forecast for 2009 ($t = 9$) is Balance($) = 1984 + 146(9) = $3298

**c.** *Note*: $t = 1$ corresponds to 2001, $t = 2$ corresponds to 2002, and so on. The estimated regression equation is

```
Balance($) = 2924 - 419 t + 62.7 tsq
```

The forecast for 2009 ($t = 9$) is Balance($) = 2924 − 419(9) + 62.7(9)$^2$ = $4232

**d.** The quadratic trend equation provides the best forecast accuracy for the historical data

**e.** Linear trend equation

**46. a.** The forecast for July is 236.97

Forecast for August, using forecast for July as the actual sales in July, is 236.97

Exponential smoothing provides the same forecast for every period in the future; this is why it is not usually recommended for long-term forecasting

**b.** The linear trend equation is

$$T_t = 149.72 + 18.451t$$

Forecast for July is 278.88
Forecast for August is 297.33

**c.** The proposed settlement is not fair since it does not account for the upward trend in sales; based upon trend projection, the settlement should be based on forecasted lost sales of $278,880 in July and $297,330 in August

**48. a.** The time series plot shows a linear trend

**b.** $T_t = -5 + 15t$

The slope of 15 indicates that the average increase in sales is 15 pianos per year

**c.** 85, 100

**50. a.**

| Quarter | Adjusted Seasonal Index |
|---------|------------------------|
| 1 | 1.2717 |
| 2 | 0.6120 |
| 3 | 0.4978 |
| 4 | 1.6185 |

*Note*: Adjustment for seasonal index $= \dfrac{4}{3.8985} = 1.0260$

**b.** The largest effect is in quarter 4; this seems reasonable since retail sales are generally higher during October, November, and December

**52. a.** Yes, a linear trend pattern appears to be present

**b.** The estimated regression equation is

Number Sold = 22.9 + 15.5 Year

**c.** Forecast in year 8 is or approximately 147 units

**54. b.** The centered moving average values smooth out the time series by removing seasonal effects and some of the random variability; the centered moving average time series shows the trend in the data

**c.**

| Quarter | Adjusted Seasonal Index |
|---------|-------------------------|
| 1 | 0.899 |
| 2 | 1.362 |
| 3 | 1.118 |
| 4 | 0.621 |

**d.** Hudson Marine experiences the largest seasonal increase in quarter 2; since this quarter occurs prior to the peak summer boating season, this result seems reasonable, but the largest seasonal effect is the seasonal decrease in quarter 4; this is also reasonable because of decreased boating in the fall and winter

Microsoft Excel 2010, part of the Microsoft Office 2010 system, is a spreadsheet program that can be used to organize and analyze data, perform complex calculations, and create a wide variety of graphical displays. We assume that readers are familiar with basic Excel operations such as selecting cells, entering formulas, copying, and so on. But we do not assume readers are familiar with Excel 2010 or the use of Excel for statistical analysis.

The purpose of this appendix is twofold. First, we provide an overview of Excel 2010 and discuss the basic operations needed to work with Excel 2010 workbooks and worksheets. Second, we provide an overview of the tools that are available for conducting statistical analysis with Excel. These include Excel functions and formulas which allow users to conduct their own analyses and add-ins that provide more comprehensive analysis tools.

Excel's Data Analysis add-in, included with the basic Excel system, is a valuable tool for conducting statistical analysis. In the last section of this appendix we provide instruction for installing the Data Analysis add-in. Other add-ins have been developed by outside suppliers to supplement the basic statistical capabilities provided by Excel. In the last section we also discuss StatTools, a commercially available add-in developed by Palisade Corporation.

## Overview of Microsoft Excel 2010

When using Excel for statistical analysis, data is displayed in workbooks, each of which contains a series of worksheets that typically include the original data as well as any resulting analysis, including charts. Figure 1 shows the layout of a blank workbook created each time Excel is opened. The workbook is named Book1, and consists of three worksheets named Sheet1, Sheet2, and Sheet3. Excel highlights the worksheet currently displayed (Sheet1) by setting the name on the worksheet tab in bold. To select a different worksheet simply click on the corresponding tab. Note that cell A1 is initially selected.

*A workbook is a file containing one or more worksheets.*

The wide bar located across the top of the workbook is referred to as the Ribbon. Tabs, located at the top of the Ribbon, provide quick access to groups of related commands. There are nine tabs shown on the workbook in Figure 1: File; Home; Insert; Page Layout; Formulas; Data; Review; View; and Add-Ins. Each tab contains a series of groups of related commands. Note that the Home tab is selected when Excel is opened. Figure 2 displays the groups available when the Home tab is selected. Under the Home tab there are seven groups: Clipboard; Font; Alignment; Number; Styles; Cells; and Editing. Commands are arranged within each group. For example, to change selected text to boldface, click the Home tab and click the Bold button in the Font group.

Figure 3 illustrates the location of the Quick Access Toolbar and the Formula Bar. The Quick Access Toolbar allows you to quickly access workbook options. To add or remove features on the Quick Access Toolbar click the Customize Quick Access Toolbar button on the Quick Access Toolbar.

The Formula Bar (see Figure 3) contains a Name box, the Insert Function button $f_x$, and a Formula box. In Figure 3, "A1" appears in the name box because cell A1 is selected. You can select any other cell in the worksheet by using the mouse to move the cursor to another cell and clicking or by typing the new cell location in the Name box. The Formula box is used to display the formula in the currently selected cell. For instance, if you had entered $=A1+A2$ into cell A3, whenever you select cell A3 the formula $=A1+A2$ will be shown

**FIGURE 1**    BLANK WORKBOOK CREATED WHEN EXCEL IS OPENED

in the Formula box. This feature makes it very easy to see and edit a formula in a particular cell. The Insert Function button allows you to quickly access all of the functions available in Excel. Later we show how to find and use a particular function.

## Basic Workbook Operations

Figure 4 illustrates the worksheet options that can be performed after right-clicking on a worksheet tab. For instance, to change the name of the current worksheet from "Sheet1" to "Data," right-click the worksheet tab named "Sheet1" and select the Rename option. The current worksheet name (Sheet1) will be highlighted. Then, simply type the new name (Data) and press the Enter key to rename the worksheet.

Suppose that you wanted to create a copy of "Sheet 1." After right-clicking the tab named "Sheet1," select the Move or Copy option. When the Move or Copy dialog box appears, select Create a Copy and click OK. The name of the copied worksheet will appear as "Sheet1 (2)." You can then rename it, if desired.

To add a worksheet to the workbook, right-click any worksheet tab and select the Insert option; when the Insert dialog box appears, select Worksheet and click OK. An additional blank worksheet titled "Sheet 4" will appear in the workbook. You can also insert a new worksheet by clicking the Insert Worksheet tab button 🔲 that appears to the right of the last worksheet tab displayed. Worksheets can be deleted by right-clicking the worksheet tab and choosing Delete. After clicking Delete a window will appear warning you that any data appearing in the worksheet will be lost. Click Delete to confirm that you do want to delete

**FIGURE 2    PORTION OF THE HOME TAB**

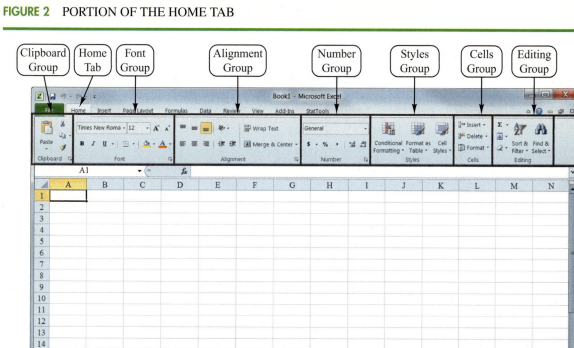

**FIGURE 3    EXCEL 2010 QUICK ACCESS TOOLBAR AND FORMULA BAR**

**FIGURE 4**   WORKSHEET OPTIONS OBTAINED AFTER RIGHT-CLICKING
ON A WORKSHEET TAB

the worksheet. Worksheets can also be moved to other workbooks or a different position in the current workbook by using the Move or Copy option.

## Creating, Saving, and Opening Files

Data can be entered into an Excel worksheet by manually entering the data into the worksheet or by opening another workbook that already contains the data. As an illustration of manually entering, saving, and opening a file we will use the example from Chapter 2 involving data for a sample of 50 soft drink purchases. The original data are shown in Table 1.

Suppose you just opened Excel and want to work with this data. A blank workbook containing three worksheets will be displayed. The soft drink data can now be entered by simply typing it into one of the worksheets. If Excel is currently running and no blank workbook is displayed, you can create a blank workbook using the following steps:

**Step 1:** Click the **File** tab
**Step 2:** Click **New** in the list of options
**Step 3:** When the Available Templates dialog box appears,
Double-click **Blank Workbook**

A new workbook containing three worksheets labeled Sheet1, Sheet2, and Sheet3 will appear.

Suppose we want to enter the data for the sample of 50 soft drink purchases into Sheet1 of the new workbook. First, we enter the label "Brand Purchased" into cell A1; then, we enter the data for the 50 soft drink purchases into cells A2:A51. As a reminder that this worksheet contains the data, we will change the name of the worksheet from "Sheet1" to "Data" using the procedure described previously. Figure 5 shows the data worksheet that we just developed.

**TABLE 1**   DATA FROM A SAMPLE OF 50 SOFT DRINK PURCHASES

| | | |
|---|---|---|
| Coca-Cola | Sprite | Pepsi |
| Diet Coke | Coca-Cola | Coca-Cola |
| Pepsi | Diet Coke | Coca-Cola |
| Diet Coke | Coca-Cola | Coca-Cola |
| Coca-Cola | Diet Coke | Pepsi |
| Coca-Cola | Coca-Cola | Dr. Pepper |
| Dr. Pepper | Sprite | Coca-Cola |
| Diet Coke | Pepsi | Diet Coke |
| Pepsi | Coca-Cola | Pepsi |
| Pepsi | Coca-Cola | Pepsi |
| Coca-Cola | Coca-Cola | Pepsi |
| Dr. Pepper | Pepsi | Pepsi |
| Sprite | Coca-Cola | Coca-Cola |
| Coca-Cola | Sprite | Dr. Pepper |
| Diet Coke | Dr. Pepper | Pepsi |
| Coca-Cola | Pepsi | Sprite |
| Coca-Cola | Diet Coke | |

**FIGURE 5**   WORKSHEET CONTAINING THE SOFT DRINK DATA

*Note: Rows 21–49 are hidden.*

Before doing any analysis with these data, we recommend that you first save the file; this will prevent you from having to reenter the data in case something happens that causes Excel to close. To save the file as an Excel 2010 workbook using the filename SoftDrink we perform the following steps:

**Step 1:** Click the **File** tab
**Step 2:** Click **Save** in the list of options
**Step 3:** When the Save As dialog box appears,
Select the location where you want to save the file
Type the filename **SoftDrink** in the **File name** box
Click **Save**

*Keyboard shortcut: To save the file, press CTRL+S*

Excel's Save command is designed to save the file as an Excel 2010 workbook. As you work with the file to do statistical analysis you should follow the practice of periodically saving the file so you will not lose any statistical analysis you may have performed. Simply click the File tab and select Save in the list of options.

Sometimes you may want to create a copy of an existing file. For instance, suppose you would like to save the soft drink data and any resulting statistical analysis in a new file named "SoftDrink Analysis." The following steps show how to create a copy of the SoftDrink workbook and analysis with the new filename, "SoftDrink Analysis."

**Step 1:** Click the **File** tab
**Step 2:** Click **Save As**
**Step 3:** When the Save As dialog box appears,
Select the location where you want to save the file
Type the filename **SoftDrink Analysis** in the **File name** box
Click **Save**

Once the workbook has been saved, you can continue to work with the data to perform whatever type of statistical analysis is appropriate. When you are finished working with the file simply click the close window button ✖ located at the top right-hand corner of the Ribbon. To access the SoftDrink Analysis file at another point in time you can open the file by performing the following steps:

**Step 1:** Click the **File** tab
**Step 2:** Click **Open**
**Step 3:** When the Open dialog box appears,
Select the location where you previously saved the file
Enter the filename **SoftDrink Analysis** in the **File name** box
Click **Open**

The procedures we showed for saving or opening a workbook begin by clicking File tab to access the Save and Open commands. Once you have used Excel for a while you will probably find it more convenient to add these commands to the Quick Access Toolbar.

# Using Excel Functions

Excel 2010 provides a wealth of functions for data management and statistical analysis. If we know what function is needed, and how to use it, we can simply enter the function into the appropriate worksheet cell. However, if we are not sure what functions are available to accomplish a task or are not sure how to use a particular function, Excel can provide assistance. Many new functions for statistical analysis have been added with Excel 2010. To illustrate we will use the SoftDrink Analysis workbook created in the previous subsection.

**FIGURE 6**   INSERT FUNCTION DIALOG BOX

*Note: Rows 21–49 are hidden.*

## Finding the Right Excel Function

To identify the functions available in Excel, select the cell where you want to insert the function; we have selected cell D2. Click the **Formulas** tab on the Ribbon and then click the **Insert Function** button in the **Function Library** group. Alternatively, click the $f_x$ button on the formula bar. Either approach provides the **Insert Function** dialog box shown in Figure 6.

The **Search for a function** box at the top of the Insert Function dialog box enables us to type a brief description of what we want to do. After doing so and clicking **Go**, Excel will search for and display, in the **Select a function** box, the functions that may accomplish our task. In many situations, however, we may want to browse through an entire category of functions to see what is available. For this task, the **Or select a category** box is helpful. It contains a drop-down list of several categories of functions provided by Excel. Figure 6 shows that we selected the **Statistical** category. As a result, Excel's statistical functions appear in alphabetic order in the Select a function box. We see the AVEDEV function listed first, followed by the AVERAGE function, and so on.

The AVEDEV function is highlighted in Figure 6, indicating it is the function currently selected. The proper syntax for the function and a brief description of the function appear below the Select a function box. We can scroll through the list in the Select a function box to display the syntax and a brief description for each of the statistical functions that are available. For instance, scrolling down farther, we select the COUNTIF function as shown in Figure 7. Note that COUNTIF is now highlighted, and that immediately below the Select a function box we see **COUNTIF(range,criteria)**, which indicates that the COUNTIF function contains two inputs, range and criteria. In addition, we see that the description of the COUNTIF function is "Counts the number of cells within a range that meet the given condition."

# Essentials of Modern Business Statistics, 5e, WEBfiles